'Compelling and highly original .
Rana Mitter, *Literary Review*

'A detailed and thought-provoking study . . . an extremely valuable
addition to the scholarship of modern revolutionary movements'
Saul David, *Daily Telegraph*

'Brilliant, superbly original . . . *Underground Asia* breaks new ground
by showing how a collective consciousness emerged among
revolutionaries on this shifting terrain . . . Though many of the
revolutionaries Harper evokes are now forgotten – or, for some Asian
nations, too inconvenient to remember – their underground stories
still echo through time' *Economist*

'Harper makes the intriguing point that as imperialism fostered
globalisation, so this same process allowed Asia's anti-colonial
activists to establish connections with each other'
Tony Barber, *Financial Times*

'A monumental and magnificent study of anti-colonial revolutionaries
who forged solidarities across the globe to mount a connected
onslaught against the British, French, and Dutch empires. Written
with verve and panache, this is riveting narrative history at its very
best that would evoke the envy of the finest novelists'
Sugata Bose, Gardiner Professor of Oceanic History
and Affairs, Harvard University

'A special kind of history writing at its very best. It is breath-taking
in its sweep, matchless in its command of diverse sources spread
across different archives, remarkable in its empathy for the lives and
emotions of forgotten men and women and for the clarity of its prose'
Rudrangshu Mukherjee, *The Wire* (India)

'A rare historian-storyteller . . . a powerful story that lends credence to
the belief that the empires were quite rattled by the audacity of these
groups of men and women who could not be repressed into
submission . . . This book has truly brought alive all those characters
who were either erased or faded away from memory and paid them a
tribute they richly deserved' Ajay Singh, *Indian Express*

30108 034611397

'Reading *Underground Asia* is like being privy to a historical particle accelerator, watching as revolutionary agents smash up against different imperial oppositions . . . The result provides an unexpected key to understanding contemporary Asian politics' Thomas Meaney, *New Yorker*

'*Underground Asia* is the most gripping work of history I have ever read. It is a truly profound meditation on the struggles for freedom that shaped modern Asia, it is an astonishing feat of archival detective work, and it is a flat-out literary masterpiece' Sunil Amrith, author of *Unruly Waters*

'A marvel of a book. I have never seen anything like it. Harper has the storyteller's gift. He makes connections across space and time and race and place that most people can't dream to emulate. No one understands the warp and weft of the absolute powder-keg explosion of the beginnings of nationalism in Asia writ large better than Tim Harper' Eric Tagliacozzo, Professor of History, Cornell University

'Magisterial . . . Harper does not simply challenge the conventional view of Vietnam's history but also other Great Man accounts of liberation struggles in different Asian countries, from Indonesia to India, the Philippines to China. He does this through life stories of intriguing individuals, downplayed or completely ignored in standard histories because their approaches diverged sharply from those of the figures now seen as the key saviors of their countries' Jeffrey Wasserstrom, *New Republic*

'A sweeping account . . . Harper's broad perspective reveals the interconnectedness of these anti-colonial struggles and their reverberations more than a century later . . . Asia scholars and students of international affairs will find this revisionist history to be of exceptional value' *Publishers Weekly*

ABOUT THE AUTHOR

Tim Harper is Professor of the History of Southeast Asia at the University of Cambridge, a Director of the Centre for History and Economics, and a Fellow of Magdalene College. He was the co-author with Christopher Bayly of two landmark Penguin books on the British Empire's experience of the Second World War in south and southeast Asia: *Forgotten Armies* and *Forgotten Wars*.

TIM HARPER

Underground Asia

*Global Revolutionaries and
the Assault on Empire*

PENGUIN BOOKS

PENGUIN BOOKS

UK | USA | Canada | Ireland | Australia
India | New Zealand | South Africa

Penguin Books is part of the Penguin Random House group of companies
whose addresses can be found at global.penguinrandomhouse.com.

Penguin
Random House
UK

First published in Allen Lane 2020
This edition published 2021
001

Text copyright © Tim Harper, 2020

The moral rights of the author and translator have been asserted

Printed and bound in Great Britain by Clays Ltd, Elcograf S.p.A.

The authorized representative in the EEA is Penguin Random House Ireland,
Morrison Chambers, 32 Nassau Street, Dublin D02 YH68

A CIP catalogue record for this book is available from the British Library

ISBN: 978–0–241–95794–3

For L.

Contents

CONTENTS

List of Illustrations and Photographic Credits

Every effort has been made to contact all copyright holders. The publishers will be pleased to amend in future editions any errors or omissions brought to their attention.

LIST OF PLATES

1. Ships in dry dock, Singapore, c.1896. *Balean/TopFoto.*
2. Sikh policeman, Nanjing Road, Shanghai, 1910s. *Gamma-Keystone/Getty Images.*
3. The 'Maniktola garden', Calcutta. *Wikimedia Commons.*
4. Khudiram Bose, 1907. *Historic Collection/Alamy.*
5. Aurobindo Ghose, 1908. *Historic Collection/Alamy.*
6. Gurdit Singh on the *Komagata Maru*, 1914. *914 Collection/Alamy.*
7. Women tobacco workers, Sumatra, c. 1914, photograph originally published in the contemporary journal *Deli Planters Vereeniging.*
8. Poster for Colonial Exhibition, Semarang, 1914. Lithograph by Albert Hahn Snr. Lithograph on paper mounted on linen, 108.5 x 82.5 cm. *Collection of National Gallery Singapore, image courtesy of National Heritage Board.*
9. Funeral procession for Mewa Singh, Vancouver, 1915. *Simon Fraser University Library Special Collections, Kohaly Collection.*
10. Maulana Barakatullah and Raja Mahendra Pratap, Mesopotamia, 1915. © *Stiftung Bibliotheca Afghanica, Bubendorf.*
11. Execution of rebel sepoys, Singapore, 1915. *Imperial War Museum, London.* © *IWM (Q 82506).*
12. Henk Sneevliet, Betsy Brouwer, their sons and servants, Semarang, c. 1919. *International Institute of Social History, Amsterdam (BG T2/732).*

29. Borodin, Zhang Tailei and Wang Jingwei, Canton, 1926. Photograph by Fu Bingchang. *Image courtesy of C.H. Foo, Y.W. Foo and Historical Photographs of China, University of Bristol (www.hpcbristol.net).*

30. The British Bund, Hankou, 1927. *PA Images.*

31. Xiang Jingyu, 1928. *Source unknown.*

32. Mas Marco Kartodikromo and his wife in Boven Digoel, 1932. *Leiden University Libraries, Royal Netherlands Institute of Southeast Asian and Caribbean Studies (KITLV 4452).*

33. Tan Malaka, 1932. Harry A. Poeze, *Tan Malaka: Strijder voor Indonesië's Vrijheid: Levens-loop van 1897 tot 1945,* 's-Gravenhage, Nijhoff, 1976, p. 426.

ILLUSTRATIONS IN THE TEXT

Frontispiece: Nguyen Ai Quoc in Paris. *Archives nationales d'outre-mer, Aix-en-Provence (File/Fond, HCI, SPCE, 364).*

p.2 Pham Hong Thai, 1924. *Archives nationales d'outre-mer, Aix-en-Provence (File/Fond, Indochine, GG, 65533).*

p.22 Phan Boi Chau, Prince Cuong De and Phan Chu Trinh in Japan, 1906. *Archives nationales d'outre-mer, Aix-en-Provence (File/Fond, INDO, RSTNF, 6661).*

p.54 An Act of Banishment: Page from a Criminal Registry, Singapore, 1914. *The National Archives, Kew (TNA, CO 273/420).*

p.96 Madame Cama in Stuttgart, 1907. *International Institute of Social History, Amsterdam (BG B9/835).*

p.134 The viceroy's State Entry into Delhi, 23 December 1912, illustration from *La Tribuna Illustrata,* January 1913. *Look and Learn/ Bridgeman Images.*

p.170 Bhagwan Singh with a samurai sword, Yokohama, 1914. *Courtesy of Surinder Pal Singh and the South Asian American Digital Archive.*

p.206 Ibrahim gelar Datuk Tan Malaka, c. 1922. *Leiden University Libraries, Royal Netherlands Institute of Southeast Asian and Caribbean Studies (KITLV 17800).*

p.240 At the gateway to India: Raja Mahendra Pratap in Afghanistan, 1915. *© Stiftung Bibliotheca Afghanica, Bubendorf.*

p.278 M.N. Roy in Mexico. Photograph reproduced in Sibnarayan Ray, *Selected Works of M.N. Roy: 1917-1922*, OUP, 1987.

p.316 Mas Marco Kartodikromo and his wife, abroad, c. 1920. *Leiden University Libraries, Royal Netherlands Institute of Southeast Asian and Caribbean Studies (KITLV 4451)*.

p.362 Calling card of Nguyen Ai Quoc. *Archives nationales d'outre-mer, Aix-en-Provence (File/Fond, HCI, SPCE, 365)*.

p.416 The Great World, Shanghai, photograph by Jack Birns, 1940s. *The LIFE Picture Collection/Getty Images*.

p.468 Front cover of pamphlet by Tan Malaka, *Indonezija i ee mesto na probuždajuščemsja vostoke* (Indonesia and its Place in the Awakening East), 1924. *International Institute of Social History, Amsterdam (1992/3905)*.

p.506 Wong Sang, the 'bobbed-haired woman'. *Archives nationales d'outre-mer, Aix-en-Provence (File/Fond, Indochine, GG, 65533)*.

p.554 Chiang Kai-shek enters Shanghai, April 1927. *SZ Photo/Scherl/ Mary Evans*.

p.616 The abandoned typewriter of Nguyen Ai Quoc, Kowloon, 1931. *Archives nationales d'outre-mer, Aix-en-Provence (File/Fond, HCI, SPCE, 365)*.

Maps

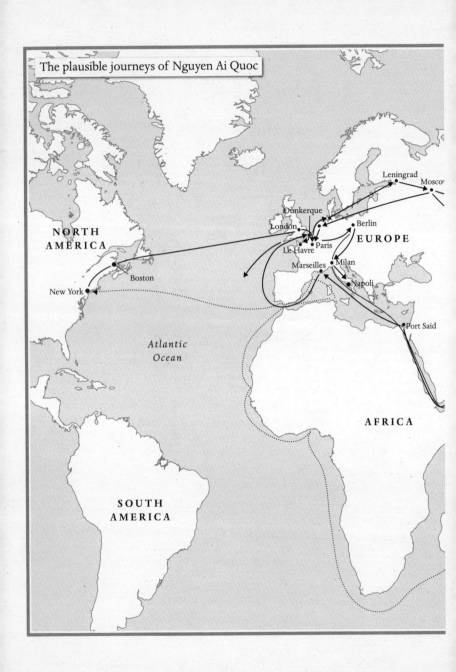

The plausible journeys of Nguyen Ai Quoc

NORTH AMERICA

New York
Boston

Atlantic Ocean

SOUTH AMERICA

Leningrad
Moscow
Dunkerque
London
Le Havre
Paris
Berlin
EUROPE
Marseilles
Milan
Napoli
Port Said

AFRICA

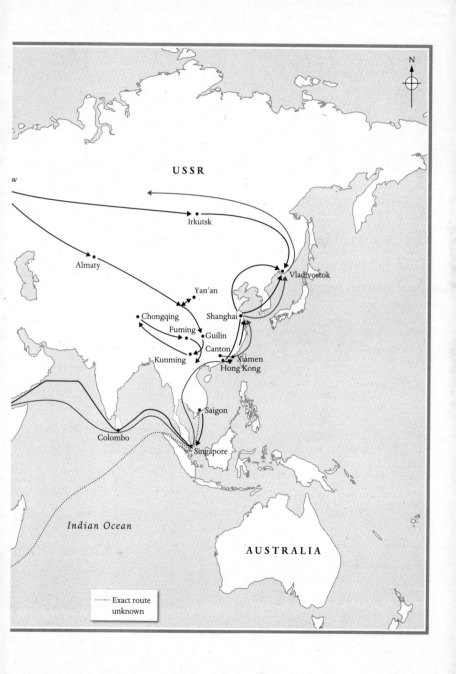

N

USSR

Irkutsk

Almaty

Yan'an

Chongqing   Shanghai

Fuming
          Guilin
          Canton
Kunming   Xiamen
          Hong Kong

Saigon

Colombo   Singapore

Indian Ocean

AUSTRALIA

Vladivostok

...... Exact route
       unknown

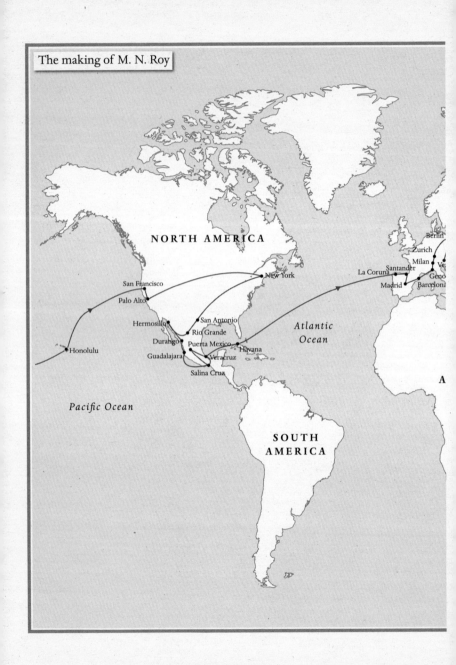

The making of M. N. Roy

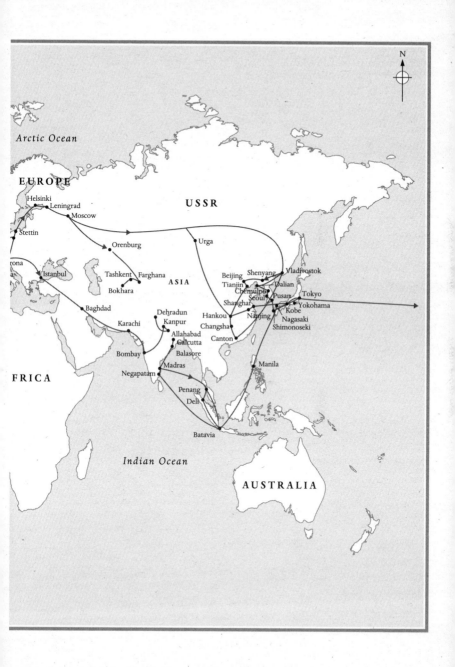

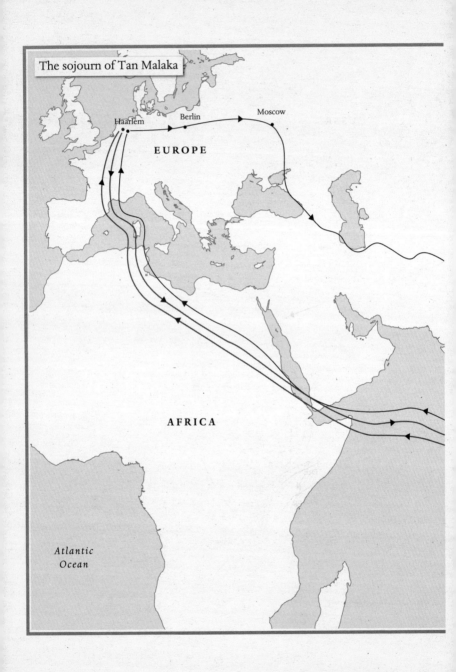

The sojourn of Tan Malaka

Haarlem Berlin Moscow

EUROPE

AFRICA

Atlantic
Ocean

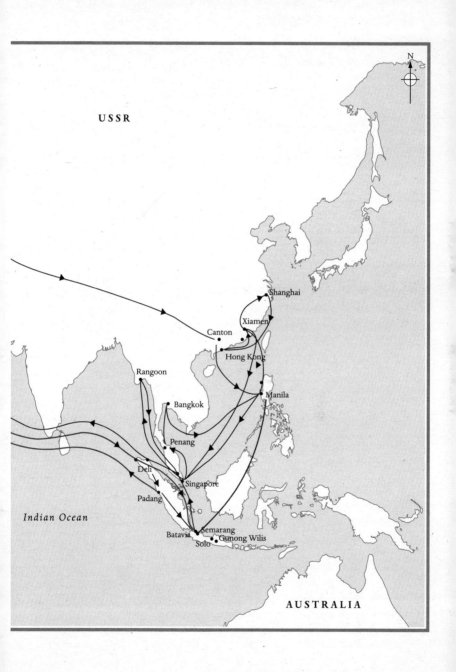

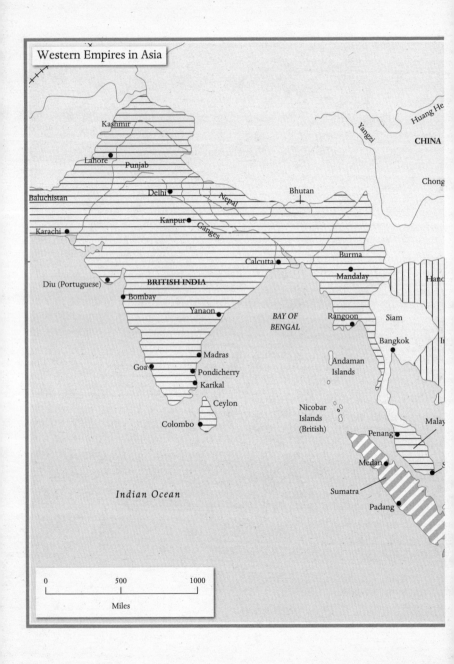

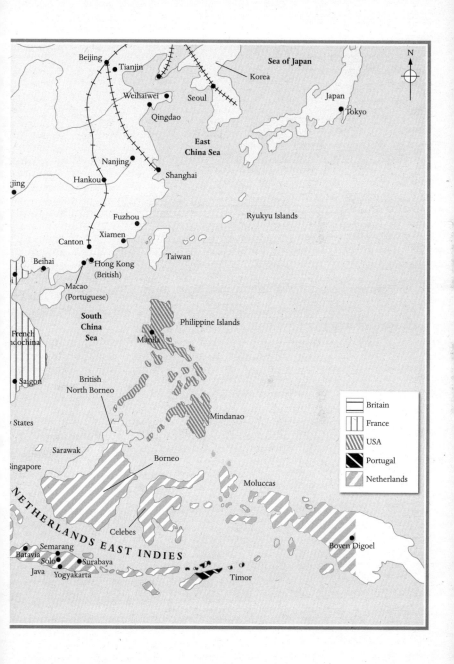

Revolutionary China

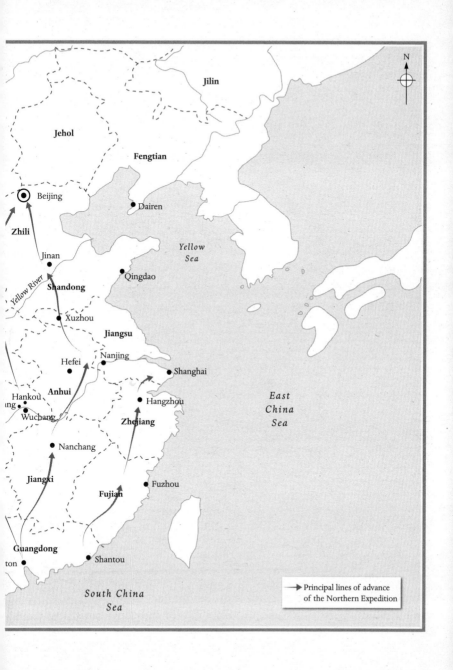

Foreword

This book tells the story of a connected wave of revolution across Asia from its beginnings in the first years of the twentieth century to a crescendo of protest, rebellion and war between 1925 and 1927. It sees the struggles for freedom from foreign domination in India, Southeast Asia and China – that is, the greater part of humanity – as a connected assault on empires. It is written from the perspective of those who took their struggle abroad, as exiles, operating over long distances, in a search for allies and in pursuit of a world revolution, which they believed Asia was destined to lead. The book's scope is therefore global in compass. Many of the pathways of Asia's revolutionaries crossed in Europe and the Americas, at the metropolitan hearts of the empires they sought to overthrow. Then, after 1920, they converged in the Soviet Union, only to return to Asia soon after, as the continent became the front line of the global revolution.

One objective of this kind of world history is to 'loosen' our sense of time and space, to shift narrative focus and to look at great events afresh.[1] Although this story encompasses the milestones of the age – the Great War, the Bolshevik revolution and the end of empires – its own watershed moments unfold rather differently, and in so doing decentre our understanding of these larger processes. Familiar, national stories might, at times, seem a little far away. The towering figures of modern Asian history – the likes of Sun Yat-sen, Gandhi, Sukarno, Mao Zedong – all play a role in this story. But they do not necessarily begin, nor end, as its most important figures. I have written from the standpoint of diverse actors, many now overlooked in national histories. I do so from the vantage-point of what they knew and saw, and what they may have believed and thought possible at the time. In telling their story, I have tried as hard as possible not to divulge too much of the hindsight of the historian. In retrospect, many might now be seen among the vanquished of Asian history. But, in their triumphs, failures and adversities, they shaped Asia's future in profound ways.

This book offers, quite deliberately and literally, an eccentric view of Asian history. It traces the insurgent geography of what I call 'underground Asia'. I try to describe the terrain revolutionaries carved out for themselves, and how certain milieus generated new ideas and strategies for action. It tells of lives that were lived at the interstices of empires, and of struggles that did not see the nation-state as its sole end or as the natural ordering of a future world. Although much divided them, often violently so, most of the principal actors in this book voiced a commitment to what the Indonesian journalist, novelist and activist Mas Marco Kartodikromo called 'the human nation of the world'. Thinkers continually stressed that they lived in an era of transition: a time and a place between – or, perhaps more accurately, besides – empire and nation. Mas Marco and his contemporaries celebrated a 'world in motion' and a 'world upside down'.[2] This evoked a vision of Asia, and of the world, that was more open than any time before or, perhaps, since.

Research for this book has taken me beyond my linguistic capacity; this has been inescapable for the story I wanted to tell. The same was also true for the people I am writing about. Most things happened in translation; the process of translation is crucial to the story, and it had – it has – its limits and its blindnesses. I have tried to be internally consistent with place names, and generally use their modern form. In the case of China this means the Pinyin, although there are exceptions: for example, I use 'Canton' for Guangzhou. Beyond China, I also use traditional forms – 'Batavia' for Jakarta, 'Calcutta' for Kolkata, and so on – where using modern names for what were at the time very distinctive colonial or semi-colonial spaces seems anachronistic.

In the case of personal names, for China I have largely opted for the Pinyin form, but retained the older romanization where to do otherwise would add little to clarity – for example, Sun Yat-sen, Chiang Kai-shek and the Kuomintang. Similarly, I have mostly followed contemporary usage for names from South and Southeast Asia. I am not a Vietnamese or Japanese language specialist, so I have, on the whole, omitted diacritics. An added challenge for the historian is the use of pseudonyms, which was endemic to clandestine struggle. For instance, the man we encounter around 1905 as Nguyen Tat Thanh becomes Seaman Ba, then Nguyen Ai Quoc, Ly Thuy and Sung Mun Cho, with many other aliases in between. He later refashions himself under the name by which he is best known to posterity. Other key examples are

Ibrahim / Tan Malaka, and Naren / the Reverend C. A. Martin / M. N. Roy. I generally use the name they were going by at the time. To aid the reader, cross-references are included in the index.

In a complex way, the work of historians mirrors that of colonial policemen as they briefly catch sight of, and often misidentify, quarries before they suddenly plunge back into the shadows. Indeed, I have drawn on the archives of the principal western colonial powers – British, French and Dutch – and those of the Shanghai Municipal Police. Their seductive, distorting nature, however, and their illusory claims to authority have long been acknowledged by historians. Police reports were often composed from the whispers of informers paid by piece rate. This was a world of professional dissimulators. Police interrogations were a choreographed affair designed to establish an implicitly agreed story, especially where prisoners turned police witness. I have tried to embed into the narrative of this book a sense of what was known or unknown, disputed or misunderstood, or, more importantly, what was believed to be true at the time. I have been very much struck by the symbiotic, often intimate, relationship between international policing and the anti-colonial underground; how the one helped bring the other into existence. Global revolutionaries obsessively tried to forge connections to advance their struggles; the police obsessively looked to uncover connections in order to prove the existence of wider conspiracies and plots. Each helped fashion the other and this drove forward events.

It is a paradox that some of the most clandestine lives of the imperial underground were some of the best documented of their time. The case files of Nguyen Tat Thanh in the Archives Nationales d'Outre Mer in Aix-en-Provence, for example, amount to several large boxes, packed with reports on the thinnest paper. They contain copies of private letters, translations of writings and ephemera, snippets of conversations and confessions of his associates and the informing of his enemies that are not extant elsewhere. These can be triangulated with the archives of international communism in Moscow, copies of which I have consulted in collections in western Europe and in published volumes, along with the remarkable amount that people wrote about themselves and others, to fix their place in these events and to draw up the roll call of martyrs. The archives of those individuals with no country have a vitally important home in libraries such as the International Institute of Social History in Amsterdam.

In writing this book, I am acutely conscious that I stand on the shoulders of many ground-breaking scholars, biographers in particular, who have traced 'despised and forgotten' lives over vast distances, and who did so at a time when it was much harder to do so than it is now. I highlight their work in the endnotes. Unlike many of them, I have benefited from online archives and powerful digital search tools. These technologies open up new possibilities for the history of global networks. But they are governed by the choices that historians make and must be set within an understanding of local contexts, the textures of place and of the visceral reality of human mobility.[3] For each connection I have chosen to follow, I know that there are others that might lead in other directions.

At the heart of the book is an attempt to trace the connections within Asia that have shaped its modern age. It steps backwards in time from the two books I wrote with Christopher Bayly that trace the connected arc of war and revolution across South and Southeast Asia after 1941.[4] War is a pivotal theme of this book also, but, in order to tell the story of an earlier era of anti-imperial struggle, I have had to range over a wider geographical compass. This book is also about empires, but seen here from their dark underside. I have tried to write this history from within and from below, at the eye level of men and women moving through strange cities and unfamiliar landscapes, and in secret. The story opens with a prelude in the summer of 1924, when some of these long journeys were about to burst into the open, and on a massive scale. It then returns to their starting points around 1905 and follows them forward chronologically and in synchronism to their terminus in 1927. Finally, an epilogue takes a longer view of the outcomes and legacies of underground Asia.

Underground Asia

Pham Hong Thai, 1924.

Prelude
On the Threshold of Free Asia
1924

HYPO-COLONY

In the summer of 1924 the border between colonial and free Asia was a 100-foot-wide canal in southern China. On one bank stood the continent's largest self-governing city, Canton; on the other was one of its oldest colonial enclaves, Shamian Island. Lying on a reclaimed sandbar of around fifty-six acres in the heart of the Chinese city, this western outpost was home to perhaps 500 Britons and 100 or so French residents, together with smaller numbers of Germans, Americans and Japanese. Ever since the Anglo-French intervention in China in 1860, the treaty port of Canton had comprised two extraterritorial concessions: one, covering about four-fifths of the island, was administered by the British, the other by the French. Each concession possessed its own bridge to the shore, guarded by Sikh and Vietnamese troops respectively. They also protected the island's grid of wide, tree-fringed boulevards interspaced with formal gardens, tennis courts and a football pitch. The streets of Shamian were lined with consulates, banks and missions which dated from the heyday of the China trade. The stately architecture resembled similar enclaves, such as Shanghai or Tianjin, if on a less grand scale. This was part of Shamian's charm. The island, as the old Asia hand Sir Ernest Satow described it in 1905, was 'the prettiest bit of Anglo-Chinese life that can be imagined'.[1]

The European steamers and gunboats anchored to the south of the island at the Shamian Bund had to navigate their way through one of the busiest inland waterways on earth, the Pearl River, which thronged with Chinese sampans, junks, huge man-powered paddle-boats, house barges and the 'flower boats', the floating brothels of erotic legend. On the north and east, Shamian's two bridges linked it to the old western suburb of Canton, with its labyrinthine markets and artisan workshops, and to a city of more than 1 million Chinese. For them, Shamian was a 'semi-banned' place: they needed permits from the Shamian town council to enter the island; even then, they could access only particular areas, and not after midnight, and they certainly could not walk on the grass. Yet Shamian was not entirely forbidden: it was a refuge in times of turmoil, a place for private banking and a destination for pleasure trips, where the Cantonese would promenade and enjoy the gardens, fascinated by the curious lives of the foreigners. However, at this time, the island had become a focus of Chinese patriotic anxiety and was virtually under siege. As one local writer put it: 'Whenever one sets foot on this island branded with a shameful mark, who, except those Chinese collaborators, would not be enflamed in his heart with anger and hatred?'[2]

The last years of the nineteenth century had seen a frenzied competition for contracts and concessions in China as the Qing government began a programme of reforms and modernization. It culminated in a further incursion in 1900, the first 'international' intervention of its kind, when troops of seven western powers and Japan marched on Tianjin and Beijing to protect their citizens and their interests during the Boxer Rebellion. In its aftermath, ten nations possessed territorial enclaves in China, including the United States of America, Italy, Belgium and the Habsburg empire, which gained a first foothold at Tianjin in 1901–2. Sun Yat-sen, a leading voice for a new, free China, was to call the city a 'hypo-colony', using a prefix borrowed from chemistry for a compound of an inferior kind, which he used to denote a degraded colony of all the western empires.[3] Although a revolution in China in 1911 had overthrown Qing rule, the western powers held tenaciously to their extraterritorial privileges which seemed, to patriots, to mock China's claims to sovereign status and to block its entry into the modern world. Many Asian intellectuals felt that the rules of the international system had been established merely to help the existing imperial powers to hold on to what they possessed and to exclude others. In 1912 China became a republic, but as its central institutions in Beijing weakened, the divided port cities became symbols of the collusion of the western powers to uphold the imperial system for all time.

Canton was not merely a border zone. In 1923 it became the seat of the newly established Nationalist Government of Sun Yat-sen. Yet, beyond the six areas Sun controlled in the south, China was still fragmented into rival alliances of military commanders – the so-called 'warlords' – who battled for the inheritance of the Qing. In early 1924 the crucial decision was taken to create an independent military base for the Nationalist Government with the founding of Whampoa Military Academy some fifteen miles outside the city. Political education was to be one of its distinctive functions, and young radicals from China, Korea and Southeast Asia flocked to enrol there. Now, as the exemplary centre of the new nation, Canton was a place of intense social experiment in the name of unity and progress, exporting ideas and practices, a beacon of free Asia.[4]

Yet there was a brittleness to this achievement. In recent years, China had experienced some of the most brutal civil wars of modern history, and there was more to come: the fighting for Shanghai and for the north from the summer of 1924 would see the mobilization of around 420,000 troops.[5] Politics was dominated by 'the purse and the sword'. To consolidate his power in the south, Sun Yat-sen had allowed 'guest armies' from other provinces into Canton, and the so-called 'bayonet thieves' ran loose in the city, robbing houses on the pretext of searching for gamblers and opium smokers. Soldiers were well known for forcibly occupying the best seats in cinemas and shows; a British theatre and Bostock's Circus were particular targets.[6] Sun Yat-sen had looked to the west for diplomatic recognition and loans in 1923. But now he was increasingly frustrated by western support for the northern militarist coalition that controlled the old imperial capital of Beijing. In mid-1924, starved of cash, Sun tried to seize control of the Canton customs, which were run principally by the British, but he had been faced down by a flotilla of twenty-one western warships. He had been expelled from Canton on two previous occasions, and intellectuals and other elites were gripped by anxiety that China might fall apart like 'a heap of sand' in the face of imperialist invasion.

Canton remained in a volatile state and there had been talk on the back-alley telegraph for weeks that Sun Yat-sen was dead. At the end of May, a Chinese newspaper editor was arrested and banished for ten years for publishing the rumour. In the face of new war taxes, the streets were full of resistance to authority: sedan-chair carriers were on strike against their licence fees. Even the pawnshops were on strike.

There were around 160 labour unions in the city. Employers were organizing their own unions and volunteer militias to back them up. The left was doing the same.[7] Although by no means was all of this aimed at the large western shipping and trading concerns, westerners feared that, should the situation deteriorate – in the words of one visiting American journalist – the guarded bridges of Shamian and 'the barbed wire entanglements along the sea wall were no more protection than a silken thread'.[8] For young radicals, they were places where (in the old saw) 'xingxing zhi huo keyi liaoyuan', 'a single spark can light a wildfire', and the deeds of a few could set an entire society – history itself – in motion.[9]

EVENING AT THE VICTORIA HOTEL

Into this tinderbox, on 19 June 1924, stepped His Excellency M. Martial Merlin, the Governor-General of French Indochina. He arrived in the evening from Hong Kong, where he had stopped on his way home from a visit to Japan and northern China. He was to attend a dinner on Shamian Island in the British Concession.

Merlin was a first-generation colonial civil servant who had risen to his current position after a long and increasingly controversial tour of duty in France's new imperial possessions in Africa. He had begun as a proponent of the policy of 'association' with native elites, the so-called évolués. But in his final post in Africa, in Senegal, he had repudiated it, with dire warnings that the évolués had become uprooted déracinés, and that France needed to restore social cohesion in the face of the 'self-interested calls and fallacious promises of professional agitators'.[10]

A principal goal of Merlin's tour of Japan had been to secure the cooperation of the Japanese authorities in curbing the political activities of Vietnamese exiles on their shores. There were reports in the Japanese press that seven Vietnamese had left Shanghai for Seoul, in Japanese-occupied Korea, and that 'a serious conspiracy' had been reported to the local police.[11] The urbane foreign affairs adviser of the Nationalist Government, Eugene Chen, was heard to say that he anticipated trouble. For this reason, Merlin left his wife and son in Hong Kong. But these warnings had not been passed on to the British authorities in Canton. Nor had they been told of the banquet in the British Concession.[12]

The Frenchman had arrived in a despatch vessel escorted by a gunboat. After a drinks party at the French consulate, the French community in Canton entertained M. Merlin at the Victoria Hotel. It was not much of a place, but it was the only hotel on Shamian. The American journalist Hallett Abend reported that 'the food, even in times of peace and plenty, was always the worst to be found in China', excepting possibly, he added, the Hotel Nicotine in Manzhouli, Manchuria.[13]

The dinner for some fifty guests took place in the hotel's lounge, its high windows open to the street. Because of the visit, the Canton government had placed stringent security on both sides of the canal. The two stone bridges that linked the island to the Chinese city were closed and guarded. There were police agents along the street, although none of them was armed. The guests sat down to dinner at 8.30 p.m.; then, ten minutes later, just as the soup was being served, a man 'rather luxuriously dressed' appeared at one of the windows. According to one eyewitness, he surveyed the scene within, 'just as anyone, a gentleman or a coolie, might do'.[14]

Suddenly, the man hurled an attaché case through the window. It landed on the table, shattering glasses and plates. After a few seconds it exploded. The blast was heard across the island. Some thought a chandelier had dropped down, or that it was a bad joke: in the chaos of the breaking tableware and glass, few had seen the plunge of the briefcase. Others sat where they were, stunned. The blast was to the left of Merlin.[15] It killed three people immediately: a young French couple who had arrived a fortnight previously, and an elderly clerk of the Banque de l'Indo-Chine. The two men were 'shockingly shredded', the woman with 'a sliced carotid artery dying in a sea of blood'.[16] Knives and forks sent flying by the blast inflicted injuries as terrible as the bomb itself; forks were stuck in the wainscoting and walls. Two people died later, the senior partner of a French silk firm and another businessman. Five other guests were seriously injured, including the deputy consul, Dr Casabianca, whose left arm was almost completely blown off. Three Chinese serving 'boys' were also wounded.[17]

A local resident called Laynaud ran after the attacker with a policeman and a cook. The assassin twice fired a revolver at his pursuers and then headed towards the French Bund, where two Parsis joined the chase, backing off when they were warned the man was armed. They then proceeded to chase the assassin in and out of the French Garden, until he was seen walking along the bund with revolver in hand. Challenged by a Sikh inspector of the French police, he hid behind a hedge. The policeman began to beat the bushes in the dark; there was another shot, and the assassin rushed out and jumped into the river near the landing steps of the French Concession. It was dark, the tide was ebbing, and there were no sampans or patrol boats around.[18]

Some thirty-six hours later, a bloated body washed up on the south side of the Pearl River. It was identified by a gun cartridge in a pocket, the same calibre as those found in the French Garden. A pocket watch on the corpse had stopped at 8.47 p.m., about the time when the assassin jumped in the river.

Merlin was unharmed, partly because he was fortuitously seated away from the briefcase. If he had been sitting at the head of the table – as might have been supposed – he would have been directly hit. Also, one of his entourage had the presence of mind to shout 'Under the table!' and thrust him to the ground just before the explosion. Uncharitable British reports had him hiding beneath the tablecloth.[19] The view of the vociferous local press in Saigon was that he had irretrievably 'lost face'. As the writer André Malraux, normally an acerbic critic of Merlin, commented: 'For the Vietnamese perhaps; to the French, he was simply being sensible.'[20]

Merlin's conduct after the incident won him few admirers. Following a night in the French consulate under close guard, he returned to the gunboat and left for Hong Kong, cancelling a planned lunch with Sun Yat-sen ostensibly to avoid attracting further attacks.[21] At the funeral for the victims, the eulogies claimed them as patriotic fallen of the Great War.[22] There was resentment that Merlin had not stayed long enough to bury them or visit the injured in hospital. In the Catholic Cathedral of the Sacred Heart of Jesus in Canton, a crucifix had fallen from its wall mounting just two hours before the attack; some saw it as a portent, or a miracle.[23]

When Merlin embarked for Saigon a few days later at Hong Kong's Blake Pier, the bund was lined with Chinese and Indian police officers standing shoulder to shoulder. Police launches with guns patrolled the water; a detachment of the East Surrey Regiment was stationed on the pier; and the sidecars of the motorcycle outriders escorting Merlin's car carried crack shots, each man a colony champion: 'no possible anarchist could have got to him except from the air'.[24]

Rumour abounded as to the identity of the assailant, and, above all, to his origins. The French would not entertain the idea that he came from their colony of Indochina; still less that he might be an educated man. Instead, in protests to the Nationalist Government, they insisted that the attacker was Chinese. They argued that he could not be Vietnamese because his feet were not disfigured by the pressure from a sandal strap between the big toe and the others, as those of a Vietnamese might be. This was a man who habitually wore western footwear, and a pair of fashionable white shoes were recovered from the corpse. Early press reports had both the assassin and the recovered corpse dressed in white shorts and shirt. But these proved mistaken. His teeth were not enamelled black, as a coolie's might be; his hair was *en brosse*. Canton officials stressed that he had 'the appearance of being at least a middle-class man'.[25] His clothes – white trousers, grey jacket – were well made locally. The label led the police to his tailor, who was interrogated along with all other known associates. When a revolver was dredged up from the riverbed, the French then maintained that he was a paid assassin, and that the three Hong Kong dollar notes in his pocket were proof of this.[26] British diplomats took up the cry that the Chinese republican government harboured 'anti-European societies of all sorts – Indians, Malays, Annamite [Indochinese], etc . . . Canton is full of these people's bomb factories.'[27]

These protests to the Canton government merely enflamed the Chinese press: after all, at no point had Merlin set foot on Chinese soil.[28] Just a few days before the attack, the new Whampoa Military Academy had formally opened. The cadets now demanded that Shamian Island be recovered from foreign rule by force. This cry was heard on the streets of the city, and most loudly from the 2,000 male and 300 female domestic servants on the small island itself. When the Shamian authorities increased security in the wake of the attack by insisting that all Chinese working on the island carry a photographic identity card, and only walk on certain streets, a strike broke out. By 6 p.m. on the evening of 15 July, only thirty servants remained with their employers, and all had left by the 17th. The sampan men and women and the stevedores came out in solidarity and would not ship or unload any goods for Shamian. At a meeting of the strikers, one labour leader was heard to demand that foreigners weighing over 150 pounds should be banned from taking rickshaws in the city, that those of them unable to swim should not ride sampans in Chinese waters, and that they should submit three photographs to the authorities in order to be allowed into the city.[29] Cooks, houseboys, even those in the European police force, all stayed off the island and picketed the bridges. It was a boycott of the entire western community. This was at some personal sacrifice for the workers: their employment on Shamian exempted them from being press-ganged into military service and sent to fight; meanwhile, the local middle classes could not access their bank accounts and the bosses lost trade with the island.[30]

The strikers, however, found wide support in the city, and a 'People's Association against the Shamian Regulations' united left and right in a common anti-imperial front, even as far as Hong Kong.[31] It drew in high officials and the military, and was funded by popular theatrical performances. The strike headquarters was a theatre and players and schoolgirls collected donations which, three weeks into the protest, were to the tune of 1,000 silver dollars a day.[32] Suddenly starved of supplies, Shamian's westerners had to be brought food by warship, and marines had to man the island's water and electricity plants, damaging them in the process. The women and children were evacuated to Hong Kong. Ironically, the key beneficiary of this was the Victoria Hotel, which offered succour for Europeans who now had no one to cook or clean for them.[33] The strike ended in a long-drawn-out compromise on 20 August when the servants paraded back to work to a salute of bells and firecrackers.[34] This wave of boycotts and strikes across the Chinese seaboard was a full dress rehearsal for some of the most pivotal moments of China's revolution and its relations with the west, that would reverberate across Asia.

A MAN WITHOUT A COUNTRY

A Chinese newspaper identified the Victoria Hotel assassin before the police did. A package was dropped into the letterbox of the *Xianxiang Bao*. It contained a photograph and the 'testament' of a man called Pham Hong Thai:

I am a Vietnamese who was born under the brutal rule of the French. Since I was young, I began to find certain approaches to resist the French and liberate my homeland. I immediately became a member of the Vietnamese Revolutionary Army after its establishment. In April of 1924, I was ordered to assassinate the Governor-General of Annam [Indochina]. We had around ten members to conduct this task. They were assigned to Japan, Beijing and Hong Kong to look for opportunities. However, due to certain hardship, I failed to succeed in the assassination until June 19 when the Governor-General arrived in Shamian, Canton. There, I was able to kill him by throwing a bomb . . . For the evil deeds he did in Vietnam, I had to kill him. However, I apologize to those others who were injured in this incident.

I will not be regretful for this deed even if I die. I wish that what I have done will make other nations understand the suffering of my people and help us.

The testament was accompanied by a letter from a Korean friend, Seo Hung-a, who had met Pham Hong Thai in Tokyo and been inspired by him, and to whom the latter had entrusted his final message before he had set out to kill Merlin.[35]

Pham Hong Thai was around twenty-four years old. At an early age he had left home in Nghe An province in north-central Vietnam for the capital, Hanoi. He turned down the opportunity to join the civil service, trained as a mechanic and worked in sundry trades, as an auto repairman and in a railway workshop (some accounts had him working variously as a 'cyclo', or rickshaw-driver, and a coal miner). In November 1918 he slipped over the hills to Laos and across the border with Siam, through a revolutionary network that stretched from central Vietnam into northeastern Siam and by sea to south China.[36] These were pathways between safe havens that more and more young radicals were taking to flee French authority. About this time, there were attempts to radicalize the young men living in settlements of exile in Siam by a 'walking teacher', Dang Thuc Hua. He set up a route for them to travel through Siam and on to China. On one count, perhaps 100 men made the journey in the 1920s, more than went to the university in Hanoi. In Siam, Pham Hong Thai headed for a village in Phichit province called Ban Dong, where there were sixty or seventy families in exile with a long anti-colonial tradition. He must have spent several years there; local tradition had it that his parents lived there, and he was remembered as 'Giai Thai' ('Willy Thai'), a typical family pet name for a young son. But the locals were close about this, even to Vietnamese outsiders. Pham Hong Thai also left a wife and son in Ban Dong. After the assassination attempt on Merlin, she was forced to flee.[37]

From Siam, Thai moved to China, where he joined a group of Vietnamese based there called the Tam Tam Xa, or the 'Society of Like Hearts'. Exposed to the radicalism of Canton, the Like Hearts repudiated the more cautious policies of the earlier generation of anti-colonial activists; they looked to direct action. High among Merlin's crimes was his attempt to silence and eliminate patriots outside Vietnam. And so it came to pass that Thai had undertaken to carry out a 'death sentence' on the Governor-General of Indochina.[38]

The patriots abroad claimed Pham Hong Thai as a martyr. First among these was the scholar and reformer turned revolutionary and exile, Phan Boi Chau. Now fifty-seven years of age, he was the most celebrated national figure of his generation. At the time the bomb was thrown, Phan Boi Chau was living in Hangzhou in China, at an even greater distance from French rule. But as he read the news his arms and legs began to shake. 'People throughout the world came to know about Vietnam and the Vietnamese revolutionary movement . . . The Russian ambassador in Beijing pounded his desk, saying, "This is what *should* happen in the cattle ranch of the capitalists!" '[39] Phan Boi Chau travelled to Canton to assess the movement and to capitalize on the moment. He wrote a memorial pamphlet which celebrated Pham Hong Thai as the latest patriot in a long heroic tradition.[40] He related how Pham Hong Thai had twice attempted to reach Merlin earlier in the evening.[41] First he had tried to rent a sampan near where Merlin was due to disembark, 'hiding in the boat like a tiger, waiting for Merlin to step on to the pier to throw his bombs'. But the Cantonese port authorities had ordered all craft, large and small, away from the pier as a security measure. Pham Hong Thai had then tried, 'with courage higher than ever', to rent a room on the second floor of the Victoria Hotel, directly above where Merlin would be, but he had been turned away. With no other option, he walked directly from the gate of the British bridge to the hotel with an assured air, posing as a photographer.[42] This would later be recalled with triumph:

He was dressed in Western clothes, wearing Western shoes, and carrying a Western cane in his hand . . . The French police who were guarding the door on both sides all thought that he was a French guest at the reception because his outfit and his deportment looked like a Frenchman, so that they suspected nothing.[43]

It was not clear that Pham Hong Thai had deliberately taken his own life by plunging into the Pearl River. But Phan Boi Chau saw it as a noble suicide and within weeks the legend of Pham Hong Thai, and his photograph, spread widely.

In his tract, Phan Boi Chau claimed that a turning point in the struggle had been reached and a new generation and new methods were coming to the fore.[44] He wrote of Pham Hong Thai as 'a man without a country since his mother's womb', that because of French colonialism he had died for a nation he had never himself experienced. But there was something more to this: the struggles of the new generation were not merely about the Vietnamese nation; in many ways their lives were lived beyond the nation, in a realm where the Vietnamese situation connected intimately with that of others across Asia.

Pham Hong Thai had followed Merlin to Japan, where he met Korean activists; they found common cause as one of the purposes of Merlin's visit to Japan was to recognize Japan's colonial occupation of Korea.[45] Thai's friend Seo Hung-a told the Chinese press that an attack was originally planned for a dinner to be held in Repulse Bay in Hong Kong, but it was called off as there was too much risk of people of other nationalities being hit.[46] Pham Hong Thai was assisted in making his bombs (a second device was later recovered) by a Russian sympathizer who taught at Whampoa Military Academy, where a growing number of the overseas Vietnamese were trying to enlist.

Pham Hong Thai's sacrifice moved the people of Canton.[47] One popular Chinese newspaper, in its leader of 24 June, called him a hero. The bomb was strong enough to electrify the whole world, it claimed, and was caused by the French treating the Vietnamese as barbarians and savages.[48] Pham Hong Thai's remains had been buried by the Chinese Water Police, but leading citizens subscribed funds for them to be reinterred. The French watched in horror as the senior Nationalist official Hu Hanmin personally prepared one of the commemorative stone tablets.[49] What is more, Pham Hong Thai was laid in a hallowed spot, next to the tomb of the 'Seventy-Two Martyrs' of the earlier 1911 uprising against the Qing, thereby making the Chinese and Vietnamese struggles a common cause against the established order of all kinds. This played on an older theme: fourteen of the '72 Martyrs' had come from British Malaya.[50] Hu Hanmin's inscription celebrated Thai as 'a man of high purpose'. He described how Thai had become convinced that only violence could shake the enemy and fire the people's revolutionary zeal.[51]

The French watched the cult of Pham Hong Thai obsessively from afar, complaining annually at the commemoration the Canton authorities allowed at his tomb on the anniversary of his death. As more Vietnamese were recruited to the radical underground via Canton, as more Vietnamese graduated from Whampoa Military Academy – as soldiers and, even more worryingly, as pilots – a visit to the shrine became a ritual of initiation. Women came too, and one of them later described an emotive scene. In front of old revolutionaries and Whampoa cadets, incense sticks were lit and speeches made. 'Pham Hong Thai, be content; be at ease in your tomb. We will emulate you and expel the foreign invaders from our land.' In a formal oath before the tomb, young men and women swore to sacrifice their life, family and property to the revolution, to pledge unquestioning loyalty to the movement, to preserve the secrecy of its work and not to join any other, under pain of death. It was like a wedding ceremony, but one that strengthened the resolve not to take a spouse but to wed oneself to the cause.[52] To the people of Canton, these rites confirmed the presence of a new anti-imperialist front of the Asian revolution.

THE BICYCLE PARTY

In 1924 many political struggles across Asia converged on Canton. It was a city of exiles, one of the few apertures in the imperial system. Nationalists, anarchists, communists, revolutionaries of all descriptions, all made their way there. It was one of the first cities in which Chinese men had cut off their queues, as a gesture of defiance to the Qing empire, and so Vietnamese, Siamese, Japanese, Koreans and others could blend in, at least to the eye of an outsider. In the words of a 1913 French report, it was a population of 'indistinguishable ethnic elements'.[53] The exiles were often men and women with no family and open to new solidarities. They were, in their own minds, and in Phan Boi Chau's words, 'suffering the same sickness'.[54] It was soon reported from the British colony of Singapore that forty Hainanese 'of the domestic servant class' had left en masse for Whampoa Military Academy. The head 'bar boy' at the Grosvenor House Hotel there was caught receiving Bolshevik literature from Canton.[55] From Shamian to Saigon to Singapore, the Asian revolution was a revolt of the houseboys.

Among the new arrivals in Canton were visitors from the Soviet Union. Following a long period of negotiation, and despairing of other alliances, in late 1923 Sun Yat-sen had accepted the aid of Soviet Russia. It came in the form of the Third Communist International, or the Comintern, which had been established by Lenin in 1919 to foster a global revolution of the proletariat, which he saw as essential to the survival of the Bolshevik regime in Russia itself by breaking it free from its encirclement by 'White' reactionary forces. To this end, the Comintern sent a series of emissaries and then a large mission to China. It was the Soviet Union's largest investment in revolution outside its own borders. The mission was headed by a veteran Bolshevik, Mikhail Borodin, whose own exile from Russia had begun after the 1905 revolution and led him to Britain, the United States and Mexico, where he carried with him the aura of being a long-term associate of Lenin. Borodin threw his support behind the founding of Whampoa Military Academy and began to refashion the Nationalists as a revolutionary party. He gave fateful advice to the local Chinese communists that they should work with the Nationalist Party and form a 'bloc within' it. The Asian revolution was entering a new phase.[56]

The old Tsarist consulate on Shamian Island had been seized by the British, so on arrival in Canton in October 1923, Borodin and his staff operated from an elegant mansion in Tungshan, an enclave where the new republican officials built their villas to mirror and eclipse those of Shamian. It became the focus for numerous comings and goings. One arrival from Moscow was a young man known as Tan Malaka, originally from the Dutch possession of Sumatra. He had arrived in December 1923, and was not so impressed by the place. 'Canton's only claims to the term "city" were the post office, some electric lighting, and three main roads.' It was 'filled with shops and businesses run on feudal lines, lined by narrow, dark streets and overflowing with pedicabs and sampans. It's true,' he conceded, 'as the adage goes, that "everything new comes from Canton". Had not the social and political revolution started there?'[57] He used Canton's resources to publish tracts aimed at his countrymen in the Netherlands East Indies – including the first blueprint for a new 'Republic of Indonesia' – putting the place of publication as 'Tokyo' to confuse the Dutch police.

In the midst of these arrivals, the gaze of the French focused on one person in particular. In November 1924 a man known as 'Ly Thuy' took up residence in 'the Borodin House'. He too had come from Moscow, ostensibly as a journalist for the Soviet news agency, ROSTA, and as an occasional translator. He was mysterious about his role; he claimed to be Chinese and wrote articles under the pseudonym of a woman to avoid identification. There was a subterranean mystique about him. A young Russian woman working as a translator to the mission later recalled:

> We jokingly called him Li An-nam (Annam was the name of the French colony in Indochina). He was thirty-six years old. He was unimpressive in appearance; there was something wrong with his lungs.
>
> I can remember his small, spare figure in a white linen suit of European cut, which hung loosely on him, his attentive somewhat sad gaze and the walk of a very tired or sick man. He spoke French, English, and Cantonese well, and knew Russian. I took Vietnamese lessons from him and he willingly taught me. He was friendly towards us but reserved and he never told us what his work was and what he had done in the past. We knew nothing about him except that for his capture the French imperialists had offered a great sum of money and that the Kuomintang government had given him political asylum. He was quite at home in Borodin's house.[58]

Ly Thuy grumbled in letters to friends in Moscow that he spent most of his time, and a good deal of his money, on Canton's Vietnamese exiles. He too was to eulogize Pham Hong Thai and seek to exploit the excitement that his martyrdom had fostered among the young Vietnamese in the city. But his political message was very different from Phan Boi Chau and the earlier radicals, and even from that of Pham Hong Thai himself. He urged the young men he sought out at Whampoa and elsewhere to turn away from the ethos of individual self-sacrifice and martyrdom to embrace revolutionary theory and party discipline.[59]

The French security service, the Sûreté Générale, had a Vietnamese informer, codename 'Pinot', who worked as a photographer in Canton.

He probably led the French to the second bomb that Pham Hong Thai had failed to explode. He also alerted them to Ly Thuy. With his cover, Pinot had ample opportunity to photograph groups of Vietnamese. One such snapshot of a group outing on bicycles gave the Sûreté a likeness of a man to the left of its centre, dressed in white, wearing a dark fedora: Ly Thuy.

By early 1925 Pinot had identified Ly Thuy as a Vietnamese. On the evidence of the photographs, and of a missing part of the man's left ear, the Sûreté then traced Ly Thuy's movements back in time and across vast distances. This led them all the way to Paris itself, and to 6 villa des Gobelins, a townhouse in a small but well-appointed side street in the *13e arrondissement*. In the summer of 1919 a man matching the description of Ly Thuy had begun to lodge there with some other Vietnamese émigrés.[60]

In June 1919 a petition started to circulate in Paris among delegations to the Versailles peace conference. One of a great many into which were decanted the hopes of entire peoples, it was headed 'Demands of the Annamite People' and was signed 'Nguyen Ai Quoc'. It was received by the president of the republic, by the US president, Woodrow Wilson, and other diplomatic missions, and by August it had reached the streets of Hanoi. It seemed clear that Nguyen Ai Quoc – 'Nguyen the Patriot' – was a pseudonym, a Vietnamese Marianne or John Bull.[61] But in the coming weeks and months, Nguyen Ai Quoc began to take a more solid form as the name was used to lobby various delegations and newspapers across Paris.

The Sûreté sent its Vietnamese agents in Paris to eavesdrop on conversations, open mail, in order to uncover Nguyen Ai Quoc's origins. The man came from a floating world that seemed to stretch across the Indian and Atlantic Oceans. There were traces of him in the United States and in England. They followed him across Paris to public meetings, newspaper offices, libraries, cafés and lodging-house bedrooms. Then, in mid-1923, they lost him. Over the coming months and years, the French authorities continued to search for him. They never wavered in their belief that he was important in some way. This surveillance and notoriety was the making of Nguyen Ai Quoc. The police of other imperial powers were enlisted to follow the man's every move for the next fifty years as he roamed across an imperial underground in which the fate of Asia was ultimately decided.

In late 1923 there was another photograph, this time taken in Moscow. This too passed through the hands of the police of all the imperial powers. In its centre was Grigory Zinoviev, the leader of the Comintern. Seated on Zinoviev's right in the photograph was the veteran Japanese anarchist and socialist Sen Katayama. Then, next to him, on the end of the front row, was Nguyen Ai Quoc, in the improvised uniform of a commissar of some kind. Behind him, third from the left, staring directly into the camera, was Tan Malaka. He had been expelled from his homeland in 1921 to the Netherlands; he too was watched by the police but had disappeared in 1922. The tall man beside him had travelled still further. He went by the name 'M. N. Roy'. His path to Moscow had begun several struggles and many identities earlier, in Bengal in 1915, and led through Southeast Asia, Japan and China to the United States. He was the first Asian recruit of Borodin, but they had originally met in Mexico City.

Nguyen Ai Quoc, Tan Malaka, M. N. Roy and others were at the heart of the greatest missionary undertaking of the modern age. In Asia nothing like it had been seen since the Jesuits attempted the conversion of India, China and Japan in the sixteenth century. There were few representatives of the colonial world at the first meetings of the Comintern. Lenin had looked instead to the working classes of the advanced industrial nations of western Europe to provide a lead, rather than the 'backward' peasantries of Asia. But the failure of the revolution in Germany in 1918–19 and the passivity of the working classes in Britain led Lenin to look to the east to address the failures of the west. Allies, particularly from Asia, were sought and by 1923 were found in growing numbers. As Moscow-trained communists returned to Asia, they attempted by their words and example to awaken vast societies and set them in motion. Their paths were to cross in the coming revolutionary struggle in China and throughout Asia.

There were many such pathways and trails laid by an entire generation in motion. Nguyen Ai Quoc, so far as anyone could say for sure, was born in 1890, Tan Malaka in 1897, M. N. Roy in 1887. They were among the first to travel in large numbers far beyond their own countries, to meet each other across Asia, Europe and the Americas, and to begin to explore what they had in common. Their itineraries might begin in Saigon, Sumatra or Calcutta, but they then dispersed across three oceans to Tokyo, Paris, Amsterdam, San Francisco, New York,

Berlin and Moscow, before converging again in Asia, in Canton, Shanghai or Singapore. If the iconic image of this age of travel was the modern splendour of the great ocean liners, these travellers often experienced its underside. Many of them – although not all of them and not all of the time – travelled as seamen, labourers, servants, entertainers, students and, most often, as exiles. They tended to travel light, often under false names and nationalities, with banned literature, illicit currency or encoded messages hidden in their luggage. They experienced a world of connections, but also a world upside down: the underbelly of the great port cities of empire where they found they were able more freely to organize and act. The sites of their struggles were the waterfront, the lodging house, the coffee shop, the clandestine printing press in the back alley.[62] They made these places centres of global awareness, and their experience of a secret underworld of empire helped shape a spectrum of radical ideas – about class and national identity, the position of women, the function of art and literature, the history of the future.

This was a time when local nationalisms were still nascent, and when the political future of the colonial world seemed uniquely open. Many of these men and women believed that the solidarities they made – born from a shared history of oppression and exploitation, and of negotiation of borders and exclusion – would prevail over the narrowness of nations and usher in a common utopian destiny. Although many were loyal disciples of Lenin and Stalin, they moulded Marxist-Leninist doctrine to Asian realities in innovative ways. And when it was unyielding, they often broke with it: such ideas were a method, and not an iron dogma. A new generation of intellectuals sought to weave together seemingly irreconcilable doctrines – anarchism, nationalism, communism, even religious revival – in the name of unity and in opposition to western imperialism. They shared a central dilemma as to how far violence could be employed for political ends and what arguments might legitimize its use. They shared as well a conviction that Asia was to lead the struggles for human freedom from subjugation and impoverishment: what Tan Malaka was to call '100 per cent independence'. He was also to give the future a name: 'Aslia' – a new unity within a world order remade. This was just one of many such visions.

The itineraries of these dangerous men and women converged repeatedly in some of the most monumental events of the twentieth century as seen from the west: the two world wars and the rise of communism. But they often experienced this history through a very different lens, a different sense of time and place, and as a different kind of story altogether: that of a contest between western empires and their most dedicated opponents, fought across the globe by a generation whose intertwined lives gave their experience a unity. Theirs were some of the first truly global lives of modern times, and their ideas were distinctive in the extent to which they were forged by the experience of global travel and exile. Many would not live to see the freedoms for which they fought; they would perish or fall by the wayside. Those who survived the tempests would witness a narrower nationalism prevail, a freedom far short of '100 per cent independence', and their footprints washed away. Yet, in many ways, they were pathfinders for a world without empire and for an Asian future.

Perhaps the French colonial officials who followed the traces of Nguyen Ai Quoc, alias Ly Thuy, alias Li Annam, had a vague premonition of this, of lurking menace and coming nemesis. All empires were prey to fears of overreach, decline and fall, and each had its inner demons. The lines the French police traced on their maps in 1919 and 1924 led back to their colony of Indochina and to the very moment of imperial fulfilment.

The voyage to the east: Phan Boi Chau, Prince Cuong De and Phan Chu Trinh in Japan, 1906.

I

In Search of a Lost Country
1905

A SWAN ESCAPED FROM ITS CAGE

On 23 February 1905 three men left the port of Haiphong, in northern Vietnam, to cross the Gulf of Tonkin. It was a short journey between empires, from French Indochina to Qing China, but for these men it was a voyage into a new epoch.

They left after dark, on a western steamer, dressed as itinerant merchants, or to at least pass as such to Frenchmen. Two of the travellers were of the mandarin class. The third was harder to place: a thick-set man in his early forties who had followed the sea between Vietnam, China and Japan, and clearly 'had seen much of the world and undergone many trying experiences'. He acted as their guide.[1]

The nearest crossing point into China was the bridge at the town of Mong Cai. But it was guarded by a French border post. For the Vietnamese, the customs and excise was perhaps the most tangible presence of the colonial order. It employed over half the European officials in Indochina, some 1,290 of them, backed by 2,000 locals and an armed militia. They were the French regime's eyes and ears in the countryside and its shock troops. The Vietnamese saw them as little more than bandits; they avoided them if ever they could, and, where they could not, confronted them with insults and blows.[2] The three travellers therefore quietly dropped off the steamer before Mong Cai, no longer under western eyes.

The Gulf of Tonkin was ringed by a mountainous hinterland that had kept states at bay for centuries and propelled human activity towards the sea. Its deep bays, hidden coves and constellations of limestone karsts, rising sheer from the waters, sheltered independent local communities and pirate brotherhoods, who were the nearest thing to a government.[3] The waters were a gateway to the long littoral of continental Asia which connected the river systems that opened up its interior and were its natural thoroughfares. The sea itself was a kind of 'vast connecting river' that stretched southwards along the coast of Vietnam into the Gulf of Siam and the Malay Archipelago and beyond to India.[4] To the east and north lay the coastal cities of China, and then the edge of the Yellow Sea, where the Tsushima Strait opened into the Sea of Japan, the three travellers' ultimate destination. For its maritime peoples – who shared much sea lore – upriver streams, river basins, estuaries and seas were a single flow of human activity, an endless series of horizons.[5]

Few people journeyed the entire length of the 'connecting river'. Most experienced Asia as a series of smaller regions, each with its own customs, its own lingua franca and secret knowledge. Goods and people moved by stages, through natural crossways, that were determined by landscape and by the winds, where one region would merge into another and its population dissolve into a melange of peoples.[6] The three travellers well knew that, even in this era of railways and steamships, it was no small thing that they 'left their ancestors' tombs, parted with their wives and children, crossed the ocean, and went to the country with which they have not been familiar for these thousands of years'.[7] Now, as European conquest erected new borders, it required a huge flight of imagination to see Asia whole.

Crossing the Gulf of Tonkin in 1905 was a dangerous undertaking. China had experienced the most destructive human conflicts of the old century, and these had spilled out into the southern seas. The Taiping Rebellion – a tempest of millenarian peasant violence against the Qing authorities – had from 1850 left a death toll in the tens of millions, and propelled migrants on a similar scale across frontiers and seas.[8] The main power in the Vietnamese borderlands was a breakaway group from these struggles, a bandit army known as the 'Black Flags' which led the resistance to the French conquest of north Vietnam.[9]

The French justified their intervention in terms of the pacification of this borderland. But the peace of western colonialism often merely added a new layer of violence to older forms, albeit one more bureaucratic and self-righteous.[10] The French conquest stemmed, but did not still, the constant flow of refugees and clandestine trade, not least in human souls: young women and children for the wealthy households of southern China or for the 'flower boats' of Canton. It was said that a young child bought for one piaster in Vietnam could fetch between 100 and 200 silver dollars in Hong Kong.[11] The French navy tried to intercept the junks that carried them, but there were cases of traffickers throwing women and children overboard as patrol boats approached to inspect. They could absorb the losses: the human trade was even more profitable than opium.[12]

The travellers' guide had fought alongside the Black Flags and knew the hidden byways of these waters. He led his companions to a fishing village, a community of Christian converts. He gave them both a crucifix to wear, to gain the villagers' acceptance, and when they sat together for a meal they blessed themselves in the Roman Catholic fashion. They were able to rent a fishing boat, and later that day to cross into Fangcheng county in China, where their guide found them shelter on a houseboat owned by an old acquaintance in the settlement of Chushan.

To stay out of sight, they needed to avoid the larger ports of the gulf and western ships and their passenger manifests. So, with a favourable wind, they used the same boat to sail to Beihai. This was the southernmost treaty port in China, and one of the smallest. Dating from 1876, it was an outpost of western extraterritorial privileges, where eight nations had a consulate, including the French. But it was well known to travellers and pirates as 'the little backdoor to China'.[13]

The leader of the three felt like 'a swan that had escaped from its cage . . . in this place there were no ears and eyes of the French!'. This was Phan Boi Chau. He was thirty-seven years of age and was stepping outside Vietnam for the first time. He poured his elation into a poem entitled 'To all comrades as I go east':

> A hero roams at large and sees man's realm.
> To posterity he will leave no shame –
> He can admire five continents with joy.
> His dreams of old are past and gone for years –
> The world begets new wonders day by day.
> These words are sent to those beyond the sea:
> Who are the ones zeal-mad and passion-drunk?[14]

From Beihai, being quite well provided with silver dollars, the pilgrims caught one of the German steamers that plied the passage to Hong

Kong. On the voyage, they established a clandestine route back to their homeland. They befriended the ship's cook, a fellow Vietnamese. Such a man knew how to hide things on board a ship, and they decided he could be trusted to smuggle letters and money.

In the freer air of the British colony of Hong Kong, with its relatively open border and its many Chinese schools and newspapers, Phan Boi Chau began to walk about in plain sight, and even to adopt the manner of a diplomatic envoy. Encouraged by the Chinese he met, he wrote to the Qing governor of nearby Canton to announce himself and to seek an audience. Was it not the case that the fates of Vietnam and China were interdependent, 'like lips and teeth'? In 'the era when the strong eats the weak's flesh', did this not demand solidarity? He waited some weeks for a reply, but none came. The servants of despotic empires, whether Qing or French, Phan Boi Chau concluded, were 'not human . . . just badgers from the same hole!'.[15]

In April 1905 the companions left Hong Kong and followed the steamer route up the coast to Shanghai. But from here larger events intervened. Two great empires, Japan and Russia, were at war; all Japanese merchant ships were requisitioned and there were no sailings. It was only on 28 May, after a Russian armada that had sailed 18,000 nautical miles from the Baltic was destroyed by a Japanese fleet off the island of Tsushima, that the party were able to cross to Japan. Their landing in Kobe was a quiet affair, and journey's end was a small guest house in Yokohama.

Phan Boi Chau spoke no word of Japanese; he was barely conversant in Chinese. His life had been lived entirely within the old imperial order of Vietnam, under the Nguyen dynasty. He was born, in 1867, into a lineage of village scholars and teachers in Nghe An province, in north-central Vietnam. His background was one of genteel poverty, from which the traditional path for betterment was through the tiers of examination for the Vietnamese imperial civil service, on the Confucian model. But now, for the first time, this future was in question.[16]

The western partition of Asia was at its final stage. The French had seized a foothold in Cochinchina, the southern territory of Vietnam, in 1861–2, on the grounds of protecting Catholic missions and with an eye to a stake in the Mekong River trade. In 1883–5, to counteract a rival British push into Upper Burma, the French extended their effective control to the north, commanding the entire seaboard of Indochina.

This necessitated a war to break the centuries-old Qing hegemony in the region. For the French, it was an opportunity to exorcise the ghost of defeat in the Prussian War of 1870–71 and the loss of Alsace-Lorraine, and to open a new field for overseas investment. But the 'Tonkin Affair' extorted a bitter price in lives, money and political reputations. It drew in around 30,000 men: veterans of earlier French imperial adventures in Algeria, Senegal and Mexico, many of them Foreign Legionnaires and men convicted by military tribunals. They were assaulted on all sides by Chinese imperial troops, the Black Flags and bandits. The French suffered 4,222 dead and wounded in fighting, and an even greater number of fatalities (5,223) from malaria, dysentery and cholera. At one point in 1885, they were losing men at a rate of twenty to twenty-five a day.[17]

In July 1885, when the fighting was all but over, a force of 1,000 soldiers was sent to the Vietnamese imperial court at Hue, under General Roussel de Courcy. He was there to present his credentials, but the expedition became a crude display of martial strength intended to disarm and humiliate the boy emperor, Ham Nghi. On the night of 4 July, led by royal officials hostile to the French, fighting erupted across the city. Thousands died, temples were desecrated and the citadel and its treasure were plundered by French troops. Tens of thousands of Vietnamese Christians were killed in retaliatory attacks launched by scholar gentry to aid the emperor as he fled Hue with his advisers. Some days later his half-brother, Dong Khanh, was raised to the throne in his stead.[18] The imperial court and bureaucracy survived as a French Protectorate, but, in the words of the visiting George Curzon, soon to be Viceroy of India, the Nguyen dynasty was reduced to 'a sort of Indian feudatory state'.[19]

Phan Boi Chau came of age at a moment when Vietnam had become a 'lost country' – a phrase that was to resonate across a generation and across Asia. This loss was deeply felt by many families in his home province. The hills of Nghe An were one of the bases from which the local gentry rallied around the fugitive emperor and his court, under the edict 'Aid the King', or *Can Vuong*, and waged a sporadic war of resistance. Nghe An gave access to the relatively safe haven of Siam, which was only two weeks away overland through Laos, across mountain paths that had been laid by traders and the wandering poor over several generations. Exiles were scattered across these hills in small camps and villages, a symbol of the possibility of escape from submission to European rule.[20]

The resistance rekindled folk memory of older patriotic struggles and fired the imagination of the young. Phan Boi Chau, then barely seventeen years old, attempted to organize his fellow students in Nghe An into an 'Army of the Examination Candidates'. This was forestalled by the arrival of French troops and quietly disbanded. It was, he later admitted, 'a childish and ludicrous patriotic game'.[21]

The French pursued the rebels across borders. The deposed emperor was captured in Laos in 1888 and sent to live out his days in distant Algeria, where in 1904 he married a daughter of the French president of the court of appeal in Algiers. The French 'pacification' of Vietnam was an undeclared war with no battles to speak of, only the spectacle of heavy columns ploughing through the countryside, burning villages, indiscriminately executing 'strays' and 'pirates' and press-ganging increasing numbers of Vietnamese as corvée labourers and auxiliary soldiers.[22] As Phan Boi Chau was to describe it, the French 'captured their wives and families, rounded up their fellow villagers, and dug up their family graves . . . One should feel pity for the dead. What crimes did they commit to justify the French violently disinterring them and chopping them up, hanging them on the city gates, of casting them into fire and water?'[23] It was only later that indiscriminate terror gave way to attempts to hold on to territory and to rule through co-opted local mandarins and village headmen. These local leaders retained a 'phantom of power' in the short term, but over time they forfeited moral standing, the sense of being the 'soul' of their community, which, as much as official status and power, was the bedrock of Confucian legitimacy. The smaller number of men who stayed aloof scorned them for their opportunism and self-interest.[24]

The memory of the rebel martyrs was kept alive in the storytelling of the villagers, and their ideals were nourished in the houses of patriotic village scholars, like Phan Boi Chau, which served as the local schools. He venerated the rebels, but he understood the depth of their failure. Tied to the care of his ailing father and his sisters, he did not leave Nghe An until the age of thirty-four, when he moved into court circles at Hue to study at the Imperial Academy. For Phan Boi Chau, scholarship now became 'a mask behind which to hide myself from people's eyes' and a means to give gravitas to his standing as a patriot.[25]

This brought him into a circle of other 'men of high purpose', who drew up a programme of 'new learning' and, in 1904, formed a Modernization Society. Phan Boi Chau flouted official censorship to read everything that was to hand. Vietnamese understandings of the west and its intellectual inheritance were absorbed principally from the 'great learning' of the Chinese-language world, with which they still shared a script, and from the writings and translations of a similar reform generation in China. Chau read books in Chinese on international politics, on the Eastern Question and on the Franco-Prussian War – anything that might illuminate the state of the world.[26]

The French seizure of Tonkin was one crest of a mighty wave of blood and steel that broke across Asia in these years. It was propelled by strategic rivalry and economic competition among the great powers. What began in Indochina, in Danang in 1858, and culminated in the creation of the Annam-Tonkin Protectorate, then struck in Mandalay in 1885, where the forces of the British Raj in India overthrew the last outpost of the kingdom of Burma. It swept down the Malay Peninsula, where, from 1874 to 1914, a constellation of nine Malay states came under British 'protection' as 'British Malaya', alongside the older trading outposts of the Straits Settlements. A vast swathe of Borneo – an area only slightly less than the land mass of Great Britain itself – was effectively in the private hands of Englishmen: the Brooke dynasty of 'white Rajahs' of Sarawak and, from 1882, a British North Borneo Company, under royal charter. Britain's Asian empire now extended from Baluchistan to the Pacific.

The Dutch overlordship of the southern archipelago radiated outwards from the settlement of Batavia on the island of Java, a foothold that dated from 1619. It was only under J. B. van Heutsz, governor-general between 1904 and 1909, that the archipelago was finally 'pacified' after some of the longest and bitterest colonial wars in Asia, particularly the struggle in Aceh, in northern Sumatra, between 1873 and 1904.[27] But the climax came in September 1906, when a Dutch force landed at Sanur beach on the island of Bali and marched on the old kingdom of Badung at Denpassar. After enduring several days of remorseless shelling, the king, his wives, children, court and retainers staged a *puputan*, or 'ending'. In a final act of defiance, they processed out of the palace in ritual array and threw themselves, singing, at the Dutch automatic weapons. 'Women opened their chests to be killed', wrote one observer, and threw golden coins at European soldiers 'as a reward for the violent death they desired from them'. To some of the young Dutchmen, this seemed like mockery. 'If the soldiers did not fire, they stabbed themselves.'[28] It was part last stand, part mass suicide. The numbers of dead were covered up at the time; over 1,000 people died, but the Balinese chroniclers trebled this number. Two years later this local apocalypse was repeated at the leading royal court of Bali, Klungkung.[29] Between 1898 and 1909, more than 200 states and chiefdoms signed a *Korte Verklaring*, or 'Short Declaration', of formal submission to the Netherlands Indies, and their myriad local coinages were supplanted by the Dutch guilder.[30] By this, Dutch paramountcy was sealed and van Heutsz was cast as the architect of a new imperial state voicing universal liberal values.

The western conquest of Asia had begun in 1498, when the Portuguese under Vasco da Gama first carried the wars against the 'Moors' into the Indian Ocean. It travelled full circle when the United States, after its acquisition of the Philippines from Spain in 1898, fought a campaign against the 'Moros', or the Muslims of the islands of the south, which dragged on until 1913. But this marked a caesura, not an ending: new fields of imperial competition were opening up in China. In Southeast Asia, Siam alone had seemingly escaped formal colonization after a resourceful programme of modernization during the reign of King Chulalongkorn from 1868 to 1910. But the kingdom could not avoid territorial concessions to the British and the French, and crippling, unequal treaties. Some among the Thai elite now saw Siam as a 'lost country' too.[31]

But how was a 'lost country' to be regained? To confront such overwhelming firepower, Phan Boi Chau concluded, would be like a child trying to fight a warrior capable of pulling the horns off wild bulls: 'How could we not be defeated?'[32] All that was left was a war of words, to recast the old system to meet new challenges. Perhaps the most compelling voice was the writer and journalist Liang Qichao, who, aged just twenty-five, was in 1898 a principal architect of one of the last major attempts by the Qing state to comprehensively revitalize itself: the Hundred Days Reform movement. After its failure, Liang wrote prolifically from exile in Japan and America. He looked beyond 'the false classics' of Confucian learning to explore the modern meanings of statehood, citizenship, freedom and truth. He broke from the worldview of China as a civilization entire in and of itself, and from a cyclical, dynastic vision of history, to see China as merely one entity within world-historical time, which progressed in linear fashion from the ancient to the medieval to the modern.[33] This allowed persuasive new comparisons to be made. 'I love Confucius,' Liang famously wrote in 1900, 'but I love the truth more. I love my elders, but I love my country more. I love my friends, but I love liberty more.'[34]

The search to recover a 'lost country' began with 'that universal response to crisis, the demand for a history to instruct the future'.[35] A new understanding of human history was gaining currency across Asia, shaped by ideas of Social Darwinism – particularly the struggle between nations for the survival of the fittest – as popularized by Herbert Spencer and others. A translation of T. H. Huxley's 1893 lecture 'On Evolution and Ethics' introduced Social Darwinism into China in 1898, and very soon after to Vietnam. For westerners, Social Darwinism fortified a sense of moral and scientific triumph, and racial hubris. Read within a 'lost country' like Vietnam, it had the force of revealed truth, exposing elemental weaknesses within Vietnamese society and history. But where the determinism of western Social Darwinism seemed to condemn weak nations to perpetual defeat, for some members of the defeated elites of Vietnam, who saw through the confusion of loss, it was a call to arms and to transform themselves into agents of historical change. In this there was an echo of the old Confucian ideal of the cultivation of the 'perfect man'. But now there were new models of conduct.[36]

One of the most discussed works of the day was a Japanese political novel from the 1880s entitled *Strange Encounters with Beautiful Women (Kaijin No Kigu)*. It was written by Shiba Shiro, who was born into a samurai family, fought on the losing side in the Meiji Restoration, but then travelled abroad and studied commerce and business in San Francisco and Philadelphia, before returning to a successful career in the new legislative assembly. Under the pen name 'Tokai Sanshi', or 'Oriental Traveller', he recounted from first-hand experience the travels of a young Japanese through the United States, Europe and Egypt, and introduced readers to a kaleidoscopic cast of contemporary revolutionaries. It was shot through with empathy for those nations that had suffered at the hands of the hegemonic powers.[37]

Vietnamese readers approached the novel through a Chinese adaption by Liang Qichao, which he began in 1898 on board the ship on which he fled China for Japan. One of Phan Boi Chau's fellow searchers for the new learning in Hue was a young man called Phan Chu Trinh. He recorded his response to *Strange Encounters with Beautiful Women* in verse:

> The scramble for survival is shaking the entire world,
> With their hearts broke, heroes and heroines meet at the Liberty Bell,
> Though his hairs already turn grey, a man of high purpose shows
>   concern for his country,
> Fashionably attired, elegant young women vow revenge on behalf of
>   their lands,
> Indignant at world affairs, they converse spiritedly,
> Indifferent to life and death, their names will go into history.[38]

Phan Chu Trinh knew such self-sacrifice at first hand. His father was a wealthy official who had perished in the Can Vuong revolt, most likely at the hands of his fellow rebels. Born in Quang Nam province in 1872, Trinh was some five years younger than Phan Boi Chau. He was quick to adopt western dress and, although he did not read French, more willing than Chau to embrace European ideals. The two men first met in Hue in early 1904, but Trinh felt that Phan Boi Chau's ideas 'did not escape from the traditional straitjacket'.[39] For Phan Chu Trinh, it was an uncomfortable truth that traditional authority was arbitrary, violent and corrupt; monarchy, 'where the laws exist for nothing', drew his most irreconcilable anger.[40] The path to reclaim the 'lost country' lay through popular sovereignty, and so the overthrow of the disempowered Vietnamese monarchy was a more urgent task even than the expulsion of the French.

But, for Phan Boi Chau, freedom from foreign domination was an overriding and unshirkable end in itself. He looked to the young Prince Cuong De, the last direct descendant of the founder of the ruling Nguyen dynasty, Gia Long, as a figurehead for the coming struggle. As the 'moral journeys' of Phan Boi Chau and Phan Chu Trinh crossed and diverged over the coming years, they personified the predicament of a generation. One path led to an open pursuit of reforming goals and, except in its intensity and temper, was not so dissimilar from that of those who chose to cooperate with the French.[41] The other was embarked upon in secret and nourished by a 1,000-year-old tradition of armed challenge to aggressors.[42]

SHARING THE SAME SICKNESS

In 1905 all paths seemed to lead to Japan. The remaking of the Japanese imperial order following the Meiji Restoration of 1868 exerted a fascination on restless minds across Asia. For Indian maharajahs, Malay sultans and Thai kings, Japan was a model for monarchical revival in the face of western encroachment. For critics of royal power, Japan was also an example of successful westernization and liberal constitutional reform. The Ottoman reformer from Egypt, Mustafa Kamil, published in 1905 an account of Japan without ever having set foot there. This book was vastly popular across the Arab world, and soon circulated in translation in the Malay Archipelago. Through it, the Arabic word *watan*, or 'nation' – as an achievement of unity and mutual purpose – entered political discourse in Southeast Asia.[43] As Phan Boi Chau put it, 'When the French came we knew nothing but France.'[44] But now, across Asia, peoples of different civilizations and faiths no longer examined themselves solely in the distorting mirror of the west.

More than any other non-western power, Japan was now a key reference point within new sets of global comparisons. Above all, at a time when martial ascendency had become the measure of the technical and moral supremacy of western civilization, Japan called this fundamentally into question. Japan's victory over China in the Sino-Japanese War in 1895, and its subsequent acquisition of the island of Taiwan, had signalled its imperial ambitions in East Asia. The euphoria of the Japanese victories against the Russian navy at Port Arthur in February 1904 and at Tsushima in May 1905 transformed a regional phenomenon into a global turning point. Where the unity and common purpose of the west had earlier seemed to cow Asian countries, Japan's victory reversed this perspective. To the Japanese, Russia was now their 'other': a country internally divided, 'backward' against most measures, and thus predestined to defeat. With this came an increasingly militant sense of Japan's destiny as 'the light of Asia', and of an Asian future for humankind.[45]

Phan Boi Chau looked not merely to Japan's inspiration but to the possibility of its active assistance. Throughout 1904, he and his friends collected funds and recruited 'secret friends' to house emissaries and transport money across Vietnam. Late that year, Chau left the Imperial Academy in Hue on the grounds of returning home to Nghe An. Once there, he restored his parents' grave and told neighbours he was return-ing to the academy. However, his aim was to vanish entirely from sight and travel to Japan. He gave his wife of fifteen years, Thai Thi Huyen, a letter of divorce, already signed by himself and a witness. This was perhaps to spare her harassment by the French authorities. He left behind their child and his two children by a secondary wife. Thai Thi Huyen's only recorded comment was: 'You are setting out to catch a tiger; the tiger has not been caught yet, but so many people have already heard what you are up to. Why is that?'[46] The answer was that Chau saw himself as the pathfinder for a larger movement of young Vietnam-ese: the *Dong-du*, or 'Journey to the East'.[47]

Pilgrims from myriad nations had already made a similar leap of faith. The gradual opening of the Trans-Siberian Railway and, from 1906, the Chinese Eastern Railway – which dipped from just east of Chita through Manchuria to Harbin and Vladivostok, branching south to Shenyang and the port of Dalian on the Yellow Sea – was a cause of friction between Russia, Japan and China. But it opened new pathways east for the peoples of Central Asia under Tsarist rule, from Persia and from Ottoman lands. It was the old Silk Road in reverse. Japan became a first haven for exiles from tumultuous events elsewhere in Eurasia. They came even from Tsarist Russia itself; or, closer to hand, from Qing China in the aftermath of the failed Hundred Days reforms in 1898; or, in the same year, from the Philippines, fleeing Asia's first anti-colonial revolution, against Spain. Central to the idea of Japan as the heart of the new Asia was its situation as a place of transit for Chinese, Japanese, Indians and Filipinos on the longer journey further east across the Pacific Ocean, to the islands of Fiji and Hawaii, and to the Americas and the Caribbean.

In 1896 there were thirteen Chinese students in Japan; by 1904 there were 1,300, and 8,000 by 1905. More than three-quarters of Chinese government scholars overseas travelled in this direction, women as well as men. From 1899, early reformers set up *Datong*, Sino-Japanese or pan-Asian 'unity' schools, which explored a new curriculum and in which, at the end of the founding school's first year, forty of the 110 students were women. In 1907 there were around 100 Chinese women students in Japan, many travelling unaccompanied; most enrolled in the model Practical Women's School in Tokyo, established by the Japanese educator and pan-Asian idealist Shimoda Utako. It was one of the clearest examples of cooperation, albeit on unequal terms – Shimoda insisted that her Chinese students wear kimonos and learn the Japanese language – and graduates pledged themselves to the great causes of educational renewal and women's progress in China, where they had an impact disproportionate to their numbers.[48] The number of students from British India in Japan – almost exclusively men – grew from only fifteen in 1903 to fifty-four in 1906 and more than 100 by 1910, many studying sciences at Tokyo University or Tokyo Higher Technology School.[49] Others came to obtain direct experience of Japanese industrial processes. Bombay and Madras silk importers set up shop in Kobe and elsewhere. The foreign students were concentrated in the Kanda district of Tokyo, where many of the private higher-education institutions and used bookstores were to be found, and here they embraced modern times. The room over the bookshop in the Chinese Students' Union echoed to the steps of ballroom dance practice.

It was here that Asian intellectuals first came to know each other, and to learn to speak to each other. Within five years of his first arrival in 1898, Liang Qichao had founded three literary journals. From an apartment above a print shop in Yokohama, and then a beach villa in Suma, he wrote under the literary pseudonym of *Ying bing*, the 'Ice Drinker', a classical allusion to cool, purposeful reflection in the heat and anxiety of the age. His exile was real and perilous – in effect, the Qing had placed a price upon his head – but it had its consolations. Unlike most émigrés, he had his wife and children with him. He had comfortable funding from a Japanese benefactor and was able to travel widely. His writing and translations were a beacon for younger men. On one estimate, in the first two decades of the twentieth century, around 80 per cent of translations of western literature into Chinese came from retranslations of earlier Japanese versions. Between 1902 and 1907, the number of Chinese literary translations exceeded original works in Japanese, and after the Meiji Restoration perhaps the most common authors translated into Japanese were Russian.[50] Japan became a prism through which ideas were refracted around Asia and beyond, crossing language worlds in increasingly complex ways.

One of Liang's dictums to achieve a more universal appeal was that young students should cast off the old literati's disdain for popular forms. 'If we are to renovate the people, we must begin by renovating fiction.'[51] It was in Liang's literary journals that texts such as *Strange Encounters with Beautiful Women* were read in serial form by Phan Chu Trinh and others in Vietnam and elsewhere. One prolific contributor was a native of Zhejiang province called Zhou Shuren. His rite of passage was typical. Some months after arriving in Japan in 1902, he cut off his queue, the symbol of submission to the Qing – an event that may have been prompted by convenience for his martial-arts training – which he celebrated with a photograph to send home. Thereafter, he sported a moustache to set off his military-style Japanese school uniform. He read Byron, Nietzsche and later many of the Russians in Japanese translation, and began to publish his own stories in the student magazines that circulated in Japan. His first major translation, from a Japanese rendering, was of Jules Verne's *From the Earth to the Moon* in 1903 (he later produced a similar version of *Journey to the Centre of the Earth*). His goal, he said, was scientific education in an entertaining form.[52]

New ideas often germinated through a style of translation that Zhou Shuren was later to call 'grabbism', borrowing without deference. It was an article of faith that words and ideas could be commandeered from the west without falling prey to the political and cultural assumptions embedded within them.[53] There was a compulsive eclecticism to this, encompassing aesthetic, high modernist visions, as well as pulp fictions of passion and intrigue. English and French detective novels were rendered into Japanese from the late 1880s. In a syndicated world, Japan was a voracious consumer of the *roman-feuilleton*, both home-grown and imported. By the turn of the twentieth century, Verne's futurism and the forensic verve of Conan Doyle's Sherlock Holmes – both heavily mediated by their translators – were among the most travelled and popular fiction of the day.[54] They circulated among Chinese populations in Southeast Asia, where they entered other Asian languages, such as Malay, the lingua franca of the archipelago.[55] The detective became a talismanic figure for this age of dissimulation. These emerging literary genres, in playful translation, had the effect of loosening time and distance, so that Chinese and Japanese intellectuals saw themselves as every bit as much of the global avant-garde as their European counterparts.[56]

As he travelled east, Phan Boi Chau entered this transcendent world of ideas. He read Liang Qichao's writings on his journey along the China coast. He acquired his address through a chance meeting on the ship from Hong Kong to Shanghai with a Chinese student returning home from the United States. One of his first acts on establishing himself in Yokohama was to write to tell Liang that they were destined to meet. 'When we are born we cry out one word and we begin to know and understand each other. But after studying books for ten years we become like members of a family related through marriage.'[57] When he visited Liang, they had no spoken language in common, but shared knowledge of the ideograms of classical Chinese script, and conversed for several hours through 'brushtalk', or calligraphy, a medium of asking questions and exchanging ideas across Asia from the earliest times.[58] Liang gave Chau a copy of his Chinese-language biography of Giuseppe Mazzini, the Italian patriot whose life and struggle was to move Asian nationalists above all others. Through Mazzini, Chau began to discern that love of country, or patriotism (ai-quoc), could be stronger than loyalty to kings and emperors.[59] But both Liang and Chau still ultimately looked to emperors, and not to the sovereignty of the people, for national redemption.

Liang's advice fixed the fate of the 'Journey to the East'. Revolt now against the French, Liang argued, was futile. He urged Phan Boi Chau to look to his country's own resources, to train his people and prime an organization within Indochina. In June 1905 Liang took Phan Boi Chau to tea with the leading Japanese patrons of the Asian nationalists in Tokyo, including Count Okuma Shigenobu, one of the foremost proponents of Meiji fiscal reform and constitutionalism, and the founder of Waseda University. It was Chau's first formal meeting with the Japanese. He was received with polite condescension. His Japanese hosts confirmed that the principal aspiration of the Vietnamese, active Japanese military support for an uprising, could not be met. Chau impressed upon them the depth of his patriotism, but in Japan he was one supplicant among many and the message he received – to 'rally the intellectuals and send them abroad' – seemed like a stock response. He left humiliated by how late the Vietnamese had come to modernization, and to Japan.[60]

From this moment, the focus of Chau's activities became the recruiting and financing of students for Japan. He poured his resolve into a pamphlet called *Viet-Nam Vong Quoc Su, History of the Loss of Vietnam* (1905). He sketched the history of Vietnamese patriotism, he attacked the façade of French protection, and the rule of 'servile' mandarins – 'immoral good-for-nothing thugs' – and appealed directly to the 'common people' by cataloguing unpopular French laws and taxes. Written in plain, direct language, and published by Liang's press, it became a catechism for the 'Journey to the East'.[61] Armed with copies of it, Chau retraced his journey back via Hong Kong to Vietnam to recruit young 'men of high purpose' from all three regions of the country. Not all of those who had originally sent him abroad were convinced by his approach. The cost was forbidding, and it was guns they wanted. But young men came forward. The first to arrive, Luong Ngoc Quyen, was the son of a reform-minded mandarin, who abandoned his own studies and turned up alone, unannounced and with only three piasters in his pocket.[62]

In early 1906 the morale of the Vietnamese in Japan was lifted by the arrival of Prince Cuong De. The French kept the royal family within Vietnam under a close watch, going so far, as Phan Boi Chau put it, as to 'check their names on the royal family tree two or three times a month, taking a roll call'. But Prince Cuong De's clandestine flight from Hue caught them unawares.[63] With his arrival in Yokohama, the Vietnamese became a more visible community, in a rented two-storey house. When Phan Boi Chau travelled to Canton to collect the prince, he was reunited there with Phan Chu Trinh, who had made the decision to travel to and learn from Japan. He too was forced to leave Vietnam in disguise, in the tattered robe and torn shoes of a ship's cook. He made it clear that he was in Japan merely as an observer. The two men resumed their dialogue over forty intense days, but their visions did not converge. The presence of Prince Cuong De in Japan reaffirmed Phan Boi Chau's commitment to monarchy, not least because it seemed to lend the Vietnamese a degree of diplomatic legitimacy as representatives of a country and not vagabonds. However, the young prince was treated by the Japanese not as a royal pretender but as a normal student, and not a particularly diligent one at that.[64] Studio photographs of Phan Boi Chau, Phan Chu Trinh and the prince in Tokyo in modern dress circulated back in Vietnam and announced their whereabouts to the French police.

For many exiles and students in Japan, the idea of 'Asia' became something more than an amorphous geographical concept. They became aware of their common experience of 'loss of country', of 'sharing the same sickness'. Yet there was no consensus as to what this might betoken. 'Pan-Asian' ideas tended to universalize their advocates' own religious or civilizational standpoint. For one of its most sublime praise-singers, the Bengali poet and sage Rabindranath Tagore, the unity of Asian civilization was based upon the ancient spiritual geography of an extended Indian Ocean world, a 'Greater India' that had less resonance the further it travelled east and into the archipelago.[65] Muslim intellectuals looked to extend the universalism of the *dar al-Islam* across Asia, from Morocco to the Moluccas. In 1889 the Ottoman Sultan Abdulhamid II – in a projection of his own influence as Caliph in the wider Islamic world – sent the *Ertugrul*, an antiquated warship, on a mission to the east. Its eleven-month odyssey across the Indian Ocean and along the Indochinese and China coast provided vivid images of the crew at prayer in mosques in colonial ports and climaxed in the high dignity of its reception in Japan. When in September 1890 the *Ertugrul* was shipwrecked off the coast of Wakayama prefecture with the loss of some 587 men, a wave of humanitarian sentiment in Japan led to the return of the seventy survivors to Istanbul in two Japanese warships. This sealed a symbolic bond between these two 'sentinels' at either end of the Eurasian land mass. Within this mutual fascination, there was a temptation for each to exoticize the other and an undercurrent of imperial competition. But the stream of Muslim travellers, many refugees from both old and new empires, from Russian Central Asia, Persia, British-occupied Egypt and India, seemed to suggest the possibility of a concerted response to the west.[66]

One of the key movers was Maulavi Barakatullah, a travelling scholar from the Indian princely state of Bhopal, who gained prominence as a proselytizer and supporter of the Ottoman Caliphate during stays in London and at the Liverpool mosque. He was active in Muslim affairs in New York, and then became a teacher of Urdu at Tokyo University where, from 1909, with a Japanese convert, Hasan Hatono Uho, he established an English-language journal called *Islamic Fraternity* that carried this message directly to Muslims in island Southeast Asia and elsewhere. It was promptly banned in India, and its publication quietly suppressed by the Japanese government after British pressure.[67] Privately, Japanese converts to Islam saw their faith as part of their duty to the emperor to extend Japan's historic mission in Asia. The Japanese who acted as patrons and publicists of the pan-Asian movement struggled to conceal their patriotic euphoria. Perhaps the most trenchant statement of Asia-as-one, certainly the most widely read in its English translation, Okakura Kakuzo's *The Ideals of the East* (1903), made clear its vision of cultural and racial hierarchy, with Japan at its apex.[68]

But if 'Asia' achieved no common transcendent meaning, there was still something perhaps more provisional to be drawn from this: a sense of Asia as a field for concerted action.[69] Patriots voiced their longing in similar phrasing and shared similar models for struggle. In mid-April 1907 about twenty Indian students in Tokyo invited Chinese students and leading Japanese – including Okuma Shigenobu – to a celebration of the seventeenth-century rebel Shivaji, a figure who had become laden with patriotic meaning. The event was widely reported in the Chinese press in Japan, which saw in Shivaji an analogy with the historic resistance of the Han people to Manchu rule. The attendees also lacerated Okuma for his moderate tone towards the British. With support from Japanese and Indian industrialists, including the Tata family of Parsi businessmen from Bombay whose interests had spread east, a Sino-Indian 'Asian Solidarity Society' was founded. At a second meeting, at a Unitarian chapel in the Kudanshita neighbourhood of Tokyo, Filipinos and Vietnamese – including Phan Boi Chau – attended and it expanded into an Asian Solidarity Association.[70] With this, it evinced a more plural understanding of Asia's shared history and culture, and embraced José Rizal, a Filipino writer, social thinker and national martyr in the resistance to Spanish rule, as the 'quintessential patriot' of the new Asian future. This was a reflection of the impact that the heroic violence of the Philippine revolution of 1898 had across Asia, carried by its own exiles. The association's stated goals, voiced in its lingua franca of classical Chinese and English, centred on 'organising all the patriots in Asia, all the peoples who have lost their countries, into one party and waiting for the time of simultaneous revolution'.[71] Along with many other writings of the moment, Phan Boi Chau's pamphlets – which circulated ever more widely in Vietnam – began to pit the 'yellow race' against the 'white race'.[72]

The Asian Solidarity Association was a shot in the dark. It was a series of meetings whose attendees were, in many cases, strangers to each other. They pledged 'to stand together like trees of the forest', but afterwards it was not clear who had been present, whom they spoke for and who would speak for the cause in the future. However, it alarmed the British enough that they entered a formal protest, the first of many, and the Japanese police stepped up their watch on exiles and dissidents.[73] For this reason, the Asian Solidarity Association also marked the beginning of the end of the émigrés' dependence on Japan.

Phan Boi Chau now turned to the Chinese for aid. In early 1906 he had a series of meetings with one of the leading figures in exile, Sun Yat-sen. Sun was sojourning in Japan while he planned his own revolutionary strategy. He too looked to recruit support from the students, particularly those from his home province of Guangdong, such as the men who were to become his two closest allies, Hu Hanmin and Wang Jingwei. His willingness to accept material support from Japanese supporters, and his overbearing, dictatorial behaviour, created tensions within the revolutionary alliance that had emerged among the Chinese students in Japan.[74] To Phan Boi Chau too, an alliance with Sun could never be an alliance of equals. Chau felt that his brush conversations with Sun were 'like groping in the dark, but not grasping the essentials'.[75] Sun offered Vietnam an imbalanced and wholly theoretical alliance. 'Asia' was a long-term speculative investment made on the haziest of understandings.

Japan could itself be a disillusioning experience. By the end of 1906 there were only around twenty Vietnamese students in the country. It was not always clear to them what they were doing there, and they struggled to connect with Japanese society. Phan Boi Chau wrote of the many kindnesses of strangers, the honesty of rickshaw men and train conductors, but of few steady friendships. Students did not initially learn the Japanese language: there were no institutions that could teach it to them. Their everyday communication with their hosts was through scribbled characters in their notebooks. It took a great deal of negotiation and expense to get them enrolled in Japanese academies. In the early months of their stay, they were reliant on gifts and loans from the wealthier Chinese.[76] Unlike the Chinese or Indians, the Vietnamese had no overseas business community to draw upon.

In these conditions, it was remarkable how many young men did come forward, more than half of them from the wealthier regions of

Cochinchina in the south. They were supported by patriotic business-men there, such as the hotelier and soap manufacturer Gilbert Chieu, who sent his own son. This took numbers by the end of 1907 to around 100. By the middle of 1908 the number of students peaked at around 200, but the well was running dry.[77] For his part, Cuong De began to assert his royal status, requiring new Vietnamese arrivals to come before him in ceremonial dress and to prostrate themselves in the trad-itional manner. His ascendency, particularly among the new arrivals from Cochinchina, and his increasing independence, began to antagon-ize Phan Boi Chau.[78] It sharpened the question of how far the expulsion of the Europeans and a restoration of royal rule would address Viet-nam's underlying weaknesses. Regional differences were deep, personal relationships strained and the Japanese winters cold. 'Loss of country' turned to homesickness.

The experience of the Chinese, too, was ambivalent. The student and translator Zhou Shuren came to despise the frivolity of student life in Tokyo and in 1904 decided to study medicine in the northern city of Sendai. He was the first Chinese person to do so and was painfully con-spicuous there. Sendai was a military city; old animosities from the time of the Sino-Japanese War of 1894–5 hung in the air, and he was on occasion singled out for racial abuse. The Russo-Japanese War of 1904–5, which many Chinese students had supported, stoked Japanese nationalist fervour on the streets and in the lecture halls. The custom after lectures was to watch lantern slides of news events. On one such occasion in 1905, a picture was shown of a Chinese about to be beheaded by Japanese soldiers as a Russian spy. Another Chinese could be seen watching the spectacle. The image was greeted by triumphant shouts of 'Banzai!' from Zhou Shuren's fellow students. He was appalled at the depiction of China as a 'weak and backward country' whose popu-lace 'can only serve to be made examples of, or to witness such futile spectacles'. It was not enough to cure the health of his people; he needed to 'change their spirit'. He quit medical school – or failed at it, some said – and soon left Japan. In such a hothouse, the choices one made, the personal crises one experienced, all carried a symbolic, even polit-ical, meaning, and were replayed in many ways: as memory, in fiction and in the testimony of others.[79]

At the very hour of Asia's re-emergence in world history, the mood within Japan changed. The liberalism of the early Meiji era was fading.

Its democracy was now dominated by powerful oligarchs; young Japanese radicals were angered by increasing 'Prussianization' and mourned a revolution unfulfilled. Japan had succumbed to what the radical journalist Kotoku Denjiro (under the pen name 'Kotoku Shusui') had dubbed, in the title of a book, 'the monster of the twentieth century': imperialism.[80] Japan sought equality in her relations with the great powers, and parity in the privileges enjoyed by the Europeans in China under the treaty port system. Above all, Japan aspired to be an empire among empires. Kotoku likened it to a plague 'which indiscriminately infects the humble and the mighty'. 'Japanese of all classes,' he wrote, 'burn with fever to join the race for empire, like a wild horse suddenly freed from its harness.'[81]

After the peace of 1905, Japan wrested the railway zone in Dalian, the principal seaport of northeast China, from Russia. Chinese students became more politicized, more critical of Japanese imperialism, and the authorities tried to curb their activities. In November 1905 there was a students' strike, led by members of the reformist Practical Women's School, during which one student activist threw himself into the sea. Some 2,000 Chinese students left Japan in protest.[82] In the same year, of the 16,530 foreign nationals who entered Japan, 1,944 of them were from Korea, and they played an important role in the émigré life of Tokyo and Yokohama.[83] In 1907 Gojong of Korea, Emperor Gwangmu, the last King of Joseon and first Emperor of Korea, was deposed, and in 1910 Korea became a colony of the Japanese empire. Koreans led protests in 1907 and 1908 at the presence of Japanese in the Asian Solidarity Association and attempted to raise the question of Japanese imperialism at international meetings.[84] A companion of Phan Boi Chau recorded a conversation with a Korean friend. 'Our two countries differ from one another as to their language, their clothing, and yet they have received the same name: they are both called "lost countries".'[85]

Just a few years earlier, in 1902, Japan had formed an alliance with Britain in East Asia, and now events were drawing her closer to France. A series of sensationalist reports in the *Écho de Paris* in January 1905, headlined 'The Yellow Peril', claimed that Japan planned to use Taiwan, now also a colony of Japan, as a base to attack the French in Indochina. By a strange osmosis of animosity and opportunism, Japan responded by strengthening ties with France. A Franco-Japanese Treaty was signed in 1907, and the French immediately used it to put pressure on Japan's Vietnamese émigrés.[86] As the Governor-General of Indochina explained it to the minister of the colonies in Paris in July 1908, the people of Vietnam could not be indifferent 'to the events occurring in this theatre of nations' when their country, because of its long border with Siam, rail links to China and sea lanes to the ports of China, Japan and Southeast Asia, lay in the middle of 'the great Far Eastern highway'.[87]

The French gathered information on the Vietnamese émigré students at home, and their spies caught up with them in Japan. In 1906 laws were passed in Vietnam to punish the fathers and elder siblings of those who had illegally left the country. In Japan, students received desperate letters from home, sometimes written with French assistance, and they were ordered by the Japanese authorities to write to their families in turn. Many of the recipients of these letters in Vietnam were arrested. The students were then advised by Japanese supporters to disband and disperse. There was hope that if they did so they might be able to remain, but the Japanese and French authorities were now cooperating closely. This drove one student to suicide in a small temple in the Koishikawa district of Tokyo. Others went underground, but most asked to return home and an expensive repatriation exercise began. By early 1909 only twenty students remained. In March, Phan Boi Chau was himself expelled and his publications were burned in front of the French consulate.[88] He fled, penniless, to China. The 'Journey to the East', as a collective endeavour, was at an end.

THE DEVIL'S SNARE

On his return visit to Vietnam to recruit students in 1905, Phan Boi Chau made a brief trip back to his home province of Nghe An. It seems that he visited an old friend, Nguyen Sinh Sac, a mandarin of the second rank a few years younger than him but of similar reforming views, who had followed a parallel path, choosing to make his way by teaching in his home village, Kim Lien. Sac had two sons and a daughter, the eldest child, who was a supporter of the movement like her brothers; it was suspected in their village that Phan Boi Chau had an unexpressed yen for her.[89] Phan Boi Chau asked the two sons to join the 'Journey to the East'. Either the boys rejected this offer, or their father did so on their behalf. But, by this time, wider horizons were shaping the minds of young Vietnamese men whether they stirred from their villages or not.

Sac's younger son was most probably born in Kim Lien in May 1890. Following Vietnamese custom, he was given a formal name on reaching adolescence: Nguyen Tat Thanh, 'He who will succeed'. In 1905, with his father's support, he entered the new French education system, at its most elementary level, in the provincial capital. In 1906 Sac took a minor position in the Board of Rites in Hue, which oversaw court ceremonial and the education system, and by late 1907 both his sons were attending the most prestigious French-Vietnamese school in Annam. Both were formally reprimanded by their teachers for their challenges to authority, and Thanh cut his hair short in the seditious modern style.[90]

This was, as Phan Boi Chau termed it, 'an epoch of transition'.[91] The imperial order in Asia was now a bewildering patchwork of multiple jurisdictions and overlapping sovereignties, directly ruled colonies of trade and settlement, protected states and smaller concessions and treaty ports. The French drew Annam, Tonkin and Cochinchina, plus the kingdom of Cambodia and the principalities of Laos – all with their hundreds of years of independent history – into a new political entity: 'French Indochina'. Small armies of officials descended in a fury of scientific mapping and gazetting, registering people and assessing land and revenue: the sun never set on the empire of the theodolite. Over a short period of time, colonial territories became a nexus of post offices, telegraph relays and inter-city telephony. By 1911 a quarter of the government budget in Indochina was spent on the salaries of 5,683 Europeans.[92]

However, the local forms of authority the Europeans tended to work through – whether mandarins, village headmen, Chinese tax-farmers and Indian clerks, or Malay sultans and Vietnamese emperors – were often less than modern. The impact of imperial rule was felt most acutely in the incompleteness rather than in the fullness of its order. In Indochina and elsewhere, the new plantations and mines were half-governed places where European managers and their native overseers were proxies for colonial law; they were heavily armed and sometimes murderous. On the new rubber estates in the 'grey lands' surrounding

Saigon – comprising some fifty-one plantations and 2 million trees by 1913 – European planters meted out their own corporal punishment and ran their own prisons.[93] White violence across colonial Asia often undermined the very rule of law from which the west claimed its legitimacy.[94] But whatever the internal contradictions, to those excluded by colonial rule it seemed a cohesive, unbreachable edifice. Even where the Europeans were dependent on traditional authority, the demands of power seemed more undiscriminating, more unrelenting and less negotiable than before. Across lands which had previously been relatively open to human mobility, an old and tested way of escaping tyranny was to avoid it, to move beyond its reach. It was now much harder to do so.[95]

This new quotient of power was felt directly across Vietnam through a host of everyday imposts, indignities and oppressions. In 1897 the new governor-general, Paul Doumer – a member of the Radical Party and later President of the Third Republic – arrived with a mandate from home to make empire pay. He embarked on a programme of great public works – roads, wharves and railways – to open up Indochina to French investment. To meet the expense, he turned to corvée labour and to other 'beasts of burden', such as taxes on salt, opium and alcohol. A state monopoly of rice liquor – a traditional staple of the Vietnamese diet – which was projected to raise 15 per cent of state revenue, cut to the core of local feeling. Like much colonial policy, it was launched in the name of science and efficiency; the intention was to oust local production with an industrialized state monopoly of liquor of a purer distillation. This was developed by a disciple of Louis Pasteur who was later a co-inventor of the tuberculosis vaccine, BCG. It symbolized the intimate alliance between French business and colonial power. But the new liquor was devoid of the subtle flavour of the local specialities. It was not only an affront to local palates, it was also seen to undermine social life, ritual celebrations and, being much stronger, public health. The new monopoly was challenged by rampant bootlegging and further violence against customs officials. In the ensuing battle of wills, the French responded with the collective punishment of entire villages. Although, for the Vietnamese elite of the towns, the drink of choice was now imported French wine, rice alcohol gave them a cause to connect with rural feeling. In the writings of Phan Boi Chau and others, the colonial liquor monopoly became an enduring symbol of oppression and of failed European 'modernization'.[96]

But the imperial project demanded that the Vietnamese engage with its values. On his return from Japan, taking advantage of a liberal interlude in French policy, Phan Chu Trinh took the lead in establishing a Free School movement, inspired by the national academies he had visited in Japan. A school was established in Hanoi, financed from the sale of a store owned by the wife of the principal. It employed traditional forms of learning but adopted a new medium for them: Vietnamese in romanized script, or *quoc ngu*. This had been pioneered by Vietnamese Catholics from as early as the seventeenth century, and rapidly gained adherents among those committed to European learning. It was a break with the use of classical Chinese and of Chinese characters, and lamented for this reason by some, but it lent itself more easily to mass literacy and to dissemination in print.[97] The school promoted the vitality of modern commerce – the literati were encouraged to break with old systems of status and to take to trade – and the power of science. Its teachers and textbooks developed the ethos that 'society' (*xa hoi*: a term itself transposed into Vietnamese from Japan, via Chinese) was based on struggle. It was built by a collective, a people, by themselves, and had to be strong to compete and survive.[98] The accession of a boy emperor, Duy Tan, in 1907 under French tutelage, made the monarchy a less potent rallying cry, and cleared the way for more radical ideas.[99] Wherever Phan Chu Trinh appeared across the country it was, in the words of one description, like he was 'giving a speech'. This signalled the arrival of a new type of public personality and public event. To underline the break with the past, wherever a new-style school was founded, people cut their hair, in some cases with the principal acting as a barber, singing the popular 'haircutting chant': 'Off with stupidity! Off with foolishness!'[100]

In March 1908 the French were confronted with what they called the *Révolte des cheveux tondus* ('revolt of the cut-hairs'). It was sparked by peasant anger with a march on the coastal town of Hoi An in central Vietnam to oppose the new taxes and, particularly, the corvée in this region. The 'deception' of indirect rule, as Phan Boi Chau termed it, was now cast aside: this was a direct confrontation with European officials. The cry was: 'Don't pay taxes to the French!' Demonstrators converged on the old port of Hoi An, and there they remained, camped outside the house of the French Resident. As more people sought to join them there were confrontations with soldiers and people killed. As the demonstrations spread down the coast to neighbouring Quang Ngai, there were sweeping arrests and summary executions. In Hue itself, peasants surrounded the house of the French Resident.[101] Young Nguyen Tat Thanh was to claim afterwards that he witnessed French troops firing on the crowd.[102]

There was more. On 27 June 200 French soldiers in Hanoi sat down to a formal banquet at the old citadel. Vietnamese cooks added 'devil's snare' – the hallucinogen *Datura stramonium* – to their rations. There was insufficient to kill them, but it sent many of them into an altered state.[103] It was the signal for a rebel from the north, De Tham, a survivor of the Can Vuong revolt who still commanded a few hundred men, to seize the capital. It was a thoroughly modern coup: there were plans to cut off the electricity, water and telegraph. The plot was betrayed when a conspirator went to confession with a French priest. The uprising was exploited from outside by the followers of Phan Boi Chau. These links were now easy for the authorities to trace. They implicated Phan Chu Trinh as well, by virtue of his sheer visibility. The new Free Schools were closed, and an entire generation of activists was rounded up, even prominent wealthy men like Gilbert Chieu.[104] Now, even to possess a map of the country was a crime.

Governor Doumer had announced in 1905: 'Truly it is time that France put on this land her stamp, which is civilization.'[105] But, for all this, colonial rule still upheld the old order. It trumpeted a vision of Franco-Vietnamese 'association', but of only a limited kind. It projected a vision of a modern future, but one that was uneven, fractured, distorted. It offered no coherent public doctrine of its own. This failure was underlined by the ferocity with which the colonial state cut down these expressions of dissent. After the incident in Hanoi, thirteen men were executed. Another two men took their own lives in prison, it was said, to escape the humiliation of the public guillotine; they had also given important information to the police.[106] The executions became a grisly public spectacle. One of the victims was taken to the port of Haiphong and paraded around the city before being despatched. Photographs of the condemned men, and their corpses, were published as a popular series of picture postcards.[107] Colonialism could not escape the logic of its own violent beginnings.

The use of capital punishment, however, caused consternation in France. So too did the widening net of oppression. Phan Chu Trinh, who had constantly argued for a more accommodating policy towards the French, received a death sentence. But his case enlisted the support of liberals in France in the *Ligue des droits de l'homme* ('League of the rights of man'), and his sentence was commuted to life imprisonment in the new penal colony of Poulo Condore, a small island fifty miles off the Mekong delta, in the South China Sea. For the first time, outside the 'Journey to the East', activists from north, south and central Vietnam came together in one place and forged a 'spiritual connection' as they broke rocks there and cut wood. Others were sent much further afield, to French Guiana and New Caledonia. As one of the most high-profile political prisoners of the French empire, Phan Chu Trinh was not confined in the prison but stayed in a fishing village on the island, where he wore his own clothes and ate his own food. In June 1910 he was released into house arrest on the mainland, at My Tho on the Mekong delta, and then permitted to go to France – with his young son, but without his wife and daughters – on a stipend of 5,400 francs a year. He travelled in the same ship as the returning governor-general and arrived in Paris in April 1911.[108]

Sometime in the months before his exile Phan Chu Trinh composed a review of his relationship with Phan Boi Chau, under the title 'A New Vietnam Following the Franco-Vietnamese Alliance'. It was written to exonerate his friends from charges of complicity in the 1908 rebellion. It was also an assessment of their role in Vietnamese history. The times were new, he argued, and the means of struggle had to be new too. But Phan Boi Chau had failed to unshackle himself from the past:

> The history of Phan Boi Chau is a sorrowful and gloomy history. It is a history full of hardship and challenge. His history is also the history of my life. His temperament is identical to mine, his aspiration is identical to mine, and his circumstances are identical to mine. Only his opinion is not identical to mine, and his conviction is just as different.[109]

Chau's commitment to armed struggle and his reckless alliance with Japan were seen now as a betrayal. Violence had shown itself to be indiscriminate and unpredictable in its effects and in the counter-terror it unleashed. In a way, it did not provoke France far enough, and merely underlined Vietnamese powerlessness. Phan Chu Trinh discerned an arrogance, an egotism, in the persona Phan Boi Chau had adopted in Japan. After they parted in Tokyo in mid-1906, they were not fated to meet again.

Violence itself was a snare. Liang Qichao's advice had been to equip intellectually the leaders of the future and build a movement for them. But what if there was no way to do this? As Phan Boi Chau himself reflected:

> With a situation as bad as this, there was no way I could keep myself from turning to the way of violence. I already knew that violence and suicide were acts committed by those of narrow learning with no ability to plan for the future. But if circumstances force us toward suicide, then I would prefer to die a violent death. For in violence there is one chance in a thousand that one might find success. In any case, as I thought it over I realized that if I were to give up violence at that time there would be nothing more worth doing.[110]

After his expulsion from Japan, he fled to Canton and Siam, where he organized remnants of his movement into settlements and farms in the central province of Phichit.[111] His search for military allies increasingly took the form of gun-running.

THE ASPHYXIA OF EMPIRE

In these quickening times, it mattered a great deal whether one was born in 1867 or 1880 or 1890. Generations had a clear sense of themselves as such, and their moments came and went in quick succession.[112] The men and women born in the years either side of 1890 were the first to experience the modern imperial age in the fullness of its design. The generation that came of age after the Russo-Japanese War shared with the one before it an impetus to move, to valorize change above stasis and to search for new, universal civilizing standards. But for them it seemed that never before had the future been so open to imaginative possibilities, yet the world so closed in practice. Faced with the asphyxia of empire, many of them could not accept the prospects that Phan Chu Trinh had seen in partial cooperation with the French. By imprisoning and exiling Trinh, the French themselves acknowledged it to be an illusion. Instead, many of this generation focused their gaze on more distant, worldly horizons.

The 'revolt of the cut-hairs' was a parting of the ways for Phan Boi Chau's old friend Nguyen Sinh Sac and his family. In 1909 Sac moved from Hue to become an assistant district magistrate in Binh Dinh province, further south. He acquired a reputation for irascible interventions in land disputes, often siding with the poor and powerless against the wealthy landlords. In 1910 he went too far in ordering a beating to be meted out to a landlord, and it was alleged that this had led to the man's death. In May, Nguyen Sinh Sac was imprisoned, demoted and dismissed, and when he was freed – the evidence against him was never compelling – he headed south to the colonial port city of Saigon and the Mekong delta, where he lived on odd jobs in internal exile in a 'lost country'. By this time, he was a target of the colonial police, as were all his family.[113]

Soon after Sac departed for Binh Dinh, his younger son, Nguyen Tat Thanh, left school. He took a series of odd jobs, teaching at reform-minded schools, as he also worked his way south to Cochinchina, and he abandoned his family name to escape the attention of the authorities. In early 1910, now around twenty years old, he was teaching in a school attached to a fish sauce factory in Phan Thiet, a bustling little port on the southeast coast. It was linked to the Modernization Society, but in these days of repression, trading took precedence over political work, and the school was soon to close. A former pupil recalled Thanh in a short vest with a high collar, a green belt and wooden shoes, and cropped hair. He taught French and Vietnamese, and in the mornings joined the rest of the staff and students in Japanese-style physical exercises. On Thursdays and Sundays he would disappear, no one knew where. One morning, in October 1910, he vanished without warning for good. He resurfaced in Saigon, at a technical school for seafarers. But, again, he did not stay in any one place for very long.[114]

In mid-1911 Nguyen Tat Thanh left his family and his name behind entirely. The sea routes around Indochina were opening up horizons beyond Asia. French shipping companies – the Messageries Maritimes and the Chargeurs Réunis – operated from Haiphong, Danang and Saigon to Yokohama, Vladivostok, Hong Kong, Bangkok, Singapore, Suez and beyond, to Marseilles, Le Havre and London. By 1914 one annual tally recorded 2,214 steamers and junks entering Vietnamese ports and 2,175 leaving.[115] It seemed that, as he moved south, Thanh had had the sea in mind all along. It may have been that his motive was to emulate the noble endeavour of Phan Boi Chau and the 'Journey to the East'. Or perhaps it was the lure of adventure. Thanh later said that he chose the journey to the west as he wanted to study Europe at first hand. For this there was Phan Chu Trinh's path to exile in Paris to follow. But Thanh did not go, as small numbers of Vietnamese were beginning to do, with a scholarship to study in France. Instead, he enlisted as a common seaman, under the name 'Ba', on board a passenger mailship of the Compagnie des Chargeurs Réunis, the *Amiral Latouche-Tréville*. Thanh then sailed from Saigon for Singapore on 5 June 1911. He would not return for thirty years.[116]

Banishment order 37/14

Issued under the Provisions of "The Prisons Enactment, 1907," Section 24.

CRIMINAL REGISTRY.

Ban Reg 54

Prison Reg. No. 2996.

Name, Alias and Father's Name   Ong Choon son of Ong Ek.

Do.   do.   in a native character

Crime stated in full   Theft of clothes valued at $5/-.

Section, Enactment, etc.   Section 380 of the penal code.

Date of Conviction   21.8.14

Place of Conviction   Seremban.

Sentence, stating Fine, etc., if any   One(1) month R.I.

Police Supervision

Name of Magistrate   H. H. Banks. Esqr:

Case No. 1191/14.

C. O
9958
Rec'd
Reg'd   1 MAR 15

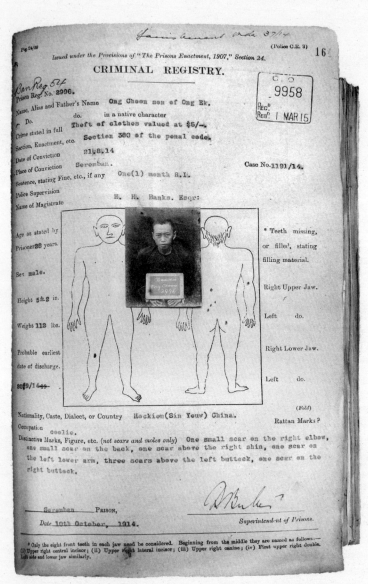

Age as stated by Prisoner 28 years.

Sex male.

Height 5 ft. 2 in.

Weight 112 lbs.

Probable earliest date of discharge.

20/9/14

Nationality, Caste, Dialect, or Country   Hockien(Sin Yeuw) China.

Occupation   coolie.

* Teeth missing, or filled, stating filling material.

Right Upper Jaw.

Left   do.

Right Lower Jaw.

Left   do.

(Fold)

Rattan Marks?

Distinctive Marks, Figure, etc. (not scars and moles only)   One small scar on the right elbow, one small scar on the back, one scar above the right shin, one scar on the left lower arm, three scars above the left buttock, one scar on the right buttock.

Seremban   PRISON,

Date 10th October, 1914.

Superintendent of Prisons.

* Only the eight front teeth in each jaw need be considered. Beginning from the middle they are named as follows:—
(i) Upper right central incisor; (ii) Upper right lateral incisor; (iii) Upper right canine; (iv) First upper right double.
Left side and lower jaw similarly.

An Act of Banishment, Singapore, 1914.

2

Fugitive Visions
1905–1909

THE WORLD, STEERAGE CLASS

Nguyen Tat Thanh stepped out into a world of clandestine movement that stretched far beyond the borders of Indochina. Phan Boi Chau called it 'the village abroad', a community created actively by migration and exile. Harassed by the French and their informers, the dispersed settlements and lodging houses of exile became forward bases in the struggle for a free Vietnam. The goal of the 'Journey to the East' was the creation of a new elite vanguard. For all the covert planning, it was executed, as Phan Boi Chau's wife Thai Thi Huyen pointed out, in plain sight. Its failure forced the movement to work within a rougher terrain, and in secret. Over the years, Phan Boi Chau and his followers learned the arts of disappearance and disguise. They nurtured networks to move money, people, illicit publications and arms; they drew on the resources of former rebels and pirates. But increasingly the connecting tissue of these networks were young Vietnamese in the most mobile of trades: seamen, cooks, laundrymen and servants ubiquitous in the service of European traders and officials. Women, too, featured within them, as wives or daughters, or posing as such; or as prostitutes, or women-without-men having the appearance of being so. They could travel more freely in some ways, they could run small businesses that might be used as fronts and act as couriers. The village abroad was often built around ties of kinship. As the movement retreated from Japan to the Chinese seaboard provinces or Siam, communities became more rooted in places of sojourn by intermarriage to locals. Their settlements evolved from being merely a place to hide, to offer a measure of security. As French policing began to claim lives, the sites of exile were given emotional force by the shrines of revolutionary martyrs. It was a homeland 'inside out'.[1] But over time these communities began to connect with others like themselves and form a world besides that of empire or nation.

Dispersed as it was, the village abroad was a curiously intimate place, where people knew each other, or of each other, or at least where one another came from. It had its own networks of information that paralleled the new colonial posts and telegraph. Rumour flew vast distances. It was into these byways that the story of Nguyen Tat Thanh became interwoven, as he made his way through them, and as the French attempted to trace his movements. The new regime in Indochina emerged out of a blizzard of papers for personal identification and restrictions on exit and entry.[2] The village abroad, like the smuggling of people and goods that surrounded it, honed skills of evasion and created a booming trade in false papers. To them were added the very different versions of himself that Nguyen Tat Thanh gave to friends and strangers, to police informers and judges. Many years later, on the few occasions when he wrote of his past, he was oblique, adopting the third person or a pseudonym, or expressing it in the form of a series of vignettes penned by imaginary fellow travellers chance-met along the road. For many Vietnamese, this was to become an exemplary tale of struggle, against which one's own patriotism and sacrifice might be measured. His life was also surrounded by the slurs and insinuations of rivals. This too was a common pattern of the life he had chosen: a 'ghost narrative' of suspicion, innuendo and hearsay. These kinds of shadows cloaked many voyagers through the world in which Nguyen Tat Thanh now travelled.[3]

In those days it was still just about possible to lose oneself. Everywhere people were on the move. For centuries the trading communities of Asia – be they Chinese, Indian Muslims, Sindhis, Arabs, Jews or others – forged family life over long distances and more securely integrated themselves through strategic alliances with local women. They adapted swiftly to imperial conditions; they followed the logic of the new steamship routes, settled in colonial port cities, exploited the new business opportunities and claimed the protection of colonial law. This was the high tide of influence for these old diasporas. They put down roots across Asia, although they still sent monies to their ancestral homes and their elders travelled there to die. In an age of national awakening, the question of their status and belonging became ever more urgent. Within these sites of sojourn, prosperity and respectability encouraged their philanthropy, and an outward-looking approach to social and religious reform.[4] People made ever longer journeys for faith. Pan-Asian sentiment was fortified by older paths of pilgrimage, such as the campaign to reclaim the site of the Buddha's enlightenment at Bodh Gaya, in Bihar, India. More Asian Muslims than ever before could afford to undertake the hajj: in 1911, 24,025 pilgrims left by steamship for Mecca from the Netherlands East Indies alone.[5] Many lingered in the holy cities of the Middle East to absorb new ideas and carry them home, or to die a little closer to God.

Young people set out in all directions to learn, not only to Japan, the obvious destination. The Islamic schools of north India, West Sumatra and southern Siam exported teachers around the archipelago. In 1899 there were 217 traditional Chinese schools in Java alone, and as the movers of the late Qing reform movement dispersed abroad there was an explosion of new-style Chinese schools in colonial cities such as Batavia, Semarang, Penang, Manila and Singapore – where the Chinese Girls' School, founded in 1899, was the first of its kind. They were linked by the itineraries of mainly Cantonese travelling educators, who instilled a keen sense of colonial inequalities and an ethos of modern self-improvement. Some, like the influential Tiong Hoa Hwee Koan School in Batavia, were not merely modelled on European schools, or schools in China, but were established by teachers who came directly from the *Datong* schools set up by the Chinese reformers in Tokyo, Yokohama and Kobe.[6] Across Southeast Asia, these, and the more improvised night schools, provided intellectual forums that previously had been entirely lacking for migrant communities mostly comprising traders and labourers.

Not only teaching but letter-writing, publishing and printing created intricate networks across Asia. In 1891 there were forty-nine private Chinese letter shops in Singapore, serviced by the junk trade; in the same year the colonial post office of the Straits Settlements handled 137,500 books coming in and 59,000 going out, as well as 1.5 million letters.[7] Mobility was one of the great spectacles of life, and some of the most ubiquitous travelling communities were the popular entertainers: the intercontinental travelling circuses, Chinese opera and musical parties, troupes of Japanese acrobats, Filipino orchestras and *vodavil*, and the magic lantern shows that plied their trade to villages, estates and mines in the countryside.[8] Through these media, new ideas and attitudes were voiced in popular forms, not least the idea of travel itself. And one did not have to travel far to experience its cultural displacements and a sense of divers connections. Sometimes, one did not have to travel at all. Even for people who never ventured into the cities, ideas from far away could be experienced near at hand.[9]

José Rizal, the Filipino patriot-martyr executed by the Spanish in 1896, was posthumously anointed at the Asian Solidarity meetings in Tokyo as a prophet for the new Asia, because he embodied this experience by his own sojourns in Hong Kong, China, Japan, western Europe and the United States between 1882 and 1892. His 1891 novel *El Filibusterismo* – a term drawn from the argot of the sea, which Rizal himself translated as 'a dangerous presumptuous patriot who will soon be hanged' – was at once an indictment of colonial life and a reflection of a Southeast Asian world consciousness as witnessed from abroad.[10] It began with a ship setting sail. This was at once a metaphor for the colonial Philippines and for escape: 'something akin to triumph over progress, a steamer that wasn't exactly a steamer per se, but an immutable organism, imperfect'. Although the ship was 'quite dirty', Rizal wrote, 'one could even imagine it as the ship of state':

> If you are still not convinced of the metaphor of the ship of state, look at the arrangement of the passengers. Brown faces and black heads congregate below decks, indios, Chinese and mestizos crammed among parcels and trunks. While up there above decks, under a canopy that protects them from the sun and seated in comfortable armchairs, are several passengers dressed European-style, friars and bureaucrats smoking fat cigars and contemplating the countryside, taking no notice, it seems, of the captain and crew's efforts to navigate the river's shoals.[11]

But 'other things were going on below'. This was how the world, for the most part, was encountered: from below deck, in steerage, sleeping on planks above the cargo, 'in the heat of the boiler, amid human steam and a pestilential smell of oil'.[12] A voyage, as one Chinese student travelling from Medan in Sumatra back to China in 1910 described it, was a constant fight for space, often involving bribery, a diet of 'coolie food' – a little rice, vegetables or salt fish – eaten standing outside the engine room, and even sleeping on deck itself with no protection from the elements.[13] Even on the most modern ships on the longest Pacific crossings, steerage passengers could expect the same amount of space 'as is usually occupied by one of the flat boxes in a milliner's store', on rows of shelves barely eighteen inches apart. The largest of the Pacific steamers, the *Oceanic*, carried 1,000 people in steerage.[14] Only Japanese ships, which were the most affordable means of travel within Asia and (from the 1890s) on the trans-Pacific run, built in some space and comfort for their Asian passengers, in family-size 'silkworm shelves'. The hold of one ship was fitted out in the style of an opium den.[15] With their opaque manifests, Japanese ships were thus the preferred choice for the clandestine traveller.

The passage carried the grim imprint of older systems of bondage. The first trans-Pacific Asian migrants had been slaves from across the Indian Ocean and Southeast Asia, the so-called *chinos*, traded on the Manila galleons in the late sixteenth and early seventeenth centuries to the slave markets of Mexico City.[16] After the gradual abolition of the Atlantic slave trade, most long-distance migrants within Asia and the Pacific travelled as notionally 'free' labour, under differing forms of 'credit-ticket', which involved paying off the cost of travel and vital necessities along the way, or indenture, signing terms of engagement for five years or more. New migrants were often recruited by members of their own communities, such as in the *kangani* system that brought labour from southern India to Malaya or Ceylon, by which a familiar foreman would return to recruit people from his home village, collecting 'head money' for their good behaviour, or holding them in debt by acting as a shopkeeper or moneylender.[17] Conditions varied vastly; journeys abroad each exacted their own unique toll of servitude to crimps and brokers. Colonial officials asked themselves how far these types of labourers were able to guard their own interests and to exercise meaningful control over their lives. In the tropical plantation colonies, migrants faced shocking death rates from malaria or dysentery in newly cleared forest, and also, in the early days, from savage corporal punishment. In Malaya before the 1910s, death rates were the highest anywhere in the British empire: in the state of Perak, in 1900 and 1901, they hovered around 142–3 in 1,000.[18] Some even argued that slavery continued to exist in the heart of modern colonies such as British Singapore by pointing to local religious discussions over its use.[19]

European labour recruitment, even when it was conducted through Asian intermediaries, drew on forms of caricature and racial imagery from earlier encounters with native peoples or African slavery. The first wave of migrants to North America were stigmatized as vectors of disease, as enemies to family life; as such they were seen as people who could not be assimilated into a white labour force. This culminated in the Chinese Exclusion Act of 1882.[20] In 1903, during his years of exile, Liang Qichao was received in New York and Washington society by the likes of J. P. Morgan and President Theodore Roosevelt. But Liang was appalled at the racism and inequalities he witnessed and their corrupting effect on the Chinese communities in the US. He quoted the Tang poet Du Fu: 'Crimson mansions reek of wine and meat, while on the road lie frozen bones. Rich and poor but a foot apart; sorrows too hard to relate.'[21]

All these shadows merged in the figure of the 'coolie'. The word appears to have originated in some long-lost form of colonial pidgin. In India the standard etymology gave it as *kuli*, from a Tamil word referring to a task; it signified individuals inseparable from their work, anonymous – a cross or an inked fingerprint in a ledger – and statusless beyond it.[22] In written Chinese, *ku li* was represented by two characters suggesting, respectively, bitterness or suffering and strength or power. In both cases, by its rendering in the English language 'coolie' became a generic term signifying perennial human bondage, a person of no family, of no name and with only a temporary status anywhere in the world at large. In the United States, by a cruel twist, the association of what became known as the 'coolie trade' with indentured labour or slavery was seen as a challenge to freedoms enshrined in the Constitution, and this became another argument for Chinese exclusion.[23] The word was despised by those who spoke for these communities, as they tried desperately to assert their free status: 'Chinese', they insisted, 'are not coolies.'[24]

Migrants everywhere lived under the constant fear of sudden displacement or banishment. This practice of medieval rulers was condemned in England by the Magna Carta of 1215, if never wholly discontinued. It was routine in the repertoire of colonial states. It was visited on Asian kings – the last Mughal emperor in 1858 and the deposed rulers of Burma in 1885, Vietnam in 1888 and 1907 and Korea in 1910 – as well as coolies. People of long residence could be suddenly expelled to some distant 'home', a point of imagined origin to which they might have few ties. This was a visceral exercise in power to cow and to shame: the life histories of the banished were recorded, their faces photographed, and the scars and other marks on their bodies mapped to guard against their return. In the Straits Settlements alone in 1914, 416 people were banished for life, and another 801 'vagrants' detained in prison, the great majority to be repatriated. Ministers denied in parliament that they used banishment to expel trade unionists from the colony.[25]

Some of the most vulnerable migrants were women. Although controls on women leaving home for overseas were often rigid, the village abroad could be a place of refuge, somewhere to seek anonymity and wage work. When restrictions on women leaving China began to lift, it became a way to live without men for certain groups of labouring women – the amahs in domestic service, or the *samsui* women, self-governing collectives of construction workers from Guangdong. They were often at the forefront of struggles against inequality. Factory work in Shanghai brought in women in large numbers from the countryside, and three-quarters of the first labour strikes there between 1895 and 1910 were initiated by women.[26] They were never just mere helpmates, or cover, or alibis for male revolutionaries, the roles in which Phan Boi Chau and others tended to see them. An early exemplar was Qiu Jin, who left her husband and family in Shaoxing, in Zhejiang province, in 1903 to study at the Practical Women's School in Tokyo, where she became an orator and leader in the student clubhouses of the city. Her poetry contained some of the first and most evocative descriptions of the new imaginative geographies of Asia:

> Heaven and earth are in darkness when the sun and moon have lost
> their vision.
> Who are the aides to the lethargic world of women?
> Jewels pawned to cross the dark blue ocean,
> Leaving my flesh and blood I step out of the last gate of the country.
> Unbinding my feet to undo the poisoned years,
> Arousing the souls of a hundred flowers to passionate movement.[27]

Qiu Jin's writings recorded not only the bodily anguish that self-emancipation and the reshaping of her feet unleashed but also the possibility of escaping the body: she habitually wore men's attire, and photographs of her in traditional and modern male dress circulated widely. The manner of her death – she was beheaded by Qing troops in July 1907 at the reforming *Datong* school she had founded on her return to Zhejiang – raised her instantly to the status of a patriotic martyr across China and overseas.[28] But other women cut their own unsung paths across these worlds and became travellers, couriers, speakers and organizers in their own right. Although they often moved in labouring communities that were overwhelmingly male, they were everywhere present in the intellectual life and political struggles of the village abroad in ways that were often hidden from view, disguised by the widespread use of male pseudonyms or expunged by the testimonies of men.[29]

These journeys often ended in betrayal and exploitation. Even in a staid colonial outpost like Hanoi, there were, on one count in 1915, an estimated 2,000 prostitutes, serving working men, soldiers and 'an explosion of pleasure-seeking' among the new Vietnamese middle class. The numbers of 'non-submissive' – unregulated or clandestine – prostitutes were hard to measure.[30] But the traffic in women across the Gulf of Tonkin was a small part of the wider picture. The presence of so many prostitutes among the few Chinese women who made it to Southeast Asia or the Americas was an added stigma to their communities. Also prevalent in major Asian cities were the Japanese *karayuki-san*: young women from poor rural families who went via Shanghai and Hong Kong to Haiphong, Saigon and Singapore, where in 1915 there were 2,000 of them in brothels and lodging houses.[31] Yet this was a small part of the total, which had grown with Japanese expansion into Korea and Manchuria after the Russo-Japanese War. A tally in 1907 gave a figure of 7,975 *karayuki-san*: some 62 per cent of them were in China, 16 per cent in North America and 14 per cent in Southeast Asia. At their peak, in 1910, there were more than 19,000 of them.[32] The euphemisms that surrounded the women 'who went to China' served to cloak the cruel underside of the new empires of trade.

In no small part, modern empires were created in an effort to realize what the British Under-Secretary of State for the Colonies, Winston Churchill, in 1908 called 'a harmonious disposition of the world among its peoples'.[33] At the cold heart of liberal visions of free trade and progress was a ruthless global and racial division of labour. Europeans monitored movement obsessively, enumerating and marshalling people towards their mines, plantations and households. Colonial regimes' ability to control subjects beyond their own borders, often in the name of exercising 'protection' over them, became a yardstick of their authority and a challenge to their prestige. Who were all these people, and to whom did they belong? Who was what they said they were, and who was not, and how could it be proven?[34] Across the Indian and Pacific Oceans, official paranoia over 'vagabondage' – the wanderings of masterless men and women – led to some of the first exercises anywhere in personal identification, directed at stowaways, destitute migrants or pilgrims. If people were stranded somewhere, who was to pay to send them 'home'?[35] And was 'home' even where they said it was? In an age of international travel, the consuls of colonial powers were tormented by people 'passing' as different nationalities and ethnicities as it suited them and by new 'crimes of mobility' that allowed the imposter, the confidence trickster, the bigamist to thrive.[36]

The issue of personal status went to the heart of the meaning of the imperial world in these years. The proliferation of jurisdictions greatly complicated legal identities. Some colonial subjects possessed citizenship which put them on a par with Europeans – such as the long-domiciled 'King's Chinese' of the Straits Settlements – others were merely 'subjects' or 'protected persons'. But an ethnic Chinese in French Indochina or the Netherlands East Indies, say, was none of these, merely an 'Asian foreigner'. This status determined what law one was subject to, the courts one had access to, the prison one might be sent to. It mattered above all for one's right to roam a global commons. In the British empire after 1870 there was a crucial incoherence, and a tightening hierarchy, between those who were 'colonially' naturalized with local, territorial effect and those who were 'imperially' naturalized with wider effect.[37] Out of a fog of ambiguity and misinformation, Asian migrants held to a common assumption that being an imperial subject of any kind brought with it an entitlement to move.[38] But as racial and ethnic exclusion grew, British imperial citizenship was defined in increasingly Anglo-Saxon terms through the 'colour line' that protected the ring of white settlement around the Pacific Ocean, epitomized by the 'White Australia' policy of 1901. The further afield people moved, the more their right to be there came into question and tested amorphous ideals of equal belonging.[39]

In this way, Nguyen Tat Thanh and others escaped into the world as sailors only to experience western power as something more insidious, systemic and world-encompassing. Sailors moved in the vanguard of the new colonial capitalism, which slowly eroded the powerful traditions of independence of the maritime communities of the Asian littoral. The China junk trade was built on family networks while, in the inland waters, men lived on their boats, and employers could not ride rough-shod over their solidarities.[40] But by the 1880s Chinese traders were investing in fleets of coastal steamers. The expansion of modern ocean-going shipping brought a new scale and standard of impersonal industrial hierarchy to shipboard life. From the 1890s German and then British shipping lines recruited from the pools of maritime labour in Hong Kong and Canton. At any one time between 1876 and 1906, perhaps 80,000 cooks, servants, deckhands and sailors served in this 'invisible merchant marine'.[41] By 1906 over half the world's trade was carried on British merchant vessels, and an estimated 39,000 'foreigners' and 42,000 'lascars' served on them, amounting to half the crew on deep-sea voyages.[42]

The term 'lascar' had been in currency for centuries, and evoked the 'motley crews' of the Indian Ocean: a world so hybrid in its circulations and lingua franca that it made little sense to speak of a man's origins. Over time, the term attached itself to specific communities with strong connections to the sea.[43] In British India, for example, the landlocked villages of Sylhet in Assam had the most extraordinary global linkages through maritime recruitment, and Sylheti sailors, the *Londoni*, were an established presence in the East End of London from as early as 1795.[44] But the right of Asians to be there came under increasing attack. By the 1900s lascars and Chinese had become a kind of sea-coolie, everywhere to be seen, but everywhere absent in terms of their status on land. Their world was divided by a 'lascar line' and subject to 'lascar' or 'Asiatic articles' that governed the waters in which they could and could not sail, according to the season, and the ports where they could not land. From 1893 lascars were restricted to voyages between fifty and sixty degrees north from October until March, ostensibly because of the cold weather, but ultimately to protect white labour. These seamen were among the first communities anywhere that had to carry dockets and papers to identify themselves.[45]

On board modern ships, seamen were ensnared within elaborate gradings based on the nature of their work, which dictated where they slept, what they ate, and whom they ate with. Against petty oppression at sea, observed the British consul at Port Said while contemplating a spate of lascar suicides in 1904, a man's only redress might be, quite literally, 'jumping ship'.[46] The lowest rungs were occupied by the galley staff and cabin boys, who grew in number with greater demands for comfort by officers and passengers. This was a world familiar to Nguyen Tat Thanh, or Seaman Ba. He worked as a cook's help, cleaning the galley, peeling vegetables and lighting the boilers, and eased his passage by assisting his fellow sailors to write home.[47]

IN THE COUNTRY OF THE LOST

As Nguyen Tat Thanh moved through the South China Sea and into the Indian Ocean in 1911, the universal revealed itself to him in a continuum of port cities. Singapore, Hong Kong, Shanghai, Batavia, Calcutta and Bombay were now some of the great choke points of human activity. Here the commanding global networks of western power – banks, shipping, telegraphs – collided with the plebeian energies of Asia's great age of movement. Notwithstanding the growing controls on departure and arrival, there were plenty of opportunities along this vast, connected waterfront across Asia, Europe, Australasia and the Americas to land illicitly, 'behind empire's back'.[48]

Many journeys across Asia passed through Singapore: in the seventy years after 1870, 11 million Chinese travelled there in order to tranship to the Netherlands East Indies and beyond, and 4 million from India made the shorter, but equally arduous, journey to it across the Bay of Bengal.[49] In the ten years before 1911, Singapore's population had grown 34 per cent to 303,321, and the annual average of migrants flowing through it was 254,000, four-fifths of them male. From Singapore, shipping, trade and people fanned out to other seaports and river harbours across the archipelago.[50] Within a few years after 1905, Singapore's new showpiece docks, its new streetlights and fans, its first electrified trams, its Cold Storage chain of emporia and cinemas blazoned a modernity that, at least in the city's more privileged spaces, was more advanced than that of the west. Amid contrasts of flamboyant wealth and crushing poverty, of darkness and light, of daily promise and danger, Asians often felt displaced. As the Islamic reformist journal of Singapore, *al-Imam*, described the city in 1907:

About a quarter of a century ago, the areas around High Street and Cross Street and their environs were inhabited mostly by Malays with a sprinkling of Arabs . . . And no sooner did wealth and progress step into these two areas then [sic] did the Malay and Muslim residents have to retreat once again further away to . . . other remote areas! If this pattern continues, and it most certainly will, the Malays and Muslims of this island will eventually have to run to Papua or to those places where the inhabitants are still naked![51]

In this other city, beyond the bunds and banks and mansions, international connections were not the preserve of a well-positioned elite, but something more protean and subterranean.

It was first to be sought in the 'native' quarters and the Chinatowns, but increasingly took form away from the older enclaves, in the half-made, semi-urban sprawl in which those excluded from the colonial city, and recent arrivals from the countryside and from overseas, tended to lodge themselves. It was an invisible city, an anti-city; darker, more dangerous and less modern. Here urban life was experienced as a series of village neighbourhoods that merged into one another in the spaces in between the international city and the Asian city, in the voids surrounding the new factory compounds and in the floating city of boats and barges moored across inlets and canals between the water and the shore – like Soochow Creek in Shanghai or the Singapore River itself – where the maritime communities of Asia had always lived. In turbulent times, these 'beggars' villages', as they were termed in Shanghai, were seen as nests of squalor, crime and disorder. But municipal government surveys also went out of their way to show that they were inhabited by relatively stable communities of working people, not itinerants or refugees.[52]

This was a townscape of lodging houses and dormitories, food stalls and cafés, fashioned for men and women with no hearth or family life of their own. Home was the cubicles in the upper storeys of the shophouses of the archipelago, and workers' dormitories – or, for 'the great class of the Unroofed', as a 1909 description of Hong Kong dubbed them, there was the rudimentary shelter to be created from barrels, rope bales and gunny bags on the waterfront, or claimed under the covered 'five-foot ways' fronting the commercial buildings.[53] People lived in an unquestioning and fluid world of pseudonym, subterfuge and fleeting encounters, where personal ties were hastily improvised. Its meeting places were the drinks and food stalls which abutted liquor and provision shops or which conducted their trade from handcarts in alleyways. In the backs of the larger coffee shops (*kopitiams*) of the Straits and the tea-houses of Shanghai or Kowloon, there was room for gambling, for popular theatre, and also for discreet meetings. These were locations for all communities to encounter one another, to settle conflicts, to learn or to read aloud.[54]

Cities in Asia became places of turbulent competition. For new arrivals in Singapore or Shanghai, finding work and housing meant dealing with waterfront overlords, labour contractors or brothel madams with connections to one of the city's gangs.[55] These were often run on ethnic lines, operated by networks across long distances. In Singapore, Chinese associations worked specialized niches, Indian and Chinese lightermen fought a long battle for control for the waterfront, and struggles between rival Chinese broke into riots in November 1906.[56] Workers, pedlars and drifters were pushed together in close proximity, sometimes in conflict, sometimes in indifference. People's sense of self was often fragile, and their lives often ended in isolation and alienation.

A rare record is provided by the case files of coroners. In Singapore, for example, they were a catalogue of everyday death and injury: of knifings in dormitories over debt or disturbed sleep; of a child's body in the wreckage of a collapsed tenement; of the frightening attrition of labour on the waterfront. In a new-forged society where women were few in number, there were many casualties in the frustrated search for affection and family life. Many people died unnamed and unclaimed. There was a case on New Year's Eve in 1913, when a Chinese man of about thirty-five years of age staggered into the police station at Telok Ayer at around 8.05 p.m. He was dressed in black trousers and jacket and a small hat, and was 'in the last gasp'. He was asked who he was but he could not answer as he had a cut jugular. There he expired, and no one was found who could speak for him, to say who he was, or who had done this and why.[57]

Of the 171 investigations by the Singapore coroner in the first three months of 1916, sixty-one of them were classified as relating to persons 'unknown'. Their remains were most frequently discovered by the roadside or in storm drains, although they were often found in the midst of the European suburbs too. Sometimes they had lain ignored for weeks: stillborn, or struck down by the omnipresent scourges of dysentery, tuberculosis and malaria, or plain worn out by exhaustion and *morbus cordis*. In the Telok Ayer case, the man had perhaps used a knife on himself, but it was never found. The case was singular only for the man having died in plain sight. More often people took their own lives seeking even the most meagre privacy: to cast themselves into the sea, or to hang from a tree in the scrub, from the underside of a bridge, or from a pipe in a prison or asylum latrine in the dead of night. Such deaths were a sombre, almost silent counterpoint to the colony's self-mythology of migrant opportunity, free enterprise and benevolent government.[58]

But, crucially, the jeopardy of everyday life also compelled individuals to live beyond their own communities. People of very different origins met for the first time and had to negotiate space, develop reciprocal services, learn from each other and, of necessity, forge a degree of trust. In these cities, the languages of status broke down and new ways of talking and naming evolved. Shifting lingua francas – the Hindustani of commerce; the *pasar Melayu*, or 'bazaar Malay', of the archipelago; or the dialect of Shanghai, exclusive to that city – acquired a new importance and began to take form in print. These were cities where a shared creole experience could create a new ethnicity in itself, such as the Betawi, who had come to be regarded as the natives of old Batavia.[59] At the very least, individuals could blur some of their ethnic and class definition, so that an educated man like Nguyen Tat Thanh could pass as a menial worker.

Thanh moved across an endless waterfront of intricate communities and long-distance communications, with its own sense of worldliness and its own solidarities. Here labour retained some of its self-governing traditions. Among the Chinese communities overseas, the world of work preserved an old ideal of brotherhood and partnership, of 'collective self-mastery', and of a rough 'democracy' that bore no debt to the traditions of the west.[60] It was no accident that sailors and dockhands were at the forefront of labour movements. During the Sino-French War of 1884–5, the prelude to the annexation of Tonkin, there was a wave of patriotic unrest on the southern China coast, fanned by sympathetic Qing officials. In early September 1884, dockers in Hong Kong refused to refit a French warship, resulting in an unprecedented boycott of the entire French community. This transcended dialect groups, guilds and gangs, and drew in the boatmen, cargo and coal carriers, rickshaw pullers and sedan-chair bearers. Waiters refused to serve French diplomats in the hotels, and any European in the street was in danger of being threatened. When boatmen were apprehended there were parades, demonstrations and violence, virtually a general strike; one man was killed and thirty arrested. The British responded with an emergency 'Peace Preservation Ordinance', which gave the colonial authorities unprecedented powers to arrest and banish people convicted of no specific crime. The revelation of popular patriotism in the face of the crisis of the Qing regime moved young revolutionaries deeply, including one student at the Hong Kong Government Central School, called Sun Yat-sen.[61]

As Sun Yat-sen gained standing as a reformer and revolutionary, and took his own struggle into exile, he was one of the first leaders to look to the resources of the village abroad. Although other late Qing intellectuals, including Kang Youwei and Liang Qichao, were equally visible, it was Sun who embraced new methods such as the boycott, which mobilized the resources of labour. Its power was seen again in Hong Kong and Canton in 1905–6 when, in response to continuing exclusionary policies in the United States, workers refused to smoke American cigarettes, women to wear American cotton clothes or rickshaw men to ferry heavy American passengers, not least the 300-pound visiting secretary of war, William Howard Taft.[62]

The life and death of a young man called Feng Xiawei came to embody the cause. He had worked in Mexico and then was refused entry to the United States because he was a manual labourer. On 16 July 1905 he took poison in front of the US consulate in Shanghai. He had gone to the consulate in Japanese dress, and on his hospital deathbed claimed to be a Filipino and an American subject. It was a new kind of martyrdom: brutal, public and wrapped in unsettling signs and significations of what it meant to be an Asian man at this time. The commemoration of Feng's death in the temples, streets and theatres of Hong Kong, Canton, Singapore, Kuala Lumpur and Manila was itself a new strategy of popular mobilization. Never before had a person of low status been mourned in this way.[63] Many of the new leaders of labour had stories similar to Feng's. One of the movers of the Canton protest, Ma Chaojuan, had worked as a mechanic in San Francisco, where he had met

Sun Yat-sen, and organized clubs for fellow mechanics in Hong Kong and Canton on his return.[64]

The movement spread to the mainly Chinese stevedores of Singapore. In 1908, in the wake of China's increasing diplomatic humiliation, anti-Japanese boycotts stretched from Canton and Hong Kong to Singapore, Manila and Honolulu. Workers refused to use Japan-made matches, and the middle classes spurned the consumer goods from Japan that were flooding shops and stores across Asia. In Malaya, pickets prevented men entering Japanese brothels. The Canton post office would only accept mail in non-Japanese-made envelopes and restaurants were shunned if they served Japanese dried mushrooms or seafood. All this benefited Chinese business, but it was only possible with the support of labour.[65] Above all, the boycott demonstrated a powerful means to cast struggle across territories and mobilize support from without.

Sun Yat-sen was constantly on the move in these years, especially after his expulsion from Japan in 1907. It was in the British settlement of Penang, in a house on Armenian Street, adjacent to the Aceh mosque and near the Chinese gangs' jetties on the waterfront, that Sun Yat-sen laid the plans for his first armed uprising in Canton in 1910. His supporters from his days in Japan, Hu Hanmin and Wang Jingwei, went on speaking tours of the small industrial towns of the Malay Peninsula and the Netherlands Indies in order to exploit the growing financial and intellectual resources of the village abroad. They trod delicately around the colonial authorities, choosing to speak using historical themes or raise funds through appeals for humanitarian relief, such as in the wake of the Fuzhou typhoon in October 1908.

Between 1908 and 1911, fifty-eight reading clubs were founded in Singapore and Malaya, and revolutionary leaders argued that travelling theatre shows which attracted labouring audiences had more impact than their speeches. One of those moved to action was Wen Shengcai, a former Qing soldier who then worked for many years in Malaya, as a factory apprentice and a tin miner in Perak. After he clashed with an English manager, and inspired by a speech by Sun Yat-sen, he returned to Canton entirely on his own initiative where he shot dead the Qing general Fu Qi in April 1911. In this, Wen was following the inspiration of Wang Jingwei himself, who became a patriotic hero after he returned to China incognito from Japan with an assassination squad and tried – and failed – to assassinate the Qing prince regent in Beijing in early 1910, with a bomb planted in a metal box on the roadside near his residence.[66] These deeds launched from overseas generated a powerful mystique which encouraged others to follow their example.

As the pathways across the village abroad connected disparate sites of exile, they began to bypass home altogether, and became interwoven with local ties of intimacy. Wang Jingwei married into a wealthy Chinese merchant family of Penang. It was a tradition of long standing for traders to take secondary wives in the places where they did business. Sun's secondary wife Chen Cuifen, who was constantly with him during his years of exile, settled in Malaya after he left, a revolutionary companion and 'second mother' to his children. Like many women, she played a silent role as a courier and assistant in revolutionary work.[67] For Sun's part, his odyssey led nationalists from other communities to seek him out for emulation and advice. He was not immune from the reach of empires, nor from their exclusions. After he made a speech at a Chinese club in Penang in November 1910 which drew attention to the vulnerability of the Chinese presence in Malaya – wine had loosened his tongue, it was said – the British ordered him to leave. No colonial territory in Asia would admit him, nor would the kingdom of Siam. He was, an English-language newspaper mocked, 'a revolutionary who does not revolute'. He was forced to flee to the west, leaving his family behind in Malaya.[68] This merely increased his standing as first citizen of the country of the lost.

As anti-imperialists began to move through the interstices of empire, they became specialists in this underworld and its shared skills. Worldliness was a set of tools that people could take from city to city as they moved long distances. To survive was to make endless small investments that might or might not pay off: a friendship from a chance meeting, the ability to mention a name, a safe place for a time, a small loan, a meal or a night on the town. These networks and connections could all too easily break down: there was always the friend or contact who never showed up, the remittance that never arrived. The everyday life of the village abroad was a constant gamble on the future. But this mobile world was more real for many than any idea of 'the nation'; it was a place where the boundary between 'home' and 'abroad' dissolved, where so much was experienced in common with others very different from oneself. To travel was to experience how one neighbourhood of the village abroad blended into another, and to see beyond national humiliation into the global.

For a time, this *was* the 'lost country' of which Asian patriots constantly spoke. It was inhabited by people – some privileged, but increasingly very ordinary – whose identities were created by travel and by these environments. The day-to-day experience of travel was constant exposure to new experiences, constant comparisons and translations, which challenged a person's understanding of the world and of power, a reservoir of lived experiences and reimaginings of society. Over time, a new type of intellectual emerged out of this, with few of the credentials of the traditional scholar, shaped principally by the world at large. Their thought was rarely systematically set down in books and tracts, but expressed in fragmentary fashion in émigré newspapers, handbills and letters, or through speech alone. Ideas were made on the move, and from sudden displacement and adaptions new fugitive visions were set in motion.[69]

This Asia was without borders. The opening of the Suez Canal in 1867 had brought the west dramatically closer. In the guise of Seaman Ba, Nguyen Tat Thanh landed in July 1911 in Marseilles, and experienced the rough cosmopolitanism of the old Mediterranean. Here he entered his first café, and for the first time was called 'monsieur' by a Frenchman. 'The French in France are all good,' he concluded. 'But the French colonialists are very cruel and inhuman.' He would touch land in ports further afield, in Madagascar, Congo, Senegal, Algeria, Tunisia, Portugal, Spain, picking up in each a postcard or matchbox as a souvenir, and soaking up impressions of colonial conditions, not least their essential similarities.[70]

In these years, it was still possible for a person to travel vast distances and leave little imprint on official ledgers or lists. When French officials came to retrace Thanh's steps, they found in their archives a letter from him, dated December 1911, addressed to the President of the Third Republic. It was a request to be enrolled in the elite École Coloniale in Paris. 'I am completely without resources and am eager to learn,' Thanh wrote. 'I would like to become useful to France in relation to my compatriots . . .'. This could have been self-abasement, as it was later seen by his enemies. Or it was an attempt to gain French training to subvert the system from within, as Phan Chu Trinh had advocated. Either way, the petition came to nothing.[71] The French acquired a postcard and a record of remittance home from Ceylon, and a note postmarked New York in 1912, but with the address 'poste restante Le Havre'. There was also a 'Ba' on the Atlantic cargo line between Le Havre, London and New York, which may well have been Thanh. From the years after 1911, there is a photograph of Nguyen Tat Thanh, perhaps on the pont Alexandre III in Paris, posing with his hat to one side, cigarette at the corner of his mouth, an umbrella on his arm, quite the dandy. Then there were the scattered hints he dropped much later: of working in Boston at the Parker House Hotel; of hearing the African-American activist Marcus Garvey speak in Harlem; stories of Rio de Janeiro and Buenos Aires. Then he seems to have settled for a while in London, taking English lessons while working, so he claimed, at the Carlton Hotel as *sous chef* to the great Auguste Escoffier. But no one ever really knew the truth of any of this.[72]

UNDER WESTERN EYES

Nguyen Tat Thanh arrived in Europe at the dying of the light of its *belle époque*, an era of unbounded confidence in the promise of a world connected and transformed. The wealth, goods and styles of Asia had never been more accessible to European publics. It was a time of great 'universal' expositions – Paris in 1900, Brussels in 1910, the Festival of Empire in London in 1911 – which brought in colonial products, and even imperial subjects, as objects of curiosity. The London extravaganza of 1911 – together with the establishment of the Imperial Institute in South Kensington, imperial-themed clubs, museums and monuments and the Imperial College of Science and Technology – marked the crescendo of attempts to fashion London into a city that better reflected its world-encompassing status. It was certainly a lure to its new colonial subjects. This was still a world of circulating monarchs, and Indian and Malay princes gravitated to the courts of Europe and took the waters at their aristocratic playgrounds, in a reprise of the old Grand Tour. This was not always a genuflexion to imperial authority. The ostentatious itineraries of one of the wealthiest of these men, the maharajah of the Malay state of Johor, took in not only the Court of St James but also the Sublime Porte in Istanbul, the Hohenzollern and Habsburg courts, as well as the imperial palace in Tokyo, in a global performance of Malay sovereignty.[73]

In the west, some Asians were virtually unassailable by virtue of their wealth and standing. In 1867 Dadabhai Naoroji, a Parsi business-man and the first Asian to be elected to the House of Commons, was able to lecture London audiences on the 'drain of wealth' and Britain's moral debt to India. The argument, as Naoroji pointed out, had a long pedigree in India, and it ran far ahead of liberal and radical critiques of empire within Britain itself – but it went unheard.[74] The Bengali sage Swami Vivekananda brought his message of reformed Hinduism, and a sharp critique of western materialism and triumphalism, to a world stage at the Parliament of World Religions in Chicago in 1893, and to lecture audiences across the United States and in Britain in 1895. Per-haps 2,000 people attended the Universal Races Congress in London in 1911. It was called originally to discuss 'the awakening of Asia', but then was broadened, at the insistence of the African-American activist and writer W. E. B. Du Bois, to encompass issues of slavery and the condition of Africa. Du Bois's book *The Souls of Black Folk* (1903) exposed the global 'colour line' as the defining problem of the new cen-tury and, in his evocation of the 'darker world', he reached across it to seek solidarity with Asian thinkers.[75] While the organizers of the congress skirted imperial controversy, it brought together voices of colonialists, colonial reformers and the colonized in a way that was unprecedented and not to be repeated for many years.[76]

Then there were the defeated and the dispossessed. The west was now seen as the safest haven for its opponents. A central paradox of empire in a liberal age was that its most enlightened, most universal principles and practices could not be universally applied to colonial societies, on the grounds of their essential 'difference'.[77] But in the imperial metropolis, it was not possible to restrict freedom of movement, expression or associ-ation in the ways that were now routine in a colony. The rules of evidence, the right to asylum, the higher thresholds for arrest and extradition were backed by judicial traditions, the relative autonomy of the universities, the press and public opinion, and the French Revolution and its values. All this could be exploited artfully.[78] Many Asians came to imperial capitals in search of justice, as what official records called 'disappointed litigants', appealing to a higher power against local oppressions. Others arrived as refugees or simply found themselves stranded: discharged sailors, aban-doned servants, itinerant traders or performers fallen on hard times. But increasingly they came as exiles.

José Rizal's two long sojourns in Europe, in 1882–7 and 1890–92, took in not only colonial Spain but also extended stays in London, Paris, Heidelberg, Berlin and Brussels. Of necessity, his fictional exposé of colonial life, *Noli Me Tangere* ('Touch Me Not', 1887), was published in Berlin and his dark *novela mundial*, *El Filibusterismo*, was published in Ghent. Already well read and thoroughly versed in Europe's ways, Rizal, his fellow Filipinos and others came not with a defeated air but to seize the continent's opportunities with a brash confidence, and to make Europe their own.[79] Sun Yat-sen's first period of exile brought him via Japan, Hawaii and the United States to London in 1896. In a curious incident, he wandered, or was enticed – it was never clear – into the *de jure* Qing territory of the Chinese legation at 40 Portland Place, from there to be bundled off to China on a capital charge. But he was released after a public campaign by English supporters which was taken up by *The Times*. The incident, and Sun's own published account of it, greatly elevated his revolutionary aura as 'the man destined to save China'.[80] After he was banished from Penang in November 1910, and persona non grata in British Malaya, Hong Kong, the Netherlands East Indies, French Indochina, Japan and Siam, the only path open for him was to London again, and from there to the United States.

In Paris in 1911, the exiled Phan Chu Trinh established himself on the margins of the republic of letters, near where rue Mouffetard, with its small publishers and bookshops, emptied into the working-class districts of the *13e arrondissement*. With his modest official stipend, he took up lodgings in the townhouse at 6 villa des Gobelins, where he worked on a 7,800-line verse translation into Vietnamese of Liang Qichao's Chinese rendering of *Strange Encounters with Beautiful Women*. Trinh moved among a small community of Vietnamese and of other Asian nationals who worked as translators or instructors in institutions such as the École des Langues Orientales.[81]

Increasingly, students added to the numbers of Asians resident in Europe. After 1890 the Qing government had encouraged its ambassadors in Paris to take 'embassy students' with them. One of them, Li Shizeng, returned to Paris with Francophile friends to open a publishing house and a soya bean factory, along with an outlet in the Marais extolling the bean's health virtues. He recruited workers from China, the first batch of sixty travelling via the newly opened Trans-Siberian Railway, for what was called 'frugal work-study': an idealized vision for creating model citizens, disciplined and aware. By 1913 there were some 242 Chinese students in Europe, most of them in France.[82] Others made their way to Berlin and Heidelberg, or to Lucerne. To Indian educators and students, German Indology and German science were vital counterweights to British scholarship in the same fields, compromised, as it was, by its role in supporting colonial rule in India.[83] But while there were barely 100 students from India in Britain in 1880, by 1910 there were between 1,000 and 1,200. That year, a parliamentary report on 'distressed' colonial subjects voiced its concern at the growing number of 'adventurers' from British India: young men 'with no very clearly defined aim', travelling under their own steam, or with rather unsteady family support.[84]

For the unbound traveller and the exile, the journey to the west could be arduous and humiliating. In September 1908 the young Indian journalist M. P. T. Acharya left his home city of Madras with a single suitcase and only 300 rupees, under a heavy cloud of suspicion and watched by the police. The question was where, if anywhere, in a world of empires was sanctuary to be found? He could travel relatively easily to the French possessions in India, the largest of which was the old port of Pondicherry, some 100 miles to the south. There he attempted to re-establish his journal, *India*. But, as its proprietor, he was liable for any offence of the paper, and although this was a different jurisdiction, there was the constant threat of extradition, or of being carried away to British territory by force, 'with the help of rowdies for whom Pondicherry was famous'. It was also not much of a place to live. Returning briefly to Madras in October for the marriage his parents had arranged, the following month Acharya travelled to Colombo by train and ferry. His next step would be irrevocable, as beyond this point he could not pay his passage home. But he was unsure whether to head east or west. His preferred route was to the Netherlands East Indies, a journey he could make more cheaply in deck class, in the tropical warmth, in the clothes he possessed. It was impossible to travel west in deck class without winter clothes. Yet there was no passage to Java, and he could not afford to stay in Colombo, a British port, with the ever-present danger of being sent home. So, almost on impulse, around late November he purchased a third-class ticket on a Japanese ship with 165 rupees of the money he had left and sailed to the Red Sea and through the Suez Canal to France.[85]

The Japanese ship served only English food, a staple boiled beef, forbidden to a Brahmin like Acharya, and so he fasted for the 22-day passage, except for the gift of an apple from the steward. Entering the Mediterranean, the air felt freer, and sailing between Sicily and Italy he communed with the ghost of Giuseppe Mazzini. Acharya disembarked in Marseilles, starving and very cold. He could see the republican trinity – *Liberté, Égalité, Fraternité* – chiselled everywhere on public buildings. He was in a country famous as a haven for refugees, but he knew that if the authorities heard he was penniless, 'all that vaunted freedom and hospitality would have vanished into air'. Through the kindness of a stranger he was given the fare to 'the city of revolutions', Paris. But it was a humiliation for a man of good family and standing to be reduced to mendicancy in shabby clothes. 'I was not accustomed to ask even for a recommendation in India from my own relatives. How dare I go down on my knees before a stranger?' Acharya approached long-distance correspondents from his days as a newspaperman, chiefly French orientalist scholars and Indian translators. But the established Indian residents of Paris, settled in comfortable middle-class homes, with a household of staff, were unsympathetic, defensive over the sacrifices they had made, and weary of giving to a constant stream of exiles. Although it had never been Acharya's intention to go to 'the English "home" ', unable to find anything to do in Paris, to London he went. An acquaintance in Paris advanced him his fare, Acharya knew, just to be free of his 'pestering'.[86]

In London, as in Paris, people created their own spaces in the city. The privileged lived in awkward proximity to servants and seamen: Lascars, Chinese, Malays and Arabs had been a presence in London for centuries in areas such as Limehouse, often lodging with Asian house-keepers who had married local wives. In 1911 there were around 1,319 Chinese in Britain, mostly in London, Liverpool and Cardiff. Most had followed the sea as stewards or cooks, like Nguyen Tat Thanh. They were literate, resourceful men – emphatically not 'coolies', but, as the *Liverpool Weekly Courier* recognized in 1906, 'the true intellectuals and progressives of their country'. However, the growing number of Chinese sailors jumping ship in Britain fuelled an ugly mood of racial panic.[87] An international seamen's strike in 1911 was in some ways a testament to the solidarities across borders, but also to growing hostility at the Asian seamen who, in Canton and elsewhere, were hired to break it. Paradoxically, this helped establish a global web of what the Cantonese called 'Chinaports' – such as the community of 300 stranded seamen in Hamburg and Bremerhaven, the Chinatowns in Rotterdam's Katendrecht district or Amsterdam's Binnen Bantammerstraat – all serviced by laundries, lodgings and eating houses, and far-roving pedlars from Zhejiang province.[88]

In the midst of this, the new wave of Asian students to London gravitated to enclaves such as 'Asia minor' in Bayswater or, more often, Fitzrovia and Bloomsbury, where the British Museum, University College and the nearby Inns of Court – the destinations of most foreign students – were to be found. Many Indians spent their time, as was intended, preparing for high office in the Raj. English civil servants on home leave or in retirement were placed *in loco parentis*. On his arrival, Acharya watched scornfully how his countrymen cultivated India-bound Englishmen with a view to future influence, grateful to mix with men they could not be seen with at home. Some were so anxious not to be seen as subversives that they did not 'care to be in any other company but their own landlord's family'.[89] These domestic situations too could open the way for intimacies impossible in Calcutta, Singapore or Hanoi. But others chafed at the chaperones and the racial snubs of landlords. Acharya's journal in Madras had carried a 'Letter from London' by a student, V. V. S. Aiyar, and so he made his way to its source: a well-appointed villa at 65 Cromwell Avenue, Highgate, north London.

'India House', as it was called, was the vision of one of the leading Indian citizens of Edwardian London, Shyamji Krishnavarma. Born in Gujarat in 1857, the year of the Indian Mutiny, he had come to England in 1879 as a protégé of the Oxford Sanskritist and evangelist Sir Monier Monier-Williams. He earned success at Balliol College, Oxford, qualified as a barrister of the Inner Temple and was even accepted as an honorary member of the United Empire Club. Returning to India, he served as *diwan*, or chief minister, of a number of princely states, and grew wealthy through investments in cotton mills in the region of Ajmer, in Rajasthan. He was every bit 'the successful prize-boy of a subject nation'. But, in 1897, disillusioned by his political career in the Indian princely states, and feeling personally betrayed by Englishmen after a series of affronts, he quit public service and left for London.

This was a year of hard choices in Indian politics. The Indian

National Congress had, since its formation in 1885, adopted an avowed 'moderate' policy towards the Raj. Now there were calls from within Congress for full *Swaraj*, or 'self-rule', backed by the new strategy of boycott. These were led by the radical trinity 'Lal-Bal-Pal': Lala Lajpat Rai in the Punjab, Bal Gangadhar Tilak from Maharashtra and Bipin Chandra Pal in Bengal. Their most dramatic manifestation came out of Bombay, where Tilak led opposition to the new invasive government powers that were adopted there in the wake of the plague of 1896–7. After the political murder of a plague official and his military escort at Poona, as they returned from a parade to mark the diamond jubilee of Queen Victoria in June 1897, Tilak was arrested on a charge of incitement and imprisoned. Krishnavarma had played a small part in Congress politics but had grown increasingly critical of it. He had also sought Tilak's aid in his own disputes with the British. He now felt a marked man. As he explained some ten years later: 'It is a folly for a man to allow himself to be arrested by an unsympathetic government and thus deprived of action when, by anticipating matters, he can avoid such evils.'[90]

'Exile', Krishnavarma also wrote, 'has its privileges.' For some years after 1897 Krishnavarma quietly enjoyed them. He took the view that the British might have robbed India, but at least their banks were solid, and he was an opportunistic investor on the London stock exchange. He was quick to read the runes from the Russo-Japanese War and made money from the issuing of new Japanese loans.[91] He moved in the outer circles of academic life, but then, out of nowhere, at the funeral of the philosopher Herbert Spencer in 1904 he made the dramatic announcement of a gift of £1,000 to the University of Oxford for a lectureship in Spencer's memory. He also launched a journal, *The Indian Sociologist*, in January 1905. Spencer was quoted on the banner-head of each issue: 'Resistance to aggression is not simply justifiable but imperative. Non-resistance hurts both altruism and egoism.' The paper took full advantage of freedom of publication in London and was an increasingly radical voice for *Swaraj*. Its initial run of 1,000 copies swiftly circulated among Indians overseas, and, to the consternation of officials, copies made their way back to India hidden in the baggage of travellers.

Krishnavarma then bought the house at 65 Cromwell Avenue, which he opened to a small fanfare in July 1905 as an alternative base for

Indian students in London. It was modelled on the adult education branch of Oxford University, Ruskin Hall. Krishnavarma established his own scholarships – loans, in effect – named after Indian heroes and martyrs, and made it a condition that holders should not join the Indian Civil Service. The speech at the opening of India House was given by H. M. Hyndman, an early follower and popularizer of the ideas of Karl Marx.[92] Hyndman threw the language of colonial paternalism back at the imperial establishment: 'It is the immoderate men, the fanatical men, who will work out the salvation of India by herself.'[93] Soon Krishnavarma heard of an 'India House' in Tokyo and in New York. The villa in Highgate was a natural base for M. P. T. Acharya, who took up free board there. Staffed by an Indian cook, a lascar and 'a Czechish refugee', it was, Acharya found, much like a bachelor hostel back home.[94]

India House gathered into its orbit some of the most talented Indian intellectuals abroad. Bhai Parmanand, from the Punjab, had been travelling in South Africa as a preacher for the Hindu reformist organization the Arya Samaj; on the recommendation of an Indian activist there, a lawyer by the name of M. K. Gandhi, he came to London. For Parmanand too, England was 'a sacred land' by virtue of its 'pure and free atmosphere'. Like many exiles of all nations, he found sanctuary in the reading room of the British Library. There he wrote a master's thesis on 'The Rise of British Power in India', the beginnings of a larger history of India. His examiners did not take to it; in any case, he had come to the view that English education was introduced to 'destroy our national consciousness'.[95]

Parmanand encountered a like mind in a fellow student from the Punjab, Har Dayal, who was studying modern history and Sanskrit at St John's College, Oxford. Har Dayal had already been talked about in his school days at St Stephen's in Delhi as one of the nimblest minds of his generation and was a protégé of Lala Lajpat Rai. Early in his time at Oxford, he made the most of the opportunity to meet thinkers such as George Bernard Shaw and Shaw's friend, the exiled Russian anarchist Peter Kropotkin. But his mood was darkened by the arrest of Lala Lajpat Rai in the Punjab in May 1907 and his banishment to Mandalay. This was a naked exercise of executive power that divided even the high imperial establishment and was a parting of the ways for many of the empire's Indian subjects. Later that year, Congress split on 'moderate' and 'extremist' lines. At the same time, with calculated impudence and characteristic impulsiveness, Har Dayal resigned his government scholarship and his place at Oxford. The man responsible for Indian students, Sir William Curzon Wyllie, was quick to point out that he was almost at the end of his three years of funding in any case. Officials were even more perplexed when he wore a dhoti and kurta about London and preached sexual renunciation and a rather strident form of Hinduism. Har Dayal was a married man, and had brought his wife, Sundar Rani, to England, to the great annoyance of her family. Now she was expecting, and her family sent her a second-class ticket to return home for a wedding. Har Dayal cashed it in for two third-class tickets and they travelled together. Their families cushioned the choices they made. Sundar Rani was the granddaughter of the Prime Minister of Patiala and, as her cousin put it, 'they were all well-off people and they took care of him'.[96] By the following year, both Har Dayal and Bhai Parmanand were back in the Punjab, disillusioned men in the epicentre of the Raj's crackdown on 'extremism'. Where Har Dayal went, 'young students flocked to hear him'.[97]

One of the first India House scholars, chosen from over 100 applicants and on the recommendation of Tilak himself, was Vinayak Savarkar, who with his two brothers had been active in western Indian politics. He carried with him from India in 1906 a biography of Mazzini, and while ostensibly studying law at Gray's Inn he spent much of his time translating it into his native Marathi. Savarkar saw in Mazzini the model for a new revolutionary personality. He fashioned himself in Mazzini's likeness, and devoted himself to instilling it in others. He shared Acharya's contempt for fellow students who became 'paying guests' of the English and thought so 'highly of the opportunity of sitting, drinking and dining with white families' and paying over the odds for it. He cultivated what he termed the more 'middle-class' students – those who were less confident and less anglicized – although he also looked to enlist a rich or princely sponsor. All this was possible in London: 'If someone organises a tea party,' he noted, 'people of all Indian provinces, grades and prestige can participate.'[98]

Meetings began to be held in relative secrecy in India House. But Savarkar was known to the police before he left India, and Scotland Yard started to watch his inner circle, a secret organization which, again inspired by Mazzini's 'Young Italy', he called *Abhinav Bharat*, or

'Young India'. One of his closest associates was Virendranath Chatto-padhyaya, a law student at the Middle Temple, from a notable Bengali literary family, and better known simply as 'Chatto'. He had failed to win an India House scholarship – 'a disappointed man', scoffed Krishnavarma – and from 1903 lived with a young Englishwoman. They opened a confectioner's shop in Shepherd's Bush in 1908, and when it failed they lived in Notting Hill as 'Mr and Mrs Chatterton' until they quarrelled and parted.[99]

For the British, it was highly impertinent of Indians to abuse in such a way the liberties of what the Viceroy of India termed 'the headquarters of the Empire'. It was even more distressing that they might find allies and sympathizers there. The Anglo-Boer War of 1899–1902 and earlier British interventions in Egypt and elsewhere had deepened the liberal and radical critique of imperialism and of the economic cartels and militarism behind it. The word itself now took on a new edge: 'house-breaking reduced to a science', as the Fabian socialist C. H. Norman defined it in 1906.[100] India House enlisted a range of British sympathizers, from Spencerites and curiosity seekers to the likes of H. M. Hyndman and Guy Aldred, an anarchist and agnostic who took on the printing of *The Indian Sociologist*. Patriots of all colonized lands drew on the words and deeds of Sinn Fein. But these people could not be relied upon. The Irish were also servants of empire, with generations of soldiers, policemen and administrators going out to India; and as an example of anti-British struggle, the stunted progress of home rule in Ireland in the 1900s was cause for dismay. It was a slogan that Indian nationalists hesitated to use.[101]

Krishnavarma's own alliances were tactical rather than a passionate meeting of minds. He lived austerely, with no interest in the bohemian pleasures of London – unlike many of his students – adhering to a strict Brahmin-like vegetarian diet that avoided onions and chillies, and dressing, as a Parisian newspaper mistook it, in 'the severe garb of an English clergyman'. Despite all Krishnavarma's munificence, some of the young men of India House thought him miserly and too quick to remind them of their obligation to him.[102] The likes of Savarkar were less interested than Krishnavarma in a British audience. For them, faced by everyday racism and condescension, and constantly confronted by their own relative disempowerment, it was a moot question as to how far such 'entanglement' with the ruling class of empire was advancing their cause.[103] Where *was* the common ground?

This was an era of congresses and manifestos – in art, literature and politics – of the discovery of the 'international' and the pursuit of the 'cosmopolitan'. All too easily, internationalism proved to be no more than a 'fantasy', the 'hypocritical private-egotistical cosmopolitanism of free trade', as the young Friedrich Engels had discovered at the 'Festival of Nations' in London in 1845.[104] But in a world where others had wealth, privilege and position, it at least offered the possibility for a well-positioned few to create some space for themselves to speak for their community on term of rare equality and to argue with dignity in the midst of indignities.[105] Across colonial Asia, not least in the port cities, outward-looking mobile elites embraced liberal cosmopolitanism as an ideal, a lifestyle and even an identity. They belonged to a small Asian middle class and a colonial public sphere that flourished though newspapers, clubs and municipal institutions such as sanitary bodies or school boards. Many remained attracted to the idea, at least, of imperial citizenship; they asked only for it to be upheld fairly.[106] Their lives were very different from those for whom worldliness was not a choice but was thrust upon them as a necessity for survival.

Some liberal and radical causes travelled further than others. Temperance leagues, women's movements, campaigns against 'white slavery' and for animal rights all swiftly found an audience and advocates in Asia, and sometimes beyond the elite. Internationalism spawned universal inter-languages, like Esperanto, which offered speakers the possibility to escape the cage of their linguistic past, and to reverse the curse of Babel.[107] Esperanto was embraced by Japanese reformers and Chinese students in Japan and Paris around 1907 – not least as a strategy to allow them to communicate with each other outside the official languages of empires. In 1908 there was a Shanghai Esperanto Society and, by 1912, a national body in China.[108]

This same mood gave rise to multiple attempts to fuse western and eastern spiritual and esoteric traditions, as they were variously understood. This in turn encouraged Asian thinkers to return to the sources of their own spiritual knowledge. As Bal Gangadhar Tilak himself acknowledged, 'we began to recognize the importance of the contents of our home only after the foreigners showed us'.[109] Theosophy – which drew in various measures on pan-racial mysticism, Anglo-Celtic radicalism and Hindu-Buddhist revivalism – was crucial to the founding spirit of the Indian National Congress in 1885 and was personified in one of its founders, Annie Besant. Theosophy found adherents among the European-educated from Ceylon to the Straits and Dutch Java. It carried with it its own vision of empire: enthusiasts saw the movement for 'imperial federation' in the 1890s as a step towards a millennial world commonwealth. For others, it was a way of ignoring empire altogether.[110] And yet openness, recognition and sympathy could not shed the insidiousness of imperial attitudes and cultural appropriation.[111]

Some Asians were drawn into the web of intimate friendships that shaped the modernist circles and salons of *fin de siècle* England and their utopian idealism, and sometimes intimacy led to long partnerships. Through this, and with particular intensity in these *belle époque* years, colonial subjects began subtly to shape metropolitan cultural life. India was a central presence in the very creation of 'Bloomsbury'; many of its writers and artists had Raj family connections, friendships with Indians and a shared aesthetic of the exotic, as seen in the formation of the Indian Society, which drew in many Bloomsbury luminaries after 1910. For some, these encounters fostered a deeper critical awareness of empire.[112] But, for Europeans, all this was easier to contemplate at home, and on a one-to-one basis, rather than under the rigid social conventions of colonial Calcutta, Singapore or Hanoi.

The high cosmopolitanism of the European tradition could be brutal to the rights of small nations and 'inferior' civilizations. The first 'Internationals' of western socialism gave the colonial question only a passing consideration. Karl Marx's own writings on imperialism, such as his reports on the Indian Mutiny for the *New York Daily Tribune*, were diffuse and of the moment, and were not widely read afterwards. His analysis of the 'Asiatic mode of production' built upon images of despotism, stagnancy and decline that were commonplace within western orientalist thought. His later work, however, showed more sympathy for the 'communal' patterns of social organization he had encountered in the writings on India of the sometime Bengal civil servant and academic jurist Henry Maine and others.[113] For Marx's followers, the ills of imperialism provoked a deeper debate as to how far the inevitable development of capital could be seen as a step towards its self-destruction. If so, was not the subjugation of what socialists, along with other western commentators, called 'the backward peoples' a necessary step – however morally abhorrent – towards this end?

The Second International was born in 1889 at the very moment of accelerated imperial expansion and competition. It was 'international' only in a European sense and its defining debates centred on how socialist parties should respond to the widening franchise in western Europe. Socialist critics of empire were more concerned by the jingoistic militarism it encouraged at home, and its capacity to distract the working class from the pursuit of class struggle. While some saw imperialism as an anathema to anyone committed to freedom, others saw it as the calling of a higher civilization which the socialist movement was bound to support. The English Fabian socialists – of which a surprising number of sympathizers were to be found in imperial civil services – saw themselves, as H. G. Wells put it, as 'Samurai': elite warriors for social improvement on the part of communities who could not manage this for themselves.[114] Seen in this way, one response to colonialist exploitation was more and better imperialism. The default position for the Second International was a conditional acquiescence in the imperial status quo.

At a Stuttgart meeting in August 1907, Madame Bhikaiji Cama – an exile from an influential Parsi family who had acted as Naoroji's secretary and was a prominent Paris-based suffragist and activist in her own right – unfurled for the first time the tricolour of India, which she, Krishnavarma and Savarkar had designed. But this symbolic act flew in the face of historical materialism's insistence on the irrelevance of what was rather contemptuously termed the 'national question'.[115] It seems she did not meet Lenin, who was present, and the International's most influential theoretician, Karl Kautsky, remembered only 'an Indian lady waving a flag'. When she raised the question of freedom for India, the British delegation, including Ramsay MacDonald, challenged her accreditation and, according to some accounts, walked out.[116]

THE BIRTH OF THE UNDERGROUND

Worldly visions of living outside empires, states and nations had, from earlier times, carried dark associations: with the quest for illicit knowledge like alchemy; with cabalistic brotherhoods; of universal tongues written in cipher; a freemasonry of the mind that was constantly stigmatized by charges of disloyalty to the established order.[117] The

'Cosmopolis' was a common place of publication by the underground printers of the Enlightenment, and 'Cosmopolite' a common pseudonym for radical writers. It signified the clandestine world of the dispossessed, belonging nowhere.[118] In the late nineteenth century the principal heirs to this tradition were the anarchists. They were a central presence in the émigré politics of Paris, and London became their principal city of refuge. They were the first to withdraw from the Internationals, after their leading thinker, the Russian Mikhail Bakunin, broke with Marx and the International Workingmen's Association in 1872, in the face of what he saw as its authoritarian tendencies. Anarchism's 'black internationals' were, by the movement's very nature, institutionally formless. No Asians attended or were invited to their few congresses, the last of which was in Amsterdam in 1907.[119] But, denied full access to the internationalism of the west, Asian travellers created their own, to which anarchist ideas seemed to speak directly.

Anarchism was mostly encountered through a broad spectrum of thought, as a path rather than a doctrine, and – for its followers – as the antithesis of a creed or dogma. The most read and translated theorist in Asia, Peter Kropotkin, defined anarchism in 1881 as a collective of individual acts. It offered a spectrum of different approaches to economic and social organization, such as mutualism, federalism, syndicalism and communism. In common with the times, most anarchists tended to identify with scientific advance and with an expanding worldly vision.[120] The most comprehensive anarchist account of the world was the nineteen-volume *Nouvelle Géographie Universelle: La Terre et les Hommes* (1876–94) of Elisée Reclus. His thought was distinctive in the way it 'provincialized' Europe as humanity's 'smallest tribe' and set an anarchist vision of the future firmly within a global context.[121] His writings also anticipated the form and scale of the new urban spaces that were emerging in Asia. For Reclus, the city was the highest form of communal life, a 'collective personality' formed by mutually supporting, contrasting neighbourhoods.[122]

Reclus's writings had a profound impact on Chinese studying in Paris, such as Li Shizeng, who translated some of them and adopted them as a foundation of work-study. The Chinese-language journal this group founded in 1907, *New Era (Xin Shiji)*, lasted three years and a hundred issues, generating translations of anarchist thought that would circulate across Asia for many years to come. Its banner-head carried an Esperanto subtitle, *La Novaj Tempoji*.[123] Leo Tolstoy's spiritual anarchism also found followers among pacifists and socialists in Japan and China at the time of the Russo-Japanese War. In the face of the futility and doubts raised by early confrontations with colonial power, anarchism spoke directly to the question of violence as a form of political struggle. And these and other issues of theory – on the forms of a future society, on attitudes to the 'nation' – were increasingly worked through in struggles beyond Europe.[124]

During the French Revolution, François-Noël Babeuf, whose writings forshadowed much later anarchist thought, had argued that in the face of an oppressive, immovable state, 'when a nation takes the path of revolution it does so because the . . . masses realize that their situation is intolerable, they feel impelled to change it, and they are drawn into motion for that end'.[125] By challenging the state's monopoly of violence, 'terror' could then acquire meaning and purpose. After the violent suppression of the Paris Commune of 1871 – in which not only anarchists fought – the argument gained currency that terror could be discriminate, proportionate even, when it was self-defence in the face of police action. Such thinking underlaid a decade of anarchist *attentats* in Europe and beyond.[126] By a different route, the populist *narodnik* tradition in Russia that culminated in the assassination of Tsar Alexander II in March 1881, struck an emotional chord in India, Japan and elsewhere. Others defended the motive for the deed, if not the deed itself. But beyond Europe, in the United States, the anarchist and feminist theorist Emma Goldman, together with Alexander Berkman – in relation to attacks such as that on the Carnegie Steel Corporation boss Henry Clay Frick in downtown Pittsburgh in July 1892 – argued that capitalists must take responsibility for their actions. The question was whom and what were to be targeted? What was the threshold of guilt or innocence?

The invention of dynamite, both as a weapon and as an idea, supported the arguments of men such as Émile Henry, the infamous perpetrator of a series of fatal bomb attacks in Paris in 1892–4, that the police's indiscriminate targeting of anarchists dictated an indiscriminate response. But despite the secret circulation of manuals for bomb-making, the construction of explosive devices was a specialized and highly dangerous affair. Most assassinations were a *coup de main* and many attempts ended in failure. They were often the work of solitary, troubled figures, dismissed as misanthropes. By the 1890s, despite the wave of violence that killed eleven people in France between 1892 and 1894, extreme nihilism had been largely disavowed in Europe. But although the 1892–4 attacks were unconnected in fact, the idea of a vast underlying conspiracy distilled many of the anxieties of a global age and was not to be dispelled. The state response conflated in the popular mind the image of 'the terrorist' and 'the anarchist', who were not at all the same thing.[127]

What also travelled was the figure of the terrorist as a modern demon, both as a theoretical ideal and as a literary type. The aesthetic of the agitator was usually that of a male, monkish ascetic, 'everything in him', as a much-travelled primer by Mikhail Bakunin put it, 'absorbed in a sole exclusive interest – in one thought – the revolution'. For initiates, this forged a sense of solidarity and heroic martyrdom. In the eyes of opponents, the anarchist was more of an individualist, an egoist, often an aristocratic type or a student, alienated and alone. Representations shaped reality: 'the propaganda of deed' demanded that an act be staged and publicized for maximum notoriety. Its effect lay as much in the anticipation as in the bomb or the bullet itself: the dread that they could puncture time and order at any moment and without forewarning. Fictional representations of the deed, such as Joseph Conrad's *The Secret Agent* (1907) and *Under Western Eyes* (1911) and, even earlier, José Rizal's *El Filibusterismo*, viewed it both from without and from within the mind of the perpetrator. These, together with a host of memoirs, generated a curious interplay of literary form and actuality.[128] In Paris, 'crime factories' churned out sensational fiction; in 1908 the journal *Le Parisien* gave over 12 per cent of its column space to it. This magnified the idea of 'investigation' in modern society, where lives were enacted in front of reporters, forensic scientists, policemen and private detectives.[129] The theme was soon taken up in the *romans-feuilletons* read in Japan and China and elsewhere.

In the anarchist panics of the 1880s and early 1890s, secret police practices became globalized. After the assassination of Tsar Alexander II in 1881, the Okhrana extended the reach of its informers and even operated freely out of its own building in Paris. New forms of censorship, anti-socialist laws and the prosecution of criminal conspiracy all widened the repertoires of state power. An 'International Conference of Rome for the Social Defence against Anarchists' in December 1898 further criminalized anarchism and entrenched the argument that it had 'no relation to politics'. It advocated new measures, such as extradition across borders for regicides. In 1903, in the wake of the assassination of President William McKinley in 1901, anarchists became the first category of person to be prohibited from entry to the United States on the grounds of political belief. A St Petersburg 'Secret Protocol for the International War on Anarchism' in March 1904 helped fashion a more standardized and professionalized police culture across the globe. As one Italian anarchist, Pietro Vasai, observed: 'The police are the same in all parts of the world'; they had become a highly mobile, specialized global labour force, identified with imperial migrants such as Sikh constables and watchmen.[130] Following the Entente Cordiale of 1904 between Britain and France, their police forces shared information on Indian and other activists across Europe, and this was soon extended to colonial territories.[131] From the landlords and brothel-keepers, pimps and prostitutes who peopled the underside of the migrant world, they recruited an undercover army of turncoats, informers and agents provocateurs. This was the same terrain that anarchists worked themselves.[132] The policing of ports and railheads was often in private hands. Security companies, such as Pinkertons, with their detectives and 'procurers', worked internationally in an extra-legal way to break strikes and seize fugitives. They enforced borders before states themselves did and fed public paranoia about the anarchist peril. In the words of Allan Pinkerton himself: 'It was everywhere, it was nowhere.'[133]

Anarchism was the quintessential ideology of exile: a state of being – displacement outside a country – which embodied the anti-nationalism of anarchist belief.[134] The aftermath of the Paris Commune sent a generation of sympathizers into exile and imprisonment across the world. Between 1864 and 1897 the French authorities despatched some 4,500 political prisoners – only twenty of them women – to New Caledonia. Many were communards of 1871, spared the firing squads to live alongside colonial rebels, Arabs and Berbers, and Vietnamese labourers. Many died there from what was diagnosed as 'nostalgia': a void of isolation and unrelieved depression.[135] More than 9 per cent of Italians lived outside Italy; among Italian anarchist editors, 20 per cent had experience of more than one country – and 40 per cent of all Italian anarchist publications were produced abroad. The mystique of many anarchists was enhanced by extended exiles far from home. Enrico

Malatesta – one of the best-known European exiles – spent time in Egypt, Argentina and Uruguay, Tunisia, the United States and England.[136]

The slogan 'Nostra patria e il mondo intero' – 'Our homeland is the whole world' – was a lived experience. Its citizenship, as it were, came not through allegiance to any formal organization, but from personal networks: from the circulation of letters, pamphlets and newspapers; from the translation of small pieces aimed at initiates as much as the masses; from encounters with people passing through on propaganda tours; and from songs and theatre.[137] These ties could prove as strong as the more visible ones of kin and kind, and resilient to the new forms of policing.[138] In this way, radical ideas oscillated around the world, endlessly syndicated and taken up, reshaped by local circumstances and exported again, so it was impossible to say who had thought of what first. It was a Pentecost rather than a movement.[139]

At the very moment that anarchist ideas began to capture the imagination of radicals in Europe, they were also at large in Asia. They were present with the first wave of Russian exiles to Japan, beginning with Mikhail Bakunin himself, who spent a month in Japan on his escape from internal exile in Siberia in 1861. Some were adept in the science of dynamite.[140] In 1874 another Russian internationalist *narodnik*, Lev Mechnikov, appeared in Japan. He arrived from the United States, competent in Japanese and with excellent introductions to the country's intellectuals from those he had met in Europe. Over the next two years, while teaching at the Tokyo School of Foreign Languages, he saw in the Meiji revolution's search for knowledge, everyday collaboration and solidarity a premonition of the general human evolution towards a cooperative civilization. He understood that Japanese use of European ideas was selective and a manifestation of a deeper communitarian ethic, rather than, as most other Europeans saw it, part of an evolutionary flow of reason and progress from the west to the east. On Mechnikov's return to Europe, his writings had a profound impact on the likes of Reclus – with whom he worked closely on the *Nouvelle Géographie Universelle* – Georgi Plekhanov and Kropotkin. This was especially true of Kropotkin's collection of essays *Mutual Aid: A Factor of Evolution* (1902), which, by a circumnavigation from east to west to east again, was reintroduced to Japan by the time of the Russo-Japanese War, and from the Japanese translated into Chinese. To many

Japanese readers it was as if Kropotkin merely explained and clarified ideals they already cherished as their own.[141]

The principal Japanese translator of Kropotkin was Kotoku Shusui, author of *Teikokushugi: Nijuseiki no kaibutsu* (1901), or *Imperialism: The Monster of the Twentieth Century* and co-founder in 1896 of the Society of the Study of Socialism. He had read Kropotkin and corresponded with him on a visit to the United States in 1905, following a prison sentence for his opposition to the Russo-Japanese War. Kotoku argued that both the war and the terms of the concluding peace treaty would lead to further imperial competition, instability and violence, and that 'true progress' lay in extending anarchist forms of mutuality and cooperation into the international sphere. He was an early enthusiast for Esperanto, and, during the relatively liberal period of Japanese politics in 1906, a founder of the Japanese Socialist Party. In the midst of the party's factionalism, the collaborative ideals of anarchism were a powerful common ground.[142] They were present too at the meeting of the Asian Solidarity Association in 1907, when Kotoku chided the Asian movements for failing to 'go beyond demands for national independence'. He urged the patriots gathered in Tokyo to go further in making anarchism the foundation of the new Asia: 'if the different revolutionary parties of Asia start to look beyond differences of race or nation they will form a grand confederation under the banner of socialism and one-worldism. The East Asia of the twentieth century will be the land of revolution.'[143]

It was almost a new dawn. Kotoku's 1901 critique of 'imperialism' had preceded and gone further than that of J. A. Hobson, Lenin and others in the west. Within a year it had been translated in Chinese and in 1906 into Korean. The Chinese organizers of the Asian Solidarity Association had embraced anarchist ideas. Even Phan Boi Chau, representing Vietnam, was part of the anarchist grouping at the meeting. He shared the euphoric mood of unity, but it is not clear how aware he was of delegates' diverse ideological positions. By no means all of them identified as anarchists or embraced the propaganda of the deed.[144]

Within three years, dark repression struck. In June 1910 a Japanese worker was arrested and accused of making bombs. The police claimed to have uncovered an extensive assassination plot against Emperor Meiji, and there was a general round-up of alleged socialists suspected of high treason. Among those snared was Kotoku, who had been working on his translation of Kropotkin's *The Conquest of Bread* (1892) at a hot-spring resort. In the trials that followed in early 1911, twenty-six conspirators were condemned to be hanged. Although twelve of the guilty were reprieved at the last moment by the emperor, another twelve were executed within three days of their sentencing. Kotoku and his lover, the journalist and feminist Kanno Sugako, were the final two to be hanged.[145]

The 'Kotoku Incident', as it became known, provoked an unprecedented press blackout with the trials held in camera. Nevertheless, in the way it polarized opinion it became the 'Dreyfus Affair of Japan'. Not all of those indicted were intellectuals, and not all the intellectuals – including Kotoku – were active in bomb-making, or even endorsed violence. For many it seemed that the only charge proven against Kotoku was that of his anarchist beliefs.[146] As the poet Ishikawa Takuboku wrote in June 1911:

> Though I used to feel quite remote from
> The sad mind of the terrorists –
> Some days recently I feel it coming close.[147]

The Japanese authorities reaffirmed the authority of the emperor as the centre of the nation, and the Special Higher Police deepened its surveillance of the thoughts of his subjects. Many socialists and anarchists withdrew from public life; some committed suicide, others fled abroad, such as the close associate of Kotoku, Sen Katayama, who moved to the United States and was soon prominent in activist circles there. By 1910 most of the Chinese anarchists in Japan had moved on to Paris, to join the schools and newspapers that were being founded for the work-study group there. The trial and executions were reported in anarchist journals in London, Paris and the Americas, as part of a worldwide attack on the anarchist idea.[148]

Kanno Sugako's involvement in the plot was more direct than Kotoku's own and went beyond acting as a courier or helpmate. She was a thinker in her own right, and many across Asia were moved by her troubled life, her 'free love' with Kotoku, and her cruel execution. In the words of a 'farewell missive' from her friend, Koizumi Sakutara, which Kanno copied as one of the final entries into her prison journal: 'How pitiful. This enlightened age derails the talented woman.'[149] The feminist circles occupied by women such as Kanno were a site for new experiments in thinking that did not see the women's movements in Europe, America or even Japan as the yardstick for female emancipation, unlike many male reformers. Moving amid them, the Chinese feminist thinker He-Yin Zhen drew on radical anarchist critiques of the state to envisage fundamentally new forms of social life, beginning with a rejection of existing forms of family and property. In her journal *Tianji Bao* (*Natural Justice*), published in Tokyo between 1907 and 1908, excerpts from *The Communist Manifesto* reached a Chinese readership for the first time – specifically, the burgeoning audience for new periodicals and translations among women.[150]

Formless and fluid this world might be, but it had its recurring and intersecting circulations, and a rhythm of its own. In his early writings, Karl Marx had a premonition of this, of the moment world history came into being: when capitalism could no longer satisfy its needs within one country, but 'chases the bourgeoisie over the whole surface of the world':

> From this it follows that this transformation of history into world history is not indeed a mere abstract act on the part of the 'self-consciousness', the world spirit, or of any other metaphysical spectre, but a quite material, empirically verifiable act, an act the proof of which every individual furnishes as he comes and goes, eats, drinks and clothes himself.[151]

In this sense, these mobile Asians abroad were among the first people to experience world history. They experienced it not as an idea but by coming and going, as workers and also as colonial subjects, in a way that brought capitalism and imperialism closer together in their worldview. Liminal spaces – locations of sudden displacement and new solidarities little understood by metropolitan elites, such as port city slums and the mining and plantation frontiers of the tropical colonies – became the foci of world-historical change. In this context, anarchism, as a doctrine of self-help and self-governance, as a vision of internationalism and of a world less patriarchal, began to insinuate itself into the village abroad, carried by the new workers of the global economy of movement, such as seamen and dockhands.[152] Anarchism was well adapted to their mixed labour forces of the waged, the unwaged and the casual, which defied the kinds of conventional 'class' analysis that was the staple of Marxist enquiry in Europe.[153] These broad coalitions had already led boycotts in Asia and would do so again in new 'general' labour unions.

Anarchists were also more willing than other radicals to give countenance to the underworld of labour. As an early anarchist newspaper
in Buenos Aires celebrated it in 1890: 'We are the vagrants, the mal-
efactors, the rabble, the scum of society, the sublime corrosive of
the present social order.' This itself was an echo of forms of protest in
the seventeenth and eighteenth centuries, during the first global age of
empire, when motley crews, slaves, drifters and pirates had combined
in a world of resistance across shorelines and oceans. It was seen at the
time by those in authority as a 'many-headed hydra' and left behind a
freewheeling vision of liberty and a folk memory of places outside
empires and their authority.[154]

Marx and Bakunin shared an image for how the radical spirit survived under the weight of capitalist oppression: the underground. Its
source was Hamlet's quip to his father's ghost: 'Well said, old mole.
Canst work i'the ground so fast? / A worthy pioneer!' This was taken
by G. W. F. Hegel as a metaphor for the spirit of the philosophy of history, which 'often seems to have forgotten and lost itself, but inwardly
opposed to itself, it is inwardly working ever forward . . . until grown
strong in itself it bursts asunder the crust of earth which divided it from
the sun, its Notion, so that the earth crumbles away'.[155] And so the idea
of the underground was taken up in this new age of empire by the kinds
of itinerant leadership that were emerging from the waterfronts and
railheads of empire, harrying, disappearing, burrowing and then resurfacing somewhere else, far away. The imperial underground now
confronted western power in Asia with the logic of its own globalism:
that it too might crumble away.

Die indische Delegierte Cama und Genosse Rana

The flag of Free India: Madame Cama in Stuttgart, 1907.

3

Empire's Inner Demons
1905–1909

ANGLO-INDIAN JERICHO

At the centre of the western condominium over Asia was the British Raj in India. It was a world system in its own right, centred not on London but on its seat of power in Calcutta. It formed the midpoint of an arc that encompassed the Indian Ocean and beyond, eastwards to Singapore and Hong Kong, down towards the southern Dominions, westwards from Bombay into the Persian Gulf and the Red Sea, and down the coast of Africa. The British occupation of Egypt in 1882 threaded new 'red routes', in the form of garrisons, post offices and telegraph relay stations, through the eastern Mediterranean and, via Malta and Gibraltar, into the home waters of the British Isles. Singapore took on a new strategic significance as the Clapham Junction of the East. This great arc helped defend the approaches to the Raj, and the Raj supplied the circulations of people that gave it a unity. Punjabi constables and watchmen guarded western interests in Southeast Asia and the foreign concessions in China. Sindhi merchants set up shop in Malta, Bukhara, Kobe and Panama, and Bengali or Malabari clerks staffed colonial secretariats, land offices and railway stations from Mombasa to Malaya. Plantation labourers recruited in Calcutta, Bombay and Madras hewed out the frontiers of human cultivation and settlement across three oceans. The 200,000 or so men in arms of the Raj garrisoned the far-flung outposts that allowed Great Britain to imagine herself a terrestrial, as opposed to a maritime, power of consequence. And it was the vastness of this domain that allowed British statesmen to think in classical 'imperial' terms. The only occasion when British sovereigns assumed an imperial style was in their guise as *Kaiser-i-Hind* – a title by which the

British claimed the inheritance of the Mughal empire, bestowed on Queen Victoria, in her absence, at the imperial Durbar, or grand levée, held in Delhi in 1877.[1] Britain's unchallenged paramountcy in Asia stabilized the entire imperial order, for a time.

But now, in the new century, the Raj was beset by political and strategic challenges, and by self-doubt. In 1904 the British geographer Halford Mackinder announced the end of 'the Columbian epoch'.[2] Western maritime conquest had reached its furthest extent; all that remained was the securing of its internal frontiers in contested border regions. In a more imaginative sense, the limits of 'human empire' had been reached, and with this came a gnawing sense of vulnerability and decay.[3] The arrival of competitors such as Germany and Japan brought new conundrums to the so-called 'Great Game', the clandestine scheming for hegemony in Central Asia. Never mere play, this was prosecuted with lethal seriousness by a growing phalanx of specialist soldiers and spies, cartographers and cryptographers.[4] Yet, in spite of this, the number of Britons governing India was famously small, around 1,000 in the Indian Civil Service, with perhaps 1,000 more in the police. Over two-fifths of the territory of the Raj, comprising some 565 princely states, was ruled by proxy. The 'steel frame' of the Raj was very uneven. It was government by smoke and mirrors, and after the attrition of decades of warfare across the arc of empire, in Egypt, Sudan, Burma and on the Northwest Frontier, there was a growing risk that the underlying trickery might be exposed. In the highest circles of the Raj it was possible to discern doubt and pessimism. Britain, the viceroy, Lord Lytton, feared in 1878, was 'losing the instinct and tact of empire'. Others foresaw the Raj being swamped by its own collaborators, the rising elites within Indian society, or, in the Darwinian language of the day, being fatally enfeebled by its own racial degeneration.[5] In truth, the Raj had never emerged from the shadow of the Indian Mutiny-Rebellion of 1857. The British lived in eternal fear of sedition among the Raj's Indian troops, especially those posted overseas, or fomented by 'mad mullahs' and *mahdis*: the Muslim outlaws – sufis, scribes and go-betweens – who moved between the various imperial constellations in Asia and the Middle East. Such men grafted a rival Muslim connectedness on to western networks of consuls, shipping lines and law, which the British never fully understood.[6] These mobile subjects mastered empire as a system before the British ever did.

The Viceroy of India after 1899, Lord Curzon – one of the most well-travelled men to hold the office – saw India as the 'pivot' of the empire, and in British rule 'the decree of providence'. He was determined to dispel all doubt as to the permanence of the Raj. Like his contemporaries J. B. van Heutsz in the Netherlands East Indies and Paul Doumer in Indochina, and in harmony with his own personality, he looked to create a more aloof, more elite imperial service, founded on racial hierarchy and administrative efficiency. Above all, he was obsessed with 'prestige', and the need to untangle what he termed the 'Supreme Government' of the Raj from the nascent public sphere in which Indian elites had begun to find a voice. By 1905 the British in India were confronted with 1,359 registered newspapers and journals with an estimated 2 million subscribers.[7] Curzon began by cutting back Indian participation in institutions within Calcutta itself, in the Calcutta Corporation and university. Then, stating his intention to 'dethrone Calcutta from its place as a centre of successful intrigue', Curzon announced in 1904 his intention to divide Bengal – British Asia's oldest province – into two separate territories.[8] The Bengal Presidency itself was one of the largest political units on earth, with a population in 1901 of 44 million, more than the Habsburg, Ottoman or Japanese empires. 'Partition' seemed to many to be an attempt to 'convert Bengal into a second Ireland' by dividing it into Hindu and Muslim majority areas.[9] This threatened the primacy of Calcutta, where a colossal proportion of the wealth of all Bengal was concentrated. More than this, the lofty arrogance of the move was seen by Bengal's political class, the English-educated intelligentsia who had most to gain and now the most to lose from the Raj, as nothing less than an assault on their entire society and culture.[10] The campaign to save the city and to save Bengal became the defining struggle of the times.

'India's shame', in the words of the novelist Bankim Chandra Chattopadhyay – who did much to shape the thoughts of educated Bengalis in this period – was that the loss of nation had brought with it the loss of the very idea of independence. Self-confidence had to be recovered through a sense of history and through India's spiritual strength. Calls for the promotion of home-grown enterprise, or *Swadeshi*, gathered momentum from the 1870s. But in 1905 this erupted into a full-scale boycott of British goods and British institutions. On the assigned day of Bengal's Partition, 16 October 1905, there were fasts, processions and mass bathing in the Ganges. Demonstrations and picketing continued over the following months. Manchester dhotis were burned, Liverpool salt was thrown into the Hooghly River.

Swadeshi set up new national-type schools – about forty of them by 1909 – run by an unprecedented movement of volunteers, and centred on a revival of *samitis*, or local brotherhoods, whose work ranged from philanthropy, education and training to enforcing boycotts and stewarding meetings.[11] These were young men committed to disciplined activities and to physical regeneration, casting off the clothing of the effeminate 'babu', the stereotypical anglicized shopkeeper or clerk in the service of the Raj. High among the humiliations of colonial rule was that, while it recruited some so-called 'martial races' into its service, it seemed to disarm and emasculate the majority. Wrestling and fighting with the *lathi*, a bamboo stick, became popular with young men of the middle class in the national schools and the *samitis*. They nurtured a collective ethos through individual acts of renunciation and service.[12] Women also attended public meetings; but, more than this, in a way that was invisible to the British, *Swadeshi* went to the heart of the home, to the handling of salt for meals, the choosing of what clothes to wear, such as the discarding of English bodices and chemises: 'Let us use rose scent instead of lavender perfume and free ourselves from stumbling in a lady shoe.'[13]

With curses, cuffs and blows, the British in Bengal inveighed against the growing 'cheek' of Indian employees and servants. An epidemic of violence by Europeans further incensed Bengali opinion and led to calls for vigilante justice against what the leading Bengali 'extremist' Bipin Chandra Pal termed 'the European criminal in India'. A horrified Archbishop of Canterbury passed on a file of cases to the viceroy. Across India between 1901 and 1905, there were 392 European assaults on Indians, twenty-seven of them fatal, compared to 251 Indian attacks on Europeans with twelve deaths.[14] The lieutenant-governor of the new province of East Bengal and Assam, Sir Bampfylde Fuller, was notorious for using his personal retinue of Gurkhas to enforce the prestige of his office and slap down the 'rudeness' of students and demonstrators.[15] 'What ails Fuller Sahib', worried the loyalist prince Sir Pertan Singh, 'that he wants to blow flies from cannon?'[16] Fuller was the target of a bungled assassination attempt, and Curzon's successor, Lord Minto, was quick to accept his resignation in August 1906.

Fuller's departure was claimed as a victory for Bengal, but it brought home the question of how far *Swadeshi* could go. There were, in the first year after the Partition, some 200 meetings in Bengal, and riots in Calcutta in October 1905. This no doubt hurt the British: there was a 25 per cent drop in the quantity of Lancashire cotton piece-goods imported into Bengal. It also hurt the peasant consumer. But it did not hurt the British enough. Bipin Chandra Pal, on a triumphal lecture tour in Madras in May 1907, reflected on the nature of British power:

> . . . what is the secret of this? The secret is hypnotism. It is hypnotism. It is *Maya* and *Maya* [magic, or illusion]. And in the recognition of the *Mayic* character of British power in India that lies the strength of the new movement. What we want is – to prove this *Maya*, to dispel this illusion, to kill and destroy this hypnotism. We have been hypnotised into the belief that, though three hundred millions we may be, yet we are weak . . . They set up one Indian against another, and then they call it their conquest. That is how they write our history.[17]

After one of these speeches, a Madras speaker stood up to advocate both the making of bombs and, in a provocative metaphor, that Indians should go abroad and return at each new moon to sacrifice 108 white lambs.[18]

Anticipating this greater struggle to come, a new type of leadership rallied around new journals, especially the Bengali *Yugantar* ('Era of Transition') and the English-language *Bande Mataram*, founded in 1905 by Bipin Chandra Pal, and named after the 'Hymn to the Mother' penned by Bankim Chandra Chattopadhyay and set to music by Rabindranath Tagore. These journals were the work of many hands, and there were multiple translations of articles between the two. In Bengali homes, they were treated 'as sacred lore'. The guiding personality of *Bande Mataram* was Aurobindo Ghose. Born in 1872, Aurobindo had the English middle name 'Ackroyd' imposed on him by his father, a committed Anglophile like so many of his generation and station. He was sent in 1879 to St Paul's School in London, before taking the top First in the Classical Tripos in his second year at King's College, Cambridge. In theory, the Indian Civil Service was open to all, but candidates had to travel to London to take the entrance examination. Aurobindo passed it in eleventh place. But the final hurdle was a horse-riding test, which Aurobindo repeatedly missed, effectively throwing the examination. This – the privilege that he had been afforded and spurned – made him a marked man.[19]

On his return to India in 1893, Aurobindo wrote scornfully of the lack of progress achieved by the Indian National Congress: 'The walls of the Anglo-Indian Jericho stand yet without a breach, and the dark spectre of Penury draws her robe over the land in greater volume and with an ampler sweep.'[20] Like Krishnavarma, he tried to carve a path outside the Raj, in the service of a princely state, in Baroda, and aligned himself with the 'extremist' circles of the Congress. But Aurobindo was one of the first to break with its 'babu' methods. In an uncompromising series of articles in *Bande Mataram* in April 1907 he laid out a programme of 'passive resistance' to the Raj, in which he refused to lay an absolute moral injunction against 'any attempt to answer violence with violence'. As in Russia, as in Ireland, 'Where the need for immediate liberty is urgent and it is a present question of national life or death on the instant, revolt is the only course.'[21]

Aurobindo's younger brother, Barindra Kumar Ghose, born in Croydon but educated in India, drew together a constellation of *samitis* of radicalized young men into something approaching a revolutionary organization. The British, increasingly obsessed with 'secret societies', began to refer to the *Yugantar* 'party'.[22] Not all *samitis* were radicalized, but they provided a mechanism for it. The most disciplined and clandestine, the Dacca Anushilan Samiti, was religiously exclusive, and adopted elaborate oaths, with a suffocating system of mutual observation to enforce them, sometimes upon the very young. To Aurobindo, in the current conditions of colonial subjugation, the idea of 'party' carried the danger of further subservience and factionalism. In language that echoed Kropotkin's teachings, he favoured a diffuse federation of bodies: an underground to prepare for 'the great rising in India, to be helped with the cannon and guns of China and Japan'.[23]

From the outset, the movement placed itself on a global plane. The vast Bengal delta was another of the great crossways of maritime Asia, part of a 'moving India' from where humans and goods travelled onwards to China and Southeast Asia, and people looked far beyond Calcutta or London for inspiration. Travellers from Bengal, like those from Vietnam and elsewhere, wrote of their 'world abroad'.[24] *Swadeshi* activists soon joined the trail of students to Japan, among them a prominent stump orator of the Dacca Anushilan Samiti called Taraknath Das. He was its chief emissary to Madras, and its first to the world abroad. In 1906, tipped off by a sympathetic policeman that he was about to be arrested, he left Madras with several others as a deck passenger on a

French ship carrying livestock via Colombo to Japan, where he later took fresh passage to the United States.[25]

Japan was in everyone's minds. As Aurobindo wrote, 'the Japanese had only to revitalize and perfect a strength that already existed. We have to create strength where it did not exist before; we have to change our natures, and become new men with new hearts, to be born again.'[26] In Calcutta, a Japanese called Murtaza promoted ju-jitsu and taught fencing at a school founded on a Japanese model in 1904 by Sarala Debi Ghosal, a niece of Tagore. To its adepts, Murtaza was the true 'fountain of *lathi* play'.[27] On public platforms, the victory of the Japanese over Russia in 1905 and the Partition agitation were claimed as a single historical moment. Newspapers campaigned for aid for Japanese sick and wounded, and children were named after Japanese leaders. *Swadeshis* were identified by their use of Japanese 'Elephant Brand' matches – ironically, the same kind that were being boycotted in China. It was also no coincidence that the Hong Kong boycott against American goods was launched just a few weeks before the *Swadeshi* campaign. Boycott was a global strategy which linked China, India and the protests against the treatment of Asian labour in South Africa led by the Durban lawyer M. K. Gandhi.[28]

In 1908 the British seized and catalogued the library of the Dacca Anushilan Samiti. Among the most borrowed of its several hundred volumes were, predictably enough, accounts of the conquest of Bengal and 'Clive the forger', histories of the 1857 rebellion and the fictions of Bankim Chandra Chattopadhyay.[29] But in this and similar libraries, to be found as far away as the remote towns of Assam, there were also books on the American War of Independence, the French Revolution, the Italian Carbonari, the Irish risings and Russian nihilism.[30] The British panicked when they came upon an account of the life of Emma Goldman, together with her portrait, circulating in Bombay.[31] For those contemplating the path of violence there was, for secrecy and method, the example of the Russian *narodniks*; for technique, the chemical manufacture of the bomb, which more patriots were sent to countries like Japan to learn; and for legitimacy, the universal argument that, by its despotism, the colonial government had betrayed the rule of law, and so one was now morally free to transgress it. In these conditions, as the *Yugantar* manual *Bartaman Rananiti* ('Modern Military Science', 1907) put it: 'the power of discriminating between right and wrong is gone. Everything is sacrificed at the feet of the goddess of liberty.' All this placed Bengal at the centre of the wildly eclectic transmission of ideas that was making anarchism part of the common culture of political movements across Asia.[32]

These ideas spoke in a variety of political tongues. The writings of the Bengali revolutionaries also looked to root their actions within South Asian ethical traditions and the language of scripture. The Bhagavad Gita, a dialogue between the warrior Arjuna and Lord Krishna on the eve of the deciding battle for the age, was a staple of the libraries of the *samitis*. It was employed by theosophists, liberals and nationalists alike as a defining statement that announced modern Hinduism to a world audience, as a political text that transcended the present moment, as a response to modernity and as a call to duty. But Lord Krishna's appeal for action against injustice in the world, in the face of all consequences, could be incendiary. It dramatized the question of war and violence in a time of capitulation and resignation by proclaiming, 'It is better to do than not to do.'[33] The dense symbolism and metaphor of the Bhagavad Gita, as woven into journals and pamphlets, bamboozled the official censors. It conjured a Manichean view of the world and promoted devotional practice in which *sakti* (divine energy) and the idea of service to the 'Mother' were powerful movers of minds.

For any campaign of violence to succeed, it needed to win popular sanction. But, the radicals understood, this did not have to amount to active support; to win tacit empathy might be enough. If the Raj was indeed an 'illusion', it would not take much to dispel it: 'How many English officials are there in each district?' asked *Yugantar* in March 1907. 'If you are determined you can put an end to English rule in one day.'[34] For some, this religious language was a dangerous 'shortcut' to mass feeling. For one Bengali Muslim, Muzaffar Ahmad, it was possible to be caught up in the 'romance' of the moment, but the Hindu diction of 'Bande Mataram', 'The Hymn to the Mother', was an obstacle to identifying fully with it: 'How could a monotheist Muslim youth utter this invocation? No Hindu Congress leader was ever able to understand this.'[35] Yet Aurobindo came to believe that it was the emphasis on 'faith' and 'selflessness' that made the Indian struggle something more than a mere imitation of the west or a nationalism in 'a purely materialistic sense'.[36]

The government of India now estimated that *Swaraj* 'had captivated the minds of fully 80 per cent of the educated Hindu population of Bengal':

> So little of the actual power of the British government had been seen in recent years in Bengal that apparently the people had forgotten or completely disbelieved in its existence. A wild idea spread among, not only the youths of the country, but even most of the older men that they had only to combine and take up lathis, revolvers and bombs to drive the English out of India in a few years.[37]

This perception of an absence of rule was a recurring nightmare for the British, particularly as Aurobindo's clarion calls came on the fiftieth anniversary of the Indian Mutiny. Their nervousness could not be hidden and reinforced the power of the symbolism that the Mutiny evoked on all sides. There were fears of a general rising in the Punjab on 10 May 1907, the day when in 1857 the sepoys had first turned their bayonets on the Raj at Meerut. Once again the rallying cry was 'Chalo Delhi!', 'To Delhi!' The old capital was under curfew.[38] The newspapers of the *Yugantar* group were slapped with a series of indictments for sedition. In July, *Yugantar*'s editor, Bhupendranath Datta, received a year's rigorous imprisonment, having infuriated the authorities by making no attempt to defend himself.[39] The fact that he was the younger brother of the world-renouncing, world-travelling Swami Vivekananda underlined to the British the complexity of the networks involved. In August Aurobindo was also arrested, and charged as editor of *Bande Mataram*. He did defend himself and, confounded by the loose collective leadership of the paper, the prosecution was unable to prove Aurobindo was responsible for its content. The case against him collapsed and an illiterate printer was convicted instead.[40] In the heated atmosphere at the trial, a young student jostled a European police inspector and was sentenced by the presiding magistrate, D. H. Kingsford, to a whipping of fifteen lashes. In this moment of looming crisis, a line was crossed.

The violence, when it came, targeted specific oppressors with indiscriminate consequences. The most spectacular attack was an attempt in December on the life of the lieutenant-governor of West Bengal, Sir Andrew Fraser. A mine was placed on the line to be travelled by his special train in Naraingarh, but he was unharmed. The most shocking act occurred on 30 April 1908 in Muzaffarpur, a quiet town in the mofussil, when two men threw a bomb into the carriage of a Mrs and Miss Kennedy, the wife and daughter of an English barrister, Pringle Kennedy, as they returned home from the local club. The daughter was killed instantly and the mother died shortly afterwards. It was a case of mistaken identity: the target was the carriage that followed behind carrying the district judge, D. H. Kingsford, who, after trying the cases against *Yugantar* and *Bande Mataram* the previous year, had been posted to the countryside, supposedly out of harm's way. Another bomb was sent to Kingsford packed into a Cadbury's cocoa tin hidden in a 1,075-page commentary on the common law. But it was delivered to his previous posting in Calcutta. The package remained unopened in his library, the detonating mechanism perished in the heat and the device only came to light more than a year later.[41]

Two suspects were observed at the scene of the Muzaffarpur attack. One was arrested nearby, and the other attracted the suspicions of an off-duty Indian police officer who was travelling in the same train carriage, by virtue of his 'suspiciously clean clothes' and new patent leather shoes. When challenged at a stop, he ran, was pursued, drew a gun and shot himself in the chest and head.[42] After a quick trial, the surviving assassin, Khudiram Bose, was sent to the gallows and became the Bengal revolutionaries' first and most hallowed martyr. The entire *Yugantar* circle was under surveillance, and there were police raids on sites across Calcutta, notably a Ghose family property at 32 Muraripukur Road, known as the 'Maniktola Garden'. The two-acre plot of overgrown brush, stagnant ponds and a cluster of fruit trees also contained an old summer house and a couple of sheds and was used by the young men of the *Yugantar* circle as a kind of ashram for their religious, political and physical training. On the morning of 2 May the police found eleven revolvers, four rifles, a shotgun and bombs hidden in an iron tank in a remote part of the garden.[43]

ACROSS THE BLACK WATER

The police pulled in and examined 222 witnesses before bringing thirty-six men to trial in the sessions court at Alipore in two batches, the first on 19 August and the second on 19 October. A number of the accused were kept in the 'Forty-Four Degree': the forty-four separate solitary cells for condemned men at Alipore jail. Central to the Indian system of criminal justice was the institution of the 'appróver'. Deriving from English common law during the reign of King Henry I in the early twelfth century, it had all but died out by the end of the fifteenth century but was never formally abolished.[44] It survived in India in the so-called 'extraordinary' trials of the Thugs in the nineteenth century. The idea was that an accused could be convicted 'by someone else's confession' – namely, that of an accomplice, who thereby could gain the promise of a pardon after the trial. It was not enough for an approver to provide an eyewitness account; his testimony had to be corroborated, or 'approved', with physical evidence. In mass trials, the approver and the prosecuting authorities worked to a kind of formula to produce a stable narrative of events, and even where the approver was doubted, judges tended to follow the detail of the case through his eyes. A canny approver knew what was required of him. The accused might compete for the role, but it was a deadly gamble. One's own guilt was exposed from the outset, and the less skilful, the less credible, might end up merely convicting themselves. For the plausible approver, it was a high price for freedom, one that was ultimately paid for with the lives of others.[45] It added a treacherous counter-current to the underground in India.

The British found their approver in Alipore jail. Arms were smuggled in and he was killed by two of his fellow accused outside the prison hospital. They were promptly tried and hanged, and the public claimed them as martyrs, a huge crowd following the bier as if they were family members. Flowers and rice were thrown by the women from the houses along the streets. This was the last funeral of its kind to be permitted, but not the last of the violence.[46] An Indian prosecutor was shot dead outside the courthouse and the Indian police officer who had led the pursuit of the Muzaffarpur killers was later gunned down on the street.

The 'Alipore Bomb Trial' opened behind barbed wire and lines of soldiers with bayonets fixed. The English chief prosecutor, Eardley Norton, who was new to India, kept a loaded revolver on top of his brief in court.[47] It was perhaps the first political show trial of its kind in the British empire. It showcased the brilliance of the Indian lawyers who exploited the situation to defend the accused. Barindra Ghose declined the privilege of a separate trial in a European court, which his birth in England and British citizenship entitled him to. He was one of the first men to admit to his guilt: in his case, it was a time-honoured tactic to throw up a smokescreen to hide men still at large, and to use the public platform of the trial 'to place the details of our workshops before the country so that others may follow in the footsteps'.[48] For the British, the trial presented an acute dilemma as to how far they were prepared to uphold the due process of law in defending their own position.

The authorities' key goal was to convict the man they saw as the 'mastermind' of this 'anarchist society', Barindra's brother Aurobindo. Privately, the viceroy was warned at an early stage that Aurobindo had remained so far in the background that a full conviction was impossible. The trial focused on a letter from Barindra to Aurobindo in December 1907: 'We must have sweets all over India ready for emergencies.' This, the prosecutors claimed, was a simple code for bombs. But Barindra retracted his confession, the approver was dead and the letter was discredited by the defence as a forgery, partly on the grounds that Barindra had signed his full name. The defence argued, and the judge was forced to agree, that no 'Europeanized' person would possibly write to his brother in this way.[49] Suspicion was cast on a key police informer who was a forger of banknotes. The police were known to fabricate evidence and, when cases collapsed, were treated indulgently by their superiors, who were anxious to preserve morale. The trial occurred in the wake of a series of recent scandals which exposed routine police extortion and torture – including by British officers – and how little was done by superiors or magistrates to prevent it. The proceedings were further confused by false and conflicting confessions.[50] In the courtroom, Aurobindo had a vision whereby the prosecuting counsel, Norton, became the Lord Krishna, who said to Aurobindo: 'Now do you fear? I am in all men and I overrule their actions and their words.'[51]

The case dragged on for 125 days. At its conclusion in April 1909, seventeen of the thirty-six accused escaped conviction by pleading their ignorance of what had gone on. On the capital charge of conspiracy to wage war against the king-emperor, the defence lawyers – chiefly C. R. Das, who was to emerge as a major force in Bengal politics – pressed the argument that Aurobindo had merely advocated passive resistance.

The two Indian assessors judged the charge unproven, and the judge – a man whom, years ago, Aurobindo had beaten into second place in the Classical Tripos in Cambridge – acquitted him. His brother Barindra, however, and his close associate Ullaskar Dutt were sentenced to death, only for their sentences to be commuted on appeal.

As a show trial, Alipore was a conspicuous failure. The rule of law remained a powerful legitimating idea, and prosecutors did not always get their way. 'Conspiracy' was not easy to prove, and courts were not always willing to go beyond what could be legally proven. Cases in which many accused were involved were often 'whittled down' by the courts at various stages. And between those who were never caught, those who were caught and not brought to trial, those who were discharged by magistrates, those who proved their innocence and those who were convicted but then acquitted by the court of appeal, retribution was somewhat diluted.[52] But, to those caught up in it, this was no justice at all. As Aurobindo explained for a Bengali readership:

> Unless one stood in the dock oneself, one cannot realise the delusive untruth of the Western penal code. It is something of a gamble, a gamble with human freedom, with man's joys and sorrows, a life-long agony for him and his family, his friends and relatives, insult, a living death. In this system there is no counting as to how often guilty persons escape and how many innocent persons perish. Once one has been involved in this gamble, this cruel, callous, reactionary social machinery, one can understand the reason for so much propaganda on behalf of Socialism and Anarchism, and their wide influence.[53]

This for Aurobindo marked a further break with the approach of Congress that still tended to see politics as a 'grand suit-at-law' and imperial justice as a higher court of appeal, a neutral third party to which Indians could address their claims. Henceforth, the Raj and its subjects confronted each other face to face, with no possibility of mediation, and the fount of justice for India was to be sought within, in what Aurobindo termed, in 1909, 'internally complete rule by the people'.[54]

The government did not pursue Aurobindo on appeal; it feared it would only allow him to 'develop into a myth'.[55] Instead, Aurobindo fashioned his own. Not only in court, but in solitary confinement in his 'ashram at Alipore', he experienced visions of visitations from Swami

Vivekananda. On his release, after a final campaign of speaking and writing in which his spiritual conversion was an increasingly central theme, Aurobindo withdrew from the political world and from the Raj. He went first to the French territory of Chandernagore, and then to French Pondicherry, and devoted himself to yoga, meditation and religious and philosophical writing.[56]

Norton, for one, regretted the whole affair. In an ideal world, he argued, Aurobindo would have 'been a valuable asset to the State', who would have gone far, say, in the educational service.[57] But, in the collective wisdom of old Raj hands, Alipore was a manifestation of a primordial truth about India: 'so easily does the hysterical East with its perverted world cults, change from simple kindly humans, to demons'.[58] The conspiracy conjured up an 'underside India' of 'every sort of half understood thing and people', dark with the threat of *thuggee* and steeped in 'the pathos of underworlds'.[59] Into this bestiary of empire was now placed the *bomb-parast*, the 'worshipper of bombs'. British observers expounded a primitive social psychology of violence. In one analysis, the Bengal trials showed 'how the Hindu student depraved and often injured by too early eroticism, turns to the suggestiveness of the murder-monger, and worships the nitro-glycerine bomb as the apotheosis of his goddess'.[60] Certainly some of the *samitis* were militant in forbidding 'undue intimacy' with women. Police reports – drawing on Sir Richard Burton's accounts of homosexuality within the circle of Socrates and the armies of ancient Thebes – analysed at length allegations of 'pederasty'.[61] Some advocated corporal punishment as an antidote. However, the vast majority of those convicted, including Barindra Ghose and Ullaskar Dutt, instead endured transportation on the SS *Maharaja* 'across the black water' and a long exile.

The shipping of convict labour to Singapore, to Sumatra, to Australia, had, in quite literal terms, laid the foundations of British Asia. But while the practice had died out elsewhere, the Andaman Islands existed for little else. Many rebels of 1857 had been sent there to get them out of India, ostensibly to relieve crowding in Indian prisons, and then as a tool of colonization. Mortality rates were high and the atmosphere was violent. The only viceroy yet to be killed in office, Lord Mayo, met his end there in 1872 at the hands of a prisoner. By 1901 there were nearly 12,000 convicts and 3,000 free or conditionally released residents. The transportation of 'seditious' prisoners had been stopped in 1906, but was resumed in 1909, after some hesitation, to isolate the new generation of revolutionaries from the 'surroundings that induced [them] to commit the crime'.[62] They were shipped in fetters with a wooden 'ticket' on an iron ring round their necks, their names replaced by a number, and landed at the Cellular Jail at Aberdeen in the settlement of Port Blair. This was a prison-within-a-prison, a 'strange harem' as Barindra described it, constructed between 1890 and 1905 on scientific lines, with a great tower, or *Goomti*, at the centre of seven radial wings of three storeys and around 690 cells designed for solitary confinement. Of the regime's effect on an inmate, Barindra wrote:

> One week would be sufficient to make him feel what another avatar felt on the cross. If he remained two years he would begin to grow his wisdom tooth anew. And if he could pass twelve years he would be disabused of all doubts as to whether by beating an ass you can turn him into a man. At least I, for one, have never come across anything that gives as much direct knowledge as a sojourn in transportation. Jesting apart, as a matter of fact, such ordeals alone are pregnant with the blessings of God.[63]

The 'seditious' prisoners were kept in the Cellular Jail longer than the norm of three to six months; some of them for two years. They were not allowed to mix with other prisoners. Their dress was marked out with 'S' for sedition or 'C' for conspiracy, and all their neck tags carried 'D' for dangerous.[64] These were men of letters, unused to manual labour of any kind, but they were expressly forbidden clerical jobs. They were given the hardest of labour, such as coir-pounding or working oil mills; these were designed to be bullock-driven, but instead men dragged round the iron cross bar that turned the cast-iron pestle. Those who could not keep pace were beaten with cudgels, and there were cases when a man was lashed to the bar and dragged along by his fellow prisoners. Punishments, such as the infamous standing handcuffs, were medieval. The diet was sparse and maggot-ridden; 'sweet water' for drinking was always scarce – no more than two cups a day – and there was little for washing. Prisoners could urinate only at three fixed times a day. They were given no books or news. Some prisoners had travelled before, but for many, like Ullaskar Dutt, it was their first voyage. The experience of displacement, he wrote, 'disturbs the partition line that exists between the earthly and the unearthly, the manifest and the unmanifest, the visible and the invisible around us'.[65] For some it led to mental breakdown, or to spiritual rapture.

Notwithstanding the widespread publicity surrounding the bomb cases, this 'Indian Bastille' flourished without a major outcry from liberals in Britain. The penal colony was shielded by its idyllic and exotic surroundings. Even Barindra described it as 'a veritable landscape painting', surrounded by 'wild' and 'savage' aboriginal peoples.[66] Colonial travelogues and photographs portrayed the Andamans as a malleable terrain, a place of scientific experiment where 'the most profligate and abandoned criminals' could work for their conditional release and 'self-sufficiency', and, by becoming orderlies and trusties, live under a system of self-surveillance. Through the infamous 'marriage parades' of women convicts, they could even be reclaimed to settled family life. 'Seditionists', however, had little hope of remission or companionship. Given the scale of the state enterprise it represented, Port Blair was perhaps not so 'isolated' as it seemed. But, as the 'king of the Black Waters', the jailer David Barry, put it in his stock speech of welcome: 'it is impossible to escape from this place. The sea surrounds it for a distance of 1000 miles.' And so, for the time being, it was still possible for the Raj to punish its opponents in secret and with impunity.[67]

Colonial policing struggled to contain empire's inner demons.[68] Its formidable apparatus of knowledge-seeking was directed increasingly at enemies within. The special branches of the Indian police expanded between 1905 and 1910 when a new Department of Criminal Intelligence (the CID) was created. Its inspectors and constables grew from 284 in 1907 to 525 in 1910, though this was still half the numbers of the political police in Paris alone. Then there was the sheer number of men needed to follow suspects: in the case of the most dangerous men there were four watchers assigned to each quarry. In Calcutta, at the height of the bombings, there were as many as 116 constables assigned to the task; in the mofussil and around the French colonial enclave of Chandernagore, there were some 487 men disguised as sweetmeat sellers, cloth merchants and money changers.[69] The number of armed police grew, as did investments in fingerprinting, photography and graphology.[70] The charge of sedition – 'exciting disaffection' against the government – had featured in the Indian penal code since 1870 and was now used more widely. It encompassed a range of sins, speech acts as well as political violence, and made little distinction as to levels of intent between the militant and the romantic patriot or between the man who threw the bomb and, in cases such as Aurobindo's, the strategist with no blood on his hands.[71] The challenge of political violence led the colonial state to make the dangerous argument that India lay in a position of exception to the idealized norms of liberal governance.[72] The Indian Criminal Law Amendment Act of 1908 strengthened the position of the prosecution in ways that restricted the right of the accused to representation, to a jury and even to being present at a trial.[73] But these measures divided and demoralized the British, and they ran into scruples at home: the Liberal secretary of state for India, John Morley, constantly reminded colonial officials that they were the 'agents of Parliament in a free country'. Ominously, there was also a sense that this repression was having a morbid effect on the police's Indian rank and file, who were unreliable, lackadaisical and often in sympathy with the students and radicals.[74]

Nor did the new measures have a conspicuous effect. Many of the sedition trials were a noisy farce, and when the British tightened controls over the newspapers this just drove the printing presses underground; publishers turned from newspapers to pamphlets that were harder to trace and easier to pass around schools and colleges.[75] The 1910 Indian Press Act demanded steep securities from all publishers and made it easier to close newspapers and periodicals down. But over the next three years, although around 200 tracts and books were banned, only fifteen deposits were forfeited and no press was seized. To intercept dangerous texts and forestall further plots, the British resorted to unwrapping packages and steaming open sealed letters, whose privacy had been a sacred principle of the Royal Mail for over a century, only to wrestle with their translation and the interpretation of the complex imagery of their contents. As the government ethnographer, now Home Secretary of India, H. H. Risley, described it in 1907: 'We are overwhelmed with a mass of heterogeneous material, some of it misguided, some of it frankly seditious, the mere bulk of which, to say nothing of its chaotic character, renders it unmanageable.'[76] By 1909 matchboxes and handkerchiefs with portraits of Indians convicted of sedition were appearing in cases of imported Japanese goods.[77] Even dhotis worn by young men in Bengal in 1910 were embroidered on the hem with a song of praise to the martyrs of Alipore.

One bomb can kill a man.
There are a lakh [100,000] of bombs in our homes.
Mother, what can the English do?

All the English could do was publish a notice in the *Calcutta Gazette Extraordinary* that such dhotis would be 'forfeited to His Majesty'.[78]

Across Bengal, the bomb seemed able to strike anywhere and at any time: it struck in a municipal cart, on the steps of St Andrew's Church, Calcutta, in coconuts packed with carding needles from jute combs, broken glass and nails, or in the preparation of sulphide of arsenic and chlorate of potash used in a series of attacks on railways in eastern Bengal. The servants of the Raj lived in conditions of fear and insecurity amid a wave of so-called 'dacoities'. On the face of it, the attacks seemed to follow old bandit methods whereby villages were surveyed in advance, targets selected and intimidated by threatening letters, and escape routes planned by boat or bus. But the mostly middle-class youths who led these political 'actions' did so for flamboyant effect – one leader favoured the piratical dress of long boots, a flowing coat bulging with weapons, and a large curved sword – and used modern firearms rather than *lathis* to terrorize entire neighbourhoods.[79] Conspiracies broken up by the police in one region materialized elsewhere across north India. In Allahabad, on 18 November 1909, two bombs in coconuts were thrown at the carriage of the viceroy, Lord Minto, outside a women's hospital and orphanage, on a street lined with children. One was deflected, injuring a sweeper, and the other hit the sword of a mounted trooper without going off. Minto did not realize what had happened: 'That was a good shot,' he exclaimed; 'he must have cut it in half.'[80] The following month a district magistrate in Nasik, Bombay Presidency, was riddled with bullets after attending the theatre. Some of those still at large in the *Yugantar* group urged restraint. War was looming between Britain and Germany, they said, and this would provide the opportunity to strike with decisive effect. But, for the younger men, 'the lure of the bomb, the prospect of immediate retaliation and breaking the morale of British administration were too tempting to wait'.[81] For these youths, the bomb was an epiphany, and revolution now a career.

One such young man was Narendra Nath Bhattacharya, who was born in March 1887 at the village of Arbelia in the Twenty-Four Parganas, the first territories of Bengal to come under East India Company control after 1757. The family was Brahmin; Naren's father was a teacher of Sanskrit in a junior high school and a hereditary high priest of an incarnation of the mother goddess of the *sakti* cult. In 1897 the family moved to Naren's mother's village, Chingripota. It was a rural region well connected to the intellectual circles of Calcutta; leading social reformers were born here, building libraries and retaining family links. Later accounts by family and friends portrayed Naren as a restless, assertive youth and, like many of his generation, a spiritual seeker.[82] Through encounters with swamis who preached Hindu revivalism, and the writings of Vivekananda, his veneration of the *sakti* took on a patriotic meaning and betokened not a withdrawal from the world but an active life of social engagement. He devoured books on revolutionary history, as well as spiritual texts. Having become caught up in the politics of the anti-Partition movement, Naren was rusticated from his school in 1905. Later that year his father died, and Naren moved to Calcutta, where he studied in the 'National College' established by Aurobindo Ghose, and its associated Bengal Technical Institute. It is not clear how serious a student he was, or might have been had the times been different. He moved between the lodgings of his brothers and members of his political circle and tried his hand at journalism.

Around this time, through a cousin from Arbelia, Naren was introduced to Barindra Ghose and drawn into the orbit of the Anushilan Samiti. He met Khudiram Bose on the eve of his departure to Muzaffapur, and the encounter marked him deeply:

> Khudiram himself was the gentlest of souls imaginable; evil passions like vengeance, malice, cruelty could not cast any shadow on the limid surface of his deep idealism. In a trance, a psychological state of the mystic *karmayogi*, he started on his fatal pilgrimage: the bomb in his box and the pistol in his pocket were not the means to destroy human life; they were as flowers with which the devotee goes to the temple to please and propitiate the god.[83]

Naren himself was initiated through a raid on the railway station at Chingripota, in which a sympathetic stationmaster was supposed to give up the keys to the safe. The man got cold feet, and so a real and violent robbery took place. Naren became known to the CID and was soon arrested, only to walk free after the court refused to believe that the sons of respectable gentlemen could be guilty of such a crime. He now ran a steel-trunk shop on Calcutta's Cornwallis Street, but was arrested again in the so-called 'Howrah Gang case' on 4 March 1910. It was, for the British, another 'practical fiasco'. When an approver changed his story, Naren and others walked free.[84] He roamed across north India, in the manner of a holy man, shadowed by the police.

It was not clear where such wanderings led. The revolutionary party, as enumerated in the police files of the men convicted, remained elite in composition. Of the 186 men eventually convicted of political crimes, nearly 90 per cent of them were men of higher caste and most were no more than twenty-five years old. Caste was no guarantee of class or status. But their occupations – overwhelmingly they were students, teachers, clerks, doctors and compounders, and even landowners – clearly identified them as members of the *bhadralok* class.[85] Their status as young 'gentlemen' was deeply unsettling to British officials: it seemed to mark the limits of India's malleability when it came to reform on a liberal model. But this was the group most alienated by the ceiling which the same policies imposed on their advancement.[86] The cult of heroism did not fully satisfy their intellectual hunger. Naren was haunted by a remark by Barindra Ghose to the effect that 'the worst of cowards could walk up to the gallows if he knew that the whole country was applauding'. Was then this idealism merely 'an expression of selfishness'?[87] *Swadeshi* had led to strikes in the cotton mills, but the great part of the population, not least the rural masses, were merely spectators to its drama. It had found its martyrs; but, as in Vietnam, the violence had not wounded the state deeply enough. Many of the attacks on high officials missed their mark – not a single European administrator had been killed – rather, the worst of the effects fell upon their Indian subordinates, or ordinary townsfolk and villagers.

The most immediate legacy of the campaign of violence was the propelling of more young men out into the world.[88] As a senior CID officer put it: 'Political *sadhus*, or missionaries tour all over India, New York and Paris; send out letters which are used for disaffection in the army and among the civil population . . .'.[89] In mid-1908 a wave of Indian activism in the telegraph industry swept through the system, from Kandahar to Moulmein in Burma, in a strike by a virtual community at the heart of the great arc of imperial communications.[90] The suspect bomb makers of western India came from a circle that had studied chemical engineering in Japan as far back as 1899: men such as Govind Narayan Potdar, who had edited an 'industrial journal' in Japan called *India House*, and was involved in ventures producing sulphuric acid and a 'Swadeshi match factory'.[91]

In the face of this, the CID became ever more tangled in rumour and lurid supposition, aggravated by the fact that some of the leads were true, or might have been. The British believed that rifles came from Japan packed in industrial merchandise. 'The Shyamji Krishnavarma of Tokyo', Maulana Barakatullah, was said to be friendly with the captains of Japanese steamers working the cargo routes to India who carried messages in cipher.[92] Weapons brought in by lascars on foreign ships were deposited in the houses of prostitutes in the new dock area at Kidderpore, where a sprawl of overcrowded workers' dwellings with the highest mortality rate in the city hemmed in this model of imperial engineering.[93] Guns also came overland along old smuggling routes across Muslim Asia. A Kabuli combined his cocaine-trafficking operation with running guns through Turkey, Persia and Afghanistan, using men disguised as lame or blind beggars.[94] One of the men arrested at the Maniktola Garden, Hem Chandra, was one of the first of the *Swadeshis* to return from Europe. He carried technical information on bombs and materials on 'general principles' of revolutionary cell organization that he had picked up in anarchist circles in Paris. There, it was said, he learned from a Russian military engineer and Sanskrit scholar called Safranski – and even, it was whispered, encountered the now legendary Emma Goldman. Before that, he had been seen at India House in London.[95]

'AT HOME' IN SOUTH KENSINGTON

As the India secretary, John Morley, warned the viceroy, Lord Minto, in June 1908, 'the ordinary square-toed English constable' was ill equipped to track 'wily Asiatics' and their 'secret societies'.[96] Nonetheless, Scotland Yard trailed the students of India House and posed as newspaper men seeking interviews, or as sympathetic Irish republicans. Shyamji Krishnavarma decamped to the relative safety of Paris in June 1907, declaring that 'England affords a safe asylum to the oppressed of all countries save India'.[97] He had the means to do so. He remained an advocate of passive resistance – of 'the modern weapon of revolution', the strike and boycott – but refused to denounce armed rebellion. He returned repeatedly to his favourite maxim from Herbert Spencer: 'Resistance to aggression is not simply justifiable but imperative.'[98] Chatto lacerated Krishnavarma in *The Times*. 'The day that I feel convinced of the necessity of political assassination and underground work I shall cease to write. I shall return to my country and put my theories into practice. But I shall certainly not seek a safe retreat within the hospitable walls of a European city.'[99]

At India House, the charismatic Vinayak Savarkar was now in charge. On 10 May 1908, the fifty-first anniversary of the outbreak of the Indian Mutiny, he threw a large jamboree for nearly 100 students from London, Oxford, Cambridge and Edinburgh. He distributed to his guests a pamphlet with the title *Oh Martyrs!* which declared the Mutiny to have been nothing less than a 'revolutionary war'. This was a first draft of his 484-page *The Indian War of Independence, 1857* (1909), researched in the library of the India Office, written in Marathi, translated into English at India House and printed overseas, in Holland. The British banned the book without seeing a single copy. But it was carried by lascars to India sewn into volumes of *The Pickwick Papers* and *Don Quixote*.[100] It was the most potent counterblast to the Raj's historical narrative of itself yet penned by an Indian. It appealed to the power of history to recover the nation, and it reminded patriots that a nation had already existed in past struggle: 'Let your love and bravery purify the Past and incite and inspire the Future.'

Such calls for revolutionary self-sacrifice were read aloud at Sunday meetings in India House to cheers and thumping of tables, followed by the singing of the 'Bande Mataram' and, on one occasion, a gramophone record of the music hall singer Harry Lauder. *The Indian Sociologist* now moved from publicizing accounts of Russian or Sinn Fein violence to openly discussing 'the ethics of dynamite', and there were lectures on 'The Making of Bombs' by a student at University College, London. Few respectable Indian students now visited the villa in Highgate. It was, observed M. P. T. Acharya, who was still in residence, 'a leper's house'. By June 1909 only two boarders remained.[101]

On the streets of London, it was easier for Indians to come face to face with the great men of the Raj. On 1 February 1909 a young Bengali resident of India House, Basundev Bhattacharya, accosted the man responsible for monitoring the students, Sir William Lee-Warner, on Pall Mall near his club, The Athenaeum. He gave Lee-Warner a letter, demanding an apology for an earlier incident when Lee-Warner had brushed aside another Indian who had tried to present him with a petition. Lee-Warner had told him, 'This is not India', and called him a 'son of a pig'. On the second confrontation, Bhattacharya alleged that Lee-Warner pushed him aside, crying, 'Get away, you dirty nigger', and struck him with an umbrella. Bhattacharya retaliated by hitting Lee-Warner on the leg with his walking stick. Lee-Warner's temper was notorious. In India some thirty years earlier, a group of Parsis had alleged assault after he tried to drive his carriage through a religious procession. He was fiercely anti-Brahmin, anti-Congress and anti-Hindu. He had recently penned a tract demanding Indian obedience in the face of empire's manifest material benefits.[102] All this came to light in court to illustrate Lee-Warner's state of mind. As Bhattacharya stated in his own defence: 'I thought it desirable that Anglo-Indian insolence should be stopped, so with the walking stick, which luckily I carried, I taught Sir William Lee-Warner better manners.'[103] He found wide sympathy. To the young Jawaharlal Nehru studying in Cambridge and writing home to his father Motilal, a leading Congress politician, Lee-Warner was simply 'a villain'. Lee-Warner's bad language, it was said, provoked the ire of King Edward VII himself when he heard of it. Bhattacharya refused to be bound over to keep the peace and was sent to Pentonville prison for a month.[104]

Shortly afterwards, on the evening of 1 July, in order to ease the atmosphere an 'at home' was hosted for students by the loyalist Indian National Association in the Jehanghir Hall of the Imperial Institute in South Kensington. Among the guests was a young Indian engineering student from University College, London, called Madan Lal Dhingra. He arrived by cab, around 9 p.m., smartly turned out in a lounge suit and blue turban. He mixed with friends and acquaintances, taking tea and eating canapés. At around 11 p.m. he was seen talking to Sir William Curzon Wyllie of the India Office in the Institute's vestibule. But then, suddenly, he drew a Colt revolver and fired four shots into him. A Parsi physician from Shanghai who tried to interpose himself between Curzon Wyllie and Dhingra was also killed. The young man then turned the gun on himself, but the safety catch had slipped on. Disarmed by bystanders, he was held down in a chair until the police arrived. He was composed – his pulse normal and regular – and said nothing except 'My specs': they had fallen off in the attack.

Madan Lal Dhingra enjoyed as many advantages of birth as was possible for a young Indian under the Raj. His father was a wealthy surgeon in Amritsar who was on friendly terms with British officials – including, it turned out, Curzon Wyllie – and acted as private physician to the Maharajah of Jammu and Kashmir. His other sons were businessmen, doctors and lawyers, and, as was the case with so many of the families of the men at India House, they lived in the English style and were vocal loyalists of empire. Madan was the second youngest son, and, to his despotic father, the most disappointing of them. He had run off to sea as a stoker on a ship for six months, and had been barred, on grounds of race, from entering Australia. Arriving in London in 1906, aged nineteen, he lived in some comfort under the supervision of one of his brothers. He stayed for periods in India House, but in April 1909 – under pressure from his parents and furnished with ample means – he shifted to rented digs at 108 Ledbury Road in Bayswater.

When the police searched his lodgings after the attack, they found a reproduction of the Russian artist Vasily Vereshchagin's painting *Suppression of the Indian Revolt* (1884), depicting the blowing of Indian rebels from British field guns; a portrait of Lord Curzon, on which was pencilled 'Heathen Dog'; and over sixty loose pistol cartridges. Dhingra came to the 'at home' by way of a shooting range above a penny arcade called 'Fairyland' on the Tottenham Court Road, where he regularly practised (an indifferent shot it was said). He stopped at a restaurant called the Indian Catering Company; there, Scotland Yard believed, he was plied with bhang. They also suspected that Dhingra had hoped to find at the reception either the secretary of state for India, Lord Morley, or Lord Curzon himself. But there had been rumours of trouble; both men were under police protection and beyond Dhingra's reach.[105]

At his trial three weeks later, despite earnest offers of assistance from the Indian community, Dhingra appointed no counsel and refused to say anything beyond a prepared statement. But this was taken from his pocket, and in court the judge would only let him speak impromptu. He stated that he refused to recognize the court's authority and attacked the 'hypocrisy' of the English. 'They pose as the champions of oppressed humanity . . . when there is terrible oppression and horrible atrocities committed in India.' These words and the written statement – published in the *Daily News* on 18 August – soon circulated across India and around the globe. Dhingra claimed martyrdom: 'A nation held down by foreign bayonet is in a perpetual state of war . . . The only lesson required in India at present is to learn how to die, and the only way to teach is by dying ourselves.' He appealed in particular to sympathizers in America and Germany.[106]

The trial lasted little more than an hour. After the verdict, and after the presiding chief justice, with little preamble, pronounced the death sentence, a King's Counsel hired by Dhingra's family to follow the case read a brief statement disassociating them from his actions and motives. 'There are no more loyal subjects of the Empire than they are.'[107] Dhingra's father in India had earlier written to Curzon Wyllie to urge him to take their son under his wing because he had fallen under the influence of India House. Curzon Wyllie in turn had written to Dhingra, but he had ignored the letter, and so it had been arranged that he be invited to the 'at home'. His family supplied stories of his eccentricities and solitariness, perhaps to try to save him from the gallows, including an incident when he clipped off the whiskers of his landlady's cat. 'A morbid, melancholy and indolent man; very vain, very susceptible to personal influence and unbalanced,' as Har Dayal later described him to the British, although at the time he hailed him as 'a hero of ancient times'.[108] But the medical officer at HM Prison Brixton found no evidence of insanity, and his landlady in Bayswater declared him to be a steady lodger, who stayed home after seven in the evenings, and attended his classes to the last. A new delinquent stereotype was born: the lonely and alienated colonial student.

Dhingra's brother was brought from Edinburgh, where he was studying, to affirm his rejection of his brother at a public meeting which had been organized for the purpose of loud demonstrations of outrage at Caxton Hall in Westminster. When members of India House spoke up for Dhingra, a fracas erupted. Savarkar was assaulted and had his spectacles broken, and Acharya jumped into the fray. On 17 August, Dhingra was despatched at Pentonville prison by the executioner Henry Pierrepoint, having walked to the gallows, it was said by British witnesses, without assistance. Savarkar and friends tried to claim his body for Hindu cremation rites. This was refused and the body was buried in the prison yard. Curzon Wyllie was memorialized in St Paul's

Cathedral and in Rajputana, where he had served for many years as a political agent. India Office officials were now guarded.

In Paris, confronted by pressmen, Krishnavarma had refused to accept any personal responsibility for the shooting. He expressed regret for the death of Sir Curzon Wyllie and denied any knowledge of Dhingra. But he also claimed Dhingra as a martyr and announced four new scholarships in his name. This equivocation did not satisfy his young former followers, and it was said that Dhingra hated him. The former Congress leader Annie Besant accused Krishnavarma of 'pushing forward only boys while remaining himself in the background'.[109] It seemed as if a division of labour had emerged whereby the intellectuals gave theoretical support to acts for which they disclaimed any personal connection. The British nevertheless issued a warrant for incitement to murder, to be acted upon should Krishnavarma set foot again in England, and he was forced to send his wife to sell the house in Highgate – which she did, at no financial loss.[110] The last issues of *The Indian Sociologist* now appeared from Paris, as did a new journal established by Madame Cama and titled *Bande Mataram* in imitation of Bipin Chandra Pal's periodical. The first issue of the new *Bande Mataram* in September 1909 was unequivocal: 'No subject nation can bring freedom without war – without a war to the knife with its alien rulers. He who tells people that this principle is wrong must be a fool or a knave.'[111] Despite being banned by the Raj, copies of these papers were carried by maritime networks via the Portuguese and French settlements into British India.

Earlier, the press had been happy to compare the likes of Krishnavarma to Mazzini; now they called for him to be placed in the dock with Dhingra. Some Englishmen saw the hypocrisy of this. The Fabian C. H. Norman argued that by denying Dhingra his statement in court the 'Anglo-Indian imperialists of today are undermining the liberties of England'.[112] One of the most powerfully placed sympathizers with Indian and Egyptian nationalists was the writer and horse breeder Wilfrid Scawen Blunt. He tackled the president of the board of trade, Winston Churchill, in private. The Cabinet, Churchill disclosed, had discussed Dhingra, and the chancellor, Lloyd George, had expressed admiration for him as a patriot. This was a view Churchill shared: 'He will be remembered 2,000 years hence, as we remember Regulus and Caractacus and Plutarch's heroes.' He went on to say, as they talked late into the night, that Dhingra's words were 'the finest ever made in the name of patriotism'. Nevertheless, Churchill approved of the prison authorities' refusal to return Dhingra's body to his friends.[113]

Scotland Yard sifted through the evidence looking for signs of a carefully prepared plot. But in the months before the killing, Dhingra had distanced himself from India House, and had not spoken at any meeting. M. P. T. Acharya told the story that Dhingra had turned up at Highgate the night before the murder as 'happy as a bird'. There was, he believed, no conspiracy. The police reluctantly came to the same conclusion, but not before Scotland Yard had called him in and offered him money to pay for his studies if he disclosed the plotters' identities. There was some evidence a friend had been on hand at the 'at home' to reinforce Dhingra's resolve, but no one had actively assisted him. However, it was enough that Dhingra had been inflamed by Savarkar's words for there now to be three police spies placed within India House. One was unmasked by Savarkar, who had also urged Archarya to take the police shilling to feed them misinformation. But the British now had a vivid picture of what was said and by whom at the secret meetings which took place in a small, shabby Indian restaurant in Red Lion Passage in Holborn. They believed that Acharya was being 'coached' as a martyr and overheard a joke made with a nod to the respective origins of Dhingra and Acharya that 'after the Punjab, Madras is next'.[114]

Savarkar himself was already banned from the India Office library, and now the Benchers of Gray's Inn refused to call him to the bar. Struck down by a bout of pneumonia, he spent much of his time in Brighton, reading on the pier, and at a convalescent home in Somerset. In early January 1910 he moved to Paris. But, without telling his friends, he returned to London on 13 March 'on some unexplained mission'. He was accompanied by Perin Naoroji, the student granddaughter of Dadabhai Naoroji: 'a very pretty and clever girl', the British reported, with radical views. Savarkar seemed to be unaware that there was a warrant out for his arrest, and he was detained immediately on arrival at Victoria station. Perin visited him in Brixton prison, under an alias, and saluted him with the 'Bande Mataram' at his committal hearing. During a dinner to mark the Parsi new year, she shocked those present by refusing to stand to drink the king's health.[115] The publishers of *The Indian Sociologist*, Arthur Horsley – who claimed not to have read its contents – and Guy Aldred – who most certainly had – were also prosecuted for sedition, one of the last times the law was invoked in the United Kingdom.

There were those at home and abroad who saw some merit to letting these radicals function in plain sight, in using liberalism as a *ruse de guerre*. But the Dhingra affair occurred in a season of spy scares and plots. A feeling of vulnerability and military unpreparedness at home was fanned by the spy novels of William Le Queux and by the warmongering of Lord Northcliffe and his newspapers. The principal targets of this were 'Germans' – waiters, clerks, barbers and servants – of whom there were around 50,000 living in Britain at the time. But it made 'aliens' of all kinds of subjects of formal and informal surveillance, and of legislation that tried to draw the line between Englishmen and others in law – such as the Aliens Bill of February 1911.[116] The Bill was not enacted as law. The Prime Minister, Herbert Asquith, moved to limit the scope of such measures and emphasize liberal reform. But Britain's prestige was being tested by the effrontery of violence in the full glare of international opinion.[117]

In June 1910 Savarkar was extradited to India under the Fugitive Offenders Act of 1881. The proceedings were controversial. The defence argued that Savarkar had never 'fled' India but had come openly to study, and that the capital charge that waited for him in India was related to offences allegedly committed in England in 1909 and so should be tried in England. These arguments were taken to appeal, only to be dismissed. Plans were hatched, with the help of some Irish prison guards, to spring Savarkar en route from Brixton prison to Bow Street magistrates' court.[118] Behind this was the youngest fellow traveller of India House, David Garnett, the seventeen-year-old son of a literary family linked to the Bloomsbury set, who had become friends with the son of Bipin Chandra Pal and the younger brother of Ullaskar Dutt, Sukhsagar. He was admitted to India House and exhilarated by Savarkar's passionate reading of his history of 1857. He also encountered the 'Byronic' Dhingra. On the strength of this, when Savarkar was arrested Garnett visited him in Brixton and then travelled to France to procure a boat for a quixotic attempt at rescue. Garnett's father was warned and rushed to Paris to bring him home.[119] In the event, Savarkar wrote his farewell to friends from his cell: 'As in some oriental play sublime, all characters, the dead as well as living, in Epilogue they meet: thus actors we innumerable all-once more shall meet on History's copious stage before the applauding audience of Humanity . . .'.[120]

On 1 July, Savarkar left Southampton on board the passenger steamer

Morea, sharing a four-berth second-class cabin with a Scotland Yard detective inspector and a British CID officer from India. The ship docked in Marseilles, where the Englishmen made entreaties to the French police not to allow a demonstration by Savarkar's friends in France. About 6.30 a.m., after they had docked, Savarkar asked to go to the water closet. The Scotland Yard man accompanied him and stood on the urinal to peer over the partition as he went into the cubicle. He was replaced by an Indian policeman, who watched Savarkar's slippers in the gap below the door, but then climbed up on the urinal to make sure he was there. He saw Savarkar's half-naked body halfway out of the porthole. As he tried to break down the door, Savarkar dropped into the water. He swam the ten or twelve feet to reach the quayside, and then he ran. The policeman dashed on deck, shouting, 'Catch him! Catch him!' Savarkar got about 200 yards before some dockhands blocked him. The Indian policeman grabbed him by the neck, helped by a steward and a gendarme who had joined in the chase. Savarkar told the gendarme: 'Take me into your custody. Assist me. Take me before a Magistrate.' But he could not speak French and the Frenchmen could not understand English. The local police commissioner later came on board, but no action was taken.[121]

Savarkar had hoped that friends from Paris – Madame Cama and her associates – would be waiting for him with a car on shore. But they were delayed. If the French policeman had spoken English, things might have turned out differently. French sympathizers, including the socialist Jean Jaurès and the grandson of Karl Marx, Jean Longuet, took up his cause, after the *Morea* had sailed on. Savarkar's case for sanctuary in France was pursued as far as the Permanent Court of Arbitration at The Hague. Much turned on who had placed hands on Savarkar and at what moment.[122] But, in a landmark ruling, and amid allegations of Anglo-French collusion, the position of the British government was upheld. By this time, though, Savarkar had already been tried and sentenced in India.

Sitting in a prison cell in Bombay, Savarkar, like Dhingra and Sinn Fein activists, refused to recognize the British court. The evidence against him was partly the testimony of letters home, of informers and of his book on the Indian Mutiny, and partly the product of surveillance across borders and over several years. Crucially, this had traced the pistol used in the murder of the district magistrate at Nasik in

December 1909 to a consignment of twenty Brownings smuggled from Europe in the luggage of India House's cook. It was disputed whether they had been procured by Savarkar or bought by someone else. But the prosecution contended that it was unnecessary to establish 'conscious concert' between each conspirator; it was enough for them to 'engage'. The judge concurred: in the eyes of the authorities, proof of conspiracy required 'no formal organisation' among plotters, merely 'a sympathy and a rapport which enabled them, as occasion rose, to get in touch with and assist each other'.[123] Savarkar was found guilty of 'the abetment of the waging of war' against the king-emperor. The manner in which the trials of former intimates of India House were conducted served as a cruel awakening for all of its circle.

In July 1911 Savarkar left for the 'prison-world' at Port Blair in the Andamans, transported for 'life' twice over, his property forfeit, his degree revoked, and with a release date of 24 December 1960. Like all inmates, he was allowed one letter home a year. 'I recalled to my mind', he noted on the eve of his transportation, 'the lives of great prisoners from Sir Walter Raleigh down to Prince Kuropatkin [Kropotkin]. Bunyan, who wrote his *Pilgrim's Progress*, had, at least, the materials to write it with. I have not with me even the end of a broken pencil.'[124] He began with six months' solitary confinement and received three punishments for writing illicit letters to other prisoners, each of a further one month's isolation. In addition he was given seven days in standing handcuffs on two occasions, ten days in cross bar fetters and four months in a chain gang. His initial appeal for clemency was rejected in September 1911.[125] Yet, by the time he wrote his first letter to his younger brother in December 1912, he had adapted to the appalling conditions. In the midst of hard, automatic manual work, he escaped into a landscape of the mind: 'My spirit avoiding all detection is out for a morning trip, and across seas and oceans, over hills and dales it roams sipping only pleasant things, and things noble, like a bee amongst the flowers.' It was as if he had 'entered a higher College for a higher study'.[126]

But this kind of escape was impossible for many to contemplate. Around 1 a.m. on 20 April 1912, one of the men convicted in the Alipore trial, Indu Bhushan Roy, tore his white cotton kurta into strips for a noose and took his own life in his cell. It was said, in a story smuggled out to the Bengal press, that he could take no more of his labour pulping the *rambash* plant, which covered his hands in vicious sores; he had asked for relief but had been abused by the overseer, Mr Barry. He was left hanging in his cell overnight before the medical superintendent arrived and he was cut down. The Port Blair authorities denied all this, and a fellow prisoner who blurted out on parade that 'Mr Barry ill-treated and tortured the Hindu who died on Saturday night!' was punished with solitary confinement.[127] The prison's deputy superintendent acted as coroner, and noted that in Roy's cell there was a book by Annie Besant, *Thought Power: Its Control and Culture* (1901), and concluded that its 'emotional nature' had probably pushed him to take his own life. Roy had also hallucinated that two of his fellow prisoners were out to kill him as an informer, and had been scheduled to return to associated confinement after three months in solitary on the day following his death.[128] Shortly afterwards, Ullaskar Dutt collapsed under the strain of the standing handcuffs, having been punished for refusing to work. The medical superintendent suspected him of malingering and administered large electric shocks. 'The pressure rose so high,' Dutt later wrote, 'as to exceed the limits of my endurance.' It led to the complete disintegration of his mental health.[129] The officials put it down to 'severe malarial infection' and then to 'melancholia'.[130]

The 'seditious' prisoners in the Cellular Jail struggled to get their complaints past Mr Barry. There was no pretence of rehabilitation or remission for them. They were denied the possibility of advancement to overseer that was available to the murderers, dacoits, rapists and thieves who lorded it over them. They complained of abusive punishment and demanded complaint books in their cells ('almost Gilbertian' was the official response).[131] There was a hunger strike, in which prisoners were force-fed and their sentences extended, followed by a labour strike. News of these reached the *Bengalee* newspaper on 8 September 1912, despite the barriers of distance and censorship. In this way, news of Ullaskar reached his father, a retired professor, who made a desperate plea to the viceroy:

> It would afford both me and Ullaskar's mother great relief if you would be so kind as to enlighten us on some points: How long has Ullaskar been insane? Could you ascertain any specific cause for his insanity? ... Ullaskar was an expert singer, and enjoyed sacred music. Has the curative effect of music – vocal or instrumental – been tried?[132]

Above all, the convicted men demanded to be given the status of 'political prisoners', rather than merely 'seditionist prisoners'. But in the feverish public and official discussion of these events, the term 'terrorism' began to be preferred to 'sedition', 'agitation' or even 'revolution' as a politico-legal category. But its precise compass and meaning were often unclear.[133] So too was the validity of violence itself. If terrorism on Indian soil often missed its targets, Dhingra had hit his mark in England, albeit perhaps not as spectacularly as he had hoped. But what else had he achieved? His actions had divided Indians abroad; their alliances with European activists led nowhere. In London, Guy Aldred, on his release from prison, launched a long, lonely campaign for Savarkar's liberation, but its implicit support for Savarkar's brand of nationalism alienated other anarchist internationalists.[134] The Indian extremists had neither created a mass organization nor had they done much for Hindu-Muslim unity. They had added to the uncertainty of the age, but how far had they advanced their vision of a free India? Savarkar's own support for violence appeared in many ways too backward-looking and increasingly like revenge for 1857, and for the recent sentencing of his brother.[135]

DOWN AND OUT IN PARIS AND TANGIER

In November 1909 the Gujarati lawyer M. K. Gandhi was heading home to Durban from London after a failed four-month mission lobbying on behalf of the civic rights of Indians in South Africa. Aboard the SS *Kildonan Castle*, he imagined a dialogue between himself (as 'Editor') and his 'Reader'. In no small part, it replayed a conversation he had had at a late-night dinner with Savarkar and his friends at the Indian restaurant in Red Lion Passage on 24 October. He had provoked anger by telling them that 'the real oppressor – the ten-headed monster – was within them and not without'. A companion of Gandhi further darkened the mood by rebuking them: how could they hope to ameliorate the condition of India if they could not serve dinner on time?[136] 'What they want', Gandhi scoffed, 'is not very Indian and not very national . . . What is the good of national spirit if they cannot protect themselves from Herbert Spencer?'[137] In the last ten years there had been little love lost between Gandhi and India House. At the time of the Anglo-Boer War, Krishnavarma had excoriated Gandhi for his support of the British: 'an attempt to purchase rights and privileges at the wicked price of ruining other people's independence'.[138]

In London, Savarkar accused him of a supplicatory approach to the British: 'He too tried to use Top Hat, Tail Coat and expensive ties.'[139] But Gandhi's advocacy in South Africa had brought him closer to the working masses than India House had ever come.

Over ten days at sea, Gandhi wrote in Gujarati on ship's stationery with a passionate urgency, fully expecting he would be arrested on his return home. When his right hand could write no more, he used his left:

> Do you not tremble to think of freeing India by assassination? What we need to do is to kill ourselves. It is a cowardly thought, that of killing others. Whom do you suppose to free by assassination? The millions of India do not desire it. Those who are intoxicated by the wretched modern civilisation think these things. Those who will rise to power by murder will certainly not make the nation happy. Those who believe that India has gained by Dhingra's act and such other acts in India make a serious mistake. Dhingra was a patriot, but his love was blind. He gave his body in a wrong way; its ultimate result can only be mischievous.[140]

On his arrival in South Africa, Gandhi published his thoughts in his multilingual Durban paper, *Indian Opinion*, one of the journals that were beginning to connect the scattered populations of Indians overseas, and later (after a Gujarati pamphlet edition was banned by the Bombay government) as a small volume in English.[141] He used his rejection of violence to fashion a path of moral conduct that would transcend the 'wretched' politics of the present civilization. This he called *satyagraha*, or 'truth-force'. To the call for martyrdom through resistance by arms, he offered the giving of one's body by a different token: 'a method of securing rights by personal suffering'.[142] It was an appeal to the supremacy of India's civilization, but it was also a rejection of many other currents of the day: the Japanese way of modernization, pan-Asianism, the lure of anarchism.[143]

By the end of 1909, all those associated with India House who were able to remove themselves beyond the reach of the Raj did so. Adrift in continental Europe, they tried with ever more urgency to connect their struggle to those of others. But it was hard to start over in a new city. For his part, Chatto was reported by the British to be 'living a life of ease' in a hotel at 92 rue de la Boétie in Paris: he was 'all talk and no work', sighed Madame Cama. His romantic entanglements were catching up with him. He had left his 'Mrs Chatterton' in dire poverty in Notting Hill, and a more current English girlfriend, a Miss Reynolds, turned up in Paris disguised as a boy.[144] Now it was harder to move around, it was women like Miss Reynolds, Perin Naoroji and Chatto's younger sister, Mrinalini (who arrived in Europe in 1911), who acted as couriers, translators or as a poste restante. Chatto and his compatriots looked to the exiles of other nations for aid, especially the Egyptians in Paris, Lyon, Vienna and Bern. In London, in January 1909, India House had hosted an 'Indo-Egyptian Club' dinner at the Imperial Hotel in Bloomsbury to honour the visit of the Egyptian reformer Mustafa Kamil, the man who had lauded the rise of Japan from Cairo a few years earlier.[145] Now the bond was more emotive. The newspaper, al-Liwa, 'The Standard', which Mustafa Kamil had founded, published a poetic eulogy 'To Dhingra, after Execution', which circulated back to India. When, in early 1910, the Coptic Christian Prime Minister of Egypt, Boutros Ghali, a key ally of the British regime, was shot, the comparison with Dhingra was instantly made. Like Dhingra, the assassin of Boutros Ghali, Ibrahim Nasif al-Wardani, was a student in London and a close reader of Herbert Spencer. In Paris, Krishnavarma put up money for an essay prize of 1,000 francs in al-Wardani's name.[146]

There was an element of parlour revolution to all this. When Chatto and others attended the soirée at the Hôtel Élysée Palace on the Champs-Élysées which opened the Egyptian National Conference in September 1910, they did so sporting rosettes and one of them wearing a fez. And at the gala that concluded the conference proceedings, which had been held in Brussels, Perin Naoroji caused a sensation by singing in Urdu, 'Oh brave young men of India quickly take up your weapons'. In fact, at the convention itself, some of the Egyptian nationalists' speeches were said to have been ghost-written or edited by Chatto and Har Dayal. But the meeting failed to endorse their calls for open revolt in Egypt, and the Indians complained of the event's 'unreality' and extravagance. Earlier that year, despite his domestic troubles, Chatto had drawn up an elaborate, theoretical scheme for an uprising in India.

It had, for the first time, many strands, and was global in compass. It was to be kindled by emissaries sent to Mecca and Karbala in order to foment support among Indian residents, and through them to reach Sunnis and Shias in India itself. For this it sought to channel pan-Islamic sympathy in Turkey, Egypt and Afghanistan. The plan also looked to enlist the backing of Sikhs living in the United States, Canada and Hong Kong, and anti-British sentiment in Nepal and China. In a new departure, it gambled on the prospect of a coming world conflict in order to persuade Germany to declare war on Britain as soon as the revolt began, and for Japan to deploy its navy on their behalf in the Indian Ocean. Reading Chatto's scheme, as they did much of the revolutionaries' secret correspondence, the British were dismissive: 'He does not seem to have considered the probable cost of these alliances.'[147] However, some now did begin to act on this grandiose vision.

Back in London, M. P. T. Acharya was hard up and, with the closure of India House, had nowhere to stay. He looked for somewhere, anywhere, to continue the anti-imperial struggle, but when he applied for a passport through Thomas Cook & Co. he was refused. He faced the major challenge of proving his identity. He then went to the India Office, where he was known, but such was the panic in the wake of the Curzon Wyllie assassination that they were reluctant to let him through its doors. He told officials plainly that he and a friend, Sukhsagar Dutt, wished to join the rebels against French colonial rule in the Rif mountains in Morocco. This was to gain experience in irregular warfare. The British gave him a passport just to be rid of him. He and Sukhsagar Dutt were lent a Winchester rifle by David Garnett; they added a Browning pistol to their armoury and were escorted to Southampton by detectives 'to wish us goodbye and good luck'. On the day Dinghra was hanged, 17 August 1909, they boarded the German steamer *Lützow*. A few weeks later, a warrant was finally issued in Britain for Acharya's arrest for fleeing Madras as an offender the year before.

On Acharya's and Dutt's arrival in Gibraltar the rifle, revolver and 300 rounds of ammunition were confiscated. Dutt baulked at boarding for Morocco and headed to Marseilles. Acharya was overheard to say that Dutt had been ordered back to London to kill Dhingra's brother. When Acharya landed in Tangier, he was alone and had only thirty shillings in his pocket. An English-speaking Arab guide latched on to him at the steamship terminal and took him to a European hotel.

Learning the purpose of Acharya's visit, the man was impressed that a Hindu would seek to support the Rif rebels, and when Acharya was unable to pay his hotel bill he settled it on his behalf and found him lodgings with a Spanish family. Acharya dallied in the Arab cafés with the tour guides, smoked their hashish and began to be drawn into the underside of the city. His new friend, Salim Atyyeh, turned out to be part of an Arab-Spanish crime syndicate that preyed on tourists. He was later secretary to the leader of the Rif rebellion, Abd el-Krim, and in 1926 would accompany him into exile on the Indian Ocean island of Réunion. The links between the underworld and political struggle impressed Acharya deeply. But without the means to get to the rebels in the mountains, he resolved to leave. Stranded in Tangier, he toyed with 'trying to become a Moor' to find work. However, in the end he had to appeal to the British consul for assistance. Now aware of Acharya's presence, the consul enlisted the aid of a French constable to have him followed every step of the way and to intercept his letters.

In late September, Acharya fled to Portugal, where there was a one-time resident of India House to offer him shelter: Dr Joaquim de Siqueira Coutinho, a native of the Portuguese colony of Goa, to whom the Marathi manuscript of Savarkar's infamous history of the Indian Mutiny had been entrusted. But here too the authorities were on to him, and he was immediately hauled up in front of the police and questioned about bomb-making. He told them he wanted to learn Portuguese in order to travel to Brazil and enlist as a soldier. This was part of an embryonic scheme to establish a colony to train fighters from India there. He was confined to his lodgings in Estoril, under orders not to leave town without telling the police. Even nearby Lisbon seemed to him to function as 'a colony of British capital'.[148] Finally, on 5 October, he took a night train to Paris. In this way, Acharya fled from one underground to another, one police interrogation to another.

The viceroy's State Entry into Delhi, 23 December 1912.

4

The Fury of Enlightenment
1909–1912

A REPUBLIC OF ASIA

The Portugal witnessed by M. P. T. Acharya in the autumn of 1909 was a country that lay in the shadow of regicide and on the edge of revolution. The following October, a republic was proclaimed, sparking labour militancy and anticlericalism, in which anarchists took to the streets of the large cities, burning town archives, opening the prisons and exhibiting an 'almost ritualistic' use of the bomb.[1] As an imperial power in Asia – in India, in China and in the archipelago – Portugal was entangled in a connected arc of protest reaching from the Mediterranean right across the land mass of Eurasia which, over the next three years or so, drew in all the colonial empires. Its beginnings might be traced to the storm of expectation arising from Japan's defeat of Russia, which fanned the fire of street demonstrations in St Petersburg. This same wind inspired patriots across Asia, and sped Phan Boi Chau's 'Journey to the East'. At the same time, in 1907, a constitutional revolution undermined the Qajar dynasty in Persia, and in 1908 the Young Turk revolution challenged Ottoman authority, if not yet the empire's underlying legitimacy.

In these years the imperial *belle époque* was beset by its hidden furies and faced a reckoning. A series of shock waves to the global economy, particularly the United States stock market panics of 1907 and 1910–11, brought acute economic uncertainty. Upheavals, from rebellion in the Rif in Morocco to the Mexican Revolution which began in 1910, exposed recognizably similar conditions of uneven industrialization, poverty and loss of autonomy. Old regimes faced a common prospect of peasant revolution and urban disorder.[2] These events were further linked by the instability of the imperial system, and the challenges faced by independent states from loss of sovereignty to western encroachment.

The crisis was experienced within new global networks and multiple translations and transpositions of ideas. It was said that the Russian Revolution of 1905 was the first to be followed 'live', as it were, by telegraph.[3] But this might also have been said for the Boxer Rebellion in China in 1900–1901. The Ottoman empire was one of the most wired-up parts of the globe, and military officers who played a role in the Young Turk Revolution of 1908 served in the imperial relay stations.[4] News agencies such as Associated Press and Reuters, with branches now in Japan and China, developed within and beyond the routes of imperial telegraphy, which meant that it was harder for states to silence news items that might spur their own subjects on to protest. The Japanese alone sent 33 million telegrams in 1913.[5] This compression of space and time gave local events, whatever their specific causes and consequences, a palpable synchronicity and a wider resonance.

The revolutions of the *belle époque* cast out fresh waves of exiles and drew others towards new revolutionary centres. Some of the Indian exiles, and not only Muslims, were drawn to the cities of the Middle East. Once such was Ajit Singh, a close follower of Lala Lajpat Rai, who made his way via the Gulf states to Persia, where, from 1906, the Qajar empire was challenged by demands for representation and a constitution. Ajit Singh jettisoned his Sikh name for a Muslim one and set up a newspaper in Shiraz: one more dangerous man on an unsettled frontier between empires. After his sojourn in Morocco, his arrest in Lisbon and return to Paris, M. P. T. Acharya went to Berlin and Munich, finding work in tea shops. However, armed with testimonials to his tea-making skills, by late 1912 he was in Istanbul to try to sow unrest among Indians gathered there for the hajj to Mecca.[6] Soon Ajit Singh would travel to Brazil, as Acharya had warned the British he himself planned to do. This itinerary was not so unusual. There were already close connections between the anarchists of the Mediterranean and the Americas, as Arab migrants and exiles carried the name of Marx (or 'Max' in the Arab transliteration) to the United States and Brazil.[7] Acharya himself left for the United States some time later.

The Middle East was an increasingly important intersection of these global pathways. By 1912 there were some 134 new periodicals in Otto-man lands. The most influential of these was the Syrian reformer Rashid Rida's *al-Manar* ('The Lighthouse'), its name echoing the say-ing of the Prophet: 'Just as the road, Islam has its beacon and lighthouse.' It was read across the eastern archipelago through rapid translation in the Arab-owned Malay newspapers of Penang and Singapore. It found a further echo in Padang, on the west coast of Sumatra, in a reformist publication called *al-Munir* ('The Radiant'), and, much to the ire of the British, in Maulana Barakatullah's *Islamic Fraternity* in Tokyo. When the Ottoman empire plunged into a disastrous war in the Balkans in 1912, Muslim papers in Singapore and elsewhere increased the number of issues in order to keep pace with the demand for news.[8] The idea of the caliphate had a powerful hold on the minds of Muslims in South and Southeast Asia. In India, the war signalled a moment of crisis for Islam, and they sent moral, financial and medical support to Turkey on an unprecedented scale. The spearhead of this campaign was *The Comrade*, a new journal launched in Calcutta in 1911 by Mohammed Ali Jauhar. 'In common parlance,' he reflected in 1913, 'the Mussalmans have arrived at the parting of ways.'[9]

This was a portentious statement. A bedrock of the British Raj in north and central India after the Mutiny of 1857 was its accommodation with Muslim elites. This was a common feature of indirect rule across vast swathes of territory from northern Nigeria, Egypt and Sudan, to the Gulf emirates and the Malay States. Not for nothing did the British empire proclaim itself, in David Lloyd George's words, 'the greatest Mahomedan power in the world'. This was central to its projection of itself as a universal empire.[10] Some French statesmen also saw the secular Third Republic as a *puissance musulmane*. In French North and West Africa and the Netherlands East Indies colonial rule at the *fin de siècle* was a Euro-Islamic condominium.[11] But now, as a new wave of Muslim activists headed west, travelling through Ottoman lands and on to Eur-ope, more began to question why India's Muslims were, in the words of the most influential of them, Abul Kalam Azad, 'mere camp followers of the British'.[12]

At home and abroad, colonial empires were confronted by new pub-lics. The religious anxieties and political demands of the age were voiced everywhere in similar terms: in calls for democratic rights and constitutions, for press freedoms and for reformed education – often beginning with the advancement of women – and through the same metaphors of darkness into light, of beacons to illuminate the path forward.[13] Above all, from the October 1910 revolution in Portugal to the 1910 Kotoku Incident in Japan, political movements shared a common language of republicanism. This was drawn from any number of wellsprings: from the constant comparison and declared affinity with the patriotic deeds of a Mazzini or of Sinn Fein; from the republican values within the education system of the colonial powers, as in the case of Phan Chu Trinh's exposure to French republican ideals in Vietnam; or through a long process of ideological adaptation that looked to fashion a new understanding of what republicanism might mean.

One of the most prolifc writers on this theme was K. P. Jayaswal from the Northwest Provinces of India. After his early studies at the University of Allahabad, he undertook graduate study of Indian literature in Oxford, and studied for the Bar at Lincoln's Inn in London. On his return to legal practice in Bengal, he wrote a scholarly 'Introduction to Hindu Polity' (1913), one of a series of essays in the *Modern Review* of Calcutta, that evoked the imagined democratic republicanism of a Vedic past, a vision of 'elective monarchy' wrapped in scriptural language. He identified no fewer than eighty-two republics in India over 2,000 years of ancient history, maintaining they possessed a sophistication that surpassed any since, whether in Switzerland or the United States of America. During his years as a law student in London, Jayaswal had been active in India House and close to Savarkar. Republicanism had been a theme of the Bengal reformers since the 1840s. Now, Jayaswal drew a line clearly in his readers' minds from ancient *samitis* to their modern reincarnation, and argued that for the patriot the 'Golden Age of his polity lies not only in the past but in the future'.[14] In a similar spirit, the Young Turk theoretician Hüseyin Cahit staked the claim that Turkey might be 'the France in the East'. Ideological boundaries were not tightly drawn, but these diverse republicanisms were linked by a shared knowledge of revolution-as-history – of 1789, or 1848 across Europe, or now Turkey and Vietnam in 1908 – and an acute sense of the present moment of crisis within the imperial system.[15] In 1912 the then Viceroy of India, Lord Hardinge, looking back to the flash fire of 'extremism' in 1907, acknowledged that the Raj had, 'in the past five years, passed . . . through something very like a revolution on a small scale'.[16]

This moment was proclaimed as a connected series of enlighten-ments. The new crossways of Asia – Calcutta, Singapore, Shanghai, Tokyo; or, for that matter, Paris, Alexandria and Istanbul – took on a fresh importance as sites of their intersection.[17] The western idea of enlightenment as the quiet triumph of reason had always been something of an illusion. Enlightenment could be violent in its first unleashing, and later brutal in its demands for conformity. For many this was a moment to speak out loud and in the open. Much that was hidden burrowed to the surface. In the Arab world and India, so-called 'secret societies' stepped briefly out into the streets. It was a time for the people's tribunes to seize government buildings and commandeer the-atres, for newspaper sellers to shout about the latest dramas on the pavements, and for the pleasure of reading satire aloud in cafés. Epochal events were re-enacted in popular theatre: in Shanghai there was a particular appetite for dramas involving assassination. It was an opportunity for new styles, for the cutting of hair and shaving of beards, and for women to be seen more in public, and even to remove their veils and unbind their feet. It was a riot of new colour: of wall posters, illustrated newspapers, commercial advertising and political cartoons. It was no coincidence that the urban landscapes of Cairo and Shanghai became stages for new media such as the cinema and the gramophone record, and for performances of vaudeville and cabaret. Egypt's historical terrain was crucial to early cinema's claims to 'rearrange time and distance'; before 1914 four companies had already filmed five versions of *Cleopatra* in Egypt. In 1913 the first Asian-made movies were shot in an open-air studio behind the Shanghai Bund: the taste, unsurprisingly, was for humorous tales of urban low life. The circulation of new kinds of entertainment professionals – Russian exhibition dancers, Filipino showbands, Indian conjurors, Ashkenazi musicians – added new layers to the world abroad.[18]

In the descriptions of suspects that were circulated over vast dis-tances by the police, the hunted men of empires were often marked out as nattily dressed *flâneurs*, or women by their styled hair. The advent of the Asian 'dandy' was not only a time for politics and polemic.[19] To the avant-garde of art and letters, it was a moment of rupture, a time to proclaim new values and new aesthetics. Modernisms in the west drew from an Asian palette, whether that of *Japonisme* or the 'Asianism' of Tagore, now a global celebrity by virtue of his 1913 Nobel Prize.[20] But these Asian 'traditions' were already exposed to the shock of the new and to the world at large, and Asian artists and writers saw themselves as part of the vanguard of modernism. Beyond the west, as the Turkish poet Ahmet Muhip Diranas later wrote of the new generation of painters in Istanbul – the celebrated salon of 1914 – modernist innovations could achieve 'a better lucidity', a form 'more plastic . . . and more artful'.[21]

But the immediate goals of this republican moment – press freedoms and constitutional advancement – were rarely secured. Empires responded with a new wave of reaction and expulsions across borders. It was long ordained that exile over ever longer distances was to be the condition for much of the intellectual life of the new century.[22] But the constant mobility of the 1890 generation – Acharya, Nguyen Tat Thanh and others – merely drew their myriad worlds closer together. The politics of the Partition of Bengal too continued to play out on a world stage. After 1905, the global underground was reinforced by hardened revolutionaries out of Russia. They announced their presence in April 1906 at a 'unity conference' held in Stockholm to try to address the deepening cleavage in the Russian social democratic movement between the Menshevik majority and the minority Bolsheviks led by Lenin. Although this was a struggle over how to respond to the crisis in Russia, the Bolshevik position caused them to be identified as the voice of internationalism. A new face among the veterans at the conference was Mikhail Borodin, a twenty-one-year-old from Latvia. He had been a target of anti-Semitic nationalism against the Jews of the Pale of Settlement, and so was drawn to the Bolsheviks' line, becoming well known to their leaders, including Lenin and Stalin. Shortly after the conference, Borodin was picked up by the Okhrana while fleeing underground from Riga to St Petersburg and given a choice between Siberia and exile in the west. On arrival in London, he put a notice in the *Daily Telegraph* offering to teach Russian in exchange for English lessons, which triggered the interest of the police. By early 1907, like many of those whom the British authorities were tracking, he found sanctuary in the United States. After a short period in Boston, he attended Valparaiso University in Indiana and then ran a school for émigrés in Chicago.[23]

For all exiles, the conflicting pulls of patriotism and their cosmopolitan existence among patriotic renegades from elsewhere was a test of faith and of doctrine. In early 1913 Stalin, now in Vienna, stated the problem in his first substantial work, *Marxism and the National Question*. He saw nations as an inescapable category of belonging but underlined the necessity for a countervailing internationalism to stamp 'an indelible impress on the whole mental life of a worker'. He forecast future national and democratic risings in Asia.[24] Also writing in early 1914, Lenin saw the 1905 Russian Revolution as 'awakening' Persia, Turkey and China. In so doing he began to link the fate of revolutionary struggles in Europe to those of Asia, as part of 'the chain of world events of *our* period in our "Orient"'.[25] But the centre of gravity of protest had already moved to Asia itself.[26]

It was in Asia that the first of the great world empires fell. On 10 October 1911, in the old walled city of Wuchang, at the confluence of the Han River with the Yangzi, a chain of revolts began which led to the collapse of the Qing empire by the end of the year. It was sudden and, by most, unforeseen. A series of reforms in the late Qing era, instituted after China's defeat in the Sino-Japanese War in 1895 and the further setback of the international intervention during the Boxer Rebellion of 1900–1901, had begun to bear fruit. It included strengthening the army, the revival of education and the stimulation of commerce, and also the creation of an element of representation within provincial assemblies. In much of this, emulation of and learning from Japan had been important. But it had allowed an upsurge of anti-Qing sentiment led by the very groups that emerged from the reforms: officers in the new army, students returning from Japan and the elites in the provinces. The Wuchang uprising triggered discontent and a cascade of smaller revolts in other cities across China: Xian, Taiyuan, Zhenjiang, Fuzhou and Nanjing.[27] These showed how a comparatively limited numbers of activists returning from overseas and, above all, overseas funds could shape events.

Sun Yat-sen was still in the United States when the Wuchang uprising occurred. But his centrality to the exiled activist networks, and his gift for raising funds, propelled him to the provisional presidency of a new republic in 1912. This was short-lived. By July 1913, after his failure to contain the rise of the military faction of Yuan Shikai, Sun returned to exile in Japan. Other Chinese abroad, such as Liang Qichao, were persuaded to come home to serve the republic. What appeared to have been a moment of crisis became a protracted struggle. The commitment to a vision for a new form of government encompassed a wide range of possible futures for China. Many of the republican thinkers to emerge were, as one observer put it, 'a bundle of contradictions'.[28] Some borrowed directly from the west; others, like Liang Qichao himself, thought that virtue was not necessarily located in the exercise of the popular will through a universal franchise or political accountability. It was to be found in a reassertion of older arguments about the centrality of personal morality and the cultivation of a sense of self-mastery among a literati who would impart the right kinds of learning to guide China to wealth and strength and to protect it from foreign incursion. In this sense, the republic was a long-term experiment in political and civic education.[29]

Outside China, the news of the fall of the Qing was received with euphoria. From his cell in the Andaman Islands, Vinayak Savarkar used the first letter he was allowed to write home to his doctor brother in late 1912 to hail it:

> How is the *Republic* of *China*? Does it not sound like *Utopia realized*? A Romance of History: Don't suppose that China's work is a day's. No! from 1850 they have been strenuously at it, though the world knows not where the Sun is making its way – till it is risen: and Persia, Portugal and Egypt? And are the Indians in South Africa successful in getting their demands?[30]

Like all the *belle époque* revolutions, the Wuchang uprising in China spilled across borders and opened new fronts in the struggle against imperialism. In Shanghai, an early consequence of the new republic was the demolishing of the walls between the Chinese city and the foreign concessions. One could now simply walk across a wide boulevard to cross jurisdictions: China and the encircling western empires were at a much closer, more combustible remove.[31]

In Hanoi, the triumph of liberty over despotism was celebrated in banners and paper lanterns hung from houses – 'To the Chinese republic! Ten thousand years!' – long before it was formally declared in Nanjing.[32] The news of the Wuchang uprising was greeted in Singapore with the burning of Qing flags and the cutting of queues – some 10,000 in Singapore and 5,000 in Penang after the revolutionaries' capture of Beijing – a rejection of servitude to the old dynastic order. Vast sums were raised for the republic under the guise of provincial 'relief funds', often by women going door to door.[33] On the Malay Peninsula, the lunar new year in 1912 was marked by a week of riots in Kuala Lumpur when Chinese began to forcibly sever the queues of their countrymen. In the violence that followed, an attempt was made to rush the central police station; the police opened fire on the crowd with fatal results: in all, twelve people were killed.[34] In another incident in November 1911, 2,000 tin miners returned to China from Malaya to fight for the revolution. They were mostly young men with no families, their fellow workers raising money for their passage.[35]

The Canton–Hong Kong connection was the foundation of western imperial interests in China. Just five days before the Wuchang uprising, on 5 October 1911, the final, Chinese section of the railway between Canton and the waterfront of Kowloon was laid, having been constructed at vast expense. But the proximity of Hong Kong to the bellwether province of the new republic shattered the peace of what was hitherto seen as a placid outpost of empire. Crowds gathered daily outside the newspaper offices in Hong Kong for news. In November a false rumour of the capture of Beijing by the revolutionaries triggered street carnivals. The British governor of Hong Kong, the conqueror of northern Nigeria, Sir Frederick Lugard, was obliged to give them free rein – a thing unheard of – and even to permit the use of firecrackers; if he checked the exuberance, Lugard realized, it would provoke bloodshed. The scale of fundraising for the revolution was immense: by 18 November it was claimed that some 1.5 million Hong Kong dollars had been raised. Refugees spilled into the British colony. In the three months from December to February 1912, looting and unrest led to fifty-one floggings of up to twenty-four lashes of the cat o'nine tails, and the police were ordered to carry revolvers. When Lugard was summoned to the great imperial Durbar in Delhi in December 1911 to welcome the new king-emperor, George V, he had to pull out.[36]

The mood in Hong Kong was still tense when Lugard stepped down in mid-1912. His successor as governor, Sir Francis Henry May, was not new to the colony. He had first come to Hong Kong in 1883, at the age of twenty-three, and had risen within ten years to be captain superintendent of police and then colonial secretary. He had fought both the first anti-western boycotts and the Asian plague pandemic that hit Hong Kong in 1894. May had been serving as governor of Fiji for the eighteen months prior to his return to Hong Kong, but the lobby for his recall and reassignment was insistent. The moment was not auspicious. In the week May arrived in Hong Kong, there were eighty-two new cases of plague, taking the annual total to 1,551 deaths, and the police continued to turn up bodies in the streets.

May disembarked with his wife and three daughters at Blake Pier, in the central district of Hong Kong, on 4 July 1912 to the thunder of a seventeen-gun salute and the stomp and cymbals of the band of the King's Own Yorkshire Light Infantry. The city fathers waited on the pier side to welcome him, and the streets were lined with around 500 troops. May's party then proceeded in two sedan chairs, each carried by eight men, down Pedder Street and Queen's Road to the City Hall, where a further three guns were fired to mark his installation as governor. Then, suddenly, in front of the post office, a man in a blue serge suit of European style strode forward pointing a revolver towards May. An Indian policeman grabbed his arm so that the shot he fired went into the bamboo frame of Lady May's chair (later this intervention was credited to a British sergeant). The assailant was subdued to cries of 'Lynch him!' Lady May, according to some local press reports, 'throughout the whole time kept a smiling face'; in others, she burst into a flood of tears. May rose from his seat and coolly brushed down his coat with his right hand, fastening on the assailant 'a half-contemptuous, half-sympathetic glance'.[37] The Indian soldiers lining the route had not moved from their position. This, to one British eyewitness, was either a 'glorious' display of discipline, or it was rather sinister. This observer had been present at the anarchist attack on the King of Spain in Paris in 1905 when a bomb was thrown at his carriage: troops there also 'never flinched, even though the air was rent with cries of "*Le Roi est mort*"'.[38]

May dismissed the attacker as a madman, although the doctor he sent to examine the man pronounced him sane. At a magistrate's hearing crowded with locals, the accused, a twenty-five-year-old whose name was given as Li Hon-hing, of no fixed abode, merely said – in quite good English – 'I did it.' At his trial, he was sentenced to life imprisonment with hard labour. The court did not trouble to establish his motive. This suggested that it was perfectly plain to the colonial authorities that their subjects would want to use violence against them. But conjecture was rife. Li's father, it was said, was a former policeman and had been imprisoned by May for corruption fifteen years earlier.

There were hints of a wider sympathy, if not conspiracy, when a letter was intercepted from Li's landlady to the effect that the attempt on May's life had 'unfortunately failed'. There was speculation that the attack was a provocation to induce foreign intervention in China. Another man was arrested, a soldier in the revolutionary army, from whom Li was said to have acquired his gun.[39] In a statement, Li denounced the governor's 'high-handed treatment' of the Chinese in Hong Kong and Fiji. Li also referred to the boycott of Hong Kong's trams when the operators refused to accept the new Chinese currency in payment. This had tested the bonds of collaboration with Chinese business figures on which the stability and wealth of the colony rested.[40] May privately told a correspondent that Li had confused Fiji (*Fei-li*) with South Africa (*Fei-zhou*), and had obviously thought May had been governor of the Transvaal and responsible for the well-publicized ill-treatment of Chinese there.[41] But the court transcript was quite clear what Li had meant. Grief and anger at the 'misery' and 'suffering' of Chinese communities overseas – and at the loss of the ideal of a more equal world – had been a staple theme of history-writing, novels, songs and dramas ever since the Hong Kong boycott movement against the exclusionary policies of the United States in 1905–6.[42]

Six years after the shooting, and with no explanation, Li Hon-hing was pardoned by May. The incident featured in *The Mystery of Dr Fu Manchu*, a serial by Sax Rohmer which ran in *Collier's* magazine from October 1912 until June 1913. This popularized the racial stereotype of the 'yellow peril' in the form of an inscrutable Chinese mastermind leading a powerful and secret international organization of assassins, and spoke to British unease at the challenge that the vision for a new China might present to their interests in Asia.

Europeans in Asia were now obsessed with the threat of assassination. After the 'revolt of the cut-hairs' in 1908, the French residents of Hanoi saw themselves as under siege – 'Civilians – why speak of civilians, since we are all soldiers?' – and the colonial government struggled to control their fear and rage. The lobby of *colons*, a growing proportion of the 15,116 French in Indochina in 1913, voiced support for Europeans taking retribution into their own hands, and even for lynch law.[43] They complained bitterly that 'because a soldier, after drinking, will beat an unfortunate rickshaw coolie, because a French woman, already unstrung by the heat, will box the ear of an insolent boy, because a police agent, exasperated by a vagabond's silence, will thrash him, a small group of metropolitans launches anathemas against us'.[44] They fought a new initiative from Paris for 'Franco-Vietnamese collaboration' which was spearheaded by the appointment of the radical politician Albert Sarraut as governor-general in 1911. In practice, however, Sarraut's gestures towards a colonial republican future were vague, and addressed to a rather idealized image of a Francophile urban elite. His policy was, he admitted, 'a double action, one political, one repressive'.[45]

In February 1913 secret reports from Hong Kong warned Sarraut to expect a concerted attack on the frontiers of Indochina. Prince Cuong De had left his comfortable exile in Shanghai for Hong Kong, where the Vietnamese revolutionaries were gathering and communicating with others in Siam.[46] On the night of 23/24 March homemade bombs were found in eight locations in Saigon and Cholon, including the stables of the governor-general's residence. They were the work of a network led by a wandering geomancer known as Phan Xich Long, who had spent time among exiles in Siam, and whose followers descended on the streets of Saigon wearing amulets believed to confer invulnerability. Phan Xich Long and many of his followers were rounded up by the police.[47] On 26 April, during the Saturday evening *apéro*, a bomb was thrown at a crowded terrace café at the Hotel Hanoi, a favoured haunt of officials and members of the military. Two soldiers were killed, and six Europeans and five Vietnamese injured, including a European lady wounded in her feet. Officials in Indochina concluded rapidly that the device came from Canton or Hong Kong.[48] *The Times* of London reported that schoolgirls from good families in these cities were being used to carry bombs to Tonkin. Vietnamese without identification cards were arrested and brought before a special commission. In all, 254 arrests were made, including a number of women. Seven people were executed.[49] An ex-Foreign Legionnaire, who had somewhat naively sold dynamite to a Chinese, was also implicated.[50] A number of leaders were tried *in absentia*, including Phan Boi Chau and Prince Cuong De.

From China, Chau formed a new revolutionary league under Prince Cuong De and acted as its 'prime minister'. But the French put pressure on the Chinese republican government, on British officials in Hong Kong and on the Siamese to chase Chau down. His whole organization, such as it was, came under attack. Arrests were made at what appeared to be a bomb-making factory in Kowloon in mid-June. The men were from Vietnam, and had arrived via Siam and elsewhere. One was a pupil at a respected Catholic school, St Joseph's College; he was transported to French Guyana.[51] Before long, Phan Boi Chau was arrested in China by a regional commander loyal to Yuan Shikai. He escaped extradition, but spent three years in a Chinese prison, and emerged a marginalized figure exiled in remote Hangzhou.[52] Prince Cuong De made a final voyage to southern Vietnam, via Singapore, hidden among the cabin boys and servants, who were tempted to turn him in for the bounty on his head. In the south, he was kept hidden by royalists, but found little mood now for an uprising and no opportunity to reveal himself to inspire one. He was smuggled out to Hong Kong in June 1913, this time for good. Later that year he arrived first in Berlin and then London, watched closely, as all exiles now were, by the police.[53]

Revolution, wrote Sarraut in 1913, was 'a vast fire that seems to cover the whole of Asia'. He believed it was a coordinated campaign with the 'double goal of "republicanizing" all of the Far East as well as Russia and nationalizing the countries in question by driving out the French, English and other Westerners from their respective positions in Asia'. This was the first time a link had been drawn from the politics of Russia to Vietnam. By stressing that the unrest was externally driven, Sarraut sought to strip it of legitimacy within Indochina itself.[54] Certainly the violence repelled many educated Vietnamese. Just two weeks after the Hanoi bomb, the journalist Nguyen Van Vinh launched a new journal in the city to cultivate the young urban constituency that Sarraut hoped to reach: 'to bring literature and learning, the blessing of French civilization, and stir them up to drown out the words of rebellion'. He himself had experienced the full force of this 'blessing' as an official guest at the Marseilles colonial exposition of 1906. The claim for the universalism of western ideas of 'civilization' remained attractive to many in Asia, not least those for whom it seemed the only realistic alternative both to what Vinh called the 'backwardness', 'superstition' and 'ossification' of Vietnamese tradition and also to the virulent racism of the *colons*.[55] This position, though, was hard to sustain in the face of the violent backlash against the bomb attacks on one side and the patriotic prestige garnered by those who had planned them on the other. But it offered enough for Sarraut and his kind to hold on to the benign fiction of colonialism's capacity to mould local political futures.

IF I WERE A DUTCHMAN

Nowhere, perhaps, was this fiction more entrenched than in the Netherlands East Indies. Here *rust en orde* ('peace and order') was a governing maxim of the colonial state and the central source of its legitimacy. It was accompanied by an expansive so-called 'ethical policy'. This was developed after 1900 to answer the charge – laid against western empires everywhere – that 'a debt of honour' was owed to the colonized. The demands of business for efficient native workers and willing consumers were fused with a 'moral calling' to provide for their health, welfare and limited enlightenment. Ethical evangelists saw the Netherlands Indies as a unique laboratory for humankind. As with the Curzon Raj in India, ideals of native advancement collided with the drive for a more racially exclusively 'European' bureaucratic order. The provision of village schools, a pillar of the policy, was on a modest scale (some 2,500 by 1912), especially measured against the practice of free schooling at the village level within the Islamic tradition embodied in the *pondok* of the Malay world and the *pesantren* of Java, both of which were illuminated by the beacons of Islamic reform from far afield.[56]

The achievements of the ethical policy were more visible in the physical infrastructure of the Indies. They were perhaps best symbolized by the Koninklijke Paketvaart-Maatschappij ('Royal Packet Navigation Company'), simultaneously a commercial and political venture and a wonder of ledgers, timetabling and technological prowess, which, by 1910, tied 223 ports across some half a million miles of sea lanes in the archipelago into the orbit of the Indies state.[57] Or, at the most mundane level, by the fact the average distance between streetlights in Batavia was a mere 200 feet in 1912, far less than in Amsterdam itself. The Netherlands Indies embodied the surreal promise of the colonial modern.[58]

It was surreal in that, alongside its technocratic achievement, the Dutch also reinforced and reinvented the archaic. In Java, the *priyayi* or lesser nobility had traditionally dominated the lower tiers of local administration. Over the course of a generation, however, there emerged in the early twentieth century a 'new *priyayi*' for whom European education and ideas had an undoubted power. This was encapsulated in the life and writings of Raden Adjeng Kartini, the young daughter of a *bupati*, or provincial head, in the old wood-carving centre of Jepara. For Kartini, an early advocate for the education of Javanese women, 'knowledge of Dutch language [was] the key which can unlock the treasure houses of Western civilization and knowledge'. Her letters to a Dutch pen-friend, first translated and published in The Hague in 1911 as *Door Duisternis tot Licht* ('From Darkness into Light') and translated into English as *Letters of a Javanese Princess* (1920), made her perhaps the most read author writing in Dutch, and the most read Asian, of her era.[59] Kartini died a few days after the birth of her first child in 1904, at the age of twenty-five.

It was young men, mostly medical students in Batavia, who in 1908 gathered the new ideas into a movement for educational uplift. Modest as its goals were, it represented a new kind of activity entirely: as one participant described it, 'One became another person, felt as if in motion, trembling throughout one's flesh and bones, one's vistas became broad, one's feelings refined, one's ideals taking on beautiful forms.' The *Budi Utomo*, or 'noble endeavour', as it was called, was led by men who were aristocratic in status and Java-centred in their worldview. But they were shaped by outside influences, such as theosophy, and the same circulating ideas and comparisons as their distant counterparts in British India and French Indochina.[60]

Long-domiciled Arab communities in cities like Semarang and Surabaya acted as a channel for modernist Islamic ideas through their schools and newspapers. The Chinese living in the Netherlands East Indies were a diverse community, some with a long creole ancestry, the so-called 'Peranakan Chinese', others were more recently arrived. There were areas of Java where, to quote one official in 1906, 'Chinese settlements have gone entirely native.'[61] But, after 1911, community leaders looked to China afresh and made generous gifts to the new republic for public causes; they gave direct support to the treasury by buying bonds for state enterprises and sent delegates to sit as representatives of the overseas Chinese in the new national assembly. At the same time, Chinese associations became more vocal within the Indies.[62] The Dutch relaxed antique rules and restrictions on Chinese dress, their travel and on new-style Chinese–Dutch schools. Chinese were exempted from making ritual obeisance to Javanese officials. But they were watched closely through a new bureau of Chinese affairs. Colonial powers across Southeast Asia feared that new ideas out of China could light the way for others.

The sheer ebullience of Java's Chinese communities in the wake of the Wuchang uprising – the street parties, the cutting of queues, the wearing of modern dress – heightened the sense of disparity between them and the rural Javanese population. In debates on the conditions of village life, Chinese petty traders and pawnbrokers were often stigmatized as a cause of native poverty, although many of them shared it. New tensions flared: there was street fighting in the port of Surabaya, with its large Chinese population, and in the capital, Batavia, shops were closed. In the old royal city of Solo, or Surakarta, a neighbourhood protection society was established by the Javanese traders and batik merchants. It grew into a wider movement for community self-help and religious revival, known from mid-1912 as the Sarekat Islam, or 'Islamic Association'. It soon spread to other towns and cities in Java. By the time of its first congress in Solo on 25 March 1913, it had forty-eight branches and 200,000 members; a year later, it had 366,916 members.[63] There was no mass organization on this scale anywhere else in colonial Asia.

To join the Sarekat Islam required oaths of loyalty and submission to its codes of conduct. While it was an open organization, members shared secret signs: a dot under a signature, a squeeze of the knuckle in a handshake, accepting a glass of water or a local clove cigarette (a *kretek*, itself a symbol of Javanese industry) in a particular manner. They adopted particular styles of dress and allegorical ways of speaking, and used signals such as coloured paper markers along a road as a call for help or a warning. Some of these practices had their origins in the initiations into Islamic sufi brotherhoods (*tarekat*) and their secret knowledge. But, as Dutch colonial officials pointed out, they also had much in common with the mutual aid associations and secret societies of the Chinese themselves, into which Javanese has been admitted in the past. Leaders of the Sarekat Islam likened it to freemasonry.[64] The Sarekat Islam soon began to intervene in the world of work. In early 1913 it encouraged members to petition employers for a day's rest on the birthday of the Prophet Muhammad; if it were not granted, they should walk out. In late February some 350 men in a Surabaya engineering factory did just that.[65]

One witness to the temper of the times was the young journalist Mas

Marco Kartodikromo, who edited the Sarekat Islam's newspaper. Marco was the epitome of the ideal colonial subject the ethical policy was trying to mould. He was born into a *priyayi* family in 1890 in central Java, part of the first generation to benefit fully from colonial education.[66] He cut his teeth as a journalist in one of the earliest Malay-language journals, the *Medan Prijaji* ('Forum for Priyayi') of Bandung. Its masthead announced it as 'the voice of all the [native] rulers, aristocrats, and intellectuals, *priyayi*, native merchants and officers as well as merchants of the subordinated people made equal [in status] with the "Sons of the Country", the Dutch East Indies'.[67]

For centuries Malay had been the lingua franca of trade and mobility across the archipelago. It was shaped by sojourners, its expression infused with other world languages such as Arabic, Sanskrit or Portuguese. But Malay was a first language for only a few, with multiple local variants and no standard spoken or written form. In the colonial period, encouraged by the Dutch who used it as a secondary language of administration, most people spoke it to some degree and could comprehend others in spite of linguistic differences; one did not so much understand Malay, as inhabit it. Malay reached beyond ethnicity and religion to embrace many of the different cultural streams of maritime Asia. A low, *pasar Melayu*, or 'market Malay', in romanized form was the medium of the presses of the Peranakan Chinese.[68] The number of periodicals in Malay published in 1913 was around eighty-eight in Java, and thirty-five outside Java, especially in the Sumatran towns of Padang and Medan, but also in the outer islands. Malay allowed writers like Marco to step outside the language of Java with its courts and old culture – its syntax of status and hierarchy – and to speak in the first person, directly, on the level, as a personality who could be followed in the pages of newsprint and who debated with readers.

The Malay language readily adapted to the fluid sense of new ideas and was enriched by a constant flow of translations. One of the first English-language texts to be rendered into Malay by a non-Dutch writer was a Sherlock Holmes tale, in which the Baker Street sleuth became the quintessential creative outsider, an apparition in times of crisis, putting the world to rights. Malay became the language for local novels of crimes of passion and of love and betrayal – often cast across racial and ethnic lines – and for new forms of reportage.[69] Marco's own serialized stories captured cameos of a world of movement; of new arrivals in the city, and the ubiquitous contrasts of light and darkness, pleasure and despair, wealth and poverty.[70] Armed with the new ways of writing and speaking, Marco began to wage what he was to call a *perang suara* – a 'war of voice' – against colonialism.

In 1912 Marco moved to Solo, which was now the centre of a vibrant anti-colonial culture and of startling new phenomena such as boycotts and public meetings. Nothing like this had been experienced before in the Netherlands East Indies. Marco described rallies as a carnival of carriages, flags and music: 'Because of the influence of the Sarekat Islam, there was no discrimination among the people, all recognized one another as brothers, not only the people who had high status but also those who had low status.'[71] Perhaps the most charismatic of the speakers was a *priyayi* engineer in Surabaya called Tjokroaminoto, who was one of the first Javanese to embrace politics as a vocation. He spoke in Malay, his voice reaching large crowds through a loudspeaker, and his baritone adopted the familiar style of recitation of the *dalang*, or puppet-master of the shadow-play. Tjokroaminoto may have placed Java at the centre of what was happening in Japan, India and China, but it was also the case that the music the crowd heard at such events was, more often than not, the Dutch royal anthem, the 'Wilhelmus', and the pledges of loyalty were not only to Islam but also to the Dutch government.[72] The Sarekat Islam was increasingly torn between those who sought Dutch protection and those who saw no future in it. To the former, the governor-general, A. W. F. Idenburg, held out a cautious hand of friendship. For the latter, the movement appeared to have hit a kind of glass ceiling by the middle of 1912.

This was broken by Ernest Douwes Dekker. In the Indies, this name had a certain power. His great-uncle was the famous author 'Multatuli' ('I have suffered much') who, long before Ernest was born, wrote one of the first critiques of the contradictions of liberal imperialism: *Max Havelaar, or, The Coffee Auctions of the Dutch Trading Company* (1860). This was a blistering exposé of the harsh labour regimes that lay behind the scientific façade of colonial capitalism. Ernest himself was born in 1879 of a Dutch father and a German-Javanese mother. He experienced anti-imperial struggle at first hand when, as a young man, he volunteered to fight with the Boers against the British in South Africa. He was caught in one of the largest mass banishments of the age when the British sent 5,089 or so prisoners to Ceylon. After his return to Java in 1903, he worked as a journalist in Batavia, where his home close by the native medical school became, in the words of his friend Soewardi Soerjaningrat, a 'clubhouse as well as reading room and library' for the Javanese students of the *Budi Utomo*.[73]

During 1909 and 1910 Ernest Douwes Dekker took his wife and children on a grand tour of Europe. Funded by an inheritance, their travels meandered through the Netherlands, Saxony, Prussia, Belgium, France, Spain, the Balearic Islands, Algiers, Italy, Switzerland, Bavaria, England, Denmark, Sweden and Norway. While they were in Paris, Douwes Dekker made a house call: he had read about Shyamji Krishnavarma in the *Straits Times* of Singapore, and 'decided to see what kind of man he was'. He visited him in his well-appointed home near the Bois du Boulogne and they talked for an hour. Although Krishnavarma continued to disclaim any responsibility for Dhingra's assassination of Curzon Wyllie in 1909, he lectured Douwes Dekker on the importance in the anti-colonial struggle of the individual act, as opposed to awakening the masses. 'I did not agree with him', Douwes Dekker later explained to the British police, and 'told him that one must first adopt the creed of democracy before trying the doctrines of anarchy'.[74]

Shortly after his return, Douwes Dekker in 1912 founded the first political party in the Netherlands East Indies. Based on two older community associations, the 'independent and progressive' Indische Partij was formed to realize the aspirations of those who, like Douwes Dekker, saw themselves as native inhabitants of the Netherlands East Indies, whether they were among the 70,000 or so resident Europeans in Java – not least the three-quarters of them who were Indies-born – or the 50,000 Indo-Europeans who were the legacy of a centuries-old creole experience. It also attracted Javanese into its orbit, beginning with Douwes Dekker's friends the journalist Soewardi Soerjaningrat and the doctor Tjipto Mangoenkoesoemo. Douwes Dekker immediately mobilized the party to fight a non-existent election campaign for a non-existent parliament, and, in the last months of 1912, its leaders embarked on a whistle-stop tour of Java, with Douwes Dekker giving speeches from the running boards of trains like an American presidential candidate. In Semarang, a stronghold of the movement, his arrival on 19 October was likened by a local newspaper to 'that of a monarch into a town' as he was carried aloft from the train while the crowd chanted, 'Long live the general!' There was talk that he was 'a reincarnation of Mohammed', a rumour Douwes Dekker did not wholly refute, 'being too much of an easterner to be able to make fun of it'. Perhaps 1,300 people attended his address in the local theatre the next day. He told the audience – which included the leaders of the Sarekat Islam – that the Indische Partij's goal was to transform the Indies 'from a colony into an independent state'.[75]

At a 'constitutional convention' in the West Java city of Bandung on Christmas Day 1912, Douwes Dekker threw the imagery of the ethical policy back in the face of the government of the Netherlands East Indies as he declared 'war' on the regime:

> Such a declaration of war is the declaration of shining light against dark-
> ness, of good against evil, of the citizen against the tyrant, of the colonial,
> tax-paying slave against the home country's tax-scraping state. Would
> that not be a feast for us? Our social battle has begun. Our national eco-
> nomic struggle has started. Where will this lead us?[76]

In an 'open letter' to Governor-General Idenburg, which he read out from various platforms, Douwes Dekker hinted darkly that should democratic means fail there were other possibilities: 'But, Excellency, I tell you, *if* one day our fist clutches a weapon – may fate forbid – it will *not* be our fault.'[77] His writings and speeches drew on the words of socialists and anarchists in Europe and Asia, summoning up the spectres of passive resistance, boycott, strike and revolution. In one flight of rhetoric, he promised to tell the people of the Indies where they could find their 'political Browning-guns'.[78] In March 1913 the party's application for legal status failed. Idenburg summoned Douwes Dekker and Tjipto Mangoenkoesoemo and, in Douwes Dekker's version of the encounter, the governor-general was emphatic that 'the Netherlands will never grant the Indies an independent national existence'. Douwes Dekker was already in trouble for libel and many of his own supporters were alienated by his language. As he had told friends in early 1912, they were 'the state-forming energy; I, the state-destroying one. They, the future men of distinction, the pioneers; I, the next exile.'[79]

The talk of 'war' caused panic. In mid-1913 the lobbyists of the European sugar industry in Surabaya spread hysterical rumours that riot and murder were about to erupt on the plantations around the city.[80] In the midst of this, colonial society in the Indies began to prepare for the centenary of the Dutch monarchy and for their own 'independence' that was to fall in November that year. On 19 July, Soewardi published a newspaper article in Dutch entitled 'Als ik eens Nederlander was' ('If I were a Dutchman', or 'If only I were a Dutchman'). In it Soewardi adopted the persona of a Dutch witness to the coming jubilee and spoke, as one Dutchman to another, of his unease that 'we' might give offence, 'commemorating our independence here in their native country which we keep in subjection'. He would forbid the natives to join the cheering and close off the area of the celebrations so they could not be seen. 'It would', he went on, 'be a tactical mistake to show this people how it should eventually celebrate its independence . . . It might cause [them] to become impudent.' Then, with teasing mock humility, Soewardi resumed his Javanese self and a soothing tone: 'But . . . I am not a Netherlander, I am only a brown-coloured son of this tropical land, a native of this Netherlands colony and I would therefore not protest . . .'. At this point, his use of the nominative first-person pronoun, *ik*, was more direct, less than humble, and altogether impudent; the humour and elegance of the writing laid bare the incongruity of the colonial condition.[81]

When the article was published as a pamphlet, Dutch readers, while affronted, did not take too much notice of its contents. But such was the tension of the moment that, when it was translated into Malay and read across the archipelago by non-Dutch, it became far more troubling. It was no longer a gentle satirical exchange between those who shared the *ik* of a Dutch education. The use of *saya*, 'I', confided to a vaster audience the absurdity of empire. The soothing tone evaporated, and the inflection became a new level of offence. Soewardi, Tjipto and Douwes Dekker were all detained. But had the essay not been translated, Soewardi's prosecutor told him in prison, he would never have been arrested. In the event, all three were initially banished into internal exile, to the outer islands of Bangka, Banda and Timor respectively. Then, as a concession, they were given leave to go into exile in Europe. Soewardi's parting words had a long echo: 'Rawé-rawé rantas, malang malang poetoeng.' 'It will be slashed to shreds, obstacles will be broken down.'[82]

All the western imperial powers resorted to banishment and exile to resolve political problems. This demanded that they work increasingly in concert to stabilize the system and to monitor the village abroad. The formidable French colonial security apparatus – beginning with the secret *police à l'extérieur* in 1912, to which later was added the Sûreté Générale – was founded explicitly to tackle the threat of the overseas Vietnamese communities (what the French called 'the nomads') along the sea routes and borders of Indochina.[83] The British stationed a Bombay policeman in London with a roving brief across Europe. Empires traded information and shared surveillance. The western powers were haunted by subterranean global spectres of all kinds – 'yellow perils', 'white slavery', 'secret societies' – which often transmitted into anxieties about entire populations, such as the Chinese in the archipelago.[84] Disillusioned though it was with the west, Japan petitioned to join the protocols of international policing when faced with Japanese anarchists abroad and those of other nations on its soil.

These developments propelled the final stage in the partition of the globe: the creation of modern borders and systems of identification, through paper, photographs and fingerprinting. Policing was increasingly personalized and targeted ideas and intentions. After 1911 the revolt of the *belle époque* seemed to subside in a succession of reactions, coups and military takeovers: the first challenges to royal absolutism in Siam – in something short of a revolution – were met in 1912 by a draconian set of *lèse-majesté* laws. Fortified in this way, the imperial order seemed to have quelled its demons. At the end of 1912 the viceroy in Calcutta, Lord Hardinge, felt confident enough to inform London that 'seditious agitation was dead'.[85]

GRAVEYARD OF EMPIRES

In the loosening of time and distance, what happened in Delhi at noon was known in London by mid-morning. On Monday 23 December 1912, as the London banks, offices and ministries were closing early for Christmas, there were rumours of a great calamity. The bustle broke out in the streets of the City before any official communication reached the India Office in Westminster. It was said that King George in Buckingham Palace heard the cries of the paper boys and sent for a newspaper.[86] On that same December morning, some 4,000 miles away, the leading men of the Raj had been absorbed in a pageant, as the Viceroy of India began his State Entry into the city of Delhi.

Just twelve months earlier, the King-Emperor George V had marked his accession to the throne with a spectacular Durbar in Delhi. He was the first reigning English monarch to visit India. The Durbar was the culmination of an imperial progress, and had been carefully choreographed earlier in the year in Windsor Great Park. In Delhi itself, a canvas city of twenty-five square miles was raised at some remove from the old Mughal city to disguise the discomforting memory of recent deathly famine. Its hastily dug lawns, rose beds and anti-malarial drainage works were there to evoke the empire's ability to render gardens from dust and wrench order from chaos. It was served by 2,500 kilowatts of power, forty miles of railway, thirty-one post offices and ten telegraph offices. A Delhi Durbar Police Act instituted thirty-three prohibitions in the temporary 'civil ward', including begging, prostitution, public bathing, bodily exposure and the exhibition of deformities.[87]

The King's State Entry on 7 December was a five-mile-long procession down the principal commercial thoroughfare of Delhi, Chandni Chowk, to the Red Fort and the encampment beyond. George insisted on entering Delhi on horseback, but being short in stature – around five foot six – the triumphal effect of this was rather lost beside the elephants of the princes. 'The truth must be told outright,' commented an official chronicler; 'the King-Emperor was not recognised as he passed.'[88] Evoking the practice of the great Mughal emperors Shah Jahan and his son Aurangzeb, King George and Queen Mary were attended over ten days by all the princes and vassals of India and Burma and greeted by 100 Indian veterans of the Mutiny of 1857. At the climax of the Durbar, on 12 December, the king-emperor and his consort sat in a vast amphitheatre of 70,000 spectators as the princes made ritual obeisance to the throne. It was one of the first iconic moments of the age of moving pictures, captured by British and Indian film companies. A careless bow that was more of a bob to the throne by one of the most illustrious of the princes, the Maharajah of Baroda – a man who had briefly funded a successor to *The Indian Sociologist* – became a major scandal after it was caught on celluloid.[89] He was vilified for his irreverence and for his association with the arch-seditionist Krishnavarma.

The next day, the monarchs appeared at the Red Fort on Shah Jahan's balcony, and it was said that half a million of their quarter of a billion Indian subjects filed past. The symbolism was carefully chosen to set British rule in India within a timeless continuum of 'Oriental despotism'.[90] In June the previous year the former Prime Minister A. J. Balfour had laid down this emphatic principle in the House of Commons: if the east was accustomed to untold centuries of absolute government, 'is it not a good thing . . . that this absolute Government should be exercised by us?'.[91] The Durbar's effect was slightly marred by false reports on 15 December in the French evening papers, and in Germany, that the king had been assassinated. There had indeed been a pledge by 3,000 or so men in Madras to kill him as soon as he landed on Indian soil, but it came to nothing.[92]

King George had insisted on using the occasion to grant a major 'boon' to India. The nature of this was a great secret until the day itself, when the king announced personally, as the final act of the Durbar, that the Partition of Bengal was reversed. At the same time, he declared that the capital of British India would move from Calcutta to what was to be called 'New Delhi'. Only a handful of people were close enough to hear him. The announcement was received less as a boon and more as a punishment. The viceroy, Lord Hardinge, had concluded, as his predecessors had, that the people of Bengal were 'born agitators', and that the high officials of the Raj should be evacuated from the heart of *Swadeshi*. The choice of the site of the old Mughal capital was also, in part, a concession to Muslim opinion. But it did not placate anybody, and, as the head of the Viceroy's Council reported, the 'scum' of Calcutta were enraged by the change and abused Lord Hardinge in the streets.[93]

For several generations the old Mughal capital, still badly damaged by the siege of 1857, had decayed. To Indians such as the Bengali writer Nabin Chandra Sen in 1892, Delhi was 'the great cremation ground of Hindu empires, the graveyard of Muslim imperium, and the playground of Fate'.[94] Har Dayal had grown up within a prosperous family here, near Chandni Chowk, and had studied in the mission school, St Stephen's. But it was a place for an ambitious young man to escape. Its population in 1911 was 229,141; Calcutta was nearly six times its size. The 'New Delhi' government enclave, however, was to be 1,290 square miles; by comparison, Washington, DC was a mere seventy square miles. A grand architectural vision had been commissioned from Edwin Lutyens, famous for his designs of English country houses and churches for garden suburbs. Land prices had begun to rise in anticipation, but by the end of 1912 little progress had been made in its execution. The purlieus of the old Red Fort had been cleared for the king's visit, but there were worries that what was now called the 'Indian Town' would encroach on imperial space, and that Delhi railway station remained 'one of the worst in the world' for the city's intended size and new importance.[95]

It was here that the viceroy arrived on 23 December 1912 for his formal State Entry. Unlike King George the previous year, he was met at the station by the biggest elephant he had ever seen, lent by the Raja of Faridkot. It was caparisoned with howdahs and saddlecloths of gold and silver that had been used by the former viceroy, Lord Curzon, in the imperial Durbar of 1903 which celebrated Edward VII's succession as king-emperor. The howdah bearer was an old man who had come all the way from his village to beg the honour, with the unlikely claim that his great-grandfather had performed the same office for Hardinge's grandfather, who was governor-general between 1844 and 1848.[96] Lord Hardinge mounted the giant beast with his wife, Winifred, at his side, and two attendants to accompany them.

The procession moved off, led by the Royal Artillery and the Enniskillen Dragoons; then came Lord Hardinge's own bodyguard and staff; and, immediately preceding the viceroy, the Imperial Cadet Corps on black chargers, resplendent in snow-leopard skins. To Hardinge's rear, his council flowed behind him on fifty carefully picked elephants. Then, somewhat diminished by having to ride on horseback this time, but still resplendent in their royal accoutrements, came the rulers of the Punjab: the Princes of Patiala, Jind, Nabha, Kapurthala, Maler Kotla, Faridkot and others. The legendary frontier cavalry of the 3rd Skinner's Horse brought up the rear.[97]

As they processed through the Queen's Gardens, from which the public were excluded, Lord Hardinge had what he described as 'a presentiment of evil'.[98] At this point, the cavalcade entered Chandni Chowk as it stretched towards the Red Fort and the *Diwan-i-Am* audience room at its heart. The street was dressed with bunting; there were people on the housetops, at the windows and peering through lattices, cheering loudly. The row of great *bodhi* trees planted down the centre of the road forced the procession to move closer to the windows. At 11.45 a.m. the viceroy passed the building of the Punjab National Bank; it was some 300 yards down Chandni Chowk, at a point halfway between the gothic Clock Tower and the Fountain. The elephant halted and there was a sudden silence.

The bomb deafened the viceroy and his wife before the sound of it could reach them. Hardinge saw his pith helmet in the road. He turned first to his wife, and saw that she was unscathed, and then to the back of the howdah, where he noticed some yellow powdery residue.

The viceroy turned again to his wife and said: 'I am afraid that was a bomb.'

'Are you sure you are not hurt?'

'I am not sure. I have had a great shock, but I think I can go on.' He felt as if someone had hit him hard in the back and poured boiling water over him.

The chief of police handed up the viceroy's helmet on the end of a lance and asked for orders. Lord Hardinge called, 'Go on!' to set the procession in train again. Fresh cheers erupted as they went on another 200 yards. It was then that Lady Hardinge realized the back of the howdah had been blown off, and that her husband was looking pale. She saw red flesh through his torn uniform. She looked round again and noticed the legs of a *jamadar* entangled in the ropes of the howdah. They belonged to the man who had been holding the state umbrella. He now hung backward.

'Do let me stop the procession,' she said, 'as I fear the man behind is dead.'[99]

The bomb had hit the pole of the state umbrella and fallen into the well of the howdah, killing the *jamadar*, Mahabir, instantly. A piece of metal was later removed from his heart. The debris subsequently revealed the device to have comprised a Wills tobacco tin charged with picric acid, packed with rusty jute carding needles and held together with wire. Indian assassins, the head of intelligence wryly observed, had 'at last secured a fairly perfect bomb'.[100] The needles had plunged into Hardinge's neck and right shoulder blade, causing a wound four inches long and exposing flesh and bone. The back of the howdah had been built thickly to support the silver sheathing, and this probably saved his life, although verdigris from the gold plating poisoned his blood.[101]

Hardinge then fainted. Or rather, as one eyewitness put it, he executed a 'gradually dignified collapse, as if he melted'.[102] Hardinge's doctor was on a following elephant and hurried to the viceroy's side, climbing from one great beast to the other to treat him.[103] Members of his staff worked in their shirt sleeves to lift him down, like a baby. They had to pile up wooden cases to reach him, the elephant being too disturbed by the bomb to kneel.

There was a stampede in the crowd. One policeman heard a cry of 'Shabash Mara!' ('Bravo, die!')[104] But in the general confusion, many bystanders simply sat down in shock. A sixteen-year-old youth, Suraj Bhan, sitting watching on a pavement in the middle of the street, had been killed instantly when a needle and silver from the howdah entered his brain.[105] The helmets of the men of the 60th Rifles lining the street were peppered with metal. At least twenty others were injured; the total was unknown as many victims never came forward.

The viceroy recovered consciousness on the pavement, and immediately gave orders that the ceremony was to continue. He then espied his Indian personal servant, who had also been on the elephant, climbing down. He was not in his scarlet dress uniform.

'What the devil do you mean by being here in khaki?' Hardinge cried. But the man did not appear to hear him. Hardinge later learned that his servant's dress uniform had been blown off in the blast, revealing the khaki kit he had worn underneath to keep warm. The man was lacerated with thirty to forty minor wounds and both his eardrums had burst. He was deafened for life. Hardinge fainted again, and was ferried in a motor car borrowed from an Indian nobleman back to the Viceregal Lodge.[106] Detachments of Skinner's Horse were sent to search the streets.

No one watching was sure what had happened. Some witnesses claimed that the bomb had been thrown from the pavement. But the balance of opinion was that it had been launched from the roof of the Punjab National Bank, a three-storey block on the north side of Chandni Chowk, densely packed with 150 or so spectators, most of them women. Several of these ladies, along with a small boy, described a muffled figure on the roof with them, holding a handkerchief by its four corners. Witnesses elsewhere in the crowd noticed that, after the explosion, some men on the roof of the bank were slow to move away.

The police were equally slow to surround the premises: the usual precaution of placing policemen in the buildings along the route had not been taken. But eventually the bank was sealed off. It was a maze of staircases and passages, and its flat roofs made for easy escape routes. Some men were arrested after they fled into the bazaar. The police chased them into a cul-de-sac, forced a door at the end of it, and two men with injuries to their faces were arrested. Four others outside the bazaar, who were 'apparently trying to evade notice', were also arrested.[107] A rumour – never really refuted – that the attacker was a man dressed as a woman gathered momentum. Women at the scene were examined by female nurses.

At the head of the procession, Sir Guy Fleetwood Wilson, the vice-president of the Viceroy's Council, continued on to the Red Fort. Mounting a white dais, he took his seat in front of the Peacock Throne and was handed a bloodied copy of Hardinge's speech. The words prepared for the viceroy rather unfortunately recalled the king-emperor's announcement of the previous year that the Great Durbar marked a new beginning for India. In front of 1,000 princes and notables, Wilson now proclaimed New Delhi as 'the definite capital of the Empire'. To the sounds of a thirty-one-gun salute, the Indian princes and imperial proconsuls remounted their horses and elephants and proceeded out through the Delhi Gate and back down Chandni Chowk.[108]

One of the princes praised Hardinge's self-restraint in not immediately ordering the troops present to attack in retaliation; that, he reminded the British, would have been the way of it in Mughal Delhi. Instead, across Delhi, shops were closed and searches began of temples, hotels, serais and railway stations. Even the street sweepers and the known 'bad characters' of the brothels and opium dens were rounded up and questioned. The Viceroy's Council gathered for an informal meeting over Christmas lunch. Sir Guy Fleetwood Wilson made the case for mass punishment: 'Delhi must be made to feel what has happened.' He abused the director of criminal intelligence, Charles Cleveland, who was currently recovering from a mauling by a leopard, and the commander-in-chief of the army. More sober minds argued against 'flurry', and prevailed.[109]

The Indian princes and the Punjab National Bank – whose office was forever linked to the attack – pledged lavish funds to the tune of a lakh of rupees for information. It did not help that the founders of the bank included the Punjabi radical politician Lala Lajpat Rai. Some of Delhi's citizens even passed a motion to pull down the building, and a large number of them accompanied the body of the attendant Mahabir as it was carried down Chandni Chowk to the Hindu cremation ghat. The Indian press denounced 'the curse of anarchism'.[110] The Indian National Congress voted for a resolution to the same effect at its session in Patna. Liberal opinion feared 'vigorous and unbending repression'.[111]

There was speculation that Muslim concern at the plight of the

Ottoman empire in the Balkan War was at the root of the attack.[112] Mohammad Ali Jauhar and his brother, seen as the leading Indian supporters of the Ottoman Caliphate, had established themselves in Delhi in 1912 to exploit its Islamic associations as a base for their activities. Just two weeks earlier, their medical mission had left for Turkey, tracing the viceroy's route in reverse from the Jama Masjid to the railway station and followed by an estimated 15,000 of the city's Muslims.[113]

From the French enclave of Pondicherry in south India, the fugitive Aurobindo Ghose wrote to friends in January 1913 about the event, using a code drawn from the tantric yoga he now practised. The only criteria for judging the deed, he argued, were the success of the venture and the failure of the *bhutas* ('ghosts': that is, the police) to foil the perpetrator. The 'experiment in the *smashana* ['cremation ground': that is, Delhi] was a daring one – but it seems to have been efficiently and skilfully carried out . . .'. Aurobindo, however, grieved for Hardinge's injuries. While he defended India's right to use violent means against the Raj, he demurred at its practical consequences.[114]

Meanwhile, as Hardinge slowly recovered from his wounds, he ordered sweets to be handed out to Delhi's schoolchildren to celebrate his escape from death.[115] From his sickbed on the veranda of the Viceregal Lodge, he presented the attendant who survived the attack with a purse of 100 rupees and a medal. Then, still tormented by neuritis and a burst eardrum, he repaired to the hill station of Dehra Dun, some 150 miles north of Delhi, for a month's rest. The secretary of state for India offered him six months' home leave, which he refused: the bomb could not be seen to disrupt the government of the Raj. He decided instead to scotch the rumours of his dire health with a time-honoured display of imperial manliness and mastery, by shooting a tiger.[116] A sequence of photographs was published nearly a year later, to dispel rumours of Hardinge's continuing ill-health, showing him bagging a buck, under the headline, 'As well and as strong as ever'.[117]

THE HUNT FOR FAT BABU

On his way up to Dehra Dun, Hardinge passed a welcoming party of loyal Indians. At the forefront was a man called Rash Behari Bose. At a public meeting in the hill town just two days previously, he had proposed a vote of condolence to Hardinge. But there was something about him that led many locals to believe that he was a police stooge. The reality was a lot more complicated.

Rash Behari was born in 1886 in Bengal's Hooghli district, but he moved around a good deal in his youth. He twice ran away from home to join the army but failed to pass muster. His schooling was erratic, much of it in the French colonial enclave of Chandernagore – some twenty-two miles north of central Calcutta – where his father, a government printer, had a house. Rash Behari worked for a time at the government press in Simla, the Himalayan summer capital of the Raj, before resigning to come to Dehra Dun in 1906. He found employment as a clerk at the Imperial Forest Research Institute, perhaps the most magnificent scientific establishment in the Raj. The Tagore family maintained a villa in the town, and Rash Behari lived in a small outbuilding in its garden, which he turned into a meeting place for restless young men. He was part of the constant flow of people, many of them travelling incognito, from Bengal through the United Provinces to Dehra Dun, and on to the Punjab or to Delhi. And he had access to acid for bomb-making and to second-hand revolvers from retired Gurkha officers living in the town. By now, his life was cloaked in rumour.

It was at a wedding that Rash Behari met one of the few survivors of the Bengal underground, Jitendra Mohan Chatterjee, who was now looking to build networks across north India. For the first time, the Bengal group came into direct contact with men such as Lala Lajpat Rai and Har Dayal, who had returned briefly to the Punjab in 1908 after resigning his scholarship at Oxford. Har Dayal set up a string of reading circles for young men, often from leading families. From Delhi, where the circle centred around the home of Amir Chand, a teacher at Har Dayal's old school, St Stephen's, they stretched as far afield as Kanpur, in a residence borrowed from an India House friend, and Lahore, where the door of the house displayed a sign saying, 'No admission to Europeans or Christians'. The young men versed themselves in English texts on the French Revolution and the revitalization of 'national history'. Har Dayal expounded in articles for the press the beginnings of his ideas of the 'social conquest': an assault on the habits of mind and the self-abasement – the 'moral bleeding' – that imperial rule had fostered among the very class of Indians in which he lived and worked, especially pleaders and civil servants. This was surrounded by a Hindu religiosity which many felt was more a badge of commitment than a product of metaphysical engagement.[118] Even so, he left behind him the image of a travelling monk, of a kind of 'political missionary' that owed much to the Christian education he had disowned. He was also now living apart from his pregnant wife, which he projected as a further act of renunciation. But, feeling under threat from the authorities, he left India again, without seeing his daughter born. Situated where he was, Rash Behari was well placed to take up the lead in his stead.[119]

In early 1911 Rash Behari went back to Chandernagore to visit his dying mother. Such marginal places were now key centres in the new map of the underground. To the British, Chandernagore was the main conduit for anarchist influences from Paris. It had only one underpaid French police officer, its mails were unmonitored and the French governor was thoroughly intimidated ever since a bomb had been thrown into his dining room in April 1908. Aurobindo Ghose had passed through Chandernagore in disguise on his secret journey to sanctuary in Pondicherry in 1910, and now one of his disciples instructed Rash Behari on the path of self-renunciation revealed in the Bhagavad Gita. It was here that the plan was hatched to strike at the heart of the Raj by killing the viceroy.[120] This fitted with the British theory that the attack on Hardinge was undertaken only after an earlier plan to assassinate the king-emperor himself the previous year was abandoned due to the high security. It was here also that Rash Behari became a paid informant of the Bengal CID.[121]

The manhunt after the attack on the viceroy was on an unprecedented scale. It was led by a police officer from the Department of Criminal Intelligence, a thirty-three-year-old Scot called David Petrie. His team grew to thirty-four men. No political subject of any consequence escaped enquiry, nor did their relatives.[122] It became an axiom that 'no detail of a suspect's life and associates is so small, that it will not eventually repay the trouble involved'.[123] But Petrie's appeal for information elicited only 'mercenary', 'malicious' and 'foolish' statements. Over the next months, however, Petrie and his team began to piece together Rash Behari's movements.

As a first step, Rash Behari returned to Dehra Dun from Chandernagore with a young man from Bengal called Basanta Kumar Biswas, who travelled as his cook and manservant. The British reported that the two men lived on 'much more intimate terms than master and servant'. Biswas was, as the British later described him, a 'friendless boy', an immature seventeen-year-old, the 'jackal' for the plan that was orchestrated by Rash Behari.[124] At this point Rash Behari took long leave from his post at the Imperial Forest Research Institute. Biswas was given a false name and caste and was infiltrated into the Popular Dispensary in Lahore as a compounder of chemicals. The two men came to Delhi on 20 December 1912, staying at the house of a merchant from Dehra Dun who knew nothing of their purpose. On the morning of Hardinge's arrival, they left the house at dawn. Biswas was dressed in pyjamas and a round cap, with a shawl to conceal the bomb. This was perhaps the origin of the reports that the assassin was dressed as a woman.

In the wake of the bombing, Rash Behari travelled back to Dehra Dun in order to denounce it roundly and publicly. This confused both local observers and the police themselves. The police in Dehra Dun cultivated him, and he was even able to gain entry to the government circuit house in which Hardinge was recuperating, it was said with a police pass. The police would ultimately conclude that Rash Behari had ingratiated himself with them as an informer 'to further the ends of his conspiracy'. As Petrie put it, they had been 'spoofed'.[125]

Biswas went back to Lahore and, on 17 May 1913, again on instructions from Rash Behari, planned another attack with an almost identical bomb. This time the target was a British official in Lahore who had been a scourge of the revolutionaries in Bengal; the aim was to kill him while he was drinking in the bar of the British Club, in Montgomery Hall. An associate passed Biswas the bomb, which had been hastily assembled in the shade of the adjoining Lawrence Gardens. This time Biswas panicked and did not throw the device; instead he left it on Library Road, in the hope a European would run over it. In the event, an Indian messenger triggered it with his bicycle and was killed. The British painstakingly recorded that the same type of quarter-pound Wills tobacco tin was used here and in an earlier failed attack in Dalhousie Square, Calcutta, in March 1911.[126]

Enquiries continued through the hot summer months of 1913. A breakthrough occurred only in November, during a raid on a house in Calcutta, on Upper Circular Road, where bomb-making equipment was found which seemed to match the materials recovered in Delhi,

Lahore and elsewhere. Remnants of the old *samiti* of Dacca were arrested, in the course of which an inflammatory leaflet written in English, called *Liberty*, was recovered. Further work by police agents revealed that it was published in Lahore, and circulated from there to Bengal and to the Northwest Frontier Province:

> Revolution has never been the work of men. It is always God's own will worked through instruments. Those who are commissioned to bring about mighty changes were full of the force of Zeitgeist. Spirit enters into them . . . The thrower of bomb on the representative of the tyrannical Government at Delhi was none else but the spirit of the Dispenser of all things Himself . . .[127]

This led to a raid on 16 February 1914 on a house in Lahore frequented by young men from Bengal. Not only were more leaflets found – and a young man studying Savarkar's book on 1857 – but also a detonator, in the shape of discoloured cotton wool in a biscuit tin. A box of belongings, which contained no clue to their owner's identity, was revealed to be Rash Behari's when one of the men arrested at the house, Dina Nath, turned approver. It was only then – nearly fifteen months after the Delhi bombing – that Petrie learned of Rash Behari Bose and Biswas for the first time. Dina Nath said he had written to Rash Behari to congratulate him on the bomb, and received a reply from him stating that it was the work of his party. He had also seen Biswas leave for Delhi a day or two before the State Entry. In late March this story was corroborated by a police informer Petrie called 'Nemo' – who, Petrie believed, had heard it from Rash Behari himself. Nemo stressed that Biswas had thrown the bomb, and from the roadside, with Rash Behari standing nearby. In the event, Biswas was arrested in Bengal, when he went home to perform the death rites for his father. The owner of the house in which Biswas and Rash Behari had stayed in Delhi when they mounted the attack later pointed Biswas out from seventeen other men in an identity parade. The police now circulated a photograph of Rash Behari with a bicycle, offering a 7,500-rupee reward for information. The approver, Dina Nath, was allowed to flee to Burma, where he had a brother in the postal department.[128]

Rash Behari spent most of 1913 and early 1914 touring north India, attempting to draw the militant networks together. Now there was talk of action on an all-India scale, a new 1857. Military garrisons became a renewed target of recruitment. In Bengal the secret organization revived, and at its centre was a rising force, Jatindranath Mukherjee. Sometime in late 1913 the two men met to work towards a longer-term goal of building militant cells and support within the British Indian Army.[129] The police got ever closer to Rash Behari. When Dina Nath was arrested, Rash Behari was also in Lahore. He fled to Delhi, then to a house in Chandernagore. On 8 March 1914 it was raided by the Calcutta police. Rash Behari was not found; as the police report sheepishly acknowledged, he was watching 'from behind a mango tree in his garden nearby'.[130] Even without Rash Behari, the British now felt that they had enough evidence for a 'Delhi-Lahore Conspiracy Case' to go to court.

The hearings ran from 21 May to 1 September, and judgment was given on 5 October. There were two trials, the first of nine defendants including Basanta Kumar Biswas, the second of Amir Chand and one other. To the judge, the defendants – apart from their 'monomania' – seemed to be 'estimable men and of blameless private life'.[131] The evidence focused on the testimony of the approver, Dina Nath, who was denounced as a scoundrel by the defence, as well as on the recovered objects and documents and the evidence of shared methods of bomb-making across India. As was argued at various stages, though, the evidence was never more than circumstantial; as one government opinion admitted: 'We will probably never prove to conviction in a court the Delhi Outrage against its actual perpetrators.'[132] But the burden of proof for 'conspiracy' had been reduced by Indian case law so that it was not necessary for it to be 'corroborated in every detail' in the face of witness testimony and circumstantial evidence. Once the approver, Dina Nath, came forward, the prosecution was able to argue successfully that the Delhi and Lahore attacks could be treated as 'one general conspiracy' which stretched back many years. A key argument of the defence was that the case was concocted by Petrie and other CID officers to cover their chagrin at failing to catch the perpetrators of the Delhi attack, hence their employing Rash Behari as a 'spy' and their 'tutoring' Dina Nath in his testimony. This was rejected. Six of the accused were found guilty: three of them were sentenced to death, and Biswas to transportation for life. He was spared the gallows on grounds of his gullibility and immaturity. The government of the Punjab, however, appealed against the decision in a bid to exact the ultimate price.[133]

For most of the rest of 1914 Rash Behari lived quietly in Benares, near the Bengali quarter of a cosmopolitan city where the up-country police had little sense of all the comings and goings. He was put in touch with a local 'young men's association', and spent his time training its members in what the authorities saw as 'a sort of catechism': 'Are you married?' 'Are you prepared to go to prison?' 'Are you prepared to lose your life?' These 'post-box youths' would spread leaflets through the mail or paste them up in the bazaar. In one raid on the organization, the police found a copy of Bolton King's *Life of Mazzini* (1911) with a passage underlined: ' "Here are we," said Jacopo Ruffini to his fellow-conspirators at Genoa, "five young, very young men, with but limited means, and we are called on to do nothing less than overthrow an established government." ' Rash Behari also imparted his knowledge of firearms and bombs; in one demonstration, variously reported as September 1913 and November 1914, a detonator in a biscuit tin went off, badly damaging the third finger on his left hand. By this he could be identified, but few who met him knew his true name: instead he was 'Satish Chander' or 'Fat Babu'.[134] He posed as a *sanyasi* – a religious mendicant – a shopkeeper, a scavenger. It was said that, in the guise of the shopkeeper, he 'borrowed' a colleague's wife as his own. It was also said that he evaded police cordons dressed as a woman; that he made a fool of one Indian officer by reading his palm; and that he duped a British policeman by travelling in a first-class railway carriage disguised as an Englishman. When the last ruse became known, it was said the officer 'could not stir out of his bungalow for a week for shame'.[135] The legend of this Lord of Misrule travelled vast distances, a harbinger of a greater struggle to come.

Bhagwan Singh with a samurai sword, Yokohama, 1914.

5

Pundits of the Seas
1912–1914

A MODERN RISHI

What happened on a Delhi afternoon was waking news in California. That day, 23 December 1912, in the university town of Berkeley, shouts were heard from a gathering of Indian students: 'Have you heard the news? What one of my men has done in India to Lord Hardinge?' Those present burst into the 'Bande Mataram', singing and 'dancing about their rooms for hours'. Two days later they held a Christmas feast in celebration; the sympathizers who attended included their fellow undergraduate Sun Ke, the son of Sun Yat-sen.[1]

The Raj had its ears everywhere. The voice that raised the cry in Berkeley was soon identified as that of Har Dayal. Officials had followed him during his days as a promising schoolboy in Delhi, an Indian Civil Service hopeful in Oxford and an India House student in London; they watched him even more closely on his sudden return to the Punjab in 1908, where he tried to rally the region's young men against the Raj. But since then he had vanished from sight, and when a secret report revealed him to be chairman of a 'Radical Club' in Berkeley 'composed of Russians, Poles and Socialists', it took them quite by surprise.[2]

The author of the report was William Hopkinson. He too was an Indian abroad, born in Delhi (like Har Dayal), in 1880, into an Anglo-Indian, Eurasian family and a Hindi-speaking world. He had enlisted in the police, and learned some Punjabi, although he could not read Gurumukhi script – as those he spied on were quick to point out. He transferred to Calcutta as an inspector at the height of the *Swadeshi* protests. But, frustrated it seems by the racial barriers to his advancement, he left India in 1907 for Canada. Here he married a respectable young stenographer who had come from Highgate, in London, and raised two young children while working in Vancouver as a store-keeper. In 1912 he was thirty-two years old: a tall man, who, despite his visible mixed heritage, pretended to be a Yorkshireman, giving his birth place as Hull, and his nationality as English, on any official forms in Canada. In truth, he was only on leave of absence from the Raj. He advised the local Canadian authorities on Indian affairs, informally at first, and then, from 1909, he became a lone secret agent in the pay of both India and Canada, with sight of confidential papers that his Canadian supervisors in the immigration authorities had no clearance to read and direct access to the Dominion's governor-general.[3]

Much of this was well known to the Indians on the west coast of America, a number of whom remembered Hopkinson from his Calcutta days. The rumour travelled that he donned a turban and fake beard to listen in on meetings. At other times he turned up in plain sight with a lady stenographer who took down his dictated translations; most likely this was his wife, who did all his confidential secretarial work. He had come down from Canada to California before, to gather information from the immigration centre at Angel's Island and to recruit the swami of the local Vedanta Society as a covert informant. In January 1913, in the aftershock of the Delhi bomb, Hopkinson returned to San Francisco.[4] He had been warned in Vancouver that this time he was a marked man, and so he registered under a pseudonym in the Argonaut Hotel, on Fisherman's Wharf.

The name of Har Dayal was new to Hopkinson. It was first whispered to him by a young student from Madras, who came to America on a scholarship offered through the Indian newspapers, only to discover to his horror that most of his fellow Indian students were 'anarchists'.[5] Hopkinson tried to insinuate himself into student circles, and paid a clerk in the Berkeley post office to open Har Dayal's mail. Meanwhile, the authorities in India opened any letters of Har Dayal's they could lay their hands on.

In the months that followed, as the police in India arrested more informants in the Delhi case, they connected the plot to the network of houses in the Punjab in which Har Dayal had set up reading circles in 1908. While the Punjabi press had portrayed him as a 'quixotic dreamer' at that time, the British now concluded that he was, in David Petrie's words, 'the presiding genius' of the whole affair.[6] His letters to India from California were key exhibits in the trial of the conspirators. Hopkinson made himself indispensable by collecting any thread of evidence that might lead back to Delhi and was despatched to London to report in person to the high officials of the India Office.

In the wake of the British arrests and trials of 'extremists' that had caused Har Dayal to abandon the Punjab, the atmosphere in the region was poisonous. 'I find myself helpless before the demon of suspicion and distrust,' wrote Lala Lajpat Rai to Har Dayal's friend Bhai Parmanand. 'I live almost alone with my books and newspaper.'[7] Bhai Parmanand had returned to the Punjab around the same time as Har Dayal to teach history at the Arya Samaj College in Lahore. In the vacations he gave lectures further afield, in south India and Burma. But a police raid on his home in 1909 uncovered dangerous documents in a box: plans for bombs and what appeared to be a draft constitution for a future independent India. Bhai Parmanand argued that the plans were a plant. But, by this time, possession even of Sir John Seeley's magisterial *Expansion of England* (1883) in Urdu translation was labelled as sedition.[8] Bhai Parmanand was bound over by a magistrate to keep the peace and lost his teaching position. The manuscript of his 'History of India', together with the notes from his research for it in the British Library, were stolen. Unable to work in any public position in India, he took third-class passage to Marseilles, and then boarded a Dutch liner for New York.

Although the Indian nationalist cause was alive in New York, the absence of an Indian business community meant it was reliant on support from a miscellany of theosophists, humanitarians and Irish nationalists centred on the circle of the *Gaelic American*, whose editor, George Freeman, took it upon himself to campaign for 'a great Asiatic revival'.[9] The interest of such patrons was fed by a taste for esoteric ideas and a market for exotic goods. The Bay of Bengal now lapped the shores of the north Atlantic in annual waves of itinerant Hooghly pedlars and sailors jumping ship in Brooklyn and Staten Island. By 1900, the *New York Times* was reporting the existence of lascars, Arabs and Malays in Lower Manhattan.[10]

But the city of New York alienated Bhai Parmanand. He was repeatedly turned away from lodging houses, he believed on account of his race. Even the swami of the New York Vedanta Society, he felt, tried to avoid meeting Indians in person. At least the British masked their racism with politeness. His earlier experience of working in South Africa, as a preacher for the Arya Samaj, led him to turn to the communities of indentured labourers from India in the Caribbean. He took ship for British Guyana, but broke his journey at Fort-de-France, in the French colony of Martinique, having learned that Har Dayal was living there.

After a few hours of asking around town, Bhai Parmanand found his old friend living the life of an ascetic. Har Dayal rented an upper room from a local woman, slept on a bare floor in the manner of the Buddha, and sustained himself with fruit and a little boiled grain and potatoes. He was preparing, he said, to found a new faith. His spiritual progress since 1908 had taken him at first to Paris, but he became disillusioned with the fractious politics of the refugees from India House in the wake of the Dhingra affair. Suffering from consumption and needing somewhere warmer and cheaper to live, he left around April 1910 for Algiers. However, North Africa disagreed with him – as did Muslim society as a whole, Bhai Parmanand surmised – and so, telling friends in Paris he was going to Djibouti to set a false trail, he set out instead for Martinique.

Har Dayal was no happier in his new Caribbean home. It was, he wrote to Madame Cama in Paris, 'a dreadful hole of a place'.[11] So in February 1911, encouraged by his meeting with Bhai Parmanand, he travelled steerage via St Thomas in the Danish West Indies and San Juan in Puerto Rico to New York. He had a fruitless spell at Harvard, and then went to Hawaii, where, he told an old schoolfriend, he meditated on Waikiki Beach. There were rumours he had spent time further afield, in Suva in Fiji, and that in Hawaii he had gone to seek Sun Yat-sen, who had studied there in his youth, and visited again as recently as March–May 1910.[12]

After his reunion with Har Dayal, Bhai Parmanand lingered in the Caribbean, preaching Hindu revival in British Guyana and Trinidad, where a genuine 'pandit from India' was something of a curiosity. But then he too travelled west, to California to enrol at Berkeley, where by early 1913 around thirty-seven Indian students were registered, attracted by the low fees, the sun and the more tolerant atmosphere. He funded his studies at the College of Pharmacy by working in a drugstore and by picking flowers at plant nurseries in the holidays.[13]

The longer journey to the east, from Asia across the Pacific to the

Americas, opened up as other paths began to close. The 'White Australia' policy from 1901 pushed migrants further across the ocean, to the Pacific northwest of the United States, and also to Canada, where the long-standing exclusion of Chinese labour led the Canadian Pacific Railway to recruit Indian construction workers in large numbers, at wages as high as two or three Canadian dollars a day. Most came from the Punjab, to escape indebtedness, the pressure on land and the long shadow of the famine years of 1899–1902. They were rarely the poorest of the poor. Migrants had to pay their own passage, a cost equivalent to mortgaging one or two acres of land. There was a tremendous amount at stake for entire families, and it was impossible for a migrant to return unless a substantial return on the investment had been earned. Many, perhaps half of them, were former soldiers: worldly, confident English-speakers with special skills. Most migrants were Sikhs, who, although only 1 per cent of the population of British India, provided 20 per cent of its military recruits. The imperial networks of the Punjab – not least its 2,000 miles of railways – made this landlocked province one of the better connected to the outside world. Some soldiers had their imaginations fired when they returned through Canada after parading at Queen Victoria's Diamond Jubilee celebrations in London in 1897 and saw great tracts of wheat like a Punjabi Cockaigne. Others were among the 3,000 Indian troops who fought in the Boxer Rebellion in China in 1900–1901, where they came into contact with Americans.[14]

Military fraternities stretched across the western and eastern rims of the great ocean, often close knit by recruitment from the same villages and service in the same units. They relied on each other and tended to travel in groups. One such was Nawab Khan from Ludhiana district. He first travelled abroad aged sixteen, when he left his home village in 1901 to join his brother, who was serving in Hong Kong. Many from the Punjab – Muslims in Nawab Khan's case, as well as Sikhs – worked as policemen or watchmen in Hong Kong or the treaty ports of China in order to raise the cash to pay for the passage to America. But Nawab Khan's lack of reading ability told against him in his efforts to find employment; he returned to India after a few months and enlisted in the 8th Cavalry, serving on the Northwest Frontier for two years. In 1906 he set out again to follow his brother to the United States, only to make it as far as Penang, where he became a soldier in the Malay States

Guides. He remained there for two years, until he returned home to marry. In December 1909 he left the Punjab for San Francisco, following what was now a long trail of young men from his village with tales of prosperity. He arrived in California in March 1910, and with the help of friends worked his way up the Pacific northwest, toiling in factories in the state of Washington before slogging on to Vancouver, Canada.[15]

Between 1905 and 1920 an estimated 12,200 Indian immigrants were recorded entering Canada and the United States.[16] The Pacific was created several times over: by the needs of capital in the sugar plantations of Hawaii and the fruit farms of California; by networks of Japanese, Korean, Chinese, Filipino and South Asian migrants; and increasingly by an imperial vision of Anglo-Saxon settlement ringing the ocean and encompassing the Indian Ocean too, as far as South Africa. Settler newspapers, white trade unions and bodies such as the Asiatic Exclusion League (from 1905) raged against 'yellow perils' and the 'tide of turban', and conflated all Asians into a kind of 'Mongolian horde'. After the first Chinese exclusions of 1882, the formal barriers to movement in North America were raised higher. Japanese migrants were restricted by a so-called 'gentleman's agreement' of 1907. On Labor Day in the same year, a white mob in Bellingham, Washington, turned on the many Indians who had found work there. Many of the migrants were locked in the police station for their own protection, and around 200 of them were chased out of town. They made their way forty miles up the railway line to British Columbia, looking for sanctuary, but walked into a further wave of anti-Asian violence that erupted in the Chinatown and Japantown of Vancouver. When the SS *Monteagle* arrived there three days later with 914 'Hindus' – mostly, in fact, Sikhs – on board, it was blocked from docking by a mob. With these obstructions to Indians entering the British Dominion of Canada, it seemed that the fundamental principle of free mobility within the empire was now in jeopardy.[17] News of this flashed around the colonial world. The vision of Canadian entrepreneurs had been central to the creation of the Imperial Penny Post of 1898 and the 'All Red' telegraph route across the Pacific in 1902. Asians abroad were some of their most enthusiastic users.[18] So what happened in Vancouver was very soon known in San Francisco, Shanghai, Durban and Lahore.

The two-way traffic with India and China helped swell the population of the village abroad, not least with the birth of new outposts, such as Manila. Many Indians exploited the right to enter the United States unhindered on production of a certificate proving six months' residence in a US overseas territory like the Philippines or Hawaii. According to one US customs estimate, a transient community of 6,000–7,000 migrants en route to North America eked out a living in Manila as night watchmen, pedlars, gamblers or conjurers at fairs. Over time, however, the Pacific passage became increasingly difficult. Two Orders in Council of 1908, re-enacted in May 1910, prohibited landing in Canada by immigrants who had not come on a non-stop passage from their country of origin. This was a condition Indians were physically unable to fulfil as the steam routes dictated that it was necessary to trans-ship en route.[19] In 1907–8, 2,623 Indians had been permitted to land in Canada. In 1908–9 there were only six.[20] In 1911–12 a renewed public backlash began to gather force and passenger companies raised prices to exclude such migrants. But when the US Senate formally blocked these 'back door entrances' in June 1913, the staging posts merely shifted to Mexico, the Panama Canal Zone and the Caribbean.[21]

For many, America did not fulfil its promise as the land of opportunity. Tensions were high in the trail of lumberyards and sawmills between San Francisco and Vancouver where many Indians found work because of an economic slump that saw men constantly being laid off. Many Indians found themselves on the streets or camped in the parks. This was the terrain of the North American 'drifter': tents and bunkhouses; camps or 'jungles' on the fringes of settlements; the street-corner 'slave market' or 'stiff town', where day-labourers were recruited.[22] But the rough sociability of this urban underworld was hard for Asian men to navigate. Their quests for companionship or intimacy were often rebuffed, as they were seen as a danger both to white women and to white men, and anathema to respectable family life.[23] In Vancouver, where the city fathers tried to keep Indians out of the city and to deport any vagrants, some 700 or more were living in shacks, and in woods outside the city limits, supported by their friends. Others made their way back down through Washington and Oregon, to the vineyards and orange groves of California. By 1913 these shifting populations meant there were three times more Indians in California than in Canada.[24]

But it was not possible to replicate Asian colonial conditions in the Americas, and the new arrivals explored its freedoms. With a collective tenacity that impressed even their most trenchant opponents, their communities grew stronger as the worlds of the lettered and labourers began to draw together for the first time. Their leaders began to invest their savings. They bought land in California: fruit orchards, rice fields in Calusa county, and potato farms such as those in Stockton belonging to Juwala Singh, who had worked his way through Panama and Mexico. And, by 1911, they owned urban property worth some half a million dollars in Vancouver and nearby Victoria. In Vancouver, wealthier Sikhs sponsored a temple and a night school – which taught politics along with the English language – and supported an attempt to make the community self-sufficient through a 'Guru Nanak Trust and Mining Company'. Striving for connections in a world of inequality, such Indians developed a vision of a constellation of free communities in the New World: an empire inside out.

These communities also became increasingly vocal in their anger at their treatment by the empire as a whole. There were instances where ex-soldiers publicly took off their medals and burned their honourable discharge certificates.[25] In 1908, unable to find vagrants to deport, and armed with the conviction of its right to redirect labour to where it was most needed in the empire, the Canadian government attempted to resettle some 1,000–1,500 Indians en masse in the tropical timber colony of British Honduras.[26] When Sikh leaders were sent there on an exploratory mission, the adviser and interpreter who accompanied them was the policeman from India, William Hopkinson. They accused him of bribery, of trying to coerce them into reporting favourably on Honduras. Despite Hopkinson's efforts on behalf of the Canadian authorities, the leaders were shocked by the conditions they found in Honduras, and at the attempt by mass 'transportation' to reduce free migrants to indentured labourers.[27]

An old opponent of Hopkinson's – codenamed 'Delta' in his diary – was among the men at the Christmas feast in Berkeley in 1912 that the secret servants of the Raj had followed for many years and over vast distances. This was Taraknath Das, who had been one of the first of the Dacca Anushilan Samiti to flee to Japan during the first euphoria of pan-Asianism. After studying at Tokyo University, he came to San Francisco, finding shelter initially within the religious networks of the

Vedanta Society. He embarked on his own kind of work-study, spending time as a laundry assistant and a hospital janitor, before eventually enrolling as a student in chemistry at Berkeley. He then worked as a customs translator for a while in Vancouver, using the job to help fellow countrymen talk their way into Canada. In 1908, after he was forced to resign his customs post, he started a bi-monthly journal, *Free Hindustan*; published first from the press room of the Socialist Party of Canada in Vancouver, it moved to Seattle when he returned to the United States later that year, and then to New York and the offices of the *Gaelic American*. Through its pages, he preached a message of republicanism and engaged Leo Tolstoy in an open correspondence on the ethics of violence. In turn, Tolstoy's 'A Letter to a Hindu' was translated into Gujarati by M. K. Gandhi on his voyage back to South Africa in 1909 and published in his *Indian Opinion* in Durban.

With the help of sympathetic patrons, Taraknath now began a course in military engineering at the private Norwich University, the military college of Vermont. He was a popular man on campus, but entreaties from the British embassy to American military men with colonial sympathies from their service in the Philippines led to questions about his suitability. He was barred from enlisting in the Vermont National Guard, and fears that he might be the first of a wave of applicants to military colleges, together with his refusal to abstain from agitation against Britain, led to his honourable discharge from Norwich University. He then studied politics and worked on a thesis on employment law at the University of Washington while labouring as a vegetable picker and making frequent visits to Berkeley. The British exerted pressure by every possible means to have him moved on again, but they were running out of steam. Taraknath revived an obscure argument of the Founding Fathers in 1790, which spoke of the 'white race' as a qualification for American citizenship, to claim that a Hindu's 'Aryan' origins entitled him to its protection.[28]

Altogether more dangerous than Taraknath, however, was his fellow guest at the Christmas feast, Har Dayal. He arrived in California from Hawaii in late 1911. With Bhai Parmanand's help, and armed with letters from Oxford and Harvard, he approached Stanford University. Founded in 1891, Stanford was already attracting students from across the Pacific and Har Dayal took full advantage of its liberal, outward-looking, non-denominational and co-educational character.[29] He gave a few talks on Hinduism, which struck the founding president of Stanford, the evolutionary biologist and peace activist David Starr Jordan, as 'remarkably clear and forceful'. Har Dayal offered to lecture on 'Indian philosophy' without pay, 'for the good of the cause', having told Jordan he had means enough to live. 'In a moment of weakness', as he later put it, Jordan accepted the offer.[30] In Palo Alto, Har Dayal entered the radical circles of the San Francisco Bay Area, including that of the writer and socialist Jack London. He began to advertise his presence in a series of articles in local journals and for the *Modern Review* of Calcutta. One such, published in March 1912, was perhaps the first extended encounter in print between an Indian intellectual and the great 'modern rishi', or 'seer', Karl Marx.

Har Dayal's short biography of Marx portrayed him not as a philosopher principally but as a campaigner against poverty and inequality. Marx's name was known in India, Har Dayal reminded his readers, for the help his grandson, Jean Longuet, had given Savarkar after he tried to jump ship in Marseilles three years earlier. Har Dayal outlined his empathy with Marx's own life of struggle: with Marx's quarrels with his father; the sacrifices of his wife, Johanna; their shared poverty in exile; and the loss of two of their children. 'India too knows this domestic strife, which makes one home dark but spreads light over the land.'[31]

But Har Dayal showed little interest in synthesizing Marx with South Asian knowledge, or even in fully explicating his writings. As with many others who were also beginning to discover Marx, it is not clear which of his works Har Dayal had read directly or were available to him. He applied his own style of 'grabbism' to what he found. He had little time for historical materialism: 'I only state this view in order to disagree with it.' Nor for class struggle: 'It is not class-selfishness, but social co-operation based on the appreciation of a higher ideal, that has been the motive force of progress at all epochs.' He showed a little more patience with the theory of surplus value. 'But,' he concluded, 'I am not interested in the stupid economics of a stupid system.'[32]

What Har Dayal took from Marx's thought above all was 'how it attacks the great evil of private property in land and capital, with its brood of money, rent, taxes, interest and profit', together with his faith in the working classes. This faith, Har Dayal argued, Marx held in common with Jesus, the Buddha, the Prophet Muhammad and Jean-Jacques Rousseau. 'The great man, who perceives that all men, even the rudest and poorest, are capable of the highest moral growth, is the saviour of society. He knows the essence of human nature. He evokes power in those who are apparently weak: he makes heroes of the scum of the earth.' Har Dayal's text was shot through with the cadences of his own mission-school education, and his own self-fashioning drew equally on the spiritual disciplines of the founder of the Jesuit order, St Ignatius of Loyola.[33]

Har Dayal cultivated his own saintly mystique as a modern rishi, having quickly grasped what one of his American friends called 'the utility of self-mortification': the exploitation of western fascination with Indian philosophy in a calculated way so as to raise India's prestige and to advance its struggle. He stayed in a small room near a railway, sleeping on the bare floor and he appeared at meetings in ragged clothes. Although, as the British pointed out, with three well-to-do brothers working as pleaders (a profession he publicly scorned), and a wealthy wife, he did not lack for funds.[34] A cameo as the syncretic philosopher 'Dyal Har' in Jack London's novel *The Little Lady of the Big House* (1915) gave him an additional, fictional lustre that would follow him around for the rest of his life.[35]

Har Dayal's classes, as Bhai Parmanand noticed, attracted 'a large number of lady students'. Some years before, in a letter written to *The Indian Sociologist* while he was in London in 1908, Har Dayal had decried attachments with western women as a 'desecration and de-nationalisation of the home'.[36] Now, in California, he began an intense relationship with a young married Swiss woman, Frieda Hauswirth, a seeming embrace of 'free love' that sent shock waves through the Indian community in the United States. Others who were drawn into his circle included a miner's daughter from Colorado, Agnes Smedley. Beguiled by an ethos that seemed 'about as distant from American life and thought as any movement can be', she identified her struggles as a woman with those of the Asians in America. Although many of the Indian students in California formed similar attachments, complaints reached the ears of students' parents and of David Starr Jordan, who wrote to Har Dayal to suggest he give up his post. Har Dayal, realizing his time at Stanford was at an end, resigned before he received the letter.[37]

Har Dayal spent the summer of 1912 in anarchist and syndicalist circles in the Bay Area, briefly meeting Emma Goldman – whose own trip to India in 1910 had been blocked by the British, but whose ideas were beginning to travel ahead of her – and the charismatic rising star of the American left, John Reed.[38] Har Dayal also gave a series of lectures to the Industrial Workers of the World, or 'Wobblies', who aspired to nothing less than a new form of society, with trade unions as 'the basis of social reorganisation'.[39] Although they set a premium on direct action, the Wobblies had failed to defend labourers of Asian origin during the pogroms of 1907. However, they did not perceive them entirely in terms of a threat, but saw them increasingly as fellow victims and looked to build sympathies and solidarities across race. When capitalism had broken the seclusion of the east, they argued, 'it compelled not only the mingling of commodities but of men also'.[40] Syndicalism, contemporary observers thought, held a particular appeal to 'the floaters', the 'immense army of unskilled or semi-skilled workers, of no fixed abode', in which Asian and other labourers toiled side by side.[41] What brought these movements together, for a season, was a vision of political education for working people. This was a great experiment of the age, furthered by what Jack London called 'the shrinkage of the planet', and its laboratories were found at the great crossroads of human mobility.[42]

By stages Har Dayal began to reach these men. He and Bhai Parmanand visited sawmill workers in the meeting rooms and town halls of Oregon and Washington: St Johns, Portland, Bridal Veil. By early 1913, with donations from men such as 'the potato king' Juwala Singh, he was able to fund Indian students in a hostel at Berkeley, echoing the practices of India House in London. Har Dayal and his associates were not alone in their endeavours. Another who sought to forge connections with the 'floaters' was an individual known as Husain Rahim, who purported to be a Muslim from Delhi who had arrived from Japan in 1910 and was now Nawab Khan's boss in Vancouver. He was active in raising money for the Canadian Socialist Party and the Wobblies, claiming class solidarity between the white workers and the Indian migrants of British Columbia. When Nawab Khan soon fell under Rahim's sway, a worried cousin turned to William Hopkinson, whom he knew from Hopkinson's days as a policeman in Bengal. Hopkinson worked on Nawab Khan, sowing seeds of doubt over Rahim's sincerity and disclosing that Rahim was not in fact a Delhi Muslim but a Hindu from Gujarat.[43] Hopkinson tried repeatedly to have Rahim deported, but without success. 'You drive us Hindoos out of Canada,' Rahim warned, 'and we will drive every white man out of India.' Instead, Rahim rose to lead the community's improvement trust. He published journals in Punjabi, which the British immediately banned from entering India, and he began 'preaching sedition', one informant reported, 'house to house'. There were even rumours, eagerly forwarded by Hopkinson, of secret bomb-making.[44]

This eventually was enough to persuade Nawab Khan to break with Rahim. Leaving Vancouver, he and his friends formed a work party that stayed together through the lumber mills of Astoria, Oregon, a beet sugar factory in Sacramento, California (until they were driven out by the malarial conditions) and the vineyards of Fresno. Although the work was hard and precarious, the group lived in a world of constant intellectual stimulation from reading and debate. In California, Nawab Khan admitted into the party a man called Ghulam Hussan, who constantly talked politics and introduced Nawab Khan to Urdu translations of *Bande Mataram* and a popular life of Garibaldi by Lala Lajpat Rai which had a huge impact on him. But Ghulam Hussan, too, was not at all what he seemed. Ghulam's failure to participate with the other Muslims in the Eid al-Fitr festival raised Nawab Khan's suspicions, as did his vagueness about his past history. Nawab Khan slowly began to piece it together.

Ghulam was in reality a Brahmin from Patiala. He had been in the United States at the time of the political agitations of 1907. This had driven him back to India, where he worked for the 'extremist' cause with Lala Lajpat Rai. He had accompanied Rai's follower Ajit Singh to Persia – where it seems he had adopted his present Muslim name – and then moved on to Istanbul and Paris, where he had worked with Madame Cama. The nature of his activities, Ghulam explained, 'obliged him at one time to be a professed Hindu, and at another time a Muslim'. For men like Ghulam, such a world of constant religious shape-shifting and relentless reinvention of the self pointed to a vision of Hindul-Muslim cooperation.

It was while they were at Sacramento that Nawab Khan was persuaded to attend a meeting in San Francisco addressing the Balkan War. The advertised speaker was a former student of the Muhammadan Anglo-Oriental College at Aligarh, but he did not appear, and instead Har Dayal spoke in his place.[45] Har Dayal's intellectual confidence impressed people, but could also alienate them. After he had been speaking for more than one and a half hours on the subject of 'the non-existence of God', his fellow speaker, the leader of the Baha'i movement, walked out with all his followers. But Nawab Khan was stirred enough to invite Har Dayal to Astoria, where his work party was now based. At the beginning of June 1913 Har Dayal arrived in a procession of hired cars bearing the words 'India' and 'Freedom' to speak to Indians and their American sympathizers at the Hindu Hotel and the Finnish Socialist Hall. He was, according to one shocked immigration inspector, 'regarded as their [the Indians'] Messiah'.[46]

Afterwards – it was a little unclear at what point in all of these meetings – a new movement coalesced. A Hindustani Association of the Pacific Coast was formed and, soon after, a centre was established at 436 Hill Street, San Francisco. It was named the 'Yugantar Ashram', after the Bengal revolutionaries, and it operated with a similar code of secrecy. But the movement was very different in the way that its strategy of lecture tours, complete with magic lantern slides and bioscope, drew thousands of unlettered labourers into its orbit. And then, on 1 November 1913, the association launched a journal: it was called *Ghadar*, or 'Mutiny'.[47]

THE WEDDING OF THE BOMB

The readership of *Ghadar* was truly global, and it was published in a polyphony of languages and scripts – Gurumukhi, Urdu, Hindi and English. While *The Indian Sociologist* and *Bande Mataram* from London and Paris and the *Free Hindustan* from New York had all travelled to some extent, *Ghadar* was carried with the mails across the Pacific to Manila and the treaty ports of China, and then via Singapore and Penang to India. Copies were hidden in the cargoes of traders and the kitbags of soldiers. They turned up in Indian garrisons across the great arc of the Indian Ocean, in East Africa, Sudan and the Middle East, wherever Indians overseas were to be found, and as far as Morocco, where they were not. The copies the British intercepted in the post showed signs of 'slow reading', having passed between many hands, then been kept and reread.[48] To try to avoid this, Chinese Canadian supporters of Sun Yat-sen circulated *Ghadar* in their mail.[49] Some fifty copies of *Ghadar* in Urdu and English ended up, via New York and the Dutch postal routes, in a Chinese medicine dispensary in the French Concession of Shanghai, where the proprietor, claiming ignorance of their content, used them to wrap bottles.[50] In small, significant ways, one neighbourhood of the village abroad now helped sustain another.

In March 1914 a box of sealed envelopes addressed to Madame Cama in Paris was confiscated by the French customs. It contained 187 copies of a pamphlet for trans-shipment to seventy-two addresses in India and another 115 addresses elsewhere across the globe. It was entitled *Shabash!* ('Bravo!'), issued from San Francisco and dated 31 December 1913: 'Price per copy: One English head'.[51] The publication was anonymous, but the British swiftly, and correctly, attributed it to Har Dayal. It declared the first anniversary of the attack on Lord Hardinge to be a 'holiday of the Bomb': 'May durbars and bombs go together till there are no more durbars on the surface of the earth.' It was a review of all the violence that had gone before and a manifesto for the greater fury that was to come. Its three sections comprised an invocation, a technical manual and a martyrology: 'the philosophy of the bomb', 'the effective bomb', and 'the exploits of the bomb'.[52]

'How can a dead nation be brought to life?' it asked rhetorically. 'How can a nation made of cotton threads be up-raised? How can the terror of the terror-stricken be got rid of? How can freedom be obtained by slaves? We give you the answer – by the "Bomb".' The bomb was stronger than the printed word, as it reached the illiterate workers and soldiers in cantonments. The power of the bomb lay in its ability to sow perpetual fear among the British 'lest at any corner, door, wall, railway coach, lavatory, from somewhere or other a bomb may fall on them . . .' The bomb of 23 December 1912 was a 'miracle'; the bomber, a philosopher. The pamphlet held all servants of the Raj culpable for the regime's oppressiveness. 'The officers of the Government must be killed, wounded and humiliated by means of bombs, guns, clubs, shoes, bricks, stones and blows.' It targeted the Raj's Indian collaborators in equal measure, pouring scorn on the 'renegade Maharajahs', and on the Indian National Congress – 'the Ali-Baba of the English thieves'. Were the British, it scoffed, to be 'placated by politeness, humility, or flattery'?

The pamphlet spoke directly to students. It likened the preparation for a bombing to that for a school examination, in which all 'the pleasures and comforts of the world' were to be foresworn. But it was also attuned to deeper South Asian traditions of sacred violence and martial memory. It sought to dispel over fifty years of failure and iniquity following the Mutiny of 1857. 'In one explosion, the seven dignities of the arrogance of the chief Lord of the Noxious Ones were broken down! . . . This bomb was the sound of the drum, was the national proclamation that the manhood of Hindustan was ready to leap on the field of battle.' The call of 'revenge for Plassey' for the first time appointed Indians overseas to the vanguard: 'Oh young men of India, travel in other countries. Go on learning the mode of making the soap which catches fire . . . If you all become pundits of the seas, and no worker for the making of bombs appears from among you, then your lives are fruitless.' To Har Dayal, as to Gandhi, the bomb epitomized a cycle of violence from which there was no escape – although the conclusions they drew from this were very different. 'Whether you perform any act you like, or do not perform it,' Har Dayal warned, 'the messenger of death of the Government is behind you.' The bomb was a self-fulfilling prophecy; its detonation proof of the oppression of India.

In such acts of violence, Har Dayal saw the moment of India's reawakening and freedom, a new *maya*, or magic. 'The bomb and the pistol are so full of magic that they can change the whole nature of man, can bring men to life, can awaken the sleeping and can destroy tyrants.' This was illustrated with historical 'proofs' ranging from tyrannicide in ancient Greece, to the death of Julius Caesar, to John Felton, the assassin of the Duke of Buckingham in 1628, the English parliamentarians and the regicide of Charles I. But, above all, Har Dayal situated the Delhi bomb in the midst of the populism and anarchism of the moment, in what he termed 'the Esperanto of revolution':

The nation that has learnt the lesson [of] the bomb is included amongst the civilised nations. Amongst Asiatic Kingdoms the appearance of the bomb has been found to be the forerunner of independence.

Observers know that Doctor Sun Yat-sen learnt the first lesson in the war of independence, that was to make bombs. It is not twenty years ago that the afore-mentioned Doctor Sahib introduced the bomb into China. And today some little time has passed since a republican Government was established in China . . .[53]

The struggle of others in Asia was the 'flare that lights the way'. 'The people of Hindustan have received full permission to stand at the table cloth of the feast of civilisation but nevertheless the right of sitting down and joining in has not been obtained.' The bomb would allow India to rejoin the world. 'At the wedding of the bomb what may I say?'

Ghadar was now a movement. But it was in no sense a political party and still less a disciplined revolutionary vanguard. Through pamphlets, periodicals and public meetings, it spread as an idea with which many 'pundits of the seas' chose to identify. Behind its collective voice, there were myriad individual Ghadars. They were brought together by a heroic reading of India's past struggle against empire and by lives constantly measured against India's progress on its quest for freedom. They shared a revolutionary eclecticism that was formed by the global terrain in which they operated and a willingness to embrace violence and its consequences. The freewheeling anarchism of exile stoked a sense of apocalyptic foreboding.[54] Not all those caught up in this activism recognized themselves as 'anarchists' – the appellation, by now, was a convenient term of abuse employed by the many state authorities charged with tracking these individuals. 'There are no anarchists in India,' Krishnavarma claimed from Paris, and with some justification. It was perhaps futile to seek for a common source, as the colonial police tried to do, and as the international obsession with 'conspiracy' demanded. In exasperation, the British continued to turn to well-worn stereotypes of the religious 'fanatic' or maladjusted adolescent.[55]

The diffuse nature of the movement also made it hard for any would-be leader to establish a sense of intellectual or political authority. Krishnavarma had assumed the position fell to him, but his star had faded. Savarkar had tried to mould men in his own revolutionary image, but he was now far out of sight, 'across the black water', in prison. Taraknath Das bemoaned the lack of leadership among the 'mass people' as he termed them: 'Where are the real people?' he asked in June 1913.[56] In so far as Har Dayal sought to provide a centre for the storm, it seemed to be a sudden tempest that came to little. His thought was passionate in its eclecticism and he was little interested in reconciling its contradictions; instead he appeared to thrive on paradox. His writings and speeches did not lay out a clear vision of the future government of a free India; rather they voiced an apocalyptic republicanism.

The moment of rupture with colonial rule was the surpassing goal. And even here Har Dayal was inconstant in his advocacy of individual terrorism.[57]

But, in the world through which he moved, nothing stayed in one shape for long, and for this Har Dayal was a fitting figurehead. His struggle was marked by the short-lived nature of his activism in India, by the brevity of his presence anywhere, the constant adaptations, and the discontinuities of his ideological affinities. It was a series of displacements rather than a journey.[58] In early 1914 an imperial web began to close around him. Orchestrated by William Hopkinson, the British campaigned to have him arrested. But it was bungled by the US authorities: they grabbed the wrong man, an illiterate labourer called Hardial Singh. They found the real Har Dayal giving a lecture at the Bohemian Hall in San Francisco on 25 March 1914 and arrested him. When he was released two days later, he jumped bail, leaving behind a $1,000 surety provided by his friends. He resurfaced in Switzerland, poste restante Lausanne, and the British once again had no idea how he managed to travel without leaving a trace.[59]

A FLARE THAT LIGHTS THE WAY

The mechanisms that linked oppression at home with racism and exclusion abroad were now laid bare. In these years the international humanitarian campaign against indentured labour reached a crescendo. Demands for its abolition were fired by moral outrage at abuses and scandals from Fiji to the Caribbean, not least at the high suicide rates that were symptomatic of the anomie, everyday brutality and sexual violence of the plantation world. It united colonial reformers such as C. F. Andrews, an associate of Gandhi's in Natal, Indian National Congress politicians and sympathetic imperial officials like no other issue before it.[60] And beside this was a wider and more elemental groundswell of anger among Indians in the world abroad: fury over broken families, and over families that could not be made, and despair at ever finding a place of one's own. Questions of identity when stepping across the territorial borders of the earth were negotiated not by individuals, but by states. To communities overseas, the Raj had not only failed to protect them but actively orchestrated their subjugation through imperial governments in Southeast Asia, Fiji, North America, Australia, South Africa and the Caribbean. This seemed to mock the appeals to imperial citizenship that were now taken up by the campaigners against indenture.

The treaty ports of China were full of people desperate to move on. In Shanghai at the end of 1912, the British estimated that there were 1,228 Indian residents, perhaps 1,000 of them Sikhs and most of the rest Muslim. Some 449 were policemen, 114 jailers, 224 watchmen working under the police and 300 watchmen for private hire. These men lodged together and supported a growing number of unemployed friends. This reserve army of jobless men undermined the confidence of the British in China in their ability to control the labour on which they relied for their security.[61] Some of the destitute and dismissed Indians made their way from the coast upriver to the port of Hankou, where 149 of them were registered in 1912, as constables for the British and German Concessions or watchmen in godowns or hulks. There were no fewer than fifty-five criminal charges levelled against them.[62] Some made their way as far as the frontier town of Harbin, running opium dens and gambling halls. Such individuals were vodka-addicted, riotous and armed, and closely enmeshed in the Chinese underworld. In a world of multiple jurisdictions and extraterritorial protections these Indian men-without-papers naturally sought the protection of the British Empire. The British consul in Harbin was 'at the end of his tether' and such aid as he could give was inadequate.[63] Many of them were in China solely as a step towards the Americas, but rumour spoke of a closing door. They found strength in men such as Bhagwan Singh Gyanee, who had been a preacher among the Sikhs settled in the state of Perak, in British Malaya, where he had a reputation for unorthodoxy. After 1910 he became a priest at the gurdwara in Hong Kong, where he created more ripples, not only for his relationships with Chinese women but for his relentless attacks on the British colonial authorities.[64] He was a new kind of leader, formed entirely by the village abroad.

Indians mobilized on both sides of the Pacific against racial exclusions. Two older Vancouver residents – Bagh Singh, a former cavalryman and a policeman in Hong Kong and Shanghai, now secretary of the Guru Nanak Trust and Mining Company, and Balwant Singh, the first priest of the city's gurdwara – waged an expensive two-year trans-Pacific campaign to bring in their wives and children, during which their families were detained and they stood to lose all they had.[65] They were eventually admitted on humanitarian grounds, but Bagh Singh's wife, Harnam, died during childbirth in January 1914 under the shadow of a deportation order, leaving behind two motherless children. The case was surrounded by ugly accusations of fraud and polygamy.[66] In 1913 Balwant Singh joined a delegation that travelled to London and the Punjab to plead the plight of the Indians in Canada. They managed to secure an informal audience with Lord Hardinge at Simla, against the advice of the governor of the Punjab, who marked down Balwant Singh as a 'dangerous revolutionary'.[67] But this, and another test case in November 1913, when a party of Indians who landed in the port of Victoria on Vancouver Island and claimed the privileges of British subjects, heightened anti-Asian hysteria and strengthened the resolve of the Canadian government to prevent further arrivals. The socialist Edward Bird, who served as counsel to the Indians, received death threats and fled town.[68] In the midst of all this, Bhagwan Singh entered British Columbia under a false name, and panicked the authorities with his angry lectures in the Vancouver gurdwara. On 13 November 1913 he was bundled in handcuffs on to a ship to be deported back to India, only for him later to abscond when it made a halt at Yokohama in Japan. This public farce was swiftly transmitted into a mood of panic in Hong Kong. 'We are shut out of Australia and New Zealand,' the Sikhs there petitioned; they believed they had one last chance to reach Canada.[69]

At this moment a deliverer appeared, or so it seemed. In January 1914 a Sikh businessman, Gurdit Singh, was visiting Hong Kong to settle a legal case with a former partner. At fifty-five years of age, he had made some money as a labour and transport contractor in British Malaya and Singapore between 1889 and 1909. He had seen the worst of the conditions of Indian labour: 'serfs at home, they are treated no better than helots abroad'. He was a well-known figure in the pathways of Indians overseas, a founder of the first community organization in the Malay state of Perak, the Khalsa Diwan Malaya, and had wide dealings with the British, including the chief secretary of Hong Kong, a man he had known in Malaya. He was smarting from a failed lawsuit in Malaya earlier against his brother over thirty-three head of cattle, in which the judge had berated him as 'entirely unworthy of credence'.

The British treatment of Asians even of 'high social standing' had revealed to him 'the utter hollowness of the equality cult of the western democracies'.[70]

Staying at the gurdwara in Hong Kong, Gurdit was deeply moved by the Sikhs gathered there who were struggling to enter Canada and who called on his aid. He resolved to give them passage himself. As he wrote later in his diary: 'Though it is time for me to rest and pass my days in peace at the age of 49 [sic], yet I have come forward to act as a judge in the affairs of our nation and country to remove disunion, to the ties of friendship, and to distinguish truth from falsehood.'[71] In March 1914, after trying unsuccessfully to hire ships from British owners in Calcutta and Singapore, and sensing a conspiracy to obstruct him, Gurdit privately chartered an ageing Clyde-built, Japanese-owned cargo steamer, named the *Komagata Maru*, for six months at a cost of 66,000 Hong Kong dollars. Gurdit Singh saw no contradiction between philanthropic patriotism and business opportunity. An advertising bill for his new 'Shri Guru Nanak Steamship Company' proclaimed that its ships would 'go around the world in future'.[72]

Gurdit Singh's stated resolve was to 'test' Canadian immigration law, not just in Canada, but to use his own resources and those of dispersed Indian communities to exploit the inconsistencies and undermine the authority of the whole system. He intended to challenge the monopoly held by the imperial state on the management of mobility. Even more fundamentally, he asserted the idea of the 'freedom of the sea' against the increasing legislation over space and time that imperial expansion had imposed on the oceans of the world. He appealed to a collective memory of India's maritime enterprise of centuries past. But Gurdit's methods were modern. Indian 'pundits of the seas' had become, by necessity, adept at navigating colonial laws across different jurisdictions, and Gurdit had acquired a reputation as a determined litigator.[73]

That said, it was not clear to those who listened to him in Hong Kong whether he would be permitted to land in Canada. Gurdit told his acquaintance, the chief secretary, that he did not believe that the Canadian government could legally bar him from entering the country. If he was wrong, he said, there were other countries to steer towards, such as Brazil. The governor of Hong Kong telegraphed Ottawa to obtain a clear statement from the Canadian government that might convince those embarking on the ship that they would not be able to land. But at this point, at least, the imperial mesh came undone. No such thing arrived in time. In the meantime, the governor had exhausted formal legal procedures to detain the ship. The passengers for the *Komagata Maru* marched in a procession from the gurdwara to the docks in high spirits, carrying before them the Granth Sahib – the Sikh holy book – which was stowed, as if in a temple, in the forecastle of the ship.[74] The ship set sail from Hong Kong on 4 April for Shanghai, with 165 passengers on board. However, there was no clear resolution as to what might be its ultimate destination.

The brio of Gurdit Singh electrified India in China. When he landed in Shanghai, Indians scrambled to raise the funds to go with him. There were reports that if he was forbidden entry into Canada 'he would return to India to turn the British out'.[75] About 350 people were on board when the ship left Shanghai, and a further couple of dozen from Manila and elsewhere joined on the next stop, at Yokohama.[76] In Japan, the *Komagata Maru* also took on copies of *Ghadar*, and the passengers heard lectures attacking the British by Bhagwan Singh, now a hunted man, and the priest Balwant Singh, who was making his own way back to Canada from his failed delegation to India. These were the most open statements of political purpose behind the voyage, but it was not clear that all the passengers shared them in equal measure. There were 376 of them: overwhelmingly Sikh men with twenty-four Muslims and twelve Hindus. There were two women, one of them the wife of an Indian army doctor hired in Hong Kong as the ship's physician, and five children, including the doctor's, and Gurdit's own seven-year-old son.[77] The Canadian newspapers shadowed the voyage of the *Komagata Maru* across the Pacific, and whipped up public hysteria at the prospect of a 'Hindu invasion'. In London, as the clouds darkened over Europe, the news that this Japanese steamship was leased by a German agent and had previously been under German ownership, sparked deeper fears of Germany's suborning of the imperial underground.

The *Komagata Maru* reached Vancouver Island on the night of 21 May 1914, and anchored in the tidal stream off the quarantine station at William Head. It was refused permission to dock and a stand-off ensued. Well-wishers from Vancouver's Indian community were chased away by immigration officers. The local response was led by William Hopkinson and the local immigration officer, Malcolm Reid, a political appointee well known for his anti-Asian views. Gurdit Singh announced to them, and to the journalists who had also come over by shore boat, 'What is done with this shipload of people will determine whether we shall have peace in all parts of the British empire.'[78] But no one was permitted to land, and a Japanese sailor attempting to swim to shore drowned.

When the *Komagata Maru* eventually entered Vancouver harbour and anchored off No. 2 berth at 11 a.m. on 23 May, a crowd gathered expectantly on the wharves and began semaphoring the men aboard, some of whom had military training in signals. Yachts and launches buzzed around the ship. The passengers stood at the taffrail in their best clothes and posed for pictures in long lines. They were, a Vancouver newspaper admitted, 'a particularly fine looking lot of men'. Gurdit Singh was applauded for his gentlemanly bearing. But stories of Gurdit's warm reception in Japan provoked the disquieting notion that the Japanese had inspired 'the idea of Asiatic conquest'.[79] Hopkinson and Reid began to fan the flames of a conspiracy theory.[80]

This was now a major imperial crisis. That same month, the director of criminal intelligence in India had identified 'the rabid discontent among the Sikhs and other Punjabis on the Pacific Coast as one of the worst features of the present political situation in India'.[81] Detailed discussions about the ship's legal status were taken up in Indian newspapers, which equated the 'un-English' attitude in Canada with that in Australia, New Zealand and South Africa.[82] With Hopkinson's aid, the identities of individual passengers were sent back to India. Such was the postal network of the Raj that the British needed only a father's name, a village or a police station and district and an identification could be made. This kind of surveillance was illegal, but the Canadian immigration service acquiesced in it all the same. It resulted in an official 'Ghadar Directory' for the Punjab of 1,030 names and addresses, listing kin, connections and sojourns overseas.[83] The government of India's overriding concern was the potential backlash if the passengers were excluded from Canada. The federal government in Ottawa was also exposed on the issue. In the Canadian parliament it was pointed out that, given so many of the men had served in the British Indian Army, 'it seems a very serious matter to deny them entrance into a British country'.[84]

Meanwhile, Reid's and Hopkinson's processing of applications to enter Canada was painfully slow, and quite deliberately so. Of the 376 passengers, twenty-two claimed to be returnees to Canada.[85] Only thirteen of them were allowed to land, on the basis that they had been in Asia 'on holiday'. But others were refused on the grounds that they had been away too long; yet more after failing the invasive medical screening to which migrants were now routinely subject. Gurdit Singh himself proclaimed loudly that he belonged to the category of merchant not migrant, but was denied entry. 'The law of immigration, which is child's play before me, I could break into pieces in court if [I] could go ashore. For this very reason I was confined in the vessel.'[86]

But the South Asian community already in Vancouver was hardened to this kind of struggle. At a public meeting in the Dominion Hall on 30 May, the men who had led them in the wake of the 1907 riots – including Balwant Singh, who was one of those granted permission to come ashore, Bagh Singh and Husain Rahim – watched as the table was piled high with ten-dollar and hundred-dollar bills. Having re-enlisted Edward Bird, the socialist lawyer who had acted for the community before, the support committee used the 66,000 Canadian dollars that had been pledged to attempt to purchase the charter of the *Komagata Maru* and to sue the government for the ship's cargo of coal which sat unloaded in its hold. There was a fresh wave of meetings: a gathering in Stockton on 3 July was attended by over 700 people, including Indians from Canada and Mexico, and an even larger meeting on 21 June included many Canadian sympathizers.[87] Bird challenged the white Canadians present to confront their prejudice; others, however, argued that the Sikhs should return to fight imperialism in their own country.

Bird turned the *Komagata Maru* into a test case against Canada's exclusion laws. He took the leading case of the passenger Munshi Singh to appeal, moving that the government had no legal right to exclude British subjects, and arguing that a common Caucasian past made 99 per cent of migrants to Canada of 'Asiatic origin'. The judges were forced to state publicly that the 'Hindu' and 'Asiatic' races were 'fundamentally different' to the 'Anglo-Saxon' and 'Celtic' races and the court upheld the government's case that a British subject in India could not be considered a native in other parts of the empire. The legal proceedings dragged on for over a month, but by 6 July that avenue of recourse had been exhausted, and deportation orders began to be issued.[88]

By now, the *Komagata Maru* floated in a miasma of waste and was short of food. Officials connived in a trade of scarce necessities over the taffrail, and Hopkinson himself was accused of taking a £20 bribe to allow supplies aboard.[89] Gurdit Singh knew well that Hopkinson was trying to turn the passengers against him, and, in a letter to his lawyer, expressed fear for his life.[90] Hopkinson and Reid put pressure on the medical officer, Dr Raghunath Singh, a military man on leave from the 8th Rajputs, who had been allowed on shore to buy food and medicines. The doctor had no desire to settle in Canada as he was anxious to rejoin his regiment in Hong Kong. He suggested that Gurdit was not the man of means he appeared to be, and that the financing of the voyage was a 'successful bluff'. Some passengers disclosed that they had put in their own money to lease the vessel, and that Gurdit had raised more money from others while they were in Japan. In a secret report supplied to Hopkinson, the doctor later claimed that, on the voyage, Gurdit Singh assumed the powers of a magistrate, and punished passengers with fatigues in the galley or carrying coal. He was, the doctor said, a 'trickster' making a good deal of money from them.[91] Hopkinson brought the doctor before H. H. Stevens, the local MP and a staunch advocate for Asian exclusion, to repeat the allegations, which Stevens in turn conveyed to the Prime Minister of Canada, Sir Robert Borden.[92] After this, Gurdit Singh had the doctor locked in his cabin. With only a handful of exceptions, the passengers' faith in Gurdit Singh remained unshaken. However, by early July, starving and with no possible legal redress remaining, some of them threatened to storm the ship's boats and go ashore.[93]

The affair was ready to explode into violence. One of Hopkinson's and Reid's informers overheard a conversation in which local Sikh supporters discussed their assassination by employing 'some roge [*sic*] whiteman from Socialist Party'.[94] In mid-July, three of them, Balwant Singh, Bagh Singh and Mewa Singh, crossed the border to the small town of Sumas, Washington. There they met Taraknath Das, who helped them buy four revolvers and 500 rounds of ammunition in order to pass them to those on board the *Komagata Maru*. When Mewa Singh attempted to cross back to Canada ahead of the others, one of the pistols and all of the ammunition were found stuffed down his trousers and in his socks, and he was arrested.[95] He was fined fifty Canadian dollars, but given a reprieve while Hopkinson coerced him to provide more information.

Then, in the early hours of 18 July, around 175 Canadian police tried to storm the *Komagata Maru*. They were met with a fusillade of coal, firebricks, hatchets and iron bars, which left twenty men in hospital. Four shots were also fired from the ship.[96] The mayor called out the militia, and the cruiser HMCS *Rainbow* – in truth, half of the Canadian navy – was ordered to Vancouver along with a British regiment. Sensation-seekers gathered in their thousands.[97] The passengers built a barricade of timbers along the rails of the ship, and there were reports of them using the ship's forge to make swords. Local Indians signalled from the shore in the military manner that if the *Rainbow* opened fire they would 'set fire to the whole city'. The repulse of the police raid and the subsequent standing down of the *Rainbow* were claimed by the passengers of the *Komagata Maru* as a decisive victory. In the chronicle penned by Gurdit's secretary, Lord Krishna's rallying cry at the defining battle of the age in the Bhagavad Gita was invoked alongside Quranic and Sikh scripture. 'This is the first instance of the kind in the history of Canada; say in the history of the world . . . the first battle between Asia and Europe over the Colour Question.'[98]

The resistance of the passengers was now termed a 'mutiny'. Fed reports of the German–Japanese connection, Prime Minister Sir Robert Borden became convinced that the *Komagata Maru* was part of 'a deliberate plot to foment sedition'.[99] In order to give credence to this, Hopkinson – it was alleged – had planted copies of *Ghadar* on board.[100] The Japanese captain of the ship, Yamamoto, whom Reid and Hopkinson suspected was a prime instrument of the conspiracy, claimed that his life would be in jeopardy if he attempted to raise steam, and so his sailors were later armed by the Canadian authorities.[101] Faced with a display of overwhelming naval firepower, the passengers began to negotiate the ship's departure. But still the affair dragged on in the full gaze of the world, as the passengers refused to leave without provisions. After a final stand-off, the Canadian authorities, unwilling to antagonize the government of India, which now expected dire repercussions at home if there was a further confrontation, relented and supplied the ship.

On the morning of 23 July the *Komagata Maru* was given fifteen minutes to raise anchor and leave. As the ship departed, at 5.30 a.m. on the morning tide, shadowed by the *Rainbow*, the Indians on deck took off their sandals and shoes to wave at the immigration officer, Malcolm Reid, who trailed in the immigration launch in case some might jump ship. As it happened, two Japanese sailors dived overboard in a bid to reach shore, but were picked up by the *Rainbow*'s lifeboat.[102] As Gurdit Singh wrote in his diary: 'Today we are giving up hopes of Vancouver from our minds, but sweet songs of the liberty of lovely India are being sung.'[103]

VANCOUVER TO BUDGE BUDGE

That same day, 23 July 1914, on the far side of the world, the Austro-Hungarian government sent an ultimatum to Serbia in response to the shooting of Archduke Franz Ferdinand in Sarajevo three and a half weeks earlier. In Germany, officers' leave was cancelled, and the ships of the British Royal Navy were ordered to their home ports. On the 28th Serbia and Austria-Hungary opened hostilities; and when Britain declared war on Germany on 4 August, so too did the viceroy, Lord Hardinge, on behalf of the Raj, without consulting Indian political leaders.

As the lights went out across Europe, the *Komagata Maru* inched across the Pacific, but it was unclear where it was headed. It passed like a ghost through the crossways of the South Asian village abroad. It arrived at Yokohama on 16 August; and then, on the 21st, it anchored at Kobe, where the Indian community led the passengers in procession through the city before they re-embarked. The vessel's Japanese owners tried to harry the passengers off the ship, but Gurdit Singh's lease ran until 3 October, and so the ship again set sail, heading for Hong Kong. The British had planned to repatriate the passengers to Calcutta from there; but when the *Komagata Maru* arrived, it found the threat of mutiny hanging over the garrison. A vagrancy law was invoked against the passengers and they were not able to land. They were now destitute and, with their original port of embarkation closed to them, officially vagabonds of the high seas. One of the passengers summed up the situation while they were still in Japan:

Brothers, this is the story of our new tyranny. They do not want us in Hong Kong. They departed us from Vancouver. They do not want us in India. They want to keep us for ever in the new Andamans, viz., the *Komagata Maru*, in the Japan waters. They have made us beggars, slaves, close prisoners in solitary confinement for an indefinite period on a steam-ship in the mid-sea; 352 human beings confined in one small sea-house cut off from all intercourse with mankind and outside world. Our children must be starving.[104]

Few of the passengers wanted to return to India. While in Japan, they had heard that the British were demanding their names, residence, caste and the name of their father before determining whether to readmit them.[105] Two Sindhi radicals had joined the ship at Yokohama, and some passengers had purchased arms from Japanese crewmen, who had acquired them in Vancouver. There were false rumours among the passengers that Aurobindo Ghose and Rash Behari Bose, no less, had secretly come aboard at Kobe.[106]

According to Captain Yamamoto, after the *Komagata Maru* steamed away from Hong Kong, Gurdit Singh began continually to speak of revolution; there were lectures every day, to which the passengers were summoned by bugle. He was also drinking a bottle of whisky every two days. The ship sailed silently past Singapore, where again no one was allowed to disembark. Gurdit was desperate to do so; he argued heatedly in Malay with a launch of fifty or sixty Singapore police, and there was nearly another violent confrontation. He tried to send a telegram urging 'Indian leaders' to meet the ship in Calcutta but, unbeknown to him, it was intercepted by the Singapore censor. He also asked to be let off secretly as they passed through the Straits of Malacca, but Yamamoto was no longer following his orders.[107] The passengers had set out as free settlers but were now effectively prisoners of war. Watching from London, Sir Arthur Conan Doyle declared the ship to be 'one more piece on Germany's worldwide board'.[108]

On 26 September the *Komagata Maru* finally arrived in the mouth of the Hooghly River in Bengal. The ship was surrounded, as was the way of it, with small local trading craft. But they were turned away by the pilot, and an armed guard was placed on board. Some of the weapons possessed by the passengers were thrown over the side. The government of Bengal decide it would use sweeping new war powers – an 'Ingress into India Ordinance' hurriedly passed on 5 September – to send most of the men back home to the Punjab in a sealed train and to arrest and detain the remainder in Bengal. A district magistrate and police officers boarded the vessel to notify the passengers of the situation and to search their luggage. One of them was the man who had led the Delhi bomb investigation, David Petrie. He did not know what to expect, but he was surprised to find no guns and only one copy of *Ghadar*. He was also taken aback at the strength of the loyalty shown to Gurdit Singh: it was clear he was their 'guru and champion of their rights'. He decided to detain only Gurdit and seven others.[109] But none of the passengers were told of their fates.

The viceroy wanted to keep the passengers of the *Komagata Maru* out of Calcutta at all costs. On 29 September the ship was permitted to land at Budge Budge, a railhead fourteen miles south of the city, and the 321 remaining passengers were finally able to disembark. They were met by British officers and a detachment of twenty-seven Punjabi police constables. The Sikhs walked in procession behind the Granth Sahib, singing as they went, to a level crossing close to the station. There they halted, many believing that the train waiting ahead for them was not for the Punjab but for Assam. Some fifty-nine of them decided they would board it, but all the others sat down around the Granth Sahib in protest. Sometime between 3 and 4 p.m., Gurdit Singh called out '*Chalo!*' ('Let's go!'), and the seated men rose.

For a moment, the British officers believed the Sikhs had resolved to board the train, but someone called 'Quick march!' and, instead of taking the turn to the station, they crossed the railway line and headed up the Calcutta road. The police followed them, unable to turn them back. The officers on the spot mobilized reinforcements of European police sergeants from Calcutta, who crowded into a motor car, a van and a fire engine. More police followed on horseback. Regular troops, 150 Royal Fusiliers, were put into thirty taxis hailed in the street. From the attempts of Gurdit Singh to send messages ahead, the British were afraid that the marchers were looking to provoke a local demonstration of support and were advancing on Calcutta to meet it. There were rumours in the city that the British had demanded that the Sikhs 'put on a *topi* and go to war' and that they had refused.[110] But, living under the new draconian war measures, the leaders of India did not rise to welcome them.

Some four or five miles along the Calcutta Road, the marchers found the way barred. Faced with a show of force, the procession turned back to Budge Budge, arriving there as the moon rose. By now, the special train had departed. Many of the Sikhs sat down within a cordon formed by the European sergeants and began their evening prayers. The police superintendent called for Gurdit Singh, and two of the sergeants moved to grab him. Fearing his arrest, the men around him jumped to their feet to protect their leader. There was a gunshot. The British later claimed it was from one of the marchers. The superintendent was hit. More shots followed in a confused mêlée in the dark as the regular soldiers began to spill from their taxis and form up on the other side of some iron railings. When the police and Sikhs began to separate, the soldiers had clear targets, and they were ordered to shoot by a magistrate present who had himself just been hit in the foot. Some 177 rounds were fired at close range. The Sikhs charged the soldiers several times with bamboo staves and swords they had snatched from the police. It was never clear how many guns they possessed; estimates were anywhere between ten and forty. Some of the British believed they were hidden in the casket holding the Granth Sahib.

When the shooting ceased, twenty-two men were dead: fifteen of the marchers, three Indian policemen (at least one of whom died from a soldier's bullet) and a superintendent, two bystanders and a British railway employee. Several police officers were injured, including David Petrie, who was shot in the left thigh and arm. Many of the marchers now dispersed into the surrounding villages. The military immediately conducted a massive sweep to gather European women and children in the area under their protection, evoking fearful memoirs of the great Mutiny. And 'mutineers' was how the *Englishman* newspaper termed them, playing on the fact that many were ex-soldiers.[111] Soon 120 had been rounded up and consigned to the notorious Alipore jail. Soldiers went round the villages announcing, to the beat of a drum, rewards of 100 rupees for each of the others; but two weeks later, thirty-nine of the Sikhs were still unaccounted for.[112] There were reports of them shaving, cutting their hair and adopting Bengali dress.[113] Gurdit Singh – his money and merchandise on the *Komagata Maru* having been seized – disappeared into the deep underground of the subcontinent.

The departure of the *Komagata Maru* from Vancouver left Indian communities across North America angry and divided by rumour and betrayals. In the weeks that followed, one of Hopkinson's informants disappeared and was later found dead in the undergrowth with his throat slit; a second was shot, ostensibly accidentally, and fatally wounded. At the latter's funeral on the evening of 5 September, a man called Bela Singh entered the Sikh temple in Vancouver and sat down next to Bagh Singh at the front. During the prayers, Bela rose with two revolvers in his hands. He opened fire on Bagh Singh and then on those who were trying to escape by leaping from the second storey of the temple's porch. Eight men were hit, many of them active campaigners for the *Komagata Maru*. Two of them died in hospital, including Bagh Singh. He left behind three orphaned young children.

Bela Singh was well known as Hopkinson's nark.[114] He had the reputation, according to one newspaper, 'of being the smartest dressed East Indian in Vancouver', with 'snowy white turban and linen collar and well-pressed blue serge suit with very modish-looking brown boots'.[115] On 21 October 1914 Hopkinson appeared at the courthouse to give mitigating evidence to the Grand Jury that Bela Singh had acted in self-defence. As Hopkinson walked along the corridor, the man he had interrogated in July for carrying arms across the border, Mewa Singh, approached him, a revolver in each hand. He shot Hopkinson point-blank through the chest. Hopkinson grabbed Mewa Singh by the thigh to drag him to the ground. Mewa struck him with a revolver butt and fired three more times into him. Mewa was seized by a janitor, and gave himself up to police. Hopkinson died some three minutes later. In prison, Mewa was 'perfectly cheerful' and 'to all intents and purpose seems glad' to have murdered Hopkinson.[116]

The trial took place just nine days later, and a local newspaper proudly claimed that it was concluded 'in the shortest time ever known in the justice in the British empire'.[117] Mewa refused counsel, and spoke through a translator, but nothing was translated for him. In his own statement he described how, after his arrest for smuggling weapons, he had been put under intense pressure by Hopkinson and Bela Singh to inform against the men leading the support for the *Komagata Maru*, including Bela's victim Bagh Singh. Mewa had acted to reclaim his honour and that of his community. The shooting by Bela had desecrated the gurdwara. Now not ten men prayed there, and Bagh Singh's children had been left orphaned. This he laid at the feet of Hopkinson, as well as detailing his extortions and tyrannies. He 'was a deceiver, both to the Government on one side, and to us Sikhs on the other, and was a blood sucker'. After Bagh Singh's murder in the gurdwara, Mewa had been threatened with death if he did not speak for Bela. He had found the pressure unbearable:

> I then thought it better to die, I will die like a man straight. These people have disgraced us altogether; they think we are nothing. Sikhs are nothing; there is nothing of us left, we are walked on. There is no judge listens to us . . . No one can do anything here except Bela Singh, Baboo Singh [his associate], Mr. Reid and Mr. Hopkinson. That is why I have killed Mr. Hopkinson and I have sacrificed my own life.[118]

For Mewa, Hopkinson was not only a symbol of local oppression but of the global failure of the Raj. It was 'as bad as if the Muhammadans had ruled us in India'. He described himself as 'a lonely man'; he had no wife, so had chosen this solitary path, and acted alone. Before he spoke, he asked for the orphaned daughter of Bagh Singh to be brought into the court to listen to him, but she could not be located in the large crowd outside. After he finished speaking he began to chant Sikh holy scripture. The defence made a half-hearted plea for manslaughter. After deliberating for ten minutes, the jury found Mewa Singh guilty of murder and he was sentenced to death.[119] The entire business had taken an hour and forty minutes. Mewa's counsel later argued for a stay of execution on the grounds that he had fallen into a fevered religious state. But a medical report from the asylum reported 'no evidence of delusions or hallucinations' nor of 'religious mania'.[120]

William Hopkinson's funeral was a massive affair, mounted at public expense. The cortège was followed by a procession of over 2,000 people, including 100 firemen, Mounties, port and postal workers, and several hundred members of the Orange Lodge. Large crowds lined the way, along with plain-clothes policemen.[121] Obituaries for 'Hoppy' focused on the children, aged two and five, he had left behind. They drew a veil over his origins; it was said that he had been taken to India as a child and raised there. The references to his father having been killed as part of the British ambassador's ill-fated mission to Kabul in 1878 set Hopkinson within a heroic Raj tradition. A Eurasian policeman had become an unlikely hero of Canada's white supremacy. His young widow, Winifred, was given a modestly well-paid position as a stenographer in the immigration department.[122]

Mewa was executed a few minutes after eight on the morning of 11 January 1915, singing, it was said, until the fatal bolt on the gallows was shot. He was bathed according to Sikh rites by Balwant Singh, who had joined him in his vigil in the early hours of the morning. Balwant had been one of several men arrested with Mewa, but Mewa's insistence that he had acted alone secured his release. Mewa's body was escorted by a procession of 370 Sikhs, slow-marching in military files the four miles to the gurdwara at Fraser Mills, where it was burned on a pyre. The city gave a special dispensation for this. As the column wound through the streets, it passed before the immigration officer Malcolm Reid, standing at the front of a small group of bystanders.[123] Shortly afterwards, Balwant Singh and his wife left Canada with their children.

In British Columbia the harassment of Indians continued, and officials received constant offers of information for money. One would-be informant went so far as to send an itemized brochure of intelligence for sale, cash down, ranging from 'a brief outline' (300 Canadian dollars) to the names of the Delhi bombers (1,000 Canadian dollars).[124] An attempt at sexual entrapment, involving a police officer and a Sikh who had already come to blows at the Bela Singh trial, collapsed in the face of revulsion at the unsavouriness of the means and allegations of bribery.[125] Bela Singh himself was attacked: he was shot at and had dynamite thrown at the boarding house where he was staying. After serving a prison sentence for another assault, and now a liability for all concerned, he was sent back to the Punjab, where he continued to inform on his countrymen.

Faced with such a hostile climate, Indians began to leave British Columbia. There were now only around 500 of them in Vancouver and no more than 700 in the whole province. Many drifted over the border. On the Pacific coast of the United States, there were stories of Indians emptying their bank accounts and booking sea passages. The traffic was not all one way. They were joined from Tokyo by the Islamic activist Maulana Barakatullah. The British embassy there had bought information from one of his 'satellites' that he was engaged in a plot to poison British officials. The authorities nearly apprehended him in

Hong Kong, after he left Japan in May 1914.[126] With him in the United States was Bhagwan Singh: 'Be not perturbed that Har Dayal has fled. We – Bhagwan Singh and I – are here to take his place and carry on his work.' In public Barakatullah pleaded for Hindu-Muslim unity; in private he spoke of the 'golden opportunity' the war presented for the cause of Indian freedom.[127]

The latter view was widely shared. At meetings in the states of California, Oregon and Washington through the spring and summer, the talk was that the looming hostilities provided an opportunity and an obligation to return to India to seduce the troops there and to redeem the solemn pledges they had made to overthrow the Raj.[128] A few days after the outbreak of conflict in Europe an 'Open Letter to the British Public by the Hindustanis of North America' circulated in Vancouver, Portland and Seattle. It argued that Indian troops were now being asked to bear the burden of fighting, as they had done in the Boxer Rebellion in China, in Tibet, in Afghanistan, the Crimea, Egypt and the Anglo-Boer War. It asked: 'If those 352 Hindustanis returning to Hong Kong can succeed in inducing at least some of their friends and relations who are now serving in the artillery, infantry, and police force, to desert their posts, what will be the moral effect of such an act?'[129] It was followed by an announcement in *Ghadar*:

WANTED

Fearless, courageous soldiers for spreading mutiny in India.

Salary:	Death
Reward:	Martyrdom and Freedom
Place:	The field of India.

Many of those who had found in the village abroad a new political understanding of the world now looked for a tide that would bring them home and to redemption. As *Ghadar* explained: 'The responsibility for tyranny is not on the neck of the tyrant, but on the oppressed, because if the oppressed people did not wish it, the oppressor could not oppress them.' So it was that, on the morning of 29 August 1914, Nawab Khan found himself on the dockside in San Francisco, looking for a man who had absconded with a large sum of cash from his comrades. His Astoria work-party friends were among sixty Ghadar men embarked on the SS *Korea*, bound for Yokohama. He had not planned to leave with them, and indeed had been working with Hopkinson to keep his friends out of the coming venture – or so he told the British some months and thousands of miles later. But just before noon, as the ship set sail, he stepped on board with only the clothes on his back. What need had he any more of clothes, his companions asked him, when they were going to their deaths?[130]

Ibrahim gelar Datuk Tan Malaka.

6

The Great Asian War
1914

A POSTCARD FROM LONDON

In the summer of 1914, after three years drifting at sea, Nguyen Tat Thanh washed ashore in England. He wrote to the exile Phan Chu Trinh at 6 villa des Gobelins in Paris, giving his address as a hotel in Ealing, west London. He told the older man that he was living among western people and learning English. He later wrote another postcard, this time from 8 Stephen Street, off the Tottenham Court Road, adopting an assured and worldly tone:

> Shooting is heard in the air, and bodies cover the ground. Five great powers are at struggle. Nine countries make war. I am reminded suddenly what I told you a few months ago, about the rumbling storm. Destiny has surprises in store for us and it is impossible to say who will win. The neutrals are still undecided and the belligerents cannot divine their intentions. In these circumstances, if someone sticks his nose into the business, he will be forced to take sides with one or the other. The Japanese apparently intend to dip a finger in the dish. I think in three or four months the fate of Asia will change, change enormously. Too bad for those who fight and are unsettled. We should stay calm.[1]

This postcard was intercepted by censors, reviving a paper chase on the part of the French, who asked their British allies for information on Vietnamese who might be sympathetic towards Germany. The British police struggled with names. They turned up two men with 'Thanh' in their names, who were assumed to be brothers. One was 'Joseph Thanh': the French Sûreté identified him as Lam Van Tu, a man from the south of the country with political connections to Prince Cuong De, whose own exile had by 1915 led him to London. This made it unlikely that 'Joseph Thanh' and the other man, identified as 'Tat Thanh', were related. Tat Thanh, it seems, had obtained an apprenticeship with the Igranic Electric Company in Bedford, an early pioneer of radio production, through his friendship with the daughter of the English family with whom he lodged.[2] But at this point the British ran out of information and interest in the inquiry.

For the French authorities, the real danger was closer to hand, at 6 villa de Gobelins itself, in the form of Phan Chu Trinh and his housemate, Phan Van Truong. Truong had arrived in Paris in 1910 and worked at first at the École des Langues Orientales as an interpreter, but his post was revoked due to his anti-French views. He then qualified to practise law, as an *avocat*, giving him a rare independent status in France. In the interim, two of his brothers had been deported for life for their part in the Hanoi bomb attack of April 1913. The housemates shared the rent of 570 francs a year, and their small circle met at a Chinese restaurant at 163 boulevard Montparnasse.[3]

Suspicion of all exiles was rising. Some of the British Indians in Paris, including Chatto, escaped to Germany, fearing arrest when King George V visited France in April 1914. Many of those who remained, including the redoubtable Madame Cama, were now detained in Vichy or as far afield as Martinique. In September 1914 Phan Van Truong and Phan Chu Trinh were both arrested and taken to the Cherche-Midi prison in the *6e arrondissement* of Paris. Built in the mid-nineteenth century as a military prison, this was where Alfred Dreyfus was held on charges of treason in 1894–5. Truong and Trinh were then interned in the notorious asylum at Bicêtre. Here prisoners were interrogated and set against each other. Truong was confronted over his friendship with Phan Chu Trinh. He was not aware it would be a crime to know Phan Chu Trinh, he told his interrogator. After all, Trinh had come to Paris at the colonial government's own expense. 'But Phan Chu Trinh is a dangerous man,' came the response. 'For sure, he has many qualities,' Truong admitted. 'He is intelligent, he is educated, he is honest, he is a kind fellow: but all that is not enough to make a conspirator.'[4]

It was impossible for the village abroad to stay out of the war, and imperial mobilization swelled its numbers. The winds that followed the *Komagata Maru* across the Pacific and Indian Oceans carried Asians on myriad new courses. As the *Komagata Maru* headed for China, the first contingent of Indians troops sailed from Bombay, less than three weeks after the outbreak of the conflict in Europe. By late October an Indian expeditionary force of 24,000 men was in Flanders, holding the line in the Lys valley. The Raj was now a pivot of the British empire's vast war effort: in the years to come, 943,000 men from India would serve overseas, and 175,000 animals, 1,855 miles of railway track, 229 locomotives and 5,989 vehicles would be sent from India to support them.[5] The British empire had no federal parliament nor central governing organ. The nearest things to it were born out of war, in the form of the Committee of Imperial Defence, formed in 1904 in the wake of the Anglo-Boer War, and the Imperial War Cabinet in 1917. The omnivorous demand for human, animal and material resources required the British empire for the first time to function effectively as an integrated system rather than as a loose and bewildering agglomeration of formal and informal jurisdictions. The ultimate physical and moral price paid for this was incalculable.

The war increased the urgency of the old questions surrounding movement across empires: who were these people, and to whom did they belong? This propelled the final stage of the division of the globe: the construction of modern borders and systems of identification, and the creation of a new relationship of people to the state as documented individuals.[6] The old concept, central to visions of imperial citizenship, of the British empire as a zone of free movement was at an end. The reverse of the coin was the displacement of people of disputed status across borders as the colonial powers resorted ever more frequently to devices such as banishment. If the acceptance of the migrant labourer had always been provisional, the war made him or her even more vulnerable. In China, a British Order in Council now allowed the British minister in Beijing to deport colonial subjects: in August 1914 the first batch of fifteen Indians was sent to Singapore.[7]

Asia's liberal experiment, such as it was, was drawing to a close. A hardening of authority, and a new spatial impress to power, soon began to be felt within colonies and at home. In the first months of mobilization, colonial subjects were visible in the metropoles in unprecedented numbers. In 1914, 48,995 Indochinese and 36,941 Chinese arrived in France, in what the left-wing journal *Humanité* called 'the foreign and colonial invasion'. In all, around 91,747 Indochinese were enlisted for the western front: 48,694 as riflemen (not only to fight but to repair roads and railways), 42,744 as general workers (drivers, mechanics, butchers, bakers, cooks, tailors, nurses) and 309 as interpreters. Many were from the troubled region of Nghe An and its neighbouring provinces in north-central Vietnam. Most were volunteers, escaping hardship and earning a bounty for their families on signing up; those with skills travelled to see France and receive technical education. These men, after passages under the harshest of conditions, docked at Marseilles, and barely glimpsed its waterfront and cafés before they were deployed to factories in other cities, such as the arsenals of Toulouse, or to the gas and shells and trench-rot of the western front. They wrote home of the wonders they had seen, and increasingly of their frustrations. Those who had enlisted to escape the indignity of their lives as labourers in Vietnam now complained that that were being treated like coolies. About one in three of their letters were censored, and as many again did not reach their destination. Those that did find their way across the ocean widened dramatically the horizons of the village at home.[8]

The call to arms – the call to empire – polarized politics at home, and divided diasporas. It was met with ostentatious outward displays of empire loyalty by many of its subjects. The leading voices within India declared for the Allied cause. The legislative council voted a £100 million contribution – more than India's annual income – which added over 30 per cent to India's public debt. The war created an acute moral dilemma for a *satyagrahi*, a follower of non-violence, such as M. K. Gandhi, who arrived in England again a few days after its outbreak. 'When thousands have come forward to lay down their lives only because they thought it their duty to do so, how could I sit still?' he wrote to a family follower. 'A rifle this hand will never fire. And so there only remained nursing the wounded . . .'.[9] He established an ambulance corps, as he had done in the Anglo-Boer War, but this time for service in France. It was partly to escape his moral predicament that Gandhi then decided to return to India. When he was feted on arrival in Bombay on 9 January 1915, many observers expected him to take up an extremist stance against the Raj. But in his first interview to *The Times of India* he offered what he called his 'unqualified' support for the war effort. Although he continued to campaign on the abuses of indenture and worked to realize *satyagraha* at his ashram in Ahmedabad, he argued that in living under a great imperial state, and seeking first partnership with and then eventual freedom from it, Indian hands must aid in its defence.[10]

In Canada there were more who hoped that participation in the war marked a new dawn of tolerance and imperial belonging, what the chronicler of the *Komagata Maru* saga called a 'Raj of brotherhood'.[11] Even in the distant Andamans, Vinayak Savarkar petitioned for a general amnesty of the prisoners, and undertook in return to 'volunteer to do any service'. The word 'volunteer' was underscored. It was hard to know how to interpret this: the letter was written in the name of advancement towards 'one Universal State', and as a test of Britain's good intentions in India. In a much later petition, which signalled a communal turn to his thought, Savarkar elaborated that his plea was motivated 'by danger that is threatening our country from the North at the hands of the fanatic hoards [*sic*] of Asia who had been the curse of India in the past . . .'. But in late 1914, with a new revolutionary challenge gathering at its borders, the Raj had no thought of an amnesty and told Savarkar this informally through the warden at Port Blair.[12]

The shooting-war had reached the shores of India. As the Battle of the Marne began far away in France, the light cruiser SMS *Emden*, part of the Imperial German Navy's East Asia Squadron under Admiral Spee, was detached from the armoured cruisers *Scharnhorst* and *Gneisenau* as they steamed across the south Pacific towards the Atlantic. It entered the waters of the neutral Netherlands Indies; then, passing through the Lombok Straits, it infiltrated the Indian Ocean and travelled up the west coast of Sumatra. The *Emden* announced its presence in early September by attacking Allied shipping. For over two months it jeopardized the British empire's island coaling stations and telegraph relay stations for the 'All Red' routes that were the strategic sinews which connected her Asian and Pacific colonies. In a surreal episode, the *Emden* was careened, coaled, provisioned and royally entertained by the coconut plantation bosses on Diego Garcia, a British-held island which had not yet heard the news of war. More ominously for the British, the cruiser threatened the prison colony of the Andamans. Defence plans were hurriedly drawn up.

The *Emden* raided Madras on 23 September, hitting the oil tanks of the Burmah Oil Company, and there was public hysteria when Britain's oldest outpost of the islands, Penang, was bombarded on 28 October.

The German ship slipped in using the *ruse de guerre* of flying Japanese flags and displaying a dummy funnel. Its torpedoes sank the Russian cruiser *Zhemchug*, leaving eighty-nine Russians dead and 123 injured, and its guns destroyed the French destroyer *Mousquet*, killing thirty *matelots*. When it was finally cornered and forced aground in the Cocos Islands in early November, survivors from the crew managed to escape by boat to Sumatra.[13] The *Emden*'s phantom-like existence stoked febrile rumours and delayed the sailing of the *Komagata Maru* from Japan for fear of it falling into the hands of Germany. The lesson was clear: if one ship could unsettle imperial networks in Asia, what might more concerted action achieve?

In Asia the conflict was developing a momentum of its own, and it was not clear that any European power would be the ultimate victor. This was the beginning of a prolonged great Asian war: a conflict that was fought on a different timescale and plane to the one which was unfolding on the western front in France and Belgium, one that was longer and perhaps ultimately bloodier. It was a war to settle the inter-twined fates of the imperial assemblages of Eurasia: Tsarist Russia, the Ottoman empire, the Qing and the great arc of the British empire reaching from the Cape to Cairo, Calcutta to Kowloon.[14] The colonial borders of Southeast Asia had been largely unchallenged since the Anglo-Dutch Treaty of 1824, but they now seemed open to revision. In October 1914 a combined task force of British, British Indian and Japan-ese troops besieged Germany's major enclave at Qingdao. The German forces, many rallied from expatriate communities across China, led a dogged resistance in which more besiegers than defenders fell. But on 7 November the settlement capitulated. It was seen, in stark contrast with the deepening stalemate on the western front, as a military tri-umph, and Qingdao was left under Japanese administration. Some 5,000 German defenders ended up in fifteen hastily constructed prisoner-of-war camps in Japan, arriving rather incongruously to the fluttering of German and Japanese flags. Bismarck's Germany had, after all, served as a model for Meiji statesmen.[15]

Japan took advantage of the embroilment in Europe to project her national trade and influence across Asia and into the Pacific. Exploiting the 1902 alliance with Britain, Japanese warships were seen everywhere in British harbours. Civilian 'sightseeing parties' gathered economic and political intelligence in Malaya and also in Indochina and in the

Netherlands Indies. British strategists knew that as the greater weight of British naval power was drawn towards the home seas, the defence of eastern sea lanes was at the mercy of Japanese goodwill. Few were under any illusions about Japan's hidden intentions. The Dutch press in the Indies saw the loss of Qingdao as a moral and racial victory at the expense of European powers and feared a pre-emptive British occupation of the Dutch outer islands.[16] It would not take much – Germany overrunning the neutral Netherlands, or the Japanese extending their occupation of German Oceania – for an overzealous rival to encamp on the borders of Australia. To forestall this, the enterprising British consul in Batavia, W. R. D. Beckett, suggested to Whitehall that parts of the Netherlands East Indies – Sumatra, Borneo and the Celebes – be partitioned between Britain and Japan. But Whitehall upheld the status quo: the Dutch at least were 'harmless'.[17]

To capitalize on this 'one in a million chance', on 18 January 1915 Japan presented 'Twenty-One Demands' to the President of China, Yuan Shikai, calling for economic privileges, rights of settlement and extraterritorial concessions. This launched a fresh wave of patriotic demonstrations across Chinese cities. The leaders of the newly established republic, for their part, sought recognition and respect among the imperial powers of the world. They saw the conflict in Europe as an opportunity to regain their lost territories, especially the German Concession at Qingdao. But the Allies denied China's entry into the war. Although officially neutral until August 1917, China began the recruitment of 'labourers as soldiers' for Europe. This became a patriotic cause like no other, as the fierce internal debates around the war extended the public spheres for newspapers and polemic.[18] Some 120,000 men were despatched to the west; in the region of another 100,000 were recruited for Tsarist Russia, for the Murmansk railway, the Baku oilfields and the coal mines of the Donets Basin. But for many of the impoverished rural labourers – most of whom came from Shandong, the old heart of the Boxer Rebellion on the eastern edge of the north China plain – it resulted in a form of debt bondage much like any other. The route to the western front for 84,244 of them was through Canada: a cynical, and secret, hiatus in the decades of exclusion.[19]

The unrelenting demand for men and resources was a massive burden on all empires. The Vietnamese landowners of French Cochinchina offered gifts and credit in return for promises of schools and citizenship. By the end of 1916 this amounted to loans of over 60 million francs and raw materials worth around 30 million. The 'economic war' could act as a stimulus to foreign trade: the trade surplus of Indochina in these years reached a peak of 442 million gold francs, the greater part of it with neighbouring countries.[20] The imperial networks across Asia were an intricately connected subsystem of the world economy, whereby the rice produced from the great river deltas of the mainland supplied the export-orientated economies of maritime Asia.[21] But soon a shortage of shipping broke down the delicate mechanisms for food supply. British prohibitions on the trade in gunny for sacking – because of its military uses – caused a near-collapse of the inter-island trade of the western archipelago in rice and other foodstuffs, as there was no other suitable material for its carriage.[22]

These were, by the vicissitudes of nature, hard years. The great floods in Tonkin in 1913 and 1915 left perhaps a quarter of its cultivable land inundated. Much of it could not be reclaimed for a generation. Rice output, and rice consumption, collapsed: in Nghe An it was down 50 per cent by 1916. Bad harvest upon bad harvest, unalleviated by the colonial state, led to famine, chronic indebtedness, looting and robbery.[23] To counter this, the colonial governments of France and Britain took on functions unprecedented in peacetime: the seizing of ships and goods on the high seas, food control in the countryside, the registration of people. In so doing they further overstretched and exposed the underlying instability of the system.

Another, inner Asian war was unfolding. It was a crisis of imperial globalism: a collision of local struggles with global networks, of which the revolutions of 1905–12 were a portent and the Battle of Budge Budge an opening salvo. The declaration of this war came perhaps on 14 November 1914, in Istanbul, when the Shaykh al-Islam of the Ottoman empire ordained *jihad* on the British and French empires. In the decades before this, the Ottoman Caliphate had intensified its spiritual sway over the Muslim subjects of European empires, which from French Morocco through the British Raj to the Netherlands Indies were the greater part of Muslims everywhere. Following the ill-fated *Ertugal* expedition of 1890, in the wake of the Boxer Rebellion in 1901 a mission was also sent by Sultan Abdulhamid II to win the allegiance of the Muslims of western China to the Caliphate. In his words:

Everyone knows that a word from the caliph, the head of the Muslims, that is I, would suffice to inflict a great harm on the English authority in India. One does not need great intelligence to realize it. If Germany, Russia, and France had accepted my help [suggestion] during the Boer War in Transvaal, they could have destroyed the fictitious English castle in India, but they failed to act on time and thus missed the opportunity.[24]

The man who led the mission was Hasan Celalettin Enver Pasha, a Polish convert known in Istanbul European circles as 'Edward'. He made no attempt to see anything beyond Shanghai, where he reportedly voiced surprise at seeing 'a city in China as advanced as Stamboul itself is', having 'thought he was coming to an entirely savage country'. When the pasha inspected an Indian regiment of the British expeditionary force in China, he told an Indian Muslim officer, 'I come from the head of your religion, the Sultan of Turkey.' 'Your Excellency,' came the reply, 'the only head that I know is the King of England.' Short of funds, the mission departed hurriedly via Nagasaki for Vladivostok and the Trans-Siberian Railway home. The British press called it a 'complete farce', and subjected it to 'politely veiled but yet not entirely repressible ridicule'.[25] But it was a reminder that other worlds underpinned the empires the west had created. In the words of one of the Raj's civil servants, there were 'secret and long forgotten currents', spiritual pathways that seemed to exist in a different space and time, and often passed through the heart of colonial cities.[26]

These hidden domains of power haunted the imagination of officials in Cairo, Delhi, Calcutta, Singapore, Hanoi and Batavia. For the British, war with Turkey revived longstanding anxieties about the Islamic networks that straddled the fault lines along the strategic land-based approaches to British India. It disturbed the post-1857 *convivencia* between the Raj and its Muslim subjects.[27] Ottoman pan-Islam invoked old notions of suzerainty in the eastern Indian Ocean and reopened the question of the nature of the Caliphate. European specialists, such as Thomas Arnold – author of *The Preaching of Islam* (1896) and a 'guru' of leading Muslim intellectuals at Government College, Lahore – and the Dutch orientalist and colonial adviser Christiaan Snouck Hurgronje, warned of the dangers of underestimating the symbolic and spiritual power of the Caliphate. But its allure on the ground was notoriously hard to assess. Its value as a distant source of authority was in some ways enhanced for those on the further edges of the Islamic world. Its rallying cry could encapsulate theological dilemmas in sharper terms. In everyday religious life, however, this perhaps mattered far less.[28] But the very possibility of pan-Islam was enough to cause security panics once Turkish and German propaganda attempted to conjure it into being across Asia and Africa.

In the years before the war, Indian radicals had looked to Japan and Istanbul for alliances. The war in the Balkans in 1912–13 was the great cause of its day for Muslim popular politics in India and led to a massive movement of funds through the Red Crescent Society, for the humanitarian relief of Ottoman subjects, and the *Anjuman-i Khuddam-i Ka'ba*, for the protection of the holy places. The British initially suspected the war as a prime motive for the bomb attack on the viceroy in Delhi in 1912. In Calcutta, pan-Islamic propaganda stirred up the Muslim working communities concentrated in areas such as the port, where urban clearances and the demolition of mosques brought an urgent sense of threat. Some leaders turned to the tactics of *Swadeshi*; others privately invoked notions of struggle and *jihad* in closed meetings and in the mosques. In September 1914 there were multiple rumours in the city of German victory; and when the Ottoman *jihad* was declared, pictures of the sultan and of the Young Turk war leader Enver Pasha circulated in the bazaars, and public prayers were offered.[29]

Now new connections were forged along old pathways from the Punjab, as young men began to withdraw from the authority of the Raj and headed to lands under Muslim rule, in Afghanistan and beyond, as a symbolic preparation for *jihad*.[30] In one sense, they crossed an old Islamic ecumene in the footsteps of the exiles of 1857. In another, they moved in very similar circuits to the Europe-based radicals (not all of whom were Muslim) who had gravitated to Persia and Istanbul before the war, such as M. P. T. Acharya.[31] Too much, perhaps, could be made of this. But there was certainly a resurgence of the deep-set paranoia of the Raj. As the veteran correspondent G. F. Abbott asked in January 1915, invoking the ghost of Percy Shelley, was this war 'a revolt of Islam'?[32]

THE BATTLE FOR THE UNDERGROUND

The village abroad was now a means to accomplish the ends of other empires. For Germany, influence within the Ottoman empire had been central to the *Weltpolitik* of Kaiser Wilhelm II since his trip to the Holy Land and entry into Jerusalem on a white charger in 1898. On the night of 30 July 1914, when he learned that Russia's mobilization would proceed, the Kaiser mooted approaches to the Indian and Islamic opponents of the British empire. Within a month, a generation of German and Austro-Hungarian oriental linguists and historians were suborned to the task, led by Max von Oppenheim, a Hittite archaeologist who had advised the Kaiser on the Middle East since 1898 and was a scion of the banking family.[33] Rapidly, German agents took advantage of the territory of neutral powers such as Spain, Siam, the United States and its colony in the Philippines to distribute calls to Muslims to resist the British and support the Ottoman Sultan and his ally 'Hadji Guillaume'. In late 1914 the British felt that they had uncovered a plot among local officers in Egypt and there were ominous desertions by Indian troops along the Suez Canal. Martial law was declared, and British and Australian troops drafted in. The Khedive of Egypt, who was away in Istanbul when war was declared, was deposed in favour of his uncle, to forestall any plotting with Istanbul, and 'loyal' imperial Muslims such as the Aga Khan and Sir Abbas Ali Baig were despatched by the foreign secretary, Earl Grey, to calm Egyptian and Indian regiments. This was described by the India Office as a 'ludicrous failure'.[34]

It was not clear in late 1914 that Indian troops had been suborned in any great numbers.[35] But fear of Islamic resistance helped launch the British further into Arab lands, in particular their fateful approaches to Hussein ibn Ali, custodian of the holy places in the Hejaz and Sharif of Mecca, and their support for his 'Arab revolt' against the Ottomans. During this, the question of a future Arab Caliphate was mooted, very much to the alarm of both Muslim opinion in India and British officials there.[36] The British built a large intelligence operation, beginning with an 'Islamic Bureau' in London – in which Thomas Arnold played a role – and then an 'Arab Bureau', based out of the Savoy Hotel in Cairo, with outposts in Jeddah and elsewhere. The Arab Bureau's gaze reached across the Indian Ocean to the Hadrami Arabs of Penang, Singapore and Java, who had long been bearers of pan-Islamic influences across the Indian Ocean, and now came under pressure to declare themselves. All of this drew the British empire deeper into an unprecedented global counter-propaganda exercise as it asserted its claim to be the world's largest Muslim power and a defender of the faith.[37]

Muddled reports of the outbreak of a revolution in India reached the small community of exiles and students in Germany. Few of them believed in it. But von Oppenheim's 'Intelligence Bureau for the East', acting through intermediaries, recruited a cluster of them into an Indian Revolutionary Committee, including Swami Vivekananda's brother Bhupendranath Datta, who had been jailed as editor of *Yugantar* in 1907. They looked to attract other celebrated figures. They ignored Krishnavarma, who was now in Geneva, and were rebuffed by Lala Lajpat Rai, who was in London at the outbreak of the war and who saw the idea of foreign patronage as demeaning.[38] But they enlisted Chatto, who was now enrolled at the University of Halle in Saxony, and M. P. T. Acharya, who had just returned from a low-key sojourn in the United States. Specialists on Islam were at a premium. Maulana Barakatullah was ferried to Berlin through the United States, his fare paid by the German consulate in San Francisco, along with others, including Taraknath Das.[39]

These were all men who had been away from India for six years or more. In Berlin, they basked in what they saw as the recognition of the government-in-exile of a 'free state'. They were now the 'Supreme General Staff of the Indian Revolution'. But in the closed conditions of blockade they had little news from India, and India had even less news of them. They struggled to maintain their standing. They were given small amounts of money at first, but then ever-increasing sums to despatch to India and East Asia through intermediaries. German aid was, for them, an opportunity to discipline a movement dispersed across three oceans. For the first time they produced centralized propaganda, and made direct contact with Indian troops in segregated prisoner-of-war camps in Germany.[40] But these would-be generals were a long way away from their troops, and it was now much harder for them to move around.

In August 1914 Har Dayal was in Geneva, reading philosophy, learning Spanish and trying 'to pick up the thread again' with his former lover Frieda Hauswirth, who had returned to Zurich. More interested in working for India than submitting to his domineering entreaties, she returned to America, and burned the letters he asked her to carry.[41] Taraknath Das urged her to stay away from Har Dayal. 'Today he brags about the emancipation of women by trapping you to his den of dreamy foolishness . . .' he wrote witheringly; 'he is a slick politician with great understanding of psychological moments.'[42] Har Dayal also corresponded with another acquaintance from his California days, a woman of around eighteen years old called Pearl Vogel, to whom he sent money for a ticket to Amsterdam, to pursue revolutionary work. When the US authorities caught up with Miss Vogel she told them 'she would prefer to have her throat cut from ear to ear than to give up her ideas'. They thought her naive, but she was astute enough to burn the letters and to try to use the money for the struggle in America. She had been living among miners in Arizona, and her 'chief aspiration', the Bureau of Investigation concluded, 'was to be a second Emma Goldman'.[43]

Har Dayal's route to Berlin – 'the Mecca of Oriental patriots of all shades of opinion', as he termed it – was via Istanbul, where he travelled in October posing as a merchant from German East Africa. In the Ottoman capital he took up with the German mission that had been sent there the month before to further a new phase in the old Great Game that had played out in Central Asia since the early nineteenth century, one in which Britain and Russia were (for now) no longer rivals but allies. The Germans and the Ottoman war minister, Enver Pasha, looked to strike at the Raj through Afghanistan, where the nominally neutral emir was said to be sympathetic to their cause. Har Dayal argued for a massive push, which would spark an uprising in India that he believed would then be supported by some 10,000 supporters from North America and 100,000 from China and the Malay Peninsula. As a token of their support for the strategy, many of the Indian exiles – Chatto, Taraknath Das, Acharya – took Muslim *noms de guerre*; Har Dayal himself became 'Professor Mirza Osman'.[44]

Har Dayal now wrote to another woman supporter from Stanford days, Ethel Dobson, to join him in Istanbul. Then he suddenly returned to Geneva on a false Turkish passport, railing against the lack of funding, consultation and autonomy from German officers in Istanbul. For their part, the Germans reported his disdain for the pan-Islamic aspect of the policy and suspected him to be a traitor. They claimed that the other Indians distrusted him too.[45] But by early February 1915 Chatto had persuaded Har Dayal to return to Berlin from Geneva, and to bring with him a new figurehead for the Afghanistan mission he had met in Switzerland: a Muslim prince called Mahendra Pratap, who had married into the ruling family of Jind in the Punjab.[46] Pratap was described by Jawaharlal Nehru on first meeting him as 'a character out of medieval romance, a Don Quixote who had strayed into the 20th century'. Yet he had an internationalist and pan-Asian outlook and was committed to the use of violent means to overthrow what he termed the 'dirty British empire'.[47] However, the exploratory expedition disguised as a travelling circus had its baggage of concealed radios and arms seized by Romanian customs officials.[48]

An army for this great enterprise was to be found in Pacific Asia. Attempts to raise it would come to be known, misleadingly, as the 'Hindu Conspiracy'. It had many movers – not all of whom were aware of each other – and its many streams flowed across three continents. Often independently of Berlin, and encouraged by the exploits of the *Emden*, German consuls, traders and adventurers still at large in Southeast and East Asia looked to exploit the resources of international cities like Shanghai and Tianjin and neutral territories such as Siam, the Philippines and the Netherlands Indies. But in the early days of the conspiracy it was German diplomats in the United States who had the funds and the opportunity to purchase arms. To coordinate these efforts for the Berlin Committee, a man called Heremba Lal Gupta was sent from the German capital to San Francisco and to Japan.[49] There were other emissaries, too, travelling through Latin America or the Middle East on neutral ships, with ill-defined missions and uncertain credentials. From the outset, foreign gold raised the stakes of deception and the possibilities of betrayal. Money for travel, like that of Pearl Vogel, was always going astray. People took assumed names, then swapped them with comrades. The talk of codes and ciphers and subterfuge fed into the spy fever of the day. It was never clear who was manipulating whom.

The South Asian communities in the United States and Canada had already taken the liberation of India into their own hands. The meetings in small Californian towns such as Oxnard and Fresno after the departure of the *Komagata Maru* in July and the SS *Korea* in August were attended by hundreds of people. They spoke, often from first-hand experience, of places like Egypt, Sudan and Burma, where many had fought for the British without the reward of rights of movement and settlement. These, British intelligence realized early on, were not merely young hotheads, but older, 'credible' men: experienced men like Nawab Khan, with long imperial service across different territories.

On the *Korea*'s long passage across the Pacific, Nawab Khan and his companions attended daily gatherings where they memorized patriotic songs. At a three-day stop in Manila there were public meetings in the opera house under the banner of Ghadar.[50] In the Malay Peninsula and Penang, they visited army cantonments and even sent a delegation to the governor; they also wired the Calcutta newspaper *Amrita Bazar Patrika*, announcing their presence. It was in Penang that they learned of the fate of the *Komagata Maru*'s men at Budge Budge from a disembarking passenger from India. In Rangoon they met two regiments about to embark for Europe, with a view to setting off a chain reaction of garrisons in revolt.

The men of the *Korea* were followed by the SS *Siberia*, which sailed for Shanghai on 5 September, and the *Mexico Maru*, which left Victoria for Hong Kong.[51] More men joined them en route, including some who had earlier been on the *Komagata Maru*. Not all of them were Indians. There was a 'Jack Sloan' who was stopped trying to enter India via Colombo. According to his criminal file in California, he was a Wobbly 'street speaker' who had done time; his real name was John Harrison, or John Henry Jenkins; he was originally from Scotland and he was an associate of Emma Goldman. He was recruited by the Indians because they thought a rebel white man would make a dramatic impact in the Punjab. No one knew what happened to him after Colombo – or, indeed, was ever quite sure who he was. There were rumours of him in Germany and Switzerland, and a sighting in New York; old friends thought he joined the army or the navy as a cook.[52]

Based on the locations of the rebel bridgeheads that were forming on the China coast, and following the logic of the routes taken by Japanese steamers to avoid British shipping, there were a variety of possible passages to India, via Singapore or Penang, Rangoon or Colombo. One plan was to build up numbers first in Shanghai, then move down to Shantou before crossing the South China Sea to Bangkok, where there were Indians working on railway construction, particularly in the south of Siam. This offered the prospect of slipping over the frontier into Burma, or of shipping via Penang to Madras or Calcutta and posing as returning migrants from Malaya. On one official count, perhaps 1,050 made the voyage from North America and Asia between August 1914 and March 1915. But the total was probably larger as the movement gathered momentum within Asia itself. The government of India processed some 3,125 returnees in Calcutta and in the Punjab: some 189 were interned, and 704 more restricted to their villages.[53] The British-led Shanghai Municipal Police began to purge their Indian rank and file and this added to the numbers of disaffected men in the ports seeking to get home.[54]

The message in the Punjab was apocalyptic: 'It is time! Plunder the treasuries! The doors of martyrdom are open.'[55] Those who made it through the British cordon threw themselves into the task of suborning garrisons and preaching among peasants. One returnee from the Straits Settlements established a society in his home village of Sangwal which ran a school and a library and raised money to build a veterinary hospital. Elsewhere in the Punjab, they preached the republican ideals they had embraced in the United States. Others turned to robberies for funds and experimented in the making of bombs. There was talk that some had learned to build airships in the jungle, and that a man called Katar Singh had studied aviation in New York. Villagers were told the Germans were about to arrive. Some were swayed by the returnees, and young men were recruited to the cause. But the reappearance of these forceful, worldly men did not immediately translate into peasant revolution, despite their rhetoric. It was by no means clear that Germany was winning the war, and the *maya* of the Raj seemed as strong as before. Many families in the region had too much to lose: their land or their employment with the Raj.[56]

Much of the initial action was uncoordinated. In November 1914 there were attempts to recruit the 23rd Cavalry stationed at Lahore, and a raid took place on a treasury at Moga in which two officials were shot dead. This was the start of a rising tide of political robberies, many on Hindu shops, and of attempts to derail trains. By January 1915 some of the men of the *Komagata Maru* were again at liberty. But police surveillance reduced them to vagrancy. When Bhai Parmanand had returned from the United States, via Paris, in December 1913, every stage of his journey from the ship in Bombay harbour to his home village was shadowed by senior police officers. He was surprised that more men had not been arrested in advance. Surely the police knew who they were? As a man of some substance, he was sought out by other returnees to change their American gold dollars, but he was scathing about their dacoit tactics. 'Did not Sivaji commit dacoities?' they retorted. 'Sivaji also plundered forts and royal treasuries,' Bhai Parmanand replied. 'Even if he committed a crime why should we repeat it?'[57] Leadership and expertise were clearly needed.

In December 1914 a herald appeared from Bengal, a man called V. G. Pingle. He was known to some of the returnees as a former engineering student at the University of Oregon who had been active in Ghadar circles in Portland, Astoria and the San Francisco Bay Area.[58] He had arrived back in India in November and now carried news of the Bengal underground to the Punjab. It was not clear on what authority he spoke, but on 25 January he brought a friend from Benares to Amritsar to advise on bomb-making. The stranger was known to those who met him as 'Fat Babu'. It was Rash Behari Bose.[59] He swiftly took command, and laid plans for a great uprising from 'Lahore to Dacca'. It would target the garrisons along the Grand Trunk Road: Meerut, Kanpur, Faizabad, Lucknow, Allahabad and Benares, where Rash Behari's own organization waited for the signal. This would trigger risings by Indian troops stationed in Southeast Asia and elsewhere. Emissaries were despatched, on foot and by bicycle; bombs were manufactured, often in brass inkpots from the Amritsar bazaar which could be thrown; and around 10,000 copies of *Ghadr di Goonj* ('Echo of Mutiny'), a distillation of the message and martyrology of Ghadar in poetry and song, were distributed. Great store was set on the making of tricolour flags and on printing declarations of war. When the frequent comings and goings from his rented house in Amritsar began to draw suspicion, Rash Behari moved himself to Lahore and the centre of the plot. Here he fixed the hour of destiny for nine days hence: 21 February 1915.

There was a tremendous urgency to this, driven by a sense of irreversible momentum, but also by fears of betrayal, that garrisons might be posted away to the front, and that the war might suddenly end. The mutiny desperately needed trained soldiers and arms. It also needed to win the province that had stayed loyal in 1857 but had led the way in 1907–8: Bengal. The Bengal leadership had prepared the ground over a longer period of time. It was highly factionalized, but its key figure was now Jatindranath Mukherjee. He was born in 1879, into a Brahmin family well connected to close-knit progressive circles; his politically aware mother and sister were strong influences on his life. He entered the University of Calcutta in 1898, and became a follower of Swami Vivekananda, following his advocacy of social work in the city and a personal regime of gymnastics and wrestling. He had met Auro-bindo Ghose in 1903 and was drawn into the *Swadeshi* movement, where he advocated a loose, clandestine organization. He worked for a while in Muzzafarpur for the English barrister Pringle Kennedy, whom he admired as a scholar and a reformer. In 1905, Pringle published the first volume of his *History of the Great Moghuls.* Jatindranath had left Kennedy's service before the bomb attack in April 1908 that took the lives of Kennedy's wife and daughter. After the clampdown that followed, he managed to combine his work as a government typist – a job Kennedy had secured for him – with the task of building a more or less permanent underground. This pro-voked a widely reported remark from Barindra Ghose: 'How can a government servant be a revolutionary?'[60]

But the scorn of Aurobindo's brother only seemed to increase the magnetism of Jatin for younger men. He had, as the police put it, built a reputation as 'a local Sandow' – a reference to the famous German bodybuilder, who had something of a cult following in Indian nation-alist circles. He acquired popular fame by killing a tiger that had terrorized his home village, and by landing blows on some boisterous English officers who had insulted him and his wife on a station plat-form in April 1908. Well known by now to the police as the 'anarchist in chief', he was arrested, and after thirteen months in Alipore jail he was tried with forty-six other militants in the so-called 'Howrah Gang case' in 1910. Lacking hard evidence, and unwilling to create another martyr, the British allowed the case to collapse in early 1911 and Jatin was released under close police surveillance. While ostensibly working as building contractor for bridges and railways, Jatin managed to evade scrutiny as he set about resurrecting his old decentralized cell-like organization. This went on to survive several crackdowns and reached out – as few other such groups did – to farmers through flood-relief work in Burdwan and Midnapur in 1913.[61]

Jatin was an inspirational presence rather than an active leader. His most dynamic lieutenant was Narendra Nath Bhattacharya, who had risen swiftly within his orbit. Naren had begun to question the selfishness and vanity of some of the revolútionary leaders, and to harbour misgivings about what their violence had achieved. But he found no hint of bluster by Jatin about his 'extensively ramified secret organisation'. Instead, he encountered real charisma: Jatin 'was kind and truthful as well as bold and uncompromising. His boldness stopped short of cruelty.'[62]

Jatin met Rash Behari Bose in late 1913 and early 1914, and a new network was set up to prepare for the promised all-India rising. Jatin's men also embarked on a series of daring robberies, to more effect. In August 1914, fifty Mauser pistols were seized from an arms dealer, and in early February 1915 there was a particularly audacious heist from the old British firm of Bird & Co., in the residential quarter of Garden Reach in Calcutta, which involved the use of motor vehicles to make away with a large haul of cash. The 'taxi dacoities' added to Jatin's legend, and the distribution of the pistols to the various gangs in Bengal boosted his authority. The police quickly began rounding up suspects for these crimes. One of the men they arrested was G. D. Birla, son of the industrialist Baldeodas. Naren also was picked up, but absconded on bail. Hunted himself by the police with renewed energy, Jatin went underground in the village of Kaptipada, some thirty miles inland from Balasore in the princely state of Mayurbhanj.

For some time, Jatin's party had scouted land to buy in the area as a long-term sanctuary removed from the iron cage of the Raj. The railway station at Balasore was a regular halt on journeys between Calcutta and the south and the junction with the main line to Bombay was within convenient reach to the north at Midnapur. There was easy access to escape into the hills: Naren himself found refuge for a time working as an overseer on a nearby estate. Fronts for messages and moving funds were set up in the form of a general trading store called Harry and Sons in Calcutta, and a cycle-shop subsidiary in Balasore dubbed the Universal Emporium.[63] This channel was an open secret, and watched by the police. But Jatin's men discovered that the watchers could be distracted; one vital bank draft was cashed by luring them, rather too easily, to the pleasures of Benares in the mango season.

Pathfinders were prepared in secret for a new journey to the East; Naren, now officially an absconder, was one of those chosen to blaze the trail. He had several suits cut for him by a master tailor to help create his disguise as a Christian pastor, 'the Revd C. A. Martin'. To one witness, 'he looked a callow youth, extremely keen and ready for adventures'. But the force of Naren's personality had won Jatin's confidence.[64] His first journey was to the Netherlands Indies, where many Indians lived and laboured. A large number of them were Sikhs, especially in the plantation centre of Deli on the east coast of Sumatra; they worked as shopkeepers or merchants, on the railway, and even as doctors on the farming estates. Ghadar newspapers were smuggled into Deli through the gurdwara or hidden in the unsupervised neutral Dutch mails that were distributed throughout the Netherlands Indies by Indian merchants.[65] Pathways and plots, global in compass, now wove their way through this natural crossway of Asia.

WAITING FOR THE JUST KING

It had been planned that, in 1914, the world would come to the Indies. On 13 August the colonial exhibition opened in Semarang, on the north coast of Java. Like much else in the civic life of the Indies, the event was billed as a showcase of 'modern refinement', a celebration of the economic achievements of the *belle époque*. From the 1870s to 1914 the contribution of the Netherlands Indies to national income rose from 2–3 to 10 per cent, and total investment into the Indies rose from no more than 200 million guilders in 1885 to 1.5 billion guilders by 1914.[66] Semarang's population had risen from 60,000 to 101,000 in the same period. Its trams and railways fanned out to the sugar factories of the hinterland, some forty-eight of them by 1905, many with their own branch lines. Although the halcyon days of sugar profits were receding, there was a lively trade in foodstuffs and native goods as the economies of the old Javanese royal cities of Yogyakarta and Solo became orientated towards Semarang. The opening of a clove cigarette factory by a Chinese businessman in nearby Kudus in 1910 turned a sleepy town into a new industrial centre, drawing in not only the labour of men but also a large number of women and children who worked in the factories.

All this was celebrated in the pavilions at the exhibition. Its centrepieces were the Machinery Hall and the Sugar Hall, but there were also displays of 'native industry': timber, petroleum, concrete, coffee-roasting, quinine, cigars and cigarettes. A special building was devoted to the new phenomenon of traffic: railways, tramways, motor cars and 'the wonders of technics'. In all, the sixty-four-acre site encompassed more than 600 yards of roadway, almost 1,200 yards of railway and 105 pavilions, along with demonstration fields, a Lunar Park and cabaret. It was a blaze of electrical illumination. Emulating the great 'universal' expositions of the *fin de siècle* – Paris in 1900 and Chicago in 1893 – and their colonial equivalents in Hanoi in 1902 and Calcutta and Allahabad in 1911, the city of Semarang promoted its international character. Its large population of Indo-Europeans and what were termed 'Foreign Asiatics' featured prominently. There was a Chinese pavilion provided by businessmen of the city, and one run by the Japanese – who held European status – as well as displays from neighbouring Western Australia and from New South Wales, and a 'native village'.[67] Semarang in many ways embodied the diversity of Indies society, but it was dominated by colonial hierarchies of law and status. And, in any case, Semarang's moment of cosmopolitan rapture had come too late.

With the declaration of war a few days beforehand, the extravaganza opened to a much smaller audience than anticipated. The Batavia-born Dutch architect and archaeologist Henri Maclaine Pont described it as 'the first large-scale expression of the Netherlands Indies conceived of as a single indivisible nation'.[68] But the 'Indies for the *Indiers*' he imagined was that of the Europeans and Indo-Europeans. The great political campaign of the previous year had exposed Dutch resistance to the idea that this might be led by others. As the journalist Mas Marco Kartodikromo put it, at Semarang the Dutch were 'showing off a perfect fake.'[69] The exhibition, by all accounts, left many unmoved. When one of the leading men of old Java, Pakubuwono X, *Susuhunan* of the neighbouring kingdom of Surakarta, came to inspect it, a court chronicler described the ruler's visit:

> The colonial exhibition
> was located south of the city proper
> on an expansive site
> in the mountain foothills
> among neatly parceled rice fields.

Pavilions were erected
along the lines of various
models: Dutch, Indies Chinese,
Chinese, Indian, Palembang, Padang, Deli, Acehnese,
Bornean, Pontianak,

Ambonese, Celebes, Bawean, Balinese,
Madurese, and Javanese, East, Central,
and West, all were created
and filled with products
from their respective regions.

But Pakubuwono chose not to examine the display of royal regalia that carried his name. Instead, he sat near the entrance of the pavilion and commanded his retainers to look on his behalf:

At thirty minutes
after nine, His Majesty
decreed to his brother:
'I want to return home now
To Hotel Salatiga.'[70]

Europeans gave their servants money so that they could attend, but even they chose to stay at home. There was considerable speculation about this. Was it that they had taken government calls to be thrifty in times of war to heart? Or did they feel alienated by the modern surroundings? The exhibition did not draw the world to the Indies, nor did colonial subjects need to see their own backwardness reflected on to them in the live exhibition of a 'native village'. But, more than this, there were rumours of dark magic; that visitors disappeared, or died suddenly on returning home.[71] Numbers tailed off, despite a halving of the ticket price. The site, on land loaned by a Chinese entrepreneur, was soon abandoned and the buildings dismantled.

Beyond the exhibition grounds, and behind the shopfronts and mansion façades of the European city, lay their antithesis: a mass of slums, back alleys and *kampungs* – villages swallowed by Semarang as it expanded. Part of the plan of the colonial exhibition was to push them aside. But here the writ of municipal administration did not run, and the trains and trams brought ever more new migrants. The *kampungs* were a waking nightmare to the city fathers, especially after an out-break of bubonic plague in 1911. A report by the chemist and urban reformer H. F. Tillema in 1913 painted a bleak picture of these over-crowded slums: crammed with between 160 and 400 people an acre, often lying under water, and acting as incubators for disease, they boasted death rates of sixty to eighty-eight in 1,000.[72]

Semarang had one of the largest concentrations of urban labour in the Indies, not least in transport and on the docks, which depended on an army of workers for the 200 or so sailing boats that ferried people and goods to the freighters in the harbour, and for the heavy lifting on the wharfs. The work was seasonal, based on circular migra-tions from neighbouring towns and villages. Labourers often slept in huts on their boats, or in cramped dormitories in the *kampungs* where, despite the constant churn of the population, village solidar-ities were forged. In July 1913 there was perhaps the first strike of port labour in the Indies, when men working for the Semarang Steam and Sail Boat Company refused to ferry goods to waiting ships without a rise in wages, an increased rice allowance and a new fish allowance. Employers could not break the strike even by offering double the usual rates to landsmen.[73] These self-governing and self-reliant village cities were also to be found in the shadow of the capital Batavia – itself a hybrid city of a 'thousand villages' – and in the *arek Surabaya*, the people from the working neighbourhoods of the East Java port of Surabaya.[74]

The new languages of journalism and the new schools of the activ-ists were beginning to reach into these worlds. Marco's short stories, and his later novel *Student Hidjo* ('Student Green'; 1919), described the rites of passage of young men newly arrived in the city from the neighbouring countryside to work or to study. Around this time, one such, a fifteen-year-old Javanese called Sukarno, came to Surabaya. He remembered it as 'a bustling, noisy port town, much like New York':

It had keen competition in commerce from the sharp Chinese plus a large influx of mariners and merchantmen who brought news from all parts of the world. It had a swollen population of young and outspoken dock-hands and repair workers. There were rivalries, boycotts, street fights. The town was seething with discontent and revolutionaries.[75]

Surabaya was, by 1915, a city of 148,710 people. With its new, paved roads and streetlights, it was a contrast between colonial planning and local improvisation; in a literal sense, between light and darkness.[76] Sukarno boarded in a small windowless room, a 'chicken coop', at the rear of a house in a *gang*, or alleyway, close to the river. There was electric light to study by, which he could not really afford, but he ate with the family and they looked after him. The house was that of the leader of the Sarekat Islam, Tjokroaminoto. Sukarno raided his landlord's library and those of the local Theosophical Society and the freemasons' lodge, retreating into an 'inner world' of conversations with Thomas Jefferson, Sidney and Beatrice Webb, Mazzini, Cavour, Marx, Engels and Rousseau. 'I lived their lives,' he recalled. 'I actually was Voltaire.' He attended the liberal, mixed-race, co-educational Dutch high school, where most of the teachers were 'ethical' – and some even anti-colonial – in outlook, and where he was encouraged to set up a debating club. But above all:

> Tjokro taught me what he was, not what he knew nor what I should be. A person with creativity and high ideals, a fighter who loved his country. Tjok was my idol. I was his student. Consciously and unconsciously he molded me, I sat at his feet and he gave me his books, he gave me his values.[77]

In Tjokroaminoto's home, Sukarno's fellow boarders would watch him stand on a table and, facing a large mirror, launch into oratory, waving his arms and tilting his head. In the back rooms of these village cities, a new type of intellectual and activist was moulded, an urban successor to the *priyayi* of the old regencies of Java.[78]

Mas Marco now headed a union of journalists, which by mid-1914 had its own mouthpiece – *Doenia Bergerak*, or 'World in Motion' – which gave a name to their times. 'If we delay in setting our people, the *bumipoetras* [sons of the soil], in motion, they will, as time passes, probably become weaker because our force will ultimately dissipate.' Through its pages, he began an assault on the ethical policy, beginning with the government's much-sanctified Welfare Commission. He satirized its claims of understanding and assumption of abundance. More directly than any writer before him, he took up the voice of the 'little people', those 'mostly living by eating once a day'. But very soon he was in deep trouble with the authorities, not least when he refused to disclose the identities behind the pseudonyms of his correspondents.[79] In March 1914 a series of *haatzaai artikelen*, or 'hate-sowing articles', were added to the penal code. Modelled on legislation in British India, they created a new kind of press offence for Mas Marco and his like to run afoul.[80]

At the outbreak of war the neutral Netherlands East Indies was left isolated in an ocean of rumour and alarm. Shipping all but ground to a halt; there was no mail for a month, and the telegraph broke down. The trams and Chinese shopkeepers refused to accept paper banknotes. At the Semarang branch of the Javasche Bank there were scuffles as it was overrun by people demanding to change their notes into silver coins. There was a shortage of bread and prices sky-rocketed: in Semarang a box of matches rose in six hours from eighty-five guilders to 200. Europeans began to hoard food while, on the plantations, their labourers' wages were not paid in full.[81] Cargo arrivals in Java dropped around 25 per cent in volume between 1914 and 1916.[82] There were bad harvests, and strikes and food riots ensued. For the first time, elites across Asia confronted the possibility of a sudden disintegration of the colonial order.[83]

In Java, one witness to all this was a thirty-four-year-old Dutchman called Henk Sneevliet. He arrived in the Indies in 1913 by a path outside the colonial establishment. He was raised and schooled in 's-Hertogenbosch, where his father worked as a clerk, cigar maker and prison warder. From 1902, aged only nineteen, Sneevliet was active in the Social Democratic Workers' Party, rising to national prominence as chairman of the Railway and Tramworkers' Union in 1910. But frustrated by the collapse of the transport workers' strike of 1911 – the first internationally organized mass walkout – and feeling a little lost, he eventually took passage for Java with his second wife, Betsy Brouwer, a teacher, and their twin sons. He took up a position with a Surabaya newspaper, and then moved to Semarang in the year of the colonial exhibition as an employee of the city's traders' association.[84]

Sneevliet's new job – with no small irony – was to trumpet the achievements of Dutch capitalism, but his free time was spent working to undermine it. He found kindred spirits among the Dutch schoolteachers and clerks often posted to outlying areas, who were diligent journalists in their spare time, tirelessly writing open letters home exposing the poverty and injustice to which they found themselves accessory. Few European critics of empire could speak with more authority on the subject. They made common cause with poor whites – sailors and soldiers in ports such as Semarang and Surabaya – and Eurasians, all of whom were excluded from the idyll of expatriate life and had little cause to defend its privileges.[85] Out of this raw material Sneevliet took a lead in forming the Indies Social Democratic Association – *Indische Sociaal-Democratische Vereeniging*, or ISDV – the first body in Asia to carry such a name. It was launched with a hearty rendition of 'The Internationale'.

The ISDV was in no sense a mass movement; it fished for support in the same small pool of Europeans and Eurasians that contained the followers of Ernest Douwes Dekker. After his banishment in 1913, a rump of them formed a new party which took its name from an arcane geographical term for the archipelago, *Insulinde*. It was energized in August 1914 by the return of Douwes Dekker's companion in exile, the Javanese doctor Tjipto Mangoenkoesoemo. On arrival in the Netherlands, Tjipto had enrolled at the University of Amsterdam, but 'days of misery and want' ruined his health, and the minister for the colonies was told he was close to death. No one wished to make a martyr of a man of such transparent civic virtue, and so Tjipto was allowed to go home. Rapidly restored to strength, he threw in his lot with Insulinde, and seemed to be the man to deliver it a mass following. Shut out from the colonial medical establishment, and unable to follow his specialist vocation as a plague doctor, Tjipto ministered to the poor of Solo, and witnessed at first hand the hardships of the war years. He turned to journalism to make ends meet, writing for Marco's *Doenia Bergerak*. But Insulinde's members were divided in their resolve to destroy an administration on which most depended for their livelihood and many for their very presence in the Indies. Tjipto attacked 'political adventurers' such as Sneevliet for their willingness to place internationalism before Indies nationalism.[86]

For his part, Sneevliet had no interest in the cult of Douwes Dekker – so-called *Dédéisme* – nor his shady doings in exile in Europe. He saw the seeds of a socialist future in the Sarekat Islam, which he cast in a historical role akin to that of the Chartists of mid-nineteenth-century England. He found an ally in Asser Baars, a twenty-two-year-old Dutch engineer teaching in the Surabaya technical school. Baars was a regular visitor to Tjokroaminoto's boarding house in Peneleh Alley, which doubled as the office of the local Sarekat Islam, where townsfolk came for help and advice. The young Sukarno – still at high school, precocious and aware – was witness to a constant stream of visitors and fellow boarders, most slightly older than him and true *arek Surabaya*, denizens of its urban villages. There was the locally born Mas Alimin Prawirodirdjo, a foster-son of the European official responsible for 'native affairs' and a leading proponent of the ethical policy, G. A. J. Hazeu. Alimin rose in prominence through his activities among the seamen and dockers and led the print workers' union. Another Javanese protégé of a leading proponent of the ethic policy was Munawar Musso. Born in 1899, and trained as a schoolteacher in Batavia, Musso was now a staunch follower of Tjokroaminoto, and seen often at his home.

A defining feature of the age of movement – *pergerakan* – in the Indies was its leaders' presence in multiple, intersecting organizations. Both Musso and Alimin followed Baars into the ISDV, yet they remained active within the Sarekat Islam. As elsewhere in Asia, such affiliations were rarely exclusive; fluidity was a stimulus to ideological experiment, and politics refused to be rigidly programmatic.[87] The impresarios of the *pergerakan* saw the struggle for the Indies as inseparable from wider affinities. In Peneleh Alley, Alimin introduced Sukarno to Marxism, and Baars ingrained in him its humanist imperative: 'Do not', he instructed Sukarno, 'have even the least sense of nationalism.'[88]

The parting words of Douwes Dekker's other fellow exile in 1913, the journalist Soewardi – 'it will be slashed to shreds, obstacles will be broken down' – were now a popular slogan. This was an era of prophecy. Around 1898 a man called Surontiko Samin began preaching in north-central Java. He spoke of a 'religion of Adam', in which each took responsibility for their own salvation. 'God', he said, 'is within me.' His followers began to withdraw from the world, from the traditional authority of village Islam, from officialdom, and to embrace a common self-sufficiency. They rejected the world of the ethical policy which placed new burdens on the rural poor, with its strains on credit, its school fees and its scientific forestry. They voiced the expectation of a time and a world in which taxes would not have to be paid and men could take teak from the forests at will. They adopted a free attitude to sexuality and to the status of women, which owed much to old fertility rites. Asked for their place of birth, it was enough for them to say: 'I was born on earth.' The movement seemed to have no links to wider currents of protest, and the Dutch complained that its followers in the villages spoke in 'riddles'. But they heard in it an intimation of peasant revolt, and in 1907 they arrested and exiled Samin to Sumatra. Yet the movement lived on; the Dutch authorities believed as many as 2,305 households were involved. It reached a peak in 1914, when villagers were faced with rumours of new taxes – on the burial of the dead and on bathing buffaloes in streams – and so they refused to pay them and claimed the land for their own.[89]

In one interpretation, Samin was a local manifestation of an old Javanese prophecy that, out of times of upheaval, a kingdom of equality would be established under the 'just king', the *ratu adil*. It had last surfaced widely in the Java War of 1825–30, in which the rebel Javanese prince Dipanegara, who had vowed to rescue the island from the Dutch, had been captured and exiled. The title of the just king was not claimed by Samin himself: under interrogation he denied it, and said only that he looked for a simple life on earth. But in the minds of many, the Sarekat Islam and its public meetings and flags intensified the millennial sense of anticipation at the coming of an *Erutjakra*, or messenger, who would usher in the age of peace, justice and abundance.[90]

The prophecy attached itself to Tjokroaminoto, and was taken up by rural propagandists who often used esoteric language to induct new members of the Sarekat Islam. People would come forward at meetings to touch Tjokroaminoto's garments or kiss his feet.[91] It was not that gullible peasants were attracted to these movements because of the prophecy. It was rather that the new spectacle of politics created an atmosphere of expectation in which prophecy was rekindled. This was stoked by police spies, who were happy to tell the Dutch what they hoped to hear: that if a movement rested on one charismatic leader, then it might quickly fall apart if he were arrested. Samin died in exile in Palembang in Sumatra in 1914. But there were followers who still believed he would soon return, with a Dutch wife and an army.[92]

A LONELY MAN IN A SMALL COUNTRY

The Dutch in the Indies resorted ever more to banishment to keep its society at bay. In 1914 the leader of the 'triad' of deportees from Java,

Douwes Dekker, lived among the small community of students from the Indies in the Netherlands. Finding little sympathy in a Dutch mother-country that was to him no homeland, Dekker took his wife, Clara, and their three little children to Switzerland, where they lived for a while just outside Geneva. But although their journey to Europe had been supported by Douwes Dekker's party, he was now chronically short of money. Then, a few days before the war broke out, he received a postcard from Krishnavarma. It was not clear how Krishnavarma was aware of Douwes Dekker's presence, but he appeared at Douwes Dekker's lodgings with Har Dayal, who was then living in a village near the French border. Douwes Dekker returned the call and found a bitter old man, feeling deserted by the Indians in whom he had invested so much of his fortune. 'He seemed', Douwes Dekker later told the British, 'quite out of Indian affairs, and was downhearted over it.' He took more to Har Dayal, who would play with his children. 'He was', Douwes Dekker observed, 'out and out an anarchist.' Har Dayal was confident that the war would weaken the British empire, but he had little good to say about the Germans: 'he strongly depreciated German discipline and militarism, their lack of originality, and confidence in others'. Through this friendship, Douwes Dekker also spent time among Egyptian exiles, at an Egyptian club, until Har Dayal disappeared on one of his missions to Istanbul.[93]

In October 1914 Douwes Dekker moved to Zurich and enrolled for a PhD in political science at the city's university. Although he had few formal qualifications, his colourful past earned him dispensation. There, in December, he was visited by Maulana Barakatullah, who had been provided with a letter of introduction by Har Dayal. They spoke nothing of India, but solely of Japan and the position of Islam there. Shortly afterwards, Douwes Dekker was summoned to a hotel to meet another friend of Har Dayal. It was Chatto. He asked Douwes Dekker to act as the agent for the publications of the Berlin India Committee, but he refused. Towards the end of January 1915 Barakatullah invited him by telegram to travel to Berlin, all expenses paid. No reason was given, although Douwes Dekker guessed the Berlin Committee was behind it. His wife advised him not to go, but they were in dire straits. He had borrowed heavily in order to book tickets to send his family back to the Indies, where at least his wife could pay her way by running a boarding house and giving lessons. Increasingly, he despaired of 'the loneliness, the whole life of worry, living like a poor workman, my wretchedness and self-accusation that I was the cause of all the misery of those, who I loved so dearly'. He was sustaining himself with morphine. Now he sensed a possible lifeline. 'From what I had seen, I felt I could easily exploit them, only if they had money. I had no idea what money that Committee had, or what their sources were.' [94]

To scent this out, Douwes Dekker left for Berlin on 25 January. He was directed to a pension in Charlottenburg kept by a Frau Beloff. There he was met by Barakatullah, before being left in the company of the secretary of the committee, a twenty-three-year-old engineering student called Chempakaraman Pillai, whom Douwes Dekker referred to as 'the Boy'. From this point onwards, the leaders of the conspiracy 'acted behind a screen', although on one occasion at a banquet he met Max von Oppenheim, the leading patron of the anti-colonial radicals in Germany. The 'Boy' explained the work of the Berlin Committee. For Douwes Dekker, it was 'only an object of study about the unbelievable naiveté of mind of this kind of revolutionists. What interested me, was to know whether they had any money. There ought to be some money for the printing, posting and distribution of their silly pamphlets.' [95] The 'Boy' tried to involve him in a scheme whereby he would lend his good word so that Indians might acquire passports from the Dutch consul in Zurich, who spoke neither Dutch nor Malay and would not ask too many questions. These were, it seemed, for a man who would bring to the Indies a 'writ' from Istanbul calling for an uprising. [96] Douwes Dekker was also asked to provide letters of introduction to friends in Java for a German agent with a Dutch passport, a man called Vincent Kraft. He added to these letters a coded message that he did not trust Kraft and neither should they. [97] 'Nonsense' it might be, but in the back bedrooms of wartime Europe a new generation of global revolutionaries was coming of age.

In December 1913, slightly before the coming of Douwes Dekker and his comrades in exile to the Netherlands, there was another, quieter arrival. For Ibrahim gelar Datoek Tan Malaka, it was his first time out of the Indies, and he was sixteen years of age. The title *gelar Datoek* signified his origins in the traditional aristocracy of the Minangkabau people of the highlands of West Sumatra. The west-coast region had been connected to the trade routes of the Indian Ocean for centuries, and its people were some of the first in the archipelago to adopt the religion of oceanic commerce and learning, Islam. And it was in the name of Islam that they had fought the Dutch interlopers who sought to control this commerce, most notably in the Padri Wars of the 1820s and 1830s. Like all these conflicts in the Indies, it was recent to folk memory, and it was briefly rekindled by a tax revolt in the highlands in 1908. The Minangkabau remained an enterprising, highly mobile people, with their own spiritual geography of the world (*alam*). It was divided between the *rantau* – that which was outside – and the *darek*, or core. The *rantau* designated both physical geography – the lowland fringes of Sumatra, as distinct from the populous highland nucleus of the Minangkabau realm – and a geography of the imagination, a *rantau* of further horizons. It was a matrilineal society, and part of the journey to manhood and marriage was the idea of sojourning abroad to aquire wealth, skills or knowledge. There was a duty to enrich and renew local custom by exposing oneself 'to the largeness of the world'.[98]

Ibrahim's education began close to home, at the government Normal School in Fort de Kock (now Bukittinggi), a Dutch administrative centre nestled in the shadow of two large volcanos. This was a rare opportunity, as the Minangkabau were heavily under-represented in the few Dutch-medium elementary schools in the region. This led to a dramatic expansion of private education. In Padang alone there were twenty-three of these establishments in 1912, as well as flourishing religious schools, with an outward-looking and entrepreneurial ethos. They were not necessarily a route to employment with the colonial regime, and graduates were beginning to emerge as its vocal critics.[99] By contrast, the Normal School was designed to train students of noble birth for careers as government doctors or teachers. There, Ibrahim's talents were spotted by the deputy director, Mr Horensma, with whom he played the cello in the school orchestra. His mentor saw in him the potential to be a teacher in a Dutch-medium school. As was the way of it, Ibrahim's village chief raised funds for his further study in the Netherlands, and his teachers and some civil servants also contributed. The family fortune, such as it was, was pledged as security against a loan to be repaid on his return to Sumatra. Together they produced an allowance of fifty guilders a month. The quintessential product of the optimism of ethical imperialism, Ibrahim travelled with the Horensma family as they headed home on leave.[100]

Ibrahim's first impressions of Europe were deeply underwhelming.

He was enrolled in the Government Teachers Training College in Haarlem and put up in a hostel attached to it. The cost was thirty guilders a month, plus eleven and a half guilders insurance. This left him little for other necessities. The institutional food – 'bread and cheese and bread and cheese' – repelled him, and though he played football keenly for a local team, his health waned. 'I didn't know how to look after myself in winter, and what I did know I didn't pay attention to.' To the annoyance of the college's director, he moved to a room in a family home. But he fell ill with tuberculosis, and struggled through his first exams. He began to feel that the process of studying for a teaching assistant's qualification was unnecessarily prolonged and difficult, and that he was unfairly disadvantaged: he had not begun to learn Dutch until the age of thirteen, and then for only a few hours a week. He met Dr Snouck Hurgronje, who rather dispiritingly questioned his ability ever to master the language well enough to teach Dutch children. His aptitude for mathematics, though, surprised his teachers, who thought Indonesians incapable of learning it. Both Ibrahim and Mr Horensma – albeit for rather different reasons – later rued the fact that he did not become an engineer. For an imperial metropole, Ibrahim decided, the Netherlands was the *smaalst* or 'narrowest' of countries, in every sense of the word: 'Everything is small, moderate, gradual.'[101]

Ibrahim had been in the Netherlands barely six months when the war broke out. At the time he was lodging in an attic room in a house on Jacobin Street, Haarlem, with a working-class family and with a Belgian refugee. With the van de Mey family, Ibrahim experienced the resilience of the European poor and was exposed to the socialist literature that circulated among them. He observed how the elder van de Mey had been 'abandoned like a sick mule' after being stricken by industrial illness, and the dull routine of his son as a lowly clerk in Amsterdam. Mrs van de Mey was 'honest, simple, and in everything filled with a humanitarian spirit at a time when the world showed no humanity toward her'.[102]

The van de Meys provided him with a degree of stability, and he filled his time with reading. The corner bookshop at the end of Jacobin Street stocked a series of 'the great thinkers of the ages'; he read, in Dutch translation, Nietzsche's *Der Wille zur Macht* (1906), 'The Will to Power', in order to understand the fury and unity of spirit of the German war effort. He then tried to enlist in the German army's

Foreign Legion, only to discover that no such unit existed. He turned inward to explore the *Umwertung aller Werte* – or 'transvaluation of all values' – within Nietzsche's thought. He also studied Horensma's old copy of Thomas Carlyle's *The French Revolution* in Dutch, which he had passed to Ibrahim as a parting gift. Later, much later, Ibrahim described the effect these books had on him:

> Politics was a *terra incognita* for me then. I neither hated nor liked it, for I knew absolutely nothing of its existence. But in that time of *Sturm und Drang*, when ideas were leaping about, hiding, turning left and right, and breaking through like dammed up water, the book *De Franche Revolutie* suddenly appeared as a resting place for my weary, questing thoughts.[103]

Here Ibrahim was: a lonely man, in a small country, in the midst of a world crisis that would make Europe look smaller than ever before.[104]

At the gateway to India: Raja Mahendra Pratap in Afghanistan.

7

Ghost Ships
1915

PANIC IN SUBURBIA

The mirror-worlds that Europe created in its tropical possessions had a
strangely humdrum, provincial air. Singapore was the seventh busiest
port in the world and a key link in the chain of settlements that ringed
the British Indian Ocean. It governed the empire within an empire of
the British Malay world. Yet for its more privileged residents, life was
an increasingly elaborate set of suburban fantasies. At only a short
remove from the boat-homes and shophouses of the waterfront Asian
city lay the wooded stretches of Tanglin Road and its Palladian villas,
and the commercial thoroughfare of Orchard Road, with its Cold Storage emporium that held the fresh beef and butter shipped from Australia
for expatriates, its animal menagerie and its new car-dealerships. A
golf course had been cleared above the new port facilities at Keppel
harbour.

With commercial steamship routes through the Suez Canal came
growing numbers of European women, and with them a facsimile of
English family life, corralled according to the rank and profession of
the men and tended by armies of amahs and houseboys. For high officials, there were the 'black-and-white' mock-Tudor raised bungalows of
Malcolm Road and Mount Pleasant. The army quarters of Portsdown
Road and Alexandra Park were sparer in style. At the top of an elaborate hierarchy were British families with four generations of residence in
Malaya. Newly arrived technical specialists and commercial men were
often cold-shouldered by Malaya's old colonial hands, who murmured
that they knew not the country and were not quite the thing socially.

Yet, for all this, the colonial elite fought to defend its superiority against the encroachments of Asian reality; in doing so, it thought of itself as 'European' as much as British. Of the 5,711 resident Europeans in Singapore in 1911, 209 were Dutch, 181 Germans and 128 French, with significant numbers of Russians, Austrians, Italians and Americans, who tended to be included in the European category. There were also 313 residents of 'unspecified' origin, along with a growing undercurrent of 'drifters'.[1] The 'British' were part of a cosmopolitan and kaleidoscopic world in which many other people – through affinity, identity or citizenship – claimed 'Britishness', including Peranakan Chinese and Arab merchants and Indian and Eurasian civil servants.[2]

To a wealthy, industrial colony such as British Malaya, the war came swiftly. The years since 1905 had seen a boom in exports: in 1914 some 1,168,000 acres of plantation produced 37.8 per cent of the world's rubber. Although the profits generated by this were shared unevenly, it created a pool of wealth from which could be drawn war taxes and 5,172,174 Straits dollars in donations to voluntary war funds and charities. Malaya financed fifty-three warplanes, 250 Chinese labourers, and a 'Malay Ford Motor Van Company' of 128 men for service in the Mesopotamian campaign, while the government and the Malay sultans subscribed to a battleship, HMS *Malaya*.[3] But all this demanded a reckoning. The sultans were showered with high honours and Asian merchants expected new recognition. In Singapore, the Straits Chinese reformer and personal physician to Sun Yat-sen, Dr Lim Boon Keng, wrote a series of essays published as *The Great War from the Confucian Point of View, and Kindred Topics* (1917). The text was a profession of imperial loyalty, a vision of empire as a prelude to a cosmopolitan world federation; but equally it was a powerful demand for Britain to apply to its colonial subjects the standards of 'civilization' and racial equality for which it claimed it was fighting.[4] On these terms, Asians and Europeans were prepared to fight for empire. The Straits Settlements possessed perhaps the longest tradition of volunteer soldiery in the tropical empire.

War with Germany deepened affinities of blood. The Germans in Malaya were themselves a diverse community of traders, physicians, hoteliers, journalists, bandleaders and missionaries.[5] Now long-term residents such as H. C. Zacharias, a British citizen, the secretary of the Selangor Club and the man who imported the first British motor car into Kuala Lumpur, were threatened with internment and the deportation of their families.[6] Ugly rumours pursued Britons suspected of 'pro-German' sympathies at every level of the colonial hierarchy, including Lady Evelyn, the wife of the governor, Arthur Young.[7] The Alien Enemies (Winding Up) Ordinance of December 1914 led to a looting of German economic interests. The Teutonia Club in Singapore (founded in 1856), the first of its kind and the envy of the British establishment, was one of the earliest prizes of war.[8] Sequestration exposed the sheer extent of commercial inroads by German businesses. It also led to an acute shortage of beer. Many Chinese traders preferred dealing with Germans as they gave longer credit and 'dealt with Asiatics and Eurasians as men to men', as one local paper told it: 'This was before the age of snobs.'[9] But by mid-1915 the trade of the Sulu islands of the southern Philippines, which had been largely in German hands, had been seized by British ships and by neutrals.[10] In the wake of the rampage of the *Emden*, German and Austrian nationals were detained in growing numbers, although some were allowed parole. Others fled. The principal German trading company in Singapore, Behn Meyer & Co., lost everything in Malaya but re-registered in Batavia, under Dutch protection. There the company's leading men, Emil and Theodore Helfferich, brothers to a minister in the Kaiser's government, attempted to mobilize the company's twenty-one ships, 500 sailors and other personnel in anti-British intrigues.[11]

This shrill emphasis on 'Britishness' was something new; behind imperial insouciance lay acute paranoia.[12] Since the late nineteenth century distinctions of 'race' were inserted into bureaucratic processes, such as the hardening of census categories, and in more militant social exclusion. Now, men who were 'noticeably Eurasian' were weeded out of government service, on the grounds, as Arthur Young explained to London, that it might interfere with 'that spirit of harmonious co-operation which is secured by unity of race and social feeling'.[13] Even before the war the local military volunteers were under strength: in Penang, men refused to join because of the preponderance of Eurasians, and the British authorities lamented the shortage of 'the better classes of European residents'.[14] The European war took away 20 per cent of the Malayan Civil Service's 'heaven-born', or forty-five British officers. In total 700 European men left the Federated Malay States during the war, and 200 of them would lose their lives.[15] Those who remained were denied leave, and this took a silent toll, with men suffering from alcoholism, hallucinations and madness. 'Going troppo', it was called: the breakdown of a brain weakened by too many 'smokes' and *stengahs*, the whisky-and-soda staple of the verandas. There was a minor epidemic of suicides. These men, the governor was later to remark, were all victims of the war.[16]

Colonial society was haunted by the spectre of weakened prestige. No fewer than twenty-one readers and translators were put to work censoring the mail.[17] The first revelations they stumbled upon, however, were the British community's own dark secrets. A schoolteacher in Ipoh – the man who brought association football to Malaya – was intercepted writing, on the suggestion of someone at his club, to a former pupil in Singapore to arrange an assignation: 'You know what I like, if you can arrange I'll pay you what you want. Do you understand I wonder, *jantan* [cock] about fifteen?' This was, the British Resident commented, a bit much, 'even for the Ipoh Club', and the man was permitted to resign 'to avoid a grievous scandal'.[18] A policeman, A. W. Hamilton, was disciplined under a rarely invoked 1909 directive forbidding the keeping of mistresses by those in colonial service. Ominously, it came after anonymous complaints from the Malay police rank and file that he was living with two women, one Malay, the other Japanese. This was indeed the case, but the officer denied impropriety, and none was proven. However, he was fined for living with his servants 'in such circumstances as to cause scandal and grave discredit to the public service'. Above all, he was punished for living in the manner of a Malay. His nickname was 'Haji' Hamilton: it emerged that he had converted to Islam in 1912 and had performed the pilgrimage to Mecca while on leave, and in his spare time he would translate Edward FitzGerald's version of *The Rubáiyát of Omar Khayyám* into Malay. White transgression exposed a complex world of Anglo-Malay intimacy beneath the surface of colonial society, and it went to the heart of British security fears.[19]

Other than the Straits Settlement Volunteers, the only available troops on the Malay Peninsula were the Malay States Guides, the unit in which Nawab Khan had served. It comprised around 399 Sikhs and 205 Indian Muslims recruited locally from the very communities from which Gurdit Singh and Bhagwan Singh had harvested their support.[20] When the *Komagata Maru* was forbidden to dock in Singapore on its way back to India, it had, the governor admitted, 'left a bad effect'. A letter circulated from the 'Men of the Guides':

> We can never forget the kindness of the Indian Government (British) for shooting and slaughtering the dead who lost their livings in India in the hopes of earning money and better livings in America from which country they were expelled, and not allowed to land and returned . . . When we have no right to walk freely on our own land then what do you want us for in other countries?[21]

The Guides refused to serve overseas in East Africa, and most were sent up-country to Taiping, in the industrial heartland of the Kinta valley in Perak, and to the environs of the federal capital, Kuala Lumpur, where the bulk of the Indian migrant population was concentrated. British officers impugned their motives: they were 'barbers, *bhisties* [water carriers], weavers', who wanted to 'lend money and make and save money'.[22] But the area was a clearing house for Ghadar's publications and its returning pilgrims from the Americas: some, including Nawab Khan, had visited military camps 'in Malay country' and dispensed advice on raiding police stations to obtain arms.[23] In mid-January 1915 a secret committee in Kuala Lumpur identified general unrest among Sikhs or Punjabi Muslims in the area. If the loyalty of the Guides could not be counted upon, the 1,000 or so Malay police would face an estimated 6,000 men likely to rebel, many of them armed with twelve-bore shotguns and Winchester rifles, while another 6,000 would offer the British no assistance. This, in turn, would provoke a break with the local Chinese, especially with a fall in the price of tin. For the first time, the British in Malaya seemed at the mercy of their colonial subjects.[24]

Singapore was a fortress, of a kind, but it had always been rather lightly defended. At the end of the nineteenth century it had the fourth smallest garrison of any British colony. The last British regiment in the region was sent to the western front in late 1914. This left 200 British artillerymen and fifty sappers holding a thin red line, along with the 5th Bengal Light Infantry, known as the 'Loyal 5th' because of its role in suppressing the 1857 rebellion.[25] There were families who had served in it throughout its long existence. Unusually, however, most of its manpower was Muslim; in general, the British tended to mix the composition of units as a bulwark against sedition. The regiment was stationed at Alexandra Barracks, overlooking the docks, and was occupied mainly with sentry duties in small units at dispersed outposts, such as watching the interned Germans at nearby Tanglin camp. It was riven by the usual longstanding enmities and factions involving internal promotions, laxness over sentry details, malingering in the infirmary and the administering of punishment fatigues. Moreover, the officers were at odds with their commander, Colonel Martin, who they felt 'stultified them'. For his part, Martin complained that his senior officers spent half the afternoon on the golf course. There was also a particularly bitter dispute involving a letter of thanks from visiting French officers, which had been hung in the mess. The colonel had taken umbrage at its referring to his daughter as 'la charmante et gracieuse Mademoiselle Martin' and had confiscated it.[26] By the time the regiment was due to embark for Hong Kong on 16 February 1915, its officers feared they had lost the respect of the men, and a number applied for transfer.

There were signs, for those who could read them.[27] Troops' letters home, intercepted by the censor, spoke in millenarian terms: 'the war is increasing day by day. There is no decrease. Germany has become Mohammedan. His name has been given as Haji Mohammed William Kaiser German. And his daughter has been married to the eldest prince of the Sultan of Turkey.'[28] The British distributed throughout Malaya 17,000 copies of a statement by the Aga Khan denouncing Turkey as a 'tool in German hands', an unprecedented act of counter-propaganda. But the sepoys in Singapore did not know who the Aga Khan was.[29] Instead, men posted outside the barracks drew their information from local mosques. An Indian preacher at Kampong Java, Nur Alam Shah, was venerated as a sufi teacher by soldiers and Malays alike. He promised the arrival of a German warship and the triumph of Islam. A local Gujarati merchant, Kassim bin Ismail Mansoor, who was close to the Malay States Guides, had written earlier to the Ottoman consul in Rangoon requesting a Turkish ship. Kassim visited the sepoys' barracks in his coach-and-four where there was, the garrison commander noted, 'an undue amount of praying'.[30] On another occasion, a sepoy spoke out in the regimental mosque: 'We should pray for the advancement of Islam and the victory of the forces of Islam.' He was rebuked for 'improper prayer'.[31] Each Christmas Day, the custom was that the men would visit and salaam their British officers. On 25 December 1914, one subaltern noted, only five came; the previous year it had been 200.[32] In London, the secretary of state for war, Lord Kitchener, had concluded that the 5th Light Infantry were 'too Mohammedan for service in Egypt', but the sepoys in Singapore did not know this, and were convinced that their redeployment to Hong Kong was a feint to send them to Egypt against the Ottomans, or even that their ship would be scuttled at sea by the British.[33] This dark talk was overheard by a Punjabi secret agent sent from India. He intended to come to his superiors in the night to report, but he was picked up off the streets by the police for suspicious behaviour and could not pass on what he knew.[34]

Then there was trouble from quite another quarter. Two days before the departure of the 5th Light Infantry, it was the eve of the lunar new year. Shortly before this the news reached Singapore that, on 18 January 1915, Japan had presented its Twenty-One Demands to China. The usual street processions and firecrackers had an angry, patriotic air. On the morning of the first day of the Year of the Rabbit – Monday 15 February – there was a parade and inspection of the 5th Light Infantry by the commanding officer in Singapore, Major-General Dudley Ridout. He gave a short speech in English to the effect that he hoped that after Hong Kong the regiment 'would have the opportunity of later going on to service'. A translation in Hindustani was read out by Colonel Martin. But the adjutant, Captain Ball, was worried that it gave the impression that there was 'no knowledge of where they were going'. So a new translation was made and entered into the vernacular order book at around 2 p.m.[35]

By this time, the officers had long dispersed. Captain Ball joined a bathing picnic at the local beach, and others headed to Punggol, a beauty spot on the north of the island. As Ball's party returned around 3 p.m., a shot was heard across the camp. Many assumed that it was a firecracker to mark the new year. But then came shouts: 'Rungga the sentry has run amok!'

'I suppose we had better go down to the lines,' Ball said. They found men charging around with rifles. The captain began to take down names and gather men. But they had no ammunition and scattered at a new burst of firing. Some sepoys were shouting, 'Ali! Ali!' – the name of the son-in-law of the Prophet Muhammad and Rightly Guided Caliph. Soldiers broke open the magazine with pickaxes and cut the military phone lines. They then broke out of the barracks. No one, it seems, thought to alert the police. One party of rebels marched towards Singapore's Chinatown, killing Britons they met on the way. There was a shoot-out near the central police station at Outram Road, where their advance into town was halted. Others headed to a nearby battery manned by Malay States Guides: they killed the British officer and foisted rifles on the Guides, but most fled into the nearby jungle. Both the innocent as well as the guilty knew that the British would not now differentiate between friend and foe.[36]

Ball led some remnants of his regiment to the volunteers' camp at Normanton for ammunition. On returning at sunset to Alexandra, they barricaded themselves in the colonel's bungalow with chests of drawers filled with earth. They found their commanding officer lying doggo. 'The mutiny', one of them observed, 'had been too much for poor Col Martin.'[37] There was some sniping through the night, but no sustained assault on the bungalow. Sailors from the sloop HMS *Cadmus* relieved them in the morning.

The largest and most resolute band of rebels headed towards the Germans at Tanglin camp. With the incarceration of the survivors from the *Emden*, the number of internees and prisoners of war there had swelled to more than 300. Many knew Singapore well and had friends in the town. Their relations with the Indian guards were cordial. Ridout later reported that the interned Germans stoked pro-Caliphate sentiment by prostrating themselves at sundown and 'pretend[ing] to recite the Koran'.[38] Certainly the previous evening, the Sunday, the sepoys who had been guarding the camp drove back to Alexandra Barracks in a lorry in elevated spirits, shouting, 'Islam, Islam!' Many of them now returned, opening fire on the British and Malay guards, killing several, and pulling Germans out of their huts, shaking their hands and again shouting, 'Islam, Islam!'[39]

One of the civilian internees, Herr Hannke, was painting in his hut. He had recently finished a portrait of the Kaiser and Franz Josef of Austria-Hungary. Each day, the sepoy responsible for the dustcart would salute them. 'Are you mad?' Hannke asked him in Malay. 'He's my King,' came the reply. That morning, the sepoy ran into the room with outstretched arms: 'Salaam, your Excellency, are you well? We will go to it . . . You will go'; and then, in English, 'Come, come.' But the Germans were divided. Some now had guns and talked of wreaking havoc on the British. Others were more frightened of the sepoys. Shortly, three British military officers turned up, in polo gear, with their ponies. They were ordered to give up their weapons, and the Germans took control of the camp. There were wild rumours that 'Kuala

Lumpur was afire! All the English people were killed in that town! Mohammedans were marching on to Singapore to help the mutineers and the forts were all taken! That German men of war were here' and that India itself was 'in full mutiny'.[40]

But, in extremis, the hierarchies of colonial status held, and the Germans protected the British as best they could. One of the *Emden*'s officers, Lieutenant Julius Lauterbach, in his highly colored account of the episode, claimed he knew that the rebels intended to head across the causeway from Singapore to the Malay Peninsula and come together with the Guides at Kuala Lumpur. But he cautioned his friends not to join them: his stated credo was 'a German officer does not fight without his uniform or in the ranks of mutineers'.[41] Nevertheless, the next morning seventeen of them, including Lauterbach and a businessman called Diehn, walked out of the camp. A few days later Diehn telegraphed the governor, Arthur Young, from Karimun Island, some forty miles to the southwest of Singapore, in the Netherlands Indies: 'Arrived safely.'[42] From here they crossed Sumatra to Padang, where the German consul paid their hotel bills; the local newspaper was edited by a German and they found shelter among veterans of the Boer War.[43]

In several days of confused fighting across Singapore Island, the mutineers killed forty-seven soldiers and civilians. Five Chinese and Malays died, but most were British men, targeted on the golf courses, or in cars and carriages.[44] The killings were far from indiscriminate: 'You Ingleesh?' a party of mutineers demanded of a European. 'No, Irish!' came the reply, and the man was set free.[45] *The Times* of London recalled the hysteria during the 1857 Indian Mutiny over the 'unspeakable things' that might befall European women. There were no reports of rape, but one British woman, a Mrs Woolcombe, was killed seemingly by accident when she threw herself in front of her husband.[46] The women and children withdrew – 'like the cinema pictures of Belgium refugees' – into a protected cordon around the exclusive Raffles and Adelphi hotels. From these favoured haunts of expatriates they were then taken on to steamers in the harbour, provoking an ugly racial fracas as Eurasian and other local women attempted to join them. Some of the women remained at sea for two weeks, furious that they could not bathe or change their linen; the normal practice in Singapore was to replace a white skirt or blouse every two hours.[47] Only on 8 March did the golf clubs reopen. In the Chinese quarters of the city, meanwhile, at the street stalls and in the theatres, people continued the new year festivities.

The *New York Times* called the uprising the greatest threat to British power in Asia since 1857.[48] And so it seemed. The British only held on to their island fortress by calling up a militia of some hundreds from a hodgepodge of European society: beachcombers, parsons, engineers, heads of firms, many of whom showed up in golfing gear or tennis whites. What swung the balance were the sailors and settlers of other nations: the numbers of European special constables were matched by 190 Japanese civilians raised by the imperial consul.[49] There were 190 seamen from the French cruiser *Montcalm*; 150 more from two Japanese cruisers; a smaller detachment from a Russian ship; and the private army of the Sultan of Johor, which headed off remnants of the sepoys trying to cross the causeway. Even here there were rumours that the Russians had fled their ships and supplied shells to them. The decision to place Russian sailors under British command, and in British khaki rather than the white uniforms of the Imperial Russian Navy, was a humiliating twist to the old Great Game.[50] At the first victory parade, French sailors took centre stage, the tricolour streaming in the breeze. Two days later, there was a parade for the Japanese, and then one for the Russians, the sailors whistling and singing as they marched.[51] Japanese pressmen noted gleefully that, for the first time, the Rising Sun flew over Singapore.[52]

A week later, 614 Indian troops were in custody; fifty-two had been killed, and around 150 were still unaccounted for. Nur Alam Shah sheltered mutineers and chided them for not bringing him arms for a general rising: 'he would have arranged to kill the Governor'. He clothed them in local garments and exhorted the Malay policemen not to arrest them.[53] Others dressed in Chinese-style clothing or attempted to blend into local Indian society by posing as cattle-herds. Twelve of them, armed with seven rifles and some 262 cartridges, were intercepted in a small rowing boat crewed by seven Javanese as they tried to escape across the Strait of Johor to the Malay Peninsula.[54] One 'ringleader' was captured 200 miles away. But most were arrested without weapons or threw them away in the jungle.[55] In August eleven men were still unaccounted for, and the Siamese police believed that two of them were in Bangkok by this point.[56]

British retribution was swift and pitiless, even though it proved nigh impossible to identify the perpetrators of specific murders, due to the need often to rely on the testimony of ladies 'not accustomed to dealing with Indians'. After a summary general court martial, 202 men were convicted: forty-three were executed and sixty-three transported for life.[57] At one of the executions, on 25 March, twenty-two men were lined up in front of a firing party of 110 local volunteers and British regulars, five men at eight paces for each condemned sepoy. In a break with local practice, it was held in public, against the walls of Outram Road prison, and a crowd of around 15,000 spectators assembled to the sound of wails from inside the prison. Many in the firing party were unaccustomed to short-range musketry; their scattered, ineffective fire had grisly results. In eight cases, death was not instant and the men had to be despatched by revolver.[58] One of the condemned, Lance Naik Ferez, tried to address those present. 'I am a German soldier,' he began. But the jailers silenced him, claiming he was *non compos mentis*.[59] Around 143 men were sent to prisons across India. The Cellular Jail in the Andamans was no longer secure; a few months earlier the political prisoners there had gone on strike to protest at the lack of remission of their sentences.[60]

On 22 April, Kassim bin Ismail Mansoor faced nine charges of high treason, one of spying and one of trying to levy war against the king, all of which he denied. Although Kassim's case was heard before a civilian court, the governor had ordered that his trial should follow the procedures of a court martial. Kassim's lawyer protested unavailingly that this was unprecedented and unjust:

[He] doubted whether there was a case on record where a civilian has been tried before a court martial. Such a trial deprived the man of the right which every man had, namely, he had been deprived of his right of trial by a ballot of jurors of his own class. He had been deprived of the right of appearing before a Judge experienced in law.[61]

Furthermore, the defence had no specific knowledge of the allegations before they entered the court.

Throughout his trial, Kassim sat on the dais where normally a jury would sit. He was a Surat-born British subject of around sixty-three or sixty-four years of age: 'a rather senile old gentleman', according to the provost marshal now administering the law in Singapore.[62] He still had a house in Surat, in Rander, and seemed to have families scattered across the Indian Ocean, including a son by a now-dead 'Rangoon wife'. He had first come to Singapore in 1884 or 1885 and was now living in Telok Ayer Street while spending the weekends at a small plantation in Pasir Panjang. Guides and sepoys were known to visit the latter address, and a mysterious figure, 'Ismail the baker', a Bengali, was said to live there, who, unfortunately for the accused, disappeared the morning after the mutiny.

The evidence against Kassim centred on his writing to his son in Rangoon, and on an epistle intended for the now non-existent Ottoman consul there. Kassim had asked for a warship to take the Malay States Guides to war, for 'the honour of us Mohammedans will continue by the existence of the Sultanate of our Islam Khalifat'. The letter, written in Gujarati with a passage in Urdu, was intercepted by the censor in Rangoon, and Kassim was seized on 23 January, along with his brother and around 600 more letters, which were translated by Indian exchange-brokers suborned to the task. Appealing to the rules of evidence for a civilian trial, Kassim's defence lawyer maintained that it could not be proved that the handwriting was his. But the court held the letters to be admissible, even though no other incriminating evidence had been found in them. The only possible crime, therefore, was forwarding a letter. There was no attempt to prove a connection with the mutiny; the provost marshal later admitted that it did not exist.[63]

The high treason charges were dismissed, but on 3 May Kassim was found guilty of passing information to the enemy and planning to wage war. After a last-minute reprieve attempt on 10 May, the death sentence was confirmed. Before Kassim's execution, it was reported in the colonial press that he had confessed to having authored these letters. He had posed to the soldiers as a man of influence and agreed to help them 'in a moment of self-esteem, stimulated by the flattery and importunities of the deluded men'. He had written frantically to tell his son not to act on the letter, but it was too late. Kassim was hanged on 31 May. It took just twelve seconds from when he entered the execution chamber to the moment he met his death.[64]

Against this background, an inquiry into the mutiny was held. It was intended to be public, but its report was never published. In general, the British blamed the affair on the lack of discipline of the men and the laxity of their commanding officer. They drew comfort from a mass meeting in early March of some 3,000 local Muslims, led by Singapore's wealthy Arab community: 'The King is considered the shadow of The Most High and our faith teaches us that to him we must give implicit obedience.'[65] But then this had always been 'a relationship of mutual benefit, attraction, and aversion'.[66] Kassim bin Ismail Mansoor embodied communities that lived family, commercial and religious life over long distances within imaginative geographies that followed colonial circulations but had a different sense of time and place. He was, the British explained, a *pinjara*, a member of a community that was noted for its 'business enterprise, thrift, loyalty and freedom from fanaticism'.[67] It was not clear how this was meant to console the colonial public.

In private, British witnesses admitted that it had been a close-run thing. There was, on the face of it, little leadership or coordination to the mutiny. But had the mutineers managed to march on the town, 'nothing would have stopped a general massacre'.[68] It was an unsettling reminder of the violence that ultimately underpinned British rule. The besetting terror was that the disorder would spill into wider society and connect to other currents of protest in the colony. The sepoys found sympathy among the Chinese communities on the island, appalled by the ragtag army the British had employed to crush the mutiny. The role of the Japanese in the suppression, and the martial law to which both Indian mutineers and Chinese launching a renewed boycott of Japanese goods were subject, brought them together in a kind of loose anti-colonial front. It focused Chinese attention on the wider international context to their struggle against Japan and to the place of a now vulnerable Britain within it. It also led Japan to reassess its relationship with other Asian nationalisms, not least with the new arrivals of exiles and those already studying in Japan itself.[69]

The British tried to silence news of the mutiny. Newspapers and letters from Singapore and Hong Kong were heavily censored and no cablegrams were sent.[70] A new Libel Ordinance and a Seditious Publications (Prohibition) Ordinance were introduced. The former extended to reports of legislative council meetings; the latter had a catch-all definition of 'bringing into contempt' the government and penalties that went as far as life imprisonment.[71] Martial law remained in place; one of its major functions was to assist the French and Dutch whose renegades were now apprehended at their request on mail ships landing in

Singapore.[72] The British were convinced that if the mutiny had spread 'there would have been a blaze throughout the Federated Malay States the effects of which might have reached the Punjab'.[73]

LAHORE TO MANDALAY

But in the Punjab the day of destiny was already at hand. The rallying cry was 'Lahore to Dacca', and there were hopes for simultaneous uprisings by Indian garrisons in Burma, Rangoon and Mandalay. But the police now had informers within the intimate circles of friendship and kin at the heart of the affair. One them, Kirpal Singh, worked his way into a meeting of the leaders at a house by the Mochi Gate of Lahore on 15 February. But he asked too many questions, and the plotters sent him on an errand out of town. Fearing exposure, they brought forward the launch of the uprising by two days, to 7 p.m. on the evening of 19 February. That morning, Kirpal returned to the house again. By the afternoon he had become afraid for his life; at 4.30 p.m. he went up to the roof of the building and signalled the police to raid it. Seven men were seized at the house, along with plans, arms and a large number of flags; others were arrested at large, including V. G. Pingle, the messenger from Bengal who had first brought Rash Behari Bose to Lahore, who was caught at Meerut with bombs in his possession. After 1857, the British had developed elaborate protocols for pre-empting incipient mutiny, and that night they turned out the regiment at Lahore, the 23rd Cavalry, to keep it busy. A few sepoys declared for Ghadar, but most of them were betrayed to the police.[74] Disaster for the British was averted, but, as the Punjab police conceded, only narrowly. The returnees had stirred up the country with the boldness and optimism of their exhortations to revolt. Their youth and message of self-sacrifice made an impression on the soldiers in the Punjab. But any cultivation of the garrisons and coordinated planning between them was compressed into a short, ten-day period in February, and did not stretch far beyond the Punjab. The rebels could not reap what they had only just sown.[75]

The Raj launched a security sweep on an unprecedented scale. In March 1915 an emergency Defence of India Act was passed. Based on the earlier home Defence of the Realm Acts, it contained a regulation allowing for detention without trial even of British subjects. Similar powers had existed before, but the new legislation stretched the meaning of how emergency powers could be used, as it also made provision for trials before special tribunals.[76] More than 1,000 print titles were banned, many relating to Muslim affairs; the British printed their own journal in the Punjab, as well as around 400,000 'loyalty' postcards with a religious message in the main Indian languages, to be distributed through booksellers and the mails.[77] In the villages, loyal Sikhs were told to watch returnees from overseas. Having been reduced to vagrants, in desperation more of these men now turned approver, or state witness.

Special tribunals tried prisoners in nine batches. The first opened at Lahore on 26 April 1915 to try sixty-one prisoners and seventeen others listed as having absconded, including Rash Behari Bose; forty-eight of them were returnees. Many of those recruited locally were schoolboys. The proceedings took place in the city's prison, its entrances guarded and sandbagged. The defendants were herded into a railed enclosure like 'dumb-drived cattle'; some were indifferent to or contemptuous of the process and used it as an opportunity to talk to each other, or to sleep in the heat of the day. When men spoke out, they were given thirty lashes for contempt of court.[78]

In English law the notion of 'conspiracy' had broadened from its early fourteenth-century origins as the infliction of a civil injury to encompass not only actual crimes but also acts far removed even from the attempt to commit such a crime. Here the Lahore tribunal judges drew directly on the precedent of the 'Delhi-Lahore Conspiracy Case' arising from the attempt to kill Lord Hardinge, when they argued that 'the criminality of the conspiracy is independent of the criminality of the overt acts'.[79] A new latitude was also given to the evidence of approvers, of which there were eight in the first trial alone. It was no longer required that their testimonies were supported by material evidence. The judges would not entertain challenges by the government-appointed defence lawyers as to the approvers' unreliability, as could be made of normal witnesses.

The most controversial of the tribunals' approvers was Nawab Khan. He had landed in Calcutta on 29 October, sailing on the *Tosha Maru* from Penang, via Rangoon. The small party of Sikhs travelling with him were detained at the docks, but Nawab Khan slipped through, only, he presumed, because he was a Muslim. Two days later he created a small sensation by arriving in his village, Halwarah in Ludhiana District, after six years away, without any luggage. For several weeks he travelled the Punjab to rally the returnees and new recruits in search of treasuries to pillage, troops to suborn and officials to assassinate. Plans were frustrated repeatedly by a lack of arms. On 15 December he returned quietly to his village, and a few days later, in 'the realisation of the utter failure, which has overshadowed all our schemes', turned himself in to the police.[80] He gave evidence that ran to seventy-two printed pages of foolscap, and was then released to gather more 'on the sly'. This account became for the court the foundational narrative of the movement in America and the return to India. Nawab Khan, the defence argued, was 'more a spy than an accomplice'. The judges regarded him as 'a vain and boastful adventurer', carried away at first by an impossible vision of Hindu and Muslim cooperation before 'a few unproductive and abortive dacoities and aimless wanderings' caused 'luke-warmness [to] set in'; but they accepted his testimony nonetheless.[81] As one of the men implicated and arrested, Bhai Parmanand, saw it: 'Many join secret societies and indulge in dreams of the power and prestige which should follow them once freedom is won; but the result too often sadly shatters their fond imaginings and forces them to contrive for the very safety of their lives.'[82]

Bhai Parmanand was on trial for his life. The British were convinced he was 'the real dangerous man', and the local mastermind of the affair.[83] The primary evidence against him was what was termed the 'continuity' of his opposition to the Raj. Bhai Parmanand had, it was true, been in California, and had become an inspiration to the younger men. But he had left the United States in December 1913. How, he asked, could he have foreseen the war or the impact of the *Komagata Maru* affair? There was, he saw, 'no escape in action, nor any in inaction'.[84] The prosecution held against him his earlier arrest in 1909, and his proscribed 'History of India': a book that had never been published as the manscript was seized at the time. It might have been researched from respectable British sources while Bhai Parmanand was in England, but it provoked the judges into a discourse on the uses and abuses of history:

No doubt a historian enjoys certain privileges. Criticism, exposure and condemnation of what is wicked or unethical; approbation of what is noble and chivalrous; and vindication of the truth are some of the privileges universally conceded to him; but he has no right, under the guise of a historical treatise, to malign, traduce, or calumniate anybody; much less a ruling race, with the object of bringing the subject of his criticism into hatred and contempt, which as a citizen owing allegiance to a Government, he has no rights to assail. He may point out the demerits of a Government, or of a race, or of an individual; but, if a historian takes up only the dark side, and studiously avoids all mention or does not even hint of any merit of the subject of his criticism, he is not a historian but a man who abuses his privileges and renders himself accountable to Government and the public.

Now there are times and times. In times of peace a dispassionate condemnation of a people or of persons, albeit they be rulers or Kings, cannot be impugned; but to rake up old things long buried and forgotten except in books, and to impress upon the subjects of a Government that it is an evil worth ridding themselves of is nothing short of sedition clothed in an ostensible historical treatise. Mutilations and distortions may be forgiven in a historian, few are free from this fault; bias may be excused as human frailty; but perversion with a sinister motive cannot be forgiven.[85]

The tribunal ruled that Bhai Parmanand was in the same 'state of mind' as in 1909, and that 'a revolutionary in 1909 [was] a revolutionary in 1915'.[86] He was sentenced to death by a majority of two judges to one. At the final hour, the sentence was commuted to transportation and forfeiture of his property. On arrival at Port Blair in the Andamans, he refused to work. For his insolence, he was struck in the chest and kicked by the head warder, Mr Barry, who then sentenced him to twenty 'stripes' and to wear bar fetters for six months.[87] In the higher reaches of the Raj establishment there was considerable unease about the verdict on Bhai Parmanand. The advocate of the government of India admitted that all the principal approvers were in agreement 'that he had no knowledge of the conspiracy'.[88]

In the first tribunal, of the men tried in person, twenty-four were sentenced to death and twenty-seven transported for life; six others were imprisoned and four were acquitted. Of the death sentences, seventeen were commuted after a campaign by their lawyers. The remaining seven – including V. G. Pingle and Katar Singh – were executed on 16

November 1915. It was reported that they put the nooses around their own necks: 'Oh Mother India! We could not remove your shackles of slavery.'[89]

The British now rounded up the village abroad. Men who had travelled and lodged and eaten and prayed together – Shanghai policemen, Hong Kong watchmen, Penang tailors and California fruit-pickers – were brought in front of 'supplementary' Lahore tribunals in 1915 and 1916. These were men who had not even landed in India, but were brought from prisons in Bangkok or Singapore or elsewhere. The testimony of the approvers and of the men themselves laid bare the complex alliances and interdependence forged in long sojourns in foreign cities. Quarrels from the new world followed the men back to the old: disagreements over gurdwara accounts; goods bought and sold; money borrowed and lent on the longest lines of credit, not least for the passage to the Americas. The British judges struggled to decipher who was betraying whom, and to what end, and seized upon these disputes to explain the motives of men who they could not imagine might have genuinely acted out of ideas or deep conviction. There were no defence witnesses from abroad, although over fifty were called by the defence.[90]

In the third tribunal, Bela Singh – Hopkinson's former nark in Vancouver, now rewarded with land in the Punjab – acted as approver. One of the men he had informed on in Canada, Balwant Singh, the priest of the Vancouver gurdwara, was also tried. After setting sail from San Francisco in January 1915 with his wife, Kartar Kaur, and their three children, Balwant left them in Singapore in order to head to Siam, and from there to India, alone. They would not meet again. Balwant fell ill in Siam, was hospitalized, arrested and sent back to Singapore, and then to Lahore. He was accused of waging or abetting war against the king-emperor in India in 1913, in Yokohama, Vancouver, Sumas and San Francisco in 1914, and Honolulu and Bangkok in 1915.[91]

Following the additional or 'supplementary' trials which dragged on into 1917, a total of 291 men were tried, forty-two of them sentenced to death, including Balwant Singh, 114 transported for life and ninety-three imprisoned.[92] Not only lives and liberty were at stake, but also the impoverishment of entire families, as the property of the convicted was in many cases forfeit to the Crown. To the reformer C. F. Andrews, this was 'a relic of the Dark Ages' and a form of 'mental torture'.[93] This took other forms. It became a tradition within the Sikh community in

1. The world, steerage class: Tanjong Pagar dock, Singapore, c. 1896.

2. Guarding the western stake in China: Sikh policeman, Nanjing Road, Shanghai, 1910s.

3. The 'Maniktola garden', Barindra Ghose's headquarters in Calcutta.

4. Khudiram Bose, executed for his role in the Muzaffarpur bomb attack of December 1907.

5. Aurobindo Ghose in Alipore Jail, 1908.

6. The *Komagata Maru*, with Gurdit Singh in white, arms aloft, 1914.

7. Working the colonial plantation in Deli, Sumatra: women tobacco workers, c. 1914.

8. Poster for Colonial Exhibition, Semarang, 1914, designed by Albert Hahn Snr.

9. Funeral possession for Mewa Singh, following his execution in Vancouver, January 1915.

10. The plot against the Raj: Maulana Barakatullah (reading) and Raja Mahendra Pratap (second from right), on a Euphrates river boat, Mesopotamia, 1915.

11. Mutiny in Singapore: mass execution of rebel sepoys outside Outram prison, March 1915.

12. At home in Semarang: Henk Sneevliet, Betsy Brouwer, their two sons and household servants, c. 1919.

13. Welcoming the delegates to the Congress of the Peoples of the East, Baku, August 1920.

14. The opening of the 2nd World Congress of the Communist International, Petrograd, July 1920. In the foreground, to Lenin's left are Maxim Gorky, M.N. Roy and the German delegate, Clara Zetkin.

15. Nguyen Ai Quoc in Moscow with delegates to the 5th World Congress of the Comintern, 1924.

16. A Sarekat Islam meeting in Kaliwoengoe, Java, including women members from Semarang, 1921.

17. Colonialism critiqued: a painted textile depicting the arrest, trial and execution of a group of Javanese, made in Central Java, c. 1920–30s.

Canada that when Balwant Singh's wife, Kartar Kaur, finally came to visit him in prison on 30 March 1917, she was told he had been executed the previous day.[94]

For all the echoes of 1857, and the invocation of its heroes and heroines, the February 1915 uprising had no visible leadership. The man who seemed anointed to provide it, Rash Behari Bose, once again eluded the police and remained deep underground. He appeared briefly in Benares where he told supporters he was heading 'to the hills'. He was spotted heading towards the coast, in Orissa, wearing a sacred thread and carrying a bundle of dhotis and some manuscripts. The underground required a large and expensive organization which only really existed in Bengal. Supporters, sometimes people of wealth and privilege, gave money when they could; print shops, empty classrooms or small stores were marked as safe houses. Women workers provided the cover of family life for fugitives, often at the cost of their own. But more often they were constantly on the run and sleeping rough; groups of young strangers in eating houses or lodgings now attracted suspicion. They were drawn into the criminal underworld of smugglers and opium dens; what one absconder called 'a sort of brotherhood of recklessness'.[95] Amid Calcutta's large populations of men with no fixed occupation, the spheres of the labour organizers and the urban *badmashes* – men experienced in violence – intersected, along with their codes and argots. The police built elaborate networks to shadow political fugitives, within which women were also informants, and brothels could be both a hideaway and a trap.[96] Many of the leaders of the Bengal radical networks, including Jatin Mukherjee, retreated to the mofussil, and this marked the beginning of a shift of political momentum to the countryside.[97]

As the arrests and trials continued, the appeals from the earlier Delhi-Lahore case also now ran their course. In the original trial, the man said to have cast the bomb at Lord Hardinge, Basanta Kumar Biswas, had been portrayed by the judge 'more as a useful tool' than as a principal and was spared death.[98] But on 10 February 1915 the appeal judge dismissed this argument for leniency as 'a very dangerous doctrine [which] would, if accepted, palliate the offence of every hired assassin'. He also dismissed the earlier concerns as to Biswas's age and capacity. Biswas, the judge confidently stated, was twenty-four years old at the time of his trial in 1914, which was only a year younger than two of the men condemned to die. He upheld the conviction and raised its tariff: Biswas was sentenced to death. David Petrie knew that it would be necessary to obtain Biswas's testimony in order to convict Rash Behari, should he be apprehended, but Biswas's execution could not be indefinitely postponed.[99] A final appeal to the Privy Council in London on 3 March was dismissed. On 8 May, three of the conspirators were executed at Delhi prison, and Biswas was hanged in Ambala central prison in the Punjab three days later. The appeal judge had been mistaken about his age: in the accounts of Biswas's life and sacrifice that soon circulated, he was revealed to be barely twenty years old.

The day after Biswas's death, another Japanese vessel, the *Sanuki Maru*, sailed from Calcutta. It arrived in Singapore on 22 May, only to leave on the same day for Shanghai and Kobe.[100] Among the passengers was a 'P. N. Thakur'. He was, to anyone who asked, the nephew and secretary of Rabindranath Tagore, travelling ahead to prepare for a visit by the sage to Japan. But 'Thakur' was an unusual spelling of the family name, and after he disembarked, the Indians he met in Tokyo were suspicious of him. They observed that Thakur carried a copy of the Bhagavad Gita. They also noticed that he had an injured left hand. One of the Indian exiles already in Tokyo was Lala Lajpat Rai, the 'Lion of the Punjab'. He had an awkward meeting with Thakur, where they fenced around the issue of the latter's identity. As Lala Lajpat Rai put it: 'I begged of him to give me no secrets, and he gave me very few.'[101] No one, it seems, 'felt bold enough to ask', although some began to guess. It was enough that Thakur was a man who had succeeded in 'foiling history'.[102]

ISLA SOCORRO TO BALASORE

Half a world away, at around 4 p.m. on 22 April 1915, an ageing Standard Oil tanker of some 1,561 tons, the SS *Maverick*, left San Pedro, California. Its captain, H. C. Nelson, and its twenty-two-year-old American supercargo, Jack Starr-Hunt, put it out that they were heading to Borneo. Instead, they charted a course south, seemingly towards Mexico.[103]

The ship's company were the usual scatterings of all nations and of none. Among them were five 'Persian' waiters, who were rather generously paid, at $30 a month. One of the cooks, a Swiss hired for high wages in San Francisco, noted that they messed alone and drank only water or lemonade. They spoke in what he recognized to be Hindustani.[104] No one aboard believed they were who they said they were. Their leader carried six $100 traveller's cheques and five suitcases packed with Ghadar leaflets.

The source of the money was traced to the German embassy in Washington, DC. Diplomats there had engaged a well-connected German businessman of San Francisco, Frederick Jensen, to purchase the *Maverick* for $13,400 and to set up a shell steamship company for the Pacific trade. Jensen had also arranged for a large quantity of arms and ammunition purchased in New York – 8,080 Springfield rifles, 2,400 carbines, 410 repeating rifles and 500 Colt revolvers – to be carried to San Diego. There they were loaded aboard a schooner, the *Annie Larsen*, which sailed on 8 March. It was headed ostensibly for Topolobampo in northwestern Mexico, and its customs papers were brokered by a man posing as an agent of the Mexican president, Venustiano Carranza, who was fighting a civil war against the forces of Pancho Villa in the north and Emiliano Zapata in the south. But in order to fool the authorities – and because the *Annie Larsen* was inadequate for a Pacific voyage – the plan was for the arms to be secretly transhipped off the coast of Mexico on to the *Maverick*, which would then steer a course for the Netherlands Indies.

Held up by repairs, the *Maverick* left some forty-five days after the *Annie Larsen*. It sailed to the rendezvous at Isla Socorro, an uninhabited shield volcano some 400 miles west from the Mexican coast. It was an arid place, with one brackish spring covered by the sea at high tide, and home only to birds that roamed as if entirely tame and some sheep which no one knew how they survived.

Anchoring off the island, the *Maverick* blew its whistle and sent out a launch. There was a campfire close to the shore, with two sailors left behind by the American schooner with a note for the *Maverick*'s captain. There was also another hidden note buried under a cairn of rocks near a sign, 'Look Here'.[105] The *Annie Larsen* had run out of water and set sail twelve days earlier for Acapulco.

The *Maverick* and its crew stayed five weeks at Isla Socorro, waiting for the *Annie Larsen* to return. They rigged up a telescope on a high peak in order to scour the sea for the schooner. The supercargo,

Starr-Hunt, killed time by shooting sheep. After two weeks, a passing American ship called and took away the two previously stranded men. But of the schooner and the arms there was no sign. Eventually, documents relating to the rendezvous with the *Annie Larsen* were cached ashore, under the cairn and in bottles left on the beach. One of the 'Persian' waiters was asked to stay but refused. As it resumed its voyage, the *Maverick* was intercepted by a pair of warships, one Australian and the other American. Before their ship was boarded, the 'Persians' burned their papers in the five suitcases, although some charred remains were later collected by an oiler, and eventually found their way to the US authorities.[106] The naval ships then let the *Maverick* go on its way.

The *Maverick* then turned back north; it was off San Diego, California, on 22 June when Captain Nelson was instructed to head for Hilo in Hawaii. There a German agent gave Starr-Hunt a sealed letter to be handed to Emil Helfferich of Behn Meyer & Co. in Batavia. In a final attempt to rendezvous with the *Annie Larsen*, the *Maverick* sailed some 900 miles southwest of Hilo to Johnston Atoll – a deserted, blasted spot, its valuable guano deposits long mined out – where another message in a bottle was left behind.[107] There had never been any prospect of the *Maverick* finding the *Annie Larsen*. The schooner's attempts to return to Isla Socorro were defeated by the lack of winds in late June. The ship vanished into the doldrums, before eventually escaping and heading north to land at Hoquiam in Washington on 29 June, where its precious cargo fell into the hands of United States customs officials.[108]

The *Maverick* sailed on from Johnston Atoll into the Celebes Sea and the waters of the Netherlands Indies. Whispers travelled through the ports of the archipelago of a ghost ship and its secret cargo. There was talk that it carried a submarine; others said that its merchandise had been unloaded on to a fleet of sampans. On 30 April – shortly after the time the *Maverick* first left San Pedro – a stranger from India arrived in Batavia. He went by the name 'C. A. Martin' and lodged at the Hotel des Indes, the best place in town. He stayed for a week and was seen in the company of the Helfferich brothers, but then he disappeared abruptly. British intelligence identified him as one of the Howrah Gang from Bengal, but they did not know quite who. It was, in fact, Narendra Nath Bhattacharya, and he was looking for the *Maverick*.[109] After an aborted attempt to reach German diplomatic representatives in China,

Martin returned quietly via Madras in June to bring the news of the ship's approach to Jatin Mukherjee and the underground. The story that circulated in Bengal was that five ships besides the *Maverick* were coming. The plan was to mobilize a loose confederation of the gangs from eastern Bengal, Balasore and Calcutta under Jatin Mukherjee's leadership, then take over the countryside before marching on to Calcutta, seizing arms, arsenals and ultimately Fort William itself. The German officers supposedly on the *Maverick* would help them raise and train armies. They calculated that there were few British units in India able to stop them. Indeed, the Raj could call on fewer than 15,000 European troops.[110]

The challenge before the underground's leaders was how to coordinate this great undertaking over vast distances. There were several strands to the enterprise: the Indians and the Germans in America; the Ghadar networks strung out between China and Siam; and German civilians, mostly in neutral Java. It also hinged on a small number of go-betweens. They were often reluctant and always unreliable. To carry news of the army that was readying itself on the eastern border of India, the Sikhs in Siam turned in mid-June to a Bengali pleader in Bangkok called Kumud Nath Mukherji. He had been in business there since before the war; he was deeply in debt on his house rent, and his creditors were threatening to take him to court. His motive, he explained to anyone who asked, was money. He was given cash and a contact in Calcutta. He travelled via Singapore, in no particular hurry, arriving in Calcutta in early July. His news was already stale. But, after some hesitation, his contact then informed him that 'the Chief' wanted to see him.

One evening, Kumud Nath was escorted out of Calcutta by tram to Kidderpore. He and his guide got out a little below Kidderpore Bridge and turned down a wide lane off the main road. After a few more turns he arrived at a rundown house, seemingly long unoccupied, and was led upstairs. There, seated on mats, were two men dressed in dhotis with silk chadors thrown over their shoulders. 'The Chief' was a serious-looking man, aged around thirty-five, Kumud Nath guessed; he was 'very dark, very thin, clean shaven, very narrow face, lips usually pursed up, has bright eyes, and has a habit of looking at you attentively when talking to you'. He had another tic of making 'sucking noises with his mouth as he spoke'. He explained to Kumud Nath that he was now part of an organization of 'watertight compartments', and that he had been chosen to deliver a message to the German Helfferich in Java, requesting that dates and times be set for receiving the ships and men at secret locations in India. Kumud Nath was also to ask for money and at least 500 German soldiers. Given further financial inducement, he agreed, and set off at his usual slow pace to Madras, Singapore and then Batavia.[111]

In the interim, Emil Helfferich and a few others were observed by the residents of Batavia to hire a motor launch and cruise in the Sunda Straits for over a week. They planned to meet the *Maverick* and offload its cargo at sea near the usual landfall for Java at Anjer. But as the *Maverick* approached Anjer, it was boarded by sailors from Dutch torpedo boats and escorted into Batavia. When it was searched on its arrival at Tanjung Priok harbour on 21 July, much to the surprise of everybody its cargo hold was empty.

The Dutch authorities had been alerted to the vessel in late June by the British consul in Batavia, W. R. D. Beckett. On 28 June, Beckett had received an anonymous letter from the town of Bandung in the interior, offering information 'which might lead to frustrate the General rising'. He was to acknowledge it by placing an advertisement in the *Nieuws van den Dag* seeking an experienced rubber planter for Perak in Malaya. In return for information, the writer demanded 500,000 florins, a passport and free passage to any part of the world.[112] Beckett's correspondent from Bandung revealed himself as a German-Swede, who dropped hints of a ship with a name beginning with 'M' and ending with 'K', and of its destination. Beckett surmised he was interested solely in money and drew up a contract for him to work as an informant, under the alias 'Orens'. But Orens had scruples enough to demand that those involved in the scheme in India 'should be spared'.[113]

Around the same time, the British deputy consul in Medan, in Sumatra, also received a letter, which denounced a man recently arrived from Europe as a German agent. Shortly afterwards, the man in question appeared before Beckett in Batavia to apply for a visa to Singapore and Hong Kong. His name was Georg Vincent Kraft, a man born in the Indies, who had enlisted in the German army. Beckett was convinced that he was a secret agent. And indeed Kraft – known as 'L31' – was the man Ernest Douwes Dekker had helped earlier that year to procure travel papers in Zurich on behalf of the Berlin India Committee and of whom he had warned friends in the Indies. Emil Helfferich had not been impressed by the way Kraft, on his arrival in Batavia, set about 'wasting money and drinking'. Kraft soon left on a trip to Shanghai; he was intercepted by the British in Singapore in August with messages pasted inside the band of a cigar, together with maps of the Bengal coast. He was recruited by them as a double agent, 'X', and allowed to 'escape' to Manila.[114]

The British then moved to pick up the crew of the *Maverick* as they were discharged and began to disperse. The supercargo, Jack Starr-Hunt, stayed on in Batavia at the Hotel der Nederlanden, at the expense of the Germans, but he was arrested in Singapore as he attempted to return to San Francisco in November.[115] No one trusted him: not Emil Helfferich, who thought him 'a gentleman at large and a ladykiller', nor Martin, who thought he was a British spy.[116] His father was a prominent lawyer in Mexico City who had been excluded from his country club as 'a hustler and a cad', his uncle was an attorney in Los Angeles and his godfather a leading banker in San Francisco.[117] On the intervention of the American authorities he was confined in some comfort at Raffles Hotel. One of the waiters on the *Maverick*, Harcharan Das, was picked up by the Siamese police in Bangkok in November; he was also sent to Singapore, and then on to Calcutta and the Punjab, where he was released into the custody of his father who was a revenue collector. Harcharan had been sincere at the beginning, he said, but the others on the ship were 'rascals'. He was paid fifty rupees a month and given the rank of deputy inspector of police, and he became a key witness at the conspiracy trials in Lahore.[118] His associates vanished into the Indian community in Manila, and then scattered across the Philippines. One was said to run a peep show in Negros Occidental in the Visayas. The *Maverick* herself was lost in a typhoon off the Philippines in August 1917.[119]

Kumud Nath Mukherji arrived in Batavia only on 8 August 1915. He was not discreet: he asked people he met on the steamer about Emil Helfferich. On arrival he set about finding his contact, a man called Abdul Selam, alias Rafiqi. For many at the time, Abdul Selam seemed to be at the heart of numerous long-distance plots. He was, it appeared, a Kashmiri, son of a noted *maulvi* of Noorpur. He was himself educated in Urdu and Arabic, a *pesh-imam*, or prayer leader, and a *hafiz*, who had memorized the holy Quran. He had been a correspondent of Lahore newspapers and a member of the noted Anjuman Hamayat Islam society, which promoted Islamic education for women. In 1903 he had gone to Burma as agent to a contractor; there he established a *waqf*, or charitable trust, for the Muslims of Rangoon and lobbied the government to restore the dignity of the tomb of the exiled last Mughal emperor, Bahadur Shah, which was located in the city. He published a paper called *al-Rafiq*, 'The Companion', but lived on the breadline, working for a while as a mail contractor for the Rangoon General Post Office, and being imprisoned for six months for debt by his landlord. It was said that around this time he taught himself English and developed a taste, as so many suspect Asians seemed to do, for dapper European dress. He was accused of misappropriating money collected for Muhammadan Anglo-Oriental College at Aligarh by the Muslim communities of Rangoon, and in July 1912 he disappeared, abandoning his wife and son. He left a note saying he intended to take his own life and that his body would not be found.[120]

The Germans in Java believed that Abdul Selam had in fact been in the service of British intelligence in Singapore. He had arrived, it was said, via Japan, and had taken to printing anti-British pamphlets and sending them to Singapore and the Malay States from Batavia. In January 1915 he had predicted the February rising in Singapore.[121] Kumud Nath had been sent to Abdul Selam because the latter was able to send telegrams from Batavia to Harry and Sons in Calcutta through a Roman Catholic convert who worked as a salesman in the shop of the well-established Sindhi firm of K. A. J. Chotirmall & Co. This placed Abdul Selam at a crucial juncture in Ghadar transoceanic communications. But Harry and Sons was now known to the British as a front for Jatin Mukherjee's network and for the man 'Martin', whom they were now hunting across the Asian seaboard.[122] They demanded that the Dutch arrest Abdul Selam and deport him into British territory. This became a legal cause célèbre, given that he had committed no crime against the Dutch. So, to resolve the problem, he was sent into internal detention at Kupang on Dutch Timor.[123]

With his contact gone, Kumud Nath kicked his heels in Java. He delivered his message to Emil Helfferich, who told him it came from Martin. This was the first Kumud Nath had heard of the name. He then made two visits up-country to visit Java's ancient Hindu temples.

On his return, Helfferich told him that Martin had arrived, travelling via Penang on Chinese and Dutch shipping, and was staying at the Grand Hotel, in room 66. It was 'the Chief' from the house in Kidderpore, who had come for the money himself. Martin learned of the loss of the *Maverick*, but still had hopes for guns from China. It was now too dangerous for him to travel with a large sum of money, so he took Kumud Nath on a trip to the hill station of Garut with its old Hindu temple and tried to persuade him to carry it to India instead. But Kumud refused to go.

In the end, a Batavian Chinese called Ong Seng Kwie was sent. He was ostensibly on his way to Calcutta to trade batik textiles for scarce gunny sacks when he was arrested by the British in Singapore in October. He endured a hard interrogation at the hands of Major-General Ridout and his now notorious chief inquisitor, Hector Kothavala, a Parsi borrowed from the Bombay police who had first come to Singapore as a Gujarati translator for the Kassim Mansoor case but had made himself so indispensable that he was kept on. At one point, Ong was taken to what he thought was his summary execution. He was eventually released in the hopes he would unwittingly lead the British to the recipient of the money. But, Emil Helfferich observed, he was never the same man again. British officials guessed that the cash was destined for the mysterious Martin.[124] Kumud Nath followed behind Ong back towards India, wanting nothing more to do with the business. But he too was arrested in Singapore. He told the British about the house in Kidderpore, 'the Chief' and the uprising that had been planned.[125] The British now had a good idea of what Martin was about, even if they did not yet know his precise identity.

In July 1915, while Emile Helfferich waited expectantly for his rendezvous with the *Maverick*, a curious expedition arrived in Manila. It was led by the American Frederick Albert Cook, who enjoyed international notoriety for his claim to have been the first man to have reached the North Pole, in 1908. He was trying to make it first to Pontianak in Borneo and then on to British India, ostensibly to hunt big game or to attempt to climb Mount Everest. With him, or travelling in the same direction, were two German-American businessmen: a Chicago silversmith and jeweller called Albert Wehde, and the more shadowy Paul Boehm, who was said to be carrying $60,000 in cash. They were supposedly on a mission to collect ethnographical curiosities for an art gallery in Chicago. They arrived in Manila at the same time as a Persian 'prince' named 'Hassan Zade' and some Indians, who all travelled on the same ship but separately, in different cabin classes.

The Indians – and the Persian – were part of a second wave of Ghadarites from San Francisco. Hassan Zade was in reality a man called Jodh Singh, who since 1907 had spent time in Penang, Vancouver, Portland, London (at India House), Berlin and latterly Rio de Janeiro, where he was recruited to return to the German capital by the India Committee. He was then sent back to the United States to lead a scheme to suborn Indian soldiers and labourers in Siam and set up military camps on the mountain border with Burma. In Manila, Jodh Singh and his followers met up with other activists in parks and exchanged messages. They also hatched a bizarre plan to kill Cook and pose in his place to infiltrate India. But at this point the party split into different groups.[126] Cook's entourage left Manila for Singapore, shooting moving pictures as it went on its way; it was for the British an unnerving presence along an unsettled maritime frontier.[127] Then Cook departed from the region as abruptly as he had arrived, this time for Japan, and thence to Siberia in order to travel overland to Copenhagen, where he joined the Ford Peace Party.[128]

That might have been that, but another ghost ship was abroad. Wehde and Boehm set out from Manila for Borneo in mid-July in a hired vessel, the *Henry S*. Its ultimate destination was Bengal. But when it was intercepted by the Dutch navy off Celebes, it had broken down and been unable to get a tow. Yet again there were no arms to be found.[129] Meanwhile, Jodh Singh and his companions travelled by way of Xiamen and Shantou to Bangkok, to set about recruiting Indians to lead into British Burma. But within a few weeks they were arrested by the Siamese authorities and locked in a prison full of Indians confined in separate cells. They managed to smuggle coded messages to each other hidden in cigarettes. Among their fellow inmates they discovered Balwant Singh, who had been captured while attempting a similar task to theirs. Jodh Singh was terrified that his father would be sent for and would formally identify him. But the British knew full well who they all were, and transferred them to Singapore for interrogation. Balwant was soon sent to Lahore to face a Special Tribunal on a capital charge; Jodh Singh remained in custody in Singapore.[130]

It was a season of wild schemes. They were conducted in a cacophony of rumour and miscommunication, many of them arising from the independent fantasies of German civilians and Indians abroad. The escapee from Tanglin internment camp in Singapore, Diehn, now worked for Behn Meyer & Co. in Deli, Sumatra; he hatched a plan to smuggle weapons to the Nicobar Islands disguised as lumber, then to storm the Andamans and liberate the Indian convicts, who would be carried to Singapore or Rangoon in order to seize them.[131] German diplomats complained that these shenanigans were an 'open secret' among dissipated expatriates, and the Helfferich brothers' houses were 'universally looked upon as the seats of secrets and espionage'. There was even a newspaper account of the whole of Diehn's affair in the *Penang Gazette and Straits Chronicle* in mid-July. The British got wind of the details through Kraft and Orens.[132] They lent the whole thing added drama by calling it the 'Christmas Day Plot'.

Imperial policemen and the rebels of 1915 shared an obsession with making connections. Yet it was unclear at the time how far the assault on the Allied empires bridged different groups of people and places. They were more often missed rendezvous, glancing encounters, intermittent conversations, partial translations; the co-presence of the spectator, the passing stranger on the quayside, the unacknowledged figure at the back of the room, the police spy on the margins of the crowd. Worldly people might share a neighbourhood but never meet, still less become a collective. The Dutch thought Abdul Selam to be an important figure, versed in many networks, a man with a significant, if veiled, past. Yet Abdul Selam's itinerary across north India, Rangoon, Singapore, Tokyo, Batavia, Medan – his intersections with nationalism, Islamism, anarchism and pan-Asianism – led nowhere in particular and came to rest in remote Kupang. Even there, he was suspected of pro-Japanese sympathies, while supplying information on Japanese intelligence activities to the Dutch.[133] A vast swirl of innuendo, denunciation, obfuscation and lies surrounded these journeys. It was given harder currency by the bluster and barter of the paid informants – Kraft, Orens, Nawab Khan and many others – who realized that their stock with the British, and their very survival, rested on the magnitude of their claims. These were then elevated to official status in telegrams and 'abstracts of intelligence' on which professional reputations were built, and, at the highest levels, the line between fact and fantasy blurred. Equally, in the madhouse of global war, the most outlandish stories might, perhaps, be true.[134]

The imperial dragnet now reached across multiple jurisdictions. The Bombay policeman Hector Kothawala was sent on missions to China and to the Philippines, running the agent Kraft, boarding ships upon the high seas.[135] Under pressure from the British, the Siamese government launched a wave of arrests and extraditions from the beginning of August 1915. With the aid of the French police in their concession in Shanghai, the British picked up Phanindra Chakravarty – a cousin and travelling companion of Naren, alias Martin, and another intimate follower of Jatin Mukherjee – who went by the implausible pseudonym of 'William Arthur Payne'. It was nine months before he was induced to confess, but when he did he laid bare many of Naren's and Mukherjee's plans.[136] A final emissary from Bengal, Pramatha Nath Mukherji – who travelled as 'Paul Michael Carr' – came to the Indies via Rangoon to attempt to keep the connection alive, but he was stranded in Semarang with no possibility of arranging transport for arms to India. He waited several months for the return of Martin, then left for Shanghai as a Muslim merchant to search for him, but to no avail. He too was intercepted by the British in Shanghai and began to talk.[137] The only major suspect outside India still at large was Martin himself. In August 1915, he left the Indies once and for all, via Manila, still carrying a large sum of money; the British believed he had either changed identities with one of the *Maverick*'s 'Persians', using the name 'Jamshed Jehangir', or was masquerading as a 'Mr White'.[138]

Back in India, Martin's fellow revolutionaries waited for their ship to come in. They had four boats moored in the Sundarbans, the tidal channels and mangroves near the Matla River. At night, the area was under water and so watchers took to the trees to shine a light to guide in the ship when it arrived.[139] Meanwhile, 100 miles west along the coast near Balasore, the paramount leader of the Bengal underground, Jatin Mukherjee, was still holed up in a house in the village of Kaptipada. To the villagers, Jatin was nothing more than a harmless forest guru.

In June, however, the British in Calcutta intercepted a seemingly innocuous telegram from Martin in Madras to comrades in the Bengali city: 'Arrived here starting tonight for Balasore expect to meet someone there'. They began to make enquiries about Bengalis in the area. They heard stories of boating expeditions where the river channels flowed into the Bay of Bengal.[140] In August, Harry and Sons in Calcutta was raided; this led the police to its subsidiary Universal Store in Balasore on 5 September; and this in turn pointed to the house at Kaptipada. Expecting to find Martin, the CID chief from Calcutta, G. C. Denham, and his Irish colleague Charles Tegart – the most feared scourges of the Bengal underground – headed down to intercept him. Arriving after dark, they spent the night in the government bungalow at Kaptipada. The man who served them dinner brought word of their presence to Jatin. When the police raided his house on 7 September they found it empty save for a map of the Sundarbans showing steamship routes, police and forest-guard posts, and a cutting from the Penang newspaper reporting the story of the *Maverick*. There were bullet holes in tree trunks from practice firing. The police had approached on a large number of elephants, and the bells on the harnesses had given them away.

Half an hour ahead of the police, Jatin and his companions disappeared into the forest, then backtracked to the station at Balasore. But it was too hazardous for them to board a train to escape, so they withdrew again into the brush. Denham and Tegart seemed to have lost them. Then, on 9 September, came news from a village called Darpal, north of Balasore: five strangers, exhausted and hungry, had requested help to cross the Burha Balong River. When villagers had demanded who they were, the strangers drew revolvers and retreated, but the villagers followed them. The intruders fired, killing one of the locals. Thinking the gunmen were Bengali dacoits – a rumour the police in the area had fed – the villagers sent news to Balasore, and armed police were called out. The strangers withdrew to higher ground, effectively a small island in the paddy fields, with a natural parapet formed by anthills. They had Mauser pistols stolen during the Calcutta taxi dacoities, converted into rifles sighted up to 1,000 yards. Here they made a last stand. In a firefight lasting some fifteen to twenty minutes, one of the five was killed outright as he exposed himself to shoot, and two others were hit. The last two stood up and raised their hands in surrender.

Jatin Mukherjee was wounded severely in the arm and lower abdomen, and was vomiting blood. He was carried carefully back to the government hospital in Balasore and operated upon. He survived the procedure and was photographed in his bed in a private room. But for the neatness of his bandages it looked like the kind of image of dead dacoits that the police were wont to display. In the morning, Jatin was well enough to speak privately to Tegart. Jatin took responsibility for the whole affair: 'All is over,' he was reported to have told him; 'Goodbye.' Shortly afterwards, Jatin was found dead. The tale attached itself to Tegart that he was the man who shot Jatin, but he was not in the paddy fields for the so-called 'Battle of Balasore'. There were dark rumours about what happened between the two men in the hospital room. In another telling of Jatin's martyrdom, he eluded the British to the last by pulling off his stitches and bandages.[141] News of this reached Martin in Manila. Jatin was, he later reflected, the 'only man I ever obeyed almost blindly'. He thought only of revenge.[142]

DISMAL NATIONALISM

Scattered assaults on empires continued across Asia. There were reports in April 1915 of a Chinese man trying to tempt the exiled Burmese prince Mingoon Min in Saigon into a rebellion in Burma and Bengal, with the promise of a throne; and that the Germans in China were recruiting Buddhist priests to preach sedition in Chinese temples in Malaya.[143] Independently of these matters, word reached Hong Kong via the Canton press that an attack was planned on British officials at a service of intercession to be held at the cathedral on 4 August.[144] A new Chinese anti-Japanese boycott broke out in Singapore, as Chinese merchants refused to ship supplies to Japanese residents in Malaya, and the situation was contained only by the continuing state of martial law. Vietnamese radicals in Siam were encouraged by the Germans to wage war on the frontiers of French Indochina. But the man most likely to lead this, Phan Boi Chau, still languished in prison in south China. Like many in this situation, he turned to poetry:

> Still the patriot, still the gentleman on the move,
> With legs tired out, I come to rest in prison.
> At once the homeless guest of the four seas,
> And a wanted man on all five continents.

He also wrote a patriotic novel and a searching memoir of his struggle.[145] He remained in contact with the outside world through his Cantonese cook, and his followers were active among local rebels and pirates in the border regions. They were encouraged by the brief reappearance of Prince Cuong De in China in 1914, although by late May the following year he had once again taken refuge in Japan. He lived quietly in Tokyo, surrounded by barely a dozen survivors of the 'Journey to the East' of ten years earlier.[146]

Tonkin was under martial law, and a state of war was extended to Cochinchina in February 1916. Governor-General Sarraut's much vaunted plans to encourage the Saigon press were placed under notice.[147] As the harshness of war conditions began to bite, in early 1916, remnants of the Can Vuong movement launched strikes on French positions along the Mekong.[148] In the early hours of 15 February 1916, a flotilla of cargo boats arrived in Saigon docks, and armed men sprang from them to attack the city prison in an attempt to break out the leader of the failed uprising of 1913, Phan Xich Long. The attack was soon rebuffed, but its scale panicked the French authorities, and provoked the execution of fifty-one men by firing squad, the leaders watching as their followers were shot six at a time, before their own turn came.[149] On the night of 2 May 1916 loyalist gentry sprang the boy emperor Duy Tan from the citadel at Hue, but only got as far as a Buddhist temple south of the city, where they were quickly overcome by Foreign Legionnaires. Duy Tan joined his father in exile on France's remote Indian Ocean outpost of Réunion. These skirmishes failed to coalesce into a concerted challenge to French rule, still less a popular uprising; the main centres of anti-colonial agitation remained abroad, in Siam, China and France itself. But they weakened still further the hold of the monarchy on Vietnamese political thinking, or at least the indignity of the treatment of the court nourished a popular sense of shared suffering.[150]

A palpable sense of millenarian expectation lingered in the air. The attackers in Saigon wore the robes and talismans of adepts of cults of invulnerability. In the Malay state of Kelantan on the east coast of the peninsula, an uprising in the isolated district of Pasir Puteh in May 1915 was inspired by a charismatic preacher called Tok Janggut, 'Old Man Beard'. Although it took the form of a tax revolt, its leaders were wealthy men defending their local prestige against interlopers. They displayed an opportunistic awareness of outside events. Captured rebels testified that the British empire was coming to an end (a view shared by the Sultan of Kelantan himself) and Singapore would fall to rebellion. European troops had fled and so it was possible to drive the white man out. The British had to rely on the uncertain loyalty of the Malay States Guides to crush the unrest. Tok Janggut was killed and his body exhibited publicly, although there were some locally who never believed in his death.[151] In a similar way, a rebellion the following year in Jambi in Sumatra was also a reaction to the recent imposts of colonial rule and ignored the local royal court; its leaders looked instead for Turkish ships and scoured the sky for the arrival by aeroplane of a leader of the Sarekat Islam – as a messiah or as a son of the 'Raja Stamboul', or Ottoman Sultan.[152] Communal riots in Ceylon in 1915 also reflected the slow spread of pan-Islamic sentiment, such as the wearing of the fez among the coastal Moors of the island, where the famous Egyptian rebel Urabi Pasha had spent his exile since 1883. Disputes over religious processions combined with economic tensions from wartime profiteering to produce whispers that Muslims were about to attack Buddhists and that the Kaiser would appear with the Buddhist reformer Anagarika Dharmapala as his high priest.[153]

There was, however, no evidence of direct German, Turkish or Indian meddling in cases like these. Local communities did not need direct external prompting to frame their actions in broader terms. Their struggles were shaped by rumour; but these rumours did not spring from nowhere: they were the product of longer-term arguments between people participating in wider networks that encompassed others far distant and often very unlike themselves. Above all, these rebellions seemed to mark the passing of the relative equilibrium and fluid tolerance of the old Indian Ocean world.

Asia's great age of movement seemed to be stilling, and its open maritime frontiers began to close. Restrictions on the embarkation of labour from India marked the first hiatus in the great human flows across Asia since the 1880s. In 1915 steamship companies across the Bay of Bengal complained that they were running at a heavy loss.[154] The only remaining passage to India was across the Northwest Frontier. The Berlin India Committee continued to pursue its apocalyptic vision of marching at the head of an army of freedom fighters through Kabul and on to the subcontinent. After the British and Russians successfully blocked the earlier, small-scale mission to Persia, on 9 April 1915 a new party – again including Mahendra Pratap and joined, this time, by Maulana Barakatullah – left Berlin for Istanbul. It was accompanied by a second group, whose leaders included Taraknath Das and M. P. T. Acharya, and whose goal was Palestine. The combined company was received in the Ottoman capital with full honours by Enver Pasha, and by the Sultan himself. Barakatullah was given a *fatwa* by the Shaykh al-Islam and letters for selected Indian princes who might be swayed into disloyalty to the Raj. Pratap's and Barakatullah's party travelled on via Baghdad and through Persia, reaching Kermanshah on 7 June. After a pause, and joined by others from Teheran, they continued to the Afghan frontier. But the Allies were alerted and the Russians blocked the roads. It was 9 August before they passed via Boshruyeh into Afghanistan, and 2 October when they finally reached Kabul.

Under pressure from Lord Hardinge in India, the Emir of Afghanistan initially detained the party, albeit in conditions of some comfort, and they became the centre of a factional battle at court. The Germans with them began to train the army. Muslim students from the Punjab had been slipping over the border into Afghanistan for some time in a flight, or *hijra*, from lands under British control into Muslim space – a sign of preparation for *jihad*. These *muhajirin* encouraged Mahendra Pratap to believe the time was ripe for general rebellion in north India. There were British officials on the frontier who also believed that any forward move on the exiles' part would find support in India. In Kabul on 1 December, Pratap declared, for the first time, a Provisional Government of Free India, with himself as president, and Barakatullah as prime minster. But the emir would not move without a German army, and by the end of May 1916 the small German military mission had departed.

The aim of the Palestinian mission, meanwhile, was to mingle with the Indian troops holding Sinai against the threat of an Ottoman thrust at Egypt. But it was hard for them to get through the lines; and, as Hindus enlisted in a Muslim cause, their commitment was less than absolute. Taraknath Das, disillusioned and pleading ill health, retired to Hebron, and by November 1915 was back in Istanbul. By this time, any hope of a successful Ottoman offensive on Egypt had evaporated. There was, for a brief moment, the opportunity to enlist the 10,000 or so Indian officers and men captured in April 1916 at the siege of Kut-al-Amara in Mesopotamia. But the troops' morale had completely collapsed, and they were divided on religious lines. Consequently, the idea of an independent 'Indian Legion' found no favour in Istanbul or Berlin.

In July 1916 the British captured missives that exposed a plot to turn Muslim opinion in India. It became known as the 'Silk Letters Conspiracy' because the documents were written on yellow silk and sown into the lining of the jacket of a courier from Kabul. This added glamour to the affair, but their contents, written in several hands, were no revelation to the British. The letters were an attempt to unite the 'many limbs' of the Islamic networks across north India, Afghanistan and the holy places within a vision of an 'Army of Islam' to drive the British from India and the Middle East.[155] Such messages, including the physical letter and its calligraphy, were an important way in which Islamic authority – a 'kingdom of words' – was projected across the Indian Ocean and the archipelago.[156]

A year earlier, in June 1915, an Indian clerk of the Standard Oil Company in Hankou, China, described how he was approached by an aristocratic Indian, in a new serge suit and pith helmet, and a German. He was sworn to secrecy on the Quran ('although they should have known that as I had my boots on and my hands were unclean, it was not binding'), then shown a photograph of the Kaiser, styled 'His Islamic Majesty', and a proclamation under the seal of the Emir of Afghanistan announcing a revolution in India in August.[157] But by July 1916 Mecca was in the hands of the British ally Sharif Hussein ibn Ali, the British had detained the leading men of north India with pan-Islamic sympathies, and the panic receded for a time.

Har Dayal was also in Istanbul in the spring and summer of 1915, his second visit. The police in San Francisco intercepted his letters to women; again he offered to pay for Ethel Dobson to join him and carry out revolutionary work.[158] But he soon abandoned Pratap and withdrew, first to Budapest and then to Berlin. By October, tiring of the 'pugilistic' squabbles within the Indian community in Berlin, he was in neutral territory in The Hague. He was alienated by the pan-Islamic thrust of German policy, not so much on communal grounds – Ghadar had after all attempted to forge unity across India's main religions – but because it was 'a fraud and a hoax, designed to impose upon credulous Muslims in distant lands', and it undermined India's autonomy in its quest for freedom. Har Dayal's own struggle reached something of an impasse in the face of what he saw as German 'megalomania': the triumph of the 'cult of Force' and 'world-conquest', driven by the 'dismal nationalism' of the age.[159]

In the long summer of 1915 assaults on empire were unleashed that had been developed over many years and vast distances out of the resources of the country of the lost. They drew on its compulsive eclecticism and constant translations. They shared an everyday internationalism that existed alongside other commitments – to faith, to political ideology or to 'nation'. Each movement depended to some extent on the assistance and cooperation of others. This was often a 'rough tolerance' at best.[160] No aid was unconditional, no ally wholly reliable, and in some cases colonial freedom fighters became hostage to the designs of other empires. They travelled under the shadow of imminent betrayal: the fragile connections across the village abroad had to be carefully cultivated. For those who moved through the crossways of Asia, this worldliness persisted because it was necessary, despite all the mistranslations, misadventures, false alliances and schisms it carried with it. But in this time of blood, belonging and martyrdom, the early visions of an Asian whole, united in suffering the same sickness, became harder to sustain. 'Dismal' they might be, but narrower nationalisms had an increasing purchase on the imaginations of colonial peoples. And the constant mobility of the Asian underground collided ever more with a deepening imperial obsession with borders and with standing still.

M. N. Roy in Mexico.

8

The New Great Game
1915–1917

ALONE IN SHANGHAI

There were now several circles to the underworld of empire. As the networks of the village abroad became an insurgent force, the warring powers fed them with gold and weapons, and they became more closely interwoven with those of organized and opportunistic crime. Drug-smugglers, people-traffickers, gun-runners gathered at every crossing point of human mobility and flourished in wartime. New waves of refugees were expelled across borders, and the centre of gravity of these connections shifted like quicksilver. Following the failure of the 'Christmas Day Plot' of 1915 in India, the front line of the proxy war in Asia shifted to the coastal areas of China, where the worlds of espionage and private enterprise embraced. The French consul in Canton, M. Beauvais, wrote resentfully of how, since 1912, he had been drawn into a 'world of secret agents' and into a compromising position with the authorities. The stakes of this were brought home when an agent was assassinated on the water in front of his consulate and left floating in a sampan.[1]

The imperial powers recruited a parallel universe of spies and informers. In Singapore, Dudley Ridout relied on Allied consuls, friendly sea captains, Asian merchants and a dubious crew of European freebooters. The British consul in Yokohama used a Muslim merchant from the Punjab to track arms shipments. Driven by the needs of empire, however, the gathering of intelligence became more formalized. Although the culture of the gentleman spy remained pervasive, Britain's new MI5 employed a disproportionate number of old Raj toughs.[2] David Petrie travelled from India with a roving brief across Southeast and East Asia, placing agents in Java, Sumatra and Manila, mostly men already used by consuls; from August 1916, as British concerns focused on a China-Tokyo-Manila nexus, he set up a regional centre in Shanghai.[3] He was put on the consular establishment as an intelligence officer; although, it was pointed out, this would be likely to draw suspicion. A Sikh agent from India, sent to identify Ghadarites tracking between Siam and China, was shot dead in Nanjing by a suspect who had managed to elude him in Bangkok.[4] The British published thick directories of the names, addresses and business interests of German and Ottoman sub-jects in areas where they had no jurisdiction, such as the Netherlands Indies and Japan, and circulated index cards of suspicious individuals to every outpost in Asia.[5] Imperial policemen were obsessed, in the argot of the eastern seas, with the 'renegadoes' of empire: those capable both of 'visiting addresses at which Europeans rarely call' and of haunt-ing the exclusive cafés and luxury hotels that only whites could enter.[6] The Great Game was rejoined; only, instead of the high Pamirs, its terrain was the back alleys and low dives of the foreign concessions in China.

Shanghai emerged at the Pentecost of modern global connections and was perhaps the only place on earth that truly deserved its reputa-tion as an 'international' city. One of the most densely populated places on earth, it was an émigré city in its most evolved form, a city of all nations, and none, and a focus of Chinese patriotic resentment. Among its multiple and growing minorities it had one of the largest Jewish populations of any city in Asia. From the turn of the century, pogroms in the Pale of Settlement drove Ashkenazi Jews towards Siberia and, following the railway line, on to Harbin and finally to Shanghai. Many travelled in conditions of poverty to which they were entirely unaccus-tomed: doctors, dentists, musicians and their families. They arrived in a city whose rules were dictated by extreme contrasts of luxury and des-pair, and governed by powerful guilds, clubs and commercial bodies. Newcomers were aided by the comfortably established Baghdadi Jew-ish community, numbering some 800 at its peak. It was so called as most of its members were born in the Ottoman empire, but they had moved across the Indian Ocean within the imperial networks of trade having been granted the legal status of 'British protected persons'. By 1914, however, given the mood of anti-alien legislation within the Brit-ish Isles and abroad, this status had become more precarious. Jews travelled alongside Russians, Georgians, Latvians, Ukrainians and

Poles, as well as increasing numbers of Chinese refugees from the civil war in the hinterland.[7] As the Ottoman war entered its last and most destructive phase, Turkish exiles also made their way by the old overland routes to Shanghai. Many sought onward passage to Southeast Asia, Australia and the United States – mirroring in reverse the Ghadar warriors returning from North America and Japan in 1915, for whom Shanghai had served as a port of entry into Asia.

The old diasporas which had dominated the port city's life faced new challenges from these influxes of humanity, and westerners' fears at the dent to their prestige from a tide of poor whites were also greatly magnified. The outbreak of the war also brought disruption to shipping, scarcity, inflation and financial insecurity. For some incomers and established citizens alike, however, these displacements were an opportunity. And by 1916, after months of global boycotts and blockades, the economy of Shanghai began to recover, even to boom, not least as a gateway to trade with Russia.

Since the 'unequal treaty' of 1860, Shanghai had been a divided city. The International Settlement, dominated by the British and the Americans, operated alongside a French Concession and the areas under Chinese control. But westerners were a small minority even in their own quarters. A census of the International Settlement in 1915 gave a foreign population of 18,519, against 620,401 Chinese; there were around 2,405 westerners and 146,595 Chinese in the French Concession; and the population of the Chinese city stood at around 1,173,653. These numbers were always in flux, and, as elsewhere in East Asia, the fastest growing foreign population appeared to be the Japanese.[8] The Shanghai Municipal Council, elected on a property-holding franchise that mirrored that of pre-1832 Britain, was responsible to no higher authority. Citizens of imperial powers with extraterritorial privileges were subject to consular courts; Chinese within the International Settlement, foreigners with no extraterritorial privileges, and civil suits against Chinese defendants were overseen by the Mixed Court, with its Chinese magistrates. The judiciary and other public bodies, not least the Shanghai Municipal Police, were increasingly dominated by Britons. As one American observed, the settlement was 'about as international as the Tower of London or Westminster Abbey'.[9] Shanghai was not a colony, but Chinese and western observers alike were all too aware that its founding charter had been signed at gunpoint.

At the onset of the war in 1914, Shanghai's European antagonists lived in uniquely close proximity. Their trade was enmeshed – as for example in the Anglo-German Brewery Limited, the creators of the staple 'Tsingtao Beer' – and their nationals served together in the Shanghai Volunteer Corps. There were those who saw the maintenance of this cosmopolis as a higher calling than the distant conflict in Europe. But soon Germans and Austrians slipped off to the defence of the German Concession at Qingdao, those who remained were expelled from the clubs and the Municipal Council, and commercial interests were mobilized for total war.[10] But yet there was little the British or French could do to counter German diplomatic intrigues unless someone actually broke the law. Shanghai became a world of stowaways, false passports, 'cloak' businesses, counterfeit coin and 'submarine' postal services, where secret messages in homemade invisible ink were scratched in empty walnut shells, and agents were equipped with exploding pencils.[11]

At the height of the crisis in 1915, a German trader, Adolphe Nielsen, was accused of smuggling arms for India. In March 1916, boxes of ammunition were found on his property in the French Concession. This brought into public view the role of the German consulate in the affair and launched a spy scare.[12] The Shanghai Municipal Police shadowed a legion of go-betweens. The blunt instrument of the German consul in Shanghai was a man called Abel Ettinger, a Yiddish-speaking Turkish subject under German protection. Before the war, he had co-owned a vulcanizing plant, which he sold to Dunlop, and a rickshaw repair shop.[13] He had since amassed $25,000 in the Bank of Territorial Development, aided by a Baghdadi Jew employee of the bank. When asked to remit funds, the banker would release only a third or half of the sum, but make the agent sign a receipt for the full amount. Ettinger traded in false passports, made using genuine paper somehow extracted from and stamped by the consulates of Spain, Britain and Norway, and ran women couriers who smuggled opium into Shanghai from up north.[14] With a mysterious Japanese accomplice, he expanded into the import of bomb-making ingredients and copies of the Ottoman declaration of *jihad*.[15] His schemes extended into Central Asia and India through a pedlar called Moses Meyer – commonly known as 'Moses of Jerusalem' – who was apprehended by the British in Peshawar and detained in Bombay.[16]

In May 1916 a Rumanian dentist called Max Kindler, who had arrived in Shanghai via Alexandria, Madras and Singapore – where he was wanted for 'cheating' – came forward to inform on Ettinger. Short of money, Kindler had got caught up in the passport forgery racket. Here he picked up word, from an unnamed Greek, of a plot by Koreans – who were becoming a connecting tissue in many of these underground networks. They planned to raid an ammunition store and blow up the railway between Harbin and Vladivostok in return for German support in their struggle against Japan.[17]

Throughout the autumn, detectives trailed Ettinger's daily progress through Shanghai from the German Club to Japanese bars, via obscure assignations in coffee shops and hotels.[18] There were tales that he stashed counterfeit coins in the chimney of his house; that he planned to sell boxes of sand to Chinese by conning them into thinking they were full of revolvers and that he was plotting to plant clockwork bombs of his own construction aboard British ships, beginning with the RMS *Empress of Russia*. A rumour circulated in the spring of 1917 that the cavernous cellars beneath the German companies and the consulate in Hongkou district were packed with explosives, so that if the Chinese or the British came for the city's German inhabitants, the International and French Settlements would be destroyed in a vast explosion.[19]

When Ettinger was tried and acquitted in mid-1917 for possession of a forged Spanish passport, the case offered what the *North China Daily News* called 'startling glimpses into the dark underworld of Shanghai'. It exposed publicly what every resident knew: the existence of a British Shanghai Intelligence Bureau, referred to coyly in the trial as a 'Shipping Office'.[20] The case against Ettinger was undermined by the revelation that the bureau's own intermediary, a man called Rothman, was in on the former's passport scheme, and that he ran a protection racket posing as a high official in the British consular service or the police in order to intimidate prostitutes and bar owners.[21] But by the time of Ettinger's trial, such machinations had been running out of steam for months. 'Respectable' Germans were weary of intrigue and of the low types associated with it. According to the 'boy' in the German Club who had been waiting on its members for a decade, they now had little money and their chits were modest. They drank beer instead of wine and had stopped tipping.[22]

In cities like Shanghai this game of shadows took on a fictive, filmic quality. The war released a kaleidoscopic cast of adventurers and spies into popular literature and cinema who came to personify many of the cultural and political obsessions of the times. John Buchan's novel *Greenmantle* (1916) was based in part on his own role in wartime propaganda and his knowledge of actual German designs on Islam in Eurasia. Fictions like this one perpetuated a mythology of white self-mastery at the edge of empire; they celebrated the thrill of disguise, but also hinted at the perils of 'passing' as a white foreigner or as an Asian native.[23] Achmed Abdullah, a hugely popular and prolific author of orientalist intrigues in the United States from 1910, and most famous for writing the screenplay of *The Thief of Bagdad* (1924), claimed descent from the Romanovs on one side and from a daughter of an Emir of Afghanistan on the other. His publisher's biography spoke of his schooling at Eton and Oxford, of soldiering with the British Indian Army on the borders of the Raj and in China, and of spying in Ottoman lands.

Such frontier dramas were often interwoven with urban exoticism and worldly glamour. The novelist Somerset Maugham worked for British intelligence in Switzerland, where he was a close observer of Indian and Egyptian intrigues. An attempt to lure Chatto out of Switzerland and capture him on French soil by exploiting his love for a Spanish dancer provided the raw substance for Maugham's story 'Giulia Lazzari' (1928), featuring the writer turned secret agent Ashenden.[24] The fantasy of the exotic female spy was fired by the tragedy of Margaretha Zelle, alias 'Mata Hari', who was feted as a *demi-mondaine*, then pilloried and executed as a spy in Paris in October 1917. With her Javanese past and photographic images of her décolletage and 'Hindu' dance, she left a deep imprint on the 'Asia' that evolved in the popular consciousness of the west. Death only added to her allure. The French censors tried to forbid the newspapers from reporting that she faced her executioner with a smile on her face. In the words of *La Petite République*: 'The bearing of the spy, with her serenity and her smile, was a form of defiance.'[25] The enigma of the female agent was a large part of the emerging mythology of the global underground.

In colonial and semi-colonial Asia, women – and more particularly women without men – were targeted obsessively by the police. In

Shanghai there was a growing public panic about vice: in 1915 it was estimated that there were 10,000 prostitutes in the International Settlement alone.[26] This was invariably conflated in public attitudes with its burgeoning nightlife. Shortly after the tango came to Shanghai in 1913, the city had seen its first nightclubs with western dancers. There was soon a boom in Russian dance hostesses in the cabarets of the so-called 'Trenches' in the Hongkou district. The black economy of this demimonde on the edge of the International Settlement would soon account for the income of a third of the Russians in Shanghai.[27] Other western women worked as ladies' companions or as secretaries; another quintessentially modern professional was the stenographer. The Special Branch of the Shanghai Municipal Police researched multiple biographies of these women with some relish, often as background for their visa applications to move on, and also because of their political importance, both as symbols of the public virtue of western expatriate society and as potential recruits to the underground.

So, while Asian women enjoyed some measure of anonymity and exemption from the surveillance by colonial police, western and Eurasian women in Asia were all the more visible and watched. When a typist from Shanghai's grandest hotel and principal romantic rendezvous, the Astor House, seemed to disappear in 1916, it sparked a continent-wide investigation. She was Miss Gwendolen Ross, the twenty-two-year-old daughter of the Canadian trade commissioner in Shanghai, J. W. Ross.[28] She travelled a great deal; she had only just returned from a trip to Hong Kong and the Manila carnival. But she came to the particular notice of the authorities, in a time when they tried to follow almost everybody, because she travelled alone, with only a Chinese amah. Her sister in Shanghai, it seems, then denounced Gwendolen for fraternizing with the Germans just as she was about to set out once more. So the British consul ordered the captain of the ship carrying her to Yokohama to keep an eye on her, setting events in motion.

British diplomats soon tracked Miss Ross down and questioned her in Tokyo. The consul there was equally suspicious. He asked the Japanese police to arrest her, but she had committed no offence on Japanese soil and they refused. Telegrams flew around Asia. What kind of young woman travelled without a proper escort? Was she really in Yokohama for a throat operation, as she claimed? Who was 'Mr Elliot', the wealthy

American who offered her work as a typist in Tokyo? And why did she travel on through Sapporo and Seoul to Vladivostok with Mr Elliot and his mother? Was she sightseeing? As Miss Ross made her way south through Dalian, Tianjin and Beijing to Shanghai, the British became convinced Miss Ross could only be a German spy. They interviewed the itinerant westerners she encountered in hotels along the way, investigating a strange cast of biscuit salesmen, cashiered drunken ex-missionaries and suspect businessmen. Officials speculated about her several presumed and illicit love affairs, all of which were denied by everyone involved. Finally, the trail of telegram messages with obscure names led them to an illegal gambling den on Honan Road, back in Shanghai. It was run by a notorious American, and Miss Ross was said to have visited it.

When Miss Ross returned to Shanghai from Beijing, the British officials in the International Settlement were waiting for her. They decided to charge her with high treason. But then a retired British policeman presented himself quite out of the blue at his country's consulate in Shanghai. He too worked at the Astor House, but he came on behalf of a very wealthy American businessman 'who must remain anonymous'. He told a totally different story to the one the authorities had pieced together. The anonymous American had got Miss Ross 'in the family way' and she had gone to Japan to procure an abortion. She could not find a doctor there, and so had tried Korea. The casino boss had telegraphed incognito to suggest names of doctors. But the British authorities were still not convinced of her innocence. By her own admission there had been no abortion. It was unnecessary, she claimed; the stress of the journey, and of the continual questioning, had caused her to miscarry in Japan. But yet she had kept on travelling at speed through Korea and on to Russia. There was still no explanation for why she had gone to Vladivostok. Was she ever pregnant? Miss Ross demanded a letter from the consul saying she was cleared of engaging in suspicious activities. He refused to provide one; instead she was given until the end of the month to leave Shanghai. She disappeared on a steamer to Manila with another American, having told the authorities she intended to marry him. The British were no closer to understanding what she was about.[29]

Preposterous as this witch hunt was, it exposed the silent undercurrents of the Asian demi-monde. Spies, renegades and revolutionaries all had their wives and lovers, who cut their own pathways across these cities and were instrumental in their own right. The émigré wife of the go-between for the Shanghai Germans, Abel Ettinger, was hounded by the police. Ettinger's would-be nemesis, Max Kindler, lived with a thirty-year-old woman called Polly De'Blinde, who fascinated the Shanghai police. She was said to have been a prostitute ten or so years previously and a barmaid at The Hague Hotel.[30] Then there was 'Mrs Lea Cox', 'known in red light circles as "Helen" ', alias 'Mrs Lea Weinschtok', alias 'Mrs Leissherps', alias 'Mrs Wise', alias 'Emma Schwartz'. She was another refugee – a 1914 arrival from Russia – and sometime companion to Adolphe Nielsen. She was imprisoned in 1916 for three months for possessing false papers, while he managed to wriggle off the hook.[31] But it was hard to say who was respectable and who was not, and who was there by choice and who was not, and these were never static categories.

Women of wealth and the highest social standing were drawn into the intrigues of the time. In 1916 Taraknath Das appeared in Shanghai, working for an 'Oriental Ancient Literature Society'. Having despaired of efforts to turn Indian troops against their officers in the Suez Canal, and suffering from sand-colic, he had travelled through neutral countries, the United States and Japan. He now endeavoured to take a lead in the attempts to enlist the support of Chinese revolutionaries for the liberation of India. But, hounded by Petrie, he soon moved to Japan. He received crucial support in his latest ventures from two wealthy American ladies whom he first met on the boat over from San Francisco: Ellen La Motte, niece of the Delaware industrialist Alfred du Pont, and Emily Chadbourne, sister of the Chicago plutocrat Charles Crane. They were moved by his experience of persecution at the hands of the British and American authorities. They too were harassed by the British, who saw them as co-conspirators, and barred from the United Kingdom, although it achieved nothing, given the ladies' social status. Officials dismissed their encounters with Taraknath as 'a story of two lonely women looking for a little excitement and adventure'.[32] But western women travelling by themselves continued to create security panics, as when the young American Amy Dudley left her home in San Diego and headed for New York in order to follow Har Dayal to Switzerland, or when an elderly lady, Mrs Edmund Calton, threatened to sell up her substantial property and assets and head to India to 'help'. These cases, too, were put down to 'nerves' or senility.[33] But these friendships reached across great distances and sustained long-range politics.[34]

In these years, long fuses were laid across empires. The one lit by the expulsion of Ernest Douwes Dekker from the Indies in 1913 still had some way to burn. During his meeting with the India Committee in Berlin at the beginning of 1915, in which he had become entangled with the fiasco involving Vincent Kraft, Douwes Dekker had proposed his own grand plan to ship arms from the United States to the Coromandel coast. It was a 'Big Lie . . . A preposterous scheme' dreamed up, with little thought of the consequences, solely as a means to escape the financial worries that had been driving him to despair. 'The motives for my lust for money', he later claimed, 'were pure.' But in time the consequences would crush him. 'It is the most difficult thing in the world to become a scoundrel. One ought to be born for that.'[35]

The India Committee told Douwes Dekker to wait in the Netherlands for instructions. They had, he realized, begun to suspect him as a spy. 'These revolutionaries tremble for shadows.' He was tempted to sell their conspiracy to the British when he was taken by his handler – the 'Boy', Chempakaraman Pillai – to the British consulate in Amsterdam to have his passport stamped. But instead he maintained the charade, and demanded payment of monthly instalments of £600 to be sent to Java, and some £3,000–£3,500 for his own expenses. He fully expected that his remittances to his wife, now back in Java, would expose his fraud, but they did not. The committee intended that Douwes Dekker should join the mission to Istanbul to meet the Shaykh al-Islam and the Sultan and receive a *fatwa* to take to Asia. But he refused to travel east via Port Said, only westwards via New York. On the Atlantic crossing, he took his plans and letters of introduction and threw them overboard. But he kept a German code book as a guide to making a potential Javanese or Malay code and carried it quite openly. 'Spy-business was not my business, I told myself.' In his own naivety, he was planning to take the money he carried and live in Singapore.[36]

In New York, 'mental and moral agony' began to consume him, and he thought of returning to the Netherlands. But, ever the world-tourist, he used his expenses to visit the Niagara Falls, then hurried to San Francisco to sail on the *Chiyo Maru* for Tokyo. The plan now was for Douwes Dekker to join the Indian conspiracy in Siam. He was astonished by the trust his new friends placed in him. Was revolution so easy? 'I don't believe they had read a history of revolution at all.' But his contact in Tokyo – 'a mistrusting utter coward' – refused to give him the address to head to in Bangkok. There was, Douwes Dekker complained, 'not a shadow of an organisation between these would-be-conspirators'. This misdirection further spurred his own treachery. Later, he was tempted to justify his actions by saying that he acted to spare his co-conspirators, to 'betray them in their illusions'. But, at the same time, he was aware that his confused motivations were also driven by vanity and a sense of personal destiny: 'The revolution has to be "made" by me.'[37]

He was eventually given a route to Bangkok via Taiwan and Xiamen on the mainland, in order to avoid British territory. But he had no intention of following it. He went instead to Shanghai, where he announced to the Berlin Committee that he would go to Singapore. He was seeking to extort the maximum amount of money from them before the inevitable rupture. He deposited the code book with the Dutch consul in a sealed package, saying that it comprised private letters from his wife. Then, on the eve of his departure to Singapore, he fell ill. Alone in Shanghai, he sat in his hotel with a loaded revolver. A vision of his wife and children stayed his hand, and the light from a paper lantern in the street seemed a benediction. He collapsed in tears, craving morphine to which on the course of his travails he had become addicted. He vowed to return to Java, repay the money, confess his betrayal to the India Committee and throw himself on the mercy of the Dutch government. In prison, he hoped, there would be rest, 'rest for the soul above all'.[38]

He left Shanghai for Hong Kong on 15 November. He was taken ill again on the ship. Morphine calmed him during the voyage, but on arrival in Hong Kong he was rushed to the Government Civil Hospital. He wrote to his wife, Clara, to tell her that he was ill with dysentery and thought only of returning home to be with her in Java, but that he could not say any more on account of the censor. In truth, he lay in a venereal ward, which deepened his torment and remorse. Reports of his presence in Hong Kong had already circulated in the Indies press, along with speculation as to who was paying his way. In his anguish, Douwes Dekker demanded a Catholic priest, not in hopes of consolation but expecting to be condemned as a sinner. Then he turned to his physician, Dr Koch, having noticed the pity in his eyes. He wrote Koch what he called a letter of 'confession': 'I am longing for pity now, as a dying man for the end of all his pains . . . I am not guiltless, but it is another, far greater guilt which torments me.' He wrote in Dutch and in English, in the language of sin, shame and repentance. He wrote 'and did not know why', nor what he would do with it.[39] His extraordinary letter passed immediately into the hands of the Hong Kong police. When, on 8 December, the British told him he was a prisoner he felt only relief that his involvement in the revolution was over. He did not believe that they would be able to convict him of any crime.

It was Vincent Kraft who first alerted the British to his movements. He had sent a telegram to Douwes Dekker in Shanghai, asking for the date of his arrival in Singapore. In Hong Kong, when the police went through Douwes Dekker's luggage, they had found only commercial samples and books 'in the socialistic line'. But he had his code book sent on from Shanghai, and so it fell into the hands of the Hong Kong police. The Dutch told the British they would like him returned to Batavia so that he could resume his exile on Timor. But instead, in mid-December, the British shipped him to Singapore for interrogation and declared their intention to intern him for the rest of the war. Like all political prisoners, he was given the impression that the sword of death hung over him by a thin thread. But although the British took his remaining $1,000 in gold from him, he was, by his own account, well treated. He was never charged, and was allowed to move around Singapore freely on parole. He spent his time writing essays on 'sexual psychology'. He gave the British the most direct testimony they had of the India Committee in Berlin, and names: not least that of the enigmatic 'Thakur', whom he had met in Tokyo.[40]

THE MERCHANT OF KOBE

In July 1915 an Indian silk merchant based in Kobe arrived back in Yokohama, having taken ship from Manila. The merchant, who called himself 'Jaimal', had been in the Sulu Islands in the southern Philippines, from where he had tried to enter Dutch Borneo. The American military had picked him up in February, suspecting he was stirring up the Moros Muslims of the region. He gave his name variously as 'Amar Singh' and 'B. S. Jakh'. But his true identity soon emerged: it was

Bhagwan Singh, returned from his recruitment for the Ghadar in the United States. He pleaded with the authorities in the Philippines that his business was elsewhere: 'I am not interested in any religious movement whatsoever,' he told the US secret service agent in the port of Zamboanga who questioned him. Rather he was involved in a scheme to liberate India: 'within a few days' the Germans would furnish him with a million rifles and there was an army of 3,000 or 4,000 men 'waiting for him in the Punjab'. Moreover, there were agents like him 'in all parts of the world wherever any of our people live'. The US authorities soon released him – he had done nothing to break the local law – but confiscated two sets of fake moustaches, some additional false hair and police and private detective badges. He returned to the Philippine capital, where he wrote about his Indian mission in the *Manila Daily Bulletin*; it soon reached British ears from US sources.[41]

In fact, Bhagwan was now one of the Asian underground's leading operatives. Secret knowledge was woven into the migrant communities through which he moved, to be shared and adapted by others. It was well known, for example, that Hong Kong was more open than Singapore, and Manila more than any other colonial port city, although it too was increasingly precarious. 'Warning,' announced *Ghadar* in August 1915. 'Never try to run against the government of the place you reside.' Manila was 'swarming with detectives' and men working for the British government. 'Don't abuse anyone and never be ready to quarrel with your fellow countrymen, but don't trust them . . .'.[42] But Manila also had a sizeable community of Indian merchants operating bazaars with branches in the southern islands – where there were numerous leakage points into British and Dutch Borneo for those travelling or working unseen on Japanese ships. And Ghadarite messages could be smuggled out of Manila in cigars, with the help of an Indian watchman in La Giralda cigar factory.[43]

Bhagwan drew on all these resources to reach Japan, where he had supporters among the Sindhis in the silk trade. He had got to know them during his time as priest at the gurdwara in Hong Kong, when they stayed there on their way to and from China. Despite Japan being one of the safer havens for members of the Asian underground, Bhagwan was tailed by a Japanese policeman as soon as he came ashore. Not long after his arrival in Yokohama in July 1915, Bhagwan attended an evening party given by the Sindhis, where he was introduced to a Mr

Thakur and told he was a medical student from Bengal on his way to the United States to study. He was hungry for news from India; he was also curious about Thakur because he was wearing both socks and gloves despite the summer heat. The two men spoke of international affairs and arranged to meet the next evening for dinner.

They began with tea, in the Japanese way. As Thakur was pouring for his guest, Bhagwan noticed a scar on the back of his left hand. This must be why he wore gloves, but how had he been injured? Then Bhagwan remembered a newspaper report of the Delhi bomb in 1912, and descriptions of the suspects. However, 'respecting the code of revolutionary ethics', he said nothing. As they walked barefoot to their table, Bhagwan noticed another scar, on the foot of Thakur.

Over dinner, Bhagwan tackled his host on the subject of revolutionaries. Had he met any? Had he, for instance, come across Rash Behari Bose of Calcutta? Thakur answered cautiously, but conceded that he had met some Ghadarites in India. He told Bhagwan that 10,000 'soldier-patriots' who had been sent back to India would not succeed in freeing their country while the war was on.

Then, at midnight, as they rose to leave, Thakur rounded on Bhagwan: 'I know you are not a silk merchant. Who are you?'

'Neither are you a student of medicine . . .' replied Bhagwan. 'If you reveal your identity, I will do likewise.'

'You start first.' After they exchanged their true names, the men embraced. It was, for Bhagwan Singh, 'a moment of ecstasy'. Rash Behari was bemused: 'I had pictured you as a six-footer Punjabi, be-turbaned and with long whiskers!' he told the bareheaded and clean-shaven Bhagwan.[44]

Shortly afterwards, Bhagwan introduced Rash Behari to Sun Yat-sen, whom he had first encountered in December 1913 during his earlier removal from Canada. Sun was in Japan to rebuild his own organization. In the underground's quest for arms and training, Sun was as much a competitor as a collaborator, but he still served as a meeting point for revolutionaries of all nations. These connections, however, were at some remove from the idealism of ten years earlier. Bhagwan, like the other Indian conspirators, also still looked to German support, turning increasingly to their consulates in the treaty ports of China. But he was trailed too closely and was too well known to travel there to meet them. Thakur was also now being watched by the Japanese police because of his association with Bhagwan, and they too had seen the injury to the third finger of his left hand.

The scar was noted by another visitor from India. Abani Mukherji had first come to Japan in 1910–11, for training in textile manufacture. He was remembered by fellow students as a 'mad-cap' militant among the fledgling artists and activists. Then Abani spent time in Germany, where he encountered socialism. He returned to the mill industry in India, but after his involvement in a strike in 1913 left him hard-up, he returned to Japan. He found the community of Indian students and traders to be smaller than it was before, less well organized and less well known to each other. But there were still powerful Japanese willing to help Asian visitors. One of them, a Japanese scholar called Ishibashi, was an old friend from Abani's days in Germany, and put him in contact with other Japanese scholars and fellow Indians. Abani also visited Sun Yat-sen on several occasions but found him to be uninterested in the recent mutiny in Singapore in February 1915 and pessimistic about the future of the Indian struggle. Through these circles Abani met Lala Lajpat Rai; he worked for a time as the older man's secretary, and showed him the Japanese sights.[45]

But then a summons came from Bhagwan Singh. The two men held a discreet rendezvous in Tokyo's Hibiya Park to size each other up. Bhagwan then paid for Abani to return to Tokyo to meet him and Thakur in their hotel. On the strength of this, Abani was recruited to be an emissary to China. He travelled to Shanghai in August 1915, staying at an Italian hotel in the French Concession. There, to his surprise, he ran into Thakur, who was ostensibly travelling incognito but went so far as to have a business card printed for his trip. Thakur told Indians resident in Shanghai that he was going back to India disguised as a sailor with arms for a rebellion.[46] Abani was asked to travel to India ahead of him with messages for the underground. But, in September, Abani was arrested in Singapore as part of a round-up of suspects.[47] He had in his possession a notebook which showed his contacts with the German legations in China, together with names and addresses.

One of Abani's inquisitors in Singapore was David Petrie. Petrie had his suspicions about Thakur; the British had got wind of a 'clever Bengali' in Shanghai at this time who stayed, over the course of three weeks, first at a hotel and then at the house of the German Adolphe Nielsen. The CID officer knew Rash Behari bore a distinctive scar from his bomb-making accident back in Benares in November 1914 (although some intelligence sources said it was from clumsily opening a railway carriage window).[48] He showed Abani a photograph of Rash Behari: it was, Abani said, 'remarkably like' him, although he was now clean-shaven. Although Abani did not tell the British at the time, he too had suspected Thakur from their first encounter, because he had known all the gossip of the leading families of Bengal, and at a subsequent gathering he had mentioned being in Dehra Dun, the starting point of the Delhi conspiracy.[49]

The British passed the photograph of Thakur and samples of his handwriting to the Japanese authorities. Throughout October, diplomats made daily visits to the Ministry of Foreign Affairs in Tokyo to press the Japanese into launching a manhunt for Rash Behari, alias Thakur. They were met with polite reserve.[50] The Japanese would not arrest people accused of 'political crimes' such as sedition, especially if they would be faced with a capital charge. Meanwhile, Rash Behari was joined back in Japan by Heremba Lal Gupta, the Berlin India Committee's emissary to the United States for overseeing the purchase of arms; he had been on the expedition of the Chicago businessmen to Manila and been sent on to acquire weapons in China. Finally, a direct British appeal to the new foreign minister, Viscount Ishii Kikujiro, persuaded the Japanese to expel the two men, and the necessary directive was signed on 27 November.

In order to arrest Rash Behari and Gupta, however, the British needed them to be sent to a British territory, but there were few direct steamers to Hong Kong. When it was realized the two men would most probably leave Japan on the French steamer *Polynesian*, which would set sail from Kobe for Shanghai within a week, a plan was concocted with the French for the British ship *Atlas* to intercept their vessel and take the men off. There was a further contingency plan to arrest and expel them from Shanghai should the *Atlas* miss the *Polynesian* on the high seas. In the event, there was time before the fugitives had to leave for them to rally Japanese public opinion, which was already hostile to the British in the light of a recent raid by them on a Japanese ship.

That evening, 27 November, a meeting to celebrate the coronation of Emperor Meiji was held at the famous Seiyoken, one of Tokyo's first western-style restaurants, which dated back to 1876. The Japanese patron was Shumei Okawa, a well-known writer on pan-Asian ideas. The speakers included Lala Lajpat Rai, who exalted Japan's role in Asia's liberation.[51] On 1 December, the day before their expulsion, Gupta and Rash Behari – who was disguised as a woman in a kimono – were shadowed by the police as they went to the house of one of the Japanese sympathizers, Professor Toyama Mitsuru. The fugitives entered the house through the garden of a neighbour, leaving their shoes on the porch. But the police dared not search the compound of such a prominent man, as they had no legal right to do so; and in the manhunt that followed they were ordered to go through the motions.[52] Abandoning their shoes, Rash Behari and Gupta were then spirited away in a fast car to the Nakamuraya bakery and restaurant, located in the commercial district of Shinjuku. Under the ownership of Aizo and Kokko Soma, the restaurant functioned as a liberal, internationalist salon; it was frequented by the blind Russian poet, anarchist and Esperantist Yakovlevich Eroshenko and young Japanese artists working in western styles, including the Somas' eldest daughter.[53] Through the intervention of a customer, the Somas agreed to shelter the two Indians. It was at great personal cost: under the terrible strain of the concealment, Madam Soma could not feed her newborn baby, which died. 'I have lost my baby,' she later reflected, 'but I got close contact with the spirit of great Mother India.'[54] Gupta soon headed back to the United States, but Rash Behari stayed on and taught the Somas how to make 'curry rice': *indo karii* became the signature dish of their restaurant, and through it entered Japanese cuisine.[55]

When Thakur originally came to Japan in May 1915, he had done so posing as the nephew and secretary of Rabindranath Tagore. Twelve months later, it was the turn of the sage himself to land in Kobe, while en route to the United States. Tagore's journey was undertaken in a manner far removed from that of the exiles. At every stage – Penang, Singapore, Hong Kong, Tagore – he was repelled by the modern sprawl of the port cities of Asia. 'On shore after shore, and port after port,' he wrote, 'man's greed mocks at heaven with hideous gestures.' His gaze was fixed on a pure vision of Asia's ancient civilizations. 'There is', he observed in Singapore, 'no uglier nightmare on earth than a ship's quay.' In Japan his dealings with Indians were confined to the merchant community, which competed with his Japanese hosts to toast his celebrity. But when his anti-materialist, anti-militaristic message was revealed in his talks, and when his admiration for Japan became admonition, public opinion turned against him.[56]

Tagore's visit exposed the underlying contempt many Japanese felt for India as a diminished, long-colonized land, and this stigma attached itself to Tagore himself. 'Slave of a defeated country' was the jeer that followed him wherever he went. As he retreated from the public eye in Japan, he wrote an attack on the 'menace' of nationalism as a closed and conservative concept, which he had been ruminating on since the outbreak of the war and which he would present in lectures in the United States. The message, however, found little favour with his own countrymen abroad.[57] But as Tagore travelled eastwards across the Pacific, he was surrounded by rumours that he too was working for what the US authorities now called the 'Hindu-German Conspiracy'. He was alarmed enough to later write directly to President Woodrow Wilson to deny any involvement in the 'secret lies and dishonest deeds of violence'.[58]

The British were no closer to apprehending Rash Behari. In December 1915 they were stung by false reports placing him in Jinan in eastern China, and a suspect Indian was picked up at Tianjin.[59] Later that month, there was a second attempt to seize Rash Behari in Tokyo. He was glimpsed, heavily disguised, getting into a rickshaw with another man outside a rented house behind a high fence in Azabu, a residential district south of central Tokyo. For over a year he had been continually on the move, but British intelligence in Japan now learned from a local agent that he had been in the house since October; he was living with a Japanese woman, her sister and a servant, and no tradesmen ever called. The man who accompanied him in the rickshaw was identified as a Japanese plain-clothes policeman, and Rash Behari's short excursions were reported to the head of the Tokyo Metropolitan Police. The British were furious at Japanese 'duplicity'.[60] The story among the Indians in Japan was that the police officer used to swim with Rash Behari at a beach in Chiba prefecture.[61] The woman he seemed close to was the eldest daughter of the Soma household, Toshiko. She and Rash Behari married in July 1918 in private, and despite the cosmopolitan-mindedness of her family it was no small step for her to do this. They had two children together, and by the time of her death in 1925 he had been granted naturalized citizenship. The case of Rash Behari would figure high on the list of grievances sent to London when the crucial question of renewal of the 1902 Anglo-Japanese Alliance was discussed in the coming years.[62]

As Rash Behari was lying low in Japan, Abani Mukherji continued to face constant interrogation by Petrie, Ridout and others at the military headquarters of Fort Canning in Singapore. In September 1916, a year after his arrest, he made a second confession, in which he admitted more of his complicity with Bhagwan Singh and Rash Behari, and gave further details of the plans they had laid. But then, the following year, he too disappeared. Abani's story was that the British let their prisoners bathe in the sea, and one day, with the help of German internees who distracted the guards, he swam underwater out into the straits. He then managed to grab the side of one of the Japanese fishing smacks that increasingly plied the area. It took him to a remote island, where he subsisted on monkey nuts and spring water until rescued by fishermen from Sumatra who took him to sanctuary in the neutral Netherlands Indies. There he passed as a local called 'Shaheer' and worked for a Dutch planter. He had been in Java before, on his way to Japan, and the Germans who met him did not trust him. There was no public mention of Abani's escape from Singapore. Perhaps, as Abani himself said, it was because everyone presumed him drowned or taken by sharks. But the extremely brief intelligence reports warning that Abani had 'broken parole' stated that he had disappeared on the morning of 7 April 1917 with a fellow prisoner known as 'Okamoto' – who was serving a sentence for criminal trespass – and that he had been wearing a black alpaca coat, white trousers and a dark felt hat when he was last seen. The Japanese consul and press in Singapore had denounced Okamoto as a scoundrel; but, behind the scenes, the British were told that he was in fact a secret agent. Others peddled a more sinister version of Abani's escape, a shadow narrative of treachery that was to follow him after he resurfaced some years later on the far side of the world, in Rotterdam.[63]

REVEREND MARTIN HEADS EAST

By the autumn of 1915 one of the few Indian conspirators still at large outside the subcontinent was Narendra Nath Bhattacharya. He had learned how to be invisible as he shifted between his two aliases, the

Reverend C. A. Martin and the equally implausible Mr White. The British were not yet aware of his identity. They had been tracing the mysterious Martin back and forth from India and through Java; they had picked up a bare whisper of his presence in the Philippines in the spring, which had made them think he had been one of the 'Persians' from the SS *Maverick*. Now, as the year drew on, they were beginning to connect Martin with Naren, whom they knew to have been a close confidant of Jatin Mukherjee and to have been involved in a series of terrorist acts in Bengal at the time of the infamous Howrah Gang in 1910–11 and the daring taxi dacoities of 1914. With Jatin now dead, Naren was the rising force in the Bengal underground and high on the suspect list of the British.[64]

After leaving the Indies for the last time in late 1915, Naren headed for Japan. On arrival, he immediately made contact with Rash Behari Bose. They had last met in India, with Jatin Mukherjee, to lay plans for the February 1915 uprising. Their re-encounter did not go well. Rash Behari preached to Naren about Japan's destiny in Asia, telling him that revolt in India without Japanese support was futile. But, Naren protested, was not Japan an ally of Britain? Japan, Rash Behari confided knowingly, was playing a longer, bigger game, and this was the real reason it had joined the war.

Unconvinced, Naren turned to Sun Yat-sen, who was still in Japan. But Sun also seemed prepared to wait upon Japan's goodwill. This rested on his hard-nosed assessment of the strength of the British in southern China. Nevertheless, Naren now exuded enough revolutionary authority to draw Sun Yat-sen into an alliance of convenience. Naren was to approach the Germans in Beijing for fresh funds to buy arms from Chinese forces in Yunnan and Sichuan opposed to Yuan Shikai. The goods would then be delivered to the Bengal revolutionaries across the northeast frontier of India. The sum involved – some 5 million silver dollars – which would pass to Sun personally on behalf of the Chinese rebels, would provide him with sufficient resources to amass the support to challenge Yuan Shikai. It was a strategy of high ambition and deep presumption: that Sun spoke for the rebels in Yunnan and Sichuan and that Naren had sufficient sway with the Germans. On the strength of it, Naren sent covert messages to Bengal to order the remnants of Jatin Mukherjee's followers to the frontier in Assam in readiness to receive the arms. But then he had a visit from the Japanese police and was warned by an emissary of Rash Behari that he had only twenty-four hours to evade extradition to Shanghai.

The afternoon after his meeting with Sun Yat-sen, Naren visited the largest department store in Tokyo. As was the custom, he took off his leather shoes at the main entrance, and put on cloth slippers in order to enter the matted interior. He never returned for his shoes, but left by another exit. Just over an hour later he was on the train to Shimonoseki, from there to head by ship to Busan and then Seoul, in Japanese-occupied Korea, on a through ticket to Shenyang across the Chinese border. This route was closely watched. At Seoul, Naren sidetracked to the nearby port of Incheon in order to cross the Yellow Sea on a Japanese cargo ship; a harsh voyage in midwinter. Naren booked passage as far as Shanhaiguan, one of the major passes in the Great Wall, in Hebei. But he quietly disembarked earlier at Dalian, took a train on a different line to Shenyang and from there booked an onward ticket to Beijing. He again got off early, at Shanhaiguan, where he stayed overnight, and then took a local train to Tianjin, which was his intended destination all along. The false ticket trails laid across northeast China assured him that he had shaken off any surveillance.

Tianjin was China's fifth largest city, perhaps its fastest growing, and was dominated by the British Concession.[65] Naren looked to make contact with the large numbers of Indians: traders, labourers and some 700 policemen under British officers with Russian and Sikh sergeants.[66] In the deadly game of chess that all fugitives played, Naren learned in advance that the railway station was just outside British extraterritorial control. However, on the platform itself he was greeted by a 'typical colonial tough'.[67]

'Good afternoon, Mr White.'

Naren ignored him and kept walking. The man fell into step beside him. 'Before you go to your destination, would you mind accompanying me for a few minutes?'

Naren asked him where and why. 'To the police station; I am Chief of the British Police.'

Naren knew that the German Concession, safe ground, was just a street in front of him. 'I am very tired after the journey and would rather go straight to a good hotel. Moreover, I believe we are not in British territory.'

'That's alright,' the policeman pulled him up. 'I know my business. Really, I may not detain you long.'

There was a car waiting, and Naren was taken to the police station. He was told he would spend the night there while the British awaited information from Japan. Dinner was ordered from the Astor Hotel, the epicentre of the social life of Tianjin's diplomatic circles.

'How did you know I was coming?' Naren finally asked.

This was met with a laugh. 'Oh, the Japanese police is very efficient. Good night.'

He was under armed guard, Sikhs initially, but these were soon replaced by British troops. In the morning he was taken before the British consul-general, sitting as a magistrate. Naren claimed to be a student travelling to England but impeded by the war. He had been given a contact in Tianjin, he said, by a fellow passenger on the boat. But he had realized his mistake. He said that he 'was frightened and wanted to return home, but desired to see a little of the world along the way'.

This time the hazard of legal process played Naren's way and, to the chagrin of the policeman, he was set free. The policeman asked him where he was heading: 'To a good hotel.' He checked in at the Astor, which – as the policeman reminded him – was in the British Concession. But he needed a hot bath and a good meal. That afternoon, Naren took a rickshaw into central Tianjin. He sensed he was being followed. He took refuge in a store, and when his pursuers repaired to a tea shop he slipped out by a side door, down a lane to the river, and took a ferry to the German Concession nearby.

When Naren finally reached the German ambassador in Beijing, Admiral von Hintze, he realized that he was merely a foil to the ambitions of others. It seemed that Sun Yat-sen was not the inspiration behind the rebellion in Yunnan and Sichuan; the Germans did not trust him and would deal directly only with the rebel leaders. For some weeks, Naren tried to broker a deal between Yunnan and the Germans in Hankou, whereby arms were to be delivered from the Sichuan city of Chengdu to Assam via the pass at Sadiya. He pleaded with the Germans that this was still India's hour, and that an army of liberators waited only for outside aid. 'Was five million dollars too much to win the possibly decisive battle?' But in the end, the 'patronizing Junker' von Hintze admitted that he lacked the power to sanction so large a sum. Only the 'supreme war lords' in Berlin could do this. And the only road to Berlin lay through the United States.

Naren ran a new gauntlet by rail from Beijing to Hankou, and by Yangzi steamer to Nanjing, where he was taken on board a German gunboat. There was another secret passenger: Bhagwan Singh. He too was heading to the Americas. Naren disliked him from the first. He had, as Naren later described it, 'picked up many of the vulgarities of the American "He-man" without losing any of the equally objectionable native qualities. He was a lusty eater and drank beer by the gallons.' (At this time Naren was teetotal and vegetarian.) They stole into Shanghai and on to a Japanese cargo ship, where they were concealed from a British search in a smuggler's hole. Naren was much oppressed by his companion, not least by his constant farting. Appalled at spending a longer journey with him, Naren jumped ship at Kobe, and took a train to Tokyo.[68] Travelling as 'Pritam Singh', Bhagwan Singh headed on to Panama. He was seen to stay at what advertised itself as the 'coolest place in Panamá' – 'Al's Place', on the Plaza Santa Ana – where he cabled around for money under various aliases. Aided by the merchants' network, he slipped into the Caribbean, eventually arriving in New York in 11 October 1916. The British received false reports from Manila, based on letters he wrote to friends there, which said that he had entered Afghanistan via Tibet.[69]

Alone in Tokyo, Mr White resumed his disguise as the Reverend C. A. Martin. A French-Indian passport supplied by the Germans provided him with the identity of a young theology student from Pondicherry heading across the Pacific and the United States to Paris to study. He donned a cross and bought a leather-bound Bible printed on rice paper and presented himself at the American consulate. Convincing the young lady official that he was hurrying to meet the start of a new semester, he acquired a visa. After a final, midnight meeting with Rash Behari Bose, he boarded the liner *Nippon Maru* at Yokohama for San Francisco.

The British, who now had an extensive espionage operation in North America, tracked several Martins across the Pacific. More often than not it was an exercise in futility. Late in 1915, for example, they had intercepted a cable from a Martin in Yokohama to Wilmington, Delaware, announcing a sailing. The British sent to Wilmington what was euphemistically termed a 'gentleman who has for many years been actively employed by HMG in New York but whose proceedings are intentionally concealed from the Ambassador'.[70] He discovered that Martin was an American working in a car assembly plant, coming home from Japan for Christmas.

On board the *Nippon Maru* the Reverend C. A. Martin himself travelled above decks, in first class. The few westerners aboard were mostly missionaries, and he had to fend off the attentions of a young lady Indian missionary. He touched at Honolulu, before landing in San Francisco on 15 June 1916 and checking into the Bellevue Hotel. The *Daily News* reported the arrival of 'a man of mystery' from China. Martin told the journalist that the situation there was one of 'unlimited chaos'. The paper speculated that he was 'either a revolutionary leader or an emissary of the British government'.[71] But no one paid much attention to its report at the time.

Within a couple of days, Naren found refuge at Stanford University in Palo Alto with Dhan Gopal Mukerji, the brother of one of his closest comrades in the Bengal underground, whom he had ordered to wait for arms on the Assam frontier. Dhan Gopal's own path, like Naren's, had led through Japan; but he had since pulled back from the anarchist circles of the San Francisco Bay Area to a relatively settled, contemplative life of poetry and metaphysics. As recently as mid-September 1915, though, the Viceroy of India, Lord Hardinge, had speculated that he was the elusive Martin and 'the Chief' of the revolutionaries.[72] Now the real Martin took a room in a boarding house run by the mother of the Palo Alto police chief.

At the urging of Dhan Gopal, Naren adopted a new identity: 'Manabendra Nath Roy', or, more simply, M. N. Roy. Manabendra Nath was a variant of his original name, a common enough device in the tradecraft of the underground. 'Roy', however, was not a caste name and signalled a break with the Hindu nationalism of the Bengal revolutionaries. The new identity was not merely a device to evade the British, it was to 'wipe out the past' altogether.[73] Jatin's death absolved Naren of obeying his order to return.

This new persona was viewed with suspicion by local Indian circles, but then they were suspicious of everybody. When Bhagwan Singh finally arrived in San Francisco from New York, he launched a bitter struggle to wrest control of the Yugantar Ashram and its funds from its local leader, Ram Chandra, in which allegations of embezzlement and

loose-living were flung around on all sides. These struggles were followed by the Indian diaspora far and wide. In China, Taraknath Das
deplored the factionalism and squandering of money and energy in
America. He wrote from Shanghai in March 1917 to criticize the time
spent debating a new Great Seal of the Hindustani Association in America: 'How many times shall I emphasize the point of our work is not
limited within the bounds of America but ours is the world movement
centered in America.' He imagined a global network of associations,
modelled on the YMCA.[74] But this vision was becoming harder to
sustain.

The war tested the open atmosphere of Stanford. Intended as a non-
sectarian research university, it found itself caught up in the wave of
anti-German feeling that swept America after the sinking of the RMS
Lusitania in May 1915, and its students joined ambulance and flying
corps. It remained one of the few universities that admitted female students.[75] Through Dhan Gopal's Irish-American girlfriend, M. N. Roy
was introduced to a twenty-three-year-old English major, now a graduate student, called Evelyn Lenora Trent. She was active in progressive
causes, and close to the wife of the president of Stanford, David Starr
Jordan. Evelyn dropped her plans to become a writer in order to follow
Roy to Europe – his goal still remained Berlin – and she sought the
intercession of Jordan for a visa.[76] But her father, a well-to-do mining
engineer from Utah and sometime adviser to the Japanese government,
accused Roy of kidnapping her and demanded his arrest.[77]

As a step to a greater freedom, in early 1917 Roy and Evelyn moved
to New York. They were followed by Evelyn's brother, who threatened
to disown her and to expose Roy in order to break up the relationship,
although what precisely he knew of Roy's past was not clear. Within a
year the couple quietly married.[78] The Roys found the Indian freedom
movement in New York in equal disarray to that of the west coast, its
leaders burning through what was left of its German funds. They were
introduced to Lala Lajpat Rai, who had also arrived in the United
States from Japan. Evelyn worked for him as a stenographer and Roy as
a research assistant, spending much of his time studying in the New
York Public Library. It was his first opportunity for a settled education
and, reading independently, his first real encounter with Karl Marx
and other socialist writers. The Roys moved constantly around the city,
staying at first in Gramercy Park and later at an apartment on West

44th Street; they used the Ceylon Restaurant on Eighth Avenue, a popular haunt of Indians in the city, as a postal address.[79] In Lala Lajpat Rai, Roy found a new mentor of sorts, and he and Evelyn were a constant presence at Lajpat's public lectures, which were rather sparsely attended by elderly Americans more interested in India's spiritual message than its politics. This was dispiriting. 'The poor old man', Roy reported to Rash Behari in Tokyo, 'is awfully homesick.'[80] But Roy's exposure to pacifist internationalism in the libraries and public lecture halls of New York was another rupture with his past. 'The idea of revolution, associated with the heroic deeds of individuals armed with pistols or bombs,' as he described it much later, 'receded from my mind.'[81]

THE PLOT AGAINST AMERICA

During the war years, New York intellectual circles were electrified by the presence of Bolshevik revolutionary exiles from Europe, such as Nikolai Bukharin and the feminist Alexandra Kollontai, who acted as an emissary for Lenin, distributing pamphlets and campaigning at socialist meetings against the war. In 1915 she had visited Chicago, where she met her old comrade Mikhail Markovich Gruzenberg, better known by his alias, Mikhail Borodin, and alerted Lenin to his presence in the United States. On 13 January 1917 Leon Trotsky arrived in New York from Barcelona. His name was not well known outside exile circles, but from his residence at the Astor Hotel, and then from rented rooms in the Bronx, he was drawn into the febrile world of Russian and German émigré politics, fundraising and espionage, and worked to enlist American followers for the anti-war cause. Then came news of the abdication of Tsar Nicholas II on 15 March. It reached Trotsky that very evening, and he was propelled on to a succession of public platforms. With the announcement of a general amnesty for political prisoners, many exiles immediately started to head back to Russia, including Trotsky. The British were watching them closely. Trotsky himself had a short spell in British detention in Amherst, Nova Scotia.[82] Others, like Borodin with his wife, Fanya, and two US-born children, were slower to give up the new life they had made.

There remained a powerful sense in which America was a gateway to a utopian future. Sen Katayama, in exile since the High Treason Incident in 1910, had been active in organizing Japanese socialists in San Francisco and Oakland, and on an earlier sojourn had set up a utopian colony for Japanese settlers in Texas. In 1916, like Roy, he moved to the more open atmosphere of New York; he came at the invitation of the Dutch Marxist S. J. Rutgers, at whose Brooklyn home he worked as a cook. For many of these émigrés, not just Roy, New York was a bridge from an inward-looking, 'dismal nationalism' to a more cosmopolitan awareness.[83] But America too was shrinking. Official tolerance for radical political movements on US soil was at an end. In his December 1915 State of the Union address, President Woodrow Wilson demanded new federal laws and, in language of unprecedented vehemence, that 'such creatures of passion, disloyalty, and anarchy must be crushed out'. During 1916, seventeen bills to support this aim were presented to Congress.[84] The British encouraged this, and their growing intelligence organization in the Americas – some eight staff and agents in New York alone, and more agents on the west coast – was supplemented by a new officer from India, the former chief of police in Dacca, Robert Nathan. He cultivated the city authorities and recruited more paid informers.[85]

In New York there was little real contact with or detailed news from India. The self-appointed leader of the independence cause in North America, Dr Chandrakanta Chakravarty, was a latecomer to it in the wake of the departure of Har Dayal and others. He had first come to New York in 1910, then left for Berlin in December 1915 to return with some $60,000 with which to despatch revolutionaries to India. He lived in high style in Manhattan with a German friend, an entrepreneur in patent medicines called Dr Ernst Sekunna, who had the ear of the German embassy. Roy visited Chakravarty at his apartment – 'rather like an exclusive club than a rich man's residence' – and mistrusted him from the first. He was struck by his habit of applying Vaseline to his scalp from a large tub he kept constantly close at hand. Not for nothing, Roy observed, was he known as 'the oily leader of the oily revolution'. Roy could not take him seriously; but, preposterous as he seemed, he could not be ignored, as he was the only real channel to the Berlin India Committee. Two months after his arrival in New York, Roy wrote to Rash Behari in Tokyo, complaining of the state of affairs. 'The Germans have lost faith in our cause,' he told him. 'Everybody is gradually slipping off the field with the small amount of money at their disposal to make his own provision for the future.'[86] Roy was not the only one to despair: Heremba Lal Gupta, now safely returned from Japan, denounced Chakravarty in a letter to a go-between in Switzerland as 'an adventurer', 'irresponsible and half-insane', not least because of his indiscretions with the women he was involved with. He was 'not only useless but spoiling the work'.[87]

In early March 1917 British agents in the United States fed the New York Police Department with a story that Chakravarty planned to bomb New York. Men from the Bureau of Investigation and the NYPD bomb squad raided Chakravarty's house on West 120th Street and arrested him with Dr Sekunna and Heremba Lal Gupta. In the basement of Chakravarty's house, they discovered stocks of pamphlets in English, Chinese, Arabic and Hindustani. There were also remnants of M. P. T. Acharya's low-profile sojourn in the United States in 1914: his British passport and his school leaving certificate from days long past in Madras; and a large number of postcards addressed to him, 'in most affectionate terms', by a German girl in Munich who signed herself 'Faschoda Marie'. On the shelves of a sub-cellar were plaster figures of John Bull 'with a villainous countenance', his paunch covered with a Union flag, holding a rope tied around the neck of a woman lying on the ground. There was a bloodstained shirt collar, said to have been worn by Chakravarty when he was attacked by a British agent with a sword-cane in Washington, DC, and kept as evidence of British oppression. There were materials relating to a medicinal compound called 'Omin Tonic Tablets' developed by Dr Sekunna, plus some chemical powders, duck shot, a demijohn of gasoline and a quart of varnish. In the garden there were two miniature fountains and a coloured mosaic of the words 'Bande Mataram'. There was, of course, no bomb.[88] The raid was relayed to the viceroy back in India in gleeful detail. Chakravarty, as the official report described it, was at home, 'lightly clad in his native costume' and 'performing an Indian dance for the delectation of his German confrère who was reclining on an Eastern divan'.[89]

During Chakravarty's interrogation, Nathan sat in silence behind a screen, passing written questions to the New York detectives. Almost immediately, inevitably, the betrayals began. The Roys were picked up on 11 March on the campus of Columbia University, after a public meeting. Roy's pivotal role in the arms plot in Asia had yet to come to light. Under questioning he admitted only that he had fled to Japan from India, via China. Of Thakur and 'Gupta', he claimed, 'all I know is from reports'. Neither the British nor the Bureau of Investigation believed him. They were inhibited from extracting more information by the fact that the interrogation occurred in the relative visibility of police headquarters. As the Bureau of Investigation agent explained in a sinister undertone, 'I was unable to press this feature at any great length but will endeavour to do so in the next day or so.' But there was confusion over the grounds of Roy's arrest and he was released.[90]

On 6 April 1917 the United States entered the war, and within a matter of hours many of the Indian leaders on the west coast were arrested. Bhagwan Singh was arrested at Naco, Arizona, as he tried to cross the Mexican border while passing as an 'English Jew, on his way to Del Rio to see his sweetheart'. In Tucson county jail in Arizona he bragged to an opium smuggler that he now had 400,000 men waiting for him in India.[91]

A fusillade of legislation was now unleashed. The first shots had, in fact, been fired a couple of months earlier with the immigration law of February 1917. This went far beyond the anarchists who had already been formally excluded from the United States since 1903 to target any-one guilty by association merely through belonging to an organization that advocated violent revolution. It also established a 'barred zone' from which Asian immigration was forbidden, aimed at Chinese and Indians. This was followed in June by the Espionage Act – bolstered in 1918 by a set of amendments known as the Sedition Act – which allowed not only the detention of enemy aliens but also the prosecution of American radicals opposed to the war such as the Wobblies. Amid public hysteria, only the conditions of war itself prevented large-scale expulsions of immigrants. A pseudo-medical jargon surrounded the official pathology of the alien 'agitator', 'anarchist' and 'terrorist', and conflated them all.[92]

All of this converged in the spectacle of the 'Hindu-German Conspiracy Case', which unfolded in the United States District Court of Northern California in San Francisco at the end of 1917. In terms of the volume of the dockets of evidence against the 105 accused, it was the largest criminal case since the foundation of the Republic. The charge they faced was of recruitment to a military expedition against a power with which the United States was at peace. The case was not clear-cut; therefore the idea of 'conspiracy' was invoked to strengthen the possibility of convictions. This was the first time it was invoked against a plot that 'permeated and encircled the whole globe'. In the trial, a Republic born from revolution, and currently fighting a war for the cause of national self-determination, prosecuted on its own soil a revolutionary movement for national self-determination.[93]

Only thirty-seven of the accused stood in the dock: others mentioned in the indictment – Har Dayal, M. P. T. Acharya and Rash Behari Bose – were listed as absconders, although there were plenty of rumours that Rash Behari Bose was travelling to San Francisco under an assumed name.[94] Some of those in the dock were also prosecution witnesses. Their names and status were marked in green on the wall map opposite them, on which the defendants' journeys across the world were traced; the rest of the accused were labelled in red. The head of the Indian CID, Sir George Denham – the man who had run Jatin Mukherjee to ground in Balasore in 1915 – was in attendance; according to one newspaper report, he was supported by more than 200 British secret policemen in California and a detective agency hired by the consulate, at a reported cost to the British government of over $2.5 million. In truth, both Denham and Nathan – under the work name 'Hale' – openly worked side by side with officers of the US Bureau of Investigation, interviewing witnesses and preparing evidence with the prosecution.[95]

The British shipped in witnesses from India and Singapore. Many were promised immunity in return for their testimony, and were hidden out of sight on a private ranch in Sonoma county.[96] Among those who took the stand for the prosecution were the approver in the Lahore case, Nawab Khan, and Harcharan Das and Jack Starr-Hunt of the *Maverick*, the latter of whom came under escort from Raffles Hotel in Singapore via Brixton prison in London. Ernest Douwes Dekker travelled from Singapore separately, escorted by a British soldier. Provided with a witness fee, he was able to stay in a private house on Bancroft Way in Berkeley, although his landlord accompanied him whenever he went out. He was introduced to the court as an 'international scoundrel' and employed to give evidence about the Berlin Committee. But he refused to testify against the movement in Java.[97]

A number of the men made passionate public appeals in court for their liberty. Bhagwan Singh insisted that he 'worked independently and not for Germany. What I did I did for humanity's sake, for the sake of 315,000,000 Hindus crushed beneath England's yoke in India.'[98] Perhaps the most dramatic testimony came from one of the 'star witnesses', one of the approvers, Jodh Singh, who had been brought from Singapore. Jodh Singh's revolutionary progress stretched across Europe, Asia and the Americas. He broke down on the stand when confronted with his comrades.[99] His appearance in court bore evidence of compulsion, of torture even. Agnes Smedley, the young radical and close associate of many of the accused, described his arrival at the court for the *Nation*, escorted by British agents, 'thin, emaciated, and weak'. When he reached the marshal's office he tore open his shirt and pulled up the sleeves of his coat: 'On his breast and on his skin were dark brown splotches – burned skin.' His 'black eyes, sunk deeply into his head gave him a fearful appearance'. They had, she said, 'lost their gleam of intelligence'.[100] But his words in court had no measure of madness about them. He was, he said, speaking under stay of execution. 'Since the Lahore and Mandalay cases have been tried, I have been put before the world as the punishment of the people convicted to death.' He attacked the legal process in India, invoking the Founding Fathers of the USA:

Gentlemen, this is the United States of America. This is a country where democratic government was established by one of the Mahatmas of the world who is known as George Washington. This is the country where men of high and low class have almost equal rights . . .

Until now I have not understood what right has the Government of the United States to bring me to this country as a prisoner without issuing any legal warrant against me, either in India or the United States, and then expect testimony in this world-wide intrigue . . .

I am used by the British government as a tool and a story-teller in the courts of the world, a mere medium of punishing the Germans and other nationalities of the world.

Confronted by the accused, he was, he said, 'ready now to share their punishment and their suffering'. His change of heart, as described by the *Oakland Tribune*, was met by the defendants rising 'to chant a weird, occult Brahmin air'. But Jodh Singh's plea for equal treatment was refused him. He was transferred to Alameda county jail and committed to an institution for the insane.[101]

But the defendants were bitterly divided by the informing and on their strategy. One of the men in the dock was Taraknath Das, who had returned voluntarily to the United States to face the charges, as an American citizen determined to exercise his rights. His backers, Ellen La Motte and Emily Chadbourne, supported his legal costs. An old friend from his earlier California days, Mrs Camille de Berri, presented herself to the British consul-general in San Francisco, offering information in return for not having to testify in court. She was sent in to induce Taraknath to plead guilty. Soon she became a confidante, filling in her own daily contact reports, turning her 'flirtation', as she termed it, to official use. She had been born in India and had first met Taraknath Das in 1914 through an interest in spiritualism and her membership of the Cosmopolitan Club in Berkeley. When he left for Germany, he had stowed copies of a Ghadar 'bomb manual' in her safe deposit box, and he sent her photographs of himself and postcards on his travels, from places as far afield as Rumania.[102] But she failed in her task. She was then put to work tracking the notorious Jack Sloan, who had travelled with Ghadar to Colombo then disappeared. 'The Hindus simply *won't* talk,' she reported. 'They seem to be scared out of their very senses.'[103]

The divisions among the Indian accused deepened during the trial. On 22 April 1918, in the courtroom during a recess, one of the defendants, Ram Singh, approached a fellow accused, the leader of the movement on the west coast, Ram Chandra. He pressed a revolver into Ram Chandra's side and fired three fatal bullets. He then raised his weapon at the US Attorney, John W. Preston, but his arm was seized by another lawyer, and a federal marshall vaulted into the aisle and shot Ram Singh down. Ram died before an ambulance arrived. He had been passed the weapon by a fellow defendant who had been allowed bail.[104]

At the end of the protracted trial, one man was acquitted, twenty-nine were convicted, two were dead and one was certified insane. The sentences ranged from sixty days to twenty-two months, the stretch handed down to Taraknath Das to serve in Leavenworth Federal Penitentiary. But the men managed to avoid repatriation to India. The issue was kept alive by a smaller-scale second trial in Chicago in 1918 which was followed avidly not only in Britain and India but also in Japan.[105]

In San Francisco, Roy's name was listed among the absconded

defendants. Earlier, in June 1917, he had been picked up again on suspicion of breaching immigration laws. Released on bail, he headed with his wife, Evelyn, to Texas, and with a false passport crossed the Mexican border on 15 June, a year to the day since his arrival in the United States. The police had hesitated; they had been watching his home address and had contrary information about his movements. In May the British had still not been clear how he had entered the United States, and were unsure of his true identity. They traced his path back to Palo Alto, where another India radical, Sailindra Nath Ghose, who had arrived via South Africa, was looking for him. Prompted by this visit, a local informant pieced together Roy's movements, although Roy had fed him a false trail with a story that he had been smuggled out of Japan in a small boat and had then gone to Turkey.[106] At 239 East 19th Street, New York, the Roys' last known address, the arrival of a friend to settle an unpaid gas bill led the Bureau of Investigation to a location in Mexico City. But even by mid-October, neither the Bureau nor Denham were quite sure where Roy had gone.[107]

Mexico had long been a draw to migrants from Asia. Overseas Chinese comprised Mexico's third largest immigrant group after migrants from the United States and Spain: in 1901 there were 13,203 Chinese in Mexico (only eighty-two of them women). They were, for the most part, a community of shopkeepers; in some regions, like Sonora in the north, they suffered vicious pogroms, but the Mexican Revolution created conditions under which they could prosper.[108] The country was a lure to Indians too. Many came via Manila, although after April 1917 the American colony of the Philippines was no longer neutral ground, leaving prospective migrants there in 'a wholesome state of "funk" '.[109] Nevertheless, the Indian network was by now well established across Central America and into the Caribbean. In Chakravarty's papers there was a plan – linked to Bhagwan Singh's brief sojourn in Panama in 1916 – to occupy Trinidad as a 'foothold into America', and if Trinidad could not be held to move into Venezuela. The Bureau of Investigation's suspect lists now included large numbers of pedlars from Panama.[110]

But Mexico was something more than another temporary haven. The Mexican Revolution, which began in 1910, was a global event as much as any other convulsion of the age and was widely followed in radical circles. Its peasant revolts were pictured as an exotic curiosity, and seen through images of barbarous medievalism, such as in John Reed's reporting for *Metropolitan Magazine*. It was Reed's first experience of insurgency. Mexico was where many Americans, and Asians too, learned their revolutionary vocabulary. By mid-1917 it had drawn in a wave of exiles, especially young Americans evading the draft. On one estimate, there were perhaps 3,000 so-called 'slackers' loitering in the Alameda, the principal public park of Mexico City, some of whom found work in the Berlitz Language School. They even had their own periodical, *Gale's Magazine*, edited by Linn A. E. Gale, who was minister to the New Thought Church of Mexico and professed support for left-wing causes. They were, as Roy described them, 'pacifists, anarcho-syndicalists, socialists of all shades': Greenwich Village in the Valley of Mexico. There were also proven trade union organizers – Wobblies – who saw in the Mexican Revolution the promise of a socialist utopia.[111]

Roy found himself well placed in such circles. He had a letter of introduction to the Mexican president, Venustiano Carranza, from David Starr Jordan. He had his wife's money and German advances: there were $6,750 and 15,000 pesos in the bank in Evelyn's name. The Roys settled in Mexico City, first at the Hotel Geneva, and then in a rented house in the Colonia Roma, to the west of the city centre. It was a barrio popular with expatriates and the Mexican elite, and Roy mixed freely with both. He acquired a taste for the style of a *salonista*, and for the 'good things of life': ice cream parlours, horse-riding, fine coffee and wine. 'And, why not say it,' Evelyn was later to reflect, 'he enjoyed the secrecy and the intrigue, in those decades of spies, plots, and secrets . . . It was charming to see him dressed in a western suit, with style, a black Quixote who lectured on the evils of British and Yankee imperialism.'[112] Some took him to be an Indian prince, and Roy, for his part, admitted to a Brahminical affinity with the old elite and shared membership of a universal intellectual aristocracy.[113] The left-wing journalist Carleton Beals described a romantic hero: 'Tall, with long, slim, expressive hands and black-white eyes that flashed frequent wrath out of a very dark face, Roy had boundless energy.'[114]

Roy's education in socialism, begun in New York, now deepened with his exposure to the Mexican Revolution. It rekindled Roy's interest in peasant politics; an understanding of how imperialism had beggared a once vital social system was an enduring legacy of his older

Swadeshi schooling. Mexico lifted this into a wider frame of reference. In many ways, what he saw in Mexico was far ahead of any European struggle. As the peasant leader Emiliano Zapata wrote in early 1918: 'We would gain a lot, human justice would gain a lot, if all the peoples of our America and all the nations of old Europe were to understand that the cause of Revolutionary Mexico and the cause of Russia are and represent the cause of humanity, the supreme interest of all the oppressed peoples.'[115]

Roy translated the anti-war text he had written in English in New York, an *Open Letter to His Excellency Woodrow Wilson*, into Spanish as a way of learning the language, and published it in pamphlet form as *El Camina Para La Paz Duradera Del Mundo*. It was a factual record of British rule in India, supported with detailed statistical appendices. He then began to work on a larger study. Notwithstanding the exotic persona that propelled him into fashionable society, Roy resisted the temptation to portray India as a mysterious 'dreamland'. In its social conditions, he argued, it was similar to Mexico. This drew the attention of socialist circles, then dominated by anarcho-syndicalists. He imbibed much of their anti-nationalism, and these ideas infused his barely formed Marxism. In the plutocratic, polyglot melting pot of Colonia Roma, M. N. Roy became a political personality and a cosmopolitan.[116]

Roy positioned himself as a useful outsider, a go-between among the émigrés. He turned over the residue of his German funds to buy a printing press for the small socialist party of Mexico to print its journal, *Lucha de los Clases* ('Class Struggle'). It had no more than twenty members and was referred to as the *cinco gatos* ('five cats'). It met in front of a shoemaker's house, and it was said that Roy rooted out old pairs of shoes for repair to help the man remain in business.[117] The Roys' largesse and their open house in Colonia Roma kept many of the exiles going; to a new trickle of Indian refugees from the United States Roy was a 'gold mine'. They were all watched closely. For cover, Roy used the name 'Manuel Mendez', but Evelyn's letters back to the States were intercepted by the authorities.

Roy's activities in Mexico centred on the struggle for social justice and the defence against American encroachment for resources, namely oil. There was little here he could do for India. But he soon attracted attention from the German embassy. Mexico had been at the heart of the Central Powers' intrigues against America, and Roy ran into old acquaintances from the Netherlands East Indies, including Jack Starr-Hunt, busy on some 'shady enterprise' having been released after the San Francisco trials. The double agent Vincent Kraft, too, was briefly in Mexico, and there were other Germans from Java 'living in grand style'.[118] The Germans approached Roy, with the covert support of the Mexican government, in one last attempt to use German gold to fund revolution in Asia. But a gift of 10,000 dollars from Mexico was rebuffed by Rash Behari Bose in Japan. By this time, Rash Behari was living alone in the Koishikawa district of Bunkyo, Tokyo, watched by the British, isolated, under close confinement, and far from well. 'These people', Rash Behari scoffed, 'are the victims of utopian ideas, which under no circumstances can be materialised.'[119] Roy's own involvement in the scheme lacked real conviction. Accompanied by Evelyn, he got as far as travelling south to the Pacific port of Salina Cruz to board a Japanese cargo ship for Asia. But the ship failed to arrive and their return to Colonia Roma – to the ideal of 'a small cosmopolitan community of free human beings' – seemed like a homecoming to Roy.[120] Soon news from Europe would send them off on another course entirely.

Mas Marco Kartodikromo and his wife, abroad, *c.*1920.

9
Victory!
1917–1919

THE HUMAN NATION OF THE WORLD

On 18 March 1917, three days after the abdication of Tsar Nicholas II, the news from St Petersburg reached Java. The next day an article appeared in a Semarang newspaper, under the headline 'Zegepraal' ('Victory'):

> Do the victory bells peal loudly enough to reach the cities and *desas* [villages] of this country? . . . Here live people who suffer and endure . . . People of Java, the Russian Revolution contains lessons for you, too! The Russian people were poor and illiterate like you; they also bore centuries of oppression. They won a victory only because of their unrelenting struggle against a government that was grounded in violence and duplicity.

The author was Henk Sneevliet. He was writing for *De Indiër*, a Dutch-language mouthpiece for the followers of Ernest Douwes Dekker, whom the government of the Netherlands Indies was conspiring to keep out of Java and out of mind in the custody of the British. Initially, few people paid Sneevliet's provocation much heed. But when his words were translated into Malay and spoke directly to a local audience in Java and beyond, they were seen as treasonous.[1]

By early 1917 the tempests of the world outside blew directly into the households of Surabaya and Semarang. Because of the global shortage of shipping between 1913 and 1920, the price of key commodities doubled, and labourers' wages did not keep pace. Wage work, for towns-people, now commanded most of their waking moments. Even in a sector like the railways, with its formal employment structures, a working day could stretch to twelve or fifteen hours for a driver or fireman – even more at peak times – with few rest days. For the larger numbers of casual workers, or those posted out of town, hours could be even longer, with no possibility of rest, not even the 'blue Mondays' stolen by factory or transport workers. There was a relentless demand from employers for the labour of women and children, and for families with very limited means there was no avoiding it. In Semarang, women did heavy lifting on building sites; they lined the rolling tables of cigarette factories and the centrifuge rooms of sugar mills, often under sweatshop conditions. Children worked in factories too, and as shoeshines on station platforms or weeders on plantations. Women and children also dominated domestic work, which accounted for around a quarter of urban employment. Added to the escalating cost of living were urban rack rents, which ate up around a quarter of a household budget in the cities of Java. This led to chronic indebtedness, most often to shopkeepers and moneylenders, who would wait at the gates of a factory to collect on payday. Then there was the foreman's cut from wages, and employers' fines for absenteeism or tardiness, which were, in the words of the transport union, 'as endemic as malaria'.[2]

As elsewhere in Asia, labour organization in Java spread outwards from the waterfront. The new networks of trains and trams generated skilled jobs for a first generation of townspeople literate in Dutch and Malay. By 1916 this amounted to around 50,000–60,000 workers, and comprised both skilled Europeans and Indonesians who toiled alongside each other on unequal wages. This was a larger body than the total number employed in the 1,823 privately owned workshops and factories in Java. The intricate hierarchies of the transport industry gave Javanese an opportunity to lead, but also exposed them to a heightened sense of racial hierarchies and discrimination. Foremen, cultivated though they were by European employers, often had intimate ties to the village city and took leadership roles in trade unions.

Sneevliet, with his wide experience of trade unionism, was instrumental in encouraging the rise of Javanese within the transport union by holding meetings in both Dutch and Malay. His chosen protégé was a young railway clerk from Surabaya called Semaoen. Already a leading member of the Federation of Railway and Tramway Personnel, Semaoen left his job in 1915, at barely sixteen years of age, to become a full-time, salaried trade unionist and moved to Semarang. The union spread from its Semarang base across Java; in the eighteen months after December 1916 it grew from 4,900 to 7,600 members, although not all paid their dues, but conversely nor were all sympathizers necessarily official members.[3] Together with Darsono Notosudirdjo, a minor aristocrat turned trade union propagandist, Semaoen took over the newspaper of the transport union, *De Volharding*, or 'Persistence'. They built up the Semarang branch of the Sarekat Islam from 1,700 to some 20,000 members. It became, effectively, the left wing of the national movement. In smoothing the rise of Javanese leaders, Sneevliet and his associate Asser Baars tried to avoid the impression that they were, as Baars put it, 'attempting to do missionary work'. However, their zealous sense of predestiny in promoting what Sneevliet called 'the social democratic religion' often had a similar effect.[4] The paranoid expatriate press laid the mounting unrest in Java at Sneevliet's feet.

Tensions were stoked in February 1917 with the return of Mas Marco Kartodikromo after nearly two years' sojourn in prison and abroad. Following the introduction of the censorious 'hate-sowing' articles of the Netherlands Indies penal code in March 1914, Marco's 'war of voice' had collided repeatedly with them. In April 1915, with an investigation hovering over and stifling him, and with the financial support of friends, Marco travelled to Singapore to enlarge his experience of the world. He stayed with the journalist M. A. Hamid – editor of an *Islamic Review* – on Minto Road. But within a few weeks the British police descended on the house to search Marco's room and seize his letters and books. He was detained, interrogated and expelled back to the Indies. Soon after his return, in July 1915, he was sentenced to nine months in Semarang prison; after a public outcry this was reduced to seven months. On his release, he left for the Netherlands, ostensibly to study, but funded by the editor of the Batavia paper *Pantjaran Warta* ('Broadcast News') as a special correspondent.[5]

From The Hague, in late 1916, Marco published a small collection of impressions and comparisons, entitled *Boekoe Sebaran Jang Pertama* ('The First Prospectus'). In it he took the uprising in Jambi earlier that year as a symptom of a wider Indies rebellion and of the colonial order on a precipice. The message was plain: 'If our government hopes for peace in the lands of the Indies, give us our equality with the

European race, thereby the hearts of the children of the Indies will surely cool.'⁶ The tone had a residue of conciliatoriness and regret which only served to underline the latent menace. The experience of abroad, and of directly witnessing Dutch democracy in action, heightened Marco's indignation, and his journey home shortly after had the air of a gathering storm. Not for nothing was the newspaper that had recently taken over the mantle of Marco's old *Doenia Bergerak* titled *Goentoer Bergerak* – 'Thunder in Motion'.

Marco's return to Batavia on 12 February 1917 was announced by him in a series of columns in *Pantjaran Warta* under the headline, 'Sama Rasa Sama Rata' – literally, 'same feeling, same level': a graceful transposition of the republican ideals of fraternity and equality into simple Malay. The articles were signed and dated as letters from his voyage to and from Europe; not in any chronological time sequence, but as despatches at large from the 'Spanish Sea', the Straits of Gibraltar, Aden and the 'Saumatra Sea'.⁷ They compared the freedoms in the Netherlands with the lack of equality before the law for natives in the Indies, and lampooned the Dutch colonial government's plans to raise a native militia to defend the Indies. Marco turned the figure of the journalist into a modern incarnation of the *satria* warriors of legend.

Marco's guerrilla war of voice summoned up a nervous excitement among his readers as to how far he might go, and how far the Dutch would be provoked. In fact, the articles got him arrested within a week of his return; and after the trial that ensued he was imprisoned again, this time for twelve months. Sneevliet and Baars took up his defence in a Press Freedom Action Committee. It sought to exploit the way that Marco's aura was enhanced by the ubiquity of his name; traders in Solo even sold 'Sigaret Djawa Merk Marco' – 'Marco' branded cigarettes celebrating the 'defender of the Javanese people' – the proceeds from which, it was claimed, would be given to his wife.⁸ Marco's sentence was again reduced, but Sneevliet lost his job, and now faced a reckoning before the courts himself for his recent 'Victory' article.

Alongside their editors-at-large, newspapers now listed their 'editors-in-prison'. In Weltevreden prison in Batavia, Marco put his slogan *sama rasa sama rata* into verse form. It spoke of prison as an epiphany: a vision of an underground nation, a hidden 'nation of bandits', from which Marco drew moral strength:

But such are of the selfsame type
As those who have in their control
Power and the wealth of men,
Yet acting in a hidden way.

There are robbers refined and crude,
There are robbers small and big,
Masked with culture and educated,
There are those who rob in error.

All of them are robbers
Demanding things by force
Uncaring of their nationhood
The human nation of the world.[9]

In prison Marco read Max Havelaar, Tolstoy and Marx, and emerged as a figure of the left. Shortly before his release, there came word of another revolution in Russia.

The news of the Bolshevik putsch in November 1917 travelled more slowly than that of the fall of the Tsar in March, and its outcome was unclear. Newspapers carried fragments of wire reports, and even in the leftist press of Semarang the names of Lenin and Trotsky were barely heard.[10] Sneevliet and Baars took it on themselves to be their heralds. On Christmas Day Baars addressed a victory speech to the people of the Indies: 'You must organize *now*, the Russian example must be followed now ... Do as in Russia and the victory is yours!'[11]

Sneevliet used his trial in early April 1918 and the immunity of the courtroom to give a nine-hour defence of socialist principles. After his acquittal, he returned from Batavia to Semarang on the 5th, when he was carried from his train like a conquering hero, in scenes reminiscent of Douwes Dekker's triumphant progress through Java five years earlier. But this time there were more Javanese in the crowds – some 3,000 to 4,000 on official estimates alone – and also, ominously, European soldiers. Sneevliet had to climb a lamp post to speak, and the police called out the fire brigade to disperse the crowd with water hoses. The scene was repeated the following day with Semaoen's return to the city. Only this time the police were ready with batons, and a planned showing of the film *Rasputin, The Black Monk*, in the central square was cancelled.[12] The next month, Semaoen and Marco founded a new newspaper in the city: *Sinar Hindia* – 'Light of the Indies'. It took up the old metaphor of darkness into light, but this time to speak, as the masthead proclaimed, on behalf of 'proletariats of all nationalities and religions'.[13] Semarang was now a Red city.

Empires were never so vulnerable as when they attempted to reform themselves. In May a *Volksraad*, or parliament, modelled on that of South Africa, opened in Weltevreden, the administrative enclave of Batavia. Half of its thirty-eight members were non-European, and they included Tjokroaminoto and Tjipto; some were appointed, and some were voted for by an electoral college of little more than 1,000 men. Yet for all this, and not withstanding the *Volksraad*'s purely consultative role, its proceedings were under immunity, and its existence gave substance to the Indies as a 'legal personality' with a unitary structure. For many of those involved, modern nationhood needed Dutch statehood – needed shared oppression by the Dutch – to come into being, until such a time as the barriers to legal equality could be dissolved. Speakers in the *Volksraad* voiced their demands for full budgetary powers and ministerial accountability in the language of self-determination that was common to the global moment inspired by Woodrow Wilson's Fourteen Points.[14] But what selfhood was to be determined in the Indies? What were its common ties, and where did its boundaries lie?

Leaders voiced very different 'nations of intent'. The rallying cry of Ernest Douwes Dekker before the war, of the Indies for the *Indier*, suddenly lost force. The word 'Indies' too closely evoked both British India and the Dutch state, as did its variant, *Insulinde*. Some preferred the term *Nusantara*, literally the 'islands within' or 'between'. It broke with the linguistic inheritance of Dutch; it was archipelagic in compass. But its origins lay in a chronicle of the world-conqueror from fourteenth-century Majapahit, Gajah Mada, and this made it too Java-centric for nationalists from the outer islands. The term 'Indonesia' had been used by early British ethnographers and then by some Dutch scholars at Leiden University to designate a wider cultural region of island Southeast Asia. Suddenly it began to acquire imaginative force. In late 1917 the exile Soewardi and others established an 'Indonesian Association of Students' at Leiden. Some of its members were Dutch, such as the Semarang-born H. J. van Mook, who had attended the same Surabaya high school as Sukarno, where his father taught. Men like van Mook expected to participate in and to lead an 'Indonesia', but they did not yet see it as a nation. Others saw 'Indonesia' as a common destiny of the island peoples, in the struggle for which Europeans, Eurasians, Chinese and Arabs might be allies but not full members. But there was also a claim for a more equal belonging, where, in Soewardi's phrase, 'whoever is a citizen of the Indonesian state is also an Indonesian'. The question of the new nation's ethnic and cultural foundations remained unresolved and untested in the Indies itself.[15]

The exiles of 1913 now began to return. Tjipto Mangoenkoesoemo had been the first, in August 1914, and after the end of the war both Soewardi and the most dangerous renegade of all, Ernest Douwes Dekker, were allowed back into Java. Officials leaned towards forgiveness in the hope that these men might counter more radical voices. But it was not clear that the famous 'triad' of 1913 still commanded popular adulation, and the situation was so changed that, as one high official put it, 'one more would not make a difference'. Douwes Dekker arrived at Tanjung Priok harbour on 22 July 1918, to be greeted by his wife and daughters, and was then whisked off by a crowd of well-wishers to a reception in the Masonic Hall in Batavia. In a newspaper article, Sneevliet scorned their expressions of gratitude to the governor-general. Douwes Dekker embarked on a new speaking tour across Java. His oratory was still full of fire and left a mark on many who heard him, including the young Sukarno. But this time, to many Javanese, Douwes Dekker's assumption that his Insulinde party spoke for all the peoples of the Indies smacked of arrogance. The socialists attacked his 'primitive' nationalism and dark mutterings about his wartime adventures cast a shadow over his homecoming.[16]

The news of the Bolshevik Revolution left the European membership of Sneevliet's small social democratic party, the ISDV, more divided than ever. Some argued, as socialists in the west did, that the Indies was 'backward'; it lacked a proletariat and was not yet ripe for revolution. But to this it could now be countered that Russia was, after all, the least industrial of European societies. Java had, too, its big industry and its capitalists, Chinese as well as European. It had its 'Red Guards', in the form of Dutch enlisted men, who now, to the alarm of government, rallied to the revolutionary cause. And with the news of the abdication of Kaiser Wilhelm in Germany on 10 November 1918, there was, for a few short weeks, the real possibility that the Netherlands itself would follow Russia and Germany, and rumours reached Batavia that Queen Wilhelmina had abdicated. Were this true, the European leaders of the ISDV looked to the 'Red Guards' in Surabaya to seize power in their name. Yet no clear signal came from the west. The uprising that followed the formation of the Communist Party of Germany on 31 December 1918 failed; its vanguard, the Spartacists, was destroyed, and its leaders, Rosa Luxemburg and Karl Liebknecht, murdered. There was no revolution in the Netherlands and the elite politicians of the Indies settled for a further promise of reform from Governor-General Idenburg.[17]

Leadership of the radical movement now slipped out of European hands. In December 1918 Sneevliet was expelled back to the Netherlands. His associate Asser Baars soon followed him. He was a Malay speaker, unlike Sneevliet, and his particular sin had been to criticize the 'rottenness' of Indies government 'in native company' and in 'ugly Malay words'. He avoided prison but lost his job, and was outcast. He succumbed to the sadness of the tropics, complaining of the 'deadly hot' of Semarang and the sapping of strength 'that is not renewed by the warm sympathy of those you are struggling to help'. Defeated by the Indies, both men went in search of the mother lode of world revolution, where Sneevliet vowed to continue to speak for colonial peoples.[18]

Local leaders no longer needed Sneevliet's voice. Semaoen and others had been willing to accept the help of Sneevliet, Baars and Dutch soldiers and sailors 'to prevent the capitalists of other countries like Japan and England from attacking our country'.[19] But they were quite clear in their minds that, although the global struggle of the working class in theory was indivisible, in practice there were in the Indies two unequal proletariats. The privileged white working class took it on themselves to speak for the 'general interest', but still expected the habits of colonial deference.[20] Their present sacrifices and imagined futures were not shared. As Marco put it in a letter of support for Sneevliet in November 1917: 'The Javanese themselves must suffer to reach their goals.'[21]

The membership of the Sarekat Islam had grown to 2.5 million people and now stretched from Java to the outer islands. In October 1918 its congress rejected 'sinful capitalism' and endorsed a 'minimum programme' that did not merely chime with the demands of revolutionary movements across the world but exceeded many of them. It called for wages in line with the cost of living; equal pay for equal work for men and women; an eight-hour day and a six-day week; paid holidays, insurance and a pension fund; free medical care and sickness pay; pre-natal and maternal leave; an end to employers' fines; and a ban on child labour. The Sarekat Islam organized large federations of labour to launch general stoppages. Semaoen and others were not willing to sub-ordinate the anti-colonial struggle to world revolution, nor to wait on outside events. There was a powerful nativism in their language of faith and fearlessness in the face of guns and hunger. Semaoen drew on the fighting traditions of old Java to dispel the fears of the militant workers of Semarang that by their actions their families might go hungry. In the wars of the ancient kings, in the rebellion of Dipanegara – the last *ratu adil*, or just king – against the Dutch in 1825–30, had not the villages risen in support and vital food and supplies been found? 'Now we must have courage and will, then with God's blessing our goal will surely be achieved.'[22]

Thus emboldened, workers now began to strike across Java. These were often walkouts led from below, which the leaders of labour or the Sarekat Islam were then summoned to investigate in an incendiary atmosphere. Industrial action was no longer confined to the cities. In central Java, in the Sarekat Islam's old heartland around Solo, the movement's leaders targeted Dutch sugar factories. Europeans called it 'terror'. But this method of protest was not new, although its rhetoric was. The head of the Sarekat Islam, Tjokroaminoto, was not alone in seeing its ideal of economic autonomy as a form of socialism. He had read Marx and adapted Islamic socialist ideas absorbed from India.[23] However, a new guiding spirit now emerged in central Java: an imam called Haji H. M. Misbach.

Misbach was born in 1876 and raised in the old Muslim quarter of Solo, close to the royal palace and the grand mosque, where he would later run a small batik workshop. He was educated in a *pesantren*, or local religious school, for the most part, with very little debt to the eth-ical policy. He entered the political world through Marco's Journalists' Union, and sought above all, as Marco put it, 'to spread Islamness with the methods of the present age'. He embodied the title of the periodical he guided, *Islam Bergerak*, or 'Islam in Motion'. He moved easily among the urban poor; he did not shun the worlds of the gamelan or the popular theatre, the thieves or the 'butterflies of the night'. He wore a simple Javanese headdress, not the Turkish-style fez or turban affected by many others who had made the pilgrimage to Mecca. He denounced the hypocrisy of those who used their religious standing to entrench their privilege or exploit their fellow Muslims. His writing style followed the familiar rhythms of Quranic recitation and exposition, but through this he brought a pious reasoning to the day-to-day experience of colonial inequality. Long before 'Tuan Marx', whose teachings Misbach respectfully referred to in his own speeches and writings, there was the example of God's Prophet Muhammad and his injunction that true Islam demanded action in the face of worldly injustice. In Misbach's injunction: 'God commands us to move together.' Adapting an image of epochal upheaval from old Java, Misbach identified the times as a 'djaman balik boeono', an 'age upside down':

> The present age can rightly be called the *djaman balik boeono* – for what used to be above is now most certainly under.
>
> It is said that in the country of Oostenrijk, which used to be headed by a king, there has now been a *balik boeono*. It is now headed by a Republic, and many bureaucrats have been killed by the Republic. A former bureaucrat only has to show his nose for his throat to be cut, and so on.

Through their own resources and vision, leaders of the *pergerakan* (movement) placed the Indies in the midst of the collapse of European empires – the 'Oostenrijk' of the houses of Hohenzollern, Habsburg and Romanov – and at the forefront of world history.[24]

This was a time of urban violence, the most savage in living memory. There were attacks on Chinese communities in the northern towns of Java, a targeting of middlemen in conditions of scarcity. The situation was not helped by Chinese being used as strike-breakers in Semarang. The worst of the unrest occurred in nearby Kudus, the centre of the clove cigarette industry, in late October 1918. Here Javanese producers faced competition from Chinese interlopers, while the mostly women workers in the town's other staple industry, batik production, endured acute labour bondage. The backdrop was the visitation of the global influenza pandemic. To drive away these evil spirits, the Chinese of the town held four nights of procession, a *danse macabre* of fire, colour and noise. The spectacle of Chinese men, some in the dress of

Europeans, others in the garb of hajis with their red Turkish fezzes, gave rise to offence. On the final night, 30 October, violence erupted when a cart carrying a Chinese in the haji dress collided with the hand-cart of a Javanese loaded with sand. A fight broke out; the mosque drums were beaten to summon people to the fray. Rumours spread which interpreted the procession as it passed the mosque as lewd dancing, and which conflated fireworks with firearms. The following evening, larger numbers gathered and attacked Chinese residences. Despite some attempts by leaders to restrain the crowd, there were ten deaths, eight of them Chinese; shops were doused with benzene and set alight and houses ransacked. Chinese families fled to Semarang and the violence looked likely to spread.[25]

The Chinese and Javanese communities had lived side by side for generations. The leaders of Javanese labour knew this, but they did not wholly condemn the violence; some leaders of the Sarekat Islam in Kudus were arrested for their part in the riot. Semaoen argued that the relative prosperity of the Chinese was bitter testimony to how impoverished and impotent the Javanese had become. 'Their hatred towards the Dutch is drowned because the Dutch are the rulers and they are strong, but the hatred towards the rich Chinese has to counter balance [it].'[26] Darsono launched a heated attack on Chinese leaders. The Peranakan Chinese Malay-language newspaper *Sin Po* claimed common cause:

> What Mr. Darsono said about the great love of the Indies Chinese for China and their nationality is true. This consciousness, however, is not the 'fault' of the Chinese. It is because they were pushed from both sides. They were forced into this kind of situation ... The Chinese today are also groaning under the oppression of capitalism.[27]

But in Semarang a charity football match for the victims was stormed by protesters.[28] The Dutch responded by strengthening urban policing. In Surabaya there were 1,358 police, working on round-the-clock shifts; the ratio of police to public was higher than in Amsterdam itself, and that was not accounting for the private security of the Chinese and wealthier Arabs.[29] In Singapore, a city with a similar ethnic composition, the British watched these developments closely.

After the influenza first struck the Netherlands Indies in June 1918, at least 1.5 million died there from the disease. It became known, with dark irony, as the '*sama rasa sama rata* illness'.[30] There were other omens, through which old prophecies spoke to changed times. A new *ratu adil* proclaimed himself in central Java, and established a small *kraton*, or palace, with his followers outside Yogyakarta. There was talk of holy war against infidels and the coming of an *imam Mahdi*.[31] On 19 May 1919 Mount Kelud in East Java erupted, spewing debris and some 50 million cubic yards of water from its crater lake. More than 5,000 lives were lost within forty-five minutes; local reports claimed fatalities were ten times higher. The region was covered in darkness, a hail of acrid dust lasted two days, and a river of boiling mud flattened the town of Blitar, engulfing the prison and the railway station. In what was seen as a prophetic act of grace, only the mosque was left standing. Seismic waves were felt as far away as Colombo.[32] Such cosmic events had always presaged rupture in 'the human nation of the world'. It was well known that Tjokroaminoto himself, the leader of the Sarekat Islam, was born in fire in 1882, just prior to the destruction of Krakatoa.

All these events seemed to implicate the Sarekat Islam and its leaders. In May 1919 a Dutch tax collector in Celebes was murdered. In July, in the fasting month, there was a confrontation in Cimareme, West Java, between police and troops and the followers of a local leader, Haji Hassan. The immediate issue was his refusal to comply with the compulsory sale of grain to the government. The situation escalated when officials and police and soldiers descended to arrest him. They were met by a group of men in white robes, armed with sticks and knives. After some negotiation, the men were persuaded to change their dress and to disperse. A few days later all of them were arrested in their own homes. On 7 July the police returned to Haji Hassans's house, to be confronted with a crowd of some 1,000–1,500 people, standing four to five deep along the sides of the road. Haji Hassan, his family and close followers remained indoors, surrounded by the police. They refused to emerge; and as they chanted the *dhikr*, or devotional remembrance of God, the roof and then the doors and windows of the house were fired upon. Haji Hassan was killed along with some six others – according to villagers' accounts – including his daughter and her week-old son. In the inquiry that followed, the officials who gave the order to fire escaped public censure; but, in private, the minister of the colonies himself admitted they had gone too far.[33]

In common with the leaders of the revolts in Kelantan in Malaya in 1915 and Jambi in 1916, Haji Hassan was a relatively wealthy man, defending his local position against the imposts of the colonial state. He and his followers were linked by membership of mystical sufi brotherhoods; by the trading of talismans conferring invulnerability; by the cult of the *ratu adil,* and by the language of holy war.[34] To the Dutch, these signs led to a deeper, darker, 'perverse' game, in which the goading of the peasants into holy war was a means to political ends. That the men involved revered Tjokroaminoto, who for some was the just king that was promised, was enough to link events in West Java to the Sarekat Islam. Dutch officials became obsessed with what they termed 'the secrets of *Afdeeling B*', an alleged 'Section B' of the Sarekat Islam, which, it was said, was preparing to launch the wholesale slaughter of officials and Chinese.[35] They feared the suborning of police and soldiers. Former boarders at Peneleh Alley – 'Red' Sarekat Islam leaders such as Alimin, Musso and Darsono – were all detained.[36] Both Douwes Dekker and Haji Misbach were arrested under powers of preventative detention for their part in the rural protests around Solo. Fear of 'Section B' provided a fresh alibi for the assault by conservative officials and industrialists on ethical imperialism. Its stigma also scared away many Javanese from the Sarekat Islam, particularly schoolteachers and minor clerks dependent on a government salary.[37]

In early 1919 Semaoen was indicted for multiple press offences and by June was in Yogyakarta prison. 'Verily,' he announced, 'prison is a gift, a place where a man can make plans for the general well-being of the world.' He used the next few months to write a novel called *Hikayat Kadiroen* ('The Story of Kadiroen'), which was published in serial form the following year. Fiction was now the genre of writing safest from censure and prison the safest place to write. Semaoen's novel was a satire of old Java, and a premonition of the future, as seen through the coming to consciousness of a young civil servant who rejects a life of status to embrace the cause of the common people as a communist activist. In the reckoning of the new science of history and in the revealed truth of Islam, a threshold had been reached.[38] No longer was the colonial *rust en orde* inviolable; neither were local hierarchies nor the cautious 'freedom and order' advocated by Tjokroaminoto.

'Wherever there is a pergerakan,' Semaoen had argued in defence of Marco in March 1917, 'tranquillity will disappear, for the pergerakan exists [precisely] because tranquillity disappears. Move and calm are two things in direct conflict.'[39] Now 'move' was on an ever larger, global scale. 'This is the end of an age,' an activist proclaims in a long speech at the heart of *Hikayat Kadiroen*, 'the realisation of which we can only have a vague conception.'[40]

REBUILDING BABYLON

The war's end, and all it portended, was marked with peculiar intensity across colonial Asia. In the industrial outpost of Kuala Lipis, deep in the interior of the Malay Peninsula, an effigy of the Kaiser was filled with Chinese crackers and burned on a high hill.[41] When the festivities to commemorate the official peace were held in Kuala Lumpur on 19–20 July 1919, they were a celebration of imperial community. Indian plantation workers were paid double time to attend, and it was an opportunity for local Sikhs to reaffirm their loyalty. But there was an 'entire absence' of Chinese, save for a few businessmen. The customary Chinese fireworks were provided by the Japanese business community. Many European residents were stung by accusations from home – real and imagined – that they had escaped the worst of the bloodshed while living in conditions of privilege and plenty. Their mood was defensive and despondent. As doggerel by a rubber planter had it:

> I work alone year in, year out;
> No leave in London town.
> And no one gives a cuss for me
> If fever puts me down.
>
> They would not take me for the front;
> My eyesight they found lacking.
> So I suppose, I can't expect
> A free show or free makin [food].[42]

There were painful public debates as to whether men who had fought in the Singapore Mutiny should wear the '1914–15 Star', especially as demobbed servicemen arrived in the colonies from Europe looking for work.[43] They reinforced the fragile façade of imperial control. At the end of the war, in the rubber industry of Malaya, there were around 1,107 European planters in charge of an Asian labour force of 181,295 spread over 577,277 acres. There was an epidemic of armed robberies, and a 'great exodus' of women and children for home once shipping again became available.[44] In many ways, the colonies were still at war. British residents demanded the continued exclusion of Germans and were shaken by reports of them escaping from the internment to which they were subject in Singapore. Peace arrived in a different time signature to the west, and victory was no victory at all.

All colonial societies were mutinous. In Tonkin, the uprising the French had feared for so long had come on 30 August 1917. It began in the largest penitentiary in the north of the country, in the town of Thai Nguyen, some forty miles north of Hanoi. Some prisoners and around 150 of their guards seized control of the prison, liberated the rest of its 200 inmates and occupied the town. Joined by 300 townsfolk, the rebels raised the five-star flag of Phan Boi Chau's revolutionary league, cut the telegraph, occupied key buildings, plundered the local treasury and waited for a general uprising to support them.

The insurgents were led by an illiterate militia sergeant, but among the political prisoners held at Thai Nguyen was Phan Boi Chau's first recruit to the 'Journey to the East', Luong Ngoc Quyen. Since 1905 he had travelled for the cause in Japan, Siam and China until, in 1915, he had been extradited from Hong Kong to Vietnam and convicted for playing a role in the 1913 bomb attack in Hanoi. The clarion call of the rebels, which Quyen seems to have penned, appealed to a tradition of border rebellion and banditry, but it was also a litany of resentment at the new taxes and indignities heaped on to the people by the French and the humiliation of the emperor. 'Our country', it said, 'has become poor and powerless like a broken thread. Suffering has taken away our final breath.' Then there was the war itself – 'they requisition our men and use them like a high wall to protect them from bullets' – and the regime at Nguyen Thai prison with its shocking mortality rate from forced labour: 192 dead in 1915, 162 in 1916 and 162 in the first half of 1917. Like the British in Singapore two years earlier, Governor-General Sarraut saw the roots of mutiny in specific local misdeeds, particularly the sadistic corporal punishments inflicted by a low-ranking provincial official called M. Darles. Prison 'isolation colonies' such as the one at Nguyen Thai were never entirely quarantined from society. They threw men of spirit together: in this case, from more than thirty different provinces. But the rebellion also drew urban literati, soldiers, bandits, mine workers, villagers, vagabonds, smugglers and draft dodgers into an army of 'the human nation of the world'. They defended Nguyen Thai against the assaults of regular troops for several days. But in the campaign to pacify the town, hundreds died on both sides.[45] In a riot on Indochina's Château d'If, Poulo Condore, in April 1918, another seventy-five Vietnamese were killed. The French-language newspapers indulged the *colons*' macabre appetite for minute accounts of the final walk of rebels to the guillotine and the manner of their dying.[46]

This paranoia over restive garrisons, insurgent prisons and secret societies spread out from the port cities of colonial Asia to where conditions of dearth were most acutely felt. In 1918 the rice crop in India failed. Exports from Burma to maritime Asia collapsed by 50 per cent in 1919; between January and July the price of Siam and Saigon rice more than doubled, and in July the government of Indochina forbade its export. Governments attempted to buy up crops and control rice stocks, but there was no quick relief, and this only made them the targets of anger which exposed their corruption and the collusion of landlords. There were arson attacks on Chinese merchants in the Philippines, amid charges of speculation.[47] In Singapore, official high-mindedness was punctured by an ugly scandal involving the supply of motorcycles, cars and fruit to the military, which became public thanks to an amateur dramatics production – a traditional medium for the expression of expatriate sentiment. It depicted the well-known manager of the International Restaurant in Raffles Arcade – a Scots-Rumanian Jew from Bombay – 'presenting a pineapple to the GOC': namely, the commander of the garrison and the deliverer of the colony in February 1915, General Ridout, who was popularly known as 'King *Kumsha*' (bribe).[48] In June there were two days of riots in Penang and rice stores were looted. But the impact of these shortages was overshadowed by the global influenza pandemic, which followed the routes of war through the port cities. In the archipelago it was known as 'Singapore fever'. In French Indochina morbidity reached 50 per cent in some areas.[49] In Europe the image of the influenza as a wind from the east was conflated with the wind of revolution.[50]

After the stasis of trench warfare and the shipping shortage, millions of people were once again on the move. Thousands of Chinese labourers returned from France; there was no question of them being allowed to remain. They travelled across Canada chiefly and the Pacific, journeying under a cloak of secrecy.[51] Whole armies were left stranded by the peace: from Arab and Czech legions in Russia to Indians almost everywhere. Over half the Allied troops in Mesopotamia – more than 250,000 men – were Indian and over a third in Palestine. An entire Indian division was captured at the siege of Kut-al-Amara, with perhaps 10,686 men taken prisoner during that campaign as a whole. On their long march deep into Ottoman territory, perhaps 1,708 of them died and 1,324 simply disappeared, 'untraced'.[52] The full agony of such losses was faced in the Punjab, which was as much a 'home front' of the war as any English county or Australian outback town. One in every twenty-seven men in the region had been mobilized: recruiting agents reverted to outright coercion when the official incentives and rewards that had dampened support for Ghadar no longer prevented it resurfacing. The end of the war brought a flood of men back into a Punjab hard hit by economic slump and by the pandemic, which took a quarter of a million lives in the province. Land was no longer available as a bounty. Families confronted the Raj in a more direct way than ever before, in search of information and the pensions owed to them.[53] All homecomings were potentially inflammatory.

The fall of 'Oostenrijk' opened a new fissure across Eurasia. The rift followed the borders established by the Treaty of Brest-Litovsk in 1918 and stretched into the debatable lands of the Caucasus, separating the new Bolshevik regime from its marshalling, encircling enemies. Across it, there were vast, deadly forced expulsions of population.[54] Meanwhile, along the borders of the Raj, old fault lines reopened and wartime plots were resumed by new players. In the first months of peace there were minor uprisings in Burma in the Kuki-Chin-speaking areas. From May 1919 the regime in Kabul found itself embroiled in what soon became known as the Third Anglo-Afghan War. And further east the defence of British India now began at the Amur River, on China's northern frontier. The Allied intervention in Russia in support of the White armies also created uncertain new front lines. Imperial troops, including men from India, were sent to the Baltic; others, from the United States' garrisons in the Philippines and from Canada, were despatched to Vladivostok, with an eye to the Arctic's resources and potential trade. The larger, stated goal of the Allied strategy, however, was the 'closing to [the Bolsheviks] the material resources of Asia, and of bringing to bear against them a part of the enormous allied manpower of that continent'.[55]

Out of this, new imperial constellations were born. The fighting in the Middle East had entrenched the British empire once again in Egypt, under a 'veiled protectorate'. It had brought the British soldiers closer to the holy cities of Islam; Mecca was governed by a British protégé, and on 11 December 1917 General Edmund Allenby made a pilgrim's entry into conquered Jerusalem, on foot, through the Jaffa Gate. One by one, the great port cities of the eastern Mediterranean – Alexandria, Salonika, Haifa – came under the control of the British and French navies before a combined force, including a single, symbolic warship from the United States, took Istanbul itself in November 1918. The French imagined the recreation of the crusader kingdom of Outremer, la Syrie integrale, while the United States and Britain eyed oil in the Gulf: the Anglo-Persian Oil Company looked to extend its state within a state at the Abadan refinery, and recruited some 1,000 men annually for the task.

For a brief moment, the British fashioned a new empire of the Levant.[56] It extended east of the Jordan valley to the Tigris and Euphrates, where British steamship companies launched into the river trade. From New Delhi, the British entertained visions of Punjabi settlers moving into the plains around the Shatt al-Arab and of rebuilding Babylon itself. The Raj dragooned labour on a pharaonic scale: as well as 295,565 combatants, some 293,152 workers went to the Ottoman provinces of Basra, Mosul and Baghdad, around 16,000 of whom were the sweepings of the prisons of the Raj, including 405 juvenile offenders from the Lahore borstal. After the end of the war, there were still 71,000 Indians in the Labour Corps in Mesopotamia, 42,000 more in the Inland Water Transport Directorate, Nepalese quarrymen and 1,000 Chinese carpenters to rebuild Basra dock.[57]

The British Indian Ocean now encompassed both the entire length of the old Swahili coast, having absorbed the German territory of Tanganyika, and also the western Pacific, where German New Guinea and the Bismarck Archipelago were now under Australian occupation. But the old sense of fragility was if anything enhanced. It was clear in New Delhi that the British Indian Army could no longer be used in peacetime to hold down this great arc. As Lord Chelmsford, who had succeeded Lord Hardinge as Viceroy of India in April 1916, argued in February 1919: 'so long as India pays . . . India must control its own Army'.[58] A redemption of the old moral debt seemed to be in the air.

These new imperial possessions were established on old principles, but they had to respond to the new global rhetoric of peace and self-determination. As the leaders of the great powers arrived for the peace conference at Versailles in January 1919, their task was to stabilize the order of the world and to fix and guarantee its borders on the principle of nationality. They gathered under the mood of expectation that had been generated by President Woodrow Wilsons's Fourteen Points outlined in January 1918. But here, too, pessimism was palpable. For many European social thinkers and moralists, the horror of industrial warfare had shaken faith in the truth and supremacy of a civilization based on the ideals of the western Enlightenment. It had also left an indelible mark on the minds of those Asian intellectuals who had led the dialogue with such European cultural values. On visiting England and France for the first time in 1919, Liang Qichao saw only bleakness, ruin and dismay: 'They are in utter despair . . . They once had a great dream about the omnipotence of science. Now their talk is filled with its bankruptcy.'[59]

For colonial subjects, this was the moment when promises of imperial belonging were supposed to translate into palpable political privileges. Pleas for the rights of small nationalities and a more egalitarian citizenship were aired through the press, through public forums and demonstrations, and through appeals that were often addressed directly to Wilson as a benign paterfamilias.[60] But there were a variety of languages of internationalism to draw upon: pacifist, Esperantist, federalist, feminist. And there was what H. G. Wells termed a 'new kind of people': a 'floating population' of legal, humanist and liberal minds committed to international bodies.[61] Some thinkers drew on their exposure to Asian thought and aspirations: Tagore's attack on narrow forms of patriotism in his *Nationalism* (1917) thrilled his admirers in the west. The new internationalism of Bolshevism shared a similar universalist vocabulary.[62] But there was a gathering distrust of received ways of being 'international', and of patrician statesmanship and its halls of mirrors.[63] M. N. Roy, in his open letter to Woodrow Wilson, published from New York and in Spanish from Mexico City, asked 'if your intention and promises to establish peace in the world are sincere':

> It is not in Europe but in the debilitated countries of Asia and Africa that the germs of war in modern times are hatched by the imperialist greed of the European nations, whose ambition throws the world into horrible convulsions causing suffering to people who are in no way to blame for the catastrophes. The panacea that can cure the evils of the world is the complete liberation of all dominated peoples and countries, not only in Europe but also in Asia and Africa. Therefore, our intention of liberating India, if successful, will not only give freedom to a fifth of the world's population which is without question their birthright, but also will prepare the way for humanity towards its goal of peace and fraternity.[64]

Roy's tone was less supplicating than mocking, and his scepticism seemed to be supported by subsequent events. In March 1919 the Philippine Legislature declared its intention to study the means of attaining liberation. A Commission of Independence went to Washington, DC. It met with soothing rhetoric, but no firm timetable for the transfer of full sovereignty was set. When Wilson said that Philippine independence was 'almost in sight', he meant that it lay on some future, far distant, retreating shore.[65]

The empire-minded struggled to comprehend 'nationalism'. British statesmen might support small nationalities at a distant remove, as in the romantic attachment to Greek independence early in the previous century. They had learned to concede 'responsible self-government' to societies that could be seen as an organic outgrowth of 'Anglo-Saxon' settlement and ancient 'Anglo-Saxon' institutions: a 'Greater Britain' encompassing the white Dominions, and, by extension, the United States. But it was a very different question when, in the case of India, or Ireland, they were presented with the demand, not merely for self-government, but for the return of original sovereignty. They mistrusted the models for this adopted by Asian leaders, whether drawn from Mazzini in Italy or Meiji-era statesmen in Japan. Nationalism was seen as a narrow vision, illegitimate in the face of the greater claims of imperial citizenship. It was the creed of babus and lawyers: a *'vakil* raj' of over-educated, frustrated and self-interested men who were not 'the natural leaders of the people'. High policy looked to elevate the 'natural leaders' – the princes, the aristocrats, the old agrarian grandees, the city notables, the merchant moguls – often cloaking them in nationalism's borrowed robes, and to give only limited succour to dissidents.[66]

Beneath all of this lay deep debates about what the concept of original sovereignty might amount to in political terms. In the case of India, although the Ghadarites had appealed to the 1857 Mutiny, they evinced no desire to return to the pre-colonial Mughal sovereignty that had been at stake in the earlier rebellion. Even the supporters of the Ottoman Caliphate appealed to a more universalist vision of Islam-in-the-world than to the last Muslim rulers of India. Gandhi's vision of a federation of village communities was more inclusive but decidedly pre-industrial. The moderate members of Congress looked to inherit directly the 'steel frame' and borders of the Raj itself. But their advocacy, together with the emerging force of the Muslim League, for Dominion status – to be on an equal footing with Canada, Australia, New Zealand and South Africa – had been rejected at the 1917 Imperial Conference in what was seen as a blatant assertion of white racial privilege.[67]

With moderates in mind, the secretary of state for India, Edwin Montagu, and the viceroy, Lord Chelmsford, introduced a limited representative element to provincial politics. This carefully calculated concession was seen as in no ways a demonstration of weakness, but as a return to the mid-nineteenth-century principle that empire was politically and financially a good deal more effective when it rested on influence, or paramountcy, and its cost was borne by others. As crisis after crisis challenged British imperial power, the words of Lord Milner in September 1920 became a steady refrain: 'But is it therefore necessary that we should own it? Is it not sufficient if we have a firm foothold there?'[68] The British empire in the Levant and Asia reverted to treaties and subsidies, and to the practice of indirect rule, often under the guise of a League of Nations 'mandate'. Any concepts of national identity contained within the idea of a 'mandate' were diminished by racial presumptions of backwardness and tutelage; and, in any case, it was not applied to the colonies of the victorious powers. In Malaya, Britain reaffirmed its commitment to the native sultans, notwithstanding the long and significant presence of Indians, Chinese and myriad other peoples in the peninsula. In 1913 the British had established land reservations for Malay ownership; now, as they contemplated political reform in the wake of war, there was a renewed emphasis on the essential Malay-centredness of government. Empire – even in its new vision of a 'Commonwealth of Nations' after 1919 – remained a vast system for the management of racial and ethnic interests: in the words of one of the makers of British Malaya, a 'huge moral-forcing system'.[69]

So, in 1919, there was no new covenant for colonial peoples. Instead, a wave of uprisings across Asia inspired anti-colonial movements which were confounded in their quest for recognition and for the right to plead their cause in Paris. It began, perhaps, in the choke point of imperial communications that was Egypt, where war-weariness and political frustration ignited into revolt. Here the main party took its popular name from the idea of a 'delegation', or *Wafd* – to the British-backed King Fuad, to the Versailles peace conference, to the world at large. The arrest of the *Wafd* leader, Saad Zaghul, on 8 March led to disturbances. The British wartime occupation of Egypt had operated under the fiction of the 'veiled protectorate'. The impact of the vast mobilization of land, water, human and animal power – 72,500 camels and 170,000 camel drivers, 46,000 horses and 15,000 mules for Allenby's campaign in Palestine alone – was felt across the region.[70] The veil had dropped, and the *fellahin* of the Nile delta now stood face to face with their European oppressors. The Egyptian spring of 1919 was increasingly defined, not by the petition and the delegation, but by the crowd, which manifested itself to Russell Pasha, the long-serving British commander of the Cairo police, as 'a solid, unified mass, capable of any violence and reckless of the consequences'.[71]

In India, the Montagu-Chelmsford reforms were introduced under the shelter of the so-called 'Rowlatt Act', specifically the Anarchical and Revolutionary Crimes Act of March 1919, which perpetuated the wartime emergency measures seemingly indefinitely. Chelmsford was confronted by Gandhi's introduction on an all-India scale of his idea of *satyagraha*, in the form of a *hartal* or stoppage in protest at the Act. The viceroy saw it from the first as an elemental challenge to British rule. Notwithstanding Gandhi's unwavering injunctions against violence, there were attacks on colonial officials. 'What a d . . . d nuisance these saintly fanatics are!' Chelmsford wrote to Montagu on 9 April.

'Gandhi is incapable of hurting a fly and is honest as the day, but he enters quite lightheartedly on a course of action which is the negation of all government . . .'.[72] The same day, Gandhi was prohibited from travelling to the Punjab and arrested. There were demonstrations on the 10th in Bombay, Ahmedabad and across the Punjab, particularly in the city of Amritsar, where troops fired on a crowd that was approaching the Civil Lines – the European garden suburb – killing twelve people. In response, five Europeans were murdered, and a woman missionary, Miss Sherwood, was beaten in the street and left for dead. The old hysteria once more engulfed the Raj, and the remaining European women and children in the city were taken into protection in the old fort. The man sent to deal with the trouble was Colonel Reginald Dyer, who had spent part of his war with the Seistan Force, intercepting the infiltration of Indian and German agents from eastern Persia into Afghanistan. On arrival in Amritsar on the 11th, Dyer declared martial law. To all intents and purposes, the city was now pacified.

Two days later, on 13 April, a crowd gathered at Jallianwala Bagh, a piece of public land a few hundred yards away from the Golden Temple of the Sikhs. It was enclosed by the high backs of houses, a low wall to one side, and approached by narrow alleyways. It had been a public gathering place for some years. That afternoon, around 20,000 people were there. Some were playing cards; others had come into town for the cattle market or a holiday; others listened to a senior lawyer of the city speak, the latest in three hours of speeches. Around 7.30 p.m., Dyer arrived with ninety Baluchi and Gurkha troops and two armoured cars. Fifty rifles swiftly formed up at the entrance to the Bagh. After thirty seconds, they were ordered by Dyer to open fire. No warning was given. They fired for ten minutes without pause, some 1,650 rounds in all. Dyer personally directed their aim where the panicked crowd was thickest, its members scrambling over each other to reach the narrow exits of the Bagh. According to the British estimate, 379 people died and 1,200 were wounded. Indian witnesses put the numbers far higher. There were, it was said, perhaps 200 bodies down one well alone. Dyer later acknowledged that had he been able to bring the machine guns on the armoured cars to bear he would have used them too. He 'would do all men to death if they were going to continue the meeting'.[73] The wounded were left to fend for themselves: 'not my business', said Dyer. For Britain and its empire, such a direct toll of civilian life had not been seen since the Morant Bay Rebellion of 1865.[74] Amritsar was, in a crucial sense, cold vengeance for the rebellion of February 1915.

The entire Punjab was once more in lockdown, and little news leaked out. One of the first Congress leaders to reach Amritsar was Jawaharlal Nehru. He had returned from his studies in England in 1912, by his own admission 'a bit of a prig with little to commend me'.[75] Amritsar changed him. He visited the Bagh and the street in which the missionary lady had been pulled off her bicycle, where Dyer had forced townspeople to crawl on their bellies and had summarily flogged suspects. Nehru and others began collecting evidence, as Congress launched its own inquiry. When he appeared before the government commission investigating the events in Amritsar, Dyer did not disguise the fact that he had made the decision to order his men to open fire before he entered the Bagh, and that he had done so with the intention of 'producing a sufficient moral effect' on the entire Punjab. This went beyond the loose conventions of British martial law across the empire. But Dyer believed he had saved India from a new Mutiny, and many Britons in India and at home agreed with him. 'It was', he told the commission, 'a merciful though horrible act and they ought to be thankful to me for doing it . . . I thought it would be doing a jolly lot of good and they would realise that they were not to be wicked.' Dyer had been born in the Punjab. He seemed to embody an entire generation of imperial manliness and all the psychological tensions masked by its habits of mastery.[76]

As Dyer left the inquiry in Lahore by sleeper train for Delhi, he bragged to his fellow passengers that he could have reduced Amritsar 'to a heap of ashes, but he took pity on it and refrained'. Jawaharlal Nehru was in the same carriage and heard it all from an upper sleeping berth. He saw Dyer get down at Delhi wearing striped pink pyjamas and a dressing gown. He was appalled by the banal callousness of the man, but saw, as Gandhi repeatedly stressed, that the real enemy was the system that produced him. In these months, Jawaharlal drew closer to the older man.[77] Both the younger Nehru and his father, Motilal, had been torn between the moderate and extremist positions. Gandhi offered them another path.

No one was prosecuted for the killings in the Bagh. In the meantime, 581 Indians were arrested in connection with the disturbances, and

108 were sentenced to death. In the public outrage that followed, these sentences were commuted, but not before eighteen men had already been hanged. To Indian observers, there had never been an equivalence between white and Indian murder. In Calcutta, the police had first confronted the urban mob in riots in the 1890s. Fearful of public opinion in Britain, they had shied away from buckshot and relied on *lathis*, or, if they fired at all, fired blanks. But as these tactics became known, a harder line was taken, using European police and troops. In the Tallah riots in Calcutta in 1897, where violence was anti-police in character, live ammunition was used indiscriminately. In one confrontation eleven people were shot dead.[78] The terrorist violence in Bengal after 1907 was justified by some as a reckoning for the silent attrition of white murder and judicial violence. What happened at Amritsar was singular only in the bluff candour of its perpetrator and the extent to which it was discussed at home.

Debates in Britain focused on the spread of 'Dyerism' at home, in a society that saw itself labouring under the brutalizing effects of war. But, for the upholders of empire, Dyer was the principal victim of the affair. Montagu warned Dyer's defenders in the Commons – as the soldier watched from the gallery – that if they backed what he termed 'terrorism', Indians would quickly see 'your rule in India as being impossible on *modern* ideas of what an Empire means'. Montagu, a Jew, was censured for saying it, in a wave of anti-Semitic comment likened by *The Times* to the Dreyfus Affair.[79] These rebellions were not the border skirmishing of a bygone empire, for which there was, on the part of Europeans, now considerable nostalgia. The echoes of mutiny brought frontier warfare to the heart of the imperial city and to the streets outside their own homes. In order to defend this world of privilege, colonial officials were confronted with the question: how far were they willing to go?[80]

BAREFOOT INTO THE STREETS

The older generation of Asian radicals had asked the same question. Some still looked to imperial law – perhaps more than they liked to recognize – and to its essential goodness as an ideal by which to hold empire to account. Others transferred their hopes to the international institutions of the League of Nations that were setting up offices in the Hôtel National in Geneva. And so, despite the near universal censorship, the 'war of voice' continued. But, in the spring of 1919, the prison mutiny in Tonkin, the 'Red Days' in Surabaya and Semarang, state killing in the Punjab, the undertow of holy violence in West Java – all defined a new era of the 'age upside down', one in which a new generation thrived and came to the fore in accelerated succession. In the Netherlands Indies, they defined themselves as *orang pergerakan*, men and women of 'movement'. They were a generation who knew of nothing else but to move. They actively sought to free themselves from ties to the Dutch colonial regime. In British India too, to throw aside a government scholarship, as Aurobindo Ghose and Har Dayal had once done to shock contemporaries, was now an established rite of passage. Many more young men and women now refused colonial education altogether. Free Schools and night schools multiplied in the moving cities of Asia. The spring of 1919 was a moment of open politics; but by the very nature of the 'upside down', what began above could very suddenly move below.[81] Following the logic of this path, the new generation stepped out into the global underground.

Across frontiers, the villages of exile and resistance prepared to receive them. In Siam, the situation of the Vietnamese communities there had turned precarious when the country abandoned its neutrality and joined the war on the side of the Allies in July 1917. Without Phan Boi Chau – who had helped some of them settle there when the Japanese authorities clamped down on 'the Journey to the East', and who was still in exile in China – they were rudderless.[82] But in 1919, one of Chau's early followers, Dang Thuc Hua, who had been expelled from Siam for his revolutionary activities in 1917, returned to the country. He now attacked Chau and Prince Cuong for their elitism, and set out personally to muster young men and women from Nghe An and neighbouring districts to make the journey to Siam, to the established haven in Phichit province. 'We must', Dang Thuc Hua declared, 'go barefoot into the streets and byways and live the life of the common people.'[83] One of his recruits was a young man called Pham Hong Thai. Some of those who later fell into the hands of the French described a well-travelled pilgrims' way; ironically, their journey was hastened by French road construction, particularly route 8, which ran some 200 miles from Nghe An through the highlands of Laos to the border with Siam.[84]

One young man who answered the call in 1920 was the twenty-year-old Le Van Phan. Inspired by a nephew of Dang Thuc Hua, he left Nghe An in a party of five men and five women. After entering Laos, they walked south for ten days to Thakek, where they crossed the Mekong into Siam. All of them fell sick with fever, and local helpers had to move them in slow stages by foot and by train on to Phichit. After some months, Le Van Phan was entrusted with a mission to reach Phan Boi Chau in China. He headed to Bangkok, and then took a British vessel to Hainan Island. There he joined some young Vietnamese émigrés travelling to Canton, where he lived with other Vietnamese for some months in the house of a Chinese lady while she taught them the language. The group then journeyed north to Hangzhou, in order that Phan Boi Chau could enrol them in a school to learn English. But Phan Boi Chau's prestige among young idealists was waning, and Le Van Phan's English improved only slowly. In search of better schooling Phan first went back to Canton and then proceeded to Hong Kong and to Tokyo. From Japan, he returned to China in 1922 with a revolver to assassinate the Vietnamese who had encouraged Chau to write a treatise that seemed to endorse Sarraut's promise of 'association'. The man, Le Van Phan was convinced, had been a government agent.[85] In southern China and Japan, the Vietnamese were ever more closely entwined within the anarchist networks that stretched along the great maritime trunk road of Asia.

Throughout 1919 the imperial powers were haunted by jinns uncorked by wartime plots. It was not clear which were the most devilish, but the humiliation of the House of Osman through the Allied occupation of Istanbul and the slow dismemberment of its ancient empire signalled the start of a long struggle of succession in Eurasia. Pan-Islam, after the war, may have been more a product of the western imagination than a policy of any Islamic power. But while the fate of the Ottoman Caliphate hung in the balance, and the continuity of 1,000 years of Indo-Persian civilization was in jeopardy, a heightened sense of the crisis of Islam was carried across Asia by pilgrims as the sea routes to Mecca reopened. It was taken up as a popular cause at public meetings throughout India and in disputations in the coffee shops of the Malay Archipelago. Britain's 'man on the inside' in Penang explained how every café acted as a political salon: those on the Magazine Road were for the Malays; those on Campbell and Chulia Streets for the Indian

Muslims and Malays. In one *muturbak*, or spiced pancake, shop, he reported, the Caliphate question and Indian home rule were discussed every evening.[86]

Turkish refugees appeared as far afield as Shanghai. They included Sami Bey, brother and companion to Esref Bey, a leader within Enver Pasha's notorious 'Special Organization' whom the British had been watching in India and had imprisoned in Malta.[87] Sami arrived with four other men in March or April 1919 having travelled from Afghanistan through Kashgar into China. The five of them seemed to be well off, though it was not clear where their money came from. Over the next months, their visitors were logged, as were their 'long walks in the settlement' and visits to the homes of Japanese. They used as a go-between the same Abel Ettinger who had been gofer to the German conspiracies in China. They were said to be waiting for news from Enver Pasha, who was himself now a fugitive. Sami would later join Enver in Tashkent.[88] But all eyes in Asia were now on Mustafa Kemal Pasha, the victor of Gallipoli, who since 30 April 1919 had led the Turkish resistance to the Allied occupation. In Malaya and the Indies, the martial, modernizing patriotism of Mustafa Kemal as a new 'champion of Islam' captivated the imagination of the *orang pergerakan*, not least the young Sukarno, who began to draw from the future Atatürk's actions a repertoire of state-making strategies.[89]

These political shifts became entangled with an international 'Red panic'. The British tended to conflate pan-Islamism and communism, seeing both of them as 'Made in Germany'.[90] British secret service agents, fired by their role in the wartime power game, looked for the first seepage of the ideas of the Russian Revolution into the eastern Mediterranean. In Istanbul, they saw Bolshevik agents in 'the low quarters of Galata and Stamboul, frequenting beer halls and coffee houses', according to one report, passing the word among 'sailors, *hamals* [porters], lower class workmen and riffraff of the city'.[91] However, in 1918 and 1919, when War Office lists of Bolsheviks were circulated by the British across their diplomatic missions in Asia, it met with a sceptical response. But already 'Bolshevik' proved a versatile term of abuse, hurled at business rivals and political enemies.[92]

The Second International had collapsed during the war in a vicious split between those who had followed the call of patriotism and those, led by Lenin in exile, who did not. But western European socialists looked to revive the old International away from Russian leadership, in what Karl Radek – an influential journalist and theorist active in the German movement and now firmly in the Bolshevik camp – called contemptuously the 'Two and a Half' International.[93] As early as 1914, Lenin had proclaimed: 'The Second International is dead, overcome by opportunism . . . long live the Third International.'[94] The first meeting of the Third Communist International, on 4 March 1919, was called in the context of appeals to western European workers and their parties for support, and in the belief that the spark of revolution would soon be set alight. Barely fifty people attended the gathering in the Kremlin in Moscow; perhaps thirty-five were 'delegates', and only twelve of them had credentials from any political group. Eight of these were Russians, including the representatives of the Communist Party, Lenin, Bukharin, Georgy Chicherin – the Commissar for Foreign Affairs – Trotsky and Zinoviev, who was elected chairman of the new organization. Its official language was German, although there was only one German delegate present, and he was instructed to oppose the new International as premature. Many of the other 'delegates' were simply exiles who happened to be in Russia at the time.[95]

Amid all the white faces at the meeting, however, there were a handful of Asian attendees. There were, in fact, plenty of Asians present in Russia, not least around 500,000 Chinese, most of whom were widely dispersed across Siberia. At the war's end, their conditions had collapsed as many of the mines and enterprises that had employed them went bust. They became vagrants in the streets of Petrograd or Omsk or Moscow, where there were some 3,000 refugees of war. Some, perhaps 40,000–50,000 of them, signed up for the Red Army; one became a personal bodyguard to Lenin.[96] One of the Chinese representatives at the Congress, who claimed to speak on behalf of his countrymen in Russia, was Liu Zerong (also known as Liu Zhazou). He had been brought as a boy to the Caucasus by his father, who had taught tea cultivation there; Liu himself had studied architectural engineering in Petrograd. He was interviewed by Lenin, and he addressed the gathering in Chinese followed by Russian. It was, he told the delegates, the first time the Chinese people had been represented at an International; and he assured them that their meeting enjoyed 'the liveliest sympathy among the Chinese people'.[97]

More than it had in the first two Internationals, the 'relentless battle against the monster of world imperialism' – as Liu called it – took centre stage.[98] The global compass of the new 'revolutionary epoch' was clear from the Congress's deliberations, and the final manifesto, drafted by Trotsky, pointed to unrest in Vietnam and strikes in India. But it was the emancipation of the working class in the imperial home countries that would dictate the future:

> The workers and peasants not only of Annam, Algiers, and Bengal, but also of Persia and Armenia, will gain their opportunity of independent existence only when the workers of England and France have overthrown Lloyd George and Clemenceau and taken State power into their own hands . . .
> Colonial slaves of Africa and Asia! The hour of proletarian dictatorship in Europe will also be the hour of your own liberation![99]

In all this, the colonial world was expected to have little voice of its own.

Across Asia, the Bolshevik Revolution did not arrive as a sudden event. There was a slow trickle of 'Bolsheviks' through Vladivostok into China. In Shanghai, a scholar of Japanese and Chinese known as Mikhail Popov, who was supposedly attached to the Red Army's general staff, appeared briefly in May 1918, and perhaps again in 1919 and 1920; and a Jewish Bolshevik called Joseph Malkin was apprehended in August 1918; but it was not clear if either man had been sent, or what authority they carried. The presence of a small delegation in the city was reported in April 1919, then it disappeared as quietly as it came. There were also rumours of Bolshevik gold. However, the intercepted men seemed to be refugees and ex-prisoners of war, Czechs mostly, who identified with the revolution rather than served as its agents.[100] Asians declared themselves 'Bolshevik' in a haphazard way, and often not as the result of any direct encounter from outside. Indeed, the term 'Bolshevik' first appeared in Bangkok as a trademark for gun caps with the word 'Bolshevikials' under a mock British royal coat of arms.[101]

The more immediate challenge to the balance of power in East Asia came not out of Russia but from Japan. British officials still resented the tacit support of the Taisho government for Indian intrigues on their home soil, and remained apprehensive of Japanese encroachment in

India and Central Asia. A central source of this security panic was the career diplomat Frank Ashton-Gwatkin, who had attended the funeral of the last ruler of the Tokugawa shogunate, Prince Tokugawa Yoshinobu, in 1913. He combined his elaborate assessments of Japan's threat to British imperial interests in Asia with a certain Japanophilia. Attached to the intelligence operation in Singapore for his expert knowledge of Japan, he spent some of his time writing a novel, *Kimono*. It was the story of an Anglo-Japanese marriage, heavy on racial stereotypes and imbued with an ominous sense of Japan's rise to power. It was published in 1921, under the pseudonym 'John Paris', to some controversy.[102] Those whose familiarity with Asia and Japan equalled Ashton-Gwatkin's, and who read his intelligence reports, worried at their 'anti-Japanese bias'.[103]

However, the Indian policeman at large, David Petrie, subscribed to the idea of the Japanese threat. He acknowledged that Ghadar's networks were almost moribund, but he believed that the old visions of pan-Asianism had left an afterglow. In 1917 the Commercial Press in Shanghai had published a sympathetic study entitled *Is Japan a Menace to Asia?* by Taraknath Das. It was immediately banned in India and the Straits Settlements but circulated widely. Meanwhile, its author continued to serve twenty-two months in Leavenworth Federal Penitentiary in Kansas. Behind all this, the British saw the guiding genius of Rash Behari Bose, although Rash Behari himself, they discovered, was no longer on the 'active list' but living under official protection in a remote coastal village near Katsuura in Chiba prefecture in Japan.[104] Fellow travellers such as the French writer Paul Richard and the 'notorious' W. W. Pearson, disciples of Aurobindo Ghose and Tagore, now beat a path to Japan. The arrival in Tokyo of the poet and playwright James Cousins, a veteran of the Abbey Theatre circle in Dublin, caused the British added consternation. He sought, via theosophy, a mystical connection between the Celtic peoples and the east, and published, in 1922, a short book on *The Cultural Unity of Asia*. A small but resourceful republic of letters, inclined to spiritualism and radicalism, continued to promote Japan's grand designs in Asia.[105]

But most worrying to the European imperial powers was the more tangible presence of Japanese within their Asian colonies, particularly what seemed a coordinated southwards push into isolated frontier zones such as Sarawak and British North Borneo and along the mighty rivers of Dutch Borneo. Here Japanese in large numbers had been visible since 1905, in pearling stations and timber camps, and as stowaways on coaling ships, scouting strategic small islands along the sea lanes.[106] The British and the Dutch colonial authorities were now obsessed with the 'sightseeing parties', educational delegations and small armies of pedlars, dentists and photographers that seemed to be at the forefront of a coordinated 'Nanyo ["south seas"] expansion'. European planters began to believe that the takeover of the Netherlands Indies was inevitable. Certainly, Japanese visiting Java were aware of the prophecy of the twelfth-century king Joyoboyo that the rule of the white men would end with the coming of the dwarfish yellow men, who would reign as long as 'a maize seed took to flower'. In a time of the 'upside down', locals were reviving it too.[107]

In Malaya, the Japanese consul estimated there were 3,000 Japanese living in Singapore and 8,000 up-country in the peninsula. In early 1918 there were around 500 arriving each month, of whom roughly half went on to the Netherlands Indies. Most of them were 'vagabond, self-styled ronin', travelling third-class, and peddling drugs and women. Liberty men from the Japanese warships that routinely visited Singapore swaggered down the middle of the streets, defying the traffic, their arrogance expressing the ' "Prussian" idea' that they were the new protectors of Singapore. Meanwhile, Japanese publications at home and abroad exalted the role of the nation's sailors and citizens in putting down the 1915 mutiny.[108] For the people of cities like Singapore, Japan was a source of cheap consumer goods. The new generation of Asian clerks obtained the cheap shirts and ties which they were forced to wear from Japanese department stores. Asian children pestered their parents for cheap Japanese toys. Asian businessmen stayed in cheap Japanese hotels. Visitors to the Japanese Commercial Museum that opened in Singapore in November 1918 wondered at its spectacle of modernity. Troupes of Japanese acrobats travelled with the circuses that went from city to city, colony to colony.

But Japan's burgeoning power could also serve as a stark contrast and a bitter affront to other Asian nations. This was keenly felt in China after the Japanese peremptory 'Twenty-One Demands' of 1915. The sudden death of Yuan Shikai in June 1916, at the age of fifty-six, weakened the hold of centralized government in China still further. The northern warlord armies still dominated the constitutional process of the Beiyang government in Beijing. After the death of Yuan Shikai, and his failed attempt to accede to the imperial throne, they had reluctantly restored the old emperor, Puyi, for twelve days in 1917. Sun Yat-sen had returned from exile in 1916 to lead a constitutional protection movement which set up a military government in Canton to challenge the northern factions. But in early 1919 it was defeated and Sun was driven back to his villa in the French Concession of Shanghai, where he consoled himself with grandiose plans for a 'second industrial revolution' by means of the construction of 100,000 miles of new railway in China.[109] Continued humiliation at the hands of foreign powers polarized politics. In early May 1918 the Beiyang government agreed to an unequal alliance with Japan. Chinese students in Tokyo met to protest and began to head home to China in disgust, angered by the weakness of their republic. Such returned students were becoming an ever-more palpable force in China: a 1917 survey reported that, out of some 1,673 of them, 1,024 claimed to have entered politics.[110]

Beijing was a tableau of the contradictions between the vision and reality of a 'new China'. Modern ministries were scattered throughout the city, indistinguishable from older residences that once dominated the cityscape. The Legation Quarter, with its high walls and barracks for the troops of many nations, was a constant reminder of the foreign intervention during the Boxer Rebellion. In the midst of it all was the brooding stillness of the Forbidden City, where fallen nobles and ministers still paraded in their sedan chairs to visit the deposed emperor, the young Puyi, and demanded the old ritual deference from shopkeepers and rickshaw men. These tensions were played out in Beijing University, or Beida, in its late imperial buildings and in the frictions between students and intellectuals who could still remember their place in the old dynastic order. Young, serious students, many from the more radical environment of the south, mocked the 'lao yeh ["milord"] gentry ways' of their seniors, their long robes and conservative attitudes.[111]

The writer and translator Zhou Shuren had returned to China from Japan in 1909. After the fall of the Qing in 1911 he worked in the Ministry of Education in Beijing. It was a fallow time for him, until his patron, Cai Yuanpei, became rector of Beida in 1917. Zhou was then drawn, reluctantly at first, into the circles of the journal *New Youth*

(*Xin qingnian*). Its guiding lights (and founders) were Chen Duxiu and Li Dazhao, Beida's dean of arts and librarian; like many of the writers who rallied to its pages, they had also spent time in Japan. Established in 1915, in the wake of Yuan Shikai's attempts to assume the monarchy, the magazine was a call to youth – in reality, elite youth – to adopt a new, more universalist culture to save the republic.

As Beida's dean of arts, Chen Duxiu oversaw the introduction of courses in Esperanto, and encouraged the students to reach out to the city with experiments in mass education. Although these efforts were not always a success, the lecture halls of Beida were often overcrowded with attendees not formally attached to the university.[112] A native of Anhui province with a gentry-official background, and with first-hand experience of the tiers of the old imperial examination system, Chen taught liberation from Confucian values and hierarchy, and a global outlook. His support for a new, strong nation was not unconditional. 'A nation's purpose', he wrote in a famous essay on 'Patriotism and Consciousness' in 1914, 'is the protection of the people's power and the seeking to increase the people's happiness and prosperity. If it does not carry out this duty the nation's existence has no special honor. Its death would not be regretted.'[113] China, given the weakness of its republican institutions, was not yet a 'true' nation. Such arguments were voiced from a position of high privilege and often extolled virtues that were drawn from Confucianism. But Chen's willingness to argue that women, workers and peasants were at the forefront of the exercise of democracy marked a clear departure from China's past. This was a lesson from the world war, and also from Chen's own disillusion at the state of governance in China, of 'these days of international powers, political horrors, the crime of private wealth, the darkness of war, the inequality of classes . . .'.[114] Such views were echoed in darkly symbolic form in a story Zhou Shuren contributed to *New Youth* in 1918 under the pen name 'Lu Xun'. Entitled 'Diary of a Madman', it tells of a man who awakens to realize that his fellow villagers have been practising cannibalism for centuries, and is then confined as a lunatic as a result of his insight.[115]

A shared animus at the old system crystallized in debates on China's place in the world. 'Warlordism', a popular pejorative term for the politics of the provincial militarists, was seen as a symptom of imperialism and the weakness of China's democracy.[116] When China's demands at

Versailles for the restoration of its territories at Qingdao were finally rejected by the European powers, the news spread through Beijing like wildfire. There was fury that Qingdao remained in Japanese hands. On the evening of 3 May 1919 students from across the city rallied at Beida's school of law. There were fiery speeches, and one student bit his finger and wrote in blood on a banner: 'Return our Qingdao'. The next morning some 3,000 students from across Beijing rallied on the square before the Tiananmen, or 'Gate of Heavenly Peace', and the threshold of the dethroned emperor. They shouted demands for an hour, wrote slogans on the joss notes ('hell banknotes') used at funerals, and recited mock funerary couplets for the ministers who had failed China so badly at Versailles. Then they marched to the Japanese legation, but soldiers and police barred the way, and they had no permit to enter. Determined to hold someone directly to account, part of the crowd surged towards the house of one of the Versailles delegates, the deputy foreign minister, Cao Rulin, who was seen to be sympathetic to Japan. Ten or so students – at least one of them a not-so-young twenty-nine years of age – broke into the house and opened its doors to the rest. They punched one of the minister's house guests – China's minister to Tokyo, who had played a role in acquiescing to Japanese demands – terrorized Cao's concubine and set fire to his bed. The rector of Beida, Cai Yuan-pei, resigned and left the city. Thirty-two students were arrested, before being released three days later. One student died, but only because the demonstration had exacerbated his tuberculosis.[117]

The students endeavoured to prove to western observers that this was a modern protest enacted in an orderly manner in the public spaces and new thoroughfares of Beijing. In the words of one leader, it was an awakening of sorts: 'a new way of doing things, applying a new method of thinking, using colloquial, easily understood language to communicate with the masses, and using effective organisational techniques . . . It embodied the progress of the age.'[118] For them it heralded a 'life or death' struggle that propelled them out into the world. The key activists were now younger, a self-conscious and exclusive generation; there was an invisible threshold by which, if one was born too early or too late, one was on the wrong side of history as they understood it. They shared a conviction that the generation before them was ill equipped for leadership and had, by its failings, relinquished such a role. But this fissure was more imaginary – and exaggerated for effect – than real.

They were somewhat selective in their self-fashioning, even in the choice of some of their intellectual inspirations, which included members of the generation in between, the generation of 'lasts and firsts'. Lu Xun was thirty-seven years old and had spent most of the last decade trapped in the bureaucratic inertia the students were challenging. Chen Duxiu was forty. He had increasing doubts about the efficacy of the students as yet another 'movement of constitutions'. Soon, however, two of his own sons would break with him and head abroad.[119]

Almost immediately, 'May Fourth' came to symbolize a rejection of the old ways and the birth of a new culture: another fury of enlightenment. Demonstrations and boycotts soon spread to the divided port cities. The moment news of the protest reached Shanghai on 5 May, a city-wide students' union was formed encompassing some sixty-one schools. It garnered wider support with the fourth anniversary of China's acquiescence to Japan's Twenty-One Demands, which fell on 9 May, and through a boycott took on a more popular dimension. By 15 June there was a five-day shutdown of the city's Japanese cotton mills in a strike involving some 30,000 labourers. Perhaps the largest single episode of violence occurred in Tokyo itself, on 7 May, when 400 demonstrating Chinese students were confronted with more than 1,000 Japanese cavalrymen; over a quarter of the protestors were injured, though none fatally.[120]

If May Fourth saw the advent of 'students' as new political and social actors, its legacy lay as much in their methods as what they thought and symbolized. The longer-term and deeper strands of activity that lay behind these events were located not only in the sites where the most prominent champions of the new ideas were to be found, but also in provincial cities away from the coast. In the cities of Wuhan, for example, the heart of the 1911 Wuchang uprising, there was an interlocking world of literary and study societies, cooperative bookstores and bodies such as the YMCA, with its hiking, singing, socializing and group discussions. These overlapped with mutual aid societies on a more radical model.[121] Similar constellations were to be found in other Chinese cities. As one young writer explained it:

As to the actions which should be undertaken once we have united, there is one extremely violent party, which uses the method 'Do unto others as

352

they do unto you' to struggle desperately to the end with the aristocrats and capitalists. The leader of this party is a man named Marx who was born in Germany. There is another party more moderate than that of Marx. It does not expect rapid results, but begins by understanding the common people. Men should all have a morality of mutual aid, and work voluntarily. As for the aristocrats and capitalists, it suffices that they repent and turn toward the good, and that they are able to work and to help people rather them harming them; it is not necessary to kill them. The ideas of this party are broader and more far-reaching. They want to unite the whole globe into a single country, unite the human race in a single family, and attain together in peace, happiness, and friendship – not friendship as understood by the Japanese – an age of prosperity. The leader of this party is a man named Kropotkin, who was born in Russia.[122]

The author was a young history teacher and review editor in Hunan province called Mao Zedong. He had recently returned from Beijing where, between August 1918 and March 1919, he had been one of the many non-students who attended classes at Beida and had worked in the university's library. Before that, he had formed part of the active circle based around the Hunan First Normal School in Changsha, a reformist teacher-training college whose curriculum combined classical Chinese pedagogy with new forms of learning that included many thinkers from the European Enlightenment. Its teachers had spent time in Japan, Germany and even Scotland, and they introduced *New Youth* to their students.[123] One of the principal acts of the Hunan group, spearheaded by Mao Zedong, had been to set up a 'Culture Books' agency in Changsha. In the absence of a 'national' press, it signed up subscribers to newspapers from Beijing and Shanghai, particularly for their literary and political supplements.[124] In an important sense, therefore, much of the intellectual substance of May Fourth had already permeated these circles.

In other places, May Fourth was distant thunder. In the interior of Fujian province, in Zhangping, only a handful of people read the newspapers in the local reading room. News of strikes and boycotts in the region, or of what happened in Beijing, normally took some time to filter through. No student had even seen a copy of *New Youth*. But then, here too, the effects of May Fourth were eventually felt. As one nineteen-year-old, Zheng Chaolin, later remembered it: 'Students who normally never stirred were now active; students who never spoke were now voluble. The reading room was crowded, current events were common knowledge, and, most important of all, the students now controlled their own association.'[125]

In the swirling currents of new thought in Fujian, a military commander called Chen Jiongming had been swayed by the anarchist-inspired work-study movement that had emerged in Paris before the war, and acted as a sponsor to students. In the years of global conflict, the movement's founder, Li Shizeng, kept alive an ideal of a humanist, republican, progressive and scientific France. On the back of the vast recruitment of 'workers as soldiers', there was now a sizeable organization down to provincial and city level in China – particularly in Hunan, Sichuan and Guangdong – that could send a smaller number of young men and women aged sixteen to twenty-five to Europe as 'students as workers'. From 1919 to 1921 more than 1,600 students were sent to France.[126]

With a contribution from his family and the county magistrate, and with a great public fanfare, in November 1919 Zheng Chaolin found himself on a work-study scholarship to Paris. He travelled from the river port of Zhangzhou to Canton, and then to Hong Kong, where he joined the Messageries Maritimes liner *Paul Lecat*, which was en route from Shanghai to Marseilles via the Indian Ocean with some 200 students on board. For the first time, Zheng met students from 'across the river'. They struck him as 'a new sort', with their portable libraries of the new learning, where he came across a copy of *New Youth* with an article 'by someone called Chen Duxiu'. 'I experienced my personal May Fourth aboard that packet-liner.'[127]

THE PACKET-LINER REVOLUTION

It was a packet-liner revolution. The news of May Fourth from Beijing spread more quickly abroad than it did to some parts of China. In the Chinese Nanyang, the 'south seas' of maritime Southeast Asia, the sense of humiliation that had goaded the crowds in Beijing or Shanghai was, if anything, experienced with a greater intensity. In Singapore, for instance, Japan was in many ways much nearer to hand, as were the everyday indignities of western imperialism. Here the growth of Japanese trade, the high visibility of Japanese warships and sailors provoked popular anger – 'very cocky and unpleasant they were', admitted one colonial policeman.[128] Singapore was an overwhelmingly Chinese society, dominated by young men, and, increasingly, young women. The city had been at the forefront of protests against Japan's Twenty-One Demands in early 1915, and knew how to organize itself. As early as 9 May 1919 the British colonial police started making arrests and moving against inflammatory publications.

On 19 June students took to the streets; they were younger than those in Beijing – fifteen or sixteen years of age – and rougher. They targeted Japanese shops and cafés, and the Japanese Commercial Museum, throwing crockery, glassware and other merchandise into the streets; the women in the Japanese brothels of Tan Quee Street were forced to do the same. Some sixteen premises were damaged and a soap factory in the north of the city was set alight. The chief of police was attacked, and shots were fired. It was the most serious disorder since the 1915 mutiny. But this time the colonial authorities – the police, the Straits Volunteers and seamen from HMAS *Sydney* – were better prepared. Martial law was proclaimed; two men were shot and killed, and another died from a bayonet wound. One of the dead was Tamil: it was not solely a Chinese mob; the anger was contagious. Around 131 people were arrested, including twelve Japanese, and twenty-one Hainanese waiters at the Europe Hotel for refusing to serve meals to Japanese guests.[129] In a futurist image, a Japanese newspaper likened the bonfires that blazed through the night to an air-raid.[130]

Riots also broke out in Penang and Kuala Lumpur, and an anti-Japanese boycott spread across colonies to the Chinese in Batavia, Semarang and Surabaya. In Penang, the protests were enflamed by rice shortages; on 22 June all the banks were shut, the volunteers were called out and machine guns readied for use.[131] Placards, posters and threatening letters spelled out a campaign of violence. A Chinese firm accused of breaking the boycott by dealing in Japanese matches from Hong Kong had a bomb placed outside its Singapore godown, which grazed a passer-by with a lead slug. In September cyclostyled leaflets appeared: 'Announcement of the Death Sentence' and 'Reasons for Throwing the Bomb'.[132] There were five more incidents of bombs and arson in Singapore over the next six months.[133] A curfew had been implemented and was lifted only on 9 September, when Chinese businesses were ordered to resume trade. But the protest took on a further symbolic dimension when, across the peninsula and in Singapore, the Chinese community also boycotted the official celebrations of the Allied victory.

For the first time, British officials in Malaya blamed 'communists'. That year, in Singapore, a school had celebrated May Day, and a Patriotic League and a Truth Society were discovered with links to a 'Bolshevist' society in Canton.[134] But the real force was the anarchist networks that had spread before and during the war from Japan and Canton through Manila. Many of those involved were followers of the leading inspiration of Chinese anarchism, Liu Shifu, known simply without his family name as 'Shifu', a homophonic pun to suggest 'master', who died in 1915. They arrived in Malaya and Singapore to work as journalists or printers or schoolteachers, and amounted, the British believed, to signs that a more concrete branch of Shifu's organization was being established in Malaya.

One of the most influential travellers was Wang Yu-ting, who had first arrived in Malaya as early as 1907, as a sixteen-year-old dockyard worker. In 1918 he had left for Red Semarang and edited an anarchist newspaper called *Truth* until he was picked up by the Dutch police and eventually banished to Hong Kong in September 1919. During his time in Malaya, Wang had introduced into Kuala Lumpur's anarchist circles a young man from Fujian who had studied in Japan called Goh Tunban. Goh established his own paper in Kuala Lumpur in March 1919, having attracted funding from patriotic Chinese businessmen and supporters of the Kuomintang, a revolutionary body created by Sun Yat-sen in exile, with his morally charged manifesto. But the journal's name, *Yiqun Bao*, indicated that it spoke for the masses, and Goh's editorials carried the clear imprint of anarchist thinking.

In fact, *Yiqun Bao* operated within a continuum that stretched from China throughout the archipelago, in which nationalist, mutualist and communist thought were given shared tongue through anarchist ideas – often quite literally so, with the promotion of Esperanto. In the words of the feminist revolutionary Zhang Ruoming, who travelled to France as a work-study scholar in 1920, it was a 'hodgepodge' of 'those who speak of "New Thought," those who say "Democracy," those who say "Marxism," those who introduce "Bolshevism" '. It sparked fierce polemics between those who sought to dissolve the state – by acts of violence if need be – and those who privileged the creation of a vanguard of the proletariat on the new Bolshevik model. But, for a moment in time, it was defined more by its creative eclecticism and, above all, by its commitment to reach out to the ordinary people and 'go barefoot into the streets'.[135]

As early as April 1919 Goh Tun-ban used *Yiqun Bao* to support the radical movement in Semarang, and on May Day he announced the goal of 'a free and happy land of mutual aid communism'. In the wake of May Fourth, he published an uncompromising series of rallying cries in open letters. Then there was a further call to action in response to the repressive acts of the colonial regimes in Malaya and elsewhere. On 29 July Goh Tun-ban was arrested along with five other Chinese writers and educators. The so-called 'six gentlemen' – the honorific signalled the high status of popular intellectuals in a society dominated by workers and small traders – became a cause célèbre that threatened further mass protest. *Yiqun Bao* published a stirring account of the police interrogation of Goh, which he most probably penned himself. When asked if he had 'ever propagated anarchism', Goh was defiant: 'Yes, I have. That ism aims to eliminate *chiangchuan* (repressive authority), cultivate humanity and benefit people the world over. It is undoubtedly the most sacred ism.'[136]

This was to be Goh's final political testament. The 'six gentlemen' were promptly banished back to China, the punishment involving brutal assumptions as to their origins or sense of belonging. Supporters gave them a heroic send-off all the way to Singapore. In Lahat, in the industrial Kinta valley of Perak, a schoolteacher called Qian Zi Yu was also arrested; he was bailed after protests, and after local Chinese raised the money for his bond, then banished. He too went off into exile in style, escorted by hundreds of his students dressed all in white, as for a funeral. Six other teachers from nearby Kampar were banished merely for giving their students a holiday to commemorate Japanese aggression against China.[137] The sites for new ideas and action had moved decisively beyond the port city sphere to the *desas*: the world of the small towns, railheads and company settlements of colonial Asia.

Ideas travelled swiftly through new forms of political communication. To the ubiquitous posters, placards, broadsheets and pamphlets were added new-style literary supplements, or one-page insets in the

Chinese-language newspapers, which had a combined circulation in Singapore of 38,000. These novel means of dissemination had already begun to adopt a vernacularized style and an updated vocabulary; as one of the leading papers, *Le Bao*, put it earlier: 'we will place the simple and pure next to the adorned and decorated . . . singing the village song is the best way to touch people.'[138] The long-distance flow of translation was speeded up; what was written in Canton or Shanghai soon appeared in Malaya or Singapore, often in Esperanto. The new political messages were even communicated through touring entertainments such as the 'Magic Lantern Lecturing Association' organized by Chinese students from Japan, whose cornucopia of provocative slides was captured by the police in Penang.[139] In Kuala Lumpur in late June 1920, a Chinese 'clown and a humorist' called Tau Phai Yun performed for several nights at a city theatre. The entertainment stopped early, and from 11.30 p.m. until midnight he gave a lecture 'advocating anarchist doctrines, abolition of capitalists and governments'. Placards appeared outside the theatre:

> We have no Fatherland, the world is our Fatherland
> Freedom means anarchy, Equality is communism,
> Anarchy is real Freedom, communism is real equality,
> We shall go forward, we shall advance, Oppose taxation;
> Oppose duties, strike work, suspend business, assassinate and revolt,
> A day's disturbance is better than ten million copies of propaganda!

The clown was last spotted heading for Calcutta.[140]

For those who made the longer journey west, to Europe, the passage often marked a radical break with the past. In late 1919 the SS *Paul Lecat* unloaded its cargo of work-study scholars in Marseilles. Eager for the excitements of Paris, the students headed to the French capital before dispersing; one popular destination was Lyon, an established centre for the silk trade. They rapidly formed cliques and societies, and churned out publications, all under the overarching umbrella of the recently formed Chinese Federation. They experienced, in Zheng Chaolin's words, 'the seriousness and radical depth of the change from being a link in someone else's chain to becoming a new-style human being'. Yet after Zheng moved to a school at Saint-Germain-en-Laye, he was surprised by what he found. Rather than a rupture with old thought and religion, he was confronted by cowled priests and French students who seemed so much less mature and perplexingly uninterested in politics, socialism or anarchism. 'Could it be that France had not yet had its May Fourth?'[141]

As the prospects of revolution receded in western Europe, the new centre of gravity in Moscow exerted its pull across the continent. In the Netherlands, in the wake of the crisis in November 1918 when it had briefly looked as if the monarchy might fall and the Indies be lost, Soviet ships put in regular appearances at Dutch ports, revolutionary propaganda began to arrive, and the news from Russia was met by many on the left with a celebratory air. Henk Sneevliet arrived back in Rotterdam in January 1919, where he returned to trade union work. He spoke with fervour of the new 'religion' for which he had acted as herald in Java, while his friend the poet Henriette Roland Holst proclaimed its 'apostles' Lenin, Trotsky and Bukharin. But, frustrated by the pace of development of the communist movement in the Netherlands in comparison to its largest colony, Sneevliet looked increasingly to Russia to advance the cause of the Indies.[142]

Ibrahim gelar Datoek Tan Malaka followed every move of this from his lodgings in Haarlem. His reading had progressed – as he described it: 'Nietzsche as thesis, Rousseau as antithesis, and finally Marx and Engels as synthesis' – and he had begun to relate it more closely to his experience of working-class poverty and his status as a colonial. A fuller understanding of his position, as he later described it, was 'a byproduct of my search for a satisfactory understanding of the Russian communist revolution'.[143] But, for Ibrahim, the dialectic took a deeply internal form:

When one's body suffers through want and one's spirit is shackled, when all roads to change and improvement are blocked, then one's heart is open, torn between the emotions of the common fate of humanity and the realization of social contradiction, between negative and positive forces. The turbulence of thesis and antithesis within me was a reflection of the external struggle taking place about me: in the typical poor household in which I lived and as an echo of the struggle throughout Europe, which together with the whole world was caught in the crucible of the First World War.[144]

By now, Ibrahim had all but abandoned his formal education. But it was colonial patronage – a fund in the name of the conqueror of Aceh, van Heutsz – that provided the loan to move his life forward with new housing in the cleaner air of the bourgeois town of Bussum, and a richer diet of vegetables and fruit. It 'lulled me to sleep and tied me body and soul to the bourgeois world'. But his political course became more fixed, and the constant appeals from his Dutch sponsors for 'gratitude' began to repel him.[145]

On 10 May 1919, there was a public discussion in Amsterdam between Sneevliet and Soewardi on the socialist and nationalist tendencies within the *pergerakan* in the Netherlands Indies. Perhaps it was here that Ibrahim first met Sneevliet. Certainly, writing as 'Ibrahim', he now began to intervene in the journal debates from this time. There was a distinct edge to his voice, whether he was invoking the German invasion of Belgium to summon the ghosts of van Heutsz's conquest of Aceh or targeting the internationalists – the socialists in particular – whose 'internationalism' did not extend to denouncing the colonial system. His friends now greeted him in the street as 'Mr Bolshevik'. As Soewardi prepared to return to the Indies, he asked Ibrahim to lead the movement in the Netherlands. But the reality of his penury overtook Ibrahim: he needed to repay the debt he owed to his village and to his Dutch sponsor and friend, Mr Horensma, for bringing him to Europe in the first place. And the entreaties of his family were calling him home.[146] 'My parents have decided that I will return to the Indies,' he wrote to a Dutch friend, Dick van Wijngaarden, on 19 September. 'They would love to see me again. In addition, my father is now old and sick.' They had threatened to stop writing to him. 'If necessary I go to my parents as a needy native for a blue Monday, to glide back out like a thief in the night.'[147]

Ibrahim secured a job on the largest tobacco plantation in Sumatra, the Senembah Maatschappij on the east coast, as assistant supervisor for the schools set up by the management for labourers' children. He was given an advance of 1,500 guilders and free passage of a kind: he was made to teach Malay en route to the outgoing director of Senembah, a Mr Janssen, and two of his relatives. He left the Netherlands with few regrets. Much later, he recalled that 'the huge unresolved conflict within myself had been enlarged and exacerbated by the "conflict" within the European society that I was leaving and the sharp contradictions of the society towards which I was headed'.[148] In debt to the amount of 4,000 guilders, but with all moral obligation to the Netherlands discharged, Ibrahim forged a new path, from which there seemed little prospect of return. It was not clear where it would lead, nor where the centre of his struggle would lie.

But, in many ways, the Indies already appeared to be surging ahead of its 'small' metropolis. As Ibrahim left Rotterdam in October 1919, a message circulated among the city's workers, brought by the seamen from the Indies who made land there: 'Wait, we in the East Indies will precede you.'[149]

A calling card.

10

To the New Mecca
1919–1921

A MAN WITH NO PAST

In the summer of 1919, the embassies and hotels in Paris remained crowded with delegates for the peace conference at Versailles. It was on 18 June, shortly before the peace treaty was signed with Germany, that yet another petition began to make the rounds, entitled 'Demands of the Annamite People' and signed 'Nguyen Ai Quoc' – 'Nguyen the Patriot'. It elicited a few polite, non-committal responses. The British Foreign Office refused categorically to acknowledge it.[1]

The demands in themselves were moderate enough. They called for freedom of the press and association; the right to education; equality under the law; and the abolition of government by decree. They asked for an amnesty for political prisoners and 'freedom of emigration' and residence overseas. In many ways, it was a *cri de cœur* of the village abroad.

There was something about the missive – its tone, its presumption in speaking directly to power – that instantly got under the skin of French officials. 'Nguyen the Patriot' was clearly a pseudonym, and, appalled by his audacity, by what they referred to continually as his 'libel', they tried to find out everything they could about the person or persons behind the name.[2]

The man responsible for watching over the Vietnamese in France was Louis Arnoux, head of the Service des Renseignements Politiques, an arm of the Sûreté Générale. He despatched one of his agents to the address from where the 'Demands' were sent, 56 rue Monsieur-le-Prince, near the boulevard Saint-Germain. He found traces of a nameless Vietnamese who had stayed there for a few weeks in June and picked up a trail that led to 6 villa des Gobelins, well known to the police since before the war as a centre of Vietnamese comings and goings. Its principal residents, the scholar-in-exile Phan Chu Trinh and the lawyer Phan Van Truong, were now released from their wartime internment, but the Sûreté remained convinced that they were at the centre of a network of revolutionaries. Phan Van Truong worked as an interpreter in the arsenal in Toulouse, where one of the largest concentrations of Vietnamese labour was stationed; he then set up in legal practice in Mainz and was busy among the Vietnamese who remained in the Rhineland. From here, the Sûreté surmised, he corresponded freely with exiles and sympathizers in Japan and China. He was the prime suspect for having written the 'Demands', or at least for translating them into decent French.[3]

But then, on 18 and 20 September, articles appeared in a Tianjin newspaper, *Yishibao*, in which its roving US correspondent interviewed in Paris a man who declared himself to be Nguyen Ai Quoc. He then suddenly took physical form, appearing, rather scruffily dressed, at political meetings and public lectures across Paris, handing out printed copies of his 'Demands', a number of which found their way to Vietnam. The stranger was initially dismissed as a stooge of Phan Chu Trinh and Phan Van Truong, but he swiftly emerged as an independent and unsettling political personality. Arnoux contrived to run into him at a meeting near the Opéra and, to find out more about him, secured him an interview with Albert Sarraut, still Governor-General of Indochina but soon to be elevated to minster of the colonies, who was in Paris at the time. Their meeting did not go well, and the following day Nguyen Ai Quoc wrote to Sarraut to complain haughtily that he had not received a satisfactory answer to his demands. Arnoux fired off enquiries to Hanoi, and sent his Vietnamese agent provocateur, codename 'Édouard', to worm his way into the man's acquaintance.

From this first encounter with metropolitan authority Nguyen Ai Quoc betrayed a practised understanding of the arts of the underground. He lied about his name: 'Nguyen Ai Quoc', and its diminutive, 'Ai', was plainly a ruse. He lied about his age: his expanding police file gave various dates of birth between 1885 and 1895. He lied about his origins: was he really the son of a businessman? But, if not, how did he feed himself? How did anybody at 6 villa des Gobelins feed themselves? According to one story, Nguyen Ai Quoc found work with Phan Chu

Trinh as a retoucher of photographs and painter of oriental 'antiques'. Another report stated that 'they seem not to engage in any well-defined occupation', but nevertheless lived quite well. There was an infuriating solidity to their presence in Paris.

Above all, Nguyen Ai Quoc lied about his movements. It seemed he had entered France only that summer, most likely mid-June, from London; lodging alone first at rue Stockholm, near the Gare Saint-Lazare, and then rue Monsieur-le-Prince.[4] But he let it drop that he had been in France before, then in London: for how long it was not clear. For six years prior to that he seemed to have been in the Americas. Nguyen Ai Quoc belonged to no one and nowhere: a man without a past. In a world in which a key measure of imperial authority was its ability to enumerate, identify and claim ownership and powers of protection over its subjects, his existence was intolerable. All the police agent Édouard managed to glean was that he had been in Vietnam during the troubles of 1908, and this had left him gripped by hatred of French rule.[5]

The surveillance was stepped up. On the evening of 3 December 1919, a Vietnamese salesman armed with samples of clothing called at 6 villa des Gobelins. He enquired after the young Vietnamese who lived there. The concierge confused matters by mispronouncing Nguyen Ai Quoc's name as 'Uyen' or 'Chuyen'. The salesman met a man he took to be a servant, called 'Toan', but left without seeing Nguyen Ai Quoc. He persisted and related all this to Arnoux, to whom he became agent 'Jean'. His reports – sometimes two of them in a day – continued into the new year and beyond, when other stool pigeons took his place.[6]

No Vietnamese, perhaps no colonial subject anywhere, was under such close scrutiny as this man. 'He often changes his name, he carefully hides his true origin, forges his accent,' Jean complained to Arnoux. They identified it as originating from the north of Annam. He spoke English quite well, and proper French. He appeared to be around twenty-eight years of age; 1m 62cm; 'skinny, bulging forehead, flared nostrils, thick lips, prominent upper'.[7] His only distinguishing mark was a scarred left ear, the result, probably, of a childhood injury.

No one was certain what he was about, yet the Sûreté insisted that he was important in some way. His interview with *Yishibao* spoke of conversations with leading Korean nationalists in the United States by means of 'brushtalk' and hinted that his 'Demands of the

Annamite People' marked the launch of a concerted propaganda campaign across the colonial world.[8] There was a particular fascination with his regular visits to the Bibliothèque Sainte-Geneviève, next to the Panthéon. Agent Jean carefully built up a log of the books he requested. He was also a subscriber to, among other things, the *Korea Review* and socialist publications such as *L'Humanité*.[9] Jean duly listed the contents of every issue received at 6 villa des Gobelins, where the 'order of the day' was 'analyse the speeches pronounced by Lenin'.[10]

In the course of trailing his *flânerie* across the city, agent Jean managed to eavesdrop on a conversation between Nguyen Ai Quoc and a friend during the interval at the theatre: 'What have you been up to these days?' he was asked. 'Always researching in books,' came the reply. This was a first hint of a purpose. Jean scribbled down the outline of the book Quoc was writing, as related by him to his friend: an anatomy of the evils of French colonialism. Thereafter, Jean and his superiors followed its progress nervously. In a curious way, the police replicated his 'slow reading' – his auto-didacticism and his radicalization – page by page. They also copied his mail, transcribed the postcards he received from distant ports, and delved into the history of everyone he met: Vietnamese, French, Irish, Korean or Chinese, many of whom exhibited a similar pattern of restive rootlessness.[11] At 6 villa des Gobelins, 'noisy nocturnal meetings' were reported. Agent Édouard was sent there to record Nguyen Ai Quoc's night-thoughts, but what he said was carefully weighed; they all knew they were being watched.[12]

Eventually, by late December 1919, and more firmly in 1920, after tracking down the man's brother and sister in Vietnam, the French seemed to settle on his likely identity. A clue had come from Édouard that his name was Nguyen Tat Thanh. This led to a family in the troubled Nghe An province who were well known to the police; to a brother jailed as a rebel; a sister notorious as a ' "*belle amie*" of pirates'; a mandarin father, cashiered for 'drunkenness, ill-treatment and brutality': rebellion for a patrimony.[13] The long journey to the west of Nguyen Tat Thanh, alias seaman Ba, begun in 1911, had finally come to its destination in Paris.

But after a year as a bohemian at large, the feeling of asphyxia that had first propelled his escape from colonial rule caught up with him. In

August 1920, Nguyen Ai Quoc was admitted to the Hôpital Cochin with an abscess in his shoulder. The Sûreté tried unsuccessfully to exploit his immobility and have the staff secretly take his photograph.[14] He had a good number of visitors, and the Sûreté tracked their movements too. After his discharge, their eyes fastened on the visits to 6 villa des Gobelins of his 'mistress', eighteen-year-old Marie Brière. She lived with her mother in rue du Faubourg-Saint-Antoine. They examined her own surpisingly extensive international correspondence and encouraged the tittle-tattle of neighbours. She had no regular work, it was reported in an insinuating tone: 'she leaves her mother's house early in the morning to come home only quite late in the night and sometimes not even at all.' She was, above all, a woman of 'extreme' social revolutionary opinions.[15]

Now the authorities wanted firm answers. The official with oversight of Vietnamese troops in France wrote to Hanoi in a series of expostulations: 'Who is he really? Who can prove it? . . . Under what circumstances has he come to Europe?'[16] Not least among the frustrations of Arnoux and others in Paris was that the government of Indochina seemed quite happy to leave him in Paris and not have to deal with such ingénues at home. On 20 September 1920, after a series of ignored requests, Nguyen Ai Quoc presented himself at the prefecture of police. In an attempt to intimidate him they had him photographed and formally interrogated. They did not get very far, and Nguyen Ai Quoc, with characteristic devilment, swiftly lodged a complaint with a human rights organization.[17]

Then, from mid-October 1920, it was reported that Nguyen Ai Quoc was living the life of a recluse.[18] The atmosphere at 6 villa des Gobelins was, by all accounts, increasingly tense. The older man, Phan Chu Trinh, did not approve of the confrontational course Nguyen Ai Quoc was embarked upon, and some of the younger Vietnamese had been scared off. Another young woman, Germaine Lambert, the French fiancée of Quoc's housemate, the 'servant', Vo Van Toan, was questioned. The ethos of what she described as the 'communistic' household at 6 villa des Gobelins was too much. Nguyen Ai Quoc had given her the house rules: earnings were to be paid into a common fund; evenings were for repairing the clothes and underwear of the inhabitants; Sunday was for laundry: he extolled blind obedience to her husband-to-be. She would sooner break up the engagement, she said, than submit to such slavery.[19] By this point, Nguyen Ai Quoc was announcing his intention to leave France.

Obsessed by the 'famous' Nguyen Ai Quoc, the 'pseudo' Nguyen Ai Quoc – 'the most active and the most determined of the adversaries of the French administration in Indochina' – by a process of symbiosis the Sûreté created a legend and allowed him to thrive on its mystique. This was the dangerous allure and political alchemy of the underground. As his *nom de guerre* suggested, there were any number of Nguyen Ai Quocs in France. Phan Van Truong was still a dangerous man, and so too in his way was Phan Chu Trinh.[20] The Service des Renseignements Politiques opened 250 files on individual Vietnamese. They were scattered across the battlefields, or as prisoners of war awaiting repatriation, or as workers: there were 9,000 Vietnamese in the state arsenal in Toulouse alone. They possessed a great web of communications: in a mere fortnight in the summer of 1920, the French postal censor read 2,227 of their 2,438 letters; 114 of them were held back. The soldiers were laconic in their correspondence, and many merely sent their addresses in an envelope. But they were frustrated by the lack of Vietnamese news and Vietnamese tobacco, and voiced admiration for the Germans for their superior organization, vitality and industry, in comparison to that of the French.[21] The capacity of these networks to make mischief was palpable.

Arnoux and others sought to build a buffer between the French public and the colonials, and prevent French tastes seeping back to undermine imperial hierarchies in Indochina. In some ways this worked. The Vietnamese labourers in France were paid lower wages and confined, in theory, to their places of employment. Even the French left was hostile to them, especially in 1917 and 1918, when they were seen as taking jobs and used as strike-breakers. But equally, a common hostility to the war brought people closer together. The cases of Marie Brière and Germaine Lambert were far from exceptional. Racial tensions ensued as other Vietnamese formed liaisons with European women who were entering the industrial workforce for the first time, and with whom they found they had much in common, not least, with demobilization, the growing hostility of white men. By the early summer of 1919, as a massive repatriation exercise, backed up by police raids, gained momentum, some Vietnamese tried to remain; 175 were still there in 1921, only to face bureaucratic pettifoggery devised to marginalize and exclude them.[22]

These tensions were seen in other European cities too. In the spring and summer of 1919, in Britain there were attacks on Arab lodging-house keepers who had married local girls, on the Chinese community in Glasgow, and three days of riots in the East End of London. The unrest spread to Liverpool, Barry, Newport and Cardiff, all congested port towns facing demobilization, unemployment and housing short-age. The Asians were immediately identified with Bolshevism, defined by the *Liverpool Courier* on 3 June 1919 as 'a typical Asiatic ideal of anarchy and rapine'. There were voices of solidarity: a mouthpiece of the Independent Labour Party argued that 'the blacks who have been subjected to this treatment are the victims of our imperialist policy and capitalist system'.[23] But mostly, colonial workers found common cause with each other and rubbed shoulders in quarters of the city they tried to make their own.

The *13ème arrondissement* in Paris, around the place d'Italie, was also home to those who had come to work and study. Chinese students and workers met people from across the colonial world in the left-wing circles of *L'Humanité* and at the public meetings which Nguyen Ai Quoc continued to haunt. He was now known to leading French social-ists, such as Karl Marx's grandson, Jean Longuet, who had rallied support in Savarkar's extradition case in 1910. Longuet recommended that Quoc read *Das Kapital*. Quoc put it about that he used it as a pil-low.[24] But he moved closer to the socialists and introduced five of the Chinese students to party work in the *13ème arrondissement*. For this reason too he was marked as the most dangerous of men, and his name travelled across this world.

Chinese students now came to France in larger numbers. The *André Lebon*, arriving in October 1920, brought them from far inland, after a long river journey from Sichuan province, and then thirty-nine days in steerage from Shanghai. Some were very young: Deng Xiaoping left home at fifteen years of age, funded by the Chongqing Chamber of Commerce, and was assigned to a private school in Bayeux, Normandy. By this time there were some 1,300 Chinese work-study students in France, twenty-one of them women. Many of their leaders were graduates of the Hunan First Normal School. The women came under the auspices of a Hunan 'Embroidery Company', a fabrication to allow acceptance of the idea of women abroad.[25] One of the Hunan students, Cai Hesen, travelled with his sister, Cai Chang, and their fifty-five-year-old mother. He formed a romantic attachment on the voyage with Xiang Jingyu, a friend of the family circle in Changsha. Xiang had already founded a new model girl's school back home in Hunan, and in France, in May 1920, she advocated, in a local French version of the famed *New Youth*, study societies, nurseries, student loan societies for women and free choice in marriage. When Cai Hesen and Xiang Jingyu 'married' in the same month, they created a prototype for a new socialist 'free love'; there were no formalities, just a picture of them sitting together holding a copy of Marx's *Das Kapital*.[26]

Beginning in 1920, the 'lost generation' of many nations embraced Paris as a world capital of art, literature and pleasure; for others it was the terminus of bitter exile. But the close-knit communities of work-study students were formed in very different conditions from the literary cafés of Montparnasse or Pigalle. Like many of the working migrants, they tended to concentrate in *quartiers* on the outskirts of the city, such as at the education association in La Garenne-Colombes, where the anarchist Li Shizeng had set up his soya bean factory before the war, and which many used as a poste restante. Others went to smaller factory towns, where Chinese workers and 'students as workers' began to live together for the first time. By the census of 1921, the Chinese population amounted to the largest non-European community in France: 13,000.[27] But for the students there was increasingly less work, and with no work there was no study. Many of the early arrivals, such as Zheng Chaolin, awoke to the fact that they 'had descended from the "petty bourgeoisie" into the "proletariat"; simultaneously – was there a connection? – I stopped thinking as a mere democrat and started thinking as a socialist, and I even started acting as a socialist'.[28] They scrutinized the news from Russia with a searing earnestness and debated it by mail with similar groups of students in China, particularly the New Citizens' Study Society in Hunan. Between 6 and 10 July 1920, a group of students gathered at a college in Montargis, south of Paris, a town where the local municipal worthies had helped support a small community of students in the hope of encouraging republican ideals in China itself. The meeting was to some extent a reading party: Cai Hesen brought over 100 western publications and these were divided up and discussed in groups. But the difficulties they faced in France raised a fundamental question for the work-study programme: how was it possible that education by itself would bring change? The founding vision behind work-study was, in the words of one student leader, Xiao Zisheng, 'anarchism – without force – a Kropotkinist-style revolution. This is more peaceful and perhaps slow; but even though slow it is peaceful.'[29] But others, witnessing at first hand a wave of labour strikes in France, drew a different conclusion. At the meeting, Cai Hesen tried unsuccessfully to form a Marxist party. In August 1920, he wrote to a classmate of his and Xiao Zisheng's from Hunan, Mao Zedong. He predicted a Kerensky-style February revolution in China: 'I believe that a few young people will take part in it, but I hope you will not do so. I hope you will prepare for a Russian October Revolution.'[30] He pointed to the new Communist International in Moscow. Mao, now back in Beijing, replied to say that he had already come to the same conclusion. In this constant exchange of letters and ideas over long distances, it was hard to say who was leading whom, or who got there first. In time, the return of the students to China would draw together the different strands of this discussion with explosive intensity.

These events posed a fundamental question about the direction and purpose of universal history. Liang Qichao and other late-Qing reformers had placed China within world-historical time and broken away from the cyclical time of the old dynastic order. This had heightened awareness of both the synchronicities and imbalances with the experience of other countries, which the many journeys to Europe had deepened. Now the Bolshevik Revolution had begun to create a new order, albeit fragile and increasingly isolated in Russia. But Russia was an Asiatic country, and stood apart from the epicentre of the birth of capitalism in western Europe. A reappraisal of China's place in time and the world followed from this. How were Asian countries to be positioned within this new world-historical moment? Did Europe always have precedence? For many voyagers, especially those who had witnessed, at first hand, the crisis of Europe during and after the Great War, the front line of the global struggle against capitalism and imperialism lay not there, but in Asia, in remote, little-known places seemingly at the wildest frontiers of human empire.

DELI: THE CITY OF GOLD

In December 1919, Ibrahim gelar Datoek Tan Malaka arrived in Medan, the principal town of Sumatra. It was a colonial outpost in the old Malay sultanate of Deli, where from the 1900s, almost overnight, the ancient rainforests of East Sumatra had become the Klondike of the age. Deforestation, railways, wharfs and export industries on a vast scale had created a state within a state in the Indies, run as a fiefdom of international capital. It was dominated not merely by Dutch tobacco-growers, who claimed 'pioneer' status, but by American firms invested in rubber, the palm oil plantations of the French-Belgian conglomerate SOCFIN, and British tea estates.[31] The region drew in vast amounts of labour, principally young men and women from Java, circulating rather than settling on rigid systems of indenture. In 1911 alone there were 50,000 arrivals from Java. By 1920, a high tide of labour recruit-ment, there were around 250,000 'contract coolies' in Deli, perhaps 50,000 more casual labourers, and nearly a third of them were women.[32] All of them – the merchant, the labourer and the cultivator – carried their dreams of prosperity, and experienced capitalism on a scale and in a concentrated form seen in few places elsewhere in Asia. Senembah Maatschappij, the tobacco plantation on which Ibrahim was to work as a schoolteacher, was one of the oldest, and larger than 90,000 acres. From here, Ibrahim saw that Deli was indeed 'a land of gold, a haven for the capitalist class, but also a land of sweat, tears, and death, a hell for the proletariat'. It had turned the Dutch, 'the gentlest people on earth', into 'a buffalo charging and trampling its enemies'.[33]

'Was there anything that Deli did not have?'[34] In the minds of the Dutch, Medan, with its scientific research stations and its tropical Art Deco architecture, was a showpiece of their ethical policy. In the face of an unforgiving physical environment, the plantation enterprises of Deli were seen as a model of preventive and curative health care. At Sen-embah Maatschappij, which promoted itself as a progressive employer, the crude mortality rate for labourers between 1890 and 1894 had averaged seventy-one per 1,000 annually, and sixty-three per 1,000 between 1895 and 1899, at a time when it employed 5 per cent of all labourers in Sumatra's plantation belt. After 1905, mortality rates declined to below ten per 1,000. But the numbers exposed the ethical policy's blind spots. The death rates were artificially low as they were based on a population of young, relatively fit migrants; the aged and infirm did not travel.[35] The Indies state generated vast ledgers of num-bers and some of the civil servants responsible for them began to voice their realization that indenture was 'modern slavery', and that Deli, with its coercion, restrictions on labour movement and settlement, had become an 'out-door prison'. The statistics also disguised the dark heart of the 'Deli system': sexual predation on the women who came to work in the tobacco factories.[36] Families, Ibrahim wrote, could 'at any time lose wife or daughter should the white boss lust after her'. Exploitation was also endemic within the high levels of prostitution and the unstable 'coolie marriages'. 'Morality, fineness? Oh, my soul. Dice, adultery, it fuels the lowest depths of humanity . . . if only they work! Your purest capitalism.'[37]

By the end of the Great War, Europeans were seized by a moral panic about the levels of violence on the plantations, which exposed them to danger and scandal at every turn: the routine striking of labourers by planters; the judicial whippings; the scragging of managers at pre-dawn roll call. Europeans closed ranks in fear of worse to come. A 1915 ordinance created offences that made legal protest or collective organization impossible; 'threats by word or posture' became punishable by a maximum of three years in prison. These punitive measures kept the powerful trade unions that had arisen in Java off the plantations of Sumatra. However, everyday forms of resistance – foot-dragging and sloppiness – were a relentless trial of strength between labourers and a growing army of Asian overseers. Between 1917 and 1924, there were 8,000–13,000 infractions of the coolie code each year; officials denied this was in any way 'political'. At the same time, in 1920, the railway workers in Medan went on strike for the first time; it was rapidly broken up and employers refused to concede that it arose from genuine economic grievances.[38] Ibrahim arrived at a moment of rising paranoia that labour agitators would infiltrate the workforce from Java and elsewhere.

His own role as a company schoolteacher was anomalous. After six years of the Netherlands, he was not to be intimidated by Dutchmen. The head office of the company had instructed its local employees 'to treat Tan Malaka like a European'. But he was repelled by their company: their lack of interest in the people of the Indies; their obsessive talk of 'salaries, bonuses, leave. Nothing else.'[39] He raged later at the 'empty-headed Dutch schlemiels . . . sitting with their big sticks in the pool room in front of their glasses of beer and whisky'.[40] In these difficult post-war years, there were growing tensions between the Europeans in employment and the 'poor whites' surviving on credit in Japanese hotels, struggling to live at the level that white prestige demanded.[41] It took him time, Ibrahim confessed in a letter to his friend Dick Wijn-gaarden in the Netherlands, to find 'some kindred spirits', one of whom was a Dutch trade union secretary. But it was hard to get involved. Ibrahim was stationed sixteen miles outside Medan, and still some 5,000 florins in debt. The parting advice of his patron, Mr Horensma, was to 'Work, study and save!', and Horensma wrote regularly to enquire about the paying-off of instalments on the money Ibrahim owed. For the first six months or so of 1920, Ibrahim sent fifty or eighty florins a month from a salary of 350 florins. He had worked, he had studied and saved, he told Horensma, but had his family to support, and taxes and insurance premiums to pay. He still had plans to travel to Java to fur-ther his education and was reliant on European goodwill to move ahead in life.[42]

Ibrahim was, he wrote soon after his arrival, 'a spectator, but a wait-ing one'. The experience of Deli soon convinced him, as he wrote to Dick in February 1920, that 'we now live in a time when differing worldviews collide'. Ibrahim had seen through ethical imperialism: he concluded that the Dutch were not interested in developing in Sumatra the higher forms of capitalism, nor in sharing its fruits. The fundamen-tal injustice of the whole system was that it rested ultimately on Asian 'erudition' and experience. As Ibrahim worked to clear his and his fam-ily's debt, he shared the sense of loss of the 'most oppressed, exploited and humiliated of my own nation'.[43] As for the job the plantation com-pany had given him, he felt it was a sham, and that he was living in a Potemkin village. But, teaching in the Malay lingua franca of the labour force of Malays and Javanese, he used his experience to reflect on the Russian model of popular workers' enlightenment. Soon he began to write for the newspapers. He kept alive the memory of his six years in the Netherlands. But his letters to his 'best friend' Dick became ever more evangelical: lectures on the evils of capitalism, airing his uncompromising reading of Marx and the necessity of the 'dictatorship of the proletariat'. Although their tone remained intimate, the two men were ideologically estranged. This was something of a pattern with all his friends, and 'It was not . . . only with white people either, that I was to experience the playing out of this *tragedy* of life' – writing later, Tan Malaka defaulted to the English word – 'that you can go through good and bad with someone, eat and drink together, and yet be on opposite sides of the barricades.'[44]

'It is impossible to speak anymore of reform', he announced to Dick on 19 May 1920. In this age of transition, it was the Russian Revolution alone that offered a forward path. It was clear to Ibrahim, from his exposure to the 'purest capitalism' in Sumatra, that the forms it took were universal:

> You should look around in Java, British India and Egypt, where millions are sacrificed at the cost of the soul, yes the lives of millions. And this is putting it mildly. I am not even mentioning child labour, the labour of women, the destruction of family life. I am not mentioning war, imperialism. And all this for the sake of surplus value, i.e. the blood of the workers.

The struggle in the Indies had not yet taken on a class aspect. It was still unsure 'in what direction it wanted to go. But when it realises that the whole of the capitalistic world is united against the colonised and the proletariat then it will extend its arms to the rest of the "world proletariat".'[45]

As Ibrahim watched and waited, in neighbouring Java the hostility between the Red and the Green – the socialist and the Islamic – wings of the Sarekat Islam led to a decisive break between them. The Indies Social Democratic Association was also divided. Its former leading light, Asser Baars, returned to Java in March 1920 to advocate a change of name for the party to break with the 'false socialisms' of Europe. At a meeting in Semarang on 23 May 1920 – a relatively subdued affair given the vigilance of the police – a new name was adopted: *Perserikatan Komunis di India* (PKI), the 'Communist Association of the Indies'. The change, it was argued, was a recognition of the leadership of the Comintern and an affirmation of the universality of its struggle. A dwindling number of Dutch members argued that the Indies lacked the readiness and the ideological 'nuance' for such a move. But the time for grumbling had passed. The new chairman and vice-chairman of the *Partai Komunis Indonesia* (PKI) were Semaoen and Darsono. Baars announced he would not seek major office in it. In their eyes, the change of name was not a change in direction: Semaoen and Darsono had been committed to mass struggle since the end of the war. In the words of one of their last remaining Dutch advocates, the tram driver and trade unionist Piet Bergsma, who had struggled in the Indies for some fifteen years and married a local girl: 'We have been Communists for a long time now.'[46] This was the first party to take the name in Asia. At the moment of its founding there was no communist party operating as an official entity in major industrial and imperial countries such as France and Italy, nor yet in Britain.

It was an easy thing in the polyglot cities of Java to speak for Mas Marco Kartodikromo's 'human nation of the world'. It was possible, on the edge of the great forests of Sumatra, to imagine a future, in Ibrahim's words, when labour might come into its own and 'people will use the forces of nature for the benefit of the whole'.[47] But now there was also the heavy task of carving new paths and building new alliances, made harder still under the gaze of the likes of Arnoux, Jean and Édouard, and, for that matter, the well-meaning Mr Horensma.[48] All this pointed to the necessity of clandestine struggle. In Moscow, to which so many eyes were turning across Asia, a new order was being built by men and women who had in many cases spent ten or fifteen years underground. Describing the founding of the Third International in 1919, Trotsky once again evoked the 'old mole' of Hegel, Marx and Bakunin. He described the scene:

> In the halls of the Courts of Justice, where weary ghosts of criminal statutes from Tsarist codices still wander, the delegates of the Third International now sit in session. Assuredly, the mole of history did not excavate poorly beneath the Kremlin walls.[49]

For those who had spent much of their lives underground, the old mole was never far away. It was present in many, perhaps contradictory ways within the new Soviet regime: it remained an ideal of freedom and commitment, but also a model for revolutionary iron discipline.[50] Lenin was heard to quip during the worst moments of the civil war in October 1919: 'Oh well, we shall have to go underground all over again!'[51] Veteran exiles were recruited to the work. One of Lenin's oldest comrades from the underground was Mikhail Borodin. He had abandoned his life in Chicago, leaving his wife and children, and in August 1918 reached Moscow via Oslo. He acted as an agent in Scandinavia, and as a man of unimpeachable revolutionary pedigree and worldly experience played a background role in the First Congress of the International. He then departed quietly, in April 1919, on a Mexican passport and, it was whispered, carrying Romanov jewels.[52]

DAYS IN THE HOTEL LUX

In August 1919, a stranger presented himself at the office of *El Heraldo de México*, in Mexico City. He had come on behalf of a travelling companion, a businessman from Chicago. He had been in Mexico only a couple of days, picked up *El Heraldo*, read its English-language section, and guessed the radical sympathies of its editor. He had come looking for socialists, and the famous 'Hindu'; by this he meant M. N. Roy.

The editor of the English section of *El Heraldo*, a 'slacker' called Charles Phillips, was given the address of a hotel, the Ritz. There the businessman introduced himself, in fluent English with an American twang, as Peter Alexandrescu. He was middle-aged, smartly suited and dignified, walked with a stick and had an unmistakable air of *Mitteleuropa*. Phillips spent a long lunch with him, discussing European music, painting and food.[53] All this was relayed to Roy and Evelyn; their Jewish-American companions-in-exile assured them that any eastern Jew was surely a Bolshevik. Phillips reported excitedly that the stranger knew all the leading Russian revolutionaries, and that he was a friend of the great Lenin himself. Phillips was shown credentials on a silk cloth sown into the businessman's coat sleeve, signed by the secretary of the Communist International, Angelica Balabanova. Roy scoffed at Phillips's credulity. The man was most likely a British or American goon.

Roy trailed the businessman at a distance about town for a morning as he went to the poste restante and visited some shops. He noted his excessive caution and sensed his vulnerability: the stigmata of the underground. Moved by the spectacle of 'a good man in some distress', he decided to give the stranger the benefit of the doubt. Roy visited Alexandrescu in his suite in the faded grand hotel, where he was received by him in a black silk dressing gown, in the style of a down-at-heel émigré rather than a messenger of misrule.

Alexandrescu confessed that he had arrived in Mexico without funds. Roy was left to pick up the restaurant bills and taxi fares from their meetings, and within days he invited the newcomer to become a guest in his house. On arrival with his baggage he announced that the name 'Alexandrescu' – and another false one, 'Brantwein' – was to be forgotten. In the United States he was known as Michael Gruzenburg, and he also used the work name of Mikhail Borodin, 'who had come to the New World as the first emissary of the newly founded Communist International'. His aura among exiles was burnished by the legend of the Romanov jewels he claimed to be carrying in the false bottom of a suitcase, for sale on the international market. As he told it, he became separated from them while in transit in New York when he passed the suitcase to a newly made ship-board friend, Henrik Luders, a Dutch trader from Port au Prince, Haiti, to carry through the US customs. But they had missed each other on the other side. Borodin first sent the intermediary who had announced him at the *El Heraldo de México* after the Dutchman, but this man only got as far as Cuba, then disappeared. Now Charles Phillips was persuaded to travel under assumed identities to Havana and Port au Prince to look for the suitcase, not being fully aware of its contents. He found Luders and the suitcase and returned it to Mexico City, but when Borodin opened the secret compartment the jewels – diamonds it was said – had vanished. Little in the story really added up. The fabled diamonds were never found and Borodin's elaborate, futile attempts to recover them cast a long shadow over his movements across the Caribbean and Atlantic.[54]

Over the next months, in return for Roy's hospitality, Borodin undertook his education, a schooling that had been truncated at every stage of his journey from Bengal in 1915. So too had Borodin's own, but he had read avidly during his years in Chicago. For Roy, it was his first encounter with a committed Bolshevik who spoke with the full authority of its revolution. Roy, much later, remembered it as a conversation between equals. He also remembered it with no mention of Evelyn's presence. As others were to point out, her role in his education, the clarity of her own thought and writing, was a major part of Roy's conversion story.[55] Either way, it marked a firm break with a militant nationalism in which he no longer placed much conviction, and with its doctrine of violence. A first sign of the rupture came when some of his companions in New York, including his friend Sailendra Ghose, who had been with him in Mexico, and Agnes Smedley became snarled up in a new wave of arrests and arraignments in the wake of the San Francisco trials. They had attempted to create a false front as the 'Indian Nationalist Party', which might win public sympathy and diplomatic immunity for those on trial. Roy now wanted nothing to do with this 'frivolous adventure'. He was slow to send funds to pay for a lawyer, and only did so out of fear that Agnes might talk. She kept her silence, but spurned his help, and was left embittered by a period of detention in the notorious 'Tombs' of the New York Police Department.[56] As for Roy: 'I had lost faith in the original mission with which I had left India. I still believed in the necessity of armed insurrection. But I had also learned to attach greater importance to an intelligent understanding of the idea of revolution. The propagation of that idea was more important than arms.'[57]

Roy had followed the news from Petrograd, as relayed in despatches by the American journalist John Reed, well known in Mexico, that were later published in book form as *Ten Days That Shook the World*. On the strength of this, a Socialist Party of Mexico was formed, with Roy as its secretary-general. Encouraged by Borodin, he trumpeted its internationalism. At a dinner party he introduced Borodin to the President of Mexico, Venustiano Carranza. A principal goal of Borodin's mission was to forge covert diplomatic connections between the Bolshevik regime and the Americans. In this he had been granted plenipotentiary powers by Moscow. But he found that Carranza's caution outweighed his anti-imperialism; he was wary of the presence of foreign members within the Socialist Party, which was a contravention of the constitution of the republic. However, through Borodin, he extended his greetings to Lenin: a small victory for Soviet covert diplomacy.[58]

With Borodin lurking in the background, on 24 November 1919 a small caucus within the Socialist Party formed the Partido Comunista Mexicano. It immediately became affiliated with the Communist International and vaunted itself as the first communist party outside Europe. This was not strictly true: the Communist Party in the United States had been founded in the midst of factional disputes in August, although much of its membership would be pushed into exile with the expulsion of 249 radicals after sweeping arrests between 7 and 25 November 1919. These were known as the 'Palmer Raids' after the attorney-general, but oversight lay in the hands of the new head of the General Intelligence Division of the Department of Justice, J. Edgar Hoover. They were a direct continuation of the investigations behind the San Francisco and Chicago trials of Indians and their wartime allies. As a number of those imprisoned in San Francisco began to be released from jail, their vision of America as a land of possibility rapidly diminished. Many had asked only for American-style democratic freedoms for India. Now they were swept up in a renewed anti-radical, anti-foreign hysteria in the United States itself. The 'Hindu-German Conspiracy' was compounded into the anti-Bolshevik scare of the 'Red Summer' of 1919. Some, like Taraknath Das, an American citizen, and Bhagwan Singh, still wanted by the British, stayed to fight India's cause from American soil. But others, including Agnes Smedley, suddenly at liberty after the charges against her were dropped, were forced overseas by continuous police harassment and constant evictions by landlords.[59]

Roy's eyes were now on the further horizons of global anti-imperial revolution.[60] Sensing that the recruitment of his new friend might offset the loss of his Tsarist treasure, Borodin told Roy he had orders to return to Moscow and urged him to follow. Roy hesitated, but was swayed by a conviction that 'the new ideal of freedom was not to be attained within national or geographical borders'.[61] He now saw a new route to India, not through China and the northeast frontiers of Assam where the wartime conspiracies had been abandoned, but by marching to the Northwest Frontier from Russia.

In early December 1919, the Roys embarked on 'a pilgrimage to the holy land of revolution'. They were, on Borodin's authority, accredited as Mexican delegates to the forthcoming Second Congress of the Communist International. For all the aura of secrecy, the voyage from the port of Veracruz to Santander, Spain, was made with quasi-official aid from the Mexican Foreign Ministry, and with diplomatic passports, as Roberto and Helen Allen. They left behind a depleted shell of a party, fought over by rival claimants, some of whom placed their faith in international alliances, others in the old anarcho-syndicalist tradition, who looked to the strength of Mexico's masses. Accusations from Mexico followed Roy to Moscow that he was an 'intriguer' and 'agent provocateur': 'We do not know if this is true or not, but if it is not, he is at least an ambitious politician only seeking personal gain and with habits and partners who are totally inconsistent with the aspirations of the working class.'[62]

Even on the run, the Roys travelled first-class and on dry land stayed in luxury hotels and dined at the best places. This was, Borodin taught, a revolutionary necessity: 'if you wanted to hide revolutionary connections . . . you had better travel first class.'[63] Roy was repelled by the bourgeois vulgarity of Europe, but he absorbed its pleasures as he travelled through Madrid, Barcelona, Genoa, Milan and Zurich.[64] Borodin had left slightly earlier, with Charles Phillips in tow, via the United States to Rotterdam. They caught up in Berlin, where in the bitter winter of January 1920 the Roys witnessed the aftermath of the Spartacist Uprising from a suite at the grand Hotel Fürstenhof on Potsdamer Platz. Roy gained access to the private salons of the factions of the German revolution, coming into contact with men like Eduard Bernstein, who worked closely with Marx himself, and those supporters of Rosa Luxemburg who were still at large. Roy forged an enduring bond with the scholarly head of the German Communist Party, August Thalheimer, and gravitated further away from the insurgent nationalism of his youth. The staunchly anti-nationalist message of Rosa Luxemburg left a deep imprint upon his own new faith. In adapting to various intellectual circles in Berlin, as in Mexico City, Roy displayed a chameleon quality.[65]

In the spring of 1920, Berlin was a waystation on new pilgrim roads. There Roy met Henk Sneevliet, on the heels of his expulsion from Java, and was impressed by his missionary-like intensity. Earlier in the year Sneevliet had been active in a transport workers' strike in the Netherlands, but in the wake of its collapse, with the help of the Comintern's west European office in Amsterdam, he was making his way east. These coeval itineraries had been set in motion long before the war. They did not always result in connections, although this was what the colonial police and, much of the time, the travellers themselves were searching for. Roy's own revolutionary journey in 1915 and 1916 throughout Southeast Asia, China and Japan was conspicuous for its absence of desired connection. Now, where Roy met old comrades, they found him inhabiting a new persona, speaking in idioms for removed from the Bengali radicalism of his not-so-distant youth, and travelling with a sophisticated American wife. But opportunities that had been missed in Asia and the United States now became possible in the intellectual forcing-houses of Europe.

In Berlin, Roy met for the first time a co-conspirator who had undertaken a long sojourn from Bengal in a strange parallel to his own, through the Netherlands Indies, Japan and China, Singapore and the United States. There was much that was opaque about Abani Mukherji, not least the circumstances of his arrest in China and his detention and flight from British custody in Singapore in 1917. The story was that he had gone to ground in the Netherlands Indies and, assisted by Indonesian radicals – quite who was never clear – he travelled to the Netherlands as a servant to a Dutchman. He was propelled towards Moscow on the good word of S. J. Rutgers, a Dutch journalist and Marxist. In the twists and turns of the underground, the endless self-fashioning and storytelling that surrounded it, there were gaps in every person's account of themselves, and fear of revolutionary justice cast a long shadow. Roy urged Abani to turn back from Moscow and prove himself in the struggle within India. But Abani knew that his story of himself had little chance of being accepted by revolutionaries in Bengal in the wake of the exposure of Rash Behari Bose in Japan, the arrest of scores of Ghadarites in Southeast Asia, and the death of Jatin Mukherjee at Balasore. In Berlin, Roy ran into more of the 'Indian derelicts of German intrigue'. The members of the Berlin Committee still clung to the fantasy of being a government-in-waiting. Bhupendranath Datta, the brother of Swami Vivekananda, had worked for the cause at its beginning as editor of *Yugantar* in Bengal, then in India House in London, in North America and in wartime exile in Germany. On finally encountering Roy in Berlin, Datta demanded that he account for the large sums of German money that had passed through his hands. But the other members of the committee, such as Virendranath Chattopadhyaya, or Chatto, and Har Dayal, were now in Sweden, and had no power to bring Roy to a reckoning.[66] Empires had fallen, the balance of the world had shifted, and Roy was now the servant of other masters. Borodin left Berlin ahead of Roy and Evelyn, to face his own reckoning in Russia.

The leaders of India in Europe had experienced similar tests of faith as had Roy. The Indian revolution was not merely a political movement but a series of philosophical experiments which moved to resolve themselves in myriad ways.[67] To Har Dayal, the experience of alliance with Germany had so deepened his aversion to the 'dismal nationalism' of the Prussian kind that he repudiated it entirely. Like many Indian radicals he feared that the triumph of moderates in India 'would not result in the establishment of independent Nation-States, but only in a change of masters'.[68] He had therefore come to see that 'the British empire in Asia and Africa is, after all, a necessary institution' as the best defence against German or Islamic invaders. By March 1919 he had written an open letter that went further: the empire, for all its inequities, was 'a fundamentally beneficent and necessary institution'. This position seemed a shocking repudiation of his past. The British seized upon his 'renunciation' with relish. It was printed and distributed in Tokyo by the British embassy to reach renegade Indians in Japan, including Rash Behari Bose, who was still in hiding. Har Dayal's bitter memoir, *Forty-Four Months in Germany and Turkey, February 1915 to October 1918* (1920), was translated into Hindi and distributed in India free of charge. He still remained an outlaw of empire, but the British pursuit of him quietly dropped back, although he was unaware of this. His scepticism and internationalism, his search for a higher 'world-state' sent him into a solitary life on neutral ground in Gothenburg, scraping a living from his lecturing on Indian art and thought that returned to the Hindu religious themes of his Oxford and London days.[69]

The gaze of other members of the Berlin Committee now turned to Moscow. Their wartime alliance with imperial Germany cast aside, Bhupendranath Datta argued that the left was the natural supporter of émigrés and that 'when one of them established a new state order through revolution, was it not natural that all left-minded persons would go there?'[70] The previous year, both Raja Mahendra Pratap, still notionally the head of the 'provisional government of India' in Afghanistan, and Maulana Barakatullah had been in Moscow. Barakatullah acted as an emissary for the new Emir of Afghanistan, Amanullah Khan, who had declared his independence from the British. They were received by Lenin on 7 May 1919, and Barakatullah was employed to accompany the new Soviet ambassador to Afghanistan and introduce him to the emir.[71] Barakatullah then embarked on speaking tours for the new propaganda bureau, Sovinterprop, harnessing his pan-Islamic message to the Soviet cause in a pamphlet on 'Bolshevism and Islam'. 'I am', he told *Izvestia* in May 1919, 'an uncompromising enemy of European capitalism in Asia, as represented by the English, above all.'[72] Their travelling companion was M. P. T. Acharya, who lingered in Moscow, where in 1921 he married a Russian-born Jewish modernist painter and illustrator, Magda Nachman, best known for her portrait of the poet Marina Tsvetaeva.[73] In this way, wartime plots were prosecuted with new alliances.

In Petrograd, the anarchist émigré and recent convert to Bolshevism Victor Serge was counting off the new arrivals. Serge had arrived in the city in early 1919, after a period in the underground in Paris, and then in detention with other suspected Bolsheviks at a prison in Précigné, where a quarter of the inmates died of influenza, compounded by the effects of hunger. He was taken under guard to Russia, via Finland, as part of a hostage exchange. He soon met the head of the Petrograd Soviet, Grigory Zinoviev, another long-time associate of Lenin and now commander of a city under siege. Serge relayed to him the demoralization of the revolutionaries in the west. 'It is easy to tell you are not a Marxist,' Zinoviev rebuked him calmly. 'History cannot stop halfway.' But in those months, it seemed to do so. The Bolshevik regime faced encirclement, incursion and war on all fronts. Treachery was in the air. The secret police, the Cheka, were everywhere. Lenin drew attention continually to the inherent instability of the peace of the capitalist powers at Versailles. In the spring of 1920, the situation was worsening again with fighting on the Polish front. In the fullness of the crisis enveloping Russia – 'face-to-face with the ruthlessness of history' – Serge decided to stand with the Bolsheviks. He was put to work in the political secretariat of the Communist International, under the direction of Zinoviev, in the vast empty rooms of the Smolny Institute, the former girls' school from where Lenin had directed the revolution in its early days, and where now a small staff prepared for the Second Congress of the Comintern.[74]

Zinoviev's rallying cry was: 'Our salvation lies in the International!' The text of the hour was Lenin's *'Left-Wing' Communism: An Infantile Disorder*, handed out to delegates in advance, in a bag, in their lodgings. It was an attempt to discipline the global movement and to make Bolshevism, and its understanding of 'the Party', its template. There was a new stringency to the conditions for admission of national movements to the Comintern, and a will if necessary to appeal over their heads to the masses. The global underground arrived in force, not all of them by invitation, travelling legally and illegally, with and without papers, through Sweden and Finland, or through the Baltic, to Petrograd and then to Moscow, often at great peril, to seek asylum. They were ex-detainees, old socialists, syndicalists, anarchists: Kropotkin himself had returned in mid-1917, and promptly withdrew in dismay to the countryside outside Moscow. Welcoming the delegates, Serge took the view that few of them were actually communists, still less Bolsheviks. 'It was obvious at first glance', he recorded, 'that here were no insurgent souls.' But one at least made an impression: 'very tall, very handsome, very dark, with very wavy hair, he was accompanied by a statuesque Anglo-Saxon woman who appeared to be naked beneath her flimsy dress'. It was 'the pockmarked Manabendra Nath Roy'.[75]

Roy and Evelyn were housed in the Guchkov Mansion overlooking the Kremlin. It had belonged to an industrialist former mayor of Moscow and war minister of the provisional government who had fled with what remained of his fortune to Paris.[76] After October 1917, most of the powerful, philanthropically minded, commercial elite who had funded the city's rapid expansion in the 1900s had taken to their heels. Moscow possessed some of the highest levels of literacy in Russia, a vibrant literary scene and more bookshops than existed in the European city of Petrograd. Serge witnessed the rising pessimism among the non-Marxist intellectuals in Russia, many of whom would soon pass into exile. Moscow itself had a transient, frontier feel; there were on average eight people crowded into each of its new apartments, a density far above European cities of comparable size. The population of Moscow was just over 2 million in February 1917. By August 1920, it had all but halved; housing had deteriorated, and mortality levels – not least through scourges such as typhus – were as they were a half-century before. To some extent this exodus was replaced by the influx of Soviet officials. When the capital moved from Petrograd to Moscow in March 1918, it was presented as a temporary war measure. But now Lenin was firmly ensconced in a small apartment in the Kremlin, emptied of its royal retainers, monks and nuns. Other mansions and banks were taken over as the offices of the revolution.[77]

In May and June 1920 there were few people in Moscow who could speak for Asia; among the Indians in the city, it was Roy who had the vital official accreditation, as the representative of the Communist Party of Mexico. As preparations advanced for the Second Congress, he became a key source of advice on conditions in Asia. His experience of India and also of China was more recent than many of his fellow émigrés. Acharya and Abani Mukherji were present for the Congress but had no vote.[78] Roy tried unsuccessfully to recruit the rest of the Stockholm group to Moscow, particularly its leading personality, Chatto. But, as they well knew, Roy wanted to centralize the Indian revolutionary organizations overseas and to submit them to Comintern control under his authority. Roy could not disguise his scorn for the old networks and their fellow travellers. In a letter to an unnamed friend in the United States, he mocked 'the same old mix-up business, without any definite underlying idea . . . the benign smile and pink tea of the liberal American professor[']s wife'; the 'stupid Indian stories written by Irishmen'.[79] In Mexico, Roy had worked in the background, in small meetings. Public speaking had never been part of the repertoire of the Bengal underground: 'we never believed words would make revolution.'[80] But now in Moscow he found himself propelled on to public platforms.

Roy's claims to authority came to rest, above all, on his obtaining the ear of Lenin. It was an established rite of passage for many overseas comrades that they 'would begin and end the story of their visit' in his large, unadorned office in the Kremlin. These audiences were conducted with punctilious timing, signalled by the blinking of a light on Lenin's desk. When it was his turn to be called to see Lenin, Roy saw a slight, unassuming man with a simple, unaffected manner. For his part, Lenin let it be known that he had expected to meet an elderly bearded sage: a Tagore or a Barakatullah. But, in the end, it was helpful to Roy's cause that, in Bolshevik terms, he was a man without a past. In their brief conversation, Lenin dismissed Mexico: it was locked in the shadow of the United States; Europe was the first concern of the revolution. But he also stressed the need to mobilize 'the oppressed and exploited masses in Asia'. Prior to the meeting he had sent Roy, 'for criticism and questions', his draft entitled 'Theses on the National and Colonial Questions', a document to be discussed at the Congress. It was passed to Roy by Lenin's confidante, Angelica Balabanova, secretary of the Communist International, with the cautionary words: 'Young man, you have reason to be proud; but don't lose your head.' Other delegates – beginning with the British representative, Jack Murphy – began to bridle at Roy's arrogance.[81]

Most of the new arrivals were settled in the Hotel Lux at 36 Tverskaya Street, and the less prestigious Hotel Bristol. The Lux was commandeered for the first two Comintern Congresses, but this arrangement became permanent. It was a jaded edifice built in 1911: 'a huge monster of a building', said one resident, 'where everything was in bad taste'. It was increasingly overrun by vermin.[82] There was a hierarchy within its six storeys, diminishing from the grand apartments on the lower floors of the building to the hutches in the upper floors. The veteran Japanese revolutionary Sen Katayama, who had evaded the Palmer Raids, arrived to a guard of honour and was given a suite of rooms in 'Oriental splendour'. However, visa conditions for later Japanese arrivals stipulated that they should not stay in the Lux. Katayama reacted strongly against these slights, especially when in early 1922 the black activist Claude McKay was kicked out of the hotel by fellow Americans.[83]

The Lux was the centre of an international organization that paralleled the Hôtel National on Lake Geneva, home of the League of Nations. Roy, in addition to his lodgings, also had rooms in the Lux as an office: it was a gathering place for the English-speakers, the Americans, John Reed and the young, already veteran revolutionary ideologue from New York, Louis Fraina, and the British delegates, Manchester-born Jack Murphy and the Glaswegian trade unionist Willie Gallacher. Evelyn was a constant presence.[84] They were joined by Henk Sneevliet, accredited as the representative of the Netherlands Indies, who became one of the first Comintern professionals, taking a work name, 'Maring', a pseudonym he had used earlier in his journalism in Java. Soon elaborate rites of passage were established whereby a recruit's individual identity was laid bare then cast aside. There was a lengthy autobiographical questionnaire, written under a 'pact of truth'; then passports were surrendered and work names allocated. A calling that might have begun more or less in the open became, by degrees, closed and subject to the disciplines of secrecy. In his official correspondence, Sneevliet referred to Comintern colleagues by their Hotel Lux room number as a simple code.[85] In the late spring of 1920, the Hotel Lux was already a place of long-term exile: a portrait of the diplomat and Norwegian explorer Fridtjof Nansen – the creator of the refugee passport that bore his name – stood next to Lenin's on its Art Nouveau façade.[86]

The winter of 1919 had been bleak and spring had been slow to arrive. War communism ruled the economy. Basic foods were scarce. There were few private traders to be found in the outdoor bazaars such as Sukharevskii market, where, in the words of the other Mexico delegate, Charles Phillips, 'shadows of men and women offered old clothing, jewellery, family silverware, icons', harried by raids of the Cheka.[87] Of over 20,000 stores in the city before the war, by June 1920 only 540 remained. Cafeterias and canteens were the main source of food, alongside illegal trade and barter, as the has-beens of the old nobility and their remaining family retainers sold heirlooms. The gold standard was passports, travel permits, forged ration cards and foreign banknotes.[88] Against this backdrop, Comintern delegates became part of a nascent Soviet elite. Party members in the city belonged to a secret cooperative, well sourced from far afield, and the central committee had its own 'Kremlin Cafeteria' in the former royal guards' mess, which served 1,100 hot meals a day.[89] Travelling around the city with the new arrivals, Serge was struck by their blindness to its quotidian reality. 'Many seemed to react like holiday-makers or tourists within our poor Republic, flayed and bleeding with the siege.'[90] Or, as Phillips put it, he was appalled by much of what they saw, but 'the evidence of purposeful, shared hardship exhilarated me'.[91]

In the face of this austerity, the Second Congress opened in a carnivalesque mood: the revolution was on parade. The delegates were sent in three special trains to Petrograd to be received on 19 July 1920 at the Smolny Institute, the British and American delegates surrounding Lenin on his arrival singing, 'For He's a Jolly Good Fellow'.[92] The opening session was staged in public at the opera house, to the strains of 'The Internationale'. The conference proper commenced in the white colonnades of the Tauride Palace, the site of the old imperial State Duma. Lenin's opening speech struck observers for its sombre, cautious tone. An informal photograph of the delegates was taken under its portico, with Roy standing tall at the centre. This image soon took on iconic status and was seized upon by the police of many nations. There were visits to the Winter Palace, and a mass rally with marching soldiers and trade unionists in front of it; a Red Mass for fallen revolutionaries at the Field of Mars, to the strains of Richard Wagner's *Götterdämmerung* from a brass orchestra; and throughout the night of 19 July, fittingly in front of the stock exchange, a great spectacle entitled 'Towards a World Commune' enacted by 4,000 soldiers. It was lit by projections from ships on the Neva. One absentee from the podium at these events was Trotsky. He was present only at the opening and closing sessions of the Congress: the rest of the time he was away at the front. A map was hung on the wall of the congress hall to show the daily progress of the Red Army.[93] The delegates returned to Moscow, and to the Kremlin, for the real business of the hour.

On the first day, the discussion turned on Lenin's 'Theses on the National and Colonial Questions'. Lenin was now persuaded that the fate of the revolution was bound to events in Asia. According to the Marxist orthodoxy, the revolution was never supposed to have begun in Russia, a country with underdeveloped capitalism, a small proletariat and a vast peasantry. Nor could it be confined to it. Its leaders looked to a global deluge beginning in the more advanced capitalist economies of western Europe. They staked their own survival on it. But the prospects for this were diminishing, especially with the failure of the Spartacist uprising in Germany in January 1919. The Bolshevik regime was under blockade. The Allied intervention was undertaken initially to keep Russia in the Great War; but, if anything, the capitulation of the Central Powers widened the scope of the incursions. Intervention in Odessa by the French was met with mutinous reaction from the sailors who hoisted the red flag: an iconic moment that reverberated in the dockyards of empire.[94] The British intervention in Murmansk and Archangel underlined the sheer scale of the undertaking. The incursions in other parts of East Asia by the United States and Japan fuelled brutal proxy wars. Under these conditions, Lenin, for pragmatic reasons if nothing else, was alert to the argument, made by Bolsheviks from Russia's own empire in Asia, that success in the west needed success in the east, not least because of the western powers' dependence on their colonies abroad. On the eve of the Congress, a Japanese journalist asked Lenin what has the greater possibility of success: communism in the east or in the west?

> At the moment, real Communism can have success only in the West. However, the West lives at the expense of the East. European imperialist powers are enriched, mainly, on the Eastern colonies. But at the same time they arm and train their colonies as fighters. And thus the West is digging itself a grave in the East.[95]

But for this to be something more than a cynical stratagem, it required a reassessment of the historical necessity of capitalism for the creation of socialism. In Zinoviev's words:

From the moment that even one country separates itself from the chains of capitalism, as Russia did, from the minute that the workers place on the agenda the question of proletarian revolution, from that moment we can say that China, India, Turkey, can and ought also to begin the struggle directly for a socialist order.[96]

Lenin himself, reflecting on the Russian experience, had begun to look to comparisons from the colonial world. More than any other Asian country, Lenin gave perhaps his most extensive thought and reading, and time for discussions with visitors, to India.[97] This found form in Lenin's draft 'Theses on the National and Colonial Questions', dated 5 June 1920. The text, as it was passed to Roy in English translation, advanced two key principles. The first was that proletarian parties in the colonial world must make some concession to 'bourgeois-democratic' forces:

The Communist International must enter into a temporary alliance with bourgeois democracy in the colonial and backward countries, but should not merge with it, and should under all circumstances uphold the independence of the proletarian movement even if it is in its most embryonic form.

While internationalism remained the 'primary and cardinal task', 'national egoism and national narrow-mindedness' were deeply entrenched and 'certain concessions' might be made to them until they could be overcome. The second principle was that in 'pre-capitalist societies' communists could and should give 'special support' to peasants' movements, while looking to draw them into a basic system of soviet organization.[98]

After meeting Lenin, Roy drew up his own Theses, which in deference he termed 'supplementary'. Roy disputed the language of the original theses: the term 'bourgeois-democratic', he argued, disguised a multitude of more or less progressive movements, and suggested indiscriminate support for all of them. In his writings from Mexico City, particularly a book, *La India, Su Pasado, Su Presente y Su Porvenir* (1918), 'India: Her Past, Present and Future', his disdain for the moderates was unwavering. The patrician leaders of the Indian National Congress had far too much respect for colonial institutions. They were no foundation for a revolutionary movement, because they believed that 'English rule is so firmly entrenched that it is impossible to work for total independence'.[99] In Roy's absence from India, and even since his departure from Mexico, however, much had changed: the leadership of Congress was in new hands and Gandhi had launched a mass *satyagraha*. But Roy's old suspicions held, as did his belief that in India – perhaps in the shape of *Yugantar*: Roy was not specific – and 'in most colonies there already exist organised socialist or communist parties, in close relation to the mass movement'.[100]

This was a second point of divergence: the assumption of the 'backwardness' of Asia. This was a residue of the older Enlightenment language of the 'Orient' as a byword for economic decline, social stasis and despotic power. It was present in the writings of Marx, within the Bolshevik leadership of the International and in the 'Red orientalism' of Soviet scholarship on Asia. The formula of words, 'the backward nations', was echoed as a mantra in the debates at the Second Congress.[101] In his remarks to the Congress, Roy stressed that the proletariat in India had recently, in the conditions of the war economy, come to the fore. In a sense, Roy cleaved closer here to Marx's insistence on the historic role of the proletariat than did Lenin, or at least to the optimism of the early Marx towards a sense of a spontaneous revolution from below. For Roy this was partly a legacy of *Swadeshi*; as he had written in Mexico, 'when the natural development of events is blocked artificially, the latent energy forces itself out and then revolution violently destroys the reactionary forces which threaten the new era'.[102] This insight was now fortified by Roy's unbending internationalism.

In a deeper sense, Roy appointed Asia to a greater role in world history and the world revolution than Lenin was willing to concede. Shortly before his departure from Mexico, he wrote in *Gale's Magazine*:

The struggle for Indian independence is not a local affair, having for its end and purpose the creation of another egoistic nationalism; the liberty of the Indian people is a factor in world politics, for India is the keystone of British Imperialism which constitutes the greatest and most powerful enemy of the Social and Economic Revolution that exists to-day.[103]

Behind this was a wider claim that India was 'destined to play a prominent role in the future of humanity'.[104] If the east was necessary for the success in the west, then the colonial world was now the wellspring of the struggle against capitalism. Behind this – and shared by intellectuals elsewhere in Asia of whom Roy was as yet unaware – was a far-reaching challenge to western-centred understandings of the direction and purpose of world history.[105]

In the opening session of the Congress on 24 June, Lenin allowed the dispute to go forward to a commission. In Lenin's graciousness, there was more than a hint of condescension. Its secretary, at Lenin's suggestion, was Sneevliet. He had impressed Lenin with his knowledge and his measured and pragmatic approach to questions of doctrine. For Sneevliet, this was a debate that had already run its course in Java in late 1918. Could Java, could Asia, pass to socialism without the full transition to capitalism? The answer he had given was that it could, if the correct proletarian direction was there. He had seen the possibility for this in the Sarekat Islam. On this larger stage he continued to extoll this approach as a means to an end. In public he steered closely to Lenin's pragmatic line. But in spirit he was closer to Roy and warned delegates that they 'had not fully understood the significance of the Oriental question'.[106] From this point onwards, Roy and Sneevliet, alias 'Maring', formed a close working relationship.

The commission conferred over two days. Late in the evening of 26 June, the issue returned to the floor of the Congress. Roy read out his slightly corrected theses, speaking now as the representative of 'British India'. He diluted the claims he had made for the existence of socialist movements in the colonies. Lenin announced that the phrase 'bourgeois-democratic' would be dropped for 'national-revolutionary'; in theory, this advocated alliance only with groups that would not actively obstruct the proletarian movement. But Lenin also made it clear that in practice this made little real difference. Sneevliet also argued that each thesis complemented the other. Revolutionary nationalism was a fact: 'we are only doing half the job if we deny this movement and play at being doctrinaire Marxists.'

Most western delegates cared little either way and, Roy noticed, were impatient to pass on to other matters. The debate soon veered away from Asia and Africa: John Reed made a long speech on the position of African Americans; there was discussion of the Irish diaspora and the plight of the Jews of the Pale. Karl Radek, a fiery, witty journalist whose stock was rising in Comintern circles, lampooned the

British delegates for their failure to support anti-imperial struggle in the colonies and their temerity in raising the issue at home in the face of working-class jingoism. Their leader, Tom Quelch, was of the view that the 'rank and file British worker' would see an attack on empire as treasonous. There was plenty of debate over the time all these testimonies took, among the few delegates who had experience of the colonial world – led by the Dutch delegate, David Joseph Wijnkoop – who argued that colonial voices needed to be heard; even if, as Radek complained, 'we will have the histories of all the different nationalities in the world to listen to'. It fell to Sneevliet, as the delegate from the Netherlands Indies, to point out that 'only on Java is there a Marxist experience and has the work been carried out in a Marxist spirit, and I should like to hope that the German delegation is just slightly interested in hearing about conditions about which we know nothing'.[107]

There was a crucial, abiding ambiguity as to the relationship of Roy's theses to Lenin's. The stenographer's minutes omitted the amendments that were made in the session. The next day, in the face of a hostile room, it fell to the Italian communist G. M. Serrati, the man who had ousted Benito Mussolini from leadership of the Italian Socialist Party in 1914, to state the perils. The definition of what constituted 'backward countries' was open to abuse; few bourgeois-national movements were truly revolutionary and alliances with them would only weaken the growth of a proletarian movement. 'The Theses' lack of clarity', he argued, 'conceals within itself the danger of giving weapons to the pseudo-revolutionary chauvinism of western Europe against truly communist international action'. Roy sprung to his feet to defend them:

In the backward countries the national revolution is a step forwards. It would be unscientific to distinguish between different kinds of revolution. All revolutions are various stages of the social revolution. The population of the exploited countries whose economic and political evolution cannot proceed, have to pass through different revolutionary phases from the European peoples. Whoever thinks that it is reactionary to help these peoples in their national struggle is reactionary himself and speaks the language of imperialism.

In the event, Serrati abstained with two others, and both Roy and Lenin's theses were passed to cheers. But behind this theoretical ambiguity lay a very practical question: at what point should the alliance with the bourgeois-nationalists be broken? This gave rise to new terms of abuse: 'leftist deviation' or 'rightist opportunism'. However, it was a question unanswerable in the abstract, only in the immediacy of the treacherous ebb and flow of revolutionary events.[108]

The unrevised words of Lenin were broadcast to the world. The 'Theses on the National and Colonial Questions' was published in *L'Humanité* on 16 and 17 July in Paris, where Nguyen Ai Quoc had been following closely the debates as to whether the French socialists should join the International:

> Why were the discussions so heated? Either with the Second, Second and a half or Third International, the revolution could be waged. What was the use of arguing then? As for the First International, what had become of it?
>
> What I wanted most to know – and this precisely was not debated in the meetings – was: which International sides with the peoples of colonial countries?

He now had an answer:

> At first, patriotism, not yet communism, led me to have confidence in Lenin, in the Third International. Step by step, along the struggle, by studying Marxism-Leninism parallel with participation in practical activities, I gradually came upon the fact that only socialism and communism can liberate the oppressed nations and the working people throughout the world from slavery.[109]

From 25 to 30 December 1920, Nguyen Ai Quoc appeared in the city of Tours, at a congress convened at a moment of great political tension and with a high sense of theatre, where the French socialist movement debated its entry to the International. Quoc, who was announced with only a small fanfare – and again with a degree of patronage – as a delegate from the colonies, declared his unconditional allegiance to the Third International and publicly shouted down Jean Longuet's anguished claims that he too had spoken for the colonized peoples. The Comintern now faced the task of reaching such men and women. In Moscow, it was Sneevliet who suggested the next steps. Moscow and Petrograd were to 'form a new Mecca of the east', to attract and to train communist hajis from Asia.

The news was slower to reach Sneevliet's former comrades in the Netherlands Indies. In 1920 they still received little direct news from Russia. The key decisions that set the path of the new Communist Party of Indonesia (PKI) were taken in a vacuum. The thesis of the Second Comintern Congress was published in the socialist paper *Het Vrije Woord* only in late November 1920, and the news that Henk Sneevliet had been there to speak for the PKI was not known until after December. In the Indies, the mood was veering against what Baars called, in his published commentary on Lenin's theses, 'that accursed, nonsensical, and narrow-minded nationalism'.[110] Mistrust focused on the likes of Douwes Dekker, who still sought to speak as sole spokesman for the 'Indies', and on the Sarekat Islam for its increasingly moderate stand. In any case, the Sarekat Islam was still haemorrhaging members in the aftermath of the 'Section B' affair and police action against its underground movement. The PKI stepped up its attacks on the Sarekat Islam's leaders: in October 1920, Darsono shocked many by accusing the saintly Tjokroaminoto of corruption. Above all, the communists in the Indies saw themselves ahead of history as it was scripted in the west. At the PKI's congress in Semarang in December 1920, the decision to join the Comintern was purely a formality. 'We have followed the Communist tactic here before there existed "orders from Moscow".'[111] But fresh instructions were on their way for a first thrust at colonial Asia.

RED *JIHAD*

The delegates from Moscow were met in Baku with bunting and fanfares. Nearby towns and villages demonstrated their loyalty to the new Soviet republic of Azerbaijan with the sacrificial slaughter of cattle and sheep which were to be transported to the city. The luminaries of the Third International – Grigory Zinoviev, Karl Radek, John Reed – had travelled south on a special train, which also served as a propaganda theatre, entertaining villagers and nomads along the route. John Reed went reluctantly, under orders from Zinoviev, and on the way back to Moscow was to be struck with the symptoms of the typhus fever which would within a few weeks claim his life. The story was that he had picked it up from a watermelon in a Dagestan marketplace. The call for a 'Congress of the Peoples of the East' in Baku was made initially for August 1920; it was addressed primarily to the peoples of western and Central Asia, but its rhetorical horizon stretched further, to 'give strength to millions and millions of the enslaved throughout the world'.[112] The Congress eventually convened on 1 September, and some 3,000 or more delegates were anticipated, which added to local anxiety at exacerbated food shortages.[113] Roy did not travel with 'Zinoviev's Circus', as he called it; he believed that it would amount to little more than a noisy demonstration against imperialism.

There was certainly plenty of noise. This was no isolated outpost of the Russian empire. Baku was a busy crossroads on an inland sea; a terminus of the Trans-Caucasus railway, although in mid-1920 the journey from Moscow took four days. Its name pronounced in American, John Reed quipped to great laughter among the crowd that greeted him, was 'Oil'.[114] By 1901, the Baku region was responsible for over half the world's output. There were in 1906, at its peak, around 300 enterprises, which were then consolidated by big firms such as Royal Dutch Shell. By 1913, Baku had a population of 214,600, with 119,330 more in the outlying industrial districts: people of multiple nationalities, nearly three-quarters of whom had been born elsewhere, mostly Russians and Armenians; only 40 per cent were women. They settled in 'company towns' along the coast, little more than shacks among the derricks, administered by the oil men and their armed guards as a private domain.[115] Baku was an early centre of highly factional revolutionary politics. In 1904 it experienced large strikes, and saw the first collective agreement between employers and workers in Russia.[116] But, with declining prices and the competition of American oil after 1909, there was a reaction, with layoffs throwing rootless men on to the streets. More radically minded Bolsheviks moved in, including the Georgian Joseph Dzhughashvili – Stalin – who acquired a reputation for hostage-taking, piracy, robbery and assassination that he struggled to shake off later. For him, after a series of arrests and jailbreaks, Baku was a gateway, as Trotsky put it, 'deep into the underground'.[117] For his part, Stalin believed that Baku had an importance equal to that of the central and northern cities.[118] Part of the reason for the choice of Baku for the Congress was its reputation as a city of refuge.

The new fault lines of imperial collapse ran through Baku. The Bolshevik Revolution and the peace of Brest-Litovsk had briefly opened western and Central Asia to German and Ottoman expansion. The German *Drang nach Osten*, or 'drive to the east', was an attempt to break the oil blockade, reap the cotton harvest in Turkistan, and further the dream of an assault on India through Afghanistan. For the Young Turk leadership it was a vital link in a 'pan-Turanic', or 'pan-Turkic', sphere of influence stretching 'from Constantinople to China', encircling British interests in Persia and India. For the British it was a defensive line, a 'gateway' to India, a line that in the eyes of the general staff was moving ever further westwards. In the last months of the war, Baku was the target of a dramatic British intervention by the 'Dunsterforce' of Lionel Dunsterville, which crossed 650 miles from Baghdad to Anzali and then proceeded to Baku by sea. Enver Pasha sent two Ottoman divisions under his half-brother Nuri Pasha, the so-called 'Army of Islam'. It ousted the Dunsterforce, only to be dislodged in turn at the Ottoman capitulation on 30 October 1918. British Indian troops then reoccupied the area, and the importance of Baku became the subject of an intense debate in London and New Delhi, led by the former Viceroy of India, Lord Curzon, now foreign secretary, over the need for a long-term British presence in the region. The military used the pipeline to the refinery at Batumi for their Black Sea fleet. The minister of war, Winston Churchill, saw it as part of 'a belt of little states' guarding the northwestern approaches to the Raj. Policy-makers couched British imperial interests in terms of a Christian defence against Islam and Bolshevik ungodliness. However, the deciding view was, in the words of the secretary of state for India, Edwin Montagu, in December 1918, that 'it would be very satisfactory if we could find some convincing argument for not annexing all the territories in the world'. Faced with overstretch and internal challenges in India itself, the British withdrew to Mesopotamia and to the defence of Anglo-Persian oil there.[119]

The British occupation was a raw memory. A key tableau of the Baku Congress was the emotive reburial of twenty-six Baku Bolshevik commissars who had been shot in 1918 in British custody. For the Bolsheviks, the Baku Congress was a feint at British India. Trotsky had taken up the language of the old Great Game in August 1919:

The sort of army which at the moment can be of no great significance in the European scales can upset the unstable balance of Asian relationships of colonial dependence, give a direct push to an uprising on the part of the oppressed masses and assure the triumph of such a rising in Asia . . . [T]he international situation is evidently shaping in such a way that the road to Paris and London lies via the towns of Afghanistan, the Punjab and Bengal.[120]

The Congress opened in parallel to trade negotiations in London. Zinoviev, as one observer put, 'knew no other means of effectively threatening the English in order to change their attitude on the blockade'.[121] In this sense, the Comintern acted as an arm of Soviet foreign policy.

The grip of the revolution was fragile. The government of the city had changed hands several times since the end of the Great War. A first Baku Commune, in 1918, had ended in bloodshed. It was succeeded by an Azerbaijani Democratic Republic, calling itself 'the first Muslim republic in the world'. This was portrayed by the Bolsheviks as Islamic reaction, but it possessed a social programme, a suffrage that extended to women, and a vision of national autonomy that evinced a socialist and Islamic internationalism. Like all small nations, it tried to make itself respectable in the eyes of Versailles. It cooperated uneasily with the Bolsheviks to these ends. The Red Army occupied Baku only on 29 April 1920, its troops wearing special armbands of red stars and crescent moons.[122] In late May, there was an anti-Soviet mutiny in the town of Ganja, crushed with several hundred summary executions, and, as the delegates gathered in Baku, fresh waves of anti-Soviet violence broke out in the countryside, much of it religion-based.[123] The forces of nationalism, Islam and communism were hard to reconcile. But the Congress now attempted to do so on a world scale.

The 'Peoples of the East' were represented, in official figures, by 1,891 delegates of thirty-seven nationalities – however they were defined – of whom 1,273 were reported communists, although many – perhaps 360 – came anonymously and did not fill in the ubiquitous official questionnaire. Among the 'nonaligned' were *khans* and *begs* who took advantage of the journey to trade carpets and leather goods. Most of the delegates were from the Caucasus and Central Asia: 105 from Turkey, forty from Afghanistan, fourteen from British India and seven from China. The British claimed the Persian delegates were pulled off the streets of Anzali. The Indians included a number of Indian troops who had deserted the army of occupation, but also M. P. T. Acharya and a more recent arrival in these parts, a Peshwari religious scholar called Abdur Rab. He had worked as a gazetteer in British India, then for the British embassy in Baghdad, and – so the story went – was left behind as their agent when war broke out. However, he embraced the Ottoman cause of pan-Islam and, upon the British occupation of Iraq, crossed over to Kabul. There he and Acharya set up an 'Indian Revolutionary Committee' working among Indians displaced between Kabul and Tashkent.[124]

The Baku Congress, as Zinoviev acknowledged, was far more representative than any hitherto in Moscow had been. It was less significant in bringing clarity to the problems of anti-colonial nationalism than for its pageantry and its symbolism. Zinoviev may have looked unprepossessing, but as John Reed's wife, Louise Bryant, observed from close at hand, he was the most photographed man in Russia, with a flair for staging spectaculars. Effigies of Lloyd George, Woodrow Wilson and Alexandre Millerand were hanged on a scaffold in the central square. There was a spectacular night procession. But the most enduring image was of men unsheathing their swords to declare *jihad*, at Zinoviev's exhortation. The Ottoman-German *jihad* of the war years was a 'monstrous deception', Zinoviev announced at the first session:

> Comrades! Brothers! The time has now come when you can set about organising a true people's holy war against the robbers and oppressors. The Communist International turns today to the peoples of the East and says to them: 'Brothers, we summon you to a holy war, above all against British imperialism!'[125]

Then there was another scene, of women in the gallery tearing off their veils. This was the problem with Zinoviev, Bryant explained: 'the effect of the second act always ruined the effect of the first'.[126] The equality of rights for women had been at the forefront of the Soviet manifestos. But it was not unopposed and not always upheld. Women had a striking visibility at Baku, not least in the comprehensive charter for 'complete equality of rights' read out from the floor of the Congress by the Turkish representative, Naciye Hanım. It was years later before the campaign became an attack on the veil. To many women's leaders in 1920, this was a distraction. 'The women in the East', argued Khaver Shabanova-Karaeva, who translated Naciye's words at the Congress, 'are not fighting merely for the right to walk in the street without wearing the chador . . .'.[127]

The most colourful entrance was that of Enver Pasha himself. He had been at the heart of the underground organization of the Committee of Union and Progress that had launched the Young Turk Revolution in 1908. He was the architect of the secret alliance with Germany that propelled the Ottoman empire into the war. As war leader, he kept a picture of Napoleon Bonaparte on his desk. Like Bonaparte he married into royalty, the daughter of the Sultan-Caliph, and saw his campaigns against Russia as his march on Moscow. The comparison with Napoleon was first made in 1908 by his colleague and future rival Mustafa Kemal, who later reflected: 'Enver took the comparison to heart and was never able to be saved from its effects.'[128] Enver came to Baku not as a delegate but as a guest. He had taken refuge in Berlin, along with much of the Ottoman high command, after the Ottoman Armistice of Mudros in 1918. There he had met Karl Radek, who was jailed there, but ran a kind of salon from his cell. With the aid of Germans happy to sabotage the Versailles peace, Enver attempted to revive the anti-British designs of the war years. To this end, he set out for Moscow in April 1919, only for his plane to be forced down on German territory. On a second attempt, on 10 October, he posed as a delegate of the Red Crescent. His new Junkers plane made an emergency landing near Kaunas, Lithuania. Although his true identity was not discovered, Enver was arrested as a spy by the British authorities and detained for two months. With the help of a German secret service agent, Enver escaped to Berlin. On 31 December 1919 he travelled with Radek on his release from prison, but the plane lasted in the air only ten minutes from take-off, before being forced to land. In late March 1920, Enver travelled as a Jewish German Communist, a 'Mr Altman'. This time he was arrested at Riga and imprisoned at Wolmer in Latvia. He seemed to have returned to Berlin in July 1920.[129] Then, finally, he travelled to Stettin, by ship to Königsberg and thence by train to the Russian border. Arriving after the Second Congress, he was placed in a house on Sofiyskaya Naberezhnaya, the embankment facing the Kremlin over the Moskva River, a guest of the Soviet government, together with Louise Bryant, who had arrived after a similar, traumatic journey.[130]

Moscow was, in an image that circulated in Ottoman circles, Enver's Elba.[131] Unable to return to Turkey, he was consumed with a vision of a new 'pan-Turanic' empire in Central Asia.[132] His mind's eye swept across the realm of Alexander the Great, embracing Turkestan, Kazakhstan and Afghanistan. He imagined marching through the Khyber Pass into India to strike a mortal blow at the British empire. Enver appeared in Baku accompanied by Dr Bahaeddin Shakir Bey, a leading figure in the 'Special Organization' of the Committee of Union and Progress, who, along with Enver, had already been court-martialled *in absentia* and sentenced to death for his role in the Armenian genocide of 1915. Enver agitated for aid to Turkey, but fulminated against the leadership of his one-time subordinate, Mustafa Kemal. This was a stern test of the 'Theses on the National and Colonial Questions'. The view was taken that, in the words of the Soviet foreign minister, Georgy Chicherin, the Comintern would facilitate the task of the national movement 'in every way, although it is not our place to enrol it in our ranks'.[133] Enver tried to speak but was refused permission, and only allowed to submit a written statement. But at a parade, Enver appeared on horseback and attempted to rally the crowd. He was asked to leave.[134] But, as Louise Bryant reflected, 'Zinoviev could not complain about Enver's shallow attitude towards Socialism since there was hardly anything Socialistic about Zinoviev's appeal for a "holy war".'[135]

The circus soon left town. Enver returned to Moscow, another exotic luminary of the social scene. 'Some future historian', Bryant observed, 'will probably call him the Don Juan of the revolution.' But with Soviet aid unforthcoming, within two years he fled to Bokhara and joined the local Muslim Basmachi rebels against the Soviet regime. In August 1922, the Soviet troops pursuing him ran into an armed party some fifty miles from the Afghan frontier. It was the festival of Eid, and it was said that on the eve he dreamed of a martyr's death. The skirmish, in the account of one American reporter, was a clash of sword and scimitar that 'resembled the combats of King Richard the Lion-hearted and his medieval knights'. In reality, it was a forlorn hope of a cavalry charge on a machine-gun nest. The Russians did not know that Enver had fallen. His corpse was left where it fell for two days, until he was recognized by a village imam. He was identified by three letters from Berlin in a woman's hand, by a notebook and scraps of orders in Turkish, and by the signet ring on his finger. Louise Bryant asked the Soviet commissioner for the east, Yakov Peters, what he knew. He had only the haziest information by telegram. The man who had seen the body had never seen Enver before. There were no letters. It was, Peters, believed, 'a trick of Enver's to sham being dead'. Bryant, like many at the time, tended to believe him. The British were plagued with rumours of his presence in the region for a year or more.[136]

In the autumn of 1920, older landscapes asserted themselves. The circulations of the Islamic world had been disrupted and distempered by the world war. One of the major consequences of the peace was their resumption, especially the pilgrim traffic to the Hejaz. There hajis were exposed to new national regimes and new religious movements. This was of great concern to the largest surviving Islamic powers: the British, French and Dutch empires. British troops had edged closer to the holy cities of Mecca and Medina, and occupied Jerusalem and the Shi'a sites of Kabala and Najaf. The feared break-up of the Ottoman empire challenged the unity of all Asia and for many Muslims was an existential crisis for Islam-in-the-world. Seen from British India, as M. A. Ansari put it, it was 'not only a question of India's honour and Freedom, but of a great struggle for the emancipation of all the enslaved Asiatic peoples from the thraldom of the West'. As such, the cause embraced non-Muslims such as Gandhi himself.[137] This challenged the *convivencia* with local Muslims which, in no small measure, guaranteed the stability of the colonial order in India. It reopened the theological question of their status under Christian British rule. At the time of the British conquest, the *ulama* of the Delhi school of Shah Abd al-Aziz and his successors argued that the British had undermined the status of Islamic law, and that India was therefore no longer an Islamic space, that is *dar al-Islam*, but outside it and in a state of conflict, *dar al-harb*. This theological position had legitimized rebellions from 1857 to the 'Silk Letters Conspiracy' of a few years earlier. It now resurfaced. It placed an injunction on the able-bodied to emigrate – or make *hijra* in the path of the Prophet and his companions' flight from Mecca to Medina in 622 – to place themselves under the *dar al-Islam* and to prepare for struggle. The *ulama* of India were divided on the question. A cautious ruling by a leading scholar of Firangi Mahal in Delhi held that *hijra* was a step of last resort rather than a binding duty on all Muslims. But in the mood of crisis this did not halt a growing exodus. Then, in late April or early May 1920, a *fatwa* was issued by Abdul

Kalam Azad. Only thirty-one years of age, he was viewed by the British and by many of his contemporaries as one of the most remarkable religious scholars of his age. He had moved in the same circles as the Indian revolutionaries in Bengal, in Europe and also – it appeared – in reformist and nationalist circles in Egypt, Istanbul and Iraq. These sojourns shaped a powerful pan-Islamic anti-colonial vision. Azad ruled that the war had made *hijra* mandatory, not upon all Muslims, but as a carefully planned venture. The British gathered evidence that he was collecting resources towards this end.[138]

The nearest 'free Muslim nation' was Afghanistan, and initially, to the discomfort of the British, the *hijra* was encouraged by Emir Amanullah Khan. His support was rhetorical rather than practical. Soon his administration was overwhelmed by the arrival of upwards of 40,000 emigrants, or *muhajirin*. Most made the journey on foot, from the United Provinces, Sind and the Frontier, but also from the Punjab and further afield. They travelled to Peshawar, and then, via a staging post in Landi Kotal, at the end of the British-held section of the Khyber Pass, crossed to Jalalabad. The area to the north of this crossing was an older *muhajirin* settlement, dating from the rebellion of Sheikh Ahmad Barelvi in the early nineteenth century. Since then, the area had seen three Anglo-Afghan wars and, in the spiritual geography of India's Muslims, was a 'gateway' to an idealized Islamic world stretching west to Istanbul, and to the *qibla* at Mecca itself. It was a frontier of constant traffic of scholars, traders and exiles. There was now, partly as a legacy of the wartime grand designs, a sizeable community of Indian experts, teachers and advisers in Kabul, clustered around the court. Many worked in modern technical fields as printers, mechanics and military men.[139] One of the *muhajirin*, Rafiq Ahmad, who set out from Bhopal sometime in May 1920, described how on arrival in Kabul he was received by the emir himself, and then invited to take tea with exiles who had travelled from another direction, M. P. T. Acharya and Abdur Rab. They urged him to travel on further, into Soviet Russia.

Rafiq and his party travelled to Jabal al-Siraj, a refugee settlement inside an old fort, in a high, fertile valley some forty to fifty miles beyond Kabul. But at this point, many of the *muhajirin* were disillusioned by their reception and asked permission to leave, ostensibly to fight in Turkey. The Afghan government was now coming to terms with the British, and its support for the *muhajirin* was cooling. A decree in August 1920 prohibited fresh entry, until those who were already in Afghanistan were settled. In practice, this encouraged the *muhajirin* to either return or move onwards. Rafiq joined a party of around eighty in attempting the dangerous journey across the Hindu Kush on foot, before the full summer thaw, to Termez, in Soviet-held territory. They reached the town in July and were welcomed with a military band. But the frontier was not yet under Red Army control and, embarking on a local river boat on the Oxus River, following the border, they were taken hostage by Turkmen rebels. Some of the group perished, but Rafiq and his companions escaped during an artillery bombardment of the rebel camp to reach the Red Army outpost at Kerki. There the group parted ways. 'Till then,' Rafiq observed, 'we could never be sure what was in the mind of the other fellow.'[140] Some headed towards Baku and Turkey, itself a dangerous journey. Some were said to have joined the local Basmachi rebels and the cause of Enver Pasha; others dispersed. Two *muhajirin* of the party who headed west, Akbar Shah and Masood Ali Shah, were among the Indian delegates at the Baku Congress, and then turned back to rejoin the others.[141] When Rafiq's party reached Bokhara, it had only been under Bolshevik control for two days. From there they travelled by rail though the ruins of medieval Islamic empires.

In 1920, the elegant old city of Tashkent was now a major military outpost of Soviet Russia; its commissars commandeered the hotels and the best provisions. The whole region was hit by desperate food shortages. It too was a strangely cosmopolitan place. There were many Austro-Hungarian prisoners of war, who provided orchestras for the cafés and restaurants. An Englishman with a troupe of performing elephants passed through on his way to Kashgar. There were also British agents at large, including in 1918 Colonel Frederick Marshman Bailey. One of the last of the Great-Gamers, his presence was no secret; the band at the most fashionable café would break off and play 'Tipperary' when he and his companions entered. Towards the end of the year he was arrested, only to escape and return disguised as a prisoner of war. His spectral presence stoked Soviet fears of counter-revolutionary activity and triggered a violent crackdown after the so-called 'January events' of 1919, an incipient *coup d'état*, quickly crushed by the increasingly brutal Cheka in the city.[142] Bailey's self-appointed role was to set up networks of couriers and agents to monitor all these comings and goings. Tashkent was a staging post for Indian traders, military deserters and the men recruited by Abdur Rab and Acharya into an Indian Revolutionary Association.[143]

Roy and Evelyn left Moscow on 20 September 1920, with Acharya, and arrived in Tashkent with a military baggage train on 1 October.[144] Roy's plan was to enlist the support of the Emir of Afghanistan and build a base for operations against the Raj through frontier people and the traders. In this obsession with conquest there was more than an echo of the old Bengali revolutionary thinking. The foot soldiers for this were to be the *muhajirin*, who were already training in Afghanistan with wooden sticks for guns.[145] But with the road to Kabul now closed, a new 'India House' was established in Tashkent. A staff of military instructors and aviators began to build up a base area for an Indian Brigade of the Red Army. Around twenty-six of the *muhajirin* joined the training. But they were short of facilities, books and Indian newspapers. Nevertheless some were trained as aviators, billeted in a monastery, where they learned air navigation, photography and topography. Like all Comintern recruits they were made to fill in questionnaires. From the eighty-four returns that were eventually collected it was clear that many were from peasant backgrounds – though some had since been soldiers – mostly from the landholding peasantry. There were also traders (14 per cent) and 'clerks' (12 per cent). Taken together, around half of the Indians had a secondary education and could be categorized in the Soviet way as 'near intellectuals'. But their ideological commitment was uncertain. 'You want one thing', Roy told them in December 1920, 'to fight the English, although many of you have no idea of how this is to be done.'[146]

It was clear to the new arrivals that there were two camps in Tashkent. Abdur Rab travelled up from Kabul and made a great show of welcoming the recruits. He resented Roy from the start as an interloper to the local networks he had built up for some time. He was senior in his exile, which had been harder than Roy's, cushioned as it was with German and now Comintern funds. Abdur Rab had no pretensions to being a Marxist. His visions for India were socialist only in the degree they evoked pre-colonial 'democratic' institutions such as the *pan-chayat*, or village council, and the egalitarianism of the frontier peoples from which he looked to recruit. Roy's ideas ran further ahead than much of the Soviet hierarchy in Moscow and Tashkent in his conviction as to India's readiness for scientific socialism. This view was already being denounced by his critics, in the new jargon, as 'infantile'.[147] Soon after Roy's arrival a decision was taken to establish a 'Communist Party of India' (CPI). There was dispute from the very beginning as to who had suggested this and why. Roy maintained that he counselled that the time was not yet ripe, that there was insufficient preparedness, and that the idea came from Abdur Rab and particularly from Acharya. For their part, they claimed precedence for their own organization, which was already working alongside Bolshevik propagandists in the region. Acharya reported to Moscow that he warned Roy that 'it would be better not to have a party so named at all than to have one composed of different sorts of people calling themselves Communists'.[148] But whoever floated the idea, once it gathered momentum Roy moved swiftly to retain the initiative, to control the process and reinforce his standing in Moscow. A first, brief meeting of the CPI took place in Tashkent at 7 p.m. in the evening of 17 October 1920. The founding members included Roy, Evelyn, who now began to sign her journalism as 'Shanti Devi', and Acharya. Abani Mukherji had arrived in Tashkent, from Moscow, via the Baku Congress. His appearance was a surprise to Roy, but he was a welcome recruit and ally. Abani was accompanied by his new Russian-Jewish wife, Rosa Fitingov, who had worked as assistant to Lenin's private secretary, Lydia Fotieva. She acted as Roy's interpreter and was the fifth member of the new party. Two of the earliest Indian Muslims to reach Russia, Muhammed Shafiq and Muhammed Ali, were also present; others were later to join, including Rafiq Ahmed and his travelling companion Shaukat Usmani.[149] Abdur Rab was excluded on Roy's insistence. There were bitter disputes over the party's legitimacy and, as a creation of exile, its authenticity.

Emissaries went out to recruit men and probe routes to India. Rafiq and Shaukat were sent separately to Andijan and Osh to meet the Sindhi traders who were known to travel there. They were beaten back by the terrain. As Rafiq pleaded: 'How could I find the way to India when snow fell all around?'[150] Instead, revolution was made by post. Missives were sent to announce the CPI's presence in Tashkent. This was also a way for exiles to reach family and friends after many years of silence. Abani Mukherji wrote to Benares, to the educationalist Shiv Prasad

Gupta, recounting his adventures and asking that news of his marriage be passed to his family:

> I am no longer a Nationalist – to make it clear to you. I tell you that I am anti-nationalist and an Internationalist. I do not believe that the driving of the English from India only will bring happiness and freedom to the Indian People. If we put Lajpat Rai in the place of [the viceroy, Lord] Chelmsford . . . the masses will not be any happier. The workers of India will go on suffering as they are doing today if not more. And by these national revolutions, the parasites of India or the intellectuals and capitalists will be the only gainers. And these cheats and adventurers have no scruple to throw the Indian people into a bloody revolution which will mean unprecedented suffering and loss of life to the masses, not to them. I do not like to be a partisan of such crime.[151]

Before he left for Tashkent, Roy wrote to Lala Lajpat Raj, now back in Lahore, entreating him to join them in Kabul. Above all they tried to reach the leaders of the failed 1915 uprising, including Rash Behari Bose who was still in exile in Japan. Roy wrote to Aurobindo Ghose, now a living saint in his ashram in the sanctuary of French Pondicherry. 'I take the liberty of imploring you to come back to active life, to take in your wise hands the direction of the revolutionary forces of India.'[152] And in January 1921 they invited Gandhi – 'Dear Comrade' – to an All-India Revolutionary Congress in Tashkent or Kabul in the summer of 1921. Many of these letters fell into the hands of the police and would visit many sorrows upon the heads of their recipients.

Work in Tashkent was consumed by the question of whether the CPI should claim the exclusive allegiance of its members. Acharya argued to remain a member of the Indian Revolutionary Association. Muslim recruits came forward 'conditional on their individual liberty to believe in God'. Utterances 'against Communism' were heard, and at the end of December Acharya was removed as chairman of the party, and then, on 24 January 1921, from all revolutionary work for 'groundless accusations against the Committee members . . . in an underhand and sneaking manner, tale-telling, back-biting and otherwise lowering the dignity of the Indian revolutionaries'.[153] The dispute had reached such an intensity that Roy and Evelyn returned to Moscow in February 1921 to defend themselves. They were faced with Zinoviev's penchant for pan-Islam and his continued employment of Abdur Rab. The Indian movement, Roy pleaded to Lenin, was 'essentially and predominantly an economic mass movement and not a welter of religious fanatics stirred up by priests and political adventurers'.[154] In Tashkent, Mukherji attacked Abdur Rab for his past work for the British in Baghdad. Acharya, Mukherji claimed, had left India as a British agent to spy on the students in London but had been dropped by the British because of his drinking.[155] On a tense frontier, and with the Cheka hovering, such allegations were potentially fatal. The Russian leadership in Tashkent reported the dispute to the Comintern leadership in March 1921. They sided with Roy. Abdur Rab was arrested – accused of making 'secret pan-Islamic propaganda' – then travelled to Moscow to plead his cause and attack Roy, but eventually withdrew quietly from the battlefield to Germany and then to Turkey.[156] But by this time, the mud-slinging had turned on Abani Mukherji himself. The Indian revolutionaries in Tashkent denounced him as a 'mere bourgeois . . . whose sole business is to seek for high living'. Similar charges were thrown at Roy: that he basked in Comintern funds, favours and travel passes.[157]

By May 1921, the Tashkent mission was closed and the remaining *muhajirin* were sent to the capital. 'Life in Moscow is something terrible,' one grumbled, 'no markets, no stores, everything belongs to the State . . .'.[158] India House in Tashkent became a 'University of the Toilers of the East' in Moscow. Within a year it had 713 students, mostly from Soviet Asia, but also seventeen of the *muhajirin* who came with Roy from Tashkent. It was formed under the auspices of the Commissar of Nationalities, Stalin, with whom Roy worked increasingly closely. It taught the history of the American and French revolutions, an understanding of capitalism, and classes on elementary Marxist theory were given by Evelyn. From April to July 1921, Evelyn travelled to Berlin, Paris and London in a final attempt to rally the Indian 'world abroad'. She found the exiles, whom she was meeting for the first time, 'knit together by common prejudices and animosities rather than by common convictions and principles, full of personal rancour and animosity towards the personnel and work of the Russian contingent'.[159] Shortly before her return, the old guard of the Indian revolution finally arrived from Berlin, including Chatto and Bhupendranath Datta. Chatto had already been barred from re-entry into Sweden and in truth had nowhere else to go. It was the first time Chatto and Roy had met. Chatto had come to Moscow around the previous November, on a fleeting low-key visit from Stockholm, but Roy was still in Tashkent.[160] Chatto and his colleagues were given passports and funds by Zinoviev and housed initially in the Hotel Lux, and then in the lesser-ranking Hotel Dresden.

Much to Roy's dismay, Chatto arrived with Agnes Smedley. Roy and Agnes could not conceal their contempt for each other. Roy, for his part, thought 'she was hysterical – a pathological case'.[161] He and Mukherji branded her a British spy: 'Think of it,' she wrote home to the United States, 'not even an *American* spy – but a British one.' She had carried papers from the radicals in New York to Chatto in Berlin, and they had become lovers. In Moscow, she lobbied on behalf of Chatto's group with skill and conviction, recounting her own considerable revolutionary record, and announcing her intention to go to India, 'where I expect to spend my life'.[162] Given their presence, Abani could not escape from the rumours that had followed him since his arrest in Shanghai in 1915 and his interrogation and escape from Singapore in 1917. He had, Chatto and others related, given lists of names and instructions from Rash Behari Bose to the British colonial authorities. If the denunciations were accepted, it would be Abani who would be answerable to the Cheka. Roy refused to disown him without compelling evidence of his treachery. But by this time, Acharya had returned from Tashkent to repeat his denunciation of the iron grip that Roy and Abani had on the party, and Abani was a liability to Roy.[163]

Behind this acrimony was the unresolved debate on Lenin and Roy's theses. The Berlin group refused to cooperate with the new Communist Party of India and demanded recognition from Moscow for their own Revolutionary Committee, although this too was a body divided among itself. Chatto lobbied to see Lenin and submitted his own theses on the Indian question. He received a written reply: 'I have read other theses with great interest. But why new theses? I will soon talk to you on this.'[164] Chatto's theses emphasized that British imperialism stood in the way of class consciousness at home, of class formation in India by keeping alive caste and religious divisions. It was also 'a permanent military menace to the security of Soviet Russia and its preservation and world-revolutionary centre'. So, not to work with national movements on – this a swipe at Roy – 'rigid Communist grounds' was 'a pathetic and stupid detachment from the Realpolitik of the world situation'.[165] But Chatto never got to see Lenin. The whole affair was put to a commission of the Comintern, which included a number of Roy's allies, such as Thalheimer, Borodin and the Dutchman S. J. Rutgers. Thalheimer likened the Berlin group to the bourgeois politicians of nineteenth-century Germany who would 'pose themselves as social democrats'. This seemed to settle the question: the commission found in favour of Roy. Bhupendranath Datta, along with most of the group, headed back to Berlin. He took his leave of Roy. He had gone further than Chatto in paying attention to building up a peasants' movement in India, and Roy had more time for him than the others.

'You stay here and take responsibility for all work. Do not feel sorry for my victory.'

'Roy, it is not true,' Datta replied. 'Neither have you won, nor am I defeated ... Now you make your career here. I make my career elsewhere.'

'The world is big enough for everybody,' Roy replied.[166]

But, under the new dispensation of doctrinal purity, with its recently learned vocabularies and codes, only the most closely initiated and adept would survive.

Later, with heavy hindsight, Victor Serge described the mood in the autumn of 1920:

> I have the feeling that this point marked a kind of boundary for us. The failure of the attack on Warsaw meant the defeat of the Russian Revolution in Central Europe, although no one saw it as such. At home, new dangers were waxing and we were on the road to catastrophes of which we had only a faint foreboding. (By 'we', I mean the shrewdest comrades; the majority of the Party was already blindly dependent on the schematism of official thinking.) From October onwards significant events, fated to pass unnoticed in the country at large, were to gather with the gentleness of a massing avalanche. I began to feel, acutely I am bound to say, this sense of a danger from inside, a danger within ourselves, in the very temper and character of victorious Bolshevism. I was continually racked by the contrast between the stated theory and the reality, by the growth of intolerance and servility among many officials and their drive towards privilege.[167]

From this point, the leaders of the Communist International in Moscow embraced a situation where historical conditions were agreed to be unfavourable in Europe. This enhanced the importance of the Asian communist leaders in Russia, but it brought for them danger and their actions might be subordinated to wider Soviet priorities. The British were aware of the visit of the Indian delegation, and the Soviets were reluctant to rock relations further in the wake of the March 1921 trade agreement with Britain. As part of its terms, overt propaganda against India came to an end.[168] Lenin had never trusted the Emir of Afghanistan. The British, he told Roy, would bombard his citadel with silver and gold bullets. Not even all the Tsar's treasure could compete with 'the super-profits from a vast colonial empire in the game of bribing this or that Asiatic court'.[169] The Soviets' flirtation with Islam, always half-hearted, began to recede, set against the imperative of securing their southern frontiers. The Soviet Union began to recognize the new regimes that surrounded it. On 28 January 1921, fifteen leaders of the Turkish Communist Party, including its leader in exile, Mustafa Subhi, were killed at sea between Trabzon and Baku, after a clandestine visit to Turkey. The assassins were partisans loyal to the new government in Ankara, and its steering hand was suspected at the time. The incident showed the dangers of bringing home a communist opposition in exile to a popular nationalist movement. It also revealed Soviet expediency. Between the two new states, the matter was quietly dropped. Less than a month later, Turkey and Soviet Russia signed a 'Treaty of Friendship and Brotherhood'. It would, Lenin announced, 'rid us of interminable wars in the Caucasus'. The following month, treaties were signed with Persia and Afghanistan. By this, the borders of revolutionary Russia and the British Raj began to stabilize.[170]

The British had nearly a century of experience in running agents on the Northwest Frontier and beyond into Central Asia. The imperial powers also spied on colonial subjects in Moscow, photographing Asian faces at parades, and recruited informers from among the students. For many of them, exile was a quest for a pathway home, and a number played a wary and dangerous double-game. Little of the expatriate power struggle in Moscow had as yet reached India. The Bolshevik Revolution remained a revolution of words. Some news of it was discernible in the counter-propaganda of the British and the scaremongering of the expatriate newspapers. It led to a shift in language: whereas in 1910 radicals had been labelled as 'extremists' or 'anarchists', they were now 'Bolsheviks', whether they claimed to be so or not.

This created a dilemma for the British authorities. Their reflex was to show a masterful response. But there was a danger that to do so might give sedition too much public credence, and result in it gaining a stronger purchase on the local imagination. There were signs that this was happening. There was, in 1919, something amounting to an anti-Bolshevik hysteria in British India, especially as to its impact on Muslim opinion. As in the war, the authorities responded with their own crude counter-propaganda. This time they prevailed on the Grand Mufti in occupied Cairo in August 1919 to issue a *fatwa*. This was ridiculed in the press in Egypt and India and merely encouraged the talk in tea shops.[171]

Not all news could be censored. In parallel to the secret diplomacy, the public declarations of the Soviet regime and its repudiation of old Tsarist treaties were widely covered in British newspapers. This news was received in India by local praise-singing of Lenin in particular, as an emblem of anti-imperialism, but also as a model of sacrifice and devotion – a 'master-spirit' as Gandhi was to call him. His writings began to filter into the bookstalls of Calcutta and Bombay.[172] In Calcutta, as the revolutionaries of the *Swadeshi* and war years retreated from view or were picked up by the police, new groups of students, often new migrants to the city, began to take stock of the world. They did so in conditions of continuing material distress, soaring food prices and high unemployment; many who came as students were forced to drop out. It pushed them into closer intimacy with the lives of the urban poor. They sought companionship in an anti-city of alleyways, in lodging houses, or 'messes', or as itinerant tutors to middle-class families. Such was the experience of Muzaffar Ahmad, a Muslim student born in 1889 on the island of Sandip in the Bay of Bengal, a literal backwater, from which he escaped to Calcutta in 1913. He spent two years as a student on a pre-graduation course, but then gave up studies and made his way in the streets and alleys around College Square, a centre for printing presses, small periodicals and a colourful pavement book market. As a still-devout Muslim, he could not find affinity with the Hindu-laden imagery of the *Yugantar* and other radicals but found it instead through wider anti-imperial struggles and activism in a Bengal Muslim Literary Society while working odd jobs such as religious teacher, slaughterhouse clerk and journalist. It was in writing a piece for the English-language *Modern Review* of Calcutta that he encountered Har

Dayal's piece on 'Karl Marx: A Modern Rishi'. By the end of the war, fragments of writings on Bolshevism were appearing in stalls in College Square, and Muzaffar was spending time among the Muslims of the port at Kidderpore, who were some of the most disaffected and mobile wage workers in the city. Many were from his home island of Sandip, and he taught for a while among the poor in a small *madrasah*.[173]

In Bombay too a small study circle, not so different from those in China, was forming. It announced itself in March 1921, when a pamphlet appeared, written in English and published at his own cost by S. A. Dange, a twenty-two-year-old student active in Congress circles. It was entitled *Gandhi vs. Lenin* and was the first of its kind published within India to link the news from Russia to a detailed critique of Congress strategy at home. It recognized what the two leaders and their ideas had in common – their assault on poverty and despotism – but set out their divergences in a series of parallel numbered theses. These began with their differing views on modernity, industrialization and mechanism, and then crucially:

4. Let all noncooperate and the edifice will fall.

4. They will never do so because the interests of the majority are allied with that of the existing tyranny. The minority alone will work out the downfall and the majority will follow.

5. Religion and nonviolence alone can do this. For religion will teach the emptiness of modern acquisitions. Violence is usurped by violence: Nonviolence will be followed by nonviolence and chaos will be prevented which is imminent upon the subversion of despotic power, as is shown by revolutions in history.

5. Tyranny will not be moved by religion and such other humane motives. Despotism will go so far as to exterminate the whole race of liberators. So it must be undermined and suppressed by its own means and ways. The chaos after the fall is temporary and men tired of the chaos soon evolve order as shown by history.[174]

In this way, the old debates on the 'snare' of violence were taken up in new terms, both in India, in a number of similar pamphlets, and across

Asia. *Gandhi vs. Lenin* soon reached M. N. Roy in Moscow, and through him engaged the interest of 'the old man' Lenin himself.[175]

Already the Raj was on high alert, seizing pamphlets and letters that were copied and sent on, or never reached their recipients. For Indian leaders scattered in Berlin or Moscow, direct channels of communication to Asia needed to be found. By the time of the Third Congress of the Comintern from 22 June to 12 July 1921, the colonial question had slipped down the agenda and, of the senior Soviet leadership, only Zinoviev attended it. Roy complained that he was given only five minutes in which to speak. But nevertheless, the Congress demonstrated that Roy was in command of the Indian revolution, and was the principal voice for Asia as a whole. But, as the old Hindustani adage went, Delhi was still far away. There were fresh attempts to cross the Hindu Kush. In Moscow, Roy began to equip Indian students to return by the old sea routes. On her visit to London, his wife Evelyn looked to recruit lascars to carry printed materials back to India.

Elsewhere, pilgrims were making their way home from the west. In early 1921, the Chinese work-study students were coming to terms with the life of a worker. At the Schneider steelworks in the commune of Le Creusot in Saône-et-Loire, working alongside other students such as Deng Xiaoping, one of them, Chen Yi, asked: 'Is it possible to transform society when a person is overwhelmed with work and lacks the strength to live and breathe?'[176] Tensions spilled over when the former president of Beijing University, Cai Yuanpei, now education minister, came to France at the end of 1920 and appeared to ignore the students, over half of whom in Paris were now unemployed. On 28 February 1921, around 400 students converged on the Chinese embassy on the rue de Babylone to petition for better conditions. The demonstration was broken up by police. The criticism was led by Zhou Enlai, the twenty-three-year-old son of a civil service family from Zhejiang province, who had arrived after a period studying in Japan and been active in study groups in Tianjin. This had given him an entrée into the circles of the leaders of the May Fourth movement in Beijing and Shanghai, and after he arrived in Marseilles in December 1920, along with another 196 students, intending to study in Edinburgh, he enjoyed a more independent status than most, as a roving European correspondent for the Tianjin paper *Yishibao*, which had earlier given a platform to Nguyen Ai Quoc. Zhou eventually settled in Paris, a few streets away from Quoc in the *13eme arrondissement*. His reports home chronicled the deep rifts with the Chinese students overseas on regional and ideological lines, such as the Marxist-inclined Montargis faction, with whom Zhou Enlai shared a deep interest in events in the Soviet Union.[177]

In the aftermath of the protests, Chinese officials and the French who had encouraged it began to withdraw their support from the work-study movement. Along with many other students, horrified by the conditions they experienced as workers and as migrant Chinese, Deng Xiaoping quit his job at the steelworks and headed back to La Garenne-Colombes, where, in the spring of 1921, around 500 students gathered for a daily handout of five francs. In the cramped conditions and stale disillusion there were fist and knife fights and five students died. In September the funding dried up.[178] At the same moment, an alternative Sino-French Institute was opened in Lyon, at Fort Sainte-Irénée, and a new batch of over 100 students were brought in, but from the elite families and not the work-study group, who assumed that the places would be open to them. On 21 September, 125 abandoned and angry students converged on the Fort demanding entry. They were detained and eventually deported, among them Cai Hesen. In this way, France finally experienced its own May Fourth. They travelled home in abject conditions, not as honourable students, returning from their studies abroad, but in disgrace. Zhou Enlai wrote a serial account of the incident that exposed the 'collusion' between the Chinese and French authorities.[179] Soon the other work-study students made their own way home, but this time via Berlin and Russia. In Moscow, China was moving to centre stage. Henk Sneevliet was lobbying to return to the Netherlands Indies or to go to British India as the Comintern's apostle. Instead, he was ordered to China as a pathfinder for perhaps the most ambitious and audacious mission of conversion to Asia since that of the Jesuit father Matteo Ricci in 1582.

The Great World, Shanghai.

II

Rebels in Rubber Soles
1921–1922

NIGHTS IN THE GREAT WORLD

The land route to China was 3,920 miles on the Trans-Siberian Railway from Moscow to the branch east of Chita where the Chinese Eastern Railway dropped through Manchuria: the shortest way to Vladivostok and the Pacific. This thin strip of track was the most contested ground of the Russian Civil War. It was a line of supply for the White shadow government in Omsk, headed by the Tsar's former war minister, Admiral Alexander Kolchak, fought over by partisans and controlled by the Czechoslovak Legion of ex-prisoners of war. In November 1919, Kolchak's forces were dislodged from Omsk, and slowly retreated along the line supported by the Japanese and US interventions in Siberia. Kolchak only reached Irkutsk on 15 January 1920, and perished at the hands of a Cheka firing squad in February after the city fell to the Red Army. A Far Eastern Republic, a nominally independent entity, arose in the power vacuum, but its control over the vast territories of the Transbaikal, Amur and Maritime regions was tenuous until the anti-Soviet forces of Ataman Semenov were defeated at Chita in November 1920. In mid-1921, Japanese forces were still encamped in Vladivostok and in May 1921 a right-wing coup there created a last White redoubt. Only with the Japanese withdrawal, the Far Eastern Republic's capture of Vladivostok in October 1922 and its dissolution into the Soviet Union did the borders of the new regime stabilize.[1]

The eastern gateway to China was the town of Harbin, which emerged at a strategic junction where the Chinese Eastern Railway branched south to the port of Dalian on the Yellow Sea to connect in Shenyang to Tianjin and Beijing. The railway was in theory a joint Russo-Chinese enterprise, but effectively it was a Russian corridor 1,700 miles long, amounting to 40 per cent of all China's railway track. It had served as a vital supply line during the Russo-Japanese War of 1904–5, when Harbin was a place of rest and recreation for Russian officers. In 1921, it was a company town of some 200,000 people with a unique pidgin-Russian as its lingua franca.[2] No one heading to China could avoid it, and the flood of refugees overwhelmed the Russian administration. Existing residents – including over 9,602 young Russians born in the city – became émigrés 'by default'; part of the growing 'flotsam of the revolution'. Harbin's population was swelled by an influx of Chinese as it became the gateway to the mines and frontier farming of Manchuria: it was fast becoming a Chinese town. Americans came to Harbin to sell their heavy agricultural machinery and saw it as a mirror of their own 'Wild West'. And so too did Japanese in greater numbers: labourers recruited from northern Kyushu, shopkeepers and prostitutes.[3] Most of the branch line south of Harbin was in Japanese hands, and there were periodic clashes with Chinese troops. The Chinese occupied Harbin in December 1917, but there were disputes over the residual international control over the Chinese Eastern Railway. Only by June 1920 did Chinese troops finally oust Russian police and railways guards and deport 300 of them back to the Soviet Union.[4] The issues of sovereignty in the region were entangled, emotive and fought over every foot of ground. They culminated in mass protests in February 1922 at the 'Thirty-Six Sheds', an area of cramped and squalid settlement for Chinese railway workers: a microcosm and metaphor for China's impoverishment and desire for change.[5]

In this moraine of dislocation and asset-grabbing, the two great revolutionary forces in Asia reached across to one another. Ten years after the Wuchang uprising, the Chinese republic was more fragile than ever. The Beiyang government sat in Beijing and enjoyed the recognition of the western powers, but limited authority within China itself. It suffered from a lack of revenue from the provinces, and the government and the rump of the National Assembly were hostages to the struggle for ascendency between the rival northern warlords. In July 1920 this erupted into war between the Zhili and Anhui cliques. Sun Yat-sen struggled to create a foothold for his revolutionary movement in the south, but he too was constrained to act in alliance with the regional warlords.[6]

The Soviet Union launched one approach to China by open, legal means and another through the illegal underground. The formal diplomacy, with the Beiyang government, was aimed at securing and fortifying Russia's geopolitical interests. The covert overtures were in the hands of the Comintern and directed at furthering the Asian revolution. They came to focus increasingly on Sun Yat-sen and the south. This *pas de deux* was often out of step. First contact with Sun Yat-sen had been made in 1918, when he telegraphed Lenin from his exile in Shanghai to express the hope for a common struggle against the European empires that encircled them both. Lenin had no illusions about what he termed the 'virginal naiveté' of Sun Yat-sen's expressed commitment to socialism, but he needed allies.[7] Soviet Foreign Minister Georgy Chicherin responded with a vow to take on the 'iron ring of bayonets by the imperialist governments that had severed contact'. But it seems that this message did not reach Sun.[8] The British and Japanese reported a string of supposed envoys: refugees, renegades or prisoners of war, most of whose credentials were uncertain. Sun's main rival in the south, the reforming regional military leader Chen Jiongming, made a first move by despatching a letter to Lenin through an ex-Tsarist officer turned freelance intelligencer called Potapov, conveying his support for Bolshevism.[9] Both sides had only the vaguest notion of what they were dealing with.

In China, as elsewhere in Asia, more had been reported about the February Revolution of 1917 than the Bolshevik takeover. The Japanese incursion in the east overshadowed the internal affairs of the new regime in Moscow. The Soviets accused the western powers of blocking information and Chinese intellectuals complained of a dearth of reading material. The Soviet capture of Irkutsk in eastern Siberia in 1918 had re-established direct telegraphic communication with China, and enabled the broadcast in March 1920 by the deputy commissar for foreign affairs, Lev Karakhan, that the Soviet Union 'has given up all the conquests made by the government of [the] Tsars'.[10] While the Soviet Union later backtracked from many of its pledges, the 'Karakhan Manifesto' was received in China with great excitement.[11] Traffic resumed westwards as Japanese and Koreans travelled via Shanghai and Harbin for a Congress of the Toilers of the East, scheduled initially for Irkutsk in November as a belated follow-through to Baku. Due to the difficulty and spiralling costs of the journey, the meeting was moved to Moscow in the new year of 1922.[12] Qu Qiubai had been part of Li

Dazhao's study circle in Beijing; he became one of the first Chinese journalists to travel to Soviet Russia and wrote two books and over sixty newspaper articles about conditions there. He soon found himself employed as a translator at the Communist University of the Toilers of the East; this marked his own initiation into the higher realms of Marxist-Leninist theory. In the spring of 1921, the first three groups of students set out from Shanghai to study there.[13]

The first official Soviet mission to China was launched by the Far Eastern Bureau of the Bolshevik party in Vladivostok. It was led by Grigory Voitinsky, a twenty-seven-year-old returned émigré who had worked as a printer and an accountant in the United States and Canada, where he was active in socialist circles. He had fought against the White armies in Siberia, was captured and sent for hard labour in Sakhalin. On his release in the autumn of 1920, he travelled by sea to Tianjin and to Beijing, posing as a journalist, with his wife and two others, one of them a Chinese interpreter. Through its Russian residents, in particular a sinologist, S. A. Polevoy, he met Li Dazhao, who had recently launched a campaign for students in the study circles of the city to 'learn' Marxism. Karl Radek was later to remark caustically that 'many of our comrades out there locked themselves up in their studies and studied Marx and Lenin as they had once studied Confucius'.[14] Certainly the Bolshevik movement in Beijing, such as it was, had little to do with urban workers. But Li Dazhao gave Voitinsky a letter of introduction to his collaborator, Chen Duxiu, who was now in Shanghai, having fled Beijing in February 1920 after being jailed for distributing political leaflets. This was Chen's first encounter with the visceral reality of modern capitalism. Here in China's most proletarian city – where in 1921 alone forty-two new factories were to open – the focus of the activism was very different.[15]

Through Chen Duxiu, Voitinsky soon gained an entrée into the radical circles in Shanghai, exploiting his cover as a journalist to feed their hunger for information. Around October or November 1920, Chen arranged an audience for Voitinsky with Sun Yat-sen in the library of Sun's house on rue Molière, a comfortable villa in the French Concession built by donations from Chinese who had made their money abroad. Sun, Voitinsky reported, was 'well-built and erect, had soft manners and very distinct gesticulations. The modesty and the cleanliness of his attire at once attracted our attention.' They discussed connecting the two revolutionary bridgeheads, and Sun suggested that the Soviets might place a powerful radio station in Vladivostok or Manchuria capable of reaching Canton.[16] On 25 November Sun left Shanghai and returned to the south, and it was here that he received his first letter from Lenin and responded via the Soviet trade mission in London. Sun's overriding priority was to consolidate the republic in Canton, and then to march out to take the north. But his position rested on a fragile alliance with Chen Jiongming, who had a more circumscribed vision of the south as an industrial 'model province', as a prelude to a more gradual, peaceful reunification of China on a federal basis. In early 1921, Voitinsky travelled with Chen Duxiu to Canton to try to get the measure of Chen Jiongming, whose past associations and support for the work-study movement had earned him the sobriquet 'the anarchist warlord'.[17] By the time he left China shortly afterwards, Voitinsky had made Bolshevik Russia a firm presence in Chinese revolutionary circles, but it was unclear precisely how it mapped on to the fluid political landscape.

After its Second Congress in June 1920, the Comintern began to set up bureaux at key crossways of the global revolutionary underground, and Henk Sneevliet was appointed to oversee the revolution in East Asia from Shanghai. His passage to China from Moscow was through Berlin to Venice, from where he had to run the gauntlet of British-held ports of the eastern Mediterranean and the Indian Ocean. He was intercepted as soon as he reached Vienna. He had stopped there to get a visa for China but was picked up by the Austrian police. The other visas inside his passport revealed his travel plans and the Austrians passed these on to the British authorities, who placed a watch on Sneevliet after he joined a Lloyd Triestina steamship, the *Acquila*, at Venice and sailed to Colombo, Penang and, finally, Singapore, on 21 May 1921, where he was forbidden to land. His cover story was that he was travelling to Japan as a journalist. This was blown, and the Dutch tried to block his entry into China. But although the major powers shared a degree of information, it was harder to persuade other governments to apprehend a person who had committed no crime on their territory. In Singapore, old comrades from Java joined Sneevliet's ship to Shanghai: Asser Baars, expelled from the Indies and off to join an engineering venture in Siberia, and Darsono, the first of the Indonesians to make his way to Moscow by the overland route.

In mid-1921, Shanghai was a vagrant city, a Nansen city, a modern Babylon. Around 5,000 Russians were living there, many of them stranded. The old Tsarist consulate on the waterfront opposite the Astor House Hotel was closed up; legal cases were left hanging in the air, valuables lodged in Chinese banks were sequestrated, and in 1921 Russian exiles were stripped of their citizenship, to become another people with no country. A good number of them drifted into an underworld of petty theft and trafficking. *Les femmes russes* were a staple of salacious newspaper reports and moral panics. In fiction and popular lore, they were a new erotic type, charged with a frisson of danger from their reputation for availability to both western and Asian men. This flouted the deepest taboos of foreigners increasingly ill at ease with themselves and their fragile status in China. These women were deeply implicated in the Bolshevik and émigré plots, imagined and real, which fed westerners' myths of them and the city.[18] This mystique was further embellished with the revival of the foreign-language press. One of the city's two Russian newspapers, *Shankhaiskaia zhizn'*, 'Shanghai Life', was seen as a centre of Bolshevik influence. The *Shanghai Gazette*, established in 1918, was an English-language mouthpiece of Sun Yat-sen's government, edited by the Trinidad-born Chinese and British national, Eugene Chen, who in 1922 became one of Sun's closest supporters and his foreign minister. He promoted Sun's anti-colonial foreign policies. The *Shanghai Gazette*'s most prominent staff writer, George Sokolsky, an American of Polish-Lithuanian extraction, who arrived from Russia in 1918, boasted of recent conversations with Lenin and Trotsky and his desire to spread Bolshevism in China. He soon became a confidant of Sun's family. The Chinese and the western press, with its more protected position, were closely entangled in terms of personnel and finances, and in the acquisition of news and its translation.[19]

The austere post-war years – the continuing currency controls, the stifling social climate – were a stimulus to escape, far abroad.[20] With the revival of long-distance shipping, a fresh wave of politically minded tourists arrived to examine what one of the most illustrious among them, Bertrand Russell, in 1920–21 defined in his book *The Problem of China*. Russell's observations and reflections on China left him perplexed – the country was in turmoil from warlords, strikes and imperialist threats – yet he was drawn to its traditional culture. There were any number of more opportunistic adventurers. In 1919, the British followed a man called Goodman, one of many similar individuals, 'giving conflicting accounts of himself and behaving in a most suspicious manner':

At the British Consulate he claimed to be an Egyptian, and said he wished to return to Egypt. As the only papers he could produce were written apparently in Arabic on dirty leaves torn from a notebook, and bearing neither seal not stamp, he was refused assistance until he could obtain proper proof. It was later discovered that he came from Tientsin [Tianjin] where he had represented himself as an American Presbyterian Missionary to the USA Consul, by whom he was rejected as an imposter.

In Shanghai he booked rooms in three different hotels, and booked a passage to Hong Kong, saying he was a banker. He also applied to the USA Consul for a passport to Hong Kong, saying he was born in New York, but has lost his papers.

He is about 5 feet 10 inches in height, heavily built, very dark, looks like an Assyrian or Hindoo and wears black clothing.[21]

Such characters populated a new genre of *romans cosmopolites*, a model being Maurice Dekobra's *La Madone des Sleepings*, or *Madonna of the Sleeping Cars* (1925), set in the world of the constantly mobile, and written in polyglossic style with knowing sketches of the denizens of the revolutionary demi-monde.[22]

In Shanghai, the underworld lay in plain sight. The city's black economy was boosted by a bonanza in the illicit arms trade as China became the destination of much of the surplus weaponry of the Great War. It was financed by the opium trade, control of which gave aspirants in the struggle for China a decisive strategic advantage. It corrupted the police and created a more or less open shadow government of urban gangs. In 1922, the French consul-general dismissed an entire police post for being on the take. The head of the Chinese detectives in the International Settlement led a double life as a gangland boss. In the five years after 1922, armed robberies rose from forty-seven to 1,458 in 1927. Police raids only had the effect of pushing rackets into a Chinese-administered city or a neighbouring concession. Criminals no less than revolutionaries exploited the different police jurisdictions. To the police, revolution was merely an extension of crime by other means.[23]

Most of the new arrivals in the city were Chinese, mainly from the northern provinces, who now accounted for around 90 per cent of the population of 3 million people. Of all the transformations of post-war Shanghai, the most visible was its emergence as a city of petty urban dwellers, of loose connections, united in their exposure to hybrid cosmopolitan tastes and new ways of speaking. These years saw the bloom of a modernity that had been seeded from the end of the nineteenth century; a form of modern life experienced in other Asian cities, in a more accelerated and intense form than that of any country in Europe, 'more plastic', 'more artful'. But Shanghai's burgeoning culture of capitalism, its consumerism, was on a scale seen in few other places.[24] Here, in the vocabulary of Bolshevism, the historic destiny of the Asian bourgeoisie would be tested as nowhere else. So too, in this 'hypo-' or 'hyper-colony', would be the authority of foreign imperialism, at the birth of its jazz age.

At the intersection of all this, and at the meeting point of Avenue Edward VII and Yu Ya Ching Road, in the open atmosphere of the French Concession, stood the Great World (*Da Shi Jie*). Founded in 1917, it was an extravaganza of the city's worldly dreaming, spread over four floors, topped by a four-storey baroque-inspired tower. The entrance was a distorting hall of mirrors. The interior was a bricolage of peep shows, modern dramatic theatre, traditional storytellers in people's home dialects, music hall and roller skating, with free beer on Sundays. Film serials showed on cheap continuous screenings late into the night, in front of perambulating pleasure-seekers who ignored the seating conventions of the regular movie theatres. There were Japanese acrobats and western dance bands. There was even an indoor zoo. In one sense, with its stalls and pavilions, curios and human curiosities, it was a pastiche reminiscent of the universal fairs and expositions: Paris of 1900 or Semarang of 1914 or the newly advertised Marseilles colonial exposition of 1922. In another, it represented the banal, everyday worldliness of the country of the lost. Here new and old residents, Chinese and foreigners, rubbed shoulders in an intimate proximity seen in few other spaces in the city. Women were seen on stage and – even more controversially – prostitutes left the old courtesan haunts to circulate, seeking clients. For many foreign arrivals, the Great World was a fantasy of the exotic and its erotic possibilities. For locals, for whom the city had been a place of darkness, it was a blaze of artificial light, a conquest of night. It was unpoliced and in the hands of the gangs, one of which ran a 'Day and Night Bank' next door. With its flexible hours it was the bank of choice for the poor and the demimonde. The Great World soon welcomed 20,000 visitors a day.[25]

'The time of the silver dollar', the fragile prosperity after the war, saw 'World fever' spread across maritime Asia. In Shanghai there was also a

'New World' (*Xin Shi Jie*), established in 1915 at the centre of a new entertainment district on Bubbling Well Road; there were 'sky gardens' – a journey by lifts to the roofs of department stores – and all this became part of the accelerated syndication of styles and attitudes to other cities of China, Hong Kong and Singapore. The 'New World' of Singapore opened in 1923 and was an open labyrinth of fantastical halls and pavilions, connected by alleyways of restaurants, hawkers and sundry stalls. Here too were theatres, nightclubs, dances and an open-air cinema. In a new *flânerie*, crowds could wander from each to each, and impresarios would attract their attention by entr'actes of boxing, magic and other 'special turns'. In a colonial city, the effect of this was even more powerful. The Singapore 'World' was a playground for all ethnic communities and income groups, a place of high and vulgar culture; a place of escape for the poor. It was a fantasia for the invisible city, in a walled enclave within the colonial quarter but outside its order and exclusions. It soon became a site for political meetings.[26]

Here the fate of the 'national bourgeoisie' was dramatized. The periodical press in Shanghai was dominated in the first two decades of the century by the sentimental fictions of the so-called 'Mandarin Duck and Butterfly' writers, so named for the motifs on their covers. The escapism of their stories seemed to signify a lack of social responsibility and promote indulgence in the pleasures of the world. This highly commercialized sphere had a total output of around 2,215 novels, 113 magazines and forty-nine newspapers and tabloids. They were a principal target of the angry young writers of the May Fourth generation, but they also fostered among readers a sense of group solidarity and utopian and republican sentiments.[27] The Shanghai 'Worlds' had their own tabloid dailies, popular with those living in the city and with students, which took up the patriotic calls of May Fourth – especially to mobilize for boycotts – if not with any consistency. Often the appeal to collective pleasure – what the screenwriter Zhou Shoujuan called a 'nation of joy' – was at odds with the ethical earnestness of the radical intellectuals.[28] The writer Lu Xun moved to Shanghai in 1927 and saw only a 'scramble for money, openness of crime, waste of spirit, and rampage of carnality . . . Was this', he asked, 'the goal of mankind?'[29] A similar repugnance at the self-seeking greed of Shanghai society deepened Chen Duxiu's conviction that only the proletariat had the organization and moral vision to 'abolish the old and institute the new'.[30]

This vision took form in other, more improvised cityscapes. A few streets away from the Great World, in the French Concession, its popular theatre and food stalls were re-enacted in the open air for even the poorest of the poor: a kaleidoscope of China on the move. Shanghai now had 800,000 urban workers, 250,000 of them in factories. Migrants brought their villages with them in the form of native place associations and returned to their villages when they could. New communities formed alongside more rooted city-dwellers, distinguished by the subtleties of choosing to communicate in Shanghai dialect as opposed to vernacular Chinese. In the words of an early publication by migrants from Zhejiang, one began by thinking of what is most intimate: 'you can call it starting with one corner. The process doesn't end here, but [one is] limited by what one knows.' But, in the aftermath of May Fourth, these small corners formed common fronts, and the likes of Mao Zedong saw in this a prototype for 'a great union of the popular masses'.[31] These communities shared a distinctive urban form and worldview in the shape of the *lilong* or alleyway houses, tucked out of sight of the new commercial thoroughfares of the city. The ubiquitous building style, the *shikumen*, or 'gates wrapped in stone', were an amalgam of elements of a traditional Chinese house, impossible to build in the pressurized land market, with the terraced housing of the industrial cities of northern England. They formed a system of tight alleyways, where people were thrown into ever-closer proximity by multiple, diminishing sub-lets, and on an increasing scale. Siwenli, built between 1914 and 1921, saw 664 units compressed into eight acres. The *shikumen* was the staple interior for the realist Shanghai cinema, especially the back bedrooms or the pavilion rooms, which fancifully evoked a tranquil garden but were usually twelve square yards off a landing, above a kitchen. This was the most transient space, popular with workers, students, artists and intellectuals. The 'pavilion room writers' of Shanghai became a by-word for intellectual intensity, social commitment and political frustration. When Lu Xun settled in Shanghai, in the Japanese-dominated enclave of Hongkou, he would call his three collections of essays of the period *Qiejieting*: a clever pun suggesting 'a pavilion room from the semi-concession'.[32]

The new politics inserted itself swiftly into these spaces. Among the shops and artisan workshops there were bookstores, places to tarry and to talk, and printing presses. They were a site of constant translation, both on an everyday level of strangers negotiating with each other and in print. There were schools and colleges in these *lilongs*; even Shanghai University was housed in an alleyway house in Zhabei district. Voitinsky's wife was active in a 'foreign-language school' off avenue Joffre that prepared students for their trips abroad: this time to Moscow. Shanghai had been an early centre of the Esperanto-speaking world, and the inter-language was a medium in which anarchist literature was distributed from Shanghai by post to the colonial cities of Southeast Asia. When the famous 'blind Russian poet' and anarchist Eroshenko arrived in Shanghai from Harbin, after his banishment from Japan, in September 1921, his lectures on Esperanto had a powerful impact. He secured a post at Beijing University, and stayed in the family home of Lu Xun, who became his translator.[33] It was impossible for the police of the foreign concessions to monitor this fully; they launched raids and confiscated materials, but urban radicals cloaked themselves in the bustle and anonymity of the alleyways. A small group emerged, the nucleus of a 'proletarian party', a self-conscious group of intellectuals, workers and teachers, journalists and translators, who spent more of their time trying to reach the real proletarians through a series of short-lived journals and by attempting to get involved in trade union organization and workers' schools. They had mixed success in crossing the cultural gulf between them and fared better with the intellectuals and students. From the French Concession, Chen Duxiu launched a more theoretical *Communist Party Monthly*, which appeared for six issues from November 1920. Students' unions began to adopt a 'cell'-like structure and infiltrate existing organizations such as the YMCA and YWCA, which many activists in Asia – including Sun Yat-sen and Ghadar leaders – saw as a model for self-cultivation, civic education and for operating across borders.[34] Shanghai was still a base for Korean radicals and disaffected Indians. The movement still carried the air of the anarchist-inflected, non-doctrinaire Pentecostalism of the global underground before the war. But to the Comintern and its new converts this now smacked of petty-bourgeois individualism.[35]

The principal theoreticians of the small group were Li Da and Li Hanjun, both students returned from Japan, where they had acquired a deeper knowledge of Marxist theory than their peers. Japan, not Russia, remained the principal source of the socialist writings translated in newspaper supplements with notes to explain their sociological vocabulary.

This reading matter increased with the revival of socialist politics in Japan in 1920, after the reaction following the 1910 Kotoku Incident and was absorbed in circles close to Sun Yat-sen as well as by the younger, more radical students. In August 1920, the first full Chinese translation of *The Communist Manifesto* appeared, with a provenance that stretched back to a Japanese edition of 1904. To this was added material in English imported from the United States, which introduced the names and the writings of Lenin and Trotsky to many Chinese readers.[36] So armed, and through their own work as translators, Li Da and others began to attack anarchist influence, not least its hostility to political discipline and to the state. Both, Li Da argued, could be used to transform production and social conditions, and his writings placed an emphasis on 'true' Marxism and the proletarian strategy as the sole path to an understanding of this. Li was a native of Hunan and his views carried weight with Mao Zedong and his circle in Changsha.[37]

Sneevliet arrived in Shanghai at the beginning of June 1921 deeply unhappy. As a European in Java, he was used to travelling with a certain status and style. Now his European bank savings had been wiped out by hyperinflation following the war, and bad hotels, hardship and harassment weighed down on him. His letters to Moscow were a constant complaint about his finances. Eventually, under the name Andresen, he settled into digs in the house of a Russian woman in Wayside Road in the International Settlement. In Java he had worked closely with local allies such as Semaoen and Darsono. But he was at something of a loss in Shanghai, with only a sketchy knowledge of the country and dependent entirely on interpreters. He based his advice, he later admitted, principally on what he saw as the successful experience of organizing trade unions and other left-wing groups within the Sarekat Islam in Java.[38] He gained his entrée into leftist circles through a Russian, Nikolsky, from the Far Eastern Bureau in Irkutsk. But the lines of authority were unclear, and Sneevliet's brief was vague. As with the proconsuls of the Dutch trading empire of old, the slowness of communications to and from Asia gave a great deal of discretion to the man on the spot. However, for every action there would later be a stern reckoning.

Sneevliet saw his primary task as instilling Comintern discipline. His first step was a first-hand report on the resolutions on the 'National and Colonial Questions' at the Second Congress. This carried weight with those who heard it. But Sneevliet's easy assumption of authority generated tensions from the outset. As Zhang Guotao, a witness to May Fourth in Beijing and now the 'small group's' chief organizer, put it: 'he saw himself coming as an angel of liberation to the Asian people.' His Comintern diction, laced with terms such as 'backwardness' and 'infantilism', betrayed a man who had lived too long as a 'colonial master'.[39] Translating the loose Comintern policy into a tactical blueprint for the Chinese situation immediately escalated tensions. In Sneevliet's analysis, an alliance with the bourgeois movement was a priority. It was also an imperative of Soviet foreign policy. In the turbulent labour politics of Shanghai, the reading of the situation, the sense of pressing need, was quite different. To the professional revolutionary, which Sneevliet had become, the only way to settle the issue was to call for a 'national congress'.

The gathering was organized by Li Da and Li Hanjun at the latter's residence in the French Concession, in the small living room of a *shikumen* house at 106 Wangzhi Road, on 23 July 1921. It brought together thirteen representatives from a variety of study circles and small groups across China for the first time. They spoke for just fifty-three party 'members'. Those present were mostly intellectuals and not hardened labour organizers. The classrooms of a nearby 'alley' girls' school were used as a dormitory for delegates from out of town: two from Beijing – including Zhang Guotao, who chaired the meeting – two from Wuhan, two from Jinan, two from Hunan – one of whom was Mao Zedong, who departed from Changsha in late June – one from Canton, one from Japan and one 'unattached'. They masqueraded, very plausibly, as students from Beida on a summer excursion.[40] They were not the only group to see themselves as a communist 'party'; there were other simultaneous groupings of Chinese in Tokyo and France who made similar claims. But it was the Shanghai meeting that was later to become known as the First Congress of the Chinese Communist Party (CCP).

Sneevliet attended under his work name, 'Maring', to speak for the Comintern and Nikolsky for the Far Eastern Bureau. But the unease at Sneevliet's presence, and his lack of understanding of China, was such that the two outsiders were absent for key debates on the party programme. The most intense discussion was over how far the party should be a working-class organization aiming for the dictatorship of the proletariat, or whether it should remain a looser study group, reaching out to students and intellectuals as a party of ideas. If the first line was followed, cooperation with the nationalists was impossible; if the second, then it was entirely feasible for members to participate in national assemblies and open public work. The path of the proletariat was a path underground. Sneevliet, on the outside of this discussion, returned to Wangzhi Road on 30 July. But, as he did so, the meeting was interrupted by a stranger at the door. It appeared to be a case of mistaken address, but the attendees guessed that it was a prelude to a French police raid. It was likely that Sneevliet was being watched and the police had caught wind of the meeting. Added to this, the next morning there was a murder in a hotel next to where the delegates were staying. The delegates scattered and reconvened on a boat at a beauty spot, the South Lake at Jiaxing, some two hours away by train, without Sneevliet. There the proletarian line was endorsed, and the party adopted an exclusive membership. The question of cooperation with Sun Yat-sen's party was deferred. There was no mention of the Comintern in the new party constitution, which was mostly culled from that of the Communist Party of the United States. The proceedings were not published, and there was considerable haziness as to what had been resolved and what remained open for discussion.

The two most prominent leaders of the movement did not attend. Li Dazhao remained in Beijing, and Chen Duxiu was away in the south, in Canton, working for Chen Jiongming as a director of public education. When Chen Duxiu returned to Shanghai around August or early September he was reluctant to meet Sneevliet, still less to concede Comintern authority or to accept its gold. When they did meet, the mood was frosty. Having spent much of his adult life fighting a closed bureaucracy, Chen Duxiu was irked by the organizational obsessions of the Leninist model, such as Sneevliet's insistence on constant reports on party work among labour. In truth, there was little new going on.[41] Relations only softened in October when Chen was arrested by the French Concession police and Sneevliet helped bail him out of prison. Thereafter, the CCP came to rely on Comintern funds. Word went out for the party to recruit members and to build a structure from the district level upwards. However, the question of relations with Sun Yat-sen's nationalists remained unresolved and gathered urgency. Sun's movement in exile, the Kuomintang, had been refounded in October 1919. It had only a few thousand members within China; its greater strength, and the source of its funding, was overseas. There were around thirty-six branches and sub-branches in British Malaya alone, based in reading rooms, clubs and clan associations.[42] But, to the communist leaders, the Kuomintang seemed the cleanest break with the vilified 'warlords'. As Sun Yat-sen became increasingly enigmatic to the European powers and more radical in his attacks on their ambitions in China, the Kuomintang also appeared to be China's strongest defence against imperialism.

In December 1921, Sneevliet set out for the south. Sun, after his return to Canton in November 1920, had by May 1921 controversially contrived his election as president of the republic. With the help of war-lord armies, he moved to establish a forward base for his northern campaign at Guilin in Guangxi province, but his plans stalled through lack of finance. Sneevliet travelled via Hankou and Changsha, the capital of Hunan, where he lectured to the youth circles in which so many of the Chinese activists in France and elsewhere had been active. Over the next two weeks, Sun and Sneevliet, his guest at Guilin, shared their experiences of struggle, their understandings of the Bolshevik Revolution and their views on Sun's national movement. They agreed that the Kuomintang needed a firm party structure, and that it should develop its military training, in order to abandon its reliance on the warlords. There seemed to be a consonance between Sun Yat-sen's notion that the Chinese masses lay under the 'slave psychology' of centuries and needed a period of 'political tutelage' under the Kuomintang and the Leninist 'dictatorship of the proletariat'.[43] Sneevliet lectured on this to Sun's cadres. Where the two men differed was over cooperation with the communists. While Sun Yat-sen was content to accept the friendship of the Soviet Union in the international arena, he still held a hope for British recognition and support in the struggle against his rivals in China itself. To Sneevliet, Sun Yat-sen was 'far more militant than Gandhi, but he thought purely along the lines of military conspiracy'. He was also wary of Sun's 'mystical' mentality.[44] Leaving Guilin, Sneevliet headed further south, and arrived in Canton on 23 January 1922. 'In Shanghai', he reported to Moscow, 'I had become very pessimistic about the movement in China and its possibilities. In the south, I became convinced that fruitful work was possible.'[45]

In Canton at that time there was a fad for rubber-soled shoes. Ten factories were set up to produce them, the largest of which turned out 1,500 pairs a day. The British consul drew attention to this in a despatch, with some puzzlement: 'The use of these soles by the modernized young Chinese is becoming almost universal.'[46] They were popular not least for running in crowds. The level of foreign investment in the city was slight compared to, say, Shanghai; the economy of Canton was dominated by light industry, often of a traditional kind, in which Chinese capital predominated: over half the value of Canton's exports lay in silk. But for centuries the Pearl River delta had been a sprawling centre of production, the final terminus of the old Silk Road. A 1923 survey of money-making enterprises in the city listed 31,802 different concerns, classified into 233 types. For example, there were twelve western-style banks, ninety-six local banks, forty-eight customs brokers, fifty-three underwriting firms and seventy-five pawnshops, with great fortress-like structures to store goods.[47] Not least of the nationalists' goals was to make Canton the epicentre of China's future economic development.

The delta was perhaps the greatest concentration of toiling humanity on earth. Comprising some 8,000 square miles, it was the densest area of settlement of the most crowded region of China, with 1,170 people per square mile. The population of Guangdong province was around 37.1 million: in 1923, perhaps half of it was urbanized, although the borders of city, town and village tended to blur into one another.[48] As the centre of gravity of politics and trade in China moved from inland cities, rivers and canals to the coast, Guangdong sat in the middle of a watery continuum facing outwards to the southern and eastern seas, and was a principal point of departure for migrants.

Canton stood at the edge of empires. Its neighbouring province, Guanxi, bordered French Indochina. Just over 100 miles to the southeast, near where the Pearl River entered the South China Sea, stood the British colony of Hong Kong. Canton was a shallow river port; Hong Kong a deep-sea ocean port. Since 1839 it had been Britain's principal gateway to China and a vital entrepôt for China itself. The British likened the dependency of the two cities to that of Manchester and Liverpool. By 1921, 90 per cent of the people of Hong Kong were natives of Guangdong, and people still travelled freely by steamer and by rail from one city to the other, 900,000 by train alone.[49] Since 1839, the British had used their foothold in China to police the maritime badlands of the delta, what they saw as nests of piracy, smuggling and trafficking in people – potential flashpoints that seemed to multiply as China's crisis deepened. Sun Yat-sen and other revolutionaries looked to Hong Kong and its wealthy businessmen as a bank to draw upon and as a bolthole.

Canton was one of the most unruly and radical of China's cities. This was led from the waterfront where, unlike Shanghai, the labour force tended to have strong local ties. Wages had not kept in line with the soaring cost of living during and after the war; sub-contractors demanded their cut of earnings, so too did the police. When alternative organizations of labourers formed to counter this, they received a crucial impetus from organizers committed to anarchist ideas of self-help. Many had come to these beliefs through travel overseas. In the city, translations of Kropotkin, Bakunin and Malatesta were more widely available than radical literature of any other kind. As a doctrine, anarchism was malleable to individual needs: it represented freedom from the state and feudal structures and a new moral purpose. It was less a systematic system of thought than a utopian horizon. Like Marxism and Leninism, it was not something passively received but elaborated on locally by men and women making sense of their alienation from the old order. The ideas of Liu Shifu, who had brought anarchism and Esperanto from Japan in 1912, were embedded in the city, and, after his death in 1915, were carried far afield by his followers. By 1918, thirty-two newspapers were operating freely there – in which the full spectra of the new politics of Asia found a new voice. Between 1922 and 1923, over seventy anarchist publications had appeared in Chinese at home and abroad, making it perhaps the most discussed ideology of its day, and Canton was the major centre for anarchist influence, especially within its labour movement. This was a major obstacle to the small party of Chinese communists who were beginning to focus their organizational efforts away from Shanghai towards the relative sanctuary of the south.[50]

Chen Duxiu's attempts to create a Leninist organization during his short sojourn in Canton earlier in 1921 had been rebuffed by local anarchists deeply suspicious of its 'dictatorial methods'. He claimed only to have founded three workers' schools, supported one strike, and identified a mere thirty-two communists in the city.[51] But it was here that Chinese Bolshevism was first encountered by British intelligence. They saw it as a strange cult in which 'filial affection was a back number and that promiscuity and free love form the height of human happiness'.[52] This image lingered in both the foreign and Chinese publics: in March 1921 the *Huazi Ribao* of Hong Kong elaborated on the 'promiscuity' of a man who 'dares to poison our youth, destroy our moral values'.[53]

When Sneevliet reached Canton, the Pearl River delta was at a standstill. Its chaotic labour conditions had spread to the British enclave in

Hong Kong, where there was a large-scale mechanics strike in 1920 and in February 1921 a Chinese Seamen's Union was formed, tightly organized around the workers' dormitories. After issuing a series of calls for revision of wages in the face of soaring inflation throughout 1921, the Union's demand for a 40 per cent rise was accompanied by a strike of seamen on 13 January 1922, on a scale that took employers and the authorities by surprise. It was led by worldly men exposed to trade unionism outside China, who experienced every day on board ship the insidious comparison with European sailors' wages and privileges. Although the causes of the strike were economic, the movement became increasingly vocal in its opposition to British and Chinese capital and to colonialism. It involved at its height some 20,000 men, and some 10,000 more – part of the same family networks and working communities – came out in Canton in a sympathy strike and in street demonstrations. There was an exodus of labourers by train to Canton, where many had families: a tactic of 'asylum' used to good effect in the earlier mechanics' strike. On 18 January some 7,000 strikers paraded in the city, and the next day pledged themselves at the memorial of the 72 Martyrs of the 1911 Revolution. The governor of Hong Kong, Reginald Stubbs, declared the union illegal and used martial law to prohibit workers leaving the colony in order to press-gang labour. Employers tried to sign on strike-breakers in Shanghai, but were rebuffed by support for the strikers among labour there and had to recruit as far afield as the Philippines and the Netherlands Indies. On 28 February, a sympathy strike rolled out from the waterfront bringing in stevedores, tram drivers, street coolies, houseboys and clerks, including the staff of Government House itself. Commerce froze and expatriate families were left marooned on the Peak, unable to fend for themselves without servants. The total number involved, from a tally by the expatriate *South China Morning Post*, was around 120,000, that is 20 per cent of the entire population of Hong Kong. On 5 March a procession of around 2,000 workers was stopped from crossing into China; jittery police and soldiers opened fire, killing five workers and injuring others. What became known as the 'Shatin Massacre', and the ensuing nationalist outrage, showed how rapidly a wage dispute could escalate into an elemental threat to colonial order. Within days of the march, labour and management had come to terms; it was a victory for organized labour and an unprecedented shock to imperial prestige.[54] In the last stages of the strike, as one British report had it: 'The delta is in chaos, no junks on the move, and the silk cocoon market, on which the main bulk of Canton's foreign trade depends, cannot be held, as it is unsafe to carry about silk or money to pay for it.'[55]

This made a deep impression on Sneevliet. Here the drive to organize labour he had failed to find in Shanghai was everywhere to be seen. The seamen's strike was not communist-led, but it goaded communist activists into taking a lead and they later claimed it as a triumph of their own initiative. Nor was the strike backed unequivocally by the Canton government.[56] But the tacit support of the city authorities confirmed Sneevliet's impression that the Kuomintang was a progressive force. He met three times with Chen Jiongming but was ultimately unconvinced by his support for 'socialism'. Chen was, Sneevliet later observed, a sort of 'Chinese Stalin', chasing a vision of 'nationalism in one province'.[57] However, once Sun Yat-sen re-established himself in the city, Sneevliet concluded that it was 'the only city in the Far East where . . . a permanent representation was possible without being bothered by the authorities'.[58] He took this news back to Shanghai, a journey by sea slowed by the aftershock of the strike in ports along the coast. The Dutch colonial authorities believed Sneevliet was behind its spread. When he arrived in Shanghai, after a side trip to Beijing, Sneevliet resumed his bitter dispute with Chen Duxiu and others. He then left to carry his impressions to Moscow, travelling back as precariously as he had arrived. The Japanese would not grant him a visa to cross by rail through south Manchuria to reach Harbin. The British, still under pressure from the Dutch, would not allow him to land in any port they controlled between Hong Kong and Port Said. In the event, he left on 24 April 1922 on a Japanese ship from Shanghai to reach Marseilles in early June.[59] But, two days earlier, the ground shifted once again. Sun Yat-sen and Chen Jiongming clashed bitterly over the necessity and funding of the northern expedition. There were attempts on Chen's life and on 22 April he withdrew from Canton with 10,000 of his troops. But Chen remained popular in the war-weary city, and the struggle between the two men reached a climax on 16 June, when Sun's presidential palace was bombarded by the forces loyal to Chen Jiongming. Sun escaped by car, on to a boat off the bund, leaving his wife, Soong Ching-ling, the second of three daughters of the Shanghai financier Charlie Soong, to flee on foot and under fire, dressed as an old peasant woman. Sun took refuge on a gunboat, and – in a move that shocked local opinion – bombarded the city, causing civilian loss of life. After five weeks, protected by his closest military aide, an officer called Chiang Kai-shek, Sun was eventually given ignominious safe passage to Hong Kong by a British warship, and then headed into exile in Shanghai.[60] Canton opinion was bitterly divided by the affair. As one paper remarked, 'Canton was originally a majestic and prosperous city. Since the return of Sun Yat-sen it has become a world of terror.'[61] Suddenly, the Asian revolution seemed to have stalled.

ISOLATION COLONIES

A new Asian underground had started to take form. However, as its travellers began to pass through Moscow or Shanghai they connected only haphazardly to the older networks of the *belle époque* and war years. They did not possess a secure foothold in the labouring communities of the world abroad. The Vietnamese pioneers of the 'Journey to the East' of 1905–7 were scattered across Siam and China; Phan Boi Chau continued to live quietly in Hangzhou, China. Of the radical leaders of the Netherlands Indies, not only Sneevliet, Baars and Darsono were in exile, the leader of the PKI, Semaoen, followed them to Moscow in late 1921. Rash Behari Bose was joined in Japan in 1922 by the erstwhile leader of the Provisional Government of Free India in Kabul, Raja Mahendra Pratap. The conspiracy trials of 1914–19 had pulled in South Asians across Southeast Asia, the Pacific and the United States. Those who had avoided prison or had received lighter sentences, such as Taraknath Das and Bhagwan Singh in the US, were forced out of the public eye; others retired to private life.

The full force of imperial retribution was felt by those languishing in a series of isolated penal colonies scattered across oceans. As the aftermath of the war unfolded, the 'seditionist' prisoners in Port Blair in the Andamans followed events through a weekly edition of *The Times* of London. There were hardly any Indian newspapers, but rumour and the tales of incoming prisoners brought word of the recent disorder in the Punjab. After some years of good behaviour, a prisoner might be allowed to write a petition for clemency. Vinayak Savarkar had been punished eight times in 1912–14 for refusing to work and possessing forbidden articles. But his behaviour over the ensuing five years, the superintendent reported, was 'very good'. He was 'always suave and polite but like his brother he has never shown any disposition to actively assist government'.[62] When the amnesty was announced in 1919 to mark the Allied victory, many prisoners appealed for release. Savarkar asked for remission of his second term of twenty-five years. 'So far from believing in the militant school of the Bukanin [sic] type, I do not contribute even to the peaceful and philosophical anarchism of a Kropotkin or a Tolstoy.'[63] He elaborated this in a letter to his brother. 'We were revolutionists under necessity and not by choice. We felt that the best interests of India as well as of England demanded that her ideals be progressively and peacefully realized by mutual help and cooperation.' The Raj was not satisfied: there was to be no remission. Savarkar had one visit over 30–31 May 1919 from his wife and brother, of one and one and a half hours respectively. Some prisoners were released to mainland prisons, others under warrant for good behaviour. In one sense, the dismal experience of captivity could reinforce a sense of the solidity of the Raj in a prisoner's mind; it left no sphere of one's physical or mental life untouched. Daily indignities wore down the mind. But, then again, violence committed, contemplated, witnessed left no one untouched.[64] In another sense, long-term imprisonment mirrored the revolutionary aesthetic adopted by many of the young men, even down to the cell-like structure that governed their lives. Savarkar saw a role for himself in the prison in fighting mental languor and promoting spiritual discipline. Fortified by a growing prison library, he read and began to write. Influenced perhaps by the ever-present tyranny of the mostly Muslim guards, the vision of the nation that emerged on paper was fashioned in Hindu terms, in defiance of external aggressions. This took form in two new histories of India, and a treatise published in 1923 entitled *Hindutva: Who is a Hindu?*[65]

Many of the radicals of the pre-war years were seeing the future in more exclusive terms. Bhai Parmanand, who remained in the public eye as one of the most controversial prisoners from the 1915 rebellion, went on hunger strike at Port Blair and was force-fed through a tube. He was released after signing a warrant that he would not take part in any anarchist activity. He had always maintained his innocence. He saw this as victory and likened his release to the fall of the Bastille. He travelled by train to Lahore, and to his wife. She was now the teacher in the family, supporting their daughters; as Bhai Parmanand told the superintendent of the prison, 'perhaps I shall do her work at home'. After a short rest in Kashmir, he attended the Congress Special Session in Calcutta on 4 September; it was a reunion with Gandhi, whom he had last seen when he had stayed in his house in the Transvaal. He now accepted him as 'a new Avatar'. He also came to the conclusion that 'the salvation of this country was possible through Hindus and Hindus alone'.[66]

As he travelled, Bhai Parmanand shared a railway carriage with a visiting British Labour politician, J. C. Wedgwood, a scion of the fine-china family, who published his version of the encounter in the *Daily Herald* under the headline, 'Hell in Andamans'. Under pressure from within India, the British authorities had already launched an inquiry, as part of a wider investigation into prison conditions. The distorted world of high prisoner mortality, 46.73 per 1,000 in 1919, routine brutality and sexual predation could not stand up to close scrutiny.[67] As a result of this, the sending of seditious prisoners to the Andamans was briefly halted, but, given the scale of the investment there, the ideal of the islands as a model settlement endured. Around 4,000 of the estimated 11,532 convicts and the 3,000 local-born persons were sent back to the mainland, but they were soon replaced in 1922 by 1,000 men serving life sentences for rebellion in south India. By 1925, their wives and families were encouraged to join them.[68] This vision of quarantine colonies was common among empires. Political prisoners from French Indochina were shipped across oceans, from French Guiana to Congo or Gabon, Madagascar or New Caledonia. There were instances of escape from French Guiana. It was harder to abscond from nearer to home, from the prison on Poulo Condore, off Saigon, or from those built in montane areas, such as the penitentiary at Lao Bao.[69] In the Netherlands Indies, the nineteenth-century practice of using convict labour in remote coal mines in West Sumatra or southeastern Borneo persisted into the 1920s. The average prison population in the Indies in 1920 was 57,006, or 106 in 100,000. Overcrowded prisons led to the creation of a new-style 'agricultural colony' at Nusa Kambangan, an island off the south coast of Java, which by 1922 held more than 3,200 convicts. All of these regimes were known for their high mortality, violent punishment and corruption, and stood ready to absorb new populations of political internees.[70]

The imperial dragnet was global in its reach, but not all-encompassing. In the face of the Bolshevik panic, a conference on 'The International

Struggle against Bolshevism' was convened in Munich in December 1920 and attracted twenty-four police officials from six European countries. But the major imperial powers, Britain and France, were absent. International criminal policing was strengthened by the formation of Interpol in 1923. But cooperation in political policing tended to be ad hoc, informal and bilateral. In the face of the wartime anarchist scares and the new Bolshevik panic, the sharing of intelligence between the British, United States and Canada was formalized in 1919.[71] On paper, a formidable coven of intelligence bodies now oversaw the secret governance of British Asia. There was the Central Security Department in London, the Intelligence Bureau of the Home Department of India, the Joint Naval and Military Intelligence Bureau in Hong Kong, the ambassadors and consuls in Bangkok, Batavia, Singora and elsewhere. In the aftermath of the Singapore Mutiny, in late 1918 a Special Branch was formed there. Learning from the Sûreté, it built up its index of fingerprints from 7,751 records in 1906 to 203,075 in 1927. In 1921 it was augmented by a new Malayan Bureau of Political Intelligence, also based in Singapore, which tracked moving targets across the region and liaised with other agencies. Its brief was explicitly political, separate from the criminal, 'except in so far as the criminal is "political" '. 'Many crimes which appear to be ordinary are afterwards seen to be "political", and vice versa.' It built up an archive of 'political' files inherited from the military. It also dabbled in counter-propaganda. It was staffed by Europeans of long standing in Asia. Its first head was an Englishman, A. S. Jelf, with twenty-two years' service in Malaya, who had worked as a counter-espionage officer for Ridout in 1917 and for MI5 in 1918. But all this did not prevent 'suicidal' turf wars between Indian intelligence and the new Secret Intelligence Service (MI6).[72] In the first annual review of its workings, the director of the Malayan Bureau of Political Intelligence complained that district officers communicated to it 'so little of the common talk of the people'. Nor in its first year did any branch of government in Malaya call on its services. The police had their own paid informers, and on these the Political Intelligence organization depended: it had none of its own, nor its own translation staff. It maintained lists of suspects and proscribed publications and a flagship monthly, *Bulletin of Political Intelligence*, printed by the 2nd Middlesex Regiment. It was an article of faith that only Europeans should handle it: the staff of the Bureau consisted of Jelf and one confidential typist: a

married European lady. Over time, the empire of ledger and list began
to catch up with the field craft of the underground.[73]

The Great Game, the 'beautiful game' of old, was to be played with
new rules. Officials in New Delhi were now chary at the thought of
swashbuckling freebooters flashing subsidy payments to potentates
beyond the borders of the Raj. Frederick Bailey, as he donned native disguise in Tashkent, inspired by the heroics of John Buchan's Richard
Hannay, admitted that he found little encouragement from on high. He
went so deep underground that he was out of contact with his superiors
entirely from October 1918 to January 1920, when he reappeared
miraculously in Meshed in Persia after he had been reported dead in
India, and the Soviets in Tashkent had given him a funeral *in absentia*
with full military honours.[74] It was increasingly unclear what such
adventures achieved. It was reported in the Bengali press that Charles
Tegart, the nemesis of Jatin Mukherjee, 'dressed as a dandy' to survey
the bazaars. But this was part of his growing myth, and in truth most
British policemen dealt with agents at a remove through local subordinates.[75] The Raj had forward posts on the overland routes to India at
Meshed and at Kashgar, in Xinjiang, from where the road to India, such
as it was, led to Gilgit, which took twenty-six days, or, via Leh, thirty-
eight days. As Roy and his associates in Tashkent had found, there were
only two plausible overland routes from Russia into India, through
Afghanistan to Peshawar or over the Pamir mountains to the Kara-
koram, where the British picked up ten men in early 1922.[76] The British
were confident that all of the *muhajirin* trained and despatched to India
overland by M. N. Roy were accounted for.[77] If an act by one person or
a few could set great revolutionary events in motion, equally the right
man at the border post, or in the harbour master's office, could stop
them in their tracks. The first line of imperial defence was the mail censor. Few Indians received letters from abroad, and the foreign mail that
arrived was all channelled through the Foreign Post Office in Bombay.
Local post offices could screen it out, even if letters were under several
covers, as the police looked first to the addresses from which they were
despatched. It became impossible, as Muzaffar Ahmad later observed,
to guide an international movement 'though the postal department'.[78]

The first Comintern emissary to get through to India from Europe was
Nalini Gupta, a man who had spent the war in Britain and had moved to
Berlin and to Moscow with Chatto's party. Alone of that group, he had

gained Roy's confidence, and his relative lack of involvement in the war-time plots perhaps recommended him as a discreet messenger. He left Berlin in mid-September 1921, travelling by sea. He tarried in Colombo for some weeks, treating an injured leg, arriving in Calcutta two days before Christmas. He brought the first direct communication from Roy to India: a manifesto, signed by Roy and Abani Mukherji, for the Congress meeting in Gandhi's home city of Ahmedabad in December 1921. In Moscow, Nalini claimed to have connections with the Bengal under-ground. But in Bengal it transpired that this acquaintance was thin. The old guard would not see him and had no reason to trust him. Some remembered that he had been involved in the Burdwan Flood Relief in 1913, as many patriotic young men were. But he was recollected more for his 'instinctive flair for fanning personal resentments'. There was talk of a statement he had given to the police back in 1914. He had had a com-fortable war, working in munitions factories in Britain. Rebuffed by the Bengal underground, he sought out the younger revolutionaries through their newspapers. Via an intermediary he met Muzaffar Ahmad, then running a periodical for workers. Muzaffar Ahmad accepted that he was what he said he was, but while Nalini seemed to know a good deal about bombs, Muzaffar was struck by his ignorance of the workings of the International, about which he and his friends were hungry for knowledge. And at every stage, the British were watching him.[79]

THE MAN WHO WOULD BE KING

All this encouraged the British in a remarkable display of imperial sangfroid. Shortly before Christmas 1921, under the eyes of press pho-tographers and captured by the wonder of Cinechrome, all the military and civilian resources of the Raj were fully mobilized on its frontier, in the Terai, on the edge of the Himalayan foothills in Nepal. About a mile from the border, Edward, Prince of Wales was going hunting. The expedition had been a year in the planning: jungle had been cleared over two seasons, with labour drafted in from across the kingdom to make a road; electric cables had been laid for huge arc lamps that were hung in the trees. A base station was set up, with streets of huge tents and its own telegraph station, manned by Gurkha signallers from Rawalpindi. There were telephone wires and field stations in the forest to report the movement of the quarry. 'No rhino was untracked,' the official account declared, 'or tiger left to itself.' The camp was dressed like a film set; even the wastepaper basket by the prince's bed was the lower joint of a rhino's leg.[80]

No more than an hour after his arrival, following a ceremonial blessing from Buddhist monks from Kathmandu, the Prince of Wales set off on the hunt. Tigers were 'ringed' by 100 elephants: some 300–400 elephants were involved in all. Soon a 9½-foot tiger was corralled, to await the prince. His first shot was a hit, but the kill went to a member of his staff. Each night buffaloes were tethered to lure the tigers to gorge themselves into somnambulance. The 'bag' during a week at the camp amounted to seventeen tigers, nine rhinoceros, two leopards and two bears.[81] The prince was accompanied by a large retinue, which included his favourite cousin, Lord Louis Mountbatten, who kept a diary. He recorded the squabbles over the kills, and the dark mood of the prince, who found the odds between man and beast unsporting and was 'too keen on his riding and polo to care much about anything else'. The whole affair cost the kingdom of Nepal around £300,000.[82]

The sport was the climax of a grand royal progress across Asia, over some 41,000 miles in eight months. The twenty-seven-year-old heir to the throne had already undertaken a series of morale-raising tours, most recently to Australia. His visit to India was postponed from 1920, because of the Amritsar Massacre and the lockdown of the Punjab. By 1921, many still felt it was unwise for him to go, but the viceroy believed it was impossible to postpone it further, as it would signal to the world that India was no longer safe for the British. Edward was to retrace the steps his father, George V, had taken ten years previously, when he was tailed by revolutionaries. For his part, the king impressed on his son 'the importance of elaborate display and pageantry in impressing the Oriental mind'.[83]

The royal progress had set forth from Portsmouth on 26 October 1921, when the prince had sailed on HMS *Renown*, with his retinue, his own printing press and sixteen drummer boys from the Royal Marine barracks at Eastney. It was reported across the empire that eleven black cats joined the ship: a good omen.[84] The ship stopped at the key strategic nodes of Britain's imperial defence: Gibraltar, Malta, Suez – where Indian troops, still in the field, lined the Canal – and Aden, where the streets were adorned with a large banner: 'Tell Daddy we are all happy under British rule.'[85] The Indian officers on duty presented the hilts of their half-drawn swords for the prince to touch, a traditional gesture of fealty and its acceptance. In India, however, provincial governors continued to warn against the visit. Gandhi in an article in *Young India* on 29 September had declared that 'it is sinful for any one, either as soldier or civilian, to serve this Government.' British intelligence itemized ninety separate attempts to interfere with Indian troops between April 1919 and September 1921, and fifty-four major instances of riot or violence in 1921 alone, many of them targeting Europeans.[86] As *Renown* approached India, the visit was a crucial test of the security of the Raj and of the loyalties of its peoples.

On the very eve of the prince's arrival in Bombay, another long imperial voyage came to an end, that of Gurdit Singh and the *Komagata Maru*. Since the battle at Budge Budge in September 1914, Gurdit Singh had gone to ground and covered vast distances by foot across India. He avoided his home territory of the Punjab, settled for a while near Baroda, working as a herbalist, then on the outskirts of Bombay as a doctor and in a shipbuilder's yard. He had come to the city to seek an audience with Gandhi, to whose teachings he now, a reluctant advocate of violence it seemed, submitted. Over three meetings in 1921 they discussed the terms of his surrender to the British. This would be, Gandhi urged, the noblest end to his odyssey, when, even under the shadow of the death sentence, and in despair at British law, he might present his cause to the world. On the afternoon of 15 November, in an event carefully stage-managed on both sides, Gurdit appeared at Sheikhupura in the Punjab and surrendered to the police in front of thousands of Sikhs gathered for the festival of the Guru Nanak. He was the final person to be arrested under the 'Ingress of India Ordinance' of 1914, just as he had earlier been its principal target. It marked a kind of ending to one campaign of the inner Asian war.[87]

The entire royal tour was a series of stations through which to reflect on the imperial sacrifices of the war years. When the Prince of Wales landed in Bombay two days later, on 17 November, he entered India through the as yet unfinished arch of the Gateway of India. At every pause on his itinerary he was confronted by ex-servicemen, many of them maimed. One of his first public acts was to lay the foundation stone of a memorial to the fallen Maratha soldier at Poona, and this was combined with a visit to the shrine of the seventeenth warrior-king

Shivaji, revered by Hindu patriots. His time in Bombay set a pattern for the next seven months: there was a naval pageant; cricket with the Parsi community and polo with the Maharajah of Rutlam's team. There were nightly balls, where the modern prince surprised guests by his willingness to shake their hands. The precedent and protocol of the Raj, he later wrote, was 'so rigid that it astonished even me'.[88]

A few days earlier, Gandhi had given notice that a civil disobedience would begin in the *taluka* of Bardoli, in Gujarat. The choice was heavy with symbolism: it was near Surat, where a British fleet had first arrived in India some 300 years earlier, and from here – or so the news was spread across north India – the British Raj would come to an end on 1 December. The police would be told to stand down and serve the people. Taxes would not be paid. This was a region where the call for *Swaraj* was beginning to mobilize the peasantry, although Bardoli was chosen as it was one of the least unruly areas where the tenet of non-violence was most likely to be adhered to.[89] On the morning of 17 November, as *Renown* approached Bombay, Gandhi entered the city to preside at a bonfire of foreign clothes – including silk saris thrown from house windows – at the Elphinstone Mills. An estimated 25,000 people assembled to launch a boycott of the royal tour: a *hartal*, or 'stoppage'. It was an opportunity to test non-cooperation as a strategy and as a vision of a political nation that united Muslims, Hindus and others. In Delhi and Calcutta most of the shops were closed. The *hartal* was enforced by a movement of 'volunteers' sporting 'Gandhi caps'. In Bombay they forcibly stopped and emptied trams carrying people southwards to welcome the prince and set some on fire. Groups who had turned out to welcome the prince – such as the Anglo-Indians and Parsis prominent in imperial service and trade – became targets: women had their saris torn and there were testimonies of rape. These communities defended themselves in turn. In five days of riots across the city, perhaps thirty people were shot dead. 'I have been shamed,' Gandhi wrote, and he embarked for the first time on a fast at his house in the city to restore order.[90] The sweep of arrests across provinces took in C. R. Das in Bengal, Lala Lajpat Rai in the Punjab and Motilal Nehru in the United Provinces. By the end of December there were perhaps 30,000 political detainees. The British authorities hesitated to make Gandhi himself a martyr. They had come to acknowledge that, to the masses, Gandhi was not merely a national hero, but 'semi-divine'. The presence of the Prince of Wales – and the large, experienced press pack at his heels – stayed their hand. Gandhi renewed his call for 'Hindu-Muslim-Sikh-Parsi-Christian-Jew unity'. He was now caught between pressure to seize the moment to push the Raj to the edge of collapse and fear that the *satyagraha* would descend further into violence. In the event, Gandhi also stayed his hand, and the Bardoli protest was postponed. However, the policy of non-cooperation was reaffirmed at the Congress session in Allahabad in the last week of December, and on 1 February 1922 Gandhi sent an ultimatum to the viceroy that it would resume on 12 February.[91]

The belief that the Raj was entering its endgame drew credence from an unprecedented wave of strikes in the textile and jute mills of Bombay and Calcutta, on the railways, the posts and telegraphs, the Calcutta tramways and the plantations of far Assam. Like the strike waves in Java, on the waterfront and in sugar factories, these disputes often began from within groups of workers, without even a visible trade union organization, with recognized leaders being called in to investigate and mediate. However, their aim was rarely to inflame the situation: as Gandhi wrote in July 1921, 'We seek not to destroy capital or capitalists but to regulate the relations between capital and labour. We want to harness capital to our side.'[92] There had also been plenty of instances of peasant unrest in the earlier non-cooperation of 1918–19, especially in the wake of Gandhi's arrest in April 1919: railway stations were attacked and telegraph wires cut. But, to Gandhi, this was a 'Himalayan miscalculation' on the part of protesters.[93] Now, in the wake of bad harvests, there was more to come. Among Muslim peasants of the south Malabar region, the so-called 'Moplahs', the resentment of tenants in the face of evictions fused with a sense of Islam being endangered. A series of confrontations with armed police developed into full-scale rebellion, with arson, killings and assaults on the symbols of the Raj. The leaders proclaimed themselves 'Khilafat Kings'. Here too there was a local mood, in the words of the governor of Madras, 'that the end of the British Raj is at hand'.[94] It was a second Amritsar, which the British met on a war footing, another sign – if it were needed – of the naked force on which their control now rested. At the time of the prince's arrival in Bombay, the military sweeps were still under way: in total 2,339 rebels were killed, 1,652 wounded; 5,955 were captured and 39,348 more surrendered – casualties on the largest scale since 1857.[95] On the night of 19 November, a closed goods wagon carrying 100 prisoners from Calicut to Madras was opened at Podanor station to find seventy of them dying of heat exhaustion and asphyxiation. The venetian blinds at the upper part of the doors were sealed with wire gauze and painted over, making them more or less airtight. The guards had ignored the shouts and banging: it was a mobile Black Hole of Calcutta.[96]

This provided a macabre backdrop to the high pomp of the royal tour. Over 100 people departed Bombay with the prince in four trains. At every stage, the official history noted the 'crouched . . . silent, intent population'.[97] More biddable crowds were shipped in from the country-side with the assistance of local landlords. In New Delhi, an estimated 20,000–25,000 of them appeared, armed with *lathis* against non-cooperators. At Lucknow, the prince's party toured the British memorials to the siege of 1857. At the tomb of its defender they were confronted by the graffito: 'Here Henry Lawrence died. May God send him straight to hell.'[98] The prince travelled onwards in a *cordon sanitaire*, in what he termed 'Gandhi's ominous shadow'.[99] The policeman David Petrie, having received renewed reports of bomb-making in the French enclave at Chandernagore, accompanied him throughout. After Bombay the royal train moved through the territories of the princely states, in homage to the new emphasis on 'indirect rule'. It was also a place of greater safety in that the states possessed unrestrained powers to arrest and detain. Indeed, it was to the Indian princes, in whom many British conservatives saw a potential third force standing between the people and Congress, that the visit became chiefly directed. Each halt was consecrated with the sacrifice of wild beasts: cheetah in Baroda, snipe on Pichola Lake in Udaipur, pig-sticking in Jodhpur, imperial sand grouse in Gujner – where one day's bag was 1,035 birds – demoiselle crane at Kodamdesar, and more tigers in Mysore. In Patiala, two panthers were taken from the zoo, doped and left beneath bushes for the prince to bag. But by this point, his enthusiasm had long flagged.[100]

The press bandwagon retreated into an *Arabian Nights* fantasy: a 'semi-mystical parade' whose excesses further inflamed Indian opinion.[101] An illuminated night pageant at Bharatpur with golden elephants, dancing horses, and camels sixteen abreast, viewed from a pavilion on a hill built especially for the occasion, cost £60,000. But in the same city

there were rumours of an attack on the prince's convoy of motor vehicles, and Lord Mountbatten rode as a decoy with a six-shooter in his
pocket. The old *maya*, or magic of the Raj, observed so close to hand,
did not fool the prince himself: he saw through the crowds of 'high-
school boys, Boy Scouts and Europeans', and well realized 'what a b.f.
[bloody fool] they had made of me'. 'I was', he wrote to the viceroy,
Lord Reading, 'not so naive as to suppose that the India won by Clive
had been saved through my exertions on the polo field of Allahabad.'
After the hunt, Christmas was spent in Calcutta, with races and a historical pageant to open the new Victoria Memorial, a 'Valhalla of the
Indian Empire', and yet another war memorial. Even loyalists criticized
the expense at a time of austerity, and those who attended the events,
as one district officer reported in Bengal, did so for 'fun and out of
curiosity, rather than out of a feeling of loyalty to the throne'.[102] Mooted
in part to acknowledge the empire's contribution to the war effort, the
visit became an opportunity to voice the damage that had been done to
ideas of imperial citizenship. And because the Crown was traditionally
a distant place for 'loyal opinion' to appeal to in the face of local
oppressions, the Crown's sudden nearness in India brought it under
closer scrutiny and it was found wanting. Royal visits were traditionally celebrated by the release of prisoners. But, as local opinion
constantly pointed out, this tour was marked by ever more arrests.
Imperial patriotism and national dissent drew closer together.[103]

On 4 February 1922, the prince was in Bhopal state, at a shooting
camp at Kachnaria, twenty-two miles from the capital, pursuing tigers,
panthers and sambar deer, and then attended a house party, amusing
himself by playing on pogo sticks.[104] Some 600 miles away, in the heart
of the United Provinces, *satyagraha* broke free of its self-imposed constraints. Chauri Chaura was a town fifteen miles east by road of
Gorakhpur junction, not far from the Nepal border: a rail halt of some
1,371 inhabitants, with a godown, a kerosene tank and a small bazaar.
It sat within a matrix of similar settlements, trading oil, animal skins
and dal, although it was its role as a cloth market that was played up
by observers steeped in the imagery of the *satyagraha* campaign. It was
a place of no large consequence, but it was locked into wider horizons:
villagers had migrated to Assam and Burma, especially to Rangoon,
and enlisted in war service. After a Congress official appeared in the
village, fired by protests at the price of wheat it embraced the campaign

for *satyagraha*. Local volunteers swore off meat and alcohol. One of the key movers, a man called Bhagwan Ahir, was a retired soldier who drilled the volunteers in the vicinity of the police station. When challenged by the police on 1 February, his contemptuous response was met with a beating. This reinforced the mood of militancy, and at a protest at the bazaar on 4 February against his maltreatment the police fired shots, at first into the air. But the seeming fact that the 'bullets have turned into water by the grace of Gandhiji' emboldened the crowd further.[105] Shots were then fired into the crowd; three people died and more were injured. The police backed into the police post, where they were locked inside. It was sprinkled with kerosene and set alight: twenty-three men died in the blaze. Gandhi denounced the 'mob'; just over a week later, on 12 February, Congress called off its national campaign, and Gandhi began another penitent fast. But the protestors had called out Gandhi's name, and the signing of the pledge of abstinence was now taken as an implication of guilt in the killings. The Raj launched what was, in effect, a large-scale exercise in collective punishment.[106]

Chauri Chaura brought *satyagraha* as a means to freedom under ever more searching scrutiny. For Gandhi, the calling of his name meant that, despite the pledges, it had been taken up by the villagers as a watchword for violence. This appalled him. If *satyagraha* was to be an act of freedom, the men of Chauri Chaura had abandoned it. This was 'the death of non-violence'. Gandhi's thoughts were not geared towards some future outcome – some horizon of liberty set ultimately at the discretion of the British, fixed, as it were, in imperial time: *satyagraha* was a goal and an end in itself, and it lived in the present.[107] To many nationalists this was precisely the problem: that the means might stifle the end. Gandhi's call to the masses was at its heart a way of disciplining them, an implicit call for restraint. For some within Congress, like the Bengal leader C. R. Das – the man who had led the defence at the Alipore Bomb Trial – this was a rejection of politics itself. For the radicals, in the prisons and the bookstalls, there was no sense in which his campaign for *Swaraj* was aimed at creating a revolutionary crisis, to push the colonial state into the abyss. As a young follower of C. R. Das, Subhas Chandra Bose, observed: 'No one could understand why Mahatma should have used the isolated incident at Chauri Chaura for strangling the movement all over the country.'[108] But equally, for the moderates, Chauri Chaura showed how quickly open defiance of the

Raj could collapse, and they were antagonized by Gandhi's failure to negotiate with its offers of reform. Sensing his vulnerability on all sides, the British had Gandhi arrested and sentenced him to six years in prison. Further afield, the Indians in Moscow looked to capitalize on this, and more emissaries from Russia began to fall into the net of the British.

For the remainder of the royal tour, the mood of the country, and that of the prince, darkened. After a ten-day side trip in Burma, he returned to Madras. There were yet more parades of pensioners, at which their war wounds seemed ever more a blandishment. By the time he finally caught up with his father's old footsteps in New Delhi on 14–21 February to open the All-India memorial to King Edward VII, the place was a wilderness. His days in the Punjab and the Northwest Frontier Province were spent mostly in the company of the military. His departure on 17 March was a relief for all concerned. After Ceylon, and a visit to the site of the holy relic of the Buddha, he entered the Straits of Malacca and the seemingly calmer waters of British Malaya.

On 28 March 1922, the prince docked off the coast and was met by a cavalcade of sultans in motor cars to whisk him off to the capital, Kuala Lumpur. Nestled among the sharply rising granite peaks of the central range of the Malay Peninsula was an empire in microcosm: a symbol of colonial capitalism's 'protean versatility' in regenerating itself.[109] Kuala Lumpur was barely a generation old, cut from the forest at a lip of land where two rivers met, which gave the town its Malay name: 'muddy confluence'. From here, the swollen brown waters of the Klang River began their final surge into the Straits of Malacca, some forty meandering miles downstream. For several generations, miners from China had opened up the small Malay state of Selangor by clearing the lowland forests to dredge the rich alluvium for tin. As the economic possibilities and competition increased, rival Chinese gangs formed alliances with rival Malay factions. The British drew from this a picture of anarchy and misrule and, in 1874, seized upon it as just cause to take the Malay rulers of the peninsula under their own 'protection', and awarded themselves the status of pioneers.

By the 1900s this process had accelerated, and drew the gaze of investors from Singapore and beyond towards the higher tracts of forest, for the planting of large plantations of rubber trees. It was a fulcrum of Asia's age of mobility. The population of Kuala Lumpur rose from only 18,000 in 1891 to 46,718 in 1911 and 80,424 in 1921, mostly with Chinese and Tamil labour. The population of the Malay Peninsula as a whole peaked in these boom years of the mid-1920s, with a colossal annual inflow of over 200,000 people a year. By the 1931 census there were 624,000 Indians, mostly Tamils from the south, and 1,700,000 Chinese in a population that had risen from 2,673,000 to 3,358,000 since 1921. In addition, of the over 594,000 Muslim Malays, who claimed special status as the indigenous people of Malaya, less than 60 per cent were residents of more than forty years' standing. The others were recent settlers from the islands of the Netherlands East Indies.[110] By the mid-1920s, Malaya's volume of trade exceeded the aggregate volume of all the other British colonies and protectorates combined. Most of the profits, however, passed through the colonial port cities of the Straits Settlements – Singapore, Penang and Malacca – where the British had had a foothold since the late eighteenth century. In terms of value of exports per head of population Malaya was the wealthiest country on earth.[111] Close to the meeting of rivers stood the Market Square, where there were Palladian shophouses with Art Deco flourishes, built by the British banks and agencies which controlled the commanding heights of the colonial economy. At the heart of the square stood Mr Zacharias's Ford dealership. Zacharias himself was gone, driven out by the ugly anti-German mood in the war. But business was good: over the previous two years the number of motor cars had trebled to 4,525, and this in a town of only 2,500 Europeans.[112] The local newspapers inveighed constantly against the new scourge of 'traffic'.

In 1922 Kuala Lumpur was one of the first cities of the empire to institute an urban plan on garden city lines: a tropical Letchworth. Kuala Lumpur's massive storm drains and its anti-malarial works, for instance, were models of municipal engineering. The streets were latticed overhead with electric and telegraph wires, and lit by brilliant electric globes, alongside the old oil lamps, which Tamil lighters still tended nightly. 'The government', a town worthy had proudly claimed a few years before, 'is an all-powerful and benevolent one. Every Resident is a Socialist in his own State.'[113] This was driven in no small part by a desire to discipline and segregate its citizens. Here, within a small grid of streets, a town of barely 100,000 souls, western dreams of dominion in Asia took something near their most complete form. All that was needed, observed one visitor, was to find it a name not so associated with mud.[114]

The visit of the Prince of Wales to Kuala Lumpur was a celebration of a return to normal times after the war. Its centrepiece was an elaborate pantomime on the sacred ground of the Padang, a former vegetable patch, a few hundred yards west of the Klang River, which served as village green, cricket pitch and Field of Mars for the British. On the Bluff above it, in a last-ditch defensible position, stood the official residencies, the messes of unmarried colonial servants and the police barracks. The Padang was surrounded by the keystones of imperial power: St Mary's Church, the police station, the government printing press, the law courts and the mock-Tudor Selangor Club with its long bar, the 'Spotted Dog', named after some resident cur, long dead. From its veranda the prince watched the torchlight procession of dancing dragons and open cars carrying local beauty queens.

Across the Padang, the club faced the long, arched galleries of the Federal Secretariat. The British ruled but the Malay rulers remained sovereign. However, as the succession of treaties of 'protection' after 1874 made clear, they were bound to accept British advice on all matters save those pertaining to 'Malay custom and religion'. As a genuflection to this, the Secretariat was built in lavish Indo-Saracenic style; the railway station to the south was an arabesque fantasia of domes and turrets, painted snow-white. 'It no more suggested an autochthonous growth', cautioned one new arrival in 1921, 'than did a "Moorish" city of laths and plaster at Earls Court or Shepherd's Bush.'[115] Something similar was staged for the prince's benefit a few days later, at a Malaya-Borneo Exhibition in Singapore. The post-war years saw a British reassertion of the 'Malay' character of the government. The British created a new role for Malay elites in the burgeoning bureaucracy. There was unease about the effect of all this on the natural rhythms of Malay life, to which aristocratic English remained curiously emotionally attached. 'We have', the high commissioner, Sir Laurence Guillemard, observed ruefully, 'bred too many clerks.'[116] Food shortage, and the post-war slump in prices, also strengthened a paternalistic and self-serving imperial view that the Malays were essentially a yeoman peasantry, happiest as subsistence farmers and fishermen, in their *kampungs*, shy of towns, shy of work, under the feudal sway of their sultans and chiefs. Their lives were a world away from, though often in thrall to, the Indian moneylender or the Chinese shopkeeper, whose communities dominated the middle reaches of the colonial economy and the wage labour opportunities of the emerging industrial economy of the towns, mines and plantations. These stereotypes were at odds with Malay histories of urban trade and the Chinese experience as pioneering farmers. But in the British imagination Malaya was, as one visitor later termed it, 'a Tory Eden', where each community knew their place. To its critics it had become a 'plural society': a mélange of peoples, where different ethnic groups were concentrated in different economic tasks; living side by side, but separately from one another. These communities mixed but never mingled and met only in the marketplace. One consequence of this was to make solidarities beyond race – in Mas Marco Kartodikromo's *sama rasa sama rata*, fraternity and equality – hard to envisage.[117]

Kuala Lumpur was still very much a Chinese town. From its early days, government revenues were entirely reliant on duty from its tin mines and revenue farmers. At one point, the Selangor State Railway was leased to Yap Ah Loy, the magnate whom the local Chinese celebrated as the true founder of the city, in order to keep it running. The local temples venerated him as a paragon of rags-to-riches endeavour in both Malaya and China; in the writings of the late-Qing reformer and intellectual Liang Qichao, he was a heroic colonizer who had his inheritance stolen from him by the British.[118] As British ambitions grew, Chinese were dislodged from key administrative roles and their leaders were consulted less often. The Chinese cemetery, where the tombs of the first settlers lay, was later to be turned into 'a first-class golf course'.[119] It was these migrants, more than the British, who created 'British Malaya', and they bore the physical cost of opening up its inhospitable terrain. Death rates from scourges such as malaria were some of the highest in the colonial world and were only slowly stabilizing. Labour was cheap, and wages at a minimum. The rubber boom created a chasm not merely between Europeans and Asians, but also among Asians themselves. Some of the most ostentatious wealth was that of the Chinese 'Kapitans' – or bosses – who controlled the trade in migrant labour. In the Market Square, Chinese shophouses encroached on the British-owned banks and merchant houses. Their narrow frontages were covered with a 'five-foot way' to shelter customers from the rain and heat; their deep interiors were partitioned and sub-let in infinite fractions to tailors, barbers, moneylenders and, smallest of all, the cubicles for workers. Surveys of similar shophouses in Singapore in 1906–17 showed an average density of 18.7 to 44.5 people a house and 635 to 1,304 people an acre.[120] These buildings were no place for stable family life and a stage for myriad small tragedies.

At daybreak on Sunday, 18 December 1921, three months before the arrival of the prince in Kuala Lumpur, three young Chinese, a man and two women, had been found hanging from a mangosteen tree in the Lake Gardens, a handkerchief twisted around each of their necks, their clothes drenched. Another girl was found semi-conscious at the foot of the tree. The dead girls, aged sixteen and eighteen, and the survivor, only fifteen, were servants from the same household, sold to Yap Loong Hin, a wealthy businessman and son of a Kapitan. They had been there for six to ten years. The young man worked as an assistant storekeeper, and lived with his brother and mother. In his pocket was a silver watch and chain, and the names of two football teams in a notebook. They were all, it seemed, local-born. Their shoes were laid out neatly on a nearby bench, and a fourth handkerchief lay nearby with a bottle of hydrochloric acid. The young man had come for the girls in the night. They had drunk the acid together, saying 'if they could not get married, they preferred to die'. Then they had jumped in the lake, the girl who survived explained, and tried to drown. When this failed, they lay on the ground. What then happened, she could not say.[121] In Kuala Lumpur, the juxtapositions of brazen wealth and poverty and alienation intensified a hunger among the young for a new ordering of society. The colonial idyll was stillborn.

The Prince of Wales reached Hong Kong on 6 April, in the wake of the largest strike in the colony's history. He was carried in a palanquin in a manner that evoked the assassin's welcome to Governor Francis May in 1912. A great pavilion was constructed in the square facing the Hong Kong Club at vast expense. But the mood remained tense, and it was only in the bosom of another, newer empire that the tensions outwardly eased. An entire squadron of light cruisers was sent to escort him to Yokohama, only four days' journey away, where he was welcomed by two more battle squadrons on the morning of 12 April 1922. There were large crowds, and dockyards, factories and temples, it was reported, emptied to greet him. He was welcomed by Hirohito, Regent of Japan (*Sessho*), to review an entire division of the Japanese Imperial

Guard. Later they played golf and hunted for ducks with nets. Here the imperial tour ended, in the wake of the signing of the Four-Power Treaty by the United States, Britain, France and Japan at the Washington Naval Conference in December 1921, which formally ended the Anglo-Japanese alliance. On 26 April a massive earthquake struck below Tokyo Bay, cracking the palace walls and sending houses tumbling into canals. The prince was travelling towards Mount Fuji at the time. But the nightclub he had visited a few nights before suffered serious damage. It was, seismologists reported, a portent for a bigger upheaval to come.[122]

WILD LEARNING

As HMS *Renown* sailed the 'vast connecting river' from the Indian Ocean, through the Straits of Malacca to China and Japan, it traced the course of the *Komagata Maru* in reverse. It was followed by whispers of rebellion: that the Chinese were planning to kidnap the prince and that overseas Indians were planning a fresh *hartal*. But, in the event, the most that happened was that one Indian in Singapore became 'very vociferous' on the morning of the prince's arrival and was locked up for the duration of his stay.[123] In the war years, the idea of these seaways as free spaces had taken a battering. The *belle époque* of the arc of port cities seemed as if it might be on the wane. Since the midnineteenth century, imperial globalism had drawn Alexandria, Aden, Bombay, Calcutta, Penang, Singapore and Hong Kong into a connected public sphere in which the universalisms of the 'four seas' came into more intimate contact.[124] This allowed their polyglot, diasporic communities to participate in a variety of Enlightenments: of the west, of the eastern Mediterranean, of East Asia. But now many of the stories they told of themselves were narratives of loss: of grief for lost influence; nostalgia for a cosmopolitan past or for the recession of the prospect of alternative futures.[125] To be sure, old imaginative geographies remained intact. The 'kingdom of words' – the world of letter-writing and calligraphy, the invocation of titles, lineages and distant sovereignties – still remained a substance of power in the archipelago. It was visible in the 'Silk Letters Conspiracy' of 1916 and the defence of the Ottoman Caliphate.[126] There were those, including

Rabindranath Tagore himself, who continued to extol the 'different universalisms' of the first, inclusive wave of pan-Asian thinking.[127] But in many ways, old connections were increasingly tempered by colonial borders, by ethnic and ideological exclusivity, and the rise of 'dismal nationalism'.

And yet, while one set of connections diminished, the cities themselves and their intricate worldly neighbourhoods endured. A new cast of intellectuals in Asia attempted to weave them together, with all the mistranslations, misadventures, false alliances and schisms this brought. Cosmopolitanism was embraced not only by the elite but taken further into society both as an ideology and even, by some, as an identity.[128] These ideas were rarely informed by the traditions of thinking about rights and hospitality that the term invoked in the European canon. They were the product of a world consciousness at work at multiple levels, not least in the banal worldliness of everyday life, of people who often did not travel very far at all. All this kept alive 'the nearness of the faraway'. Even where a narrower nationalism grew in strength, it took on many of the features of a world that was already deeply creole.[129] In the wake of immigration controls and surveillance, the initiative passed into non-elite hands and so dropped somewhat out of view.

A hidden empire of protest was rendered visible by circulating symbols. 'Gandhi caps', national calendars and associated iconography travelled across the archipelago. It was hard to tell where they originated from: propaganda labelled 'Made in Japan' might in fact come from Madras or China, and its signs became embedded in localities in surprising ways. There was a sensation in Province Wellesley in Malaya in December 1921 when a spider was rumoured to have spun the words 'Mahatma Kand', seemingly to signify Gandhi. The police had to break up crowds of spectators, and there was at least one copycat incident. An Amritsar paper reported that 'On banana leaves there appear the figures of Mahatma Gandhi, Mohamed Ali and Shaukat Ali', the leaders of the Khalifat movement. The British saw in this the hand of the millionaire son of a Sikh businessman of Kedah. Three more apparitions occurred in Perak in April the following year. They were swiftly destroyed by the police, but the third in particular, on a piece of wasteland near the Sikh temple and the Tamil settlement, attracted hundreds of visitors, with tradesmen and educated clerks 'solemnly riding in carriages to the scene'. Carvings appeared on benches. The signs were clear to all: Gandhi was in prison and must not be forgotten.[130]

This was a world bristling with intellectual resources. In the face of the shackles on open meetings and the press, these energies found an outlet in popular education. In addition to the mission schools and modernizing *madrasahs*, there was a boom in private schools, many of them unlicensed or unregistered by colonial governments. These 'wild schools', as they were called by the Dutch, soon far outstripped colonial provision. Gandhi's *satyagraha* was above all a means for popular instruction. New ideas lodged themselves at the heart of colonial institutions. A leading Malay educator of the day, Haji Abdul Majid bin Zainuddin, was a teacher at the Malay College Kuala Kangsar, in the state of Perak, a school aimed at turning elite Malays, and some commoners, into second-tier civil servants, with training in western table manners and team sports. Outwardly loyal to the empire, Abdul Majid was an advocate for Malay recruitment into colonial armies and served as the British government's representative in Mecca, partly in an intelligence role. But in a memoir in English, perhaps the first of its kind, he described a many-layered life:

> I was convinced that, coming as I did from a life of having associations with people of the 'Old World' straight into the life under the changed conditions of the 'New World', I would be the best person to advise the educational authorities how or in what form that education should be to give the best results to the Malays in their condition of being transformed from their ideals of the old into those of the new world.

He did this by exploiting the logic of British education policy in very specific ways, so that his support for military recruitment became an attempt to recover the martial spirit of the Malays. At the Malay College, he observed that religious instruction for the boys, on a Sunday, followed the model of Bible classes in English public schools, and that this offered new possibilities to expand the realm of religious instruction of the Malay elite, which had hitherto been confined to Quranic recitation. Abdul Majid used the opportunity to launch modernist reading classes and recruit a new generation of reformist religious teachers.[131]

His home, Kuala Kangsar, was a small town; a royal seat with many palaces and mausoleums, but also a new kind of strategic marketplace, a *pekan*, situated in the heavily industrial Kinta valley: Malaya's Ruhr. Its economic geography thrust Chinese tin miners, Indian rubber tappers and Malay rice farmers and smallholders from the lower river plain into close proximity as never before.[132] It was Malaya's most urbanized area, not only in the growth of its residents but in the thousands of others making a short journey to town to walk its streets and use its shops, services and entertainments. Its wider connections were measured in the rise in number of money orders and post and telegraphic offices: in the state of Perak alone, from six serving eleven other settlements in 1889 to eleven serving an additional twenty-six centres in 1891. By the 1921 census, 27 per cent of the population of the Federated Malay States and Straits Settlements could be classified as 'urban', but virtually all were in settlements with fewer than 5,000 souls, and few of these had more than ten European residents.[133] A new kind of public sphere emerged at a remove from that of the larger port cities, in local newspapers, law courts, networks of clubs, schools and philanthropy, and early quasi-democratic institutions such as school management and sanitary boards.[134] In this Kuala Kangsar was typical of many inland small towns which became centres of publishing and popular entertainments. A number of key modernist Malay periodicals of the 1920s came from smaller towns like Kuala Pilah, or Seremban – including *Majallah Guru*, a formative journal by and for schoolteachers – and in Malacca, Johore Bahru and elsewhere.[135] Circles of friendships across communities were fostered by the unavoidable intimacy of school life, shared work and the constant inspiration of translation, argument and negotiation. They helped carry political ideas across the rural-urban divide, which was never hard and fast in a context where the rural and urban livelihoods brushed against each other and were connected far and wide by constant comings and goings.[136]

Here traditions of free education and 'slow reading' were very strong. The greatest collective achievement of the Chinese communities was the massive expansion – through philanthropy and sacrifice – of grassroots education. By 1924, 564 Chinese schools were established in Malaya and Singapore with an enrolment of 27,476 pupils. Most of these provided a primary education to a maximum of six years. But, in 1919, the first secondary school, the Chinese High School, was founded in Singapore by the businessman and philanthropist Tan Kah Kee, and in 1922 the Chung Ling School was expanded into a high school by a group of businessmen with explicit links to supporters of Sun Yat-sen; six more were soon to follow. No longer did parents have to send children back to China to study. There were also new schools for women – a crucial early experiment was in Kuala Lumpur – fuelled by growing networks of highly committed schoolteachers and alumni associations.[137] Informal reading clubs and night schools extended further into labouring worlds. These self-help schools were especially associated with those from the coastal districts of Hainan. A survey in Singapore in 1927 calculated that 42 per cent of the working population in shops and coffee shops and restaurants heralded from the island; some 14 per cent of those worked on ships and boats and 12 per cent were employed by foreigners, mostly as domestic servants. It estimated that each percentile represented about 120 persons. They worked in around 200 coffee shops, especially ones which doubled as lodging houses. They were quite isolated from other groups of Chinese, who saw them as an unstable community, lacking family life. Poor and often illiterate, they were ardent supporters of self-help. According to a 1931 survey published in Haikou, the capital of Hainan, twenty-six night schools were founded by the Hainanese community in Singapore between 1914 and 1929, most of them after 1924. The British viewed these as especially pernicious reading rooms for anarchist and socialist materials and saw the Hainanese as ripe for sedition: in the words of one policeman, as 'a celibate and cliquish clan ready made for the job'.[138] To the British, all Chinese were more or less culpable. As the Kuomintang spread its influence in Malaya and Singapore, officials likened its 'lodge' structure and oaths to freemasonry. They also lamented the scale of resources remitted to Sun Yat-sen's movement: by 1920, some 400,000 Straits dollars. They conflated the challenging syntax of the Chinese language with the complexities of new political ideologies.[139] These anxieties were compounded by the prose of the new *Bulletin of Political Intelligence*: indirect, allusive, insinuating reports – in the words of a 1922 issue – of activity 'in various guises, whose objects are uncertain but yet give no cause for definite suspicion, and it is difficult to prevent the feeling that more is going on under the surface than we are actually aware of'.[140] Chinese societies were targets of a swingeing round of legislation.

Armed with their immigration logs and card indexes, the British traced life histories across long distances. Many of these centred around Kuala Lumpur, where the legacy of the 'six gentlemen' expelled in 1919 remained strong. They believed that communists worked in schools such as the Chung Wa School, at Setepak on the outskirts of the town. The headmaster had come from Shanghai and put about a paper in praise of the German Spartacists. A new journal, *Nanyang* [*South Seas*] *Critique*, was published in early 1923. It founders had links to British North Borneo and Dutch Java. One of the key personalities was Lei To Wang, alias Lei Hui Chau, a Cantonese educated in Nanjing and at Beijing University. He had experience of political work in Shanghai and been involved in the Hong Kong seamen's strike. Between 1922 and 1924 he made use of eight different aliases to teach in schools across the Malay Peninsula and was instrumental in disseminating literature from China. His work with the *Nanyang Critique* and the night schools drew the attention of the police, and he fled to Siam only to reappear again in Penang. He was arrested and deported in May 1924. Others came from further afield, including a man called Han Kuo Hsiang, whose diary and letters detailed training at Chita and Moscow in 1922. In January 1923 he was arrested in the International Settlement of Shanghai, but made his way to Canton. He later became active in consumers' and workers' unions, reaching out to workers in mining districts around Kuala Lumpur, until he fled again, this time to Medan in Sumatra.[141]

Malaya was one of several crossways of a new long-distance itinerary that connected colonial Asia, running from the Netherlands East Indies via Siam and French Indochina to Canton, Shanghai and now to Russia. The other principal axis of the Malay world was West Sumatra, the homeland of Ibrahim Tan Malaka. As a source of intellectual leadership within Indonesia, with its private Islamic schools and maritime connections to the Middle East, it now rivalled Central Java, particularly in the way its thinkers sought to weave together Islam, nationalism and the new communist ideas. In the Minangkabau heartland, particularly influential were the Islamic Sumatra Thawalib schools of Padang Panjang, especially the modernist teacher Zainuddin Labai el Junusiah, who founded in 1918 a mirror to Rashid Rida's famous reforming newspaper called *al-Munir*. Graduates of this circle visited Java and fell under the spell of the 'Red' Haji Misbach, and even before the foundation of the PKI in Semarang students set up a 'Boffet Merah', or 'Red canteen', in the schools in Padang Panjang, which, like Semarang itself, was now seen as a Red town. Traders took the new Islamist ideas along the railway to the weaving town of Silungkang and the environs of the Ombilin coal mine, a place of servitude for many convicts.[142]

Ibrahim himself had, he confessed to his friend in the Netherlands, Dick Wijngaarden, been initiated, 'very secretly', into Islamic mysticism. He dismissed it now as 'hocus-pocus or trickery or both'. He believed still in the virtue enjoined by the Prophet Muhammad:

> But when his followers came out of the desolate desert and entered fertile lands and prosperous cities, then the well-known recipe came into vogue again: peace between the owners of property and the powerful and the exploited . . .
>
> I am all for virtue. But first we must prepare the soil in which virtue can grow and ripen. Virtue and peace are in my opinion only possible by way of revolution. And in fact the materialist Marx has really an idealistic background. But in the first place whatever obstructs virtue and peace must be destroyed.[143]

His time on the east-coast plantations was coming to an end. Although in some measure he found friendship there and understanding, the management's fiction that he would be treated as a European was unworkable. He knew they disapproved of the entire project of educating common labourers. He was met with slights on the tennis court and confrontations in the classroom with the head teacher. In developing the local schools, he had got to know the families who came to his house and was 'caught between the society of the Dutch mad with tropical fever and that of the contract coolies'. His bosses suspected him of writing for the local press under a pseudonym, 'Pontjo Drio', and of being in league with striking railway workers in Deli. He was writing, but under his own name, as Tan Malaka. His first pamphlet, *Sovjet atau Parlement?*, 'Soviet or Parliament?', was first of a series of writings to address the form a free Indonesia might take. He had earned enough finally to repay most of his debt to his old teacher, Horensma, and to his village. He resigned and in July 1921 left Sumatra with a first-class steamer ticket to Java.

A battle for the soul of the Indies movement was under way, and at its heart lay the status of knowledge. As the possibilities for open politics constricted, education became a principal field for activism. Mas Marco Kartodikromo led a renewed 'war of voice' with what the Dutch categorized as *batjaan liar* – or 'wild publications'. He moved away from the polemics surrounding race that had been so damaging, by promoting a new vocabulary of commonality: the idea of *anak Hindia*, the children of the Indies, privileging the *kromo*, or common-ers, as well as strong female characters in a modern, urban milieu. Dutch educationalists went to extraordinary lengths to stem this tide. They published their own modern reading in the new idiom of Indo-nesian Malay, albeit in a less 'low' form, an 'original' variant from the royal court of Riau islands, a literary centre just south of Singapore. This counter-propaganda was led by Marco's old adversary, D. A. Rinkes; an earlier polemical exchange between them had got Marco thrown in prison. Rinkes now headed the *Balai Pustaka*, a 'Palace of Reading', which published approved reading on a scale without prece-dent in the colonial world. By 1923 it had 623 libraries, although some were no more than a cupboard in a school classroom, as well as travelling libraries, fifty-eight salesmen and travelling bookstalls. In 1920 there were 1 million registered borrowings. [144] It was the last flourish of the ethical policy. It even departed from its own high standards to pub-lish a journal in Malay, *Pandji Poestaka*, 'Banner of Literature', that to some extent mimicked the 'wild' press. The PKI leader, Musso, declared this to be 'not good for the colonised'. It was aimed 'at misleading peo-ple's thoughts in a gentle and systematic way'.[145] The PKI began to commission reading materials, mirroring in many ways the didactic prac-tices of the *Balai Pustaka*, on socialism and the 'new science'. This led to the first full translation of Marx and Engels's *The Communist Manifesto* in 1923.

One of the reasons Semaoen departed Indonesia for Russia in December 1921 was to recruit Moscow-trained intellectuals for this kind of work. But in producing what Musso called 'the necessary books, our own storybooks', the PKI's increasingly dogmatic class line began to collide with the more open message necessary for a united anti-colonial front with the Sarekat Islam.[146] A conflict was under way between the imperatives of unity and ideology, inclusiveness and party discipline, religious orthodoxy and a more secular, materialist world-view. These were disputed in an escalation of personal attacks, and invective portraying the Sarekat Islam leaders as hypocritical 'servants of the capitalists' and Communists as the 'enemy in the armpit' or the 'thief inside the hut'.[147]

Ibrahim was swiftly propelled to the front rank of the PKI leadership 'through the door of education'. After a brief visit to Horensma in Batavia, he headed directly to Yogyakarta and met most of the leading figures of the movement: Tjokroaminoto, Semaoen, Darsono and Marco. Of all of them, he alone had had a formal education overseas. In the midst of increasingly personalized attacks, he was accepted as a welcome outsider. His status as a non-Javanese drew attention to the movement's pan-archipelagic nature. Ibrahim attended the Sarekat Islam conference in Surabaya in October 1921, when the issue of the relationship of Islam and communism came to a head. The Central Sarekat Islam leadership attempted to instil discipline on the issue. The main mover of this, and the leader of the 'Green', more pious wing, was Haji Agus Salim, a religious scholar who had worked closely with the orientalist Snouck Hurgronje at the Dutch consulate in Jeddah, and more recently with Rinkes. Salim acknowledged, as Haji Misbach – now in prison – had argued before him, that before Marx there was Muhammad, and that the essence of Marx's ideas could be found in the holy Quran. But Salim repudiated the necessity of class struggle to argue that Islam was a basis on which to strive for the equality of all classes in the national struggle, and also the source of its internationalism. Here Ibrahim tried to mediate, pointing out that communism and Islam had been allies in the recent past elsewhere in Asia and could again be in the future. 'A schism of this sort, taking place in a period of reaction, would be exceedingly difficult for the people.'[148] But the schism occurred, and the PKI was formally expelled from the Sarekat Islam, although the ties between the two movements did not dissolve overnight.

Ibrahim regretted the split and was ambivalent about 'the slippery ground of politics'.[149] Java was an alien environment for him, and he fell ill from the tuberculosis that was to dog him over the coming years. He focused his energies on building the kind of school for workers' children that was impossible on the plantations of Sumatra. He headed to Semarang, staying in Semaoen's house, and was given charge of the Sarekat Islam school in the city. He set out the principles of the new *sekolah rakyat*, or people's schools, in an illustrated pamphlet: *SI Semarang dan Onderwijs*, 'Sarekat Islam Semarang and Education'. It made clear his indebtedness to Soviet mass education. But it also placed its faith in the spirit of Indonesian youth: 'These are the children who understand the feeling of independence because they want to rise up, but they cannot.'[150] They were more popularly termed the 'Tan Malaka schools', and by this form of his name Ibrahim became universally known, and something of a talisman. He also established himself as the party's principal theoretician. Initially reticent at putting himself at the front of public platforms, his reputation grew among the trade unionists: the print workers, the oil workers and the railway and transport workers. After Semaoen left the Indies for the Netherlands and for Moscow, at the party's Semarang conference at Christmas 1921, Tan Malaka – dragged to the podium, in his own account – spoke for six hours on the need for unity and continued to press the common cause of Islam and communism, in a way that now went against the grain of Comintern thinking. After the public session, and aged only twenty-five, he was elected chairman of the party. He began to argue for a broad campaign on civil liberties, targeting especially the *exorbitante rechten*, the reserves of 'extraordinary powers' held by a colonial governor-general.[151] They had initially been deployed against religious rebels but were now used in a more naked way against opponents whom the more specific offences of conspiracy or sedition, or 'hate-sowing', could not ensnare.[152]

The 'period of reaction' of which Tan Malaka spoke was well under way. With the failure of rice crops in Burma and Thailand, prices shot up in Java. The communists, he argued, had to show that 'they had not been talking with their mouths alone, but also with their hearts'.[153] The test came with an issue that was both material and deeply symbolic. The pawnshop had for decades been seen as a central way to fight rural indebtedness to the Chinese petty traders. A project of the ethical policy had been to establish government-operated pawnshops across Java and Madura, which became a valuable source of employment of lower-ranking officials. It spoke to the objectives of the Sarekat Islam, and was a draw for the most able and educated men in the colony other than the teachers and bureaucrats. It was the most unionized sector, with some 2,700 members in their own Indonesian union, largely under the sway of the radicals within the Sarekat Islam.[154] They faced a challenge to their hard-won status from the policy of retrenchment of the new governor-general, Dirk

Fock, who tried to compel them to resume manual labour. While the angry reaction of the workers seemed a regressive attitude to some of the radicals, equally it could be seen as racial discrimination. As the refrain went:

> A warning,
> Do you want to become a slave?
> Do you want to be ordered around like a dog, if you do not
>   want to carry a rice steamer, a gong, or a great chest?
> Do you want to lose your worth as a person, and become a
>   worthless stooge?
> Do you want to live a more wretched existence than a goat?
> If so enquire at the Pawnshop Service.[155]

The strike began from below in Yogyakarta. It split the Sarekat Islam leadership, but the PKI threw its support into it, as a step towards setting up a broad labour front. Tan Malaka campaigned for a general strike. For the government, too, it was a symbolic confrontation: it saw the action as a concerted campaign of subversion. Public assemblies were banned, and troops and the militia called out.[156]

In the midst of this, on Sunday, 13 February 1922, Tan Malaka visited the second *sekolah rakyat* in Bandung, a large, clean building in ample grounds. Bandung was an altogether more prosperous city than Semarang, and Tan Malaka felt it was even too good for the workers' children of the city. He was met by a Dutch colonial agent who asked him to leave the building as there was a strike meeting of the Bandung branch of the railway workers taking place. He bristled at this: 'In point of fact I have the right to throw anyone out of here, since we own this building.' But he agreed not to enter the room. At noon, a police car returned with the same agent. 'Respectfully and with apparent sadness', Tan Malaka later recalled, he was asked to get in and sit between two senior officers. He was taken to Bandung prison, and held without visitors until he was transferred via the police station back to Semarang. The junior policeman who had arrested him told him: 'I regret your leaving because . . . the pupils need you.'[157]

Tan Malaka's leadership of the PKI had lasted less than two months. His interrogation lasted less than five minutes. The questions were carefully scripted in advance, in several drafts, to incriminate him following a Moscow line dictated by Henk Sneevliet. Tan Malaka's responses were a repeated refrain: 'Of that, I do not wish to comment.'[158] This was of no matter: the outcome was preordained. He was held under *exorbitante rechten* and was to be banished to the Outer Islands, to Kupang on Dutch Timor, where the anti-British activist Abdul Selam had ended up during the war. Tan Malaka petitioned to be sent to the Netherlands. This was granted, but the authorities were determined that his departure would be a quiet affair. He was to travel with Piet Bergsma, one of the last of the Dutch members of the PKI, who was expelled. His brother, who was with him in Semarang, was sent home to warn his parents that although his ship would dock in Padang, they should not travel to meet it: he would not be allowed to see them. He had made one visit home during his return from the Netherlands and received their blessing for the choices he had made. These were now irrevocable. Tan Malaka left behind him a sense of lost opportunity. After his ship sailed, Marco and two other friends fasted and visited Mount Lawu, straddling East and Central Java, a holy site within Javanese mysticism, as a cleansing ritual to give them inner strength to face the future. Tan Malaka left no immediate political heirs within the movement, but the seeds of a legend that anointed him as its once and future king.

Tan Malaka sailed at almost the same moment as Sneevliet left Shanghai. Sneevliet wrote ahead that Tan Malaka should travel with him to 'Mecca', his code for Moscow. But the Communist Party leadership in the Netherlands, headed by David Wijnkoop, who had championed the colonial question in Moscow and was now beginning to take up the issue at home, had other plans for him. They claimed him as one of their own: a man who had learned his communism as a student in the Netherlands; an educator who could light the way for others. As the *Tribune* thundered announcing his arrival, 'Time will show that the People will have the power to take Malaka and the others out of exile.'[159] On May Day 1922, Tan Malaka was feted in the trading hall of the Diamantbeurs, the Diamond Exchange in Amsterdam. Darsono had addressed the Dutch party the previous year, but this was one of the few times in which an 'inlander', or native, had stood on an open public platform in the Netherlands. When he spoke, the press reported – not a little condescendingly – it was a very different kind of speech altogether: 'an eastern-coloured, sometimes warm-hearted, then passionate, always lively outpouring', yet delivered in 'vivid, very pure

Dutch'. It was a bitter testimony of conditions under Dutch rule: of 'deep and terrible degeneration, where the main institutions are prisons, pothouses and brothels'. Tan Malaka attacked the sham of the extra-judicial powers that had banished him: 'legal authority has been brought and is being maintained with the bayonet'. In 'the sarcasm and the scorn in the voice with which Malaka uttered these words', it was reported, 'one felt and heard the three centuries of domination of the Indies'.[160]

Tan Malaka's appeal to human rights became a repeated refrain. To capitalize on the public sympathy, the Communist Party put forward his name in third place on their slate of candidates in the general election. Campaigning was already under way, and Tan Malaka was introduced as the candidate of the tens of millions of Dutch subjects in the Indies. He spoke in twenty-two towns and cities, in some places more than once. On their shared appearances he was given precedence by Wijnkoop, and gained public popularity. As a local newspaper in Arnhem commented wryly: 'The East Indies issue is infinitely more important than anything that happens in the small Netherlands.'[161] To many who came to hear him, the 'brown brother' was merely an exotic sideshow. The anti-communist press stigmatized him for being part of 'the banned underworld', and it did not help matters that he was revealed to be twenty-six years of age (he was in fact twenty-five, but claimed not to be sure), under the threshold of thirty years for election to the chamber. In the event, the party gained two seats; Tan Malaka polled 5,211 votes, but he was third on the party list and not elected. He had not expected to be. The Communist Party's enthusiasm for the Indies soon receded.[162] Tan Malaka's political career in the Netherlands was as short-lived as it had been in the Indies. He left quietly, sometime in August, for Berlin, lodging there with Darsono, who had found the city's intellectual culture more congenial than that of the Netherlands. They were joined for a while by another young student from West Sumatra, Mohammad Hatta. They parted after two months not knowing when next they would meet: Darsono was to return to Java, and Hatta would continue to rise in student circles. Tan Malaka resumed his writing, on education in Indonesia and the relationship between Islam and Bolshevism. In October, supplied with funds by Darsono, he finally reached 'Mecca'. But he came not as a supplicant. He was one of the first of the Asian communists to arrive as an ideologue in his own right, whose Marxism was honed from afar: in his experience among the plantation coolies of East Sumatra, the 'wild' schools and trade unions of Java. At home, he was not seen as a 'westernized' intellectual who had become distanced from his culture. As he was later to enjoin his young followers:

> You must not yield to the Westerners in analytical thinking, honesty, enthusiasm, and readiness for any sacrifice . . . Admit in all honesty that you will and must learn from the Westerners . . . Only when your society has produced men who are better than a Darwin, a Newton, a Marx, or a Lenin, then you can be proud . . .[163]

In his mind's eye, Tan Malaka resumed the tradition of migration of his Minangkabau heritage known as *merantau*: the young man's quest to expose himself 'to the largeness of the world' and return with useful wisdom.[164] But this time there was little prospect of a homecoming. 'Under such conditions,' he later wrote, 'many a faith is broken; exiles return in secrecy and silence, kill themselves, or live demoralized as animals. Seldom are we able to hold firm to our original beliefs, desires and faith.'[165]

Tan Malaka, *Indonesia and its Place in the Awakening East*, Moscow, 1924.

12

The Next World War
1922–1924

BERLIN TO KANPUR

M. N. Roy had now been in exile for seven years. He moved to Berlin in April 1922 to be somewhat closer to the maritime routes to India. Unlike Tan Malaka, Roy became well established in the more exclusive political salons of the city. After the claustrophobia of Moscow and Tashkent, Roy embraced Berlin's more open atmosphere, its dissenting Marxist traditions and its afternoon cafés. In Berlin, Roy was also closer to his enemies. He and Evelyn were under constant pressure from British agents, and among the Indian émigrés old quarrels were prosecuted with renewed intensity. Roy's claims to head a central revolutionary organization outside India had been challenged by competitors in the United States, Japan, Afghanistan and Europe. Communist ideas that travelled and connected people in many ways followed these older networks.[1] But, in Berlin, Roy told Moscow in July, the atmosphere was 'vicious': he was surrounded by 'intellectual anarchists' obsessed by intrigue, with no sense of discipline. Roy's rival, Chatto, formed his own Indian Revolutionary Council, to which Abani Mukherji defected, alleging Roy's misuse of Comintern funds. This body was itself a house divided – into what Roy termed the 'Chatto group' and the '[Bhupendranath] Datta group' – but it continued to plan sedition on a global scale; it acquired secret funds from Moscow and successfully evinced an air of menace to the Raj.[2] Agnes Smedley reported in December 1921 to a friend in the United States that they were 'followed night and day by British spies'. Just two weeks previously, she said, there was an attempt to poison Chatto as he sat with friends in an Islamic restaurant, by putting arsenic in his hot chocolate. She carried a pistol she had brought from New York.[3]

The world abroad had its intimate enmities, and Roy and Smedley's went back to their encounter in the United States.[4] A few years later, in 1929, Smedley wrote an autobiographical novel about her experiences, *Daughter of Earth*. In one scene, the protagonist, Marie, describes her rape at the hands of an Indian nationalist in New York and how it left her feeling violated, ashamed and alone. In the novel, Marie marries his political rival, only for her assailant to spread rumours that she had seduced him. The assailant in the novel was perhaps an amalgam of individuals; but he was named 'Juan Diaz', which seemed to nod to Roy's sojourn in Mexico. The novels and memoirs that were now appearing featuring the wartime underground had many occlusions and omissions. By this point, Chatto was himself a character in a short story by Somerset Maugham. Fiction was a distorting two-way mirror through which the world saw the underground and the underground saw itself.[5] But in Berlin in 1922, the rumours of infidelity were real enough; they were designed to wound and humiliate Chatto, and some of them pointed to Roy. Smedley's relationship with Chatto became acrimonious and, she later claimed, abusive. Their open-handed way of living – their free house for émigrés – was undermined by the hyperinflation that hit the Weimar Republic after 1921. Smedley's physical and mental health deteriorated, and she spent spells in a north German sanatorium and a Berlin hospital.[6] She and Chatto finally parted ways in early 1925 and she left for China. Chatto confessed in a letter to Jawaharlal Nehru that his nerves were left in a terrible condition, and his work was ineffective due to 'private difficulties of long-standing'.[7] By this time, the Roys' marriage was also at breaking point – the tales of infidelity hurt Evelyn too – and rumours were abroad that she was 'an agent of Scotland Yard'.[8]

Roy maintained his ascendency among the exiles by virtue of his superior resources and official status. In November 1922, he was appointed a candidate member of the Comintern's Executive Committee and granted another £120,000 for Indian work. But any authority he possessed in India was exercised solely through the written word. In May 1922 he set up a newspaper published ostensibly from five European cities – Berlin, Paris, London, Zurich and Rome – called *Vanguard*, and later, in a further, futile attempt to confuse the British, *Advance*

Guard, with its place of publication given as Dublin. Until January 1924 it was in fact printed in Berlin. From here, Roy also published a book-length analysis of *India in Transition* and a shorter polemic, echoing Lenin's *What Is To Be Done?*, called *What Is It We Want? India in Transition* was printed in English, Russian and German. The first copies reached India in June 1922 and most of them fell into British hands before they found Indian readers. But it was not long before paraphrased excerpts appeared in mainstream newspapers such as *Amrita Bazar Patrika* of Calcutta.[9]

India in Transition was begun in Moscow in the autumn of 1921, in the first rush of anticipation following the launch of Gandhi's non-cooperation movement. The text was completed in March 1922, after its sudden collapse. Its title page recorded that it was written 'in collaboration' with Abani Mukherji, whose chief contribution seems to have been its detailed statistical apparatus. It followed the example of Marx and Plekhanov, but also of the imperial gazetteers, in its detailed account of land-holding and inventories of agricultural resources, and in its fascination with sheer scale (it detailed 150 billion bovines in India in 1919, 19.5 billion ploughs and 5 billion carts).[10] The book was, in one sense, an attempt to develop the argument, *contra* Lenin and others, that India was relatively advanced in its class formation and in the awakening of its workers. In another, it did more than try to impose Leninist categories on Indian realities. Like Tan Malaka, although they were to differ in many other respects, Roy sought to bring scientific rigour and a sense of immanent rupture to his history of India. His persistent critique of nationalists – including his former *Swadeshi* self – was that they looked 'not to begin a new life, with a new vision, but to revive the old'. In this, Roy perhaps had absorbed something of the futurist thinking of Berlin in 1920 and 1922, which was also evident in the works of its other resident Indian intellectuals.[11] He argued that the consciousness of the peasants and workers was in many ways ahead of the elite. 'The mass movement', Roy stressed, 'cannot always be kept within the limits set by the bourgeoisie.'[12] Evelyn elaborated on this in a series of searching critiques of Gandhi:

... when the masses were ready to surge ahead in the struggle, and Mr. Gandhi vainly sought to hold them back; they strained and struggled in the leading-strings of Soul-Force, Transcendental Love and Non-violence,

torn between their crying earthly needs and their real love for this saintly
man whose purity gripped their imagination and claimed their loyalty . . .
Mr. Gandhi had become an unconscious agent of reaction in the face of
a growing revolutionary situation.[13]

Similar views were voiced within the small groups of communists in
India.

As in China, in their early days these circles were aware of one
another, but not in direct contact. There was now a committed group
in Calcutta gathered around Muzaffar Ahmad. In Bombay, the success
of S. A. Dange's pamphlet *Gandhi vs. Lenin* led him to be invited to
run the large private library of the millionaire flour-mill owner and
socialist R. B. Lotvala and to use it to import radical writings. Lotvala
also financed a new periodical in Bombay called *The Socialist*. Lotvala's place in the movement was akin to that of Shyamji Krishnavarma
in London and Paris; he was a patron rather than an active participant.
But Lotvala was more decisive in his support of young radicals and outspoken in his critique of Gandhi's 'irrational, superstitious and suicidal
traits'.[14] There was also an independently minded group in Madras led
by M. Singaravelu, a sixty-two-year-old lawyer who had in early life
embraced the socially engaged Buddhism of Dharmapala and then
trade union activism.[15] He led the Madras *hartal* against the Prince of
Wales's visit, which had shocked Gandhi with its militancy. A college
professor called Ghulam Hussain was recruited in Kabul and given
money to set up an Urdu newspaper in Lahore called *Inqilab*, or 'Revolution'. Of the original Moscow *muhajirin*, only Shaukat Usmani had
managed to return to India as an active agent, reaching Bombay on a
Persian passport in September 1922. He then went underground in the
United Provinces.

All Roy could do, at this stage, was write to people to assert his central authority, give doctrinal direction and recruit men to Moscow.
Another purpose of his letters was the 'excommunication' of Abani
Mukherji, who headed from Hamburg to India in December 1922, on
his own mission, and with his own letters of introduction from the
Berlin group. Again, most of Roy's letters were intercepted. They were
usually photographed by the police, although some originals were kept
for study by the 'Examiner of Questioned Documents', for angularity,
pen pressure, idiosyncrasies of spelling and other marks by which the

expert eye might distinguish one hand from another. The police had six documents that they were reasonably sure of being Roy's, being written in the presence of other witnesses, amounting to 100 lines of text. Then there was his typewriter and its imperfections: mathematically, the Examiner explained, two typewriters with the same defects could not be found among fewer than 270 million machines. Most of the letters opened with 'My dear Comrade' and were signed 'R', although some were disguised as personal letters, signed with his birth name, 'Naren', including one addressed to 'My dear Mama'.[16] Roy's mother had died in 1908.

The first of Roy's emissaries from Europe to India, Nalini Gupta, returned to Germany in May 1922. He had left Calcutta in March as a common sailor. But he was not up to the subterfuge and jumped ship in Colombo, cabling contacts in Calcutta and Germany for funds. Once back in Berlin, he inflated his accomplishments and his assessment of the size of the communist organization in Bengal. He had also left behind promises of money he could not honour. The communist movement had yet to gain any strong purchase in the trade unions or within Congress itself, and, in any case, the wave of organization from below of 1919–21 had ebbed. The All-India Trades Union Congress, founded in October 1920, owed its origins to India's participation in the new International Labour Organization; its leaders cleaved closely to the model of the British Trade Union Congress and tried to steer unions away from the anti-imperial struggle. They rarely intervened directly in labour disputes. Their tenacious presence, and the weakness of the organization they led, made it hard for communist sympathizers to subvert and suborn the unions.[17] The organization of *kisan sabhas*, or cultivators' associations, in north India had also receded in the face of landlord hostility, police pressure and Congress calls for restraint. In the face of this, Roy's goal was to set up an open-front workers' party with a secret 'communist nucleus'. British postal censors picked up a worrying remark from Nalini Gupta: 'Work on old revolutionary lines should be continued and that terrorism should be resorted to achieve the objective.'[18] The British authorities believed in the second half of 1922 that the calls to violence from Berlin were becoming more unequivocal. As the *Vanguard* put it in its 1 December 1922 issue, while there were perils to premature violent action, 'it is altogether erroneous to think that there can be such a thing as a non-violent revolution, no matter how peculiar and abnormal the situation in India may be'. The British worried less about the small numbers of activists at large, who were well known to the police, than they did that the movement might connect to the old terrorist underground: where newspapers slipped into India, so too might guns. They intercepted an ominous early letter from Muzaffar Ahmad to Roy: 'There is no fear of our work being hampered by your old friends. Moreover, we would get much from them.'[19]

More radical voices were being heard within Congress itself. In particular, C. R. Das, who was newly released from prison, seemed willing to step up civil disobedience. He argued that Congress should seek entry into the reformed colonial councils that had been boycotted in 1921, 'to tear the mask from off the face' and wreck them from within. Roy tried in vain to attract Das to the Comintern cause and to induce his close follower, the young firebrand Subhas Chandra Bose, to visit Moscow or Berlin. Roy appealed directly to Congress with a 'Programme' for complete national independence addressed to its annual session in December 1922 at Gaya in Bihar, near the site of the Buddha's enlightenment at Bodh Gaya. Das was to chair the session. The number of delegates had declined from the previous year – from 4,728 to 3,848 – reflecting the large number in prison and the general demoralization after the collapse of non-cooperation. Singaravelu came from Madras to speak for the 'Programme':

> Beware you rich men, beware you big men, remember all our sorrows and our toils . . . Remember that Indian labour has awakened. They are wide awake and are coming steadily and surely to their rights to save the world.[20]

But both Singaravelu and C. R. Das ultimately reaffirmed their support for non-violence. 'Council Entry', which was to Roy something of an irrelevance, was defeated. Das and Motilal Nehru established a new Swaraj Party as a more political, programmatic wing of Congress to contest the council elections. But it was clear that it could not function as the mass party Roy was seeking.[21] Gaya was, for Roy, a historic missed opportunity. In the event, some 549 copies of Roy's 'Programme' were seized at Gaya post office, although its publication by Reuters allowed for a wave of publicity in Indian newspapers.[22]

The strain between open and underground politics now came to a head. On 9 March 1923, Roy wrote to Shaukat Usmani, his principal mobile agent: 'we have five centres to link up.' His impatience was palpable: 'I do not say that all these people are all that is desired; but we will have to work with the viable material.' But the steel cage of the Raj was closing in on them. In September 1922 a number of returning *muhajirin* were put on trial at Peshawar, the first of a new series of 'Conspiracy Cases'. Shaukat Usmani lay low and eluded the police for a time, but he was eventually arrested on 9 May 1923, while working as a schoolmaster, 'Hamid Ahmad', at the Muslim National School in Kanpur in the United Provinces.[23] This was the cue for a 'simultaneous' round-up of the other regional leaders, including Muzaffar Ahmad, S. A. Dange, Ghulam Hussain and M. Singaravelu, who was later released on grounds of ill health. Ghulam was reprieved by the forcefulness with which he recanted his actions. Roy's emissary, Nalini Gupta, was also arrested. He had arrived back in India via Persia on 12 June, in ignorance it seems of the arrests, and then took refuge in Dacca until his arrest in Calcutta in late December. As Muzaffar Ahmad told it, he then made a long police statement over nine days, 'mixing fact and fiction in the manner of the Arabian nights'. His testimony, which was not disclosed at the time, gave the British the confidence to launch a further conspiracy trial.[24] The name of M. N. Roy, 'the notorious Indian Communist', was high on the charge sheet and secured him a visibility within India he was struggling otherwise to attain.

The men in British hands were put on trial at Kanpur in March 1924. The location was controversial. None of the accused heralded from the city, and no real crime had been committed there. But the prosecutors insisted that Shaukat Usmani had been arrested there as a 'primary agent' of an 'All-India' conspiracy, directly connected to Roy and linked to both Dange and Muzaffar Ahmad. In Kanpur the accused were to be tried by assessors; they demanded trial in Bombay or Calcutta, where they would have the benefit of a jury, 'more impartially inclined to new ideas, principles and methods . . . hence our desire to be tried in such a culturally tolerant atmosphere'.[25]

More than this, the presiding judge was the same man who had the previous year sentenced 172 men to death in the Chauri Chaura case in a single day. Within the exhibits of evidence were articles attacking him personally. For both sides, Kanpur had a symbolic significance as a site of one of the bloodiest episodes of 1857, and of one of its most notorious instances of drumhead justice.

But, as with previous conspiracy trials, in private the British admitted to considerable uncertainty as to whether the evidence would stick. The prosecution relied on documents that had passed through many hands, letters that had been copied, with the originals destroyed. It could be argued that the writings of S. A. Dange, for example, were 'not anti-British': their principal target was the bourgeois leadership of Congress and their unfitness to inherit power. Nor was it clear that the accused by themselves represented a particular threat. But, as the head of the Intelligence Bureau, Lieutenant-Colonel Cecil Kaye, saw it: 'Even the most insignificant insects . . . are often dangerous foci of infection.' Kaye was supremely confident that decisive action on his part would work 'to discredit and we hope, to destroy – Roy's organisation'.[26] The men were held under the notorious Regulation III of 1818, which allowed for detention without trial on political grounds.[27] They were treated according to strict new rules, isolated from other prisoners but protected from corporal punishment. In Alipore jail, Muzaffar Ahmad was given books, mostly on political economy: Adam Smith, Henry Sidgwick, R. C. Dutt's two-volume *Economic History of British India* (1902–4), the Scottish theologian and sociologist Robert Flint and Thomas Nixon Carvar, the Harvard professor best known at the time for his work on rural economics.[28] But when the detainees appeared in court, the sight of the chafing of fetters on Shaukat Usmani from the time of his arrest a year before exposed the reality of their confinement. As he wrote in November 1923 from his prison in Peshawar: 'I have not, so much as, been given to understand the offence I am charged with.'[29] As proceedings dragged on, public outrage deepened. Roy argued his defence through the newspapers, denouncing 'the methods of the machine gun and the Star-Chamber'.[30] Some of the most cutting and forensic analysis of the trial came from the pen of Evelyn. Kanpur was unique, she wrote, in that, unlike the earlier conspiracy trials, 'it is not based on any terrorist act nor plot to use armed force', but on people 'who openly profess to be socialists or communists'.[31] The verdicts were delivered to an empty courtroom on 20 May 1924: Muzaffar Ahmad, S. A. Dange, Shaukat Usmani and Nalini Gupta were each imprisoned for four years. Their confinement together at Kanpur prison had finally brought the regional leaders of the Indian communist movement together. Beyond its walls, 'the word "Bolshevik" began to be read and uttered all over India, from Assam to Bombay and from the Himalayas to Cape Comorin'. But the acute stress, suspicion and self-doubt of the trial pulled the men apart.[32]

Plots and quarrels begun in Moscow and Berlin continued to play out across vast distances. The workers' international was sustained by the world 'below decks', by couriers recruited from seamen working from the bases of the main European shipping companies in Hamburg, London, Marseilles and Rotterdam. This was perhaps the most direct form of cooperation in the anti-colonial struggle with the western communist parties. In Britain, a key intermediary was an Indian member of the Communist Party of Great Britain, Shapurji Saklatvala, the son of a Parsi merchant family of Bombay, related to the Tata family, who became an early member of the Communist Party of Great Britain, winning the parliamentary seat of Battersea North in the 1922 general election. Roy employed another party member, Charles Ashleigh – who had served time in the United States for crimes of violence – to sail to Bombay with messages for S. A. Dange. He was deported a few days after his arrival in late September 1922. A German sailor from Hamburg, one F. Schmidt, was also arrested in Bombay carrying ten copies of *India in Transition* and thirty-six of *What Do We Want?* after being entrapped by a false 'S. A. Dange', impersonated by a police officer of the new 'Bolshevik Branch'.[33]

In the midst of all this, Roy's bête noire, Abani Mukherji, continued to live a charmed life. He made it to Calcutta again on 31 December 1922, after stowing away for fifty-two days under an unlit ship's boiler and in the coal bunker. He went on to Madras to meet Singaravelu and later claimed that he was responsible for writing the manifesto of Singaravelu's Labour-Kisan [Peasant] Party, a body designed to work within Congress, and launched on May Day 1923. It became the most visible manifestation of Indian radicalism, much of the rest of which was deep underground. Abani was sheltered by the Bengal veterans of the early anarchist underworld, both by the Anushilan Samiti group in Dacca and the *Yugantar* leaders in Calcutta, who saw him as a surer source of arms than Roy himself. In the repressive political atmosphere, and even as those sent 'across the black water' in 1908 began to be released, the tactic of terror was beginning to reassert itself. Fresh armed robberies in Bengal in 1923 and early 1924, and a bomb attack in central Calcutta, seemed a prelude to something more. There were two attempts on the life of Charles Tegart, whose fame and notoriety personified for many British policing in India; one of them, in January 1924, killed a British bystander. The trial and execution of the perpetrator reignited public debate on the ethics of violence and on the need for repressive laws. In October 1925, one of the key protagonists in this, the Swaraj Party leader, Subhas Chandra Bose, experienced his first detention and exile in Burma.[34] The wheel of radicalism was turning again in the Punjab, on many of its old sites. Lala Lajpat Rai, returned from New York, and Bhai Parmanand, released from the Andamans, were active in a new 'Tilak School of Politics' in which a new generation of activists emerged, often drawn from families of those who had been active ten or fifteen years earlier. These young people were less travelled, but no less worldly; learning and reading kept the inspirations from far away near at hand.[35] Through all this, Abani remained at liberty. He claimed the police were only alerted to his presence when the Comintern statement on his expulsion came into their hands: 'I was betrayed in a brutal way.'[36] But he could not escape the shadow narrative that surrounded him: that the British were happy to leave him at large to run Roy down. This had some effect. 'The Boss and family are living as princes', one letter to Europe accused, '. . . and the boys here – real, sincere workers are starving.'[37]

EUROPE IS NOT THE WORLD

But Europe was closing as a field of action. Many of the Asians who had arrived there during the war were starting to head home. In March 1923 there were 2,945 Vietnamese civilians in France, but by May of the following year this had dropped to 1,239, of whom 227 were released military men, some 500 of them domestic servants, along with 355 *navigateurs* and 177 students. All Vietnamese students now had to be approved by the governor-general and tended to be from relatively wealthy southern families. All were subject to increasing formal and informal surveillance: by the end of the decade, of the 5,000 Vietnamese in France, 3,675 would have a dossier in the ministry. Nguyen Ai Quoc chastised the students for spending too much time in the billiard halls and nightclubs.[38] Freewheeling exiles like Quoc were fewer in number and somewhat isolated. In July 1921, he moved to a hotel room in a working-class area of the *17ème arrondissement*, at 9 impasse Compoint, where he worked next door as a retoucher of photographs. This marked the end of the communal living at 6 villa des Gobelins. One likely reason for the move was the intensity of the police scrutiny of the house after Quoc's appearance at the Tours conference of the French Communist Party. The Vietnamese had a good idea who the informers were. The police reported 'violent' late-night discussions in the weeks before Quoc's departure. His former housemate and mentor, Phan Chu Trinh, did not follow Quoc on his path towards Marxism. But he and Phan Van Truong continued to meet with Quoc and attend many of the same meetings. Quoc joined the Intercolonial Union, a body which brought him in contact with nationalists from Réunion, Madagascar, Dahomey and the French Caribbean. He spent more and more of his time on its newspaper, *Le Paria*, and published more short, sharp indictments of colonial rule, drawing heavily on comparisons from the ports of call of his seafaring years.[39] But it was not clear to whom they were principally addressed. In February 1922, Phan Chu Trinh wrote to Nguyen Ai Quoc from Marseilles:

> From East to West, from Antiquity to the present day, no one has acted as you have, in staying abroad on the pretext that your country is full of traps . . . To awaken the people, so that our compatriots will engage in combat against the occupiers, it is indispensable to be there . . . Following your method you have sent articles to the press here to incite our compatriots . . . But this is vain. Because our compatriots can't read French or even *quoc ngu* [romanized script]; they are incapable of understanding your articles!

Phan Chu Trinh was lobbying to return home. 'I am an exhausted horse who can no longer gallop,' he told Quoc; 'you are a fiery stallion.'[40] His son, who had travelled with him to Paris, had returned to Vietnam the previous year, only to die of tuberculosis. Trinh, it was widely reported, was never the same again. Exile and grief had left him muted.

Phan Chu Trinh was in Marseilles to work as a photographer for the colonial exposition of 1922 and on hand to witness another royal progress. The Emperor of Vietnam, Khai Dinh, was visiting the spectacle at vast expense. In the eyes of many Vietnamese overseas, this merely served to parade his subjection and Vietnam's national humiliation. The emperor came to Paris to visit a replica of a Vietnamese communal house built in the botanic garden in the Bois de Vincennes to commemorate the Vietnamese fallen of the Great War.[41] Phan Chu Trinh poured his frustration into an open letter to him in literary Chinese. For Trinh, the position he adopted back in Tokyo in 1906 still held: the first enemy of freedom was the old order. He laid seven charges against 'this demon' ruler – from 'reckless promotion of autocratic monarchy' to 'shady deals behind the present visit to France' – and called on the emperor to pass judgment on himself. 'The day is certainly not far away when monarchy will be washed away in the deluge', he wrote, '. . . during the Great War, thirty-eight kings, including three great emperors, were murdered by their people.'[42] Nguyen Ai Quoc wrote a play which was performed showing antique workers – one of his trades at the time – constructing a bamboo dragon: a clear metaphor for the emperor's hollow crown. In the following months, police watchers reported an endless whirl of appearances by Nguyen Ai Quoc at political meetings in Paris and its suburbs. In December 1922 he too was in Marseilles, for the first Congress of the French Communist Party, still fulminating against the costs of the exposition: 'Indo-China alone had to pay 12 million . . . the famous reproduction of the Angkor Wat palaces required 8,000 cubic metres of timber at 400 or 500 francs a metre. Total: 1,200,000 to 1,500,000 francs!' In Marseilles, two plain-clothes policemen attempted to seize him. Albert Sarraut, now minister for the colonies, still believed he could co-opt Quoc.[43] 'We shall', Quoc mocked in an open letter to Sarraut in *Le Paria*, 'publish every morning a bulletin of our movements . . . Besides our timetable is quite simple and unchanging':

Morning: from 8 to 12 at the workshop.
Afternoon: in newspaper offices (leftist, of course) or at the library.
Evening: at home or attending educational talks.
Sundays and holidays: visiting museums or other places of interest.
There it is![44]

On 13 June 1923, Nguyen Ai Quoc left his room in impasse Compoint without any luggage. He let it be known that he was taking a brief holiday in Savoie. But at the end of the month his friends at the Intercolonial

Union were still awaiting his return. Phan Chu Trinh suspected foul play. He wrote angrily to one of the Vietnamese police informers: 'Why did you betray him? . . . where did you incite him to go?' On 11 October Sarraut reported to Hanoi that Quoc was in Moscow. He had travelled as a Chinese businessman to Hamburg, and there took a Baltic steamer to Petrograd. It was not clear how he had got there: whether he was sent with Intercolonial Union funds, whether he had been recruited, or whether he had acted out of sheer audacity, determined, as in 1919, to take his demands directly to those in power.[45]

Quoc had shown an uncanny ability to move easily between the worlds of the intellectuals and the workers' cafés, while cultivating – he was the son of a mandarin, after all – his own plebeian identity. After Quoc's departure, the politics of the Vietnamese in Paris further fragmented. The workers began to form their own organizations, led by the cooks and household servants in 1922, followed in 1923 by the manual workers in assorted trades from mechanics to the retouchers of photographs.[46] For the Chinese students in France, the protest at Lyon and the expulsions of September 1921 had also brought home the need for workers and intellectuals to cooperate more closely. In the course of 1922, a small group began to meet in Paris to this end. It included Zhou Enlai and Zhao Shiyan, a participant in the May Fourth movement who, exceptionally, had worked as a factory labourer. In June 1922, in the shade of the Bois de Boulogne, renting chairs from a nearby café, they formed a European branch of the Chinese Communist Youth Corps, with branches also in Germany and Belgium, a party by any other name which placed itself under the Chinese Communist Party in China. In November 1922, Zhao Shiyan received a letter from Chen Duxiu urging him to downplay work within Europe and create a 'Russian pipeline' to send members there for training. In early 1923, twelve students left for the Communist University of the Toilers of the East in Moscow, including Zhao himself. Zhou Enlai organized the visas from Berlin and, moving between cities, honed his skills as a journalist. He gave the youngest of the work-study students, Deng Xiaoping, a job printing the party newspaper in Paris, *Red Light*, in the little commune of anti-colonial revolutionaries that had formed around the place d'Italie and encouraged him to open a soya bean factory. The two men worked side by side for nearly two years. All this encouraged Deng to write home to repudiate his family, turn down the marriage that had been arranged for him and embrace revolution as a vocation. Friendships forged in these years cast a long shadow.[47] For Deng Xiaoping too the journey back to the east was through Moscow.

Tan Malaka arrived in Moscow around October 1922, shortly before the Fourth World Congress of the Comintern. He was not the first Indonesian to reach Moscow. Darsono and Semaoen had left Java ahead of him. Darsono had travelled with Henk Sneevliet and Asser Baars and was present at the Third Congress of the Comintern in mid-1921, although he was not listed as an official delegate, and had then moved on to Berlin. There was considerable speculation at home as to why Semaoen had left, and indeed whether he had actually gone to Moscow at all. He most likely travelled to deepen his knowledge, encouraged by others to expose himself to more orthodox Marxist thinking. His route took him through China and he attended the Congress of the Toilers of the East when it was initially convened in Irkutsk in November 1921, and then when it was relocated to Moscow in January and February 1922. Being unable to speak either lingua franca of the Comintern, English or German, he was a muted witness to events, although he produced a detailed report on conditions in Indonesia. He joined a small delegation of Asian leaders that met Lenin and drew encouragement from the Soviet leader's defence of the New Economic Policy, that Moscow would allow communist movements in Asia considerable latitude in the face of local conditions. He returned to Java in late May, but at a rally to welcome him home in Semarang he startled the audience of 3,000 people by reporting that the situation and the needs in Russia were very different, and that 'we are not so foolish as to imitate the Communists there'. Tan Malaka, still in the Netherlands, expressed his shock at what Semaoen was reported to have said. But when he himself reached Moscow he was struck by the same mood of permissiveness.[48]

At the main sessions of the Fourth Congress in Moscow from 9 November to 5 December 1922, the assessment of the world revolution was bleak; in Karl Radek's words, 'the proletariat was in retreat'. As a result, more attention was paid to conditions in Asia, if not to Asian delegates, than at the Third Congress sixteen months earlier. In the two days allocated to Asia, Tan Malaka spoke out, in German, for an alliance between communism and Islam based on his experience with the Sarekat Islam:

We have been asked at public meetings: 'Are you Muslims – yes or no? Do you believe in God – yes or no?' And how did we answer? 'Yes,' I said, 'when I stand before God I am a Muslim, but when I stand before man I am not a Muslim [loud applause], because God said there are many Satans among men!' [loud applause.] And so, with the Qur'an in our heads we inflicted a defeat on their leaders . . .

On the world stage, he argued, 'pan-Islam' signified 'the liberation struggle against the different imperialist powers of the world'. His bravado had an impact on all who heard him. He joined a protest of the Asian delegates against the lack of time allocated to their affairs, and in open session rebuked the chair who tried to rein him in: 'I come from the Indies; I travelled for forty days. [Applause.]'[49]

Tan Malaka's pragmatic position echoed the kind of alliance being advocated by Sneevliet in China, and by the Chinese delegates at the conference, including Chen Duxiu, who sat with Tan Malaka and Roy on a commission to examine what the Comintern still termed the 'eastern question'. Roy remained sceptical about reliance on either pan-Islam or nationalists within the united front: 'The experience of the last two years has proven that this front cannot be achieved under the leadership of the bourgeois parties. We must develop our parties in these countries, in order to take over the leadership and organisation of this front.'[50] Soon, Tan Malaka reflected later, the 'chasm between the *abstract* and the concrete, between theory and practice, became visible'.[51] In Java, the alliance between the Sarekat Islam and the PKI was already disintegrating. Tan Malaka was put to work writing his own gazetteer-like description of conditions in Indonesia. In June 1923, his position within the Comintern was formalized. His rapid rise in status was a matter of concern and dispute among the leadership in Java and at large in the world. As Piet Bergsma, a former sergeant in the Netherlands East Indies army, who had been exiled with Tan Malaka from the Indies, commiserated with Semaoen back in Java: 'you know how it goes: if someone at such a congress fills the whole congress with speeches, the delegates are so grateful that they reward the speaker with a position in the executive.'[52]

Neither Tan Malaka, nor Nguyen Ai Quoc who arrived after the Congress, expected to stay long in Moscow. The novelty of a voice out of Asia had passed. Asian leaders were no longer garlanded as the tribunes of their peoples. There were in 1924 over 1,000 students at the Communist University of the Toilers of the East, where Nguyen Ai Quoc took classes, his only experience of higher education. The Comintern was now more bureaucratized, a 'general staff' of world revolution, and he was put to work in its Eastern Department. It was some time before Quoc, even with his persistence, got to meet anyone of importance, and his requests for a meeting with Zinoviev went unanswered. He worked in the same way as he had in Paris: firing off memoranda on Indochinese affairs, attending meetings, cold-calling on officials, writing for journals such as *Inprecor* and completing the book he told friends he was working on in Paris, *Le Procès de la Colonisation Française*. He became an advocate for deeper Comintern involvement in peasant politics in Asia.[53] He was reported in *Pravda* in October 1923 as speaking at an International Peasants' Congress, saying that the International could not live up to its name 'until it encompasses the peasant masses of the entire East, especially those of colonial countries'.[54] But there was no private audience with Lenin, which he had ardently hoped for. In May 1923, Lenin had suffered a severe stroke. Visibly frail, he had made an appearance at the Comintern World Congress in November to defend his New Economic Policy. Now a 'left opposition' led by Trotsky was pitted against the 'triumvirate' of Stalin, Lev Kamenev and Zinoviev, who was seen by many as a likely successor to Lenin. The Comintern was drawn into this struggle, and events in Asia would be decisive to its outcome.

Roy remained at the centre of these deliberations, but he too was looking for a way home. In February 1924 he wrote to the new British Prime Minister, Ramsay MacDonald, 'as a socialist and representative of the British proletariat', demanding that he be allowed to return to India. The letter was sent from Zurich through his friend and lawyer Dr Christian Hitz-Bay. He invoked the Raj's general amnesty of 1919: 'my political views have undergone a radical change since I left India in 1915.' He received no reply, only a warrant for his arrest as a fugitive.[55] In April 1924 Roy was expelled from Germany, which, for all the intrigues, was the most stable home he and Evelyn had had since Mexico City. They spent an increasing amount of time apart, Evelyn constantly moving apartments in Paris, with Roy away on secret business. Later that year, Roy was to reflect from Paris on his relentless campaign since mid-1920 to recentre the vision of world revolution away from the west. In an essay entitled 'Europe Is Not the World', he wrote that Lenin had rescued Marxism from old thinking that had neglected the colonies and that was 'more imperialist than Marxist':

> Not only the final overthrow of Capitalism, but the immediate necessity
> of an effective resistance to the capitalist offensive demand that this Pro
> letarian Unity must transcend European limits and become a World Unity.
> The partisans and pioneers of proletarian unity should liberate themselves
> from the quasi-imperialist traditions of the Second International, and
> organise themselves into a true International, giving real significance to
> the historic slogan 'Workers of the World Unite'.[56]

Yet the personal cost of this was heavy. He and his friends and lovers were, Roy later wrote, 'the wandering Jews of the twentieth century'.[57]

FIRST FALLING LEAVES

In late March 1923, Henk Sneevliet wrote bitterly to Bukharin from Shanghai. 'The situation is such that it cannot go on. I have hardly any personal friends, mainly because I lead the existence of an Ahasverus [Ahasuerus].' He had abandoned stable relationships and lucrative posts in the Netherlands and Java for the cause. But he lacked a definite attachment to any one movement. He had asked to work with his closest comrade, Roy, but had been sent instead to China in 1921. His domestic situation was disastrous: he had lost money on his arrest in Vienna and had ever since been locked in dispute – over accounting for the £4,000 he had been given for the trip – with Comintern clerks who knew nothing of the high cost of living as a European in the colonies. He had failed to support his wife and two boys, who remained in Java after his expulsion in 1918. His wife, Betsy, now forty-three years old, had made ends meet as a teacher, but now needed to bring the boys on home leave to the Netherlands. Because of her marriage to Sneevliet, and charges relating to her handling illegal literature, she would be unable to return to Java. Moreover, following a three-week stay in Moscow in the summer of 1922, Sneevliet had fallen in love with a twenty-six-year-old factory worker, Sima Lvovna Zholkovskaya, a Bolshevik Party member from the illegal period. They had travelled to China together, sharing a third-class billet, and she was now pregnant with his child. Sneevliet asked to return to Europe, to work with Roy, to see his two boys, 'and explain to my first wife, in a way that would give her the least pain, that I love another woman and live with her'.[58]

Sneevliet had returned to China in August 1922 with the task of enforcing the will of the Comintern as he understood it. On 29–30 August he met the Chinese Communist Party leaders on the West Lake in Hangzhou. For the first time, the leading personalities of the movement from home and abroad were gathered in one place, many of whom had not attended the Party Congress in Shanghai the previous year. Li Dazhao travelled from Beijing; Chen Duxiu had returned to Shanghai from the south; Cai Hesen was back in China following his expulsion from France for his part in the student demonstration in Lyon. By all accounts the meeting was tense. Sneevliet declared that party members should join the Kuomintang and act as a 'bloc within' its various bodies. Not all present were convinced by the strategy, including Chen Duxiu, but Sneevliet pressed his argument in his abrasive, commissarial way, and, invoking Comintern discipline, carried the meeting. Afterwards, Li Dazhao met with Sun Yat-sen in Shanghai to secure his agreement to the first communists joining the Kuomintang; these included Chen Duxiu, Cai Hesen and Li himself. But Sneevliet could no longer claim a monopoly of Comintern wisdom. Cai Hesen's extensive experience of Europe made him disinclined to defer to Moscow on issues of revolutionary internationalism. Chen Duxiu returned from the Fourth Congress in Moscow at the end of 1922 with a concession from the central leadership that, while the 'bloc within' remained the priority, the Chinese Communist Party should nevertheless retain its own organization and undertake its own educational efforts among the masses. Moscow also endorsed the importance of work among the peasantry in general terms. Sneevliet returned to Moscow briefly between late December 1922 and early January 1923 to fight his corner. He rejected the notion that 'approximately 250 Chinese communists' alone could build a mass organization. Without cooperation with the nationalists, they were 'a meaningless sect'.[59]

But a series of local experiments were already under way towards building the party through workers' education. A group around Zhang Guotao approached the concentrations of proletarians in northern China, particularly in Shanghai and – working through an alliance of convenience with the regional warlord Wu Peifu – on the Beijing to

Hankou railway, where a young Beida graduate, Deng Zhongxia, travelled as a train inspector to reach the working communities along the railway lines. Outside the oppressive political atmosphere of Beijing, he helped establish a model school at Changxindian, a railway town ten miles to the south of the capital, to instil in them a 'sense of common interest and discipline'. He and his fellow student workers adapted their scholarly persona to the new work and taught class struggle and anti-imperialism in colloquial language and through everyday analogies.[60] Perhaps the most successful initiative – accounting for a fifth of paid-up Chinese Communist Party members at the time – was at Anyuan, a settlement of 13,000 coal miners and 1,000 railwaymen on the mountainous border between Hunan and Jiangxi provinces. It was led by a group from Hunan that included Mao Zedong, who was working at the time as a schoolteacher in the provincial capital, Changsha, and two returnees from overseas: Li Lisan, expelled from France in 1921, and Liu Shaoqi, one of the first Chinese students to be sent to Moscow. Mao had never set foot overseas, and his own rural childhood in the region made him particularly well placed to translate the revolutionary message to the workforce and to refashion himself as a new kind of scholar. As at Changxindian, the emphasis was not on doctrinaire Marxism, but on a more elemental call for dignity and equality under the slogan, 'Once beasts of burden, now we will be human.' It was pursued through workers' night schools, cooperatives and Red cultural activities – art, film and drama – and when successful strike action was launched at Anyuan in 1922, it was preceded by careful negotiation with the local triads – who held real power in the region – to maintain discipline and to avoid the snare of violence.[61] Unknown to the central party leadership, there was another experiment from below led by a returned student from Waseda University in Japan, Peng Pai, who set up a peasant association in Haifeng in the eastern coastal region of Guangdong province, where his family were prominent landowners.[62] Over time, the workers of Anyuan would return to their homes in Hunan and Jiangxi and take the lead in establishing peasant associations of their own.

All this was undertaken in plain sight and was dependent on the tacit toleration of local warlords and the alliance with the Kuomintang. But Sun Yat-sen was an uncertain ally. Only his ejection from Canton by forces loyal to Chen Jiongming had persuaded him to endorse the alliance with the Communists. In February 1923, with the support of outside troops – so-called 'guest armies' – Chen Jiongming was ousted from the city and withdrew into the northeast of Guangdong province. Sun Yat-sen was able to return to establish a new government. Before he left Shanghai, after a series of meetings at the Palace Hotel and at Sun's mansion, on 26 January 1923 Sun signed a treaty of cooperation with the new Soviet ambassador, Adolph Joffe, the man who had led the Soviet delegation at Brest-Litovsk. Sun's foreign affairs adviser, Eugene Chen, lauded it as a breach in the encirclement by the 'Anglo-Latin conquerors' that would elevate Sun to the status of a global leader. But, as Joffe was fully aware, Sun hoped that the western powers might ultimately support his goals.[63] Many of his closest aides bitterly opposed the policy of cooperation with the Communists. His son, Sun Ke, a graduate of the University of California at Berkeley and Columbia University, newly appointed as mayor of Canton, sought investment from Hong Kong. Even before the announcement of the Sun-Joffe Manifesto, Eugene Chen laid plans with the British for a visit by Sun to the colony on his return journey to Canton. Arriving on 17 February, Sun was warmly received by the governor and spoke to staff and students at the University of Hong Kong, his 'intellectual birthplace', of his respect for British parliamentary institutions.[64]

Sneevliet returned to Canton in late April 1923. Since his departure a year earlier, the transformation of Canton into a modernist showpiece, begun in the late Qing period and continued by Chen Jiongming, had gathered momentum. The old city walls had come down in 1920–21 to make way for modern roads – some twenty-six miles by 1922 – with trams and motor cars. Old temples and monasteries were commandeered as offices and hospitals by the city authorities. The west end of the Canton Bund was dominated by the twelve-storey Sun Company building, which housed the Hotel Asia, a department store and a roof garden: a symbol of the city as it was now promoted to the outside world. In the battle for ideas, the lines were not yet definitively drawn. What many thinkers had in common was the idea of a new science for society. For the leadership of the Kuomintang, the potential of Canton as a city of futuristic vision was limitless. Here they might try to manage and discipline its citizens in ways that had never been attempted by the Qing empire, which demanded only obedience, the observance of hierarchy and orthodoxy, and that at a distance. Sun Ke, as mayor, set up a municipal administration on the new eight-storeyed city bund; streets were widened into boulevards, parks and schools built. This remodelling of the city produced a civil police force unique in its scale in China, with several hundred officers and 4,000 constables.[65]

The garden suburb of Tungshan, beside the Canton–Kowloon railway line, with its mission schools and villas, became an enclave for elites, and was also popular with foreigners. Much of the investment for expansion came from those returning from overseas. Canton's public works were designed above all to educate and reform the people. But in spite of all this, Greater Canton remained a pre-modern sprawl of workshops and artisans' shops and its multiple forms of transport were dependent on human labour. According to estimates at the time, only 12.5 per cent of its vast workforce could be considered industrial workers; labour was still dominated by guilds and the mentalities of locality, kin and clan.[66] But, in many ways, Canton was the apogee of the village cities of Asia, on the edge of empires and of modernity. Its improvised enclaves were a place of transit for a surge of new arrivals from the countryside and abroad, an invitation to lose old markers of origin and to forge new solidarities.

Canton was a magnet for adventurers and speculators. On 19 October 1922, there were six bomb attacks in the city and suburbs. Two struck hotels: young women, it was said, came in with a handbag, took a room, then left, the explosion occurring shortly afterwards. Room 7 in the Oriental Hotel was hit, and several rooms blown through on the third floor of the Hotel Asia. The latter was just opposite the Canton steamer wharf, and described by British intelligence as a 'hotbed of intrigue', handy for 'stolen visits'.[67] A bridge and a newspaper office were also targeted. A forty-eight-year-old doctor working at the Republican Hospital, Maximillian de Colbert, was arrested. A 'stout active man with a Hohenzollern moustache', he had acted as chief surgeon to Sun Yat-sen's northern campaign. The military authorities, who initially apprehended him and claimed to have been watching him for some time, uncovered bomb cases, secret notes and photographs of government officials targeted for assassination. De Colbert was said to have had three secret meetings with Sun Yat-sen while he was exiled from the city, and trained protégé assassins by throwing rubber balls. The doctor's son, 'fearing for his father', led the military to 100 pounds of dynamite hidden under some rubbish in his laboratory. The doctor's interpreter was also arrested. De Colbert claimed the empty shells were souvenirs from Flanders and that the recovered bombs had been found by his children playing in the streets. He possessed chemical compounds as he was setting up a modern sanatorium. There was much confusion over his origins and, hence, over his claims to exterritorial legal privilege. He was born in Aachen, and supposedly brought up in Belgium; he qualified as a medical doctor in Germany and had worked in the United States in rural Wisconsin in 1917–19.[68] He spoke German, French, English and Russian, none of them, it was said, very well. His story, as he told it, was that he had organized a relief mission in Canada for Armenia after the armistice, travelling by camel to Kars. But his funds were lost in a dubious foreign exchange deal and he and his family had to make their way to Samara and Bokhara.[69] He maintained that he then fled the Bolsheviks and ended up in Vladivostok in 1920. His wife was American, and de Colbert claimed American citizenship as well, but the US consul hesitated to intervene. At various times he said he was German and British. When questioned, he answered: 'Yes, I am an anarchist. But there are four types of anarchists, and I am one of the Tolstoy type, doing educational work.'[70] De Colbert was interred in the same cell as his interpreter, and it was late December before the case came to Chinese justice. In January 1923 he was released by the district court on lack of evidence. His interpreter died in prison. There was no resolution of the questions as to whether the incidents were related or who might be behind them. The whole bizarre affair seemed to be symptomatic of a deepening struggle between anarchists, communists and nationalists for the soul of the city. In the months to come there would be many more unexplained deaths.

Violence was endemic within Canton and across the whole province. In Guangdong there were still around 150,000 men in arms, most of them ragged and hungry, and in the aftermath of war large swathes of the delta region were under the local sway of an underworld of bandit gangs.[71] Peasants and townsmen, rich and poor alike, were hit by a host of new taxes as Sun Yat-sen sought to rebuild his regime. Sun's position came under renewed assault in early 1923, as the armies of neighbouring provinces who had helped him regain Canton now turned on him and Cheng Jiongming launched a new offensive. Sun's desperate need for material aid pulled him behind the Soviet alliance. This was provided in the form of 2 million Mexican silver dollars. There was a deepening sense, too, that the revolution needed a period of military rule to secure itself, a view that, to a number of Sun's advisers, had been borne out by the Red Army, in which some 10,000 Chinese had fought while in Russia.[72] In this period, Sun and Sneevliet met often. But despite his advocacy for the alliance, Sneevliet felt that Sun's military situation was desperate and he planned his own escape from the city. As he told a colleague in Shanghai, 'the soldiers of Sun will one day or the other be defeated . . . When Sun has to leave, I have to take care not to stay here one day longer.' Sneevliet sent his companion, Sima, ahead of him on the long, dangerous journey through Manchuria, but he himself tarried to make a final attempt to convince the communist leaders of the need for the alliance with the Kuomintang.[73]

Between 12 and 20 June 1923 the party leaders convened for the first time in Canton, in a modest house near Sneevliet's more ambassadorial residence in Tungshan, for their Third Congress. It was the only place they could meet openly, under Sun's protection. The mood was grim. The 'little Moscows' established in scattered communities of industrial workers across China had come under attack. The first leaf to fall was in October 1922, when a strike within the 30,000 labour force with the largely British-owned coal mine at Kailuan was put down when Indian guards and Chinese police fired on a crowd.[74] Then, a strike on the Beijing to Hankou railway ended on 7 February 1923 in a bloodbath of thirty-seven workers at the hands of the forces of Wu Peifu. Zhang Guotao, instrumental in the early organization of the party and the railway workers, reported that the heads of four labour leaders were hung from telegraph poles at the railway station at Changxindian. This was a profound shock to the leaders, the end of what quickly became seen as a 'golden era' of labour mobilization. It also marked the breakdown of cooperation with the warlords in the north.[75] In Shanghai, harassment by the police in the International Settlement drove the party deep underground. Chen Duxiu lamented that cadres 'often do not have complete faith in the party'; regional leaders had little sense of a 'party' at all. In the face of these setbacks, Sneevliet argued that the revolutionary potential of the Kuomintang was closer to the ideal than that even of the Sarekat Islam in Java, and that the Chinese Communist Party should enter it en masse. But Sneevliet then faced accusations that he wanted to dissolve the party entirely. This was baffling to Sneevliet, who was – he thought it was clear – playing a long game. But there was little reason for the others to share his faith in it. Mao Zedong told the gathering that the party should cut its own path with the peasantry. The 'bloc within' strategy prevailed, only by Chen Duxiu's casting vote. The newly elected central committee, with Chen as its chair and Mao as its secretary, quickly and quietly returned to Shanghai.[76] As Sneevliet made plans to return to 'Mecca', he wrote again to Bukharin to complain that the Comintern's Executive 'still revel in fantasies about the mass party, ours, in China'.[77] Sun Yat-sen offered Sneevliet the opportunity to stay, employed within the Kuomintang as a full-time adviser. He was also offered a smaller role running the Soviet news agency, ROSTA, in Canton. Both would have stabilized his finances, but Sneevliet was disillusioned with Sun and with the Comintern, and with his capacity to shape events further.[78]

Passing through Shanghai, Sneevliet ran into Chiang Kai-shek, who was also travelling to Moscow. Chiang was born into a merchant family of rural Zhejiang in 1887 and escaped its constraints and an unhappy arranged marriage through his attempts to win a scholarship to study at a military school in Japan. Initiated there from 1907 into the tight-knit circles of revolution-minded cadets, and after two years in a Japanese artillery regiment, he returned secretly to Shanghai in late 1911 to join the Wuchang uprising. He became actively involved in Sun Yat-sen's operations against Yuan Shikai. Shuttling between Shanghai and Japan between 1912 and 1918, Chiang displayed an ability to cultivate personal networks among the business elite and its dark underbelly, the urban gangs of Shanghai. He developed an antipathy to capitalism but was very willing to use its resources to advance the revolution. He was military adviser to Sun Yat-sen during his first attempt to set up a regime in Canton in 1918.[79] He surprised Sun – surprised everyone – by responding swiftly to Sun's plea for help when Chen Jiongming's troops seized the presidential palace in Canton in June 1922. As they headed into exile together, the two men forged what Chiang was later to describe as 'a wordless rapport'. Chiang was feared and mistrusted in equal measure by the other, older members of Sun's entourage, in his own words, for being 'wild and ungovernable'. Chiang's outsider's air and reputation for unpredictability endured. But through growing self-discipline, and self-cultivation by reading, he positioned himself as one of Sun's most steadfast followers.[80]

Chiang's moment arrived when he travelled with an introduction to Lenin from Sun that named him as Sun's 'most trusted' deputy. Chiang proceeded behind Sneevliet, but the two men spent a good deal of time together in Moscow, as Chiang was there for three months inspecting military facilities. Trotsky told Chiang that the Soviet Union would not send troops into China, but weapons, money and military advisers. He urged him not to rely on military force alone: 'a good newspaper is better than a bad division'.[81] Chiang was impressed with Trotsky's candour. He was impressed too with aspects of the new society, especially the youth organizations, but recorded in his diary that many Soviet high officials were 'cads and rascals'. His meeting with Zinoviev and the Comintern Executive did not go well. He told them the Chinese revolution was one that happened in stages and he was not in a position to openly embrace Bolshevism and class struggle. Chiang was stung by the 'superficial and unrealistic' Comintern communiqué that was issued after the meeting, which urged an opposite course: 'It considers itself the centre of the world revolution, which is really too fabricated and arrogant.'[82] Nevertheless, Chiang's visit raised Comintern hopes for their alliance with the Kuomintang, and Chiang remained deeply impressed by the promise of material aid.

At Harbin, Sneevliet also met the entourage of a newly formed mission en route to Sun Yat-sen. It was led by Michael Borodin. Since his return from Mexico, Borodin had continued to work underground as a Comintern talent scout. He had recently returned from a visit to Britain, as 'Georg Braun/George Brown', a Czech or a Yugoslav, travelling from Hamburg to Grimsby on 15 July 1922. He was arrested on a tip-off from Scotland Yard on 22 August, only two and a half hours after his arrival in Glasgow, with £38 in his pocket but no documentation, just as he was about to begin a lecture at the Labour College. The police identified him as 'a Communist emissary' after gleaning from him a long, unverifiable story of complex ancestry, dubious nationality, constant movement and an unconvincing cover which involved research on urban motion: traffic, underground railways, the flow of crowds along thoroughfares and the provision of public toilets. He was deported after serving six months in HM Prison Barlinnie in Scotland.[83] Several months after his return to Moscow he was chosen, ahead of Voitinsky, to lead the expedition to China. This surprised some, but he had a formidable reputation as a 'missionary' for Bolshevism. He spoke English well, so could speak directly to Sun Yat-sen, and he claimed that they had come across each other in his Chicago days, although it was not clear that Sun remembered this.

From Harbin, Borodin travelled swiftly on to Shanghai and by steamer to Canton, managing to bypass Hong Kong, where the British were watching for him. He was welcomed on the day of his arrival by Sun Yat-sen as 'China's Lafayette'. On 15 October he spoke beside Sun on several platforms in the city, the first occasions in some time that Sun had appeared at public gatherings. It was the first time too that the people of Canton had seen a veteran Russian Bolshevik.[84] Borodin moved swiftly to reorganize the Kuomintang along Leninist lines. He won his spurs in mid-November at a moment when Sun was preparing once more to go into exile, and the forces of Chen Jiongming looked likely to break through in the north and advance on Canton. Borodin urged mass resistance; Kuomintang cadres were despatched to the front and the line held. The Borodin mansion in Tungshan became a new centre of gravity within the republic. Borodin's wife, Fanya, acted as his secretary, and as a new model of a woman in political life, her credentials burnished by the story – as recounted later by Soong Mei-ling, sister-in-law to Sun Yat-sen – that she was related to Buster Keaton.[85] Borodin gathered Asian co-workers around him. Like Sneevliet before him, Borodin knew no Chinese. His principal assistant was Zhang Tailei, an activist from Tianjin, who, based on rather dubious credentials, had spoken for China at the Third Congress of the Comintern in 1921. He was an ardent follower of the Moscow line. Another ally and scribe was Qu Qiubai, a journalist who had reported from Moscow and taught Chinese to some of the Soviet advisers who came with Borodin. When he came down to Canton from Shanghai in January 1924, it provoked the caustic observation that Borodin 'treats our party just as if we were a provider of interpreters'.[86] In many ways, international communism was a mighty translation machine. Qu was indeed a brilliant renderer of Russian Marxist and sociological texts into Chinese in its newly emerging modern form.[87] Like all translation, this was a creative process. By accident or design, Chinese party translations of Lenin's theses on the 'National and Colonial Questions' of 1920 tended to amplify the language of M. N. Roy's 'supplementary' theses and the need to confront the national bourgeoisie more immediately and cultivate the peasantry.[88] To this end, cadres began to reappear in Canton and to recruit from the powerful waterfront unions and from men banished from places like British Malaya.[89]

The new alliance was sealed at the first Congress of the Kuomintang, which opened in Canton on 20 January 1924. Although the official tally of members of the Chinese Communist Party amounted to less than 10 per cent of the Kuomintang, they provided twenty-three of the 165 delegates who attended the sessions. Borodin had been part of the commission that had drawn up its programme between late October and mid-January. This was seen as a major statement of intent: an attempt to shift the party away from the personal forms of authority which characterized Sun's leadership to more formal, statist adminis-tration.[90] The meeting exposed cleavages within the Kuomintang. These came to be understood in terms of the Kuomintang 'right' and the Kuomintang 'left', labels which were in many ways adopted by out-siders to make sense of a very fluid situation and complex moral and intellectual journeys.[91] But they were also taken up as cudgels by the main protagonists themselves. In the centre of the Kuomintang 'left' was Wang Jingwei. His revolutionary credentials were, on first scru-tiny, unimpeachable: he had been an adjutant to Sun Yat-sen during his years in Southeast Asia after 1905 and had attempted by his own hand to assassinate the Qing prince regent in 1910. During a second sojourn overseas after 1912, Wang was active in the anarchist work-study movement in France, although he himself did not live as a worker. His experience of the Great War left him with a deep mistrust of militarism and a belief in 'human co-existence'. Wang was naturally inclined to scholarship more than politics, but was pulled into the latter's epicentre by Sun Yat-sen on his return to China in 1919.[92] In his stay overseas he had married the daughter of a wealthy merchant of Penang, Chen Bijun, who bore him six children, the eldest two having been born in France. It was said in Canton that everyone in the city walked on rub-ber soles from her trees and many mistrusted his professed 'socialist credentials'.[93] But Borodin and his allies now relied on them for the success of their strategy.

Tensions surfaced at a celebratory banquet on the very first evening of the Congress, when a Kuomintang delegate demanded that if the com-munists were sincere, they should leave their party. Li Dazhao attempted to reassure the conference that 'we join this party as individuals not as a body. We may be said to have dual party membership.'[94] But they were largely seen as subordinates, and in an early session, when Mao Zedong and Li Lisan began to speak, many Kuomintang veterans 'looked askance . . . as if to ask: "where did these two young unknowns come from? How is it they have so much to say?" '[95]

On 25 January, Sun Yat-sen, again with Borodin at his side, dramatically took to the stage at the Congress to announce that Lenin had died on 21 January. Sun delivered an emotional eulogy. The conference was adjourned for three days, and the city was decked in mourning. A wave of grief swept through Asia. This was not brought into being by the affiliates of Moscow, but was something spontaneous, embraced by declared communists and non-communists alike. Across India, newspapers repeated the refrain, in the words of a Hindi paper of Allahabad, that the 'world's greatest man of the age has passed away from this world'. M. Singaravelu, who formed the Labour Kisan Party in India, led a week of mourning: 'by his death workers of the world lost their great Teacher and Redeemer'. It also revived the comparison with Gandhi, who was still in a British prison, and the question of violence. For some, the contrast had diminished, as one Kannada-language account put it: 'Lenin hated violence as much as Gandhiji. But he did not believe in licking the hand that holds the sword like a coward.' For others, Lenin had died a true *sanyasi*.[96]

In Moscow, Nguyen Ai Quoc queued for hours in Red Square finally to see the great man; Quoc's toes, it was said, were permanently blackened by frostbite. In December 1923 he had settled into the Hotel Lux. He was becoming better known in Comintern circles but complained of sharing a small room with four or five others and campaigned for separate quarters for the leaders from Asia. But nearly four years from the first debates on the 'National and Colonial Questions' there was impatience at the lack of progress that had been made in communicating with the human masses of Asia. As Quoc told the Fifth Congress: 'I am here in order to continuously remind the International of the colonies and to point out that the revolution faces a colonial danger as well as a great future in the colonies.' He laid out figures to convey its scale, for populations, investments, acres of lands in North Africa, equatorial Africa, Madagascar. He lambasted the European parties for their lack of action on the colonial question: comrades who 'give me the impression that they wish to kill a snake by stepping on its tail'.[97] He was increasingly impatient: he had, he said, been nine months in Moscow and six of them waiting. Then he was told to join Borodin, who was 'an old Bolshevik versed in the ways of the underground'.[98]

THE BIRTH OF ASLIA

Ten years after the outbreak of the war in Europe, there were many signs that the next world conflict was coming. But it was to be unleashed at a moment when the revolutionary tide in the west was ebbing, and its field would be Asia. At the anniversary of the February revolution Zinoviev reminded his audience that:

> The revolution will turn from a European revolution into a world revolution only in the measure that the hundred million human masses of the East will rise. The East is the main reserve of a world revolution . . . The proletarian revolution is aiming first of all at English imperialism.[99]

He returned to this theme through the year. At the Fifth Comintern Congress in July 1924, he stated that the Treaty of Versailles and the last imperialist war was pregnant with 'a new imperialist war'.[100]

The bunds and bridges that marked the limits of extraterritorial privileges for foreigners in China had become the front line for the assault on empire. When, on 19 June 1924, Pham Hong Thai threw his bomb into the dining room of the Hotel Victoria in Shamian, the city of Canton came out on strike against the entire European community. Perhaps it could have happened anywhere, but in these months it was Canton that took on a special significance as the beacon for a free Asia. Around Borodin was a growing band of revolutionaries from all nations. One of them was a Korean former anarchist known as Kim San, who had embraced communism during a sojourn in Beijing. To Kim, the veteran Bolshevik was 'a rock in a wild sea of inexperienced youth and enthusiasm'.[101] The frenzy of life in the city was fuelled by the expectation that Sun Yat-sen would commit to the launching of a great northern expedition, to cut his way out of the southern enclave and reunite China.

It was, in the words of one Indian writer, an 'ecliptic time'.[102] A fore-taste of this came with the arrival, in April 1924, of the poet and sage

Rabindranath Tagore. He had been invited by the Beijing Lecture Society, presided over by the reformer and intellectual Liang Qichao,
following its earlier hosting of the philosophers John Dewey and Bertrand
Russell. Tagore's pan-Asian, spiritual cosmopolitanism was confronted
with a new mood and by a new generation. Many Chinese intellectuals
of the reform and May Fourth eras had drawn inspiration from Tagore
at some point in their lives. Chen Duxiu, for instance, had translated
some of his verse. But the protests were led by a younger group of intellectuals, many recently returned from Japan and exposed to anarchist
thought there, for whom the generation of May Fourth already seemed
distant and aloof. Guo Moruo was a returnee who had studied for
many years in Japan in the Medical School of Kyushu Imperial University and married a Japanese woman. An avid reader of Spinoza, Goethe
and Tagore, he had abandoned medicine for literature and on his return
to Shanghai had, with kindred spirits, formed a 'Creation Society'.
It challenged the older generation's near-monopoly on the printing
presses – the influential Commercial Press controlled 30–40 per cent of
the city's literary output at the time – and championed a new, socially
engaged, internationalist style. 'If you are sympathetic with revolution,'
Guo wrote, 'the works you create or appreciate will be revolutionary
literature, speaking in the name of the oppressed class.'[103] Guo Moruo
had devoured and translated Tagore as a student in Japan, but now, as
he told it, his evolving responses to Tagore were stations on his journey
towards materialism: 'My spiritual ties with Tagore were snapped . . . I
thought Tagore was a nobleman, a sage, and I was an ordinary mortal
of little worth. His world was different from mine. I had no right to be
there.' With Tagore's presence in China, there was a danger that the
youth might be similarly seduced by his reification of the 'oriental' and
distracted by his spiritualism.[104]

Tagore reached Hong Kong in early April 1924. Through a messenger, Sun Yat-sen invited him to Canton, but Tagore, travelling behind
schedule, pressed on to Shanghai and Beijing. Few questioned Tagore's
anti-colonial credentials. In Shanghai, he criticized Britain's continued
deployment of troops from India in China.[105] But Tagore's visit to the
last emperor, Puyi, in the Forbidden City further antagonized his critics. There was growing mistrust of the motives of his hosts. Lu Xun,
who heard him speak in Beijing, satirized their wearing of 'Indian caps'
on the stage: they treated Tagore as if he was 'a living god'.[106] In

Hankou, Tagore was met with shouts and placards at a lecture out-side the Supporting Virtue Middle School: 'Go back, slave from a lost country!' 'We don't want philosophy, we want materialism!' He left acknowledging that the gulf between him and his audience was unbridgeable.[107] The worries that a new generation in China would be seduced by Tagore's spiritual passivity proved to be unfounded. An opinion poll was commissioned of students at Beijing University and 1,007 responded, 725 of whom favoured 'people's revolution':

Which country is China's true friend? Russia: 497; United States: 107; Neither of the two: 226; Both: 12; No opinion: 253.

What political party or system do you favour? Socialism: 191; Sun Yat-sen's party: 153; Democracy: 69; Federal Republic: 40; 'Good gov-ernment': 14; Revolutionary party: 13.

Who is the greatest man in the world [outside China]? Lenin: 227; Wilson: 51; Bertrand Russell: 24; Tagore: 17; Einstein: 16; Trotsky: 12; Kaiser Wilhelm II: 12; Washington: 11; Harding: 10; Lincoln: 9; John Dewey: 9; Bismarck: 9; Gandhi: 9; Tolstoy: 7; Marx: 6, etc.[108]

In the coming months, many of these university students made their way to Canton.

At the centre of this was the foundation, with Soviet money, of a military academy at Whampoa, some miles south of the city. It was to provide an independent military cadre for the Kuomintang, as had been urged by Sneevliet and others from the outset, but it also became a means for its commandant, Chiang Kai-shek, to cultivate his leader-ship style, as he emerged as the leading force within what was an increasingly militarized regime. Chiang was a strong believer in the discipline and rigidity that military training provided. But physical resilience was insufficient, and an important function of Whampoa was political education. It was a measure of the ideological fluidity of the moment that when the first classes began in June 1924, one of the commissar-instructors in political economy was Zhou Enlai, who had returned from the communist organization in France. Soviet advisers also led classes. These included around twenty-five Koreans and between ten and fifteen Vietnamese, and recruits also came from the Chinese night schools in Malaya and Singapore. The academy was a forcing-house for bodily discipline, revolutionary élan and personal networks: the 'Intimacy, Fraternity, Dexterity, Sincerity' of its motto. Chiang Kai-shek took his maxim – 'the lives of all the cadets at Whampoa are ultimately one life' – as a licence to cultivate men whose loyalty would be to him. A high number of the first cohort of recruits came from Shanghai, through Chiang's connections with the city's business elite and criminal underworld.[109] Meanwhile, Zhou Enlai created a caucus of military officers loyal to the Chinese Communist Party. This emphasis on leadership training went further than previous experiments in Asia, such as the Tan Malaka schools. A Peasant Movement Training Institute was also set up in July in Canton in an old Confucian temple with a class of thirty-eight students, mostly from Guangdong, and led by Peng Pai. Over the next two years, this Institute would educate over 800 peasants from increasingly further afield, many coming from the mines of Anyuan, and they gained practical experience in the Guangdong countryside.[110]

Tan Malaka had arrived in Canton in December 1923, after a long, clandestine journey that sowed the seeds of a vision of unity of the maritime world of Asia. On his journey into European exile, bullied by drunken Dutchmen, the Chinese sailors on board his ship had stepped in to protect him. They were followers of Sun Yat-sen; they knew his situation and shared his views. These solidarities now helped him move freely across Asia. They were also at the heart of the sojourns of his own people, the Minangkabau, in the largeness of the world, across the Indian Ocean, to Ceylon and Madagascar: 'Guided by the moon and the stars, sailing in their tiny boats, they were protected by their wits, and their spirit of community and mutual co-operation in both good times and bad. And even the ocean became only a lake in their eyes.'[111] Now he gave the vision a name, 'Aslia': a nation for the peoples without a country, within a new socialist world system. In Canton he was put to work with the seafarers. Reasonably fluent in the lingua franca of the Comintern in Europe, German, he possessed neither of the common tongues of radicalism in Asia, Chinese and English. For his propaganda work he adopted a kind of 'basic English' with a limited vocabulary of some 800 or so words, which he later conflated with the pacifist C. K. Ogden's global interlanguage, which was to be brought to China by I. A. Richards, a fellow of Magdalene College, Cambridge, in 1929.[112] His journal, *The Dawn*, was produced by a Chinese printer with no knowledge of western languages and, Tan Malaka complained, with insufficient Latin type for the task. Despite his work with the sea-farers, he was out of touch with events in Indonesia and, in the relative extremes of the climate in southern China, his tuberculosis worsened. An Indonesian visitor, his only contact with home for an entire year, found him bedridden in an 'outlying quarter' of the city.[113] But his major achievement came in June 1924, in the first Pan-Pacific Labour Congress in Canton. For the first time, it brought together Asia's global waterfront, sailors and dockers fanning out from China, Japan, Singapore, Malaya, Indonesia, Siam, the Philippines and India in intri-cate cross-cutting webs, re-energizing links that stretched across the Pacific.[114]

The entire seaboard of Asia seemed about to catch fire. In the middle of 1924 there were a reported twenty-eight pirate gunboats roaming the water approaches to Canton, and most of the tow-boats to delta ports such as Dongguan and Xiangshan had stopped sailing.[115] To the north, fighting threatened the river and rail connections of Shanghai: the ultimate prize of the warlords of the north, not least because of the profits of the drugs trade. In August 1924 the Huangpu River was vul-nerable, and the foreign powers determined to bring in their own warships. A flotilla of several nations anchored off the bund, and a military cordon was thrown around the city beyond its treaty bor-ders. Fighting itself – and the press-ganging of labour – reached the Chinese city and by the end of September there were perhaps half a million Chinese refugees in the International Settlement; masterless men and women roamed the surrounding countryside and spilled into the city, 8,000 or so of them occupying the railway carriages and wait-ing rooms of the Northern Station. In December fighting erupted again; much of the country around Shanghai was ransacked and violence and looting once more spread into the suburbs. Like the bomb thrown at M. Merlin, it brought the brutal reality of war to the doorsteps of the privileged foreigners.[116]

On 12 November 1924 a flurry of letters from Canton to Moscow announced another new arrival. He wrote to apologize for his sudden departure from Moscow and to give his new address as the office of the Soviet news agency, ROSTA. He swiftly ensconced himself in the Boro-din House. He used the identity of Ly Thuy, feigned a Chinese ethnicity, and wrote sometimes under the pseudonym of a woman, but concerned himself principally with the Vietnamese communities in the city. 'I haven't seen anyone yet,' he complained. 'Everyone here is busy about Dr Sun going north.'[117] It took a couple of months before the French Sûreté confirmed that Ly Thuy was indeed their old quarry, Nguyen Ai Quoc.

The same evening there was a military parade to bid farewell to Sun Yat-sen, as he left Canton to resolve the fate of the Chinese revolution. He went at the invitation of the northern warlord, Feng Yuxiang, whose forces had seized Beijing the previous month. One of Feng's first acts was to remove the titles and privileges of the imperial families, of the last Qing emperor, eighteen-year-old Puyi, and to evict him from the Forbidden City, where he had lived in seclusion with a diminishing retinue of eunuchs and tutors since the fall of the dynasty in 1912.[118] For Sun, this seemed to open a path for him to regain the national pre-eminence he had lost in his wilderness years of exile and isolation in the south. He had, of late, become impatient with the 'radical drift' of Canton politics and his mind turned towards the higher arena. In September he left Canton for Shaoguan, on the border with Hunan province, to prepare for a new expedition to the north to unify China. His plans stalled when his commanders were slow to rally to him. Chiang Kai-shek believed the position in Canton itself was not secure enough to allow this. Now, Sun stopped only briefly back in Canton as he left to achieve by diplomacy the 'great central revolution' that he had failed to achieve by arms.[119] As Sun passed through Shanghai, the local leaders of the Kuomintang organized clamorous civic receptions. His insistent anti-imperialist message and his call for a new national assembly caught the popular mood, and it seemed that he might regain the momentum to restore past glories and the presidency of the republic.[120]

The air of predestination intensified when, between Shanghai and Tianjin, Sun made a short visit to Japan. In a speech at a girls' school in Kobe on 28 November he invoked the vision of pan-Asianism first raised by the exiles in Japan twenty years earlier: the call for solidarity between peoples suffering the same sickness of imperial domination. Those who had taken a stand against empire during the world war – men such as Rash Behari Bose and Prince Cuong De – still lived in exile in Japan, awaiting their hour. The horrors of the Great War had undermined faith in western 'civilization' and its claims to universal standards, among both European and Asian intellectuals. 'Asianism' revived as a counterweight to its materialism and rapacious violence.[121] But Sun Yat-sen had always put the struggle for China first. In his

Three Principles of the People, written after the first Kuomintang Congress in 1924, Sun warned that 'the European idea of cosmopolitanism is but the doctrine of "might is right" in disguise', and therefore 'unless the spirit of nationalism is well-developed, the spirit of cosmopolitanism is perilous'.[122] He seemed to place his faith in the 'universalism' of Chinese thought – its historic traditions of peaceful reciprocity – and to distance himself from his earlier declared affinity for western socialism.[123] His attacks on British imperialism electrified his Japanese audience. But in Kobe, in his peroration Sun also questioned the motives of his hosts: 'Will Japan become the hunting dog of the Western Rule of Might or the bulwark of the Eastern Rule of Right?' These last words were redacted in many Japanese newspapers, as Sun's ideological legacy became contested on all sides.[124]

For months there had been rumours of Sun's failing health. Many of his key aides, including his de facto deputy in the south, Hu Hanmin, counselled against the journey to Beijing. They feared it was a trap to confer recognition on his northern warlord rivals at the expense of Sun's own claims to lead China. Many of his allies on the left were opposed to negotiating with warlords, however patriotic or progressive their professed intentions. Sun's generals had yet to achieve a monopoly of force within Guangdong's own borders. There was a long and bitter stand-off in Canton itself between government forces and the so-called 'paper tigers', the mercenary militias employed by the city merchants to protect their fortified warehouses and break strikes. When their ability to import arms was obstructed on 10 October 1924, fighting broke out and some 3,000 houses and shops – according to the estimate of the Electric Company – in the traders' district to the west of the old walled city were left in flames. People who tried to escape were shot at from the rooftops. Refugees fled into the western concessions on Shamian Island. From behind its defences, the cries of those caught in the flames could be heard through the night. Perhaps 200–300 merchant volunteers were killed and 100 soldiers, many shot for looting. The civilian death toll was unclear. The city merchants never forgave Sun. He was, one Chinese newspaper cried, 'bringing us all to our total destruction'. As a foreigner who witnessed it commented, 'I am convinced that it will be impossible for Sun Yat-sen to ever return here.'[125]

In Sun's absence, Canton was threatened by a fresh offensive by Chen Jiongming from the east. Sun ascribed both crises to the machinations of the foreign powers. His government survived in no small part by virtue of its ability to mobilize the cadets training at Whampoa Military Academy. In 1925, around 2,500 graduates passed through its gates, many of them to fight alongside Soviet advisers in the breakout spring 'eastern expedition' against Chen Jiongming. These cadets gathered valuable war booty and vital experience of using political propaganda to enlist farmers and labourers as guides, spies and porters.[126] The Soviet advisers, of whom there were around forty by this time, were transfixed by a looming power struggle within the Kuomintang. They complained of Chiang's increasing hauteur; his temper, procrastination and evasiveness. But they had little reason to doubt his commitment to revolution. When Mikhail Borodin was asked by one of his subordinates, 'How far will Chiang Kai-shek go with us?', he replied: 'Why shouldn't he go with us?'[127]

On Sun Yat-sen's arrival in Beijing on 31 December 1924, his old friend the president of Beijing University, Cai Yuanpei, turned out the student cadets to escort him in triumph from the railway station, attended by the representatives of some 500 civic associations. But, in a twist of fate, Sun was taken seriously ill in Tianjin. His condition worsened a few days after his arrival in Beijing and he moved from the Hôtel de Pékin to the Rockefeller-funded Peking Union Medical College Hospital. A small circle of advisers closed around him, led by Wang Jingwei, who travelled as his secretary, Borodin, who had journeyed separately to join him in Beijing, and the communists Li Dazhao and Zhang Guotao. As Sun ebbed in late February 1925, a political will and testament was drafted by Wang Jingwei, with a 'letter of farewell' to the Soviet leadership pledging alliance, approved by Borodin. They were the only two aides allowed at his bedside. With the help of Sun's wife, Soong Ching-ling, the letters were signed by Sun on 11 March, together with a will bequeathing his property to her. Sun died the next day. The documents named no successor. Sun was not a 'party' leader in any conventional sense, but the embodiment of a revolution; nor, despite Borodin's best efforts, was the Kuomintang yet a fully formed 'political party' in the Bolshevik image.[128]

Sun's prestige soared on his passing: there were solemn vigils in cities across China in which emotions blended with rituals from the new cult of Lenin.[129] Sun asked to be buried, like Lenin, close to the people and a bronze and crystal glass-fronted coffin was ordered from Russia. A plan to requisition the Hall of Supreme Harmony within the Forbidden City was quietly dropped. Instead, Sun lay for three weeks in Beijing's Central Park, adjacent to Tiananmen Square. When the coffin arrived it proved to be an inadequate manufacture of tin and glass, and Sun's embalmed body was laid to rest in a simple wooden casket. The private funeral ceremony – amid further controversy – was a Christian service, insisted on by the American-educated Soong Ching-ling, and featuring Sun's favourite hymn: 'Abide With Me'.[130] His body was then laid in the Temple of the Azure Clouds in the Western Hills, along with the empty tin casket.

As with Lenin, news of Sun's death was a catalyst to grief across the globe: he was the 'father of the nation', and, together with Gandhi, the best-known face of Asia. As Tan Malaka, a witness to this in Canton, observed, before Sun's passing many in the city had called him an 'empty cannon': 'it was really only after he had died that I saw respect and even praise given to Dr Sun.' Tan Malaka had met Sun when he first arrived in the city. He could not subscribe completely to Sun's vision, especially his critiques of Marxism and his lifelong faith in Japan as the 'light of Asia'. But he admired Sun for his perseverance, his awareness that there would be constant reversals on the path to revolution, and, above all, as 'a fugitive who had many "strategies" and who had friends everywhere'.[131] In the Netherlands Indies there were memorial services in Semarang, Surabaya and Bandung, attended by Javanese as well as Chinese, and after speeches celebrating the friendship of Sun and Lenin, the government forbade a similar demonstration of solidarity in the capital, Batavia.[132] In Singapore mourners converged on the 'Happy Valley' amusement park in Tanjong Pagar, where the Prince of Wales had opened the Malaya-Borneo exhibition three years earlier. Over two days, an estimated 100,000 people filed past 2,000 commemorative scrolls and a life-sized portrait of Sun. This was almost on the scale of the crowds in Beijing itself. The British saw this as an insidious challenge to their authority.[133] Even the quietest corners of colonial Asia felt the impact of these events.

The 'bobbed-hair woman'.

13

Anarchy Loosed
1925–1926

THE BOBBED-HAIR WOMAN

At a quarter to eleven on Friday morning, 23 January 1925, the world revolution came to Kuala Lumpur. It was an otherwise slow day. The main barometer of the life of the town, the rubber price, was falling and the market sluggish. Around the Market Square the banks and businesses were closing early as people prepared for the Chinese New Year holiday. The Year of the Ox was to be announced by firecrackers at midnight, a grudging concession by British officials to the local lords of misrule.

In the late-morning bustle, a young Chinese woman made her way towards the government bungalows at the lower end of the High Street. She was alone, dressed in a white jacket, black skirt, white shoes and white stockings. She was carrying a small briefcase.

She was a striking presence. For one thing, she was not wearing a hat, as any respectable woman would do. But more than this, her hair was trimmed very short, in the modern style. There were few women of any kind to be seen in Kuala Lumpur. European women tended to come out rarely to this part of town, and then only in long dresses and hats and veils. It was a town of thrusting young men, the majority of them Chinese from the southern provinces. In the previous decade, only about one in fourteen Chinese arrivals in the Federated Malay States had been women. Many of those had been trafficked – shipped via Shanghai, Saigon, Bangkok and North Borneo to avoid detection – and were to be found in the brothels of the High Street.[1] There were twenty-six Chinese brothels and eleven Japanese brothels in Kuala Lumpur with an estimated 326 known inmates. The 'Protector of

Chinese' in KL, Daniel Richards, had overseen 144 admissions in the Federal Home for Women and Girls in 1924.[2]

The protector's office was on the High Street, a short walk from the Market Square, past the gambling booths and the barred, open windows of Chinatown and the heavily painted women within. The door of the office was just opposite that of the local chief of police. The girl opened it and peered in, then entered. She stood, flushed in the face, in front of Daniel Richards and his junior, Wilfred Blythe, who were seated at a table.

'There is someone threatening me,' she said in Cantonese dialect, the patois of the town, or so it seemed to Blythe's ears. Richards asked what it was all about and she offered him the briefcase, saying that a friend had told her to give it to him.

As she placed it on the table, Richards saw two ridges on the case, as if a tin had been squeezed into it. As she appeared to fumble with the catch, Richards noticed that there did not seem to be one on the case. She then withdrew her hands and stepped back slightly. She turned and spoke again, but almost immediately there was a loud explosion.

A four-foot hole was blown in the table, the baize-green public works curtains of the office were pitted with holes and the floor was covered with shreds of paper and plaster. In the remnants of the case could be seen a switch and a single-cell battery, together with nails and fragments of a tin which bore the words 'Sperry Pure Rolled Oats'.

The girl staggered out of the office, turned around, walked two or three paces then fell over on her back, blood on her mouth, at the feet of a shocked Chinese clerk.[3]

Richards was rushed to the European hospital, the girl to the general hospital, both unconscious.[4] Astonishingly, both of them were alive. The bomb was lightly packed and, there being little resistance, the force of the explosion was weakened.[5] Later accounts claimed that the girl had thrown herself beneath furniture to escape the worst of the blast.[6] Richards, however, lost the use of one hand. The girl was kept under guard for five days as the shards of metal in her forearms and face were removed; her torso was badly scarred by puncture wounds.[7] The doctor who treated her remarked that throughout she remained calm and collected and, he was careful to add, she showed no signs of insanity.

'The bobbed-hair woman', as she rapidly became known, was the most sensational local news story for years – at least since 1911, when a housewife, Ethel Proudlock, had shot dead her lover, claiming he had tried to rape her, an incident which only the previous year Somerset Maugham had turned into a short story, 'The Letter'. But this case, by contrast, seemed to be a motiveless crime.

There was speculation that it was a crime of passion, to avenge a dead lover. The female assassin driven by 'filial piety, contained sexuality, and sublimated passion' was a familiar type in public debate in China, not least in the avenging daughters of the sentimental 'Mandarin Ducks and Butterflies' fiction.[8] But the girl made no appeal to public sympathy. Nor did she make recourse to well-travelled arguments that her feminine passion had overwhelmed her reason.

The colonial public was chilled by her exacting premeditation. The 'bobbed-hair woman' had arrived in Kuala Lumpur only that morning. Some reports said that she came from Canton; others that she was from Penang, and fluent in Malay.[9] They were, above all, obsessed by the way she looked. She appeared in court on 29 January, her arm still in a sling. 'She has', intoned the *Straits Times*, 'a singularly masculine appearance. Her hair is bobbed particularly short. She is of dark complexion, has a scar near the right temple.'[10]

No single event heralded the arrival of the Asian revolution so much as the advent of the 'Modern Girl'. Across Asia, women were suddenly visible on the city streets, working in shops and factories, taking public transport, talking in a direct way, raising their hemlines, rouging their cheeks, crossing their legs in public and – above all – cutting their hair. The year 1925 was when the 'Modern Girl' became a global phenomenon, and in this the women of Asia took the lead. Letters to readers' pages in local newspapers hotly debated the question, 'To bob or not to bob?' Many people, and not all of them men, expressed outrage at what they saw as decadent, brazen and masculine behaviour. There were stories of 'bobbed-hair riots' as far away as Mexico City, of rival 'anti-bobbed-hair leagues' and 'bobbed-hair defence leagues'.[11]

From Shanghai to Tokyo to Penang, the 'Modern Girl' – in Chinese *modeng gou'er*, in Japanese *modan garu*, or *moga*, in Malay *wanita moden* – suggested a cosmopolitan awareness that shocked and inspired people in equal measure. Such was the speed with which new ideas syndicated around Asia that it was impossible to say which had come from where, or who had thought of it first. What was certain was that it was no longer the west that was leading the way with things new.[12]

The 'Modern Girl' was increasingly linked to a dangerous, disordered modernity; to nihilism and to anarchism.[13] As one expatriate journal put it: 'The now notorious "bobbed-haired" lady might just as well have turned up in Venezuela or Tibet for all the relation that her "mission" had to events in Malaya . . . Politics virtually do not exist in this country.'[14] The *Straits Times* brayed for a system of 'identity tickets' to indicate who was a loyal subject of His Majesty King George V and who was not.[15] There were suddenly other sightings of 'strange' young women in Kuala Lumpur.[16]

At a subsequent court appearance, in late February, her name was given as 'Wong Sang'. As she waited for her case to be called, she continually glanced at the crowd and seemed to exchange smiles with spectators. Reporters noted the calmness, even disinterestedness, with which she walked to the dock. She listened to the charge with a smile. Her interest only seemed to be aroused when the police chief held in his hand a photograph taken 'evidently when she was much younger and before she bobbed her hair'. She kept staring at the photograph until it was hidden from view.[17]

At the root of the case was her 'new style'. As the sole official statement on the case put it: 'The woman who was self-educated and educated in opposition to the wishes of her parents is obsessed with an idea of grievance against the world in general.'[18] Her trial came to the Kuala Lumpur Assizes two months after the event, on 23 March, delayed due to Richards's stay in hospital. Wong Sang entered the courtroom with complete composure and, with what the court reporter called 'a complacent smile', as she took the dock she surveyed the court and gallery.[19]

The room lacked ornament. There was a raised and partitioned area for the judge and his three assessors, in the absence of trial by jury, and a large semicircular table for the counsel. The capacious dock was guarded by Sikh policemen, who were rotated every half-hour. Where the jury would sit in an English court there was the high chair for the interpreters, like that 'used by umpires at tennis'. The proceedings, which were entirely in English, broken by hurried translation, were rarely understood by the accused, and the testimony rarely understood directly by the judge. The whole affair resembled a military court martial.[20]

When asked to plead, Wong Sang said only that she had nothing to say. She briefed no counsel and called no witnesses. The judge pressed her to explain herself.

'I admit I brought the bomb to the Protectorate,' she told him in the flat tones of the court interpreter. 'I admit that I did wrong. I plead guilty. I ask for leniency. I have a very bad temper': this was said with a smile. 'I have repented for what I have done.'

'You say you have a very bad temper,' the judge ventured further. 'I do not know whether you wish to explain that. Is it that you have some ill-feeling?'

'I do not wish to say anything beyond what I have already stated.'

His lordship then turned to the deputy public prosecutor to ask him to speak in her defence: 'This woman has not as far as I can see told us the motives as to why she did this: have enquiries been made?'

'Some political reasons, my lord.'

'Has she said so?'

'Yes, she has – several times. She has got some weird notions about the brotherhood of man and other things.'

'Was she born in Penang?'

'Yes, my lord, but she has been in Canton. Her father was banished from this country and later killed in Canton. She has made some very broad statements as to her opinions on political questions – very loose, wild sort of anarchical statements, but there is no definite statement against Mr Richards personally.'[21]

She was sentenced to ten years' rigorous imprisonment. As he delivered the sentence, the judge rebuked her.

'After having told the authorities in prison or hospital, I don't know where, that you did this for political reasons you ask me to be lenient with you on the ground that you have a bad temper, and that is about all the assistance we can get. It is impossible for me to be lenient with you even though you are a woman, because you have committed such a particularly cruel and dastardly crime. You, therefore, must be rigorously imprisoned for ten years.'[22]

The press reported 'that eternal smile' as the verdict was read to her. They were shocked at the court's leniency, even though such long sentences were relatively rare.

In the west, when such dangerous individuals were brought to trial, legal process had by the later nineteenth century increasingly demanded some form of confession or self-revelation. Even in this colonial parody of the law – where the accused had no representation and called no witnesses – there seemed to be a similar expectation that the accused 'really ought to speak a little about themselves, if they want to be judged'. But the 'bobbed-hair woman' had remained silent. She had evaded the crucial question: 'Who are you?'[23]

And there the case of the 'bobbed-hair woman' seemed to rest. The British government in London only heard about the bomb three months later when the injured Richards arrived home on leave. The colonial secretary, Leo Amery, rebuked the governor for taking so long to report it. 'A complete adequate description of it in a telegram would have been hard to compile,' the governor, Sir Laurence Guillemard, explained somewhat weakly, 'and might have given a more serious complexion to the affair than was really warranted.' He added that the press had shown 'a very creditable reticence' about the case.[24]

The Malayan government was so unforthcoming about the affair that there was mounting public speculation that information was being withheld, and that what was first reported as 'a daughter's vendetta' might indeed be political. The independently minded mouthpiece of the new Asian middle class, the *Straits Echo* of Penang, hinted that before going to Kuala Lumpur the woman had been 'looking for somewhat higher game'.[25]

In prison Wong Sang said a little more. It took several days before the police could, as a secret report put it, overcome her 'great reticence' and extract her original name. The means by which they did so was not put to paper. They discovered that the name Wong Sang was entirely fictitious; the British translated it to mean 'Life's Victim'. Her name was variously given as Wong Sau Ying, or Wong So Ying. She was twenty-six years old at the time of the incident. She came not from Penang, as reported, but from China, and had spent time in Beijing and Shanghai. Her prison record gave her calling, or occupation, as 'artist'.[26]

The story about her father was also false. In 1919 she was living in Malaya, in Penang, with a lover called Mak Peng Chho who was known to the police as an anarchist. In some accounts she was his mistress, in others his wife. In 1919 their house was raided by the police, part of the famous case of the 'six gentlemen': the mass banishment of schoolteachers and journalists. The police found pamphlets relating to a Chinese anarchist society, but Mak had escaped arrest and fled to

China. He returned in May 1923 but was banished to China in July of the same year, after the police had once again found in his possession a pamphlet on *Anarchism and Communism*, printed in Kuala Lumpur, and letters explaining the difficulties of carrying out propaganda in Southeast Asia. When Mak was deported back to Hokshan, Canton, with Wong Sang, he had been caught and shot on the orders of the local Chinese district magistrate in February 1924.[27]

Wong Sang had indeed been after 'higher game': the governor himself. She told her police interrogators that she was a 'universalist' and had chosen to assassinate Guillemard because he represented 'a system which hinders the progress of the world'. She had brought the bomb materials from China and purchased an electric battery in Singapore. Another male comrade, Yat Mun, was to shoot him with a pistol. They had tracked the governor on his tour of the peninsula. First, she waited with her suitcase on Penang golf course, but stood at the wrong tee and missed him. She then boarded his train to KL, but he got off early at Kuala Kangsar to meet the local sultan. Having lost him, Wong Sang had to act against lesser prey and was left to do so alone.[28] Her male accomplice was never found.

All this was hidden from the public at the time.[29] But four years later, a policeman at the heart of the case recorded the story for a police magazine, adopting the *nom de plume* 'Rambler', a nodding allusion perhaps to Dr Johnson. A few days after the bomb, Rambler was staying on local leave at a 'Japanese inn' in the nearby rubber town of Seremban, where 'he had his Suki Yaki amidst a series of gossips with other lodgers. He touched on the incident of the Kuala Lumpur bomb case saying that now bobbed-hair women were becoming a danger to society. One of the lodgers said that he had seen a Chinese bobbed-hair woman living at 3 Short Street, Singapore.'[30]

Singapore was an altogether larger, brasher and more cosmopolitan world, where it was much easier than Kuala Lumpur or Penang for a young Chinese woman to lose herself. The number of Chinese women entering the Straits Settlements had growing dramatically: 27,753 arrived from China in 1924, up over 5,000 on the previous year.[31] On returning to Singapore at the end of January 1925, Rambler made enquiries at the address. It was a Japanese lodging house in an area where there were a number of Japanese brothels. Rambler discovered that the bobbed-hair woman who had been seen there was not Wong Sang but another

Chinese girl named Leong Soo, who had left for Hong Kong a few weeks earlier. But it turned out that her room was occupied briefly by Wong Sang, who was identified by the lodging-house keeper from a police photograph. He told Rambler that Leong Soo had been brought to the house from a nearby Chinese school on Middle Road. The headmaster of the school was interrogated, and it was learned that Leong Soo was living with – the term used was 'kept by' – a man called Leung Man. The police knew him as an anarchist. He had been associated with the 1919 disturbances and banished from Malaya. He had returned in late 1923, working as a schoolteacher at Middle Road.[32]

Rambler went undercover. He took to wandering around Short Street wearing a Malay *baju* and *sarong*, grilling rickshaw pullers as to whether they had seen a bobbed-hair girl. One of them came forward. Rambler immediately gave him five Straits dollars and ordered him to carry him to where he had taken the girl. The rickshaw man pulled him to a photographic shop, which she had visited in the company of a Chinese youth. Rambler demanded that the shopkeeper hand him the negatives of the photographs they had taken together, but they were no longer there. The rickshaw puller then took him to a room in yet another Japanese lodging house which the girl later visited. 'Rambler took courage, and entering the room without any ceremony' stumbled on one Simon Yapp, who was interrogated and produced a photograph of Leong Soo. When the room was searched, letters from her from Hong Kong were also found. It turned out that Simon Yapp, too, was a lover of Leung Soo, and engaged to marry her.[33]

The Hong Kong police were then involved. There was a report in the Chinese newspapers in late March 1925 that a bobbed-hair woman had, on instructions from the Singapore police, been intercepted off a steamer that ran between Canton, Hong Kong and Shanghai. She had with her only a leather handbag, a box and some correspondence which the Chinese press described as of 'sweetness like unto honey'. It was Leong Soo. She was brought back to Singapore under escort and the Hong Kong authorities told the press nothing more about her.[34] When Leong Soo was interviewed in Singapore, it transpired that she had been sent away to Hong Kong as she was thought by the men to be unreliable. She was, Rambler concluded, 'a woman of weak intellect'.

Wong Sang was at the centre of a web of intimacy, entangled over long distances. Under further interrogation she admitted to the police that she had known the other woman, Leung Soo, in Hong Kong. In Singapore, Leung Soo had lived as the mistress of Leung Man. But it turned out that Wong Sang was by that time married to Leung Man and she told the police that she had travelled to Malaya to find him. She arrived in Singapore on 2 December 1924, on the SS *Katshang*, and stayed with a second associate, Lok Ngai Man, at the Chinese school.

The police closed in on Leung Man. He worked as an agent of the Nanyang Film Company, one of the popular travelling cinema shows that toured the small towns and villages of the region. He had a business partner, Wang Yu-ting, who also had a long police record: he had earlier been banished from the Netherlands East Indies. These two men were well used to avoiding the police and soon got wind of Rambler's enquiries, so an attempt by Rambler to waylay Leung Man on his business travels up the peninsula failed when his partner laid on a car to spirit him away.

Rambler then laid a trap for Leung Man in Singapore. On 5 February 1925 Rambler appeared at his office, in 'coolie dress', with a bogus letter for him, claiming that he had been sent by a Chinese businessman from nearby Johor to organize a film for the coolies on his rubber estate. Evidently fooled by the disguise, one of Leung Man's employees called his boss from a back room, 'and thus Rambler was able to lay hands on him'. Under arrest, Leung Man said nothing other than that he was an anarchist. He was banished to China for a second time.

Lok Ngai Man was arrested in an elaborate international sting. Rambler had word from Penang that he was connected to a certain shop in Singapore, and so a bogus money order, under a false name, sent from a fake address, was delivered to him care of the shop. The idea was that Lok Ngai Man would have to come to the shop to collect the order, and he would then have to visit the General Post Office in order to cash it. The GPO was alerted to the order, and Rambler waited to pounce. In the event the target was not in Singapore, and the letter was forwarded to him in China. He, in turn, sent back the money order to a friend and asked him to cash it for him. His luckless friend was arrested. A search of his lodgings yielded 'a group photograph of the anarchist party'. Lok Ngai Man bolted to Singora in southern Siam.[35]

A conspiracy was unmasked that stretched across the Netherlands East Indies, Malaya, Siam, Hong Kong and China. It drew on the cooperation of the police of several colonial powers. Over the next few weeks, months and years, arrests were made of a region-wide network. A first trail led to a group of local anarchists. The police knew about them through an agent of the Chinese Protectorate who was in touch with the Kuala Lumpur leaders, and who in February 1924 visited Penang, where they held a meeting. They were men from a variety of industrial towns of Malaya's west coast: a fitter from Kampar, a mechanic from Ipoh, the secretary of the car hire guild, a tailor from Seremban and three shop assistants from a goldsmith's in Penang. Another delegate came from Siam, but was arrested in Penang with a very detailed account of bomb-making in his possession and banished to Canton. The meeting was, in any case, not so secret: it was even reported in a Canton anarchist journal, with the Esperanto title *La Printempa Tondro*, 'Spring Thunder'. And it was not clear, even to detectives who were eager to unravel a large conspiracy, that this meeting had authorized the Kuala Lumpur attack. The thrust of the discussion in Penang had, on the contrary, been about extending propaganda and building an underground movement. This local group they were following seemed to be at odds with the new arrivals from China.

What was different about Wong Sang and her associates was their commitment to acts of individual violence. This was broadcast in imported pamphlets celebrating the life of the Japanese anarchist Osugi Sakae, who had been killed by a policeman the previous year. His life had been marked by a passionate libertarianism and experiments in 'free love', inspired in turn by the writings of anarchist femme fatale Emma Goldman, arrested and deported from the United States during the Red scare in 1919.[36] In their raids, the police intercepted alarming tracts. The main recipient was the Kuala Lumpur newspaper *Yik Khuan Po*. Most of them came from the Soviet news agency, ROSTA; there were reports from China and Moscow, but also manuals that explained communism in a Chinese context. One such, *Communism and China*, came from a Hong Kong press, and claimed that a communist state could be achieved in less than ten years, without the need for a period of capitalism. There were translations of anarchist classics such as Kropotkin's *Anarchist Morality*, and detailed descriptions of how to make a bomb. Some were printed in Kuala Lumpur at the press of the *Yik Khuan Po*, along with appeals to mark events from May Day to the commemoration of the founding of the Illuminati in 1776 by Adam

Weishaupt. They were manifestos for a new age. As one journal, *The Bright*, put it in May 1924:

> How can liberty be procured? Plainly speaking the saying 'If Liberty is wanted there must be bloodshed', is, I believe recognised by all who travel along the glorious path of liberty, for no reformation can be effected by means of empty talk. This is truth in all ages. Let us refer to history, either Chinese or Western. It is nothing but a record of so many bloodsheds.
>
> Without going into the remote periods, let us take some instances from modern times. There is the American War of Independence of 1776, there is the Third Republic of France; there is the overthrow of the Manchu [Qing] dynasty by China: then there is the establishment of the Soviet by Russia. Which of these is not the result of bloodshed?
>
> Not only social reform requires bloodshed, but the same thing is true of the birth of a child. Look at a woman's travail: she must shed her blood when her child is born. From this it may be clearly seen that bloodshed is inevitable in social reform.
>
> So we may loudly declare: 'If you want liberty, I invite you all to hasten to shed blood.'[37]

Eventually the trail led back to Canton in late 1924, when Wong, by compulsion, conviction or in despair, had become the catalyst to a conspiracy.

On 24 November 1924, the French information service in Canton had learned of the departure of a Chinese woman from the city, 'Wong San', on the P&O steamer *Sardinia*. It was said that she had in her possession gun-cotton and several pints of fulminate of mercury (some said several quarts), and that she intended to carry them to Bangkok or Singapore. The French believed that she was under orders to commit an act of violence, but that she had the initiative to choose the place and the victim. The French had passed this on to the British police in Hong Kong, where the ship was due to stop. In fact, a report had appeared in *The China Mail* in late November 1924 about a 'bobbed-hair woman' with a birthmark above her eye, sought by the Hong Kong Police, under the front-page headline: 'Have you seen her?'[38] The British had scrutinized passengers on the Canton steamer, but no trace of the girl was found, nor was her destination clear. The scare had ended with the departure of the *Sardinia* from Hong Kong.[39] It was much later, after the Kuala Lumpur bomb, in May 1925, that the Siamese government identified her as the bomber, by her short hair and the birthmark above her eye. From this the trail led to her being a member of an anarchist society, 'Chan She' of Canton, where she was known as the mistress of its leader, Mak Peng Chho.[40]

The bomb was reported across southern China. On 10 February 1925 an article appeared in a Canton newspaper, the *Yin Cheong Po*, attributed to a Kuala Lumpur correspondent, entitled 'The assassination of the Protector of Chinese in Kuala Lumpur'. It mistakenly recorded the deaths of both Richards and Wong Sang. But it also hinted at a motive for the attack:

> The duty of the Protector is to protect the Chinese, but in reality this officer restricts the talents of the overseas Chinese, and superintends their social organisations.
>
> If any devoted men come to Malaya to instruct and guide the people, he looks on them as extremists. He devises means to detect their movements, and finds fault with them in order to punish them according to the law. For instance in the last few years, numerous innocent schoolteachers and editors have been arrested and banished; and all sorts of restrictions have been brought into force.
>
> Even newspapers and correspondence, brought into or sent out from the State, must be censored by the members of the said Protectorate before they can be delivered to the consignees.
>
> Our Overseas Chinese are subject to the unreasonable oppression and have to bear it, and keep their mouths shut.[41]

The French security police in colonial Indochina, the Sûreté Générale, opened a file labelled '*La femme au coton poudre*': 'the gun-cotton woman'. In a rare, and rather strained, attempt at cooperation, the British Special Branch in Singapore passed the photographs captured by Rambler to the Sûreté Générale in Hanoi. The Hong Kong police let the main French agent in southern China, codename 'Noël', read their own file. The Sûreté had a long-term informer working in Canton: a Vietnamese, working undercover as a photographer, codenamed 'Pinot'. It was he who had first got wind of Wong Sang and her journey from loose talk among Vietnamese émigrés in Canton. It was never really clear to what extent Pinot was the Sûreté's man, or whether he was peddling them partial truths and misinformation. But nevertheless, in one of their clandestine meetings, on the Canton–Hong Kong overnight steamer, Pinot confronted Noël with troubling questions and scenarios. If Wong Sang had wanted revenge, why had she not taken it out on the man who had killed her lover in Canton? Where was she ultimately heading? He suggested that her real destination was French Indochina. Pinot's rationale was that it was merely by chance that Wong Sang was in Kuala Lumpur, and that she could easily have travelled on to Indochina.

Noël was far from convinced that Pinot was telling him the complete truth.[42] But all the same, given the stakes, he could not rule out the possibility that Vietnamese anarchists in Canton had heard of her mission and might have tried to persuade her to go to Indochina, and that she only went to Malaya as it was more familiar to her. He discovered that there were photographs of Wong Sang circulating among Vietnamese political exiles in Canton. Pinot easily obtained one for him from a well-known Vietnam exile by claiming that he wanted it as a 'souvenir' of a woman who had done an exemplary deed.[43] All this suggested the most volatile synergies across different anarchist groups, undiscriminating in their use of terror.

The French did not confide their own fears to the British. But, with Wong Sang's photograph in their possession, the Sûreté began to trace back the footsteps of the 'gun-cotton woman' to the much bigger conspiracy that had begun some months earlier, at the principal fault line between China and the west. The French believed that the patterns of bomb-making had much in common, and that the bobbed-hair woman in Kuala Lumpur had applied the method and the ideals of the Pham Hong Thai affair. In these months, from when Pham Hong Thai threw his bomb and Wong Sang detonated hers, and across Asia, a great assault on empire was under way. But it little resembled the revolution imagined by seasoned veterans in Moscow and elsewhere. It recalled questions that had first been posed in the debates of the 'Journey to the East' in 1905. How far could individual acts of defiance and violence usher in a new world, or did they merely hark back to the old? And even if their immediate targets were clear, who would ultimately pay the price? As Nguyen Ai Quoc began to identify and cultivate the Vietnamese revolutionaries in Canton, he met a man whose exile dated back thirty years. 'The sole goal of this man is to avenge his country and his family who were massacred by the French,' he wrote to Moscow. 'He doesn't know anything of politics and even less of mass organising. I have demonstrated the necessity of having something organised and the uselessness of the agitation without any base.'[44]

There was a steady trickle of new arrivals from Vietnam, many from the troubled province of Nghe An. Some enlisted at Whampoa, others studied at the Peasant Leadership Training Institute. By the middle of 1925, Ly Thuy had established himself as the dominant personality among them, and on the back of the strike-boycott set up, with Russian funds, a weekly paper called *Thanh Nien*, or 'Youth'. This was part of a broader 'League of Oppressed Peoples' formed out of the radical flot-sam and jetsam of Canton. In letters to Moscow, Ly Thuy referred to the circle around *Thanh Nien* as a 'Vietnamese Kuomintang'. *Thanh Nien* was organized into a training school, which grew to operate out of a three-storey building near the Communist Party headquarters; Ly Thuy later claimed that seventy-five students passed through it. There were guest lectures from the Russians and communist cadres such as Zhou Enlai from Whampoa and Peng Pai, and, as in Paris and Mos-cow, Ly Thuy embarked on a relentless round of political meetings and receptions. But Ly Thuy's policy was cautious: like Borodin's, it was geared towards building organizational strength through what became known as a 'Revolutionary Youth League', and turned away from the old obsession with military plots.[45] Known as teacher 'Vuong', he led the ceremonial visits to the grave of Pham Hong Thai. But, in a revolutionary primer, he berated the patriotic anarchism of the earlier movement: 'Because they do not comprehend developments elsewhere in the world, our people do not know how to compare, how to formulate a strategy. When it is not time to act, they do; when it is time to act, they don't.'[46] Graduates of these classes made their way back to Tonkin via the old revolutionary networks and pathways, and a chosen few set out for Moscow. Ly Thuy, M. N. Roy, Tan Malaka and other pathfinders of global revolution needed to convey hard-won experience to a new generation of young men and women who were leading the insurrection in the world abroad: the products of wild learning in all its creativity and passion, unpredictable and indiscriminate in their fury.

THE BATTLE OF NANJING ROAD

In these conditions, the acts of an individual or a few could produce a sudden alchemy. Local grievances over the conditions of life and work escalated rapidly into anger at China's national humiliation. The edges of empire in Shanghai were frayed as skirmishes between the troops of rival warlord cliques reached the outskirts of the city and refugees spilled into the streets in their tens of thousands. Curbed by strict policing, the labour scene had been relatively quiet since 'the first strike high tide' of the seamen's dispute in 1922. Nevertheless, led by veterans of the ill-fated Hankou–Beijing railway workers' strike, such as Zhang Guotao and Deng Zhongxia, underground newspapers began to circulate among the Shanghai workers speaking to them directly in *baihua*, or colloquial language. Even as the communists' united front with the nationalists took solid form in Canton, the Shanghai leaders placed their faith in a social revolution led by the urban workers. In early 1925, the currents of historical necessity seemed to be running in their direction.[47] On 2 February, fifty male workers were sacked at a Japanese textile mill in the west of the city, Naigai Wata Kaisha's Shanghai Mill No. 8. They had complained when a Japanese supervisor kicked and slapped two female Chinese workers, one of whom was a child. Women workers were brought in from the countryside to replace them, company-disciplined, and supposedly more pliant. Six men were arrested when they returned to collect money owed to them. There were walkouts at all the company's mills and by 18 February twenty-two Japanese factories and 40,000 or so workers were involved. Many of the mills were in the Chinese city, but the protest engulfed densely industrialized areas such as Xiaoshadu in the International Settlement, on a scale never before seen. There was intimidation and violence on both sides: when shots were fired to disperse a crowd at the Toyota mill, a car was stopped and its Japanese passengers were beaten; one was the factory manager, who later died. He too had been accused of kicking a female factory hand in the stomach.[48]

The crowd at the Toyota mill was led by a female teacher, and, for the first time, students were everywhere to be seen among the striking workers. The number of institutions of higher education in China doubled from twenty-four in 1923 to fifty in 1925; student enrolment rose from 500 in 1910 to over 25,000 in 1925, and most of these private schools and colleges were concentrated in Beijing and Shanghai. Shanghai University was founded in 1922, out of the Southeast Normal College. It was not a nationalist creation in the sense that Whampoa was, but it became overnight a centre of militant politics. Situated originally in makeshift accommodation in the factory district of Zhabei, and then from February 1924 in the International Settlement, it was a 'back-alley college' in the sense of its hastily improvised curricula and precarious funding from student fees. But it also was a manifestation of the worldly urban milieu within which it was situated. It recruited teaching staff – typically on short tenures – on the recommendation of key personalities such as Li Dazhao, from the wave of work-study students returning from France – including Cai Hesen, the Hunanese intellectual leader of the Montargis group – and from Moscow, such as the visionary head of the sociology department, Qu Qiubai, and Borodin's adviser and translator, Zhang Tailei.[49] For the first time, the energies of the returnees from the world abroad were focused in one place and to one end.

Cai Hesen's fellow student Zheng Chaolin returned from France in late 1924 and shared an alley house on Moulmein Road with him. Cai Hesen and his wife Xiang Jingyu – the formidable head of the Communist Party's women's bureau – lived upstairs, with the recently widowed Qu Qiubai. Zhang Tailei's mother, wife and child occupied a ground-floor room, and Li Lisan and his pregnant wife stayed in a guestroom. Li was also a work-study student who had been expelled from France after the protest in Lyon in 1921. Now twenty-five years old, Li was already seasoned in labour activism from the disputes at the Anyuan mines in his home province of Hunan and the Beijing–Hankou railway. 'Li Lisan was a false name,' Zheng Chaolin explained, 'created just a few hours before it was made public; if the Xiaoshadu workers had seen this Li Lisan, they would have recognised him as Li Cheng, another false name; if the Anyuan miners had seen him, they would have recognised him as Li Longzhi, which was his real name.' There were two maidservants, one of whom, 'Auntie Long', had accompanied Mao Zedong from Hunan, and stayed on when he returned to his home province. The house was a sweatshop for writing, proofreading and translation, and, with the clandestine visits of Chen Duxiu and others, the venue for meetings of the party central committee. Zheng Chaolin would retire discreetly to a neighbouring bedroom to overhear them discuss everything from 'a National Government to comrades' love entanglements', some of which, like that of Cai Hesen and Xiang Jingyu, were formed over long distances, since their sea voyage to Paris; others were new-forged in the forced intimacy of the alleyways of Shanghai. Soon the marriage of Cai Hesen and Xiang Jingyu, and the party itself, would be torn apart by Xiang's affair with a returned student from Moscow, Peng Shuzhi.[50]

For the mostly elite women who chose to follow its path, the Communist Party was a means of escape from stifling provincial family situations; an invitation to abandon arranged marriages and to live according to free choice. For many of them, their departure from their families was an act from which there was no return. In the flood of literary translations there was a particular appetite for Ibsen, which popularized the dilemma of Nora in A Doll's House, and the questions, as posed by Lu Xun in a famous lecture to a women's college in Beijing in 1923: 'What happens after Nora walks out?'; 'What did Nora take with her apart from her awakened mind?'[51] In one sense, these women found that, having left home, their personal status within the party remained largely dependent on that of the men they cohabited with. In another, their lives and dress – not least their bobbed hair – signalled a level of bohemianism that was rather exclusive to Shanghai, and which, even within its transgressive air, set them apart from those they sought to lead. Even here the activist Yang Zhihua caused a scandal in 1924 when she announced her divorce in a newspaper, prior to marrying Qu Qiubai. Soon the Moulmein Road ménage would move to Seymour Road, to be closer to the university, and the party central committee began to hold its meetings in the industrial district of Zhabei.[52]

Whereas other translators of Marxism in the city, such as the party founding member, Li Da, drew principally from Japanese texts, Qu Qiubai's ideas seemed closer to the source. His years in Moscow, his proficiency in Russian and rare access to key texts gave him, as he modestly acknowledged, a rather serendipitous standing as a 'Marxist theorist'. A prodigious translator himself, he championed the use of colloquial, unadorned language – as opposed to its literary, archaic forms – so as not to smooth out the 'foreignness' of ideas. Through the act of translation, he sought to create new language to reflect the social realities of the present age. In his lectures at Shanghai

University – published as *Outline of Social Philosophy* (1924) – Qu attempted to chart a vision of the revolution as an intellectual project.[53] In his classes there were many students whose radical politics had led them to leave their home provinces; they tended to come from further afield than students at other colleges in the city, and also from abroad, from Southeast Asia and Korea. Despite offering practical training for jobs in the modern city, Shanghai University was increasingly defined by its political activism. Staff and students shared a commitment to reach into alleyway society through public lectures by leading intellectuals, an astonishing volume of published lectures and primers, and above all through workers' education.[54] By no means were all of those involved members of the Communist Party, but a number of the key movers were, or were at least tied to youth groups close to it, such as the Socialist Youth League, which had 180 members in the city in 1924.

In late 1924 and early 1925 there were several programmes by which students set up night schools to teach workers to read and write in Chinese and in English, as well as workers' recreation clubs, with chess, table tennis, music or opera, often in a satirical vein. They were forums for debate that mirrored and rivalled established Christian bodies such as the YMCA and YWCA, against which there was a deepening cultural backlash. Xiang Jingyu had stayed somewhat aloof from the women's rights movement of the previous few years, believing that it was impossible to achieve emancipation within a corrupt political system. Now she used her new newspaper supplement, *Funü zhoubao*, 'Women's Weekly', to urge feminist activists within bodies like the YWCA to work with women labourers: 'Were Jesus living today, he would surely be leading the oppressed Chinese people to wage intense struggles against the foreign powers and warlords.' Her students sought out the women in Japanese silk mills, whose hothouse conditions – such as the boiling vats for the softening process – seemed to encapsulate a capitalist hell on earth. When the walkouts began, party intellectuals seized the opportunity to make their presence felt in the workplace by leading marches and collecting strike pay. Yang Zhihua – herself the daughter of a silk merchant of Zhejiang – would dress as a mill worker and meet secretly with the factory women by posing as pilgrims at the Jade Buddha temple.[55]

The February 1925 strikes in Shanghai were not, as the press alleged, the result of 'orders from Moscow'. In private, the Shanghai Municipal

Police acknowledged that their roots lay in real economic grievances and a 'slow reading' of left-wing texts. In a police raid at Shanghai University in December 1924, 189 books on 'extreme socialism' were seized, bringing the police tally since May 1918 to 1,202. The communists had 'rushed in' after the mill dispute was well under way, the police noted, at a point when it was 'virtually broken'.[56] Li Lisan led a small group of party specialists to strengthen workers' resolve, a Shanghai Cotton Mills Union was formed, and a wider spectrum of clubs and societies were mobilized in a Strikes Support Committee. Where party workers had previously found it hard to break through labourers' loyalties to native place associations and the power of the neighbourhood gangs, in the spring of 1925 they were presented with a wave of patriotism which they turned into an initiation in mass action. The slogans used were simple but effective: 'Oppose Japanese beating people'; 'Isn't this a terrible insult to the citizens of the Republic of China?'; 'Furthermore, they often call us "worthless" and "slaves without a country".'[57] The blows of Japanese factory managers were seen as being at one with humiliations at the hands of the western imperialists and an inevitable consequence of unequal treaties and foreign privilege.

Japanese employers retaliated by sacking strikers and placing a ban on trade unions. In the early evening of 15 May at Mill No. 7, the night shift was locked out by management and charged the gates. The Sikh watchmen and Japanese foremen panicked: shots were fired and seven people were hit. One of them, a twenty-year-old worker called Gu Zhenghong, died a few days later. The news of his 'martyrdom' from a Japanese bullet on Chinese soil was spread, in the face of press censorship, by street speeches. On 24 May, some 5,000–10,000 people gathered for a memorial event in the shadow of a mill in Zhabei. It was a remarkable show of strength by the alleyway communities of the city. Student leaders came from the International Settlement with their night-school pupils, and a number were apprehended by the Shanghai Municipal Police. When Zheng Chaolin and a friend arrived, they provoked considerable suspicion by wearing western suits. They saw that, on the platform, Li Lisan wore the blue shirt and trousers of the workers.[58] Popular anger fused with opposition to four new ordinances of the Municipal Council, including an unpopular attempt to regulate publications and a reforming measure to tackle child labour. But the Council's very right to legislate over Chinese was now challenged.[59]

The arrested students were to be tried in the Mixed Court, which was widely scorned for its bias against Chinese, and this led the students to carry their protest for the first time into the heart of the International Settlement.

The next Saturday morning, 30 May, Nanjing Road was bustling with shoppers, gawkers and pleasure seekers. The commercial thoroughfare was a symbol of the city's burgeoning consumer society and of an electric modernity on a scale unmatched anywhere else in Asia. Nanjing Road was lined with large department stores; some, like Sincere or Wing On, served the Chinese, while others were aimed more exclusively at westerners, such as Whitelaw's and Lane, Crawford & Co., with its 200-foot glass frontage and slogan 'For the Classes rather than the Masses'.[60] Workers and students thronged in the area, then launched into speeches and street dramas re-enacting the events of recent days. It was a 'war of voice' designed to flood the international city, planned with military precision. The students arrived in small bicycle brigades, and, at different access points to the city centre, split up to speak and hand out leaflets to shoppers. Then, when the police appeared, they scattered like birds. The officer on duty in the area, a Welshman, Edward Everson, witnessed two of these waves. When, around 2 p.m., he made some arrests, the news travelled by bicycle, bells ringing, and the student brigades converged on Louza police station, just off Nanjing Road. By 3.30 p.m. the crowd outside had grown from a few hundred to perhaps 2,000: according to witnesses, an equal number of students and workers. Louza police station was a well-known flashpoint; it had been set alight in riots twenty years earlier. Its police were an equal measure of Chinese and Sikhs. Students followed Everson into the station, demanding that their friends be released, or that they too should be arrested. There were scuffles and the demonstrators were turned out into the street, some of them bloodied. The mood of the crowd darkened. It flowed to the department store opposite, but the police were soon pushed back to their station. Fearing his command would be overrun, Everson shouted, in crude Chinese, a threat to open fire. No one seemed to hear him. Then the police let loose two volleys, killing four people in the crowd outright and injuring nine others, five of whom later died. By the end of the day, twelve people had been killed and many more injured.[61]

'Yes, certainly I fired to kill,' Everson told a court a few days later.

'In the event of danger to life and property, the order is to shoot to kill.'[62] This defiant, deadly reflex was at one with instances of white panic in India and elsewhere. Western residents rallied behind the police and mobilized as volunteer soldiers to protect their property. There was a painful attempt to justify and dismiss the incident in the House of Commons in London by the secretary for overseas trade, Arthur Samuel, when questioned by the Labour MP George Lansbury:

> Mr Samuel: I do not agree it is true that those who were shot were shot in the back. While it is quite true to say they were unarmed, it is also a fact that it was a very large and murderous crowd—
>
> Mr Lansbury: How do you know? You were not there.
>
> Mr Samuel:—that the crowd tried to rush the police station, which was full of arms, and that if they had obtained those arms, there is no doubt greater bloodshed would have taken place.[63]

But this was no backwoods riot, no dark defile; it occurred in full view of the glass palaces of Nanjing Road. In Shanghai there was no possibility of locking down an entire city or province as there had been after Amritsar in April 1919. It was no longer possible to kill protesters in private. The event was soon broadcast globally and provoked a 'Hands off China' campaign by the British left.[64] Chinese testimonies were corroborated by the witness of missionaries and formidable women labour activists such as Eleanor Hinder and Adelaide Anderson, who reported first-hand on the dire factory conditions in Zhabei.[65] The tragedy threw a spotlight on the Gilbertian governance of the 'hypo-colony'. The police commissioner, Kenneth McEuan, was nowhere to be found on the day. Although trouble was in the air, he had embarked on a stately progress to the horse races, via the Shanghai Club on the bund and the Lawn Bowls club, and then on to his golf club where, sometime in the late afternoon, news reached him of gunshots.[66]

Zhang Guotao arrived by steamer from Canton at around 6 p.m. that evening to find 'the entire city of Shanghai ⋯ seething with anger'. He had been in Beijing on May Fourth, but the depth of popular feeling he experienced over the coming days and weeks, he believed, far exceeded that of 1919. He went to his house in Zhabei to find the communist leaders in the city gathering there, gripped, much as anyone else, by patriotic fury.[67] The next day, more people came on to the streets; police used fire hoses to disperse them and there were more deaths. A 'shop-strike' boycott was announced for 1 June, and the city merchants – who had an equal contempt for the Municipal Council and the Mixed Court – threw their support behind it. In truth, they had little choice but to do so. The waterfront was the first area to shut down; the department stores held out but were compelled to close by the moral force of popular indignation. The protest differed from May Fourth and the seamen's strike of 1922 in its scale – strikes occurred in over 200 workplaces involving some 200,000 labourers, many staying out in conditions of great hardship for three months – but also in the lead taken by political parties. The communists now set up a General Labour Union, representing all trades, at the helm of which was Li Lisan, who cut an increasingly prominent figure in the city. He attempted to deepen the wedge between the gangs and the workers and managed in Zhabei to negotiate underworld protection for strike leaders. However, over time, the big gangs fought back to shore up their influence.[68] Li was dragged before a local strongman and forced to call him 'chief'. But, for the moment, there was an epiphany of unity. The strike-boycott was supported by an equal number of small traders, some 150,000–200,000 of whom closed shop. Local capitalists had much to gain: no one now wanted to smoke British American Tobacco's 'Great Britain' cigarettes, the daily sales of which dropped to a tenth of their earlier level as people moved to local brands. The newspapers kept going but stopped publishing their 'arse-end': the supplements of gossip and scandal. Zheng Chaolin worked on a new political publication called *Hot Blood Daily*, which ran for twenty days until the police closed down the print shop. All the while, 'foreign troops patrolled the silent streets, as if before a great enemy'.[69]

JUNE DAYS

The average age of the killed and wounded was only twenty-two to twenty-three years. Like May Fourth, 'May Thirtieth' defined a generation. In its aftershock of literary and artistic memorialization, the figure of the woman protester stood out in her modern dress and short hair: a 'Joan of Arc' for China.[70] The funerals of the 'martyrs', especially the students, exceeded any previous event in their scale and emotional intensity. No one had died on May Fourth. Now, at every turn, there were symbols of red: in street theatre and in print; in the parades of the shirts of the victims, with the bloodstained bullet holes clearly in their back; and in the heavy spring showers that could not seem to wash the blood off the streets. The violence appalled many May Fourth intellectuals, some of whom retreated into private despair.[71] Hu Yuzhi was a translator and publisher at the Commercial Press; he was an ardent Esperantist who wrote prolifically on the 'Indian revolution' and its inspiration, Gandhi. He genuflected to the changed mood:

> Violence is the most striking characteristic of our time. In revolutionary periods violence is most prevalent. There are some who believe that revolution can be accomplished without violence. However, quiet revolutions, revolutions of the spirit are lies. Today, the task of revolution is to demolish obstacles and for this, violence is our only means.[72]

It seemed that what Marx, writing in 1848, termed 'the revolutionary point of departure' had arrived.

The nerves of the Europeans of Canton had yet to recover from Pham Hong Thai's bomb attack and the walkout at Shamian the previous summer. On 21 June 1925, their coolies and servants abandoned their posts once again. The American journalist Hallett Abend stepped off the Hong Kong steamer to find the two bridges to the Chinese city guarded by concrete bunkers and pill boxes and the entire perimeter of the island enclosed by sandbags and barbed wire. Soldiers clutched machine guns and hand grenades and watched for snipers on the bund. Most of the women had left. Such was the totality of the boycott that there was 'not a newspaper, not an orange, not a cigarette, not a letter or even a clean sheet of paper'. The Hotel Victoria slumped into sudden decline, the rooms 'mildewed and damp'. As he tried to cross the bridge into the Chinese city, Abend was rebuked by a Chinese contact for wearing shorts: they were the stigmata of the despised Englishmen.[73] A procession was announced for 23 June. Permission for it to enter the Shamian concessions was refused, and the British consul-general complained to the Chinese authorities that students were drawing lots as to who would have first call on martyrdom. The marchers were a mixed body of students, workers and a contingent from Whampoa, led by

Zhou Enlai. At around 2.30 p.m., as the procession passed along the Shaji, the embankment on the north side of the creek across from the British Concession, shots were fired. The crowd began to run, and, in the confusion, it was hard to say from where first fire had come. The British commander, a naval officer, claimed that soldiers in the procession had turned and fired as they approached parallel to the Hotel Victoria. British troops returned fire with Lewis guns; the consul-general ordered a ceasefire, but there were further exchanges over the next hour or so. One French civilian was killed. Estimates of the dead on the Chinese side were at least fifty-two, with over 100 cadets, students and children wounded, many trampled in the stampede of the crowd. The next day, a British resident and local Volunteer, H. R. Burge, shot himself in his room in the Canton Club. The press reported that it was 'fairly unlikely' that this was linked to killings on the Shaji, but there were also witnesses who swore they saw a civilian firing first from the first floor of the Hotel Victoria. In the following days, the Europeans lodged counter-claims that it was Russians who had begun the shooting. To justify the fatalities, they declared that the incident was a planned aggression. The creek was lined with sampans, the British pointed out, so it would have been the work of a moment for the Chinese troops to storm the island.[74]

The Whampoa cadets now argued for a full-scale assault, and the Russians reasoned that even if the attempt failed and Canton itself was lost, this might be enough to ignite the rest of China. The republican government braced itself for a retaliatory attack: it reinforced the southern forts, such as Whampoa, and positions along the railway line towards Hong Kong. The bridges were mined and the river approaches to the city packed with ships and rafts in the hope of seizing any attacking vessel. Over the next few days the streets were full of angry crowds, and no westerner dared step out into them. The British reinforced the island with two platoons of Indian troops. But there were reports of Indian troops elsewhere in China refusing to fire on Chinese, and of Sikh policemen in Hong Kong resigning in shame and offering their services to the Chinese government in Canton. By the time they reached the Punjab in August, these reports had become a rumour that 300 troops had been shot for failing to fire on a crowd in Hong Kong. The ghost of Ghadar was abroad.[75] The image of British troops and civilians taking potshots with impunity from Shamian to the mainland seemed to encapsulate all that was abominable about China's semi-colonial status. The image of Whampoa cadets in uniform protecting the crowd evinced all that was noble about the new, martial republic.

Many of those who marched on the Shaji had come from Hong Kong. When a boycott of all British goods began in the colony, perhaps 80 per cent of the shops closed and there was a run on the banks. 'The harbour was full of lifeless steamers,' reported one Russian adviser arriving in Hong Kong shortly after the Shaji killings; the city itself 'a military camp'.[76] Few Chinese ships were permitted to sail and only then to transport some 250,000 strikers, that is 45 per cent of the entire Chinese population of Hong Kong, to Canton. Among them were many students; in the leading government school, Queen's College, numbers fell by half. Temples, gambling houses and brothels were converted into dormitories and dining houses to receive them. Some 2,000 strike pickets underwent instruction at Whampoa; they intercepted smugglers in the delta and patrolled the waterfront in semi-military khaki, sporting white panama hats and red bandannas. A 'labour college' was established to train a large strike bureaucracy: effectively a 'Government No. 2' that symbolized the Communist Party's new ascendency in the city. As much as 5 million silver dollars was raised in strike funds, over half of which came from the Canton government itself. The Beida graduate and labour organizer Deng Zhongxia arrived in Hong Kong on 6 June and set up a small communist nucleus within the strike committee. Their impact, working through the more conservative Hong Kong labour leaders, was wholly disproportionate to their numbers – they were no more than a dozen in all – and neither was it visible to the workers within Hong Kong.[77] The cumulative effect of the action was immense: the colony's total trade halved, the stock market lost 40 per cent of its value, and public reporting of financial figures was suspended for the period. The British responded in kind, by banning the export to Canton of foodstuffs, fuel and gold, all of which, with British gunboats in the delta, deepened the air of imperialist menace.[78]

As news broke of the shooting on the Shaji, a group of young students arrived in Beijing from Russia. Among them was twenty-year-old Vera Vladimirovna Vishnyakova, a fresh graduate of the Oriental Institute in Vladivostok. The journey had been tense: their ship had been aggressively searched at Moji by the Japanese authorities, and Vera

Vladimirovna's close-cropped hair and worker's cap had marked her as a Bolshevik. Reaching the treaty port of Zhifu, they had run into the boycott. All the divided cities were under siege. In the Legation Quarter of Beijing western diplomats hid behind their high walls, the British guarded by Indian soldiers, the French by Indochinese. When the Beijing students marched in protest, all the embassy servants, amahs and chauffeurs walked out. The rickshaw men carried signs: 'No English or Japanese'. Vera Vladimirovna found that the Russians, billeted in the Chinese-run Hotel Central, were in turn 'boycotted in bourgeois society' by the staff of the other legations.[79] It was much the same everywhere: incidents following May Thirtieth were reported in thirty-eight towns and cities. In Hankou, a Japanese was left for dead in a storm drain, and armed expatriate volunteers fired on crowds surging into the British Concession, killing four protesters at the scene and four more who died later. In Nanjing, Royal Marines from HMS *Durban* were alleged to have fired on strikers at a British-run export company, the Ho Chi Egg Factory, causing more deaths. This was rejected by the British, who blamed the gunfire on the Chinese police. At this point their denial counted for little. Far inland, at Chongqing, a small detail of sailors from a gunboat used bayonets on a crowd. A corpse was found near the scene and paraded through the city, although it was unclear whether it was a product of the incident or not. Where there was no bloodshed, students would smear themselves in red paint. In Tianjin they formed a 'Kneel and Wail Corps' for displays of public grief, in the manner of professional funeral mourners. To the British, it seemed as if they were being taken hostage by schoolchildren. Seen from another angle, as Deng Zhongxia wryly observed, had only workers been killed, who would have given a damn?[80]

The strike-boycott provoked a western show of strength on a scale that had not been seen in China since the Boxer Rebellion. The Boxers were on everyone's minds. The issue of a 'Boxer indemnity' had stoked Chinese patriotic feeling in the months before the Nanjing Road and Shaji tragedies. In Shanghai, British, American, Italian and Japanese troops landed, and the Americans came under gunfire near the 'New World' on the evening of 2 June: some 3,500 rounds were exchanged and, again, there was a dispute about the numbers killed in the crossfire. Nanjing Road was cordoned off and Shanghai University occupied by troops.[81] Foreigners were in a state of panic. American missionaries, scattered across China, often outside the western concessions, were an exposed target. But pan-imperial unity was hard to sustain. Some of the missionaries – such as the YMCA – were sympathetic to the strikers. Declaring that 'we are Chinese', they sought to distance themselves from extraterritorial rights and privileges that had been acquired by force.[82]

In Shanghai, the Japanese moved swiftly and pragmatically to pay compensation to the families of dead strikers. In the months that followed, the strike-boycott became an open-ended campaign directed with particular venom towards the British empire.[83] The governor of Hong Kong, Reginald Stubbs, responded with an increasingly hard line. He refused to accept that the boycott was in any sense a protest against working conditions within the colony: it was an external attack, engineered by the Bolsheviks in Canton. However, his claims that the workers acted only as a result of 'intimidation' belied the depth of feeling, and the communists' small numbers, at least in the early days.

Peasants in the delta soon felt the full fury of the pickets: in July two women were killed carrying goods into Hong Kong. Stubbs saw Canton as a nest of pirates of old. He nursed fantasies of British gunboats bringing the city to submission and asked Whitehall to despatch a cruiser. He also argued that the British should throw their weight behind the northern warlords and offered HK$100 million to finance it. Whitehall would go only so far, but an aircraft carrier, HMS *Hermes*, arrived; a state of emergency was declared, and the local expatriate volunteer soldiers were called out. There was a crackdown on the Hong Kong press, which previously had enjoyed some latitude, and, in an unprecedented attempt to cultivate local public opinion, encouraged by 'loyal Chinese', a 'Counter-propaganda Bureau' was set up. A former pirate and officer of Chen Jiongming was hired to recruit a secret force of over 150 'special police' to intimidate labour organizers.[84]

The waterfront war soon spread to Southeast Asia. In Canton, in the wake of his role in the first Pan-Pacific Labour Congress of the previous year, Tan Malaka continued to build networks in seamen's unions through an English-language publication, *The Dawn*. In the Indies itself the Communist Party secretly collected funds to support the Shanghai strike, as a means of expanding its influence among the local Chinese.[85] The Shanghai newspapers reported that student emissaries had been sent to Singapore and Penang. As one student from

Guangxi province extolled to a friend in Malaya: 'Even the pupils of the elementary schools go out and lecture. Everyone knows the injustice of the massacre of workmen and students by the English and Japanese. We all hate the English and Japanese.' Printed matter – including graphic photographs of the victims of May Thirtieth – flooded in, hidden in private shipments and the baggage of travellers, often through the Bangkok mails from the north. There were violent clashes when the famous English Harmston's Circus was picketed in the Netherlands Indies and as it toured the industrial towns of Perak in Malaya.[86]

Following Wong Sang's attack on the Chinese Protectorate in Kuala Lumpur in January 1925, the British continued to trace anarchist pathways across Southeast Asia and to contemplate drastic measures against them. When, in June 1925, the Kuomintang, under the ascendant leadership of Wang Jingwei, declared itself the sole authority within the republic and its forces a 'National Revolutionary Army', the British Cabinet responded the following month by taking the decision to ban the Kuomintang in Singapore and Malaya. The police launched raids on night schools and reading rooms across Singapore. Canton was now an outlaw regime.[87] But it was also divided.

The Soviet mission was engulfed in an atmosphere of deepening tension and paranoia. After a series of military victories in June 1925, the threat from Chen Jiongming began to lift, although it was not until a second 'eastern expedition' and the fall of the port of Shantou in December that the Kuomintang could claim fully to control Guangdong province. Under its principal architect, and a key sympathizer with the Communist Party, Liao Zhongkai, the regime's financial position stabilized. Military needs drove fiscal reform, and, in turn, military force was needed to enforce new taxes.[88] This was a delicate balancing act: memories of the confrontation with the merchants the previous year were still bitter. Then, on 20 August, Liao Zhongkai was shot three times in broad daylight on the steps of the Kuomintang central committee headquarters. His wounds proved fatal. The orations at Liao's funeral blamed his murder on the long arm of British imperialism. But Hu Hanmin, who smarted from being outflanked by Wang Jingwei and Borodin in the matter of Sun Yat-sen's political inheritance, was implicated through a relative and went into exile to Moscow. The right wing of the Kuomintang remained unreconciled to the united front with the communists. In November 1925, they convened around

Sun Yat-sen's temporary resting place, the temple in the Western Hills of Beijing, to pledge themselves to his memory. A number of them established a 'Sunist Study Society' that looked to anchor Sun's thought in the Confucian tradition and to further distance it from western socialism. Their reaction to the death of Liao Zhongkai was to assert that China 'did not need Communism' and they demanded Borodin's recall.[89] In Canton, Borodin rode in a car with Chinese soldiers with Mauser machine guns perched on its running boards. Right-wing sympathizers met at a 'Culture Society' – known locally as the 'Madmen's Club' – to drink, gamble and grumble.[90] Meanwhile, Chiang Kai-shek – himself seen as a rough interloper by Kuomintang elders – continued to cement his independent power base within the military command. Chiang too was increasingly resentful of Wang Jingwei's ascendancy and of Russian moves to postpone what he saw as the fulfilment of the revolution and his debt of honour to Sun Yat-sen: the northern expedition to reunify China.

The confrontation with the westerners shifted the balance of power within China. The Soviet Union was emboldened to extend its influence within the fractious warlord politics of the north. Vera Vladimirovna's first posting after her arrival in Beijing was to a mission at Kalgan, a spur of the Great Wall of China. It was a base of Feng Yuxiang, the 'Christian General' as he was known to the western press, who had brought Sun Yat-sen to Beijing earlier in the year. He was of peasant background but had risen swiftly through the military ranks in the last years of the Qing empire. He was baptized as a Christian around 1914, and between 1918 and 1920, while stationed in northern Henan province, built a close relationship with the Canadian Protestant revivalist Jonathan Goforth. Troops were baptized by Goforth en masse, as many as 500 on one visit – the story was that it was done by a fire hose – and there were said to be 5,000 converts in the ranks by 1920. Feng's regime of Bible study and hymn-singing also led missionaries to style him the 'Cromwell of China'. Others saw this as an opportunistic ploy to attract western support. But, for Feng, Christianity offered a path to national salvation through its physical and mental training and ethos of self-sacrifice. His troops were the most highly trained in China, besides the Whampoa recruits: a *Guominjun*, a new model 'National People's Army'.[91] The events of May Thirtieth drove him to adopt a more militant anti-imperial stance, and of all the warlords he was cultivated most assiduously by the Russians. They invested substantially in their mission at Kalgan; its head, V. M. Primakov, had participated in the storming of the Winter Palace, and some forty-two personnel were sent there by November 1925, some of them recruited from the refugees in Shanghai. Feng was sold light tanks and almost 3.5 million roubles worth of artillery.[92]

When Vera Vladimirovna first encountered Feng he was already a well-known face from the newspapers. She was struck by the simplicity of his dress – he wore the tunic of an ordinary soldier – and his palpable charisma. But he soon began to suffer military reverses against a coalition of the dominant warlords, Wu Peifu and Zhang Zuolin. Soviet material aid was increased. Because of the Russian association, Feng was now known as the 'Red General', and the war in the north was portrayed as an anti-Bolshevik crusade. It was clear, Vera Vladimirovna observed, that the reason for failure 'was not in the military but in the political field'. The Kalgan mission was unable to build the personal ties that Borodin had acquired in the south. In January 1926, Feng decide to 'retire' to study and experience work as a common labourer. This was a traditional method of temporary withdrawal from public life. But Feng's retreat led to Moscow.[93] Feng was met in Soviet Russia with military honours, feted by the likes of Trotsky, and visited schools and factories to speed his education. The Soviet mission believed that the fate of the revolution in the south was tied to that of Feng in the north.[94]

In February 1926, Vera Vladimirovna was sent to Canton to reinforce Borodin's mission. She settled into life in Tungshan, the small enclave of modern villas in a malarial zone close to the river, just south of the Canton–Hong Kong railway line. Borodin's staff in Canton had swollen to over fifty, supplied by Russian vessels shuttling directly to and from Vladivostok. Most were young – the eldest was forty – and some of the women teachers and translators and military men began family life there. Vera Vladimirovna met her future husband, a military man, V. M. Akimov. She worked in the intelligence department, translating newspaper reports. In parallel to other expatriate communities life centred around a club, with a dining room, billiard room and a small library. Though she eagerly explored the temples and artisan quarters of the old city, she did not once set foot on Shamian Island, and seldom saw any of its inhabitants, save when British residents would drive to the club to peer inside to gawk at the infamous 'savage' Russians. Notwithstanding her attendance at the endless public commemorations and rallies, Vera Vladimirovna 'rarely came into contact with the people'. Tensions were such that she and the others were under orders 'to avoid any kind of idle talk and accusations to the effect that we were spreading Red propaganda'.[95]

It was around this time that Vera Vladimirovna first encountered another mysterious lodger in the Borodin House, the rather shabby and unhealthy 'Li Annam'. 'We knew nothing about him except that for his capture the French imperialists had offered a great sum of money.'[96] Ly Thuy's quiet, authoritative and galvanizing presence became known across the village abroad. As was the way with many long-term exiles from Vietnam in southern China, he married a young Cantonese woman, known among the Vietnamese as Tang Tuyet Minh, who moved into the Borodin House with him and worked as a midwife.[97]

In his own exile in Hangzhou, Phan Boi Chau got to hear of Ly Thuy, and then divined his true identity, and an association that went back to Chau's friendship with Ly Thuy's mandarin father. They exchanged letters. In early 1925 Phan Boi Chau wrote:

> Aside from you, who else is there to entrust this responsibility of replacing me to. I left the country when I was almost forty and I can't escape the experience of my studies – thus my ideas now are the same as they were formerly. You have studied widely and been to many more places than Uncle – ten times, a hundred times more. Your ideas and your plan surpass mine – will you share one or two tasks with me?[98]

But they were not to meet. On 2 July 1925, Phan Boi Chau arrived at the Northern station in the International Concession in Shanghai, travelling from Hangzhou. He planned to catch a sailing to Canton, there to commemorate the first anniversary of the martyrdom of Pham Hong Thai. He later put what transpired into verse:

> When at Shanghai's North Station I arrived
> I knew not what my enemies contrived.
>
> A car drew up; four men stood in the way
> With ill intent; I was their destined prey.

One push – and I am helpless in the car!
It starts! The French Concession is not far.

My body's caged with an iron fence
Like pigs and chickens – there's no difference!

Moving swiftly across jurisdictions, the car drew up on the waterfront, and Chau was taken aboard a French warship. His secretary, it seems, was reporting his movements to the police.[99] But there was a ghost narrative of rumour that Ly Thuy himself was the informer. In truth, he had little to gain from this, and Phan Boi Chau never denounced him, which was the usual way of things.[100] In Hanoi, in November 1925 Chau was tried for his role in the 1913 bomb attacks that had killed Frenchmen at the 'evening prayer' of the *apéro* hour. On his transfer from Hanoi to Hue, his train stopped at the town of Vinh in his home province of Nghe An. His wife met him briefly on the station platform; they were not to meet again.[101]

There was another homecoming. In early 1925, Phan Chu Trinh returned to Vietnam after fourteen years in Paris. He settled in Saigon, campaigned for the release of Phan Boi Chau, and embarked on writing a series of public lectures on republican themes. But, by the end of the year, his deteriorating health – the tuberculosis that had followed him through his exile – prevented him travelling to Hanoi to address the university and to meet Phan Boi Chau in Hue. The news of his death in Saigon on the morning of 24 March 1926 stirred powerful demonstrations of public mourning such as no commoner had ever before commanded. The French tried by every means to suppress them. For the Sûreté, Phan Chu Trinh's death was an opportunity to retrace in their mind's eye the voyages of such a man: to review where he had been, whom he had been associated with, who was most outspoken in their grief and to reflect on what might come next. For his old associates, led by his Paris housemate Phan Van Truong, his funeral was an occasion to emulate and surpass that of Sun Yat-sen. Alongside the chief mourners, thousands came who had never met Phan Chu Trinh in person, and more still were present in the calligraphic banners: the grief of scholars, businessmen, monks and hermits, memorials sent by the Kuomintang and others far beyond the borders of Vietnam. Parallel rites were held in every province. In Hue they were led by Phan Boi Chau, who resumed the dialogue that they had left unfinished in Japan

in 1905, when Trinh had challenged Phan Boi Chau's support for mon-
archism. 'The more I think about what he said, the more I feel he is
right. I know that what I considered or what I examined is nothing as
compared to his thought! If he were still alive, we would ask him to
lead us.'[102]

But in Vietnam, too, events were increasingly driven by youth. An
underground *Jeune Annam*, 'Young Annam', movement was formed
illegally just two days before the funeral, members of which acted as
ushers in their yellow armbands. In the procession there was also a new
prominence for women. Phan Chu Trinh had not been a visible public
presence for nearly a generation. But for men and women born in the
new century, his passing was a watershed. They were also protesting
the arrest on the morning after Trinh's death of a law student who had
returned from a trip to Paris on the same ship as Phan Chu Trinh. Born
in 1900, Nguyen An Ninh was the son of an author and translator from
Cholon. In his long schooling in France, Ninh had absorbed many
anarchist ideas, and on his initial return in 1923 imported them into a
French-language journal called *Cloche fêlée*, 'Broken Bell', echoing
Baudelaire; its mission was 'a discordant sound', 'pamphleteering to
the point of breaking'. It was the most radical, iconoclastic voice yet to
be raised from within Vietnam. Nguyen An Ninh's provocative deployment of the European avant-garde, together with his adoption of simple
Vietnamese peasant dress, made him a literary sensation overnight.
Cloche fêlée was unrelenting in its exposure of the corruption and
scandals that rocked colonial society in this period, calling it to account
by its own professed republican ideals. It was worldly in its references:
Nguyen An Ninh was a devotee of Tagore and was acclaimed in *Cloche
fêlée*'s lively letters page as 'the Gandhi of Vietnam'. The French
authorities harassed its printers and subscribers, who, disconcertingly,
were most numerous among civil servants and schoolteachers. But in its
brief run of just over two years, *Cloche fêlée* became a lodestone for an
educated generation seeking a better meaning from Vietnam's own
traditions, or – as Nguyen An Ninh came close to arguing – rejecting
them altogether. There was a questing eclecticism to his thought, and
an individualism and ambivalence in his attitude to revolutionary discipline and to violence. His views seemed to harden: in February 1925
he wrote that 'against a modern organisation of oppression we must
oppose a modern organisation of resistance'. In the wake of Phan Chu

Trinh's funeral, in the 30 March 1926 issue of *Cloche fêlée* Phan Van Truong began to publish a serial version of *The Communist Manifesto*. All this provided a critical commentary to an unprecedented and compressed concatenation of events: the national mourning, the death of the emperor, Khai Dinh, labour unrest and school strikes, often sparked by French attempts to obstruct or censor the lamentation of the young. And for many students their truancy led them to abandon their studies altogether and travel to Canton.[103]

A THUNDERBOLT TO CLEAN THE AIR

In the midst of the June Days, Tan Malaka quietly left Canton. His months there had been marked by increasing frustration. In early 1925, he wrote to the Governor-General of the Indies to demand permission to return to Java to rest in a hill station in a gentler climate. He announced that his beliefs were unchanged. He was told that he would have to take internal exile to some unspecified outpost of the outer islands, other than Kupang on Dutch Timor, itself proverbial for its isolation. This was a fate he had rejected in 1922 in favour of Europe, and rejected again now, accusing the government of bad faith: 'there are still plenty of places outside Kupang, such as Atapupu, Purukcau and others, where Kupang would still be heaven.' The government had allowed Soewardi, Douwes Dekker and Tjipto Mangoenkoesoemo to return, he wrote; how much more they must now fear the hold the communists had on the people. Such was his impertinence that the Malay newspapers that printed his reply were prosecuted.[104]

Taking a step closer to home, he travelled to Singapore in April or May 1925, but then was recalled to Canton. The British were monitoring ever more closely the comings and goings from Canton and Shanghai and had an alert out for an 'Iguen' [Nguyen] and a 'Malaka'.[105] Tan Malaka then looked to the Philippines for sanctuary. He had got to know the five Filipino delegates to the Pan-Pacific Labour Conference. He was an intense admirer of José Rizal, celebrated across the islands as the 'first Malay', and this fortified his sense of their common destiny. He took to learning the local variant of Malay, Tagalog, from a young woman, a Miss Carmen, who ran a hostel for Filipinos in Canton. Tan Malaka took advice from its residents and departed quietly in July

1925 for Manila, as a stowaway, bluffing his way – as variously a returning student or as an itinerant boxer – with no papers. He settled with Miss Carmen's family in Santa Mesa, a barrio on the outskirts of Manila, as 'Elias Fuentes'.[106] He would soon advise the new *Partido Obrero*, or labour party of the Philippines, which had hitherto taken its lead from its colonial metropole, the United States, encouraging it to adopt a similar 'minimum program' to that of the communists in Indonesia, and to steer itself into the currents of Asian internationalism.[107]

Shortly before he left, in April 1925, Tan Malaka published a short book in Dutch, *Naar de Republiek Indonesia*, 'Towards the Indonesian Republic'. Like Nguyen An Ninh, he chose to write in the colonial language to target the younger intellectuals at home. Composed towards the end of 1924, the tract, like much of the literature of the hour, was full of foreboding for what Tan Malaka termed 'an impending Pacific war' between the western imperial powers, led now by the United States, 'even more terrible than the last war'. He had a premonition that the construction of the new Singapore naval base, begun in 1923, would become its flashpoint. He had no illusions about Japan's role in the struggle: 'Asia for the Asians' meant 'Asia under the heel of Japan.'[108]

Tan Malaka's use of the term 'Indonesia' had become increasingly common since it was first taken up by the students in the Netherlands in 1919. It had official standing from the Malay speech used in the colonial *Volksraad*. But for many it signified a broader territory than that of the Netherlands East Indies: an archipelagic world that spanned the Straits to encompass the Malay Peninsula and also the Philippines. It was used definitively in May 1924 in the name of the PKI – *Partai Komunis Indonesia* – to complete its passing into the hands of local leadership. But discussion of the form of Indonesia, a 'nation of intent', as a future free state, as a future democracy, was uncertain and inconclusive.[109] For the first time, Tan Malaka outlined a republican vision for a free Indonesia: sovereign, federal, with a universal franchise. At the heart of the programme was a revolutionary popular democracy:

> The Indonesia National Assembly must be convened by ourselves and not by our enemies. The Indonesian national assembly will undoubtedly be created in a time of violent physical, economic, or political clash, like local revolt, general strike, and mass demonstrations. This will become the climax of our labours. The creation of an Indonesian National

Assembly is a life or death problem in our struggle for *merdeka* [freedom], a matter of 'to be or not to be' in our fight against the holders of political and economic power.

The expression of the popular will was to be initiated by the Sarekat Rakyat, the broad front organization of the PKI that Tan Malaka advocated in his brief time as its leader in 1922. He appointed a special role to the young intellectuals he was principally addressing: the task of struggle and tasting the 'delicious[ness] of social work with the masses'. He promised a hard road: 'the land is dark, difficult, and full of poison, that is the road to independence'. For the intellectual it was a call to a battle against the untruths and distortions of power, and 'the silence of life as an individual in a capitalist society'. But, against this, he offered perhaps the clearest vision yet of the fruits of struggle:

> In the atmosphere of an independent Indonesia, intellectual and social energy will blossom faster and better. Great wealth accumulated by the labour of Indonesians will remain in our country. Knowledge, otherwise controlled and distorted for the benefit of the Dutch capitalists, will soon blossom for the use and benefit of Indonesian society. Art and libraries will find new ground on which to take root. Even more certain, Indonesia will soon grow in the field of economics, intellect, and culture . . .[110]

Revolution was an act of collective will:

> We have the courage to say this, not because we want to promise paradise to all men, but to stress their independence.[111]

Tan Malaka's book was printed at large in the world; a second edition claimed to be published from Tokyo to confuse the censors – it came, in fact, out of Manila. Its circulation in the Indies was limited, but copies entered through the schools and print networks of Sumatra.

Naar de Republiek Indonesia was dedicated with heavy sarcasm to the Governor-General of the Indies after March 1921, Dirk Fock. It was a call to arms in the face of the crackdown by the Dutch authorities: 'The sweet-talking ethical voice has now been changed for a rubber stick and a clanging sword.'[112] Fock, like Martial Merlin in Indochina, was a progressive turned conservative: a defender of big business and fiscal stringency. This had first made itself felt in the crushing of the pawnshop workers' strike in early 1922, and the arrest and banishment of Tan Malaka himself. But during Tan Malaka's exile in Europe, Russia and China, the crackdown extended to a range of what were termed 'anti-terrorist' measures. An early trial of strength came as the Indies slid into recession from late 1922, with mounting industrial tension, particularly in the most organized sector: the railway workers who faced layoffs and cuts in wages. A strike in May 1923 threatened to paralyse the train and tram network in Central and East Java. Police and troops were called out; 8,265 State Railway workers who went on strike were summarily sacked and their families evicted from their tied housing, and 120–40 of them were arrested under a catch-all provision of the penal code banning incitement or encouragement of strikes. Caught in a pincer movement between the government and employers, they stood to lose everything, jobs, homes, shop credit; only 1,596 were re-employed. The Indies' most proud and powerful union – once led by Sneevliet and Semaoen – was to all intents and purposes crushed.[113] Many of the dismissed workers found a home in the communist-led Sarekat Rakyat.[114]

Yet, for all this, the Netherlands Indies' legendary *Beamtenstaat*, or bureaucracy, was not perhaps as strong as it appeared. To British observers, it remained a weak link in the chain of imperial control across Asia. The final colonial class of 1919 of the army consisted of one man. When a job notice came up asking for an ex-officer, eighty-five serving officers applied for it. By late 1926 it would be reported in the *Java Bode*, or 'Java Messenger', that while there had been 39,039 soldiers and 10,055 armed police at the beginning of the decade, there were only 31,691 soldiers and 2,500 policemen in late 1926. The actual available strength was only about 9,000 men to guard 3,100 miles of railways and tramways.[115] The Dutch watched their native soldiers very closely. In the military, the mere possession of a pamphlet meant dismissal, a heavy price for soldiers who had no other forms of income. Cantonments were off-limits to all outsiders, although women were often used to distribute political literature. In Tan Malaka's writing, as in that of Ly Thuy, violence was a revolutionary necessity. But it was imagined as the suborning of military garrisons, the solidarity of general stoppages, the unstoppable momentum and moral force of the mass demonstration. If carefully planned and executed, it was perhaps not so bloody or violent at all. As Semaoen was reported to have said in a speech on Semarang on 1 April 1923:

> Our attitude . . . if a revolution does break out – I said if, not, come, let us make a rebellion tomorrow – is that we must urge our trade union not to kill any white people, but merely put them in jail, as hostages, so that the white people cannot use bombs against us. This way, we will ensure there is no destruction and no killing, but imprisonment only with an undertaking to send them all home. Further, 100 white people can be exchanged for 100 rifles, 10,000 white people for a warship. In this way there will be no bloodshed and we will be able to be free.[116]

This was too much for the Dutch. Semaoen's arrest and banishment in May 1923 were the immediate *casus bellum* for the railway strike, but also allowed the Dutch to justify the ferocity of their suppression of it. A range of measures were used to prevent the young gathering in numbers: people under eighteen were forbidden to join associations or demonstrate and subject to restrictions on residence. In Sumatra, where there were large garrisons of migrant Javanese labourers on the estates, there was a regulation that a resident of one district might not travel to another without permission. In Langsa, in northern Sumatra, this led to the round-up of the entire communist organization. But it could equally have a counterproductive result. The arrests rendered Langsa uninhabitable for party leaders and displaced them further south along the east coast. Sympathetic Dutch schoolmasters were shipped home and native teachers were transferred to obscure positions, but this too carried with it the danger of spreading the Bolshevik 'contagion'.[117] Such imagery became a self-fulfilling prophecy.

The Red and the 'Green' currents within the Sarekat Islam moved further apart than ever. The influential religious organization in the Indies, the Muhammadiyah, ruled that communism and Islam were incompatible. The leading voice of the Islamicists in the Sarekat Islam, Haji Agus Salim, adopted a quietist policy, following the path of the Prophet Muhammad, in *hijrah*, withdrawal, in this instance from colonial institutions. Salim was attacked by Red leaders as a 'Dutch haji'. Leaders who had taken a seat in the *Volksraad* bore the brunt of the vitriol.[118] Tjokroaminoto was accused of turning the Sarekat Islam into a 'lawyer bureau' and of using it to his own corrupt ends. The purchase of an expensive new car figured prominently in these charges, as did his new wife, a stage actress from Solo. Many of the younger men who had first come together in his house in Peneleh Alley in Surabaya broke with him: Alimin and Musso were firmly in the orbit of the PKI; their arrest and time in prison after the 1919 'Section B' affair radicalized them. Sukarno, now studying in Bandung Technical Institute, had married one of Tjokroaminoto's daughters and looked after the family during Tjokroaminoto's own preventive arrest from late August 1921 to April 1922. The marriage did not last – Sukarno had fallen in love with his landlady in Bandung – but, at a public meeting there, he defended Tjokroaminoto against cries from a hostile hall: 'Tjokro wants to be king!', 'Where's the money of Tjokro's Sarekat Islam gone?'[119] However, Sukarno was influenced increasingly by the radical nationalism of Douwes Dekker and Tjipto, and embarked on an independent path, which was elaborated in his October 1926 essay 'Nationalism, Islam and Marxism'. Here he appealed to the shared egalitarian and anti-capitalist goals of nationalism and Islam, and to a 'young' Asian Marxism which might embrace them in 'friendship and support'. He called not for an Islamic or proletarian millennium, but all-surpassing national unity, and for a charismatic 'chief leader' to act as its champion.[120]

The PKI still operated as an open political party and held meetings in plain sight. The party moved from being a 'bloc within' the Sarekat Islam to the dominant anti-colonial organization, imposing itself on the Red Sarekat Islam, in a way that ran ahead of the plans that were being laid for it in Moscow and, indeed, the 'bloc within' established by the communists in China. The main vehicle for this united front remained the trade unions and the Sarekat Rakyat. Neither were synonymous with the PKI. But they were a conduit through which propaganda, literacy classes and political training were delivered. Darsono was sent back to the Indies from Moscow and worked behind the scenes to try to strengthen central party control over an organization that was rapidly expanding beyond Java, to Sumatra and pockets in the outer islands. The movement took on distinct local inflections. Haji Misbach remained the dominant personality in Central Java. After his release from prison, his communism became more pronounced, and his attacks on capitalism, imperialism and on other Islamic leaders – the 'use of tricks by the methods of *fitnah* [disunity/unrest], oppression, exploitation and so on' – became ever more religiously charged.[121] In West Java, the scene of the most serious unrest in 1919, the movement drew on village-level sufi brotherhoods. In West Sumatra, it was embedded in the modernist religious schools. In the northern port cities of Java, it retained a more secular plebeian outlook.

By the end of 1924, the sense of trepidation and expectancy had reached fever pitch and became entangled with the rekindled twelfth-century prophecy of King Joyoboyo which foretold the armies that would herald the coming of the *ratu adil*, the just king. During and after the Great War, this was associated with the growing Japanese presence in the archipelago; it now attached itself to Soviet Russia and to the PKI.[122] Tan Malaka tried to dispel this kind of talk. Referring to the violence in West Java in 1919 he wrote: 'Not because of oaths, talismans, magic voices, or dark symptoms of feudalism which for a long time became a crutch for people's lives, did the people of Priangan rebel, but because of clear rights and consciousness as human beings'.[123] But the prophecy remained a powerful one, particularly in the rural areas into which the party was extending its influence. In Ternate, in the Moluccas, a local PKI organizer was a descendant of Prince Dipanegara, a claimant of the mantle of the just king during the 1825–30 rebellion that loomed large in nationalist mythology.[124] The sense of imminent violence was hard to talk down. There was a series of bomb attacks in Java in the aftermath of the 1923 railway strike. These targeted not merely symbols of Dutch rule, but also members of the Javanese aristocracy who cooperated with the colonial regime. There were attacks on trains, on buildings belonging to the royal courts of Solo. Mostly spectacularly, on 17 October a bomb was thrown at the Mangkunegaran Palace; more bombs soon followed, targeting a car and the houses of two court officials; two others failed to explode.[125] Darsono broke cover to condemn the methods of anarchism: 'I pay homage to people who have demonstrated the courage to want to deliver mankind by these methods. But the bombings cannot be approved by the Communists and they do not accord with the political line of the Communists.' It was not clear who was behind them. The attacks led to further arrests, which further jeopardized the party's ability to operate above ground. One of those arrested was the man behind the first Malay translation of *The Communist Manifesto*, Partondo; another was Haji Misbach.[126]

Heavily guarded, in July 1924 Haji Misbach took a slow boat to

18. The Prince of Wales and Chinese community leaders at the Malaya-Borneo Exhibition, Singapore, March 1922.

19. Anti-Japanese demonstrations in Shanghai, 1932, the year in which the rising tide of popular protest sparked Japanese military intervention in the city.

20. Pathfinders of the Comintern in Asia: M.N. Roy stands behind Grigory Zinoviev in the centre; on the far left Tan Malaka stands behind Nguyen Ai Quoc, 1922.

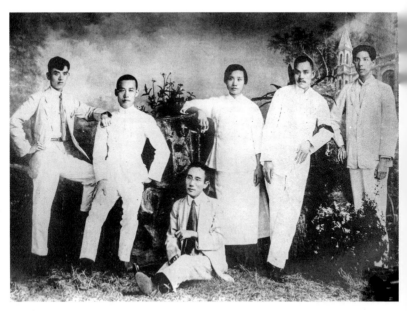

21. 'The anarchist group', Singapore, c. 1924: a photograph in police hands.

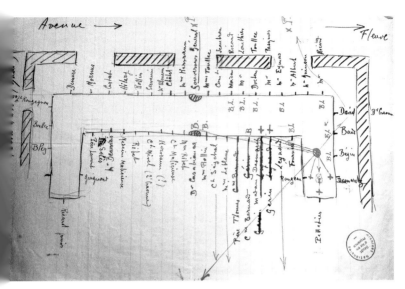

22. Seating plan for dinner at the Hotel Victoria, Canton, showing the impact of Pham Hong Thai's bomb, June 1924.

23. Vietnamese students and Whampoa cadets at the tomb of Pham Hong Thai, c. 1925.

24. Shamian island in the wake of Pham Hong Thai's bomb, showing the bridges between the French and British concessions and the old city of Canton, 1924.

25. The bicycle party: Nguyen Ai Quoc, alias Ly Thuy, in Canton, c. late 1924.

26. The Shaji incident, 23 June 1925:
before and after.

27. Ibid.

28. Students salute the cortège of Sun Yat-sen, Beijing, March 1925.

29. Borodin in Canton, second from the left, with his aide, Zhang Tailei, and Wang Jingwei to his left, 1926.

30. Liberated China: the British Bund, Hankou, after its seizure following riots, January 1927.

31. Xiang Jingyu, head of the Women's Bureau of the Chinese Communist Party, executed by the Kuomintang in Hankou, 1928.

32. Mas Marco Kartodikromo and his wife in Boven Digoel, shortly before his death, 1932.

33. From jail to jail: Tan Malaka in British custody in Hong Kong, 1932.

Monokwari on the northern coast of west New Guinea. His wife and three children accompanied him. Banishment to Europe – as had been the case with Douwes Dekker, Soewardi, Tjipto, Tan Malaka and Semaoen – was no longer an option; nor to Mecca, for which Misbach had hoped. He recorded a diary of the voyage: 'as long as the world is still in chaos, and as long as I am alive, I will continue to move, unbowed. May my brothers be ready to take this as a mirror.' Over the coming months he penned a powerful series of articles on 'Islamism and Communism', which were posted to his newspaper in Solo, *Medan Moeslimin*, or 'Muslim Arena'. A central theme was the sinful, corrupting force of capital, which brought greed and strife into the world. Into this he wove a dialectic drawn from Marx: 'the spirit of capital is so evil that it sows the seeds of hatred and courage. [Communism] is created by capitalism itself and is summoned up by capitalism solely in order to oppose it.' The writings stopped shortly before Misbach's wife, Sorojo, died of malaria in July 1925. There was a campaign to raise money to send Misbach to Europe; the Communist Party of Holland put him up as a candidate for the Second Chamber, as they had done for Tan Malaka. But the funds were insufficient, or did not reach him, and he remained, with his children, in failing health in West Guinea.[127]

The tide of hatred and of courage continued to rise. At the end of December 1924, a final public conference of the PKI was held in Yogyakarta. The walls of the halls were a blaze of red flags and delegates wore red armbands, and alongside the portraits of Marx and Lenin were those of the exiled leaders Tan Malaka and Semaoen. Graduates of Tan Malaka's school in Semarang sang 'The Internationale'.[128] At this time the PKI claimed thirty-six branches with 1,140 members, and the Sarekat Rakyat thirty-one sections with 31,124 members.[129] The PKI's open leaders began to rotate as they each took their turn in preventative detention. The conference was led by a schoolteacher, Aliarcham. He declared the party a 'dangerous' organization, and announced the creation of a more dispersed, cell-like organization – so-called 'ten-men groups' – to prepare for 'illegal' activity.[130] Darsono and Alimin were already underground. The meeting announced a dismantling of the Sarekat Rakyat: it was too large, too open to petty-bourgeois influence and too apt to lurch into undisciplined acts of terror. The policy turned back to expanding the party itself to 3,000 members within the industrial workforce: there were sixty-five sections by May 1926, and the Sarekat

Rakyat still continued to grow. It was a decisive break with the national movement, and also a break with the leadership abroad and the Comintern's injunction to form an 'independent national revolutionary party'. At this point Stalin himself, in a speech, singled out the PKI as suffering from 'leftist deviation'. The problem was, as the PKI leaders tried to tell Moscow, political conditions no longer allowed for open, legal struggle. The pressure from its own followers was intense. This came to the fore in a strike on the Semarang waterfront in August 1925, which was seen by the party as a test of strength. A local leader, a man called Soegiris, was heard to say: 'At last we are on the brink of what we have waited for for so long. At last we shall be able to follow the noble example of our friends in China and treat the insolence of the foreigner and the capitalist as it deserves to be treated.' And later, at his house: 'If the Europeans want a bloodbath, they can have it.'[131] The movement was mobilizing from below, in response to repression and in anticipation of more to come. The Dutch feared it was enlisting local criminal elements – men adept in violence – to this end.[132]

The leadership of the party was scattered halfway across the world. From April 1924, both Sneevliet and Semaoen were in Amsterdam. Around this time, the International Seamen's Union in Amsterdam established an Indonesian wing and recruited sailors plying between the Netherlands and the Indies in Rotterdam Lloyd and the Netherlands Steamship Company. The sailors connected directly to Surabaya, where a combined union of dockers and seamen was founded to control the waterfront, with members from all the major ports of the archipelago. But the old friendship between Semaoen and Sneevliet became strained when the work for Java in Holland was drawn into the orbit of Dutch socialism. Semaoen complained bitterly of Dutch comrades' possessive and paternalist attitude towards Indonesian communism; their 'ruling-race-superior-fancy'; their preference for sending Dutch communists to the Indies, who were unable to work illegally, rather than training Javanese in Moscow. Of Sneevliet he wrote to the Eastern Department in Moscow, in imperfect but eloquent English, on 15 November 1924:

I am sorry to be obliged to fight against comrade Maring, because he was the comrade, who was my teacher when I was a boy in our movement . . . Comrade Maring tell you, that he was the former of the Social-democratic-Union in Indonesia and worked many years (4 years) there, but he forget to tell you, that he did not speak the languages of our people and that his popularity was caused only by my propaganda ... comrade Maring speaks as an old teacher about our YOUNG movement. Yes, our movement is till now young, but it is not a little child more, it is a big young man with independent character, who will not be a child of the Dutch, but only the child of the Leninism ... Please help us keep away every *sectarisch* [sectarian] Dutch comrades from the rank of the Indonesian revolutionists.

For his part, Sneevliet complained of being excluded from Indonesian affairs, and of the 'absolutely wicked' attitude of Semaoen.[133] He lobbied to return to China: 'I want to do real work,' he complained, 'and not all kind of preparatory work which is often nothing else than experimenting.'[134] He took leave from March to the end of June 1924 to campaign to get his new Russian wife, Sima Lvovna Zholkovskaya, and their young daughter into the Netherlands.[135] 'After my expulsion [from Java], for 5 years I knew the pleasures of wandering around alone. Now I yearn strongly to have both my Sima's with me.'[136] He was not to travel east again. Nor was Semaoen in the foreseeable future. He was still only twenty-four years of age. He returned to Moscow to advise on the direction of the revolution, but with precious little information on events at home to hand.

Meanwhile, Tan Malaka attempted to guide the movement from afar. In late September 1925 he was in Chiang Mai, northern Siam, living as 'Haji Hassan'. He wrote to a comrade, Budisutjitro, who had travelled to the Pan Pacific Labour Conference in Canton in 1924. He sent two photographs of himself, one to be forwarded to his ageing parents, and passed a message to a friend to visit them on his behalf. He had been in exile for over three years and was still only twenty-eight years of age. He was in poor health, but the easier climate and the rains in Chiang Mai helped: 'I feel fresh,' he wrote, 'and have strength to work and am optimistic. A week's drought suffices to disturb my health again. But not as formerly. And when it is frightfully warm here we can go to the hills for a short while. Otherwise, there is nothing.' He continued:

But I fear that it will only be in name, with the quality of thinking alone, measuring its own strength, working alone and performing useless work. And the blown up ball becomes soft again when there is no support from outside. We must thus be patient and wait until the kernel comes from below. This is only a question of time and our work is first of all to educate; so also in other places, although this education often seems of necessity to be coupled with '*aksi*' [action]. But the '*aksi*' can only bear fruit when the inner strength in a State is sufficient. Not until there is sufficient inner strength can we bear the risk of the '*aksi*' and if necessary, take strength from outside.

The word *aksi* was Tan Malaka's own coinage, from the English, for revolutionary action. The letters were written partly in cipher, and the contents ostensibly related to trade. References to chocolate might indicate strikes, and rice, arms. Talk of the Quran referred not to religious authority but to communist theory, and of religious teachers to the Comintern. Unbeknown to their recipients, these kinds of letters were intercepted by Dutch intelligence and copied and sent to the British consul.[137]

The policing across borders was a distorting mirror to a movement that had embedded itself, beyond the Netherlands Indies, in the trading world of the Straits of Malacca – the heart of 'Aslia' – with its relatively open connections from Medan to Penang to Singapore and other smaller outposts of the islands. There was a constant trickle of arms through Singapore and Siam, and there were many reasons why both Indonesians and increasingly heavily armed Europeans might want to own them illegally. The movement had a safe house at Onan Road in the Katong area on the east coast of Singapore, and in Arab Street, the centre of comings and goings from the archipelago, where often its intermediaries worked as pilgrim brokers. The hajj to Mecca itself began a conduit of ideas; there was considerable anxiety when Tjokroaminoto performed the hajj in 1925 that he would return radicalized by the experience. Communist activists, particularly those identifying with Tan Malaka, increasingly used Singapore and the Federated Malay States as a safe haven, blending relatively seamlessly into the Malay population there. The British drew comfort from an intercepted letter in cipher from Tan Malaka from a visit to Singapore and Penang in November 1925 which described the Malays as 'all conservative in the manner of their living and thinking . . . if one looks for a movement from the FMS, it is not to be sought from the side of the Malays. It will certainly come from the Chinese and Klings [Indians], whatever sort of movement it may be.'[138]

But, for the British, who relied on the Malays as policemen, soldiers and officials, the presence of radicals within a growing influx of Indonesian settlers in the southern and west coast states became a constant anxiety, and Tan Malaka himself a spectral presence. He was in Singapore in November and again in December, shuttling between there and Penang. But the house in Onan Street was compromised and the contact there unreliable, so he decamped to a shophouse at 709 North Bridge Road, a row of food shops behind the main mosque, where Semaoen was thought to have been sheltered in 1922. In mid-January 1926 Tan Malaka was spotted again in Penang, and then withdrew to Chiang Mai and then back to the Philippines, probably by way of Bangkok or Singapore. He tended to travel by boat wherever possible for economy and security.[139]

His letters betrayed his awareness that the Dutch repression was gathering momentum. But he was probably unaware of a party conference on Christmas Day 1925 at Prambanan, the site of the ninth century Hindu temple complex, a few miles outside Yogyakarta and on the road to Solo, where a second gathering was held with trade unionists over the following two days. Both were shadowed by the police to make sure no 'meeting' occurred: delegates instead went to the parks and to the cinema. There the decision was taken to move into open rebellion against the Dutch. But it was taken in the full light of weaknesses in the PKI. With an eye to China, the leaders looked to the Comintern for support, and the leadership outside the Indies. The plan was for a general strike to announce the bid for power, and also to measure support for it. There was considerable dispute about what precisely was to be the timing of the revolution – whether May, June or July 1926: it was unclear – and news of the meeting was slow to be carried outside Java. The meeting was held under the chairmanship of Sardjono, and in the absence of most key leaders. Aliarcham was arrested and banished to West Guinea, and Darsono was given the option of banishment overseas – the final occasion on which such a boon was granted. He headed under guard to Singapore and Shanghai, but from there made his way to Moscow. Alimin had fled to Singapore to contact Tan Malaka, who was still seen as the oracle of the revolution and the fount of Comintern authority.[140]

The two men met in Singapore and Alimin followed shortly behind Tan Malaka to Manila. He found Tan Malaka incapacitated once again by tuberculosis. There they received a letter from Budisutjitro with news of the Prambanan meeting, informing them that he had arrived in Singapore with other leaders, including Musso and Sardjono. Tan Malaka was appalled by the decision to rebel: the party and the Sarekat Rakyat was ' "really and truly" not strong enough to carry out a general national action (let alone an international one)'.[141] He won Alimin over to his way of thinking, or so he believed. He urged a full party conference in Singapore to resolve the situation but was unable to travel there immediately. Musso reacted with anger: 'he thinks he's the boss.' The old issue of the extent of Tan Malaka's Comintern credentials resurfaced. Musso declared that Tan Malaka and himself were to travel to Moscow to gain Soviet support for the rebellion. Towards the end of February, Alimin returned to Singapore armed with written 'theses' from Tan Malaka, and under a commitment to speak forcibly for him in his absence. In a sense Tan Malaka had outlined his own objections in his *Naar de Republiek Indonesia*: the need for care and time to build an organization from below. A further tract, *Semangat Moeda*, or 'The Spirit of Youth', explicitly ruled out a 'putsch'.[142]

On his return to Singapore, Alimin met with the waiting leaders, many of whom were now impatient to return home, in a shed in a banana plantation in Geylang Serai. However, the 'theses' were not read to the gathering; Tan Malaka's reasoning was not revealed, and his objections were brushed aside. Promises were made, with no foundation, of active support from Moscow, and on 13 March 1926 Alimin and Musso left, first for Shanghai, and then for Russia. Alimin wrote to Manila to tell Tan Malaka that there was to be no conference in Singapore and that his 'theses' had been rejected. Tan Malaka waited two months for this news to arrive. He scrambled to obtain a false passport and travelled to Singapore, still ill, as 'Hasan Gozali', from Mindanao. When he reached the refuge in Geylang Serai in early June, only the local caretaker was there. They found the 'theses' still hidden in the suitcase Alimin had travelled with from Manila. They forwarded them to Java, but the rump of the party leadership had already moved out of Batavia to the more open city of Bandung to finalize their plans for what Tan Malaka termed 'a thunderbolt to clean the air'.

Chiang Kai-shek enters Shanghai, April 1927.

14

The Long March of the Underground
1926–1927

BENEATH THE WALLS OF WUCHANG

The spring of 1926 came with a sudden urgency and the promise of insurrection. In China, the communist revolutionaries had stepped out of the back alleys, with their hidden printing presses and pavilion room meetings, to establish a major stake in what was effectively an independent state and an army. But, as in Indonesia, there was a mounting sense that a revolutionary moment might be missed, and with fatal consequences. In February 1926, Borodin was summoned from Canton to Beijing to be called to account by a visiting Soviet commission headed by the veteran Bolshevik A. S. Bubnov. To an American newspaperman who spoke with him, Borodin appeared 'tired, out of sorts and ready to go back to Moscow'.[1] The charge hovered over him that he was moving far too slowly. He had little choice but to agree. 'Canton', he told them, was a 'kind of Tower of Babel in which it is possible to get lost completely.' Confined there for much longer, the revolution would 'rust out'. Borodin knew that, despite his misgivings, he had to throw his weight decisively behind the long-promised northern expedition.[2]

In Beijing, Borodin was witness to a protest on 18 March against further foreign encroachment. The leading communist in the city, Li Dazhao, led a march to deliver a petition to the administrative headquarters of the Beiyang government. It was met by its troops, who turned guns and bayonets on the demonstrators, killing forty-seven of them and injuring hundreds more. Li Dazhao narrowly escaped and took sanctuary in the Soviet embassy. Most of those killed were, once again, students. Among them was Liu Hezhen, from the Beijing Women's Normal

College at which Lu Xun taught. This was, Lu Xun wrote, 'the darkest day since the founding of the Republic'. His eulogy for her spoke of the moral imperative that the sacrifices of the younger generation, and of women in particular, placed upon the old: 'Those who drag on their ignoble existence amid pale bloodstains will vaguely make out faint glimmers of hope; true warriors will tread onward with even greater resolve.'[3] But Lu Xun had also, since May Thirtieth, been deeply uneasy about the relentless 'praise of blood and iron' by the new generation of writers, and their dogma that literature itself must be the tool of revolution, or it would be its enemy. The principal advocates of literature for revolution, Guo Moruo and other members of the Creation Society, were making their way from Shanghai to Canton, to enlist in its service by teaching at the National Canton University.[4] In 1925 it was renamed Sun Yat-sen University, a move that precipitated mass resignations in the face of political intrusion into academic life. The Kuomintang, led by its military, was becoming a formidable state propaganda machine.[5]

One of the youngest of its new recruits was Zhu Qihua. He came from Zhejiang province and had worked for a short time for a newspaper in Shanghai, where he was witness to the Battle of Nanjing Road. Shortly afterwards, barely seventeen years of age, he ran the strike blockade, travelling from Shanghai via the Portuguese colony of Macao to Canton, drawn by its revolutionary energy. He found a billet in the garden suburb of Tungshan, where his bedside reading was *Sex Histories* – a series of explicit personal stories on the model of the sexologist Havelock Ellis – whose publication in Shanghai that year had caused such a sensation that crowds queuing to buy it had to be dispersed by fire hose. The book's author, Zhang Jingsheng, known as China's 'Dr Sex', was a graduate of the anarchist work-study movement in Paris who combined a utopian blueprint for Chinese cities with an iconoclastic vision of social change. To Zhu Qihua, Canton was the future realized. He was captivated by the city's 'combination of modern civilisation and Nature's untamed beauty', and the sight of young women at school and in uniform seemed to promise freedom from sexual repression. He felt admiration and desire 'so overwhelming it made me forget the revolution and the suffering of the oppressed masses. I would scold myself for giving in to my petty bourgeois failings.' Zhu was put to work in the military affairs department of the Kuomintang central committee, to prepare for war.[6]

More young men and women were beginning to return from Moscow armed with a grounding in Marxist high theory and the dark arts of insurgency. The first students from China had studied at the Lenin School and at the Communist University of the Toilers of the East, but in 1925 candidates were recruited for a new Sun Yat-sen University in Moscow, established by the Russians to mirror Whampoa Military Academy. Some 340 students were chosen through a highly competitive process in Canton, Shanghai, Beijing and Tianjin, of whom around sixty were women. The first intake comprised nationalist and communist students in equal measure: the united front in microcosm. On arrival in Moscow, the students were given new clothes and, as in the case of Comintern agents, new work names. They lived in relatively comfortable seclusion in a former palace of an aristocrat near the Kremlin. The first rector of the university was the charismatic Karl Radek, who taught a formative course on the history of the Chinese revolutionary movement, as seen through Comintern eyes. The fifteen-year-old son of Chiang Kai-shek, Chiang Ching-kuo, found himself in the same class as Deng Xiaoping, who had been sent to Moscow after his activism in Paris had finally exhausted the tolerance of the French authorities. Chiang, Deng and their fellow students followed an austere regime of group discussion and self-criticism in which their aptitude and attitudes were closely monitored; character reviews were pinned on the walls and their letters screened. The university's obsession with inner, ideological transformation was likened by some to Jesuitical training.[7] For the students, it was a unique opportunity to reflect on the nature of the new revolutionary personality. In the dormitories and canteens, doctrinal disputes and intimate relationships were taken up with a passionate intensity. Here it was possible for Chiang Ching-kuo to embark on a two-year affair with the daughter of the 'Christian General', Feng Yuxiang, who had travelled with her father to Moscow, and for male students to form long-term attachments with Russian women. The forcing-house of Moscow created powerful ties and animosities within the Communist Party and the united front.[8]

One visitor to the university was Stalin, who gave a very long speech to the students in early 1925. One of those present was Chen Bilan, a passionate advocate of women's rights from Beijing. She complained that his grating Georgian accent brought an 'onset on our nerves', and she and a friend sneaked out of the hall surreptitiously.[9] The students inevitably took sides in the deepening power struggle within the Krem-lin. In 1923, Stalin had formed a ruling 'triumvirate' with Kamenev and the founding impresario of the Comintern, Zinoviev. But now Zinoviev, with his influence waning, had joined Trotsky in a 'united opposition' to Stalin. Trotsky had never before been so keenly inter-ested in Asian affairs; the revolution in the west had taken precedence. But now policy in China was a principal fault line between the two camps. Stalin held to his conviction that 'the USSR is the base of the world revolutionary movement and this revolutionary movement can-not be defended and promoted unless the USSR is defended.' Trotsky and Zinoviev voiced a commitment to 'proletarian internationalism'.[10] Under the influence of Radek, and given their own internationalist out-look, many of the Chinese students in Moscow gravitated towards Trotsky, including Chen Bilan, who was among the first of them to head back to China following the call of May Thirtieth. She took up work with the Shanghai journal *Women's Weekly* (*Funü zhoubao*), which had previously been edited by Xiang Jingyu who, in turn, headed in the opposite direction to Moscow, in the wake of her affair with Peng Shuzhi. Chen Bilan now embarked on a relationship with Peng, who, despite his part in the scandal, continued to rise in the party lead-ership.[11] These tangled relationships intensified the debate in China as to how long the fragile alliance between the Kuomintang and the Com-munist Party should, or could, endure.[12]

In Canton, conflicts flared on almost a daily basis. A group of techno-cratically minded officials attempted to stabilize the regime, among them the Harvard-educated T. V. Soong, the elder son of the Shanghai financier Charlie Soong, and brother to Sun Yat-sen's widow, Soong Ching-ling. As finance minister from September 1925, he attempted to collect taxes more directly by ousting tax-farmers and other intermedi-aries and enhancing the role of the new central bank. Tax receipts rose fourfold in 1926.[13] But at the same time this put additional pressure on the merchants, bitter in the aftermath of the conflagration in the city the previous October, and frustrated with the continuing strike-boycott of Hong Kong. One of the goals of the strike-boycott had been to divert trade to Canton, but now there were scores of ships stranded at their river moorings and even Borodin admitted that the boycott was a double-edged sword. The strike pickets on the waterfront were a thorn in the side of the police and the military. Restaurant owners took down the signs that offered special discounts to strikers. By the end of December 1925, perhaps 100,000 strikers had drifted back to Hong Kong, and negotiations began quietly with British officials to break the impasse.[14] But, in the meantime, pickets continued to harass and blackmail western business interests; on 10 March 1926 they even blockaded the Canton hospital and its American staff. This was part of a renewed wave of violence directed at mission stations across southern China. The US consul in Canton saw it as a coordinated plan by a Kuomintang government 'entirely under the control of radical elements bent on destroying the work of Christians in this part of the world'. He urged US military intervention to protect them.[15] There were signs from every quarter that a drive against communist influence was under way. In late 1925, communists had mobilized rural support for the eastern campaign and built peasant associations in Guangdong in its wake. But now Kuomintang rightists, many of them under the sway of the conservative Sun Yat-sen Study Society, withdrew their military protection over them, and the despised 'bad gentry and local bullies' began to reassert themselves.[16]

The united front depended on the goodwill of the Kuomintang 'left'. Its dominant personality, Wang Jingwei, basked in his status as the recipient of Sun Yat-sen's final political testament. After the banishment of his rival, Hu Hanmin, in August 1925, Wang, still only forty-two years old, consolidated his authority as chair of the Kuomintang's Central Executive. This was resented by his rivals, and few of the communist leaders were convinced of the steadfastness of their 'petty bourgeois' ally. 'His hair glittered from brilliantine', observed Vera Vladimirovna of her first encounter with Wang Jingwei, and he seemed all too aware of 'his reputation as a humbler of female hearts'.[17] As another of the Russians put it, Wang Jingwei 'looked like a spoiled actor playing the title role of a lover'.[18]

In the midst of Kuomintang factionalism, Chiang Kai-shek was still seen to occupy the middle ground and as a necessary ally for the Comintern. But in early 1926, all the chatter in Canton was that the commandant of Whampoa Military Academy had been sidelined by Wang. It was also well known that Chiang was antagonized by the bullish arrogance of the Soviet military advisers and their resistance to launching the northern expedition and the fulfilment of Sun Yat-sen's legacy. In early March, during Borodin's continued absence from the city, Vera Vladimirovna heard that Chiang had demanded that Russians living across the street from his villa in Tungshan be evicted.[19] Then, over the next few days, she was caught up in a perplexing sequence of events.

The pride of the Kuomintang's small navy was the gunboat *Zhongshan*, on which Sun Yat-sen had escaped Canton in 1921. On 18 March 1926 its communist captain received orders to sail from the city and position the ship offshore from Chiang's headquarters at Whampoa. This was preceded by a flurry of telephone calls from Wang Jingwei's wife to Chiang's wife, Chen Jieru, soliciting Chiang's whereabouts. Guessing, or having been tipped off, that there was a sinister intent behind this, Chiang booked a seat on a Japanese steamer to join his army in the field, but then decided to stay and took shelter in a cement factory.[20] He was convinced, or so he claimed, that the sailing of the *Zhongshan* was the opening gambit of a plot to topple him and carry him into exile to Vladivostok. On 20 March he declared martial law. His soldiers marched into the offices of the Soviet advisers, including Bubnov and his commission, who were visiting the city, removing their regular guards and holding them under house arrest. Communist instructors at Whampoa were rounded up. Chiang's enemies claimed that he had engineered the provocation himself by ordering the *Zhongshan* to move. Certainly Chiang Kai-shek moved with speed and precision, and the Russians had no inkling of what was about to happen. The deeper truth of the affair was never clear, and such was the gathering fog of mistrust, miscommunication and paranoia there may well have been no plot at all.[21] But the immediate issue of events was plain enough. Wang Jingwei resigned his posts abruptly, his wife pleaded his ill health, and they disappeared from the city, later to appear in Shantou and Hong Kong. The British suspected he travelled through Singapore in May with his wife as 'Wong Tsao Min'.[22] He later resurfaced in France. For the time being, Chiang Kai-shek was master of the situation.

Borodin hurried back from Beijing by a long, slow route. To evade the encirclement of Canton by the northern warlords and the western powers, he travelled first by car and camel through Outer Mongolia to the Trans-Siberian Railway, then on to Vladivostok and by Russian steamer to Canton. To save his mission, and with characteristic pragmatism, he made major concessions to Chiang Kai-shek. An offending senior Russia adviser was sent home, the strike pickets were disarmed, and communist representation was reduced within Kuomintang decision-making bodies.[23] The Russians and detained communists were soon released and, publicly at least, Chiang appeared to brush the matter aside. He also moved to clip the wings of the Kuomintang right wing. His ultimate price was the Russian support he needed for the northern expedition, and for his appointment as its commander-in-chief.

The '20 March Incident' was seen, in the words of one of the Russians, as 'a dress rehearsal for a counterrevolutionary coup'.[24] The Communist Party saw that Wang Jingwei and the Kuomintang left had done nothing to protect them. As Borodin's aide and interpreter, Zhang Tailei, asked in exasperation: 'who are the Kuomintang's left wing? Chang Kai-shek is not . . . There is no left wing.'[25] Chen Duxiu seemed vindicated in his insistence that the Communist Party central committee remain at arm's length in Shanghai, and the two revolutionary centres moved further part. Chen also raised the question as to whether the party should now operate as a 'bloc without' the Kuomintang. The northern expedition, he argued, would be 'carried out by a motley crew of military adventurers and politicians interested in achieving their own private ambitions'.[26] Zhang Guotao was sent from Shanghai to investigate and to smooth over relations with Chiang. He was disconcerted by what he saw and heard. 'To speak frankly,' Borodin confided to him in May, 'the CCP appears fated to play the role of a coolie in the Chinese revolution.' The role of 'foreman', Borodin added, was not one he would seek. He spoke from his own ambivalence about the northern expedition, but the word got out that he had said that party members should 'act as coolies' for the Kuomintang. 'I still believed Borodin was an old hand,' Zhang reflected later, 'with greater knowledge; and with the all-powerful Comintern behind him, he was not to be taken on the same level as Maring [Sneevliet]'. However, Zhang warned Borodin, as he had Sneevliet before him, that his words 'smacked a little of the colonialists'.[27]

From this point onwards, all the energies and resources of Canton were diverted to preparations for war. On one reckoning, the total weaponry despatched from Russia for the northern expedition amounted to twenty-four aircraft, 157 field guns, forty-eight mountain artillery pieces, 128 mortars, 295 medium machine guns and around 74,000 rifles.[28] A fresh shipment arrived in May 1926 along with a new chief

Russian military adviser, Vasily Blyukher, a hero of the Red Army, known by his work name 'General Galen' after his Harbin-born wife, Galena, who worked as his secretary. He had arrived earlier, in October 1924, but when the heat of the south opened his war wounds, and after constant friction with Borodin, he had withdrawn to the north of China.[29] Blyukher enjoyed an equal prestige to Borodin for his role in suppressing the merchant militias in October 1924 and in the victorious eastern campaign that followed it. Soon 'Galen's' true identity leaked out, and this only enhanced his standing. He was pivotal to the revolution's grand strategy. The main obstacle, Blyukher argued, was that British control of rail and sea communications through Hong Kong prevented the revolution from reaching central and northern China. It needed to transfer the base of its political work to central China: to the three cities of Wuhan, and the Yangzi. The analogy was made with the role of the inland town of Ankara in the success of the Turkish national revolution of 1919–23; however, Wuhan was already a major metropolis, known to westerners as the 'Chicago of the east'.[30] Blyukher favoured a single thrust against the warlord Wu Peifu in Hunan, en route to Wuhan. From this bridgehead he looked to strike north to link up with the forces of Feng Yuxiang and then to march on Beijing. Cadres trained in Canton would set up civil administrations and peasant associations in the army's wake. Blyukher placed great value on speed and on the inculcation of revolutionary élan through oath-taking and the veneration of martyrs.[31] Other Soviet advisers were less convinced of the military readiness of the Kuomintang but saw the northern expedition as a necessary consequence of the building of an army some 100,000 strong, consuming five-sixths of the budget of the Canton government. As Bubnov put it, 'a national revolution cannot remain entrenched in the south of China.'[32]

For Chiang Kai-shek, this was an appointment with destiny. He was now at the centre of military planning and commander-in-chief of the National Revolutionary Army. He was deferential to Blyukher – on the march their practice was to dine together every evening – but his own vision of the campaign was for a second front through Jiangxi towards the lower Yangzi and the cities of Nanjing, Hangzhou and Shanghai, where he hoped for financial backing. This region was under the nominal control of a former subordinate of the warlord Wu Peifu, Sun Chuanfang. For the time being Chiang waited on events, and endeavoured to keep Sun Chuanfang out of the conflict. A separate line of assault was prepared from the port of Shantou through the coastal provinces. Many returned students from Japan, France and Moscow, communist and Kuomintang, enlisted as political officers attached to the military units. Their very presence marked a break with old ways of war. More often than not, they paid for the supplies they used and rallied popular support through speeches and propaganda. Women took up medical work and set up women's associations in captured areas. These were important ways in which the National Revolutionary Army (NRA) attempted to distinguish itself from warlord armies. It also exploited local hostility to the northern troops; many of the NRA troops in the vanguard and their commanders were from Hunan. But the NRA was in no way a unitary force. At its core were men trained and led by Whampoa officers, but other armies were the product of earlier alliances with regional warlords, including troops from Guangxi, and the forces already in Hunan of the 'Buddhist General', Tan Shengzhi, which, in an alliance at the eleventh hour, became the Eighth Army of the NRA. A unit of committed communists operated along the front as an 'independent regiment'.[33]

In June, Canton began to empty of soldiers, as they boarded trains north. The railway line ran only as far as Shaoguan on the northern border of Guangdong, leaving a 250-mile gap before the base of the line that ran south of Changsha, the capital of Hunan province. From Shaoguan, the mountain passes into Hunan had to be crossed by foot in the summer heat, a journey of a week or more, and then riverboats were needed. This was the route taken by the Taiping rebels in 1851. Some 1,500 of the Canton strike pickets enlisted as baggage carriers, although the military planners had hoped for more. A formal mobilization order was issued on 1 July, encompassing perhaps 100,000 men. Progress proved swifter than expected; being more lightly equipped than their counterparts, the revolutionary forces depended on speed. The late-spring floods impaired the communications of Wu Peifu and, by 11 July, his forces evacuated the provincial capital of Changsha, which fell to Tan Shengzhi. Chiang Kai-shek joined the army there on 11 August. The weary troops were boosted by defections and local peasants seeking paid work as porters, and by mid-August the combined NRA forces stood at the Miluo River, poised to press into Hubei and on to Wuhan. Chiang staked everything on a swift, combined offensive before Wu Peifu was able marshal a counter-attack with his reserves. In the event, Wu's troops abandoned their defensive positions and fell back on the three cities. The fiercest fighting was along the railway line to Wuchang, where the land corridor between the Yangzi and the mountains created a 'funnelling' effect characteristic of military campaigns in China. The revolutionary armies were aided by the sabotaging activities of the railway workers. The key Dingsi Bridge was considered unassailable from the south, but peasants led soldiers through the shallow water to attack it from behind. Of its 10,000–11,000 northern army defenders, only a third managed to escape.[34]

The northern expedition had a wildfire quality. There were uprisings in many cities at the armies' approach, and these were seen as vital to the consolidation of the victories.[35] One of the senior political officers was the writer Guo Moruo. He marched behind the brutal fighting along the final stretch of railway towards Wuchang. The lakes surrounding the approaches to the city, an inspiration to poets of old, were full of corpses. The local farmers came forward with food, water and wine; ahead of them the morale of the warlord troops – hungry and isolated – had collapsed. Guo saw naked bodies tied to trees. They were brigade commanders of Wu Peifu. Wu had returned to the front on 25 August and, incensed at the failure of his commanders to hold the key bridges, had ordered his mercenary Big Sword Corps to execute them in front of his officers. 'Hastily fleeing for his life,' Guo mused, 'he still had the leisure to administer capital punishment.' It was said that, after the loss of the strategic bridge at Hesheng, Wu Peifu retreated with his personal guard by train, his locomotive mowing down soldiers fleeing along the line.[36] The NRA also conformed to old methods of negotiation and co-option, granting a measure of local autonomy to those who opened their gates, so much so that in August Borodin complained that Chiang Kai-shek was seeing the expedition as purely a military matter and that it was losing its revolutionary edge.[37]

But, even to hostile western observers, it was clear that this campaign was different from the warlord conflicts of the previous ten years. 'A novel feature of this expedition', The Times of London explained to its readers, 'is that it is the enterprise not of a general merely, not of an individual, but of a party, and that it has achieved its victories not by arms only, but by discipline and by propaganda.'[38] Tensions with the western powers rose as the expedition approached the heartland of British and American commercial and cultural influence in inland China. There were in the late 1920s over 13,000 manufacturing and commercial enterprises in Wuhan, including cotton mills and the principal factory of British American Tobacco. The city of Hankou, in particular, with its bund and foreign concessions, had undergone much of the same process of modernization as Canton. It was, in high-water season, navigable by ocean-going ships, and its trade in the agricultural products of Henan and Hubei – sesame seed, pulses, cotton and animal tallow – had grown dramatically after 1906 with the railway connection to the coast. Wuhan was also a major centre for education. It sent a disproportionate number of students to Japan and to France and was itself home to many technical and mission schools.[39] Its citizens braced themselves for the onslaught of the southern army. But then, overnight, Hanyang and Hankou became open cities. The ironworks and arsenal at Hanyang fell without a fight when its garrison commander switched allegiance on 6 September, and Wu Peifu himself evacuated Hankou the following day with 294 carloads of troops and retreated along the Beijing–Hankou railway, leaving behind his famous art collection and his new, custom-built armour-plated Rolls-Royce.[40]

On 1 September, Guo Moruo was still on the southern bank of the Yangzi, pressing on to Wuchang, and fully expecting to eat lunch in a capitulated city. The villagers he passed on the way, waiting to enter to sell their wares, told him the city had already fallen. Wuchang was an old imperial administrative centre, sacred within nationalist mythology as the site of the first anti-Qing uprising on 10 October 1911. It was protected by walls that dated from the thirteenth century, up to fifteen to twenty feet thick in places, with nine city gates, some of them screened by outside marketplaces and suburbs. As Guo hastened forward with the advance troops to join battle, they found that the gates were now closed and mounted with the guns of the northern army, and that there were no defending troops on the outside. They had made 'a charge against empty air'. 'Even today in the twentieth century,' Guo reflected, 'an old city wall from feudal times and a gate of two iron-clad wooden leaves were making their power felt, just as were the evil remnants of China's feudalism.'[41]

The gates of Wuchang withstood the light artillery of the attackers, who expected surprise sorties from the defenders, but none came. A

400-strong 'dare-to-die' corps was formed, and Guo helped requisition bamboo ladders for them; many were old, broken and sawn off short. In the early hours of 3 September the forlorn hope was launched, and was met from the high walls with bullets and grenades. At daylight, from his improvised propaganda workshop in an arts college beyond the walls, Guo made his way to the front line. He came upon Chiang Kai-shek, Blyukher and the front-line general, Zhang Fakui, morosely surveying the scene. The attack had failed. A second attempt on the walls was made on 5 September. Again, reports spread through the ranks that the city was taken. As Guo observed, the stakes were high: 'the unit that first broke into the city would naturally have control over Wuchang and even over the entire province of Hubei'. He was deeply shaken by the loss of a close comrade, a student newly returned from Russia, who was hit by a bullet at a temple used as an observation post outside the Pin-yang gate. The attackers had no option but to starve the city into submission. Tunnels were dug to undermine the walls, but they either caved in or surfaced short. It was a medieval siege scene but for the drone of Russian spotter planes flying low to bombard the defenders, sometimes with high explosive and at other times with propaganda leaflets.[42] The city commander hunted revolutionaries within the walls, and the head of a woman student activist was hung over one of the city gates.[43]

The siege was chronicled by American missionaries within the city, not all of whom were hostile to the attackers, and they opened their schools to casualties.[44] Reuters syndicated lurid reports that starving civilians were 'eating female babies'; that the notorious 'Red Spear' bandits had offered to join the siege and that they were joined by 400 of 'the original Boxers'.[45] Guo saw no evidence of cannibalism, but the city folk were driven to eat cats, dogs, rats, roots and bark. The Yangzi boatmen attempted to rescue the women and children. On 3 October, the gate was opened to allow perhaps 20,000 or 30,000 people to escape, and newspapers reported that 200 women were trampled underfoot in the crush to reach the boats.[46] By this time, a month into the siege, the will of the defending troops was broken: from the wall, they begged cigarettes and food off the besiegers. Confronted with the outbreak of cholera, the commanders inside began to negotiate. On the morning of the fifteenth anniversary of the 10 October 1911 Wuchang uprising, and after forty days under siege, the city finally capitulated.

The news came to Hankou in the middle of a great rally at the race-course, and crowds surged through the streets into the night. The next day, Guo Moruo entered Wuchang: 'the doors of all the shops were closed and the inhabitants were all as emaciated and haggard as mummies'.[47] There were few, if any, deaths from starvation, but bodies of the defenders still lay in the streets, and those of the attackers at the foot of the walls.[48] In the coming months, the new rulers of the city would pull down the ancient fortifications, so that a siege of this kind could never be repeated.

These events marked the refoundation of Wuhan as a Red city. The British who were barricaded in their concession in Hankou were confronted with a wave of labour disputes, graphic anti-imperial wall-posters and Kuomintang troops attempting to march along the hallowed ground of the bund. Zhang Guotao was one of the first of the communist leaders to enter the city, to witness the reawakening of student and trade union activism that had lain dormant since the brutal suppression of the railway strike by Wu Peifu in 1923, when Zhang himself had fled the city in secret. Old scores were settled. Other leading communists came in the baggage train of the armies and by steamer from Shanghai. The unions took over the 'New World' amusement park; its theatres played by night, but by day its halls staged rallies and meetings. The new masters of the city displayed a vogue for lavish victory banquets, at which, Zhang noted, 'even the big bosses of industry and trade would shout: "Long live the world revolution"'. He threw himself into the task of establishing another 'Government No. 2' of labour organizations in the manner of the strike-boycott in Canton in 1925.[49] Guo Moruo set up a propaganda bureau in the Nanyang Brothers Tobacco company. Schools were swiftly established to train cadres, including a branch of Whampoa Military Academy in Wuchang. Women came from the progressive schools of Hunan to enlist as soldier cadets. They had a 'song of struggle':

> Study quickly, quickly drill,
> Strive to lead the people.
> Feudal shackles – smash them all,
> Smash romantic dreams.
> Fulfil the people's revolution
> Wonderful, wonderful women!

Twenty-year-old Xie Bingying, like many of them, had abandoned her family in Changsha and the marriage they had arranged for her. She wrote a diary of the transformative experience of academy life, its rough discipline and political awakening, that reached a wide readership as a newspaper serial, and then, in 1930 in English translation, as *Diaries of a Chinese Amazon*.[50]

In Wuhan, as in Canton, the struggle for China swiftly intersected with that of others in Asia. Leaflets in English called on foreign seamen to join the revolution.[51] The Indian constables of the Hankou Municipal Police were prominent participants at political meetings. There was a giddy sense that a revolution was possible, that 'communism' now actually existed in Wuhan. The Hankou Bund was the new front line of the struggle against the imperial powers. Royal Marines were landed from British warships to defend the entrances to the British Concession, and more troops were promised. European volunteer soldiers openly carried arms, and the British consul was terrified that the 'club bar element' might panic and provoke a bloodletting.[52] The revolution was to be accomplished under the guns of the foreign warships anchored in the Yangzi, which were now trained on the city.

THE COMING OF THE JUST KING

As the armies of the Chinese revolution launched themselves northwards, the emissaries from Indonesia, Alimin and Musso, travelled to Shanghai and hurried overland to Russia. They reached their 'Mecca' only in July 1926, blaming the delay on Tan Malaka, and what they saw as his prevarication in the face of a revolutionary moment. They had ignored his advice and came seeking a mandate for revolt and material aid. They were asked to fill in a written questionnaire, as was the procedure for foreign supplicants, and were then summoned before a commission chaired by M. N. Roy, who was back in the Hotel Lux and at the heart of the Comintern's decision-making.

Darsono had arrived ahead of them after his banishment under the Dutch emergency powers. His first-hand report to the Comintern in May had made modest requests for a Comintern representative to be sent 'in order to study the conditions there' and for a conference overseas, 'preferably in China'.[53] It was agreed to send a 'Comrade Miller' to Java to wean the Indonesian party from its 'leftist deviation'. It was never clear who 'Miller' was – he was most likely a Chinese student at the Communist University of the Toilers of the East – and disputes over his ability to assess the situation, especially whom he should listen to, delayed his departure.[54] All this was now set aside. Alimin and Musso claimed that the revolutionary high tide had been reached. On 22 July 1926, the two men appeared before the commission, along with the Indonesian leader-in-exile, Semaoen, and Darsono. They outlined a plan of action. The revolt would begin with a general strike, led by the transport workers. This would provoke large-scale repression, which, in turn, would spark a general uprising. Alimin and Musso challenged their rivals' understanding of the situation: Tan Malaka – and, for that matter, Semaoen and Darsono – were 'erroneous: they underestimated the capacity and power of the party'.[55] They claimed 8,000 members, with another 100,850 in the Sarekat Rakyat and 23,195 trade unionists under their direct control. Of the members, they estimated 30 per cent were factory workers, 40 per cent 'semi-intellectuals, mostly small-bureau officials', 2 per cent were 'semi-intellectuals', 0.1 per cent 'big intellectuals'; the remainder were peasants.[56]

Roy and a British communist, Jack Murphy, grilled them on their level of military preparedness. 'We have our colonels,' Alimin declared breezily. Pressed on this, he said they had six officers, but, he admitted, 'we cannot reach them.'[57] There were fourteen army barracks in the Netherlands East Indies where there was a one-to-five-man 'active nucleus' but it was hard to be sure because of the close surveillance: the soldiers' trunks were searched routinely, and few were able to attend meetings. Alimin also claimed that the police were 'all on our side'. But yet the party had only 300–400 pistols. For Roy, this was not enough: 'we cannot begin an insurrection depending on loose political influence. We must have some sort of nuclei.' Above all, there was scepticism as to how the party could possibly survive the initial wave of repression that was supposed to trigger the uprising. Alimin replied by saying that the communist leaders in the Netherlands Indies 'do not believe there can be a prepared revolution only on paper. They believe that the spontaneous factor will be a very big one.' It would not, he argued, take much to achieve a transfer of power.[58]

This raised more questions as to the nature of the future revolutionary regime. As Roy put it: 'you are not raising questions of power? You are not raising the question of the State? Have you a plan for this?' For Alimin, this was not a question for the present moment:

> In every revolution, we cannot explain so clearly. We cannot make a clear programme. We are sure we can capture the whole population and after that we will make a political programme. Of course, as soon as the time comes, if we are ready, we have the power in our hands. It is easy to explain the revolution.

Semaoen countered. 'On this point they are weak', he said:

> This programme has not grown in the head of one or a few comrades but comes really from the movement. The question of the power of the state is not combined with the question of the form we have to take on it and in connection with this comrades have not discussed this clearly. They think the Comintern is powerful enough to do anything, if there is a revolt, the Comintern will help and everything will be alright. They think the Comintern will send comrades, and with their help, everything will be alright.

Yet, Semaoen himself was forced to concede, 'I have underestimated the situation.' It seemed clear that the insurrection would occur, whether the Comintern willed it or not. As Alimin put it, they 'cannot disapprove all insurrection, because it is the logical result of the general situation, hence [the] decision in December 1925 to "organize" the insurrection on big scale'. 'Anarchist rebellion [was] prevailing here', he went on, and there would be 'confusion in our whole party' if followers were not given the word to rebel. Plans had already been laid for guerrilla action in the event of a negative reaction from Moscow. 'We ask here for only a positive or a negative answer from the Comintern. If possible, support, if not there will be terror ... What are you doing about it now?'[59]

All Roy could do was to ask for more information and more careful consideration. The revolt required a leap of faith on all sides. The Comintern did not want to appear to be a brake on a popular movement, but neither could it be seen to have endorsed a failed rebellion. For the old Bolshevik Russian members on the commission, the situation seemed analogous to Russia in 1903–4: the beginning of a long process of struggle to get the people to identify with the party. With this in mind, Semaoen submitted a counterproposal to build up a 'national bloc'. Parliamentarianism had been discredited by the Dutch *Volksraad*. Nor were the Indonesian people ready to endorse a Soviet-style 'dictatorship of the proletariat'. Therefore, Semaoen argued for a legislative assembly based on an indirect franchise for men and women – the mechanism was unclear – in order to instil a 'national democratism' that would be distinct from western-style parliamentary bodies with their histories of schism. Semaoen imagined this as 'a "pure" national system', uncompromised by any foreign power, and as such it would rally the Indonesian masses around it.[60] This echoed Tan Malaka's outline for an 'Indonesian National Assembly' in *Naar de Republiek Indonesia*, but Tan Malaka was no longer a point of reference. The plan was contrary to the mood of the leadership in Java, as Semaoen admitted: 'there is also among the comrades a kind of desperate spirit'; a fatalistic view that 'we have to make it [a revolt] and if we lose, we lose'.[61]

Inevitably, in the headquarters of its general staff, the Comintern orthodoxy prevailed. The Indonesian party was to adhere to the same line as the party in China, and work within a nationalist front organization. For this, it needed to operate legally. But the Indonesian leaders were still reeling from the shock of the arrests and banishments of the summer of 1925, and of the sudden end of a long period of open struggle. The fact of the repression, the Indonesians stressed, made the Comintern line impossible to follow. The Dutch had 'simply lost their heads'. They were 'trying fascism, etc., there is more espionage than anything else'.[62] However, the overarching position, that locally as well as globally the time was not ripe, was reinforced by a meeting with Stalin himself, its ultimate arbiter. But then a further problem arose, the near-impossibility of communicating the will of Moscow to Java. 'Comrade Miller', whoever he was, only got as far as Paris, Roy told Semaoen, and then was recalled. Musso and Alimin were kept in Moscow for 'training'. Musso tried, unsuccessfully it seems, to send a cable through a secret channel. But it was early October 1926 before he and Alimin set out for Singapore, where Tan Malaka was anxiously awaiting their return.[63]

Tan Malaka warned against a 'putsch' in ever sharper terms. At a meeting in Solo in June 1926, the few senior party leaders still at large affirmed that the party was ready to strike and was waiting only for the return of Alimin and Musso with guidance from Moscow. But its acting supremo, Suprodjo, decided to travel to Singapore to meet Tan Malaka, and returned to Java via Dutch Borneo, carrying with him Tan Malaka's views. They left the leadership in Java divided and paralysed. It sought to postpone the revolt rather than countermand and disavow it. In response, there was a wave of violence from below, seemingly with the intent of forcing the central leadership's hand. There were attacks on village heads in Sumatra, a bomb stash was found in Bandung, devices were thrown at a fairground in Surabaya. On 10 September there were more arrests in central Java, after the chairman of the Solo district court was shot as he stood on the porch of his home. Among those placed in detention was Mas Marco Kartodikromo, who had come to the fore as a declared communist after the arrest and banishment of Haji Misbach. He now suffered the same fate. Interrogations by the police yielded information about a secret 'dictatorial organization' of the party that was charged with planning and directing the revolt. They were well aware of the movements of Tan Malaka and of the mission of Alimin and Musso. Confident in what it knew, the Dutch government stayed its hand in launching a general repression which the communists believed would provoke a popular uprising.[64]

No orders arrived from Moscow. The outbreak of the revolt that was long promised, the advent of the just king of legend, came from below. Militant leaders in Batavia sent emissaries to carry orders to revolt across Java, bypassing the cautious central committee based in Bandung. Their mood was: 'they had to be utterly ashamed of themselves for not having done anything so far.' The Dutch believed that the party 'wanted to prove its activity to the Comintern by a spectacular deed'.[65] In the event, some branches answered the call and others did not. The cell structure set up the previous year allowed local groups to act independently of each other, in a seemingly spontaneous combustion. It began on the night of 12 November in Batavia, where the local revolutionaries were convinced that once the capital fell, so would the entire Netherlands East Indies. Word went out that the railway workers were to strike and armed bands attacked the telephone exchange, Glodok prison, where many of their leaders had been held, and a police barracks. Chinese agricultural workers from the surrounding areas joined them. But there was little coordination; there was no mutiny in the barracks, and the affair was over by morning.[66] One Dutch railway official was killed. That night there were also gatherings in the urban *kampungs* of Solo. However, the local leaders, such as Marco, were in prison, and the police were deployed in advance. When they arrested twenty-two people in one *kampung*, and others drowned in a canal trying to escape, those gathered elsewhere in the city went quietly back to their homes. The largest confrontation was in the village of Boyolali, where a crowd attacked the house of a local district chief, and many took up the cry of holy war. But, again, the police were ready and there were 428 arrests in Boyolali alone.[67]

It was not in the big cities but in the countryside of West Java, in Banten, that what one British observer called 'a kind of guerrilla war' got under way.[68] This was not the poorest region of Java, but one where a heightened religiosity – from expanded Islamic schooling and the experience of the hajj – fed utopian visions of freedom. Much of this was expressed through religious brotherhoods and religious gurus said to possess secret knowledge. Men undertook rituals of invulnerability, fasting and spiritual preparation for holy war. Rebellion here was undertaken in the name of Islam, and communism seemed to be a way of advancing Islam-in-the-world. It was a path to martyrdom and to paradise, as well as to *sama rasa sama rata*, the earthly blessings of freedom and equality, such as free rice and free transport in cars and trains. A guru in north Banten, Hadji Selah – one of more than thirty active in the PKI – belonged to a long lineage of rebels: his father and grandfather had died in the anti-government rebellions of 1888 and 1850 and he too was killed in 1926. Yet even here there was a sense that the world outside would propel the rebellion to victory, and this expectation of success was vital to the sanction of holy war. The source of deliverance was not Russia, nor Japan, nor even China, but the arrival of the airplanes of Mustafa Kemal's Turkish republic and the inspiration of the Rif rebels in Morocco. The real worry for the Dutch was not the scale of the rebellion itself, but the sheer extent to which others in the region waited on events, gauging its likelihood of success. There were rumours that regents themselves, the principal local officials, were watching which way the wind blew, and one was suspended from duty. The rebellion took the form of scattered attacks on telephone wires and on officials' houses. There were no bombs, no seizures of towns, and the forces of colonial order soon prevailed.[69]

Emissaries from Java also reached Sumatra. For a year or so, the west-coast region had been on the edge of open revolt. The communist movement had achieved a breadth of support among school students, and here the personal sway of Tan Malaka, a local boy, was at its strongest, and his writings circulated clandestinely. The depth of feeling had intensified after arrests in late 1923 of leading local figures, particularly the Mecca-trained Haji Datuk Batuah, who was seen as Tan Malaka's representative and had brought the teachings of Haji Misbach to West Sumatra. The centres of the movement were the Red town of Padang Panjang, a mountain crossroads for trade and Islamic learning, and the nearby weaving centre of Silungkang, where small traders faced hard times but also, through their trade and sales catalogues, possessed wide international connections. In these highlands, activists looked to the large concentration of coal-mine workers at Ombilin for support.[70] From its roots as a local debating club, the Sarekat Rakyat had grown from the middle of 1924 to early 1925 from 158 to 884 members. When the party took the decision to dismantle it, most of those involved became provisional members of the party itself and underwent instruction in its principles. Lecture courses offered a Marxist narrative of local social and economic developments, set within a global history of the struggles of workers and peasants. The response to this was mixed: the Dutch reported falling attendance and people sleeping through the classes.[71] But they also offered distinctive arguments about the relationship of communism to Islam. The PKI's central leadership in Java encouraged a policy of religious neutrality, and the journals that appeared transiently in Pandang Panjang – with titles such as *Pemandangan Islam* ('Islamic Landscape') and *Djago-Djago* ('Champions') – continually contrasted the 'impure' practices of capitalism with the Islamic ideal. The capitalism in question was that of the international system and the big western combines: 'capitalism, in short, is the science of large-scale theft of plunder'.[72] From his sojourn in the Philippines, Tan Malaka highlighted the impact of American capital in buttressing the world order; this allowed small traders and entrepreneurs, as well as radical students and teachers, to unite under slogans such as 'freedom from taxation' and 'equality for all'.[73]

But the main targets of 'wild education' were the peasants. A dedicated peasant organization known as the Sarekat Tani was formed and football or martial arts clubs were also mobilized. As illegal activities grew, 'ghost' or 'black' *sarekats* drew on local men for robberies, attacks on officials, tarring of houses, vandalism of crops and the slashing of rubber trees. These local acts of violence escalated as the party made its preparations for revolt, and drew on a long-established clandestine trade in arms – used commonly to protect crops from pests – mostly smuggled by traders and seamen through Singapore. The purchase of party membership cards became seen as a potent form of protection. All of this accelerated the police round-ups, and – as forecast by Alimin – opposition to the mounting 'reaction' became the principal rallying cry of the movement.[74] In June 1926, a major eruption of Mount Merapi, a volcano which overshadowed Padang Panjang and the whole region, was seen by locals as the 'forerunner of a great confusion and commotion that would happen in the future'.[75]

But Tan Malaka still called for restraint and commanded leaders to withdraw to Singapore, Penang or the Malay States. Some thirty or so leaders went underground in response.[76] But others stayed, ready to follow the orders from Java, and to mount an uprising. The crucial signal arrived on 5 November, in the form of a simply coded telegram. This was couched as a trader's request for a set number of consignments – of batik, for example – with their number indicating the date of the uprising. But the intellectuals who led the party in West Sumatra, loyal to Tan Malaka, argued that the message did not have the full sanction of the party, and local bodies were ordered to wait on events in Java. This seeming obstruction, and the mobilization of police and troops, was a further provocation to others. Over the next few weeks, with a frantic series of journeys by bus and train across the highlands, local parties tried to coordinate their plans to rebel with those of others in neighbouring towns. In the meantime, the leaders were either being picked off by the police or fled to British Malaya. In the midst of this highly combustible confusion, word came to Silungkang that the revolution would be launched on 1 January 1927. This was an echo of an earlier call for action which continued to circulate, and was linked to a rumour that the Russians would arrive in support. As such, it carried authority. People mobilized in full knowledge of the failures in Java, and in the face of more arrests of the local leadership, but in the hope that the mutiny of the small military garrison at Sawahlunto might tip the balance. In the words of a Dutch report, 'their whole frame of mind was directed towards the coming revolution'.[77]

At midnight on New Year's Eve 1926, Dutch officials and the managers of the Ombilin mine were celebrating at a small dance hall in Silungkang. This was the moment to seize the garrison and open the local prison. The rebel leaders gathered above a restaurant facing the town square, while their supporters ate and drank lemonade downstairs. They were waiting for confirmation by messenger from Padang Panjang that this was the appointed hour. But no one came. A man called Kamaruddin, alias Manggulung, described in a Dutch report as 'the most infamous of Silungkang gamblers', swayed the mood. 'All we do is talk, talk and once again talk. We are having an endless string of meetings, but nothing else . . . We will go on meeting until nothing comes of the whole rebellion. We can no longer go back. Whoever wants to stop us now gets killed.'[78] But the Dutch had advance word and made further, key arrests. Rallying to Silungkang, a column of peasants set upon Dutch troops, killing their commander, one of two Dutchmen to die. But other groups descending on the town were attacked or scattered. The revolt collapsed into vendetta assaults on petty officials, stationmasters and teachers. Families were bitterly divided. One local official was killed by his own nephew. Another official, who conducted the arrests, had a brother who had led the uprising in Batavia. The fury and futility of the violence exposed the lack of guiding leadership, but also the scale of the anger at the arrests that had precipitated it in the first place. These continued in ever-widening circles. In Sawahlunto alone there were around 3,000 arrests; 1,363 people were tried, and this resulted in three death sentences, including one for Kamaruddin, alias Manggulung, who had led the killing of a local teacher. In addition, perhaps 100 rebels were killed in the affray itself. Very soon, many of the prisoners would join others from Java in exile in the outer islands of the archipelago.[79]

The Dutch government swiftly commissioned a series of post-mortems on the rebellion. It was obsessed by the Moscow connections, and worked ever more closely with the British to trace them to their source. The British were given a list of suspects: Indians of Surabaya who worked for a sugar broker; dubious go-betweens in Canton; batik traders carrying digitalin to poison the governor-general and other key officials using their Javanese servants.[80] On their return from Moscow, Alimin and

Musso were arrested by the British colonial police in Kota Tinggi, Johor, in the south of the Malay Peninsula on 18 December 1926, and then taken to Singapore. They had arrived via Bangkok, travelling on Chinese passports issued in Canton, carrying US$2,500 between them.[81] In the lock-up in Kota Tinggi they were very surprised to be visited by a Dutch policeman, who, with two Indonesian assistants, was operating freely in Singapore. Yet the police cordon had its weak points. Attempts to banish Alimin and Musso to the Netherlands Indies were given a stay of execution. After a split vote, members of the Singapore Executive Council were unconvinced of the case against them committing any crime on the soil of British Malaya: they were, in effect, being extradited for a political offence, and this the Council was unwilling to permit.[82] The Dutch government wanted the matter handled quietly. It considered the PKI and the Sarekat Rakyat to be illegal organizations, but was unwilling to prosecute anyone belonging to them, to avoid the spectacle of a show trial.[83] In the end the British security chief provided the two fugitives with travel documents on the understanding that they would not return, and they left for Canton.[84] The PKI leadership was now deep underground or cast into exile. Tan Malaka was back in Manila, adrift from the PKI and adrift from Moscow.

What was striking about the whole affair was that it did not see social revolution on any large scale in the main centres of PKI activity, in the concentrations of industrial labour in the cities of Semarang and Surabaya. Nor did it capture the heartland which Tan Malaka saw as strategically vital to any successful revolution in the Netherlands East Indies, the Solo valley of central Java. From start to finish, it was the expression of raw anger in seemingly more peripheral pockets of the countryside. As colonial analyses repeatedly pointed out, it was rarely led by the poorest of the poor. The report on the events in West Sumatra, by a committee led by a noted sociologist, Dr Bertram Schrieke, portrayed a backward and isolated society experiencing a crisis of modernity, whereby old village ties were weakened and new types of association had a compensating lure. Communism, in an influential image, was a movement led by the 'socially stranded', and as such easily descended into mere anarchism.[85] Schrieke was not blind to its worldliness – this was another local movement that followed the spread of the railway, packet-liners, posts and telegraphy – but he underestimated the depth of its wild learning and the harshness of colonial economic conditions, as seen in widening income disparities and the high burden of colonial taxation on the poor.[86]

In the euphoria of the fall of the cities of Hunan and Hubei to the armies of the south, a similar investigation was under way. Mao Zedong had returned to his home county of Xiangtan, in Hunan, in 1925. Floods, poor harvests and spiralling food costs brought famine conditions in many areas. That summer peasants attacked granaries and major landlords. But their leaders had been driven underground and Mao had returned to the south, to head the Peasant Leadership Training Institute in Canton. However, some ninety of its graduates headed home to Hunan. Now, in the wake of the military victories, peasant associations sprang up spearheaded by the poor, demanding rent reductions, the lowering of the price of rice and representation in the new local governments that were being set up. A congress in Changsha claimed to represent a million members. There were, for the first time, confiscations of land. The upheavals asked new questions of the form that revolutionary violence might take, and of its necessity. The Communist Party leaders, including Chen Duxiu, called for a stepping-up of work among the peasants. But they were not ready for violence on this scale. In early 1927, Mao travelled in the most affected districts and wrote for the party leadership a 'Report on an Investigation of the Peasant Movement in Hunan':

> In a few months the peasants have accomplished what Dr Sun Yat-sen wanted, but failed, to accomplish in the forty years he devoted to the national revolution. This is a marvellous feat never before achieved, not just in forty, but in thousands of years. It's fine. It is not 'terrible' at all. It is anything but 'terrible'. 'It's terrible!' is obviously a theory for combating the rise of the peasants in the interests of the landlords ... No revolutionary comrade should echo this nonsense. If your revolutionary viewpoint is firmly established and if you have been to the villages and looked around, you will undoubtedly feel thrilled as never before. Countless thousands of the enslaved – the peasants – are striking down the enemies who battened on their flesh. What the peasants are doing is absolutely right, what they are doing is fine![87]

The peasants, Mao reported, had their own sense of revolutionary justice, of 'keeping account', and in this Mao and other Communist Party leaders began increasingly to place their faith. The Vietnamese Ly Thuy was fascinated. He followed the debate closely in his role as a rapporteur for the Comintern, and Vietnamese took courses in the Peasant Leadership Training Institute in Canton, when Mao Zedong served as its director in early 1926 preparing cadres for the work in Hunan and Hubei.[88] In the autumn of 1926 and early 1927, however, it was unclear that revolutionary leaders had managed to speak for the peasantry or to channel their sense of injustice and anger, and most of them still looked to the industrial workers of the towns. Events in Indonesia and in China deepened debates over the applicability of models for revolution that came from Moscow, to which most of them, in this crucial hour, still looked for guidance.

FAITH AND TREASON IN DOOMED CITIES

'Anti-Bolshevism' was now a driving force of western foreign policy. Moscow's relations with Great Britain were at their lowest ebb since the recall of M. N. Roy from Tashkent in 1921. They had been antagonized by the fraudulent 'Zinoviev letter', published in the *Daily Mail*, which seemed evidence of Soviet interference in the British general election of October 1924, and the Comintern's fanning of anti-British agitation during the course of the strike-boycott and northern expedition in China. In Russia, there was a conviction that there was a concerted attempt by the capitalist powers to draw the Soviet Union into a new and terrible war. Comintern strategy, Soviet foreign policy and the struggle for the Kremlin were becoming inexorably entangled.[89] The revolutionary events of 1925 and 1926 demanded that the questions first raised in 1920 be posed with new urgency. Was Asia the key to the 'permanent revolution'? Or, if the most pressing concern was to shore up the Soviet Union, was the paramount goal to inflict the maximum damage on the imperial powers through alliance with nationalists? This was often stated as a stark choice between 'deepening' or 'widening' the revolution, but rarely was it so clear-cut. The positions struck by the Comintern Executive were frequently contradictory. By the time its directives reached Asia they had invariably been overtaken by events or wrongly or wilfully misinterpreted by the men on the spot. The flow of information to Moscow was erratic and often served to conceal the scale of the crisis or advance partisan positions.[90] Asian leaders had their own body of revolutionary theory and precedents and were confronted by the volatile new reality of peasant insurrection. Comintern leaders drew upon a grand vista of comparisons, but events in China began to overshadow all else. In Moscow, the seventh Executive Committee Plenum of the Comintern in November and December 1926 advocated a 'solid revolutionary bloc' in China. By this time Zinoviev had been forced out. Stalin reiterated his faith that the Chinese Communist Party could turn the Kuomintang into a 'genuine people's party', and argued for more emphasis on organizing the peasantry. All this placed Leninist theory under the most extreme pressure and acted as a wedge in the body politic of the Soviet Union itself.[91]

M. N. Roy took on a larger role in the direction of the Asian revolution at a time when his capacity to influence events in India waned. The Kanpur trials of 1924 cast a long shadow. In their aftermath, a Communist Party had been created within India without sanction from Moscow. It was led by a man known by the pseudonym of Satyabhakta, who, it later transpired, had been a suspect in the Kanpur case because of his role in a 'Socialist Book Shop' in Kanpur, which had prompted him to begin a correspondence with one of those convicted of conspiracy, S. A. Dange. While the trial in the city was still under way, he announced in Kanpur the formation of an 'Indian Communist Party'. Satyabhakta argued that the conspiracy case had shown that belief in communism was in itself legal and hoped to evade arrest by declaring his party free from Comintern influence. On the strength of this he organized a conference in Kanpur in October 1925, at the same time as a session of the Indian National Congress. It attracted figures such as M. Singaravelu and Muzaffar Ahmad, who had recently been released from prison on account of his tuberculosis. It was, by all accounts, not much of an affair, held 'in an old tent of miserable dimensions and dimly lit by a few oil lamps'. Many of the 500 attendees came and went with no credentials of any kind and suspected each other of being police spies. When some of them tried to obstruct the Congress meeting by lying prostrate at its entrance, it ended, as the policeman David Petrie gleefully reported, in a 'brawl'.[92] Satyabhakta insisted that the new organization be called the 'Indian Communist Party', to differentiate it from the existing Communist Party of India. But he had no standing with those he had invited and the move was defeated. He left the meeting in high dudgeon. There remained a divide between those, like Muzaffar Ahmad – who saw the Kanpur meeting as 'entirely a childish affair' – who were committed to internationalism, and therefore to underground work, and those who sought a nation-based, open movement within India. The internationalists ultimately managed to dominate the Communist Party of India, but this body had a disputed lineage with the party founded in Tashkent four years previously.[93]

Roy's monopoly of the movement was further challenged by the attempt of the Communist Party of Great Britain to claim control of political work in Britain's colonies. Roy bridled at their arrogant assumption that 'since they have not done anything in India, nothing whatsoever exists there'.[94] Added to this, the formation of the League Against Imperialism in Brussels in February 1927, and Jawaharlal Nehru's role in it, created a new focus for international anti-colonial activism. Roy's old rival in the Indian revolutionaries' Berlin Committee, Chatto, was appointed its secretary.[95] Roy continued to work, by mail and through journals, towards the creation of a workers' and peasants' party, with a 'veiled' underground organization within it, on the Chinese model, or on that of what the Comintern mission in China hoped to accomplish. The ripest opportunity to achieve this seemed to be in Bengal, and it was to this that Muzaffar Ahmad gravitated on his return to Calcutta. But Roy was uneasy that the Communist Party of India would remain 'a small sect without any influence unless it can find a broader organisational apparatus through which it can function'.[96]

The signs were that the underground was fatally weakened. The veteran early recruit to Soviet pan-Islamism, Maulana Barakatullah, in May 1926 surveyed the events of the last few years. He told the Comintern leadership that the drive to lead revolution from outside India had failed. 'The whole thing', he declared, 'falls into the hands of the English agents with the only result that the true Indian revolutionaries are being exposed and put to all sorts of trouble by the police.' It was an 'open secret' that all political parties were compromised by informers and only open, legal work was possible.[97] Large sums of money went missing; some of it, along with membership lists, was intercepted by the police, including false ones drawn up to impress scrutineers in Moscow.[98] Roy's feud with Abani Mukherji continued. After his trip to

India Abani had managed to re-establish himself in Moscow, and even gained an audience with Stalin. Roy warned that rumours continued to circulate about Abani, and that he was still in touch with a known British agent in Paris: 'our illegal condition in India requires a special watch concerning suspicious characters.'[99] Then, in early 1926, some Ghadar veterans came to Moscow and were surprised to see Abani there. They too revived the charges that had been made against him during the war. Roy's own emissary, Nalini Gupta, retained his earlier optimism as to the size of the movement in India and of his centrality to it. He was, he told Roy in January 1927, 'trying to make a conspiracy case soon'. But he was forced to admit that 'all work is now at a standstill . . . How long can one go on with "bogus" and "bluff"? There is not a single fellow who can organise. The objective is only money.'[100]

Roy petitioned Stalin directly to be allowed to return to India, but the 'big boss', he confided to a colleague, 'is very keen on my going East instead of where I want to go'. Stalin had told Roy that it would be possible to further the ends of both revolutions if he were to go to China. For a moment it seemed as if the grand strategy that Roy had tried to set in motion ten years earlier – to raise an army from the Indians in China to march on the borders of the Raj – might yet have its day. Roy looked for agents to approach soldiers and policemen in the employ of the British or the foreign concessions to rally them, and so that he could take some of them with him.[101] After the first meeting of the League Against Imperialism, Barakatullah reminded the Russians that 'there were thousands of Indian ex-soldiers in California, USA, in China, in Malaya and other countries, who could easily become missionaries of revolution.' But the Ghadar revival he had in mind was to be under his own and Jawaharlal Nehru's leadership.[102] In the event, Roy left Moscow in a hurry, on 20 January 1927, and went to China with a party of Comintern grandees headed to Canton for a second Pan-Pacific Congress of Labour. He sent out a flurry of invitations, but the government of India refused to issue visas to Canton, and he travelled without any delegates from India.[103] With him was the veteran British communist Tom Mann, seventy years of age, the American party leader Earl Russell Browder, the French leader Jacques Doriot, and Solomon Lozovsky, who represented the Red International of Trade Unions, or Profintern. They sailed in mid-February from Vladivostok directly to Canton with around thirty returning students from Moscow.[104] Roy was also accompanied by a German party member, Louise Geissler, with whom he had been living in Berlin for some months.

The last years in Europe had been desperately lonely and unhappy for Evelyn Roy. She and Roy had been apart much of the time, she mostly in France. 'I was so weary of being hunted from place to place, from country to country, of having to hide and always to be surrounded by a terrible fog of suspicion and fear, and to have others suspect and fear me. All this had become intolerable.'[105] She left Europe and returned to the US. In August 1925 she reached Chicago, and after a hostile reception from the American communist movement, at the end of the year she was back in California living with her parents. They welcomed her return, but not her politics, and others of her family and friends would have nothing to do with her. She had lost her citizenship, and it was made clear to her that if she took up political activities in the United States she would be deported. It was impossible for her to find employment, until she began to make a modest income as a freelance writer:

> I was restless, unhappy and frightfully disorientated. I belonged neither to my old life or the new one I had left it for – then there was personal heartache . . . I was accused of being a spy, a renegade, a defalcator of funds, of having abandoned my husband and the movement after having bled them dry, etc. etc. Quite naturally, I found myself alone . . . I have become, what Roy predicted when I left Europe, lost to the movement.[106]

When she and Roy parted, his intentions were unclear. She wrote a series of letters offering to return. They were sent through one of the two friends they had in common, Henk Sneevliet, via a cover name, 'Jack Horner'; the other was Borodin, far away in China. In her last months in Europe, Evelyn and Sneevliet had exchanged letters regularly, and Evelyn had become drawn into Sneevliet's own domestic difficulties. He was out of favour with the Comintern but had been joined in the Netherlands by his 'two Simas': his Russian second wife and their daughter. His first wife, Betsy, had also returned from Java with his two boys; she was unable to find work, and in a bad way.[107] Sneevliet was Evelyn's one remaining link to a secret world she had inhabited now for nine years.

After three months in the US, reliving events in her mind, she came to accept that Roy had wanted to be free of her, perhaps as early as 1921. Roy refused to countenance her return to Europe: she was to stay in the United States or go to China. She found it hard to leave her aged mother for a second time:

> Once I have left here I will be condemned to wander about in strange lands and the rest of my life without even the reason I have before to justify such an existence of having been married and held to follow my husband . . .
>
> If I had ever been in India, or could even go there, it might be different, but always it has been pure theoretical abstraction to me. The only living link was my husband. When this link was broken only the abstraction remained, and I was so tired of abstract theories.[108]

She divorced Roy in the autumn of 1926. The last letter to 'dear N' was written on Christmas Day, as she waited to have dinner with the family at home for the first time in ten years:

> I am watching events in the east with great interest and sometimes wish I was there to observe at close hand the developments which reach here only in distorted form. But I am not yet ready to forsake my moorings and to set sail once more on an uncharted sea.[109]

Her final letter was unanswered and rested among Sneevliet's private papers; it seems he was unable to forward it.

Roy's mission to China had been requested by Chiang Kai-shek. After the fall of Wuhan, Chiang's relationship with Borodin deteriorated sharply. With the three cities under military occupation, Chiang unilaterally launched a strike east towards the lower Yangzi, against Sun Chuanfang. He took the Whampoa units of his First Corps to attack Nanchang, the capital of Jiangxi province. Chiang captured the city on 19 September, but was pushed back only days later, and his troops were badly mauled. It took a coordinated offensive planned by Blyukher to tip the balance, and by the time Nanchang finally fell on 8 November, the National Revolutionary Army had lost 15,000 men killed or wounded in Jiangxi alone. Chiang's martial reputation was at a low ebb.[110] However, his position was strengthened by the Eastern Route Army, which included the remaining Whampoa troops, after a general loyal to him, He Yingqin, brought the coastal province of Fujian under Kuomintang control. On 20 December, Chiang ordered an onward advance into Zhejiang.[111] There were now two heads to the revolution: in Wuhan and at Nanchang, where Chiang and Blyukher took up residence in separate wings of the former provincial governor's residence. The air was tense with plots, and the intimacy of their earlier relations was at an end.[112]

By the time Roy and his party reached Canton, most of the Soviet mission had left the city for Wuhan. Borodin travelled ahead, arriving on 10 December, accompanied by Sun Yat-sen's widow, Soong Ching-ling, Eugene Chen and other Kuomintang luminaries. He established a new Borodin House in Hankou in the premises of the Nanyang Tobacco Company. Vera Vladimirovna set out in a second party with Fanya Borodina and her youngest son, Norman, in the first week of December. They travelled through Jiangxi by barge and palanquin, the bearers cursing at the ample frames of the revolution's elite.[113] Zhu Qihua travelled with them. He had formed his own views on grand strategy. The revolution should not go 'hither and thither like a field headquarters and thus be dependent on the moves of the army'. Its base in Canton was not secure and taking Wuhan 'would be at the price of losing Canton'. His opinion went unheard. In the meantime, there were the sleeping arrangements of the women cadres, which 'consumed our minds and had been our main topic of conversation' over seven days of sailing on the North River. He discovered that six out of eleven of his close comrades had brought Zhang Jingsheng's *Sex Histories* with them in their kitbags. They reached Nanchang at the year's end and were received by Chiang Kai-shek at a formal dinner. There he announced that the defeat of imperialism would be accomplished in 1,000 days, 'or you, comrades, may cut off my head'. Zhu Qihua had heard similar speeches at Whampoa, and they had 'become something of a joke. A revolution', he observed solemnly, 'is not fortune-telling.'[114]

With the triumphal entry of the Kuomintang government into Wuhan on 1 January 1927, it was proclaimed the new capital of China. A long procession of troops snaked through the crowded streets of Hanyang and Hankou to the cry of 'Down with British Imperialism'. At a firework display held on the waterfront, a crowd in carnivalesque mood clashed with the Royal Marines guarding the British Concession;

there was a bayonet charge and three Marines had their weapons seized. A leaflet circulated demanding that the barricades and barbed wire come down, and that the foreign warships leave the city. To calm the situation, the Royal Marines withdrew, and disarmed the local expatriate Volunteers. On the evening of 4 January, the crowds broke down the barricades, and, with their own Chinese and Sikh police no longer to be relied upon, the British handed control to the local police under the Kuomintang, who effectively occupied the British Concession. Vera Vladimirovna arrived in the city to find the barricades now guarded by strike pickets, the foreign banks and businesses closed, and the bund and backstreets swollen with crowds. She settled into the small Soviet colony that sprang up in the former Russian Concession. The place was still haunted by White refugees and older residents who traded in the 'brick tea' popular in Russia. She wore the dress of an emancipated Chinese woman, with a high blouse, black skirt and bobbed hair, and worked as host for a growing number of Soviet delegations that came and went as the new regime – now claiming authority over seven provinces and 200 million people – announced itself to the world.[115]

It did so first at the nearest foreign enclave to Hankou, the small British Concession downriver at Jiujiang, a centre for the tea trade and a staging post of missionary activity since 1858. On 7 January it too was overrun by protestors, and the British community of around three dozen males, with women, children and their amahs, fled on to the houseboats they used for summer excursions on the lakes. British sailors shifted the silver and cushions of the consul's house on to a British frigate, HMS *Wyvern*, and the flotilla operated as a 'floating concession' in the Yangzi.[116] This was now a major international crisis, but the fait accompli also gave the Wuhan regime diplomatic leverage as negotiations began between Eugene Chen and the British diplomat Owen O'Malley, which resulted, on 19 February 1927, in the first formal recession of British extraterritoriality in China. In both Hankou and Jiujiang this was achieved, in the eyes of one American missionary, with only 'a few bruises and scratches on each side'. In Hankou, many of the British enterprises were based outside the concession in any case, and they were still protected by the warships at anchor along the bund. But equally, the missionary realized, 'the background of the drama staged that winter afternoon stretched for a thousand miles along the roads and waterways of China'.[117] A cortège passed through the streets of Hankou to mark the death of British imperialism. News of this was received in the western press with growing hysteria, especially as some 450 British women and children fled to ships on the Yangzi, leaving their menfolk holed up in the headquarters of the Asiatic Petroleum Company on the bund. With the Yangzi now at a low level, this was no longer something the British could easily face down with battlecruisers. The stakes rose as the Eastern Route Army approached Hangzhou and came within striking distance of Shanghai.[118]

But then there was the question posed by Chen Duxiu: 'Why should we clamour over it and what kind of agitation should we develop when the aggressors were not the English, but the Chinese?'[119] Chiang Kai-shek had insisted that the capital remain with him at Nanchang and refused to submit to the authority of Wuhan. By basing himself in a quiet 'city of officials' with its conservative ways, Chiang Kai-shek had effectively insulated himself from the popular passions and industrial activism that had been unleashed in Wuhan. Zhu Qihua found Nanchang 'depressing'. On his arrival there, he killed time with Mao Zedong hunting for Tang-dynasty tiles as souvenirs in the city's ruined pavilions. There was not much else to do. He was put to work in the political department headed by Guo Moruo. Reports of its achievements, Zhu realized, had been much exaggerated. There was little urgency to the work; it was as if the revolution had already been accomplished. Zhu and Mao attended an event to mark the second anniversary of the death of Lenin: 'If we were in Canton we would be holding big rallies, but here in Nanchang the commemorative event made hardly a ripple.'[120] A few days after the formal transfer of government, Chiang Kai-shek came reluctantly to Wuhan and was received, pointedly, at a vast rally at the Hankou racetrack. At a banquet that followed it, Borodin gave deep offence to Chiang by making a barbed jibe about 'warlordism' within the ranks of the Kuomintang. This was, he admitted, a mistake.[121] In an effort to ease tensions, it was agreed after the fall of Wuchang to recall Wang Jingwei from exile in Europe. But Chiang also extended his hand towards the financiers of Shanghai.

As the British refugees from Hankou reached Shanghai, China's largest city prepared for a reckoning. After the heady June Days of 1925, the communist organization in the city had lost ground in the face of repression. But in the long summer of 1926 there was a fresh wave of strikes, led by the mill workers and supported by the Communist Youth Leagues. Encouraged by the fall of Wuchang and the first assault on Nanchang, and feeling that Shanghai was soon to capitulate, there was an attempt in the early hours of 24 October 1926 by local nationalist leaders to take over the Chinese-controlled areas of the city. It was swiftly crushed. But in February 1927, a more concerted attempt was made to set up a 'citizens' government', calling for civil liberties and free trade unions. It was inspired, in part, by the Paris Commune, and the lived experience of migrant workers from Shanghai who had returned from France after the world war. It was backed by armed pickets, perhaps 2,000 of them, many of them unemployed workers who had lost their jobs through participating in earlier strike actions.[122]

The National Revolutionary Army's capture of Hangzhou on 18 February was the signal for a general strike involving 420,970 people in nearly 6,000 workplaces. With only the remnants of Sun Chuan-fang's troops defending Shanghai, the people prepared to welcome the armies of Chiang Kai-shek. On 22 February, the communist leadership in the town decided to turn this into an uprising. It was signalled at 6 p.m. by rounds from a rebel gunboat targeting the two city arsenals; one of them, at Jingnan, fell to the pickets, but they were unable to hold it. The commander of the city garrison, Li Baozhang, loyal to Sun Chuanfang, sent out a judge with two swordsmen to mete out summary justice to strikers by beheading. This got under way before the strike, but between 19 and 23 February the General Labour Union claimed there were at least forty executions. The severed heads were put on display, and press images, flashed across the world, shocked Chinese and westerners alike. However, unlike in June 1925, the small business-men and merchants did not rally in support of the strike. This in turn led to reprisal killings of perhaps nineteen of them by so-called 'dog-beating squads'. The struggle for the city had unleashed its violent underworld.[123]

As Chiang's forces edged ever closer to Shanghai's suburbs, on 21 and 22 March there was a third attempt to take control of the Chinese city, this time led by Chen Duxiu and Zhou Enlai, who had returned in the midst of the February revolt. This time police stations were seized, and pickets were firmly established in a number of areas, particularly Zhabei, in support of a devolved city government.[124] This was part of a wider bid to forestall Chiang Kai-shek and to precipitate the creation of a 'left' Kuomintang government.[125] A young Russian émigré described the scene in the International Settlement:

> There was no recognising it: all the houses were beflagged, crowds milled about, undisguised joy shone on all faces, red bands decorated sleeves. Again there were orators, surrounded by throngs of excited people, at street corners. Many men and women were weeping. Now and again a demonstration of several dozen or a hundred people marched past, and the crowd would give way to it. It was strange to see in the midst of it all patrols of foreign volunteers, looking very military with steel helmets pulled low over their brows . . . For the moment it was victory.[126]

Then, as the Kuomintang forces occupied the city, and the notorious Li Baozhang was absorbed into their ranks, came an uneasy hiatus. There were at this point over 22,000 western regular troops guarding the foreign concessions in Shanghai, including two British divisions and forty-two warships anchored in the Huangpu River.[127]

Roy followed these events from Canton. His delegation stayed on the bund, in the Oriental Hotel, where Tom Mann looked in 'wonderment' at the tall buildings, 'the large amount of street traffic and the brilliancy of the electric lights'.[128] But the situation in the city was much changed. The danger of clashes with British gunboats on the Yangzi alarmed the Kuomintang leadership, and fear for their rearguard in Canton propelled the ending of the strike-boycott in October 1926. In the absence of communist leaders in the north, reaction was in the air in the south: there were arrests of pickets; many went underground, and the remaining families of the Soviet advisers started to head home.[129] Lu Xun had arrived in January to take up a post at Sun Yat-sen University. He found that 'everything is at a standstill; nothing has been achieved'. As he told the Whampoa cadets shortly afterwards, even the literature published in Canton was still very traditional:

> . . . which confirms that this society has yet to feel the impact of revolution. With neither paeans for the new nor dirges for the old, Guangdong remains what it was ten years ago. What is more, there is nary a complaint or protest. We do see trade unionists taking part in demonstrations, but they do so with government permission, not because they are opposing oppression. Thus, this is but revolution by imperial decree.[130]

There was indeed no shortage of public rallies. Roy and his party were paraded at meetings of uniformed and armed strike pickets and visited the graves of the Shaki demonstrators. But they were a long way from the front line, and the aeroplane that was to have carried them there broke down.

After sixteen days in Canton, Roy and his party set out by the long overland route. It was their first encounter with peasant China. On the trail they gathered testimonies of trade unionists being arrested and assassinated by forces loyal to Chiang Kai-shek. Both Tom Mann and Earl Browder published vivid accounts of what they saw.[131] Roy entered Changsha on 1 April, to a mass reception, and then Hankou by train on 3 April. On his arrival in the city, Tom Mann counted the ships of war anchored two abreast off the city: there were now ten British, ten American, three French and seven Japanese. Incongruously, in the midst of the revolution, western sailors walked with a swagger in the streets. In Hankou, Roy was reunited with his old friend Borodin, who introduced him to the Chinese leaders as a man 'very much respected by Lenin'. But soon Roy and Borodin were locked in intense disagreement. Borodin argued that the campaign should be broadened by a march on Beijing; Roy countered that this would leave them exposed to the militarists and to Chiang Kai-shek, and that first it should be deepened.

Outside Wuhan, the Kuomintang right was calling openly for a break with the left. A wide body of interests – the Sun Yat-sen Study Society, key military commanders, Shanghai capitalists and the representatives of the western powers – converged in their conviction that tensions with the west must be reduced and the regime re-established on foundations of good order, and not perpetual social struggle. Chiang offered himself as the only man who could achieve this. On 23 March, the northern expedition and the foreign powers had collided at Nanjing. After Nanjing was occupied rioting broke out, and the American president of the university was killed. British and American warships bombarded the city. Chiang blamed the violence on communist units. Few believed him. Chiang quietly entered the French Concession of Shanghai on 26 March, travelling on the *Zhongshan*, and laid his plans. He moved military units with communist loyalties out of Nanjing. In a sense, the ground had been prepared over many years. Not only the Shanghai financiers, but the leaders of its black economy, the

'Green Gang', watched the northern expedition and weighed its implications for Shanghai, and for their own interests. Chiang Kai-shek offered reassurances, to the extent of drawing the gangs into his secret organization. The gang formed themselves into a 'Mutual Advancement Society' and laid their own plans.[132]

In the midst of this, on 1 April, the lost leader of the Kuomintang left, Wang Jingwei, arrived secretly in Shanghai. He had come from Moscow, and complained that on the train journey east the Russians had treated him like a prisoner. Zhou Enlai tried to prevent him from meeting Chiang Kai-shek, but Wang was received soon after his arrival at Sun Yat-sen's mansion in the French Concession. Afterwards, Chiang issued a statement that he would confine his authority to military affairs and that Wang would be in charge of political and Kuomintang party affairs. Wang was affronted by Chiang's presumption in allocating responsibilities in this way. He also signed a joint declaration written by Chen Duxiu that news of their alliance might scotch rumours of a coup or counter-coup from either the left or the right. Wang left quietly for Wuhan to a hero's homecoming.[133]

Despite this outward show of unity, in retrospect all the signs were there of an imminent showdown. In Moscow on 6 April *Pravda* quoted Chiang as affirming that 'Wang Jingwei is my teacher and my friend'. But only the previous day, Stalin had declared that the Kuomintang right could be 'squeezed out like a lemon and then flung away'. The international war scare was at its height and, in Moscow, Stalin was convinced the British were attempting to drag him into a decisive conflict.[134] In Hankou, Roy was planning to travel to Shanghai to meet Chiang, although few thought this was a good idea.[135] In the event, first fire came not in Shanghai, but in Beijing, on 6 April, when forces of the northern warlord, Zhang Zuolin, entered the sacrosanct precincts of the Legation Quarter without a warrant and, significantly, without a protest from the western diplomatic missions. They raided the grounds of the Soviet embassy. Its staff hurriedly began to burn their secret papers, but many documents were captured, water-damaged, to be translated and published in a sensational way to show, if further evidence were needed, the extent of 'secret diplomacy' and Soviet aid. Li Dazhao, one of the first and most eminent scholars in China to embrace Marxism, had taken sanctuary in a house in the embassy grounds, but was now dragged from his desk and arrested, along with his wife and two daughters. A few days later, he was brought before a court and sentenced to death.[136]

In Shanghai, all the rumours were of immanent violence. On the night of 11 April, the leader of the 'Green Gang', Du Yuesheng, invited the leader of the General Labour Union, Wang Shouhua, to dinner in his mansion in the French Concession. Wang placed a man outside the door, to sound the alarm if he failed to reappear in two hours. Wang was never seen again. There was a sound of a bugle and an answering sound of a siren from a gunboat in the Huangpu River. In the hours that followed on 12 April, 1,500 soldiers and gangsters moved against the main picket positions in the workers' districts of Zhabei, Nanshi and Pudong, east of the river. Many issued out of the French Concession, and although the fighting threatened to break through the barriers and barbed wire that protected the foreign concessions, it was concentrated in the Chinese city. The next day, the general strike resumed. The gangs acted as the shock troops for Chiang's capture of the city. They knew exactly where to find the communist leaders. The British and French police had their ties to the underworld and were aware of the crackdown in advance; the French supplied 500 rifles, and the British safe passage.[137]

The squeeze was also put on the city's businessmen in the form of kidnappings and extortion, what the journalist George Sokolsky called 'anti-communist terrorism'.[138] Regular troops fired on crowds in the open; in one incident alone in Baoshan Road, Zhabei, over 100 people were killed. There was a heroic defence of the key communist redoubts, such as the building of the Commercial Press. Li Lisan and other leaders hurriedly arrived from Hankou to salvage the organization and had no choice but to take it underground.[139] The number killed in Shanghai on that day and over the months that followed was 3,000–4,000 communists and 20,000 others, and there were perhaps an equal number of arrests.[140] Roy abandoned all plans to visit Chiang Kai-shek and denounced him as 'an instrument of imperialism, a murderer of workers and peasants, and a traitor to the people'.[141] This cry was taken up in the streets of Wuhan. On 18 April Chiang Kai-shek, now ensconced in Nanjing, established a new national government, drawing Kuomintang officials into his orbit.

The repression was repeated with remorseless savagery in other cities. The local military commander in Canton, Li Jishen, made his move just three days after the showdown in Shanghai, on Good Friday, 15 April. Under a curfew, 2,000–3,000 labour activists were arrested, as well as university students. Around sixty communists were executed at the East Parade ground.[142] The Korean Kim San witnessed the public execution on 18 April of three propaganda workers, one of them a woman, Lu Liu Mei, 'very pretty, with short bobbed hair, thick and glossy black'. They were first paraded through the streets on rickshaws, singing 'The Internationale', before being shot by a squad of soldiers. He would later remember how one of the men stopped to tie his shoelace and thinking, 'he wants to live a few seconds longer.' Many more were killed in secret: Kim estimated a death toll of 200 students at Sun Yat-sen University alone.[143] Then, on 28 April, together with nineteen other arrested Chinese, Li Dazhao was executed in Beijing. His family were released, but only to read in a newspaper the following day that he had been killed by the despised Qing method of strangulation.[144]

These events had their echoes overseas. In the heady days of the uprisings in Shanghai, on 12 March 1927 in Singapore there was a large rally at Happy World Amusement Park to mark the second anniversary of Sun Yat-sen's death. At the previous year's commemoration there had been forty-one arrests, many of them resulting in severe prison terms. The colony's police had continued to raid and close night schools, and so the rally became a general protest against the British government. The crowd began to march on the city centre but was stopped by police outside the Kreta Ayer police station. Scuffles broke out and, as in Nanjing Road on 30 May 1925, the crowd threatened to storm the police station. On the orders of the British officer in charge the police fired into the crowd, killing two people instantly; four others died of their injuries the next day. The incident, and the neutral, absolving inquiry into it, provoked a new wave of protests.[145] The repression in China itself spread to Southeast Asia, as the Kuomintang distributed lists of names of suspected communists to its branch members. Communist organizers sent to Singapore were steadily picked up by the police. Soon a new wave of political exiles from China would reach Singapore.[146]

Zheng Chaolin had been at the heart of the fighting in Shanghai. His revolutionary journey had begun, along with many of his friends, on the packet ship to Marseilles. It now continued on the Yangzi steamer to Hankou. His companions posed as 'fish shop owners', 'fruit sellers', 'tea traders', sleeping with their faces hidden: the surviving leadership of the communist party in Shanghai. Most of them had lost comrades, friends or family, and they were openly at odds over strategy. Chen Duxiu was deeply shaken by what he had witnessed there and by the death of his eldest son, Chen Yannian. Attacked on all sides, he was gripped by 'the ogre of melancholy'.[147] On 27 April, the party's Fifth Congress began in Wuhan with very few delegates from Shanghai, Canton or Beijing. The opening sessions were held in a school in Wuchang, but the real business was done in secret, on the outskirts of Hankou. Chen Duxiu was entirely isolated, and his leadership was mostly ceremonial. Zheng saw that Borodin and Roy and those closest to them 'were the congress's puppeteers'.[148]

But then, as Zhang Guotao described it, Roy 'plunged the various meetings of the CCP in an abyss of extensive theoretical debate'.[149] In a discourse delivered over several days in advance of the Congress that clearly reflected Stalin's thinking, Roy rebuked party leaders: 'The Chinese revolution will either win as an agrarian revolution or it will not win at all.' But he also, following the 'big boss', urged against pursuing a peasant strategy so far as to destroy the united front.[150] Over the next few days in the Congress, as the nuances of these positions were thrashed out, Chen Duxiu emerged as a convenient scapegoat for past mistakes and the present crisis. It mattered little that Chen had, in fact, supported work among the peasants and had tried to balance the need to follow Comintern advice with retaining as much independence for the party as possible.[151] There was a sense that he was an intellectual of an old stamp who had stood apart from the institution-building in Canton and Wuhan and from the rank and file.[152] The more immediate power struggle was between Roy and Borodin; or rather, in the absence of a clear hierarchy of command, it was an open-ended argument. As Cai Hesen wryly observed, 'Borodin has suggested methods but has no principles whereas Roy has set forth the principles but has not brought forth any method.'[153]

That spring of 1927, in the midst of this crisis, Wuhan revealed itself, in Tom Mann's words, as 'the most significant expression of the world's revolutionary movement'.[154] As he enthused to an Australian comrade, 'the actual revolution is in progress here'. The city saw a fantasia of meetings, processions and performance. Mann tallied that he addressed 188 meetings in his time there and attended many more.[155] Red Wuhan also inspired a small 'galaxy' of western observers to make the precarious journey up the Yangzi. These included Anna Louise Strong and Arthur Ransome, who were already famed for their reports on the Russian Revolution, and Vincent Sheean of the *Chicago Tribune*, who had recently secured a major scoop in interviewing Abd el-Krim, the leader of the Rif rebellion. Their reports focused on the personalities and human drama of the revolution. Many of their despatches, such as Ransome's savage piece for the *Manchester Guardian* on the 'Shanghai mind' – a British community who 'seemed to have lived in a comfortable but hermetically sealed and isolated glass case since 1901' – were the first drafts of history.[156]

The visitors were assembled into a salon presided over by Rayna Prohme, an American socialist and journalist. She had come to China with her husband, William Prohme, to edit the *People's Tribune*, established by Eugene Chen in Beijing as the English-language mouthpiece of the regime, to counter the lurid reports of revolutionary excess that swamped the Shanghai press. She was a flamboyant figure, well known in Wuhan for her striking red hair and skilfully managed introductions to the new republican elite. Few of the visitors were committed communists, but most sympathized with a vision of a 'new China' and were hypnotized by the epic drama that was unfolding before them. They saw the regime through the eyes of Anglophone figures such as Eugene Chen and Soong Ching-ling. Chen was born in Trinidad in the British Caribbean and his wife, Aisy, was of mixed French and African descent. He had fallen under Sun Yat-sen's spell while studying as a lawyer in London, and as Sun's English secretary did much to elevate the oratorical impact of his statements to the west. Within the Wuhan regime, he worked through a Chinese interpreter and was, as Vincent Sheean put it, 'probably the best known of all Chinese leaders to the world outside, and one of the least known among the Chinese'.[157]

But, increasingly, it was Soong Ching-ling, who, as Madame Sun Yat-sen, came to embody the regime in the eyes of the world at large, and, to many, within China itself. As she overcame a natural shyness in the public eye, it became clear that she had played a major role in sustaining Sun Yat-sen in his later years. She carefully curated his legacy to become widely seen as the moral conscience of the revolution. In a typical image, Nordahl Grieg, the Norwegian poet and playwright, who travelled to Wuhan as a war correspondent, described her as 'a complete Chinese Madonna'.[158] Grieg and the other writers who frequented the Prohmes' apartment in the Mission Building or the German Beer Garden swiftly published travelogues and memoirs, all of which helped cultivate a cosmopolitan, romantic aura around the struggle.[159] 'It was', as one seasoned journalist noted, 'more like an excited lot of college freshmen than a real revolution complete with blood.' Prohme admitted at the time that they shared 'a lack ... in mental preparation for true understanding of the tremendous things happening about us'.[160]

At the centre of this drama, Borodin stepped out of the revolutionary shadows in which he had lived for so long. He was seen about town, riding in the bullet-proof car left behind by Wu Peifu, or on horseback on the bund, until he fell and broke his arm. In the crucial days of the summer of 1927, he was also bedridden with malaria. His insurrectionary glamour impressed fellow travellers and sceptics alike. After meeting Borodin, Grieg shut himself in his room for a week to write a play about him titled *Barabbas*, a retelling of the New Testament that juxtaposed the pacifist, Jesus Christ, with the violent rebel. Like many admirers, Grieg saw in Borodin a unique depth of vision: 'His tactics are quieter, not aiming at little concessions or an immediate victory. His game is one of centuries.'[161] Rayna Prohme was Borodin's chief propagandist; as she wrote to a friend in the US, he was the only man 'who grasps the significance of forces, personalities, who sees the whole movement here in big historic terms. He has the power of throwing on his searchlight and making things stand out in bold relief, so the irrelevant disappears.'[162] Borodin's mystique had been heightened when, on 28 February, his wife, Fanya, was intercepted on one of the Russian steamers, the *Pamyat Lenina*, which had plied between Vladivostok and Canton, and now sailed the Yangzi to Wuhan. It was boarded off Nanjing, and Fanya, two couriers and the Russian crew were held captive by the northern warlord Zhang Zuolin at Jinan, Shandong. She refused to say who she was, but the raiding party included White Russian mercenaries and she was identified.[163] Those who called on Borodin to offer their condolences were moved by his remarkable stoicism. Other Soviet diplomats bristled at his high status. In a 'letter from Shanghai' of March 1927, later published by Trotsky, some complained that 'the question of Borodin has become one of the main questions in this conflict'. They blamed the reverses since the '20 March Incident' on his policy: 'like every petty bourgeois revolutionist, he is subject to very great vacillations'.[164] He was increasingly attacked as a freelancer, or as 'a Napoleon', and opponents on all sides demanded his recall.[165] M. N. Roy, a secret emissary, kept to the shadows.

The foreign press, wrote Zhu Qihua, 'painted the situation in Wuhan as a reign of confusion and terror. But we in Wuhan saw the situation as a preview of the ideal future of humanity.'[166] Its most visible manifestation was the role of women, of whom Zhu no longer spoke with prurience but with deep respect. Soong Ching-ling created an independent public platform for herself on the issue of women's rights, alongside He Xiangning, who had been a target along with her husband, Liao Zhongkai, when he was assassinated in Canton in August 1924.[167] They advocated the abolition of bondage in the home, rights of inheritance, a right to divorce and to free choice in marriage. The two women were prominent within the Kuomintang left, but communist women's leaders pushed further with a political programme centred on women's education and the training of party workers. The Hankou women's union became a powerful body in the city and gave protection to fleeing wives, domestic slaves and prostitutes. It granted divorces on its own authority. The everyday spectacle of women in uniform, carrying arms and, more generally, wearing new dress and adopting new roles and postures lay at the forefront of the movement. Its effects were visible not only in official edicts commanding the unbinding of feet, but also in individual women choosing to leave home, to walk dirty streets in simple straw sandals and to cut their hair. This was a key symbol of the 'ideal future of humanity'.[168] As one male missionary observer put it: 'Without exception they had bobbed their hair, an act which branded them unalterably as revolutionaries'. It was, he acknowledged, 'not to be done except by people of courage and resolution'.[169] The movement had already been taken into the countryside in Guangdong, and now was a central feature of the military campaigns in Hunan and Hubei. It struck at the roots of traditional patriarchy, the culture and codes and notions of kin, that were the local foundations of the old order. The Qing state and its successors had hitherto failed or hesitated to penetrate it. The decision to take the revolution into the heart of the household, especially on the question of divorce, and the heightened contrasts between the status and deportment of urban activists and peasant women, proved incendiary. There were reports of forcible hair-cutting, and, on one occasion, a delegation of men from a nearby village descended on Hankou in protest: 'If we wanted our women's hair cut we can do it ourselves.'[170]

Images of wildness and abandon travelled in bizarre ways. International Women's Day had already been marked with parades in Canton. In 1926, Vera Vladimirovna had appeared to great applause in Chinese dress, in a cameo illustrating China reaching out to the Soviet Union. Theatre and dance were major ways in which the message of women's emancipation was taken to the masses.[171] On 8 March 1927, International Women's Day was celebrated in Hankou by some 25,000 women. But then a variety of reports described an incident whereby between eight and eighteen women appeared bare-breasted or clad in the flimsiest of materials. In some accounts, it was said that they were women who had been denied admission to the branch of Whampoa Military Academy in Wuchang. These protests were valid enough: many of the women who were accepted were of good family and some education. Those who had neither felt excluded. In other versions of the tale, they were prostitutes hired by reactionaries to appear topless to discredit the cause. Leading literary figures in Shanghai, including Lu Xun's brother, Zhou Zuoren, waded into the debate to declare the stories 'nonsense', but this only served to highlight the passions they had unleashed.[172] In advance of the May Day parade of 1927 there were press rumours of a 'Naked Women's Parade'. In the event, most visible at the rally were the blue cotton blouses and trousers of the women factory workers and the stumbling of women who had unbound their feet.

In the midst of this, the adopted daughter of the famous Isadora Duncan, Irma, appeared in Hankou with her 'Duncan Dancers' to give a demonstration of avant-garde style. This was reported eagerly as 'barefoot dancing'. Irma Duncan arrived after a long tour through the Soviet Union, where she had met Borodin. She travelled to Hankou at the request of the Soviet embassy to soothe tensions, as she described it, and was welcomed at the dockside by Fanya Borodin and Soong Ching-ling in person. She agreed to perform in a Chinese venue, the World of Bloody Flower Theatre.[173] The women military cadets were in the audience. Xie Bingying described the scene:

Under pale green light a group of strong, energetic, and youthful women, all draped in blood-red silk, sang, 'How we have suffered the pains of slavery and labour!' Their lively synchronized steps and their strong singing roused the passion of all who watched them, and the audience joined in and loudly sang, 'The blazing stove completely dried our blood and sweat . . .'.[174]

The Wuhan Spring reached its apogee with the Pan Pacific Labour Conference, which was finally held on 19 May. Alimin attended for Indonesia on his own peregrination across Asia, in exile. There were delegates from most parts of Asia. Yet there were also crucial absences, notably from India. But it was an inceasingly rare open demonstration of pan-Asian solidarity. The meeting also laid the foundations of the beginning of a new underground with the networks of seafarers across the great ocean.[175]

There was still hope that the revolution would triumph by force of arms. In late April a new northern expedition was launched towards Henan, in an attempt to break out of Wuhan, principally along the Hankou–Beijing railway, and link up with Feng Yuxiang. Feng had returned from Moscow supplied with 31,500 rifles, 51 million small arms rounds, 272 machine guns, sixty artillery pieces and ten planes. He also travelled with cadres from Sun Yat-sen University, among whom was Deng Xiaoping, returning to China after nearly a decade in France and Russia. The campaign in May resulted in Wuhan gaining Henan, but with heavy losses and without the decisive breakthrough to Beijing. Feng, quite literally, stood at a crossroads. He had a foothold on the Hankou–Beijing railway and also access to the Longhai line that ran west to east to the coast and connected to Shanghai and Nanjing. He had a fateful choice of allies to make.[176]

In the midst of the fighting, in Henan the peasant programme was prosecuted with particular intensity. Xie Bingying and the other newly graduated women cadets from Wuchang participated in the summary trials and executions of 'bad gentry and local bullies'. Here, too, resistance surfaced, some of it led by the local men of violence, the Red Spears, especially against the policies aimed at women. Zhu Qihua travelled in the Henan expedition in the propaganda department and experienced at first hand the difficulty of gaining information and trust from villagers:

If you asked the head of a household for the number of people in his family, he would suspect you of trying to collect the head tax; if you asked him how much land he owned, he would suspect you of trying to collect the land tax; if you asked how many men and women were in his family, he would think you were planning communal marriage.[177]

But, even in the case of the Red Spears, Zhu believed, 'we could lead them on to a shining path, if only we could stay on in Henan.'[178] He got as far as Kaifeng but then, to his bafflement, the expedition came to a halt and he was recalled. Zhu was led to question what it had all achieved. Back in Hankou the opulence of his office in the Nan-yang Tobacco Company shocked him: walking through its garden 'we felt we were being wafted into some retreat in southern Europe; never would we have imagined this grandeur in the barren land of Henan.'[179]

The campaign had left Wuhan undefended. On Zhu's return in late May the city was in mourning at the so-called 'Horse Day Massacre': on 21 May a local Kuomintang commander had turned on the peasant associations in Changsha, slaughtering their members. Women were marked out as targets. Even generals on the Kuomintang left could not be relied upon. The regime, in so far as it had ever existed as a united revolutionary force, was disaggregating. Due to the western blockade of the Yangzi, trade was at a standstill; in Wuhan there were bankruptcies, and by June Borodin estimated that there were 170,000–200,000 unemployed workers in the city. The value of its banknotes was all but wiped out; government expenditure exceeded income by a multiple of fifteen. Chiang established his rival regime in Nanjing and drew Kuomintang leaders into its service. The Wuhan revolution failed to consolidate itself as a state. No soviet was declared, nor a commune. There was no nationalization of industry, and for western and local capital it was, more or less, business as usual. The fragile alliance with the Kuomintang and the presence of western gunboats on the Yangzi would not permit otherwise.[180]

In a sense, the capture of Wuhan had always been seen by communists as a 'partial revolution', a stepping stone to a 'proletarian hegemony'.[181] But many were shocked by the lack of progress. Zheng Chaolin, after fleeing Shanghai and the April Massacre, was put to work in the party organization in Hubei. He was appalled by the party's 'complete lack of any base in the Hankou workers'. The business of revolution was driven by informal meetings of activists; this had worked well in the days of the Shanghai Commune, but in Wuhan there were few mechanisms to put its resolutions into effect. And now the party was preparing to go underground once more.[182] What many critics of the northern campaign had feared had actually come to pass: the revolution had abandoned a relatively secure coastal base for one in landlocked isolation and with few stable foundations on which to build an enduring regime. 'A mere two months,' reflected Zhu Qihua, 'but all brightness, all hope was fading.'[183]

At Wuhan the fate of the Asian revolution, the future of the world revolution, seemed to hang in the balance. In Moscow the fall of Shanghai had been greeted with euphoria and celebrations by the Chinese students. Then, as the news of 12 April reached them, they were thrown into turmoil. The seventeen-year-old son of Chiang Kai-shek, Chiang Ching-kuo, made a statement: 'Chiang Kai-shek was my father and my revolutionary friend. He has now become my enemy. A few days ago, he died as a revolutionary and arose as a counter-revolutionary.' Over the next few months, 239 Nationalist students left the university. Chiang Ching-kuo remained; some saw him as a hostage of the Soviet regime.[184] In May, as the power struggle in Moscow reached a new intensity, the Comintern gave orders for land seizures and called for new leadership for the Kuomintang. It was not clear how this was to be achieved and on what scale. Then, on 1 June, new instructions came from Stalin to Borodin and to Roy in the form of a telegram.

This message was subject to disputes over its translation, its interpretation and, in the absence of its publication at that time, speculation about its contents by those who had not read it. As a checklist of action it had an unreal quality: it was in effect an order for a full-scale counterattack on Chiang Kai-shek. Crucially, it contained an order to try reactionary generals: the word used, at least in the Chinese rendering, was to 'liquidate' them.[185] The central committee of the party agreed that it was impossible to carry out these instructions; the cooperation with Kuomintang allies within the Wuhan regime was too fragile to allow it. At this point, it might have been quietly bypassed. But then Roy invited Wang Jingwei to his apartment and showed him the telegram. The next day he gave Wang a copy to translate, subject to a few adjustments. According to one account from within Wang's inner circle, when Wang showed it to Eugene Chen and other colleagues they were aghast at its implications. In Chen's words: 'this means war between the Kuomintang and the Communist Party'. To them it seemed a fundamental breach of the agreement made by Joffe and Sun Yat-sen in Shanghai in 1922.[186]

At the time and afterwards, Roy's indiscretion surpassed all understanding. Perhaps he was expecting to galvanize Wang Jingwei into taking a more radical position: that the Kuomintang left was so dependent on the united front it would have to follow Stalin's lead. Maybe he believed that the counter-revolution was already so far under way that there was little option but to hand over an ultimatum. Or did he assume, as Zhang Guotao later reflected, that 'by his lone action he could prove the correctness of his views and the incorrectness of the views of Borodin and others'.[187] Roy later argued that he had no choice. He claimed that what was in the telegram had already been told to Wang Jingwei as he passed through Moscow on his return journey, and that some gesture of good faith was needed.[188] Shortly afterwards, Zhu Qihua attended a military parade only to hear Wang Jingwei denounce the 'conspiracy' from the rostrum. In a moment of stunned silence, Wang told the assembled troops that Roy had shown him a telegram in Russian and revealed its contents. Now, he said, Roy had disappeared: 'Who knows, he may already be dead.' The cadets cursed under their breath; some were in tears. It was, they believed, 'the beginning of the end'.[189]

Borodin wrote immediately to Moscow to demand Roy's recall. Roy remained in Hankou and continued to attend meetings, but he had no allies, and those who looked to Moscow for a lead tended to place their faith in Borodin's ability to salvage the situation.[190] All eyes were on Feng Yuxiang. He had been welcomed as a new Kemal Atatürk in Moscow and showered with arms. On 4 June, Wang Jingwei and a delegation from Wuhan travelled to meet him at Zhengzhou in Henan. Borodin, still stricken with malaria, stayed behind. The alliance was made, but in private it was agreed that its price was a break with the communists. Feng now joined the chorus for Borodin's expulsion from China. This was met by Borodin with disbelief: 'he is still with us. I am sure – he stays with Hankou.' Then news was brought to Borodin by a Swedish journalist of Feng's meeting with Chiang Kai-shek on 20 and 21 June. Feng had sided with forces of

THE LONG MARCH OF THE UNDERGROUND

order, and the promise of financial support that a depleted Wuhan regime could no longer offer.[191] All that remained to Borodin was the negotiation of safe conduct out of China for the Soviet advisers and their families, and the release of his wife, who was on trial in Beijing for her life. Stalin received the news phlegmatically. 'It's not worth arguing with Wuhan over Borodin (if Wuhan wants to remove him),' he told Bukharin. But such was the scale of the Soviet investment in China – its largest in any overseas undertaking – that Stalin continued to argue 'it is worth giving Wuhan an extra 3–5 million – but only with some assurance that Wuhan will not surrender to the tender mercies of Nanjing, with our money wasted for nothing.'[192]

In mid-July Borodin withdrew to the missionary rest station of Guling. In his absence, further repression was unleashed. With him were Li Lisan and Qu Qiubai, who seemed to be Moscow's anointed heir to the leadership of the Chinese Communist Party. The journalists Anna Louise Strong and Rayna Prohme travelled with Borodin. One evening, Prohme wrote to a friend, they drank 'two bottles of champagne, two of medoc and one of white wine – to the whispered, standard stock tales of a love affair, with hints at pregnancy, etc., etc., etc.'. In Guling, Borodin conceded that the situation was hopeless.[193] After a brief return to Wuhan, on 27 July he was seen off at Hankou station with full honours and a letter of commendation from Wang Jingwei to the Soviet leadership. Many of the journalists left with him. With a price on his head, he avoided Shanghai and travelled as far as Shensi, and his party made the long journey across the Gobi in the motor cars they had taken with them by train. Roy, Louise Geissler and a smaller party travelled separately by car via a northwest route to Ningxia and then to Ulan Bator. At the eleventh hour, Fanya Borodin was released by a Beijing judge. In fury, Zheng Chaolin launched a search for her across the city. She was hidden by an old resident, a reclusive Russian scholar of languages, and then escaped by sea to Japan and to Vladivostok. The judge too fled to Japan.[194] The other Russians were left to run the gauntlet along the Yangzi on British steamers, where they behaved as if they were strangers to one another. At one point, Vera Vladimirovna passed herself off as a cabaret girl. But then, in Shanghai, on a chance encounter at a cinema, she and her husband were recognized by Chiang Kai-shek himself. He chose to turn a blind eye.[195]

NO HARVEST BUT A THORN

In the chaos of the encircling repression in China, the communist leaders still looked to what Li Lisan termed 'a great display of power' and to establish a new revolutionary centre. Plans were laid for a 'southern expedition' to recapture Canton, either by crossing to Changsha and retracing the route of the northern expedition to the Guangdong railway, or by heading directly for the coast and the East River area. There, Haifeng, the home district of the former head of the Peasant Leadership Training Institute, Peng Pai, was the last remaining 'little Moscow', where there were armed peasants' associations. While Peng Pai was away serving the revolution in Wuhan his brother had seized power locally, executing officials loyal to the Kuomintang. This uprising was some way from the main front and was easily crushed. But the movement retreated to the villages, where, Peng Pai argued, the remnants of the communist forces on the Yangzi would find a warm welcome.[196]

On 27 July 1927 a Front Committee was created to lead the breakout from Wuhan, headed by Zhou Enlai. The forces potentially at its disposal were concentrated in and around Nanchang: units of the Second Front Army under the command of party members, or close sympathizers, and their political commissars, who had good reason to believe that they too would be the target of a violent purge. Among the most important of these were He Long, who had served under the front-line general Zhang Fakui in the northern expedition, and Zhu De, an associate of Zhou Enlai's from his days in Germany. This hastily organized coalition amounted to 20,000–30,000 men. There was hope that some of the larger forces of Zhang Fakui would join the uprising. The date for an uprising was set for 1 August. At the last minute, the party central committee, still in Hankou, urged caution. This was prompted by the arrival of a successor to Borodin, the thirty-year-old Beso Lominadze, a man with no experience of China, but who, as a fellow Georgian, was known to be close to Stalin. Zhang Guotao was sent to deliver this message, but the leaders gathering in Nanchang argued that the purge was already extending to the National Revolutionary Army: 'the arrow was already on the bowstring and must be shot.'[197] In the early hours of 1 August, rebel troops, identified by their red scarves, moved to key positions in the city, seized 'counter-revolutionaries', and disarmed hostile units. The Front Committee included some of the party's most experienced organizers, such as Zhang Guotao, Li Lisan, Peng Pai and also, as head of the propaganda work, Guo Moruo. Zhu Qihua was back in Nanchang and working under him. Such was the reluctance to entirely abandon the Moscow line that the revolt was launched under the banner of the Kuomintang, or rather in the name of the 'Continuation of the Orthodox Kuomintang'. Although political slogans in the city spoke of land redistribution, this was a military putsch, and not a social revolution. 'Hardly anyone was on the streets,' noted Zhu Qihua morosely. 'Rather than having gone through a revolutionary coup, Nanchang looked as if it had suffered a bandit rampage.'[198] News of the plan was leaked by a junior officer in advance, and forces loyal to Wuhan or Nanjing were quick to mobilize to meet it, including those of Zhang Fakui, and the rebels were unable to hold on to the city. By 5 August, the 'Front Committee' left Nanchang with some 20,000 troops.[199]

They became 'men in the wilds', out of contact with Hankou and beyond the reach of newspapers. Travelling by mountain roads, with few horses and waggons, the soldiers were each burdened with 250–300 rounds of ammunition. Rumours travelled ahead of them that they would seize wives and communal property, and so no peasants came forward to act as porters. It was impossible for them to buy food or drink; the paper money they had taken from Nanchang, some $700,000, was useless. After three days, perhaps a third of the men had deserted or fallen ill at the wayside, many from drinking ditch water. Although there was no fighting, mortars and some 30,000 rounds of ammunition were lost. After taking the town of Ruijin in Jiangxi, they tarried for a week, learning from the Shanghai newspapers of the widening repression of the left. Harried increasingly by Kuomintang and allied warlord forces, only half the original force crossed into Fujian, reaching the city of Changting on 3 September. In Ruijin and Changting, the 'Front Committee' tried to establish 'worker and peasant political authorities' and wrestled with issues of land redistribution and the treatment of landlords and merchants. But no consistent policy emerged as to what threshold of land was to be redistributed, and the forces fell back on the practice of demanding cash contributions from landlords and merchants.[200] No peasant uprisings accompanied the long march.

Encouraged by the last of the senior Russian instructors at Whampoa, Michael Kumanin, the leaders decided not to take the mountain route to Guangdong, but to aim for the coast.[201]

A wave of fear and panic travelled ahead of the small army as it moved down the Han River. Stories of its confiscations of food and money were carried by traders and missionaries fleeing ahead of the army as it approached the treaty port of Shantou, the largest on the southern China coast after Hong Kong. Merchants fled with their moveable wealth and there were bomb attacks in the city, and executions of trade union leaders in response. In part due to the factionalism in the Kuomintang forces in the area, the communists managed to occupy the city largely unopposed on 20 September. It was for Zhou Enlai a second coming: he had been the city's civil governor when it first fell to the nationalist forces in December 1925. There were one French, two US, three British and three Japanese warships moored off the city, and Japanese sailors landed to protect their commercial interests and consulate. A Shantou Commune was declared, and in the assumption that all was lost at Hankou a 'revolutionary committee' established itself in the Industrial Normal School, with a declared programme of land redistribution. Zhao Enlai became head of the city government, and Guo Moruo was rather grandly styled its 'commissar of foreign affairs'. They waited on the hope of being supplied with Soviet arms by sea. The commune established control over looters by summary executions and began to raise money from the remaining merchants. But the burden of this fell unevenly, and there were few local allies to carry out a full-scale insurrection. One seaman was heard to say, in a widely reported remark: 'These are the troops of a third Chiang Kai-shek.' The commune still acted in the name of the 'Orthodox Kuomintang', so as not to alarm the western powers. On 28 September there was an assault from Kuomintang marines from a gunboat, and the fracas on the waterfront, with Japanese troops caught in the crossfire, created an explosive situation.[202] With the city effectively under blockade, the rebels were caught 'like fish in a kettle'.[203] In truth, they were no longer a powerful fighting force. 'If the imperialists had called our bluff', Zhu observed, 'we would have been quite helpless.' There was a week of respite for the exhausted men and women. But the townspeople, Zhu noted, 'kept their distance, casting icy glances our way, with not a whit of empathy'.[204]

On 30 September, the commune was attacked by land and, in the largest pitched battle of the campaign, which raged for two days and nights at the town of Tangkeng, 2,000 of the remaining communist forces were killed or wounded. In the midst of this, Zhang Tailei arrived with word from the party central committee, now in hiding in Shanghai, to say that the united front had reached a final break and to order the rump of the troops into rural Guangdong. As one of them observed, 'the only thing was to flee and become bandits.'[205] The senior leaders tried to break through to Haifeng, but they were separated under heavy fire on 6 October. Many took ship to Shanghai, or, in the case of Zhou Enlai and other leaders, to Hong Kong. The five Russians travelling with them were unable to enter the British colony and travelled to Xiamen, where they were arrested. The leaders received severe censure for their part in the uprising: 'a purely military adventure without calling upon the broad peasant [masses] to arise was bound to fail.'[206]

In the final major party meeting in Wuhan on 7 August Chen Duxiu was removed as party leader *in absentia*, and a new group around the Moscow-trained Qu Qiubai put into effect a plan for the Nanchang uprising to be supported by peasant revolts during the coming autumn harvest in Hunan, Hubei and Guangdong. Mao Zedong was at the meeting. To Mao there was a need to recognize a deep historical shift. For this new era, Mao reversed the famous virtues as inscribed by Confucius:

> . . . a revolution is not a dinner party, or writing an essay, or painting a picture, or doing embroidery; it cannot be so refined, so leisurely and gentle, so temperate, kind, courteous, restrained and magnanimous. A revolution is an insurrection, an act of violence by which one class overthrows another. A rural revolution is a revolution by which the peasantry overthrows the power of the feudal landlord class. Without using the greatest force, the peasants cannot possibly overthrow the deep-rooted authority of the landlords which has lasted for thousands of years.[207]

But projected numbers of peasants in arms for the uprisings were inflated at every level: by the provincial leadership to the central committee in Wuhan, and by the central committee to Moscow. Although a land programme was part of the rallying cry, the principal objective of the uprising was to 'surround' and recapture the cities. Mao saw his home province of Hunan and home city of Changsha as the epicentre of the Chinese revolution, and that 'the seizure of Changsha and the land revolution are one and the same thing.'[208] There were few successes, and the uprisings fizzled out by mid-September. Mao narrowly evaded execution by a local militia in Hunan. His response, perhaps his intention all along, was to take what was left of the uprising away from the cities and deeper into the mountainous country on the Jiangxi border.[209]

The final rural redoubt was in east Guangdong, in Haifeng, and its neighbouring county, Lufeng, known as 'Hailufeng'. Peng Pai returned to the region, after lying low in Hong Kong, by 11 November, and was joined by 1,400 stragglers from Nanchang. The presence of a small army allowed Peng Pai to go further than anyone had before. Under the slogans 'All land to the peasants' and 'All land deeds to the fire', a soviet was declared. On 18 November some 311 delegates, about 60 per cent of them peasants, 30 per cent workers and 10 per cent soldiers, gathered in the 'Red Square' of Haifeng town, which was decorated with portraits of Marx and Lenin. Peng Pai declared: 'Our aim is not for success in Haifeng alone, but throughout Guangdong, all over China, in the whole world!' This was followed by the singing of 'The Internationale' and firecrackers. According to the account of one Italian missionary priest, when the army arrived with prisoners Peng Pai seized a long knife and took the first head. Under his leadership the commune began to channel peasant anger, peasant justice, into the service of 'Mr Su', as the soviet was known locally.[210]

Spurred by the example of the Hailufeng soviet, plans were laid in secret for an uprising in Canton. It was a product of rage at the repression and encouraged by the central leadership in Shanghai and the return to the city from Shanghai of Borodin's key collaborator, Zhang Tailei. The city was under the control of Zhang Fakui. He had remained loyal to Wang Jingwei and had led the counter-attack against the Nanchang uprising. In October and November, Wang Jingwei himself returned to Canton and ordered the closing of the remnants of the strike organization. Then Zhang Fakui was ousted by the previous ruler of the city, Li Jishen, who had been cultivating a position as a regional strongman as well as independent ties to the British in Hong Kong.[211] This power struggle was an opportunity. In December 1927, the bulk of Zhang Fakui's 'Ironsides' were some way outside the city, and the communist leadership manged to enlist the support of men from the Fourth Army's cadet regiment. This gave them the means to launch an uprising on the night of 11 December. The next day, a soviet of workers and peasants was declared. It rallied support from the workers of the waterfront who had led the 1925 strike-boycott, and, wearing red sashes, they constituted its 'Red Guards'. Very swiftly, public buildings were seized, some 2,000 police and other officials arrested, and the city was brought under Soviet control. Tungshan was evacuated of Europeans, and HMS *Moorhen* carried western refugees to Hong Kong. However, although remaining residents of Shameen island retreated in panic behind their sandbags and barbed wire, even the Hong Kong press was forced to admit that westerners were left unharmed. In the uprising between 200 and 300 people died, and this was reported in Hong Kong and worldwide as a ruthless slaughter. Kim San was among the 220 Koreans in the city who threw themselves into the revolt. He attended an emotional meeting on the site where the students had been executed in April. Yet, despite the anger, he was struck by the reluctance of the communards to execute the enemies of the revolution.[212]

A multivalent struggle for control of the Chinese revolution began. The city was surrounded by the hostile forces of both Zhang Fakui and Li Jishen, who bided their time. The Soviet leaders waited for the countryside to come to its aid, and for the Kuomintang soldiers to switch sides. But their plans for how this might be achieved seemed to have little substance, and their numbers were pitifully small. It was as if, as in Java, they believed that the act of revolution itself would provoke a show of strength and optimism, that it would triumph against all odds. But the position of the communists in the city was already weakened by the exodus of leadership for the northern expedition. Many of the strikers who had enlisted as porters for its armies died or were abandoned by the wayside. Following the oppression in the spring, more strike pickets had drifted back to Hong Kong or faded into the countryside after the dormitories were closed in November. The anti-communist unions that had been such a feature of the labour struggles before 1925 were again in the ascendency. Kim noted the 'generosity and discipline' of the communards; but also the unwillingness of the students to put themselves directly in the line of fire. The students and workers seemed to have drifted apart. As Zhang Tailei wrote to the central leadership on 8 December, he hoped to hold on for two weeks: 'Our leadership ability is weak; I hope elder brother Enlai can join us right away.' But Zhou Enlai was defeated in Shantou, and Zhang himself was killed leaving the meeting that declared the soviet. Too soon, as Kim put it, 'a sense of failure crept up like a low-lying fog'.[213]

The following day, 13 December, the encircling forces moved in, unleashing 'white terror' with a savagery that appalled even hostile western observers: as many as 6,000 communards were killed. In the midst of this, the Russian consulate put up its shutters and its skeleton Russian and Chinese staff defended it with revolvers until they were forced to open its gates; a number were arrested, bound and paraded through the streets, with signs around their necks inviting mob violence towards them. Around seventeen of them, including the vice-consul, were later shot; only four bodies were recovered. The Russian survivors were eventually deported, destitute and humiliated, via Hong Kong; the consulate was sacked, and the Soviet mission was at an end.[214] Those left behind faced far worse. They had no clear plan for retreat. When the assault on the bund began there was a last-ditch defence from the upper floors of the high-rise buildings.[215] A Hong Kong businessman described to the *China Mail* 'wild-eyed women' leading the crowds, under the headline 'girl fanatics run amok'. Later, women with bobbed hair were summarily executed as Bolsheviks.[216]

Canton's 'Red weekend' lasted only sixty hours. On 13 December, along with many others, including fifteen fellow Koreans, Kim San left Canton. They made a slow journey cross-country to Hailufeng, reaching relative safety by 7 January 1928. As a useful outsider, Kim San was appointed to a revolutionary court. He was taken aside by Peng Pai:

> We must kill more, not less, in case of question . . . The peasants are a hundred times less cruel than the landlords, and they have killed very, very few in comparison. The peasants know what is necessary for self-defence, and if they do not destroy their class enemies they will lose morale and have doubt in the success of the revolution. This is their duty and yours.[217]

Kim San oversaw the sentencing but asked to be relieved. The party killed with guns, but the peasant killings were brutal. They would cut off the ears and gouge out the eyes of cruel landlords. Kim saw the roots of peasant anger and reasoned over its sense of proportion. The landlords had tortured men in the same fashion. 'The people want to kill only three', he was told. 'If these three had power, they would kill 3,000.' He remembered the three young students he had seen executed in Canton in April. He slept in a Catholic church and read the New Testament, and drew on his reading of Tolstoy of his anarchist days: 'Where was there light to illuminate these dark things?' The violence stayed with him. 'Yet', he later reflected, from another war:

> . . . a man fighting in civil war must formulate his personal philosophy to make such things endurable. I could suffer such a fate more easily than to have to do the same to others, but I do not oppose this. I know that the question is only who is being killed. The ruling class began this killing; they have carried it on for generations. We only fight with their own weapons.[218]

Hailufeng did not have the military resources to withstand the onslaught of stronger, better-supplied Kuomintang forces. In early February 1928 an attempt by the soviet to take Shantou failed, and ended in summary executions.[219] On 29 February, thousands died in an attack on a mass meeting. By March most of the rebel towns of the region had fallen, villages were torched, and food stores destroyed. In early May a final attempt to recapture Haifeng town failed, and the communist troops – only 300 of the 2,000 who had come from Canton remaining – and the leaders, including Peng Pai, dispersed.

After the repression of the spring and summer of 1927, Chiang Kai-shek resigned his command, but this was a tactical retirement and he was recalled by the new year. A new phase of the northern expedition was launched that finally took Beijing on 8 June 1928. But, to signal the break with the past, the new capital was established on 10 October 1928 at Nanjing, where Sun Yat-sen's remains were permanently interred. Chiang abandoned his second wife, Chen Jieru, and made an alliance with the family of the financier Charlie Soong by marrying Soong Ching-ling's younger sister, Soong Mei-ling. This arranged marriage of capital and military power was something more than symbolic. It sealed a series of realignments. Throughout the northern expedition, and now on his recall, Chiang had proved adept at drawing on his financial networks; these weathered his military setbacks and were crucial to his eventual ascendency.[220] Relations with the western powers stabilized. The regime remained revolutionary in its rhetoric; the Kuomintang 'left' were never wholly excised. But party theoreticians sought to uncouple the 'national' from the 'social' revolution, to give intellectual grounding to the necessity for the communists to be liquated because their class struggle challenged the ideal of national unity across classes.[221] Yet China was not fully united in territorial terms, and regional cliques still wielded great power. The campaign in the north brought Chiang's armies into confrontation with Japanese troops in Manchuria. A new phase of the struggle for Asia was just beginning.

The first, great Asian revolution had ended as it began, in a wave of exile. The Vietnamese Ly Thuy appeared to have disappeared from Canton in April 1927, as soon as the arrests and executions began. His wife did not know where he had gone. By June he was back in Moscow and had reassumed his previous identity, Nguyen Ai Quoc. He was one of the first to report first-hand on conditions in China.[222] Over the coming months, many of the Asian communist leaders arrived in Moscow: Alimin, Musso, Li Lisan, Qu Qiubai, Cai Hesen, Zhou Enlai. For the Chinese Communist Party Moscow was the only safe place to hold a meeting, and there, in July 1928, the party's Sixth Congress would continue the long post-mortem on the events since the First Party Congress in Shanghai in 1921. Borodin and Roy returned to an uncertain reckoning. There were other fellow travellers from Wuhan, many of the western journalists, and Eugene Chen and Soong Ching-ling, whose own abrupt departure, and denunciation of the capitulation to militarism, marked the symbolic end of the Wuhan dream. The Borodin circle held a last, brief reunion at the new Moscow Crematorium in late November for the funeral of Rayna Prohme, who died suddenly in Moscow of encephalitis. There was a red flag draped over the coffin, and speeches in Chinese, Russian and English. Borodin himself stayed away. 'On principle,' he told Vincent Sheean the next day, 'he never went to funerals.' In the face of loss, 'there is no use in anything unless we take the long view. Remember that.'[223]

Others experienced a different kind of exile in the deep underground of Asia itself. Many, by a variety of routes, ended up in Shanghai.[224] After the fall of Hailufeng, Kim San managed to escape on a small boat to Hong Kong, and from there relied on the kindness of strangers and the network of Korean ginseng traders to make his way to Shanghai. After the rout at Shantou, Guo Moruo fled to Japan and resurfaced, quietly, in Shanghai, ill with typhus, and embarked on a translation of *Faust*. Supplied with foreign banknotes, Zhu Qihua was able to acquire some peasant clothes and make for Hong Kong, with enough cash to be measured up for a new civilian suit at the Wing On store. By the end of the year, he too was 'a drifter in the Shanghai concession'.[225] Deng Xiaoping, who made his way to the city after the collapse at Wuhan, lived as a wealthy trader to deflect suspicion.[226] Others existed in conditions of the most appalling poverty. For Xie Bingying the road to Shanghai was via her hometown, where she was imprisoned by her family, only to escape to a hand-to-mouth existence in the city, until she found some work in a bookshop and earned a few royalties from her war diary. On the morning it was published she had not eaten for four days.[227]

These were the fortunate ones. Peng Pai reached sanctuary in Shanghai, only to be exposed by a former follower from Hailufeng and executed in August 1929. It was hard to tally how many had perished. What was clear was that the cruellest violence was against women. The women's leader and companion to Cai Hesen, Xiang Jingyu, had refused to leave Hankou and was arrested there. Her sister-in-law, Cai Chang, who had travelled with her brother and Xiang to France to study, was an underground witness to the counter-revolutionary killings in Wuhan. As she told it, before Xiang was shot in the execution grounds, she began to speak. 'The soldiers put stones in her mouth and wound a leather strap around her chin, then they beat her before she was killed.' Elsewhere it was worse, she said: girls were stripped and mutilated to taunts – 'you have your free love now!' – and where men and women were beheaded together, 'their heads were exchanged on their bodies'. In Hubei and Hunan, as in Guangdong, bobbed-hair women were singled out for execution.[228]

Wong Sang was incarcerated in Kuala Lumpur's notorious Pudu prison. There were around nine women there, of 1,194 prisoners at the end of 1924.[229] It was built like a 'medieval castle', with inside courts 'neat as a Cambridge lawn' against the bare, high, slitted walls. The women were held in 'a small private house surrounded by its own trim garden' under the supervision of an Anglo-Indian matron, passing the hours with crotchet-work and sewing.[230] Wilfred Blythe visited Wong Sang there. She had been crossed in love, she told him. The world was a 'wicked place and must therefore become Communist'.[231] She was, it was said, 'a source of considerable trouble to the matron and others'. In 1926 she appealed for remission in the usual way: at the time 'she did not realise the seriousness of the crime'. But the government took grim satisfaction in dismissing the appeal: 'I am only too glad', wrote Richards's successor in May 1926, 'to see that she is finding the prospect of serving the balance of her sentence as irksome.'[232] After one of these occasions, almost two years to the day after her sentencing, as a newspaper reported it, she was 'tired of herself and her efforts'. On 25 March 1927 she got up at about 3 a.m., took a bath towel, tied one end around her neck and the other through a bar of the only window to her cell and jumped down. She was found around 4 a.m.; a verdict of 'asphyxia by hanging' was recorded.[233] But even in this the public record was unreliable, or so it appeared to Wilfred Blythe. He took a cutting of the brief newspaper report for his own research, but he corrected the details. She had, he wrote, hanged herself with her own hair.[234]

The abandoned typewriter of Nguyen Ai Quoc, Kowloon, 1931.

Epilogue
Out of Exile

LIVING IN NORMAL TIME

In Kuala Lumpur, a semblance of calm was restored. But the case of the bobbed-hair woman was not forgotten. The police maintained a small museum in which fragments of the bomb, and a (no doubt apocryphal) queue of hair torn off the head of a worker in the blast, were on display.[1] The principal victim, Daniel Richards, returned some months later to a humdrum career that lasted another ten years. Across Asia, it seemed that the long crisis sparked by the first violent assaults on empire in the wake of the Russo-Japanese war had been extinguished and order restored. British residents in Malaya resumed their tropical idyll, presiding over an economic and racial hierarchy in which, in their mind's eye, each community knew its place, and politics was the work of disruptive outsiders. The government honed its formidable powers to arrest and banish 'undesirables'. Between 1928 and 1931, the annual number of banishments from British Malaya averaged 1,500 and continued to rise after that.[2] Wilfred Blythe, the bobbed-haired woman's other target, become one of the empire's leading authorities on the Chinese underworld; he developed a pathology of the Chinese as being innately conspiratorial, governed by what he later termed a 'secret society complex'.[3] In this way, in the imperial imagination the distinction between the political and the criminal was dissolved, often into the shadowy figure of the terrorist or assassin. The repertoire and vocabulary of state violence developed in this period proved to be one of its most ubiquitous legacies.

The myth of the absence of politics was shared across colonial Asia. The Dutch in the Indies called this period the *zaman normal*, a return to 'normal time', or rather the pretence of it.[4] Normal time revived the illusion that colonial governments could dictate political futures. Imperial regimes never provided an adequate answer to the question as to what precisely was on offer for colonial subjects who still sought to work within the system and its laws. The reality was, in most cases, far less than was offered earlier. The ideal of an imperial citizenship had been fatally undermined by racial exclusion and by the war. Reform plans for British India, mooted in a series of meetings between Gandhi and the viceroy, Lord Irwin, in 1931, gestured towards constitutional reform. But by the time they were finally implemented in 1935, by a Conservative government, they had become a tactic of 'holding India to the empire'.[5] Colonial policy often sought to revive royal legitimacy, as in the case of Vietnam through the young emperor, Bao Dai, who returned in 1932. Many British in Asia still believed the Malay sultans and Indian princes to be the natural leaders of the people. The colonialism of the 1930s was shot through with nostalgia, for an exotic *Indochine* of the imagination, for the 'real' Malaya, for the 'Tempo Doeloe', the luminous 'olden times' of colonial Java.[6] This was a way by which European expatriates faced their racial anxieties, distanced themselves from the violence of colonial rule and its consequences, and grieved for a world they had themselves destroyed.[7]

If a façade of order was restored, it was only because it was buttressed by the armoury of emergency or 'exorbitant' powers that colonial regimes had accumulated during the crisis years and now retained in perpetuity.[8] They put a face to the enemy, and worked ever more in concert to maintain a *cordon sanitaire* against the 'contagion' of Bolshevism. In the months after the uprising in the Netherlands Indies, its head of intelligence, A. E. van der Lely, steadily embellished a narrative that it was ordered directly by Moscow, and that Tan Malaka was its messenger. To the British in India Tan Malaka was 'the Roy of Javanese Communism', and they saw M. N. Roy himself, despite having what David Petrie termed a 'singularly barren record', as the most capable and 'dangerous enemy of capitalism, landlordism and imperialism'.[9] The French remained obsessed by the search for the enigmatic Nguyen Ai Quoc. The various colonial intelligence services produced strikingly similar hierarchical organizational charts of international communism. In 1928, the Malayan Bureau of Political Intelligence identified thirteen tiers, rising from local 'cells' to the controlling body; those drawn by the French and Dutch led them from the villages of Tonkin or Java directly back to Moscow Centre. The world was redrawn in two camps fighting a constant, secret battle for influence – insinuating, subverting, suborning – a 'cold' or 'perpetual war' in all but name.[10] By 1928, it seemed to be one that the imperial powers were winning. The spaces in between, the places of sanctuary exploited by global revolutionaries, were ever fewer and more constricted.

After the failure of the 1926–7 uprisings in Java and Sumatra, Tan Malaka made his way to Bangkok, where from its relative neutrality he tried to rally the underground around a new Partai Republik Indonesia (PARI). It distanced itself from both the Comintern and the defeated PKI: its watchwords were 'self-help' and 'pan-Malayan' solidarity. But the British and Dutch were rounding up his associates on both sides of the Straits of Malacca. In early August 1927, seeking a place of greater safety, Tan Malaka returned to the Philippines as 'Hasan Gozali'. The British and Dutch governments lobbied the US authorities in Manila for his apprehension and extradition.[11] On the evening of 12 August 1927, as Tan Malaka strolled on the Jones Bridge, after leaving the office of the newspaper *El Debate*, he was arrested and immediately placed under interrogation. But he was experienced in the shadow-boxing of such encounters; he realized that the Manila police had no evidence of his activities in Singapore and Siam and assumed he had been in the Philippines throughout the previous two years. He therefore pleaded that he was merely an indigent journalist – when his pockets were turned out he had only ten Singapore dollars and two pesos to his name – and claimed refugee status. He gave a reasonably accurate account of his life story, but denied any involvement with international communism or with politics in the Philippines.[12] Meanwhile, leading public figures, including the president of Manila University, who had given him food and shelter, mobilized in his defence. The president of the Senate, Manuel L. Quezon, the man who had led the failed independence mission to Washington DC in 1919, insisted that 'political refugees should find ample protection under the American Flag'.[13] When the police, elated by their success in apprehending Tan Malaka, revealed that they were acting on information from the Dutch government, this backfired, provoking expressions of fury at the evidence of imperial collusion. Tan Malaka had committed no crime in the Philippines and was arrested without a warrant. To the nationalist press:

Tan Malaka might be a Filipino patriot, of the generation of José Rizal, come to life. His sufferings today were the sufferings that our leaders of the movements of '96 and '98 endured in alien lands. We thus understand him, the processes of his thoughts, and the ideals that give him strength through all his misadventures.[14]

Tan Malaka revealed that, in the manner of Rizal, he was writing a novel to expose the sufferings of colonial rule. However, siding with the colonial government, the *New York Times* rejected the comparison: Rizal 'never sailed under false colors, fought in the open and not a single soul can accuse him of deceit or duplicity'.[15]

All this only served to burnish Tan Malaka's aura as the ghostly, all-powerful 'red Javanese'.[16] The arrest presented him with his first public platform since his time in the Netherlands. Asked at a customs bureau hearing if he was a Bolshevik, he replied: 'Theoretically yes, but the aim must be subject to the limitations existing in each country.'[17] Elaborating this ambiguity, he later announced: 'I am not a Bolshevik. If love for one's country shows tendency towards Bolshevism, then call me a Bolshevik.'[18] Produced in court after an application for a writ of habeas corpus, Tan Malaka, 'very serene', 'wearing a white suit, with a pair of tan shoes and pink socks', achieved immediate celebrity. His diminutive figure was instantly recognizable in press photographs, sandwiched between police officers in court, or, after his release on bail, about town in the company of Filipino leaders. In flesh and blood he seemed a wholly benign figure. Political cartoons mocked official caricatures of him as a desperado. A conference was planned at which Tan Malaka promised to give a full account of himself. He was swiftly rearrested on a lesser charge of illegal entry, and, after a late-night meeting with Tan Malaka's lawyer on 22 August, the American acting governor of the Philippines ordered his expulsion, thus avoiding the farce of a trial in open court. The next morning, Tan Malaka left Manila on a Filipino-owned ship, the *Susana*, to the treaty port of Xiamen in Fujian province, China. Unlike his departure in exile from Java to the Netherlands in 1922, he was allowed to make a speech from the gangway: he denounced the 'hidden forces' working against him and declared that 'the cause of 60,000,000 Javanese is the cause of 12,000,000 Filipinos'.[19] Although he had avoided extradition to the Netherlands Indies, it was well known that the police of the small international concession at Xiamen were ready to intercept him. But the trap was sprung too soon and, at Xiamen, with the connivance of the ship's captain, Tan Malaka evaded the police search, slipped over the side into a Chinese inspection boat and went into hiding, saved once again by the international solidarities of the waterfront.[20]

Some months later, Tan Malaka wrote to Manuel Quezon from the 'Chinese Interior'. The letter was delivered by hand by a Chinese businessman of the Philippines, who had facilitated his escape and lodged him under the protection of a powerful local figure just north of Xiamen.[21] In the letter, Tan Malaka reviewed the past and future struggle of the 'Malayan peoples', among which he placed those of the Philippines. Colonial rule had left them divided and defeated, but in the six years since his return from Europe he had observed how the Malay language had drawn the diverse communities of the archipelago together as 'Malaysia as one body'. Although the revolts in Indonesia had ended in failure, people in Sumatra had acted in solidarity with those of Java, and Christians had shown sympathy with Muslims. Because of their geographical position and mineral resources, Indonesia and Malaya were destined to play a similar paramount role in Asia as had Britain in the industrializing west, but, unlike the British modus operandi, the goal of 'pan-Malayanism' would be attained without war or conquest. Even under current conditions there were steps towards the 'federalist idea which can be put into practice'. Quezon, Tan Malaka respectfully acknowledged, had pursued independence by 'pure diplomatic means', but what if his people were 'forced to the "next" available weapon'? 'You are now reaching a crossroad Mr Quezon: on the right hand a peaceful and level way, with a colourless end, however on the left hand a mountain upward, which lead[s] to victory, prosperity and glory of the Malayan peoples.'[22] It took nearly a year for the letter to reach Quezon and for him to reply. ''I sympathise cordially with your national aspirations, since your cause and mine are the same,' he wrote, '. . . I am sorry to say, however, that I can do absolutely nothing for you.'[23] There was no certainty that Tan Malaka received the letter. His messengers were scattered across maritime Asia, hounded ever more closely by the police. A handful of disciples made their way secretly to Xiamen to be tutored by him. But their ability to influence events in Indonesia was limited.[24]

As the revolutionary flotsam and jetsam from Canton, Shantou, Java and Sumatra dispersed, they slowly began to resurface in colonial territories that had largely stood aloof from events of 1926 and 1927. In Hong Kong there was an influx of some 200 political refugees from the collapse of the Canton commune, dodging police inspections at entry points and raids on hideouts. An underground railroad, organized hastily in a mood of rancour and recrimination, was able to feed and clothe them and help them to escape onwards or to find employment. For a time Hong Kong was the headquarters of the Communist Party in Guangdong, although, due to constant police harassment, offset only by bribery, this contributed little to building the movement within the colony itself.[25] However, in Singapore and Malaya fugitives were able to inject experienced leadership into the local movement. They worked to repeat the united-front strategy that had failed in China through a Nanyang, or South Seas, General Labour Union – organized across different trades – and a Youth League.[26] They put about aggressive propaganda advocating 'Red terror' to combat the 'White terror' of the Kuomintang and the British police. In February 1928, leading members of the new Kuomintang government, including its chief diplomatist, C. C. Wu, together with Sun Ke and Hu Hanmin, passed through Singapore on their way to Europe. As they were feted at the Chinese Chamber of Commerce on Hill Street a gunman opened fire at C. C. Wu, hitting the noted Straits Chinese reformer Lim Boon Keng. The man responsible was a veteran of the Canton commune who had broken out of jail there and taken flight to Singapore.[27] The police drew a direct connection between him and the group behind Wong Sang's bomb in Kuala Lumpur three years earlier. There were also still a large number of Indonesian communists floating around the British-controlled side of the Straits of Malacca, lying low as teachers and traders, or housed in seamen's lodges. The Singapore Special Branch was alarmed when these strands began to connect as Malay-speaking Chinese started to mingle with internationalist-minded Malays. From Shanghai, inspired by the radical line brought back from Moscow by Li Lisan in 1930, the Chinese party began to see that the strength of the Nanyang movement lay in building bridges with other national struggles, in the expectation of leading them.[28]

Soon the Comintern sent out new emissaries. In November 1927, Ly Thuy, reassuming his identity as Nguyen Ai Quoc, was in Paris, perhaps not fully aware of the degree to which the Sûreté were following his movements. Anti-communist hysteria had taken hold in France itself, and Quoc shied away from old comrades. He passed through Brussels and Berlin, destitute and directionless. Then, in late April 1928, Quoc was given Comintern funds to return to Asia, and the following month travelled though Switzerland to take ship from Italy. He returned to the oldest settlements of the Vietnamese village abroad in Siam. From here there were well-trodden pathways through Bangkok to Hong Kong. Although the object of his mission was vague, Quoc brandished his Comintern status and began to gather together those who had graduated from his Revolutionary Youth League training in Canton, now scattered across Vietnam, Siam and China. Quoc's approach was, as it had ever been, cautious. His presence and his credentials did not go unchallenged. Many Vietnamese activists who had been witness to the Canton commune and Hailufeng soviets argued for a more aggressive policy. Quoc was seen as high-handed, and his past work dismissed for its 'patriotic parochialism'.[29] Critics pointed to the harder line that was coming down from Moscow and Li Lisan in Shanghai, and they set up a new organization within Vietnam. Quoc managed to bring the various factions together in Hong Kong in a meeting between 3 and 7 February 1930. There he finally established a Vietnamese Communist Party and drew up a basic programme.[30] But it was pre-empted by a groundswell of strikes and demonstrations.

The disturbances began in Cochinchina in late January 1930 and were followed by a garrison mutiny at Yen Bai in Tonkin in February, led by a nationalist group, which was savagely repressed. After widespread May Day protests, the revolt became increasingly concentrated in Nguyen Ai Quoc's home province of Nghe An and neighbouring Ha Tinh, a region known as Nghe Tinh. In the eyes of many observers, it was a traditional peasant protest: the global economic slump was beginning to bite, taxes had continued to rise, and the poor sought the restoration of lands and entitlements. But it was also a decisive break with the past, fired by the increased mobility of the young and the arrival of highly literate communist cadres who were emboldened to set up village-level party cells. By September, they began to seize government offices, attack the warehouses of the hated alcohol monopoly, and establish village soviets. The French authorities deployed Foreign Legionnaires and airpower: in one airborne attack on demonstrators at a railway station near the provincial capital of Vinh, 174 people were killed and many more injured.[31] The French also employed older punitive measures, such as torching villages, as well as ever-denser regimes of population registration and control of movement. In a brief lull, in the face of the controversy the repression had provoked in France, the soviets launched a second wave of more murderous attacks on officials. But they had neither arms nor military training, and in the face of immanent famine the resistance began to crumble. On one estimate that excludes those who died of starvation or in camps, 1,200 Vietnamese perished at the hands of the colonial government; the rebels themselves were responsible for around 200 deaths, only one of whom was a Frenchman.[32] These sudden, incendiary events were eulogized by the party as a 'revolutionary high tide'. Parallels were drawn with Marx's verdict on the Paris Commune of 1871: it was bound to fail, yet a necessary prelude to something larger.[33] But in many ways, not least in its anarchist ethos, it was the last, broken wave of the disturbances of 1925–27 across Asia.[34]

Nguyen Ai Quoc stood at a remove from this upheaval. He regretted that the movement was dominated by doctrinaire intellectuals who had failed to build a broader anti-imperial front. He was summoned by the Comintern from Hong Kong to Shanghai, where its Far Eastern Bureau was reasserting its authority and rebuilding its clandestine organization.[35] He was censured for his scepticism. The Bureau renamed the Vietnamese Communist Party the Indochinese Communist Party, to reflect the entirety of the French territories, and to distance it from Quoc's emphasis on national struggle. Quoc himself was despatched on a brief mission down the Malay Peninsula to attend one of the series of meetings of the Nanyang communist leaders, out of which was founded the Malayan Communist Party in April 1930. Quoc brought the message that the Chinese leaders of the party needed to work more closely with the Malays and Indonesians and overcome the ethnic fragmentation that Tan Malaka had identified in 1925.[36] But the lines of communication were fragile. As early as the following spring, the Malayan party wrote plaintively to their Vietnamese comrades: 'we [have] practically ceased our relationship for a year already . . . How sad it is.'[37]

In April 1931, a new man arrived in Singapore from Moscow. Travelling on a stolen French passport in the name of 'Serge Lefranc', he checked into the best place in town, Raffles Hotel, and, throwing around the 22,000 gold dollars he was carrying, set up a flat in New Mansions, Oxley Rise, and an office at Winchester House on Collyer

Quay as a seller of sawmill tools and wines. 'Lefranc' had travelled from Vladivostok, calling first in Shanghai and then Hong Kong, where he stayed at the Savoy Hotel. His real name, the police soon discovered, was Joseph Ducroux. His revolutionary pedigree stemmed from the fact that he was bilingual in French and English, having worked for Thomas Cook in Paris and Marseilles, where he had come to the attention of both the French and British authorities for his support for the Rif rebels in Morocco and for his obstructed attempts to visit India. He then went to Moscow and was employed by the Comintern in two minor missions to China. He had worked with M. N. Roy, and his assignment to Singapore, he later claimed, was part of a plan to chart a new passage to India for the Comintern.[38]

In Hong Kong, his first task was to meet with Nguyen Ai Quoc: 'a man of about forty years old at the time', as Ducroux described him, 'slender, very alert, almost beardless, with a serious and concentrated face'. Ducroux was struck by his intensity and his immaculate French, and saw in him the timeless paragon of a monkish ascetic absorbed solely in the struggle for freedom.[39] The French police surmised that the two men had known each other in 1922–23 in France, when Ducroux was active in the Young Communists. Ducroux then made an oddly brief visit to Saigon and Hanoi, his first experience of a French colony, and arrived in Singapore, via Manila, in late April 1931. His mission lasted less than six weeks. The Singapore Special Branch had been tipped off by the French and watched Ducroux from the moment of his arrival. They staked out his office by renting the room opposite, suborned his servants and intercepted all his letters, including those to Quoc in Hong Kong. They were written in invisible ink of rice water, easily revealed by a tincture of iodine, employing a thin pseudonym that did not fool anyone.[40] Ducroux was arrested on 1 June 1931 and his trial, the first of a European for communist subversion, was a local sensation. He was sentenced to eighteen months in jail; he began an appeal, but it was withdrawn and he was banished to Saigon, where he was promptly rearrested by the French authorities. Ducroux denied giving information to the police in Singapore, beyond disclosing his true identity; he was anxious to avoid unpleasant repercussions for the owner of his stolen passport, Serge Lefranc, a poultry dealer in Seine-et-Oise.[41]

The Special Branch did not need Ducroux's confession. After his arrest they rounded up and placed on trial some sixteen suspected communists, a number of whom had visited him and others who shared their lodgings.[42] These included a close lieutenant of Tan Malaka. In Saigon, the Sûreté were able to arrest in one fell swoop almost the entire central leadership of the Indochinese Communist Party, which had relocated to the city in response to the Nghe Tinh soviets. Most explosively of all, on 15 June 1931, Ducroux's telegrams to Shanghai led the Municipal Police to arrest their recipient, 'Hilaire Noulens', and his wife, and raid eight PO Boxes, seven other addresses, ten apartments and two offices. This exposed bank accounts and a cache of over 1,300 documents which provided hitherto elusive evidence of the legendary 'Moscow gold'. Expenditure amounted to £9,500 a week, moving across Asia, as well as a monthly subvention to the Chinese Communist Party of 25,000 gold dollars. Hilaire Noulens first claimed for himself and his wife Belgian citizenship, then Swiss, under the name 'Ruegg'. Their true identity – Yakov Rudnik, a Georgian, and his Russian wife, Tatyana Moiseenko – was not publicly revealed at the time. They were sentenced to death by a Chinese court on 17 August 1932, but, in the face of a hunger strike by the Noulens from jail cells in Nanjing and an international campaign led by the League Against Imperialism, enlisting figures such as Albert Einstein, H. G. Wells and Madame Sun Yat-sen, this was later commuted to life imprisonment.[43] This personal drama masked the extent to which there were other betrayals at work, and that the real force of the backlash, including ninety-five more raids and 276 arrests, fell on the Noulens's local associates in Shanghai. Among those arrested was one of China's earliest communists, Cai Hesen, who was betrayed in Hong Kong and swiftly extradited to Canton, where he was nailed to the wall of his cell and beaten and bayonetted to death. This provoked no international outcry. The 'Noulens Affair' was, for the British, a vindication of their anti-Bolshevik paranoia and of their adoption of the dark arts of secret policing.[44]

But colonial governments did not always agree on who were the most dangerous persons, nor on how far they would bend their rule of law to assuage the fears of their allies. This was tested by the arrest on 6 June 1931 in Hong Kong of a 'Sung Man Cho'. The man had been staying in a small apartment on Nathan Road, in Kowloon, a popular haunt for local business travellers, leased under the name T. V. Wong, and travelling on a Chinese republican passport. He was accompanied by a 'niece', 'Li Sam', who was arrested and detained with him. The press soon reported what the police well knew: that Sung was Nguyen Ai Quoc. An elaborated pantomime unfolded. Under questioning, Sung denied his true identity, and claimed instead to be a Chinese business-man from Guangdong. The arresting officers of Joseph Ducroux from Singapore, and members of the Sûreté from Saigon, travelled to Hong Kong to hold a secret conclave. Swayed by the argument of the French government that if Quoc were at liberty he would be a threat to all European possessions in Asia, the colonial secretary in London agreed that he should be deported to French Indochina. At this time, execu-tions of the leaders of the Yen Bai Mutiny and summary killings of Nghe Tinh rebels were still under way. However, a Vietnamese com-rade in Hong Kong got word to a sympathetic English lawyer, Frank Loseby, who took on the case. The funds forwarded for the defence by International Red Aid and the League Against Imperialism were a rare public demonstration of the reach of the Comintern. With consummate artistry, Quoc seized the opportunity of a banishment inquiry hearing to make the charge, in calm and fluent English, that he had been inter-rogated by the French Sûreté in a British prison. The circulation of the old surveillance photographs from his Parisian days had alerted him to their presence in the British colony. Loseby then made an application for a writ of habeas corpus.[45]

The legal position of the Hong Kong government was weak. There were no legal grounds for Nguyen Ai Quoc's arrest, nor for his irregular extradition for a non-extraditable offence. The Hong Kong government would have been happy to allow the French to pick him up as he tried to leave Hong Kong. But Quoc claimed right of refuge as a political offender, and demanded to be deported to a place of his own choosing. During the hearing, which began on 31 July 1931, much was made of the irregularity of Quoc's arrest and interrogation, but ultim-ately, in mid-September, the court dismissed the application and upheld a deportation order. Loseby was granted permission to appeal to the Privy Council in London. Throughout the case there was a creative ambiguity as to his identity. No one believed that 'Sung Man Cho' was who he said he was. Like Tan Malaka in Manila, he deliberately pro-voked and confused the court with contrary claims as to his identity as a Chinese businessman and as a Vietnamese patriot. In the event, in July 1932 the counsel for the British government, the socialist Stafford Cripps, advised his clients to settle the case before it reached open court. It was, Cripps argued, better to let Sung Man Cho, upon whom the French had no legitimate claim, go on his way than face an incendiary case involving the prisoner of conscience Nguyen Ai Quoc. Under the terms of the deal, Quoc was allowed to leave on his own terms. The problem remained as to where he might go. There seemed to be nowhere that was willing to take him, and Quoc trusted no one. He announced that he would travel to England, but only got as far as Singapore, and was turned back to Hong Kong. Then it was reported in the *Daily Worker* and elsewhere that Quoc had died. He had succumbed in the British prison hospital to the tuberculosis that had afflicted him for so long. Meanwhile, a man in traditional scholar's dress, who had been lodging at the Chinese YMCA in Kowloon, boarded a ship for Shantou. This was the night of 25 January 1933, lunar New Year's Eve, a time for family and fireworks, and no one noticed he had left, nor the connivance of British officials in his departure.

Prior to his departure, Nguyen Ai Quoc spent eighteen months in the prison on Hong Kong Island and in hospital. By his own admission he was well treated. But, on his arrest, his lodgings and his possessions were seized and photographed. They passed to the Sûreté, and into their extensive archive of Quoc, itemized down to every fragment in his notebooks: jottings for articles, coded lists of contacts, lists of names, of the sailors mostly, who were the real connecting threads of the vast conspiracy. For all the talk of the profligate spending of Russian gold, Quoc recorded his expenses in meticulous detail. There was evidence of intense subterranean industry; his typewriter was photographed as it was found, in mid-sentence of an article on 'Indochina May First biggest in the world'.[46] The exhibits were a tableau of the solitary life of the underground. At this point, Quoc had been travelling almost constantly for twenty-three years, and of all the ports of call on the way, he had stayed longest in Hong Kong. He was almost entirely cut off from his home region. His father had recently died; his brother and sister had been released from French custody, but were closely watched, and his contact with them by letter was very sporadic. It was said that the wife he left behind in Canton came to Hong Kong to see him. He had written to her some time earlier, with formal affection. Besides the 'niece' arrested with him, there was another female companion in Hong Kong, Nguyen Thi Minh Khai. She played a major role in party communications and was arrested before him and extradited to China.

Of the 'niece', little was said publicly at the time. She was Ly Ung Thuan, the wife of a Vietnamese comrade, also an active member of the organization.[47] She claimed Chinese nationality and was quietly allowed to depart. Minh Khai and Ly Ung Thuan were at once further evidence of the relative invisibility, but also of the ubiquity and tenacity, of women revolutionaries in the struggle for Asia.

A few weeks after the arrests in Singapore, Shanghai and Hong Kong, on 21 July 1931 the police in Bombay raided a flat in Wylie Street. It had been staked out by plain-clothes men sleeping on the street for some time. Their quarry, a 'Dr Mahmud', had eluded them for weeks, and there had been a number of failed attempts to seize him. In truth, they had been searching for the man – whether under the names of 'Reverend Martin', Mr White or M. N. Roy – on and off for over twenty years.

For Roy, the impotence of exile had become too much. Upon his return to Moscow from China in 1927, he had fallen from favour. Stalin's displeasure was not yet fatal, but he was now in full control: Trotsky was in exile, and Borodin was in the wilderness. In early 1928, with the help of Louise Geissler and Russian friends, Roy crossed the Soviet border, in secret, at night. He returned to Berlin, the city where he had been happiest. 'Had I been in the least, even indirectly, guilty of any treacherous act,' he wrote, 'I would not leave Moscow with my head on my shoulders.'[48] Nevertheless, he immediately set to defending himself, principally in a book, *Revolution and Counter-Revolution in China*, which ran to 689 pages when it eventually saw publication.[49] Louise Geissler faded from his life, though not from Indian affairs: she acted as the companion for the wife of Jawaharlal Nehru, Kamala, when she sought medical treatment in Switzerland, and their daughter Indira.[50]

In Berlin, Roy began a relationship with Ellen Gottschalk, the daughter of a US diplomat of German origin. She was born in Paris in 1904, grew up mostly in Cologne, and on leaving home at a young age became active in the communist movement, and later with the German opposition and Roy's circle in Berlin, where they met in 1928.[51] During this period Roy's reputation came under constant attack. In his absence from Moscow, delegates from India denounced him at the Sixth World Congress of the Comintern in 1929 as 'a person completely unknown in India'. For his advocacy for the united front he was declared a 'rightist opportunist'; the following year he was expelled from the Comintern and denounced as a renegade.[52] In Berlin he lived with other outcasts, including his old friend August Thalheimer. But then, in mid-November 1930, against the advice of all his friends and after an idyllic holiday with Ellen in Merano, Italy, he left for India. He travelled as a Muslim, Dr Mahmud, through Istanbul, then Iran, arriving in Karachi on 11 December. For once he was about two months ahead of the police.

He returned to a charged political atmosphere. In March 1930, Congress had launched a new civil disobedience; a second wave of terrorism continued in Bengal and in the Punjab and reopened the question as to the circumstances in which the Raj should be resisted by force. Gandhi's spiritually inspired, village-based self-sufficiency vied with a vision of an industrial future favoured by Jawaharlal Nehru, Subhas Chandra Bose and the Congress socialists. Roy was determined to shape these debates. Initially, the circles of young radicals he met in Bombay and elsewhere did not know who he was, but the British police who tracked him were very clear that his presence was a catalyst to a growing band of supporters. However, a brief visit to the United Provinces brought home to Roy the limits to what he could achieve without an organization and unable publicly to reveal his identity. In March 1931 he met secretly with Jawaharlal Nehru and Subhas Chandra Bose at the Congress convention in Karachi, to encourage them to draw up a minimum social and economic programme. But the attacks on him in Moscow soon followed him to India and helped speed his capture.[53] The underground was already on trial, at a fresh conspiracy case at Meerut begun in March 1929. This was the product of months of harassment and surveillance – a high-stakes 'cat and mouse game' through the streets of Calcutta and Bombay – involving not only the Indian leadership – the recidivist S. A. Dange, Shaukat Usmani and Muzaffar Ahmad and others – but also British activists who had arrived to assist them in Roy's absence.[54] In a strange repertory of oppression, the policeman who had mastered the hunt for 'Fat Babu' and for Roy from 1912, David Petrie, again played a key role. Roy was not brought before the court in Meerut, although he was a constant presence in the exhibits of evidence.[55] He was thrown into the district jail in Kanpur in a resumption of the conspiracy trial there, at which he had been listed as 'absconded' some seven years earlier.

The documents captured in the June raids in Shanghai carried within them fragmentary details of the Comintern's fresh mission to India, by way of the revolutionary road from China to Burma that Roy, as 'Revd

Martin', had tried to open in 1916. This time they featured an agent codenamed 'Thomas'.[56] Tan Malaka, too, had tired of his isolation near Xiamen and had drifted up to Shanghai. After over four years of estrangement, as 'Thomas', he was drawn back into the orbit of the Comintern, or at least the fringes of it. His movements in this period left few traces. By his own account, Shanghai heralded a reawakening. As was his habit, he gravitated to the fringes of the city, the settlements of the new arrivals, places of constant transit, where he lived as a Filipino. Tan Malaka saw a city in transition, torn apart by frequent violence, ever more defined by gangsterism, rackets and the international politics of exclusion. But, in the midst of the poverty and turbulence of everyday life, he was inspired by the solidarities he found, which reaffirmed his faith in a new Asia.[57] But, when Alimin finally caught up with him in a room in Shanghai's Zhabei district, he found that Tan Malaka's health had collapsed. A substantial sum of money was made available for his treatment. Both Alimin and the Comintern, it seems, were unaware of Tan Malaka's new party, PARI, and his heresy in the intervening years.[58] But by this time Shanghai was no longer a refuge: on 28 January 1932 the city was engulfed by war. Tan Malaka was witness to the Japanese incursion that marked a new phase of imperial aggression, and he lost what little he owned.

On the run once again, Tan Malaka travelled to Hong Kong. There, in October 1932, he was grabbed one night in the street close to his hotel in Kowloon. The police of six nations had a claim on him. Officers travelled from Singapore to interview him, and to tell him of his close friends they had arrested there. His case followed a similar pattern to that of Nguyen Ai Quoc, but initially in secret. Failing to contact Quoc's lawyer, Frank Loseby, Tan Malaka managed to get in touch with the radical Independent Labour Party leader, James Maxton, who on 14 March 1933, somewhat belatedly, asked in the House of Commons about his whereabouts.[59] Sympathizers in the Netherlands, without news of their former parliamentary candidate for four years, took up a campaign against his extradition to the Indies. But by this time Tan Malaka was long gone. As with Quoc, the local authorities had no grounds on which to hold him, and in the end they had little choice but to let him go. Both men had argued 'that there was no safer place for them the world over than just where they were, in the Gaol in Hong Kong'. Only the 'loosely guarded' door to China remained open to them.[60] In February 1933, Tan Malaka outlined his case to Madame Sun Yat-sen and her China League for Civil Rights. Thrice imprisoned by three colonial regimes, by virtue of the 'secret agreement' between them, he now stood on a precipice:

> It was as if I was facing a bridge of hair, over which the Moslem has to pass in the day of judgement, to reach the end, the heaven where the houris, the maiden[s] are dwelling with big, round eyes as of doves ...
> Beneath the inferno I stand in the British gaol. At the end of the hair bridge was Shanghai, not with the big dove-like eyes of the houris, but with the eagle-like eyes of the Settlement police. The extreme end might be worse than the British gaol. Again I must stop. The way or ways of my escape has to remain in the open.[61]

The letter was addressed from South America, but it was posted from Manila, and was delivered not to Madame Sun in Shanghai but straight into the hands of the Dutch consul. Tan Malaka was lying low once again, very ill, in rural Fujian province, with a family with connections to the Philippines – his final, fragile link to the world abroad.[62] The revolution was now a waiting game.

THE ORCHESTRA AT THE WORLD'S END

Had Tan Malaka fallen into the hands of the Dutch, his likely destination, along with 1,308 of over 4,500 people sentenced for their part in the uprisings in the Netherlands Indies and many of their families, was a forest clearing 280 miles upstream on the Digoel River in West Guinea. This region was seen by some Europeans as the final frontier of empire: a new Transvaal, a 'New Australia-New America' of future white settlement. But for Asians it marked the uttermost boundary of the Indies, the extremity of Asia, and, for many who were sent there, the end of the world itself.[63]

The first internees began to arrive in early 1927. Among them was Aliarcham, who had briefly led the PKI on its path to revolt. He was one of the first to die there. Boven Digoel was a harsh, malarial environment. Beyond the cleared area of the camp lived forest peoples who had no, or very little, contact with other human beings. Tales of their savagery were embellished to keep the new arrivals confined to camp. In practice, some of the forest peoples came to the camp to work and to be observed by the ethnographers who formed part of the Dutch garrison. But for most settlers, the trees held only terror. Most were townsmen and townswomen from regions of Java where the forests had long disappeared. Very few of those who tried to flee found their way overland to the nearest border: the Australian-administered territories of Papua and New Guinea. Those who did were returned promptly into Dutch custody.

Boven Digoel was not, strictly speaking, a prison. The only fences were those built around the small garrison. The governor-general, Jonker de Graeff, was opposed to capital punishment and had angered expatriate opinion by refusing to confirm death sentences. To him, the camp was an expression of mercy: a far outpost of ethical imperialism, with better street lighting and medical facilities than many settlements of Java itself. The government's stated intention was that those who were sent there would be allowed to live reasonably freely. Or, as Mas Marco Kartodikromo paraphrased it when he heard of it from his prison cell in Java: 'Look at this, Indonesian people! These Communists in Boven Digoel cannot organize their own community, and their situation is one of chaos.'[64] To Mohammad Hatta, now returned from his sojourn overseas, 'the ethical-coax-policy of Governor-General de Graeff is, in essence, ethical force':

> His 'ethics' conveys that he has purposely selected one of the unhealthiest spots in the archipelago, where malaria and cholera are prevalent, as a concentration camp for his political adversaries, who, notwithstanding the Indian penal provisions that were worded as pliably as possible, could not be prosecuted under the law.[65]

There was a constant, one-way traffic into the camp. It became an Indies in miniature, as the first internees from Java were joined by Sumatrans and others, including supporters of Tan Malaka's PARI organization, trawled in from across Asia. Dutch officials distinguished between the 'recalcitrant', the 'half-hearted' and the 'well-meaning'. But in practice these categories ran into each other. More significant was the separation between the main settlement, Tanah Merah, named after its infertile 'red earth', and the Tanah Tinggi, the 'higher land', which was a place of punishment, of banishment beyond banishment.

Later, non-Communists, Islamists and 'intellectuals' were sent to Boven Digoel. In 1935, Hatta himself was to be banished there.

Boven Digoel was termed an 'isolation colony', a means to keep the contagion of political belief at bay. But it was not entirely adrift from the world. It was serviced by Chinese river traders, a small administration with its co-opted officials, and its many spies. When Mas Marco Kartodikromo arrived in June 1927, in shackles, he described the process of settlement in letters to a Javanese newspaper. Each person was given a space of two square yards to sleep and another to store their belongings; one small mosquito net, a small mat, a small sheet, a blunt cleaver, an axe head, hoe and spade, all without a handle, and a fortnightly food ration of rice, beans, dried fish, rancid meat, salt, sugar and tea. The settlers who were, in official parlance, 'willing to work' were paid for their manual labour; others were given only a small allowance and, it was believed, had less prospect of eventual return. Some of the internees brought their families; children would be born in Boven Digoel. But it was no place for family life. There were six or seven men to every married woman and tales of promiscuity soon circulated back into the world. The stories were true, wrote Mas Marco, and might be true anywhere, but Boven Digoel was 'a pocket-sized place that does not match the number of its inhabitants. It is also the case that a situation like that is deliberately set up to cause harm.'[66]

The camp had no lack of chroniclers: it was home to some of the most educated and luminous Indonesians of the age. They launched publishing and translation and set up language schools. The few visitors to Digoel were taken aback to hear so much Dutch and English spoken. In the evenings there was jazz, a cinema show and an orchestra, a gamelan modelled by a court musician from Solo, Pontjopangrawit, who was among the first batch of detainees. Its *bonangs*, or rows of gongs, were improvised from a variety of tin cans and, eventually, iron food drums. Later arrivals from Sumatra brought the instruments for an *orkes Melayu* for Malay opera. All this was reported by journalists from Java and the Netherlands as further evidence of the return of normal time.[67] But as conditions deteriorated, morale dissipated, monotony and ennui took a heavy toll, and this activity was more a way of simply keeping going. Mas Marco kept writing, until an article dated 9 December 1932. At its close he shifted from Indonesian, the language he had done so much to shape, to Dutch, perhaps that his voice might reach the Netherlands too:

> Reader, here I stop this history. This is just one history, just one fairy tale, just one *sprookje*, just one strange event where civilization ends on the fringes of society. O you, intellectuals and nationalists, we ask that you be mild in your judgement on us exiles, the rubbish of your society, the political exiles in Digoel. To you Indonesians we address these words. Contemplate, for what we have struggled and suffered. Remember what we have sacrificed for Mother Indonesia.[68]

He died in March 1932 from malaria. There is a photograph of him, near the end, with his wife, emaciated, barely recognizable. Boven Digoel marked the grotesque, bitter death of 'ethical' imperialism.

In a century of exile, Boven Digoel was one of its cruellest manifestations: internal to the Indies, but irretrievably distant. But in colonial Asia in the 1930s such places multiplied, a premonition of the new camps that were opening in Europe. The British penal settlement of the Andamans was recommissioned in 1932 for political prisoners. Poulo Condore, off the coast of Cochinchina, expanded to receive the communists arrested in the Nghe Tinh uprisings. Some prisoners seized the opportunity to claim an education they would or could not complete as free subjects, or, indeed, living an underground existence. In prison, the Vietnamese communists perfected their techniques of cell-like organization, their propaganda, newspapers and political classes. By this time, some of the warders were themselves implicated.[69] Even in China, where most of the captured senior communist leaders were swiftly executed, those who survived, or were arrested later, were given a measure of preferential treatment, particularly given their high profile in the eyes of the world, and as penal reform became an important aspect of the Kuomintang's modernization programme. Chen Duxiu was able to write and receive visitors in Longhua jail in Shanghai after his arrest and his thirteen-year sentence in 1932. But this was a rare case, and Chiang Kaishek intervened personally to forbid warders to pass on news of political prisoners.[70]

In Kanpur jail, M. N. Roy was first permitted to write to Ellen on 11 August 1931. He was allowed one page, and, as always, replies were infrequent and tortuously slow to arrive:[71]

So here I am lodged in a quiet country-town jail as an 'A class prisoner' – a distinction which entitles one to 'comforts' including about 60 pfennigs worth of food a day. You can imagine I should be remembering the restaurants and cafes of Berlin for food and drink, if for nothing else . . .

In this letter, nothing much can be written about. We can talk about the weather. It is already two weeks that I am in. I am arrested in connection with a case which took place seven years ago – at the time of the fatal Fifth World Congress [of the Communist International]. The Government does not seem to be in a hurry about the trial. It is uncertain when it will begin, and it will surely drag on and on when it does begin. So I must settle down with something serious to do. First, I must prepare the defence, which I shall conduct personally. Then, I shall utilise the time 'to improve my mind', if the wherewithal be available. Good books are not easily available. Could you ask August [Thalheimer] to suggest some suitable books? They should preferably be in English; otherwise there will be difficulty in getting them. They must be procured abroad, and sent straight to me in jail. At last, I have a permanent and very safe address. Everything will reach me. Do send me from time to time some intellectual food. It is very rare in this country.[72]

The presence of the censor at his shoulder left little place for intimacy. It was sought through discussion of books, and in Roy's yearning for news of the cosmopolitan life he had led for so many years: the cool autumn in Berlin; its sociability – the 'Café am Zoo', the 'Jester' and the 'Gerold am Knie'krug of Muenchener at the Wilhelmshallen' – New Year and champagne at Kempinski's, Rhineland in the spring, St Moritz in high summer.[73] Remembering their final holiday together, the Alps became a vision of Utopia: 'I don't think the new world of ours will be a large Merano,' he told Ellen, 'but certainly we shall see to it that it is better than this miserable one.' He missed 'grand music' and was haunted by the memory of Paul Robeson's spirituals. He doubted he would ever see Europe again.

The first package of books arrived in mid-October 1931: a fresh copy of Gibbon's *Decline and Fall of the Roman Empire*; Friedrich Albert Lange on materialism, and novels, 'to make up for my negligence of childhood'.[74] Roy was scathing, for the most part, of the literary production of India, although he admired Sarat Chandra Chatterjee's, *Shesh Prashna* ('The Final Question', 1931). He enjoyed most the detective novels of S. S. Van Dine, featuring the dilettantish, polymath detective Philo Vance: 'I might have been someone like him, if I were an idle rich, and escaped being someone else.'[75] He filled his letters with long reading lists, confident that friends in Europe and America would subscribe to his education. His study plan sustained him for many years. He began with a history of materialism, 'to prepare the ground for a materialist interpretation of Indian religion, philosophy and culture'.[76] By December, he finished a long essay on the historical role of Islam. Most of these writings were later published. But, as Roy concluded, 'Jail is not a university . . . Prison cells or barracks are not expected to be studies.'[77]

Roy received a sentence of twelve years. His defence had rested on the illegitimacy of the Raj, and not on a refutation of the detailed evidence of his activities and intentions. It was harsh measured against the other sentences at Kanpur and was later reduced to six years. Over this stretch of time, prison was a constant battle for status and for one's health.[78] In early 1932 Roy was in the Central Prison at Bareilly, downgraded by the sentencing judge to 'B Class' status. 'B Class' prisoners, Roy observed, were not allowed handkerchiefs. He resorted to wiping his nose on his sleeve, he told Ellen, 'like the President of USSR'. Roy used his letters to justify to friends in Berlin his decision to return: 'I did not lose my head.' 'To work in India, one must be an Indian, having regard for the Indian mentality.' But his experience of everyday India in the life of the jail showed how far he had travelled away from it. In October 1933 in Bareilly, Roy acquired a companion in his cell. He found little sympathy for him:

> Really, the chap is harmless, after all. He simply cannot be anything but himself – the product of a decayed civilisation awaiting a much delayed burial. This country needs a Kemal Pasha, to begin with, to chop off the ridiculous tufts on the heads; to make the wearing of fierce moustaches punishable as a culpable homicide; to drive the pampered, idle, gossiping, but outrageously maltreated women out in the streets to work down their fat or cure their anaemia, and to free themselves from the malignant curse of suppressed passion; to prohibit the chanting of rigmarole in a language which few understand; and to do many other similar things.[79]

These defiant musings disguised the deterioration of his health. News of it came to Ellen in the form of a note inserted by the prison superintendent,

for her to confine her letters to 'light and domestic matters'.[80] There
were cruel rumours in the British press that he was living comfortably in Burma. Roy was only allowed to write to say he was better.
In Europe, Ellen, and, in America, Roy's ex-wife, Evelyn, marshalled
international support for his appeal as it travelled, in vain, to the Privy
Council in London.

Roy lived the watershed moments of these years as much as he possibly could. He felt the rise of fascism keenly. His books and papers,
stored in a publisher's cellar in Berlin, were seized when the Nazis came
to power, and Ellen had to flee to Paris. Like Tan Malaka, he saw the
colonial situation as a premonition of fascism. He had arguably witnessed in China a foretaste of what was to come. 'There is not one
patented brand of Fascism,' he told Ellen. 'It may have different forms
and come in devious ways.'[81] He followed the deepening schisms on the
left and the purges in the Soviet Union. In a coded way he asked about
'the Sentimental Dutchman', Henk Sneevliet, now 'a follower of the
Lion', Trotsky.[82] Roy had already experienced at first hand the suspicion and denunciations of spies, saboteurs and Trotskyites. Now the
Comintern was simultaneously a witness, a participant and a victim to
the Great Terror.[83] Foreign communists were especially vulnerable: on
one list of executions during the purges, eighty-three of the victims had
an address at the Hotel Lux.[84] Roy's old rival Virendranath Chattopadhyaya, 'Chatto', was executed in 1937; so too was Roy's nemesis
Abani Mukherji, by then a professor of political economy at Moscow
University. In the spring of 1934, Vera Vladimirovna ran into her 'Li
Annam', Nguyen Ai Quoc, on the staircase of the Institute of World
Politics and Economy. They exchanged addresses, but they did not
meet again; it was too dangerous to draw attention to their shared
past.[85] Quoc had only recently returned to Russia; his standing at this
time was very unclear. Like Roy, he fully expected to be held accountable for his part in the failures in China and Southeast Asia. He was
investigated but left unpunished. Unlike Roy, he had not set himself up
as an oracle. As Vietnam sank lower in the priorities of the Comintern,
and the Comintern loomed lower in the priorities of the Soviet Union,
he survived when many others did not, sidelined as a mature student at
the Stalin School.[86]

These dark years were a time of stasis, isolation and estrangement.
Roy had few visitors: friends were either in jail themselves, or unable to

travel for days to see him. He began a series of discussions with leaders of the Indian National Congress, and on his early release in November 1936 he was met at the prison gate by Congress supporters, to be feted and garlanded as he travelled to a Congress meeting at Faizpur. There he was elected to its governing body and welcomed as a veteran of the freedom struggle by Jawaharlal Nehru himself, who offered his homes in Allahabad and Delhi for his recuperation. Roy was, after all, as Subhas Chandra Bose later remarked, 'a popular and attractive figure with a halo around his name'. It seemed that his hour had come. But as Roy stepped out of the shadows, many within Congress, particularly on the left, feared that his 'Royists' would establish a secret party within Congress, as Roy had attempted to do from Berlin ten years earlier. Some refused to believe he was a nationalist at all.[87] Roy, launching criticisms at all sides, did little to disabuse them. Despite their cordial relationship, Nehru concluded that Roy would demand a 'compete break with the past' and was 'utterly out of touch with realities in India today'. For twenty years Roy had had little opportunity to truly experience them, and his most steadfast commitment had been to a struggle on a global plane. He had broken entirely with the Hindu patriotism of his *Swadeshi* youth in Mexico in 1917.[88] Gandhi, for his part, would have nothing to do with Roy and his anti-religion: he saw Roy as 'enemy number one'.[89]

Across colonial Asia, in normal times, the only possible open national politics was more tempered, less international and far less than the 'complete break with the past' proposed by the likes of Roy. In 1937, Tan Malaka left his rural isolation in Fujian province and travelled to Singapore. He noted a growth of ethnic enclaves on the island, and contrasted it to his earlier sojourn in 1927, when Singapore seemed to be a more open, inclusive urban landscape.[90] In the inter-war years, faced with the growing policing of movement and the hardening of territorial boundaries, the massive flows of people that had dominated Asian history for a century or more began to ebb. Colonial sociologists of empire reported greater ethnic tensions, and the emergence of more segmented, 'plural' societies. The persecution of Bolshevism impacted equally on the politics of open, democratic socialism. It rendered any politics across ethnicity, on class lines, more difficult, if not impossible.[91] It also worked to discredit and to limit the possibilities of outside alliance. In these conditions across Asia, in this absence, more territorial, more exclusive, ethnic and religious nationalisms expanded to fill the breach. In China, although it never entirely shed its 'left', nor its technocratic reforming goals, the Kuomintang turned decisively away from social revolution to become a more corporatist, conservative and martial entity.[92] In Indonesia, although Sukarno himself was arrested, tried, imprisoned and spent most of the 1930s in prison or internal exile, the open political field was dominated by his populist Partai Nasional Indonesia and its successor, Partindo, and their insistence on 'Indonesia' as the basis of the political community.[93] In Vietnam, communism had to compete in the countryside with synthetic and revivalist religious movements such as the Cao Dai and the Buddhist millenarianism of the Hoa Hao.[94]

And yet the closeness of things far away, and the allure of global influences, endured. As colonial censorship hardened, the legend of the underground was perpetuated through fiction and film, particularly in 'wild literature'. In the Netherlands Indies, *roman picisan* ('ten-cent', or pulp fiction) and *roman politik* were hugely popular; around 400 such titles were published between 1938 and 1942 from provincial towns such as Medan, Bukittinggi and Solo. They were set in a futurist, subterranean world of trickery, evasion and betrayal. One popular series, authored by Matu Mona, featured the *Padjar Merah Indonesia*, or the Scarlet Pimpernel of Indonesia. The tales were set in a thinly disguised parallel universe of the Indonesian exiles in Europe, the Soviet Union, Bangkok, Singapore, Manila, Shanghai and elsewhere, and featured characters such as 'Mussotte', 'Aliminsky' and 'Darsonov'. The Pimpernel himself was a man of multiple aliases and magical powers, whose clandestine international organization allowed him to appear at crucial moments to challenge injustice and reveal truth. He was also in very poor health. The stories betrayed an uncanny knowledge of the secret movements of Tan Malaka and added to the existing myths of his shape-shifting powers, sexual abstinence and global friendships. The preface of the second book told of how Matu Mona drew inspiration for the story at the Raffles Library in Singapore, a known haunt of Tan Malaka. The books were a gateway to an 'anti-world' where the fictive and non-fictive were in constant interplay.[95] This sense of plots real and unhatched or awakening slumber was palpable, and evoked the older millenarian expectation of the 'just king'. In Java, as Japanese influence reasserted itself it heralded the fulfilment of the prophecy of the twelfth-century King Joyoboyo: that the rule of the white man would end with the coming of the dwarfish yellow men who would reign as long as 'a maize seed took to flower'.[96]

FIERCE BIRTHS, AND DEATHS . . .

On Saturday, 14 August 1937, a bomb landed outside the Great World in Shanghai, killing 1,047 people and injuring 303 more. The amusement palace had been distributing free food and drink to city dwellers under siege. The bomb was from a Chinese plane and had been aimed at the Japanese cruiser *Izumo*. The *Izumo* had fought at the Battle of Tsushima in 1905 and now bombarded Shanghai from the Huangpu River. Other bombs exploded outside the Cathay and Peace Hotels. They marked the beginning of the end of the international city. Chiang Kai-shek had chosen Shanghai to make a stand because of the presence there of western residents and the major news agencies. Over the coming weeks his wife, Soong Mei-ling, would make a radio address in English to broadcast the city's plight to the world.[97] The events in China in the summer of 1937 marked an escalation of the long struggle for the succession to the western imperial order. The Great Asian War could trace its beginnings to 1914, when Japanese troops were committed to the siege of Qingdao; it intensified with the Japanese invasion of Manchuria in 1931 and became global in compass after Japan launched its push to the south and across the Pacific on 8 December 1941. It was longer and bloodier than the European war, claiming 24 million lives in Japanese-occupied Asia, the lives of 3 million Japanese, and 3.5 million more in India through war-related famine. In the twelve years after 1937 the foreign concessions in China would be swept away, the British Raj and the Japanese empire would fall; so too would Chiang Kai-shek, and new revolutionary regimes would arise in China, Vietnam and Indonesia.

From its earliest stages, the Great Asian War absorbed many of the struggles of the Asian underground. It came to Singapore early, with the arrival of political refugees, many of them from Shanghai. This represented an unprecedented influx of intellectuals: writers transformed local newspapers; artists discovered in the archipelago new utopian possibilities; teachers took their radical outlook into small-town schools. Tan Malaka was at the heart of this, teaching English in a Chinese school in Singapore, living in a Chinese neighbourhood with Chinese friends, and with a Chinese passport. A second united front in China from 1937 brought the old adversaries, Chiang Kai-shek's Kuomintang and the Chinese Communist Party, into an uneasy alliance. In Singapore, Malaya and elsewhere, the movement of 'National Salvation' was a catalyst to a new mass politics. The communist underground had hitherto failed to recover from the arrests of 1931. It now seized the opportunity to widen its support in schools, cultural circles and trade unions. By 1939, as many as 700 associations, with over 40,000 members and ten times as many sympathizers, came together to enforce a new boycott of the Japanese and rekindle the spirit of May Thirtieth. The poet Yu Dafu, a one-time associate of Guo Moruo, declared on his arrival in exile in Singapore that 'there should be no dividing line between politicians, the military and the intellectuals'.[98] But the young men and women who heeded his call to struggle tended to come from a more insular, small-town milieu: they were a different generation, with a very different experience of the world. Over time, they gave the movement a local rootedness within Malaya and a purchase in the countryside it had hitherto lacked.[99]

For some of the older generation, Japan's vision for a 'Greater East Asia' still carried emotive force. When Japan effectively occupied Indo-china after the fall of France in 1940, Prince Cuong De campaigned to be its ruler, but in vain. When Singapore fell to the Japanese on 15 February 1942, and large numbers of Indian troops fell into their hands, it was Rash Behari Bose who travelled south to provide civilian leadership for an Indian National Army, to fight in Burma alongside Japan for the liberation of India. Rash Behari was soon to pass the mantle to the man M. N. Roy had repeatedly tried to win to his cause: Subhas Chandra Bose, whose road to Singapore, after his exile from India in 1941 to evade the British, was through an Axis underground from Berlin and Tokyo. In Singapore, Bose rallied the Indians overseas on a scale never seen before; his platform oratory was equally an inspiration to others. But Japanese pan-Asianism after 1941 was in a very different key to the radical internationalism of the 1920s and 1930s. The 'New Asia' had the imperial palace in Tokyo as its perpetual political and spiritual nucleus. Nevertheless, many Asian nationalists seized the opportunity of the Japanese occupation to advance their own cause.

They adopted a martial militancy grounded in an emotive appeal to youth, to blood and sacrifice, drawing on older memories of anti-colonial resistance. Subhas Chandra Bose's movement followed many pathways of the old revolutionary networks across Asia, drawing in South Asians across class and across religion from Tokyo, Singapore and Bangkok. The military goal of attacking Assam through Burma revived the central objective of the Ghadarites in 1915 and the Comintern in 1931. Subhas Chandra Bose's writings and speeches echoed older pan-Asianisms and the idea of Asia as a place for concerted action against empire. The veteran Rash Behari Bose lived long enough to see the proclamation of a provisional government of Azad Hind in Singapore on 21 October 1943 and died in Tokyo on 21 January 1945.

The British did everything in their power to prevent news of the Indian National Army from reaching India. The new global conflict widened the fissures in Indian politics. In September 1939, the viceroy, Lord Linlithgow, took India into the war, as his predecessor Lord Hardinge had done in 1914, without consulting a single Indian. After 1942, Congress withdrew its cooperation with the Raj, and most of its senior leadership went to jail. The Quit India disturbances in 1942 were the most elemental challenge to the Raj since 1857. But not all followed its logic of resistance. In May 1940, Roy held a 'study camp' at the house he had taken with Ellen after she joined him in India, in Dehra Dun, in the Himalayan foothills, at some remove from the main centres of national politics. There Roy argued, from the logic of his own long struggle, that the global fight against fascism must take precedence. But when he stood for the presidency of Congress in 1940 on the basis of this policy, he was beaten by 183 to 1,864 votes by another global revolutionary from Bengal, Abul Kalam Azad, standing on a platform of non-cooperation. Roy's sworn enemies, the Communist Party of India, came to the same position as Roy after the termination of the Molotov-Ribbentrop Pact in June 1941. Both groups – by standing aside at this high water of anti-colonial protest – played a high political price. Roy was expelled from Congress and founded his own Radical Democrat Party. There was a moment in early 1944, when the new viceroy, Lord Wavell, considered him for a seat on his Council, when he might have joined the mainstream of politics. Wavell was well briefed on Roy's past: 'has been a Bengal terrorist', he noted in his diary, 'a worker for Germany, Indian representative of the Comintern, expelled from France, imprisoned in India'. But Roy overplayed his hand, and Wavell concluded that he was still viceroy 'and did not propose to be vice-Roy'.[100] In Dehra Dun, although he wrote prolifically, producing far-sighted blueprints for India's economic development and federal governance, Roy was largely a bystander to the great events of the end of empire in South Asia. It was Azad who led Congress until 1946 and, on 15 August 1947, became the first education minister of independent India, in the government of the man Roy still referred to as 'the Harrow Boy', Jawaharlal Nehru.

Political futures were now determined by the issue of war. In China, the rural strategy set in motion by Mao Zedong in Jiangxi in the aftermath of the failure of the Nanchang Rebellion was strengthened after a second Long March in 1934–5 to the base area of Yan'an in the north. This allowed the party to emerge after the end of the united front in 1945 with the peasant support and military resources finally to take back the cities. Across East and Southeast Asia, the sudden collapse of Japanese rule in Southeast Asia in August 1945 was merely a hiatus before a new, deciding wave of civil war and anti-colonial rebellion, led by groups that had also built up their own military resources, whether under Japanese tutelage as in Indonesia or through guerrilla warfare in Malaya, Vietnam and the Philippines. Although some of the leaders of these struggles had links to the global underground of the first decades of the century – Zhou Enlai and Deng Xiaoping proved to be consummate political survivors – the rise to paramountcy of Mao within the Communist Party represented the playing-out of his long struggle against the so-called 'Moscow faction'. Many of those who inherited power had, by fate or by design, little direct connection to the pre-war village abroad. The leader of the Malayan Communist Party who took it into open rebellion against the British in 1948, Chin Peng, was born in Malaya in 1924.

In a more fundamental way, this period marked the end of an era of imperial globalization. In many ways, the kinds of connections that had made the Asian underground possible were broken. In Japanese-occupied Asia, long-distance shipping all but ground to a halt; the posts were erratic and in some places there was a virtual blackout on international news for three and a half years. Borders became battle fronts. During the Japanese occupation the largest migrations were compelled, as in the conscription of forced labour, or *romusha*, for railway projects; of women for sexual slavery in so-called 'comfort stations'; or in the flight of refugees from devastated areas. At the war's end travel, trade and remittance resumed. There was a cascade of internationalist sentiment. Migrant communities raced to restore ties with their homelands. But, in the longer term, the great political upheavals in India and China turned inward. The partition of South Asia in 1947, the establishment of the People's Republic of China and the retreat of the Kuomintang regime to Taiwan in 1949 raised harder borders, and gave these journeys a new finality.[101] As Roy saw it, the new territoriality embraced even the left. Echoing Lenin's comments on the Baku Conference of 1920, he wrote in 1952: 'Asian communism is nationalism painted red, the means becomes the end.'[102]

In early 1941, the long journey of Nguyen Ai Quoc finally led home. He had, after years in the wilderness, been permitted to leave Moscow for China in 1938. Travelling via Mao Zedong's base area in Yan'an, he acted as a liaison officer with the Vietnamese in southern China, writing reports, producing propaganda, travelling constantly, including to Chiang Kai-shek's capital at Chongqing to report to the party representative there, Zhou Enlai. When, after the fall of France, Indochina came under the effective occupation of the Japanese, he gathered a group of radicals and communists in Guilin for a new training programme and, over Chinese New Year 1941, they took their skills to the border area. On 8 February 1941, after thirty years abroad, Quoc crossed the way-marker into Tonkin, to set up a secret base in a cave near Pac Bo in Cao Bang province, a mountainous, ungoverned area into which the party had already made substantial inroads. There he was able finally to launch his long-range, broad-front strategy and build a coalition of national resistance, led by the communists but called a League for the Independence of Vietnam, the Viet Minh. As the Communist Party within Vietnam was hit hard by repression at the hands of the Vichy government, Quoc urged caution. He remained in the background and took on a new identity, 'Ho Chi Minh', or 'He Who Enlightens'.

In August 1942 he made for Chongqing for news of the international situation, but was again arrested by a Chinese regional military commander in Guanxi province in September and held in eighteen different prisons and then house arrest until his release in March 1944. This further burnished his legend. By the time of his return to Cao Bang after nearly two years, the base area had expanded. This was the work of many hands, but, by August 1944, the French had discovered that the man behind its propaganda, Ho Chi Minh, was none other than Nguyen Ai Quoc. The connection was made by the head of the Sûreté, Louis Arnoux, the very same man who had tracked him down in Paris in 1919, when he had sent his insolent demands for freedom to President Woodrow Wilson.[103] Crucially, the remaking of Quoc, from the son of a mandarin to a plebeian, from a cosmopolitan into a patriot – his training and guidance, his ability to read the international situation, his revolutionary charisma – helped the Viet Minh to seize its moment and declare a provisional government in Hanoi on 2 September 1945 with Ho Chi Minh at its helm.[104] But this was only a beginning.

Tan Malaka was in Singapore in 1942 at its fall and was witness to the worst horrors of the Japanese occupation. He was present at the screening and mass killings of Chinese men and was lucky to escape with his life. He left for Penang to take advantage of the lapse in border controls and from there crossed to Medan in Sumatra. He felt like Rip Van Winkle, awakening after twenty years. But his mystique, as a once and future king, travelled before him. As he browsed a bookstall in the market, the seller sidled up to him: 'This is a good book and it's very popular.' It was *Padjar Merah*, by Matu Mona. The seller added: 'You know, Tan Malaka is in Padang. He spoke today in the Padang Square. He has a high position with the Japanese army.'[105] These stories were everywhere, so he had no option but to abandon his plans to visit his parents' graves and travel on, again via Penang, by steamer and by sailing *prahu* to Java. He settled for a while in one of the outer kampongs of Batavia, so that he could travel into the city to use the museum library at Gambir and write. With the resources available to him and from memory he wrote, he calculated in 720 hours, his magnum opus, a philosophical work entitled *Madilog: Materialisme, Dialektika dan Logika*, 'Madilog: Materialism, Dialectic and Logic'. It was no less than an attempt to rewrite Marx, as if Marx were writing from within an Indonesian, Islamic or, more particularly, a Minangkabau world view.[106] It was a lesson in the purpose and power of reason, to instruct the young people of Indonesia. War conditions and political propaganda privileged the spirit and strength of youth, or *pemuda*, over the elite bureaucratic finesse of the *zaman normal*. Thousands of *pemuda* were recruited into armed militias, led by Sukarno, who had emerged from internal exile to national pre-eminence under the Japanese. In the later stages of the war, Tan Malaka worked at a labour camp in west Java and saw more of its most brutal war conditions amongst the coerced workers, the *romusha*. It was here that he encountered Sukarno, who visited the camp. Tan Malaka was unimpressed by Sukarno's cautious, mendicant approach to the struggle for freedom, and although they spoke, Tan Malaka did not reveal his identity.

Still living under a borrowed name, Tan Malaka was back in Batavia, now Jakarta, on 17 August 1945, when Sukarno and Hatta stepped forward to declare the Indonesian republic of which Tan Malaka had been the prophet. The radicalized *pemuda* became its vanguard. Tan Malaka was inspired by their zeal. 'We are', announced the writers of the self-styled Generation of 1945, 'the heirs to world culture.' But the worldview of most of them had been shaped from within Indonesia itself during the slump of the 1930s and the dearth and isolation of war. Tan Malaka tried to reach them, initially in vain. The republic began to arm itself, and the *pemuda* militias formed the core of a *Tentara Nasional Indonesia* (TNI), an Indonesian National Army. But it soon became clear that the Netherlands was determined to reoccupy the Indies at any cost, using the British, who had reoccupied Singapore in September 1945, as their proxy. Believing that a firm show of popular resistance was needed to forestall the imminent landing of British troops, Tan Malaka approached a friend from his days in the Netherlands, now acting as foreign minister. He then met, in secret, with the new president, Sukarno. At the end of the meeting, believing that the British were likely to arrest him, Sukarno told Tan Malaka that if he and his deputy, Hatta, were unable to act, Tan Malaka should lead the republic in their place. This message was repeated at a second meeting. These private undertakings formed the basis of a formal Political Testament, to which, at Hatta's insistence, four other names were added after Tan Malaka's. There would later be much controversy over the intent and status of this Testament. But it is clear that Tan Malaka viewed it as wholly binding.[107]

To test the leadership's resolve to resist the British, Tan Malaka suggested it hold massive 'ocean' rallies in the cities. The largest was on 19 September, when a crowd of 200,000 people gathered in Ikeda Square in Jakarta, many armed with sharpened bamboo staves. Sukarno, increasingly worried about provoking the Japanese or the Allied troops, tried to prevent the assembly. But, in a moment of supreme political theatre, he arrived on the rostrum and, in a short speech, demonstrated his control over the masses by persuading the crowd to disperse without violence. To Tan Malaka it was clear that Sukarno had not tried to inspire the crowd to action, 'but to request the masses to "have faith" and "obey" and to order them to go home'.[108] On 1 October Tan Malaka left Jakarta in disgust, never to return, and headed east. Rumours of his presence flew ahead of him, and there were sightings of 'false' Tan Malakas across Java and Sumatra. British intelligence believed that he was in peninsular Malaya, and behind the foundation of a new radical nationalist party there.

Instead, he was a witness to the aftermath of the British occupation of the city of Surabaya in October 1945. British and Indian occupying troops were resisted street by street; tanks were confronted by the people from the urban kampungs, the *arek Surabaya*, armed with bamboo staves and knives. Thousands perished. Sukarno again appealed for order and calm. But, moved by the city's sacrifice, on 3 January 1946 Tan Malaka finally revealed himself at a large 'people's congress' at Purwokerto in Central Java. He announced a 'minimum programme' for the revolution, under the cry: 'One hundred per cent independence'. This was defined as the immediate departure of all foreign troops from Indonesian soil, a people's government, and the people's ownership of the economy. It set a new yardstick for freedom movements across Southeast Asia, and his *Persatuan Perjuangan*, or 'Struggle Union', rallied *pemuda* and radicals from a wide spectrum of other bodies. But it was too much for the new government, who were now seeking to negotiate with the British and Dutch. In March 1946 Tan Malaka was jailed for a fourth time, this time by the Indonesian republic.[109] One of the TNI officers responsible for his arrest described their reasoning:

Tan Malaka lived more than twenty years in exile, in jail, or in hiding. He lived in a world full of ideas, a troubled world of dreams and fantasies of a utopia. It was a solitary world. Because of this, it should not be surprising if he did not always think or act on the basis of the reality of the situation and atmosphere of the time. Furthermore, he was surrounded by radical followers . . . who thought nothing of the consequence of his radicalism . . . [and] wanted to spread their own radical ideas through

Tan Malaka, who had been cut off too long from the struggle of the Indonesian people.[110]

Tan Malaka wrote prolifically, critiquing the national leadership, and on his memoir, *Dari Penjara ke Penjara*, 'From Jail to Jail'.

This was Tan Malaka's longest stretch behind bars. By the time of his release eighteen months later, in September 1948, the republic was in crisis. It had been pushed back by a Dutch 'police action' into smaller pockets of territory, with its capital now at Yogyakarta. Tan Malaka was also confronted by old adversaries. On 11 August 1948 Musso came out of exile in Moscow, by aeroplane via Prague and New Delhi, secretly at first, although not for long. He still, as his old housemate from Surabaya days, Sukarno, observed, possessed the air of a *jago*, or street fighter.[111] Alimin had arrived ahead of Musso, although a visit to Ho Chi Minh in Hanoi had tempered his approach. At every opportunity, Musso invoked his Moscow credentials as he attempted to revive the old PKI on a militant platform called a 'New Road for the Indonesian Republic'. To Musso, Tan Malaka was a Trotskyite renegade. As they refought the debates of 1926 and 1927, Tan Malaka established a *Partai Murba*, a proletarian party, but failed to regain the momentum he had lost during his time in jail.

The cleavages within the revolution came to a head on 18 September, when leftist troops seized the central Javanese town of Madiun. Musso decided to support them. In a radio broadcast the next morning Sukarno decried it as a 'coup'. Replying by the same medium ninety minutes later, Musso condemned Sukarno as a Japanese collaborator, and for releasing the 'criminal' Tan Malaka. He announced that Madiun was 'a signal to the whole people to wrest the powers of the state into their own hands'. But the communists were unprepared for a full revolt, and republican forces and Muslim militias crushed them within ten days. Musso died with perhaps 10,000 others in the mopping-up operation.[112]

Tan Malaka wanted nothing to do with the affair. But events thrust him centre stage. In December a further Dutch 'police action' took Yogyakarta, and Sukarno and Hatta were captured. Tan Malaka headed east and sought the protection of a militant, brutal fighter called Sabarudin and his notorious Battalion 38, in the village of Blimbing. There, on a battered typewriter, he continued to attempt to rally the revolutionary forces under his leadership. He invoked the Political Testament of 1 October 1945, claiming that, now Sukarno and Hatta were under arrest, the mantle of the revolution fell to him. But he was outcast on all sides, a target of both the Dutch special forces in the area and the TNI, who had no truck with his alliance with a renegade battalion. On 19 December 1948 Tan Malaka was arrested by a TNI company and held at a village ten miles from Blimbing. On 21 February 1949 the camp came under attack from the Dutch; the prisoners were abandoned and began to flee. Slowed by a wounded leg, Tan Malaka struggled towards a TNI post at Selapanggung. He was identified by its commander, who decided he was too dangerous to remain at large. Like so many in those days of chaos and violence, Tan Malaka faced summary military justice and was shot the same day, at the foot of nearby Mount Wilis.[113] The Indonesian revolution, like all revolutions, was quick to eat its own.

AND DREAMS, AND VISIONS, AND DISENCHANTMENT

To the victor, the mausoleum in a city square: to the vanquished, the shallow grave in the woods. Many of those with whom Tan Malaka's path crossed during his years of exile met a violent end. After eluding the Nazi occupiers of the Netherlands for two years, Henk Sneevliet was shot alongside other members of the Dutch resistance in the Amersfoort concentration camp on 12 April 1942. Sneevliet's comrade of his Java days, Asser Baars, died in Auschwitz in 1944. Sneevliet's successor in China, Mikhail Borodin, survived the purges and the war as editor of the English-language *Moscow News*, only to be arrested in a fresh purge in 1949 and die in a gulag in 1951. His one-time ally, Chen Duxiu, was released from prison in 1937, but he too was outcast from the party he had led and died in obscurity in 1942, after working for a time as a schoolteacher near Chongqing. Chen's successor, Li Lisan, after the collapse of the 'revolutionary high tide' in 1931, was sent on a long period of rehabilitation in Moscow. He returned to play a central role in the foundation of the People's Republic in 1949. But, after the Sino-Soviet split of 1956, his past told against him and he perished in the Cultural Revolution in 1967. His Russian wife, Lisa Kishkin, survived him, a citizen of China.

The hybrid family histories of the Asian revolution were one of its most enduring legacies. Musso was survived by children from two Russian wives and a son in Indonesia born before his departure in 1926. Musso's fellow exiles, Semaoen and Darsono, returned to Indonesia after independence to careers in public service. They played no role in the revival of a 'new' PKI after 1954. Alimin was the last of the old guard to remain with the party and was one of its staunchest critics. A scholar who interviewed him in Jakarta in 1960 described him as 'old, senile, ailing, lonely, and no longer visited by party members'.[114] Alimin died in 1964, in the midst of the party's final push for power, before its destruction in 1965–6 in slaughter and detentions on a massive scale.

The moral journeys of this generation took very different paths. Of the members of India House, Har Dayal's trajectory was unique in that, obstructed by the British, he never returned to India. He did, however, return to London, and completed a doctoral thesis in 1932 at the School of Oriental and African Studies. He died in Philadelphia in 1939 while on a lecture tour. Vinayak Savarkar returned from the Andaman Islands, his prison writings travelling ahead of him, and became a foundational thinker for Hindutva, or Hindu nationalism. When his old adversary Gandhi was assassinated in 1948 at the hands of a Hindu extremist – an event which had parallels to the Dhingra affair that had bitterly divided them nearly forty years earlier – Savarkar stood trial, and was acquitted, for his alleged role in it. By contrast, his closest associate in London, M. P. T. Acharya, lived in Berlin and Amsterdam after he left Moscow and the Communist Party of India and moved back to anarchist internationalism. He was allowed to return to India in 1935, where from Bombay he continued to write on anarchist and pacifist themes, and where the paintings by his Russian wife, Magda Nachman, were much sought after by the city's elite.[115] The friend who travelled with Acharya in 1910 to Morocco and turned back, Sukhsagar Datta, brother to the convicted terrorist Ullaskar, worked as a doctor in Bristol, was active in Labour Party politics, and died there in 1967, after nearly sixty years in the UK.[116]

The origins of many of these choices can be seen in the radical movement from its earliest inception. Ghadar charted paths to anarchism, nationalism, communism, Islamism and Sikh militancy.[117] Many of the British empire's most-wanted men in 1915–17 remained committed to international causes and what one writer has described as 'the hard slog of forging and sustaining alliances across an uneven and unequal geo-political field'.[118] Taraknath Das and Bhagwan Singh stayed in America after serving the prison terms handed down in 1918 at the San Francisco conspiracy trial. Taraknath Das married an American supporter, Mary Keatinge Morse, herself a founding member of the National Association for the Advancement of Colored People, and became a professor at Columbia and Georgetown Universities. Bhagwan Singh also lectured widely on India and spiritual themes. He was invited to return by the independent government of India in 1958 and died in Chandigarh in 1962. In a way, M. N. Roy too abandoned active politics, or was left outside them, and took a more scholarly path. While in prison, he wrote to a friend:

> I came to the conclusion that civilised mankind was destined to go through another period of monasticism, where all the treasures of past wisdom, knowledge and learning will be rescued from the ruins to be then passed on to a new generation engaged in the task of building a new world and a new civilisation.[119]

Largely alienated from the intellectual circles in Bengal and elsewhere, he surrounded himself in Dehra Dun with a small circle of 'Royists' and devoted himself to a Radical Humanist Movement. Visitors observed, however, that to the end of his life Roy kept a photograph of Stalin on his mantelpiece. He survived the old man by less than a year: after two years of illness following a bad fall, he died on 25 January 1954. The national press carried brief obituaries. His wife Ellen continued to organize his movement and to edit its mouthpiece, *The Radical Humanist*, from Dehra Dun, until her beaten, dead body was discovered on the morning of 14 December 1960. From the long police investigation and resulting prosecutions, there were signs that it was a political murder, but the mystery of its motive was never really solved.[120] Roy's first wife, Evelyn, remarried and lived quietly in California until her death in 1970, reluctant in later life to talk publicly of her role in the world revolution, and unmentioned in the memoirs Roy published in the *Radical Humanist* in his last years.

Most of these men and women lived long enough to write histories of their lives and times. They maintained a global web of correspondence, reliving encounters from long ago. But, for some, the underground was a dark cave from which they did not return – like those who perished in Stalin's purges – or left behind only the slightest traces. This web of infinite connections was a fragile one that could all too easily break, or never even fuse together at all. To go overseas was always a battle against being forgotten. The work of memorial was central to the village abroad from its very beginnings. The first histories of Ghadar were martyrologues, which shaped future waves of anti-colonial violence. The landscape of the Punjab is dotted with shrines to the men of 1915. 'India House' is reconstructed in a memorial park over fifty-two acres at Shyamji Krishnavarma's birthplace in Mandvi in Gujarat. In Vancouver, Mewa Singh, the assassin of W. C. Hopkinson, is to this day commemorated annually, and for Canada the *Komagata Maru* has become a potent symbol for national reflection. In a quieter way, Vietnamese visitors to the modern city of Canton still visit the tomb of Pham Hong Thai, to pause there to bow in homage to his memory, but as a patriotic martyr, not an anarchist internationalist. In a similar way, sites such as that of the Nanchang uprising and the Canton commune are commemorated as the birthplace of the People's Liberation Army, or as a step, or misstep, along China's revolutionary road.

For many years, the memory of the global underground dissolved into national stories. In this sense it remained a lost country: a history of revolutionary failure, or of something that did not happen. But, as it re-emerges, the view from the underground shifts our understanding of larger events in significant ways. Bhagwan Singh later insisted that the Ghadar mutiny was a close-run thing. Had there been arms from Germany, had the German troops in China not 'been lost us' when they were marched into captivity at the fall of Qingdao, had leaders within India not actively recruited for the British, events may have played out very differently. As it stood, he argued, it was Ghadar, in its stimulus to action, to repression, that brought a 'mass awakening' to India: 'it was these shocks of [the] Indian Army's disloyalty and undependability that convinced the British that India cannot be held against her will' and, by its propaganda overseas, 'destroyed the moral justification of British Rule in India'.[121] Despite the illusion of 'normal time' in the 1930s, the foundations of empire were fatally undermined. This view is borne out by much later scholarship.[122] In China, too, the events of 1923–7 can be seen as the beginning of a decades-long cycle of military violence that 'unmade' and remade the nation and extorted a horrendous toll from its people.[123]

Seen from the underground, time is loosened further, and the history of what later became known as the 'global Cold War' takes on a longer duration, with its beginnings in the Bolshevik panic across empires in the 1920s, or even back in the earlier struggle against international anarchism. This protracted conflict is a window on the experience of human movement in the twentieth century, its ebbs and flows, surveillance and obstruction. Some ten years after the fall of the Berlin Wall, an installation by the artist Arnold Dreyblatt displayed a 'mirror archive' of around 4,000 intelligence documents drawn from multiple sources, including the archive of the Shanghai Municipal Police, seemingly relating to an individual called 'T' (born in Hungary in 1879, died in Shanghai in 1943). 'T' is revealed to be a composite life of the multiple individual names in the files, which are shown redacted and cross-referenced to suggest strange, aimless, subversive journeys across America and Eurasia. 'T' becomes an Everyman whose obscure purposes are followed by the police of many countries. The archival fragments are constantly cut up, reorganized and redisplayed so that 'any desire to recover an original moment of intention or of action or of observation or of inscription or of transmission (and the multiplication of possible starting points already testifies to a crisis of determination) gives way . . . to other fascinations'.[124] Part of the purpose of this kind of history is to reveal a sea of stories that other historians will navigate in their own ways.

Some of these led to later internationals: the 1947 Asian Relations Conference in Delhi, held in the full heat of the freedom struggles in India, Indonesia and Vietnam, or the Afro-Asia Conference in Bandung in April 1955, where Sukarno and Zhou Enlai dominated a new world stage. But Bandung was more a meeting of established nation states than a common front of peoples. Perhaps the most important legacies of the old Asian underground were the internationals it spawned outside of states – of trade unionists, artists or scientists – that are now once again coming into historical focus.[125] Equally significant were the ways in which old networks of smuggling people, funds and arms across the borders of Indochina, across the Straits of Malacca, sustained the Vietnamese and Indonesian revolutions at their most vulnerable moments.[126] In a strange twist of fate, the internees from Boven Digoel, evacuated to

Australia in 1943, played a pivotal supporting role in this by coordinating by aerogram a global boycott of Dutch shipping.

The underground of 1905–27 was a singular moment in time. As an anarchist chronicler described it:

> There was besides a constant exchange of ideas from country to country by translations of questions of more than local interest. In this way every good pamphlet became very soon known internationally, and this sphere of intellectual exchange ranged from Portugal to China and New Zealand, and from Canada to Chile and Peru. This made every formal organisation, however loose and informal it was, really unnecessary; to such an extent one of the purposes of organisation, international friendly relations, was already realised in these happy years when the globe seemed to have become a single small unit, while today it is split up and scattered into atoms, separated from each other in a worse degree than in the darkest mediaeval times; at least this is so in the greater part of the European continent at present, and is supported in dumb submission.[127]

The 'today' of the passage was 1924, the crescendo of this revolutionary age. For all its partings of ways and divergent destinies, several shared qualities drew these stories together and made them something more than the sum of their parts. Foremost among these was patience. The pathfinder, Phan Boi Chau, published a memoir in 1940, from his house arrest in Hue. 'My history', he wrote, 'is entirely a history of failure, and the maladies that have caused this failure are indeed obvious.' He was, he admitted, excessively self-confident, overly open with others, impetuous in his judgements: 'on many occasions, because of small things a big plan failed'. 'All the same,' he continued, 'I do not venture to say that there is nothing of which I can be proud.' Here he listed his audacity, his ability always to remember 'a good thought', and above all his optimism: 'I always look forward to reaching the goal, and achieving victory at the last moment; even though the means and strategies may change, I am not distressed.'[128]

This extraordinary fortitude came from a conviction that revolutionaries stood at, and had a unique perception of, the defining moment of the age, when there was a possibility of them acting as an agent of elemental change whereby the previously disempowered – the ordinary worker or peasant, women, even the poorest of the poor – might reach for a new future. They constituted, in the Indonesian term, an *aliran*, an unstoppable wave of collective consciousness. Across the terrains of exile – cities and neighbourhoods – this vision gathered force and conviction as revolutionaries shared resources and skills, forged alliances, or were simply witness to each other, drawing strength from a sense of co-presence.[129] These places were a fertile ground for radical new ideas. The political thought of the underground emerged in motion; it was fluid, instinctively eclectic and endlessly creative in its work of translation. The most fertile minds did not remain doctrinal Marxists for long. Ideas were not principally to be found in philosophical treatises, although these certainly existed, as in Tan Malaka's *Madilog*, written as a treasury of hard-won wisdom. They were often published in mosquito journals that rapidly came and went, or as pamphlets whose only later traces were often in police archives; or they were spoken and taught. At the heart of the underground was a worldwide experiment in mass education, in political instruction, in creating a 'new culture' and a new type of popular intellectual – what was termed in China a 'Red literati'. They shared a premonition that Asia lay at the forefront of human futures, and that, however much they adapted its learning, in M. N. Roy's phrase, Europe was not the world.

They shared too a pervading dilemma over the means for achieving these futures, over the necessity of political violence, its temptations and its costs. Asia's first age of revolution ended as it had begun, in violence and trauma. The question of its ethics remained unresolved. In the spring of 1949, Jawaharlal Nehru visited the town of Muzaffarpur, where Khudiram Bose had thrown the bomb at the carriage of Mrs Kennedy and her daughter on 29 April 1908 killing them both, and arguably setting in motion a long cycle of terror and repression. Nehru refused a request from local political worthies to lay the foundation stone of the town's martyr's memorial to Khudiram, on the grounds that 'the principle of non-violence was involved'. Just over a year had passed since the assassination of Mahatma Gandhi. Writing at the time, M. N. Roy observed that even a couple of years earlier Nehru would not have been so weighed down with the burdens of state to refuse such a task. The prime minister of India, Roy claimed, was a beneficiary and 'not morally entitled to be censorious about acts of violence prompted by selfless idealism'. Nationalists in power continued to commit mass violence; as Roy had seen at first hand in China in 1927, it was the direct consequence of these earlier acts. To Roy, 'one can never be a nationalist and yet be sincere in the profession of non-violence'. Roy recalled how, over forty years earlier, in April 1907, he had met Khudiram on the very eve of his 'fatal pilgrimage' to Muzaffarpur. He had as long ago as 1917, in Mexico, repudiated the religious violence of his youth, as he had later that of Leninism, for the methods of reason and cultural transformation espoused within Radical Humanism. But Roy still held that the claims to idealism of Khudiram and the first generation of martyrs was such that 'the grandeur of their selflessness outshines the smallness of their mistakes'.[130] After 1927, for that matter after 1949, the cycle of imperial and revolutionary violence unleashed around 1907 had a long way to run.

But, for all this, by 1927 there was a sense of the passing of an old guard and the rise of new leaders, more dogmatic thinking and iron party discipline. Already by the 1920s, in orthodox Stalinist circles, the term 'anti-nationalism' was a term of abuse reserved for anarchists, Trotskyites and bourgeois internationalists. Vera Vladimirovna-Akimova had to wait some forty years to write of her experiences in Canton and Wuhan in 1926 and 1927. She explained that she wrote not just for herself, but so that 'other voices which are now stilled forever would resound'. It was a testimony of a 'remarkable' moment of Sino-Soviet friendship: remarkable because it no longer was a possibility.[131] As her translator noted, her richly evocative memoir 'reads like a roll call of the dead', a history of loss, of lives robbed of their historical salience.[132] Such loss is omnipresent in the writing on this era of Asian connections: the mourning of old elites for bygone influence; a grieving for lost cities and vanished neighbourhoods – the closure of Shanghai to Tan Malaka, or Berlin or Colonia Roma to Roy – for loss of mobility itself.[133] This is not merely a tolling for lost friends, family and comrades, nor for liberty, for what was destroyed. For the underground, there is a particular cadence to this loss, a grief for that which people were unable to build, for a lost heterotopia. But as another witness to this, Walter Benjamin, wrote from a similar time but another place, a moment of loss is also a 'moment of danger' at which future possibilities can be grasped.[134] In this, the image of the underground carries its specific sense of mutability and mobility, of the possibility of new places, new beginnings and new struggles: the 'old mole' of history, burying, burrowing and resurfacing elsewhere.

For many decades after his death in Java, Tan Malaka was a spectral presence in Indonesia. He was never forgotten. In 1963 Sukarno remembered his debt to him, and declared him officially a 'national hero'. But after the fall of Sukarno and the bloody crushing of the leftist movement, he remained a 'lonely' and problematic figure. In 1991, a three-volume English-language translation of his memoirs appeared, but it was little read outside a circle of specialist scholars of Indonesia. It was only with the restoration of democracy in 1999 that Tan Malaka re-emerged as 'the forgotten father of the republic'; his works were republished and became popular with a new generation of politicized youth. His image was seen on posters and T-shirts, a Che Guevara for Nusantara. The slower work of academic history had an important role to play in this, with the publication in the Netherlands in 2007 of a 2,194-page study of his life and times based on multiple archives and interviews over many years, entitled *Verguisd en Vergeten*, 'Despised and Forgotten'. As its author, Harry Poeze, observed, it was completed at the moment when Tan Malaka's times were vanishing from the memory of living; such a study would not be possible again. It soon made a larger impact in Indonesian translation.

As it did so, in 2009 a grave was opened at the foot of Mount Wilis in East Java. A portrait of Tan Malaka in middle age was placed over a makeshift *attap* tomb. The 'lonely revolutionary' had left no heirs, but a surviving cousin raised the possibility of DNA testing, and of reinterring his remains in the heroes' cemetery in the capital, Jakarta, or in his Minangkabau homeland. The science, however, was inconclusive.[135] In 2011 a theatre production opened in Jakarta called *Opera Tan Malaka*. It was staged in Soviet-era constructivist style, with a libretto by Goenawan Muhamad, one of Indonesia's leading writers. But an attempt to hold the production in East Java was blocked by the authorities. Tan Malaka remained an uncertain, dangerous presence. In the opera that bears his name, Tan Malaka does not appear. As the narrator tells it: 'I disappear therefore I exist. I am present. Tan Malaka will not die in this story. Maybe that is what I need to say.'[136] These words are an echo of Tan Malaka's own, to his British interrogators in his cell in Hong Kong in the summer of 1932: 'Remember this. My voice will be louder from the grave than ever it was while I walked the earth.'[137]

Notes

ABBREVIATIONS

ANM	Arkib Negara Malaysia
ANOM	Archives Nationales d'Outre-Mer
GOI	Government of India
IISH	International Institute of Social History
IOR	India Office Records
MBPI	Malayan Bulletin of Political Intelligence
NAI	National Archives of India
NARA	National Archives and Records Administration (USA)
NL-HaNA	Nationaal Archief, Den Haag
SMP	Records of the Shanghai Municipal Police
SNA	National Archives of Singapore
TNA	The National Archives

FOREWORD

1. Rudolf Mrázek, *Engineers of Happy Land: Technology and Nationalism in a Colony*, Princeton, NJ, Princeton University Press, 2002, p. xv.

2. Takashi Shiraishi, *An Age in Motion: Popular Radicalism in Java, 1912–1926*, Cornell, NY, Cornell University Press, 1990, is a seminal influence on this study.

3. E.g. Lara Putnam, 'The Transnational and the Text-Searchable: Digitized Sources and the Shadows They Cast', *American Historical Review*, 121/2 (2016), pp. 377–402.

4. Christopher Bayly and Tim Harper, *Forgotten Armies: The Fall of British Asia, 1941–45*, London, Allen Lane, 2004, and *Forgotten Wars: The End of Britain's Asian Empire*, London, Allen Lane, 2007.

PRELUDE: ON THE THRESHOLD
OF FREE ASIA (1924)

1. Sir Ernest Mason Satow and Ian Ruxton, *Sir Ernest Satow's Private Letters to W. G. Aston and F. V. Dickins: The Correspondence of a Pioneer Japanologist from 1870 to 1918*, London, Routledge, 2008, p. 226.
2. These arguments, and the quotation, are drawn from Virgil K. Y. Ho, *Understanding Canton: Rethinking Popular Culture in the Republican Period*, Oxford, Oxford University Press, 2005, pp. 50–53.
3. For Tianjin as 'hypo-' and 'hyper-colony' see Ruth Rogaski, *Hygienic Modernity: Meanings of Health and Disease in Treaty-Port China*, Berkeley, University of California Press, 2004, p. 21.
4. Michael Tsang-Woon Tsin, *Nation, Governance, and Modernity in China: Canton, 1900–1927*, Stanford, CA, Stanford University Press, 2000.
5. I have taken this summary figure from Arthur Waldron, 'War and the Rise of Nationalism in Twentieth-Century China', *Journal of Military History*, 57/5 (1993), pp. 87–104, at p. 98. Issues of scale and the industrialization of war are discussed at more length in Waldron's *From War to Nationalism: China's Turning Point, 1924–1925*, Cambridge, Cambridge University Press, 2003, esp. pp. 53–71.
6. TNA, FO 228/3276, 'Canton Intelligence Report, March Quarter, 1921'.
7. Hans J. van de Ven, *From Friend to Comrade: The Founding of the Chinese Communist Party, 1920–1927*, Berkeley, University of California Press, 1992, pp. 156–7.
8. Dorothy Dix, *My Joy-Ride Round the World*, London, Mills & Boon, 1922, p. 129.
9. For this phrase, Yoshihiro Ishikawa, *The Formation of the Chinese Communist Party*, New York, Columbia University Press, 2013, p. 14.
10. Alice L. Conklin, *A Mission to Civilize: The Republican Idea of Empire in France and West Africa, 1895–1930*, Stanford, CA, Stanford University Press, 1997, pp. 190–92.
11. *The Japan Times*, 21 May 1924.
12. TNA, FO 371/10293, Bertram Giles, Consul-General Canton, to Peking, 27 June 1924.
13. Hallett Abend, *My Years in China, 1926–1941*, London, John Lane, 1944, p. 14.
14. ANOM, INDO/GGI/65533, 'The Canton Outrage. Protection of the Shameen', *Hong Kong Daily Press*, ? June 1924. The date is not legible on my copy.
15. Ibid., Le Capitaine de Frégate Seychal à le Contre-Amiral Commandant les Forces Navales en Extrême-Orient, 22 June 1924.
16. Ibid., M. Beauvais, Gérant du Consulat de France à Canton à de Fleuriau, Ministre Plénipotentiaire, China, 21 June 1924.

17. *China Mail*, 21 June 1924; *North China Herald*, 18 June 1924.

18. ANOM, INDO/GGI/65533, 'The Canton Outrage. Protection of the Shameen', *Hong Kong Daily Press*, ? June 1924.

19. See the *Canton Phenomenon*, 21 June 1924.

20. As translated and cited in Richard A. Cruz, 'André Malraux: The Anticolonial and Antifascist Years', PhD thesis, University of North Texas, 1996, p. 113.

21. *Canton Phenomenon*, 21 June 1924.

22. *Hong Kong Daily Press*, 24 June 1924.

23. *China Mail*, 26 June 1924.

24. As reported in the *North China Herald*, 12 July 1924.

25. *China Mail*, 23 June 1924.

26. *Hong Kong Daily Press*, 24 June 1924.

27. TNA, FO 371/10293, L. Collier, Minute, 4 September 1924.

28. Lorraine M. Paterson, 'A Vietnamese Icon in Canton: Biographical Borders and Revolutionary Romance in 1920s Canton', in Caroline S. Hau and Kasian Tejapira (eds), *Traveling Nation-Makers: Transnational Flows and Movements in the Making of Modern Southeast Asia*, Singapore, NUS Press, 2011, pp. 69–70.

29. *China Mail*, 18 July 1924.

30. Ibid., 24 July 1924.

31. Yuan-tsung Chen, *Return to the Middle Kingdom: One Family, Three Revolutionaries, and the Birth of Modern China*, New York, Union Square Press, 2008, p. 129; Daniel Y. K. Kwan, *Marxist Intellectuals and the Chinese Labor Movement: A Study of Deng Zhongxia (1894–1933)*, Seattle, University of Washington Press, 1997, pp. 107–8.

32. *China Mail*, 29 July 1924; ibid., 30 July 1924; ibid, 7 August 1924.

33. For the Victoria Hotel see Jonathan Fenby, *Chiang Kai Shek: China's Generalissimo and the Nation He Lost*, London, Simon & Schuster, 2009, p. 71; *North China Herald*, 2 August 1924.

34. *China Mail*, 20 August 1924.

35. I have used the account and the translation in Hwang Eunshil, ' "Sharing the Same Predicament": Mutual Perceptions and Interactions between Korean and Vietnamese Intellectuals, 1900–1925', PhD thesis, National University of Singapore, 2016, pp. 126–8.

36. Doan-Bich, *Famous Men of Vietnam*, 3rd edn, Hanoi, Vietnam Council on Foreign Relations, 1970, p. 37.

37. Private collection, Interviews by Andrew Hardy and Đào Thế Đúc, Chiang Mai, 22 and 25 July 2004. Shared and quoted by kind permission of Andrew Hardy. See also: 'Gặp người con trai liệt sỹ Phạm Hồng Thái', http://cand.com.vn/Phong-su-tu-lieu/Gap-nguoi-con-trai-liet-sy-Pham-Hong-Thai-171649/ (last accessed 25 August 2019).

38. Doan-Bich, *Famous Men of Vietnam*, p. 37.

39. Phan-Bội-Châu, *Overturned Chariot: The Autobiography of Phan-Bội-Châu*, trans. Vinh Sinh and Nicholas Wickenden, Honolulu, University of Hawaii Press, 1999, p. 253.

40. ANOM, INDO/GG/65533, 'Histoire de Pham Hong Thai', a translation of the work marked 'Secret'.

41. *China Mail*, 24 June 1924.

42. David G. Marr, *Vietnamese Anticolonialism, 1885–1925*, Berkeley, University of California Press, 1971, p. 257.

43. Phan-Bội-Châu, *Overturned Chariot*, p. 256.

44. Marr, *Vietnamese Anticolonialism*, pp. 75–7.

45. Doan-Bich, *Famous Men of Vietnam*, p. 37.

46. *China Mail*, 26 June 1924.

47. Kwan, *Marxist Intellectuals*, p. 93.

48. As reported in *Hong Kong Daily Press*, 26 June 1924.

49. ANOM, INDO/GGI/65533, Governor-General Monguillot to Minister of Colonies, 23 May 1925.

50. Png Poh-seng, 'The Kuomintang in Malaya, 1912–1941', *Journal of Southeast Asian History*, 2/1 (1961), pp. 1–32, at p. 7.

51. Hue-Tam Ho Tai, *Radicalism and the Origins of the Vietnamese Revolution*, Cambridge, MA, Harvard University Press, 1992, pp. 66–7.

52. Hue-Tam Ho Tai, *Passion, Betrayal, and Revolution in Colonial Saigon: The Memoirs of Bao Luong*, Berkeley, University of California Press, 2010, p. 50.

53. Paterson, 'A Vietnamese Icon in Canton', pp. 64–95, esp. description and quotation at pp. 67–8. This essay is an excellent dissection of the multiple meanings of the incident as seen at the time.

54. Quoted by Firuta Motoo, 'Vietnamese Political Movements in Thailand: Legacy of the Dong-Du Movement', in Vinh Sinh (ed.), *Phan Bôi Châu and the Dông-du Movement*, New Haven, CT, Yale University Press, 1988, pp. 150–81, at p. 150.

55. TNA, CO 537/931, MBPI, April 1925.

56. Dan N. Jacobs, *Borodin: Stalin's Man in China*, Cambridge, MA, Harvard University Press, 1981; and see later chapters below.

57. The 'adage' he quotes is a Chinese saw. All quotations are from Tan Malaka, *From Jail to Jail*, trans. and ed. Helen Jarvis, Athens, Ohio University Center for International Studies, 1991, vol. II, p. 109.

58. Vera Vladimirovna Vishnyakova-Akimova, *Two Years in Revolutionary China, 1925–1927*, trans. Steven I. Levine, Cambridge, MA, Harvard University Press, 1971, p. 229.

59. Pierre Brocheux, *Ho Chi Minh: A Biography*, Cambridge, Cambridge University Press, 2007, pp. 29–39.

60. Sophie Quinn-Judge, *Ho Chi Minh: The Missing Years, 1919–1941*, London, Hurst, 2003, pp. 69–80.

61. For this point, Tai, *Radicalism and the Origins of the Vietnamese Revolution*, p. 69.

62. See Sunil S. Amrith and Tim Harper, 'Introduction' in Harper and Amrith (eds), *Sites of Asian Interaction: Ideas, Networks and Mobility*, Cambridge, Cambridge University Press, 2014, pp. 1–9.

1. IN SEARCH OF A LOST COUNTRY (1905)

1. The account of the journey comes from Phan-Bội-Châu, *Overturned Chariot: The Autobiography of Phan-Bội-Châu*, trans. Vinh Sinh and Nicholas Wickenden, Honolulu, University of Hawaii Press, 1999, pp. 80–83. The guide was Tang Bat Ho.

2. Gerard Sasges, 'State, Enterprise and the Alcohol Monopoly in Colonial Vietnam', *Journal of Southeast Asian Studies*, 43/1 (2012), pp. 133–57; statistics (for 1908) on pp. 142, 152; Philippe Le Failler, 'Village Rebellions in the Tonkin Delta, 1900–1905', in Gisèle Bousquet and Pierre Brocheux (eds), *Viêt-Nam Exposé: French Scholarship on Twentieth Century Vietnamese Society*, Ann Arbor, University of Michigan Press, 2002, pp. 61–86, esp. pp. 62, 72.

3. Wensheng Wang, *White Lotus Rebels and South China Pirates: Crisis and Reform in the Qing Empire*, Cambridge, MA, Harvard University Press, 2014, pp. 94–6.

4. Li Tana, 'A View from the Sea: Perspectives on the Northern and Central Vietnamese Coast', *Journal of Southeast Asian Studies*, 37/1 (2006), pp. 83–102; for the 'vast connecting river', Charles Wheeler, 'Re-thinking the Sea in Vietnamese History: Littoral Society in the Integration of Thuận-Quảng, Seventeenth–Eighteenth Centuries', *Journal of Southeast Asian Studies*, 37/1 (2006), pp. 123–53, at p. 140, illuminated in a workshop discussion in Hong Kong in December 2010.

5. Zaharah binti Haji Mahmud, 'The Malay Concept of *Tanah Air*: The Geographer's Perspective', in Danny Wong Tze Ken (ed.), *Memory and Knowledge of the Sea in Southeast Asia*, Kuala Lumpur, Institute of Ocean and Earth Sciences, University of Malaya, 2008, pp. 5–14.

6. Isabel Hofmeyr has written of the 'cross-cutting diasporas' of the Indian Ocean in 'The Complicating Sea: The Indian Ocean as Method', *Comparative Studies of South Asia, Africa and the Middle East*, 32/3 (2012), pp. 584–90.

7. Phan Chu Trinh, as cited in Masaya Shiraishi, 'Phan Boi Chau and Japan', *South East Asian Studies* [Kyoto], 13/3 (1975), pp. 427–40, at p. 430.

8. For a recent study see Stephen R. Pratt, *Autumn in the Heavenly Kingdom: China, the West and the Epic Story of the Taiping Civil War*, London, Atlantic Books, 2013.

9. Bradley Camp Davis, *Imperial Bandits: Outlaws and Rebels in the China–Vietnam Borderlands*, Seattle, University of Washington Press, 2016, pp. 32–7.

10. Ibid., pp. 16–17.

11. Nicolas Lainez, 'Human Trade in Colonial Vietnam', in David W. Haines, Keiko Yamanaka and Shinji Yamashita (eds), *Wind over Water: Migration in an East Asian Context*, New York, Berghahn Books, 2012, pp. 21–35, at p. 23; Julia Martínez, 'Trafficking in Women and Children across the China Sea', in Emma Christopher, Cassandra Pybus and Marcus Rediker (eds), *Many Middle Passages: Forced Migration and the Making of the Modern World*, Berkeley, University of California Press, 2007, pp. 204–23.

12. Micheline Lessard, ' "Cet Ignoble Trafic": The Kidnapping and Sale of Vietnamese Women and Children in French Colonial Indochina, 1873–1935', *French Colonial History*, 10/1 (2009), pp. 1–34, at p. 17.

13. A. R. Agassiz, 'From Hai-Phong in Tong-King to Canton, Overland', *Proceedings of the Royal Geographical Society*, New Monthly Series, 13/5 (1891), pp. 249–64, at p. 263.

14. 'Three Poems by Phan Boi Chau', trans. Huynh Sanh Thong, in Sính Vĩnh (ed.), *Phan Bôi Châu and the Dông-du Movement*, New Haven, CT, Yale University Press, 1988, pp. 182–92, at p. 184.

15. Châu, *Overturned Chariot*, p. 83; Shiraishi, 'Phan Boi Chau and Japan', p. 433.

16. For biographies of Phan Boi Chau see William J. Duiker, 'Phan Boi Chau: Asian Revolutionary in a Changing World', *Journal of Asian Studies*, 31/1 (1971), pp. 77–88; Yves Le Jariel, *Phan Boi Chau (1867–1940): Le Nationalisme Vietnamien Avant Ho Chi Minh*, Paris, L'Harmattan, 2008.

17. Pierre Brocheux and Daniel Hémery, *Indochina: An Ambiguous Colonization, 1858–1954*, Berkeley, University of California Press, 2010, pp. 57–8; Michael P. M. Finch, *A Progressive Occupation? The Gallieni–Lyautey Method and Colonial Pacification in Tonkin and Madagascar, 1885–1900*, Oxford, Oxford University Press, 2013, pp. 89–90, 99.

18. Brocheux and Hémery, *Indochina*, pp. 48–52.

19. George N. Curzon, 'Journeys in French Indo-China (Tongking, Annam, Cochin China, Cambodia): Conclusion', *The Geographical Journal*, 2/3 (1893), pp. 193–210, at p. 206.

20. Firuta Motoo, 'Vietnamese Political Movements in Thailand: Legacy of the Dong-Du Movement', in Vĩnh (ed.), *Phan Bôi Châu and the Dông-Du Movement*, pp. 150–81, at pp. 151–2.

21. Châu, *Overturned Chariot*, p. 53.

22. Charles Fourniau, 'Colonial Wars before 1914: The Case of France in Indochina', in Jaap A. de Moor and Hendrik L. Wesseling (eds), *Imperialism and War: Essays on Colonial Wars in Asia and Africa*, Leiden, Brill, 1989, pp. 72–86; Finch, *A Progressive Occupation?*, chs. 3–4.

23. Phan Boi Chau, 'The History of the Loss of the Country (1905)', in George E. Dutton, Jayne Susan Werner and John K. Whitmore (eds), *Sources of Vietnamese Tradition*, New York, Columbia University Press, 2012, pp. 342–53, at p. 345.

24. J. Kim Munholland, '"Collaboration Strategy" and the French Pacification of Tonkin, 1885–1897', *Historical Journal*, 24/3 (1981), pp. 629–50, quotation at p. 644, fn. 70; David G. Marr, *Vietnamese Anticolonialism, 1885–1925*, Berkeley, University of California Press, 1971, pp. 82–3.

25. Châu, *Overturned Chariot*, p. 59.

26. Mark Bradley, 'Becoming Van Minh: Civilizational Discourse and Visions of the Self in Twentieth-Century Vietnam', *Journal of World History*, 15/1 (2004), pp. 65–83.

27. For an overview see Nicholas Tarling, 'Political Structures in the Nineteenth and Early Twentieth Centuries', in Tarling (ed.), *The Cambridge History of Southeast Asia*, vol. II, Cambridge, Cambridge University Press, 1993, pp. 79–130.

28. Jhr. H. M. van Weede, 'The Balinese *Puputan*' (1908), translated in Tineke Hellwig and Eric Tagliacozzo (eds), *The Indonesia Reader: History, Culture, Politics*, Durham, NC, Duke University Press, 2009, pp. 262–4.

29. Clifford Geertz, *Negara: The Theatre State in Nineteenth-Century Bali*, Princeton, NJ, Princeton University Press, 1981; for the numbers, p. 141.

30. David P. Chandler and David J. Steinberg (eds), *In Search of Southeast Asia: A Modern History*, Honolulu, University of Hawaii Press, 1987, p. 202.

31. Shane Strate, *The Lost Territories: Thailand's History of National Humiliation*, Honolulu, University of Hawaii Press, 2015.

32. Chau, 'History of the Loss of the Country', p. 345.

33. Tang Xiaobing, *Global Space and the Nationalist Discourse of Modernity: The Historical Thinking of Liang Qichao*, Stanford, CA, Stanford University Press, 1996. Discussions of Liang's historical significance start with Joseph Levenson, *Liang Ch'i-ch'ao and the Mind of Modern China*, Cambridge, MA, Harvard University Press, 1953. For Liang in a wider context see Pankaj Mishra, *From the Ruins of Empire: The Revolt against the West and the Remaking of Asia*, London, Penguin, 2012, ch. 2.

34. Quoted in Peter Zarrow, *After Empire: The Conceptual Transformation of the Chinese State, 1885–1924*, Stanford, CA, Stanford University Press, 2012, p. 58.

35. Here I borrow John Lonsdale's dictum, and acknowledge an enduring intellectual debt. See John Lonsdale, 'Anti-Colonial Nationalism and Patriotism in Sub-Saharan Africa', in John Breuilly (ed.), *The Oxford Handbook of the History of Nationalism*, Oxford, Oxford University Press, 2013, pp. 318–37, at p. 320.

36. Bradley, 'Becoming Van Minh'; Hue-Tam Ho Tai, *Radicalism and the*

Origins of the Vietnamese Revolution, Cambridge, MA, Harvard University Press, 1992, pp. 20–22.

37. Atsuko Sakaki, *Obsessions with the Sino-Japanese Polarity in Japanese Literature*, Honolulu, University of Hawaii Press, 2006, pp. 158–9.

38. Bradley, 'Becoming Van Minh'; Sính Vĩnh, ' "Elegant Females" Re-encountered: From Tōkai Sanshi's *Kajin No Kigü* to Phan Châu Trinh's *Giai Nhân ky Ngô Dien Ca* ', in K. W. Taylor and John W. Whitmore (eds), *Essays into Vietnamese Pasts*, Ithaca, NY, Southeast Asia Program Publications, 1995, pp. 195–206, quotation at p. 202.

39. Vĩnh Sính, 'Introduction', to Sính (ed.), *Phan Châu Trinh and His Political Writings*, Ithaca, NY, Southeast Asia Program Publications, 2009, p. 16.

40. Phan Chu Trinh, 'Monarchy and Democracy (1925)', in Dutton, Werner and Whitmore (eds), *Sources of Vietnamese Tradition*, p. 377.

41. For the 'moral journey' of Southeast Asian elites see Romain Bertrand, 'The Long Moral Journey of the *Priyayi*: State-Formation Processes and the Moral Economy of Self-Denial in Java, 17th–20th century', unpublished workshop paper, Cambridge, 2006.

42. Marr, *Vietnamese Anticolonialism*, esp. p. 121.

43. Michael F. Laffan, 'Making Meiji Muslims: The Travelogue of 'Ali Ahmad al-Jarjawi', *Far Eastern History*, 22 (2001), pp. 145–71.

44. Tran My-Van, 'Japan through Vietnamese Eyes (1905–1945)', *Journal of Southeast Asian Studies*, 30/1 (1999), pp. 126–46, at p. 129.

45. For an overview and analysis see Cemil Aydin, *The Politics of Anti-Westernism in Asia: Visions of World Order in Pan-Islamic and Pan-Asian Thought*, New York, Columbia University Press, 2007. For Japanese attitudes to Russia see Naoko Shimazu, ' "Love Thy Enemy": Japanese Perceptions of Russia', in John W. Steinberg et al (eds), *The Russo-Japanese War in Global Perspective: World War Zero*, Leiden, Brill, 2005, pp. 365–84.

46. Vinh, 'Introduction' to Châu, *Overturned Chariot*, pp. 27–8.

47. Duiker, 'Phan Boi Chau: Asian Revolutionary in a Changing World', pp. 77–88.

48. Chae-Jin Lee, *Zhou Enlai: The Early Years*, Stanford, CA, Stanford University Press, 1994, pp. 76–7; Paul J. Bailey, 'Globalization and Chinese Education in the Early 20th Century', *Frontiers of Education in China*, 8/3 (2013), pp. 398–419; Craig A. Smith, 'The Datong Schools and Late Qing Sino-Japanese Cooperation', *Twentieth-Century China*, 42/1 (2017), pp. 3–25; Joan Judge, 'Talent, Virtue, and the Nation: Chinese Nationalisms and Female Subjectivities in the Early Twentieth Century', *American Historical Review*, 106/3 (2001), 765–803.

49. Harald Fischer-Tiné, 'Indian Nationalism and the "World Forces": Transnational and Diasporic Dimensions of the Indian Freedom Movement on the Eve of the First World War', *Journal of Global History*, 2 (2007), pp. 325–44, at pp. 328–9.

50. Shu-mei Shih, *The Lure of the Modern: Writing Modernism in Semicolonial China, 1917–1937*, Berkeley, University of California Press, 2001, p. 16, fn. 41; Sho Konishi, *Anarchist Modernity: Cooperatism and Japanese–Russian Intellectual Relations in Modern Japan*, Cambridge, MA, Harvard University Press, 2013, p. 5.

51. Quoted in William A. Lyell, *Lu Hsün's Vision of Reality*, Berkeley, University of California Press, 1976, p. 65.

52. David E. Pollard, *The True Story of Lu Xun*, Hong Kong, Chinese University Press, 2002, pp. 22–5.

53. Shih, *Lure of the Modern*, pp. 85–6; discussed in Lydia H. Liu, 'Translingual Practice: The Discourse of Individualism between China and the West', in Tani E. Barlow (ed.), *Formations of Colonial Modernity in East Asia*, Durham, NC, Duke University Press, 1997, pp. 83–112, at p. 109.

54. Graham Law and Norimasa Morita, 'Japan and the Internationalization of the Serial Fiction Market', *Book History*, 6 (2003), pp. 109–25; Mark Silver, *Purloined Letters: Cultural Borrowing and Japanese Crime Literature, 1868–1937*, Honolulu, University of Hawaii Press, 2008; Eva Hung, 'Giving Texts a Context: Chinese Translations of Classical English Detective Stories, 1896–1916', pp. 151–75; David E. Pollard, 'Jules Verne, Science Fiction and Related Matters', in Pollard (ed.), *Translation and Creation: Readings of Western Literature in Early Modern China, 1840–1918*, Amsterdam, J. Benjamins, 1998, pp. 177–207.

55. Doris Jedamski, 'Translation in the Malay World: Different Communities, Different Agendas', in Eva Hung and Judy Wakabayashi (eds), *Asian Translation Traditions*, Northampton, MA, St. Jerome Publishing, 2005, pp. 211–45. Jedamski draws on Claudine Salmon, *Literature in Malay by the Chinese of Indonesia: A Provisional Annotated Bibliography*, Paris, Éditions de la Maison des Sciences de l'Homme, 1981.

56. I have taken up this recurring theme from Rudolf Mrázek's brilliant *Engineers of Happy Land: Technology and Nationalism in a Colony*, Princeton, NJ, Princeton University Press, 2002, p. xvi.

57. From Phan Boi Chau's 'Prison Notes', in David G. Marr (ed.), *Reflections from Captivity: Phan Boi Chau's Prison Notes & Ho Chi Minh's Prison Diary*, Athens, Ohio University Press, 1978, p. 30.

58. Christopher T. Keaveney, *Beyond Brushtalk: Sino-Japanese Literary Exchange in the Interwar Period*, Hong Kong, Hong Kong University Press, 2008, pp. 2–9.

59. Vinh, 'Introduction' to Chau, *Overturned Chariot*, p. 10. For Mazzini see C. A. Bayly and Eugenio F. Biagini (eds), *Giuseppe Mazzini and the Globalisation of Democratic Nationalism, 1830–1920*, Oxford, Oxford University Press for the British Academy, 2008.

60. Chau, *Overturned Chariot*, pp. 87–91.

61. It is translated in part as 'The History of the Loss of the Country (1905)',

in Dutton, Werner and Whitmore (eds), *Sources of Vietnamese Tradition*, pp. 342–53.

62. Peter Zinoman, 'Colonial Prisons and Anti-Colonial Resistance in French Indochina: The Thai Nguyen Rebellion, 1917', *Modern Asian Studies*, 34/1 (2000), pp. 57–98, at pp. 62–3.

63. Chau, 'History of the Loss of the Country', p. 344.

64. Tran, 'Japan through Vietnamese Eyes', p. 131, and Tran My-Van, *A Vietnamese Royal Exile in Japan: Prince Cuong De (1882–1951)*, London, Routledge, 2013, pp. 49–50.

65. For this idea see Sugata Bose, *A Hundred Horizons: The Indian Ocean in the Age of Global Empire*, Cambridge, MA, Harvard University Press, 2006, esp. ch. 7.

66. For these encounters see Renée Worringer, *Ottomans Imagining Japan: East, Middle East, and Non-Western Modernity at the Turn of the Twentieth Century*, Basingstoke, Palgrave Macmillan, 2014, pp. 87–9; Selçuk Esenbel and Inaba Chiharu (eds), *The Rising Sun and the Turkish Crescent: New Perspectives on the History of Japanese Turkish Relations*, Istanbul, Bogaziçi University Press, 2003; Selçuk Esenbel, 'Japan's Global Claim to Asia and the World of Islam: Transnational Nationalism and World Power, 1900–1945', *American Historical Review*, 109/4 (2004), 1140–70; Nile Green, 'Shared Infrastructures, Informational Asymmetries: Persians and Indians in Japan, c.1890–1930', *Journal of Global History*, 8/3 (2013), pp. 414–35, and 'Forgotten Futures: Indian Muslims in the Trans-Islamic Turn to Japan', *Journal of Asian Studies*, 72/2 (2013), pp. 611–31.

67. For Barakatullah's early career in England see Brent D. Singleton, 'Sheikh Abdullah Quilliam's International Influence: America, West Africa, and Beyond', in Jamie Gilham and Ron Geaves (eds), *Victorian Muslim: Abdullah Quilliam and Islam in the West*, Oxford, Oxford University Press, 2017, pp. 128–30; NAI, Home Department, Political A, Proceedings, December 1912, No. 34, British Ambassador Tokyo to Foreign Secretary, 19 October 1912. For Hasan Hatono Uho see Renée Worringer, 'Hatono Uho, *Asia in Danger 1912*', in Sven Saaler and Christopher W. A. Szpilman (eds), *Pan-Asianism: A Documentary History, 1850–1920*, Lanham, MD, Rowman & Littlefield, 2011, pp. 149–60.

68. There is a large current literature on these prophets of an 'Asian century'. Besides other works cited in this section, I have found particularly helpful: Prasenjit Duara, 'Asia Redux: Conceptualizing a Region for Our Times', *Journal of Asian Studies*, 69/4 (2010), pp. 963–83, enlarged in *The Crisis of Global Modernity: Asian Traditions and a Sustainable Future*, Cambridge, Cambridge University Press, 2014; Carolien Stolte and Harald Fischer-Tiné, 'Imagining Asia in India: Nationalism and Internationalism (ca. 1905–1940)', *Comparative Studies in Society and History*, 54/1 (2012),

pp. 65–92; Sanjay Subrahmanyam, 'One Asia, or Many? Reflections from Connected History', *Modern Asian Studies*, 50/1 (2016), pp. 5–43, whose cautious reading of this question, esp. pp. 39–43, I tend to share.

69. This paragraph draws on Rebecca E. Karl, 'Creating Asia: China in the World at the Beginning of the Twentieth Century', *American Historical Review*, 103/4 (1998), pp. 1096–1118.

70. B. R. Deepak, 'The Colonial Connections: Indian and Chinese Nationalists in Japan and China', *China Report*, 48/1–2 (2012), pp. 147–70; Aravind Ganachari, *Nationalism and Social Reform in a Colonial Situation*, Delhi, Kalpaz Publications, 2005, pp. 142–3.

71. As quoted in Shiraishi, 'Phan Boi Chau and Japan', p. 439.

72. George Dutton, ' "Society" and Struggle in the Early Twentieth Century: The Vietnamese Neologistic Project and French Colonialism', *Modern Asian Studies*, 49/6 (2015), pp. 1994–2021, at p. 2005.

73. Fischer-Tiné, 'Indian Nationalism and the "World Forces"', p. 336.

74. Marie-Claire Bergère, *Sun Yat-sen*, Stanford, CA, Stanford University Press, 2000, pp. 143–7.

75. Châu, *Overturned Chariot*, pp. 133–4.

76. Tran, 'Japan through Vietnamese Eyes', at pp. 130–31.

77. I have used the numbers from Marr, *Vietnamese Anticolonialism*, pp. 142–3, fn. 71. On the finances see Tran, *A Vietnamese Royal Exile in Japan*, pp. 49–53.

78. Agathe Larcher-Goscha, 'Prince Cuong Dê and the Franco-Vietnamese Competition for the Heritage of Gia Long', in Bousquet and Brocheux (eds), *Viêt-Nam Exposé*, pp. 191–5.

79. Maruyama Noboru, 'Lu Xun in Japan', in Leo Ou-fan Lee (ed.), *Lu Xun and His Legacy*, Berkeley, University of California Press, 1985, pp. 226–35; and see the discussion in Eva Shan Chou, ' "A Story about Hair": A Curious Mirror of Lu Xun's Pre-Republican Years', *Journal of Asian Studies*, 66/2 (2007), pp. 421–59.

80. Fred G. Notehelfer, 'Kotoku Shusui and Nationalism', *Journal of Asian Studies*, 31/1 (1971), pp. 31–9.

81. From the translation by Robert Thomas Tierney, *Monster of the Twentieth Century: Kotoku Shusui and Japan's First Anti-Imperialist Movement*, Berkeley, University of California Press, 2015, p. 139.

82. Judge, 'Talent, Virtue, and the Nation', pp. 792–3.

83. Edward W. Wagner, *The Korean Minority in Japan, 1904–1950*, New York, International Secretariat, Institute of Pacific Relations, 1951, p. 9.

84. Tierney, *Monster of the Twentieth Century*, p. 119.

85. Truong Buu Lam (ed.), *Colonialism Experienced : Vietnamese Writings on Colonialism, 1900–1931*, Ann Arbor, University of Michigan Press, 2000, pp. 81, 206.

86. Tran, *A Vietnamese Royal Exile in Japan*, p. 42.

87. Louis Alphonse Bonhoure's report of 4 July 1908, as quoted by his governor-general, Albert Sarraut, in 1913, in Christopher E. Goscha, *Thailand and the Southeast Asian Networks of the Vietnamese Revolution, 1885–1954*, London, Routledge, 1998, p. 41.

88. Marr, *Vietnamese Anticolonialism*, pp. 145–6.

89. Phan Bội Châu, *Overturned Chariot*, p. 29.

90. This account is based on two outstanding scholarly biographies: William J. Duiker, *Ho Chi Minh: A Life*, New York, Hyperion, 2000, pp. 15–45; Pierre Brocheux, *Ho Chi Minh: A Biography*, Cambridge, Cambridge University Press, 2007, pp. 1–7.

91. Phan Bội Châu, *Overturned Chariot*, p. 43.

92. Brocheux and Hémery, *Indochina*, p. 82.

93. Ibid., p. 127; Martin J. Murray, '"White Gold" or "White Blood"? The Rubber Plantations of Colonial Indochina, 1910–40', *Journal of Peasant Studies*, 19/3–4 (1992), pp. 41–67.

94. See, generally: Martin J. Wiener, *An Empire on Trial: Race, Murder, and Justice under British Rule, 1870–1935*, Cambridge, Cambridge University Press, 2008; Elizabeth Kolsky, *Colonial Justice in British India: White Violence and the Rule of Law*, Cambridge, Cambridge University Press, 2011.

95. James C. Scott, *The Moral Economy of the Peasant: Rebellion and Subsistence in Southeast Asia*, New Haven, CT, Yale University Press, 1976, pp. 94–6; see also Lam (ed.), *Colonialism Experienced*.

96. Erica J. Peters, 'Taste, Taxes, and Technologies: Industrializing Rice Alcohol in Northern Vietnam, 1902–1913', *French Historical Studies*, 27/3 (2004), pp. 569–600.

97. Hoang Ngoc Thanh, '*Quoc Ngu* and the Development of Modern Vietnamese Literature', in Walter Francis Vella (ed.), *Aspects of Vietnamese History*, Honolulu, University Press of Hawaii, 1973, pp. 191–236.

98. Bradley, 'Becoming Van Minh', pp. 67–73; Dutton, '"Society" and Struggle in the Early Twentieth Century', pp. 1994–2021.

99. Tai, *Radicalism and the Origins of the Vietnamese Revolution*, pp. 26–7.

100. Vĩnh, 'Introduction' to Vĩnh (ed.), *Phan Châu Trinh and His Political Writings*, pp. 21–2.

101. For the revolt see Marr, *Vietnamese Anticolonialism*, pp. 185–94.

102. Sophie Quinn-Judge, *Ho Chi Minh: The Missing Years, 1919–1941*, London, Hurst, 2003, pp. 21–2.

103. Erica J. Peters, *Appetites and Aspirations in Vietnam: Food and Drink in the Long Nineteenth Century*, Lanham, MD, AltaMira Press, 2011, p. 51.

104. Marr, *Vietnamese Anticolonialism*, pp. 185–94.

105. Vĩnh, 'Introduction' to Vĩnh (ed.), *Phan Châu Trinh and His Political Writings*, p. 6.

106. *Straits Times*, 30 October 1908.

107. Michael G. Vann, 'Of Pirates, Postcards, and Public Beheadings: The

Pedagogic Execution in French Colonial Indochina', *Historical Reflections/Réflexions Historiques*, 36/2 (2010), pp. 39–58.

108. Vĩnh, 'Introduction' to Vĩnh (ed.), *Phan Châu Trinh and His Political Writings*, pp. 24–5; for Trinh's exile see Phút Tấn Nguyễn, *A Modern History of Viet-Nam (1802–1954)*, Saigon, Nhà sách Khai-Trí, 1964, pp. 342–7. See Lorraine M. Paterson. 'French Guiana, Ethnoscapes of Exile: Political Prisoners from Indochina in a Colonial Asian World', *International Review of Social History*, 63/S26 (2018), pp. 89–107.

109. Vĩnh (ed.), *Phan Châu Trinh and His Political Writings*, p. 44.

110. Discussed in Nguyen Khac Kham, 'Discrepancies between Nguc Trung Thu and Phan Bội Châu Nien Bieu in Their Records of Some Important Events of the Dông-du Movement: A Few Preliminary Remarks and Tentative Re-interpretation', in Vĩnh (ed.), *Phan Bôi Châu and the Dông-du Movement*, pp. 37–43.

111. Motoo, 'Vietnamese Political Movements in Thailand', p. 152.

112. For an influential example of the discussion of 'generations' in this context see Vera Schwarcz, *The Chinese Enlightenment: Intellectuals and the Legacy of the May Fourth Movement of 1919*, Berkeley, University of California Press, 1986, pp. 23–9.

113. For the father's and son's journeys south see Duiker, *Ho Chi Minh*, pp. 38–41.

114. Hoài Thanh et al., *Days with Ho Chi Minh*, Hanoi, Foreign Languages Publishing House, 1962, pp. 35–7.

115. See Lessard, ' "Cet Ignoble Trafic" ', p. 18.

116. For Seaman 'Ba' see Tran Dan Tien, *Glimpses of the Life of Ho Chi Minh: President of the Democratic Republic of Vietnam*, Hanoi, Foreign Languages Publishing House, 1958, pp. 5–6. Although presented as a series of anecdotes from contemporaries, this work is generally accepted to have been written by Ho Chi Minh himself.

2. FUGITIVE VISIONS (1905–1909)

1. Here I warmly acknowledge my debt to Christopher E. Goscha's pioneering *Thailand and the Southeast Asian Networks of the Vietnamese Revolution, 1885–1954*, London, Routledge, 1998, quotation at p. 5. Phan Boi Chau used the term 'village abroad' in 1917: ibid., p. 40.

2. For these regimes see Ilsen Abont, 'Surveillance des identités et régime coloniale en Indochine, 1890–1912', *Criminocorpus: Revue d'histoire de la justice, des crimes et des peines,* May 2011, http://criminocorpus.revnes. org/417.

3. For 'ghost narratives' see Julie Pham, 'Revolution, Communism and History in the Thought of Tran Van Giau', PhD thesis, University of Cambridge,

2007, esp. pp. 10–17, employed here with her kind permission. For a reflection on representations of Ho Chi Minh see Patricia M. Pelley, *Postcolonial Vietnam: New Histories of the National Past*, Durham, NC, Duke University Press, 2002, pp. 157–60.

4. Engseng Ho, *The Graves of Tarim: Genealogy and Mobility across the Indian Ocean*, Berkeley, University of California Press, 2006; Sunil S. Amrith, *Migration and Diaspora in Modern Asia*, Cambridge, Cambridge University Press, 2011.

5. Tineke Hellwig and Eric Tagliacozzo (eds), *The Indonesia Reader: History, Culture, Politics*, Durham, NC, Duke University Press, 2009, p. 191; Eric Tagliacozzo, *The Longest Journey: Southeast Asians and the Pilgrimage to Mecca*, New York, Oxford University Press, 2013; John Slight, *The British Empire and the Hajj, 1865–1956*, Cambridge, MA, Harvard University Press, 2015.

6. For the Indies see Leo Suryadinata, 'Indonesian Chinese Education: Past and Present', *Indonesia*, 14 (1972), pp. 49–71, figure at p. 51; Didi Kwartanada, 'The Tiong Hoa Hwee Koan School: A Transborder Project of Modernity in Batavia, *c.* 1900s', in Siew-Min Sai and Chang-Yau Hoon (eds), *Chinese Indonesians Reassessed: History, Religion and Belonging*, London, Routledge, 2013, pp. 27–44.

7. Mark R. Frost, 'Asia's Maritime Networks and the Colonial Public Sphere, 1840–1920', *New Zealand Journal of Asian Studies*, 6/2 (2004), pp. 63–94, at pp. 79, 81.

8. Laura Noszlopy and Matthew Isaac Cohen, 'Introduction: The Transnational Dynamic in Southeast Asian Performance', in Noszlopy and Cohen (eds), *Contemporary Southeast Asian Performance: Transnational Perspectives*, Newcastle upon Tyne, Cambridge Scholars Publishing, 2010, pp. 1–24.

9. For 'the nearness of the faraway' see Sumit K. Mandal, 'Introduction: Global Conjunctions in the Indian Ocean', *Indonesia and the Malay World*, 41/120 (2013), pp. 143–5.

10. Benedict Anderson, *Under Three Flags: Anarchism and the Anti-Colonial Imagination*, London, Verso, 2005, p. 59, fn. 11; John Nery, *Revolutionary Spirit: José Rizal in Southeast Asia*, Singapore, Institute of Southeast Asian Studies, 2011. For the maritime use of the term 'filibuster' see James Mark Purcell, 'Melville's Contribution to English', *PMLA*, 56/3 (1941), pp. 797–808, at p. 806.

11. José Rizal. *El Filibusterismo*, trans. Harold Augenbraum, London, Penguin, 2011, pp. 1–2.

12. Ibid., p. 12.

13. SNA, Oral History Interview, Tan Ee Leong (December 1979–January 1980).

14. Robert J. Schwendinger, 'Chinese Sailors: America's Invisible Merchant Marine, 1876–1905', *California History*, 57/1 (1978), pp. 58–69, quotation at p. 65.

15. Robert Barde and Wesley Ueunten, 'Pacific Steerage: Japanese Ships and Asian Mass Migration', *Pacific Historical Review*, 73/4 (2004), pp. 653–60.
16. Tatiana Seijas, *Asian Slaves in Colonial Mexico: From Chinos to Indians*, Cambridge, Cambridge University Press, 2014.
17. For this debate see, *inter alia*: Hugh Tinker, *A New System of Slavery: The Export of Indian Labour Overseas, 1830–1920*, London, Oxford University Press, 1974; David Northrup, *Indentured Labor in the Age of Imperialism, 1834–1922*, Cambridge, Cambridge University Press, 1995.
18. There is a vast literature on this. For a summary of the situation in the Bay of Bengal see Sunil Amrith, *Crossing the Bay of Bengal: The Furies of Nature and the Fortunes of Migrants*, Cambridge, MA, Harvard University Press, 2013, pp. 114–32. For the statistics see Ralph Shlomowitz and Lance Brennan, 'Mortality and Indian Labour in Malaya, 1877–1933', *Indian Economic and Social History Review*, 29/1 (1992), pp. 57–75.
19. Georg Stauth, 'Slave Trade, Multiculturalism and Islam in Colonial Singapore: A Sociological Note on Christian Snouck Hurgronje's 1891 Article on Slave Trade in Singapore', *Asian Journal of Social Science*, 20/1 (1992), pp. 67–79.
20. Gary Y. Okihiro, *Margins and Mainstreams: Asians in American History and Culture*, Seattle, University of Washington Press, 2014, pp. 39–48.
21. For this journey see Pankaj Mishra, *From the Ruins of Empire: The Revolt against the West and the Remaking of Asia*, London, Penguin, 2012, ch. 2.
22. Jan Breman and E. Valentine Daniel, 'Conclusion: The Making of a Coolie', *Journal of Peasant Studies*, 19/3–4 (1992), pp. 268–95.
23. Shih-shan H. Tsai, 'American Involvement in the Coolie Trade', *American Studies*, 6/3 (1976), pp. 52–8.
24. See also the useful discussion of the terms in Kornel Chang, 'Coolie', in Cathy J. Schlund-Vials, Linda Trinh Võ and K. Scott Wong (eds), *Keywords for Asian American Studies*, New York, NYU Press, 2015, pp. 37–9, from which the quotation is drawn; Philip A. Kuhn, *Chinese among Others: Emigration in Modern Times*, Lanham, MD, Rowman & Littlefield, 2008, pp. 210–18.
25. Straits Settlements, *Report for 1914*, Singapore, HMSO, 1915, pp. 20–21; TNA, CO 273/420, 'List of Persons Deported Under Orders of Banishment During the Month of December 1914'; *House of Commons Debates*, 25 February 1914, vol. LVIII, cc. 1749–50. For the colonial practice of banishment more generally see Michael Powell, 'The Clanking of Medieval Chains: Extra-Judicial Banishment in the British Empire', *Journal of Imperial and Commonwealth History*, 44/2 (2016), pp. 352–71; Robert Aldrich, 'Imperial Banishment: French Colonizers and the Exile of Vietnamese Emperors', *French History and Civilization*, 5 (2014), pp. 123–33.
26. Elizabeth J. Perry, *Shanghai on Strike: The Politics of Chinese Labor*, Stanford, CA, Stanford University Press, 1993, p. 60.

27. Yan Haiping, *Chinese Women Writers and the Feminist Imagination, 1905–1948*, London, Routledge, 2006, pp. 33–68, quotation at p. 42.

28. Ibid.; Louise Edwards, *Women Warriors and Wartime Spies of China*, Cambridge, Cambridge University Press, 2016, pp. 40–75.

29. Kazuko Ono, *Chinese Women in a Century of Revolution, 1850–1950*, Stanford, CA, Stanford University Press, 1989; Lydia H. Liu, Rebecca E. Karl and Dorothy Ko (eds), *The Birth of Chinese Feminism: Essential Texts in Transnational Theory*, New York, Columbia University Press, 2013, esp. pp. 42–8.

30. Isabelle Tracol-Huynh, 'The Shadow Theater of Prostitution in French Colonial Tonkin: Faceless Prostitutes under the Colonial Gaze', *Journal of Vietnamese Studies*, 7/1 (2012), pp. 10–51, at p. 16.

31. Frédéric Roustan, 'Mousmés and French Colonial Culture: Making Japanese Women's Bodies available in Indochina', *Journal of Vietnamese Studies*, 7/1 (2012), pp. 52–105; James Francis Warren, *Ah Ku and Karayuki-San: Prostitution in Singapore, 1870–1940*, Singapore, Oxford University Press, 1993.

32. Kazuhiro Oharazeki, *Japanese Prostitutes in the North American West, 1887–1920*, Seattle, University of Washington Press, 2016, pp. 16, 25–30.

33. Isaiah Friedman, *The Question of Palestine, 1914–1918: British-Jewish-Arab Relations*, London, Routledge & Kegan Paul, 1973, p. 7. For this theme over a longer duration see Richard Drayton, 'The Collaboration of Labour: Slaves, Empires, and Globalizations in the Atlantic World, *c.* 1600–1850', in A. G. Hopkins (ed.), *Globalization in World History*, London, Pimlico, 2002, pp. 98–114.

34. I have drawn here on Amy Elizabeth Robinson's fascinating 'Tinker, Tailor, Vagrant, Sailor: Colonial Mobility and the British Imperial State, 1880–1914', PhD thesis, Stanford University, 2006. See also Renisa Mawani, *Across Oceans of Law: The Komagata Maru and Jurisdiction in the Time of Empire*, Durham, NC, Duke University Press, 2018.

35. Valeska Huber, *Channelling Mobilities: Migration and Globalisation in the Suez Canal Region and Beyond, 1869–1914*, Cambridge, Cambridge University Press, 2013, pp. 272–305; Slight, *The British Empire and the Hajj*, ch. 2.

36. Lawrence M. Friedman, 'Crimes of Mobility', *Stanford Law Review*, 43/3 (1991), pp. 637–58.

37. Christopher E. Goscha, 'Widening the Colonial Encounter: Asian Connections inside French Indochina during the Interwar Period', *Modern Asian Studies*, 43/5 (2009), pp. 1189–1228; Natasha Pairaudeau, *Mobile Citizens: French Indians in Indo-China, 1858–1954*, London, NIAS Press, 2015. For the British case see Rieko Karatani, *Defining British Citizenship: Empire, Commonwealth and Modern Britain*, London, Frank Cass, 2003, esp. pp. 50–58.

38. Robinson, 'Tinker, Tailor, Vagrant, Sailor', pp. 34–5.

39. For this see Marilyn Lake and Henry Reynolds, *Drawing the Global Colour Line: White Men's Countries and the Question of Racial Equality*, Cambridge, Cambridge University Press; Duncan Bell, 'Beyond the Sovereign State: Isopolitan Citizenship, Race and Anglo-American Union', *Political Studies*, 62/2 (2014), pp. 418–34.

40. Hans K. Van Tilburg, *Chinese Junks on the Pacific: Views from a Different Deck*, Gainesville, University Press of Florida, 2007.

41. Lars Amenda, ' "Chinese Quarters": Maritime Labour, Chinese Migration and Local Imagination in Rotterdam and Hamburg, 1900–1950', in Vanessa Künneman and Ruth Mayer (eds), *Chinatowns in a Transnational World: Myths and Realities of an Urban Phenomenon*, London, Routledge, 2012, pp. 45–61; Schwendinger, 'Chinese Sailors', p. 62. For maritime industrialization and globalization see Michael B. Miller, *Europe and the Maritime World: A Twentieth-Century History*, Cambridge, Cambridge University Press, 2012.

42. Leon Fink, *Sweatshops at Sea: Merchant Seamen in the World's First Globalized Industry, from 1812 to the Present*, Chapel Hill, University of North Carolina, 2011, pp. 88, 133.

43. For lascar origins see Aaron Jaffer, *Lascars and Indian Ocean Seafaring, 1780–1860: Shipboard Life, Unrest and Mutiny*, Woodbridge, Boydell Press, 2015, pp. 10–12.

44. Anne Kershen, *Strangers, Aliens and Asians: Huguenots, Jews and Bangladeshis in Spitalfields 1666–2000*, London, Routledge, 2004, pp. 36–8.

45. Gopalan Balachandran, 'Making Coolies, (Un)making Workers: "Globalizing" Labour in the Late-19th and Early-20th Centuries', *Journal of Historical Sociology*, 24/3 (2011), pp. 266–96, and his *Globalizing Labour? Indian Seafarers and World Shipping, c. 1870–1945*, New Delhi, Oxford University Press, 2012; Ali Raza and Benjamin Zachariah, 'To Take Arms across a Sea of Trouble: The "Lascar System", Politics, and Agency in the 1920s', *Itinerario*, 36/3 (2012), pp. 19–38.

46. Ravi Ahuja, 'Mobility and Containment: The Voyages of South Asian Seamen, c.1900–1960', *International Review of Social History*, 51/S14 (2006), pp. 111–41, at pp. 136–7.

47. Dân Tiên Trần, *Glimpses of the Life of Ho Chi Minh: President of the Democratic Republic of Vietnam*, Hanoi, Foreign Languages Publishing House, 1958, pp. 6–7.

48. Devleena Ghosh, 'Under the Radar of Empire: Unregulated Travel in the Indian Ocean', *Journal of Social History*, 45/2 (2011), pp. 497–514, at p. 509.

49. For numbers see Adam McKeown, 'Global Migration, 1846–1940', *Journal of World History*, 15 (2004), pp. 155–89. For Asia's 'age of movement' more generally see Amrith, *Migration and Diaspora in Modern Asia*.

50. W. G. Huff, *The Economic Growth of Singapore*, Cambridge, Cambridge University Press, 1994, p. 153.

51. Alwi bin Alhady, *The Real Cry of Syed Shaykh Al-Hady, with Selections of His Writings by His Son Syed Alwi Al-Hady*, ed. Alijah Gordon, Kuala Lumpur, Malaysia Sociological Research Institute, 1999, pp. 183-4.

52. Christian Henriot, 'Slums, Squats, or Hutments? Constructing and Deconstructing an In-Between Space in Modern Shanghai (1926-65)', *Frontiers of History in China*, 7/4 (2012), pp. 499-528.

53. W. K. Chan, *The Making of Hong Kong Society: Three Studies of Class Formation in Early Hong Kong*, Oxford, Clarendon Press, 1991, pp. 153-4.

54. Lai Ah Eng, 'The Kopitiam in Singapore: An Evolving Story about Migration and Cultural Diversity', Asia Research Institute, working paper no. 132 (2010); Ying-Kit Chan, 'Kopitiams in Singapore: Consuming Politics', *Asian Survey*, 53/5 (2013), pp. 979-1004.

55. For an exemplary study see Perry, *Shanghai on Strike*, pp. 50-52.

56. Stephen Dobbs, *The Singapore River: A Social History, 1819-2002*, Singapore, NUS Press, 2003, pp. 41-2.

57. SNA, Coroner's Inquest and Inquiries, Microfilm AD010, 'Information of Witnesses taken and acknowledged on behalf of our Sovereign Lord the King touching the death of a male Chinese, Unknown, aged about 35 years at Mortuary General Hospital', 1 January 1914.

58. For the statistics see SNA, Coroner's Inquest and Inquiries, Microfilm AD067, 'Coroner's Cases Record Book, 1916-1925'. Any historian using this remarkable source does so inspired by the 'atmospheric truth and drama' of the work of James Francis Warren; see his 'Rickshaw Pullers, Prostitutes and "Pirates": Researching and Writing about Southeast Asia and the People without History', *Taiwan Journal of Southeast Asian Studies*, 1/1 (2004), pp. 1-17.

59. Jacqueline Knorr, *Creole Identity in Postcolonial Indonesia*, Oxford, Berghahn Books, 2014.

60. Wang Tai Peng, *The Origins of Chinese Kongsi*, Petaling Jaya, Pelanduk Publications, 1994; Carl A. Trocki, *Opium and Empire: Chinese Society in Colonial Singapore, 1800-1910*, Ithaca, NY, Cornell University Press, 1990.

61. Ming K. Chan, 'Labor and Empire: The Chinese Labor Movement in the Canton Delta, 1895-1927', PhD thesis, Stanford University, 1977, pp. 18-21; Lewis M. Chere, 'The Hong Kong Riots of October 1882: Evidence for Chinese Nationalism?', *Journal of the Hong Kong Branch of the Royal Asiatic Society*, 20 (1980), pp. 54-65.

62. For Taft see John M. Carroll, *A Concise History of Hong Kong*, New York, Rowman & Littlefield, 2007, p. 77.

63. Sin-Kiong Wong, 'Die for the Boycott and Nation: Martyrdom and the 1905 Anti-American Movement in China', *Modern Asian Studies*, 35/3 (2001), pp. 565-88.

64. For this and background on the labouring worlds of this period see Daniel Y. K. Kwan, *Marxist Intellectuals and the Chinese Labor Movement: A*

Study of Deng Zhongxia (1894–1933), Seattle, University of Washington Press, 1997, p. 73.

65. Hu Wen, 'To Forge a Strong and Wealthy China? The Buy-Chinese Products Movement in Singapore, 1905–7', MA dissertation, National University of Singapore, 2004, pp. 15–19.

66. Yen Ching Hwang, *The Overseas Chinese and the 1911 Revolution, with Special Reference to Singapore and Malaya*, Kuala Lumpur, Oxford University Press, 1976, pp. 115–24, 283; Edward S. Krebs, *Shifu: Soul of Chinese Anarchism*, Lanham, MD, Rowman & Littlefield, 1998, pp. 65–6, 75; Yin Cao, 'Bombs in Beijing and Delhi: The Global Spread of Bomb-Making Technology and the Revolutionary Terrorism in Modern China and India', *Journal of World History*, 30/4 (2019), pp. 559–89.

67. Khoo Salma Nasution, *Sun Yat Sen in Penang*, Penang, Areca Books, 2008.

68. Yen, *The Overseas Chinese and the 1911 Revolution*, pp. 134–5; Lee Lai To, 'The Attitude of the Straits Government towards Sun Yat-sen in 1900–11', in Lee (ed.), *The 1911 Revolution: The Chinese in British and Dutch Southeast Asia*, Singapore, Heinemann Asia, 1987, pp. 35–47.

69. Here I have found helpful Roxanne Euben, *Journeys to the Other Shore: Muslim and Western Travelers in Search of Knowledge*, Princeton, NJ, Princeton University Press, 2006, pp. 11–13.

70. Trần, *Glimpses of the Life of Ho Chi Minh*, pp. 8–9.

71. Sophie Quinn-Judge, *Ho Chi Minh: The Missing Years, 1919–1941*, London, Hurst, 2003, p. 24.

72. For all these possibilities, in addition to the preceding reference, see William J. Duiker, *Ho Chi Minh: A Life*, New York, Hyperion, 2000, ch. 2; Pierre Brocheux, *Ho Chi Minh: A Biography*, Cambridge, Cambridge University Press, 2007, pp. 9–11, and Daniel Hémery, *Ho Chi Minh: De l'Indochine au Vietnam*, Paris, Éditions Gallimard, 1990.

73. Tim Harper, 'The Malay World, Besides Empire and Nation', *Indonesia and the Malay World*, 41/120 (2013), pp. 273–90.

74. J. V. Naik, 'Forerunners of Dadabhai Naoroji's Drain Theory', *Economic and Political Weekly*, 36/46–7 (2001), pp. 4428–32; Vikram Visana, 'Vernacular Capitalism, Capitalism, and Anti-Imperialism in the Political Thought of Dadabhai Naoroji', *Historical Journal*, 59/3 (2016), pp. 775–97.

75. Bill V. Mullen and Cathryn Watson (eds), *W. E. B. Du Bois on Asia: Crossing the World Color Line*, Jackson, University Press of Mississippi, 2005.

76. Susan D. Pennybacker, 'The Universal Races Congress, London Political Culture, and Imperial Dissent, 1900–1939', *Radical History Review*, 92 (2005), pp. 103–17; Christian Geulen, 'The Common Grounds of Conflict: Racial Visions of World Order, 1880–1940', in Sebastian Conrad and Dominic Sachsenmaier (eds), *Conceptions of World Order: Global Moments and Movements, 1880s–1930s*, London, Palgrave Macmillan, 2007, pp. 69–96.

77. Elizabeth Kolsky, 'Codification and the Rule of Colonial Difference: Criminal Procedure in British India', *Law and History Review*, 23/3 (2005), pp. 631–83.

78. Nicholas Owen, 'The Soft Heart of the British Empire: Indian Radicals in Edwardian London', *Past and Present*, 220 (2013), pp. 143–84.

79. For an inspiring exploration of the world of these novels see Anderson, *Under Three Flags*, esp. ch. 3. For 'claiming' Europe see the equally rich essay by Resil B. Mojares, 'The Itineraries of Mariano Ponce', in Caroline S. Hau and Kasian Tejapira (eds), *Traveling Nation-Makers: Transnational Flows and Movements in the Making of Modern Southeast Asia*, Singapore, NUS Press, 2011, pp. 32–63, at pp. 37–8.

80. Marie-Claire Bergère, *Sun Yat-sen*, Stanford, CA, Stanford University Press, 2000, pp. 61–8; J. Y. Wong, *The Origins of an Heroic Image: Sun Yatsen in London, 1896–1897*, Oxford, Oxford University Press, 1986, quotation at p. 296.

81. Sinh (ed.), *Phan Châu Trinh and His Political Writings*, Ithaca, NY, Southeast Asia Program Publications, 2009, pp. 27–33.

82. Paul J. Bailey, 'Cultural Connections in a New Global Space: Li Shizeng and the Chinese Francophile Project in the Early Twentieth Century', in Lin Pei-yin and Weipin Tsai (eds), *Print, Profit, and Perception: Ideas, Information and Knowledge in Chinese Societies, 1895–1949*, Leiden, Brill, 2014, pp. 17–39; Chae-Jin Lee, *Zhou Enlai: The Early Years*, Stanford, CA, Stanford University Press, 1994, p. 77.

83. Kris Manjapra, *Age of Entanglement: German and Indian Intellectuals across Empire*, Cambridge, MA, Harvard University Press, 2014, pp. 46–55.

84. *Report of the Committee on Distressed Colonial and Indian Subjects, Cd. 5133*, London, HMSO, 1910, esp. pp. 16–17.

85. M. P. T. Acharya and B. D. Yadav, *M. P. T. Acharya: Reminiscences of an Indian Revolutionary*, New Delhi, Anmol Publications, 1991, pp. 67–81, quotation at p. 67; C. S. Subramanyam, *M. P. T. Acharya: His Life and Times: Revolutionary Trends in the Early Anti-Imperialist Movements in South India and Abroad*, Madras, Institute of South Indian Studies, 1995, pp. 95–9.

86. Acharya and Yadav, *M. P. T. Acharya*, quotations at pp. 72, 75, 80.

87. Sascha Auerbach, *Race, Law, and 'The Chinese Puzzle' in Imperial Britain*, London, Springer, 2009, esp. ch. 2; G. Benton and E. Gomez, *The Chinese in Britain, 1800–Present: Economy, Transnationalism, Identity*, London, Springer, 2007, pp. 84–5.

88. Amenda, ' "Chinese Quarters" ', pp. 45–61.

89. Acharya and Yadav, *M. P. T. Acharya*, quotation at p. 84.

90. Harald Fischer-Tiné, *Shyamji Krishnavarma: Sanskrit, Sociology and Anti-Imperialism*, New Delhi, Routledge, 2014, pp. 26–37; Indulal Yajnik,

Shyamaji Krishnavarma: Life and Times of an Indian Revolutionary (1934), Bombay, Lakshmi Publications, 1950, pp. 97–8.

91. Ibid., pp. 274–5.

92. For India House in this and preceding paragraphs see Fischer-Tiné, *Shyamji Krishnavarma*; Alex Tickell, 'Scholarship Terrorists: The India House Hostel and the "Student Problem" in Edwardian London', in Rehana Ahmed and Sumita Mukherjee (eds), *South Asian Resistances in Britain, 1858–1947*, London, Continuum, 2012, pp. 3–18.

93. As cited in A. C. Bose, *Indian Revolutionaries Abroad, 1905–1922: In the Background of International Developments*, Patna, Bharati Bhawan, 1971, p. 16.

94. Acharya and Yadav, *M. P. T. Acharya*, p. 82; Subramanyam, *M. P. T. Acharya*, pp. 102–4.

95. Bhai Parmanand, *The Story of My Life*, Lahore, The Central Hindu Yuvak Sabha, 1934, pp. 31–5.

96. Emily C. Brown, *Har Dayal: Hindu Revolutionary and Rationalist*, Tucson, University of Arizona Press, 1975, pp. 36–44, quotation from Gobind Behari Lal at p. 44.

97. As quoted in Amiya K. Samanta (ed.), *Terrorism in Bengal: A Collection of Documents on Terrorist Activities from 1905 to 1939*, vol. V: *Terrorists outside Bengal Deriving Inspiration from and Having Links with Bengal Terrorists*, Calcutta, Government of West Bengal, 1995, p. vi.

98. Vinayak Chaturvedi, 'A Revolutionary's Biography: The Case of V D Savarkar', *Postcolonial Studies*, 16/2 (2013), pp. 124–39, gives a fascinating dissection of Savarkar's third-person biography, *Life of Barrister Savarkar by Chitra Gupta*, Madras, B. G. Paul & Company Publishers, 1926. I have used quotations from a translation of Savarkar's later Marathi memoir, *Inside the Enemy Camp*, translation of *Shatruchya Shibiraat* (1965), pp. 46–7. Text from http://savarkar.org/en/encyc/2017/5/22/Inside-the-Enemy-Camp.html (last accessed 20 May 2020).

99. Nirode K. Barooah, *Chatto: The Life and Times of an Anti-Imperialist in Europe*, New Delhi, Oxford University Press, 2004, p. 11; 'Criminal Intelligence Office: Circular No. 2, Political of 1913: Bombay Police Commissioner's Office File No. 3120/H.', in Government of Bombay, *Source Material for a History of the Freedom Movement in India: Collected from Bombay Government Records*, vol. II: *1885–1920*, Bombay, Government Printing, Publications and Stationery, 1958, pp. 515–16.

100. Gregory Claeys, *Imperial Sceptics: British Critics of Empire, 1850–1920*, Cambridge, Cambridge University Press, 2010, p. 218.

101. Michael Silvestri, '"The Sinn Fein of India": Irish Nationalism and the Policy of Revolutionary Terrorism in Bengal', *Journal of British Studies*, 39/4 (2000), pp. 454–86, at p. 465.

102. Fischer-Tiné, *Shyamji Krishnavarma*, pp. 87–93.

103. This theme is explored in Manjapra, *Age of Entanglement*, esp. pp. 16–21.

104. Friedrich Engels, 'The Festival of Nations in London' (1845), in Karl Marx and Friedrich Engels, *Collected Works*, vol. VI: *1845–48*, London, Lawrence & Wishart, 1976, pp. 3–14, at p. 3.

105. T. N. Harper, 'Globalism and the Pursuit of Authenticity: The Making of a Diasporic Public Sphere in Singapore', *Sojourn: Journal of Social Issues in Southeast Asia*, 12/2 (1997), pp. 261–92, at p. 275.

106. See Frost, 'Asia's Maritime Networks'; Su Lin Lewis, *Cities in Motion: Urban Life and Cosmopolitanism in Southeast Asia, 1920–1940*, Cambridge, Cambridge University Press, 2016; Sukanya Banerjee, *Becoming Imperial Citizens: Indians in the Late-Victorian Empire*, Durham, NC, Duke University Press, 2010; Lynn Hollen Lees, 'Being British in Malaya, 1890–1940', *Journal of British Studies*, 48/1 (2009), pp. 76–101.

107. E. James Lieberman, 'Esperanto and Transnational Identity: The Case of Dr Zamenhof', *International Journal of the Sociology of Language*, 20 (1979), pp. 89–107; Natasha Staller, 'Babel: Hermetic Languages, Universal Languages, and Anti-Languages in Fin de Siècle Parisian Culture', *Art Bulletin*, 76/2 (1994), pp. 331–54, at p. 354.

108. Gregor Benton, *Chinese Migrants and Internationalism: Forgotten Histories, 1917–1945*, London, Routledge, 2007, pp. 92–102; Gerald Chan, 'China and the Esperanto Movement', *Australian Journal of Chinese Affairs*, 15 (1986), pp. 1–18, at pp. 3–4.

109. John Bramble, *Modernism and the Occult*, London, Palgrave Macmillan, 2015, p. 24.

110. I am indebted here to conversation with Romain Bertrand. See also: Nicholas Goodrick-Clarke, *The Western Esoteric Traditions*, Oxford, Oxford University Press, 2008, pp. 211–28; C. A. Bayly, 'Ireland, India and the Empire, 1780–1914', *Transactions of the Royal Historical Society*, 10 (2000), pp. 377–97, at p. 394; Frost, 'Asia's Maritime Networks', pp. 90–92.

111. Gauri Viswanathan, 'The Ordinary Business of Occultism', *Critical Inquiry*, 27/1 (2000), pp. 1–20.

112. Leela Gandhi, *Affective Communities: Anticolonial Thought, Fin-de-Siècle Radicalism, and the Politics of Friendship*, Durham, NC, Duke University Press, 2005; Elleke Boehmer, *Indian Arrivals, 1870–1915: Networks of British Empire*, Oxford, Oxford University Press, 2016, esp. pp. 412–22. In an important reappraisal, published as this book was going to press, Priyamvada Gopal argues that, for many British liberals and radicals, such encounters, and events in India and elsewhere were 'a kind of pedogogical watershed' that transformed their views of empire; see *Insurgent Empire: Anticolonial Resistance and British Dissent*, London, Verso, 2019, at p. 205.

113. Gareth Stedman Jones, 'Radicalism and the Extra-European World: The

Case of Marx', in Duncan Bell (ed.), *Victorian Visions of Global Order: Empire and International Relations in Nineteenth-Century Political Thought*, Cambridge, Cambridge University Press, 2008, pp. 186–214.

114. Julie Pham, 'J. S. Furnivall and Fabianism: Reinterpreting the "Plural Society" in Burma', *Modern Asian Studies*, 39/2 (2005), pp. 321–48.

115. Leszek Kolakowski, *Main Currents of Marxism: Its Origins, Growth and Dissolution*, vol. II: *The Golden Age*, Oxford, Oxford University Press, pp. 1–30; Claeys, *Imperial Sceptics*, pp. 137–40.

116. Quoted in Panchanan Saha, *The Russian Revolution and the Indian Patriots*, Calcutta, Manisha Granthalaya, 1987, pp. 48–9.

117. Margaret C. Jacob, *Strangers Nowhere in the World: The Rise of Cosmopolitanism in Early Modern Europe*, Philadelphia, University of Pennsylvania Press, 2006.

118. Tom Genrich, *Authentic Fictions: Cosmopolitan Writing of the Troisième République, 1908–1940*, Oxford, Peter Lang, 2004, pp. 21–2.

119. Constance Bantman, 'Internationalism without an International? Cross-Channel Anarchist Networks, 1880–1914', *Revue Belge de Philologie et d'Histoire*, 84/4 (2006), pp. 961–81.

120. For a general introduction to (mostly) western anarchism see Peter Marshall, *Demanding the Impossible: A History of Anarchism*, Oakland, CA, PM Press, 2010; Carl Levy, 'Anarchism, Internationalism and Nationalism in Europe, 1860–1939', *Australian Journal of Politics and History*, 50/3 (2004), pp. 330–42.

121. Federico Ferretti, ' "They Have the Right to Throw Us Out": Élisée Reclus' *New Universal Geography*', *Antipode*, 45/5 (2013), pp. 1337–55. As Ferretti notes, others have made the comparison with the writing of Dipesh Chakrabarty over a century later: see esp. Chakrabarty's *Provincializing Europe: Postcolonial Thought and Historical Difference*, Princeton, NJ, Princeton University Press, 2000.

122. John P. Clark and Camille Martin (eds), *Anarchy, Geography, Modernity: The Radical Social Thought of Elisée Reclus*, Lanham, MD, Lexington Books, 2004, pp. 72–4.

123. Arif Dirlik, 'Vision and Revolution: Anarchism in Chinese Revolutionary Thought on the Eve of the 1911 Revolution', *Modern China*, 12/2 (1986), pp. 123–65, at pp. 126–7.

124. For this point and a challenge to Eurocentrism in histories of anarchism see Steven Hirsch and Lucien van der Walt (eds), *Anarchism and Syndicalism in the Colonial and Postcolonial World, 1870–1940: The Praxis of National Liberation, Internationalism, and Social Revolution*, Leiden, Brill, 2010, esp. the editors' introduction. For a similar review see also Carl Levy, 'Social Histories of Anarchism', *Journal for the Study of Radicalism*, 4/2 (2010), pp. 1–44.

125. David E. Apter, 'Notes on the Underground: Left Violence and the

National State', *Daedalus*, 108/4 (1979), pp. 155–72, quotation from Babeuf at p. 159.

126. Martin A. Miller, 'The Intellectual Origins of Modern Terrorism in Europe', in Martha Crenshaw (ed.), *Terrorism in Context*, Philadelphia, Pennsylvania State University Press, 1995, pp. 27–62.

127. For a useful introduction see Olivier Hubac-Occhipinti, 'Anarchist Terrorists of the Nineteenth Century', in Gérard Chaliand and Arnaud Blin (eds), *The History of Terrorism: From Antiquity to Al Qaeda*, Berkeley, University of California Press, 2007, pp. 113–31.

128. Bill Melman, 'The Terrorist in Fiction', *Journal of Contemporary History*, 15/3 (1980), pp. 559–76.

129. Dominique Kalifa, 'Criminal Investigators at the Fin-de-Siècle', *Yale French Studies*, 108 (2005), pp. 36–47.

130. Richard Bach Jensen, *The Battle against Anarchist Terrorism: An International History, 1878–1934*, Cambridge, Cambridge University Press, 2013; Mathieu Deflem, *Policing World Society: Historical Foundations of International Police Cooperation*, Oxford, Oxford University Press, 2002; Clive Emsley, 'The Policeman as Worker: A Comparative Survey, *c.*1800–1940', *International Review of Social History*, 45/1 (2000), pp. 89–110. For Vasai see Lucia Carminati, 'Alexandria, 1898: Nodes, Networks, and Scales in Nineteenth-Century Egypt and the Mediterranean', *Comparative Studies in Society and History*, 59/1 (2017), pp. 127–53, at p. 136.

131. Daniel Brückenhaus, *Policing Transnational Protest: Liberal Imperialism and the Surveillance of Anti-Colonialists in Europe, 1905–1945*, New York, Oxford University Press, 2017, pp. 9–12.

132. See, for example, Charles van Onselen, 'Jewish Police Informers in the Atlantic World, 1880–1914', *Historical Journal*, 50/1 (2007), pp. 119–44.

133. Martin A. Miller, *The Foundations of Modern Terrorism*, Cambridge, Cambridge University Press, 2013, p. 126. See also Katherine Unterman, 'Boodle over the Border: Embezzlement and the Crisis of International Mobility, 1880–1890', *Journal of the Gilded Age and Progressive Era*, 11/2 (2012), pp. 151–89.

134. Important recent reassessments are: Maia Ramnath, *Decolonizing Anarchism: An Antiauthoritarian History of India's Liberation Struggle*, Oakland, CA, AK Press, 2012; Constance Bantman and Bert Altena (eds), *Reassessing the Transnational Turn: Scales of Analysis in Anarchist and Syndicalist Studies*, New York, Routledge, 2015.

135. Alice Bullard, 'Self-Representation in the Arms of Defeat: Fatal Nostalgia and Surviving Comrades in French New Caledonia, 1871–1880', *Cultural Anthropology*, 12/2 (1997), pp. 179–212.

136. Davide Turcato, 'Italian Anarchism as a Transnational Movement, 1885–1915', *International Review of Social History*, 52/3 (2007), pp. 407–44.

137. Ibid.

138. I am thinking here of Mark S. Granovetter, 'The Strength of Weak Ties', *American Journal of Sociology*, 78/6 (1973), pp. 1360–80. For an elaboration of this see Andrew Hoyt, 'Active Centers, Creative Elements, and Bridging Nodes: Applying the Vocabulary of Network Theory to Radical History', *Journal for the Study of Radicalism*, 9/1 (2015), pp. 37–59.

139. Bruce Nelson used this image of Pentecost to describe the unionization of maritime labour in the 1930s: see his *Workers on the Waterfront: Seamen, Longshoremen, and Unionism in the 1930s*, Urbana, University of Illinois Press, 1988, p. 2.

140. Yin Cao, 'Bombs in Beijing and Delhi', pp. 586–7.

141. Sho Konishi, *Anarchist Modernity: Cooperatism and Japanese–Russian Intellectual Relations in Modern Japan*, Cambridge, MA, Harvard University Press, 2013, esp. pp. 29–73 and ch. 3; John Crump, *The Origins of Socialist Thought in Japan*, London, Routledge, 2010.

142. George M. Beckmann and Genji Okubo, *The Japanese Communist Party, 1922–1945*, Stanford, CA, Stanford University Press, 1969, pp. 1–7; Thomas A. Stanley, *Ōsugi Sakae, Anarchist in Taishō Japan: The Creativity of the Ego*, Cambridge, MA, Harvard University Press, 1982.

143. Quoted in Robert Thomas Tierney, *Monster of the Twentieth Century: Kotoku Shusui and Japan's First Anti-Imperialist Movement*, Berkeley, University of California Press, 2015, pp. 119–21.

144. See Hue-Tam Ho Tai, *Radicalism and the Origins of the Vietnamese Revolution*, Cambridge, MA, Harvard University Press, 1992, pp. 58–62; and, for a more cautious view, see Daniel Hémery's review of Tai's study, *Journal of Southeast Asian Studies*, 24/2 (1993), pp. 461–3.

145. Ira L. Plotkin, *Anarchism in Japan: A Study of the Great Treason Affair, 1910–11*, Lewiston, ME, Edwin Mellen Press, 1990.

146. For the Dreyfus analogy see Peter F. Kornicki, 'General Introduction', in Kornicki (ed.), *Meiji Japan*, vol. I: *The Emergence of the Meiji State*, London, Routledge, 1998, pp. xiii–xxxiii, at p. xxviii. For the trial itself see Plotkin, *Anarchism in Japan*.

147. Yukinori Iwaki, 'Ishikawa Takuboku and the Early Russian Revolutionary Movement', *Comparative Literature Studies*, 22/1 (1985), pp. 34–42, at p. 39.

148. Tanaka Mikaru, 'The Reaction of Jewish Anarchists to the High Treason Incident', in Masako Gavin and Ben Middleton (eds), *Japan and the High Treason Incident*, London, Routledge, 2013, pp. 80–88.

149. For this remarkable prison testament see Mikiso Hane, *Reflections on the Way to the Gallows: Rebel Women in Prewar Japan*, Berkeley, University of California Press, 1988, pp. 51–74, quotation at p. 74.

150. Liu, Karl and Ko (eds), *The Birth of Chinese Feminism*, pp. 1–48; Rebecca Karl, 'Feminism in Modern China', *Journal of Modern Chinese History*, 6/2 (2012), pp. 235–55.

151. Karl Marx and Frederick Engels, *The German Ideology Part One*, ed. C. J. Arthur, London, Lawrence & Wishart, 1970, p. 58. The preceding quotation is from Gareth Stedman Jones (ed.), *The Communist Manifesto*, London, Penguin, 2002, p. 223.
152. Levy, 'Social Histories of Anarchism', esp. pp. 15–16.
153. A subject central to recent debates on 'global labour history': see Marcel van der Linden, 'The Promise and Challenges of Global Labor History', *International Labor and Working-Class History*, 82 (2012), pp. 57–76, at pp. 63–4, and the responses to this article in the same issue.
154. For these themes see Geoffroy de Laforcade, 'Federative Futures: Waterways, Resistance Societies and the Subversion of Nationalism in the Early 20th-Century Anarchism of the Río de la Plata Region', *Estudios Interdisciplinarios de América Latina y el Caribe*, 22/2 (2011), pp. 71–96; Jose C. Moya, 'The Positive Side of Stereotypes: Jewish Anarchists in Early-Twentieth-Century Buenos Aires', *Jewish History*, 18/1 (2004), pp. 19–48; and Peter Linebaugh and Marcus Rediker's inspiring *The Many-Headed Hydra: Sailors, Slaves, Commoners, and the Hidden History of the Revolutionary Atlantic*, Boston, MA, Beacon Press, 2000.
155. Jesse Cohn, *Underground Passages: Anarchist Resistance Culture 1848–2011*, Oakland, CA, AK Press, 2015, p. 4; Peter Stallybrass, ' "Well Grubbed, Old Mole": Marx, Hamlet, and the (Un) Fixing of Representation', *Cultural Studies*, 12/1 (1998), pp. 3–14.

3. EMPIRE'S INNER DEMONS (1905–1909)

1. Sugata Bose, *A Hundred Horizons: The Indian Ocean in the Age of Global Empire*, Cambridge, MA, Harvard University Press, 2006; Thomas R. Metcalf, *Imperial Connections: India in the Indian Ocean Arena, 1860–1920*, Berkeley, University of California Press, 2007.
2. H. J. Mackinder, 'The Geographical Pivot of History', *The Geographical Journal*, XXIII/4 (1904), pp. 421–44, at p. 421.
3. Rosalind Williams, *The Triumph of Human Empire: Verne, Morris, and Stevenson at the End of the World*, Chicago, IL, University of Chicago Press, 2013.
4. James L. Hevia, *The Imperial Security State: British Colonial Knowledge and Empire-Building in Asia*, Cambridge, Cambridge University Press, 2012, esp. pp. 11–14.
5. Ronald Hyam, *Britain's Imperial Century, 1815–1914*, 2nd edn, London, Macmillan, 1993, p. 190. See also Jon Wilson, *India Conquered: Britain's Raj and the Chaos of Empire*, London, Simon & Schuster, 2016.
6. Seema Alavi, ' "Fugitive Mullahs and Outlawed Fanatics": Indian Muslims in Nineteenth-Century Trans-Asiatic Imperial Rivalries', *Modern Asian Studies*, 45/6 (2011), pp. 1337–82, quotation at p. 1342.

7. N. Gerald Barrier, *Banned: Controversial Literature and Political Control in British India, 1907–1947*, Columbia, University of Missouri Press, 1974, p. 9.

8. Rajat K. Ray, *Social Conflict and Political Unrest in Bengal, 1875–1927*, Delhi, Oxford University Press, 1985, p. 148.

9. Hiren Chakrabarti, *Political Protest in Bengal: Boycott and Terrorism, 1905–18*, Calcutta, Papyrus, 1992, p. 93.

10. David Ludden, 'Spatial Inequity and National Territory: Remapping 1905 in Bengal and Assam', *Modern Asian Studies*, 46/3 (2012), pp. 483–525.

11. Ray, *Social Conflict*, p. 155.

12. Sikata Banerjee, *Make Me a Man! Masculinity, Hinduism, and Nationalism in India*, Albany, State University of New York Press, 2012, pp. 70–72. For 'service' see the discussion in Sugata Bose, 'The Spirit and Form of an Ethical Polity: A Meditation on Aurobindo Ghose's Thought', *Modern Intellectual History*, 4/1 (2007), pp. 129–44.

13. For this point see Tanika Sarkar, 'Political Women: An Overview of Modern Indian Developments', in Bharati Ray (ed.), *Women of India: Colonial and Post-Colonial Periods*, New Delhi, SAGE, 2005, pp. 541–63, at pp. 550–53. Quotation from S. N. Amin, *The World of Muslim Women in Colonial Bengal, 1876–1939*, Leiden, Brill, 1996, p. 130.

14. Ray, *Social Conflict*, p. 138–9; Prithwindra Mukherjee, *The Intellectual Roots of India's Freedom Struggle (1893–1918)*, London, Routledge, 2018, p. 159; Jordanna Bailkin, 'The Boot and the Spleen: When Was Murder Possible in British India?' *Comparative Studies in Society and History*, 48/2 (2006), pp. 462–93, at pp. 469–70, 487–8.

15. Cited in David Gilmour, *The Ruling Caste: Imperial Lives in the Victorian Raj*, London, Pimlico, 2007, p. 254.

16. John Buchan, *Lord Minto: A Memoir*, London, T. Nelson & Sons, 1924, p. 237.

17. Bipinchandra Pal, *Swadeshi and Swaraj: The Rise of New Patriotism*, Calcutta, Yugayatri Prakashak, 1954, pp. 141–2.

18. R. C. Majumdar, *History of the Freedom Movement in India*, vol. II, Calcutta, Firma, 1963, p. 296.

19. Peter Heehs, *The Lives of Sri Aurobindo: A Biography*, New York, Columbia University Press, 2013.

20. Aurobindo Ghose, 'New Lamps for Old – 1' (1893), in Aurobindo, *The Complete Works of Sri Aurobindo*, vols VI–VII: *Bande Mataram: Political Writings and Speeches, 1890–1908*, Sri Aurobindo Ashram Press, Pondicherry, 2002, p. 15.

21. Aurobindo Ghose, 'The Doctrine of Passive Resistance, III: Its Necessity' (April 1907), in ibid., p. 278.

22. Chakrabarti, *Political Protest in Bengal*, p. 102.

23. H. L. Salkeld, 'Anushilan Samiti Dacca, Part I', in Amiya K. Samanta (ed.),

Terrorism in Bengal: A Collection of Documents on Terrorist Activities from 1905 to 1939, vol. II: *Origin, Growth and Activities of the Organisations like Anushilan Samiti, Jugantar Party, Dacca Shri Sangha and Other Such Organisations*, Calcutta, Government of West Bengal, 1995, pp. 1–74, at p. 30, and quotation at p. 73; Mukherjee, *The Intellectual Roots of India's Freedom Struggle*, pp. 143–4. For Kropotkin see Maia Ramnath, *Decolonizing Anarchism: An Antiauthoritarian History of India's Liberation Struggle*, Oakland, CA, AK Press, 2012, p. 49.

24. Iftekhar Iqbal, 'The Space between Nation and Empire: The Making and Unmaking of Eastern Bengal and Assam Province, 1905–1911', *Journal of Asian Studies*, 74/1 (2015), pp. 69–84. For Ramananda Chatterjee's description of the 'world abroad' see Kris Manjapra, *Age of Entanglement: German and Indian Intellectuals across Empire*, Cambridge, MA, Harvard University Press, 2014, esp. p. 42.

25. Tapan K. Mukherjee, *Taraknath Das: Life and Letters of a Revolutionary in Exile*, Calcutta, National Council of Education, Bengal, Jadavpur University, 1998, pp. 5–7.

26. Aurobindo Ghose, 'Bhawani Mandir' (1905), in Aurobindo, *The Complete Works*, vols VI–VII, p. 86.

27. *Amrita Bazar Patrika*, 10 February 1912.

28. See Sumit Sarkar's classic study, *The Swadeshi Movement in Bengal, 1903–1908*, New Delhi, People's Publishing House, 1973, pp. 28–9. For external influences generally see Peter Heehs, 'Foreign Influences on Bengali Revolutionary Terrorism, 1902–1908', *Modern Asian Studies*, 28/3 (1994), pp. 533–56.

29. H. L. Salkeld, 'Anusihlan Samiti Dacca, Part II', in Samanta (ed.), *Terrorism in Bengal*, vol. II, esp. pp. 91–5.

30. Jogesh Chandra Chatterji, *In Search of Freedom*, Calcutta, Firma K. L. Mukhopadhyay, 1967, p. 26.

31. NAI, Home Department, Political B, June 1909, Nos 19/21, Commissioner of Police, Bombay to Director CID, 17 March 1909.

32. I draw here on two important studies: Ramnath, *Decolonizing Anarchism*, quotation at p. 55; Manjapra, *Age of Entanglement*, esp. p. 42.

33. Shruti Kapila and Faisal Devji (eds), *Political Thought in Action: The Bhagavad Gita and Modern India*, Cambridge, Cambridge University Press, 2013, esp. the editors' introduction, pp. ix–xv, and C. A. Bayly, 'India, the Bhagavad Gita and the World', pp. 1–24, quotation at p. 18.

34. Quoted and assessed in Partha Chatterjee, *The Black Hole of Empire: History of a Global Practice of Power*, Princeton, NJ, Princeton University Press, 2012, p. 285.

35. Sukla Sanyal, 'Legitimizing Violence: Seditious Propaganda and Revolutionary Pamphlets in Bengal, 1908–1918', *Journal of Asian Studies*, 67/3 (2008), pp. 759–87; Muzaffar Ahmad, *Myself and the Communist Party of India, 1920–1929*, Calcutta, National Book Agency, 1970, p. 12.

36. In a speech in Bombay on 19 January 1908, as quoted and discussed in Bose, 'The Spirit and Form of an Ethical Polity', pp. 35–6.

37. F. C. Daly, *First Rebels: Strictly Confidential Note on the Growth of the Revolutionary Movement in Bengal*, Calcutta, Riddhi, 1981, p. 16.

38. Sukhbir Choudhary, *Peasants' and Workers' Movement in India, 1905–1929*, New Delhi, People's Publishing House, 1971, pp. 13–15.

39. NAI, Home Department, Political A, August 1907, No. 239, Minute by H. A. Adamson, 30 July 1907.

40. NAI, Home Department, Political A, January 1908, Nos 34–7, esp. Appendix, cutting from *The Englishman*, 'Bande Mataram Sedition Case', 24 September 1907.

41. For the account of the arrests and trial that follows, I have drawn on the definitive study, Peter Heehs, *The Bomb in Bengal: The Rise of Revolutionary Terrorism in India, 1900–1910*, New Delhi, Oxford University Press, 1993, esp. pp. 143–65.

42. W. Sealy, 'Connections with the Revolutionary Organisation in Bihar and Orissa, 1906–1916' (7 September 1917), in Amiya K. Samanta (ed.), *Terrorism in Bengal, vol. V: Terrorists outside Bengal Deriving Inspiration from and Having Links with Bengal Terrorists*, Calcutta, Government of West Bengal, 1995, pp. 13–14.

43. Heehs, *The Bomb in Bengal*, pp. 155–61.

44. Frederick C. Hamil, 'The King's Approvers: A Chapter in the History of English Criminal Law', *Speculum*, 11/2 (1936), pp. 238–58. I am grateful to Mitra Sharafi for sharing her thoughts on this.

45. Kim A. Wagner, 'Confessions of a Skull: Phrenology and Colonial Knowledge in Early Nineteenth-Century India', *History Workshop Journal*, 69 (2010), pp. 27–51, esp. at p. 44. See also: Sandria B. Freitag, 'Crime in the Social Order of Colonial North India', *Modern Asian Studies*, 25/2 (1991), pp. 227–61, at pp. 238–9; Shahid Amin, *Event, Metaphor, Memory: Chauri Chaura, 1922–1992*, Berkeley, University of California Press, 1995, pp. 74–93.

46. Majumdar, *History of the Freedom Movement*, vol. II, p. 261.

47. See Norton's foreword to Bejoy Krishna Bose, *The Alipore Bomb Trial*, Calcutta, Butterworth & Co., 1922, pp. i–vi, at pp. iii–iv.

48. NAI, Home Department, Political A, May 1908, No. 150, Appendix: statement of Barindra Kumar Ghose, 3 May 1908.

49. Heehs, *The Bomb in Bengal*, pp. 197–217; A. G. Noorani, *Indian Political Trials, 1775–1947*, New Delhi, Oxford University Press, 2005, pp. 137–62.

50. Amiya K. Samanta, 'Introduction' to Samanta (ed.), *Terrorism in Bengal, General Trend of the Terrorist Movement in Bengal from 1907 to 1939*, I: Calcutta, Government of West Bengal, 1995, pp. i–xvi, at pp. v–ix; Sumanta Banerjee, *The Wicked City: Crime and Punishment in Colonial Calcutta*, New Delhi, Orient Blackswan, 2009, pp. 390–92, 447–54; Anupama Rao, 'Problems of Violence, States of Terror: Torture in Colonial

India', *Interventions*, 3/2 (2001), pp. 186–205; Deanna Heath, 'Bureaucracy, Power and Violence in Colonial India', in Peter Crooks and Tim Parsons (eds), *Empires and Bureaucracy from Late Antiquity to the Modern World*, Cambridge, Cambridge University Press, 2016, pp. 364–90.

51. Aurobindo Ghose, the 'Uttarpara Speech' (made in May 1909 after his release), in Aurobindo, *The Complete Works of Sri Aurobindo*, vol. VIII: *Karmayogin: Political Writings and Speeches, 1909–1910*, Sri Aurobindo Ashram Press, Pondicherry, 1997, pp. 3–12, at p. 7.

52. James C. Ker, *Political Trouble in India, 1907–1917* (1917), Calcutta, Editions Indian, 1960, pp. 11–12.

53. Aurobindo Ghose, 'Tales of Prison Life' (1909–10), in Aurobindo, *Writings in Bengali Translation*, Pondicherry, All India Press, 1991, p. 311. I have taken this from an online edition, available at https://motherandsriaurobindo.in/_StaticContent/SriAurobindoAshram/-09%20E-Library/index.php (last accessed 20 April 2020).

54. I draw here on Mithi Mukherjee, *India in the Shadows of Empire: A Legal and Political History (1774–1950)*, Oxford, Oxford University Press, 2009, pp. 140–45, quotations at pp. 140 and 143.

55. Heehs, *The Lives of Sri Aurobindo*, p. 192.

56. Ibid.

57. Norton, foreword to Bose, *The Alipore Bomb Trial*, p. vi.

58. George Fletcher MacMunn, *The Indian Social System: Castes, Tribes, Religions, and Crime*, London, Discovery Publishing House, 1933, pp. 218–19.

59. Ibid., pp. 11, 13. These types are elaborated further in MacMunn, *The Underworld of India*, London, Jarrolds, 1933.

60. Ibid., p, 218.

61. J. E. Armstrong, 'An Account of the Revolutionary Organisations in Eastern Bengal with Special Reference to the Dacca Anushilan Samiti' (1917), in Samanta (ed.), *Terrorism in Bengal*, vol. II, pp. 393–95. Valentine Chirol also shuddered at 'the worst forms of sensuality' in his *Indian Unrest*, London, Macmillan, 1910, p. 101.

62. This background is drawn chiefly from Aparna Vaidik, *Imperial Andamans: Colonial Encounter and Island History*, Basingstoke, Palgrave Macmillan, 2010, quotation at p. 52; L. P. Mathur, *History of the Andaman and Nicobar Islands, 1756–1966*, Delhi, Sterling Publishers, 1968, pp. 196–200, quotation at p. 199.

63. Barindra Kumar Ghose, *The Tale of My Exile*, Pondicherry, Arya Office, 1922, quotation at pp. 50–51.

64. Clare Anderson, 'Fashioning Identities: Convict Dress in Colonial South and Southeast Asia', *History Workshop Journal*, 52 (2001), pp. 152–74, esp. pp. 165–7.

65. Ullaskar Dutt, *Twelve Years of Prison Life*, Calcutta, Arya Publishing House, 1924, p. 37. Gentlemanly Tourists: Political Violence and the Colonial State

in India, 1919–1947, Cambridge, Cambridge University Press, 2017, pp. 64–9, 73–9. See also David Arnold, 'The Self and the Cell: Indian Prison Narratives as Life Histories', in Arnold and Short Blackburn (eds), *Telling Lives in India: Biography, Autobiography, and Life History,* Bloomington, Indiana University Press, 2004, pp. 29–53; Durba Ghosh, *Gentlemanly Terrorists: Political Violence and the Colonial State in India, 1919–1947,* Cambridge, Cambridge University Press, 2017, pp. 64–9, 73–9. See also David Arnold, 'The Self and the Cell: Indian Prison Narratives as Life Histories', in Arnold and Short Blackburn (eds), *Telling Lives in India: Biography, Autobiography, and Life History,* Bloomington, Indiana University Press, 2004, pp. 29–53.

66. Ghose, *The Tale of My Exile,* p. 43.

67. For reflections on this see Choi Chatterjee, 'Imperial Incarcerations: Ekaterina Breshko-Breshkovskaia, Vinayak Savarkar, and the Original Sins of Modernity', *Slavic Review,* 74/4 (2015), pp. 850–72. For colonial visions of the islands see Clare Anderson, Madhumita Mazumdar and Vishvajit Pandya, *New Histories of the Andaman Islands: Landscape, Place and Identity in the Bay of Bengal, 1790–2012,* Cambridge, Cambridge University Press, 2015.

68. Norman Cohn, *Europe's Inner Demons: The Demonization of Christians in Medieval Christendom,* rev. edn, London, Pimlico, 1993. This echo was suggested to me by Carl Watkins.

69. NAI, Home Department, Political B, April 1912, Nos 144–5, C. J. Stevenson-Moore to Secretary of the Government of India, 14 March 1912.

70. Richard J. Popplewell, *Intelligence and Imperial Defence: British Intelligence and the Defence of the Indian Empire, 1904–1924,* London, Frank Cass, 1995, pp. 65–72.

71. Janaki Bakhle, 'Savarkar (1883–1966), Sedition and Surveillance: The Rule of Law in a Colonial Situation', *Social History,* 35/1 (2010), pp. 51–75, at pp. 68–9.

72. See the discussion by John Pincince, 'De-centering Carl Schmitt: The Colonial State of Exception and the Criminalization of the Political in British India, 1905–1920', *Política Común,* 5 (2014).

73. Arun Mukherjee, *Crime and Public Disorder in Colonial Bengal, 1861–1912,* Calcutta, K. P. Bagchi, 1995, pp. 194–8.

74. Quoted in Barrier, *Banned,* p. 24.

75. Shukla Sanyal, *Revolutionary Pamphlets, Propaganda and Political Culture in Colonial Bengal,* Delhi, Cambridge University Press, 2014, pp. 133–9.

76. Barrier, *Banned,* pp. 16–53, quotation at p. 16, statistics at p. 55.

77. Clare Anderson, *Legible Bodies: Race, Criminality and Colonialism in South Asia,* Oxford, Berg, 2004, pp. 160–61.

78. Christopher Pinney, 'Iatrogenic Religion and Politics', in Raminder Kaur and William Mazzarella (eds), *Censorship in South Asia: Cultural Regulation from Sedition to Seduction,* Bloomington, Indiana University Press, 2009, pp. 29–62, quotations at pp. 40–41.

79. Mukherjee, *Crime and Public Disorder in Colonial Bengal*, pp. 180–85.

80. NAI, Home Department, Political A, January 1910, Nos 143–53, report to India Office, 16 December 1909.

81. Majumdar, *History of the Freedom Movement*, vol. II, quotation at p. 263, drawn originally from Judugopal Mukherjee's Bengali memoir, *Bipladi Jibaner Smriti*, Indian Associated Publishers, Calcutta, 1956.

82. Samaren Roy, *M. N. Roy: A Political Biography*. New Delhi, Orient Longman, 1997, pp. 1–2.

83. As recalled in M. N. Roy, 'Nationalism and Non-violence', *The Radical Humanist*, XIII/15 (17 April 1949), pp. 167–8.

84. For Roy's early life see Sibnarayan Ray, *In Freedom's Quest: A Study of the Life and Works of M. N. Roy (1887–1954)*, vol. I: *1887–1922*, Calcutta, Minerva Associates, 1998; Samaren Roy, *The Restless Brahmin: Early Life of M. N. Roy*, Bombay: Allied, 1970; J. C. Nixon, 'Account of the Revolutionary Organisations in Bengal Other Than the Dacca Anushilan Saimiti' (1917), in Samanta (ed.), *Terrorism in Bengal*, vol. II, pp. 501–652, at p. 539.

85. Leonard Gordon, *Bengal: The Nationalist Movement, 1876–1940*, New York, Columbia University Press, 1974, pp. 136–44.

86. Ghosh, *Gentlemanly Terrorists*, pp. 3–7.

87. M. N. Roy, *Men I Met* (1968), Delhi, Ajanta Publications, 1981, p. 1.

88. For an insightful analysis see Dilip Menon, 'The Many Spaces and Times of Swadeshi', *Economic and Political Weekly*, 47/42 (2012), pp. 44–52.

89. Quoted in John Richard Pincince, 'On the Verge of Hindutva: V. D. Savarkar, Revolutionary, Convict, Ideologue, *c.* 1905–1924', PhD thesis, University of Hawaii at Manoa, 2007, p. 36.

90. Deep Kanta Lahiri Choudhury, 'India's First Virtual Community and the Telegraph General Strike of 1908', *International Review of Social History*, 48/S11 (2003), pp. 45–71.

91. 'Govind Narayan Potdar', from Bombay Secret Abstract No. 7 of 1910 in Government of Bombay, *Source Material for a History of the Freedom Movement in India: Collected from Bombay Government Records*, vol. II: *1885–1920*, Bombay, Government of Bombay, 1967, pp. 532–5.

92. Ibid., Aravind Ganachari, *Nationalism and Social Reform in Colonial Situation*, Delhi, Kalpaz Publications, 2005, p. 143.

93. Suchetana Chattopadhyay, *An Early Communist: Muzaffar Ahmad in Calcutta, 1913–1929*, New Delhi, Tulika Books, 2011, pp. 39–40.

94. Majumdar, *History of the Freedom Movement*, vol. II, pp. 263, 269–70 for arms.

95. For Hem Chandra and the Russia to Paris connection see Maia Ramnath, *Decolonizing Anarchism: An Antiauthoritarian History of India's Liberation Struggle*, Oakland, CA, AK Press, 2012, pp. 62–8. For a recent account of these circulations see Yin Cao, 'Bombs in Beijing and Delhi: The Global Spread of Bomb-Making Technology and the Revolutionary

Terrorism in Modern China and India', *Journal of World History*, 30/4 (2019), pp. 559–89.

96. Morley to Minto, 4 June 1908, quoted in Barrier, *Banned*, p. 37.

97. Indulal Yajnik, *Shyamaji Krishnavarma: Life and Times of an Indian Revolutionary* (1934), Bombay, Lakshmi Publications, 1950, p. 98.

98. Ibid., pp. 225, 232–3.

99. *The Times*, 19 March 1909, quoted in Yajnik, *Shyamaji Krishnavarma*, p. 264.

100. Carolien Stolte, 'Orienting India: Interwar Internationalism in an Asian Inflection, 1917–1937', PhD thesis, Leiden University, 2013, p. 141; Barrier, *Banned*, p. 62.

101. M. P. T. Acharya and B. D. Yadav, *M. P. T. Acharya: Reminiscences of an Indian Revolutionary*, New Delhi, Anmol Publications, 1991, pp. 83–4; Vishwa Nath Datta, *Madan Lal Dhingra and the Revolutionary Movement*, New Delhi, Vikas, *c.* 1978, p. 23.

102. Niraja Gopal Jayal, *Citizenship and Its Discontents: An Indian History*, Cambridge, MA, Harvard University Press, 2013, pp. 115–20.

103. *The Times*, 12 February 1909.

104. *House of Commons Debates*, 4 March 1909, vol. I, cc. 1698–9W.

105. For the narrative of events I have followed see Datta, *Madan Lal*, esp. pp. 34–6 and 44–58. For 'Fairyland' see Ann Basu, *Fitzrovia, The Other Side of Oxford Street: A Social History 1900–1950*, Stroud, The History Press, 2019, ch. 6.

106. *The Times*, 24 July 1909. For the written statement see Wilfrid Scawen Blunt, *My Diaries: Being a Personal Narrative of Events, 1888–1914*, vol. II, New York, Alfred A. Knopf, 1922, p. 443.

107. *The Times*, 24 July 1909.

108. Emily C. Brown, *Har Dayal: Hindu Revolutionary and Rationalist*, Tucson, University of Arizona Press, 1975, p. 75.

109. Yajnik, *Shyamaji Krishnavarma*, pp. 270–72, 284, 296.

110. NAI, Home Dept, Political A, Proceedings, May 1910, No. 135, C. J. Stevenson-Moore, 'The revolutionary group', 25 January 1910.

111. Yajnik, *Shyamaji Krishnavarma*, p. 273.

112. C. H. Norman, 'Imperialism and Indian Patriotism', *The New Age*, 5/13 (29 July 1909), p. 264.

113. Blunt, *My Diaries*, vol. II, pp. 253 (on Krishnavarma and Mazzini), 277–8.

114. Acharya and Yadav, *M. P. T. Acharya*, p. 92; 'History Sheet of Virendranath Chattopadhyaya', in Samanta (ed.), *Terrorism in Bengal*, vol. V, p. 332.

115. 'Memorandum on the Anti-British Agitation among Natives of India in England and the Continent of Europe, Part IV' (12 October 1911), in Samanta (ed.), *Terrorism in Bengal*, vol. V, p. 436.

116. David French, 'Spy Fever in Britain, 1900–1915', *Historical Journal*, 21/2 (1978), pp. 355–70.

117. Simon Ball, 'The Assassination Culture of Imperial Britain, 1909–1979', *Historical Journal*, 56/1 (2013), pp. 231–56.

118. J. C. Kher, 'Virendra Chattopadhyaya', Criminal Intelligence Office: Circular No. 2 Political of 1913, Government of Bombay, *Source Material for a History of the Freedom Movement*, vol. II, p. 516.

119. As related in David Garnett's memoir, *The Golden Echo*, London, Chatto & Windus, 1953.

120. V. Savarkar, 'Fare-Well', in Savarkar, *An Echo from Andamans: Letters Written by Br. Savarkar to his Brother Dr Savarkar*, Nagpur, Vishvanath Vinyak Kelkar, 1924, unpaginated.

121. 'Happening of the Escape and Recapture', a summary of the statements of the officers involved, in Government of Bombay, *Source Material for a History of the Freedom Movement*, vol. II, pp. 448–50.

122. Pincince, 'On the Verge of Hindutva', pp. 244–9.

123. 'Extract from Special Bench Judgement Given on Pages 153 to 182 of Secret Abstract 1911, CID Bombay', in Government of Bombay, *Source Material for a History of the Freedom Movement*, vol. II, pp. 395–436, quotation at p. 406.

124. Bakhle, 'Savarkar (1883–1966), Sedition and Surveillance'; quotation from Vinayak Savarkar, *My Transportation for Life* (1950), Bombay, Veer Savarkar Prakashan, 1984, p. 7.

125. 'Jail History Ticket of V. D. Savarkar', in Government of Bombay, *Source Material for a History of the Freedom Movement*, vol. II, pp. 478–81.

126. Vinayak Savarkar to Narayanrao Savarkar, 15 December 1912, in Savarkar, *An Echo from Andamans*.

127. NAI, Home Department, Political B, October 1912, No. 64, 'Copy of letter dated 4 May 1912 from Capt F. A. Barker, Medical Superintendent, Jail District, Port Blair to chief superintendent, Port Blair'.

128. Ibid., May 1912, No. 60, 'Inquest into the death of convict 3155, Indu Bhusan Roy, a prisoner in the Cellular Jail', 29 April 1912.

129. R. C. Majumdar, *Penal Settlement in Andamans*, New Delhi, Publications Division, Government of India, 1975, pp. 199–204; [Guy Aldred] 'Life in the Andamans', *Herald of Revolt*, 2/10 (October 1912); Dutt, *Twelve Years of Prison Life*, p. 76.

130. NAI, Home Department, Political B, December 1912, Nos 11–31, Superintendent Port Blair to Dvijadas Datta, 28 September 1912, Statement of Ullaskar Dutt's case'.

131. Ibid., Nos 11–31, Extract from the Diary of the Overseer, Cellular Jail, dated 28 July 1912.

132. Ibid., No. 15, Dvijadas Datta to Secretary to the Government of India, 16 September 1912. This was drawn to my attention by Cathy Scott-Clark and Adrian Levy, 'Survivors of Our Hell', *Guardian*, 23 June 2001.

133. For the genealogy of the term 'terrorism', both within India and globally, see Joseph McQuade, 'Terrorism, Law, and Sovereignty in Late Colonial India, 1897–1946', PhD thesis, University of Cambridge, 2017. For 'political prisoners' see Pincince, 'De-centering Carl Schmitt'.

134. Ole Birk Laursen, 'Anarchist Anti-Imperialism: Guy Aldred and the Indian Revolutionary Movement, 1909–14', *Journal of Imperial and Commonwealth History*, 46/2 (2018), pp. 286–303.

135. These arguments were made at the time, but see also Jyotirmaya Sharma, 'History as Revenge and Retaliation: Rereading Savarkar's The War of Independence of 1857', *Economic and Political Weekly*, 42/19 (2007), pp. 1717–19.

136. 'Memorandum on the Anti-British Agitation among Natives of India in England, Part III', 19 September 1910, in Samanta (ed.), *Terrorism in Bengal*, vol. V, pp. 312–13.

137. 'London' (after 18 September 1909), later published in *Indian Opinion*, in *The Collected Works of Mahatma Gandhi* (e-edn), New Delhi, Publications Division Government of India, 1999, vol. X, p. 106.

138. Yajnik, *Shyamaji Krishnavarma*, p. 241.

139. V. V. Savarkar, *Inside the Enemy Camp*, translation of *Shatruchya Shibiraat* (1965), p. 47. Text from http://savarkar.org/en/encyc/2017/5/22/Inside-the-Enemy-Camp.html (last accessed 20 May 2020).

140. M. K. Gandhi, 'Hind Swaraj', in Anthony J. Parel (ed.), *Gandhi: Hind Swaraj and Other Writings*, new edn, Cambridge, Cambridge University Press, 2009, pp. 75–6. For the journey and his anticipated arrival, letter to Manilal Gandhi, 24 November 1909, in *Collected Works of Mahatma Gandhi*, vol. X, p. 317. For the background and a commentary see Ramachandra Guha, *India before Gandhi*, London, Penguin, 2013, and Shruti Kapila, 'Gandhi before Mahatma: The Foundations of Political Truth', *Public Culture*, 23/2 (2011), pp. 431–48.

141. Isabel Hofmeyr, *Gandhi's Printing Press*, Cambridge, MA, Harvard University Press, 2013.

142. Quotation from Gandhi, 'Hind Swaraj', in Parel (ed.), *Gandhi: Hind Swaraj*, p. 88.

143. Jonathan Hyslop, 'An "Eventful" History of *Hind Swaraj*: Gandhi between the Battle of Tsushima and the Union of South Africa', *Public Culture*, 23/2 (2011), pp. 299–319, at pp. 307–8.

144. 'Criminal Intelligence Office: Circular No. 2, Political of 1913', in Government of Bombay, *Source Material for a History of the Freedom Movement*, vol. II, p. 517.

145. Kristin Shawn Tassin, 'Egyptian Nationalism, 1882–1919: Elite Competition, Transnational Networks, Empire, and Independence', PhD thesis, University of Texas at Austin, 2014, pp. 115–42.

146. Noor-Aiman I. Khan, *Egyptian-Indian Nationalist Collaboration and the British Empire*, New York, Palgrave Macmillan, 2011, pp. 38–47.
147. 'Memorandum on the Anti-British Agitation among Natives of India in England and the Continent of Europe, Part IV', 12 October 1911, in Samanta (ed.), *Terrorism in Bengal*, vol. V, pp. 410–11, 415–19.
148. For this and the preceding paragraph, Acharya and Yadav, *M. P. T. Acharya*, pp. 108–12; C. S. Subramanyam, *M. P. T. Acharya: His Life and Times: Revolutionary Trends in the Early Anti-Imperialist Movements in South India and Abroad*, Madras, Institute of South Indian Studies, 1995, pp. 106–9; 'Memorandum on the Anti-British Agitation among Natives of India in England, Part III', in Samanta (ed.), *Terrorism in Bengal*, vol. V, pp. 396–7; NAI, Home Dept, Political B, Proceedings, December 1909, No. 37, 'Movements of M. P. Triumalaichari'.

4. THE FURY OF ENLIGHTENMENT (1909–1912)

1. Douglas L. Wheeler, *Republican Portugal: A Political History, 1910–1926*, Madison, University of Wisconsin Press, 1999, esp. pp. 57–8.
2. In this section I am revisiting an argument made by Eric Hobsbawm, *The Age of Empires*, London, Pantheon, 1987, pp. 274–301. See also John Mason Hart, *Revolutionary Mexico: The Coming and Process of the Mexican Revolution*, new edn, Berkeley, University of California Press, 1998, esp. pp. 187–234.
3. Charles Kurzman, *Democracy Denied, 1905–1915: Intellectuals and the Fate of Democracy*, Cambridge, MA, Harvard University Press, 2008, p. 3.
4. Bernard Lewis, *The Emergence of Modern Turkey*, 2nd edn, London, Oxford University Press, 1968, pp. 185–6.
5. Gordon M. Winder, 'London's Global Reach? Reuters News and Network, 1865, 1881, and 1914', *Journal of World History*, 21/2 (2010), pp. 271–96; Daqing Yang, *Technology of Empire: Telecommunications and Japanese Expansion in Asia, 1883–1945*, Cambridge, MA, Harvard University Press, 2010, p. 59.
6. A. C. Bose (ed.), *Indian Revolutionaries Abroad, 1905–1927: Select Documents*, New Delhi, Northern Book Centre, 2002, pp. 120–21.
7. Ilham Khuri-Makdisin, 'Fin-de-Siècle Egypt: A Nexus for Mediterranean and Global Radical Networks', in James L. Gelvin and Nile Green (eds), *Global Muslims in the Age of Steam and Print*, Berkeley, University of California Press, 2013, pp. 78–100.
8. Umar Ryad, 'A Printed Muslim "Lighthouse" in Cairo: al-Manār's Early Years, Religious Aspiration and Reception (1898–1903)', *Arabica*, 56 (2009), pp. 27–60; Michael Laffan, *Islamic Nationhood and Colonial Indonesia: The Umma below the Winds*, London, Routledge, 2003, esp.

pp. 142-78; A. C. Milner, 'The Impact of the Turkish Revolution on Malaya', *Archipel*, 31 (1986), pp. 117-30.

9. See the fascinating interpretation by Faridah Zaman, 'Beyond Nostalgia: Time and Place in Indian Muslim Politics', *Journal of the Royal Asiatic Society*, 27/4 (2017), pp. 627-47; *The Comrade* is cited at p. 634.

10. Feisal Devji, 'Islam and British Imperial Thought', in David Motadel (ed.), *Islam and the European Empires*, Oxford, Oxford University Press, 2014, pp. 254-68, at p. 267.

11. There is a large, nuanced literature on this, for which there is a useful review by David Motadel, 'Islam and the European Empires', *Historical Journal*, 55/3 (2012), pp. 831-56. See also the other essays in Motadel (ed.), *Islam and the European Empires*. For my own account of the Euro-Islamic condominium see T. N. Harper, 'Empire, Diaspora and the Languages of Globalism, 1850-1914', in A. G. Hopkins (ed.), *Globalization in World History*, London, Pimlico, 2002, pp. 141-66.

12. K. H. Ansari, 'Pan-Islam and the Making of the Early Indian Muslim Socialists', *Modern Asian Studies*, 20/3 (1986), pp. 509-37, quotation from Azad at p. 512.

13. Kurzman, *Democracy Denied*.

14. J. P. Sharma, *Republics in Ancient India, c. 1500 BC to c. 500 BC*, Leiden, Brill, 1968, pp. 2-5; Ram Sharan Sharma, *Aspects of Political Ideas and Institutions in Ancient India*, Delhi, Motilal Banasidass, 1996 edn, pp. 4-6; 'History Sheet of Kashi Prasad Jayaswal', in Amiya K. Samanta (ed.), *Terrorism in Bengal: A Collection of Documents on Terrorist Activities from 1905 to 1939*, vol. V: *Terrorists outside Bengal Deriving Inspiration from and Having Links with Bengal Terrorists*, Calcutta, Government of West Bengal, 1995, pp. 385-6. For early republicanism see C. A. Bayly, *Recovering Liberties: Indian Thought in the Age of Liberalism and Empire*, Cambridge, Cambridge University Press, 2011, pp. 110-11.

15. Peter Zinoman, *Vietnamese Colonial Republican: The Political Vision of Vu Trong Phung*, Berkeley, University of California Press, 2013, pp. 4-9; Banu Turnaoğlu, *The Formation of Turkish Republicanism*, Princeton, NJ, Princeton University Press, 2017, pp. 115-37, quotation at p. 127. For republicanism more generally see Maia Ramnath, *Haj to Utopia: How the Ghadar Movement Charted Global Radicalism and Attempted to Overthrow the British Empire*, Berkeley, University of California Press, 2011, esp. p. 122.

16. F. A. Eustis and Z. H. Zaidi, 'King, Viceroy and Cabinet: The Modification of the Partition of Bengal, 1911', *History*, 49/166 (1964), pp. 171-84, at p. 175.

17. Leila Tarazi Fawaz and C. A. Bayly (eds), *Modernity and Culture: From the Mediterranean to the Indian Ocean*, New York, Columbia University Press, 2002; Tim Harper and Sunil Amrith (eds), *Sites of Asian Interaction: Ideas, Networks and Mobility*, Cambridge, Cambridge University Press, 2014.

18. Zaid Fahmy, *Ordinary Egyptians*, Stanford, CA, Stanford University Press, 2011; Meng Yue, *Shanghai and the Edges of Empires*, Minneapolis, University of Minnesota Press, 2006, esp. pp. 106–35, for assassinations, p. 118. For film see Antonia Law, 'The Curse of the Pharaoh, or How Cinema Attracted Egyptomania', in Matthew Bernstein and Gaylyn Studlar (eds), *Visions of the East: Orientalism in Film*, London, I.B. Tauris, 1997, pp. 69–88; Zhen Zhang, *An Amorous History of the Silver Screen: Shanghai Cinema, 1896–1937*, Chicago, IL, University of Chicago Press, 2005, p. 66–7.

19. Rudolf Mrázek, *Engineers of Happy Land: Technology and Nationalism in a Colony*, Princeton, NJ, Princeton University Press, 2002, p. 153.

20. I draw, in particular, on Jean-Michel Rabaté, *1913: The Cradle of Modernism*, Oxford, Blackwell, 2007.

21. Quoted in Kaya Ozsezgin, *İbrahim Çallı*, Istanbul, Yapi Kredi Yayinlari, 1993, p. 207.

22. Edward W. Said, 'Reflections on Exile', in *Reflections on Exile and Other Essays*, Cambridge, MA, Harvard University Press, 2000, pp. 173–86.

23. Dan N. Jacobs, *Borodin: Stalin's Man in China*, Cambridge, MA, Harvard University Press, 1981, pp. 16–36.

24. J. V. Stalin, *Marxism and the National Question* (1913), https://www.marxists.org/reference/archive/stalin/works/1913/03a.htm (last accessed 6 September 2018).

25. V. I. Lenin, *The Right of Nations to Self-Determination* (1913), in Lenin, *Collected Works*, vol. XX, Moscow, Progress Publishers, 1964, p. 406.

26. Allen S. Whiting, *Soviet Policies in China, 1917–1924*, Stanford, CA, Stanford University Press, 1954, p. 18.

27. For a summary of the scholarship see Joseph W. Esherick, 'Reconsidering 1911: Lessons of a Sudden Revolution', *Journal of Modern Chinese History*, 6/1 (2012), pp. 1–14.

28. Edmund S. K. Fung, *The Intellectual Foundations of Chinese Modernity: Cultural and Political Thought in the Republican Era*, Cambridge, Cambridge University Press, 2010, quotation, from Fu Sinian, at p. 15.

29. I follow here Leigh Jenco, 'What Is "Republican" about Republican Chinese Thought (1895–1949)?', in Jun-Hyeok Kwak and Leigh Jenco, *Republicanism in Northeast Asia*, London, Routledge, 2014, pp. 85–108.

30. V. Savarkar to Narayanrao Savarkar, 15 December 1912, in Savarkar, *An Echo from Andamans: Letters Written by Br. Savarkar to his Brother Dr Savarkar*, Nagpur, Vishvanath Vinyak Kelkar, 1924.

31. Zhang, *An Amorous History of the Silver Screen*, pp. 45–6.

32. Fernand Farjenel, *Through the Chinese Revolution*, London, Duckworth & Co., 1915, p. 10.

33. Ching Fatt Yong, 'An Historical Turning Point: The 1911 Revolution and Its Impact on Singapore's Chinese Society', in Lai To Lee and Lee Hock Guan (eds), *Sun Yat-Sen, Nanyang and the 1911 Revolution*, Singapore,

Institute of Southeast Asian Studies, 2011, pp. 148–69; Yen Ching Hwang, *The Overseas Chinese and the 1911 Revolution, with Special Reference to Singapore and Malaya*, Kuala Lumpur, Oxford University Press, 1976, pp. 263, 286.

34. J. G. Butcher, 'Towards the History of Malayan Society: Kuala Lumpur District, 1885–1912', *Journal of Southeast Asian Studies*, 10/1 (1979), pp. 104–18; Patrick Morrah, 'The History of the Malayan Police', *Journal of the Malayan Branch of the Royal Asiatic Society*, 36/2 (1963), pp. 1–172, at p. 114.

35. Yen, *The Overseas Chinese and the 1911 Revolution*, p. 285.

36. Fung Chi Ming, 'Governorships of Lugard and May: Fears of Double Allegiance and Perceived Disloyalty', in Lee Pui-tak (ed.), *Colonial Hong Kong and Modern China: Interaction and Reintegration*, Hong Kong, Hong Kong University Press, 2005, pp. 69–88.

37. *Hong Kong Telegraph*, 4 July 1912; *Singapore Free Press and Mercantile Advertiser*, 18 July 1912.

38. Eyewitness report in the *Hong Kong Telegraph*, 4 July 1912.

39. N. J. Miners, 'The Attempt to Assassinate the Governor in 1912', *Journal of the Hong Kong Branch of the Royal Asiatic Society*, 22 (1982), pp. 279–84; *Hong Kong Telegraph*, 6 July 1912.

40. Ibid., 18 July 1912; John M. Carroll, *Edge of Empires: Chinese Elites and British Colonials in Hong Kong*, Cambridge, MA, Harvard University Press, 2005, pp. 126–32.

41. Sir Francis May to G. E. Morrison, 11 August 1912, in Hui-Min Lo (ed.), *The Correspondence of G. E. Morrison, 1912–1920*, Cambridge, Cambridge University Press, 1978, pp. 17–18.

42. Yue, *Shanghai and the Edges of Empires*, pp. 123–5.

43. Michael G. Vann, 'Of Pirates, Postcards, and Public Beheadings: The Pedagogic Execution in French Colonial Indochina', *Historical Reflections/Réflexions Historiques*, 36/2 (2010), pp. 39–58, quotation at p. 41. For numbers see Marie-Paule Ha, *French Women and the Empire: The Case of Indochina*, Oxford, Oxford University Press, 2014, p. 124.

44. Article in *L'Avenir du Tonkin*, 18 October 1912, quoted in John Laffey, 'Imperialists Divided: The Views of Tonkin's *Colons* before 1914', *Histoire Sociale/Social History*, 10/19 (1977), pp. 92–113, at p. 111.

45. For a useful discussion see Philippe M. F. Peycam, *The Birth of Vietnamese Political Journalism: Saigon, 1916–1930*, New York, Columbia University Press, 2012, pp. 40–43, quotation at p. 41.

46. Ministère des Affaires Étrangères, La Courneuve, Nouvelle Série, Indochine/12, 'Consul Général de France, Hong Kong to M. Jonnart, Ministre de Affaires Étrangères', 24(?) February 1913.

47. R. B. Smith, 'The Development of Opposition to French Rule in Southern Vietnam 1880–1940', *Past and Present*, 54 (1972), pp. 94–129; Jonathan Krause, 'Rebellion and Resistance in French Indochina in the First World

War', *Journal of Imperial and Commonwealth History* (published online 25 December 2019), pp. 1–31, at pp. 3–5.

48. Ministère des Affaires Étrangères, La Courneuve, Nouvelle Série, Indochine/12, Sarraut telegram, 26 April 1913.

49. *Straits Times*, 20 May 1913; David G. Marr, *Vietnamese Anticolonialism, 1885–1925*, Berkeley, University of California Press, 1971, pp. 220–21; Micheline Lessard, 'More than Half the Sky: Vietnamese Women and Anti-French Activism, 1858–1945', in Wynn Wilcox (ed.), *Vietnam and the West: New Approaches*, Ithaca, NY, Southeast Asia Program Publications, 2010, pp. 91–106, at p. 95.

50. *Straits Times*, 14 June 1913.

51. Ministère des Affaires Étrangères, La Courneuve, Nouvelle Série, Indochine/12, 'Consul Général de France à Hong Kong', 23 June 1913.

52. Hue-Tam Ho Tai, *Radicalism and the Origins of the Vietnamese Revolution*, Cambridge, MA, Harvard University Press, 1992, pp. 62–3.

53. Tran My-Van, *A Vietnamese Royal Exile in Japan: Prince Cuong De (1882–1951)*, London, Routledge, 2013, pp. 79–84.

54. As quoted by J. Kim Munholland, 'The French Response to the Vietnamese Nationalist Movement, 1905–14', *Journal of Modern History*, 47/4 (1975), pp. 655–75, at p. 674.

55. Neil L. Jamieson, *Understanding Vietnam*, Berkeley, University of California Press, 1995, pp. 68, 72–5.

56. M. C. Ricklefs, *Polarizing Javanese Society: Islamic and Other Visions, c. 1830–1930*, Singapore, NUS Press, 2007, pp. 49–57.

57. J. N. F. M. à Campo, *Engines of Empire: Steamshipping and State Formation in Colonial Indonesia*, Hilversum, Verloren, 2002, statistics at pp. 595, 600.

58. Mrázek, *Engineers of Happy Land*, p. 93. I also draw on Eric Tagliacozzo, 'The Indies and the World': State Building, Promise, and Decay at a Transnational Moment, 1910', *Bijdragen Tot de Taal-, Land- En Volkenkunde*, 166/2–3 (2010), pp. 270–92.

59. Raden Adjeng Kartini, *Letters of a Javanese Princess*, as quoted and discussed in R. E. Elson, *The Idea of Indonesia: A History*, Cambridge, Cambridge University Press, 2009, p. 8.

60. Ulbe Bosma, 'Citizens of Empire: Some Comparative Observations on the Evolution of Creole Nationalism in Colonial Indonesia', *Comparative Studies in Society and History*, 46/4 (2004), pp. 656–81. For the quotation, *Toward a Glorious Indonesia: Reminiscences and Observations of Dr. Soetomo*, ed. Paul W. van der Veur, trans. Suharni Soemarmo and Paul van der Veur, Athens, Ohio University Centre for International Studies, 1987, p. 65.

61. The Siauw Giap, 'Group Conflict in a Plural Society', *Revue du Sud-Est Asiatique*, 1 (1966), pp. 1–31 and 185–217, quotation at p. 187.

62. Lea E. Williams, *Overseas Chinese Nationalism: The Genesis of the Pan-Chinese Movement in Indonesia, 1900–1916*, Glencoe, IL, Free Press, 1960; Peter Post, 'The Kwik Hoo Tong Trading Society of Semarang, Java: A Chinese Business Network in Late Colonial Asia', *Journal of Southeast Asian Studies*, 33/2 (2002), pp. 279–96.

63. Azyumardi Azra, 'The Indies Chinese and Sarekat Islam', *Studia Islamika*, 1/1 (1994), pp. 26–53.

64. The Siauw Giap, 'Group Conflict in a Plural Society', at pp. 209–17.

65. John Ingleson, *In Search of Justice: Workers and Unions in Colonial Java, 1908–1926*, Singapore, Oxford University Press, 1986, pp. 64–5.

66. For Mas Marco see Henri Chambert-Loir, 'Mas Marco Kartodikromo (c. 1890–1932) ou l'Éducation Politique', in Pierre-Bernard Lafont and Denys Lombard (eds), *Littératures Contemporaines de l'Asie du Sud-Est*, Paris, L'Asiathèque, 1974, pp. 203–14; Hendrik M. J. Maier, *We Are Playing Relatives: A Survey of Malay Writing*, Leiden, KITLV Press, 2004, pp. 157–202.

67. Takashi Shiraishi, *An Age in Motion: Popular Radicalism in Java, 1912–1926*, Ithaca, NY, Cornell University Press, 1990, p. 34. For this publication see also Ahmat Adam, *The Vernacular Press and the Emergence of Modern Indonesian Consciousness (1855–1913)*, Ithaca, NY, Southeast Asia Program Publications, 1995, pp. 113–21.

68. H. M. J. Maier, 'From Heteroglossia to Polyglossia: The Creation of Malay and Dutch in the Indies', *Indonesia*, 56 (1993), pp. 37–65. For this theme, and much else see Joel S. Kahn, *Other Malays: Nationalism and Cosmopolitanism in the Modern Malay World*, Singapore, Singapore University Press, 2006.

69. Adam, *The Vernacular Press and the Emergence of Modern Indonesian Consciousness*, pp. 188–9; Doris Jedamski, 'Genres of Crime Fiction in Indonesia', in Bob Hering (ed.), *Pramoedya Ananta Toer 70 Tahun: Essays to Honour Pramoedya Ananta Toer's 70th Year*, Stein, Edisi Sastra Yayasan Kabar Seberang, 1995, pp. 167–89; Doris Jedamski, 'Popular Literature and Postcolonial Subjectivities: Robinson Crusoe, the Count of Monte Cristo and Sherlock Holmes in Colonial Indonesia', in Keith Foulcher and Tony Day (eds), *Clearing a Space: Postcolonial Readings of Modern Indonesian Literature*, Leiden, KITLV Press, 2002, pp. 19–47.

70. Mas Marco Kartodikromo, *Three Early Indonesian Short Stories*, trans. and ed. Paul Tickell, Clayton, Monash University, Department of Indonesian and Malay, 1981. Such was the efficacy of pseudonym that one of the stories here is wrongly attributed to Marco; apparently it is by his comrade Sumantri.

71. Quotation from Mas Marco Kartodikromo's novel *Student Hidjo* (1919), in Shiraishi, *An Age in Motion*, p. 65.

72. Shiraishi, *An Age in Motion*, p. 59–66. For the theatre see Bob Hering, *Soekarno, Founding Father of Indonesia: A Biography, 1901–1945*, Leiden, KITLV Press, 2003, p. 39.

73. For a summary life see Paul W. van der Veur, 'E. F. E. Douwes Dekker: Evangelist for Indonesian Political Nationalism', *Journal of Asian Studies*, 17/4 (1958), pp. 551–66, quotation at p. 552.

74. NL-HaNA, Koloniën: Openbaar Archief, Vb 27-7-1916, 25, 'Statement: E. F. E. Douwes Dekker', Singapore, 24 January 1916.

75. Paul W. van der Veur, *The Lion and the Gadfly: Dutch Colonialism and the Spirit of E. F. E. Douwes Dekker*, Leiden, KITLV Press, 2006, pp. 188–99.

76. Ibid., p. 199.

77. Van der Veur, 'E. F. E. Douwes Dekker', p. 555.

78. Kees van Dijk, *The Netherlands Indies and the Great War, 1914–1918*, Leiden, KITLV Press, 2007, pp. 48–9.

79. Van der Veur, *The Lion and the Gadfly*, p. 204.

80. Ingleson, *In Search of Justice*, pp. 69–70.

81. This essay has been much discussed, but see esp. James T. Siegel, *Fetish, Recognition, Revolution*, Princeton, NJ, Princeton University Press, 1997, pp. 26–7. I have drawn quotations from C. L. M. Penders (ed. and trans.), *Indonesia: Selected Documents on Colonialism and Nationalism, 1830–1942*, St Lucia, University of Queensland Press, 1977, pp. 232–3.

82. Ibid., pp. 59–60.

83. Christopher E. Goscha, *Thailand and the Southeast Asian Networks of the Vietnamese Revolution, 1885–1954*, London, Routledge, 1998, p. 42; Ministère des Affaires Étrangères, La Courneuve, Nouvelle Série, Indochine/13, 'Consul Général de France à Hong Kong à Sarraut', 13 July 1913.

84. Eric Tagliacozzo, 'Kettle on a Slow Boil: Batavia's Threat Perceptions in the Indies' Outer Islands, 1870–1910', *Journal of Southeast Asian Studies*, 31/1 (2000), pp. 70–100.

85. Charles Hardinge, *My Indian Years, 1910–1916: The Reminiscences of Lord Hardinge of Penshurst*, London, J. Murray, 1948, p. 79.

86. IOR, Mss Eur A97, the Revd Oliver George Lewis, letter of 28 July 1970.

87. James R. Ryan and Nicola J. Thomas, 'Landscapes of Performance: Staging the Delhi Durbars', in Julie F. Codell (ed.), *Power and Resistance: The Delhi Coronation Durbars*, London, Mapin Publishing, 2012, pp. 46–69, at pp. 54–5.

88. John Fortescue, *Narrative of the Visit to India of Their Majesties King George V and Queen Mary, and of the Coronation Durbar held at Delhi, 12th December 1911*, London, Macmillan & Co, 1912, pp. 121–3.

89. Stephen Bottomore, ' "Have you seen the Gaekwar Bob?" Filming the 1911 Delhi Durbar', *Historical Journal of Film, Radio and Television*, 17/3 (1997), pp. 309–45.

90. Alan Trevithick, 'Some Structural and Sequential Aspects of the British Imperial Assemblages at Delhi: 1877–1911', *Modern Asian Studies*, 24/3 (1990), pp. 561–78; Julie Codell, 'On the Delhi Coronation Durbars, 1877, 1903, 1911', *BRANCH: Britain, Representation and Nineteenth-Century*

History, http://www.branchcollective.org/?ps_articles=julie-codell-on-the-delhi-coronation-durbars-1877-1903-1911 (last accessed 10 September 2018); Robert E. Frykenberg, 'The Coronation Durbar of 1911: Some Implications', in R. E. Frykenberg (ed.), *Delhi through the Ages: Selected Essays in Urban History, Culture, and Society*, Delhi, Oxford University Press, 1986, pp. 369–90.

91. A. P. Thornton, *The Imperial Idea and Its Enemies: A Study in British Power*, London, Macmillan, 1959, p. 360.

92. Indulal Yajnik, *Shyamaji Krishnavarma: Life and Times of an Indian Revolutionary* (1934), Bombay, Lakshmi Publications, 1950, p. 301; Arun Chandra Guha, *First Spark of Revolution: The Early Phase of India's Struggle for Independence, 1900–1920*, Bombay, Orient Longman, 1971, p. 324.

93. Eustis and Zaidi, 'King, Viceroy and Cabinet', pp. 171–84; IOR, Mss Eur E224/2B, Guy Fleetwood Wilson, letter of 19 February 1912.

94. Quoted and discussed in Sandeep Banerjee and Subho Basu, 'The City as Nation: Delhi as the Indian Nation in Bengali *Bhadralok* Travelogues 1866–1910', in Crispin Bates and Minoru Mio (eds), *Cities in South Asia*, London, Routledge, 2015, pp. 125–41, at p. 136.

95. Narayani Gupta, *Delhi Between Two Empires, 1803–1931: Society, Government and Urban Growth*, New Delhi, Oxford University Press, 1998, pp. 175–81; 'Attack on the Viceroy', editorial, *The Times of India*, 25 December 1912.

96. IOR, Mss Eur A97, the Revd Oliver George Lewis, letter of 28 July 1970.

97. *The Times of India*, 24 December 1912.

98. In what follows, I am drawing chiefly on Hardinge, *My Indian Years*, pp. 79–81, and Lady Hardinge's account, as reported in the *New York Times*, 9 February 1913.

99. *New York Times*, 9 February 1913.

100. IOR NEG 10612: GOI Home Department, Proceedings, December 1914, No. 11: 'C. R. Cleveland to all CID Departments', 5 January 1913.

101. IOR/L/P&J/6/1216, file 183, 'GOI to Lord Crewe', 26 December 1912, Enclosure No. 2, 'Medical Report on the Condition of His Excellency the Viceroy'; *The Times of India*, 25 December 1912.

102. IOR Mss Eur E224/2B, 'Guy Fleetwood Wilson to Lord Stamfordham', 26 December 1912.

103. As recalled, in a family tradition, by the doctor's daughter, in Joyce Westrip and Peggy Holroyde, *Colonial Cousins: A Surprising History of Connections between India and Australia*, Kent Town, Wakefield Press, 2010, p. 360.

104. *Amrita Bazar Patrika*, 27 December 1912.

105. Only the Indian press thought to name the victims, and then much later: *Amrita Bazar Patrika*, 28 April 1914.

106. Ibid., 29 December 1912.

107. Michael O'Dwyer, *India as I Knew It, 1885–1925* (1925), New Delhi, Mittal Publications, 1988, p. 170.

108. *The Times*, 24 December 1912; ibid., 25 December 1912.

109. NAI, Home Department, Political A, March 1913, No. 108, Wilson to Secretary of State, 26 December 1912; IOR, Mss Eur E224/2B, Guy Fleetwood Wilson to Lucas, 14 January 1913.

110. *The Tribune* (Lahore), 1 January 1913.

111. 'The Delhi Crime', editorial, *The Times of India*, 24 December 1912.

112. *The Times of India*, 27 December 1912.

113. As reported in *The Comrade*, 14 December 1912; quoted and discussed in Zaman, 'Beyond Nostalgia', pp. 632–5.

114. Peter Heehs, *The Lives of Sri Aurobindo: A Biography*, New York, Columbia University Press, 2013, p. 237.

115. Gupta, *Delhi between two Empires*, p. 197.

116. Hardinge, *My Indian Years*, p. 83.

117. Elahe Haschemi Yekani, *The Privilege of Crisis: Narratives of Masculinities in Colonial and Postcolonial Literature, Photography, and Film*, Frankfurt, Campus Verlag, 2011, pp. 91–2.

118. Har Dyal (Dayal), *Social Conquest of the Hindu Race and Meaning of Equality*, San Francisco, Hindustan Gadar Party, n.d. (1913).

119. For details on Har Dayal's return to India see Emily C. Brown, *Har Dayal: Hindu Revolutionary and Rationalist*, Tucson, University of Arizona Press, 1975, pp. 48–57.

120. The fullest account of Rash Behari's early years is Uma Mukherjee, *Two Great Indian Revolutionaries: Rash Behari Bose and Jyotindra Nath Mukherjee*, Calcutta, Firma K. L. Mukhopadhyay, 1966, pp. 97–105. For the CID see Bimanbehari Majumdar, *Militant Nationalism in India and Its Socio-Religious Background, 1897–1917*, Calcutta, General Printers & Publishers, 1966, p. 117.

121. IOR NEG 10612: GOI Home Department, Proceedings, December 1914, No 11: R. H. Craddock, 22 August 1913.

122. Here I draw on Petrie's full summary: IOR NEG 10612: GOI Home Department, Proceedings, December 1914, No 11: 'Report on the Delhi Bomb Investigation', 8 November 1914. For Petrie himself see Richard J. Popplewell, *Intelligence and Imperial Defence: British Intelligence and the Defence of the Indian Empire, 1904–1924*, London, Frank Cass, 1995, pp. 80–82.

123. W. Sealy, 'Connections with the Revolutionary Organisation in Bihar and Orissa, 1906–1916', 7 September 1917, in Samanta (ed.), *Terrorism in Bengal*, vol. V, pp. 3–4.

124. James C. Ker, *Political Trouble in India, 1907–1917* (1917), Calcutta, Editions Indian, 1960, p. 329.

125. Mukherjee, *Two Great Indian Revolutionaries*, pp. 110–11; Majumdar,

Militant Nationalism in India, p. 119, discussed in Amiya K. Samanta, 'Introduction' to Samanta (ed.), *Terrorism in Bengal: A Collection of Documents on Terrorist Activities from 1905 to 1939*, vol. I, Calcutta, Government of West Bengal, 1995, pp. viii–xiii.

126. IOR NEG 10612: GOI Home Department, Proceedings, December 1914, No 11, 'Brief note on the bomb outrages in India in the past few years'.

127. Reproduced in P. S. Ramu, *Rash Behari Bose: A Revolutionary 'Unwept, Unhonoured and Unsung'*, New Delhi, Freedom Movement Memorial Committee, 1998, p. 32.

128. IOR NEG 10612: GOI Home Department, Proceedings, December 1914, Secret, No 11: 'Question of the treatment of the approver in the Delhi-Lahore Conspiracy Case', 5 November 1914.

129. Mukherjee, *Two Great Indian Revolutionaries*, pp. 118–19.

130. Ibid, p. 120.

131. Dharmavira, *Lala Har Dayal and Revolutionary Movements of His Times*, New Delhi, India Book Co., 1970, p. 170.

132. 'Delhi Conspiracy Case, Order', Lord Nubuleo(?), 8 March 1915, in Nahar Singh and Kirpal Singh (eds), *Struggle for Free Hindustan*, vol. III: *Delhi-Lahore Conspiracy, 1912–1915*, New Delhi, Atlantic Publishers & Distributors, 1987, pp. 495–6. This seems to be a submission to the judicial committee of the Privy Council in London.

133. 'Note on the Lahore Conspiracy by Mr C. Stead', in Singh and Singh (eds), *Struggle for a Free Hindustan*, vol. III, pp. 86–7; judgment, 10 February 1915, in ibid., pp. 335–445; IOR NEG 10612: GOI Home Department, Proceedings, December 1914, No 11: 'Report on the Delhi Bomb Investigation', 8 November 1914.

134. A. M. Nair, *An Indian Freedom Fighter in Japan*, New Delhi, Vikas, 1985, pp. 54–5; Government of India, *Sedition Committee, 1918, Report*, Calcutta, Superintendent Government Printing, India, 1918, p. 133; the injury is also discussed in Mukherjee, *Two Great Indian Revolutionaries*, p. 116, who gives the date earlier as September 1913.

135. Dharmavira, *I Threw the Bomb*, Delhi, Orient Paperbacks, 1979, p. 53.

5. PUNDITS OF THE SEAS (1912–1914)

1. Dharmavira, *Lala Har Dayal and Revolutionary Movements of His Times*, New Delhi, India Book Co., 1970, p. 171.

2. TNA, FO 115/1731, 'W. C. Hopkinson to W. W. Cory, Minister of the Interior', 11 January 1913.

3. A biography is to be found at 'Hopkinson, William Charles (1880–1914)', http://komagatamarujourney.ca/node/14691 (last accessed 20 May 2020). This, and other documents cited in this chapter, are taken from Simon

Fraser University's excellent web resource, 'Komagata Maru: Continuing the Journey', http://komagatamarujourney.ca/. For Hopkinson's role see Hugh J. M. Johnston, *The Voyage of the 'Komagata Maru': The Sikh Challenge to Canada's Colour Bar*, Delhi, Oxford University Press, 1979, pp. 1–2, 7–9, and slightly enlarged in his 'The Surveillance of Indian Nationalists in North America, 1908–1918', *British Columbia Studies*, 78 (1988), pp. 3–27. See also Richard J. Popplewell, *Intelligence and Imperial Defence: British Intelligence and the Defence of the Indian Empire, 1904–1924*, London, Frank Cass, 1995, p. 152; and the summary and press cuttings in NAI, Home Dept, Political A, January 1915, Nos 3–6.

4. TNA, FO 115/1731, 'Governor-General to James Bryce', 11 January 1913. For the disguise see Seema Sohi, *Echoes of Mutiny: Race, Surveillance, and Indian Anticolonialism in North America*, Oxford, Oxford University Press, 2014, p. 40. For Hopkinson's career see NAI, Home Dept, Political A, January 1915, Nos 3–6, C. R. Cleveland, minute, 7 December 1914.

5. TNA, FO 115/1731, 'W. C. Hopkinson to W. W. Cory, Minister of the Interior', 11 January 1913.

6. Popplewell, *Intelligence and Imperial Defence*, p. 87; F. C. Isemonger and J. Slattery's comprehensive 1919 report of the whole affair, *An Account of the Ghadr Conspiracy, 1913–1915*, reprinted Meerut, Archana Publications, 1988, begins its narrative with Har Dayal: see pp. 1–3. For the British view see NAI, Home Dept, Political A, July 1913, No. 4, 'Har Dayal'.

7. *Amrita Bazar Patrika*, 13 January 1910. For the mood at the time see Neeti Nair, *Changing Homelands: Hindu Politics and the Partition of* India, Cambridge, MA, Harvard University Press, 2011, pp. 27–30.

8. *Amrita Bazar Patrika*, 17 January 1910.

9. A. C. Bose, *Indian Revolutionaries Abroad, 1905–1922: In the Background of International Developments*, Patna, Bharati Bhawan, 1971, pp. 37–42.

10. Vivek Bald, *Bengali Harlem and the Lost Histories of South Asian America*, Cambridge, MA, Harvard University Press, 2013, ch. 3, and at p. 117.

11. 'Memorandum on the Anti-British Agitation among Natives of India in England and the Continent of Europe, Part IV', 12 October 1911, in Amiya Samanta (ed.), *Terrorism in Bengal: A Collection of Documents on Terrorist Activities from 1905 to 1939*, vol. V: *Terrorists outside Bengal Deriving Inspiration from and Having Links with Bengal Terrorists*, Calcutta, Government of West Bengal, 1995, p. 433.

12. There is an air of legend about Har Dayal's alleged encounter with Sun Yat-sen. For Waikiki see Harish K. Puri, *Ghadar Movement: Ideology, Organisation and Strategy*, Amritsar, Guru Nanak Dev University Press, 1983, p. 56. For Fiji see TNA, FO 115/1779, Washington to Grey, 7 May 1914.

13. The account of Bhai Parmanand's movements is drawn from his *The Story of My Life*, Lahore, The Central Hindu Yuvak Sabha, 1934, pp. 38–60. For student numbers see Bose, *Indian Revolutionaries Abroad*, p. 57.

14. Parmanand, *The Story of My Life*, pp. 43–5; Sucheta Mazumdar, 'Colonial Impact and Punjabi Emigration to the United States', in Lucie Cheng and Edna Bonacich (eds), *Labor Immigration under Capitalism: Asian Workers in the United States before World War II*, Berkeley, University of California Press, 1984, pp. 316–36; Puri, *Ghadar Movement*, pp. 19–23.

15. NAI, Home Dept, Political B, March 1915, No. 37, 'Statement Made by Nawab Khan, Raikat, Ludhiana'.

16. Mazumdar, 'Colonial Impact and Punjabi Emigration to the United States', pp. 316–36; Madhavi Thampi, 'Indian Soldiers, Policemen and Watchmen in China in the Nineteenth and Early Twentieth Centuries', *China Report*, 35/4 (1999), pp. 403–37.

17. See, for example, Kornel Chang, 'Circulating Race and Empire: Transnational Labor Activism and the Politics of Anti-Asian Agitation in the Anglo-American Pacific World, 1880–1910', *Journal of American History*, 96/3 (2009), pp. 678–701. For Bellingham see Sohi, *Echoes of Mutiny*, pp. 25–7. For a general introduction see Gary Y. Okihiro, *Margins and Mainstreams: Asians in American History and Culture*, Seattle, University of Washington Press, 2014.

18. Robert M. Pike, 'National Interest and Imperial Yearnings: Empire Communications and Canada's Role in Establishing the Imperial Penny Post', *Journal of Imperial and Commonwealth History*, 26/1 (1998), pp. 22–48.

19. See the appeal of 11 December 1911 to the Canadian Cabinet by Sikh representatives, in Malwinderjit Singh Waraich and Gurdev Singh Sidhu (eds), *Komagata Maru: A Challenge to Colonialism: Key Documents*, Chandigarh, Unistar, 2005, pp. 19–20.

20. Nayan Shah, *Stranger Intimacy: Contesting Race, Sexuality and the Law in the North American West*, Berkeley, University of California Press, 2012, p. 198.

21. Ibid., pp. 203–4.

22. Charles Ashleigh, 'The Floater', *International Socialist Review*, 15/1 (1914), pp. 34–8.

23. For a powerful account of this see Shah, *Stranger Intimacy*, esp. ch. 3.

24. Johnston, *The Voyage of the 'Komagata Maru'*, pp. 2–4.

25. Bose, *Indian Revolutionaries Abroad*, pp. 48–53; Peter Campbell, 'East Meets Left: South Asian Militants and the Socialist Party of Canada in British Columbia, 1904–14', *International Journal of Canadian Studies*, 20 (1999), pp. 35–65, at p. 45.

26. Michael P. Hanagan, 'An Agenda for Transnational Labour History', *International Review of Social History*, 49/3 (2004), pp. 455–74, at p. 462; for the suggested numbers see Puri, *Ghadar Movement*, pp. 34–5.

27. Sohi, *Echoes of Mutiny*, pp. 38–40; TNA, FO 228/2701, 'Judgement in Second Supplementary Lahore Conspiracy Case', 5 January 1917, p. 57.

28. I have relied here on Tapan K. Mukherjee's exemplary, *Taraknath Das: Life and Letters of a Revolutionary in Exile*, Calcutta, National Council of Education, Bengal, Jadavpur University, 1998; and Ronald Spector, 'The Vermont Education of Taraknath Das: An Episode in British-American Relations', *Vermont History*, 48/2 (1980), pp. 89–95.

29. Margo Baumgartner Davis and Roxanne Nilan, *The Stanford Album: A Photographic History, 1885–1945*, Stanford, CA, Stanford University Press, 1989, p. 42.

30. TNA, FO 115/1908, David Starr Jordan to Irving Winslow, Harvard, 19 October 1915, forwarded to British Ambassador, Washington, 28 December 1915.

31. Har Dayal, 'Karl Marx: A Modern Rishi', *Modern Review*, March 1912, pp. 273–86, quotation at p. 276.

32. Ibid., quotations at pp. 282–3.

33. Ibid., quotation at p. 285.

34. Bhai Parmanand, *The Story of My Life*, pp. 41–61; NAI, Home Dept, Political A, July 1913, No. 4, 'Har Dayal'.

35. Emily C. Brown, *Har Dayall: Hindu Revolutionary and Rationalist*, Tucson, University of Arizona Press, 1975, pp. 97–112.

36. Harald Fischer-Tiné, *Shyamji Krishnavarma: Sanskrit, Sociology and Anti-Imperialism*, New Delhi, Routledge, 2014, pp. 87–8.

37. Ruth Price, *The Lives of Agnes Smedley*, Oxford, Oxford University Press, 2005, pp. 45–7; Parmanand, *The Story of My Life*, p. 61; TNA, FO 115/1908, David Starr Jordan to Irving Winslow, Harvard, 19 October 1915, forwarded to British Ambassador, Washington, 28 December 1915.

38. On Emma Goldman and India see J. Daniel Elam, 'The "Arch Priestess of Anarchy" Visits Lahore: Violence, Love, and the Worldliness of Revolutionary Texts', *Postcolonial Studies*, 16/2 (2013), pp. 140–54.

39. Bruce Nelson, *Workers on the Waterfront: Seamen, Longshoremen, and Unionism in the 1930s*, Urbana, University of Illinois Press, 1988, quotation at p. 10.

40. David Struthers, '"The Boss Has No Color Line": Race, Solidarity, and a Culture of Affinity in Los Angeles and the Borderlands, 1907–1915', *Journal for the Study of Radicalism*, 7/2 (2013), pp. 61–92, quotation at p. 64.

41. Ashleigh, 'The Floater', quotation at p. 35.

42. Campbell, 'East Meets Left', pp. 37–8. See also Steven Hirsch and Lucien van der Walt (eds), *Anarchism and Syndicalism in the Colonial and Postcolonial World, 1870–1940: The Praxis of National Liberation, Internationalism, and Social Revolution*, Leiden, Brill, 2010, particularly the editors' introduction.

43. NAI, Home Dept, Political B, March 1915, No. 37, 'Statement Made by Nawab Khan, Raikat, Ludhiana'.

44. Campbell, 'East Meets Left', pp. 46–50, quotation at p. 46; Kornel S. Chang, *Pacific Connections: The Making of the U.S.-Canadian Borderlands*, Berkeley, University of California Press, 2012, pp. 117–36.

45. NAI, Home Dept, Political B, March 1915, No. 37, 'Statement Made by Nawab Khan, Raikat, Ludhiana'.

46. NAI, Home Dept, Political B, March 1915, No. 37, 'Statement Made by Nawab Khan, Raikat, Ludhiana'; Isemonger and Slattery, *An Account of the Ghadr Conspiracy*, pp. 13–17; TNA, FO 115/1779, 'Acting Inspector Portland Oregon to Charles H. Reilly, Immigration Inspector', 14 January 1914.

47. For this see Puri, *Ghadar Movement*, pp. 63–7.

48. See Isabel Hofmeyr, *Gandhi's Printing Press: Experiments in Slow Reading*, Cambridge, MA, Harvard University Press, 2013.

49. John Price and Satwinder Bains, 'The Extraordinary Story of the Komagata Maru: Commemorating the One Hundred Year Challenge to Canada's Immigration Colour Bar', *The Asia-Pacific Journal: Japan Focus*, 11/29/1 (July 2013), p. 3, http://apjjf.org/2014/11/29/John-Price/4149/article.html (last accessed 20 May 2020). See also Daniel Rosenberg, 'The IWW and Organization of Asian Workers in Early 20th Century America', *Labor History*, 36/1 (1995), pp. 77–87.

50. SMP, IO/426, Chief Detective Inspector to Captain Superintendent of Police, 23 June 1916.

51. TNA, FO 115/1779, 'Note on the despatch of seditious literature from the USA to Paris', 21 March 1914.

52. I am aware of two official translations through which the British read this document. One is in typescript form; the other, more polished, is typeset and was circulated marked 'secret'. I am quoting from the rawer version as the British first read it: TNA, FO 115/1779, 'The rare gift of the use of the Bomb', original published 31 December 1913. For the text and its context see Dharmavira, *Lala Har Dayal*, pp. 171–9.

53. This quotation, along with the others in this and the two preceding paragraphs, is taken from TNA, FO 115/1779, 'The rare gift of the use of the Bomb'.

54. Compelling studies of Ghadar are: Maia Ramnath, *Haj to Utopia: How the Ghadar Movement Charted Global Radicalism and Attempted to Overthrow the British Empire*, Berkeley, University of California Press, 2011; Maia Ramnath, *Decolonizing Anarchism: An Antiauthoritarian History of India's Liberation Struggle*, Oakland, CA, AK Press, 2012, esp. pp. 70–77. On its limitations as a revolutionary vanguard see Harish K. Puri, 'Revolutionary Organization: A Study of the Ghadar Movement', *Social Scientist*, 9/2–3 (1980), pp. 53–66.

55. For general thoughts on this see Janaki Bakhe, 'Putting Global Intellectual

History in Its Place', in Samuel Moyn and Andrew Sartori (eds), *Global Intellectual History*, New York, Columbia University Press, 2013, pp. 228–53, esp. pp. 231–5.

56. For this point I am grateful to Polly O'Hanlon; see Mukherjee, *Taraknath Das*, p. 46.

57. As argued by Puri, *Ghadar Movement*, pp. 104–16.

58. I draw here on Benjamin Zachariah, 'A Long, Strange Trip: The Lives in Exile of Har Dayal', *South Asian History and Culture*, 4/4 (2013), pp. 574–92; and, for Har Dayal's life as a biography of 'disruption', Shruti Kapila, 'Self, Spencer and Swaraj: Nationalist Thought and Critiques of Liberalism, 1890–1920', *Modern Intellectual History*, 4/1 (2007), pp. 109–27, at p. 121.

59. TNA, FO 115/1779, 'Hopkinson to W. W. Cory', 3 May 1914; ibid., 'British Ambassador, Washington, to Earl Grey', 7 May 1914.

60. See the classic work of Brij Lal, 'Veil of Dishonour: Sexual Jealousy and Suicide on Fiji Plantations', *Journal of Pacific History*, 20/3 (1985), pp. 135–55; and Hugh Tinker, *A New System of Slavery: The Export of Indian Labour Overseas, 1830–1920*, Oxford, Oxford University Press, 1974.

61. TNA, FO 228/2299, 'Asst. Superintendent (Sikhs), Shanghai Municipal Police to Captain Superintendent, Shanghai Municipal Police', 2 December 1912.

62. TNA, FO 228/2299, 'Consul-General, Hankow, to Sir J. N. Jordan, Peking', 28 January 1913; ibid., 9 October 1913.

63. TNA, FO 228/2299, 'Acting Consul, Harbin, to Chargé d'Affaires, Peking', 26 September 1910; ibid., 29 July 1911; ibid., 2 August 1911.

64. TNA, FO 228/2299, 'C. McI. Messer, "Bhagwan Singh"', 17 May 1915.

65. Sarjeet Singh Jagpal, *Becoming Canadians: Pioneer Sikhs in Their Own Words*, Vancouver, Harbour Publishing, 1994, p. 30.

66. For the earlier test case of one Jara Singh see Waraich and Sidhu (eds), *Komagata Maru*, pp. 30–31; Shah, *Stranger Intimacy*, pp. 212–16. Slurs against Bagh Singh were made in the trial of Mewa Singh, below.

67. Isemonger and Slattery, *An Account of the Ghadr Conspiracy*, pp. 3–9; Michael O'Dwyer, *India as I Knew It: 1885–1925* (1925), Delhi, Mittal Publications, 1988, p. 191.

68. J. Edward Bird, *Memoirs*, Chilliwack, J. Edward Bird, 1939, pp. 88–93.

69. United States Department of Immigration, 'Daniel J. Keefe to A. Warner Parker, Bureau of Immigration, Washington', 27 December 1913, accessed from http://komagatamarujourney.ca/node/12544 (last accessed 20 May 2020).

70. Gurdit Singh, *Voyage of Komagata Maru, or, India's Slavery Abroad*, New Delhi, Unistar and Punjab Centre for Migration Studies, 2007, p. 58; R. C. Edmond, JC, 'Copy of the Judgement in a Civil Suit Brought against Gurdit Singh, Civil Suit No. 170-13', in Ananda Bhattacharyya (ed.),

Remembering Komagata Maru: Official Reports and Contemporary Accounts, New Delhi, Manohar, 2017, pp. 142–4.

71. 'Translation of a Diary Belonging to Gurdit Singh', in Bhattacharyya (ed.), *Remembering Komagata Maru*, p. 141.

72. For the text of the advertisement headed 'Congratulations' see Waraich and Sidhu (eds), *Komagata Maru*, pp. 36-38.

73. For the legal aspect see Renisa Mawani, 'Law and Migration across the Pacific: Narrating the *Komagata Maru* outside and beyond the Nation', in Karen Dubinsky, Adele Perry and Henry Yu (eds), *Within and Without the Nation: Canadian History as Transnational History*, Toronto, University of Toronto Press, 2016, pp. 253–75. This essay is expanded upon in Mawani's essential *Across Oceans of Law: The Komagata Maru and Jurisdiction in the Time of Empire*, Durham, NC, Duke University Press, 2018; for a summary of Gurdit's stand against 'juridicification' see p. 5.

74. Johnston, *The Voyage of the 'Komagata Maru'*, pp. 28–9; D. Petrie, 'Note on the Budge-Budge Riot', 8 October 1914, in Waraich and Sidhu (eds), *Komagata Maru*, pp. 215–24.

75. 'Special Tribunal (Lahore Conspiracy Case), Judgement', 13 September 1915, in Waraich and Sidhu (eds), *Komagata Maru*, p. 89.

76. United States Department of State, 'American Consul General, Shanghai, to William J. Bryan, Secretary of State, Washington', 21 April 1914, accessed from http://komagatamarujourney.ca/node/12102.

77. O'Dwyer, *India as I Knew It*, p. 170.

78. *Vancouver Daily Province*, 22 May 1914.

79. Ibid., 23 May 1914; ibid., 27 May 1914.

80. Johnston, *The Voyage of the 'Komagata Maru'*, p. 100.

81. Library and Archives Canada, RG7-G-21, vol. 205, file 332, vol. 12 (b), 'Supplementary Note by C. R. Cleveland, Director of Criminal Intelligence, India, re. Har Dayal's Involvement in Bomb Gangs in India', 11 May 1914, accessed from http://komagatamarujourney.ca/node/10043 (last accessed 20 May 2020).

82. Mawani, 'Law and Migration'.

83. TNA, FO 115/1779, 'W. C. Hopkinson to W. Corry', 30 April 1914. For the extent of the postal networks of the Raj see Devyani Gupta, 'The Postal System of British India, c. 1830–1920', PhD thesis, University of Cambridge, 2016. The remarkable 'Ghadar Directory' has been reprinted: Nahar Singh and Kirpal Singh (eds), *Struggle for Free Hindustan*, vol. IV: *Ghadr Directory (Punjab Section): 1913–1915*, New Delhi, Atlantic Publishers, 1996.

84. 'The Hon'ble Mr Gasgrain, Senate', 26 May 1914, in Waraich and Sidhu (eds), *Komagata Maru*, p. 22.

85. Library and Archives Canada. RG7-G021, vol. 211, file 332 B, 'Extract from William C. Hopkinson, Immigration Inspector, to William W. Cory,

Deputy Minister of the Interior. Copy', 27 May 1914, accessed from http://komagatamarujourney.ca/node/13751 (last accessed 20 May 2020).

86. 'Gurdit Singh to Mr Sato', 10 June 1914, in Waraich and Sidhu (eds), *Komagata Maru*, p. 44.

87. NAI, Home Dept, Political A, October 1915, No. 91, 'Special Tribunal, Lahore Conspiracy Case, Judgment in re King Emperor versus Anand Kishore and Others', 13 September 1915, part III A (1), p. 7.

88. For a discussion of the issues of law, race and hierarchy in the appeal case see Mawani, *Across Oceans of Law*, pp. 131–41.

89. Extract from W. C. Hopkinson to Malcolm R. J. Reid, 3 July 1914, accessed from http://komagatamarujourney.ca/node/12097; 'A Manuscript Giving a History of the Voyage of the SS *Komagata Maru*, Written in Gurmukhi, Apparently in the Handwriting of Daljit Singh', in Bhattacharyya (ed.), *Remembering Komagata Maru*, pp. 151, 159. Daljit Singh was Gurdit's secretary; the allegations are repeated in other passengers' testimonies.

90. Waraich and Sidhu (eds), *Komagata Maru*, p. 51.

91. 'From Colonial Office Archives, Short Precis of Dr. Rughunath Singh's Report, by Lieut. Col. D. D. Phillott', 6 August 1914, p. 2, accessed from http://komagatamarujourney.ca/node/12089 (last accessed 20 May 2020).

92. City of Vancouver Archives, Henry Herbert Stevens fonds, 'Conversation between H. H. Stevens, M.P., and Dr. Rughunath Singh, Held at the Office of the Canadian Immigration Department, Vancouver, with Inspector Hopkinson also Present at the Commencement of the Conversation', 18 June 1914, accessed from http://komagatamarujourney.ca/node/473 (last accessed 20 May 2020). For Stevens's stance in parliament see his speech of 8 June 1914, in Waraich and Sidhu (eds), *Komagata Maru*, pp. 27–8.

93. City of Vancouver Archives, Henry Herbert Stevens fonds, 'Account of the Meeting of the Committee Appointed by the Passengers Who Have Taken the Matter out of Gurdit Singh's Hands', 9 July 1914, accessed from http://komagatamarujourney.ca/node/461 (last accessed 20 May 2020).

94. Ibid., 'Copy of conversation between Hindus re Reid and Hopkinson', 8 July 1914, accessed from http://komagatamarujourney.ca/node/134 (last accessed 20 May 2020).

95. 'Statement of Mewa Singh, Son of Nand Singh, Village of Lopoke, District of Amritsar, India', 1 July 1914, accessed from http://komagatamarujourney.ca/node/10307 (last accessed 20 May 2020).

96. City of Vancouver Archives, Henry Herbert Stevens fonds, 'W. D. Scott to Malcolm R. J. Reid re *Rainbow* Securing Landing on *Komagata Maru*', 19 July 1914, accessed from http://komagatamarujourney.ca/node/5 (last accessed 20 May 2020).

97. City of Vancouver Archives, Neil Gilchrist fonds, 'Neil Gilchrist Diary – 1914' entry for 21 July 1914, accessed from http://komagatamarujourney.ca/node/15765 (last accessed 20 May 2020).

98. 'A Manuscript Giving a History of the Voyage of the SS *Komagata Maru*', in Bhattacharyya (ed.), *Remembering Komagata Maru*, pp. 161–3.

99. 'H. H. Stevens to Sir Robert Borden', 19 July 1914, in Waraich and Sidhu (eds), *Komagata Maru*, pp. 61–2; 'Borden to Governor-General', 21 July 1914, ibid., p. 69.

100. 'A Manuscript Giving a History of the Voyage of the SS *Komagata Maru*', in Bhattacharyya (ed.), *Remembering Komagata Maru*, p. 158. Again, this charge appears in other passenger testimonies.

101. City of Vancouver Archives, Henry Herbert Stevens fonds, 'Copy of Letter from Captain Yamamoto to Vancouver Chief of Police, Requesting Assistance', 18 July 1914, accessed from http://komagatamarujourney.ca/node/162 (last accessed 20 May 2020).

102. Johnston, *The Voyage of the 'Komagata Maru'*, pp. 90–91.

103. 'Extracts from Notebook No. 1 (Diary Taken from Gurdit Singh's Box)', in Bhattacharyya (ed.), *Remembering Komagata Maru*, p. 123.

104. 'An Account in English of the Tyranny over *Komagata Maru* Passengers in Kobe', in Bhattacharyya (ed.), *Remembering Komagata Maru*, p. 140.

105. 'Financial Secretary, Punjab, to Secretary of Government of India, Commerce and Industry Dept', 23 August 1914, in Waraich and Sidhu (eds), *Komagata Maru*, pp. 101–2.

106. 'Statement of Bhan Singh', in Bhattacharyya (ed.), *Remembering Komagata Maru*, p. 84.

107. 'Statement of Captain Yamamoto', 3 October 1914, in Waraich and Sidhu (eds), *Komagata Maru*, p. 171–4.

108. As reported in the *Modern Review* of Calcutta, in Bhattacharyya (ed.), *Remembering Komagata Maru*, p. 614.

109. D. Petrie, 'Note on the Budge-Budge Riot', 8 October 1914, in Waraich and Sidhu (eds), *Komagata Maru*, pp. 214–25.

110. 'Speech of Amar Nath', in Waraich and Sidhu (eds), *Komagata Maru*, p. 169.

111. As reported in *Amrita Bazar Patrika*, 2 October 1914.

112. See the official account, 'J. G. Cummings to Secretary to the Government of India', 12 October 1914, in Waraich and Sidhu (eds), *Komagata Maru*, pp. 126–45.

113. *Amrita Bazar Patrika*, 8 October 1914.

114. 'Khalsa Diwan Society Diary, Vancouver', p. 21, accessed from http://komagatamarujourney.ca/node/9834 (last accessed 20 May 2020); *News Advertiser*, 6 September 1914.

115. *Vancouver Daily Province*, c. 4 December 1914, accessed from http://komagatamarujourney.ca/node/8989 (last accessed 20 May 2020).

116. Library and Archives Canada, RG76, vol. 561, file 808722, part 2, 'Reid to Scott, Department of the Interior, Vancouver', 22 October 1914, accessed from http://komagatamarujourney.ca/node/11050 (last accessed 20 May 2020).

117. *Vancouver World*, 11 January 1915.

118. Ibid.

119. 'Vancouver Fall Assizes, 'In the Court of Oyer & Terminer & General Gaol Delivery, Vancouver Fall Assizes (Before the Honorable Mr. Justice Morrison), Vancouver, B.C., 30 October 1914, Rex vs Mewa Singh (Murder)', accessed from http://komagatamarujourney.ca/node/10326 (last accessed 20 May 2020). See also Johnston, *The Voyage of the 'Komagata Maru'*, p. 131.

120. 'J. G. MacKay, Acting Superintendent, Insane Asylum, New Westminster, to Charles J. Doherty, Minister of Justice, re Mental Condition of Mewa Singh', 5 January 1915, accessed from http://komagatamarujourney.ca/node/10191 (last accessed 20 May 2020).

121. *Vancouver World*, 26 October 1914.

122. Johnston, 'The Surveillance of Indian Nationalists', pp. 19–20; see also the press cuttings in NAI, Home Dept, Political A, January 1915, Nos 3–6.

123. Melanie Hardbattle, 'Radical Objects: Photo of Mewa Singh's Funeral Procession, 1915', History Workshop Online, 19 December 2013, http://www.historyworkshop.org.uk/radical-objects-photo-of-mewa-singhs-funeral-procession-1915/, quoting the *New Advertiser*, 14 January 1915 (last accessed 20 May 2020).

124. City of Vancouver Archives, Henry Herbert Stevens fonds, 'Copy of Letter from M. L. Rustum to the British Consul in San Francisco, Offering Information for Sale re Indian Revolutionary Party', 25 January 1915, accessed from http://komagatamarujourney.ca/node/208 (last accessed 20 May 2020).

125. Shah, *Stranger Intimacy*, pp. 80, 220.

126. TNA, FO 228/2299, 'Lord Kilmarnock (Tokyo)', 19 June 1914.

127. NAI, Home Dept, Political B, March 1915, No. 37, 'Statement Made by Nawab Khan, Raikat, Ludhiana'.

128. NAI, Home Dept, Political A, October 1915, No. 91, 'Special Tribunal, Lahore Conspiracy Case, Judgment in re King Emperor versus Anand Kishore and Others', 13 September 1915, part III A, pp. 6–9.

129. In the *Vancouver Province*, 8 August 1914, in Waraich and Sidhu (eds), *Komagata Maru*, p. 103.

130. NAI, Home Dept, Political B, March 1915, No. 37, 'Statement Made by Nawab Khan, Raikat, Ludhiana'. For the call see Puri, *Ghadar Movement*, p. 151.

6. THE GREAT ASIAN WAR (1914)

1. 'Lettre à Phan Chu Trinh', London, July 1914, in Alain Ruscio (ed.), *Ho Chi Minh: Textes 1914–1969*, Paris, Éditions L'Harmattan, 1990, p. 21; discussed in Sophie Quinn-Judge, *Ho Chi Minh: The Missing Years, 1919–1941*, London, Hurst, 2003 p. 25.

2. TNA, FO 370/668, 'Under-Secretary of State, Foreign Office to French Ambassador', 8 September 1915; Quinn-Judge, *Ho Chi Minh*, pp. 26–7.

3. ANOM, SLOTFOM III/29, No. 21567, 'Phan-Van-Truong', Paris, 19 November 1919; ibid., 'Résident Supérieur du Tonkin au Gouverneur Général', 26 August 1919.

4. Phan Văn Tru'ò'ng, *Une Histoire de Conspirateurs Annamites à Paris, Ou, La Vérité Sur l'Indochine* (1925–6), Montreuil, Insomniaque, 2003, pp. 133–4.

5. Aravind Ganachari, 'First World War: Purchasing Indian Loyalties: Imperial Policy of Recruitment and "Rewards" ', *Economic and Political Weekly*, 40/8 (2005), pp. 779–88, at p. 779.

6. John Torpey, *The Invention of the Passport: Surveillance, Citizenship and the State*, Cambridge, Cambridge University Press, 1999; Adam M. McKeown, *Melancholy Order: Asian Migration and the Globalization of Borders*, New York, Columbia University Press, 2008.

7. TNA, FO 228/2740, 'Secret Abstract of Intelligence', August 1917.

8. Tyler Stovall, 'The Color Line behind the Lines: Racial Violence in France during the Great War', *American Historical Review*, 103/3 (1998), pp. 737–69, at pp. 741–2; quotation from *Humanité*, ibid., at p. 760; Xu Guoqi, *Strangers on the Western Front: Chinese Workers in the Great War*, Cambridge, MA, Harvard University Press, 2011; Pierre Brocheux and Daniel Hémery, *Indochina: An Ambiguous Colonization, 1858–1954*, Berkeley, University of California Press, 2010, p. 302.

9. 'Letter to Maganlal Gandhi', 18 September 1914, *The Collected Works of Mahatma Gandhi* (e-edn), New Delhi, Publications Division Government of India, 1999, vol. XIV, p. 290.

10. For Gandhi and the war see Judith Brown, *Gandhi: Prisoner of Hope*, New Haven, CT, Yale University Press, 1989, pp. 96–8.

11. 'A Manuscript Giving a History of the Voyage of the SS *Komagata Maru*, Written in Gurmukhi, Apparently in the Handwriting of Daljit Singh', in Ananda Bhattacharyya (ed.), *Remembering Komagata Maru: Official Reports and Contemporary Accounts*, New Delhi, Manohar, 2017, p. 165.

12. NAI, Home Department, Political B, November 1914, 'Petition of V. D. Savarkar Enclosed in Chief Commissioner of the Andamans to Secretary of the Government of India', 3 October 1914. For the later petition see 'Savarkar to Chief Commissioner of the Andamans', 30 March 1920, Government of Bombay, *Source Material for a History of the Freedom Movement in India: Collected from Bombay Government Records*, vol. II, *1885–1920*, Bombay, Government of Bombay, 1967, pp. 272–6, at p. 274.

13. For the 1914–18 war as a global conflict see Hew Strachan, *The First World War*, vol. I, *To Arms*, Oxford, Oxford University Press, 2003, pp. 479–80.

14. Michael A. Reynolds, *Shattering Empires: The Clash and Collapse of the*

Ottoman and Russian Empires 1908–1918, Cambridge, Cambridge University Press, 2011; Tim Harper, 'A Long View on the Great Asian War', in David Koh Wee Hock (ed.), *Legacies of World War II in South and East Asia*, Singapore, ISEAS, 2007, pp. 7–20.

15. Sandra Barkhof, 'Renegotiating the Yellow Peril: Cultural and Physical Displacement in the German Colony in China during the First World War', in Sandra Barkhof and Angela K. Smith (eds), *War and Displacement in the Twentieth Century: Global Conflicts*, London, Routledge, 2014, pp. 151–67, at pp. 161–2; Frederick R. Dickinson, *War and National Reinvention: Japan in the Great War, 1914–1919*, Cambridge, MA, Harvard University Asia Center, 1999, p. 117.

16. S. L. van der Wal, 'The Netherlands as an Imperial Power in South-east Asia in the Nineteenth Century and After', in J. S. Bromley and E. H. Kossmann (eds), *Britain and the Netherlands in Europe and Asia*, London, Macmillan,1968, pp. 191–206, at p. 196.

17. Nicholas Tarling, ' "A Vital British Interest": Britain, Japan, and the Security of Netherlands India in the Inter-War Period', *Journal of Southeast Asian Studies*, 9/2 (1978), pp. 180–218, at pp. 187–8.

18. Xu Guoqi, *China and the Great War: China's Pursuit of a New National Identity and Internationalization*, Cambridge, Cambridge University Press, 2005.

19. Xu, *Strangers on the Western Front*, esp. pp. 55–79 for Canada; Paul J. Bailey, ' "An Army of Workers": Chinese Indentured Labour in First World War France', in Santanu Das (ed.), *Race, Empire and First World War Writing*, Cambridge, Cambridge University Press, 2011, pp. 35–52.

20. Brocheux and Hémery, *Indochina*, p. 175.

21. Christopher Baker, 'Economic Reorganization and the Slump in South and Southeast Asia', *Comparative Studies in Society and History*, 23/3 (1981), pp. 325–49.

22. SNA, GD/C/21, 'Young to Bonar Law', 25 August 1916.

23. For a summary, Kimloan Vu-Hill, *Coolies into Rebels: Impact of World War I on French Indochina*, Paris, Les Indes Savantes, 2011, pp. 27–8.

24. Kemal H. Karpat, *The Politicization of Islam: Reconstructing Identity, State, Faith, and Community in the Late Ottoman State*, New York, Oxford University Press, 2001, p. 233. See also Deniz Ulke Aribogan, 'Open the Closed Window to the East: Turkey's Relations with East Asian Countries', in İdris Bal (ed.), *Turkish Foreign Policy in Post-Cold War Era*, Boca Raton, FL, Brown Walker, 2004, pp. 401–20, at p. 406.

25. *North China Herald*, 26 June 1901.

26. See Engseng Ho, *The Graves of Tarim : Genealogy and Mobility across the Indian Ocean*, Berkeley, University of California Press, 2006. The quote from the Rowlatt Report appears in Suchetana Chattopadhyay, 'Jihad at Wartime?', *South Asian History and Culture*, 7/2 (2016), pp. 155–74 at p. 169.

27. Francis Robinson, 'The British Empire and the Muslim World', in Wm Roger Louis and Judith Brown (eds), *The Oxford History of the British Empire*, vol. IV: *The Twentieth Century*, Oxford, Oxford University Press, 1999, pp. 398–420; David Motadel (ed.), *Islam and the European Empires*, Oxford, Oxford University Press, 2014.

28. Martin van Bruinessen, 'Muslims of the Dutch East Indies and the Caliphate Question', *Studia Islamika*, 2/3 (1995), pp. 115–40; Eric Tagliacozzo, 'Kettle on a Slow Boil: Batavia's Threat Perceptions in the Indies' Outer Islands, 1870–1910', *Journal of Southeast Asian Studies*, 31/1 (2000), pp. 70–100.

29. Chattopadhyay, 'Jihad at Wartime?', pp. 155–74.

30. For a summary see K. H. Ansari, 'Pan-Islam and the Making of the Early Indian Muslim Socialists', *Modern Asian Studies*, 20/3 (1986), pp. 509–37.

31. Faridah Zaman, 'Revolutionary History and the Post-Colonial Muslim: Re-Writing the "Silk Letters Conspiracy" of 1916', *South Asia: Journal of South Asian Studies*, 39/3 (2016), pp. 626–43, at p. 640. For the old dispersal see Seema Alavi, *Muslim Cosmopolitanism in the Age of Empire*, Cambridge, MA, Harvard University Press, 2015.

32. G. F. Abbott, 'A Revolt of Islam?', *Quarterly Review*, 223/442 (1915), pp. 66–77.

33. Thomas G. Fraser, 'Germany and Indian Revolution, 1914–18', *Journal of Contemporary History*, 12/2 (1977), pp. 255–72.

34. Jacob M. Landau, *The Politics of Pan-Islam: Ideology and Organization*, Oxford, Clarendon Press, 1990; Humayun Ansari, 'Making Transnational Connections: Muslim Networks in Early Twentieth-Century Britain', in Nathalie Clayer and Eric Germain (eds), *Islam in Inter-War Europe*, London, Hurst & Co., 2008, pp. 31–63, at p. 35.

35. David Omissi, 'Europe through Indian Eyes: Indian Soldiers Encounter England and France, 1914–1918', *English Historical Review*, 122/496 (2007), pp. 371–96.

36. Conor Meleady, 'Negotiating the Caliphate: British Responses to Pan-Islamic Appeals, 1914–1924', *Middle Eastern Studies*, 52/2 (2016), pp. 182–97.

37. For this see John Slight, *The British Empire and the Hajj, 1865–1956*, Cambridge, MA, Harvard University Press, 2015, and the essays in Motadel (ed.), *Islam and the European Empires*.

38. Fraser, 'Germany and Indian Revolution', p. 258.

39. TNA, FO 228/2299, 'Lord Kilmarnock (Tokyo)', 19 June 1914.

40. Kris Manjapra, *Age of Entanglement: German and Indian Intellectuals across Empire*, Cambridge, MA, Harvard University Press, 2014, pp. 88–9.

41. Emily C. Brown, *Har Dayal: Hindu Revolutionary and Rationalist*, Tucson, University of Arizona Press, 1975, pp. 169–77; Harald Fischer-Tiné, 'The Other Side of Internationalism: Switzerland as a Hub of Militant Anti-Colonialism, (c. 1910–20)', in Patricia Purtschert and Harald Fischer-

Tiné (eds), *Colonial Switzerland: Rethinking Colonialism from the Margins*, Basingstoke, Palgrave Macmillan, 2015, pp. 221–58.

42. 'A Maui Woman Witness in the Hindu Cases', *Maui News*, 4 January 1918.

43. NARA, M1085, Bureau of Investigation, Old German Files, Case 8000-1396, p. 432, E. M. Blanford report, 24 January 1918 for 29 December 1917; this file was accessed from https://www.fold3.com/, https://www.fold3.com/document/1991052/ (last accessed 20 May 2020).

44. Prithwindra Mukherjee, *The Intellectual Roots of India's Freedom Struggle (1893–1918)*, London, Routledge, 2018, p. 233.

45. 'Herbert Mueller to A. C. Bose', 18 March 1956, in A. C. Bose (ed.), *Indian Revolutionaries Abroad, 1905–1927: Select Documents*, New Delhi, Northern Book Centre, 2002, p. 145.

46. For an account drawing on German sources see Nirode K. Barooah, *Chatto: The Life and Times of an Indian Anti-Imperialist in Europe*, New Delhi, Oxford University Press, 2004, pp. 43–52.

47. For Pratap see Carolien Stolte, ' "Enough of the Great Napoleons!" Raja Mahendra Pratap's Pan-Asian Projects (1929–1939)', *Modern Asian Studies*, 46/2 (2012), pp. 403–23, quotations at pp. 406–7.

48. A vivid account is Peter Hopkirk, *On Secret Service East of Constantinople: The Plot to Bring down the British Empire*, Oxford, Oxford University Press, 1994, p. 86.

49. Giles T. Brown, 'The Hindu Conspiracy, 1914–1917', *Pacific Historical Review*, 17/3 (1948), pp. 299–310; Fraser, 'Germany and Indian Revolution', pp. 255–72; Don Dignan, *The Indian Revolutionary Problem in British Diplomacy, 1914–1919*, New Delhi, Allied Publishers, 1983.

50. TNA, FO 228/2701, 'Judgement in Second Supplementary Lahore Conspiracy Case', 5 January 1917.

51. 'German Intrigues', Foreign Office note, 27 August 1915, in Bose (ed.), *Indian Revolutionaries Abroad*, pp. 148–9; NAI, Home Dept, Political A, October 1915, No. 91, 'Special Tribunal, Lahore Conspiracy Case, Judgment in re King Emperor versus Anand Kishore and Others', 13 September 1915, 'The Return to India', pp. 1–3.

52. NARA, M1085, Bureau of Investigation, Old German Files, Case 8000-1396, p. 114, 'Jack Sloan'; ibid., p. 155, C. J. Scully report, 5 March for 18 February 1918; ibid., p. 433, Dave Gershon report, 12 September for 12 September 1917.

53. For a summary of these crossings see Maia Ramnath, *Haj to Utopia: How the Ghadar Movement Charted Global Radicalism and Attempted to Overthrow the British Empire*, Berkeley, University of California Press, 2011, p. 51.

54. TNA, FO 228/2299, 'Consul-General Shanghai to Peking', 23 April 1915.

55. NAI, Home Dept, Political A, October 1915, No. 91, 'Special Tribunal,

Lahore Conspiracy Case, Judgment in re King Emperor versus Anand Kishore and Others', 13 September 1915, pp. 29–31.

56. F. C. Isemonger and J. Slattery, *An Account of the Ghadr Conspiracy, 1913–1915* (1919), reprinted Meerut, Archana Publications, 1988, pp. 96–7, 105.

57. Bhai Parmanand, *The Story of My Life*, Lahore, The Central Hindu Yuvak Sabha, 1934, pp. 70–72.

58. Ramnath, *Haj to Utopia*, p. 31, for Pingle, and pp. 52–7.

59. James C. Ker, *Political Trouble in India, 1907–1917* (1917), Calcutta, Editions Indian, 1960, pp. 344–5.

60. Samaren Roy, *The Restless Brahmin: Early Life of M. N. Roy*, Bombay, Allied, 1970, pp. 33–4.

61. For Mukherjee's early career see 'Connections with the Revolutionary Organisation in Bihar and Orissa, 1906–1916', 7 September 1917, in Amiya K. Samanta (ed.), *Terrorism in Bengal: A Collection of Documents on Terrorist Activities from 1905 to 1939*, vol. V: *Terrorists outside Bengal Deriving Inspiration from and Having Links with Bengal Terrorists*, Calcutta, Government of West Bengal, 1995, p. 63. For a biography see Mukherjee, *The Intellectual Roots of India's Freedom Struggle*, esp. pp. 136–95, quotation at p. 190.

62. M. N. Roy, *Men I Met* (1968), Delhi, Ajanta Publications, 1981, pp. 2, 4.

63. 'Connections with the Revolutionary Organisation in Bihar and Orissa', in Samanta (ed.), *Terrorism in Bengal*, vol. V, p. 61.

64. Amarendra Narh Chattopadhyaya, 'My Reminiscences of Naren', in Sibnarayan Ray (ed.), *M. N. Roy, Philosopher-Revolutionary: A Symposium*, Calcutta, Renaissance Publishers, 1959, pp. 5–7; Roy, *The Restless Brahmin*, p. 91.

65. NL-HaNA, Koloniën: Openbaar Archief, Vb, 18-11-1915, 35, 'Beckett to General Secretary Buitenzorg', 20 September 1915; ibid., Vb, 20-8-1915, 35, '"Memorandum" enclosed in W. R. D. Beckett to General Secretary Buitenzorg', 29 June 1915.

66. J. Thomas Lindblad, 'Economic Aspects of the Dutch Expansion in Indonesia, 1870–1914', *Modern Asian Studies*, 23/1 (1989), pp. 1–24.

67. *The Colonial and International Exhibition at Semarang, 14 August–13 November 1914*, n.p. (*c*.1914).

68. Joost Coté, 'Towards an Architecture of Association: H. F. Tillema, Semarang and the Discourse on the Construction of Colonial Modernity', in P. Nas (ed.), *The Indonesian Town Revisited*, Münster, LIT Verlag, 2002, pp. 319–47, at p. 336.

69. Rudolf Mrázek, 'From Darkness to Light: Optics of Policing in Late-Colonial Netherlands East Indies', in Vicente Rafael (ed.), *Figures of Criminality in Indonesia, the Philippines, and Colonial Vietnam*, Social Science Research Council (US), Ithaca, NY, Southeast Asia Program Publications, 1999, p. 32.

70. As translated and discussed in John Pemberton, *On the Subject of 'Java'*, Ithaca, NY, Cornell University Press, 1994, pp. 119–20.

71. Joost Coté, ' "To See Is to Know": The Pedagogy of the Colonial Exhibition, Semarang, 1914', *Paedagogica Historica*, 36/1 (2000), pp. 340–66.

72. James L. Cobban, 'Kampungs and Conflict in Colonial Semarang', *Journal of Southeast Asian Studies*, 19/2 (1988), pp. 266–91.

73. John Ingleson, 'Life and Work in Colonial Cities: Harbour Workers in Java in the 1910s and 1920s', *Modern Asian Studies*, 17/3 (1983), pp. 455–76.

74. For Surabaya see William H. Frederick, 'Hidden Change in Late Colonial Urban Society in Indonesia'. *Journal of Southeast Asian Studies*, 14/2 (1983), pp. 354–71.

75. Cindy Adams, *Sukarno: An Autobiography as Told to Cindy Adams*, Hong Kong, Gunung Agung, 1965, p. 34. I was alerted to this by the discussion in Chiara Formichi, *Islam and the Making of the Nation: Kartosuwiryo and Political Islam in Twentieth-Century Indonesia*, Leiden, KITLV Press, 2012, p. 20.

76. For a vivid summary see Marieke Bloembergen, 'The Dirty Work of Empire: Modern Policing and Public Order in Surabaya, 1911–1919', *Indonesia*, 83 (2007), pp. 119–50.

77. Adams, *Sukarno*, p. 38.

78. Bob Hering, *Soekarno, Founding Father of Indonesia: A Biography, 1901–1945*, Leiden, KITLV Press, 2002, pp. 4–9 for Sukarno's class background, and pp. 73–8 for Tjokro's house and schooling.

79. The translated quotations are from Ahmat Adam, 'Radical Journalism and Press Persecution in Java, 1914–18', *Jebat*, 20 (1992), pp. 91–105, at pp. 95 and 97.

80. Hendrik M. J. Maier, 'Forms of Censorship in the Dutch Indies: The Marginalization of Chinese-Malay Literature', *Indonesia* (1991), pp. 67–81, at p. 70; Adam, 'Radical Journalism and Press Persecution in Java'.

81. This is drawn from Kees van Dijk's outstanding *The Netherlands Indies and the Great War, 1914–1918*, Leiden, KITLV Press, 2007, pp. 125–64.

82. 'Statistiek van de Scheepvaart in Nederlandsch-Indie over het Jaar 1916', *Koloniale Studien*, 1/2 (1916–17), pp. 14–15.

83. This is a major theme of van Dijk, *The Netherlands Indies and the Great War*. For the 'age of strikes' see John Ingleson, *In Search of Justice: Workers and Unions in Colonial Java, 1908–1926*, Singapore, Oxford University Press, 1986; Takashi Shiraishi, *An Age in Motion: Popular Radicalism in Java, 1912–1926*, Ithaca, NY, Cornell University Press, 1990. For a summary of the general unrest see Adrian Vickers, *A History of Modern Indonesia*, Cambridge, Cambridge University Press, 2005, p. 46.

84. Tony Saich and Fritjof Tichelman, 'Henk Sneevliet: A Dutch Revolutionary on the World Stage', *Journal of Communist Studies*, 1/2 (1985), pp. 170–93, which draws on Tichelman's *Henk Sneevliet. Een Politieke Bio-*

grafie, Van Gennep, Amsterdam, 1974. See also Max Perthus, *Henk Sneevliet. Revolutionair-Socialist in Europa en Azië*, Nijmegen, Social-istiese Uitgeverij Nijmegen, 1976.

85. Michael C. Williams, 'A Socialist in the Indies: Review of Joop Morrien, "'Aroen' Jan Stam, Rebel in Indonesie en Nederland"', *Indonesia*, 42 (1986), pp. 119–20.

86. Van Dijk, *The Netherlands Indies and the Great War*, quotations at pp. 71 and 480.

87. Ibid., pp. 455–9; Ruth T. McVey, *The Rise of Indonesian Communism*, Ithaca, NY, Cornell University Press, 1965, pp. 16–20. The fluidity of ideas and attachments is a central argument of Shiraishi, *An Age in Motion*.

88. Hering, *Soekarno*, p. 41.

89. The Siauw Giap, 'The Samin and Samat Movements in Java: Two Examples of Peasant Resistance', *Journal of South-East Asia and the Far East*, 1/2 (1967), pp. 303–10, and 2/1 (1968), pp. 107–13; Harry J. Benda and Lance Castles, 'The Samin Movement', *Bijdragen Tot de Taal-, Land- En Volk-enkunde*, 125/2 (1969), pp. 207–40, at p. 212; Victor T. King, 'Some Observations on the Samin Movement of North-Central Java: Suggestions for the Theoretical Analysis of the Dynamics of Rural Unrest', *Bijdragen Tot de Taal-, Land- En Volkenkunde*, 129/4 (1973), pp. 457–81. For the forest conflicts see Nancy Lee Peluso, *Rich Forests, Poor People: Resource Control and Resistance in Java*, Berkeley, University of California Press, 1994, pp. 69–72.

90. For the *ratu adil* see Sartono Kartodirdjo, 'Agrarian Radicalism in Java: Its Setting and Development', in Clare Holt (ed.), *Culture and Politics in Indonesia*, Ithaca, NY, Cornell University Press, 1972, pp. 71–125, at pp. 92–7. See also Peter Carey, *The Power of Prophecy: Prince Dipana-gara and the End of an Old Order in Java, 1785–1855*, Leiden, KITLV Press, 2007. This section of my book takes its title from ch. 10 of this remarkable work.

91. Summarized by Azyumardi Azra, 'The Indies Chinese and the Sarekat Islam', *Studia Islamika*, 1/1 (1994), pp. 26–53, at pp. 41–2.

92. Takashi Shiraishi, 'Dangir's Testimony: Saminism Reconsidered', *Indonesia*, 50 (1990), pp. 95–120, at p. 115.

93. NL-HaNA, Koloniën: Openbaar Archief, Vb 27-7-1916, 25, 'Statement: E. F. E. Douwes Dekker', Singapore, 24 January 1916.

94. TNA, FO 371/2784, 'The Confession of Douwes Dekker in Connection with Indian Sedition', Douwes Dekker to Dr Kock, Superintendent of the Government Civil Hospital Hong Kong, 11 December 1915.

95. Ibid.

96. Bose (ed.), *Indian Revolutionaries Abroad*, p. 139.

97. NL-HaNA, Koloniën: Geheim Archief, Vb 3-4-1919 X2, 'United States of America vs. Frans Bopp et al.', p. 32.

98. Wang Gungwu 'Migration Patterns in History: Malaysia and the Region', *Journal of the Malaysian Branch of the Royal Asiatic Society*, 58/1 (1985), pp. 43–57; Tsuyoshi Kato, 'Rantau Pariaman: The World of Minangkabau Coastal Merchants in the Nineteenth Century', *Journal of Asian Studies*, 39/4 (1980), pp. 729–52; Rudolf Mrázek, 'Tan Malaka: A Political Personality's Structure of Experience', *Indonesia*, 14 (1972), pp. 1–48.

99. Elizabeth E. Graves, *The Minangkabau Response to Dutch Colonial Rule in the Nineteenth Century*, Ithaca, NY, Cornell University Press, 1981, pp. 140–44.

100. Harry A. Poeze, *Tan Malaka: Strijder voor Indonesië's Vrijheid: Levensloop van 1897 tot 1945*, 's-Gravenhage, Nijhoff, 1976, pp. 10-14.

101. Tan Malaka, *From Jail to Jail*, trans. and ed. Helen Jarvis, Athens, Ohio University Center for International Studies, 1991, vol. I; for the smallness of the Netherlands see p. 17.

102. Ibid., p. 25.

103. Ibid., p. 26.

104. For this image see Ibrahim Alfian, 'Tan Malaka: The Lonely Revolutionary', *Prisma*, 8 (1977), pp. 16–36.

7. GHOST SHIPS (1915)

1. Walter Makepeace, Gilbert E. Brooke and Roland St J. Braddell (eds), *One Hundred Years of Singapore* (1921), Singapore, Oxford University Press, 1991, vol. I, p. 361.

2. Tim Harper, 'The British "Malayans"', in Robert Bickers (ed.), *Settlers and Expatriates: Britons over the Seas*, Oxford, Oxford University Press, 2010, pp. 233–68. See also Lynn Hollen Lees, 'Being British in Malaya, 1890–1940', *Journal of British Studies*, 48/1 (2009), pp. 76–101.

3. Sir Charles Lucas (ed.), *The Empire at War*, London, Oxford University Press, 1926, vol. V, pp. 398–401.

4. Discussed in T. N. Harper, 'Globalism and the Pursuit of Authenticity: The Making of a Diasporic Public Sphere in Singapore', *Sojourn: Journal of Social Issues in Southeast Asia*, 12/2 (1997), pp. 261–92.

5. TNA, CO 273/420, 'Young to Secretary of State 20 October 1914'; ibid., 'List of Prisoners of War on Parole in the Federated Malay States', enclosure to secret despatch of 21 January 1915.

6. J. M. Gullick, *A History of Kuala Lumpur, 1857–1939*, Kuala Lumpur, MBRAS, 2000, p. 234.

7. TNA, CO 273/423, 'Copy of Letter from Federated Malay States Dated 19 August 1917'.

8. Mark Emmanuel, 'Trading with the Enemy: Economic Warfare against

Germany in the Straits Settlements, 1914–1921', BA (Hons) academic exercise, National University of Singapore, 1996, p. 15.

9. *Malaya Tribune*, 20 May 1916.

10. SNA, COD/C/61, M. P. Smith (Vice-Consul, Manila), 'Memorandum on the Foreign Trade of Mindanao and Sulu, Philippine Islands', July 1915.

11. Sharon Siddique, 'Early German Commercial Relations to Singapore', in *Southeast Asia and the Germans*, Tübingen, Erdmann, 1977, pp. 178–9.

12. Makepeace, Brooke and Braddell (eds), *One Hundred Years of Singapore*, introduction by C. M. Turnbull, vol. I, pp. v–xiii, and vol. I, p. 466.

13. SNA, GD/C/18, 'Arthur Young to Harcourt', 19 August 1914.

14. SNA, COD/C/58, 'Report on the Penang Volunteers, 1911–12'; S. H. Wilson, 'Remarks by the Overseas Defence Committee', 3 January 1913; SNA, COD/C/59, 'Straits Settlements: Report on the Singapore Volunteer Corps 1912'; 'Remarks by the Overseas Sub-Committee of the Committee of Imperial Defence', 7 June 1913.

15. Robert Heussler, *British Rule in Malaya: The Malayan Civil Service and its Predecessors, 1867–1942*, Westport, CT, Greenwood Press, 1981, p. 135.

16. Harper, 'The British "Malayans"', pp. 250–53.

17. SNA, GD/C/20, 'R. J. Wilkinson to Andrew Bonar Law', 22 November 1915.

18. SNA, GD/C/21, 'Letter to "Sayer"', 7 November 1916; ibid., 'Verbal Statement Made to Mr Oliver Marks', in 'Young to Bonar Law', 12 December 1916.

19. Ibid., 'Report of Committee of 11 April 1916'.

20. Gerard McCann, 'Sikhs and the City: Sikh History and Diasporic Practice in Singapore', *Modern Asian Studies*, 45/6 (2011), pp. 1465–98.

21. As cited and discussed in Khoo Kay Kim, 'The Beginnings of Political Extremism in Malaya, 1915–1935', PhD thesis, University of Malaya, Kuala Lumpur, 1973, p. 8. See also TNA, CO 273/423, 'Governor, Straits Settlements, to Secretary of State for the Colonies', 19 August 1915.

22. SNA, GD/C/20, Lt. Col. G. H. B. Lees, 'Short History of the Malay States Guides from 16 March 1914 to date'.

23. NL-HaNA, Koloniën: Geheim Archief, Vb 3-4-1919 X2, 'United States of America vs. Frans Bopp et al.', pp. 89–90, evidence of Nawab Khan.

24. TNA, FCO 141/16954, 'Local Northern Indians: Minutes of a Committee Held at Kuala Lumpur on 14 January 1915'; TNA, CO 273/423, 'Telegram from Governor, Straits Settlements, to Secretary of State for the Colonies', 24 July 1915.

25. For the defence of Singapore see Malcolm H. Murfett, John N. Miksic, Brian P. Farrell and Chiang Ming Shun, *Between Two Oceans: A Military History of Singapore from 1275 to 1971*, 2nd edn, Singapore, Marshall Cavendish Editions, 2011, pp. 119–29.

26. TNA, FCO 141/16534, 'Additional statement by Col. Martin regarding Capt. Hall, Thursday 6 May 1915, Court of Inquiry, Forty-Second Day'.

27. For the following narrative of the Singapore Mutiny I have followed Nicholas Tarling's essay ' "The Merest Pustule": The Singapore Mutiny of 1915', *Journal of the Malaysian Branch of the Royal Asiatic Society*, 55/2 (1982), pp. 26–59, and R. W. E. Harper and Harry Miller, *Singapore Mutiny*, Singapore, Oxford in Asia Paperbacks, 1985, esp. pp. 120, 133–6. I have also drawn on my earlier article, 'Singapore, 1915, and the Birth of the Asian Underground', *Modern Asian Studies*, 47/6 (2013), pp. 1–30, with kind permission of the editor and Cambridge University Press. Since it went to press other studies have been published that emphasize the mutiny's global resonances: Heather Streets-Salter, 'The Local Was Global: The Singapore Mutiny of 1915', *Journal of World History*, 24/3 (2013), pp. 539–76, expanded as *World War One in Southeast Asia: Colonialism and Anticolonialism in an Era of Global Conflict*, Cambridge, Cambridge University Press, 2017; Itty Abraham, ' "Germany Has Become Mohammedan": Insurgency, Long Distance Travel, and the Singapore Mutiny, 1915', *Globalizations*, 12/6 (2015), pp. 913–27; Ooi Keat Gin, 'Between Homeland and "Ummah": Re-visiting the 1915 Singapore Mutiny of the 5th Light Infantry Regiment of the Indian Army', *Social Scientist*, 42/7–8 (2014), pp. 85–94.

28. T. R. Sareen, *Secret Documents on Singapore Mutiny, 1915*, New Delhi, Mounto Publishing House, 1995, p. 730.

29. Enclosures on ANM, HCO 1585/1914; TNA, FCO 141/16539, 'Young to Viceroy', 20 February 1915.

30. TNA, CO 273/423, Major-General Dudley Ridout, 'Reference to Report Signed by General Houghton on 11 May 1915, Marked "X" '.

31. TNA, FCO 141/16534, 'Col. Hav. Mahboub, C. Company, 5th Light Infantry, Court of Inquiry, Friday 19 March 1915, Third Day'. For Kassim see Heather Streets-Salter, *World War One in Southeast Asia,* pp. 30–31.

32. TNA, FCO 141/16534, 'Statement of Lt. W. G. Strover, 14 April 1915, Court of Inquiry, Wednesday 27 April 1915, Thirty-Sixth Day'.

33. For the fear of scuttling see ibid., 'Testimony of Mauzuddin, C. Company, Court of Inquiry, Wednesday 7 April 1915, Nineteenth Day'.

34. TNA, CO 273/423, 'Maj.-Gen. Dudley Ridout to Secretary, War Office', 26 August 1915.

35. TNA, FCO 141/16534, 'Statement of Capt. L. Ball, 14 April 1915, Court of Inquiry, Monday 26 April, Thirty-Fifth Day'.

36. See, for example, ibid., 'Lance Hav. Hans Raj, Court of Inquiry, Thursday 18 March 1915, Second Day'.

37. Edwin A. Brown and Mary Brown, *Singapore Mutiny: A Colonial Couple's*

Stirring Account of Combat and Survival in the 1915 Singapore Mutiny, Singapore, Monsoon Books, 2015, p. 65.

38. TNA, CO 273/423, Major-General Dudley Ridout, 'Reference to Report Signed by General Houghton on 11 May 1915, Marked "X"'.

39. TNA, FCO 141/16534, 'Testimony of Captain W. H. Adams, Ordnance Officer, Court of Inquiry, Saturday 27 March, Tenth Day'.

40. Ibid., 'Statement by Herr Hannke, 2 March 1915, Court of Inquiry, Monday 29 March, Twelfth Day'.

41. Lowell Thomas, *Lauterbach of the China Sea: The Escapes and Adventures of a Seagoing Falstaff*, Garden City, NY, Doubleday, Doran & Co., 1930, p. 114.

42. TNA, CO 273/420, 'Governor, Straits Settlements, to Secretary of State for the Colonies', 3 March 1915.

43. SNA, COD/C/61, 'Donald R. Woods to Consul-General, Batavia', 1 May 1915.

44. TNA, CO 273/420, 'Letter from Unidentified Correspondent', Singapore, 24 February 1915.

45. Capt. T. M. Winsley, *A History of the Singapore Volunteer Corps, 1854– 1937, Being also an Historical Outline of Volunteering in Malaya*, Singapore, Govt Printing Office, 1938, p. 64.

46. Christine Doran, 'Gender Matters in the Singapore Mutiny', *Sojourn: Journal of Social Issues in Southeast Asia*, 17/1 (2002), pp. 76–93, esp. p. 80.

47. Brown and Brown, *Singapore Mutiny*, p. 90.

48. *New York Times*, 2 May 1915.

49. TNA, CO 273/420, 'Governor, Straits Settlements, to Secretary of State for the Colonies', 25 February 1915.

50. Karen A. Snow, 'Russia and the 1915 Indian Mutiny in Singapore', *South East Asia Research*, 5/3 (1997), pp. 295–315.

51. *Straits Times*, 26 February 1915.

52. Tarling, ' "The Merest Pustule" ', p. 26.

53. Sareen, *Secret Documents*, pp. 616–17, and discussed by K. van Dijk, 'Religion and the Undermining of British Rule', in R. Michael Feener and Terenjit Sevea (eds), *Islamic Connections; Muslim Societies in South and Southeast Asia*, Singapore, ISEAS, 2009, pp. 109–33, at pp. 125–6; TNA, FCO 141/16534, 'Ridout to Young', 8 May 1915.

54. TNA, CO 273/420, W. G. Maxwell, 'Narrative', n.d. (24 February 1915); TNA, FCO 141/16534, Court of Inquiry, Monday 22 March 1915, Fifth Day.

55. TNA, FCO 141/16534, 'Testimony of Sepoy Dost Mohamed Khan, Court of Inquiry, Tuesday 30 March, Thirteenth Day'.

56. Harper and Miller, *Singapore Mutiny*, pp. 172–90; TNA, FCO 141/16538, 'H. Dening to Young', 3 August 1915.

57. TNA, CO 273/423, 'Court of Inquiry', enclosed in 'Governor, Straits Settlements, to Secretary of State for the Colonies', 19 August 1915.

58. Harper and Miller, *Singapore Mutiny*, pp. 195–204; TNA, FCO 141/16530, Ridout, minute, 27 March 1915.

59. TNA, FCO 141/16534, 'Testimony of Lt Morrison, Court of Inquiry, Monday 19 April 1915, Twenty-Ninth Day'.

60. L. P. Mathur, *History of the Andaman and Nicobar Islands, 1756–1966*, Delhi, Sterling Publishers, 1968, pp. 205–6.

61. 'The High Treason Charge', *Malaya Tribune*, 24 April 1915.

62. Major A. M. Thompson, '1915 Mutiny of an Indian Regiment in Singapore', appendix to H. Schweizer-Iten, *One Hundred Years of the Swiss Club and the Swiss Community of Singapore, 1871–1971*, Singapore, Swiss Club, 1981, pp. 422–33, at p. 427.

63. *Straits Times*, 22, 23 and 24 April 1915; *Malaya Tribune*, 22 April 1915. The fullest published account of the Kassim Mansoor trial is Alijah Gordon, 'Riau: The Milieu of Syed Shaykh's Formative Years and the Aspirations of the Subjugated *Umma*', in Alwi bin Alhady, *The Real Cry of Syed Shayk al-Hady, with Selections of His Writings by His Son Syed Alwi Al-Hady*, ed. Alijah Gordon, Kuala Lumpur, Malaysian Sociological Research Institute, 1999, pp. 1–68, at pp. 24–31.

64. *Straits Times*, 31 May 1915; *Malaya Tribune*, 31 May 1915.

65. Ibid., 9 March 1915.

66. Engseng Ho, 'Empire through Diasporic Eyes: A View from the Other Boat', *Comparative Studies in Society and History*, 46/2 (2004), pp. 210–46, at p. 212.

67. *Malaya Tribune*, 31 May 1915.

68. TNA, CO 273/420, Letter from unidentified correspondent, Singapore, 4 March 1915.

69. A central argument of Sho Kuwajima, *Indian Mutiny in Singapore, 1915*, Calcutta, Ratna Prakashan, 1991.

70. TNA, FCO 141/16536, 'Young to Governor of Hong Kong', 19 February 1915.

71. C. F. Yong, 'The British Colonial Rule and the Chinese Press in Singapore, 1900–1941', *Asian Culture*, 15 (1991), pp. 30–37, at p. 31.

72. Thompson, '1915 Mutiny of an Indian Regiment in Singapore', p. 428.

73. SNA, GD/C/24, 'Commandant Malay States Guides to DAAG Aden Brigade', 10 December 1916, in 'Young to Walter Long', 17 October 1918.

74. James C. Ker, *Political Trouble in India, 1907–1917* (1917), Calcutta, Editions Indian, 1960, pp. 337–8.

75. Harish K. Puri, *Ghadar Movement: Ideology, Organisation and Strategy*, Amritsar, Guru Nanak Dev University Press, 1983, pp. 88, 160–62.

76. A. W. B. Simpson, 'Round up the Usual Suspects: The Legacy of British Colonialism and the European Convention on Human Rights', *Loyola Law Review*, 41/4 (1996), pp. 629–711.

77. N. Gerald Barrier, *Banned: Controversial Literature and Political Control in British India, 1907–1947*, Columbia, University of Missouri Press, 1974, pp. 75–6.

78. Bhai Parmanand, *The Story of My Life*, Lahore, The Central Hindu Yuvak Sabha, 1934, pp. 19–27.

79. NAI, Home Dept, Political A, October 1915, No. 91, 'Special Tribunal, Lahore Conspiracy Case, Judgment in re King Emperor versus Anand Kishore and Others', 13 September 1915, part II A, p. 10.

80. NAI, Home Dept, Political B, March 1915, No. 37, 'Statement Made by Nawab Khan, Raikat, Ludhiana'.

81. NAI, Home Dept, Political A, October 1915, No. 91, 'Special Tribunal, Lahore Conspiracy Case', esp. pp. 8, 14–15.

82. Parmanand, *The Story of My Life*, p. 74.

83. Budheswar Pati, *India and the First World War*, New Delhi, Atlantic Publishers & Dist., 1996, p. 121.

84. Parmanand, *The Story of My Life*, p. 88.

85. NAI, Home Dept, Political A, October 1915, No. 91, 'Special Tribunal, Lahore Conspiracy Case, Judgment in re King Emperor versus Anand Kishore and Others', 13 September 1915, 'Parma Nand, Bhai', pp. 9–10.

86. 'The Case of Bhai Parmanand', from the *Punjabee*, reprinted in the *Leader* (Allahabad), 26 September 1915.

87. Parmanand, *The Story of My Life*, pp. 149–50.

88. 'The Sad Case of Bhai Parmanand', *Amrita Bazar Patrika*, 29 November 1919.

89. See the account in Sohan Singh Josh, *Baba Sohan Singh Bhakna: Life of the Founder of the Ghadar Party*, New Delhi, People's Publishing House, 1970, pp. 54–8.

90. NAI, Home Dept, Political A, October 1915, No. 91, 'Special Tribunal, Lahore Conspiracy Case, Judgment in re King Emperor versus Anand Kishore and Others', 13 September 1915, part I, p. 8.

91. Hugh J. M. Johnston, *Jewels of the Qila: The Remarkable Story of an Indo-Canadian Family*, Vancouver, UBC Press, 2011, p. 94.

92. For the supplementary trials see the judgments in TNA, FO 228/2701. For the numbers see Puri, *Ghadar Movement*, p. 167.

93. Parmanand, *The Story of My Life*, pp. ix–x.

94. Sohan Singh Pooni, 'Pen-Profiles of the Renowned Ghadarites of Canada-America' at http://www.globalsikhstudies.net/pdf/stockeng/sohan2.pdf (last accessed 19 September 2018).

95. Arun Chandra Guha, *First Spark of Revolution: The Early Phase of India's Struggle for Independence, 1900–1920*, Bombay, Orient Longman, 1971, pp. 396–8.

96. Sumanta Banerjee, *The Wicked City: Crime and Punishment in Colonial*

Calcutta, New Delhi, Orient Blackswan, 2009, pp. 340–56 and, for women, pp. 483–6.

97. Joya Chatterji, *Bengal Divided: Hindu Communalism and Partition, 1932–47*, Cambridge, Cambridge University Press, 1994, pp. 55–103.

98. *The Tribune* (Lahore), 9 October 1914.

99. See the judgment, 10 February 1915, in Nahar Singh and Kirpal Singh (eds), *Struggle for Free Hindustan*, vol. III: *Delhi–Lahore Conspiracy, 1912–1915*, New Delhi, Atlantic Publishers & Distributors, 1987, pp. 335–445, quotation at p. 444; IOR NEG 10612: GOI Home Department, Proceedings, December 1914, No. 11: 'Report on the Delhi Bomb Investigation', 8 November 1914.

100. J. G. Ohsawa, *The Two Great Indians in Japan: Sri Rash Behari Bose and Netaji Subhas Chandra Bose*, vol. I, Calcutta, Sri K. C. Das, 1954, pp. 4–5.

101. Bimanbehari Majumdar, *Militant Nationalism in India and Its Socio-Religious Background, 1897–1917*, Calcutta, General Printers & Publishers, 1966, p. 129.

102. A. M. Nair, *An Indian Freedom Fighter in Japan*, New Delhi, Vikas, 1985, pp. 55–6.

103. There have been a number of accounts of this affair. For two more recent research studies see Kees van Dijk, *The Netherlands Indies and the Great War 1914–1918*, Leiden, KITLV Press, 2007, pp. 333–7; Streets-Salter, *World War One in Southeast Asia*, pp. 111–41.

104. TNA, FCO 141/16063, 'Statement of Georg Strub', 1 August 1915.

105. NL-HaNA, Koloniën: Geheim Archief, Vb 3-4-1919 X2, 'United States of America vs. Frans Bopp et al.', p. 200.

106. Ibid., pp. 76–7, 136.

107. NL-HaNA, Koloniën: Geheim Archief, Vb 26-11-1915 C14, W. R. D. Beckett, 'Memorandum', 5 October 1915.

108. Thomas G. Fraser, 'Germany and Indian Revolution, 1914–18', *Journal of Contemporary History*, 12/2 (1977), pp. 255–72.

109. TNA, FCO 141/16063, W. R. D. Beckett telegram, 30 July 1915.

110. NL-HaNA, Koloniën: Geheim Archief, Vb 3-4-1919 X2, 'United States of America vs. Frans Bopp et al.', p. 18; Leonard A. Gordon, 'Portrait of a Bengal Revolutionary', *Journal of Asian Studies*, 27/2 (1968), pp. 197–216, at p. 212.

111. NARA, M1085, Bureau of Investigation, Old German Files, Case 8000-1396, copy of the statement of Kumud Nath Mukherji.

112. NL-HaNA, Koloniën: Geheim Archief, Vb 17-8-1915 F11, 'Beckett to Hulshof Pol', 29 June 1915.

113. TNA, FCO 141/16063, 'Beckett to Earl Grey', 30 July 1915.

114. Ibid.; TNA, FCO 141/16127, 'Ridout to War Office', 25 February 1916; Peter Hopkirk, *On Secret Service East of Constantinople: The Plot to*

Bring down the British Empire, Oxford, Oxford University Press, 1994, pp. 189–90.

115. NL-HaNA, Koloniën: Geheim Archief, Vb 10-1-1918, cutting from the *San Francisco Examiner*, 24 May 1917.

116. E. Helfferich to A. C. Bose, n.d., in Bose, *Indian Revolutionaries Abroad: Select Documents*, New Delhi, Northern Book Centre, 2002, p. 156.

117. William Schell, Jr, *Integral Outsiders: The American Colony in Mexico City, 1876–1911*, Wilmington, DE, SR Books, 2001, p. 19.

118. NL-HaNA, Koloniën: Geheim Archief, Vb 3-4-1919 X2, 'United States of America vs. Frans Bopp et al.', Eckhart H. von Schack et al., report of trial, pp. 80, 84–5.

119. TNA, FO 228/2740, 'Indian Society, Philippine Islands Branch', 6 October 1916; John Price Jones and Paul Merrick Hollister, *The German Secret Service in America, 1914–1918*, Boston, MA, Small, Maynard, 1918, p. 281.

120. NL-HaNA, Koloniën: Geheim Archief, inv. Nr. Vb 26-11-1915 C14, Sita Ram, Inspector of Police, 'Report', 30 July 1915.

121. E. Helfferich to A. C. Bose, n.d., Bose, *Indian Revolutionaries Abroad: Select Documents*, p. 158.

122. TNA, CO 273/447, 'Supplement VI of 1 February 1916'.

123. Van Dijk, *The Netherlands Indies and the Great War*, pp. 330–31.

124. TNA, FCO 141/16064, 'Ridout to Beckett', 12 November 1915; ibid., 'Ridout to Chief of General Staff, Simla', 28 October 1915; E. Helfferich to A. C. Bose, n.d., in Bose, *Indian Revolutionaries Abroad: Select Documents*, pp. 153–8. For Kothavala see Richard J. Popplewell, *Intelligence and Imperial Defence: British Intelligence and the Defence of the Indian Empire, 1904–1924*, London, Frank Cass, 1995, p. 263.

125. The arrests and statements are described in detail in Streets-Salter, *World War One in Southeast Asia*, pp. 121–9.

126. For Jodh Singh see Maia Ramnath, *Haj to Utopia: How the Ghadar Movement Charted Global Radicalism and Attempted to Overthrow the British Empire*, Berkeley, University of California Press, 2011, pp. 82–8. For the plot against Cook see Jones and Hollister, *The German Secret Service in America*, p. 259.

127. TNA, FCO 141/16057, various enclosures.

128. TNA, CO 273/447, 'Supplement VI of 1 February 1916'.

129. TNA, FCO 141/16063, W. R. D. Beckett telegram, 30 July 1915.

130. NARA, M1085, Bureau of Investigation, Old German Files, Case 8000-1396, p. 8, copy of the statement, untitled and undated, but identifiable from its contents as Sukumar Chatterjee's.

131. TNA, FCO 141/16064, 'Ridout to Beckett', 12 November 1915; R.S., 'The German Plot', 25 August 1915, in Bose, *Indian Revolutionaries Abroad*, pp. 150–52.

132. TNA, FCO 141/16127, 'Karl Gehrmann to German Consulate, Shanghai (as Intercepted by Kraft)', n.d.

133. NL-HaNA, Koloniën/Geheim Archief, inv. nr. Vb 30-3-1916 D5, H. J. Vermeer, 'Eenige Opmerkingen omtrent den Japanschen Inlichtingsdienst in Oost-Azië (Verkregen door Gesprekken met den Britisch-Indischen banneling A. Selam, te Koepang)', 22 November 1915.

134. For an inspirational evocation of this see Michael B. Miller, *Shanghai on the Métro: Spies, Intrigue, and the French between the Wars*, Berkeley, University of California Press, 1994, esp. pp. 69–89.

135. For his career see NAI, Home Dept, Political A, January 1920, Nos 129–50(a).

136. TNA, FCO 141/16064, 'Ridout to Beckett', 27 October 1915.

137. NL-HaNA, Koloniën: Geheim Archief, Vb 27-9-1918 F9, 'The Dutch East Indies and the Ghadar trial', *c.* August 1918; ibid., Vb 3-4-1919 X2, 'United States of America vs. Frans Bopp et al.', pp. 149–53.

138. NARA, M1085, Bureau of Investigation, Old German Files, Case 8000-1396, p. 940, E. M. Blanford report, 23 August for 18 August 1917.

139. TNA, CO 273/447, 'Supplement VI of 1 February 1916'.

140. Samaren Roy, *The Restless Brahmin: Early Life of M. N. Roy*, Bombay, Allied, 1970, p. 78.

141. For the death of Jatin see NAI, Home Dept, Political A, Nos 48–61, C. R. Cleveland, 'Notes in the Criminal Intelligence Office', 13 September 1915; ibid., G. C. Denham, 'Note on Further Enquiry at Balasore and the Arrest of the Kobtipada Party', 12 September 1915; Prithwindra Mukherjee, *The Intellectual Roots of India's Freedom Struggle (1893–1918)*, London, Routledge, 2018, pp. 262–76; Guha, *First Spark of Revolution*, pp. 393–4.

142. M. N. Roy, *M. N. Roy's Memoirs* (1960), Delhi, Ajanta Publications, 1985, p. 35.

143. SNA, COD/C/60, 'Consul, Saigon to Secretary of State', 21 April 1915; TNA, FO 228/2740, 'Enemy Activities, Shanghai', 12 September 1916.

144. TNA, FO 115/1907, 'May to Bonar Law', 13 August 1915.

145. David G. Marr, *Vietnamese Anticolonialism, 1885–1925*, Berkeley, University of California Press, 1971, p. 226.

146. Tran My-Van, *A Vietnamese Royal Exile in Japan: Prince Cuong De (1882–1951)*, London, Routledge, 2013, pp. 95–7.

147. Philippe M. F. Peycam, *The Birth of Vietnamese Political Journalism: Saigon, 1916–1930*, New York, Columbia University Press, 2012, pp. 60–67.

148. Christopher E. Goscha, *Thailand and the Southeast Asian Networks of the Vietnamese Revolution, 1885–1954*, London, Routledge, 1998, pp. 43–4; Streets-Salter, *World War One in Southeast Asia*, pp. 185–209.

149. Milton Osborne, 'The Faithful Few: The Politics of Collaboration in Cochinchina in the 1920s', in Walter Francis Vella (ed.), *Aspects of Vietnamese History*, Honolulu, University Press of Hawaii, 1973, pp. 160–90, at p. 165.

150. Firuta Motoo, 'Vietnamese Political Movements in Thailand: Legacy of the Dong-Du Movement', in Vinh Sinh (ed.), *Phan Boi Chau and the Dong-Du Movement*, New Haven, CT, Yale University Press, 1988, pp. 150–81, at p. 153.

151. J. de V. Allen, 'The Kelantan Rising of 1915: Some Thoughts on the Concept of Resistance in British Malayan History', *Journal of Southeast Asian History*, 9/2 (1968), pp. 241–57; Cheah Boon Kheng, *To' Janggut: Legends, Histories, and Perceptions of the 1915 Rebellion in Kelantan*, Singapore, Singapore University Press, 2006. For Tok Janggut's alleged survival see the article in the *New Straits Times*, 30 December 2015, '100 Years after "Death", Tok Janggut's Descendants Claim He Was Not Killed by British'.

152. Elsbeth Locher-Scholten, *Sumatran Sultanate and Colonial State: Jambi and the Rise of Dutch Imperialism, 1830–1907*, Ithaca, NY, Southeast Asia Program Publications, 2004, pp. 267–73.

153. Kumari Jayawardena, 'Economic and Political Factors in the 1915 Riots', *Journal of Asian Studies*, 29/2 (1970), pp. 223–33; Ameer Ali, 'The 1915 Racial Riots in Ceylon (Sri Lanka): A Reappraisal of Its Causes', *South Asia: Journal of South Asian Studies*, 4/2 (1981), pp. 1–20; A. P. Kannangara, 'The Riots of 1915 in Sri Lanka: A Study in the Roots of Communal Violence', *Past and Present*, 102 (1984), pp. 130–65.

154. National Maritime Museum, Greenwich, BIS/7/20, 'Letter from Agents, BISN Singapore, to Controller of Labour, FMS', 4 October 1915. I am grateful to Sunil Amrith for this reference.

155. Saul Kelly, ' "Crazy in the Extreme"? The Silk Letters Conspiracy', *Middle Eastern Studies*, 49/2 (2013), pp. 162–78; Faridah Zaman, 'Revolutionary History and the Post-Colonial Muslim: Re-Writing the "Silk Letters Conspiracy" of 1916', *South Asia: Journal of South Asian Studies*, 39/3 (2016), pp. 626–43.

156. Jane Drakard, *A Kingdom of Words: Language and Power in Sumatra*, Shah Alam, Oxford University Press, 1999.

157. TNA, FO 228/2299, 'A Statement by Mahomet Azim, aged 30', Hankou, 12 June 1915.

158. NARA, M1085, Bureau of Investigation, Old German Files, Case 8000-1396, p. 27, Don S. Rathbun report, 5 November for 2 November 1917.

159. Emily C. Brown, *Har Dayal: Hindu Revolutionary and Rationalist*, Tucson, University of Arizona Press, 1975, p. 185; Har Dayal, *Forty-Four Months in Germany and Turkey, February 1915 to October 1918: A Record of Personal Impressions*, London, P. S. King, 1920, quotations esp. pp. 10, 38.

160. Christopher MacEvitt, *The Crusades and the Christian World of the East: Rough Tolerance*, Philadelphia, University of Pennsylvania Press, 2008, pp. 21–6.

8. THE NEW GREAT GAME (1915–1917)

1. Centre des Archives Diplomatiques de Nantes, Pékin, Série A, 513PO/A, 'Beauvais à M. Boppe, Ministre de France en Chine', 26 August 1918.
2. Richard J. Popplewell, *Intelligence and Imperial Defence: British Intelligence and the Defence of the Indian Empire, 1904–1924*, London, Frank Cass, 1995, p. 219 for MI5, and, generally, pp. 258–96.
3. TNA, FCO 141/15521, Ridout, 'Memorandum on Mr Petrie's Appointment', 21 April 1916; TNA, FCO 141/15522, Ridout memorandum, 25 May 1916.
4. TNA, FCO 141/15527, Ridout minute, 23 August 1916; TNA, FCO 141/15528, Ridout cipher cable, 3 March 1917.
5. TNA, FO 228/2740, *1916 List of Germans, Austrians and Turks and Pro-Enemy Residents in the Netherlands East Indies*, Singapore, Government Printing Office, 1917; ibid., 'Enemy Subjects in Tokyo, Yokohama and Kobe', 13 July 1917; ibid., 'China Command Subject List, Compiled at Hong Kong', March 1917.
6. On the etymology of 'renegado' see James Mark Purcell, 'Melville's Contribution to English', *PMLA* 56/3 (1941), pp. 797–808, at p. 804.
7. Marcia R. Ristaino, *Port of Last Resort: The Diaspora Communities of Shanghai*, Stanford, CA, Stanford University Press, 2001; Sarah Abrevaya Stein, 'Protected Persons? The Baghdadi Jewish Diaspora, the British State, and the Persistence of Empire', *American Historical Review*, 116/1 (2011), pp. 80–108.
8. Shanghai Municipal Council, *Report for the Year 1916*, Shanghai, Kelly & Walsh, 1917, p. 59A; Christian Henriot, *Scythe and the City: A Social History of Death in Shanghai*, Stanford, CA, Stanford University Press, 2016, pp. 13–14.
9. For a summary see Nicholas R. Clifford, *Shanghai, 1925: Urban Nationalism and the Defense of Foreign Privilege*, Ann Arbor, Center for Chinese Studies, University of Michigan, 1979, pp. 20–21, quotation at p. 33.
10. Robert Bickers, *Getting Stuck in for Shanghai: Putting the Kibosh on the Kaiser from the Bund: The British at Shanghai and the Great War*, London, Penguin, 2014, esp. the section 'Extreme Cosmopolites'; Kathryn Meyer, 'Trade and Nationality at Shanghai upon the Outbreak of the First World War, 1914–1915', *International History Review*, 10/2 (1988), pp. 238–60; Tobit Vandamme, 'The Rise of Nationalism in a Cosmopolitan Port City: The Foreign Communities of Shanghai during the First World War', *Journal of World History*, 29/1 (2018), pp. 37–64.
11. TNA, FO 228/2740, 'E', 4 November 1916, for walnut shells; ibid., 'E: 146', 12 March 1917, for exploding pencils.

12. Vandamme gives a succinct account in 'The Rise of Nationalism in a Cosmopolitan Port City', pp. 55–9.

13. SMP, IO/821, various attachments.

14. SMP, IO/301, Chief Detective Inspector to Captain Superintendent of Police, 15 May 1916; ibid., DSI P. H. Reeves, 'Suspected storing of smuggled opium', 26 April 1916.

15. SMP, IO/544, report, 2 October 1916.

16. SMP, IO/144, Chief Detective Inspector to Chief Detective Officer, 27 July 1915.

17. SMP, IO/1265, Statement of Max Kindler 8 June 1917.

18. SMP, IO/626, 'Result of a watch kept on the movements of Ettinger from 25 September to 3 October', 4 October 1916.

19. SMP, IO/491, CID report, 12 March 1917; TNA, FO 228/2740, 'Enemy Activities, Shanghai', 12 September 1916.

20. SMP, IO/503, undated note; SMP, IO/214, miscellaneous reports; *North China Daily News*, 14 June 1917.

21. SMP, IO/3844, Capt SP to Consul-General Shanghai, 30 March 1917.

22. SMP, IO/923, DSI Brewster, 'The German, Nielsen', 13 March 1917.

23. On 'passing' see Yumna Siddiqi, *Anxieties of Empire and the Fiction of Intrigue*, New York, Columbia University Press, 2007, pp. 119–20.

24. Popplewell, *Intelligence and Imperial Defence*, pp. 229–30. I was alerted to this connection by Catherine Merridale.

25. Quoted and discussed in Françoise Navet-Bouron, 'La Censure et la Femme pendant la Première Guerre Mondiale', *Guerres Mondiales et Conflits Contemporains*, 198 (2000), pp. 43–51, at pp. 45–6. For Mata Hari's legacies see Matthew Isaac Cohen, 'Dancing the Subject of "Java": International Modernism and Traditional Performance, 1899–1952', *Indonesia and the Malay World*, 35/101 (2007), pp. 9–29.

26. Christian Henriot, *Prostitution and Sexuality in Shanghai: A Social History, 1849–1949*, Cambridge, Cambridge University Press, 2001, p. 117.

27. Andrew Field, *Shanghai's Dancing World: Cabaret Culture and Urban Politics, 1919–1954*, Hong Kong, Chinese University Press, 2010, p. 27, 39–43.

28. The account of Miss Ross is drawn from enclosures in TNA, FO 228/2673.

29. I have been unable to find any further reference to her, save a report on the sudden death in early July 1926 of Dr John W. Ross, a sixty-nine-year-old widower of Brockville, Ontario, at a boarding house in Woodstock, New York, where he was on holiday. The *Kingston Daily Freeman* of 9 July 1926 reported that he was accompanied by his daughter, Miss Gwendolen Ross, and was also survived by 'one son in China'. Ross was a medical examiner for an insurance firm who was an energetic promotor of Canadian flour, lumber and other commodities as trade commissioner from 1914 until his retirement in 1925; see John D. Meehan, *Chasing the Dragon in Shanghai: Canada's Early Relations with China, 1858–1952*, Vancouver, UBC Press, 2011, p. 40.

30. SMP, IO/503, enclosures.

31. SMP, IO/941, DSI Silver, 'Mrs Lea Cox at request of American authorities per DSP', 30 April 1919.

32. Tapan K. Mukherjee, *Taraknath Das: Life and Letters of a Revolutionary in Exile*, Calcutta, National Council of Education, Bengal, Jadavpur University, 1998, pp. 105-7.

33. TNA, FO 115/1908, 'British consul San Francisco to British Ambassador, Washington', 17 September 1915.

34. Kumari Jayawardena, *The White Woman's Other Burden: Western Women and South Asia during British Rule*, London, Routledge, 1995.

35. What follows is drawn from Dekker's police interrogation and his confession in Hong Kong. NL-HaNA, Koloniën: Openbaar Archief, Vb 27-7-1916, 25, 'Statement: E. F. E. Douwes Dekker', Singapore, 24 January 1916; TNA, FO 371/2784, 'The Confession of Douwes Dekker in Connection with Indian Sedition', Douwes Dekker to Dr Kock, Superintendent of the Government Civil Hospital Hong Kong, 11 December 1915.

36. Ibid.

37. Ibid.

38. Ibid.

39. Ibid.

40. Paul W. van der Veur, *The Lion and the Gadfly: Dutch Colonialism and the Spirit of E. F. E. Douwes Dekker*, Leiden, KITLV Press, 2006, pp. 322–6.

41. NL-HaNA, Koloniën: Geheim Archief, Vb 3-4-1919 X2, 'United States of America vs. Frans Bopp et al.', pp. 99–100; NARA, M1085, Bureau of Investigation, Old German Files, Case 8000-1396, pp. 123–7, Customs Secret Agent Zamboanga report, 13 February 1915 and 1 March 1915, in E. M. Blanford report, 9 August for 8 August 1917.

42. TNA, FO 115/1908, translation from *Ghadar*, 29 August 1915; ibid., 'Memorandum', Acting British Consul Manila, 14 October 1915.

43. TNA, FO 228/2740, 'Indian Society, Philippine Islands Branch', 6 October 1916.

44. The account of this meeting, and the quotations, are taken from *Presidential Address Delivered by Dr Bhagawan Singh, 75th Birthday Anniversary of Rashbehari Basu*, Calcutta, Mahajato Sadan, 25 May 1960, South Asian American Digital Archive (SAADA), https://www.saada.org/item/20120806-928 (last accessed 17 May 2020).

45. Gautam Chattopadhyay, *Abani Mukherji: A Dauntless Revolutionary and Pioneering Communist*, New Delhi, People's Publishing House, 1976, pp. 10–12, 43.

46. NARA, M1085, Bureau of Investigation, Old German Files, Case 8000-1396, p. 46, interrogation of the Shanghai watchman Tehl Singh, in E. M. Blanford report, 15 August 1917 for 10 August 1917.

47. TNA, FCO 141/16111, 'Ridout to Tokyo', 14 October 1915.

48. Ibid., 'Ridout to CGS Simla', 9 October 1915.

49. Ibid., 'Ridout to Tokyo', 14 October 1915; TNA, FO 228/2703, 'Abani Nath Mukherji: Supplementary Statement', Singapore, 7 September 1916.

50. TNA, FCO 141/16109, 'Conyngham Greene to Grey', 5 January 1916.

51. T. R. Sareen, *Indian Revolutionaries: Japan and British Imperialism*, New Delhi, Anmol Publications, 1993, pp. 27–8.

52. TNA, FO 228/2702, 'Sir William Conyngham Greene to Sir Edward Grey', 5 January 1916.

53. Helen Hardacre, 'Asano Wasaburo and Japanese Spiritualism in Early Twentieth-Century Japan', in Sharon Minichiello (ed.), *Japan's Competing Modernities: Issues in Culture and Democracy, 1900–1930*, Manoa, University of Hawaii Press, 1998, pp. 133–53, at p. 137.

54. Quoted in J. G. Ohsawa, *The Two Great Indians in Japan: Sri Rash Behari Bose and Netaji Subhas Chandra Bose*, vol. I, Calcutta, Sri K. C. Das, 1954, p. 83.

55. Lizzie Collingham, *Curry: A Tale of Cooks and Conquerors*, New York, Oxford University Press, 2006, pp, 252–3.

56. Stephen N. Hay, *Asian Ideas of East and West: Tagore and His Critics in Japan, China, and India*, Cambridge, MA, Harvard University Press, 1970, quotations at pp. 60–61.

57. Ibid., pp. 58–77. I draw here on the discussion by Mark R. Frost, ' "Beyond the Limits of Nation and Geography": Rabindranath Tagore and the Cosmopolitan Moment, 1916–1920', *Cultural Dynamics*, 24/2–3 (2012), pp. 143–58, esp. pp. 145–6.

58. Tagore to Wilson, 9 May 1918, in Krishna Dutta and Andrew Robinson (eds), *Selected Letters of Rabindranath Tagore*, Cambridge, Cambridge University Press, 1997, pp. 198–9.

59. TNA, FO 228/2702, 'Sir William Conyngham Greene to Sir Edward Grey', 5 January 1916.

60. TNA, FCO 141/15530, 'C. J. Davidson to D. Petrie', 24 January 1917.

61. A. M. Nair, *An Indian Freedom Fighter in Japan*, New Delhi, Vikas, 1985, pp. 55–7.

62. Sareen, *Indian Revolutionaries*, p. 42.

63. Chattopadhyay, *Abani Mukherji*, pp. 13–16; TNA, FO 228/2740, 'E 154: Abani Mukherji', 18 April 1917. For Okamoto see TNA, FO 228/3211, Straits Settlements, Secret Abstract of Intelligence, February 1918. For the doubts about Abani see A. C. Bose, *Indian Revolutionaries Abroad, 1905–1922: In the Background of International Developments,* Patna, Bharati Bhawan, 1971, p. 157; Muzaffar Ahmad, *Myself and the Communist Party of India, 1920–1929*, Calcutta, National Book Agency, 1970, pp. 199–254.

64. Ibid.

65. Here I have drawn on Gail Hershatter's classic *The Workers of Tianjin, 1900–1949*, Stanford, CA, Stanford University Press, 1993.

66. Francis Clifford Jones, *Shanghai and Tientsin, with Special Reference to Foreign Interests*, San Francisco, CA, American Council, Institute of Pacific Relations, 1940.

67. In this account of Roy in China, I follow M. N. Roy, *M. N. Roy's Memoirs* (1960), Delhi, Ajanta Publications, 1985, pp. 8–13.

68. Ibid., pp. 14–17.

69. NL-HaNA, Koloniën: Geheim Archief, Vb 3-4-1919 X2, 'United States of America vs. Frans Bopp et al.', pp. 55–8; TNA, FO 228/2740, 'Indian Society, Philippine Islands Branch', 24 December 1916.

70. TNA, FO 115/1908, 'Consulate-General NY to Washington', 4 December 1915; ibid., 'Consul-General Philadelphia to London', 10 December 1915.

71. Innaiah Narisetti, *Evelyn Trent Alias Shanthi Devi*, Hyderabad, V. Komala, 1995, p. 8; NARA, M1085, Bureau of Investigation, Old German Files, Case 8000-1396, p. 84, note headed 'Martin'.

72. NAI, Home Dept, Political A, Nos 48–61: Viceroy to Secretary of State, 15 September 1915.

73. Samaren Roy, *M. N. Roy: A Political Biography*, New Delhi, Orient Longman, 1997, p. 14.

74. Mukherjee, *Taraknath Das*, pp. 98–9; NARA, M1085, Bureau of Investigation, Old German Files, Case 8000-1396, p. 141, Taraknath Das to General Secretary, the Hindustani Association, Berkeley, 22 March 1917, in E. M. Blanford report, 8 August for 2 August 1917.

75. Margo Baumgartner Davis and Roxanne Nilan, *The Stanford Album: A Photographic History, 1885–1945*, Stanford, CA, Stanford University Press, 1989, pp. 159–66.

76. For a short biography see Narisetti, *Evelyn Trent*. For context see Jayawardena, *The White Woman's Other Burden*, esp. ch. 17.

77. Dhan Gopal Mukerji, *Caste and Outcast* (1923), Stanford, CA, Stanford University Press, 2002, p. 261.

78. NARA, M1085, Bureau of Investigation, Old German Files, Case 8000-1396, pp. 413–14, E. M. Blanford report, 6 April for 31 March 1917.

79. Narisetti, *Evelyn Trent*, p. 14.

80. NARA, M1085, Bureau of Investigation, Old German Files, Case 8000-1396, p. 114, intercepted 'letter from Mahendra Nath Roy to Tokio'.

81. Roy writing in 1953, as quoted and discussed in Kris Manjapra, *M. N. Roy: Marxism and Colonial Cosmopolitanism*, New Delhi, Routledge India, 2010, pp. 32–3.

82. Richard B. Spence, 'Hidden Agendas: Spies, Lies and Intrigue Surrounding Trotsky's American Visit of January–April 1917', *Revolutionary Russia*, 21/1 (2008), pp. 33–55.

83. For a rich account of this transformation in Borodin's case see Lisa A. Kirschenbaum, 'Michael Gruzenberg/Mikhail Borodin: The Making of an International Communist', in Choi Chatterjee, Steven G. Marks, Mary

Neuburger and Steven Sabol (eds), *The Global Impacts of Russia's Great War and Revolution, Book 2: The Wider Arc of Revolution, Part 1*, Bloomington, IN, Slavica Publishers, 2019, pp. 337–65. I am grateful to Professor Kirschenbaum for sending it to me.

84. Daniel Patrick Moynihan, *Secrecy: The American Experience*, New Haven, CT, Yale University Press, 1999, p. 89.

85. Keith Jeffery, *MI6: The History of the Secret Intelligence Service, 1909–1949*, London, Bloomsbury, 2010, pp. 112–13.

86. Roy, *Memoirs*, pp. 33–4; NARA, M1085, Bureau of Investigation, Old German Files, Case 8000-1396, p. 85, note headed 'Martin'.

87. Ibid, pp. 67–70, H. L. Gupta to M. Albourge, Montreux, postmarked New York 16 November 1916, in E. M. Blanford report, 14 August for 8 August 1917.

88. Ibid., pp. 958–60, L. S. Perkins report, 10 March for 7 March 1917. For Sekunna's medicine see 'Omin Tonic Tablets', https://www.si.edu/object/nmah_1298577.

89. James C. Ker, *Political Trouble in India, 1907–1917* (1917), Calcutta, Editions Indian, 1960, pp. 259–60. As cited and discussed in: Sibnarayan Ray, *In Freedom's Quest: A Study of the Life and Works of M. N. Roy (1887–1954)*, vol. I: *1887–1922*, Calcutta, Minerva Associates, 1998, pp. 50–51, and Popplewell, *Intelligence and Imperial Defence*, pp. 248–51.

90. NARA, M1085, Bureau of Investigation, Old German Files, Case 8000-1396, pp. 912–23, 'Statement of Mahendra Nath Roy, New York', 13 March 1917; ibid., p. 366, name redacted to Storey, 10 April 1917; ibid., pp. 949–52, William M. Offley to A. B. Bielaski, Chief, Bureau of Investigation, 11 March 1917.

91. NL-HaNA, Koloniën: Geheim Archief, Vb 3-4-1919 X2, p. 108; NARA, M1085, Bureau of Investigation, Old German Files, Case 8000-1396, p. 3, A. A. Hopkins report, 10 May for 10 May 1917; ibid., p. 509 E. M. Blanford report of 4 September 1917 for 3 September 1917.

92. John Higham, *Strangers in the Land: Patterns of American Nativism, 1860–1925*, New Brunswick, NJ, Rutgers University Press, 2002, pp. 202–22; Kathy E. Ferguson, 'Discourses of Danger: Locating Emma Goldman', *Political Theory*, 36/5 (2008), pp. 735–61.

93. Joan M. Jensen, 'The "Hindu Conspiracy": A Reassessment', *Pacific Historical Review*, 48/1 (1979), pp. 65–83.

94. NARA, M1085, Bureau of Investigation, Old German Files, Case 8000-1396, p. 39, E. M. Blanford report, 15 August for 10 August 1917.

95. For excellent summaries of the proceedings see Mukherjee, *Taraknath Das*, pp. 115–39 and Seema Sohi, *Echoes of Mutiny: Race, Surveillance, and Indian Anticolonialism in North America*, Oxford, Oxford University Press, 2014, pp. 184–92.

96. NARA, M1085, Bureau of Investigation, Old German Files, Case 8000-1396, p. 14, Don S. Rathbun report, 6 November for 5 November 1917.

97. NL-HaNA, Koloniën: Geheim Archief, Vb 3-4-1919 X2, 'United States of America vs. Frans Bopp et al.', pp. 34–6; Paul W. van der Veur, *The Lion and the Gadfly: Dutch Colonialism and the Spirit of E.F.E. Douwes Dekker*, Leiden, KITLV, 2006, pp. 369–71.

98. *Oakland Tribune*, 30 April 1918.

99. Sohi, *Echoes of Mutiny*, p. 189. See also Gajendra Singh's important recent study, 'Jodh Singh, the *Ghadar* Movement and the Anti-Colonial Deviant in the Anglo-American Imagination', *Past and Present*, 245 (2019), pp. 187–219, which has more to say about his fate and the essential rationale of 'the irrationalities of his psychosis'.

100. Ruth Price, *The Lives of Agnes Smedley*, Oxford, Oxford University Press, 2005, p. 106.

101. 'Bomb Plots', *Evening Post* (Wellington), 30 January 1918. I was led to this powerful testimony by a blogpost by Sanyasi, 'The Madness of Jodh Singh: Patriotism and Paranoia in the US, 1913 and 2013' (2013), https://www.chapatimystery.com/archives/the_madness_of_jodh_singh_patriotism_and_paranoia_in_the_us_1913_and_2013.html (last accessed 3 January 2020). This is expanded in Rohit Chopra, 'The Madness of Jodh Singh: Patriotism and Paranoia in the Ghadar Archives', *Socialist Studies/Études Socialiste*, 13/2 (2018), pp. 81–96. For the report on his reception in court see *Oakland Tribune*, 27 November 1917.

102. NARA, M1085, Bureau of Investigation, Old German Files, Case 8000-1396, p. 3, E. M. Blanford report, 17 August for 15 August 1917.

103. Ibid., p. 653, Camille de Berri report, 27 December for 7(?) September 1917.

104. *Oakland Tribune*, 23 April 1918.

105. TNA, FO 228/3211, 'Secret Abstract of Intelligence', August 1918.

106. NARA, M1085, Bureau of Investigation, Old German Files, Case 8000-1396, p. 879, E. M. Blanford report, 30 August for 31 August 1917.

107. Ibid., p. 168, A. Marr to J. Storey; ibid., p. 791, A Marr (NYC) to Storey, 22 June 1917; ibid., p. 202, J. F. Kropidlowski (NYC) report, 16 October for 12 October 1917; ibid., p. 636, P. Pigniuolo report, 13 July for 12 July 1917.

108. Evelyn Hu-DeHart, 'On Coolies and Shopkeepers: The Chinese as *Huagong* (Laborers) and *Huashang* (Merchants) in Latin America/Caribbean', in Wanni W. Anderson and Robert G. Lee (eds), *Displacements and Diasporas: Asians in the Americas*, New Brunswick, NJ, Rutgers University Press, 2005, pp. 78–111, at pp. 89–95; Grace Delgado, *Making the Chinese Mexican: Global Migration, Localism, and Exclusion in the U.S.–Mexico Borderlands*, Stanford, CA, Stanford University Press, 2013, esp. chs. 3–4.

109. TNA, FO 228/2740, Straits Settlements, Secret Abstract of Intelligence, August 1917.

110. NARA, M1085, Bureau of Investigation, Old German Files, Case 25680, p. 592-3, fragment entitled 'Trinidad'.

111. Dan La Botz, 'American "Slackers" in the Mexican Revolution: International Proletarian Politics in the Midst of a National Revolution', *The Americas*, 62/4 (2006), pp. 563-90. For Gale see Charles Shipman, *It Had To Be Revolution: Memoirs of an American Radical*, Ithaca, NY, Cornell University Press, 1993, pp. 72-3.

112. As quoted in Daniela Spenser, *Stumbling Its Way through Mexico: The Early Years of the Communist International*, Tuscaloosa, University of Alabama Press, 2011, p. 42. For Roy's time in Mexico see Ray, *In Freedom's Quest*, vol. I, pp. 54-64.

113. Roy, *Memoirs*, pp. 163-4.

114. Carleton Beals, *Glass Houses: Ten Years of Free-Lancing*, Philadelphia, PA, J. B. Lippincott Company, 1938, p. 44.

115. Quoted in Spenser, *Stumbling Its Way through Mexico*, p. 36. For the lasting legacy of *Swadeshi* in Roy's thought see Andrew Sartori, *Bengal in Global Concept History: Culturalism in the Age of Capital*, Chicago, IL, Chicago University Press, 2008, pp. 225-8.

116. Roy, *Memoirs*, p. 76. On Roy's transformation in Mexico see also Manjapra, *M. N. Roy*, pp. 35-9.

117. John Patrick Haithcox, *Communism and Nationalism in India: M. N. Roy and Comintern Policy, 1920-1939*, Princeton, NJ, Princeton University Press, 1971, p. 8; Beals, *Glass Houses*, p. 50.

118. Roy, *Memoirs*, p. 26.

119. TNA, FO 228/3211, Straits Settlements, Secret Abstract of Intelligence, June 1918; Bose, *Indian Revolutionaries Abroad, 1905-1927: Select Documents*, New Delhi, Northern Book Centre, 2002, p. 228.

120. Roy, *Memoirs*, p. 165.

9. VICTORY! (1917-1919)

1. As quoted and discussed in Frances Gouda, *Dutch Culture Overseas: Colonial Practice in the Netherlands Indies 1900-1942*, reprint edn, Jakarta, Equinox Publishing, 2008, p. 64.

2. John Ingleson, *In Search of Justice: Workers and Unions in Colonial Java, 1908-1926*, Singapore, Oxford University Press, 1986, pp. 26-41, quotation at p. 41.

3. Ibid., p. 15.

4. Ruth T. McVey, *The Rise of Indonesian Communism*, Ithaca, NY, Cornell University Press, 1965, p. 13, quotation at p. 20.

5. Ahmat Adam, 'Radical Journalism and Press Persecution in Java, 1914-1918', *Jebat*, 20 (1992), pp. 91-105, at p. 98. This is expanded in his 'Mas

Marco Kartodikromo Dalam Perjuangan "Sam Rata Sama Rasa"', *Jurnal Kinabalu*, 3 (1997), pp. 1–34.

6. Mas Marco, 'Tentoe Koerang Senang!!!', in *Boekoe Sebaran Jang Pertama*, 's-Gravenhage, Pertjaja Berani, 1916, pp. 5–8, at p. 7.

7. NL-HaNA, Koloniën: Openbaar Archief, Vb. 8-11-1917 36, I: Saumatra Sea, 6 January (14 February 1917); II: 1 January, Gibraltar Straits (15 February); III: Spanish Sea 7 January (16 February); IV: no place (17 February).

8. Adam, 'Mas Marco Kartodikromo Dalam Perjuangan "Sam Rata Sama Rasa"', p. 14.

9. Translated and discussed in Takashi Shiraishi, *An Age in Motion: Popular Radicalism in Java, 1912–1926*, Ithaca, NY, Cornell University Press, 1990, pp. 88–9.

10. Soe Hok Gie, *Di Bawah Lentara Merah: Riwayat Sarekat Islam Semarang, 1917–1920*, Jakarta, Franz Fanon Foundation, 1990, p. 12.

11. McVey, *The Rise of Indonesian Communism*, p. 29.

12. Kees van Dijk, *The Netherlands Indies and the Great War, 1914–1918*, Leiden, KITLV Press, 2007, pp. 552–3.

13. Rianne Subijanto, 'Enlightenment and the Revolutionary Press in Colonial Indonesia', *International Journal of Communication*, 11 (2017), pp. 1357–77, quotation at p. 1361–2.

14. For thoughtful summaries see Bob Hering, *Soekarno, Founding Father of Indonesia: A Biography, 1901–1945*, Leiden, KITLV Press, 2002, pp. 44–8; R. E. Elson, *The Idea of Indonesia: A History*, Cambridge, Cambridge University Press, 2009, pp. 6–7, 15–19.

15. Ibid., pp. 21–35, quotation at p. 25; Hering, *Soekarno*, p. 78. Rustam Sani, 'Melayu Raya as a Malay "Nation of Intent"', in H. M. Dahlan (ed.), *The Nascent Malaysian Society*, Kuala Lumpur, UKM, 1976, pp. 25–38.

16. Van Dijk, *The Netherlands Indies and the Great War*, pp. 484–5; Paul W. van der Veur, *The Lion and the Gadfly: Dutch Colonialism and the Spirit of E. F. E. Douwes Dekker*, Leiden, KITLV Press, 2006, pp. 376–9, 392–8, quotation at p. 378.

17. McVey, *The Rise of Indonesian Communism*, p. 29.

18. Van Dijk, *The Netherlands Indies and the Great War*, p. 551; McVey, *The Rise of Indonesian Communism*, p. 35.

19. *Sinar Hindia*, 18 November 1918, as cited in Henk Maier, 'Introduction: Written in the Prison's Light: *The Story of Kadirun*', in Semaoen, *The Story of Kadirun*, trans. Ian Campbell et al., ed. John H. McGlynn, Jakarta, The Lontar Foundation, 2014, p. xiii.

20. Ingleson, *In Search of Justice*, pp. 83–4.

21. IISH, Henk Sneevliet papers, inv. no. 51, Marco Kartodikromo to Henk Sneevliet, 23 November 1917.

22. 'Kesimpulan Laporan Rahasia, 6 Maret [March] 1919', in Arsip Nasional Republik Indonesia, *Sarekat Islam Lokal, Penerbitan Sumber-Sumber*

Sejarah No. 7, Jakarta, Arsip Nasional Republik Indonesia, 1975, pp. 172–7, at p. 176.

23. For this see Al Makin, 'Haji Omar Said Tjokroaminoto: Islam and Socialism (Indonesia, 1924/1963)', in Björn Bentlage et al. (eds), *Religious Dynamics under the Impact of Imperialism and Colonialism: A Sourcebook*, Leiden, Brill, 2016, pp. 249–64. A major new study by Oliver Crawford sheds fresh light on this subject: "The Political Thought of Tan Malaka', PhD thesis, University of Cambridge, 2018.

24. Shiraishi, *An Age in Motion*, pp. 127–37, quotations at pp. 128, 134, 193. The last is also discussed by Benedict R. O'G. Anderson, 'Language, Fantasy, Revolution: Java, 1900–1950', in Daniel S. Lev and Ruth Thomas McVey (eds), *Making Indonesia*, Ithaca, NY, Southeast Asia Program Publications, 1996, pp. 26–40, at p. 33–4.

25. 'Surat Kepada Penasehat Urusan Cina di Betawi, 15 November 1918', in Arsip Nasional Republik Indonesia, *Sarekat Islam Lokal*, pp. 155–69; The Siaw Giap, 'Group Conflict in Plural Society', *Revue du Sud-Est Asiatique*, 1 (1966), pp. 20–31 and 185–217.

26. Van Dijk, *The Netherlands Indies and the Great War*, p. 547.

27. 'Sedikit Perkatahan boeat Toean Darsono', *Sin Po*, 21 November 1918, translated in Leo Suryadinata (ed.), *Political Thinking of the Indonesian Chinese, 1900–1995: A Sourcebook*, Singapore, National University of Singapore Press, 1997, pp. 10–16, at pp. 15–16.

28. TNA, FO 228/3211, Straits Settlements, Secret Abstract of Intelligence, December 1918.

29. Marieke Bloembergen, 'The Dirty Work of Empire: Modern Policing and Public Order in Surabaya, 1911–1919', *Indonesia*, 83 (2007), pp. 119–50, at p. 130.

30. Van Dijk, *The Netherlands Indies and the Great War*, p. 466.

31. Sartono Kartodirdjo, *Protest Movements in Rural Java: A Study of Agrarian Unrest in the Nineteenth and Early Twentieth Centuries*, Singapore, Oxford University Press, 1973, pp. 98–103.

32. Jan J. Nossin, 'Volcanic Hazards in Southeast Asia', in Avijit Gupta (ed.), *The Physical Geography of Southeast Asia*, Oxford, Oxford University Press, 2005, pp. 250–74, at p. 256. For summaries of the press reports see *Malay Weekly Mail*, 29 May and 5 June 1919.

33. Elsbeth Locher-Scholten, 'State Violence and the Police in Colonial Indonesia, circa 1920: Exploration of a Theme', in Freek Colombijn and J. Thomas Lindblad (eds), *Roots of Violence in Indonesia: Contemporary Violence in Historical Perspective*, Leiden, KITLV Press, 2002, pp. 81–104, at pp. 81–5 and 89.

34. Chusnul Hajati, 'The Tragedy of Cimareme: The Resistance of Haji Hasan to the Colonial Power in 1919', *Studia Islamika*, 3/2 (1996), pp. 56–84.

35. 'Het Garoet-Drama en de Afdeeling B', *De Indische Gids*, 42/1 (1920), pp. 449-57, at pp. 456 and 458.

36. William A. Oates, 'The Afdeeling B: An Indonesian Case Study', *Journal of Southeast Asian History*, 9/1 (1968), pp. 107-16; Michael Laffan, *The Makings of Indonesian Islam: Orientalism and the Narration of a Sufi Past*, Princeton, NJ, Princeton University Press, 2011, pp. 209-11.

37. Michael C. Williams, *Sickle and Crescent: The Communist Revolt of 1926 in Banten*, Athens, Ohio University Press, 1990, pp. 14-15.

38. Henk Maier, 'Introduction: Written in the Prison's Light: *The Story of Kadirun*', in Semaoen, *The Story of Kadirun*, trans. Ian Campbell et al., ed. John H. McGlynn, Jakarta, The Lontar Foundation, 2014, p. xiv.

39. Shiraishi, *An Age in Motion*, quotation at p. 101.

40. Semaoen, *The Story of Kadirun*, p. xxii.

41. *Malay Weekly Mail*, 10 April 1919.

42. 'Billy', 'The Trials of a "Volunteer"', *Malay Weekly Mail*, 31 July 1919.

43. *Malay Weekly Mail*, 17 April 1919.

44. 'Planters and the War', *Malay Weekly Mail*, 1 May 1919.

45. Peter Zinoman, 'Colonial Prisons and Anti-Colonial Resistance in French Indochina: The Thai Nguyen Rebellion, 1917', *Modern Asian Studies*, 34/1 (2000), pp. 57-98, quotations at p. 65, figures at p. 90.

46. Milton Osbourne, 'The Faithful Few: The Politics of Collaboration in Cochinchina in the 1920s', in Walter Francis Vella (ed.), *Aspects of Vietnamese History*, Honolulu, University Press of Hawaii, 1973, pp. 160-90, at p. 166.

47. Lim Teck Ghee, *Peasants and Their Agricultural Economy in Colonial Malaya, 1874-1941*, Kuala Lumpur, Oxford University Press, 1977, pp. 120-22; Paul H. Kratoska, 'The British Empire and the Southeast Asian Rice Crisis of 1919-1921', *Modern Asian Studies*, 24/1 (1990), pp. 115-46, esp. pp. 129-31; Yoshihiro Chiba, 'The 1919 and 1935 Rice Crises in the Philippines: The Rice Market and Starvation in American Colonial Times', *Philippine Studies*, 58/4 (2010), pp. 523-56.

48. SNA, GD/C/24, F. S. James to Lord Milner, 20 October 1919, and enclosures.

49. Kirsty Walker, 'The Influenza Pandemic of 1918 in Southeast Asia', in Tim N. Harper and Sunil S. Amrith (eds), *Histories of Health in Southeast Asia: Perspectives on the Long Twentieth Century*, Bloomington, Indiana University Press, 2014, pp. 61-71.

50. Tyler Stovall, *Paris and the Spirit of 1919: Consumer Struggles, Transnationalism, and Revolution*, Cambridge, Cambridge University Press, 2012, p. 111.

51. Xu Guoqi, *Strangers on the Western Front: Chinese Workers in the Great War*, Cambridge, MA, Harvard University Press, 2011.

52. Heather Jones, 'Imperial Captivities: Colonial Prisoners of War in Germany and the Ottoman Empire, 1914-1918', in Santanu Das, *Race, Empire*

and First World War Writing, Cambridge, Cambridge University Press, 2011, pp. 175–93, at pp. 177–8.

53. Tan Tai Yong, *The Garrison State: Military, Government and Society in Colonial Punjab, 1849–1947*, London, SAGE, 2005, pp. 98–140.

54. Rogers Brubaker, 'Aftermaths of Empire and the Unmixing of Peoples', in Karen Barkey and Mark von Hagen (eds), *After Empire: Multiethnic Societies and Nation-Building – the Soviet Union and the Russian, Ottoman and Habsburg Empires*, London, Routledge, 1997, pp. 155–80; Nesim Şeker, 'Demographic Engineering in the Late Ottoman Empire and the Armenians', *Middle Eastern Studies*, 43/3 (2007), pp. 461–74.

55. Gaddis Smith, 'Canada and the Siberian Intervention, 1918–1919', *American Historical Review*, 64/4 (1959), pp. 866–77, quotation at p. 867.

56. As conceptualized in an important recent study by Daniel MacArthur-Seal, 'Britain's Levantine Empire, 1914–1923', PhD thesis, University of Cambridge, 2014.

57. Radhika Singha, 'Finding Labor from India for the War in Iraq: The Jail Porter and Labor Corps, 1916–1920', *Comparative Studies in Society and History*, 49/2 (2007), pp. 412–45; Priya Satia, 'Turning Space into Place: British India and the Invention of Iraq', in Eric Tagliacozzo, Helen F. Siu and Peter C. Perdue (eds), *Asia Inside Out: Connected Places*, Cambridge, MA, Harvard University Press, 2015, pp. 273–301, figures at pp. 283–4.

58. Keith Jeffery, ' "An English Barrack in the Oriental Seas"? India in the Aftermath of the First World War', *Modern Asian Studies*, 15/3 (1981), pp. 369–86, quotation at pp. 375–6.

59. Vera Schwarcz, *The Chinese Enlightenment: Intellectuals and the Legacy of the May Fourth Movement of 1919*, Berkeley, University of California Press, 1986, p. 12; Xu Guoqi, *Asia and the Great War: A Shared History*, Oxford, Oxford University Press, 2016, esp. pp. 227–31; Michael Adas, 'Contested Hegemony: The Great War and the Afro-Asian Assault on the Civilizing Mission Ideology', *Journal of World History*, 15/1 (2004), pp. 31–63.

60. Erez Manela, *The Wilsonian Moment: Self-Determination and the International Origins of Anticolonial Nationalism*, Oxford, Oxford University Press, 2007.

61. Glenda Sluga, *Internationalism in the Age of Nationalism*, Philadelphia, University of Pennsylvania Press, 2013, esp. pp. 11–44, quotations at p. 32.

62. Ibid., p. 42.

63. A point well made by Ali Raza, Franziska Roy and Benjamin Zachariah (eds), *The Internationalist Moment: South Asia, Worlds, and World Views, 1917–1939*, New Delhi, SAGE, 2015, in their introduction, pp. xvii–xix.

64. M. N Roy, 'Open Letter to His Excellency Woodrow Wilson, President of the United States of America' (1917), in Sibnarayan Ray (ed.), *Selected Works of M. N. Roy*, vol. I: *1917–1922*, Delhi, Oxford University Press, 1987, pp. 67–83, at p. 82.

65. Emily S. Rosenberg, 'World War I, Wilsonianism, and Challenges to U.S. Empire', *Diplomatic History*, 38/4 (2014), pp. 852–63. Wilson's 'almost in sight', of course, exemplifies Dipesh Chakrabarty's famous formulation that such lines of argument 'consigned Indians, Africans, and other "rude" nations to an imaginary waiting room of history': Chakrabarty, *Provincializing Europe Postcolonial Thought and Historical Difference*, Princeton, NJ, Princeton University Press, 2000, p. 8.

66. I have here drawn on A. P. Thornton, *The Imperial Idea and Its Enemies: A Study in British Power*, London, Macmillan, 1959.

67. I am grateful to Simon Winder for this point. For a discussion of reform see Mithi Mukherjee, *India in the Shadows of Empire: A Legal and Political History (1774–1950)*, Oxford, Oxford University Press, 2009, esp. pp. 134–6.

68. John Gallagher, 'Nationalisms and the Crisis of Empire, 1919–1922', *Modern Asian Studies*, 1/3 (1981), pp. 355–68, quotation at p. 361.

69. As quoted in Syed Hussein Alatas, *The Myth of the Lazy Native: A Study of the Image of the Malays, Filipinos and Javanese from the 16th to the 20th Century and Its Function in the Ideology of Colonial Capitalism*, London, Frank Cass, 1977, p. 46.

70. Kristian Coates Ulrichsen, *The Logistics and Politics of the British Campaigns in the Middle East, 1914–22*, London, Springer, 2010, pp. 143–8.

71. W. J. Berridge, 'Object Lessons in Violence: The Rationalities and Irrationalities of Urban Struggle during the Egyptian Revolution of 1919', *Journal of Colonialism and Colonial History*, 12/3 (2011), https://doi.org/10.1353/cch.2011.0025.

72. Judith M. Brown, *Gandhi's Rise to Power: Indian Politics, 1915–1922*, Cambridge, Cambridge University Press, 1972, p. 174.

73. Nick Lloyd, *The Amritsar Massacre: The Untold Story of One Fateful Day*, London, I.B. Tauris, 2011, is sympathetic to the government of India. For more critical analysis see Jon Wilson, *India Conquered: Britain's Raj and the Chaos of Empire*, London, Simon & Schuster, 2016, ch. 13; Helen Fein, *Imperial Crime and Punishment: The Massacre at Jallianwala Bagh and British Judgment, 1919–1920*, Honolulu, University of Hawaii Press, 1977.

74. Kim A. Wagner, ' "Calculated to Strike Terror": The Amritsar Massacre and the Spectacle of Colonial Violence', *Past and Present*, 233 (2016), pp. 185–225. This question is debated at more length in his new book, *Amritsar 1919: An Empire of Fear and the Making of a Massacre*, New Haven, CT, and London, Yale University Press, 2019.

75. Jawaharlal Nehru, *Towards Freedom: The Autobiography of Jawaharlal Nehru*, New York, John Day, 1941, p. 39.

76. Derek Sayer, 'British Reaction to the Amritsar Massacre, 1919–1920', *Past and Present*, 131 (1991), pp. 130–64, quotations at pp. 145–6; Purnima Bose, *Organizing Empire: Individualism, Collective Agency, and India*, Durham, NC, Duke University Press, 2003, p. 36.

77. Nehru, *Towards Freedom*, pp. 49–50.

78. Subho Basu, 'Strikes and "Communal" Riots in Calcutta in the 1890s: Industrial Workers, Bhadralok Nationalist Leadership and the Colonial State', *Modern Asian Studies*, 32/4 (1998), pp. 949–98.

79. Jon Lawrence, 'Forging a Peaceable Kingdom: War, Violence, and Fear of Brutalization in Post-First World War Britain', *Journal of Modern History*, 75/3 (2003), pp. 557–89, quotation at p. 575. See also the discussion in Neil James Mitchell, *Democracy's Blameless Leaders: From Dresden to Abu Ghraib, How Leaders Evade Accountability for Abuse, Atrocity, and Killing*, New York, New York University Press, 2012, ch. 4.

80. Martin Thomas, '"Paying the Butcher's Bill": Policing British Colonial Protest after 1918', *Crime, Histoire et Sociétés/Crime, History and Societies*, 15/2 (2011), pp. 55–76.

81. Here I am generalizing from Shiraishi, *An Age in Motion*.

82. Thanyathip Sripana, 'Tracing Ho Chi Minh's Sojourn in Siam', *Southeast Asian Studies*, 2/3 (2013), pp. 527–58, at p. 532.

83. Christopher E. Goscha, *Thailand and the Southeast Asian Networks of the Vietnamese Revolution, 1885–1954*, London, Routledge, 1998, pp. 43–6; Hue-Tam Ho Tai, *Radicalism and the Origins of the Vietnamese Revolution*, Cambridge, MA, Harvard University Press, 1992, pp. 63–4, quotation at p. 64.

84. Sripana, 'Tracing Ho Chi Minh's Sojourn in Siam', p. 533.

85. Centre des Archives Diplomatiques de Nantes, Pékin, Série A, 513PO/A, Fond 291 Bis, 'Extraits de Déclarations Faites à la Direction de la Sûreté Générale Indochinoise par l'Annamite, Le Van Phan Dit Hong Son', *c.* January 1933. Le Van Phan's victim was Phan Ba Ngoc, son of a noted official. For a discussion of this affair see David G. Marr, *Vietnamese Anticolonialism, 1885–1925*, Berkeley, University of California Press, 1971, pp. 239–40; Truong Buu Lam, *Colonialism Experienced: Vietnamese Writings on Colonialism, 1900–1931*, Ann Arbor, University of Michigan Press, 2000, p. 101.

86. ANM, Selangor Confidential 112/25, W. H. Lee Warner to W. G. Maxwell, 15 January 1923.

87. Benjamin C. Fortna, *The Circassian: A Life of Eşref Bey, Late Ottoman Insurgent and Special Agent*, Oxford, Oxford University Press, 2016, pp. 135–40, 255.

88. TNA, FO 371/5356, Secret Abstracts of Intelligence, Straits Settlements, for December 1919.

89. Michael Laffan, *Islamic Nationhood and Colonial Indonesia: The Umma below the Winds*, London, Routledge, 2003, p. 210; A. C. Milner, 'The Impact of the Turkish Revolution on Malaya', *Archipel*, 31 (1986), pp. 117–30. For Sukarno's later writings on the Turkish revolution and Atatürk see his *Under the Banner of Revolution* (1966), Jakarta, Yayasan Bung Karno, 2005.

90. Johan Mathew, 'Spectres of Pan-Islam: Methodological Nationalism and British Imperial Policy after the First World War', *Journal of Imperial and Commonwealth History*, 45/6 (2017), pp. 942–68.

91. Cited in Bülent Gökay, *Soviet Eastern Policy and Turkey, 1920–1991: Soviet Foreign Policy, Turkey and Communism*, London, Routledge, 2006, pp. 15–16.

92. For such a list see TNA, FO 262/1419, Ridout to HM Ambassador, Tokyo, 21 August 1919.

93. Patrizia Dogliani, 'The Fate of Socialist Internationalism', in Glenda Sluga and Patricia Clavin (eds), *Internationalisms: A Twentieth-Century History*, Cambridge, Cambridge University Press, 2016, pp. 38–60, at pp. 48–9.

94. As quoted in Duncan Hallas, *The Comintern*, new edn, Chicago, IL, Haymarket Books, 2008, p. 12.

95. James von Geldern, *Bolshevik Festivals, 1917–1920*, Berkeley, University of California Press, 1993, p. 178.

96. Gregor Benton, *Chinese Migrants and Internationalism: Forgotten Histories, 1917–1945*, London, Routledge, 2007, pp. 22–5; Mark O'Neill, *From the Tsar's Railway to the Red Army*, London, Penguin Specials, 2016.

97. Liu Shaozhou, 'Report on China', in John Riddell (ed.), *Founding the Communist International: Proceedings and Documents of the First Congress, March 1919*, New York, Anchor Foundation, 1987, pp. 204–6, at p. 206.

98. Ibid.

99. [Leon Trotsky], 'Manifesto of the Communist International to the Proletariat of the Entire World', 6 March 1919, in Jane Degras (ed.), *The Communist International, 1919–1943: Documents*, vol. I: *1919–1922*, London, Oxford University Press, 1956, pp. 38–47, at p. 43.

100. Liu Jianyi, 'The Origins of the Chinese Communist Party and the Role played by Soviet Russia and the Comintern', PhD thesis, University of York, 2000, pp. 70–77; Yoshihiro Ishikawa, *The Formation of the Chinese Communist Party*, New York, Columbia University Press, 2013, pp. 84–91. For Maikin see TNA, FO 228/3211, Straits Settlements, Secret Abstract of Intelligence, September 1918.

101. TNA, FO 371/5350, Straits Settlements Secret Abstract of Intelligence, March 1920.

102. Keith Hamilton, 'Gwatkin, Frank Trelawny Arthur Ashton (1889–1976)', *New Oxford Dictionary of National Biography*, https://doi.org/10.1093/ref:odnb/64923; Richard J. Popplewell, *Intelligence and Imperial Defence: British Intelligence and the Defence of the Indian Empire, 1904–1924*, London, Frank Cass, 1995, p. 283. For British anxieties see Antony Best, *British Intelligence and the Japanese Challenge in Asia, 1914–1941*, London, Springer, 2002, pp. 22–48.

103. TNA, FO 228/3211, British Minister, Peking, to Consul, Canton, 28 March 1919.

104. Ibid., Straits Settlements Secret Abstract of Intelligence, April 1918.
105. TNA, FO 262/1419, 'James Cousins', in Secretary Government of India to HM Ambassador Tokyo, 17 October 1919. For the context see Cemil Aydin, *The Politics of Anti-Westernism in Asia: Visions of World Order in Pan-Islamic and Pan-Asian Thought*, New York, Columbia University Press, 2007, pp. 121–4.
106. Eric Tagliacozzo, 'Kettle on a Slow Boil: Batavia's Threat Perceptions in the Indies' Outer Islands, 1870–1910', *Journal of Southeast Asian Studies*, 31/1 (2000), pp. 70–100, at pp. 85–6.
107. For the prophecy see Colin Wild and P. B. R. Carey (eds), *Born in Fire: The Indonesian Struggle for Independence: An Anthology*, Athens, Ohio University Press, 1986, pp. 9–10.
108. TNA, FO 228/3211, Straits Settlements, Secret Abstract of Intelligence, December 1917, January 1918, February 1918, March 1918.
109. Richard Louis Edmonds, 'The Legacy of Sun Yat-Sen's Railway Plans', *China Quarterly*, 111 (1987), pp. 421–43.
110. Marilyn A. Levine, *The Found Generation: Chinese Communists in Europe during the Twenties*, Seattle, University of Washington Press, 1993, p. 23.
111. Zhang Guotao, *The Rise of the Chinese Communist Party, 1921–1927: Volume One of the Autobiography of Chang Kuo-t'ao*, Lawrence, University Press of Kansas, 1971, pp. 40–44.
112. Timothy B. Weston, *The Power of Position: Beijing University, Intellectuals, and Chinese Political Culture, 1898–1929*, Berkeley, University of California Press, 2004, esp. pp. 114–81; Fabio Lanza, *Behind the Gate: Inventing Students in Beijing*, New York, Columbia University Press, 2010.
113. Lee Feigon, *Chen Duxiu, Founder of the Chinese Communist Party*, Princeton, NJ, Princeton University Press, 1983, p. 149.
114. Hans J. van de Ven, *From Friend to Comrade: The Founding of the Chinese Communist Party, 1920–27*, Berkeley, University of California Press, 1991, p. 17.
115. For a recent translation and introduction to the story see Lu Xun, *The Real Story of Ah-Q and Other Tales of China: The Complete Fiction of Lu Xun*, trans. and ed. Julia Lovell, London, Penguin, 2009.
116. Edward A. McCord, 'Warlords against Warlordism: The Politics of Anti-Militarism in Early Twentieth-Century China', *Modern Asian Studies*, 30/4 (1996), pp. 795–827.
117. Schwarcz, *The Chinese Enlightenment*, pp. 11–23; Weston, *The Power of Position*, pp. 175–81.
118. Zhang, *The Rise of the Chinese Communist Party*, p. 63.
119. Levine, *The Found Generation*, 1993, pp. 16–23; van de Ven, *From Friend to Comrade*, p. 17.
120. Joseph T. Chen, *The May Fourth Movement in Shanghai: The Making of a Social Movement in Modern China*, Leiden, Brill, 1971, esp. pp. 74–84;

Elizabeth J. Perry, *Shanghai on Strike: The Politics of Chinese Labor*, Stanford, CA, Stanford University Press, 1993, pp. 69–70.

121. Shakhar Rahav, *The Rise of Political Intellectuals in Modern China: May Fourth Societies and the Roots of Mass-Party Politics*, Oxford, Oxford University Press, 2015; Wen-hsin Yeh, *Provincial Passages: Culture, Space, and the Origins of Chinese Communism*, Berkeley, University of California Press, 1996.

122. Mao Zedong, 'The Great Union of the Popular Masses', pt 1, 21 July 1919, in Stuart Schram (ed.), *Mao's Road to Power: Revolutionary Writings, 1912–49*, vol. I: *The Pre-Marxist Period, 1912–1920*, reprint edn, London, Routledge, 2015, pp. 378–90, at p. 380.

123. Liyan Liu, 'The Man Who Molded Mao: Yang Changji and the First Generation of Chinese Communists', *Modern China*, 32/4 (2006), pp. 483–512.

124. Stephen R. Platt, *Provincial Patriots: The Hunanese and Modern China*, Cambridge, MA, Harvard University Press, 2007, pp. 189–91.

125. Zheng Chaolin, *An Oppositionist for Life: Memoirs of the Chinese Revolutionary Zheng Chaolin*, trans. and ed. Gregor Benton, Atlantic Highlands, NJ, Humanities Press, 1996, p. 2.

126. Paul Bailey, 'The Sino-French Connection: the Chinese Worker-Student Movement in France, 1902–1928', in David S. G. Goodman, *China and the West: Ideas and Activists*, Manchester, Manchester University Press, 1990, pp. 75–102, at pp. 82–8; Levine, *The Found Generation*, figure at p. 11.

127. Zheng Chaolin, 'A Consciousness Awakes', in Gregor Benton (ed.), *Prophets Unarmed: Chinese Trotskyists in Revolution, War, Jail, and the Return from Limbo*, Leiden, Brill, 2014, pp. 172–212, at p. 173.

128. René Onraet, *Singapore: A Police Background*, London, Dorothy Crisp and Co., 1947, p. 122.

129. This account draws on Lee Ting Hui, *Chinese Schools in British Malaya: Policies and Politics*, Singapore, South Seas Society, 2006, pp. 42–3; *Singapore Free Press and Mercantile Advertiser*, 2 July 1919 and 27 June 1919.

130. Yoji Akashi, 'The Nanyang Chinese Anti-Japanese and Boycott Movement, 1908–1928', *Journal of the South Seas Society*, 23 (1968), pp. 69–96, at pp. 73–5.

131. NARA, 846.d.00, Logan (Singapore) to Secretary of State, 23 June 1919.

132. TNA, FO 371/3816, Secret Appendix to War Diary of the General Staff, Straits Settlements Command for September 1919: 'Suspected Persons'.

133. TNA, FO 371/5356, Secret Abstract of Intelligence, Straits Settlements, for December 1919 and February 1920.

134. Lee, *Chinese Schools in British Malaya*, p. 43.

135. Arif Dirlik, *Anarchism in the Chinese Revolution*, Berkeley, University of California Press, 1991, pp. 148–96, esp. p. 149 for anarchism as a 'tongue'; Levine, *The Found Generation*, p. 30–31, quotation at p. 30.

136. C. F. Yong, *The Origins of Malayan Communism*, Singapore, South Seas Society, 1997, pp. 14–28, quotations at pp. 24 and 28.

137. Lee, *Chinese Schools in British Malaya*, pp. 43–5.

138. David L. Kenley, *New Culture in a New World: The May Fourth Movement and the Chinese Diaspora in Singapore, 1919–1932*, London, Routledge, 2003, quotation at pp. 78–9.

139. TNA, FO 371/3816, Secret Abstract of Intelligence, Straits Settlements, for August, 1919.

140. TNA, FO 371/5356, Secret Abstract of Intelligence, Straits Settlements, for July 1920.

141. Zheng Chaolin, 'A Consciousness Awakes', quotations at pp. 177–8 and 190. For the context, Levine, *The Found Generation*, pp. 99–103.

142. Gerrit Voerman, 'The Formative Years of the Communist "Moral Community" in the Netherlands, 1917–30', in Kevin Morgan, Gidon Cohen and Andrew Flinn (eds), *Agents of the Revolution: New Biographical Approaches to the History of International Communism in the Age of Lenin and Stalin*, Bern, Peter Lang, 2005, pp. 221–44, at pp. 226 and 234.

143. Tan Malaka, *From Jail to Jail*, trans. and ed. Helen Jarvis, Athens, Ohio University Center for International Studies, 1991, vol. I, p. 27.

144. Ibid., p. 25.

145. Ibid., p. 28.

146. Harry A. Poeze, *Tan Malaka: Strijder Voor Indonesië Vrijheid: Levensloop van 1897 tot 1945*, 's-Gravenhage, Nijhoff, 1976, pp. 53–6.

147. Ibid., pp. 74–5.

148. Tan Malaka, *From Jail to Jail*, vol. I, pp. 53–6.

149. TNA, FO 262/1419, Secret Abstract of Intelligence, October 1919.

10. TO THE NEW MECCA (1919–1921)

1. Minutes on FO 698/209/6, reprinted in Robert L. Jarman and K. Elizabeth Evans (eds), *Vietnam under French Rule, 1919–1946: The Nationalist Challenge and the Japanese Threat*, vol. I: *1919–1939*, Cambridge, Cambridge Archive Editions, 2017, pp. 96–7.

2. This account draws on Sophie Quinn-Judge, *Ho Chi Minh: The Missing Years, 1919–1941*, London, Hurst, 2003, pp. 11–28; William J. Duiker, *Ho Chi Minh: A Life*, New York, Hyperion, 2000, pp. 57–77. For the 'libel', ANOM/HCI/SPCE/364, 'Sûreté Générale Saigon à Hanoi', 22 July 1919.

3. ANOM, SLOTFOM III/29, 'Ministre des Colonies à M. Tirard, Haut-Commissaire de la République Française dans les provinces du Rhin', 16 June 1920.

4. ANOM/HCI/SPCE/364, L. Arnoux, 'Rapport de la Sûreté Genérale', September 1919.

5. ANOM/HCI/SPCE/364, 'De Guesde au Gouverneur-Général Hanoi', 29 December 1919.

6. ANOM/HCI/SPCE/364, 'Note de Jean', 10 December 1919.

7. ANOM/HCI/SPCE/364, 'Service de Renseignements à Hanoi', 5 December 1919.

8. Quinn-Judge, *Ho Chi Minh*, pp. 18–19.

9. ANOM/HCI/SPCE/364, 'Service de Renseignements au GG Indochine', 29 December 1919.

10. ANOM/HCI/SPCE/364, Devèze report, 23 October 1920.

11. For example, ANOM/HCI/SPCE/364, 'Note de la Préfecture de Police: Wang (Tsojo-se-Ming)', 30 January 1920.

12. ANOM/HCI/SPCE/364, 'Service de Renseignements à Hanoi', 5 December 1919.

13. ANOM/HCI/SPCE/364, 'Note: Renseignement sérieux', Hanoi, 8 March 1911; see also 'Renseignements complémentaires sur la famille de Nguyen-Tat-Thanh' and his Sûreté file.

14. ANOM/HCI/SPCE/364, Devèze report, 14 August 1920.

15. ANOM/HCI/SPCE/364, Devèze report, 27 August 1920; Devèze report, 6 November 1920.

16. ANOM/HCI/SPCE/364, Guesde au Préfet de Police, Hanoi, 17 August 1920.

17. Quinn-Judge, *Ho Chi Minh*, p. 30.

18. ANOM/HCI/SPCE/364, Devèze report, 16 October 1920.

19. ANOM/HCI/SPCE/364, Devèze report, 12 October 1920.

20. ANOM/HCI/SPCE/364, 'Nguyen Tat Thanh dit Nguyen Ai Quoc'.

21. ANOM, SLOTFOM III/29, 'Rapport d'ensemble sur les opérations du Contrôle Postal exécutées du 26 Juillet au 9 août 1920 sur les correspondances des Tirailleurs Indo-Chinois des T.M. 28 – 56 – 75 – 197 – 396 – 487 et 793', 15 August 1920.

22. Tyler Stovall, 'The Color Line behind the Lines: Racial Violence in France during the Great War', *American Historical Review*, 103/3 (1998), pp. 737–69; Tyler Stovall, *Paris and the Spirit of 1919: Consumer Struggles, Transnationalism, and Revolution*, Cambridge, Cambridge University Press, 2012, pp. 111–41, numbers of Vietnamese at p. 127; Erica J. Peters, 'Resistance, Rivalries, and Restaurants: Vietnamese Workers in Interwar France', *Journal of Vietnamese Studies*, 2/1 (2007), pp. 109–43.

23. Neil Evans, 'Across the Universe: Racial Violence and the Post-war Crisis in Imperial Britain, 1919–25', in Diane Frost (ed.), *Ethnic Labour and British Imperial Trade: A History of Ethnic Seafarers in the United Kingdom*, London, Routledge, 1995, pp. 59–88, quotations at pp. 63, 59.

24. For an excellent study of Paris in this period that begins with these connections see Michael Goebel, *Anti-Imperial Metropolis: Interwar Paris and the Seeds of Third World Nationalism*, Cambridge, Cambridge University Press, 2015, pp. 1–2; see also Michael Goebel, ' "The Capital of the Men

without a Country": Migrants and Anticolonialism in Interwar Paris',
American Historical Review, 121/5 (2016), pp. 1444–67.

25. Cai Chang, 'The proletarian revolutionary spirit will shine forever – In memory of Comrade Cai Hesen, an outstanding leader of our party in the early days', in *China Report: Red Flag* (Beijing), 6, 18 March 1980, pp. 38–43.

26. Andrea McElderry, 'Woman Revolutionary: Xiang Jingyu', *China Quarterly*, 105 (1986), pp. 95–122.

27. Stovall, *Paris and the Spirit of 1919*, pp. 118–19; Elizabeth J. Perry, 'From Paris to the Paris of the East and Back: Workers as Citizens in Modern Shanghai', *Comparative Studies in Society and History*, 41/2 (1999), pp. 348–73, at p. 352.

28. Zheng Chaolin, 'A Consciousness Awakes', in Gregor Benton, *Prophets Unarmed: Chinese Trotskyists in Revolution, War, Jail, and the Return from Limbo*, Leiden, Brill, 2014, pp. 172–212, at p. 188.

29. Hans J. van de Ven, *From Friend to Comrade: The Founding of the Chinese Communist Party, 1920–1927*, Berkeley, University of California Press, 1992, pp. 46–7, quotation at p. 47.

30. For the letter see Catherine Gipoulon, 'De Montargis à Pékin, en quête d'un plan pour la révolution: une lettre de Cai Hesen à Mao Zedong (13 Août 1920)', *Extrême-Orient Extrême-Occident*, 2 (1983), pp. 139–49.

31. For a classic study see Ann Laura Stoler, *Capitalism and Confrontation in Sumatra's Plantation Belt, 1870–1979*, Ann Arbor, University of Michigan Press, 1995, pp. 17–22, quotation at p. 22.

32. J. Thomas Lindblad, 'Coolies in Deli: Labour Conditions in Western Enterprises in East Sumatra, 1910–1938', in Vincent J. H. Houben and J. Thomas Lindblad (eds), *Coolie Labour in Colonial Indonesia: A Study of Labour Relations in the Outer Islands, c.1900–1940*, Wiesbaden, Otto Harrassowitz Verlag, 1999, pp. 51–3.

33. Tan Malaka, *From Jail to Jail*, trans. and ed. Helen Jarvis, Athens, Ohio University Center for International Studies, 1991, vol. I, p. 43.

34. Ibid.

35. A. J. Gooszen, *A Demographic History of the Indonesian Archipelago, 1880–1942*, Leiden, KITLV Press, 1999, pp. 200–201.

36. Stoler, *Capitalism and Confrontation*, pp. 21–5.

37. Tan Malaka to Dick Wijngaarden, 4 August 1920, reprinted in Harry A. Poeze, *Tan Malaka: Strijder Voor Indonesië Vrijheid: Levensloop van 1897 tot 1945*, 's-Gravenhage, Nijhoff, 1976, p. 107.

38. Stoler, *Capitalism and Confrontation*, pp. 47–70. See also Jan Breman, *Taming the Coolie Beast: Plantation Society and the Colonial Order in Southeast Asia*, Delhi, Oxford University Press, 1989. For the debate see Jan Breman, 'New Thoughts on Colonial Labour in Indonesia', *Journal of Southeast Asian Studies*, 33/2 (2002), pp. 333–9 and the response by Vincent J. H. Houben and J. Thomas Lindblad, 'Houben/Lindblad Reply to

Jan Breman's Review Article "New Thoughts on Colonial Labour in Indonesia"', *Journal of Southeast Asian Studies*, 33/3 (2002), pp. 559–60.

39. Tan Malaka to Dick Wijngaarden, 16 February 1920, reprinted in Poeze, *Tan Malaka*, p. 105.

40. Tan Malaka, *From Jail to Jail*, vol. I, p. 45.

41. Ann Laura Stoler, 'Rethinking Colonial Categories: European Communities and the Boundaries of Rule', *Comparative Studies in Society and History*, 31/1 (1989), pp. 134–61, at pp. 151–2.

42. Tan Malaka to Horensma, 1 September 1920 and 31 December 1920, reprinted in Poeze, *Tan Malaka*, pp. 100, 102.

43. Tan Malaka, *From Jail to Jail*, vol. I, p. 48.

44. Ibid., p. 59.

45. Tan Malaka to Dick Wijngaarden, 4 August 1920; I have taken and slightly adapted the translation of this letter in C. L. M. Penders (ed. and trans.), *Indonesia: Selected Documents on Colonialism and Nationalism, 1830–1942*, St Lucia, University of Queensland Press, 1977, p. 279.

46. Ruth T. McVey, *The Rise of Indonesian Communism*, Ithaca, NY, Cornell University Press, 1965, pp. 50–52. For a brief biography of Pieter Bergsma see https://socialhistory.org/bwsa/biografie/bergsma (in Dutch).

47. Tan Malaka to Dick Wijngaarden, 19 May 1920, in Poeze, *Tan Malaka*, p. 106.

48. I echo here Manu Goswami's description of the 'hard slog' of interwar internationalist politics, 'Imaginary Futures and Colonial Internationalisms', *American Historical Review*, 117/5 (2012), pp. 1461–85, at p. 1464.

49. Leon Trotsky, 'Great days', *Pravda*, 6 March 1919, in John Riddell (ed.), *Founding the Communist International: Proceedings and Documents of the First Congress, March 1919*, New York, Anchor Foundation, 1987, p. 303.

50. Lars T. Lih, *Lenin Rediscovered: What Is to Be Done? In Context*, Leiden, Brill, 2006, p. 472.

51. Victor Serge, *Memoirs of a Revolutionary*, New York, NYRB, 2012, p. 109.

52. Dan N. Jacobs, *Borodin: Stalin's Man in China*, Cambridge, MA, Harvard University Press, 1981, pp. 49–58.

53. Here I have cleaved closest to Phillips's first-hand account, Charles Shipman, *It Had to Be Revolution: Memoirs of an American Radical*, Ithaca, NY, Cornell University Press, 1993, pp. 82–33, and also *M. N. Roy's Memoirs* (1960), Delhi, Ajanta Publications, 1985, pp. 177–195.

54. Shipman, *It Had to Be Revolution*, pp. 86–9. For an account of the episode and Borodin's cultivation of his mystique see Lisa A. Kirschenbaum, 'Michael Gruzenberg/Mikhail Borodin: The Making of an International Communist', in Choi Chatterjee, Steven G. Marks, Mary Neuburger and Steven Sabol (eds), *The Global Impacts of Russia's Great War and Revolution, Book 2: The Wider Arc of Revolution, Part 1*, Bloomington, IN, Slavica Publishers, 2019, pp. 337–65, at pp. 360-3.

55. E.g. Muzaffar Ahmad, *Myself and the Communist Party of India, 1920–1929*, Calcutta, National Book Agency, 1970, p. 31.

56. Ruth Price, *The Lives of Agnes Smedley*, Oxford, Oxford University Press, 2005, pp. 64–82, quotation at p. 70.

57. Ibid., p. 220. For an interesting analysis of this part of Roy's career see Zaib un Nisa Aziz, 'Passages from India: Indian Anti-Colonial Activism in Exile, 1905–20', *Historical Research*, 90/248 (2017), pp. 404–21.

58. Lazar S. Kheifets and Viktor L. Kheifets, 'The Mexican Link in Spanish Communism: Michael Borodin's Mission to the Western Hemisphere in 1919–20 and the Creation of the Communist Party of Spain', *International Newsletter of Communist Studies Online*, XVI (2010), no. 23, pp. 79–88.

59. See Seema Sohi's excellent *Echoes of Mutiny: Race, Surveillance, and Indian Anticolonialism in North America*, Oxford, Oxford University Press, 2014, pp. 197–204.

60. Here I follow Daniela Spenser, *Stumbling Its Way through Mexico: The Early Years of the Communist International*, Tuscaloosa, University of Alabama Press, 2011, pp. 49–53.

61. Roy, *Memoirs*, p. 217.

62. Quoted in Spenser, *Stumbling Its Way through Mexico*, p. 59.

63. Shipman, *It Had to Be Revolution*, p. 90.

64. Roy, *Memoirs*, p. 231.

65. Kris Manjapra writes of his capacity to thrive in a 'fractious, amorphous intellectual landscape', *M. N. Roy: An Intellectual Biography of M. N. Roy*, New Delhi, Routledge India, 2010, p. 40.

66. Roy, *Memoirs*, quotation at p. 68.

67. A point made by J. Daniel Elam, 'Echoes of Ghadr: Lala Har Dayal and the Time of Anticolonialism', *Comparative Studies of South Asia, Africa and the Middle East*, 34/1 (2014), pp. 9–23.

68. Emily C. Brown, *Har Dayal: Hindu Revolutionary and Rationalist*, Tucson, University of Arizona Press, 1975, p. 219.

69. Ibid., pp. 218–36, quotation at p. 222. For the continuities in his thought see Shruti Kapila, 'Self, Spencer and Swaraj: Nationalist Thought and Critiques of Liberalism, 1890–1920', *Modern Intellectual History*, 4/1 (2007), pp. 109–27, at pp. 120–24.

70. Excerpt from Bhupendranath Dutta's Bengali memoir, *Aprakasita Rajnitik Itihash*, in Jyoti Basu (ed.), *Documents of the Communist Movement in India*, vol I: *1917–1928*, Calcutta, National Book Agency, 1997, pp. 96–7.

71. 'Mahendra Pratap on interview with Lenin', ibid., pp. 112–13.

72. As quoted in M. A. Persits, *Revolutionaries of India in Soviet Russia: Mainsprings of the Communist Movement in the East*, Moscow, Progress Publishers, 1983, p. 48.

73. For this remarkable life see Lina Bernstein, 'The Great Little Lady of the Bombay Art World: An Episode from an Émigré Life: The Russian Art-

ist Magda Nachman', in Christoph Flamm, Roland Marti and Ada Raev (eds), *Transcending the Borders of Countries, Languages, and Disciplines in Russian Émigré Culture*, Cambridge, Cambridge Scholars, 2018, pp. 143-58.

74. Serge, *Memoirs*, esp. pp. 84, 86.

75. Serge, *Memoirs*, p. 124.

76. William Gleason, 'Alexander Guchkov and the End of the Russian Empire', *Transactions of the American Philosophical Society*, 73/3 (1983), pp. 1-90, at pp. 77-8.

77. James H. Bater, 'St Petersburg and Moscow on the Eve of Revolution', in Daniel H. Kaiser (ed.), *The Workers' Revolution in Russia, 1917: The View from Below*, Cambridge, Cambridge University Press, 1987, pp. 20-57.

78. See the discussion of this, G. Adhikari, 'General Introduction', in G. Adhikari (ed.), *Documents of the History of the Communist Party of India*, vol. I: *1917-22*, New Delhi, People's Publishing House, 1971, pp. 30-32.

79. 'Letter from (?) to "Lord Byron" dated 5 Feb 1920 [Moscow]', in Purabi Roy, Sobhanlal Datta Gupta and Hari S. Vasudevan (eds), *Indo-Russian Relations, 1917-1947: Select Documents from the Archives of the Russian Federation, Part 1, 1917-1947*, Calcutta, Asiatic Society, 1999, vol. I, pp. 10-13. The author is in all probability Roy and the letter appears to have been written much later than February 1920.

80. Roy, *Memoirs*, p. 127.

81. Alfred Rosmer, *Lenin's Moscow*, London, Pluto Press, 1971, pp. 43-4; Roy, *Memoirs*, pp. 335-47. For his arrogance see Sibnarayan Ray (ed.), *Selected Works of M. N. Roy*, vol. II: *1923-1927*, Delhi, Oxford University Press, 1989, p. 17.

82. Rosmer, *Lenin's Moscow*, p. 92.

83. For this see Joy Gleason Carew, *Blacks, Reds, and Russians: Sojourners in Search of the Soviet Promise*, New Brunswick, NJ, Rutgers University Press, 2008, pp. 19-20.

84. Shipman, *It Had to Be Revolution*, p. 106.

85. See Brigitte Studer's excellent *The Transnational World of the Cominternians*, Basingstoke, Palgrave Macmillan, 2015, pp. 75-7, 131. However, her evidence is drawn mostly from the 1930s rather than the early years.

86. Hans Fredrik Dahl, *Quisling: A Study in Treachery*, Cambridge, Cambridge University Press, 1999, p. 45.

87. Shipman, *It Had to Be Revolution*, p. 105.

88. Robert Wohl, *French Communism in the Making, 1914-1924*, Stanford, CA, Stanford University Press, 1966, quotation at pp. 174 and 180-84.

89. Timothy J. Colton, *Moscow: Governing the Socialist Metropolis*, Cambridge, MA, Harvard University Press, 1998, pp. 116-19, 124-5, 757 for population numbers.

90. Serge, *Memoirs*, p. 121.

91. Shipman, *It Had to Be Revolution*, p. 105.

92. Rosmer, *Lenin's Moscow*, p. 65.

93. James von Geldern, *Bolshevik Festivals, 1917–1920*, Berkeley, University of California Press, 1993, pp. 178–99.

94. For this see Christoph Giebel, *Imagined Ancestries of Vietnamese Communism: Ton Duc Thang and the Politics of History and Memory*, Seattle, University of Washington Press, 2004.

95. Quoted in Allen S. Whiting, *Soviet Policies in China, 1917–1924*, Stanford, CA, Stanford University Press, 1954, p. 18.

96. As cited in Stephen White, 'Colonial Revolution and the Communist International, 1919–1924', *Science and Society*, 40/2 (1976), pp. 173–93, at pp. 180–81.

97. As observed by M. A. Persits, *Revolutionaries of India*, p. 278.

98. Much has been written on this debate. For a useful summary analysis see Tony Saich, *The Origins of the First United Front in China: The Role of Sneevliet (Alias Maring)*, vol. I, Leiden, Brill, 1991, pp. 12–25. I have followed his account of Sneevliet's role. See also John Patrick Haithcox, *Communism and Nationalism in India: M. N. Roy and Comintern Policy, 1920–1939*, Princeton, NJ, Princeton University Press, 1971, pp. 11–19.

99. M. N. Roy, 'India: Her Past, Present and Future', in Sibnarayan Ray (ed.), *Selected Works of M. N. Roy*, vol. I: *1917–1922*, Delhi, Oxford University Press, 1987, pp. 85–153, at p. 147.

100. M. N. Roy, 'Original Draft of Supplementary Theses on the National and Colonial Questions', in Ray (ed.), *Selected Works of M. N. Roy*, vol. I, pp. 164–8, at p. 167.

101. Michael Kemper, 'Red Orientalism: Mikhail Pavlovich and Marxist Oriental Studies In Early Soviet Russia', *Die Welt Des Islams*, 50/3 (2010), pp. 435–76.

102. Roy, 'India: Her Past, Present and Future', p. 153.

103. M. N. Roy, 'Hunger and Revolution in India', in Ray (ed.), *Selected Works of M. N. Roy*, vol. I, pp. 155–8, at p. 158.

104. Roy, 'India: Her Past, Present and Future', p. 153.

105. Eurocentrism is hardwired into the general histories of the Comintern and world communism. But for recent counter-currents see Stephen A. Smith, 'Introduction: Towards a Global History of Communism', in Stephen A. Smith (ed.), *The Oxford Handbook of the History of Communism*, Oxford, Oxford University Press, 2014, pp. 1–33; Vijay Prashad, *The Darker Nations: A People's History of the Third World*, New York, The New Press, 2008.

106. Saich, *The Origins of the First United Front in China*, vol. I, pp. 12–15.

107. 'Minutes of the Second Congress of the Communist International, Fifth Session', 28 July 1920, https://www.marxists.org/history/international/comintern/2nd-congress/ch05.htm (last accessed 27 May 2020).

108. Whiting, *Soviet Policies in China*, pp. 50–51.

109. Bernard B. Fall (ed.), *Ho Chi Minh: On Revolution, Selected Writings, 1920–66*, London, Pall Mall Press, 1968, pp. 6–7.

110. Harry J. Benda and Ruth T. McVey (eds), *The Communist Uprisings of 1926–1927 in Indonesia: Key Documents*, Jakarta, Equinox Publishing, 2009, pp. 97–8.

111. McVey, *Rise of Indonesian Communism*, pp. 61–75.

112. The best introduction to the episode remains Stephen White, 'Communism and the East: The Baku Congress, 1920', *Slavic Review*, 33/3 (1974), pp. 492–514, quotation at p. 498. For Reed see Serge, *Memoirs*, p. 127.

113. Cosroe Chaqueri, 'The Baku Congress', *Central Asian Survey*, 2/2 (1983), pp. 89–107, at p. 105.

114. John Riddell (ed.), *To See the Dawn: Baku, 1920: First Congress of the Peoples of the East*, New York, Pathfinder, 1993, p. 57.

115. Ronald Grigor Suny, *The Baku Commune, 1917–1918: Class and Nationality in the Russian Revolution*, Princeton, NJ, Princeton University Press, 1972, pp. 3–27.

116. Christopher Rice, 'Party Rivalry in the Caucasus: SRs, Armenians and the Baku Union of Oil Workers, 1907–08', *The Slavonic and East European Review*, 67/2 (1989), pp. 228–43.

117. Ronald Grigor Suny, 'Labor and Liquidators: Revolutionaries and the "Reaction" in Baku, May 1908–April 1912', *Slavic Review*, 34/2 (1975), pp. 319–40; Ronald Grigor Suny, 'A Journeyman for the Revolution: Stalin and the Labour Movement in Baku, June 1907–May 1908', *Soviet Studies*, 23/3 (1972), pp. 373–94.

118. Robert Service, *Stalin: A Biography*, London, Pan Macmillan, 2010, pp. 76–8, 81.

119. John Fisher, ' "On the Glacis of India": Lord Curzon and British Policy in the Caucasus, 1919', *Diplomacy and Statecraft*, 8/2 (1997), pp. 50–82, quotation from Churchill at p. 56; Sean Kelly, 'How Far West? Lord Curzon's Transcaucasian (Mis)Adventure and the Defence of British India, 1918–23', *International History Review*, 35/2 (2013), pp. 274–93, quotation from Montagu at p. 281. On the role of oil see Matthew Ghazarian, 'Obstruction as Power: Rethinking Britain's Caucasus Occupation 1918–20', *International History Review*, 39/4 (2017), pp. 654–66.

120. Cited in Kheifets and Kheifets, 'The Mexican link in Spanish Communism', p. 81.

121. Ibid., p. 158.

122. Michael G. Smith, 'Anatomy of a Rumour: Murder Scandal, the Musavat Party and Narratives of the Russian Revolution in Baku, 1917–20', *Journal of Contemporary History*, 36/2 (2001), pp. 211–40, at p. 228.

123. Tadeusz Swietochowski, *Russian Azerbaijan, 1905–1920: The Shaping of National Identity in a Muslim Community*, Cambridge, Cambridge University Press, 1985, pp. 187–90.

124. For Abdur Rab see G. Adhikari (ed.), 'General Introduction', *Documents of the History of the Communist Party of India*, vol.1, p. 17.

125. Riddell (ed.), *To See the Dawn*, p. 78.

126. Louise Bryant, *The Mirrors of Moscow*, New York, Thomas Seltzer, 1923, p. 35.

127. Douglas Taylor Northrop, *Veiled Empire: Gender and Power in Stalinist Central Asia*, Ithaca, NY, Cornell University Press, 2004, p. 80.

128. For an insightful biographic portrait see Şuhnaz Yilmaz, 'An Ottoman Warrior Abroad: Enver Paşa as an Expatriate', *Middle Eastern Studies*, 35/4 (1999), pp. 40–69; also Glen W. Swanson, 'Enver Pasha: The Formative Years', *Middle Eastern Studies*, 16/3 (1980), pp. 193–9; Charles D. Haley, 'The Desperate Ottoman: Enver Paşa and the German Empire: II', *Middle Eastern Studies*, 30/2 (1994), pp. 224–51.

129. I have here relied on the thorough reconstruction by Masayuki Yamauchi, *The Unromantic Exiles: Istanbul to Berlin – Enver Pasha 1919–1920*, Tokyo, Secretariat of the Research Project 'Urbanism in Islam', 1989, pp. 8–12.

130. H. G. Wells, *Russia in Shadows*, London, Hodder and Stoughton, 1920, p. 126; Bryant, *Mirrors of Moscow*, p. 157.

131. This image was used at the time; Haley, 'The Desperate Ottoman', p. 242.

132. Bryant, *Mirrors of Moscow*, p. 150; 'A Letter to Max Eastman in New York, From Louise Bryant in Moscow', 14 November 1920, published in *The Liberator* (New York), vol. IV, no. 2 (February 1921), pp. 11–12.

133. Chaqueri, 'The Baku Congress', p. 96.

134. Rosmer, *Lenin's Moscow*, p. 88.

135. Bryant, *Mirrors of Moscow*, p. 158.

136. Louis Fischer, 'The End of Enver Pasha', *The Virginia Quarterly Review*, 6/2 (1930), pp. 232–9; Bryant, *Mirrors of Moscow*, pp. 161–2; Yilmaz, 'An Ottoman Warrior Abroad', pp. 60–61; S. R. Sonyel, 'Enver Pasha and the Basmaji Movement in Central Asia', *Middle Eastern Studies*, 26/1 (1990), pp. 52–64, at pp. 61–3.

137. Quoted in Carolien Stolte and Harald Fischer-Tiné, 'Imagining Asia in India: Nationalism and Internationalism (ca. 1905–1940)', *Comparative Studies in Society and History*, 54/1 (2012), pp. 65–92, at p. 73.

138. Ayesha Jalal, 'Striking a Just Balance: Maulana Azad as a Theorist of Transnational *Jihad*', *An Intellectual History for India*, 4/1 (2007), pp. 95–107; Faridah Zaman, 'Revolutionary History and the Post-Colonial Muslim: Re-Writing the "Silk Letters Conspiracy" of 1916', *South Asia: Journal of South Asian Studies*, 39/3 (2016), pp. 626–43.

139. Thomas Wide, 'The Refuge of the World: Afghanistan and the Muslim Imagination, 1880–1920', DPhil, University of Oxford, 2014; Nile Green, 'The Trans-Border Traffic of Afghan Modernism: Afghanistan and the Indian "Urdusphere"', *Comparative Studies in Society and History*, 53/3 (2011), pp. 479–508.

140. A version of Rafiq's account appears in Muzaffar Ahmad, *The Communist Party of India and Its Formation Abroad*, National Book Agency, 1962, quotation at p. 27.

141. For Indians at Baku see Adhikari (ed.), 'General Introduction', *Documents of the History of the Communist Party of India*, vol. I, p. 48.

142. F. M. Bailey, *Mission to Tashkent*, London, Jonathan Cape, 1946, detail from p. 32.

143. Lina Bernstein, 'Indian Nationalists' Cooperation with Soviet Russia in Central Asia: The Case of M. P. T. Acharya', in A. Barker, M. E. Pereira, M. T. Cortez, P. A. Pereira and O. Martins (eds), *Personal Narratives, Peripheral Theatres: Essays on the Great War (1914–18)*, Cham, Switzerland, Springer, 2018, pp. 201–14.

144. There have been various versions of the timing of this journey, but the Comintern archive makes it quite clear; see 'Letter of (?) [Roy] dated 4 October to Ya. Z. Suritz' and his report, in Roy et al. (eds), *Indo-Russian Relations, 1917–1947*, pp. 82–5.

145. Naeem M. Qureshi, 'From Pan-Islamism to Communism: The Russian Connection to the Indian *Muhajirin*, 1920–1924', *Journal of South Asian and Middle Eastern Studies*, 32/1 (2008), pp. 30–61.

146. Persits, *Revolutionaries of India*, pp. 81–3.

147. There is much material on this moment. Persits, *Revolutionaries of India*, written in the Soviet period and with early access to Soviet archives, is hostile to Roy, and gives an interesting account of Rab's views on pp. 57–61.

148. Acharya to the ECCI, 30 January 1930, quoted in Persits, *Revolutionaries of India*, p. 192.

149. For the continuities and connections see Kris Manjapra, 'Communist Internationalism and Transcolonial Recognition', in Sugata Bose and Kris Manjapra (eds), *Cosmopolitan Thought Zones: South Asia and the Global Circulation of Ideas*, London, Palgrave Macmillan, 2010, pp. 159–77; Carolien Stulte, 'Uniting the Oppressed Peoples of the East: Revolutionary Internationalism in an Asian Inflection', in Raza Ali, Franziska Roy and Benjamin Zachariah (eds), *The Internationalist Moment: South Asia, Worlds, and World Views, 1917–1939*, London, SAGE, 2015, pp. 56–85.

150. Ahmad, *The Communist Party of India and Its Formation Abroad*, p. 30.

151. 'Letter from (?) [Abani Mukherji] dated 30 December 1920 to Shiva Prasad Gupta [Benares]', in Roy et al. (eds), *Indo-Russian Relations, 1917–1947*, pp. 44–50, at pp. 46–7.

152. 'Letter of (?) [M. N. Roy] dated 12 August 1920 to Arabinda Ghose', in ibid., pp. 27–30.

153. 'Copy of Letter of Provisional All India Central Revolutionary Committee Dated 24 January 1921 to M. P. T. Acharya Removing Him from Membership of the Committee', in ibid., pp. 57–8.

154. 'Letter from (?) to V. I. Lenin regarding differences with G. Zinoviev and

Abdur Rabb Barq on the Indian question', 19 March 1921, Moscow, in ibid., pp. 60–62.

155. 'Minutes of a meeting of Indian revolutionaries dated 3 April 1921 at Tashkent', in ibid., pp. 62–74.

156. 'Copy of Telegram dated 14 March 1921, sent by Carl Steinhardt and D. Zetkin to the Small Bureau of Comintern', in ibid, pp. 59–60.

157. 'Resolutions of the IRA, Tashkent dated 27 April 1921 on allegations against the activities of M. N. Roy and Abani Mukherji', in ibid., p. 66.

158. Persits, *Revolutionaries of India*, p. 94.

159. 'Evelyn Roy's signed report of trip to Germany, France and England dated 7 August 1921', in Roy et al. (eds), *Indo-Russian Relations, 1917–1947*, pp. 92–5, quotation at p. 93.

160. There are conflicting reports of Chatto's first visit. He later (1934) drew a veil over the journey, although credible evidence exists for it; see Nirode K. Barooah, *Chatto: The Life and Times of an Anti-Imperialist in Europe*, New Delhi, Oxford University Press, 2004, pp. 158–9; and his 'Letter to the Mandate Commission dated 25 June 1921' mentions a meeting with Karakhan 'in Moscow' in November and December 1920, in Roy et al. (eds), *Indo-Russian Relations, 1917–1947*, pp. 101–3.

161. Roy, *Memoirs*, p. 488.

162. Barooah, *Chatto*, p. 170; 'Agnes Smedley's signed forwarding letter ... dated 5 August 1921 to the Small Bureau of Comintern', in Roy et al. (eds), *Indo-Russian Relations, 1917–1947*, pp. 86–92, quotation at p. 88.

163. For a defence of Abani see Gautam Chattopadhyay, *Communism and Bengal's Freedom Movement*, vol. I: *1917–29*, New Delhi, People's Publishing House, 1970, pp. 24–8.

164. 'Virendranath Chattopadhyaya's speech [1934]', in G. Adhikari, *Documents of the History of the Communist Party of India*, vol. I: *1917–22*, New Delhi, People's Publishing House 1971, pp. 85–7.

165. Barooah, *Chatto*, pp. 163–6.

166. Basu (ed.), *Documents of the Communist Movement in India*, p. 103.

167. Serge, *Memoirs*, pp. 112–13.

168. Barooah, *Chatto*, p. 160.

169. Roy, *Memoirs*, p. 493.

170. Bülent Gökay, *Soviet Eastern Policy and Turkey, 1920–1991: Soviet Foreign Policy, Turkey and Communism*, London, Routledge, 2006, pp. 23–30, quotation at p. 30.

171. Joel Beinin and Zachary Lockman, *Workers on the Nile: Nationalism, Communism, Islam, and the Egyptian Working Class, 1882–1954*, Cairo, American University in Cairo Press, 1998, pp. 139–40.

172. Devendra Kaushik and Leonid Mitrokhin (eds), *Lenin: His Image in India*, Delhi, Vikas, 1970; Veena Choudhury, *Indian Nationalism and External*

Forces (1920–47), Delhi, Capital Publishing House, 1984, Gandhi quotation at p. 41.

173. See the richly evocative study by Suchetana Chattopadhyay, *An Early Communist: Muzaffar Ahmad in Calcutta, 1913–1929*, New Delhi, Tulika Books, 2011, pp. 7–43.

174. S. A. Dange, 'Gandhi vs. Lenin' (excerpts), in Adhikari (ed.), *Documents of the History of the Communist Party of India*, vol. I, pp. 288–9.

175. Sir Cecil Kaye, *Communism in India, with Unpublished Documents from National Archives of India (1921–1924)*, compiled and edited by Subodh Roy, Calcutta, Editions India, 1971, p, 19.

176. Alexander Pantsov and Steven I. Levine, *Deng Xiaoping: A Revolutionary Life*, Oxford, Oxford University Press, 2015, p. 26.

177. Chae-Jin Lee, *Zhou Enlai: The Early Years*, Stanford, CA, Stanford University Press, 1994, pp. 152–7.

178. Pantsov and Levine, *Deng Xiaoping*, pp. 25–7.

179. See esp. Marilyn A. Levine, *The Found Generation: Chinese Communists in Europe during the Twenties*, Seattle, University of Washington Press, 1993, pp. 121–31; Hu Hua, *The Early Life of Zhou Enlai*, Beijing, Foreign Languages Press, 1980, pp. 88–9.

11. REBELS IN RUBBER SOLES (1921–1922)

1. Laura Engelstein, *Russia in Flames: War, Revolution, Civil War*, Oxford, Oxford University Press, 2018, pp. 417–44.

2. Mark Gamsa, 'Harbin in Comparative Perspective', *Urban History*, 37/1 (2010), pp. 136–49.

3. Olga Bakich, 'Russian Emigrés in Harbin's Multinational Past: Censuses and Identity', in Dan Ben-Canaan, Frank Grüner and Ines Prodöhl (eds), *Entangled Histories: The Transcultural Past of Northeast China*, London, Springer, 2014, pp. 83–100, at p. 88; Joshua A. Fogel, 'The Japanese and the Jews: A Comparative Analysis of their Communities in Harbin, 1898–1930', in Robert Bickers and Christian Henriot (eds), *New Frontiers: Imperialism's New Communities in East Asia, 1842–1953*, Manchester, Manchester University Press, 2000, pp. 88–108.

4. Blaine R. Chiasson, *Administering the Colonizer: Manchuria's Russians under Chinese Rule, 1918–29*, Vancouver, UBC Press, 2010, ch. 3, esp. p. 48.

5. James Carter, 'Struggle for the Soul of a City: Nationalism, Imperialism, and Racial Tension in 1920s Harbin', *Modern China*, 27/1 (2001), pp. 91–116.

6. For this see Arthur Waldron, 'The Warlord: Twentieth-century Chinese Understandings of Violence, Militarism, and Imperialism', *American Historical Review*, 96/4 (1991), pp. 1073–1100; Edward A. McCord, *The*

Power of the Gun: The Emergence of Modern Chinese Warlordism, Berkeley, University of California Press, 1993.

7. Allen S. Whiting, *Soviet Policies in China, 1917–1924*, Stanford, CA, Stanford University Press, 1954, quotation at p. 22, pp. 110–11.

8. Xenia Joukoff Eudin and Harold H. Fisher (eds), *Soviet Russia and the West, 1920–1927: A Documentary Survey*, Stanford, CA, Stanford University Press, 1957, p. 217.

9. Yoshihiro Ishikawa, *The Formation of the Chinese Communist Party*, New York, Columbia University Press, 2013, pp. 90–91. For an exhaustive list of reported contacts see Liu Jianyi, 'The Origins of the Chinese Communist Party and the Role Played by Soviet Russia and the Comintern', PhD thesis, University of York, 2000, pp. 67–119.

10. Li Yu-ning and Michael Gasster, 'Ch'u Ch'iu-Pai's Journey to Russia, 1920–1922', *Monumenta Serica*, 29 (1970), pp. 537–56; Karakhan text as quoted in Robert T. Pollard, *China's Foreign Relations, 1917–1931*, London, Macmillan, 1933, p. 126.

11. Whiting, *Soviet Policies in China*, pp. 29–33.

12. George M. Beckmann and Genji Okubo, *The Japanese Communist Party, 1922–1945*, Stanford, CA, Stanford University Press, 1969, pp. 39–45.

13. Elizabeth McGuire, *Red at Heart: How Chinese Communists Fell in Love with the Russian Revolution*, New York, Oxford University Press, 2017, pp. 74–5; Stephen A. Smith, *A Road Is Made: Communism in Shanghai, 1920–1927*, London, Routledge, 2000, pp. 18–19.

14. Whiting, *Soviet Policies in China*, p. 96.

15. Jean Chesneaux, *The Chinese Labor Movement, 1919–1927*, Stanford, CA, Stanford University Press, 1968, p. 157.

16. Eudin and Fisher (eds), *Soviet Russia and the West, 1920–1927*, p. 218.

17. Leslie H. Dingyan Chen, *Chen Jiongming and the Federalist Movement: Regional Leadership and Nation Building in Early Republican China*, Ann Arbor, University of Michigan Press, 1999, esp. pp. 97–109.

18. For the legal situation see Pollard, *China's Foreign Relations*, pp. 153–5. For an indispensable general survey see Marcia R. Ristaino, *Port of Last Resort: The Diaspora Communities of Shanghai*, Stanford, CA, Stanford University Press, 2001.

19. Bryna Goodman, 'Semi-Colonialism, Transnational Networks and News Flows in Early Republican Shanghai', *China Review*, 4/1 (2004), pp. 55–88. For Sokolsky see TNA, FO 371/3816, 'Secret Appendix to War Diary of the General Staff, Straits Settlements Command for September 1919: Suspected Persons'.

20. Paul Fussell, *Abroad: British Literary Traveling Between the Wars*, Oxford, Oxford University Press, 1979.

21. TNA, FO 371/3816, 'Secret Appendix to War Diary of the General Staff, Straits Settlements Command for September 1919: Suspected Persons'.

22. Tom Genrich, *Authentic Fictions: Cosmopolitan Writing of the Troisième République, 1908–1940*, Oxford, Peter Lang, 2004, pp. 93–141.

23. Brian G. Martin, *The Shanghai Green Gang: Politics and Organized Crime, 1919–1937*, Berkeley, University of California Press, 1996, pp. 30–35; Frederic Wakeman, *Policing Shanghai, 1927–1937*, Berkeley, University of California Press, 1995, pp. 6–8.

24. For example, Leo Ou-fan Lee, *Shanghai Modern: The Flowering of a New Urban Culture in China, 1930–1945*, Cambridge, MA, Harvard University Press, 1999; Wen-Hsin Yeh, *Shanghai Splendor: Economic Sentiments and the Making of Modern China, 1843–1949*, Berkeley, University of California Press, 2007; Alexander Des Forges, *Mediasphere Shanghai: The Aesthetics of Cultural Production*, Honolulu, University of Hawaii Press, 2007.

25. For the 'Worlds' see Zhen Zhang, *An Amorous History of the Silver Screen: Shanghai Cinema, 1896–1937*, Chicago, IL, University of Chicago Press, 2005, pp. 58–64. For the world fair comparisons and much else besides see Meng Yue, *Shanghai and the Edges of Empires*, Minneapolis, University of Minnesota Press, 2006, pp. 183–206; see also Andrew Field, *Shanghai's Dancing World: Cabaret Culture and Urban Politics, 1919–1954*, Hong Kong, Chinese University Press, 2010, *passim*. For the underside of this see Christian Henriot, *Prostitution and Sexuality in Shanghai: A Social History, 1849–1949*, Cambridge, Cambridge University Press, 2001.

26. Wong Yunn Chii and Tan Kar Lin, 'Emergence of a Cosmopolitan Space for Culture and Consumption: The New World Amusement Park – Singapore (1923–70) in the Interwar Years', *Inter-Asia Cultural Studies*, 5/2 (2004), pp. 279–304. For 'World Fever' see Zhang, *An Amorous History of the Silver Screen*, p. 58.

27. Perry Link, 'Traditional-Style Popular Urban Fiction in the Teens and Twenties', in Merle Goldman (ed.), *Modern Chinese Literature in the May Fourth Era*, Cambridge, MA, Harvard University Press, 1977, pp. 327–50, at p. 337.

28. For this see Lam Nga Li, 'New World, *New World Daily* and the Culture of Amusement in early Republican Shanghai', PhD thesis, Hong Kong University of Science and Technology, 2015, quotation at p. 29.

29. Lu Hanchao, *Beyond the Neon Lights: Everyday Shanghai in the Early Twentieth Century*, Berkeley, University of California Press, 1999, p. 10.

30. Lee Feigon, *Chen Duxiu, Founder of the Chinese Communist Party*, Princeton, NJ, Princeton University Press, 1983, pp. 157–60.

31. Bryna Goodman, *Native Place, City, and Nation: Regional Networks and Identities in Shanghai, 1853–1937*, Berkeley, University of California Press, 1995, esp. pp. 197, 258.

32. Lu, *Beyond the Neon Lights*, p. 368, fn. 101. See also Chenlan Zhao, 'From Shikumen to New-style: A Re-reading of Lilong Housing in Modern

Shanghai', in James Madge and Andrew Peckham (eds), *Narrating Architecture: A Retrospective Anthology*, London, Routledge, 2006, pp. 453–78.

33. Mark Gamsa, *The Chinese Translation of Russian Literature: Three Studies*, Leiden, Brill, 2008, pp. 242–5.

34. Hans J. van de Ven, *From Friend to Comrade: The Founding of the Chinese Communist Party, 1920–1927*, Berkeley, University of California Press, 1992, pp. 59–64. For the 'Y', Charles A. Keller, 'The Christian Student Movement, YMCAs, and Transnationalism in Republican China', *Journal of American-East Asian Relations* 13 (2004), pp. 55–80.

35. Smith, *A Road Is Made*, pp. 24–5.

36. A principal argument of Ishikawa, *The Formation of the Chinese Communist Party*, pp. 7–8, 24–39 and *passim*.

37. Nick Knight, *Li Da and Marxist Philosophy in China*, London, Routledge, 1996, ch. 3.

38. Harold R. Isaacs and Albert Treint, 'Documents on the Comintern and the Chinese Revolution', *China Quarterly*, 45 (1971), pp. 105–6. For an elaboration of this, and of the importance of Sneevliet's role, see Dov Bing, 'Sneevliet and the Early Years of the CCP', *China Quarterly*, 48 (1971), pp. 677–97.

39. Tony Saich, *The Origins of the First United Front in China: The Role of Sneevliet (alias Maring)*, Leiden, Brill, 1991, pp. 32–3; Michael Williams, 'Sneevliet and the Birth of Asian Communism', *New Left Review*, 123 (1980), pp. 81–90.

40. For the account of the meeting in this paragraph and the following I have drawn chiefly on van de Ven, *From Friend to Comrade*, pp. 85–97, and Ishikawa, *The Formation of the Chinese Communist Party*, pp. 227–93.

41. Lee, *Chen Duxiu*, pp. 164–5.

42. C. F. Yong and R. B. McKenna, *Kuomintang Movement in British Malaya, 1912–1949*, Singapore, National University of Singapore Press, 1990.

43. Shao Chuan Leng and Norman D. Palmer, *Sun Yat-sen and Communism*, New York, Praeger, 1960, pp. 48–50.

44. Isaacs and Treint, 'Documents on the Comintern and the Chinese Revolution', p. 104.

45. 'Report of Comrade H. Maring to the Executive', 11 July 1922, in Tony Saich (ed.), *The Rise to Power of the Chinese Communist Party: Documents and Analysis*, Armonk, NY, M. E. Sharpe, 1996, p. 28.

46. TNA, FO 228/3276, 'Canton Intelligence Report, December Quarter, 1922'.

47. For the detail see Wilbur C. Martin, 'Problems of Starting a Revolutionary Base: Sun Yatsen and Canton, 1923', *Bulletin of the Institute of Modern History* (Taipei), 2/4 (1971), p. 8.

48. For a detailed study see Ming K. Chan, 'Labor and Empire: The Chinese Labor Movement in the Canton Delta, 1895–1927', PhD thesis, Stanford University, 1977.

49. Daniel Y. K. Kwan, *Marxist Intellectuals and the Chinese Labor Movement: A Study of Deng Zhongxia (1894–1933)*, Seattle, University of Washington Press, 1997, pp. 54–5.

50. For this see Arif Dirlik, *Anarchism in the Chinese Revolution*, Berkeley, University of California Press, 1991.

51. Kwan, *Marxist Intellectuals and the Chinese Labor Movement*, p. 86.

52. TNA, FO 228/3276, 'Canton Intelligence Report, March Quarter, 1921'.

53. Issue of 17 March 1921, cited in Chen, *Chen Jiongming*, p. 128.

54. For the strike see Chan Wei Kwan, *The Making of Hong Kong Society: Three Studies of Class Formation in Early Hong Kong*, Oxford, Clarendon Press, 1991, pp. 166–91; Jean Chesneaux, *The Chinese Labor Movement, 1919–1927*, Stanford, CA, Stanford University Press, 1968, pp. 180–85; for events in Canton see Chen, *Chen Jiongming*, pp. 146–7.

55. TNA, FO 228/3276, 'Canton Intelligence Report, June Quarter, 1922'.

56. For this see Ming K. Chan, 'Hong Kong in Sino-British Conflict: Mass Mobilization and the Crisis of Legitimacy, 1912–26', in Ming K. Chan (ed.), *Precarious Balance: Hong Kong between China and Britain, 1842–1992*, London, Routledge, 1997, pp. 27–57, at pp. 43–4.

57. Isaacs and Treint, 'Documents on the Comintern and the Chinese Revolution', pp. 100–115, at p. 103.

58. H. Maring 'Explanatory Memorandum', 11 July 1922, in Tony Saich and Benjamin Yang (eds), *The Rise to Power of the Chinese Communist Party: Documents and Analysis*, Armonk, NY, Sharpe, 1996, p. 33.

59. Saich (ed.), *The Rise to Power of the Chinese Communist Party*, pp. 90–91.

60. Chen, *Chen Jiongming*, pp. 165–206; Marie-Claire Bergère, *Sun Yat-sen*, Stanford, CA, Stanford University Press, 2000, pp. 299–303.

61. *Huazi Ribao*, 14 July 1921, cited in Chen, *Chen Jiongming*, p. 221.

62. H. D. Special Volume no. 60-D (a) of 1919, quoting a report from the superintendent, Port Blair, in Government of Bombay, *Source Material for a History of the Freedom Movement, vol. 11*, p. 464.

63. A. G. Noorani, 'Savarkar's Mercy Petition', *Frontline*, 22/7 (12–15 March 2005), https://frontline.thehindu.com/the-nation/article30204154.ece (last accessed 22 May 2020).

64. 'Jail History Ticket of V. D. Savarkar, in Government of Bombay, *Source Material for a History of the Freedom Movement*, vol. II, pp. 478–81.

65. There is a large literature on this, but focusing on the prison context see Choi Chatterjee, 'Imperial Incarcerations: Ekaterina Breshko-Breshkovskaia, Vinayak Savarkar, and the Original Sins of Modernity', *Slavic Review*, 74/4 (2015), pp. 850–72, esp. pp. 862–4; Vinayak Chaturvedi, 'Rethinking Knowledge with Action: V. D. Savarkar, the Bhagavad Gita, and Histories of Warfare', *Modern Intellectual History*, 7/2 (2010), pp. 417–35, esp. pp. 425–30.

66. Bhai Parmanand, *The Story of My Life*, Lahore, The Central Hindu Yuvak Sabha, 1934, pp. 174, 180, 187.
67. Government of India, *Report of the Indian Jails Committee (1919–1920)*, vol. I, Simla, Government Press, 1920, esp. pp. 296, 277–8. Discussed in Aparna Vaidik, *Imperial Andamans: Colonial Encounter and Island History*, Basingstoke, Palgrave Macmillan, 2010, pp. 169–73, for 'cult' p. 172. For colonial perceptions see Manju Ludwig, 'Murder in the Andamans: A Colonial Narrative of Sodomy, Jealousy and Violence', *South Asia Multidisciplinary Academic Journal*, 2013, https://doi.org/10.4000/samaj.3633 (last accessed 23 May 2020), and for distinctions of dress see Clare Anderson, *Legible Bodies: Race, Criminality and Colonialism in South Asia*, Oxford, Berg, 2004, p. 179.
68. Taylor C. Sherman, 'From Hell to Paradise? Voluntary Transfer of Convicts to the Andaman Islands, 1921–1940', *Modern Asian Studies*, 43/2 (2009), pp. 367–88.
69. Peter Zinoman, *The Colonial Bastille: A History of Imprisonment in Vietnam, 1862–1940*, Berkeley, University of California Press, 2001; Lorraine M. Paterson, 'Ethnoscapes of Exile: Political Prisoners from Indochina in a Colonial Asian World', *International Review of Social History*, 63/S26 (2018), pp. 89–107.
70. Matthias van Rossum, 'The Carceral Colony: Colonial Exploitation, Coercion, and Control in the Dutch East Indies, 1810s–1940s', *International Review of Social History*, 63/S26 (2018), pp. 65–88, at pp. 83–7.
71. Mathieu Deflem, *Policing World Society: Historical Foundations of International Police Cooperation*, Oxford, Oxford University Press, 2002, p. 123.
72. Ban Kah Choon, *Absent History: The Untold Story of Special Branch Operations in Singapore 1915 to 1942*, Singapore, Raffles, 2001, pp. 74–84; fingerprinting, p. 66; TNA, FO 371/8053, 'Malayan Bureau of Political Intelligence, Report on First Year (1922)', October 1922.
73. TNA, FO 371/8053, 'Malayan Bureau of Political Intelligence, Report on First Year (1922)', October 1922.
74. As argued by L. P. Morris, 'British Secret Missions in Turkestan, 1918–19', *Journal of Contemporary History*, 12/2 (1977), pp. 363–79. For a more sympathetic interpretation of Bailey's role see Peter Hopkirk, *Setting the East Ablaze: On Secret Service in Bolshevik Asia*, Oxford, Oxford University Press, 1986.
75. Michael Silvestri, 'The Thrill of "Simply Dressing Up": The Indian Police, Disguise, and Intelligence Work in Colonial India', *Journal of Colonialism and Colonial History*, 2/2 (2001), p. 25.
76. Richard J. Popplewell, *Intelligence and Imperial Defence: British Intelligence and the Defence of the Indian Empire, 1904–1924*, London, Frank Cass, 1995, pp. 309–16.
77. Sir Cecil Kaye, *Communism in India, with Unpublished Documents from*

National Archives of India (1921–1924), compiled and ed. Subodh Roy, Calcutta, Editions India, 1971, pp. 14–15.

78. Muzaffar Ahmad, *Myself and the Communist Party of India, 1920–1929*, Calcutta, National Book Agency, 1970, pp. 288–9.

79. Muzaffar Ahmad, *The Communist Party of India and Its Formation Abroad*, Calcutta, National Book Agency, 1962, pp. 112–15, quotation at p. 114; Kaye, *Communism in India*, p. 7.

80. B. C. Ellison, 'HRH The Prince of Wales shoots in India in 1921 and 1922 – Part 1', *Journal of the Bombay Natural History Society*, 28/3 (1922), pp. 675–97, at p. 673.

81. Ibid. For the film see http://www.colonialfilm.org.uk/node/207.

82. Philip Ziegler (ed.), *The Diaries of Lord Louis Mountbatten 1920–1922: Tours with the Prince of Wales*, London, Collins, 1987, pp. 220–21.

83. Edward Windsor, *A King's Story: The Memoirs of the Duke of Windsor*, London, Putnam, 1951, p. 163.

84. *Straits Times*, 24 October 1921.

85. Lord Kinross, *The Windsor Years: The Life of Edward, as Prince of Wales, King, and Duke of Windsor*, London, Penguin Books, 1980, p. 107.

86. NAI, Home Department, Political No. 303 of 1921, Appendix 1: 'Tabulated statement of attempts to tamper with Indian Troops', 11 October 1921; Appendix II: Notable instances of disorder during the war 1921.

87. See Renisa Mawani, *Across Oceans of Law: The* Komagata Maru *and Jurisdiction in the Time of Empire*, Durham, NC, Duke University Press, 2018, pp. 206–11, for the observation about the Ingress law, pp. 205–6.

88. Windsor, *A King's Story*, p. 174.

89. NAI, Home Department, Political No. 303 of 1921, 'Extract from the report of the Sind CID dated 12 November 1921'. For Bardoli see David Hardiman, *Peasant Nationalists of Gujarat: Kheda District 1917–1934*, Delhi, Oxford University Press, 1981, pp. 151–55.

90. Dinyar Patel, 'Beyond Hindu-Muslim Unity: Gandhi, the Parsis and the Prince of Wales Riots of 1921', *The Indian Economic and Social History Review*, 55/2 (2018), pp. 221–47.

91. D. A. Low, 'The Government of India and the First Non-Cooperation Movement – 1920–1922', *Journal of Asian Studies*, 25/2 (1966), pp. 241–59.

92. Quoted in Rajnarayan Chandavarkar, *The Origins of Industrial Capitalism in India: Business Strategies and the Working Classes in Bombay, 1900–1940*, Cambridge, Cambridge University Press, 2002, p. 413.

93. Hardiman, *Peasant Nationalists of Gujarat*, p. 138.

94. Robert L. Hardgrave, 'The Mappilla Rebellion, 1921: Peasant Revolt in Malabar', *Modern Asian Studies*, 11/1 (1977), pp. 57–99, quotation at p. 75.

95. Ibid.; D. N. Dhanagare, 'Agrarian Conflict, Religion and Politics: The Moplah Rebellions in Malabar in the Nineteenth and Early Twentieth Centuries', *Past and Present*, 74 (1977), pp. 112–41.

96. Hardgrave, 'The Mappilla Rebellion, 1921', p. 90.

97. *The Prince of Wales' Eastern Book: A Pictorial Record of the Voyages of HMS 'Renown' 1921–22*, St Dunstan's, London, 1922, n.p.

98. Ziegler (ed.), *The Diaries of Lord Louis Mountbatten*, p. 212.

99. Windsor, *A King's Story*, p. 169.

100. *The Prince of Wales' Eastern Book.*

101. Chandrika Kaul, *Reporting the Raj: The British Press and India, c. 1880–1922*, Manchester, Manchester University Press, 2003, pp. 230–39, quotation at p. 137.

102. Amiya K. Samanta, Introduction to Amiya K. Samanta (ed.), *Terrorism in Bengal: A Collection of Documents on Terrorist Activities from 1905 to 1939*, Calcutta, Government of West Bengal, 1995, vol. I, pp. i–xvi, at pp. x–xi.

103. Hilary Sapire, 'Ambiguities of Loyalism: The Prince of Wales in India and Africa, 1921–2 and 25', *History Workshop Journal*, 73 (2012), pp. 37–65.

104. Ziegler (ed.), *The Diaries of Lord Louis Mountbatten*, pp. 250–51.

105. See Shahid Amin's classic *Event, Metaphor, Memory: Chauri Chaura, 1922–1992*, Berkeley, University of California Press, 1995, quotation at p. 16.

106. Ibid.

107. I here draw on the insight of Faisal Devji, *The Impossible Indian: Gandhi and the Temptation of Violence*, Cambridge, MA, Harvard University Press, 2012, esp. pp. 93–7.

108. Rakhahari Chatterji, 'The Swarajist Revolt: A Forgotten Chapter of Indian Movement', *The Indian Journal of Political Science*, 29/4 (1968), pp. 398–404, Bose quotation at p. 400.

109. Victor Kiernan, 'Modern Capitalism and its Shepherds', *New Left Review*, 183 (1990), pp. 75–94, at p. 87.

110. C. A. Vlieland, 'The Population of the Malay Peninsula: A Study in Human Migration', *Geographical Review*, 24/1 (1934), pp. 61–78. Vlieland was the architect of the 1931 census of Malaya.

111. Ibid.

112. This account is drawn from J. M. Gullick, *A History of Kuala Lumpur, 1857–1939*, Kuala Lumpur, MBRAS, 2000, pp. 226, 234–5, 251; Chong Seck-Chim, 'The Development of Kuala Lumpur District', *Malayan Journal of Tropical Geography*, 3/1 (1954), pp. 48–50.

113. Goh Ban Lee, *Urban Planning in Malaysia: History, Assumptions, and Issues*, Petaling Jaya, Tempo Publ., 1991, p. 36.

114. John Dill Ross, *The Capital of a Little Empire: A Descriptive Study of a British Crown Colony in the Far East*, Singapore, Kelly & Walsh, 1898, p. 37.

115. Victor Purcell, *The Memoirs of a Malayan Official*, London, Cassell, 1965, p. 94.

116. William R. Roff, *The Origins of Malay Nationalism*, New Haven, CT, and London, Yale University Press, 1967, p. 118.

117. See the important exchange between Paul H. Kratoska, 'Rice Cultivation and the Ethnic Division of Labour in British Malaya', *Comparative Studies in Society and History*, 24/2 (1982), pp. 280–314, and Lim Teck Ghee, 'British Colonial Administration and the "Ethnic Division of Labour" in Malaya', *Kajian Malaysia*, 1/2 (1984), pp. 28–66. See also K. S. Jomo, *A Question of Class: Capital, the State, and Uneven Development in Malaya*, Singapore, Oxford University Press, 1986; Sumit K. Mandal, 'Transethnic Solidarities, Racialization and Social Equality', in Edmund Terence Gomez (ed.), *The State of Malaysia: Ethnicity, Equity and Reform*, Routledge, London, 2004, ch. 9.

118. Sharon A. Carstens, 'From Myth to History: Yap Ah Loy and the Heroic Past of Chinese Malaysians', *Journal of Southeast Asian Studies*, 19/2 (1988), pp. 185–208.

119. W. Robert Foran, *Malayan Symphony; Being the Impressions Gathered During a Six Months' Journey through the Straits Settlements, Federated Malay States, Siam, Sumatra, Java and Bali*, London, Hutchinson & Co., 1935, p. 82.

120. Brenda S. A. Yeoh, *Contesting Space in Colonial Singapore: Power Relations and the Urban Built Environment*, Singapore, Singapore University Press, 2003, p. 138.

121. *Malay Weekly Mail*, 12 January 1922.

122. Joshua Hammer, *Yokohama Burning: The Deadly 1923 Earthquake and Fire that Helped Forge the Path to World War II*, New York, Simon & Schuster, 2006, pp. 22–3.

123. FO 371/8053, MBPI, April 1922.

124. T. N. Harper, 'Empire, Diaspora and the Languages of Globalism, 1850–1914', in A. G. Hopkins (ed.), *Globalization in World History*, London, Pimlico, 2002, pp. 141–66; Mark R. Frost, 'Asia's Maritime Networks and the Colonial Public Sphere, 1840–1920', *New Zealand Journal of Asian Studies*, 6/2 (2004), pp. 63–94. See also Ilham Khuri-Makdisi, *The Eastern Mediterranean and the Making of Global Radicalism, 1860–1914*, Berkeley, University of California Press, 2010.

125. Will Hanley, 'Grieving Cosmopolitanism in Middle East Studies', *History Compass*, 6/5 (2008), pp. 1346–67.

126. Jane Drakard, *A Kingdom of Words: Language and Power in Sumatra*, Shah Alam, Oxford University Press, 1999.

127. See Sugata Bose, *A Hundred Horizons: The Indian Ocean in the Age of Global Empire*, Cambridge, MA, Harvard University Press, 2006; Sugata Bose and Kris Manjapra (eds), *Cosmopolitan Thought Zones: South Asia and the Global Circulation of Ideas*, London, Palgrave Macmillan, 2010; Cemil Aydin, *The Politics of Anti-Westernism in Asia: Visions of World Order in Pan-Islamic and Pan-Asian Thought*, New York, Columbia University Press, 2007.

128. See esp. Su Lin Lewis, *Cities in Motion: Urban Life and Cosmopolitanism in Southeast Asia, 1920–1940*, Cambridge, Cambridge University Press, 2016.

129. A central theme of Joel S. Kahn, *Other Malays: Nationalism and Cosmopolitanism in the Modern Malay World*, Singapore, Singapore University Press, 2006.

130. TNA, FO 371/8053, MBPI, April 1922; MBPI, May 1922.

131. William R. Roff (ed.), *The Wandering Thoughts of a Dying Man: The Life and Times of Haji Abdul Majid Bin Zainuddin*, Kuala Lumpur, Oxford University Press, 1978.

132. Salma Nasution Khoo and Abdur-Razzaq Lubis, *Kinta Valley: Pioneering Malaysia's Modern Development*, Perak Darul Ridzuan, Perak Academy, 2005.

133. Lim Heng Kow, *The Evolution of the Urban System in Malaya*, Kuala Lumpur, University of Malaya Press, 1978, pp. 46–7.

134. Lynn Hollen Lees, *Planting Empire, Cultivating Subjects: British Malaya, 1786–1941*, Cambridge, Cambridge University Press, 2017.

135. T. N. Harper, *The End of Empire and the Making of Malaya*, Cambridge, Cambridge University Press, 1999, pp. 287–80.

136. Tim Harper, 'The Malay World, Besides Empire and Nation', *Indonesia and the Malay World*, 41/120 (2013), pp. 273–90.

137. Yen Ching-hwang, 'Historical Background', in Lee Kam Hing and Tan Chee Beng (eds), *The Chinese in Malaysia*, Kuala Lumpur, Oxford University Press, 2000, p. 26.

138. Leung Yuen Sang, 'The Singapore Hainanese and their Political Orientation during the Inter-war Period', in Nixia Wu Lun and Chiyan Zheng (eds), *Liang Ci Shi Jie Da Zhan Qi Jian Zai Yazhou Zhi Hai Wai Hua Ren*, Hong Kong, Chinese University of Hong Kong, 1989, pp. 203–18; René Onraet, *Singapore: A Police Background*, London, Dorothy Crisp and Co., 1947, p. 111.

139. TNA, CO 537/905, D. Beatty, 'Memorandum on the "Kwo Min Tang" in Malaya', 13 December 1921.

140. TNA, FO 371/8053, MBPI, March 1922.

141. TNA, CO 537/925, MBPI, September 1924.

142. Audrey R. Kahin, 'The 1927 Communist Uprising in Sumatra: A Reappraisal', *Indonesia*, 62 (1996), pp. 19–36, at pp. 22–30.

143. Tan Malaka to Dick Wijngaarden, 6 January 1921, in C. L. M. Penders (ed. and trans.), *Indonesia: Selected Documents on Colonialism and Nationalism, 1830–1942*, St Lucia, University of Queensland Press, 1977, p. 283.

144. Doris Jedamski, 'Balai Pustaka: A Colonial Wolf in Sheep's Clothing', *Archipel*, 44 (1992), pp. 23–46.

145. Musso quoted in Hilmar Farid and Razif, 'Batjaan liar in the Dutch East Indies: A Colonial Antipode', *Postcolonial Studies*, 11/3 (2008), pp. 277–92, at p. 282.

146. Ibid.

147. Takashi Shiraishi, *An Age in Motion: Popular Radicalism in Java, 1912–1926*, Ithaca, NY, Cornell University Press, 1990, pp. 226–7.

148. Ruth T. McVey, *The Rise of Indonesian Communism*, Ithaca, NY, Cornell University Press, 1965, p. 107.

149. Tan Malaka, *From Jail to Jail*, trans. and ed. Helen Jarvis, Athens, Ohio University Center for International Studies, 1991, vol. I, p. 68.

150. T. Malaka, *SI Semarang dan Onderwijs*, Semarang, S.I. School, November 1921, p. 7.

151. I have here followed Ruth T. McVey, *The Rise of Indonesian Communism*, pp. 103–7, 113–20, quotation at p. 107.

152. Robert Cribb, 'A System of Exemptions: Historicizing State Illegality in Indonesia', in Edward Aspinall and Gerry van Klinken (eds), *The State and Illegality in Indonesia*, Leiden, KITLV Press, 2011, pp. 31–44.

153. McVey, *The Rise of Indonesian Communism*, p. 121.

154. John Ingleson, *In Search of Justice: Workers and Unions in Colonial Java, 1908–1926*, Singapore, Oxford University Press, 1986, pp. 87–9.

155. Ibid., p. 113.

156. Akira Nagazumi, 'Pawnshop Strikes of 1922 and the Indonesian Political Parties', *Archipel*, 8 (1974), pp. 187–206.

157. Tan Malaka, *From Jail to Jail*, vol. I, pp. 71–2.

158. The transcript is in NL-HaNA, Koloniën: Geheim Archief, Vb 29 April 1922 G4.

159. *De Tribune*, 29 and 31 March 1922, reported in Harry A. Poeze, *Tan Malaka: Strijder voor Indonesië's Vrijheid: Levensloop van 1897 tot 1945*, 's-Gravenhage, Nijhoff, 1976, p. 183.

160. The proceedings of this meeting are reported in ibid., pp. 185–7.

161. *Arnhemsche Courant*, 13 June 1922, as quoted in ibid., p. 195.

162. Ibid., p. 209.

163. For this perception see Yuji Suzuki, 'Tan Malaka: Perantauan and the Power of Ideas', in Leonard Y. Andaya, Charles A. Coppel and Yuji Suzuki, *People and Society in Indonesia: A Biographical Approach*, Clayton, Monash, Monash University, 1977, pp. 31–50, at p. 36 and p. 48, citing *Massa Actie/Mass Action* (1946).

164. Rudolf Mrázek, 'Tan Malaka: A Political Personality's Structure of Experience', *Indonesia*, 14 (1972), pp. 1–48, at p. 4. He is quoting Taufik Abdullah.

165. Tan Malaka, *From Jail to Jail*, vol. I, p. 79.

12. THE NEXT WORLD WAR (1922–1924)

1. For this see Kris Manjapra, 'Communist internationalism and transcolonial recognition', in Sugata Bose and Manjapra (eds), *Cosmopolitan Thought*

Zones: South Asia and the Global Circulation of Ideas, Basingstoke, Palgrave Macmillan, 2010, pp. 159–77. See also Manu Goswami, 'Imaginary Futures and Colonial Internationalisms', *American Historical Review*, 117/5 (2012), pp. 1461–85 and Ali Raza, Franziska Roy and Benjamin Zachariah (eds), *The Internationalist Moment: South Asian Worlds, and World Views, 1917–1939*, London, SAGE, 2015.

2. Roy to Eastern Secretariat, 30 July 1922, in Purabi Roy, Sobhanlal Datta Gupta and Hari S. Vasudevan (eds), *Indo-Russian Relations, 1917–1947: Select Documents from the Archives of the Russian Federation, Part 1, 1917–1947*, Calcutta, Asiatic Society, 1999, pp. 160–62.

3. Nirode K. Barooah, *Chatto: The Life and Times of an Indian Anti-Imperialist in Europe*, New Delhi, Oxford University Press, 2004, p. 188.

4. M. N. Roy, *M. N. Roy's Memoirs* (1960), Delhi, Ajanta Publications, 1985, p. 488.

5. For the various interpretations see Purnima Bose, 'Transnational Resistance and Fictive Truths: Virendranath Chattopadhyaya, Agnes Smedley and the Indian Nationalist Movement', *South Asian History and Culture*, 2/4 (2011), pp. 502–21.

6. Ruth Price, *The Lives of Agnes Smedley*, Oxford, Oxford University Press, 2005, pp. 61, 103–20.

7. Barooah, *Chatto*, p. 242.

8. Roy to Secretary, Eastern Section, 11 September 1922, in Roy et al. (eds), *Indo-Russian Relations, 1917–1947*, p. 170.

9. Sibnarayan Ray, *In Freedom's Quest: A Study of the Life and Works of M. N. Roy (1887–1954)*, vol. I: *1887–1922*, Calcutta, Minerva Associates, 1998, pp. 146–51.

10. M. N. Roy, 'India in Transition', in Sibnarayan Ray (ed.), *Selected Works of M. N. Roy*, vol. I: *1917–1922*, Delhi, Oxford University Press, 1987, p. 241.

11. Here I follow Kris Manjapra's insightful reading, *M. N. Roy: An Intellectual Biography of M. N. Roy*, New Delhi, Routledge India, 2010, pp. 48–51.

12. Roy, 'India in Transition', p. 374.

13. Evelyn Roy, 'The Debacle of Gandhism', *The Communist Review*, 3/7 (November 1922), accessed via Marxist Internet Archive, https://www.marxists.org/history/international/comintern/sections/britain/periodicals/communist_review/1922/07/gandhism.htm.

14. Maia Ramnath, *Decolonizing Anarchism: An Antiauthoritarian History of India's Liberation Struggle*, Oakland, CA, AK Press, 2012, pp. 134–40, quotation at p. 137.

15. Ravi Vaitheespara and Rajesh Venkatasubramanian, 'Beyond the Politics of Identity: The Left and the Politics of Caste and Identity in Tamil Nadu, 1920–63', *South Asia: Journal of South Asian Studies*, 38/4 (2015), pp. 543–57, at pp. 550–52.

16. NAI, Home Department, Political No. 1112 of 1932, A. Hamilton, 'Judgment [King Emperor vs. M. N. Roy']', 9 January 1932.

17. Rajnarayan Chandavarkar, *Imperial Power and Popular Politics: Class, Resistance and the State in India, 1850–1950*, Cambridge, Cambridge University Press, 1998, pp. 94–5; Sanat Bose, 'Communist International and Indian Trade Union Movement (1919–1923)', *Social Scientist*, 8/4 (1979), pp. 23–36.

18. NAI, Home Department, Political No. 261 of 1924, 'Proceedings detailing the circumstances in which it was found necessary to issue warrants under Regulation III of 1818 . . .', n.d.

19. NAI, Home Department, Political No. 261 of 1924, Muzaffar Ahmad to Roy 21 March 1923, intercepted by the British.

20. G. Adhikari (ed.), *Documents of the History of the Communist Party of India*, vol. II, New Delhi, People's Publishing House, 1974, p. 236.

21. For the numbers see Gopal Krishna, 'The Development of the Indian National Congress as a Mass Organization, 1918–1923', *Journal of Asian Studies*, 25/3 (1966), pp. 413–30, at p. 418. For Swaraj see Rakhahari Chatterji, 'The Swarajist Revolt: A Forgotten Chapter of Indian Movement', *Indian Journal of Political Science*, 29/4 (1968), pp. 398–404; Srabani Rai Chaudhuri, 'The Swarajist Interlude in Bengal: Paradox of a Strange Amalgam', *Indian Journal of Political Science*, 51/2 (1990), pp. 42–59.

22. NAI, Home Department, Political No. 261 of 1924, 'Indian Communists 21 November 1922–10 May 1913'.

23. NAI, Home Department, Political No. 261 of 1924, Cecil Kaye, note, 10 December 1923; NAI, Home Department, Political No. 1112 of 1932, A. Hamilton, 'Judgment [King Emperor vs. M. N. Roy']', 9 January 1932.

24. Muzaffar Ahmad, *The Communist Party of India and Its Formation Abroad*, Calcutta, National Book Agency, 1962, pp. 346–8, quotation at p. 346; Adhikari (ed.) *Documents of the History of the Communist Party of India*, vol. II, pp. 274–8.

25. NAI, Home Department, Political No. 261 of 1924, 'A Petition to H.E. the Governor-General from the accused in KE vs. Dange and others'.

26. NAI, Home Department, Political No. 261 of 1924, Cecil Kaye, notes of 27 July 1923 and 3 August 1923.

27. NAI, Home Department, Political No. 261 of 1924, 'Case for the use of Regulation III against Shaukat Usmani, Singaravelu, Ghulam Hussain, S. A. Dange and Muzaffar Ahmad, Communist Agents now in India'.

28. NAI, Home Department, Political No. 261 of 1924, 'Rules of the Treatment of Special Division Prisoners'; 'Detention of Muzaffar Ahmad under Regulation III of 1818', 11 July 1923.

29. NAI, Home Department, Political No. 261 of 1924, C. E. Peters to Secretary

Government of India, 23 May 1924; 'Copy of the Petition dated 22 November 1923 from State Prisoner Shaukat Usmani . . .'.

30. M. N. Roy, 'The White Terror', *International Press Correspondence (Inprecor)*, 4/23 (3 April 1924), pp. 214–15.

31. Evelyn Roy, 'Will the British Labour Government Stand for This?', *Inprecor*, 4/25 (17 April 1924), pp. 231–3.

32. For the divisions see Ahmad, *The Communist Party of India*, esp. pp. 359–60, quotation at p. 380.

33. NAI, Home Department, Political No. 261 of 1924, Commissioner of Police No. B1125, report, 3 January 1923.

34. Durba Ghosh, *Gentlemanly Terrorists: Political Violence and the Colonial State in India, 1919–1947*, Cambridge, Cambridge University Press, 2017, pp. 98–107.

35. Chris Moffat, *India's Revolutionary Inheritance: Politics and the Promise of Bhagat Singh*, Cambridge, Cambridge University Press, 2019, pp. 23–48.

36. Gautam Chattopadhyaya, *Abani Mukherji, A Dauntless Revolutionary and Pioneering Communist*, New Delhi, People's Publishing House, 1976, pp. 25–36; Abani Mukherji, 'General Indian Situation during my One and Half Year's Stay There', in Roy et al. (eds), *Indo-Russian Relations, 1917–1947*, pp. 189–91.

37. Samaren Roy, *M. N. Roy: A Political Biography*, New Delhi, Orient Longman, 1997, p. 100.

38. Daniel Hémery, 'Du patriotisme au marxisme: l'immigration vietnamienne en France de 1926 à 1930', *Le Mouvement Social*, 90 (1975), pp. 3–54, at pp. 6–7; Scott McConnell, *Leftward Journey: The Education of Vietnamese Students in France, 1919–1939*, New Brunswick, Transaction, 1989, pp. 27–39.

39. William J Duiker, *Ho Chi Minh: A Life*, New York, Hyperion, 2000, pp. 74–84.

40. Sophie Quinn-Judge, *Ho Chi Minh: The Missing Years, 1919–1941*, London, Hurst, 2003, pp. 37–8.

41. Robert Aldrich, 'Colonial Kings in the Metropole: The Visits to France of King Sisowath (1906) and Emperor Khai Dinh (1922)', in Robert Aldrich and Cindy McCreery (eds), *Royals on Tour: Politics, Pageantry and Colonialism*, Manchester, Manchester University Press, 2018, pp. 125–45.

42. Vinh Sinh (ed.), *Phan Châu Trinh and His Political Writings*, Ithaca, NY, Southeast Asia Program Publications, 2009, p. 100.

43. Ho Chi Minh, *Selected Works of Ho Chi Minh*, vol. I, Hanoi, Foreign Languages Publishing House, 1961, p. 16.

44. Bernard B. Fall (ed.), *Ho Chi Minh on Revolution: Selected Writings, 1920–66*, London, Pall Mall Press, 1967, pp. 16–17.

45. Quinn-Judge, *Ho Chi Minh*, pp. 40–42, quotation at p. 41.

46. Erica J. Peters, 'Resistance, Rivalries and Restaurants: Vietnamese Workers

in Interwar France', *Journal of Vietnamese Studies*, 2/1 (2007), pp. 109–43; The Anh Nguyen, 'How Did Ho Chi Minh Become a Proletarian? Reality and Legend', *Asian Affairs*, 16/2 (1985), pp. 163–9.

47. Marilyn A. Levine, *The Found Generation: Chinese Communists in Europe during the Twenties*, Seattle, University of Washington Press, 1993, pp. 151–8; Chae-Jin Lee, *Zhou Enlai: The Early Years*, Stanford, CA, Stanford University Press, 1994, pp. 161–4.

48. Ruth T. McVey, *The Rise of Indonesian Communism*, Ithaca, NY, Cornell University Press, 1965, pp. 126–38, quotation at p. 134. For Semaoen's report see Ruth McVey and Comrade Semaun, 'An Early Account of the Independence Movement', *Indonesia*, 1 (1966), pp. 46–75.

49. John Riddell (ed.), *Toward the United Front: Proceedings of the Fourth Congress of the Communist International, 1922*, Leiden, Brill, 2011, pp. 261–4.

50. Ibid., p. 694.

51. Tan Malaka, *From Jail to Jail*, trans. and ed. Helen Jarvis, Athens, Ohio University Center for International Studies, 1991, vol. I, p. 94.

52. McVey, *The Rise of Indonesian Communism*, p. 205.

53. The fullest reconstruction of Nguyen Ai Quoc's time in Moscow is Duiker, *Ho Chi Minh*, pp. 87–104.

54. E. V. Kobelev, *Ho Chi Minh*, Moscow, Progress Publishers, 1989, p. 63.

55. Sibnarayan Ray, *In Freedom's Quest: A Study of the Life and Works of M. N. Roy (1887–1954)*, vol. II: *The Comintern Years, 1922–27*, Calcutta, Minerva Associates, 2002, pp. 60–63.

56. M. N. Roy, 'Europe Is Not the World', *Inprecor*, 4/90 (31 December 1924), pp. 1045–6.

57. M. N. Roy, *Fragments of a Prisoner's Diary: Letters from Jail*, Calcutta, Renaissance Publishers, 1943, p. 59.

58. H. Maring to Bukharin, 21 March 1923, in Tony Saich, *The Origins of the First United Front in China : The Role of Sneevliet (Alias Maring)*, vol. II, Leiden, Brill, 1991, pp. 475–80.

59. Ibid., pp. 137–8.

60. Zhang Guotao, 'Report of the Beijing Communist Group' (July 1921), in Tony Saich (ed.), *The Rise to Power of the Chinese Communist Party: Documents and Analysis*, Armonk, NY, M. E. Sharpe, 1996, pp. 19–24; Daniel Y. K. Kwan, *Marxist Intellectuals and the Chinese Labor Movement: A Study of Deng Zhongxia (1894–1933)*, Seattle, University of Washington Press, 1997, pp. 22–4, 29–30; David Strand, *Rickshaw Beijing: City People and Politics in the 1920s*, Berkeley, University of California Press, 1993, pp. 145–7.

61. Elizabeth J. Perry, 'Reclaiming the Chinese Revolution', *Journal of Asian Studies*, 67/4 (2008), pp. 1147–64; and *Anyuan: Mining China's Revolutionary Tradition*, Berkeley, University of California Press, 2012.

62. Fernando Galbiati, *P'eng P'ai and the Hai-Lu-Feng Soviet*, Stanford, CA, Stanford University Press, 1985, pp. 168–9.

63. Allen S. Whiting, *Soviet Policies in China, 1917–1924*, Stanford, CA, Stanford University Press, 1954, pp. 181–207. For Chen see Shao Chuan Leng and Norman D. Palmer, *Sun Yat-sen and Communism*, New York, Praeger, 1960, pp. 64–5.

64. F. Gilbert Chan, 'An Alternative to Kuomintang-Communist Collaboration: Sun Yat-Sen and Hong Kong, January–June 1923', *Modern Asian Studies*, 13/1 (1979), pp. 127–39.

65. Wilbur C. Martin, 'Problems of Starting a Revolutionary Base: Sun Yatsen and Canton, 1923', *Bulletin of the Institute of Modern History* (Taipei), 2/4 (1971), pp. 1–63.

66. For the republican city see Michael Tsin, 'Canton Remapped', in Joseph W. Esherick (ed.), *Remaking the Chinese City: Modernity and National Identity, 1900–1950*, Honolulu, University of Hawaii Press, 2000, pp. 19–29; Johnathan A. Farris, *Dwelling on the Edge of Empires: Foreigners and Architecture in Guangzhou (Canton), China*, Hong Kong, Hong Kong University Press, 2004, ch. 4; Virgil K. Y. Ho, *Understanding Canton: Rethinking Popular Culture in the Republican Period*, Oxford, Oxford University Press, 2005, esp. pp. 9–42. For labour see Ming K. Chan, 'The Realpolitik and Legacy of Labor Activism and Popular Mobilization in 1920s Greater Canton', in Mechthild Leutner et al. (eds), *The Chinese Revolution in the 1920s: Between Triumph and Disaster*, London, RoutledgeCurzon, 2002, pp. 187–221, at p. 188; Chan cites Deng Zhingxia's 1927 survey.

67. TNA, FO 228/3276, 'Canton Intelligence Report, December Quarter, 1922'.

68. *Syracuse Herald*, 26 October 1922.

69. *North China Herald*, 26 March 1921.

70. *Hong Kong Telegraph*, 23 October 1922.

71. Helen F. Siu, *Agents and Victims in South China: Accomplices in Rural Revolution*, New Haven, CT, and London, Yale University Press, 1989, pp. 4–95.

72. Hans J. van de Ven, *War and Nationalism in China, 1925–1945*, London, RoutledgeCurzon, 2003, pp. 69–71.

73. Sneevliet to Wilde, 30 May 1923, in Saich, *The Origins of the First United Front in China*, pp. 488–91.

74. Tim Wright, *Coal Mining in China's Economy and Society 1895–1937*, Cambridge, Cambridge University Press, 1984, pp. 184–6.

75. Zhang Guotao, *The Rise of the Chinese Communist Party, 1921–1927: Volume One of the Autobiography of Chang Kuo-t'ao*, Lawrence, University Press of Kansas, 1971, p. 286; the image of 'first falling leaves' is his.

76. Hans J. van de Ven, *From Friend to Comrade: The Founding of the Chinese*

Communist Party, 1920–1927, Berkeley, University of California Press, 1992, pp. 106–7; Zhang, *The Rise of the Chinese Communist Party*, pp. 296–312.

77. Sneevliet to Bukharin, 31 May 1923, in Saich, *The Origins of the First United Front in China*, p. 496.

78. Ibid.

79. For Chiang's early life see Jay Taylor, *The Generalissimo: Chiang Kai-Shek and the Struggle for Modern China*, Cambridge, MA, Harvard University Press, 2009, ch. 1; Jonathan Fenby, *Chiang Kai Shek: China's Generalissimo and the Nation He Lost*, part I, London, Hachette UK, 2009, chs 1–3.

80. Pichon P. Y. Loh, *The Early Chiang Kai-Shek: A Study of his Personality and Politics, 1887–1924*, New York, Columbia University Press, 1971, Chiang diary quotation at p. 64; for the Canton coup see pp. 69–73.

81. David R. Stone, 'Soviet Arms Exports in the 1920s', *Journal of Contemporary History*, 48/1 (2013), pp. 57–77, at p. 69.

82. Taylor, *The Generalissimo*, pp. 43–4; Yang Tianshi, 'Perspectives on Chiang Kaishek's Early Thought from his Unpublished Diary', in Leutner et al. (eds), *The Chinese Revolution in the 1920s*, pp. 77–97, at pp. 90–91.

83. TNA, HO 382/2, Inspector Ewen McCaskill, 'Michael Borodin alias Georg Braun alias George Brown', 7 September 1922.

84. Aleksandr Ivanovich Cherepanov, *As Military Adviser in China*, Moscow, Progress, 1982, pp. 29–30.

85. Mei-ling Soong, Madam Chiang, *Conversations with Mikhail Borodin*, London, Free Chinese Centre, 1978, p. 4.

86. Quoted in Ishikawa Yoshihiro, 'The Chinese National Revolution and the Eighth ECCI Plenum: Exploring the Role of the Chinese delegate "Chugunov"', in Roland Felber, A. M. Grigoriev, Mechthild Leutner and M. L. Titarenko (eds), *The Chinese Revolution in the 1920s*, pp. 141–55, at p. 148.

87. For Zhang's role see Cherepanov, *As Military Adviser in China*, p. 45, and for his background Yoshihiro Ishikawa, *The Formation of the Chinese Communist Party*, New York, Columbia University Press, 2013, pp. 209–20. For Qu see Elizabeth McGuire, *Red at Heart: How Chinese Communists Fell in Love with the Russian Revolution*, New York, Oxford University Press, 2017, p. 71; Tani Barlow, ' "History's Coffin Can Never Be Closed": Qu Qiubai Translates Social Science', *Boundary* 2, 43/3 (2016), pp. 253–86.

88. Alexander Pantsov, *The Bolsheviks and the Chinese Revolution, 1919–1927*, Curzon Press, Richmond, 2000, pp. 66–9.

89. Kwan, *Marxist Intellectuals and the Chinese Labor Movement*, pp. 88–91; TNA, CO 537/925, MBPI, September 1924.

90. George T. Yu, *Party Politics in Republican China: The Kuomintang, 1912–1924*, Berkeley, University of California Press, 1966, pp. 171–5.

91. A point made by Michael G. Murdock, 'Exploiting Anti-Imperialism:

Popular Forces and Nation-State-Building During China's Northern Expedition, 1926–1927', *Modern China*, 35/1 (2009), pp. 65–95.

92. For this see Zhiyi Yang, 'A Humanist in Wartime France: Wang Jingwei during the First World War', *Poetica*, 49 (2017/18), pp. 163–92.

93. Vera Vladimirovna Vishnyakova-Akimova, *Two Years in Revolutionary China, 1925–1927*, Cambridge, MA, East Asian Research Center, Harvard University, 1971, p. 206.

94. Pantsov, *The Bolsheviks and the Chinese Revolution*, p. 64.

95. Zhang, *The Rise of the Chinese Communist Party*, p. 332.

96. Devendra Kaushik and Leonid Mitrokhin (eds), *Lenin: His Image in India*, Delhi, Vikas, 1970, pp. 90, 92, 99, 105.

97. See *Inprecor*, 4/55, 4 August 1924, pp. 577–8.

98. Kobelev, *Ho Chi Minh*, p. 76.

99. David Petrie, *Communism in India 1924–1927, edited with an Introduction and Explanatory Notes by Mahadevaprasad Saha*, Calcutta, Editions Indian, 1972, p. 3.

100. 'For the Tenth Anniversary of the Imperialist War', *Inprecor*, 4/43, 18 July 1924.

101. Kim San and Nym Wales, *The Song of Ariran: The Life Story of a Korean Rebel*, New York, John Day, 1941, pp. 79–82, quotation at p. 86.

102. Harsha Dutt, 'Rabindranath Tagore and China', *Indian Literature*, 55/3 (263) (2011), pp. 216–22, at p. 219.

103. Yin Zhiguang, *Politics of Art: The Creation Society and the Practice of Theoretical Struggle in Revolutionary China*, Leiden, Brill, 2014, esp. pp. 56–85; Wang-chi Wong, *Politics and Literature in Shanghai: The Chinese League of Left-wing Writers, 1930–1936*, Manchester, Manchester University Press, 1991, quotation at p. 14.

104. Sisir Kumar Das, 'The Controversial Guest: Tagore in China', *China Report*, 29/3 (1993), pp. 237–73, quotation at p. 253.

105. For Tagore and Indian troops see Sugata Bose, *His Majesty's Opponent: Subhas Chandra Bose and India's Struggle Against Empire*, Cambridge, MA, Harvard University Press, 2011, p. 263.

106. Das, 'The Controversial Guest: Tagore in China', quotation at p. 263.

107. Stephen N. Hay, *Asian Ideas of East and West: Tagore and his Critics in Japan, China, and India*, Cambridge, MA, Harvard University Press, 1970, p. 181.

108. Ibid., pp. 237–8.

109. Yan Xu, *The Soldier Image and State-building in Modern China, 1924–1945*, Lexington, University Press of Kentucky, 2019, pp. 27–52, quotation at p. 41; Lincoln Li, *Student Nationalism in China, 1924–1949*, Albany, NY, State University of New York Press, 1994, p. 28.

110. Gerald W. Berkley, 'The Canton Peasant Movement Training Institute', *Modern China*, 1/2 (1975), pp. 161–79.

111. Tan Malaka, *From Jail to Jail*, vol. I, p. 41.

112. Rodney Koeneke, *Empires of the Mind: I. A. Richards and Basic English in China, 1929–1979*, Stanford, CA, Stanford University Press, 2004.

113. TNA, FO 371/11084, J. Crosby, 'Notes on the national movement and on the political situation in the Netherlands East Indies generally', 30 April 1925.

114. Josephine Fowler, 'From East to West and West to East: Ties of Solidarity in the Pan-Pacific Revolutionary Trade Union Movement, 1923–1934', *International Labor and Working-Class History*, 66/1 (2004), pp. 99–117.

115. 'Kuangtung's unsettled state', *North China Herald*, 5 July 1924.

116. The classic study of these wars is Arthur Waldron, *From War to Nationalism: China's Turning Point, 1924–1925*, Cambridge, Cambridge University Press, 1995.

117. Ho Chi Minh Museum, Hanoi, Nguyen Ai Quoc to Comintern, dated Canton, 12 November 1924.

118. James E. Sheridan, *Chinese Warlord: The Career of Feng Yü-Hsiang*, Stanford, CA, Stanford University Press, 1966, pp. 136–7, 146.

119. Marie-Claire Bergère, *Sun Yat-sen*, Stanford, CA, Stanford University Press, 2000, pp. 339, 350, 395–8.

120. Arthur Waldron, *From War to Nationalism: China's Turning Point, 1924–1925*, Cambridge, Cambridge University Press, 1995, pp. 223–6.

121. Prasenjit Duara, 'The Discourse of Civilization and Pan-Asianism', *Journal of World History*, 12/1 (2001), pp. 99–130.

122. Leonard Shihlien Hsü, *Sun Yat-Sen: His Political and Social Ideals*, Los Angeles, University of Southern California Press, 1933, p. 225.

123. Bergère, *Sun Yat-sen*, pp. 369–70.

124. Torsten Weber, *Embracing 'Asia' in China and Japan: Asianism Discourse and the Contest for Hegemony, 1912–1933*, Basingstoke, Palgrave Macmillan, 2017, quotation at p. 206. See also Craig A. Smith, 'Chinese Asianism in the Early Republic: Guomindang Intellectuals and the Brief Internationalist Turn', *Modern Asian Studies*, 53/2 (2019), pp. 582–605.

125. *Shuntian Shibao*, 23 November 1924, quoted in Leslie H. Dingyan Chen, *Chen Jiongming and the Federalist Movement: Regional Leadership and Nation Building in Early Republican China*, Ann Arbor, University of Michigan Press, 1999, pp. 227–8, quotation at p. 245. Chen also cites the *Hong Kong Telegraph*, 17 October 1924; I quote its reportage more fully here.

126. Aleksandr Ivanovich Cherepanov, *As Military Adviser in China*, Moscow, Progress, 1982, p. 83; C. Martin Wilbur and Julie Lien-ying How (eds), *Missionaries of Revolution: Soviet Advisers and Nationalist China, 1920–1927*, Cambridge, MA, Harvard University Press, 1989, pp. 144–5.

127. Cherepanov, *As Military Adviser in China*, p. 211.

128. James R. Shirley, 'Control of the Kuomintang after Sun Yat-Sen's Death', *The Journal of Asian Studies*, 25/1 (1965), pp. 69–82.

129. Suggested by David Strand, *An Unfinished Republic: Leading by Word and Deed in Modern China*, Berkeley, University of California Press, 2011, pp. 283–4.

130. Henrietta Harrison, *The Making of the Republican Citizen: Political Ceremonies and Symbols in China 1911–1929*, Oxford, Clarendon Press, 2000, pp. 133–46; Bergère, *Sun Yat-sen*, pp. 395–407; Lian Xi, 'Western Protestant Missions and Modern Chinese Nationalist Dreams', *East Asian History*, 32/33 (2006/7), pp. 199–216, at p. 211.

131. Tan Malaka, *From Jail to Jail*, pp. 100–103.

132. TNA, FO 371/11084, J. Crosby, 'Notes on the national movement and on the political situation in the Netherlands East Indies generally', 30 April 1925.

133. C. F. Yong and R. B. McKenna, *Kuomintang Movement in British Malaya, 1912–1949*, Singapore, NUS Press, 1990, pp. 40–41.

13. ANARCHY LOOSED (1925–1926)

1. Sharon M. Lee, 'Female Immigrants and Labor in Colonial Malaya, 1860–1947', *International Migration Review*, 23/2 (1989), pp. 309–31. For Kuala Lumpur in this period see Ng Seo Buck, 'Some Recollections of Kuala Lumpur Fifty Years Ago', *Malayan Historical Journal*, 1/1 (1954), pp. 29–32.

2. 'Report of the Secretary for Chinese Affairs for the Year 1924', *Federated Malay States Gazette*, 1 May 1925, p. 1.

3. TNA, CO 717/14, 'In the Magistrates Court at Kuala Lumpur, Criminal Case No. 580 of 1925: the deposition of Liew Kim Wah', 27 February 1925.

4. *Straits Times*, 26 January 1925.

5. Ibid., 28 January 1925.

6. As reported to a French agent: ANOM, INDO/GG/65533, Mission Noël Note no. 130, 'Canton centre de production de bombes pour attentats dans pays voisins', 7 March 1925.

7. ANM, Selangor Secretariat, 2066/1926, 'Wong Sang: Extract from the Nominal Record, no. 9339, Pudu'.

8. Eugenia Lean, *Public Passions: The Trial of Shi Jianqiao and the Rise of Popular Sympathy in Republican China*, Berkeley, University of California Press, 2007, p. 41, quote at p. 47. Lean explores a later, celebrated case of a female assassin of a warlord in Tianjin. I am grateful to Lily Chang for this reference.

9. *Straits Times*, 26 January 1925.

10. *Straits Times*, 30 January 1925.

11. *The Singapore Free Press and Mercantile Advertiser*, 19 September 1924.

12. Su Lin Lewis, 'Cosmopolitanism and the Modern Girl: a Cross-Cultural Discourse in 1930s Penang', *Modern Asian Studies*, 43/6 (2008), pp. 1385–

1419. See also the Modern Girl Around the World Research Group, *The Modern Girl Around the World: Consumption, Modernity, and Globalization*, Durham, NC, Duke University Press, 2009; Francesca del Lago, 'Crossed Legs in 1930s Shanghai: How "Modern" the Modern Woman?' *East Asian History*, 19 (2000), pp. 103–44.

13. Sarah E. Stevens, 'Figuring Modernity: The New Woman and the Modern Girl in Republican China', *NWSA Journal*, 15/3 (2003), pp. 82–103.

14. *Malayan Saturday Post*, 14 February 1925.

15. 'Forewarned', editorial, *Straits Times*, 19 January 1925.

16. *Siam Observer*, 2 February 1925.

17. *Straits Times*, 28 February 1925.

18. Ibid.

19. *Straits Times*, 24 March 1925.

20. R. H. J. Sydney, *Malay Land: 'Tanah Malayu': Some Phases of Life in Modern British Malaya*, London, C. Palmer, 1926, pp. 122–4.

21. *Straits Times*, 24 March 1925.

22. 'A daughter's vendetta', *The Canton Gazette*, 2 April 1925.

23. Michel Foucault, 'About the Concept of the "Dangerous Individual" in 19th-century Legal Psychiatry', *International Journal of Law and Psychiatry*, 1/1 (1978), pp. 1–18, at pp. 1–2.

24. TNA, CO 717/14, Sir L. M. Guillemard to Leo Amery, 23 April 1925. The affair has also received scant attention from historians; exceptions are the late Khoo Kay Kim and Ranjit Singh Malhl, 'Malaysia: Chinese Anarchists Started Trade Unions', *Sunday Star* (Kuala Lumpur), 12 September 1993, and C. F. Yong, *The Origins of Malayan Communism*, Singapore, South Seas Society, 1997, pp. 32–4.

25. *Siam Observer*, 20 March 1925.

26. ANM, Selangor Secretariat, 2066/1926, 'Wong Sang: Extract from the Nominal Record, no. 9339, Pudu'.

27. TNA, CO 717/14, A. M. Goodman to Secretary to the Government, Federated Malay States, 5 February 1925; TNA, CO537/930, MBPI, March 1925.

28. *Straits Times*, 18 May 1928. See the account in R. B. McKenna, 'Sir Laurence Guillemard and Political Control of the Chinese in Singapore, 1920–26', *Journal of the South Seas Society*, 49 (1994), pp. 10–33, at p. 22.

29. Little has been written about this affair, although it was highlighted by Kim and Malhl, 'Malaysia: Chinese Anarchists Started Trade Unions'.

30. The account that follows, unless otherwise indicated, is taken from 'Rambler's Reminiscences', *Malayan Police Magazine* (August 1929).

31. ANM, Selangor Secretariat, 2542/1925, Straits Settlements, 'Annual Report of the Protector of Chinese for the Year 1924'.

32. TNA, CO 537/930, MBPI, March 1925.

33. Ibid.

34. *China Mail*, 30 March 1925.
35. TNA, CO 537/930, MBPI, March 1925.
36. TNA, CO 537/932, MBPI, May 1925.
37. 'The "Bright" Magazine No. 1, dated 1 May 1924, "Liberty and Blood" (Composed by To Shang)', Appendix A1 to A. M. Goodman, 'Anarchism among Chinese in British Malaya', 26 January 1925, TNA, CO 717/14.
38. *China Mail*, 27 November 1924.
39. *Straits Times*, 28 January 1925; ANOM, INDO/GG/65533, 'Attendat de Kuala-Lampur', dated Hanoi, March 1928.
40. ANOM, INDO/GG/6553, Gerardin, Le Chargé d'Affaires de France au Siam au Gouverneur Général de l'Indochine, 16 May 1925.
41. TNA, CO 537/930, MBPI, March 1925.
42. ANOM, INDO/GG/65533, Annex No. 1A la, Mission Noël Note no. 144 (Extrait A), 2 and 3 March 1925.
43. Ibid., Mission Noël Note no. 130, 'Canton centre de production de bombes pour attentats dans pays voisins', 7 March 1925.
44. Sophie Quinn-Judge, *Ho Chi Minh: The Missing Years, 1919–1941*, London, Hurst, 2003, p. 78.
45. The development of the Thanh Nien is detailed in ibid., pp. 72–85, 90–105.
46. David G. Marr, *Vietnamese Tradition on Trial, 1920–1945*, Berkeley, University of California Press, 1984, p. 375.
47. Daniel Y. K. Kwan, *Marxist Intellectuals and the Chinese Labor Movement: A Study of Deng Zhongxia (1894–1933)*, Seattle, University of Washington Press, 1997, pp. 35–51.
48. For the industrial setting see Sherman Cochran, *Encountering Chinese Networks: Western, Japanese, and Chinese Corporations in China, 1880–1937*, Berkeley, University of California Press, 2000, pp. 105–9. The indispensable study is S. A. Smith, *A Road Is Made: Communism in Shanghai, 1920–1927*, Richmond, Curzon, 2000, pp. 76–8.
49. Wen-Hsin Yeh, *The Alienated Academy: Culture and Politics in Republican China, 1919–1937*, Cambridge, MA, Harvard University Press, 2000, pp. 129–61.
50. I have drawn here on Zheng Chaolin, 'Before and After May Thirtieth', in Gregor Benton, *Prophets Unarmed: Chinese Trotskyists in Revolution, War, Jail, and the Return from Limbo*, Leiden, Brill, 2014, pp. 225–8, quotation on Li Lisan at p. 248; Zhang Guotao, *The Rise of the Chinese Communist Party, 1921–1927: Volume One of the Autobiography of Chang Kuo-t'ao*, Lawrence, University Press of Kansas, 1971, pp. 486–8.
51. Translated in Lu Xun, *Jottings Under Lamplight*, ed. Eileen J. Chang and Kirk A. Denton, Cambridge, MA, Harvard University Press, 2017, pp. 256–62.
52. For Yang Zhihua see Christina K. Gilmartin, *Engendering the Chinese*

Revolution: Radical Women, Communist Politics, and Mass Movements in the 1920s, Berkeley, University of California Press, 1995, pp. 141–3.

53. Nick Knight, *Marxist Philosophy in China: From Qu Qiubai to Mao Zedong, 1923–1945*, Dordrecht, Springer Science & Business Media, 2006, esp. pp. 32–3. For a reinterpretation see Tani Barlow, ' "History's Coffin Can Never Be Closed": Qu Qiubai Translates Social Science', *Boundary* 2, 43/3 (2016), pp. 253–86.

54. Yeh, *The Alienated Academy*, pp. 129–61.

55. For Xiang Jingyu see Gilmartin, *Engendering the Chinese Revolution*, pp. 86–95; for Yang Zhihua see Smith, *A Road Is Made*, p. 79.

56. *Shanghai Times*, 19 March 1925; Shanghai Municipal Police, CID 10381/1925, 'Japanese Mill Strike and Bolshevism', n.d.

57. Richard W. Rigby, *The May 30 Movement: Events and Themes*, Canberra, Australian National University Press, 1980, pp. 24–7.

58. Benton, *Prophets Unarmed*, pp. 242–3.

59. For this see Rigby, *The May 30 Movement*, pp. 32–3.

60. Antonia Finnane, *Changing Clothes in China: Fashion, History, Nation*, New York, Columbia University Press, 2007, pp. 134–5; Sherman Cochran (ed.), *Inventing Nanjing Road*, Ithaca, NY, Cornell University Press, 2000.

61. This account draws on Rigby, *The May 30 Movement*; Jeffrey N. Wasserstrom, *Student Protests in Twentieth-Century China: The View from Shanghai*, Stanford, CA, Stanford University Press, 1991, pp. 96–101; Nicholas R. Clifford, *Spoilt Children of Empire: Westerners in Shanghai and the Chinese Revolution of the 1920s*, Middlebury, VT, Middlebury College Press, 1991, pp. 97–107; Tiina Helena Airaksinen, *Love Your Country on Nanjing Road: The British and the May Fourth Movement in Shanghai*, Helsinki, Renvall Institute, 2005.

62. Robert Bickers, *Empire Made Me: An Englishman Adrift in Shanghai*, London, Allen Lane, 2003, p. 165.

63. *House of Commons Debates*, 15 June 1925, vol. 185, cc. 27–36.

64. Tom Buchanan, *East Wind: China and the British Left, 1925–1976*, Oxford, Oxford University Press, 2012, pp. 30–33. For a discussion of attitudes to force see Martin Thomas, *Violence and Colonial Order: Police, Workers and Protests in the European Colonial Empires, 1918–1940*, Cambridge, Cambridge University Press, 2012, esp. pp. 75–8.

65. Sophie Loy-Wilson, ' "Liberating" Asia: Strikes and Protest in Sydney and Shanghai, 1920–39', *History Workshop Journal*, 72 (2011), pp. 74–102.

66. For McEuan see Isabella Jackson, *Shaping Modern Shanghai: Colonialism in China's Global City*, Cambridge, Cambridge University Press, 2018, pp. 144–5; for the response of Shanghailanders see Clifford, *Spoilt Children of Empire*, pp. 108–9. The term Gilbertian was used at the time; see e.g. Catherine Ladds, *Empire Careers: Working for the Chinese Customs Service, 1854–1949*, Manchester, Manchester University Press, 2016.

67. Zhang, *The Rise of the Chinese Communist Party*, p. 426.

68. B. G. Martin, *The Shanghai Green Gang: Politics and Organized Crime, 1919–1937*, Berkeley, University of California Press, 1996, pp. 85–6; Hans J. van de Ven, *From Friend to Comrade: The Founding of the Chinese Communist Party, 1920–1927*, Berkeley, University of California Press, 1992, pp. 154–5.

69. Benton, *Prophets Unarmed*, pp. 247–8. For BAT see Rigby, *The May 30 Movement*, p. 145.

70. See the penetrating discussion in S. A. Smith, *Like Cattle and Horses: Nationalism and Labor in Shanghai, 1895–1927*, Durham, NC, Duke University Press, 2002, pp. 92–115; for women see Gilmartin, *Engendering the Chinese Revolution*, pp. 131–8.

71. For a brilliant discussion of this see Vera Schwarcz, *The Chinese Enlightenment: Intellectuals and the Legacy of the May Fourth Movement of 1919*, Berkeley, University of California Press, 1986, pp. 154–63.

72. Ibid., quotation at p. 162. For Gandhi see Brian Tsui, 'Decolonization and Revolution Debating Gandhism in Republican China', *Modern China*, 41/1 (2015), pp. 59–89.

73. Hallett Abend, *My Years in China, 1926–1941*, London, Lane, 1944, pp. 11–13.

74. *Papers Respecting the First Firing in the Shameen Affair of June 23, 1925*, London, HMSO, 1926; David Clive Wilson, 'Britain and the Kuomintang, 1924–28: A Study of the Interaction of Official Policies and Perceptions in Britain and China', PhD thesis, School of Oriental and African Studies (University of London), 1973, pp. 222–5.

75. Madhavi Thampi, 'Indian Soldiers, Policemen and Watchmen in China in the Nineteenth and Early Twentieth Centuries', *China Report*, 35/4 (1999), pp. 403–37, at p. 433–4; David Petrie, *Communism in India 1924–1927, edited with an Introduction and Explanatory Notes by Mahadevaprasad Saha*, Calcutta, Editions Indian, 1972, p. 191.

76. General Bluikker, 'Conditions at Canton after the events in Shameen on 23 June 1925', in C. Martin Wilbur and Julie Lien-ying How (eds), *Missionaries of Revolution: Soviet Advisers and Nationalist China, 1920–1927*, Cambridge, MA, Harvard University Press, 1989, pp. 506–7.

77. On the Canton organization see Robert James Horrocks, 'The Guangzhou-Hongkong strike, 1925–1926: Hongkong Workers in an Anti-Imperialist Movement', PhD thesis, University of Leeds, 1994, pp. 118–40, 153–4, 202. On the Communist Party in Hong Kong see Chan Lau Kit-ching, *From Nothing to Nothing: The Chinese Communist Movement and Hong Kong, 1921–1936*, Hong Kong, Hong Kong University Press, 1999, pp. 53–64.

78. Ming K. Chan, 'Hong Kong in Sino-British Conflict: Mass Mobilization and the Crisis of Legitimacy, 1912–26', in Ming K. Chan (ed.) *Precarious*

Balance: Hong Kong between China and Britain, 1842–1992, London, Routledge, 1997, pp. 45–52. For the pickets see Vera Vladimirovna Vishnyakova-Akimova, *Two Years in Revolutionary China, 1925–1927*, Cambridge, MA, East Asian Research Center, Harvard University, 1971, pp. 191–2.

79. Vishnyakova-Akimova, *Two Years in Revolutionary China*, pp. 2, 24, 47; Rigby, *The May 30 Movement*, p. 68.

80. Rigby, *The May 30 Movement*, pp. 63–74; Wasserstrom, *Student Protests in Twentieth-Century China*, pp. 113, 349.

81. Rigby, *The May 30 Movement*, pp. 41–2.

82. Karen Garner, *Precious Fire: Maud Russell and the Chinese Revolution*, Amherst, University of Massachusetts Press, 2009, pp. 70–74.

83. TNA, FO 228/3291, Intelligence report for Shanghai Consular District, for six months ended 30 September 1925.

84. John M. Carroll, *Edge of Empires: Chinese Elites and British Colonials in Hong Kong*, Cambridge, MA, Harvard University Press, 2005, pp. 135–46; Michael B. Share, *Where Empires Collided: Russian and Soviet Relations with Hong Kong, Taiwan, and Macao*, Hong Kong, Chinese University Press, 2007, pp. 65–6; on intimidation see Chan, *From Nothing to Nothing*, p. 60.

85. IISH, Archief Komintern-PKI/2, 'Report of Comrade Darsono to India Sub-Secretariat, 6 May 1926'.

86. TNA, FO 371/11698, MBPI, October–November 1925.

87. C. F. Yong and R. B. McKenna, 'The Kuomintang Movement in Malaya and Singapore, 1925–30', *Journal of Southeast Asian Studies*, 15/1 (1984), pp. 91–107.

88. For this see Hans J. van de Ven, *War and Nationalism in China, 1925–1945*, London, RoutledgeCurzon, 2003, pp. 88–92.

89. For a recent study see David Bowles, 'Finding the Way: Guomindang Discourse, Confucius, and the Challenges of Revolutionary Traditionalism in China, 1919–1934', unpublished D.Phil., University of Oxford, 2016, pp. 97–103, quotation at p. 99.

90. For the 'madmen' see Horrocks, 'The Guangzhou-Hongkong Strike, 1925–1926', p. 140.

91. This account is taken from Paul P. Mariani, 'China's "Christian General" Feng Yuxiang, the Evangelist Jonathan Goforth and the Changde Revival of 1919', *Studies in World Christianity*, 20/3 (2014), pp. 238–58.

92. TNA, FO 228/3291, Intelligence report for Shanghai Consular District, for six months ended 30 September 1925; David R. Stone, 'Soviet Arms Exports in the 1920s', *Journal of Contemporary History*, 48/1 (2013), pp. 57–77, at p. 70.

93. Vishnyakova-Akimova, *Two Years in Revolutionary China*, pp. 104–16. See the account of the advisers in the north in C. Martin Wilbur, *The*

Nationalist Revolution in China, 1923–1928, Cambridge, Cambridge University Press, 1984, pp. 42–4.

94. James E. Sheridan, *Chinese Warlord: The Career of Feng Yü-Hsiang*, Stanford, CA, Stanford University Press, 1966, pp. 199–202.

95. Vishnyakova-Akimova, *Two Years in Revolutionary China*, p. 231.

96. Ibid., pp. 228–9.

97. William J. Duiker, *Ho Chi Minh: A Life*, New York, Hyperion, 2000, p. 143.

98. As quoted in Quinn-Judge, *Ho Chi Minh*, p. 127.

99. Phan-Bội-Châu, *Overturned Chariot: The Autobiography of Phan-Bội-Châu*, trans. Vinh Sinh and Nicholas Wickenden, Honolulu, University of Hawaii Press, 1999, pp. 260–63.

100. Duiker, *Ho Chi Minh*, pp. 126–8; Quinn-Judge, *Ho Chi Minh*, pp. 75-77.

101. Vinh Sinh, Introduction to Châu, *Overturned Chariot*, pp. 26–7.

102. Ibid., p. 39.

103. For Nguyen An Ninh see Hue-Tam Ho Tai, *Radicalism and the Origins of the Vietnamese Revolution*, Cambridge, MA, Harvard University Press, 1992, pp. 72–87, quotation at p. 84; Philippe M. F. Peycam, *The Birth of Vietnamese Political Journalism: Saigon, 1916–1930*, New York, Columbia University Press, 2012, pp. 121–31.

104. NL-HaNA, Koloniën, Geheim Archief, 2.10.36.51, inv. nr. Vb 5-11-1925 A16, Tan Malaka to Governor-General Foch, 16 April 1926.

105. TNA, FO 371/11698, MBPI, October–November 1925.

106. This paragraph is drawn from Tan Malaka, *From Jail to Jail*, trans. and ed. Helen Jarvis, Athens, Ohio University Center for International Studies, 1991, vol. I, pp. 109–15. For an interesting discussion of Tan Malaka and Rizal see John Nery, *Revolutionary Spirit: José Rizal in Southeast Asia*, Singapore, Institute of Southeast Asian Studies, 2011, pp. 129–36.

107. Jim Richardson, *Komunista: The Genesis of the Philippine Communist Party, 1902–1935*, Honolulu, University of Hawaii Press, 2011, pp. 78–93.

108. Geoffrey C. Gunn, *Tan Malaka's Naar de 'Republiek Indonesia': A Translation and Commentary*, 2015, Jakarta, PT. Badak Merah Semesta, p. 84.

109. R. E. Elson, *The Idea of Indonesia: A History*, Cambridge, Cambridge University Press, 2009, pp. 26–47. For 'nation of intent' see Rustam Sani, 'Melayu Raya as a Malay "Nation of Intent"', in H. M. Dahlan (ed.), *The Nascent Malaysian Society*, Kuala Lumpur, UKM, 1976, pp. 25–38.

110. Gunn, *Tan Malaka's Naar de 'Republiek Indonesia'*, pp. 97–8.

111. Ibid., p. 54.

112. Ibid., pp. 9, 33.

113. John Ingleson, ' "Bound Hand and Foot": Railway Workers and the 1923 Strike in Java', *Indonesia*, 31 (1981), pp. 53–87.

114. IISH, Archief Komintern-PKI/1, 'Replies on the questions made by the Indonesian Commission and the National Secretariat', July 1926.

115. TNA, FO 271/12515, 'Increase in the Army – a plan', *Java Bode*, 16

December 1926, translated in Malaya Command Intelligence, 26 January 1927.

116. Ingleson, ' "Bound Hand and Foot" ', p. 70.

117. TNA, FO 371/11084, Charles M. Marling (The Hague) to Austen Chamberlain, 5 January 1925; 'Notes on the native movement and on the political situation in the Netherlands East Indies generally', enclosure in Consul-General Crosby's No. 52 Confidential of 4 May 1925.

118. M. C. Ricklefs, *Polarizing Javanese Society: Islamic and Other Visions, c. 1830–1930*, Singapore, NUS Press, 2007, pp. 236–7.

119. Bob Hering, *Soekarno, Founding Father of Indonesia: A Biography, 1901–1945*, Leiden, KITLV Press, 2002, p. 101. For the Peneleh circle see Budi Setyarso et al., *Tjokroaminoto: Freedom's Leading Light*, Jakarta, Tempo Publishing, 2013.

120. 'Nationalism, Islam and Marxism', in Sukarno, *Under the Banner of Revolution*, Jakarta, Yayasan Bung Karno, 2005, pp. 1–22.

121. Takashi Shiraishi, *An Age in Motion: Popular Radicalism in Java, 1912–1926*, Ithaca, NY, Cornell University Press, 1990, p. 258.

122. Ruth T. McVey, *The Rise of Indonesian Communism*, Ithaca, NY, Cornell University Press, 1965, pp. 180–81.

123. Gunn, *Tan Malaka's Naar de 'Republiek Indonesia'*, p. 34.

124. McVey, *The Rise of Indonesian Communism*, p. 183.

125. George D. Larson, *Prelude to Revolution: Palaces and Politics in Surakarta, 1912–1942*, Dordrecht, Foris, 1987, p. 126.

126. Shiraishi, *An Age in Motion*, pp. 277–8.

127. This is movingly told in ibid., pp. 280–98, quotations at pp. 284, 289. For his wife's passing see enclosures in NL-HaNA, Koloniën, Geheim Archief, 2.10.36.51, inv. nr. Vb 27-12-26 B20.

128. Shiraishi, *An Age in Motion*, pp. 246–7.

129. TNA, FO 371/12696, A. E. van der Lely, 'Report on the Indonesian Communist Party', January 1927.

130. Harry J. Benda and Ruth T. McVey, *The Communist Uprisings of 1926–1927 in Indonesia: Key Documents*, Ithaca, NY, Cornell University Press, 1960, p. 1.

131. TNA, FO 371/11698, MBPI, October–November 1925.

132. Benda and McVey, *Communist Uprisings of 1926–1927 in Indonesia*, p. 3.

133. IISH, Archief Komintern-PKI/10, Semaoen to Eastern Department of Comintern, 15 November 1924. For colonial attitudes and for Sneevliet's response see McVey, *The Rise of Indonesian Communism*, pp. 251, 254.

134. IISH, Archief Komintern-PKI/10, Sneevliet to Comrade Gregory, 29 April 1924.

135. IISH, Archief Komintern-PKI/10, Sneevliet to Petroff, 9 June 1924.

136. Sneevliet to Clara Zelkin, 23 April 1924, in Tony Saich, *The Origins of the*

First United Front in China: The Role of Sneevliet (Alias Maring), Leiden, Brill, 1991, p. 718.

137. This letter appears in TNA, FO 371/11698, enclosures in J. Crosby to Sir Austen Chamberlain, 28 November 1925. It is reprinted with annotations in Harry A. Poeze, *Tan Malaka: Strijder voor Indonesië's Vrijheid: Levensloop van 1897 tot 1945*, 's-Gravenhage, Nijhoff, 1976, pp. 301–2.

138. MBPI, October 1926, printed and discussed in Cheah Boon Kheng, *From PKI to the Comintern, 1924–1941: The Apprenticeship of the Malayan Communist Party: Selected Documents and Discussion*, Ithaca, NY, Southeast Asia Program Publications, 1992, p. 51.

139. For his movements see Poeze, *Tan Malaka*, pp. 303–8.

140. The account in this and the following paragraphs draws on McVey, *The Rise of Indonesian Communism*, pp. 315–33; Tan Malaka, *From Jail to Jail*, vol. I, pp. 133–8; Poeze, *Tan Malaka*, pp. 308–13.

141. Quoted in McVey, *The Rise of Indonesian Communism*, p. 139.

142. Ibid., p. 317.

14. THE LONG MARCH OF THE UNDERGROUND (1926–1927)

1. Randall Gould, *China in the Sun*, New York, Doubleday, 1946, p. 33.

2. Dan N. Jacobs, *Borodin: Stalin's Man in China*, Cambridge, MA, Harvard University Press, 1981, p. 195.

3. 'Roses without Blooms Part II' and 'In Memory of Liu Hezhen', in Lu Xun, *Jottings Under Lamplight*, Cambridge, MA, Harvard University Press, 2017, pp. 72–4, 74–8, quotations at pp. 74 and 78.

4. Gloria Davis, *Lu Xun's Revolution: Writing in a Time of Violence*, Cambridge, MA, Harvard University Press, 2013, pp. 22–130.

5. John Fitzgerald, *Awakening China: Politics, Culture, and Class in the Nationalist Revolution*, Stanford, CA, Stanford University Press, 1996, pp. 270–73.

6. Zhu Qihua, *China 1927: Memoir of a Debacle*, Hong Kong, MerwinAsia, 2013, pp. 8–13. For Zhang see Leon Rocha, 'A Utopian Garden City: Zhang Jingsheng's "Beautiful Beijing"', in Toby Lincoln (ed.), *The Habitable City in China: Urban History in the Twentieth Century*, Basingstoke, Palgrave Macmillan, 2017, pp. 143–68; Howard Chiang, *After Eunuchs: Science, Medicine, and the Transformation of Sex in Modern China*, New York, Columbia University Press, 2018, pp. 141–7.

7. Yueh Sheng, *Sun Yat-Sen University in Moscow and the Chinese Revolution: A Personal Account*, Lawrence, University of Kansas, 1971; for the Jesuit comparison see Klaus-Georg Riegel, 'Transplanting the Political Religion of Marxism-Leninism to China: The Case of the Sun Yat-sen University in Moscow (1925–30)', in Karl-Heinz Pohl (ed.), *Chinese Thought*

in a Global Context: A Dialogue Between Chinese and Western Philosophical Approaches, Leiden, Brill, 1999, pp. 327–58. For the intensity of regimes of self-criticism see Stanford University, Hoover Institution Archives, Peng Shu-tse and Zhen Bilan papers, box/folder 3/8 and 3/9, 'My Memoirs', *c.*1981, chs 8 and 9, with thanks to Rachel Leow.

8. For an engaging account of this see Elizabeth McGuire, 'Sino-Soviet Romance: An Emotional History of Revolutionary Geopolitics', *Journal of Contemporary History*, 52/4 (2017), pp. 853–73, expanded in *Red at Heart: How Chinese Communists Fell in Love with the Russian Revolution*, New York, Oxford University Press, 2018.

9. Stanford University, Hoover Institution Archives, Peng Shu-tse and Zhen Bilan papers, box/folder 3/10, 'My Memoirs', *c.*1981, ch. 10, p. 7.

10. Alexander Pantsov, *The Bolsheviks and the Chinese Revolution, 1919–1927*, Richmond, Curzon Press, 2000, p. 82.

11. Cheng Yingxiang and Claude Cadart, 'Vies parallèles et mouvementées de Peng Shuzhi et Chen Bilan', *Perspectives Chinoises*, 46/1 (1998), pp. 37–43.

12. Gregor Benton, 'Moscow's Sun Yat-Sen University', in Benton (ed.), *Prophets Unarmed: Chinese Trotskyists in Revolution, War, Jail, and the Return from Limbo*, Leiden, Brill, 2014, pp. 47–59.

13. Edward R. Slack, *Opium, State, and Society: China's Narco-Economy and the Guomindang, 1924–1937*, Honolulu, University of Hawaii Press, 2001, pp. 73–8.

14. Robert James Horrocks, 'The Guangzhou-Hongkong Strike, 1925–1926: Hongkong Workers in an Anti-Imperialist Movement', PhD thesis, University of Leeds, 1994, pp. 199–207, 210–13.

15. Jenkins to MacMurray, 14 April 1926, United States Department of State, *Papers Relating to the Foreign Relations of the United States, 1926*, vol. I, Washington, DC, US Government Printing Office, 1941, p. 704.

16. Hans J. van de Ven, *From Friend to Comrade: The Founding of the Chinese Communist Party, 1920–1927*, Berkeley, University of California Press, pp. 170–73.

17. Vera Vladimirovna Vishnyakova-Akimova, *Two Years in Revolutionary China, 1925–1927*, Cambridge, MA, Harvard University Press, 1971, p. 209.

18. A. I. Cherepanov, *As Military Adviser in China*, Moscow, Progress, 1982, p. 42.

19. Vishnyakova-Akimova, *Two Years in Revolutionary China*, p. 210.

20. Hsu-Hsin Chang and Ramon H. Myers (eds), *The Storm Clouds Clear Over China: The Memoir of Ch'en Li-Fu, 1900–1993*, Stanford, CA, Hoover Institution Press, 1994, pp. 28–9.

21. I follow here Hans van de Ven's analysis of the episode, which interrogates fresh documentary evidence, *War and Nationalism in China, 1925–1945*, London, RoutledgeCurzon, 2003, pp. 101–4. But see the earlier forensic

study by Tien-Wei Wu, 'Chiang Kai-Shek's March Twentieth Coup d'Etat of 1926', *Journal of Asian Studies*, 27/3 (1968), pp. 585–602, which sees more of a Communist-inspired plot.

22. TNA, FO 371/11698, MBPI, May 1926.

23. Jacobs, *Borodin*, pp. 203–7.

24. Marc Kasanin, *China in the Twenties*, Moscow, Central Department of Oriental Literature, 1973, p. 183.

25. Quoted by Horrocks, 'The Guangzhou-Hongkong Strike, 1925–1926', p. 213.

26. Lee Feigon, *Chen Duxiu, Founder of the Chinese Communist Party*, Princeton, NJ, Princeton University Press, 1983, pp. 189–90.

27. Zhang Guotao, *The Rise of the Chinese Communist Party, 1921–1927: Volume One of the Autobiography of Chang Kuo-t'ao*, Lawrence, University Press of Kansas, 1971, pp. 519, 512. For the afterlife of 'coolie' statement see Wu Jimin, 'Purgatory: The Chinese Trotskyists' Ordeal and Struggle', in Benton, *Prophets Unarmed*, p. 69.

28. David R. Stone, 'Soviet Arms Exports in the 1920s', *Journal of Contemporary History*, 48/1 (2013), pp. 57–77, figures at pp. 70–73.

29. 'Extract from the Report "Journey to Canton in October 1925", by A. Khmelev', in C. Martin Wilbur and Julie Lien-ying How, *Missionaries of Revolution: Soviet Advisers and Nationalist China, 1920–1927*, Cambridge, MA, Harvard University Press, 1989, pp. 523–5.

30. Shakhar Rahav, *Seeds of Radicalism in a Hinterland Metropolis*, Oxford, Oxford University Press, 2015, p. 165.

31. Jan J. Solecki, 'Blücher's "Grand Plan" of 1926', *China Quarterly*, 35 (1968), pp. 18–39.

32. E.g. Cherepanov, *As Military Adviser in China*, p. 222; Bubnov is quoted at p. 212.

33. Van de Ven, *War and Nationalism*, p. 105. For women in the northern expedition see Christina K. Gilmartin, *Engendering the Chinese Revolution: Radical Women, Communist Politics, and Mass Movements in the 1920s*, Berkeley, University of California Press, 1995, pp. 175–81.

34. This paragraph draws on Donald A. Jordan, *The Northern Expedition: China's National Revolution of 1926–1928*, Honolulu, University of Hawaii Press, 2018, pp. 77–90; C. Martin Wilbur, *The Nationalist Revolution in China, 1923–1928*, Cambridge, Cambridge University Press, 1984, pp. 55–9. For speed see Chi Man Kwong, *War and Geopolitics in Interwar Manchuria: Zhang Zuolin and the Fengtian Clique during the Northern Expedition*, Leiden, Brill, 2017, pp. 145–9.

35. Michael G. Murdock, 'Exploiting Anti-Imperialism: Popular Forces and Nation-State-Building During China's Northern expedition, 1926–1927', *Modern China*, 35/1 (2009), pp. 65–95.

36. Kuo Mo-Jo and Josiah W. Bennett, 'A Poet with the Northern Expedition',

Far Eastern Quarterly, 3/1 (1943), pp. 5–36, at pp. 29–30. For the executions see Jordan, *The Northern Expedition*, pp. 91–2.

37. Trampedach, 'Chiang Kai-shek between Revolution and Militarism, 1926/27', in Roland Felber, A. M. Grigoriev, Mechthild Leutner and M. L. Titarenko (eds), *The Chinese Revolution in the 1920s: Between Triumph and Disaster*, London, Routledge, 2002, p. 130.

38. 'British Interests in China', *The Times*, 13 October 1926.

39. Stephen R. MacKinnon, 'Wuhan's Search for Identity in the Republican Period', in Joseph Esherick (ed.), *Remaking the Chinese City: Modernity and National Identity, 1900 to 1950*, Honolulu, University of Hawaii Press, 1999, pp. 161–73; Ning J. Chang, 'Tension within the Church: British Missionaries in Wuhan, 1913–28', *Modern Asian Studies*, 33/2 (1999), pp. 421–44; Rahav, *Seeds of Radicalism in a Hinterland Metropolis*, pp. 13–45.

40. McMurray to Secretary of State, 8 September 1926, in United States Department of State, *Papers Relating to the Foreign Relations of the United States, 1926*, vol. I, Washington, DC, US Government Printing Office, 1941, p. 625.

41. Kuo Mo-Jo and Josiah W. Bennett, 'A Poet with the Northern Expedition', *Far Eastern Quarterly*, 3/2 (1944), pp. 144–71, quotations at p. 152.

42. Kuo Mo-Jo and Josiah W. Bennett, 'A Poet with the Northern Expedition', *Far Eastern Quarterly*, 3/3 (1944), pp. 237–59, quotation at p. 245.

43. Gilmartin, *Engendering the Chinese Revolution*, p. 181.

44. For missionary accounts see Karen Garner, *Precious Fire: Maud Russell and the Chinese Revolution*, Boston, University of Massachusetts Press, 2009, pp. 77–8. For US consular accounts see Meyer to Secretary of State, 8 October 1926, 12 October 1926, in United States Department of State, *Papers Relating to the Foreign Relations of the United States, 1926*, vol. I, pp. 645, 647.

45. See for example in *The Sydney Morning Herald*, on 30 September 1926.

46. *People's Tribune*, Beijing, 9 October 1926.

47. Kuo Mo-Jo and Josiah W. Bennett, 'A Poet with the Northern Expedition', *Far Eastern Quarterly*, 3/4 (1944), pp. 361–80, quotation at p. 371.

48. Ibid., p. 374.

49. Zhang, *The Rise of the Chinese Communist Party*, pp. 547–52, quotations at p. 547; for the New World see Tom Mann, 'What I Saw in China', London, National Unity Movement, 1927, p. 18.

50. Xie Bingying, *A Woman Soldier's Own Story: The Autobiography of Xie Bingying*, New York, Columbia University Press, 2001, for the song see p. 65.

51. For leaflets see the *People's Tribune*, 12 October 1926.

52. David Wilson, 'Britain and the Kuomintang, 1924–28: A Study of the Interaction of Official Policies and Perceptions in Britain and China', PhD, SOAS, 1973, p. 471.

53. IISH, Archief Komintern-PKI/2, 'Report of Comrade Darsono to India Sub-Secretariat, 6 May 1926'.
54. IISH, Archief Komintern-PKI/2, 'Minutes of the Indian Sub-Secretariat, 6 May 1926'; ibid., 'Minutes of the National Secretariat for India and Indonesia, 3 June 1926'. Alexander Pantsov identifies him as Hu Jiansan, *Bolsheviks and the Chinese Revolution*, p. 250, fn. 131.
55. IISH, Archief Komintern-PKI/1, 'Strictly Confidential: Indonesian Conference, July 22 1923 [*recte* 1926]'; IISH, Archief Komintern-PKI/2, 'Discussion at meeting of Indonesian Sub-secretariat July 29 1926'.
56. IISH, Archief Komintern-PKI/1, 'List of enrolled members of Party Kommunist Indonesia with at least 10 months course'.
57. Ibid., 'Strictly Confidential: Indonesian Conference, July 22 1923 [*recte* 1926]'; IISH, Archief Komintern-PKI/2, 'Discussion at meeting of Indonesian Sub-secretariat July 29 1926'.
58. IISH, Archief Komintern-PKI/1, 'Strictly Confidential: Indonesian Conference, July 22 1923 [*recte* 1926]'.
59. Ibid.
60. IISH, Archief Komintern-PKI/32, Semaoen, 'National Front'; ibid., 'Something after the Discussion in the British Sub-Secretariat of 3/6/26'.
61. IISH, Archief Komintern-PKI/2, 'Discussion at meeting of Indonesian Sub-secretariat July 29 1926'.
62. Ibid.
63. Ruth T. McVey, *The Rise of Indonesian Communism*, Ithaca, NY, Cornell University Press, 1965, pp. 336–40. For 'Miller', IISH, Archief Komintern-PKI/3, 'Report of comrade Semaoen to British Secretariat Meeting of 8 March 1927'.
64. 'The Governor General's Report of January 1927', in Harry J. Benda and Ruth T. McVey (eds), *The Communist Uprisings of 1926–1927 in Indonesia: Key Documents*, Ithaca, NY, Cornell University Press, pp. 10–11. For the issue of the Dutch response see also McVey, *The Rise of Indonesian Communism*, p. 327.
65. TNA, FO 371/12696, A. E. van der Lely, 'Report on the Indonesian Communist Party', January 1927.
66. Harry J. Benda, 'The Communist Rebellions of 1926–1927 in Indonesia', *Pacific Historical Review*, 24/2 (1955), pp. 139–52.
67. George D. Larson, *Prelude to Revolution: Palaces and Politics in Surakarta, 1912–1942*, Dordrecht, Foris, 1987, pp. 131–2.
68. Acting Consul-General to Sir Austen Chamberlain, 27 November 1926, TNA, FO 371 12696.
69. 'The Bantam Report', in Benda and McVey (eds), *Communist Uprisings of 1926–1927 in Indonesia*, esp. pp. 41–8. A definitive study is Michael C. Williams, *Communism, Religion, and Revolt in Banten*, Athens, Ohio, Ohio University Center for International Studies, 1990.

70. For the locale see Audrey R. Kahin, 'The 1927 Communist Uprising in Sumatra: A Reappraisal', *Indonesia*, 62 (1996), pp. 19–36, and her *Rebellion to Integration: West Sumatra and the Indonesian Polity, 1926–1998*, Amsterdam, Amsterdam University Press, 1999, pp. 31–49.

71. 'The Course of the Communist Movement on the West Coast of Sumatra, Part I (Political Section), Report of the Investigation Committee appointed under the Governmental Decree of February 13, 1927, No. 1a', reprinted in Benda and McVey (eds), *Communist Uprisings of 1926–1927 in Indonesia*, pp. 104–8, statistics at pp. 104–5.

72. 'The course of the Communist Movement on the West Coast of Sumatra', p. 111.

73. Ibid., pp. 107–14.

74. Ibid., esp. pp. 100–103, for arms pp. 120–21, among peasants pp. 123–5.

75. Muhamad Radjab, 'Village Childhood (The Autobiography of a Minangkabau Child)', in Susan Rodgers (ed.), *Telling Lives, Telling History: Autobiography and Historical Imagination in Modern Indonesia*, Berkeley, University of California Press, 1995, pp. 251–2.

76. TNA, FO 371/12696, A. E. van der Lely, 'Report on the Indonesian Communist Party', January 1927.

77. 'The Course of the Communist Movement on the West Coast of Sumatra', p. 169.

78. Ibid., pp. 176–7.

79. Kahin, 'The 1927 Communist Uprising in Sumatra', pp. 29–34.

80. J. Crosby to Austen Chamberlain, 28 April 1927, TNA, FO 371 12696.

81. 'The Governor General's Report of January 1927', in Benda and McVey (eds), *Communist Uprisings of 1926–1927 in Indonesia*, p. 8.

82. TNA, FO 371/12697, L. N. Guillemard to Leo Amery, 30 April 1927.

83. TNA, FO 371/12697, J. Crosby to Sir Austen Chamberlain, 7 May 1927.

84. Anne L. Foster, *Projections of Power: The United States and Europe in Colonial Southeast Asia, 1919–1941*, Durham, NC, and London, Duke University Press, 2010, pp. 31–3.

85. Later published in translation, 'The Course of the Communist Movement on the West Coast of Sumatra'.

86. See Akira Oki, 'Economic Constraints, Social Change, and the Communist Uprising in West Sumatra (1926–27): A Critical Review of B. J. O. Schrieke's West Coast Report', in Lynn L. Thomas and Franz von Benda-Beckmann (eds), *Change and Continuity in Minangkabau: Local, Regional, and Historical Perspectives on West Sumatra*, Athens, Ohio University Press, 1985, pp. 207–34.

87. Mao Zedong, 'Report on an Investigation of the Peasant Movement in Hunan', in *Selected Works of Mao Tse-Tung*, vol. I, Oxford, Pergamon Press, 1965, p. 27.

88. Sophie Quinn-Judge, *Ho Chi Minh: The Missing Years, 1919–1941*, London, Hurst, 2003, pp. 86–90.

89. For this background see Jon Jacobson, *When the Soviet Union Entered World Politics*, Berkeley, University of California Press, 1994, pp. 216–20.

90. For this point see Robert C. North and Xenia J. Eudin, *M. N. Roy's Mission to China: The Communist-Kuomintang Split of 1927*, Berkeley, University of California Press, 1963, p. 59.

91. For the twists and turns of Comintern policy see Pantsov, *The Bolsheviks and the Chinese Revolution, 1919–1927*; also Bruce Elleman, *Moscow and the Emergence of Communist Power in China, 1925–30: The Nanchang Uprising and the Birth of the Red Army*, London, Routledge, 2009.

92. David Petrie, *Communism in India 1924–1927, edited with an Introduction and Explanatory Notes by Mahadevaprasad Saha*, Calcutta, Editions Indian, 1972, p. 164.

93. For Muzaffar Ahmad's account see Muzaffar Ahmad, *The Communist Party of India and Its Formation Abroad*, Calcutta, National Book Agency, 1962, pp. 407–13, quotation at p. 411.

94. Roy to Petrov, 30 December 1925, in Purabi Roy, Sobhanlal Datta Gupta and Hari S. Vasudevan (eds), *Indo-Russian Relations, 1917–1947: Select Documents from the Archives of the Russian Federation, Part 1, 1917–1947*, Calcutta, Asiatic Society, 1999, pp. 205–6.

95. Daniel Brückenhaus, *Policing Transnational Protest: Liberal Imperialism and the Surveillance of Anticolonialists in Europe, 1905–1945*, Oxford, Oxford University Press, 2017, pp. 142–9. For a recent study see Michele L. Louro, *Comrades against Imperialism: Nehru, India, and Interwar Internationalism*, Cambridge, Cambridge University Press, 2018, esp. pp. 17–120.

96. John Patrick Haithcox, *Communism and Nationalism in India: M. N. Roy and Comintern Policy, 1920–1939*, Princeton, NJ, Princeton University Press, 1971, p. 49.

97. Maulana Barakatullah to Radowski, from Berlin, 6 May 1926, Roy et al. (eds), *Indo-Russian Relations, 1917–1947*, pp. 218–19.

98. Haithcox, *Communism and Nationalism in India*, p. 48.

99. M. N. Roy to Presidium ECCI, 20 May 1925; Roy to Central Control Commission of the Communist Party of the Soviet Union, 4 August 1926, in Roy et al. (eds), *Indo-Russian Relations, 1917–1947*, pp. 212–13, 219–22.

100. Copy of letter from Nalini Gupta marked January 1927 to M. N. Roy, in Roy et al. (eds), *Indo-Russian Relations, 1917–1947*, p. 223.

101. Copy of M. N. Roy's letter to Maurice dated 8 January 1927, in Roy et al. (eds), *Indo-Russian Relations, 1917–1947*, p. 229.

102. Barakatullah's signed note for Comintern 29 February 1927, ibid., pp. 232–4.

103. Petrie, *Communism in India*, p. 204.

104. University of Warwick, papers of Tom Mann, 334/3/6/47, Letter from China Sea to his wife, Elsie Mann, 15 February 1927, https://cdm21047.contentdm.oclc.org/digital/collection/russian/id/3215/rec/9 (last accessed 19 August 2019).

105. Hoover Insitution Archives, Evelyn Trent papers, Accession No. 71023-8M.16, box 1, Evelyn Trent to 'Jack Horner' (Sneevliet), 23 March (1924).

106. Ibid.

107. Ibid., Sneevliet to Evelyn Trent, 30 September 1925.

108. Ibid., Evelyn Trent to 'Jack Horner' (Sneevliet), 23 March [1924].

109. Ibid., Evelyn Trent to 'N' (M. N. Roy), 25 December 1926.

110. Van de Ven, *War and Nationalism*, pp. 106–7.

111. For the eastern campaign see Peter Worthing, *General He Yingqin: The Rise and Fall of Nationalist China*, Cambridge, Cambridge University Press, 2016, pp. 58–71.

112. Kasanin, *China in the Twenties*, p. 196.

113. Vishnyakova-Akimova, *Two Years in Revolutionary China*, pp. 261–3.

114. Zhu, *China 1927*, pp. 17–18, 19, 29.

115. Vishnyakova-Akimova, *Two Years in Revolutionary China*, pp. 281–3. For a description see Kasanin, *China in the Twenties*, p. 244.

116. P. H. Munro-Faure, 'The Kiukiang Incident of 1927', *Journal of the Hong Kong Branch of the Royal Asiatic Society*, 29 (1989), pp. 61–76; Edmund S. K. Fung, 'The Chinese Nationalists and the Unequal Treaties 1924–1931', *Modern Asian Studies*, 21/4 (1987), pp. 793–819.

117. Herbert Owen Chapman, *The Chinese Revolution, 1926–27: A Record of the Period under Communist Control as Seen from the Nationalist Capital*, Hankow, London, Constable & Co., 1928, pp. 33–5.

118. For a vivid account of foreigners' reactions see Nicholas Clifford, *Spoilt Children of Empire: Westerners in Shanghai and the Chinese Revolution of the 1920s*, Middlebury, VT, Middlebury College Press, 1991.

119. Quoted and discussed in North and Eudin, *M. N. Roy's Mission to China*, pp. 46–7.

120. Zhu, *China 1927*, quotations at pp. 52, 58.

121. North and Eudin, *M. N. Roy's Mission to China*, p. 47.

122. For the uprising see S. A. Smith, *A Road Is Made: Communism in Shanghai, 1920–1927*, Richmond, Curzon, 2000, pp. 156–66; Elizabeth J. Perry, 'From Paris to the Paris of the East and Back: Workers as Citizens in Modern Shanghai', *Comparative Studies in Society and History*, 41/2 (1999), pp. 348–73, at pp. 355–9.

123. Smith, *A Road Is Made*, pp. 156–66.

124. Perry, 'From Paris to the Paris of the East and Back', pp. 357–9.

125. Van de Ven, *War and Nationalism*, pp. 117–18.

126. Sam Ginsbourg, *My First Sixty Years in China*, Beijing, New World Press, 1982, p. 53.

127. Smith, *A Road is Made*, p. 154.
128. Mann, 'What I Saw in China', p. 4.
129. Van de Ven, *From Friend to Comrade*, p. 196.
130. Quoted in Davis, *Lu Xun's Revolution*, pp. 45, 36.
131. Mann, 'What I Saw in China', pp. 9–12; for Browder's account see Earl Browder, *Civil War in Nationalist China*, Chicago, Labor Unity Publishing Association, 1927.
132. Brian G. Martin, *The Shanghai Green Gang: Politics and Organized Crime, 1919–1937*, Berkeley, University of California Press, 1996, pp. 86–91.
133. Zheng Chaolin, *An Oppositionist for Life: Memoirs of the Chinese Revolutionary Zheng Chaolin*, trans. and ed. Gregor Benton, Atlantic Highlands, NJ, Humanities Press, 1996, pp. 262–3; van de Ven, *War and Nationalism*, pp. 117–18. For an account of the meeting see T'ang Leang-li, *The Inner History of the Chinese Revolution*, London, George Routledge & Sons, 1930, pp. 265–6.
134. North and Eudin, *M. N. Roy's Mission to China*, p. 57–8. For the war scare see Jacobson, *When the Soviet Union Entered World Politics*, pp. 217–32.
135. Ibid., p. 60.
136. Maurice J. Meisner, *Li Ta-Chao and the Origins of Chinese Marxism*, Cambridge, MA, Harvard University Press, 1967, pp. 257–9.
137. Frederic Wakeman, *Policing Shanghai, 1927–1937*, Berkeley, University of California Press, 1995, pp. 122–4. For the British and French see Elizabeth J .Perry, *Shanghai on Strike: The Politics of Chinese Labor*, Stanford, CA, Stanford University Press, 1993, pp. 90–91.
138. Parks M. Coble, *The Shanghai Capitalists and the Nationalist Government, 1927–1937*, Cambridge, MA, Council on East Asian Studies, Harvard University, 1980, p. 32.
139. Smith, *A Road Is Made*, pp. 200–205.
140. Figures from van de Ven, *War and Nationalism*, p. 119.
141. North and Eudin, *M. N. Roy's Mission to China*, pp. 60–62, 185.
142. Michael Tsang-Woon Tsin, *Nation, Governance, and Modernity in China: Canton, 1900–1927*, Stanford, CA, Stanford University Press, 2000, pp. 71–90, at pp. 169–70.
143. Kim San and Nym Wales, *The Song of Ariran: The Life Story of a Korean Rebel*, New York, John Day, 1941, pp. 88–9.
144. Meisner, *Li Ta-Chao and the Origins of Chinese Marxism*, pp. 257–9.
145. C. F. Yong, *The Origins of Malayan Communism*, Singapore, South Seas Society, 1997, pp. 75–8.
146. FO371/13215, R. Onraet, 'The Kuo Min Tang in Malaya, July–December 1927', 17 March 1928.
147. Zheng, *Oppositionist for Life*, pp. 106–7; Zhang, *The Rise of the Chinese Communist Party*, p. 619.

148. Zheng, *Oppositionist for Life*, p. 120.

149. Zhang, *The Rise of the Chinese Communist Party*, p. 617.

150. North and Eudin, *M. N. Roy's Mission to China*, p. 165.

151. Van de Ven, *War and Nationalism*, pp. 11–13.

152. Lee, *Chen Duxiu*, pp. 192–5.

153. Quoted in Zhang Guangyu, 'M. N. Roy in Wuhan', *China Report*, 24/1 (1988), pp. 81–97, at p. 89.

154. Milly Bennett, *On Her Own: Journalistic Adventures from San Francisco to the Chinese Revolution, 1917–1927*, London, M. E. Sharpe, 1993, p. 193.

155. Neville Kirk, *Transnational Radicalism and the Connected Lives of Tom Mann and Robert Samuel Ross*, Oxford, Oxford University Press, 2017, p. 106.

156. Arthur Ransome, 'The Shanghai Mind', *Manchester Guardian*, 2 May 1927, and see Nicholas R. Clifford, 'A Revolution Is Not a Tea Party: The "Shanghai Mind(s)" Reconsidered', *Pacific Historical Review*, 59/4 (1990), pp. 501–26; Robert Bickers, 'Shanghailanders: The Formation and Identity of the British Settler Community in Shanghai 1843–1937', *Past and Present*, 159 (1998), pp. 161–211.

157. Vincent Sheean, *Personal History*, Garden City, NY, Garden City Publishing Co., 1937, p. 205.

158. As cited by Harald S. Naess in his Introduction to Grieg's 'Our Power and Our Glory', in Soya, Walentin Chorell, Davíð Stefánsson frá Fagraskógi, Nordahl Grieg, Pär Lagerkvist, *Five Modern Scandinavian Plays*, New York, Twayne Publishers, 1971, p. 128.

159. The most immediate and colourful account of this circle is Bennett, *On Her Own*. But see also Jacobs, *Borodin*, pp. 260–62.

160. Gould, *China in the Sun*, quotations at pp. 69, 71.

161. Naess, in Soya et al., *Five Modern Scandinavian Plays*, p. 284.

162. Prohme to Helen Freeland, 19 March 1927, in Baruch Hirson and Arthur J. Knodel, *Reporting the Chinese Revolution: The Letters of Rayna Prohme*, ed. Gregor Benton, London, Pluto Press, 2007, p. 75.

163. Wilbur and How, *Missionaries of Revolution*, p. 392.

164. 'The letter from Shanghai', appendix to Leon Trotsky, *Problems of the Chinese Revolution*, New York, Paragon Book, 3rd edn., 1966, pp. 408, 406.

165. Michael B. Share, *Where Empires Collided: Russian and Soviet Relations with Hong Kong, Taiwan, and Macao*, Hong Kong, Chinese University Press, 2007, p. 70–71.

166. Zhu, *China 1927*, p. 84.

167. Michael E. Lestz, 'The Soong Sisters and China's Revolutions', in Yvonne Yazbeck Haddad and Ellison Banks Findly (eds), *Women, Religion, and Social Change*, New York, SUNY Press, 1985, pp. 177–96, at p. 383.

168. I draw here on Elisabeth Croll's classic, *Feminism and Socialism in China*, London, Routledge, 1980, pp. 121–30.

169. Chapman, *The Chinese Revolution, 1926–27*, pp. 85–7.
170. Croll, *Feminism and Socialism in China*, pp. 130, 138–46, quotation at p. 144. I also have in mind the idea of the 'cultural nexus'; see Prasenjit Duara, *Culture, Power, and the State: Rural North China, 1900–1942*, Stanford, CA, Stanford University Press, 1991, pp. 4–6, 15–41.
171. Fitzgerald, *Awakening China*, pp. 284–5.
172. Chia-lin Pao Tao, 'The Nude Parade of 1927: Nudity and Women's Liberation in China', in Shanshan Du and Ya-chen Chen, *Women and Gender in Contemporary Chinese Societies: Beyond Han Patriarchy*, Lanham, MD, Lexington Books, 2013, pp. 171–84. This article suggests that more research is needed on this episode.
173. Irma Duncan, *Duncan Dancer, an Autobiography*, Middletown, CT, Wesleyan University Press, 1966, pp. 285–99, quotation at p. 275.
174. Xie, *A Woman Soldier's Own Story* p. 71.
175. Josephine Fowler, 'From East to West and West to East: Ties of Solidarity in the Pan-Pacific Revolutionary Trade Union Movement, 1923–1934', *International Labor and Working-Class History*, 66/1 (2004), pp. 99–117.
176. Chi, *War and Geopolitics in Interwar Manchuria*, pp. 168–76; Jordan, *The Northern Expedition*, pp. 149–51.
177. Zhu, *China 1927*, p. 124.
178. Ibid., p. 123.
179. Ibid., p. 158.
180. A point made cuttingly by Sheean, *Personal History*, pp. 217–24.
181. For this see Fitzgerald, *Awakening China*, p. 176.
182. Zheng, *An Oppositionist for Life*, pp. 228–9.
183. Zhu, *China 1927*, quotation at p. 164.
184. Jay Taylor, *The Generalissimo's Son: Chiang Ching-Kuo and the Revolutions in China and Taiwan*, Cambridge, MA, Harvard University Press, 2009, p. 43.
185. The text remained disputed afterwards; North and Eudin, *M. N. Roy's Mission to China*, p. 107 fn.
186. T'ang, *The Inner History of the Chinese Revolution*, pp. 280–81.
187. Zhang, *The Rise of the Chinese Communist Party*, p. 639.
188. M. N. Roy, *My Experiences in China*, Bombay, Renaissance Publishing Company, 1938, p. 55.
189. Zhu, *China 1927*, pp. 172–6, quotations at p. 176.
190. Jacobs, *Borodin*, p. 269–71.
191. James E. Sheridan, *Chinese Warlord: The Career of Feng Yü-Hsiang*, Stanford, CA, Stanford University Press, 1966, pp. 228–32, quotation at p. 229.
192. Stalin to Molotov and Bukharin, 27 June 1927, in Lars T. Lih, Oleg V. Naumov and Oleg Khlevniuk (ed.), *Stalin's Letters to Molotov, 1925–1936*, New Haven, CT, Yale University Press, 1996, p. 137.

193. Prohme to Helen Freeland, 6 August 1927, and to her sister Gracie, 7 August 1927, in Hirson and Knodel, *Reporting the Chinese Revolution*, pp. 81, 83.

194. The story is told by Sheean, *Personal History*, pp. 255-8.

195. Vishnyakova-Akimova, *Two Years in Revolutionary China*, p. 328.

196. For the background see Fernando Galbiati, *P'eng P'ai and the Hai-Lu-Feng Soviet*, Stanford, Stanford University Press, 1985.

197. 'Chang Kuo-t'ao's Report', in C. Martin Wilbur, 'The Ashes of Defeat', *China Quarterly*, 18 (1964), pp. 3–54, at p. 32.

198. Zhu, *China 1927*, pp. 217–18.

199. For the background to the uprising see Marcia R. Ristaino, *China's Art of Revolution: The Mobilization of Discontent, 1927 and 1928*, Durham, NC, Duke University Press, 1987, pp. 21–30.

200. Zhu, *China 1927*, p. 35.

201. J. Guillermaz, 'The Nanchang Uprising', *China Quarterly*, 11 (1962), pp. 161–8.

202. Laura M Calkins, 'Recapturing an Urban Identity: Chinese Communists and the Commune at Shantou, 1927', *Studies on Asia*, series IV, 1/2 (2011), pp. 35–73.

203. 'Chang Kuo-t'ao's Report', in Wilbur, 'The Ashes of Defeat', p. 33.

204. Zhu, *China 1927*, p. 252.

205. 'Chou I-ch'un's Report', in Wilbur, 'The Ashes of Defeat', p. 30.

206. 'Chang T'ai-lei's Report: The Experiences of the "August 1st Incident", the Cause of Defeat, and the Future', in Wilbur, 'The Ashes of Defeat', p. 37.

207. Mao Zedong, 'Report on an Investigation of the Peasant Movement in Hunan', in *Selected Works of Mao Tse-Tung*, vol. I, p. 28.

208. Roy Hofheinz, 'The Autumn Harvest Insurrection', *China Quarterly*, 32 (1967), pp. 37–87, at p. 84.

209. Ibid., esp. pp. 61–6; Ristaino, *China's Art of Revolution*, pp. 56–74; for more on Mao at this period see Alexander V. Pantsov and Steven I. Levine, *Mao: The Real Story*, New York, Simon & Schuster, 2013, pp. 185–215.

210. Galbiati, *P'eng P'ai and the Hai-Lu-Feng Soviet*, esp. pp. 277–82.

211. Kit-ching Lau Chan, 'Hong Kong in Sino-British Diplomacy, 1926–45', in Ming K. Chan (ed.), *Precarious Balance: Hong Kong Between China and Britain, 1842–1992*, London, M. E. Sharper, 1994, pp. 71–90, at pp. 73–4.

212. San and Wales, *The Song of Ariran*, pp. 91–104.

213. Ibid., p. 101.

214. Share, *Where Empires Collided*, pp. 75–7.

215. *China Mail*, 14 December 1927.

216. *China Mail*, 13 December 1927. The story of fate of the bobbed-hair women seems to have its origin in a *Ta Kung Pao* report of 19 December 1927, cited in Harold Isaacs, *The Tragedy of the Chinese Revolution*, Stanford, Stanford University Press, 1951, p. 290.

217. San and Wales, *The Song of Ariran*, p. 107.

218. Ibid., p. 110.
219. Mayer to Secretary of State, 21 March 1928, United States Department of State, *Papers Relating to the Foreign Relations of the United States, 1928*, vol. II, Washington, DC, U.S. Government Printing Office, 1928, p, 127.
220. For this see van de Ven, *War and Nationalism*, pp. 125–8.
221. This 'decoupling' is a major theme of Brian Tsui, *China's Conservative Revolution: The Quest for a New Order, 1927–1949*, Cambridge, Cambridge University Press, 2018, esp. pp. 26–67.
222. Quinn-Judge, *Ho Chi Minh*, pp. 106–10.
223. Sheean, *Personal History*, quotation at p. 302.
224. Patricia Stranahan, *Underground: The Shanghai Communist Party and the Politics of Survival, 1927–1937*, Lanham, MD, Rowman & Littlefield, 1998, esp. ch. 1.
225. Zhu, *China 1927*, p. 304.
226. Alexander Pantsov and Steven I. Levine, *Deng Xiaoping: A Revolutionary Life*, Oxford, Oxford University Press, 2015, pp. 52–5.
227. Xie, *A Woman Soldier's Own Story*, pp. 193–4.
228. Helen Foster Snow, *Women in Modern China*, Beijing, Foreign Languages Press, 1967, p. 271.
229. 'Report on the Prisons for the Year 1924', *Federated Malay States Gazette*, 10 July 1925, p. 1.
230. R. H. J. Sydney, *Malay Land: 'Tanah Malayu': Some Phases of Life in Modern British Malaya*, London, C. Palmer, 1926, pp. 177–21.
231. Victor Purcell, *Memoirs of a Malayan Official*, London, Cassell, 1965, p. 158.
232. ANM, Selangor Secretariat, 2066/1926, Petition, forwarded by District Superintendent of Prisons, 13 April 1926; Protector of Chinese, minute, 1 May 1926.
233. ANM, Selangor Secretariat, 146/1927, Prisons Office to Secretary of British Resident, Selangor, 25 March 1927; *Malayan Daily Express*, 26 March 1927.
234. *Straits Times*, 25 March 1927; ANOM, INDO/GG/65533, French Legation Bangkok to Hanoi, 20 June 1927. The last observation comes from School of Oriental and African Studies, London, Wilfred Blythe papers, PPMS 31/File 15, 'Background note', n.d.

EPILOGUE: OUT OF EXILE

1. *Straits Times*, 14 February 1928.
2. Alun Jones, 'Internal Security in British Malaya, 1895–1942', PhD thesis, Yale University, p. 129.

3. W. J. Blythe, *The Impact of Chinese Secret Societies in Malaya: A Historical Study*, London, Oxford University Press, 1969.

4. Takashi Shiraishi, 'A New Regime of Order: The Origin of Modern Surveillance Policies in Indonesia', in James T. Siegel and Audrey Kahin (eds), *Southeast Asia Over Three Generations: Essays Presented to Benedict R. O'G. Anderson*, Ithaca, NY, Cornell University Press/SEAP Publications, 2003, pp. 47–74, at p. 47; Abidin Kusno, *The Appearances of Memory: Mnemonic Practices of Architecture and Urban Form in Indonesia*, Durham, NC, Duke University Press, 2010, pp. 182–200.

5. Carl Bridge, *Holding India to the Empire: The British Conservative Party and the 1935 Constitution*, New York, Envoy, 1986.

6. For French colonial cultures see Kathryn Robson and Jennifer Yee, *France and 'Indochina': Cultural Representations*, Lanham, MD, Lexington Books, 2005; Panivong Norindr, *Phantasmatic Indochina: French Colonial Ideology in Architecture, Film, and Literature*, Durham, NC, Duke University Press, 1996.

7. On this see Renato Rosaldo's brilliant essay, 'Imperialist Nostalgia', *Representations*, 26 (1989), pp. 107–22.

8. A. W. Brian Simpson, 'Round up the Usual Suspects: The Legacy of British Colonialism and the European Convention on Human Rights', *Loyola Law Review*, 41/4 (1996), pp. 629–711; and for legacies see John Reynolds, *Empire, Emergency and International Law*, Cambridge, Cambridge University Press, 2017; and on the idea of terrorism see the forthcoming work by Joseph McQuade.

9. Home Department, Government of India, *India and Communism, Revised up to the 1 January 1935*, Simla, Government of India Press, pp. 106, 168.

10. A point well made by Heather Streets-Salter, 'The Noulens Affair in East and Southeast Asia: International Communism in the Interwar Period', *Journal of American-East Asian Relations*, 21/4 (2014), pp. 394–414.

11. Anne L. Foster, *Projections of Power: The United States and Europe in Colonial Southeast Asia, 1919–1941*, Durham, NC, Duke University Press, 2010, pp. 35–7; for more details of the arrest see *Manila Bulletin*, 15 August 1927.

12. Tan Malaka, *From Jail to Jail*, trans. and ed. Helen Jarvis, Athens, Ohio University Center for International Studies, 3 vols, 1991, vol. I, pp. 139–45.

13. *Manila Bulletin*, 16 August 1927.

14. *The Tribune*, 16 August 1927, quoted in Harry A. Poeze, *Tan Malaka: Strijder Voor Indonesië's Vrijheid: Levensloop van 1897 Tot 1945*,'s-Gravenhage, Nijhoff, 1976, p. 372.

15. *New York Times*, 16 August 1927, quoted in Poeze, *Tan Malaka*, p. 383.

16. Takashi Shiraishi, 'Policing the Phantom Underground', *Indonesia*, 63 (1997), pp. 1–46, esp. pp. 3–9.

17. *Manila Bulletin*, 16 August 1927.

18. Quoted in Poeze, *Tan Malaka*, p. 371.

19. Ibid., pp. 372–87.

20. Tan Malaka, *From Jail to Jail*, vol. I, pp. 149–59.

21. Philippines National Library, MLQ papers, series II, box 30, reel 11, Tan Malaka to Manuel L. Quezon, 1 May 1928.

22. Ibid., Tan Malaka to Manuel L. Quezon, 25 April 1928.

23. Ibid., Quezon to Tan Malaka, 1 April 1929.

24. Shiraishi, 'Policing the Phantom Underground'.

25. Chan Lau Kit-ching, *From Nothing to Nothing: The Chinese Communist Movement and Hong Kong, 1921–1936*, London, Hurst, 1999, pp. 95–125.

26. For a 'third wave' of Chinese activism see C. F. Yong, *The Origins of Malayan Communism*, Singapore, South Seas Society, 1997, p. 121. See also an important new study which appeared as this book was going to press: Anna Belogurova, *The Nanyang Revolution: The Comintern and Chinese Networks in Southeast Asia, 1890–1957*, Cambridge, Cambridge University Press, 2019, esp. pp. 32–47.

27. Yong, *The Origins of Malayan Communism*, pp. 113–14.

28. Described in depth in Belogurova, *The Nanyang Revolution*, pp. 48–80.

29. Tuong Vu emphasizes the bureaucratic nature of the tensions in *Vietnam's Communist Revolution: The Power and Limits of Ideology*, Cambridge, Cambridge University Press, 2016, pp. 65–67, Ha Hoy Tap quotation at p. 72.

30. Sophie Quinn-Judge, 'Ideological Influences on the Revolutionary High Tide: The Comintern, Class War and Peasants', *South East Asia Research*, 19/4 (2011), pp. 685–710.

31. There is a large literature on this in English. In addition to other cited articles, see William J. Duiker, 'The Red Soviets of Nghe-Tinh: An Early Communist Rebellion in Vietnam', *Journal of Southeast Asian Studies*, 4/2 (1973), pp. 186–98; James C. Scott, *The Moral Economy of the Peasant: Rebellion and Subsistence in Southeast Asia*, New Haven, CT, and London, Yale University Press, 1976; Pierre Brocheux, 'Moral Economy or Political Economy? The Peasants Are Always Rational', *Journal of Asian Studies*, 42/4 (1983), pp. 791–803; Martin Bernal, 'The Nghe-Tinh Soviet Movement 1930–1931', *Past and Present*, 92 (1981), pp. 148–68.

32. Bernal, 'The Nghe-Tinh Soviet Movement 1930–1931', figures at pp. 160–61.

33. As discussed by Bruce M. Lockhart, 'The Nghệ Tĩnh Movement in Communist Party Historiography', *South East Asia Research*, 19/4 (2011), pp. 711–35.

34. I invoke here the classic by Roy Hofheinz Jr, *The Broken Wave: The Chinese Communist Peasant Movement, 1922–1928*, Cambridge, MA, Harvard University Press, 1977.

35. Patricia Stranahan, *Underground: The Shanghai Communist Party and the Politics of Survival, 1927–1937*, Lanham, MD, Rowman & Littlefield, 1998.

36. Yong, *The Origins of Malayan Communism*, p. 130. There is considerable debate on the circumstances of the party's funding; for an assessment of the evidence see Fujio Hara, 'The Malayan Communist Party as Recorded in the Comintern Files', Singapore, ISEAS Working Paper no. 1, 2016, pp. 48–59.

37. ANOM, Indo HCI/SPCE 369, Enclosure 1, G. Gorton to Nadaud, 2 June 1931.

38. Laurent Metzger, 'Joseph Ducroux, a French Agent of the Comintern in Singapore (1931–1932)', *Journal of the Malaysian Branch of the Royal Asiatic Society*, 69/1 (1996), pp. 1–20.

39. I draw here on an excerpt of Ducroux's unpublished memoir, headed 'Singapour' and dated 16 September 1970. This is from the personal collection of Sophie Quinn-Judge and I am most grateful to her for providing me with a copy.

40. ANOM, Indo HCI/SPCE 365, 'Lettre écrite à encre sympathique (eau de riz) et révélée avec de la teinture d'iode étendue d'eau, envoyée de Singapour par Ducroux dit Lefanc, à T.V. Wong, alias Nuuyen-Ai-Quoc, à Kowloon no. 186 Tam-Kau Road, rédigée en français'. For the surveillance see 'Alleged Communistic Activities', *Singapore Free Press*, 20 June 1931.

41. Metzger, 'Joseph Ducroux'; *Straits Times*, 18 July 1931.

42. 'European Red Sent to Prison', *Malaya Tribune*, 23 June 1931.

43. Frederick S. Litten, 'The Noulens Affair', *The China Quarterly*, 138 (1994), pp. 492–512; Streets-Salter, 'The Noulens Affair in East and Southeast Asia', pp. 394–414; 'Death Sentence on Noulenses', *Straits Times*, 20 August 1932.

44. For this see esp. Streets-Salter, 'The Noulens Affair in East and Southeast Asia'. For the death of Cai Hesen see Liyan Liu, *Red Genesis: The Hunan First Normal School and the Creation of Chinese Communism, 1903–1921*, New York, SUNY Press, 2012, p. 208.

45. This paragraph and the next are based on Dennis J. Duncanson, 'Ho-Chi-Minh in Hong Kong, 1931–32', *The China Quarterly*, 57 (1974), pp. 84–100 and documents collected by the Ho Chi Minh Museum and published in an English edition ed. by Lady Borton and Trinh Ngoc Thai, *The Legal Case of Nguyen Ai Quoc (Ho Chi Minh) in Hong Kong, 1931–1933 (Documents and Photographs)*, Hanoi, National Political Publishers/Ho Chi Minh Museum, 2006. I am grateful to John Carroll for giving me a copy.

46. These artefacts are to be found in ANOM, Indo HCI/SPCE 365.

47. William J. Duiker, *Ho Chi Minh*, New York, Hyperion, 2000, pp. 198–9, 207.

48. M. N. Roy, *My Experiences in China*, Calcutta, Renaissance Publishers, 1945, p. 53.

49. M. N. Roy, *Revolution and Counter-Revolution in China*, Calcutta, Renaissance Publishers, 1946.

50. Sonia Gandhi (ed.), *Two Alone, Two Together: Letters Between Indira Gandhi and Jawaharlal Nehru, 1922–1964*, New Delhi, Penguin Books India, 2004, p. 95.

51. Sibnarayan Ray (ed.), *The World Her Village: Selected Writings and Letters of Ellen Roy*, Calcutta, Ananda, 1979, pp. 1–46.

52. M. N. Roy, *Memoirs*, Bombay, Allied Publishers, pp. 581–3.

53. E.g. Government of India, *India and Communism*, pp. 162–9.

54. Suchetana Chattopadhyay, *An Early Communist: Muzaffar Ahmad in Calcutta*, Tulika Books, Delhi, 2011, pp. 217–24, at p. 219.

55. For a contemporary account see Lester Hutchinson, *Conspiracy at Meerut*, London, Allen & Unwin, 1935. See the collection edited by Michele L. Louro and Carolien Stolte, 'Introduction: The Meerut Conspiracy Case in Comparative and International Perspective', *Comparative Studies of South Asia, Africa and the Middle East*, 33/3 (2013), pp. 310–15.

56. TNA, FO1093/92, 'The Noulens Case', 7 March 1932, p. 36.

57. Abidin Kusno, 'From City to City: Tan Malaka, Shanghai and the Politics of Geographical Imagining', *Singapore Journal of Tropical Geography*, 24/3 (2003), pp. 327–39. This article has been for me a seminal influence.

58. Poeze, *Tan Malaka*, pp. 414–17.

59. *House of Commons Debates*, 14 February 1933, vol. 274, cc. 835–6W.

60. TNA, FO 372/2913, William Peel, Governor of Hong Kong to Under-Secretary of State for the Colonies, 16 August 1933.

61. Letter from Tan Malaka to the China League for Civil Rights, February 1933, in Poeze, *Tan Malaka*, p. 572.

62. Tan Malaka's own account of these years is rich in local colour, but sparse in most other respects, Tan Malaka, *From Jail to Jail*, vol. 11, pp. 53–90; Poeze, *Tan Malaka*, pp. 447–50.

63. This account draws on seminal work by Takashi Shiraishi, 'The Phantom World of Digoel', *Indonesia*, 61 (1996), pp. 93–118, and Rudolf Mrázek, *Sjahrir: Politics and Exile in Indonesia*, Ithaca, NY, Cornell University Press/SEAP Publications, 1994, pp. 129–53; Rudolf Mrázek, 'Boven Digoel and Terezín: Camps at the Time of Triumphant Technology', *East Asian Science, Technology and Society: An International Journal*, 3 (2009), pp. 287–314.

64. Mas Marco Kartodikromo, 'Community of Exiles in Boven Digul', in Tineke Hellwig and Eric Tagliacozzo, *The Indonesia Reader: History, Culture, Politics*, Durham, NC, Duke University Press, 2009, p. 275.

65. Greta O. Wilson (ed.), *Regents, Reformers, and Revolutionaries: Indonesian Voices of Colonial Days, Selected Historical Readings, 1899–1949*, Honolulu, University Press of Hawaii, 1978, p. 139.

66. Mas Marco Kartodikromo, 'Community of Exiles in Boven Digul', pp. 276, 279.

67. Margaret J. Kartomi, *The Gamelan Digul and the Prison Camp Musician who Built it: An Australian Link with the Indonesian Revolution*, Rochester, NY, University of Rochester Press, 2003; Rudolf Mrázek, 'Thick Whisper and Thin Victory: Concentration Camps' Contribution to Modern Acoustics', *Social Text*, 33/1 (122) (2015), pp. 1–25.

68. Mas Marco Kartodikromo, *Pergaulan Orang Buangan Di Boven Digoel*, Jakarta, KPG, 2002, pp. 177–8.

69. Peter Zinoman, *The Colonial Bastille: A History of Imprisonment in Vietnam, 1862–1940*, Berkeley, University of California Press, 2001, esp. pp. 200–239.

70. Frank Dikötter, *Crime, Punishment and the Prison in Modern China*, London, Hurst, 2002, p. 2901.

71. My reading of these letters has been informed by Kris Manjapra, 'The Impossible Intimacies of M. N. Roy', *Postcolonial Studies*, 16/2 (2013), pp. 169–84.

72. M. N. Roy, *Fragments of a Prisoner's Diary*, vol. III: *Letters from Jail*, Dehra Dun, Indian Renaissance Association, 1943, pp. 1–2.

73. Ibid., p. 22.

74. Ibid., p. 6.

75. Ibid., p. 12.

76. Ibid., p. 26.

77. Ibid., p. 21.

78. For context see Taylor Sherman, *State Violence and Punishment in India*, Cambridge, Cambridge University Press, 2009, pp. 93–110.

79. Roy, *Fragments of a Prisoner's Diary*, p. 70.

80. Ibid., p. 21.

81. Ibid., p. 37.

82. Ibid., pp. 54, 49.

83. W. J. Chase, *Enemies within the Gates?: The Comintern and Stalinist Repression, 1934–1939*, New Haven, CT, and London, Yale University Press, 2002.

84. Brigitte Studer, *The Transnational World of the Cominternians*, Basingstoke, AIAA, 2015, p. 137 and *passim*.

85. Vera Vladimirovna Vishnyakova-Akimova, *Two Years in Revolutionary China, 1925–1927*, Cambridge, MA, Harvard University Press, 1971, p. 229.

86. Sophie Quinn-Judge, *Ho Chi Minh: The Missing Years, 1919–1941*, London, Hurst, 2003, pp. 200–219.

87. John Patrick Haithcox, 'Left Wing Unity and the Indian Nationalist Movement: M. N. Roy and the Congress Socialist Party', *Modern Asian Studies*, 3/1 (1969), pp. 17–56.

88. Kris Manjapra, *M. N. Roy: An Intellectual Biography of M. N. Roy*, New

Delhi, Routledge India, 2010, pp. 151-61; the quotation from Nehru is at p. 152.

89. Haithcox, 'Left Wing Unity and the Indian Nationalist Movement', p. 45.

90. Tan Malaka, *From Jail to Jail*, vol. II, pp. 102-12.

91. My thinking on this has been shaped by Sumit K. Mandal, 'Transethnic Solidarities, Racialisation and Social Equality', in Mandal and Terence Gomez (eds), *The State of Malaysia: Ethnicity, Equity and Reform*, London, RoutledgeCurzon, 2002, pp. 49-78.

92. For a recent summary see Brian Tsui, *China's Conservative Revolution: The Quest for a New Order, 1927-1949*, Cambridge, Cambridge University Press, 2018.

93. For the triumph of this concept see R. E. Elson, *The Idea of Indonesia: A History*, Cambridge, Cambridge University Press, 2008.

94. For the latter see Hue-Tam Ho Tai, *Millenarianism and Peasant Politics in Vietnam*, Cambridge, MA, Harvard University Press, 1983.

95. Noriaki Oshikawa, ' "Patjar Merah Indonesia" and Tan Malaka: A Popular Novel and a Revolutionary Legend', in Takashi Shiraishi (ed.), *Reading Southeast Asia: Translation of Contemporary Japanese Scholarship on Southeast Asia*, Ithaca, NY, Cornell University Press, 2000, pp. 9-39.

96. For this see Peter Carey, 'Myths, Heroes and War', in Peter Carey and Colin Wild (eds), *Born in Fire: The Indonesian Struggle for Independence: An Anthology*, Athens, Ohio University Press, 1986, pp. 6-11.

97. For this I am grateful to Hans van de Ven; see his magisterial *China at War: Triumph and Tragedy in the Emergence of the New China, 1937-1945*, London, Profile, 2017, and also Rana Mitter, *China's War with Japan, 1937-45: The Struggle for Survival*, London, Allen Lane, 2013.

98. Yeo Song Nian and Ng Siew Ai, 'The Japanese Occupation as Reflected in Singapore-Malayan Chinese Literary Works after the Japanese Occupation (1945-49)', in Patricia Lim Pui Huen and Diana Wong (eds), *War and Memory in Malaysia and Singapore*, Singapore, ISEAS, 2000, pp. 106-22.

99. This section draws on themes of Christopher Bayly and Tim Harper in *Forgotten Armies: The Fall of British Asia, 1941-1945*, London, Allen Lane, 2004.

100. Penderel Moon (ed.), *Wavell: The Viceroy's Journal*, London, Oxford University Press, pp. 51, 55.

101. For this see Christopher Bayly and Tim Harper, *Forgotten Wars: The End of Britain's Asian Empire*, London, Allen Lane, 2007.

102. Samaren Roy, *The Twice-Born Heretic: M. N. Roy and Comintern*, Calcutta, Firma KLM, 1986, p. 188.

103. For an elegant summary of Ho Chi Minh's movements in this period see Pierre Brocheux, *Ho Chi Minh: A Biography*, Cambridge, Cambridge University Press, 2007, and for Arnoux pp. 84-5.

104. David G. Marr, *Vietnam 1945: The Quest for Power*, Berkeley, University of California Press, 1997.

105. Tan Malaka, *From Jail to Jail*, vol. III, p. 122.

106. Until recently the only extended English-language account of this work was Rudolf Mrázek, 'Tan Malaka: A Political Personality's Structure of Experience', *Indonesia*, 14 (1972), pp. 1–48. But see the important new interpretation by Oliver Crawford, 'The Political Thought of Tan Malaka', PhD thesis, University of Cambridge, 2018, esp. ch. 5.

107. H. A. Poeze, 'Soekarno's political testament', in H. A. Poeze and A. Liem (eds), *Lasting Fascination: Essays on Indonesia and the Southwest Pacific to Honour Bob Hering*, Stein, Yayasan Kabar Seberang, 1998, pp. 291–305.

108. Tan Malaka, *From Jail to Jail*, vol. III, p. 100.

109. For Tan Malaka and the revolution see Benedict Anderson, *Java in a Time of Revolution: Occupation and Resistance, 1944–1946*, Ithaca, NY, Cornell University Press, 1972, pp. 269–83.

110. Aboe Bakar Loebis, 'Tan Malaka's Arrest: An Eye-Witness Account', *Indonesia*, 53 (1992), pp. 71–8.

111. For an engaging profile see Budi Setyarso et al., *Musso and the Madiun Movement*, Jakarta, Tempo Publishing, 2013.

112. Ann Swift, *The Road to Madiun: The Indonesia Communist Uprising of 1948*, Singapore, Equinox, 2010, Musso quotation at pp. 159–60. For the importance of Moscow see Harry A. Poeze, 'The Cold War in Indonesia, 1948', *Journal of Southeast Asian Studies*, 40/3 (2009), pp. 497–517.

113. The definitive account is Harry A. Poeze, *Verguisd en Vergeten: Tan Malaka, de Linkse Beweging En de Indonesische Revolutie, 1945–1949*, 3 vols, Leiden, KITLV, 2007, especially vol. III, pp. 1393–494. I am grateful to Anne-Isabelle Richard for providing an English-language summary of Poeze's findings on Tan Malaka's death.

114. Donald Hindley, *The Communist Party of Indonesia: 1951–1963*, Berkeley, University of California Press, 1966, pp. 105–6.

115. These essays have been republished in M. P. T. Acharya, ed. Ole Laursen, *We Are Anarchists: Essays on Anarchism, Pacifism, and the Indian Independence Movement, 1923–1953*, Chico, California, AK Press, 2019.

116. For a brief biography see http://www.open.ac.uk/researchprojects/makingbritain/content/sukhsagar-datta (last accessed 25 September 2019).

117. A central theme of Maia Ramnath, *Haj to Utopia: How the Ghadar Movement Charted Global Radicalism and Attempted to Overthrow the British Empire*, Berkeley, University of California Press, 2011. See also Neeti Nair, 'Bhagat Singh as "Satyagrahi": The Limits to Non-Violence in Late Colonial India', *Modern Asian Studies*, 43/3 (2009), pp. 649–81; Chris Moffat, *India's Revolutionary Inheritance: Politics and the Promise of Bhagat Singh*, Cambridge, Cambridge University Press, 2019.

118. Manu Goswami, 'Imaginary Futures and Colonial Internationalisms',

American Historical Review, 117/5 (2012), pp. 1461-85, quotation at p. 1464.

119. Roy, *The Twice-Born Heretic*, pp. 189-90.

120. Tapan Ghosh, 'Ellen Roy Murder case', in Ray (ed.), *The World Her Village*, pp. 159-77.

121. Letter from Bhagwan Singh Gyanee to Jagjit Singh, 18 June 1956, Bhagwan Singh Gyanee Materials, South Asian American Digital Archive, https://www.saada.org/item/20120805-916 (last accessed 12 August 2020).

122. For example, for the Indian army as a theme of the end of empire see Bayly and Harper, *Forgotten Armies* and *Forgotten Wars*.

123. Hans van de Ven, *War and Nationalism in China, 1925-1945*, London, RoutledgeCurzon, 2003, p. 296.

124. Arnold Dreyblatt and Jeffrey Wallen, 'Hands on the Document: Arnold Dreyblatt's T. Archive', in Sonja Neef, José van Dijck and Eric Ketelaar (eds), *Sign Here!: Handwriting in the Age of New Media*, Amsterdam, Amsterdam University Press, 2006, pp. 134-49, quotation at p. 142. The online version is, alas, no longer available, but see https://www.dreyblatt.net/installation#/tmail-1999/ (last accessed 16 September 2019).

125. See Su Lin Lewis and Carolien Stolte, 'Other Bandungs: Afro-Asian Internationalisms in the Early Cold War', *Journal of World History*, 30/1-2 (2019), pp. 1-19, and the other articles in this special issue.

126. Christopher E. Goscha, *Thailand and the Southeast Asian Networks of the Vietnamese Revolution, 1885-1954*, London, Routledge, 1998; Yong Mun Cheong, *The Indonesian Revolution and the Singapore Connection, 1945-1949*, Leiden, KITLV, 2003.

127. Max Nettlau, *Errico Malatesta: The Biography of an Anarchist*, New York, Jewish Anarchist Federation, 1924, p. 59. I was alerted to this passage by Davide Turcato, 'Italian Anarchism as a Transnational Movement, 1885-1915', *International Review of Social History*, 52/3 (2007), pp. 407-44, and here quote it more fully.

128. Phan Boi Chau, *Overturned Chariot: The Autobiography of Phan Boi Chau*, Honolulu, Hawaii University Press, 1999, pp. 45-6.

129. I first encountered this idea in Verne A. Dusenbery, 'Diasporic Imagings and the Conditions of Possibility: Sikhs and the State in Southeast Asia', *Sojourn: Journal of Social Issues in Southeast Asia*, 12/2 (1997), pp. 226-60; John Urry, 'Mobility and Proximity', *Sociology*, 36/2 (2002), pp. 255-74.

130. M. N. Roy, 'Nationalism and Non-violence', *The Radical Humanist*, 13/15 (17 April 1949), pp. 167-8.

131. Vishnyakova-Akimova, *Two Years in Revolutionary China*, p. xvii.

132. Ibid., p. viii. A provocative account of loss of salience in another context has shaped my thinking: Christine Stansell, 'Louise Bryant Grows Old', *History Workshop Journal*, 50/1 (2000), pp. 156-80.

133. Will Hanley, 'Grieving Cosmopolitanism in Middle East Studies', *History Compass*, 6/5 (2008), pp. 1346–67.

134. I am paraphrasing here Volker Braun on the fall of the German Democratic Republic: 'What I never had is being torn from me,' as quoted and discussed by Charity Scribner, 'Left Melancholy', in David L. Eng and David Kazanjian (eds), *Loss: The Politics of Mourning*, Berkeley, University of California Press, 2003, pp. 300–319, quotation at p. 300; for Benjamin see also Eng and Kazanjian, 'Introduction: Mourning Remains', ibid., pp. 1–28.

135. Asvi Warman Adam, 'Tomb of Tan Malaka, finally', *The Jakarta Post*, 17 February 2014.

136. Prodita Sabarini, 'Tan Malaka: An Opera of Absence', *The Jakarta Post*, 7 May 2011.

137. Tan Malaka, *From Jail to Jail*, vol. II, p. 49.

Principal Archival Sources

FRANCE

Archives Nationales d'Outre-Mer, Aix-en-Provence

Indo/GG	Gouverneur-Général Indochine
Indo/HCI/SPCE	Haut-Commissaire de France pour l'Indochine, Service de Protection du Corps Expéditionnaire Français en Indochine
SLOTFOM	Ministère des Colonies, Service de liaison avec les originaires des territoires français d'outre-mer

Ministère des Affaires étrangères et européennes, La Courneuve
  Nouvelle Série, Indochine

Centre des Archives Diplomatiques, Nantes
  Pékin, Légation, Série A

INDIA

National Archives of India, New Delhi
  (Accessed via http://nationalarchives.nic.in/content/abhilekh-patal)
  Home Department, Political A
  Home Department, Political B

MALAYSIA

Arkib Negara Malaysia, Kuala Lumpur
  High Commissioner's Office

Selangor Confidential Files
Selangor Secretariat Files

THE NETHERLANDS

Nationaal Archief, Den Haag
Ministerie van Koloniën:
Koloniën: Openbaar Verbaal, 1901–53 (NL-HaNA, 2.10.36.04)
Koloniën: Geheim Archief, 1901–40 (NL-HaNA, 2.10.36.51)

International Institute of Social History, Amsterdam
Henk Sneevliet Archive
Archief Komintern-Partai Komunis Indonesia

THE PHILIPPINES

National Library of the Philippines, Manila
Manuel L. Quezon papers

SINGAPORE

National Archives of Singapore
Straits Settlements Records:
Confidential Despatches from Secretary of State to the Straits
Settlements (COD/C)
Confidential Despatches to the Secretary of State (GD/C)
Coroner's Court:
Coroner's Cases Record Book, 1916–25
Coroner's Inquest and Inquiries
Oral History Department:
Interview, Tan Ee Leong
Overseas Records:
Oriental and African Studies, London, Wilfred Blythe papers,
PPMS 31/File 15 (microfilm copy)

UNITED KINGDOM

The National Archives, Kew

CO 273	Straits Settlements Original Correspondence
CO 537	Confidential General and Confidential Original Correspondence
CO 717	Malay States Original Correspondence
FCO 141	Records of Former Colonial Administrations: Migrated Archives
FO 115	Embassy and Consular Archives: United States of America: General Correspondence
FO 228	Embassy and Consular Archives: China: Correspondence, Series I
FO 262	Embassy and Consular Archives: Japan (1905–40)
FO 370	Library and the Research Department: General Correspondence 1906–66
FO 371	Political Departments: General Correspondence 1906–66
FO 372	Treaty Department: General Correspondence from 1906
FO 1093	Permanent Under-Secretary's Department: Registered and Unregistered Papers
HO 382	Aliens Department: Aliens Personal Files

India Office Records and Private Papers, British Library, London

Mss Eur A97	Oliver George Lewis papers
Mss Eur E224	Personal and Official Papers of Sir Guy Fleetwood Wilson
IOR NEG 10612	Government of India Home Office Proceedings (microfilm)
IOR/L/PJ/	Judicial and Public Department Files

UNITED STATES OF AMERICA

The National Archives and Records Administration (NARA)
M1750, Records of the Shanghai Municipal Police

(accessed via https://www.gale.com)
    SMP IO Files (1916–29)
M1085, FBI Cases, 1909–21
(accessed via https://www.fold3.com)
    Old German Files, Case 8000-1396

Stanford University, Hoover Institution Library and Archives
    Peng Shu-tse and Zhen Bilan papers
    Evelyn Trent papers

Acknowledgements

This has been a long road. The story told here began to take form as a final-year special subject in the History Faculty in Cambridge between 2009 and 2012. I am grateful to all those who made teaching 'From Shanghai to Java: The Asian Underground' such a rewarding experience, and I hope, if they read this, they will recall some of our classes in it. But the starting point lies in my early days of research in Universiti Malaya, Kuala Lumpur, where conversations with Jomo K. S., Lim Teck Ghee, Loh Wei Leng and others led me towards the rich seams that lie buried beneath established national histories.

A journey of this kind can only be accomplished with the help of others. Research and writing began within a series of collaborative projects, particularly 'Sites of Asian Interaction: Networks, Ideas, Archives' between 2010 and 2014. It was set in motion by an inspirational meeting in Dubai in 2008, organized with Sunil Amrith. I am indebted to all those involved, and also to the editor of *Modern Asian Studies* and Cambridge University Press for permission to draw on a 2013 essay from our edited collection. This was the first of a fruitful series of conversations that Sunil and I shared, with colleagues in Penang on port city connections – made possible by Think City, Hamdan Abdul Majeed, Neil Khor, Loh Wei Leng, Khoo Salma Nasution and Shahridan Faiez – and in a project on histories of health, which led me to explore further the visceral experience of mobility in Southeast Asia, particularly through a workshop in Yogyakarta hosted by Bambang Purwanto and his colleagues at Universitas Gadjah Mada. These initiatives were supported by the Social Science Research Council, the Isaac Newton Trust and the China Medical Board, for which special thanks are due to Lincoln Chen.

Above all, this study was made possible by the Joint Centre for History and Economics in Cambridge and Harvard. I am deeply grateful to Emma Rothschild for her enthusiasm and faith in my own work and for creating such rich conditions in which new research ideas and connections can flourish. I also wish to thank Inga Huld Markan for her help over the years; Mary-Rose Cheadle, especially for her editorial support on the manuscript, and Amy Price and Kaye Morris. For the last decade and more, the expanding international community of the Centre has been a constant stimulus.

The later stages of the writing were supported and enriched by the EU-FP7 project 'SEATIDE: Southeast Asia – Trajectories of Inclusion, Dynamics of Exclusion' (2012–16), led by the École française d'Extrême-Orient, in which, for my part, education and mobility were a crucial concern. I learned a great deal from Yves Goudineau, Elisabeth Lacroix, Tomas Larsson, Pietro Matsina, Natasha Pairaudeau, Franciscus Verellen, Sylvia Vignato and all who attended our meetings in Chiang Mai, Hanoi, Yogyakarta and Brussels, especially, over the longer run, Sumit Mandal and Andrew Hardy, a fellow-traveller for over thirty years now.

I have wandered down unfamiliar paths and a great many people have been generous with insights, information and encouragement. I think especially of Seema Alavi, Tom van den Berge, Romain Bertrand, Marieke Bloembergen, John Carroll, Chua Ai Lin, Bradley Davis, Rohit De, Faisal Devji, Mark Frost, Christopher Goscha, Ayesha Jalal, Michael Laffan, Kris Manjapra, Sophie Quinn-Judge, Anne-Isabelle Richard, Mitra Sharafi, Henk Schulte Nordholt, Noelle Rodriguez, Amartya Sen, Carolien Stolte, Syed Husin Ali, Teresa Encarnacion Tadem, Eric Tagliacozzo, Tan Tai Yong, Adrian Vickers, C. J. Wee Wan-ling and Danny Wong. I am also grateful to participants at seminars and lectures in Berlin, Cambridge, Harvard, Hong Kong, Leicester, Leiden, Nottingham, Oxford, Singapore and Tufts, and the generous hospitality and support of Sugata Bose in Boston and Kolkata. I have also benefited from a sense of co-presence with a growing body of scholars seeking to retrace these worldly lives whom I have not had the opportunity to meet, but whose work I greatly admire.

I have been fortunate in being able to draw on archives in many countries, at a time when this was easier than it is at present. These institutions are listed above. I am also grateful to staff at the National Library of Singapore, the library of the Institute of Southeast Asian Studies, Singapore, the collection of the Koninklijk Instituut voor Taal-,

Land- en Volkenkunde, now in Leiden University Library, the Widener Library of Harvard University, Cambridge University Library and the library of the Centre of South Asian Studies, Cambridge. I am especially thankful to students and colleagues I have worked closely with over these years who have taken time to discuss ideas and help me locate sources. These include Aditya Balasubramanian, Oliver Crawford, Devyani Gupta, Rachel Leow, Su Lin Lewis, Joseph McQuade, Daniel-Joseph Macarthur-Seal, Louise Moschetta, Jacob Norris, Julie Pham, Max Reibman, John Slight, Michael Sugarman, Kirsty Walker and Faridah Zaman. Natasha Pesaran and Frances O'Morchoe undertook more extensive research in Cambridge and London, and Grace Lee En Xin and Gayne Lim in Singapore.

Over the years, many colleagues and friends in Cambridge have shaped my thinking, offered wise counsel and strengthened my resolve. These include: Susan Bayly, Amira Bennison, Annabel Brett, the late Raj Chandavarkar, Joya Chatterji, Chris Clark, Gary Gerstle, Iza Hussin, Peter Mandler, Polly O'Hanlon, Amanda Power, David Reynolds, Sujit Sivasundaram, Christina Skott, Gareth Stedman Jones, Megan Vaughan, Hans van de Ven, David Washbrook and Carl Watkins. And amongst them, none more so than my teacher, collaborator and friend, the late Chris Bayly.

The final period of writing fell at a time when I served as Chair of the History Faculty in Cambridge. I am particularly thankful to Elizabeth Haresnape for her support and good humour, and also to Liz Partridge, Joanna Pearson, Emma Spary, Alexandra Walsham and Nicki Kindersley. Magdalene College, under two exceptional Masters, Duncan Robinson and Rowan Williams, continues to provide an environment in which work can be done.

Friends in Kuala Lumpur – especially Oommen and Seok Lian, Sue and Terence, Kanna and Jacqie – continue to offer a harbour for me. Closer to home, Andrew Gibbs, Jo Hornsby, Tomas Larsson and Stuart Martin have helped maintain my morale and Iain Fraser and Will Rhys-Davies have kept me active.

I owe special thanks to Sunil Amrith, Lily Chang, Leigh Denault, Andrew Hardy, Emma Rothschild and Samita Sen, who brought their expertise to bear in reading sections of the manuscript, and also to the two anonymous readers of Harvard University Press. Any errors or missteps are entirely of my own making.

Simon Winder is the most patient, encouraging and imaginative of editors, and kept the faith when my own was flagging. I owe a tremendous amount to him. I am also grateful to Andrew Gordon of David Higham Associates and Ian Malcolm at Harvard University Press for their confidence in me. The raw manuscript was transformed by a brilliant team at Penguin: Ruth Pietroni's and Eva Hodgkin's oversight, Kit Shepherd's and Linden Lawson's meticulous, sympathetic copy-editing, Cecilia Mackay's resourceful picture research, and also by the design team at Harvard University Press.

This book was completed during a time of personal loss and in loving memory of Collette (1934–2014) and Norman Harper (1931–2019), who have been with me all along.

Finally, all journeys, even the longest and hardest, carry with them a hope of home, and this one could not have been accomplished but for the home we have made, and the love and the strength that I find there.

Index

ALLEN LANE
an imprint of
PENGUIN BOOKS

Also Published

Lisa Miller, *The Awakened Brain: The Psychology of Spirituality and Our Search for Meaning*

Michael Pye, *Antwerp: The Glory Years*

Christopher Clark, *Prisoners of Time: Prussians, Germans and Other Humans*

Rupa Marya and Raj Patel, *Inflamed: Deep Medicine and the Anatomy of Injustice*

Richard Zenith, *Pessoa: An Experimental Life*

Michael Pollan, *This Is Your Mind On Plants: Opium—Caffeine—Mescaline*

Amartya Sen, *Home in the World: A Memoir*

Jan-Werner Müller, *Democracy Rules*

Robin DiAngelo, *Nice Racism: How Progressive White People Perpetuate Racial Harm*

Rosemary Hill, *Time's Witness: History in the Age of Romanticism*

Lawrence Wright, *The Plague Year: America in the Time of Covid*

Adrian Wooldridge, *The Aristocracy of Talent: How Meritocracy Made the Modern World*

Julian Hoppit, *The Dreadful Monster and its Poor Relations: Taxing, Spending and the United Kingdom, 1707-2021*

Jordan Ellenberg, *Shape: The Hidden Geometry of Absolutely Everything*

Duncan Campbell-Smith, *Crossing Continents: A History of Standard Chartered Bank*

Jemma Wadham, *Ice Rivers*

Niall Ferguson, *Doom: The Politics of Catastrophe*

Michael Lewis, *The Premonition: A Pandemic Story*

Chiara Marletto, *The Science of Can and Can't: A Physicist's Journey Through the Land of Counterfactuals*

Suzanne Simard, *Finding the Mother Tree: Uncovering the Wisdom and Intelligence of the Forest*

Giles Fraser, *Chosen: Lost and Found between Christianity and Judaism*

Malcolm Gladwell, *The Bomber Mafia: A Story Set in War*

Kate Darling, *The New Breed: How to Think About Robots*

Serhii Plokhy, *Nuclear Folly: A New History of the Cuban Missile Crisis*

Sean McMeekin, *Stalin's War*

Michio Kaku, *The God Equation: The Quest for a Theory of Everything*

Michael Barber, *Accomplishment: How to Achieve Ambitious and Challenging Things*

Charles Townshend, *The Partition: Ireland Divided, 1885-1925*

Hanif Abdurraqib, *A Little Devil in America: In Priase of Black Performance*

Carlo Rovelli, *Helgoland*

Herman Pontzer, *Burn: The Misunderstood Science of Metabolism*

Jordan B. Peterson, *Beyond Order: 12 More Rules for Life*

Bill Gates, *How to Avoid a Climate Disaster: The Solutions We Have and the Breakthroughs We Need*

Kehinde Andrews, *The New Age of Empire: How Racism and Colonialism Still Rule the World*

Veronica O'Keane, *The Rag and Bone Shop: How We Make Memories and Memories Make Us*

Robert Tombs, *This Sovereign Isle: Britain In and Out of Europe*

Mariana Mazzucato, *Mission Economy: A Moonshot Guide to Changing Capitalism*

Frank Wilczek, *Fundamentals: Ten Keys to Reality*

Milo Beckman, *Math Without Numbers*

John Sellars, *The Fourfold Remedy: Epicurus and the Art of Happiness*

T. G. Otte, *Statesman of Europe: A Life of Sir Edward Grey*

Alex Kerr, *Finding the Heart Sutra: Guided by a Magician, an Art Collector and Buddhist Sages from Tibet to Japan*

Edwin Gale, *The Species That Changed Itself: How Prosperity Reshaped Humanity*

Simon Baron-Cohen, *The Pattern Seekers: A New Theory of Human Invention*

Christopher Harding, *The Japanese: A History of Twenty Lives*

Carlo Rovelli, *There Are Places in the World Where Rules Are Less Important Than Kindness*

Ritchie Robertson, *The Enlightenment: The Pursuit of Happiness 1680-1790*

Ivan Krastev, *Is It Tomorrow Yet?: Paradoxes of the Pandemic*

Tim Harper, *Underground Asia: Global Revolutionaries and the Assault on Empire*

John Gray, *Feline Philosophy: Cats and the Meaning of Life*

Priya Satia, *Time's Monster: History, Conscience and Britain's Empire*

Fareed Zakaria, *Ten Lessons for a Post-Pandemic World*

David Sumpter, *The Ten Equations that Rule the World: And How You Can Use Them Too*

Richard J. Evans, *The Hitler Conspiracies: The Third Reich and the Paranoid Imagination*

Fernando Cervantes, *Conquistadores*

John Darwin, *Unlocking the World: Port Cities and Globalization in the Age of Steam, 1830-1930*

Michael Strevens, *The Knowledge Machine: How an Unreasonable Idea Created Modern Science*

Owen Jones, *This Land: The Story of a Movement*

Seb Falk, *The Light Ages: A Medieval Journey of Discovery*

Daniel Yergin, *The New Map: Energy, Climate, and the Clash of Nations*

Michael J. Sandel, *The Tyranny of Merit: What's Become of the Common Good?*

Joseph Henrich, *The Weirdest People in the World: How the West Became Psychologically Peculiar and Particularly Prosperous*

Leonard Mlodinow, *Stephen Hawking: A Memoir of Friendship and Physics*

David Goodhart, *Head Hand Heart: The Struggle for Dignity and Status in the 21st Century*

Claudia Rankine, *Just Us: An American Conversation*

James Rebanks, *English Pastoral: An Inheritance*

Robin Lane Fox, *The Invention of Medicine: From Homer to Hippocrates*

Daniel Lieberman, *Exercised: The Science of Physical Activity, Rest and Health*

Sudhir Hazareesingh, *Black Spartacus: The Epic Life of Touissaint Louverture*

Judith Herrin, *Ravenna: Capital of Empire, Crucible of Europe*

Samantha Cristoforetti, *Diary of an Apprentice Astronaut*

Neil Price, *The Children of Ash and Elm: A History of the Vikings*

George Dyson, *Analogia: The Entangled Destinies of Nature, Human Beings and Machines*

Wolfram Eilenberger, *Time of the Magicians: The Invention of Modern Thought, 1919-1929*

Kate Manne, *Entitled: How Male Privilege Hurts Women*

Christopher de Hamel, *The Book in the Cathedral: The Last Relic of Thomas Becket*

Isabel Wilkerson, *Caste: The International Bestseller*

Bradley Garrett, *Bunker: Building for the End Times*

Katie Mack, *The End of Everything: (Astrophysically Speaking)*

Jonathan C. Slaght, *Owls of the Eastern Ice: The Quest to Find and Save the World's Largest Owl*

Carl T. Bergstrom and Jevin D. West, *Calling Bullshit: The Art of Scepticism in a Data-Driven World*

Paul Collier and John Kay, *Greed Is Dead: Politics After Individualism*

Anne Applebaum, *Twilight of Democracy: The Failure of Politics and the Parting of Friends*

Sarah Stewart Johnson, *The Sirens of Mars: Searching for Life on Another World*

Martyn Rady, *The Habsburgs: The Rise and Fall of a World Power*

John Gooch, *Mussolini's War: Fascist Italy from Triumph to Collapse, 1935-1943*

Roger Scruton, *Wagner's Parsifal: The Music of Redemption*

Roberto Calasso, *The Celestial Hunter*

Benjamin R. Teitelbaum, *War for Eternity: The Return of Traditionalism and the Rise of the Populist Right*

Laurence C. Smith, *Rivers of Power: How a Natural Force Raised Kingdoms, Destroyed Civilizations, and Shapes Our World*

Sharon Moalem, *The Better Half: On the Genetic Superiority of Women*

Augustine Sedgwick, *Coffeeland: A History*

Daniel Todman, *Britain's War: A New World, 1942-1947*

Anatol Lieven, *Climate Change and the Nation State: The Realist Case*

Blake Gopnik, *Warhol: A Life as Art*

Malena and Beata Ernman, Svante and Greta Thunberg, *Our House is on Fire: Scenes of a Family and a Planet in Crisis*

Paolo Zellini, *The Mathematics of the Gods and the Algorithms of Men: A Cultural History*

Bari Weiss, *How to Fight Anti-Semitism*

Lucy Jones, *Losing Eden: Why Our Minds Need the Wild*

Brian Greene, *Until the End of Time: Mind, Matter, and Our Search for Meaning in an Evolving Universe*

Anastasia Nesvetailova and Ronen Palan, *Sabotage: The Business of Finance*

Albert Costa, *The Bilingual Brain: And What It Tells Us about the Science of Language*

Stanislas Dehaene, *How We Learn: The New Science of Education and the Brain*

Daniel Susskind, *A World Without Work: Technology, Automation and How We Should Respond*

John Tierney and Roy F. Baumeister, *The Power of Bad: And How to Overcome It*

Greta Thunberg, *No One Is Too Small to Make a Difference: Illustrated Edition*

Glenn Simpson and Peter Fritsch, *Crime in Progress: The Secret History of the Trump-Russia Investigation*

Abhijit V. Banerjee and Esther Duflo, *Good Economics for Hard Times: Better Answers to Our Biggest Problems*

Gaia Vince, *Transcendence: How Humans Evolved through Fire, Language, Beauty and Time*

Roderick Floud, *An Economic History of the English Garden*

Rana Foroohar, *Don't Be Evil: The Case Against Big Tech*

Ivan Krastev and Stephen Holmes, *The Light that Failed: A Reckoning*

Andrew Roberts, *Leadership in War: Lessons from Those Who Made History*

Alexander Watson, *The Fortress: The Great Siege of Przemysl*

Stuart Russell, *Human Compatible: AI and the Problem of Control*

Serhii Plokhy, *Forgotten Bastards of the Eastern Front: An Untold Story of World War II*

Dominic Sandbrook, *Who Dares Wins: Britain, 1979-1982*